BY WILL DURANT

The Story of Philosophy

Transition

The Pleasure of Philosophy

Adventures in Genius

BY WILL AND ARIEL DURANT

THE STORY OF CIVILIZATION

1. *Our Oriental Heritage*
2. *The Life of Greece*
3. *Caesar and Christ*
4. *The Age of Faith*
5. *The Renaissance*
6. *The Reformation*
7. *The Age of Reason Begins*
8. *The Age of Louis XIV*
9. *The Age of Voltaire*
10. *Rousseau and Revolution*
11. *The Age of Napoleon*

The Lessons of History

Interpretation of Life

A Dual Autobiography

THE STORY OF CIVILIZATION: 6

THE
REFORMATION

A History of European Civilization from
Wyclif to Calvin: 1300-1564

By Will Durant

MJF BOOKS
NEW YORK

Published by MJF Books
Fine Communications
POB 0930
Planetarium Station
New York, NY 10024-0540

Library of Congress Catalog Card Number 92-82058
ISBN 1-56731-017-6

This edition published by arrangement with Simon & Schuster Inc. This edition
is identical to that published by Simon & Schuster Inc.

Manufactured in the United States of America

MJF Books and the MJF colophon are trademarks of Fine Creative Media, Inc.

10 9 8 7 6 5 4 3 2

TO LOUIS, MOLLIE, AND ERIC

To the Reader

THE prospective reader deserves a friendly notice that *The Reformation* is not quite an honest title for this book. An accurate title would be: "A History of European Civilization Outside of Italy from 1300 to 1564, or Thereabouts, Including the History of Religion in Italy and an Incidental View of Islamic and Judaic Civilization in Europe, Africa, and Western Asia." Why so meandering a thematic frontier? Because Volume IV *(The Age of Faith)* in this "Story of Civilization" brought European history only to 1300, and Volume V *(The Renaissance)* confined itself to Italy, 1304–1576, deferring the Italian echoes of the Reformation. So this Volume VI must begin at 1300; and the reader will be amused to find that Luther arrives on the scene only after a third of the tale has been told. But let us privately agree that the Reformation really began with John Wyclif and Louis of Bavaria in the fourteenth century, progressed with John Huss in the fifteenth, and culminated explosively in the sixteenth with the reckless monk of Wittenberg. Those whose present interest is only in the religious revolution may omit Chapters III-VI and IX-X without irreparable loss.

The Reformation, then, is the central, but not the only, subject of this book. We begin by considering religion in general, its functions in the soul and the group, and the conditions and problems of the Roman Catholic Church in the two centuries before Luther. We shall watch England in 1376–82, Germany in 1320–47, and Bohemia in 1402–85, rehearsing the ideas and conflicts of the Lutheran Reformation; and as we proceed we shall note how social revolution, with communistic aspirations, marched hand in hand with the religious revolt. We shall weakly echo Gibbon's chapter on the fall of Constantinople, and shall perceive how the advance of the Turks to the gates of Vienna made it possible for one man to defy at once an emperor and a pope. We shall consider sympathetically the efforts of Erasmus for the peaceful self-reform of the Church. We shall study Germany on the eve of Luther, and may thereby come to understand how inevitable he was when he came. In Book II the Reformation proper will hold the stage, with Luther and Melanchthon in Germany, Zwingli and Calvin in Switzerland, Henry VIII in England, Knox in Scotland, and Gustavus Vasa in Sweden, with a side glance at the long duel between Francis I and Charles V; and other aspects of European life in that turbulent half-century (1517–64) will be postponed in order to let the religious drama unfold itself without confusing delays. Book III will look at 'the strangers in the gate": Russia and the Ivans and the Orthodox Church; Islam and its challenging creed, culture, and power; and the struggle of the Jews to find Christians in Christendom. Book IV will go "behind the scenes" to study the law and economy, morals and manners, art and music, literature and science and philosophy of Europe in the age of Luther. In Book V we shall make an experiment in empathy—shall attempt to view the Reformation from the standpoint of the imperiled Church; and we shall be forced to admire the calm audacity with which she weathered the encompassing storm. In a brief epilogue we shall try to see the Renaissance and the Reformation, Catholicism and the Enlightenment, in the large perspective of modern history and thought.

It is a fascinating but difficult subject, for almost every word that one may write about it can be disputed or give offense. I have tried to be impartial, though I know that a man's past always colors his views, and that nothing is so irritating as impartiality. The reader should be warned that I was brought up as a fervent Catholic, and that I retain grateful memories of the devoted secular priests, and learned Jesuits, and kindly nuns who bore so patiently with my brash youth; but he should note, too, that I derived much of my education from lecturing for thirteen years in a Presbyterian church under the tolerant auspices of sterling Protestants like Jonathan C. Day, William Adams Brown, Henry Sloane Coffin, and Edmund Chaffee; and that many of my most faithful auditors in that Presbyterian church were Jews whose thirst for education and understanding gave me a new insight into their people. Less than any man have I excuse for prejudice; and I feel for all creeds the warm sympathy of one who has come to learn that even the trust in reason is a precarious faith, and that we are all fragments of darkness groping for the sun. I know no more about the ultimates than the simplest urchin in the streets.

I thank Dr. Arthur Upham Pope, founder of the Asia Institute, for correcting some of the errors in the chapters on Islam; Dr. Gerson Cohen, of the Jewish Theological Seminary of America, for checking the pages on the Jews; my friend Harry Kaufman of Los Angeles for reviewing the section on music; and, *pleno cum corde*, my wife for her unremitting aid and illuminating comments at every stage in our co-operative labor on this book.

If the Reaper will stay his hand, there will be a concluding Volume VII, *The Age of Reason*, which should appear some five years hence, and should carry the story of civilization to Napoleon. There we shall make our bow and retire, deeply grateful to all who have borne the weight of these tomes on their hands, and have forgiven numberless errors in our attempt to unravel the present into its constituent past. For the present is the past rolled up for action, and the past is the present unrolled for our understanding.

Los Angeles, May 12, 1957

WILL DURANT

1. Dates of birth and death are usually omitted from the text, but will be found in the Index.

2. The religious standpoint of authors quoted or referred to in the text is indicated in the Bibliography by the letters C, J, P, or R, for Catholic, Jewish, Protestant, or rationalist.

3. Passages intended for resolute students rather than for the general reader are indicated by reduced type.

4. To make this volume an independent unit some passages from *The Renaissance*, on the history of the Church before the Reformation, have been summarized in the opening chapter.

5. The location of works of art, when not indicated in the text, will usually be found in the Index under the artist's name. The name of a city will, in such allocations, be used to indicate its leading gallery, as follows:

Amsterdam—Rijksmuseum
Augsburg—Gemäldegalerie
Barcelona—Museum of Catalan Art
Basel—Offentliche Kunstsammlung
Bergamo—Accademia Carrara
Berlin—Kaiser-Friedrich Museum
Bremen—Kunsthalle
Brussels—Museum
Budapest—Museum of Fine Arts
Chicago—Art Institute
Cincinnati—Art Museum
Cleveland—Museum of Art
Colmar—Museum Unterlinden
Cologne—Wallraf Richarts Museum
Copenhagen—Statens Museum for Kunst
Detroit—Institute of Art
Frankfurt—Städelsches Kunstinstitut
Geneva—Musée d'Art et d'Histoire
The Hague—Mauritshuis
Leningrad—Hermitage
Lisbon—National Museum
London—National Gallery
Madrid—Prado
Milan—Brera
Minneapolis—Institute of Arts
Munich—Haus der Kunst
Naples—Museo Nazionale

New York—Metropolitan Museum of Art
Nuremberg—Germanisches National Museum
Philadelphia—Johnson Collection
Prague—State Gallery
San Diego—Fine Arts Gallery
Stockholm—National Museum
Toledo—Museum of Art
Vienna—Kunsthistorisches Museum
Washington—National Gallery
Worcester—Art Museum

The galleries of Florence will be distinguished by their names, Uffizi or Pitti, as will the Borghese and Galleria Nazionale in Rome.

6. This volume will reckon the crown, the livre, the florin, and the ducat of the fourteenth and fifteenth centuries at $25.00 in the money of the United States in 1954; the franc and the shilling at $5.00; the *écu* at $15.00; the mark at $66.67; the pound sterling at $100.00. These equivalents are loose guesswork, and repeated debasements of the currencies make them still more hazardous. We note that in 1390 a student could be boarded at Oxford for two shillings a week;[1] about 1424 Joan of Arc's horse cost sixteen francs;[2] about 1460 a maid in the service of Leonardo da Vinci's father received eight florins a year.[3]

Table of Contents

TABLE OF CONTENTS

BOOK V: THE COUNTER REFORMATION: 1517–65

List of Illustrations

THE page number referred to in the captions is for a discussion of the particular subject or the artist, and sometimes both.

The author wishes to express his gratitude to the following organizations for certain illustrative materials used in this book:

French Embassy Press and Information Bureau; German Tourist Office; The Library of the Metropolitan Museum of Art; The Library of the New York Academy of Medicine; Spanish Tourist Office; Swiss National Tourist Office; Turkish Information Bureau.

BOOK I

FROM WYCLIF TO LUTHER

1300–1517

CHAPTER I

The Roman Catholic Church

1300-1517

I. THE SERVICES OF CHRISTIANITY

RELIGION is the last subject that the intellect begins to understand. In our youth we may have resented, with proud superiority, its cherished incredibilities; in our less confident years we marvel at its prosperous survival in a secular and scientific age, its patient resurrections after whatever deadly blows by Epicurus, or Lucretius, or Lucian, or Machiavelli, or Hume, or Voltaire. What are the secrets of this resilience?

The wisest sage would need the perspective of a hundred lives to answer adequately. He might begin by recognizing that even in the heyday of science there are innumerable phenomena for which no explanation seems forthcoming in terms of natural cause, quantitative measurement, and necessary effect. The mystery of mind still eludes the formulas of psychology, and in physics the same astonishing order of nature that makes science possible may reasonably sustain the religious faith in a cosmic intelligence. Our knowledge is a receding mirage in an expanding desert of ignorance. Now life is rarely agnostic; it assumes either a natural or a supernatural source for any unexplained phenomenon, and acts on the one assumption or the other; only a small minority of minds can persistently suspend judgment in the face of contradictory evidence. The great majority of mankind feel compelled to ascribe mysterious entities or events to supernatural beings raised above "natural law." Religion has been the worship of supernatural beings —their propitiation, solicitation, or adoration. Most men are harassed and buffeted by life, and crave supernatural assistance when natural forces fail them; they gratefully accept faiths that give dignity and hope to their existence, and order and meaning to the world; they could hardly condone so patiently the careless brutalities of nature, the bloodshed and chicaneries of history, or their own tribulations and bereavements, if they could not trust that these are parts of an inscrutable but divine design. A cosmos without known cause or fate is an intellectual prison; we long to believe that the great drama has a just author and a noble end.

Moreover, we covet survival, and find it hard to conceive that nature should so laboriously produce man, mind, and devotion only to snuff them out in the maturity of their development. Science gives man ever greater powers but ever less significance; it improves his tools and neglects his purposes; it is silent on ultimate origins, values, and aims; it gives life and history no meaning or worth that is not canceled by death or omnivorous time. So men prefer the assurance of dogma to the diffidence of reason; weary of perplexed thought and uncertain judgment, they welcome the guidance of an authoritative church, the catharsis of the confessional, the stability of a long-established creed. Ashamed of failure, bereaved of those they loved, darkened with sin, and fearful of death, they feel themselves redeemed by divine aid, cleansed of guilt and terror, solaced and inspired with hope, and raised to a godlike and immortal destiny.

Meanwhile, religion brings subtle and pervasive gifts to society and the state. Traditional rituals soothe the spirit and bind the generations. The parish church becomes a collective home, weaving individuals into a community. The cathedral rises as the product and pride of the unified municipality. Life is embellished with sacred art, and religious music pours its mollifying harmony into the soul and the group. To a moral code uncongenial to our nature and yet indispensable to civilization, religion offers supernatural sanctions and supports: an all-seeing deity, the threat of eternal punishment, the promise of eternal bliss, and commandments of no precariously human authority but of divine origin and imperative force. Our instincts were formed during a thousand centuries of insecurity and the chase; they fit us to be violent hunters and voracious polygamists rather than peaceable citizens; their once necessary vigor exceeds present social need; they must be checked a hundred times a day, consciously or not, to make society and civilization possible. Families and states, from ages before history, have enlisted the aid of religion to moderate the barbarous impulses of men. Parents found religion helpful in taming the willful child to modesty and self-restraint; educators valued it as a precious means of disciplining and refining youth; governments long since sought its co-operation in forging social order out of the disruptive egoism and natural anarchism of men. If religion had not existed, the great legislators—Hammurabi, Moses, Lycurgus, Numa Pompilius—would have invented it. They did not have to, for it arises spontaneously and repeatedly from the needs and hopes of men.

Through a formative millennium, from Constantine to Dante, the Christian Church offered the gifts of religion to men and states. It molded the figure of Jesus into a divine embodiment of virtues by which rough barbarians might be shamed into civilization. It formulated a creed that made every man's life a part, however modest, of a sublime cosmic drama; it bound each individual in a momentous relation with a God Who had created him, Who had spoken to him in sacred Scriptures, Who had therein given him a moral code, Who had descended from heaven to suffer ignominy and death in atonement for the sins of humanity, and Who had founded the Church as the repository of His teaching and the earthly agent of His power. Year by year the magnificent drama grew; saints and martyrs died for the creed, and bequeathed their example and their merits to the faithful. A hundred forms—a hundred thousand works—of art interpreted the drama and made it vivid even for letterless minds. Mary the Virgin Mother became "the fairest flower of all poesy," the formative model of feminine delicacy and maternal love, the recipient of the tenderest hymns and devotions, the in-spirer of majestic architecture, sculpture, painting, poetry, and music. An impressive ceremony raised daily, from a million altars, the mystic and exalting solemnity of the Mass. Confession and penance purified the contrite sinner, prayer comforted and strengthened him, the Eucharist brought him into an awesome intimacy with Christ, the last sacraments cleansed and anointed him in expectation of paradise. Rarely had religion developed such artistry in its ministrations to mankind.

The Church was at her best when, by the consolations of her creed, the magic of her ritual, the nobler morality of her adherents, the courage, zeal, and integrity of her bishops, and the superior justice of her episcopal courts, she took the place vacated by the Roman Imperial government as the chief source of order and peace in the Dark Ages (approximately 524–1079 A.D.) of the Christian world. To the Church, more than to any other institution, Europe owed the resurrection of civilization in the West after the barbarian inundation of Italy, Gaul, Britain, and Spain. Her monks developed waste lands, her monasteries gave food to the poor, education to boys, lodging to travelers; her hospitals received the sick and the destitute. Her nunneries sheltered mateless women and directed their maternal impulses to social ends; for centuries the nuns alone provided schooling for girls. If classic culture was not completely lost in the illiterate flood, it was because monks, while allowing or causing many pagan manuscripts to perish, copied and preserved thousands of them, and kept alive the Greek and Latin languages in which they were written; it was in ecclesiastical libraries, at St. Gall, Fulda, Monte Cassino, and elsewhere, that the humanists of the Renaissance found precious relics of brilliant civilizations that had never heard the name of Christ. For a thousand years, from Ambrose to Wolsey, it was the Church that trained Western Europe's teachers, scholars, judges, diplomats, and ministers of state; the medieval state rested on the Church. When the Dark Ages ended —say with the birth of Abélard—it was the Church that built the universities and the Gothic cathedrals, providing homes for the intellect, as well as for the piety, of men. Under her protection the Scholastic philosophers renewed the ancient attempt to interpret human life and destiny by reason. Through nine centuries almost all European art was inspired and financed by the

Church; and even when art took a pagan color the popes of the Renaissance continued their patronage. Music in its higher forms was a daughter of the Church.

Above all, the Church at her zenith gave to the states of Europe an international moral code and government. Just as the Latin language, taught in the schools by the Church, served as a unifying medium for the scholarship, literature, science, and philosophy of diverse nations, and just as the Catholic —i.e., universal—creed and ritual gave religious unity to a Europe not yet divided into sovereign nationalities, so the Roman Church, claiming divine establishment and spiritual leadership, proposed herself as an international court, to which all rulers and states were to be morally responsible. Pope Gregory VII formulated this doctrine of a Christian Republic of Europe; the Emperor Henry IV recognized it by submitting to Gregory at Canossa (1077); a century later a stronger emperor, Frederick Barbarossa, after a long resistance, humbled himself at Venice before a weaker pope, Alexander III; and in 1198 Pope Innocent III raised the authority and prestige of the papacy to a point where for a time it seemed that Gregory's ideal of a moral superstate had come to fulfillment.

The great dream broke on the nature of man. The administrators of the papal judiciary proved human, biased, venal, even extortionate; and the kings and peoples, also human, resented any supernational power. The growing wealth of France stimulated her pride of national sovereignty; Philip IV successfully challenged the authority of Pope Boniface VIII over the property of the French Church; the King's emissaries imprisoned the aged Pontiff for three days at Anagni, and Boniface died soon afterward (1303). In one of its basic aspects—the revolt of secular rulers against the popes— the Reformation there and then began.

II. THE CHURCH AT NADIR: 1307–1417

Throughout the fourteenth century the Church suffered political humiliation and moral decay. She had begun with the profound sincerity and devotion of Peter and Paul; she had grown into a majestic system of familial, scholastic, social, international discipline, order, and morality; she was now degenerating into a vested interest absorbed in self-perpetuation and finance. Philip IV secured the election of a Frenchman to the papacy, and persuaded him to move the Holy See to Avignon on the Rhone. For sixty-eight years the popes were so clearly the pawns and prisoners of France that other nations gave them a rapidly diminishing reverence and revenue. The harassed pontiffs replenished their treasury by multiple levies upon the hierarchy, the monasteries, and the parishes. Every ecclesiastical appointee was required to remit to the papal Curia—the administrative bureaus of the papacy—half the income of his office for the first year ("annates"), and thereafter annually a tenth or tithe. A new archbishop had to pay to the pope a substantial sum for the pallium—a band of white wool that served as the confirmation and insignia of his authority. On the death of any cardinal, archbishop, bishop, or abbot, his personal possessions reverted to the papacy. In the interim between the death of an ecclesiastic and the installation of his successor, the popes received the net revenues of the benefice, and were accused of pro- longing this interval. Every judgment or favor obtained from the Curia expected a gift in acknowledgment, and the judgment was sometimes dic- tated by the gift.

Much of this papal taxation was a legitimate means of financing the central administration of a Church functioning, with diminishing success, as the moral government of European society. Some of it, however, went to fatten ecclesiastical paunches, even to remunerate the courtesans that crowded Avignon. William Durand, Bishop of Mende, submitted to the Council of Vienne (1311) a treatise containing these words:

> The whole Church might be reformed if the Church of Rome would begin by removing evil examples from herself . . . by which men are scandalized, and the whole people, as it were, infected. . . . For in all lands . . . the Church of Rome is in ill repute, and all cry and publish it abroad that within her bosom all men, from the greatest even unto the least, have set their hearts upon covetousness. . . . That the whole Christian folk take from the clergy pernicious examples of gluttony is clear and notorious, since the clergy feast more luxuri- ously . . . than princes and kings.[1]

"Wolves are in control of the Church," cried the high Spanish prelate Álvaro Pelayo, "and feed on the blood" of the Christian flock.[2] Edward III of England, himself an adept in taxation, reminded Clement VI that "the suc- cessor of the Apostles was commissioned to lead the Lord's sheep to pasture, not to fleece them."[3] In Germany papal collectors were hunted down, im- prisoned, mutilated, strangled. In 1372 the clergy of Cologne, Bonn, Xanten, and Mainz bound themselves by oath not to pay the tithe levied by Greg- ory XI.

Amid all complaints and revolts the popes continued to assert their abso- lute sovereignty over the kings of the earth. About 1324, under the patronage of John XXII, Agostino Trionfo wrote a *Summa de potestate ecclesiastica* in reply to attacks on the papacy by Marsilius of Padua and William of Ock- ham. The power of the pope, said Agostino, is from God, Whose vicegerent he is on earth; even when he is a great sinner he must be obeyed; he may be deposed by a general council of the Church for manifest heresy; but short of this his authority is second only to God's, and transcends that of all earthly potentates. He may dethrone kings and emperors at will, even over the protests of their people or the electors; he may annul the decrees of secular rulers, and may set aside the constitutions of states. No decree of any prince is valid unless the pope gives it his consent. The pope stands higher than the angels, and may receive equal reverence with the Virgin and the saints.[4] Pope John accepted all this as following logically from the generally conceded establishment of the Church by the Son of God, and acted on it with adamantine consistency.

Nevertheless the flight of the popes from Rome, and their subservience to France, undermined their authority and prestige. As if to proclaim their vassalage, the Avignon pontiffs, in a total of 134 nominations to the college of cardinals, named 113 Frenchmen.[5] The English government fumed at the loans of the popes to the kings of France during the Hundred Years' War, and connived at the attacks of Wyclif upon the papacy. The Imperial electors in Germany repudiated any further interference of the popes in the election of kings and emperors. In 1372 the abbots of Cologne publicly agreed that "the Apostolic See has fallen into such contempt that the Catholic faith in these parts seems to be seriously imperiled."[6] In Italy the Papal States—Latium, Umbria, the Marches, the Romagna—were seized by *condottieri* despots who gave the distant popes a formal obeisance but kept the revenues. When Urban V sent two legates to Milan to excommunicate the recalcitrant Visconti, Bernabò compelled them to eat the bulls—parchment, silken cords, and leaden seals (1362).[7] In 1376 Florence, quarreling with Pope Gregory XI, confiscated all ecclesiastical property in its territory, closed the episcopal courts, demolished the buildings of the Inquisition, jailed or hanged resisting priests, and called upon Italy to end all temporal power of the Church. It became clear that the Avignon popes were losing Europe in their devotion to France. In 1377 Gregory XI returned the papacy to Rome.

When he died (1378) the conclave of cardinals, overwhelmingly French but fearful of the Roman mob, chose an Italian as Pope Urban VI. Urban was not urbane; he proved so violent of temper, and so insistent upon reforms uncongenial to the hierarchy, that the reassembled cardinals declared his election invalid as having been made under duress, and proclaimed Robert of Geneva pope. Robert assumed office as Clement VII in Avignon, while Urban persisted as pontiff in Rome. The Papal Schism (1378-1417) so inaugurated, like so many of the forces that prepared the Reformation, was conditioned by the rise of the national state; in effect it was an attempt by France to retain the moral and financial aid of the papacy in her war with England. The lead of France was followed by Naples, Spain, and Scotland; but England, Flanders, Germany, Poland, Bohemia, Hungary, Italy, and

Portugal accepted Urban, and the divided Church became the weapon and victim of the hostile camps. Half the Christian world held the other half to be heretical, blasphemous, and excommunicate; each side claimed that sacraments administered by priests of the opposite obedience were worthless, and that the children so baptized, the penitents so shriven, the dying so anointed, remained in mortal sin, and were doomed to hell—or at best to limbo—if death should supervene. Expanding Islam laughed at disintegrating Christendom.

Urban's death (1389) brought no compromise; the fourteen cardinals in his camp chose Boniface IX, then Innocent VII, then Gregory XII, and the divided nations prolonged the divided papacy. When Clement VII died (1394) the Avignon cardinals named a Spanish prelate to be Benedict XIII. He offered to resign if Gregory would follow suit, but Gregory's relatives, already entrenched in office, would not hear of it. Some of Gregory's cardinals abandoned him, and called for a general council. The King of France urged Benedict to withdraw; Benedict refused; France renounced its allegiance to him, and adopted neutrality. While Benedict fled to Spain his cardinals joined with those who had left Gregory, and together they issued a call for a council to meet at Pisa and elect a pope acceptable to all.

Rebellious philosophers, almost a century before, had laid the theoretical foundations of the "conciliar movement." William of Ockham protested against identifying the Church with the clergy; the Church, he held, is the congregation of all the faithful; that whole has authority superior to any part; it may delegate its authority to a general council of all the bishops and abbots of the Church; and such a council should have the power to elect, reprove, punish, or depose the pope.[8] A general council, said Marsilius of Padua, is the collected wisdom of Christendom; how should any one man set up his own intellect above it? Such a council, he thought, should be composed not only of clergymen but also of laymen chosen by the people.[9] Heinrich von Langenstein, a German theologian at the University of Paris, applied (1381) these ideas to the Papal Schism. Whatever logic there might be, he argued, in the claims of the popes to supremacy, a crisis had arisen from which logic offered no escape but one: only a power outside the papacy, and superior to the cardinals, could rescue the Church from the chaos that was destroying her; and that authority could only be a general council.

The Council of Pisa met on March 25, 1409. It summoned Benedict and Gregory to appear before it; they ignored it; it declared them deposed, elected a new pope, Alexander V, bade him call another council before May 1412, and adjourned. There were now three popes instead of two. Alexander did not help matters by dying (1410), for his cardinals named as his successor John XXIII, the most unmanageable man to mount the pontifical chair since the twenty-second of his name. Governing Bologna as papal vicar, this ecclesiastical *condottiere*, Baldassare Cossa, had permitted and taxed everything, including prostitution, gambling, and usury; according to his secretary he had seduced 200 virgins, matrons, widows, and nuns.[10] But he had money, and an army; perhaps he could conquer the Papal States from Gregory, and so reduce him to impecunious abdication.

John XXIII delayed, as long as he could, the calling of the council decreed at Pisa. When he opened it at Constance on November 5, 1414, only a fraction had arrived of the three patriarchs, twenty-nine cardinals, thirty-three archbishops, 150 bishops, 300 doctors of theology, fourteen university delegates, twenty-six princes, 140 nobles, and 4,000 priests who were to make the completed council the largest in Christian history, and the most important since the Council of Nicaea (325) had established the trinitarian creed of the Church. On April 6, 1415, the great gathering issued a proud and revolutionary decree:

> This holy synod of Constance, being a general council, and legally assembled in the Holy Spirit for the praise of God, for ending the present Schism, and for the union and reform of the Church in its head and members ... ordains, declares, and decrees as follows: First, it declares that this synod ... represents the Church Militant, and has its authority directly from Christ; and everybody, of whatever rank or dignity, including also the pope, is bound to obey this council in those things that pertain to the faith, to the ending of this Schism, and to a general reform of the Church in its head and members. Likewise it declares that if anyone ... including also the pope, shall refuse to obey the commands, statutes, ordinances ... of this holy council ... in regard to the ending of the Schism or to the reform of the Church, he shall be subject to proper punishment ... and, if necessary, recourse shall be had to other aids of justice.[11]

The Council demanded the abdication of Gregory XII, Benedict XIII, and John XXIII. Receiving no answer from John, it accepted the presentation of fifty-four charges against him as a pagan, oppressor, liar, simoniac, traitor, lecher, and thief; sixteen other accusations were suppressed as too severe.[12] On May 29, 1415, it deposed him. Gregory was more pliant and subtle; he agreed to resign, but only on condition that he should first be allowed to reconvene the council on his own authority. So reconvened, the council accepted his resignation (July 4). To further attest its orthodoxy, it burned at the stake (July 6) the Bohemian reformer, John Huss. On July 26 it declared Benedict XIII deposed; he settled in Valencia, and died there at ninety, still holding himself pope. On November 17, 1417, an electoral committee chose Cardinal Ottone Colonna as Pope Martin V. All Christendom acknowledged him, and the Papal Schism came to an end.

The victory of the council in this regard defeated its other purpose—to reform the Church. Martin V at once assumed all the powers and prerogatives of the papacy. Playing off each national group of delegates against the others, he persuaded them to accept a vague and innocuous minimum of reform. The council yielded to him because it was tired. On April 22, 1418, it dissolved.

III. THE TRIUMPHANT PAPACY: 1417–1513

Martin reorganized the Curia to more effective functioning, but could find no way to finance it except by imitating the secular governments of the age and selling offices and services. Since the Church had survived for a century without reform, but could hardly survive a week without money, he concluded that money was more urgently needed than reform. In 1430, a year before Martin's death, a German envoy to Rome sent his prince a letter that almost sounded the theme and tocsin of the Reformation:

> Greed reigns supreme in the Roman court, and day by day finds new devices . . . for extorting money from Germany. . . . Hence much outcry and heartburnings. . . . Many questions in regard to the papacy will arise, or else obedience will at last be entirely renounced, to escape from these outrageous exactions by the Italians; and this latter course, as I perceive, would be acceptable to many countries.[18]

Martin's successor faced the accumulated problems of the Apostolic See from the background of a devout Franciscan friar ill equipped for statesmanship. The papacy had to govern states as well as the Church; the popes had to be men of affairs with at least one foot in the world, and could rarely afford to be saints. Eugenius IV might have been a saint had not his troubles embittered his spirit. In the first year of his pontificate the Council of Basel proposed again to assert the supremacy of general councils over the popes. It assumed one after another traditionally papal function: it issued indulgences and dispensations, appointed to benefices, and required annates to be sent to itself instead of to the pope. Eugenius ordered it to dissolve; instead it declared him deposed, and named Amadeus VIII, Duke of Savoy, as Antipope Felix V (1439). The Papal Schism was renewed.

To complete the apparent defeat of the papacy, Charles VII of France convened an assembly of French prelates, nobles, and lawyers, which proclaimed the superior authority of general councils and issued the Pragmatic Sanction of Bourges (1438): ecclesiastical offices were henceforth to be filled through election by the local clergy, but the king might make "recommendations"; appeals to the papal Curia were forbidden except after exhausting all judicial avenues in France; and annates were no longer to be sent to the pope. In effect the Sanction established an independent Gallican Church and made the king its master. A year later a diet at Mainz adopted resolutions aiming at a similar national church in Germany. Bohemia had already separated itself from the papacy. The whole edifice of the Roman Church seemed about to collapse.

Eugenius was rescued by the Turks. As the Ottomans came ever nearer to Constantinople, the Byzantine government decided that the Greek capital was worth a Roman Mass, and that a reunion of Greek with Latin Christianity was an indispensable prelude to winning military or financial aid from the West. Greek prelates and nobles came in picturesque panoply to Ferrara, then to Florence, to meet the Roman hierarchy summoned by the Pope (1438). After a year of argument an accord was reached that recognized the authority of the Roman pontiff over all Christendom; and on July 6, 1439, all the members of the conference, with the Greek emperor at their head, bent the knee before that same Eugenius who had seemed, so recently, the most despised and rejected of men. The concord was brief, for the Greek clergy and people repudiated it; but it restored the prestige of the papacy, and helped to bring the new schism, and the Council of Basel, to an end.

A succession of strong popes, enriched and exalted by the Italian Renaissance, now raised the papacy to such splendor as it had not known even in the proud days of Innocent III. Nicholas V earned the admiration of the humanists by devoting Church revenues to the patronage of scholarship and art. Calixtus III established that genial custom of nepotism—giving offices to relatives—which became a pillar of corruption in the Church. Pius II, brilliant as author and barren as pope, struggled to reform the Curia and the monasteries. He appointed a commission of prelates reputed for integrity and piety to study the shortcomings of the Church, and to this commission he made a frank confession:

> Two things are particularly near my heart: the war with the Turks and the reform of the Roman court. The amendment of the whole state of ecclesiastical affairs, which I have determined to undertake, depends upon this court as its model. I purpose to begin by improving the morals of ecclesiastics here, and banishing all simony and other abuses.[14]

The committee made laudable recommendations, and Pius embodied them in a bull. But hardly anybody in Rome wanted reform; every second functionary or dignitary there profited from some form of venality. Apathy and passive resistance defeated Pius, while the abortive crusade that he undertook against the Turks absorbed his energy and his funds. Toward the end of his pontificate he addressed a final appeal to the cardinals:

> People say that we live for pleasure, accumulate wealth, bear ourselves arrogantly, ride on fat mules and handsome palfreys . . . keep

hounds for the chase, spend much on actors and parasites and nothing in defense of the faith. And there is some truth in their words: many among the cardinals and other officials of our court do lead this kind of life. If the truth be confessed, the luxury and pomp of our court is too great. And this is why we are so detested by the people that they will not listen to us, even when we say what is just and reasonable. What do you think is to be done in such a shameful state of things? . . . We must inquire by what means our predecessors won authority and consideration for the Church. . . . We must maintain that authority by the same means. Temperance, chastity, innocence, zeal for the faith . . . contempt of earth, the desire for martyrdom exalted the Roman Church, and made her the mistress of the world.[15]

Despite the labors of popes like Nicholas V and Pius II, and of sincere and accomplished ecclesiastics like Cardinals Giuliano Cesarini and Nicholas of Cusa, the faults of the papal court mounted as the fifteenth century neared its end.[16] Paul II wore a papal tiara that outweighed a palace in its worth. Sixtus IV made his nephew a millionaire, entered avidly into the game of politics, blessed the cannon that fought his battles, and financed his wars by selling church offices to the highest bidders. Innocent VIII celebrated in the Vatican the marriages of his children. Alexander VI, like Luther and Calvin, thought clerical celibacy a mistake, and begot five or more children before subsiding into reasonable continence as a pope. His gay virility did not stick so sharply in the gullet of the time as we might suppose; a certain clandestine amorousness was then accepted as usual in the clergy; what offended Europe was that Alexander's unscrupulous diplomacy, and the ruthless generalship of his son Caesar Borgia, rewon the Papal States for the papacy and added needed revenues and strength to the Apostolic See. In these policies and campaigns the Borgias used all those methods of stratagem and death which were soon to be formulated in Machiavelli's *Prince* (1513) as indispensable to founding a powerful state or a united Italy. Pope Julius II out-Caesared Borgia in waging war against rapacious Venice and the invading French; he escaped whenever he could from the prison of the Vatican, led his army in person, and relished the rough life and speech of martial camps. Europe was shocked to see the papacy not only secularized but militarized; yet it could hardly withhold some admiration from a mighty warrior miscast as a pope; and some word went over the Alps about the services of Julius to art in his discriminating patronage of Raphael and Michelangelo. It was Julius who began the building of the new St. Peter's, and first granted indulgences to those who contributed to its cost. It was in his pontificate that Luther came to Rome and saw for himself that "sink of iniquity" which had been Lorenzo de' Medici's name for the capital of Christendom. No ruler in Europe could any longer think of the papacy as a moral supergovernment binding all the nations into a Christian commonwealth; the papacy itself, as a secular state, had become nationalistic; all Europe, as the old faith waned, fell into national fragments acknowledging no supernational or international moral law, and doomed to five centuries of interchristian wars.

To judge these Renaissance popes fairly we must see them against the background of their time. Northern Europe could feel their faults, since it financed them; but only those who knew the exuberant Italy of the period between Nicholas V (1447–55) and Leo X (1513–21) could view them with understanding lenience. Though several of them were personally pious, most of them accepted the Renaissance conviction that the world, while still for so many a vale of tears and devilish snares, could also be a scene of beauty, intense living, and fleeting happiness; it did not seem scandalous to them that they enjoyed life and the papacy.

They had their virtues. They labored to redeem Rome from the ugliness and squalor into which it had fallen while the popes were at Avignon. They drained marshes (by comfortable proxy), paved streets, restored bridges and roads, improved the water supply, established the Vatican Library and the Capitoline Museum, enlarged the hospitals, distributed charity, built or repaired churches, embellished the city with palaces and gardens, reorganized the University of Rome, supported the humanists in resurrecting pagan literature, philosophy, and art, and gave employment to painters, sculptors, and architects whose works are now a treasured heritage of all mankind. They squandered millions; they used millions constructively. They spent too much on the new St. Peter's, but hardly more in proportion than the kings of France would spend on Fontainebleau and Versailles and the châteaux of the Loire; and perhaps they thought of it as transforming scattered crumbs of evanescent wealth into a lasting splendor for the people and their God. Most of these popes in private lived simply, some (like Alexander VI) abstemiously, and resigned themselves to pomp and luxury only as required by public taste and discipline. They raised the papacy, which had so lately been scorned and destitute, to an impressive majesty of power.

IV. THE CHANGING ENVIRONMENT

But while the Church seemed to be growing again in grandeur and authority, Europe was undergoing economic, political, and intellectual changes that slowly undermined the structure of Latin Christianity.

Religion normally thrives in an agricultural regime, science in an industrial economy. Every harvest is a miracle of the earth and a whim of the sky; the humble peasant, subject to weather and consumed with toil, sees supernatural forces everywhere, prays for a propitious heaven, and accepts a feudal-religious system of graduated loyalties mounting through vassal, liege lord, and king to God. The city worker, the merchant, the manufacturer, the financier, live in a mathematical world of calculated quantities and processes, of material causes and regular effects; the machine and the counting table dispose them to see, over widening areas, the reign of "natural law." The growth of industry, commerce, and finance in the fifteenth century, the passage of labor from the countryside to the town, the rise of the mercantile class, the expansion of local to national to international economy—all were of evil omen for a faith that had fitted in so well with feudalism and the somber vicissitudes of the fields. Businessmen repudiated ecclesiastical restraints as well as feudal tolls; the Church had to yield, by transparent theological jugglery, to the necessity of charging interest for loans if capital was to expand enterprise and industry; by 1500 the old prohibition of "usury" was universally ignored. Lawyers and businessmen more and more replaced churchmen and nobles in the administration of government. Law itself, triumphantly recapturing its Roman Imperial traditions and prestige, led the march of secularization and day by day encroached on the sphere of ecclesiastical regulation of life by canon law. Secular courts extended their jurisdiction; episcopal courts declined.

The adolescent monarchies, enriched by revenues from commerce and industry, freed themselves day by day from domination by the Church. The kings resented the residence, in their realms, of papal legates or nuncios who acknowledged no authority but the pope's, and made each nation's church a state within the state. In England the statutes of Provisors (1351) and Praemunire (1353) sharply restricted the economic and judicial powers of the clergy. In France the Pragmatic Sanction of Bourges was theoretically abrogated in 1516, but the king retained the right to nominate archbishops, bishops, abbots, and priors.[17] The Venetian Senate insisted on appointing to high ecclesiastical office in all Venetian dependencies. Ferdinand and Isabella overrode the popes in filling many ecclesiastical vacancies in Spain. In the Holy Roman Empire, where Gregory VII had maintained against Henry IV the papal right of investiture, Sixtus IV conceded to the emperors the right of nomination to 300 benefices and seven bishoprics. The kings often misused these powers by giving church offices to political favorites, who took the revenues—but ignored the responsibilities—of their abbacies and sees.[18] Many ecclesiastical abuses were traceable to such secular appointees.

Meanwhile the intellectual environment of the Church was changing, to her peril. She still produced laborious and conscientious scholars; but the schools and universities that she had founded had raised up an educated minority whose thinking did not always please the saints. Hear St. Bernardino, toward 1420:

Very many folk, considering the wicked life of monks and friars, nuns and secular clergy, are shaken by this; nay, oftentimes, they fail in faith, and believe in nothing higher than the roofs of their houses, not esteeming those things to be true that have been written concerning our faith, but believing them to have been written by the cozening invention of men, and not by God's inspiration. . . . They despise the sacraments . . . and hold that the soul has no existence; neither do they . . . fear hell nor desire heaven, but cling with all their hearts to transitory things, and resolve that this world shall be their paradise.[19]

Probably the business class was the least pious; as wealth mounts, religion declines. Gower (1325?–1408) claimed that the merchants of England cared little about the hereafter, saying, "He who can get the sweetness of this life, and lets it go, would be a fool, for no man knoweth whither or by what way we go" after death.[20] The failure of the Crusades had left a slowly fading wonder why the God of Christendom had permitted the victory of Islam, and the capture of Constantinople by the Turks refreshed these doubts. The work of Nicholas of Cusa (1432) and Lorenzo Valla (1439), in exposing the "Donation of Constantine" as a forgery, damaged the prestige of the Church and weakened her title to temporal power. The recovery and publication of classical texts nourished skepticism by revealing a world of learning and art that had flourished long before the birth of that Christian Church which, at the Fifth Council of the Lateran (1512–17), had denied the possibility of salvation outside her fold: *nulla salus extra ecclesiam*.[21] The discovery of America, and the widening exploration of the East, revealed a hundred nations that with apparent impunity ignored or rejected Christ, and had faiths of their own as positive, and as morally efficacious, as Christianity. Travelers returning from "heathen" lands brought some rubbing of strange creeds and rituals with them; these alien cults touched elbows with Christian worship and belief, and rival dogmas suffered attrition in the market place and the port.

Philosophy, which in the thirteenth century had been the handmaid of theology, devoting itself to finding rational grounds for the orthodox faith, liberated itself in the fourteenth century with William of Ockham and Marsilius of Padua, and in the sixteenth became boldly secular, flagrantly skeptical with Pomponazzi, Machiavelli, and Guicciardini. Some four years before Luther's Theses Machiavelli wrote a startling prophecy:

Had the religion of Christianity been preserved according to the ordinances of the Founder, the state and commonwealth of Christendom would have been far more united and happy than they are. Nor can there be a greater proof of its decadence than the fact that the nearer people are to the Roman Church, the head of their religion, the less religious are they. And whoever examines the principles on which that religion is founded, and sees how widely different from those principles its present practice and application are, will judge that her ruin or chastisement is near at hand.[22]

V. THE CASE AGAINST THE CHURCH

Shall we recapitulate the charges made by loyal Catholics against the Church of the fourteenth and fifteenth centuries? The first and sorest was that she loved money, and had too much of it for her own good.* In the *Centum Gravamina*, or Hundred Grievances, listed against the Church by the Diet of Nuremberg (1522), it was alleged that she owned half the wealth of Germany.[23] A Catholic historian reckoned the Church's share as a third in Germany and a fifth in France; [24] but a procurer-general of the *Parlement* calculated in 1502 that three quarters of all French wealth was ecclesiastical.[25] No statistics are available to check these estimates. In Italy, of course, one third of the peninsula belonged to the Church as the Papal States, and she owned rich properties in the rest.†

Six factors served to accumulate lands in the possession of the Church. (1) Most of those who bequeathed property left something to her as "fire insurance"; and as the Church controlled the making and probating of wills, her agents were in a position to encourage such legacies. (2) Since ecclesiastical property was safer than other property from ravage by bandits, soldiers, or governments, some persons, for security, deeded their lands to the Church, held them as her vassals, and surrendered all right to them at death. Others willed part or all of their property to the Church on condition that she should provide for them in sickness or old age; in this way the Church offered disability insurance. (3) Crusaders had sold—or mortgaged and forfeited—lands to ecclesiastical bodies to raise cash for their venture. (4) Hundreds of thousands of acres had been earned for the Church by the reclamation work of monastic orders. (5) Land once acquired by the Church was inalienable—could not be sold or given away by any of her personnel except through discouragingly complex means. (6) Church property was normally free from taxation by the state; occasionally, however, kings reckless of

---

* "One cause of the downfall of the German Church lay in her enormous riches, the unhealthy growth of which aroused on the one side the envy and hatred of the laity, and on the other had a most deleterious effect on the ministers of the Church themselves."—Pastor (C), *History of the Popes*, VII, 293.

† In any society the majority of abilities is contained in a minority of men; therefore, sooner or later, the majority of goods, privileges, and powers will be possessed by a minority of men. Wealth became concentrated in the Church in the Middle Ages because she served vital functions and was herself served by the ablest men. The Reformation, in one aspect, was a redistribution of this naturally concentrated wealth by the secular appropriation of ecclesiastical property or revenues.

damnation forced levies from the clergy, or found legal dodges to confiscate some portion of ecclesiastical wealth. The rulers of northern Europe might have grumbled less about the riches of the Church if the income therefrom, or the multifarious contributions of the faithful, had remained within the national boundaries; they fretted at the sight of northern gold flowing in a thousand streamlets to Rome.

The Church, however, looked upon herself as the chief agent in maintaining morality, social order, education, literature, scholarship, and art; the state relied upon her to fulfill these functions; to perform them she needed an extensive and expensive organization; to finance this she taxed and gathered fees; even a church could not be governed by paternosters. Many bishops were the civil as well as the ecclesiastical rulers of their regions; most of them were appointed by lay authorities, and came of patrician stock accustomed to easy morals and luxuries; they taxed and spent like princes; sometimes, in the performance of their multiple functions, they scandalized the saints by donning armor and lustily leading their troops in war. Cardinals were chosen rarely for their piety, usually for their wealth or political connections or administrative capacity; they looked upon themselves, not as monks burdened with vows, but as the senators and diplomats of a rich and powerful state; in many instances they were not priests; and they did not let their red hats impede their enjoyment of life.[26] The Church forgot the poverty of the Apostles in the needs and expenses of power.

Being worldly, the servants of the Church were often as venal as the officials of contemporary governments. Corruption was in the mores of the time and in the nature of man; secular courts were notoriously amenable to the persuasiveness of money, and no papal election could rival in bribery the election of Charles V as emperor. This excepted, the fattest bribes in Europe were paid at the Roman court.[27] Reasonable fees had been fixed for the services of the Curia, but the cupidity of the staff raised the actual cost to twenty times the legal sum.[28] Dispensations could be had from almost any canonical impediment, almost any sin, provided the inducement was adequate. Aeneas Sylvius, before becoming pope, wrote that everything was for sale in Rome, and that nothing could be had there without money.[29] A generation later the monk Savonarola, with the exaggeration of indignation, called the Church of Rome a "harlot" ready to sell her favors for coin.[30] Another generation later, Erasmus remarked: "The shamelessness of the Roman Curia has reached its climax." [31] Pastor writes:

> A deep-rooted corruption had taken possession of nearly all the officials of the Curia. . . . The inordinate number of gratuities and exactions passed all bounds. Moreover, on all sides deeds were dishonestly manipulated, and even falsified, by the officials. No wonder that

there arose from all parts of Christendom the loudest complaints about the corruption and financial extortions of the papal officials.[32]

It was unusual for impecunious merit to mount in the Church of the fifteenth century. From the moderate fee charged for priestly ordination to the enormous sums that many cardinals paid for their elevation, nearly every appointment required the clandestine lubrication of superiors. A favorite papal device for raising funds was to sell ecclesiastical offices, or (as the popes saw the matter) to appoint to sinecures or honors, even to the cardinalate, persons who would make a substantial contribution to the expenses of the Church. Alexander VI created eighty new offices, and received 760 ducats ($19,000?) from each of the appointees. Julius II formed a "college" or bureau of 101 secretaries, who together paid him 74,000 ducats for the privilege. Leo X nominated sixty chamberlains and 141 squires to the papal household, and received from them 202,000 ducats.[33] The salaries paid to such officials were looked upon, by giver and recipient, as endowment policy annuities; but to Luther they seemed the rankest simony.

In thousands of cases the appointee lived far away from the benefice—the parish or abbacy or episcopacy—whose revenues supported his labor or luxury; and one man might be the absentee beneficiary of several such posts. So the active Cardinal Rodrigo Borgia (Alexander VI to be) received from a variety of benefices an income of 70,000 ducats ($1,750,000?) a year; and his furious foe, Cardinal della Rovere (later Julius II), held at one time the archbishopric of Avignon, the bishoprics of Bologna, Lausanne, Coutances, Viviers, Mende, Ostia, and Velletri, and the abbacies of Nonantola and Grottaferrata.[34] By this "pluralism" the Church maintained her major executives, and, in many instances, scholars, poets, and scientists. So Petrarch, sharp critic of the Avignon popes, lived on the sinecures that they granted him; Erasmus, who satirized a hundred ecclesiastical follies, regularly received Church pensions; and Copernicus, who did most damage to medieval Christianity, lived for years on Church benefices involving a minimum of distraction from his scientific pursuits.[35]

A more serious charge than pluralism was laid against the personal morality of the clergy. "The morals of the clergy are corrupt," said the Bishop of Torcello (1458); "they have become an offense to the laity."[36] Of the four orders of friars founded in the thirteenth century—Franciscans, Dominicans, Carmelites, Augustinians—all but the last had become scandalously lax in piety and discipline. The monastic rules formulated in the fervor of early devotion proved too rigorous for a human nature increasingly freed from supernatural fears. Absolved by their collective wealth from the necessity of manual labor, thousands of monks and friars neglected religious services, wandered outside their walls, drank in taverns, and pursued amours.[37] A fourteenth-century Dominican, John Bromyard, said of his fellow friars:

> Those who should be the fathers of the poor . . . covet delicate food and enjoy morning sleep. . . . Very few vouchsafe their presence at matins or Mass. . . . They are consumed in gluttony and drunkenness . . . not to say in uncleanliness, so that now the assemblies of clerics are thought to be brothels of wanton folk and congregations of play-actors.[38]

Erasmus repeated the charge after a century: "Many convents of men and women differ little from public brothels." [39] Petrarch drew a favorable picture of discipline and devotion in the Carthusian monastery where his brother lived, and several convents in Holland and Western Germany retained the spirit of study and piety that had formed the Brethren of the Common Life and produced *The Imitation of Christ*.[40] Yet Johannes Trithemius, Abbot of Sponheim (*c.* 1490), denounced the monks of this Rhenish Germany with violent hyperbole:

> The three vows of religion . . . are as little heeded by these men as if they had never promised to keep them. . . . The whole day is spent in filthy talk; their whole time is given to play and gluttony. . . . In open possession of private property . . . each dwells in his own private lodging. . . . They never fear nor love God; they have no thought of the life to come, preferring their fleshly lusts to the needs of the soul. . . . They scorn the vow of poverty, know not that of chastity, revile that of obedience. . . . The smoke of their filth ascends all around.[41]

Guy Jouenneaux, a papal commissary sent to reform the Benedictine monasteries of France, turned in a gloomy report (1503): Many monks gamble, curse, haunt inns, carry swords, gather riches, fornicate, "live the life of Bacchanals," and "are more worldly than the mere worldling. . . . Were I minded to relate all those things that have come under my own eyes, I should make too long a tale of it." [42] In the growing disorder of the monasteries a great number of them neglected those admirable works of charity, hospitality, and education which had entitled them to public trust and support.[43] Said Pope Leo X (1516): "The lack of rule in the monasteries of France and the immodest life of the monks have come to such a pitch that neither kings, princes, nor the faithful at large have any respect left for them." [44] A recent Catholic historian sums up the matter, as of 1490, with possibly excessive severity:

> Read the innumerable testimonies of this time—historical anecdotes, rebukes of moralists, satires of scholars and poets, papal bulls, synodal constitutions—what do they say? Always the same facts and the same complaints: the suppression of conventual life, of disci-

pline, of morals. . . . Prodigious is the number of monastic robbers and debauchees; to realize their disorders we must read the details revealed by judicial inquiry as to the internal state of the majority of the great abbeys. . . . The abuses among the Carthusians were so great that the order was in ill repute almost everywhere. . . . Monastic life had disappeared from the nunneries. . . . All contributed to transform these asylums of prayer into centers of dissipation and disorder.[45]

The secular clergy, if we take a lenient attitude toward concubinage, present a better picture than the friars and monks. The chief sin of the simple parish priest was his ignorance,[46] but he was too poorly paid and hard worked to have funds or time for study, and the piety of the people suggests that he was often respected and loved. Violations of the sacerdotal vow of chastity were frequent. In Norfolk, England, out of seventy-three accusations of incontinence filed in 1499, fifteen were against clergymen; in Ripon, out of 126, twenty-four; in Lambeth, out of fifty-eight, nine; i.e., clerical offenders numbered some 23 per cent of the total, though the clergy were probably less than 2 per cent of the population.[47] Some confessors solicited sexual favors from female penitents.[48] Thousands of priests had concubines; in Germany nearly all.[49] In Rome it was assumed that priests kept concubines; and some reports estimated the prostitutes there at 6,000 in a population not exceeding 100,000.[50] To quote again a Catholic historian:

> It is not surprising, when the highest ranks of the clergy were in such a state, that among the regular orders and secular priests vice and irregularities of all sorts should become more and more common. The salt of the earth had lost its savor. . . . But it is a mistake to suppose that the corruption of the clergy was worse in Rome than elsewhere; there is documentary evidence of the immorality of the priests in almost every town in the Italian peninsula. . . . No wonder, as contemporary writers sadly testify, the influence of the clergy had declined, and in many places hardly any respect was shown for the priesthood. Their immorality was so gross that suggestions in favor of allowing priests to marry began to be heard.[51]

In fairness to these lusty priests we should consider that sacerdotal concubinage was not profligacy, but an almost universal rebellion against the rule of celibacy that had been imposed upon an unwilling clergy by Pope Gregory VII (1074). Just as the Greek and Russian Orthodox Church, after the schism of 1054, had continued to permit marriage to its priests, so the clergy of the Roman Church demanded the same right; and since the canon law of their Church refused this, they took concubines. Bishop Hardouin of Angers reported (1428) that the clergy of his diocese did not count concubinage a sin, and that they made no attempt to disguise their use of it.[52] In Pomerania, about 1500, such unions were recognized by the people as reasonable, and were encouraged by them as protection for their daughters and wives; at public festivals the place of honor was given as a matter of course to priests and their consorts.[53] In Schleswig a bishop who tried to outlaw the practice was driven from his see (1499).[54] At the Council of Constance Cardinal Zabarella proposed that if sacerdotal concubinage could not be suppressed, clerical marriage should be restored. The Emperor Sigismund, in a message to the Council of Basel (1431), argued that the marriage of the clergy would improve public morals.[55] Aeneas Sylvius was quoted by the contemporary historian Platina, librarian of the Vatican, as saying that there were good reasons for clerical celibacy, but better reasons against it.[56] The moral record of the pre-Reformation priesthood stands in a better light if we view sacerdotal concubinage as a forgivable revolt against an arduous rule unknown to the Apostles and to the Christianity of the East.

The complaint that finally sparked the Reformation was the sale of indulgences. Through the powers apparently delegated by Christ to Peter (Matt. 16:19), by Peter to bishops, and by bishops to priests, the clergy were authorized to absolve a confessing penitent from the guilt of his sins and from their punishment in hell, but not from doing penance for them on earth. Now only a few men, however thoroughly shriven, could rely on dying with all due penances performed; the balance would have to be paid for by years of suffering in purgatory, which a merciful God had established as a temporary hell. On the other hand, many saints, by their devotion and martyrdom, had earned merits probably in excess of the penances due to their sins; Christ by his death had added an infinity of merits; these merits, said the theory of the Church, could be conceived as a treasury on which the pope might draw to cancel part or all of the temporal penalties incurred and unperformed by absolved penitents. Usually the penances prescribed by the Church had taken the form of repeating prayers, giving alms, making a pilgrimage to some sacred shrine, joining a crusade against Turks or other infidels, or donating money or labor to social projects like draining a swamp, building a road, bridge, hospital, or church. The substitution of a money fine (*Wehrgeld*) for punishment was a long-established custom in secular courts; hence no furore was caused by the early application of the idea to indulgences. A shriven penitent, by paying such a fine—i.e., making a money contribution—to the expenses of the Church, would receive a partial or plenary indulgence, not to commit further sins, but to escape a day, a month, a year in purgatory, or all the time he might have had to suffer there to complete his penance for his sins. An indulgence did not cancel the guilt of sins; this, when the priest absolved a contrite penitent, was forgiven in the confessional. An indulgence, therefore, was the remission, by the Church, of part or all of the temporal (i.e., not eternal) penalties incurred by sins whose guilt had been forgiven in the sacrament of penance.

This ingenious and complicated theory was soon transformed by the simplicity of the people, and by the greed of the *quaestiarii*, or "pardoners," commissioned or presuming to distribute the indulgences. As these purveyors were allowed to retain a percentage of the receipts, some of them omitted to insist on repentance, confession, and prayer, and left the recipient free to interpret the indulgence as dispensing him from repentance, confession, and absolution, and as depending almost entirely upon the money contribution. About 1450 Thomas Gascoigne, Chancellor of Oxford University, complained that

> sinners say nowadays: "I care not how many evils I do in God's sight, for I can easily get plenary remission of all guilt and penalty by an absolution and indulgence granted me by the pope, whose written grant I have bought for four or six pence, or have won as a stake for a game of tennis [with the pardoner]." For these indulgence-mongers wander over the country, and give a letter of pardon, sometimes for two pence, sometimes for a draught of wine or beer . . . or even for the hire of a harlot, or for carnal love.[57]

The popes—Boniface IX in 1392, Martin V in 1420, Sixtus IV in 1478—repeatedly condemned these misconceptions and abuses, but they were too pressed for revenue to practice effective control. They issued bulls so frequently, and for so confusing a variety of causes, that men of education lost faith in the theory, and accused the Church of shamelessly exploiting human credulity and hope.[58] In some cases, as in the indulgences offered by Julius II in 1510 or by Leo X in 1513, the official wording lent itself to the purely monetary interpretation.[59] A Franciscan friar of high rank described with anger how chests were placed in all the churches of Germany to receive payments by those who, having been unable to go to Rome for the jubilee of 1450, could now obtain the same plenary indulgence by money dropped in the box; and he warned the Germans, a half-century before Luther, that by indulgences and other means their savings were being drained off to Rome.[60] Even the clergy complained that indulgences were snaring into papal coffers contributions that might otherwise have been secured for local ecclesiastical uses.[61] Again a Catholic historian sums up the matter with admirable candor:

> Nearly all abuses connected with indulgences rose from this, that the faithful, after frequenting the sacrament of penance as the recognized condition for gaining the indulgence, found themselves called on to make an offering of money in proportion to their means. This offering for good works, which should have been only accessory, was in certain cases made into the chief condition. . . . The need of money, instead of the good of souls, became only too often the end of the i -

dulgence. . . . Though in the wording of the bulls the doctrine of the Church was never departed from, and confession, contrition, and definitely prescribed good works were made the condition for gaining the indulgence, still the financial side of the matter was always apparent, and the necessity for making offerings of money was placed most scandalously in the foreground. Indulgences took more and more the form of a monetary arrangement, which led to many conflicts with the secular powers, who were always demanding a share of the proceeds.[62]

Almost as mercenary as the sale of indulgences was the acceptance or solicitation, by the clergy, of money payments, grants, legacies, for the saying of Masses supposed to reduce a dead soul's term of punishment in purgatory. Large sums were devoted to this purpose by pious people, either to relieve a departed relative or friend, or to shorten or annul their own purgatorial probation after death. The poor complained that through their inability to pay for Masses and indulgences it was the earthly rich, not the meek, who would inherit the kingdom of heaven; and Columbus ruefully praised money because, he said, "he who possesses it has the power of transporting souls into paradise." [63]

A thousand other grievances swelled the case against the Church. Many of the laity resented the exemption of the clergy from the laws of the state, and the dangerous lenience of ecclesiastical courts to ecclesiastical offenders. The Nuremberg Diet of 1522 declared that no justice could be had by a lay plaintiff against a clerical defendant before a spiritual tribunal, and warned that unless the clergy were subjected to secular courts there would be an uprising against the Church in Germany; [64] the uprising, of course, had then already begun. Further complaints alleged the divorce of religion from morality, the emphasis laid on orthodox belief rather than on good conduct (though the Reformers were to be in this particular greater sinners than the Church), the absorption of religion in ritual, the useless idleness and presumed sterility of monks, the exploitation of popular credulity through bogus relics and miracles, the abuse of excommunication and interdict, the censorship of publications by the clergy, the espionage and cruelty of the Inquisition, the misuse, for other purposes, of funds contributed for crusades against the Turks, and the claim of a deteriorated clergy to be the sole administrators of every sacrament except baptism.

All the foregoing factors entered into the anticlericalism of Roman Catholic Europe at the beginning of the sixteenth century. "The contempt and hatred of the laity for the degenerate clergy," says Pastor, "was no mean factor in the great apostasy." [65] A London bishop complained in 1515 that the people "be so maliciously set in favor of heretical pravity that they will . . . condemn any cleric, though he were as innocent as Abel." [66] Among laymen, Erasmus reported, the title of clerk or priest or monk was a term of bitter insult.[67] In Vienna the priesthood, once the most desired of all careers, received no recruits in the twenty years preceding the Reformation.[68]

Throughout Latin Christendom men cried out for a "reform of the Church in head and members." Passionate Italians like Arnold of Brescia, Joachim of Flora, and Savonarola of Florence had attacked ecclesiastical abuses without ceasing to be Catholics, but two of them had been burned at the stake. Nevertheless, good Christians continued to hope that reform might be accomplished by the Church's loyal sons. Humanists like Erasmus, Colet, More, and Budé dreaded the disorder of an open break; it was bad enough that the Greek Church remained resolutely apart from the Roman; any further rending of "the seamless robe of Christ" threatened the survival of Christianity itself. The Church tried repeatedly, and often sincerely, to cleanse her ranks and her courts, and to adopt a financial ethic superior to the lay morality of the times. The monasteries tried again and again to restore their austere rules, but the constitution of man rewrote all constitutions. The councils tried to reform the Church, and were defeated by the popes; the popes tried, and were defeated by the cardinals and the bureaucracy of the Curia. Leo X himself, in 1516, mourned the utter inefficacy of these endeavors.[69] Enlightened churchmen like Nicholas of Cusa achieved local reforms, but even these were transient. Denunciations of the Church's shortcomings, by her enemies and her lovers, excited the schools, disturbed the pulpits, flooded the literature, mounted day by day, year by year, in the memory and resentment of men, until the dam of reverence and tradition burst, and Europe was swept by a religious revolution more far-reaching and profound than all the political transformations of modern times.

CHAPTER II

England: Wyclif, Chaucer, and the Great Revolt

1308-1400

I. THE GOVERNMENT

ON February 25, 1308, Edward II, sixth king of the house of Plantagenet, in a solemn coronation before the hierarchy and nobility assembled in Westminster Abbey, took the oath that England proudly requires of all her sovereigns:

> *Archbishop of Canterbury*: Sire, will you grant and keep, and by your oath confirm, to the people of England, the laws and customs to them granted by the ancient kings of England, your righteous and godly predecessors, and especially the laws, customs, and privileges granted to the clergy and people by the glorious King St. Edward your predecessor?
>
> *King*: I grant them and promise.
>
> *Archbishop*: Sire, will you keep toward God and Holy Church, and to clergy and people, peace and accord in God, entirely, after your power?
>
> *King*: I will keep them.
>
> *Archbishop*: Sire, will you cause to be done, in all your judgments, equal and right justice and discretion, in mercy and truth, to your power?
>
> *King*: I will do so.
>
> *Archbishop*: Sire, do you grant to hold and to keep the laws and righteous customs which the community of your realm shall have chosen, and will you defend and strengthen them to the honor of God, to the utmost of your power?
>
> *King*: I grant and promise.[1]

Having so sworn, and being duly anointed and consecrated with holy oils, Edward II consigned the government to corrupt and incompetent hands, and devoted himself to a life of frivolity with Piers Gaveston, his Ganymede. The barons rebelled, caught and slew Gaveston (1312), and subordinated Edward and England to their feudal oligarchy. Returning in disgrace from his defeat by the Scots at Bannockburn (1314), Edward solaced himself with a new love, Hugh le Despenser III. A conspiracy of his neglected wife, Isabella of France, and her paramour, Roger de Mortimer, deposed him (1326); he was murdered in Berkeley Castle by Mortimer's agent (1327); and his fifteen-year-old son was crowned as Edward III.

The noblest event of this age in English history was the establishment (1322) of a precedent that required the consent of a national assembly for the validity of any law. It had long been the custom of English monarchs, in their need, to summon a "King's Council" of prominent nobles and prelates. In 1295 Edward I, warring at once with France, Scotland, and Wales, and most earnestly desirous of cash and men, instructed "every city, borough, and leading town" to send two burgesses (enfranchised citizens), and every shire or county to send two knights (minor nobles), to a national assembly that would form, with the King's Council, the first English Parliament. The towns had money, which their delegates might be persuaded to vote to the king; the shires had yeomen (freeholders), who would make sturdy archers and pikemen; the time had come to build these forces into the structure of British government. There was no pretense at full democracy. Though the towns were—or by 1400 would be—free from feudal overlordship, the urban vote was confined to a small minority of propertied men. The nobles and clergy remained the rulers of England: they owned most of the land, employed most of the population as their tenants or serfs, and organized and directed the armed forces of the nation.

The Parliament (as it came to be called under Edward III) met in the royal palace at Westminster, across from the historic Abbey. The archbishops of Canterbury and York, the eighteen bishops, and the major abbots sat at the right of the king; half a hundred dukes, marquises, earls, viscounts, and barons sat on his left; the Prince of Wales and the King's Council gathered near the throne; and the judges of the realm, seated on woolsacks to remind them how vital the wool trade was to England, attended to advise on points of law. At the opening of the session the burgesses and knights— later known as the Commons—stood uncovered below a bar that separated them from the prelates and lords; now for the first time (1295) the national assembly had an Upper and a Lower House. The united houses received from the king or his chancellor a *pronunciatio* (the later "speech from the throne") explaining the subjects to be discussed and the appropriations desired. Then the Commons withdrew to meet in another hall—usually the chapter house of Westminster Abbey. There they debated the royal proposals. These deliberations ended, they delegated a "speaker" to report the result to the Upper House, and to present their petitions to the king. At the close of the sessions the two houses came together again to receive the reply of the sovereign, and to be dismissed by him. Only the king had the authority to summon or dissolve the Parliament.

Both houses claimed, and normally enjoyed, freedom of debate. In many cases they spoke or wrote their minds vigorously to the ruler; on several oc-·casions, however, he had a too audacious critic jailed. In theory the powers of Parliament extended to legislation; in practice most of the statutes passed had been presented as bills by the royal ministers; but the houses often submitted recommendations and grievances, and delayed the voting of funds till some satisfaction was obtained. The only weapon of the Commons was this "power of the purse"; but as the cost of administration and the wealth of the towns grew, the power of the Commons rose. The monarchy was neither absolute nor constitutional. The king could not openly and directly change a law made by Parliament or enact a new one; but through most of the year he ruled without a Parliament to check him, and issued executive decrees that affected every department of English life. He succeeded to the throne not by election but by pedigree. His person was accounted religiously sacred; obedience and loyalty to him were inculcated with all the force of religion, custom, law, education, and ceremonious oath. If this might not suffice, the law of treason directed that a captured rebel against the state should be dragged through the streets to the gallows, should have his entrails torn out and burned before his face, and should then be hanged.[2]

In 1330 Edward III, eighteen, took over the government, and began one of the most eventful reigns in the history of England. "His body was comely," says a contemporary chronicler, "and his face was like that of a god"; [3] till venery weakened him he was every inch a king. He almost ignored domestic politics, being a warrior rather than a statesman; he yielded powers to Parliament amiably so long as it financed his campaigns. Through his long rule he bled France white in the effort to add her to his crown. Yet there was chivalry in him, frequent gallantry, and such treatment of the captured French King John as would have graced King Arthur's court. After building the Round Tower of Windsor with the forced labor of 722 men, he held a Round Table there with his favorite knights; and he presided over many a chivalric joust. Froissart tells a story, unverified, of how Edward tried to seduce the lovely Countess of Salisbury, was courteously repulsed, and staged a tournament in order to feast his soul on her beauty again.[4] A charming legend tells how the Countess dropped a garter while dancing at court, and how the King snatched it up from the floor, and said, *Honi soit qui mal y pense*—"Shame to him who evil thinks of it." The phrase became the motto of that Order of the Garter which Edward founded toward 1349.

Alice Perrers proved less difficult than the Countess; though married, she yielded herself to the avid monarch, took large grants of land in return, and acquired such influence over him that Parliament registered a protest. Queen Philippa (says her fond pensioner Froissart) bore all this patiently, forgave him, and, on her deathbed, asked him only to fulfill her pledges to charity, and, "when it shall please God to call you hence, to choose no other sepulcher, but to lie by my side." [5] He promised "with tears in his eyes," returned to Alice, and gave her the Queen's jewelry.[6]

He waged his wars with energy, courage, and skill. War was then rated the highest and noblest work of kings; unwarlike rulers were despised, and three such in England's history were deposed. If one may venture a slight anachronism, a natural death was a disgrace that no man could survive. Every member of the European nobility was trained to war; he could advance in possessions and power only by proficiency and bravery in arms. The people suffered from the wars but, till this reign, had rarely fought in them; their children lost the memory of the suffering, heard old knightly tales of glory, and crowned with their choicest laurels those of their kings that shed the most alien blood.

When Edward proposed to conquer France, few of his councilors dared to advise conciliation. Only when the war had dragged on through a generation, and had burdened even the rich with taxes, did the national conscience raise a cry for peace. Discontent neared revolution when Edward's campaigns, passing from victory to failure, threatened the collapse of the nation's economy. Till 1370 Edward had profited in war and diplomacy from the wise and loyal service of Sir John Chandos. When this hero died, his place at the head of the King's Council was taken by Edward's son, the Duke of Lancaster, named John of Gaunt from the Gant or Ghent where he had been born. John carelessly turned the government over to political buccaneers who fattened their purses at the public expense. Demands for reform were raised in Parliament, and men of good will prayed for the nation's happy recovery through the King's speedy death. Another of his sons, the Black Prince—named probably from the color of his armor—might have brought new vigor to the government, but in 1376 he passed away while the old King lingered on. The "Good Parliament" of that year enacted some reform measures, put two malfeasants in jail, ordered Alice Perrers from court, and bound the bishops to excommunicate her if she returned. After the Parliament dispersed, Edward, ignoring its decrees, restored John of Gaunt to power and Alice to the royal bed; and no bishop dared reprove her. At last the obstinate monarch consented to die (1377). A son of the Black Prince succeeded to the throne as Richard II, a lad of eleven years, amid economic and political chaos, and religious revolt.

II. JOHN WYCLIF: 1320–84

What were the conditions that led England, in the fourteenth century, to rehearse the Reformation?

Probably the morals of the clergy played only a secondary role in the drama. The higher clergy had reconciled itself to celibacy; we hear of a Bishop Burnell who had five sons,[7] but presumably he was exceptional. Wyclif, Langland, Gower, and Chaucer agreed in noting a predilection, among monks and friars, for good food and bad women. But the Britons would hardly have created a national furore over such deviations, already hallowed by time, or about nuns who came to services with their dogs on leash and their pet birds on their arms,[8] or monks who raced through their incoherent prayers. (The humorous English assigned to Satan a special assistant to collect all syllables dropped by "graspers, leapers, gallopers, mumblers, fore-skippers, and fore-runners" in such syncopated devotions, and allotted the sinner a year in hell for each ignored or trampled syllable.[9])

What gnawed at the purse nerves of laity and government was the expanding and migratory wealth of the English Church. The clergy on several occasions contributed a tenth of their income to the state, but they insisted that no tax could be laid upon them without the consent of their convocations. Besides being represented in the Upper House of Parliament by their bishops and abbots, they gathered, directly or by proctors, in convocations under the archbishops of Canterbury and York, and determined there all matters dealing with religion or the clergy. It was usually from the ranks of the clergy, as the best-educated class in England, that the king chose the highest officials of the state. Suits of laymen against clergymen, touching Church property, were subject to the king's courts, but the bishops' courts had sole jurisdiction over tonsured offenders. In many towns the Church leased property to tenants and claimed full judicial authority over these tenants, even when they committed crimes.[10] Such conditions were irritating, but the major irritant was the flow of wealth from the English Church to the popes—i.e., in the fourteenth century, to Avignon—i.e., to France. It was estimated that more English money went to the pope than to the state or the king.[11]

An anticlerical party formed at the court. Laws were passed to make ecclesiastical property bear a larger and steadier share in the expenses of government. In 1333 Edward III refused to pay any longer the tribute that King John of England had pledged to the popes in 1213. In 1351 the Statute of Provisors sought to end papal control over the personnel or revenues of English benefices. The First Statute of Praemunire (1353) outlawed Englishmen who sued in "foreign" (papal) courts on matters claimed by the king to lie under secular jurisdiction. In 1376 the Commons officially complained that papal collectors in England were sending great sums of money to the pope, and that absentee French cardinals were drawing rich revenues from English sees.[12]

The anticlerical party at the court was led by John of Gaunt, whose protection enabled John Wyclif to die a natural death.

The first of the English reformers was born at Hipswell, near the village of Wyclif, in north Yorkshire about 1320. He studied at Oxford, became professor of theology there, and for a year (1360) was Master of Balliol College. He was ordained to the priesthood, and received from the popes various benefices or livings in parish churches, but continued meanwhile to teach at the University. His literary activity was alarming. He wrote vast Scholastic treatises on metaphysics, theology, and logic, two volumes of polemics, four of sermons, and a medley of short but influential tracts, including the famous *Tractatus de civili dominio*. Most of his compositions were in graceless and impenetrable Latin that should have made them harmless to any but grammarians. But hidden among these obscurities were explosive ideas that almost severed Britain from the Roman Church 155 years before Henry VIII, plunged Bohemia into civil war, and anticipated nearly all the reform ideas of John Huss and Martin Luther.

Putting his worse foot forward, and surrendering to Augustine's logic and eloquence, Wyclif built his creed upon that awful doctrine of predestination which was to remain even to our day the magnet and solvent of Protestant theology. God, wrote Wyclif, gives His grace to whomever He wishes, and has predestined each individual, an eternity before birth, to be lost or saved through all eternity. Good works do not win salvation, but they indicate that he who does them has received divine grace and is one of the elect. We act according to the disposition that God has allotted to us; to invert Heraclitus, our fate is our character. Only Adam and Eve had free will; by their disobedience they lost it for themselves and for their posterity.

God is sovereign lord of us all. The allegiance that we owe Him is direct, as is the oath of every Englishman to the king, not indirect through allegiance to a subordinate lord, as in feudal France. Hence the relationship of man to God is direct, and requires no intermediary; any claim of Church or priest to be a necessary medium must be repelled.[13] In this sense all Christians are priests, and need no ordination. God holds dominion over all the earth and the contents thereof; a human being can justly hold property only as His obedient vassal. Anyone who is in a state of sin—which constitutes rebellion against the Divine Sovereign—loses all right of possession, for rightful possession ("dominion") requires a state of grace. Now it is clear from Scripture that Christ intended His Apostles, their successors, and their ordained delegates to have no property. Any church or priest that owns property is violating the Lord's commandment, is therefore in a state of sin, and consequently cannot validly administer the sacraments. The reform most needed in Church and clergy is their complete renunciation of wordly goods.

As if this were not troublesome enough, Wyclif deduced from his theology a theoretical communism and anarchism. Any person in a state of grace shares with God the ownership of all goods; ideally everything should be held by the righteous in common.[14] Private property and government (as some Scholastic philosophers had taught) are results of Adam's sin (i.e., of human nature) and man's inherited sinfulness; in a society of universal virtue there would be no individual ownership, no man-made laws of either Church or state.[15] Suspecting that the radicals, who were at this time meditating revolt in England, would interpret this literally, Wyclif explained that his communism was to be understood only in an ideal sense; the powers that be, as Paul had taught, are ordained by God, and must be obeyed. This flirtation with revolution was almost precisely repeated by Luther in 1525.

The anticlerical party saw some sense, if not in Wyclif's communism, at least in his condemnation of ecclesiastical wealth. When Parliament again refused to pay King John's tribute to the pope (1366), Wyclif was engaged as *peculiaris regis clericus*—a cleric in the service of the king—to prepare a defense of the act.[16] In 1374 Edward III gave him the rectory of Lutterworth, apparently as a retaining fee.[17] In July 1376, Wyclif was appointed to the royal commission sent to Bruges to discuss with papal agents the continued refusal of England to pay the tribute. When John of Gaunt proposed that the government should confiscate part of the Church's property, he invited Wyclif to defend the proposal in a series of sermons in London; Wyclif complied (September 1376), and was thereafter branded by the clerical party as a tool of Gaunt. Bishop Courtenay of London decided to attack Gaunt indirectly by indicting Wyclif as a heretic. The preacher was summoned to appear before a council of prelates at St. Paul's in February 1377. He came, but accompanied by John of Gaunt with an armed retinue. The soldiers entered into a dispute with some spectators; a fracas ensued, and the bishop thought it discreet to adjourn. Wyclif returned unhurt to Oxford. Courtenay dispatched to Rome a detailed accusation quoting fifty-two passages from Wyclif's works. In May, Gregory XI issued bulls condemning eighteen propositions, mostly from the treatise *On Civil Dominion*, and ordered Archbishop Sudbury and Bishop Courtenay to inquire whether Wyclif still held these views; if he did they were to arrest him and keep him in chains pending further instructions.

By this time Wyclif had won the support not only of John of Gaunt and Lord Percy of Northumberland but of a large body of public opinion as well. The Parliament that met in October was strongly anticlerical. The argument for disendowment of the Church had charms for many members, who reckoned that if the King should seize the wealth now held by English bishops, abbots, and priors, he could maintain with it fifteen earls, 1,500 knights, 6,200 squires, and have £20,000 a year left for himself.[18] At this time France was preparing to invade England, and the English treasury was almost empty; how foolish it seemed to let papal agents collect funds from English parishes for a French pope and a college of cardinals overwhelmingly French! The King's advisers asked Wyclif to prepare an opinion on the question "Whether the Realm of England can legitimately, when the necessity of repelling invasion is imminent, withhold the treasure of the Realm that it be not sent to foreign parts, although the pope demand it under pain of censure and in virtue of obedience to him?" Wyclif answered in a pamphlet that in effect called for the severance of the English Church from the papacy. "The pope," he wrote. "cannot demand this treasure except by way of alms. ... Since all charity begins at home, it would be the work not of charity but of fatuity to direct the alms of the Realm abroad when the Realm itself is in need of them." Against the contention that the English Church was part of, and should obey, the universal or Catholic Church, Wyclif recommended the ecclesiastical independence of England. "The Realm of England, in the words of Scripture, ought to be one body, and clergy, lords, and commonalty members of that body." [19] This anticipation of Henry VIII seemed so bold that the King's advisers directed Wyclif to make no further statements on the matter.

The Parliament adjourned on November 28. On December 18 the embattled bishops published the condemnatory bulls, and bade the chancellor of Oxford to enforce the Pope's order of arrest. The university was then at the height of its intellectual independence. In 1322 it had assumed the right to depose an unsatisfactory chancellor without consulting its formal superior, the Bishop of Lincoln; in 1367 it had thrown off all episcopal control. Half of the faculty supported Wyclif, at least in his right to express his opinions. The chancellor refused to obey the bishops, and denied the authority of any prelate over the university in matters of belief; meanwhile he counseled Wyclif to remain in modest seclusion for a while. But it is a rare reformer who can be silent. In March 1378, Wyclif appeared before the bishops' assembly at Lambeth to defend his views. As the hearing was about to begin, the Archbishop received a letter from the mother of King Richard II deprecating any final condemnation of Wyclif; and in the midst of the proceedings a crowd forced its way in from the street and declared that the English people would not tolerate any Inquisition in England. Yielding to this combination of government and populace, the bishops deferred decision, and again Wyclif went home unhurt—indeed, triumphant. On March 27 Gregory XI died, and a few months later the Papal Schism divided and weakened the papacy, and the whole authority of the Church. Wyclif resumed the offensive, and issued tract after tract, many in English, extending his heresies and revolt.

He is pictured to us in these years as a man hardened by controversy and made puritan by age. He was no mystic; rather, a warrior and an organizer; and perhaps he carried his logic to merciless extremes. His talent for vituperation now disported itself freely. He denounced the friars for preaching poverty and accumulating collective wealth. He thought some monasteries were "dens of thieves, nests of serpents, houses of living devils." [20] He challenged the theory that the merits of the saints could be applied to the rescue of souls from purgatory; Christ and the Apostles had taught no doctrine of indulgences. "Prelates deceive men by feigned indulgences or pardons, and rob them cursedly of their money. . . . Men be great fools that buy these bulls of pardon so dear." [21] If the pope had the power to snatch souls from purgatory, why did he not in Christian charity take them out at once? [22] With mounting vehemence Wyclif alleged that "many priests . . . defile wives, maidens, widows, and nuns in every manner of lechery," [23] and demanded that the crimes of the clergy should be punishable by secular courts. He excoriated curates who flattered the rich and despised the poor, who easily forgave the sins of the wealthy but excommunicated the indigent for unpaid tithes, who hunted and hawked and gambled, and related fake miracles.[24] The prelates of England, he charged, "take poor men's livelihood, but they do not oppose oppression"; they "set more price by the rotten penny than by the precious blood of Christ"; they pray only for show, and collect fees for every religious service that they perform; they live in luxury, riding fat horses with harness of silver and gold; "they are robbers . . . malicious foxes . . . ravishing wolves . . . gluttons . . . devils . . . apes"; [25] here even Luther's language is forecast. "Simony reigns in all states of the Church. . . . The simony of the court of Rome does most harm, for it is most common, and under most color of holiness, and robs most our land of men and treasure." [26] The scandalous rivalry of the popes (in the Schism), their bandying of excommunications, their unashamed struggle for power, "should move men to believe in popes only so far as these follow Christ." [27] A pope or a priest "is a lord, yea, even a king," in matters spiritual; but if he assumes earthly possessions, or political authority, he is unworthy of his office. "Christ had not whereon to rest His head, but men say this pope hath more than half the Empire. . . . Christ was meek . . . the pope sits on his throne and makes lords to kiss his feet." [28] Perhaps, Wyclif gently suggested, the pope is the Antichrist predicted in the First Epistle of the Apostle John,[29] the Beast of the Apocalypse,[30] heralding the second coming of Christ.[31]

The solution of the problem, as Wyclif saw it, lay in separating the Church from all material possessions and power. Christ and his Apostles had lived in poverty; so should his priests.[32] The friars and monks should return to the full observance of their rules, avoiding all property or luxury;[33] priests "should with joy suffer temporal lordship to be taken from them"; they should content themselves with food and clothing, and live on freely given alms.[34] If the clergy will not disendow themselves by a voluntary return to evangelical poverty, the state should step in and confiscate their goods. "Let lords and kings mend them" and "constrain priests to hold to the poverty that Christ ordained." [35] Let not the king, in so doing, fear the curses of the pope, for "no man's cursing hath any strength but inasmuch as God Himself curseth." [36] Kings are responsible to God alone, from Whom they derive their dominion. Instead of accepting the doctrine of Gregory VII and Boniface VIII that secular governments must be subject to the Church, the state, said Wyclif, should consider itself supreme in all temporal matters and should take control of all ecclesiastical property. Priests should be ordained by the king.[37]

The power of the priest lay in his right to administer the sacraments. Wyclif turned to these with a full anticipation of Luther and Calvin. He denied the necessity of auricular confession, and advocated a return to the voluntary public confession favored by the early Christians. "Privy confession made to priests . . . is not needful, but brought in late by the Fiend; for Christ used it not, nor any of His Apostles after Him." [38] It now makes men thralls to the clergy, and is sometimes abused for economic or political ends; and "by this privy shriving a friar and a nun may sin together." [39] Good laymen may absolve a sinner more effectively than wicked priests; but in truth only God can absolve. In general we should doubt the validity of a sacrament administered by a sinful or heretical priest. Nor can a priest, good or bad, change the bread and wine of the Eucharist into the physical body and blood of Christ. Nothing seemed to Wyclif more abominable than the thought that some of the priests whom he knew could perform such a God-creating miracle.[40] Like Luther, Wyclif denied transubstantiation, but not the Real Presence; by a mystery that neither pretended to explain, Christ was made "spiritually, truly, really, effectively" present, but along with the bread and wine, which did not (as the Church taught) cease to exist.[41]

Wyclif would not admit that these ideas were heretical, but this theory of "consubstantiality" alarmed some of his supporters. John of Gaunt hurried over to Oxford, and urged his friend to say no more about the Eucharist (1381). Wyclif rejected the advice, and reaffirmed his views in a *Confessio* dated May 10, 1381. A month later social revolution flared out in England, and frightened all property owners into discountenancing any doctrine that threatened any form of property, lay or ecclesiastical. Wyclif now lost most of his backing in the government, and the assassination of Archbishop Sudbury by the rebels promoted his most resolute enemy, Bishop Courtenay, to the primacy of England. Courtenay felt that if Wyclif's conception of the Eucharist were allowed to spread, it would undermine the prestige of the clergy, and therefore also the foundation of the Church's moral authority. In May 1382, he summoned a council of clergy to meet at the Blackfriars' Convent in London. Having persuaded this assembly to condemn twenty-four propositions which he read from Wyclif's works, he sent a peremptory command to the chancellor of Oxford to restrain the author from any further teaching or preaching until his orthodoxy should be proved. King Richard II, as part of his reaction to the uprising that had almost deposed him, ordered the chancellor to expel Wyclif and all his adherents. Wyclif retired to his living at Lutterworth, apparently still protected by John of Gaunt.

Embarrassed by the admiration expressed for him by the priest John Ball, a chief protagonist of the revolt, Wyclif issued several tracts dissociating himself from the rebels; he disclaimed any socialist views, and urged his followers to submit patiently to their terrestrial lords in the firm hope of recompense after death.[42] Nevertheless he continued his pamphleteering against the Church, and organized a body of "Poor Preaching Priests" to spread his Reformation among the people. Some of these "Lollards" * were men of meager schooling, some were Oxford dons. All went robed in black wool and barefoot, like the early friars; all were warmed with the ardor of men who had rediscovered Christ. Theirs was already the Protestant emphasis on an infallible Bible as against the fallible traditions and dogmas of the Church, and on the sermon in the vernacular as against a mystic ritual in a foreign tongue.[48] For these lay priests, and for their literate hearers, Wyclif wrote in rough and vigorous English some 300 sermons and many religious tracts. And since he urged a return to the Christianity of the New Testament, he set himself and his aides to translate the Bible as the sole and unerring guide to true religion. Till that time (1381) only small portions of Scripture had been rendered into English; a French translation was known to the educated classes, and an Anglo-Saxon version, unintelligible to Wyclif's England, had come down from King Alfred's time. The Church, finding that heretics like the Waldensians made much use of the Bible, had discouraged the people from reading unauthorized translations,[44] and had deprecated the creedal chaos that she expected when every party should make and color its own translation, and every reader be free to make his own interpretation, of the Scriptural text. But Wyclif was resolved that the Bible should be available to any Englishman who could read. He appears to have translated the New Testament himself, leaving the Old Testament to Nicholas Hereford and John Purvey. The whole was finished some ten years after Wyclif's death.

* Probably from Middle Dutch *lollaerd*, from *lollen*, to mutter, murmur, mumble (prayers?); cf. *lull*.

The translation was made from Jerome's Latin version, not from the Hebrew of the Old Testament or the Greek of the New. It was not a model of English prose, but it was a vital event in English history.

In 1384 Pope Urban VI summoned Wyclif to appear before him in Rome. A different summons exceeded it in authority. On December 28, 1384, the ailing reformer suffered a paralytic stroke as he was attending Mass, and three days later he died. He was buried in Lutterworth, but by a decree of the Council of Constance (May 4, 1415) his bones were dug up and cast into a near-by stream.[45] Search was made for his writings, and as many as were found were destroyed.

All the major elements of the Reformation were in Wyclif: the revolt against the worldliness of the clergy, and the call for a sterner morality; the return from the Church to the Bible, from Aquinas to Augustine, from free will to predestination, from salvation by works to election by divine grace; the rejection of indulgences, auricular confession, and transubstantiation; the deposition of the priest as an intermediary between God and man; the protest against the alienation of national wealth to Rome; the invitation to the state to end its subordination to the papacy; the attack (preparing for Henry VIII) on the temporal possessions of the clergy. If the Great Revolt had not ended the government's protection of Wyclif's efforts, the Reformation might have taken form and root in England 130 years before it broke out in Germany.

III. THE GREAT REVOLT: 1381

England and Wales had in 1307 a population precariously estimated at 3,000,000—a slow increase from a supposed 2,500,000 in 1066.[46] The figures suggest a sluggish advance of agricultural and industrial techniques—and an effective control of human multiplication by famine, disease, and war—in a fertile but narrow island never meant to sustain with its own resources any great multitude of men. Probably three fourths of the people were peasants, and half of these were serfs; in this regard England lagged a century behind France.

Class distinctions were sharper than on the Continent. Life seemed to re-volve about two foci: gracious or arrogant lordship at one end, hopeful or resentful service at the other. The barons, aside from their limited duties to the king, were masters of all they surveyed, and of much beyond. The dukes of Lancaster, Norfolk, and Buckingham had estates rivaling those of the Crown, and the Nevilles and Percys had hardly less. The feudal lord bound his vassal knights and their squires to serve and defend him and wear his "livery." * Nevertheless one might rise from class to class; a rich merchant's daughter could catch a noble and a title, and Chaucer, reborn, would have been startled to find his granddaughter a duchess. The middle classes assumed such manners of the aristocracy as they could manage; they began to address one another as *Master* in England, *Mon seigneur* in France; soon every man was a *Mister* or *Monsieur*, and every woman a *Mistress* or *Madame*.†

Industry progressed faster than agriculture. By 1300 almost all the coal-fields of Britain were being worked; silver, iron, lead, and tin were mined, and the export of metals ranked high in the nation's foreign trade; it was a common remark that "the kingdom is of greater value under the land than above." [47] The woolen industry began in this century to make England rich. The lords withdrew more and more lands from the common uses formerly allowed to their serfs and tenants, and turned large tracts into sheep en-closures; more money could be made by selling wool than by tilling the land. The wool merchants were for a time the wealthiest traders in England, able to yield great sums in loans and taxes to Edward III, who ruined them. Tired of seeing raw wool go from England to feed the clothing industry of Flan-ders, Edward (1331 f.) lured Flemish weavers to Britain, and through their instruction established a textile industry there. Then he forbade the export of wool and the import of most foreign cloth. By the end of the fourteenth century the manufacture of clothing had replaced the trade in wool as the main source of England's liquid wealth and had reached a semi-capitalistic stage.

The new industry required the close co-operation of many crafts—weav-ing, fulling, carding, dyeing, finishing; the old craft guilds could not arrange the disciplined collaboration needed for economical production; enterprising masters—entrepreneurs—gathered diverse specializations of labor into one organization, which they financed and controlled. However, no such factory system arose here as in Florence and Flanders; most of the work was still done in small shops by a master, his apprentices, and a few journeymen, or in little rural mills using water power, or in country homes where patient fingers plied the loom when household chores allowed. The craft guilds fought the new system with strikes, but its superior productivity overrode all opposition; and the workers who competed to sell their toil and skill were increasingly at the mercy of men who furnished capital and management. Town proletarians "lived from hand to mouth . . . indifferently clad and housed, in good times well fed, but in bad times not fed at all." [48] All male

---

* Livery was originally, in Anglo-French, *livrée*, a delivery or allowance of provisions or clothing, made by a lord to a vassal. In time the clothing took on the character of a uniform worn by the clients of a great man in the pomp of his retinue. Guilds adopted the custom and proudly wore their distinctive livery at their meetings and in their parades. Such habits gave color to "Merrie England."

† The last two titles have undergone further evolution.

inhabitants of English cities were subject to conscription of their labor for public works, but rich men could pay for substitutes.[49] Poverty was bitter, though probably less extreme than in the early nineteenth century. Beggars abounded, and organized to protect and govern their profession. Churches, monasteries, and guilds provided a limping charity.

Upon this scene the Black Death burst as not only a catastrophic visitation but almost as an economic revolution. The English people lived in a climate more favorable to vegetation than to health; the fields were green the year round, but the population suffered from gout, rheumatism, asthma, sciatica, tuberculosis, dropsy, and diseases of eyes and skin.[50] All classes ate a heavy diet and kept warm with alcoholic drinks. "Few men now reach the age of forty," said Richard Rolle about 1340, "and fewer still the age of fifty." [51] Public sanitation was primitive; the stench of tanneries, pigsties, and latrines sullied the air; only the well-to-do had running water piped into their homes; the majority fetched it from conduits or wells and could not waste it on weekly baths.[52] The lower classes offered ready victims for the pestilences that periodically decimated the population. In 1349 the bubonic plague crossed from Normandy to England and Wales, and thence a year later into Scotland and Ireland; it returned to England in 1361, 1368, 1375, 1382, 1390, 1438, 1464; all in all it carried away one Englishman out of every three.[53] Nearly half the clergy died; perhaps some of the abuses later complained of in the English Church were due to the necessity of hastily impressing into her service men lacking the proper qualifications of training and character. Art suffered; ecclesiastical building almost stopped for a generation. Morals suffered; family ties were loosed, sexual relations overflowed the banks within which the institution of marriage sought to confine them for social order's sake. The laws lacked officers to enforce them, and were frequently ignored.

The plague collaborated with war to quicken the decline of the manorial system. Many peasants, having lost their children or other aides, deserted their tenancies for the towns; landowners were obliged to hire free workers at twice the former wage, to attract new tenants with easier terms than before, and to commute feudal services into money payments. Themselves forced to pay rising prices for everything that they bought, the landlords appealed to the government to stabilize wages. The Royal Council responded (June 18, 1349) with an ordinance substantially as follows:

> Because a great part of the People, and especially of Workers and Servants, late died of the pestilence, and many . . . will not serve unless they receive excessive wages, and some rather willing to beg in idleness than by Labour to get their Living; We, considering the grievous Discommodity which, of the lack especially of Plowmen and such Labourers, may hereafter come, have upon deliberation and treaty

with the Prelates and the Nobles, and Learned Men assisting us, of their mutual Counsel ordained:

1. Every person able in Body and under the Age of sixty Years, not having [wherewith] to live, being required, shall be bound to serve him that doth require him, or else [be] committed to the Gaol, until he find Surety to serve.

2. If a Workman or Servant depart from Service before the time agreed upon, he shall be imprisoned.

3. The old Wages, and no more, shall be given to Servants. . . .

5. If any Artificer or Workman take more wages than were wont to be paid, he shall be committed to the Gaol. . . .

6. Victuals shall be sold at reasonable prices.

7. No person shall give anything to a Beggar that is able to labour.[54]

This ordinance was so widely disregarded by employers and employees that Parliament issued (February 9, 1351) a Statute of Labourers, specifying that no wages should be paid above the 1346 rate, fixing definite prices for a large number of services and commodities, and establishing enforcement machinery. A further act of 1360 decreed that peasants who left their lands before the term of their contract or tenancy expired might be brought back by force, and, at the discretion of the justices of the peace, might be branded on the brow.[55] Similar measures, of increasing severity, were enacted between 1377 and 1381. Wages rose despite them, but the strife so engendered between laborers and government inflamed the conflict of classes, and lent new weapons to the preachers of revolt.

The rebellion that ensued had a dozen sources. Those peasants who were still serfs demanded freedom; those who were free called for an end to feudal dues still required of them; and tenants urged that the rent of land should be lowered to four pence ($1.67?) per acre per year. Some towns were still subject to feudal overlords, and longed for self-government. In the liberated communities the workingmen hated the mercantile oligarchy, and journeymen protested against their insecurity and poverty. All alike—peasants, proletarians, even parish priests—denounced the governmental mismanagement of Edward III's last years, of Richard II's earliest; they asked why English arms had so regularly been beaten after 1369, and why such heavy taxes had been raised to finance such defeats. They particularly abominated Archbishop Sudbury and Robert Hales, the chief ministers of the young king, and John of Gaunt as the front and protector of governmental corruption and incompetence.

The Lollard preachers had little connection with the movement, but they had shared in preparing minds for the revolt. John Ball, the intellectual of the rebellion, quoted Wyclif approvingly, and Wat Tyler followed Wyclif in demanding disendowment of the Church. Ball was the "mad priest of

Kent" (as Froissart called him) who taught communism to his congregation, and was excommunicated in 1366.[56] He became an itinerant preacher, denouncing the wicked wealth of prelates and lords, calling for a return of the clergy to evangelical poverty, and making fun of the rival popes who, in the Schism, were dividing the garments of Christ.[57] Tradition ascribed to him a famous couplet:

> *When Adam delved and Eve span*
> *Who was then the gentleman?* [58]

—i.e., when Adam dug in the earth and Eve plied the loom, were there any class divisions in Eden? Froissart, though so fond of the English aristocracy, quoted Ball's alleged views at sympathetic length:

> My good friends, matters cannot go on well in England until all things shall be in common; when there shall be neither vassals nor lords, when the lords shall be no more masters than ourselves. How ill they behave to us! For what reason do they thus hold us in bondage? Are we not all descended from the same parents, Adam and Eve? And what can they show why they should be more masters than ourselves? ... We are called slaves, and if we do not perform our service we are beaten. .... Let us go to the King and remonstrate with him; he is young, and from him we may obtain a favorable answer; and if not we must ourselves seek to amend our condition.[59]

Ball was thrice arrested, and when the revolt broke out he was in jail.

The poll tax of 1380 capped the discontent. The government was nearing bankruptcy, the pledged jewels of the king were about to be forfeited, the war in France was crying out for new funds. A tax of £100,000 ($10,000,-000?) was laid upon the people, to be collected from every inhabitant above the age of fifteen. All the diverse elements of revolt were united by this fresh imposition. Thousands of persons evaded the collectors, and the total receipts fell far short of the goal. When the government sent new commissioners to ferret out the evaders, the populace gathered in force and defied them; at Brentwood the royal agents were stoned out of the town (1381), and like scenes occurred at Fobbing, Corringham, and St. Albans. Mass meetings of protest against the tax were held in London; they sent encouragement to the rural rebels, and invited them to march upon the capital, to join the insurgents there, and "so press the King that there should no longer be a serf in England." [60]

A group of collectors entering Kent met a riotous repulse. On June 6, 1381, a mob broke open the dungeons at Rochester, freed the prisoners, and plundered the castle. On the following day the rebels chose as their chief Wat Tegheler, or Tyler. Nothing is known of his antecedents; apparently he was an ex-soldier, for he disciplined the disorderly horde into united action, and won its quick obedience to his commands. On June 8 this swelling multi-tude, armed with bows and arrows, cudgels, axes, and swords, and receiving recruits from almost every village in Kent, attacked the homes of unpopular landlords, lawyers, and governmental officials. On June 10 it was welcomed into Canterbury, sacked the palace of the absent Archbishop Sudbury, opened the jail, and plundered the mansions of the rich. All eastern Kent now joined in the revolt; town after town rose, and local officials ran be-fore the storm. Rich men fled to other parts of England, or concealed them-selves in out-of-the-way places, or escaped further damage by making a contribution to the rebel cause. On June 11 Tyler turned his army toward London. At Maidstone it delivered John Ball from jail; he joined the caval-cade, and preached to it every day. Now, he said, would begin that reign of Christian democracy which he had so long dreamed of and pled for; all social inequalities would be leveled; there would no longer be rich and poor, lords and serfs; every man would be a king.[61]

Meanwhile related uprisings occurred in Norfolk, Suffolk, Beverly, Bridgewater, Cambridge, Essex, Middlesex, Sussex, Hertford, Somerset. At Bury St. Edmund the people cut off the head of the prior, who had too stoutly asserted the feudal rights of the abbey over the town. At Colchester the rioters killed several Florentine merchants who were believed to be cut-ting in on British trade. Wherever possible they destroyed the rolls, leases, or charters that recorded feudal ownership or bondage; hence the townsfolk of Cambridge burned the charters of the University; and at Waltham every document in the abbey archives was committed to the flames.

On June 11 a rebel army from Essex and Hertford approached the north-ern outskirts of London; on the twelfth the Kent insurgents reached South-wark, just across the Thames. No organized resistance was offered by the adherents of the King. Richard II, Sudbury, and Hales hid in the Tower. Tyler sent the King a request for an interview; it was refused. The mayor of London, William Walworth, closed the city gates, but they were re-opened by revolutionists within the town. On June 13 the Kent forces marched into the capital, were welcomed by the people, and were joined by thousands of laborers. Tyler held his host fairly well in leash, but ap-peased its fury by allowing it to sack the palace of John of Gaunt. Nothing was stolen there; one rioter who tried to filch a silver goblet was killed by the crowd. But everything was destroyed; costly furniture was thrown out of the windows, rich hangings were torn to rags, jewelry was smashed to bits; then the house was burned to the ground, and some jolly rebels who had drunk themselves to stupor in the wine cellar were forgotten and con-sumed in the flames. Thereafter the army turned on the Temple, citadel of the lawyers of England; the peasants remembered that lawyers had written the deeds of their servitude, or had assessed their holdings for taxation; there too they made a holocaust of the records, and burned the buildings to the ground. The jails in Newgate and the Fleet were destroyed, and the happy inmates joined the mob. Wearied with its efforts to crowd a century of revenge into a day, the multitudes lay down in the open spaces of the city, and slept.

That evening the King's Council thought better of its refusal to let him talk with Tyler. They sent an invitation to Tyler and his followers to meet with Richard the next morning at a northern suburb known as Mile End. Shortly after dawn on June 14 the fourteen-year-old King, risking his life, rode out of the Tower with all of his council except Sudbury and Hales, who dared not expose themselves. The little party made its way through the hostile crowd to Mile End, where the Essex rebels were already gathered; part of the Kent army followed, with Tyler at its head. He was surprised at the readiness of Richard to grant nearly all demands. Serfdom was to be abolished throughout England, all feudal dues and services were to end, the rental of the tenants would be as they had asked; and a general amnesty would absolve all those who had shared in the revolt. Thirty clerks were at once set to work drawing up charters of freedom and forgiveness for all districts that applied. One demand the King refused—that the royal ministers and other "traitors" should be surrendered to the people. Richard replied that all persons accused of misconduct in government would be tried by orderly process of law, and would be punished if found guilty.

Not satisfied with this answer, Tyler and a selected band rode rapidly to the Tower. They found Sudbury singing Mass in the chapel. They dragged him out into the courtyard and forced him down with his neck on a log. The executioner was an amateur, and required eight strokes of the ax to sever the head. The insurgents then beheaded Hales and two others. Upon the Archbishop's head they fixed his miter firmly with a nail driven into the skull; they mounted the heads on pikes, carried them in procession through the city, and set them up over the gate of London Bridge. All the remainder of that day was spent in slaughter. London tradesmen, resenting Flemish competition, bade the crowd kill every Fleming found in the capital. To determine the nationality of a suspect he was shown bread and cheese and bidden name them; if he answered *brod und käse*, or spoke with a Flemish brogue, he forfeited his life. Over 150 aliens—merchants and bankers—were slain in London on that day in June, and many English lawyers, tax collectors, and adherents of John of Gaunt fell under the axes and hatchets of indiscriminate vengeance. Apprentices murdered their masters, debtors their creditors. At midnight the sated victors again retired to rest.

Informed of these events, the King returned from Mile End and went, not to the Tower, but to his mother's rooms near St. Paul's. Meanwhile a large number of the Essex and Hertford contingents, rejoicing in their charters of freedom, dispersed toward their homes. On June 15 the King sent a modest message to the remaining rebels asking them to meet him in the open spaces of Smithfield outside Aldersgate. Tyler agreed. Before keeping this rendezvous, Richard, fearing death, confessed and took the Sacrament; then he rode out with a retinue of 200 men whose peaceful garb hid swords. At Smithfield Tyler came forward with only a single companion to guard him. He made new demands, uncertainly reported, but apparently including the confiscation of Church property and the distribution of the proceeds among the people.[62] A dispute ensued; one of the King's escort called Tyler a thief; Tyler directed his aide to strike the man down; Mayor Walworth blocked the way; Tyler stabbed at Walworth, whose life was saved by the armor under his cloak; Walworth wounded Tyler with a short cutlass, and one of Richard's squires ran Tyler through twice with a sword. Tyler rode back to his host crying treason, and fell dead at their feet. Shocked by what seemed to them plain treachery, the rebels set their arrows and prepared to shoot. Though their numbers were reduced, they were still a substantial force, reckoned by Froissart at 20,000; probably they could have overwhelmed the King's retinue. But Richard now rode out bravely toward them, crying out, "Sirs, will you shoot your king? I will be your chief and captain; you shall have from me that which you seek. Only follow me into the fields without." He rode out slowly, not sure that they would heed or spare him. The insurgents hesitated, then followed him, and most of the royal guard mingled in their midst.

Walworth, however, turned sharply back, galloped into the city, and sent orders to the aldermen of its twenty-four wards to join him with all the armed forces they could muster. Many citizens who at first had sympathized with the revolt were now disturbed by the murders and pillage; every man who had any property felt his goods and his life to be in peril; so the Mayor found an impromptu army of 7,000 men rising at his command as if out of the earth. These he led back to Smithfield; there he rejoined and surrounded the King, and offered to massacre the rebels. Richard refused; the rebels had spared him when he was at their mercy, and he would not now show himself less generous. He announced to them that they were free to depart in safety. The Essex and Hertford remnants rapidly melted away; the London mutineers disappeared into their haunts; only the Kent contingent stayed. Their passage through the city was blocked by Walworth's armed men, but Richard ordered that no one should molest them; they marched off in safety, and filed back in disorder along the Old Kent Road. The King returned to his mother, who greeted him with tears of happy relief. "Ah, fair son, what pain and anguish have I had for you this day!" "Certes, Madam," the boy answered. "I know it well. But now rejoice and praise God, for today I have recovered my heritage that was lost, and the realm of England too." [63]

Fig. 1—POL DE LIMBURG: *The Month of October*, a miniature from *Les Très Riches Heures du Duc de Berry*.
Musée Condé, Chantilly

Fig. 3—HUBERT AND JAN VAN EYCK: *The Virgin,* detail from *The Adoration of the Lamb.* Church of St. Bavon, Ghent

PAGE 131

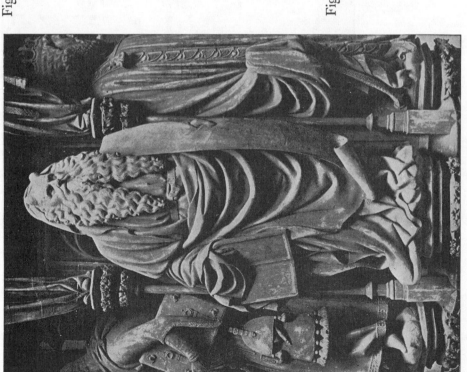

Fig. 2—CLAUS SLUTER: *Moses.* Museum, Dijon

PAGE 131

Fig. 4—Hubert and Jan van Eyck: *The Adoration of the Lamb*. Church of St. Bavon, Ghent

PAGE 131

Fig. 5—*King's College Chapel* (interior), Cambridge   PAGE 119

Fig. 6—*Chapel of Henry
VII*, Westminster
Abbey, London
PAGE 838

Fig. 7—*House of Jacques
Cœur*, Bourges
PAGE 79

Fig. 8—ROGIER VAN DER WEYDEN: *Portrait of a Lady*. National Gallery of Art, Washington, D.C. (Mellon Collection)

PAGE 134

Fig. 9—MATTHIAS GRÜNE-WALD: *The Crucifixion*, detail from the *Isenheim Altarpiece*. Museum, Colmar

PAGE 310

Fig. 10—ALBRECHT DÜRER: *Portrait of Hieronymus Holzschuher.* Kaiser Friedrich Museum, Berlin

PAGE 314

Fig. 11—HANS HOLBEIN THE YOUNGER: *Erasmus.* Louvre, Paris

PAGE 290

Fig. 12—ALBRECHT DÜRER: *The Four Apostles* (at left: John and Peter; at right: Mark and Paul). Haus der Kunst, Munich

PAGE 318

Fig. 13—LUCAS CRANACH: *Martin Luther*. The John G. Johnson Art Collection, Philadelphia

PAGE 836

Fig. 14—*Luther Memorial*, Worms

PAGE 361

Fig. 15—ALBRECHT DÜRER: *Philip Melanchthon*. Museum of Fine Arts, Boston

PAGE 349

Fig. 16—RENÉ BOYVIN: *Calvin*. Bibliothèque Publique et Universitaire, Geneva

PAGE 476

Fig. 17–*Reformation Monument*, Geneva   PAGE 489

Fig. 18–*Chateau of Francis I*, Chambord   PAGE 824

Fig. 19–*Gallery of Francis I*, Fontainebleau   PAGE 825

Fig. 20—*Church of St. Maclou*, Rouen

Fig. 21—TITIAN: *Charles V at Mühlberg*. Prado, Madrid
PAGE 454

Fig. 22—MICHEL CO-LOMBE: *St. George and the Dragon*. Louvre, Paris
PAGE 98

Fig. 23—JEAN GOUJON: *Water Nymphs*, from *Fountain of the Innocents*. Louvre, Paris

Fig. 24–JEAN CLOUET: *Francis I*. Louvre, Paris

PAGE 830

Probably under the prodding of the Mayor who had saved him, Richard on that same June 15 issued a proclamation banishing from London, on pain of death, all persons who had not lived there for a year past. Walworth and his troops searched streets and tenements for such aliens, caught many, killed several. Among these was one Jack Straw, who confessed, presumably under torture, that the men of Kent had planned to make Tyler king. In the meantime a deputation from the Essex insurgents arrived at Waltham and demanded of the King a formal ratification of the promises he had made on June 14. Richard replied that these had been made under duress, and that he had no intention of keeping them; on the contrary, he told them, "Villeins you are still, and villeins you shall remain"; and he threatened dread vengeance on any man who continued in armed rebellion.[64] The angry deputies called upon their followers to renew the revolt; some did, but these were cut down with great slaughter by Walworth's men (June 28).

On July 2 the embittered King revoked all charters and amnesties granted by him during the outbreak, and opened the way to a judicial inquiry into the identity and actions of the main participants. Hundreds were arrested and tried; 110 or more were put to death. John Ball was caught at Coventry; he fearlessly avowed his leading role in the insurrection, and refused to ask pardon of the King. He was hanged, drawn, and quartered; and his head, with those of Tyler and Jack Straw, replaced those of Sudbury and Hales as adornments of London Bridge. On November 13 Richard laid before Parliament an account of his actions; if, he said, the assembled prelates and lords and commons wished the serfs to be freed, he was quite willing. But the members were nearly all landowners; they could not admit the right of the King to dispose of their property; they voted that all existing feudal relations should be maintained.[65] The beaten peasants returned to their plows, the sullen workers to their looms.

IV. THE NEW LITERATURE

The English language was becoming by slow stages a fit vehicle for literature. The Norman invasion of 1066 had stopped the evolution of Anglo-Saxon into English, and for a time French was the official language of the realm. Gradually a new vocabulary and idiom formed, basically Germanic, but mingled and adorned with Gallic words and turns. The long war with France may have spurred the nation to rebel against this linguistic domination by an enemy. In 1362 English was declared to be the language of law and the courts; and in 1363 the chancellor set a precedent by opening Parliament with an English address. Scholars, chroniclers, and philosophers (even till Francis Bacon) continued to write in Latin to reach an international audience, but poets and dramatists henceforth spoke the speech of England.

The oldest drama extant in English was a "mystery"—a dramatic representation of a religious story—performed in the Midlands, about 1350, under the title of *The Harrowing of Hell*, which staged a duel in words, at the mouth of hell, between Satan and Christ. In the fourteenth century it became customary for the guilds of a town to present a cycle of mysteries: a guild would prepare a scene, usually from the Bible, carry the setting and the actors on a float, and act the scenes on temporary stages built at populous centers in the city; and on successive days other guilds would present later scenes from the same Biblical narrative. The earliest such cycle now known is that of the Chester mysteries of 1328; by 1400 similar cycles were presented in York, Beverly, Cambridge, Coventry, Wakefield, Towneley, and London. As early as 1182 the Latin mysteries had developed a variety called the "miracle," centering around the miracle or sufferings of some saint. About 1378 another variety appeared—the "morality" —which pointed a moral by acting a tale; this form would reach its peak in *Everyman* (*c.* 1480). Early in the fifteenth century we hear of still another dramatic form, doubtless then already old: the interlude, not a play between plays but a *ludus*—a play or show—carried on between two or more actors. Its subject was not restricted to religion or morality, but might be secular, humorous, profane, even obscene. Minstrel troupes played interludes in baronial or guild halls, in town or village squares, or in the courtyard of a frequented inn. In 1348 Exeter raised the first-known English theater, the first European building, since classic Roman structures, specifically and regularly devoted to dramatic representations.[66] From the interludes would evolve the comedies, and from the mysteries and moralities would develop the tragedies, of the lusty Elizabethan stage.

The first major poem—one of the strangest and strongest poems—in the English language called itself *The Vision of William Concerning Piers the Plowman*. Nothing is known of the author except through his poem; assuming that this is autobiographical, we may name him William Langland and place his birth near 1332. He took minor orders, but never became a priest; he wandered to London and earned something short of starvation by singing Psalms at Masses for the dead. He lived dissolutely, sinned with "covetousness of eyes and concupiscence of the flesh," had a daughter, perhaps married her mother, and dwelled with them in a hovel in Cornhill. He describes himself as a tall, gaunt figure, dressed in a somber robe befitting the gray disillusionment of his hopes. He was fond of his poem, issued it thrice (1362, 1377, 1394), and each time spun it out to greater length. Like the Anglo-Saxon poets, he used no rhyme, but alliterative verse of irregular meter.

He begins by picturing himself as falling asleep on a Malvern hill, and seeing in a dream a "field full of folk"—multitudes of rich, poor, good, bad, young, old—and amid them a fair and noble lady whom he identifies with Holy Church. He kneels before her and begs for "no treasure, but tell me how I may save my ʳoul." She replies:

> When all treasures are tried, Truth is best. . . .
> Whoso is true of his tongue, and telleth naught but that,

> And doeth the works therewith, and willeth no man ill,
> He is a god by the gospel . . . and like to Our Lord.[67]

In a second dream he visions the Seven Deadly Sins, and under each head he indicts the wickedness of man in a powerful satire. For a time he abandons himself to cynical pessimism, awaiting an early end of the world. Then Piers (Peter) the Plowman enters the poem. He is a model farmer, honest, friendly, generous, trusted by all, working hard, living faithfully with his wife and children, and always a pious son of the Church. In later visions William sees the same Piers as the human Christ, as Peter the Apostle, as a pope, then as vanishing in the Papal Schism and the advent of Antichrist. The clergy, says the poet, are no longer a saving remnant; many of them have become corrupt; they deceive the simple, absolve the rich for a consideration, traffic in sacred things, sell heaven itself for a coin. What is a Christian to do in such a universal debacle? He must, says William, go forth again, over all intervening institutions and corruptions, and seek the living Christ Himself.[68]

Piers the Plowman contains its quota of nonsense, and its obscure allegories weary any reader who lays upon authors the moral obligation to be clear. But it is a sincere poem, flays rascals impartially, pictures the human scene vividly, rises through touches of feeling and beauty to a place second only to the *Canterbury Tales* in the English literature of the fourteenth century. Its influence was remarkable; Piers became for the rebels of England a symbol of the righteous, fearless peasant; John Ball recommended him to the Essex insurgents of 1381; as late as the Reformation his name was invoked in criticizing the old religious order and demanding a new.[69] In ending his visions, the poet returned from Piers the pope to Piers again the peasant; if all of us, he concluded, were, like Piers, simple, practicing Christians, that would be the greatest, the final revolution; no other would ever be needed.

John Gower is a less romantic poet and figure than the mysterious Langland. He was a rich landowner of Kent who imbibed too much scholastic erudition, and achieved dullness in three languages. He, too, attacked the faults of the clergy; but he trembled at the heresies of the Lollards, and marveled at the insolence of peasants who, once content with beer and corn, now demanded meat and milk and cheese. Three things, said Gower, are merciless when they get out of hand: water, fire, and the mob. Disgusted with this world, worried about the next, "moral Gower" retired in old age to a priory, and spent his closing year in blindness and prayer. His contemporaries admired his morals, regretted his temper and his style, and turned with relief to Chaucer.

V. GEOFFREY CHAUCER: 1340–1400

He was a man full of the blood and beer of Merrie England, capable of taking in his stride the natural difficulties of life, drawing their sting with a forgiving humor, and picturing all phases of the English scene with a brush as broad as Homer's, a spirit as lusty as Rabelais'.

His name, like so much of his language, was of French origin; it meant shoemaker, and probably was pronounced *shosayr;* posterity plays tricks with our very names, and remembers us only to remake us to its whim. He was the son of John Chaucer, a London vintner. He won a good education from both books and life; his poetry abounds in knowledge of men and women, literature and history. In 1357 "Geoffret Chaucer" was officially listed in the service of the household of the future Duke of Clarence. Two years later he was off to the wars in France; he was captured, but was freed for a ransom, to which Edward III contributed. In 1367 we find him a "yeoman of the King's Chamber," with a life pension of twenty marks ($1,333?) a year. Edward traveled much with his household at his heels; presumably Chaucer accompanied him, savoring England as he went. In 1366 he married Philippa, a lady serving the Queen, and lived with her in moderate discord till her death.[70] Richard II continued the pension, and John of Gaunt added ten pounds ($1,000?) annually. There were other aristocratic gifts, which may explain why Chaucer, who saw so much of life, took little notice of the Great Revolt.

It was a pleasant custom of those days, which admired poetry and eloquence, to send men of letters on diplomatic missions abroad. So Chaucer was deputed with two others to negotiate a trade agreement at Genoa (1372); and in 1378 he went with Sir Edward Berkeley to Milan. Who knows but he may have met ailing Boccaccio, aging Petrarch? In any case, Italy was a transforming revelation to him. He saw there a culture far more polished, lettered, and subtle than England's; he learned a new reverence for the classics, at least the Latin; the French influence that had molded his early poems yielded now to Italian ideas, verse forms, and themes. When finally he turned to his own land for his scenes and characters, he was an accomplished artist and a mature mind.

No man could then live in England by writing poetry. We might have supposed that Chaucer's pensions would keep him adequately housed, fed, and clad; after 1378 they totaled some $10,000 in the money of our time; besides, his wife enjoyed her own pensions from John of Gaunt and the King. In any case, Chaucer felt a need to supplement his income by taking various governmental posts. For twelve years (1374–86) he served as "controller of the customs and subsidies," and during that time he occupied lodgings over the Aldgate tower. In 1380 he paid an unstated sum to Cecilia Chaumpaigne for withdrawing her suit against him for rape.[71] Five years later he was appointed justice of the peace for Kent; and in 1386 he had himself elected to Parliament. It was in the intervals of these labors that he wrote his poetry.

He describes himself, in *The House of Fame*, as hurrying home after he had "made his reckonings," and losing himself in his books, sitting "dumb as a stone," and living like a hermit in all but poverty, chastity, and obedience, and setting his "wit to make books, songs, and ditties in rime." In his youth, he tells us, he had written "many a song and lecherous lay." [72] He translated Boethius' *De consolatione philosophiae (The Consolation of Philosophy)* into good prose, and part of Guillaume de Lorris' *Romaunt de la rose* into excellent verse. He began a number of what may be called major minor poems: *The House of Fame, The Book of the Duchess, The Parliament of Fowls,* and *The Legend of Good Women;* he anticipated us in being unable to finish them. They were ambitious yet timid tentatives, frank imitations, in theme and form, of Continental origins.

In his finest single poem, *Troilus and Criseyde,* he continued to imitate, even to translate; but to 2,730 lines that he lifted from Boccaccio's *Filostrato* he added 5,696 lines of other provenance or coined in his own mint. He made no attempt to deceive; he repeatedly referred to his source, and apologized for not translating it all. Such transfers from one literature to another were considered legitimate and useful, for even well-educated men could not then understand any vernacular but their own. Plots, as Greek and Elizabethan dramatists felt, were common property; art lay in the form.

Despite all discounts, Chaucer's *Troilus* is the first great narrative poem in English. Scott called it "long and somewhat dull," which it is; Rossetti called it "perhaps the most beautiful narrative poem of considerable length in the English language"; [73] and this too is true. All long poems, however beautiful, become dull; passion is of poetry's essence, and a passion that runs to 8,386 lines becomes prose almost as rapidly as desire consummated. Never were so many lines required to bring a lady to bed, and seldom has love hesitated, meditated, procrastinated, and capitulated with such magnificent and irrelevant rhetoric, and melodious conceits, and facile felicity of rhyme. Only Richardson's Mississippi of prose could rival this Nile of verse in the leisurely psychology of love. Yet even the heavy-winged oratory, the infinite wordiness, the obstructive erudition obstinately displayed, fail to destroy the poem. It is, after all, a philosophic tale—of how woman is designed for love, and will soon love B if A stays too long away. It has one character livingly portrayed: Pandarus, who in the *Iliad* is the leader of the Lycian army in Troy, but here becomes the exuberant, resourceful, undiscourageable go-between to guide the lovers to their sin; and thereby hangs a word. Troilus is a warrior absorbed in repelling the Greeks, and scornful of men who, dallying on soft bosoms, become the thralls of appetite. He falls deliriously in love with Criseyde at first sight, and thereafter thinks of nothing else but her beauty, modesty, gentleness, and grace. Criseyde, after waiting anxiously through 6,000 lines for this timid soldier to announce his love, falls with relief into his arms, and Troilus forgets two worlds at once:

> All other dredes weren from him fledde,
> Both of the siege and his salvacioun.[74]

Having exhausted himself in achieving this ecstasy, Chaucer hurries over the bliss of the lovers to the tragedy that rescues it from boredom. Criseyde's father having deserted to the Greeks, she is sent to them by the angry Trojans in exchange for the captured Antenor. The brokenhearted lovers part with vows of everlasting fidelity. Arrived among the Greeks, Criseyde is awarded to Diomedes, whose handsome virility so captivates his captive that—*qual plum' in vento*—she surrenders in a page what before had been hoarded through a book. Perceiving which, Troilus plunges into battle seeking Diomedes, and finds death on Achilles' spear. Chaucer ended his amorous epic with a pious prayer to the Trinity, and sent it, conscience-stricken, to "moral Gower, to correct of your benignitee."

Probably in 1387 he began *The Canterbury Tales*. It was a brilliant scheme—to join a varied group of Britons at the Tabard Inn in Southwark (where Chaucer himself had emptied many a tankard of ale), ride with them on their vacation pilgrimage to the shrine of Becket at Canterbury, and put into their mouths the tales and thoughts that had gathered in the traveled poet's head through half a century. Such devices for stitching stories together had been used many times before, but this was the best of all. Boccaccio had assembled for his *Decameron* only one class of men and women; he had not made them stand out as diverse personalities; Chaucer created an innful of characters so heterogeneously real that they seem truer to English life than the stuffed figures of history. They live and very literally move, they love and hate, laugh and cry; and as they jog along the road we hear not merely the tales they tell but their own troubles, quarrels, and philosophies.

Who will protest at quoting once more those spring-fresh opening lines?

> Whan that Aprille with his shoures sote
> The droghte of Marche hath perced to the rote,
> And bathed every veyne in swich licour,
> Of which vertu engendred is the flour,
> Whan Zephyrus eek with his swete breeth
> Inspired hath in every holt and heeth
> The tendre croppes, and the yonge sonne
> Hath in the Ram his halfe cours y-ronne,
> And smale fowles maken melodye,
> That slepen al the night with open yë; ...
> Thanne longen folk to goon on pilgrimages ...
> To ferne halwes, couthe in sondry londes ...

> In Southwerk at the Tabard as I lay
> Redy to wenden on my pilgrimage
> To Canterbury with ful devout corage,
> At night was come in-to that hostelrye
> Wel nyne and twenty in a companye,
> Of sondry folk, by aventure y-falle
> In felawshipe, and pilgrims were they alle,
> That toward Canterbury wolden ryde.*

Then, one after another, Chaucer introduces them in the quaint sketches of his incomparable Prologue:

> A Knyght ther was, and that a worthy man,
> That fro the tyme that he first bigan
> To ryden out, he loved chivalrye,
> Trouthe and honour, fredom and curteisye . . .
> At mortal batailles hadde he been fiftene,
> And foughten for our feith at Tramissene . . .
> And though that he were worthy, he was wys,
> And of his port as meke as is a mayde.
> He never yet no vileinye ne sayde
> In al his lyf, unto no maner wight;
> He was a verray parfit gentil knyght.

And the Knight's son:

> . . . a yong Squyer,
> A lovyere, and a lusty bacheler . . .
> So hote he lovede, that by nightertale [count of nights]
> He sleep namore than dooth a nightingale.

And a Yeoman to serve the Knight and the Squire; and a most charming Prioress:

> Ther was also a Nonne, a Pioresse,
> That of hir smyling was ful simple and coy;
> Hir gretteste ooth was by sëynt Loy [St. Louis];
> And she was cleped madame Eglentyne.
> Ful wel she song the service divyne,
> Entuned in hir nose ful semely . . .
> She was so charitable and pitous
> She wolde wepe, if that she sawe a mous
> Caught in a trappe, if it were deed or bledde.
> Of smale houndes had she, that she fedde
> With rosted flesh or milk and wastel-breed;

---

* Sote is sweet; rote, root; eek, also; holt, farm; yë, eye; ferne, distant; halwes (hallows), shrines; couthe, known. In scanning Chaucer's lines most now silent e's are pronounced, as in French verse; and many words of French lineage (matter, courage, honor, voyage, pleasant, etc.) are accented on the final syllable.

> But sore weep she if oon of hem were deed . . .
> Of smal coral aboute her arm she bar
> A peire of bedes, gauded al with grene;
> And ther-on heng a broche of gold ful shene,
> On which ther was first write a crowned A,
> And after, *Amor vincit omnia* [Love conquers all].

Add another nun, three priests, a jolly monk "that lovede venerye" (i.e., hunting), and a friar unmatched in squeezing contributions out of pious purses:

> For thogh a widow hadde noght a sho [shoe],
> So plesaunt was his *In principio*,
> Yet wolde he have a ferthing, er he wente.

Chaucer likes better the young student of philosophy:

> A Clerk ther was of Oxenford also,
> That un-to logik hadde longe y-go.
> As lene was his hors as is a rake,
> And he nas nat right fat, I undertake;
> But loked holwe, and ther-to soberly.
> Ful thredbar was his overest courtepy,
> For he had geten him yet no benefyce,
> Ne was so worldly for to have offyce.
> For him was lever have at his beddes heed
> Twenty bokes, clad in black or reed,
> Of Aristotle and his philosophye,
> Than robes riche, or filthele, or gay sautrye . . .
> Of studie took he most cure and most heed.
> Noght o word spak he more than was nede . . .
> Souninge in moral vertu was his speche,
> And gladly wolde he lerne, and gladly teche.*

There was also a "Wife of Bath," of whom more anon, and a poor Parson, "riche of holy thoght and werke," and a Plowman, and a Miller, who "hade on the cop [top] of his nose a werte, and ther-on stood a tuft of heres reed as the bristles of a sowes eres"; and a "Maunciple" or buyer for an inn or a college; a "Reeve" or overseer for a manor; and a "Somnour" or server of summonses:

> He was a gentil harlot [rogue] and a kinde;
> A bettre felawe sholde men noght finde.
> He wolde suffre, for a quart of wyn,
> A good felawe to have his concubyn
> A twelf-month, and excuse him atte fulle.

---

* Nas was not; holwe, hollow, thin; courtepy, short coat; sautrye, psaltery or harp; souninge, sounding.

With him

> .. rood a gentil Pardoner ...
> His wallet lay biforn him in his lappe,
> Bret [brim] ful of pardouns come from Rome al hoot [hot].

And there was a Merchant, and a Man of Laws, a "Frankeleyn" or free-holder, a Carpenter, a Weaver, a Dyer, a "Tapier" or upholsterer, a Cook, and a Shipman. And there was Geoffrey Chaucer himself, standing shyly aside, "large" (fat) and difficult to embrace, and "looking forever upon the ground as if to find a hare." And not least was mine host, owner of the Tabard Inn, who vows he has never entertained so merry a company; indeed, he offers to go with them and be their guide; and he suggests—to pass the fifty-six miles away—that each of the pilgrims shall tell two tales going and two on the return, and that he who tells the best "shal have a super at our aller cost" (a supper at the general expense) when they reach the inn again. It is agreed; the moving scene of this *comédie humaine* is set; the pilgrimage begins; and the courtly Knight tells the first story—of how two dear friends, Palamon and Arcite, see a lass gathering flowers in a garden, fall equally in love with her, and contend in a fatal joust for her as the complaisant prize.

Who would believe that so romantic a pen could turn in a line from this chivalric fustian to the scatophilic obscenity of the Miller's Tale? But the Miller has been drinking, and foresees that his mind and tongue will slip to their wonted plane; Chaucer apologizes for him and himself—he must report matters honestly—and he invites the chaste reader to skip to some story "that toucheth gentillesse . . . moralitee, and holinesse." The Prioress's Tale begins on a sweetly religious note, then recounts the bitter legend of a Christian boy supposedly slain by a Jew, and how the provost of the town dutifully arrested its Jews and tortured a number of them to death. From such piety Chaucer passes, in the prologue to the Pardoner's Tale, to a sharp satire on relic-mongering peddlers of indulgences; this theme will be centuries old when Luther trumpets it to the world. Then, in the prologue to the Wife of Bath's Tale, our poet reaches the nadir of his morals and the zenith of his power. It is a riotous protest against virginity and celibacy, put into the bawdy mouth of an expert on matrimony, a woman who has had five husbands since she was twelve years of age, has buried four of them, and looks forward to a sixth to assuage her youth:

> God bad us for to waxe and multiplye ...
> But of no nombre mencioun made he,
> Of bigamy or of octogamye;
> Why sholde men speke of it vilainye?
> Lo, here the wyze king, dan [lord] Salomon,
> I trowe he hadde wyves mo than oon;

> As, wolde God, it leveful were to me
> To be refresshed half so ofte as he! . . .
> Alas, alas, that ever love was synne!

We shall not quote her physiological confessions, nor their masculine counterpart in the Somnour's Tale, wherein Chaucer stoops to study the anatomy of flatulence. The air is cleared when we come to the fable of the ever obedient Griselda in the Oxford Cleric's Tale; neither Boccaccio nor Petrarch had told so well this legend dreamed by some harassed male.

Of the fifty-eight stories promised in the Prologue Chaucer gives us only twenty-three; perhaps he felt, with the reader, that 500 pages were enough, and that the well of his inventiveness had run dry. Even in this bubbling stream there are muddy passages, which the judicious eye will overleap. Nevertheless, the slow, deep current carries us buoyantly along and gives forth an air of freshness as if the poet had lived along green banks rather than over a London gate—though there, too, the Thames was not far to seek. Some of the paeans to outdoor beauty are stereotyped literary exercises, yet the moving picture comes alive with such naturalness and directness of feeling and speech, such revealing firsthand observation of men and manners, as rarely may be found between the covers of one book; and such a cornucopia of images, similes, and metaphors as only Shakespeare would again provide. (The Pardoner "mounts the pulpit, nods east and west upon the congregation like a dove on a barn gable.") The East Midland dialect that Chaucer used became through him the literary language of England: a vocabulary already rich enough to express all graces and subtleties of thought. Now for the first time the speech of the English people became the vehicle of great literary art.

The material, as in Shakespeare, is mostly secondhand. Chaucer took his stories anywhere: the Knight's Tale from Boccaccio's *Teseide*, Griselda from the *Decameron*, and a dozen from the French *fabliaux*. The last source may explain some of Chaucer's obscenity; however, the most fetid of his tales has no known source but himself. Doubtless he held, with the Elizabethan dramatists, that the groundlings must be given a bawdy sop now and then to keep them awake; he made his men and women talk as matched their rank and way of life; besides, he repeats, they had drunk much cheap ale. For the most part his humor is healthy—the hearty, lusty, full-bodied humor of well-fed Englishmen before the Puritan desiccation, marvelously mixed with the sly subtlety of modern British wit.

Chaucer knew the faults, sins, crimes, follies, and vanities of mankind, but he loved life despite them, and could put up with anybody who did not sell buncombe too dearly. He seldom denounces; he merely describes. He satirizes the women of the lower middle classes in the Wife of Bath, but he relishes her biological exuberance. He is ungallantly severe on women; his mordant quips and slurs reveal the wounded husband revenging with his pen the nightly defeats of his tongue. Yet he speaks tenderly of love, reckons no other boon so rich,[75] and fills a gallery with portraits of good women. He rejects the gentility that rested on birth, and calls only him "gentil that doth gentil deeds." But he distrusts the fickleness of the commons, and counts any man a fool who hitches his fortunes to popularity or mingles with a mob.

He was largely free from the superstitions of his time. He exposed the impostures of alchemists, and though some of his storytellers bring in astrology, he himself rejected it. He wrote for his son a treatise on the astrolabe, showing a good grasp of current astronomic lore. He was not a very learned man, for he liked to display his learning; he swells his pages with large patches of Boethius, and makes even the Wife of Bath quote Seneca. He mentions some problems of philosophy and theology, but shrugs his shoulders at them helplessly. Perhaps he felt, like any man of the world, that a prudent philosopher will not wear his metaphysics on his sleeve.

Was he a believing Christian? Nothing could exceed the ruthlessness and coarseness of his satire on the friars in the prologue and body of the Somnour's Tale; such darts, however, had more than once been aimed at the brothers by men of orthodox piety. Here and there he raises a doubt of some religious dogma: no more than Luther could he harmonize divine foreknowledge with man's free will; [76] he makes Troilus expound determinism, but in an epilogue he rejects it. He affirms his belief in heaven and hell, but notes at some length that those are bournes from which no attesting traveler returns.[77] He is disturbed by evils apparently irreconcilable with an omnipotent benevolence, and makes Arcite question the justice of the gods with reproaches as bold as Omar Khayyám's:

> O cruel goddes, that governe
> This world with binding of your word eterne,
> And wryten in the table of athamaunt [adamant]
> Your parlement, and your eterne graunt,
> What is mankind more un-to yow holde [your estimation]
> Than is the sheep that rouketh [huddles] in the folde?
> For slayn is man right as another beste,
> And dwelleth eke in prison and areste,
> And hath sicknesse, and great adversitee,
> And ofte tymes giltiless, pardee!
> What governaunce is in this prescience,
> That giltinesse tormenteth innocence? . . .
> And when a beest is dead he hath no peyne,
> But man, after his death, must weep and pleyne . . .
> Th'answere of this I lete to divynis [divines].[78]

In later years he tried to recapture the piety of his youth. To the unfinished *Canterbury Tales* he appended a "Preces de Chaucer." or Prayer of Chaucer, begging forgiveness from God and man for his obscenities and worldly vanities, and proposing "unto my lyves ende . . . to biwayle my giltes, and to study to the salvacioun of my soule."

In those last years his joy in life yielded to the melancholy of a man who in the decay of health and sense recalls the carefree lustiness of youth. In 1381 he was appointed by Richard II "Clerk of our Works at our Palace of Westminster" and other royal residences. Ten years later, though he was little more than fifty, his health seems to have broken down; in any case, his tasks proved too much for his strength, and he was relieved of his office. We do not find him in any later employment. His finances failed, and he was reduced to asking the King for six shillings eight pence.[79] In 1394 Richard granted him a pension of twenty pounds a year for life. It was not enough; he asked the King for a yearly hogshead of wine, and received it (1398); and when, in that year, he was sued for a debt of fourteen pounds he could not pay it.[80] He died on October 25, 1400, and was buried in Westminster Abbey, the first and greatest of the many poets who there again bear the beat of measured feet.*

VI. RICHARD II

"For God's sake let us sit upon the ground and tell sad stories of the death of kings." [81]

"Richard II," says Holinshed, "was seemely of shape and favour, and of nature good enough, if the wickednesse and naughtie demeanour of such as were about him had not altered it. . . . He was prodigal, ambitious, and much given to pleasure of the bodie." [82] He loved books, and helped Chaucer and Froissart. He had shown courage, presence of mind, and judicious action in the Great Revolt; but after that enervating crisis he lapsed into enervating luxury and left the government to wasteful ministers. Against these men a powerful opposition formed, led by Thomas, Duke of Gloucester, Richard, Earl of Arundel, and Henry Bolingbroke, grandson of Edward III. This faction dominated the "Merciless Parliament" of 1388, which impeached and hanged ten of Richard's aides. In 1390 the King, still a youth of twenty-three, took active charge, and for seven years he governed constitutionally —i.e., in harmony with the laws, traditions, and chosen representatives of the nation.

The death of Richard's Bohemian Queen Anne (1394) deprived him of a wholesome and moderating influence. In 1396 he married Isabelle, daugh-

---

* His burial there may have been due not to his poetry but to his being at his death a tenant of Abbey property.

ter of Charles VI, in the hope of cementing peace with France; but as she was a child of only seven years, he spent his substance on male and female favorites. The new Queen brought a French retinue to London, and these brought French manners, perhaps French theories of absolute monarchy. When the Parliament of 1397 sent Richard a bill of complaint against the extravagance of his court, he replied haughtily that such matters were outside the jurisdiction of Parliament. He demanded the name of the member who had proposed the complaint; Parliament, cowed, condemned the proponent to death; Richard pardoned him.

Soon thereafter Gloucester and Arundel suddenly left London. Suspecting a plot to depose him, the King ordered their arrest. Arundel was beheaded, Gloucester was smothered to death (1397). In 1399 John of Gaunt died, leaving a rich estate; Richard, needing funds for an expedition to Ireland, confiscated the Duke's property, to the horror of the aristocracy. While the King was restoring peace in Ireland, Gaunt's exiled son and disinherited heir, Henry Bolingbroke, landed in York with a small army that rapidly grew, as powerful nobles joined his cause. On returning to England, Richard found his reduced forces so outnumbered, friends falling away from him in panic, that he surrendered his person and throne to Bolingbroke, who was crowned as Henry IV (1399). So ended the Plantagenet dynasty that had begun with Henry II in 1154; so began the Lancastrian dynasty that would end with Henry VI in 1461. Richard II died in prison at Pontefract (1400), aged thirty-three, perhaps from the winter rigor of his confinement, possibly slain, as Holinshed and Shakespeare thought, by servants of the new King.

CHAPTER III

France Besieged

1300-1461

I. THE FRENCH SCENE

THE France of 1300 was by no means the majestic realm that today reaches from the Channel to the Mediterranean, and from the Vosges and Alps to the Atlantic. On the east it reached only to the Rhone. In the southwest a large area—Guienne and Gascony—had been added to the English crown by the marriage of Henry II to Eleanor of Aquitaine (1152); in the north England had taken the county of Ponthieu, with Abbeville; and though the English kings held these lands as fiefs of the French monarchs, they maintained over them an effectual sovereignty. Provence, the Dauphiné, and Franche-Comté ("free county") belonged to the Holy Roman Empire, whose heads were usually Germans. The French kings ruled indirectly, through their close kin, the princely appanages of Valois, Anjou, Bourbon, and Angoulême. They ruled directly, as royal domains, Normandy, Picardy, Champagne, Poitou, Auvergne, most of Languedoc, and the Ile-de-France the "island" of north central France centering about Paris. Artois, Blois, Nevers, Limoges, Armagnac, and Valentinois were governed by feudal lords who alternately lip-served and fought the kings of France. Brittany, Burgundy, and Flanders were French fiefs, but they were, as Shakespeare called them, "almost kingly dukedoms," behaving as virtually independent states. France was not yet France.

The most vital and volatile of the French fiefs at the opening of the fourteenth century was the county of Flanders. In all Europe north of the Alps only Flanders rivaled Italy in economic development. Its boundaries fluctuated confusingly in time and space; let us denote it as the region enclosing Bruges, Ghent, Ypres, and Courtrai. East of the Scheldt lay the duchy of Brabant, then including Antwerp, Mechlin (Malines), Brussels, Tournai, and Louvain. To the south of Flanders lay the independent bishoprics of Liége and Cambrai, and the county of Hainaut, around Valenciennes. Used loosely, "Flanders" included Brabant, Liége, Cambrai, and Hainaut. On the north were seven little principalities roughly composing the Holland of today. These Dutch regions would not reach their flowering till the seventeenth century, when their empire would stretch, so to speak, from

Rembrandt to Batavia. But already in 1300 Flanders and Brabant throbbed with industry, commerce, and class war. A canal twelve miles long joined Bruges to the North Sea; a hundred vessels sailed it every day, bringing merchandise from a hundred ports in three continents; Aeneas Sylvius ranked Bruges among the three most beautiful cities in the world. The goldsmiths of Bruges made up an entire division of the town's militia; the weavers of Ghent provided twenty-seven regiments of its armed forces, which totaled 189,000 men.

The medieval guild organization, which had dowered the craftsman with the dignity of freedom and the pride of skill, was now giving way, in the textile and metal industries of Flanders and Brabant, to a capitalist system * in which an employer supplied capital, materials, and machinery to shopworkers paid by the piece and no longer protected by the guild. Admission to a guild became ever costlier; thousands of workers became journeymen —day laborers—who went from town to town, from shop to shop, getting only temporary employment, with wages that forced them to live in slums and left them little property beyond the clothes they wore.[1] Communistic ideas appeared among *prolétaires* and peasants; the poor asked why they should go hungry while the barns of barons and bishops creaked with grain; and all men who did not work with their hands were denounced as parasites. The employers in their turn complained of the risks their investments ran, the uncertainty and periodicity of supplies, the foundering of their cargoes, the fluctuations of the market, the tricks of competitors, and the repeated strikes that raised wages and prices, unsettled the currency, and narrowed some employers' profits to the edge of solvency.[2] Louis de Nevers, Count of Flanders, sided too strongly with the employers. The populace of Bruges and Ypres, supported by the neighboring peasantry, rose in revolt, deposed Louis, plundered abbeys, and slew a few millionaires. The Church laid an interdict upon the revolted regions; the rebels nevertheless forced the priests to say Mass; and one leader, stealing a march of 450 years on Diderot, vowed he would never be content till the last priest had been hanged.[3] Louis appealed to his liege lord, the French king; Philip VI came, defeated the revolutionary forces at Cassel (1328), hanged the burgomaster of Bruges, restored the count, and made Flanders a dependency of France.

France in general was much less industrialized than Flanders; manufacturing for the most part remained in the handicraft stage; but Lille, Douai, Cambrai, and Amiens echoed the textile busyness of the near-by Flemish towns. Internal commerce was hampered by bad roads and feudal tolls, but

---

* We may define capital as goods or funds used to produce goods for consumption; a capitalist as an investor or provider of capital; capitalism as an economic system or process dominated by capitalists.

favored by canals and rivers that constituted a system of natural highways throughout France. The rising business class, in alliance with the kings, had attained by 1300 to a high position in the state and to a degree of wealth that shocked the land-rich, money-poor nobility. Merchant oligarchies ruled the cities, controlled the guilds, and jealously restricted production and trade. Here, as in Flanders, a revolutionary proletariat simmered in the towns.

In 1300 an uprising of poor peasants, known to history as *Pastoureaux*—shepherds—surged through the cities as in 1251, gathering resentful *prolé-taires* in its wake. Led by a rebel monk, they marched southward, mostly barefoot and unarmed, proclaiming Jerusalem as their goal. Hungry, they pillaged shops and fields; resisted, they found weapons and became an army. In Paris they broke open the jails and defeated the troops of the king. Philip IV shut himself up in the Louvre, the nobles retired to their strongholds, the merchants cowered in their homes. The horde passed on, swelled by the destitute of the capital; now it numbered 40,000 men and women, ruffians and pietists. At Verdun, Auch, and Toulouse they slaughtered all available Jews. When they gathered in Aiguesmortes, on the Mediterranean, the seneschal or sheriff of Carcassonne surrounded them with his forces, cut off their supplies, and waited till all the rebels had died of starvation or pestilence except a few, whom he hanged.[4]

What kind of government was it that left France at the mercy of greedy wealth and lawless poverty? In many ways it was the ablest government in Europe. The strong kings of the thirteenth century had subjected the feudal lords to the state, had organized a national judiciary and administration with a trained civil service, and had on occasion summoned an Estates- or States-General: originally a general gathering of estate owners, then a consultative assembly of delegates from the nobility, the clergy, and the burgesses or middle class. All Europe admired the French court, where powerful dukes, counts, and knights mingled with silk-robed women in elegant festivities and graceful cuckoldry, and clashing jousts in glittering tournaments sustained the glamour of chivalry. King John of Bohemia called Paris "the most chivalrous residence in the world" and avowed that he could not bear to live outside it.[5] Petrarch, visiting it in 1331, described it less romantically:

> Paris, though always inferior to its fame, and much indebted to the lies of its own people, is undoubtedly a great city. To be sure, I never saw a dirtier place, except Avignon. At the same time it contains the most learned men, and is like a great basket in which are collected the rarest fruits of every country. There was a time when, from the ferocity of their manners, the French were reckoned barbarians. At present the case is wholly changed. A gay disposition, love of society, ease and playfulness in conversation, now characterize them.

They seek every opportunity of distinguishing themselves, and make war against all cares with joking, laughing, singing, eating, and drinking.[6]

Philip IV, despite his quasi-piratical confiscations from Templars and Jews, bequeathed an almost empty treasury to his son (1314). Louis X died after a brief reign (1316), leaving no heir but a pregnant wife. After an interval his brother was crowned as Philip V. A rival faction sought the throne for Louis' four-year-old daughter Jeanne; but an assembly of nobles and clergy issued the famous ruling (1316) that "the laws and customs inviolably observed among the Franks excluded daughters from the crown."[7] When Philip himself died sonless (1322), this ruling was repeated to bar his own daughter from the throne, and his brother was proclaimed king as Charles IV.* Very probably the decisions aimed also to exclude from the succession the sister of Philip IV, Isabelle, who had married Edward II of England and had borne Edward III (1312). The French were resolved that no English king should rule France.

When Charles IV died without male issue (1328) the direct line of Capetian kings came to an end. Edward III, who had become King of England the year before, presented to the assembled aristocracy of France his claim to the French throne as a grandson of Philip IV and the most direct living descendant from Hugh Capet. The assembly denied his claim on the ground that Edward's mother could not transmit to him a crown from which she herself had been excluded by the rulings of 1316 and 1322. The barons preferred a nephew of Philip IV, a count of Valois; so Philip VI began that Valois dynasty which ruled France till Henry IV inaugurated the Bourbon line (1589). Edward protested, but in 1329 he came to Amiens and did homage, and pledged full loyalty, to Philip VI as his feudal lord for Gascony, Guienne, and Ponthieu. As Edward grew in years and wile, he repented his homage, and dreamed again of sitting on two thrones at once. His advisers assured him that the new Philip was a weakling, who planned to leave soon on a crusade to the Holy Land. It seemed a propitious time to begin the Hundred Years' War.

II. THE ROAD TO CRÉCY: 1337–47

In 1337 Edward formally renewed his claim to the French crown. The rejection of his claim was only the proximate cause of war. After the Norman conquest of England, Normandy had for 138 years belonged to the English

---

* The assumption that these two decrees referred to a law of the Salic Franks prohibiting the inheritance of land by women is now generally rejected;[8] the inheritance of land by women had long since become ordinary in France.

kings; Philip II had reconquered it for France (1204); now many English nobles of Norman descent could look upon the coming war as an attempt to regain their motherland. Part of English Guienne had been nibbled away by Philip IV and Charles IV. Guienne was fragrant with vineyards, and the wine trade of Bordeaux was too precious a boon to England to be lamely lost merely to defer by a few years the death of 10,000 Englishmen. Scotland was a burr in England's side; and the French had repeatedly allied themselves with Scotland in its wars with England. The North Sea was full of fish; the English navy claimed sovereignty in those waters, in the Channel, in the Bay of Biscay, and it captured French ships that flouted this first proclamation of English rule over the waves. Flanders was a vital outlet for British wool; English nobles whose sheep grew the wool, English merchants who exported it, disliked the dependence of their prime market on the good will of the King of France.

In 1336 the Count of Flanders ordered all Britons there to be jailed; apparently Philip VI had recommended this as a precaution against English plots. Edward III retaliated by ordering the arrest of all Flemings in England and forbidding the export of wool to Flanders. Within a week the Flemish looms stopped for lack of material; workers darkened the streets crying for employment. At Ghent artisans and manufacturers united in renouncing allegiance to the count; they chose an alleged brewer, Jacob van Artevelde, as governor of the city, and approved his policy of seeking the friendship and wool of England (1337). Edward lifted the embargo; the count fled to Paris; all Flanders accepted Artevelde's dictatorship and agreed to join England in war on France. On November 1, 1337, Edward III, following the custom of chivalry, sent to Philip VI a formal declaration that after three days England would begin hostilities.

The first major encounter of the Hundred Years' War was a naval engagement off the Flemish coast at Sluis (1340), where the English navy destroyed 142 of the 172 vessels in the French fleet. Later in that year Joan of Valois, sister of Philip and mother-in-law of Edward, left her convent at Fontenelle and induced the French King to commission her as an emissary of peace. Proceeding through many perils to the camp of the English leaders, she won their consent to a conference, and her heroic mediation persuaded the kings to a nine-month truce. By the efforts of Pope Clement VI peace was maintained till 1346.

During this lucid interval class war seized the stage. The well-organized weavers of Ghent were the aristocracy of labor in the Lowlands. They denounced Artevelde as a cruel tyrant, an embezzler of public funds, a tool of England and the *bourgeoisie*. Artevelde had proposed that Flanders should accept the Prince of Wales as its ruler, and Edward III came to Sluis to confirm the arrangement. When Artevelde returned from Sluis to Ghent his house was surrounded by an angry crowd. He pleaded for his life as a true Flemish patriot, but he was dragged into the street and hacked to death (1345).[9] The weavers established a proletarian dictatorship in Ghent, and sent agents through Flanders to urge the workers to revolt. But the Ghent fullers fell out with the weavers, the weavers were deposed and many of them were massacred, the people tired of their new government, and Louis de Male, now Count of Flanders, brought all its cities under his rule.

The truce having expired, Edward III invaded and devastated Normandy. On August 26, 1346, the English and French armies met at Crécy and prepared for a decisive battle. Leaders and men on both sides heard Mass, ate the body and drank the blood of Jesus Christ, and asked His aid in dispatching one another.[10] Then they fought with courage and ferocity, giving no quarter. Edward the Black Prince earned on that day the praise of his victorious father; Philip VI himself stood his ground till only six of his soldiers were left on the field. Thirty thousand men, in Froissart's loose estimate, died in that one engagement. Feudalism almost died there, too: the mounted chivalry of France, charging gallantly with short lances, stopped helpless before a wall of long English pikes pointed at their horses' breasts, while English bowmen on the wings scattered death among the chevaliers. The long heyday of cavalry, which had dawned at Adrianople 968 years before, here began to fade; infantry came to the fore, and the military supremacy of the aristocracy declined. Artillery was used at Crécy on a small scale, but the difficulties of moving and reloading it made it more troublesome than effective, so that Villani limited its usefulness to its noise.[*][11]

From Crécy Edward led his army to the siege of Calais, and there employed cannon against the walls (1347). The town held out for a year; then, starving, it accepted Edward's condition that the survivors might leave in peace if six principal citizens would come to him with ropes around their necks and the keys of the city in their hands. Six so volunteered, and when they stood before the King he ordered them beheaded. The Queen of England knelt before him and begged for their lives; he yielded to her, and she had the men escorted to their homes in safety. The women stand out with more credit than the kings in history, and fight bravely a desperate battle to civilize the men.

Calais became now, and remained till 1558, a part of England, a strategic outlet for her goods and troops upon the Continent. In 1348 it rebelled; Edward besieged it again, and himself, incognito, fought in the assault. A French knight, Eustace de Ribeaumont, twice struck Edward down, but was overpowered and made prisoner. When the city had been retaken, Edward

---

[*] It was already a century old, for cannon had been used by the Berbers at Sidgilmessa in 1247.[12]

entertained his noble captives at dinner; English lords and the Prince of Wales waited on them, and Edward said to Ribeaumont:

> Sir Eustace, you are the most valiant knight in Christendom that I ever saw attack an enemy. . . . I adjudge to you the prize of valor above all the knights of my court.

Removing from his head a rich chaplet that he wore, the English King placed it upon the head of the French chevalier, saying:

> Sir Eustace, I present you with this chaplet . . . and beg of you to wear it this year for love of me. I know that you are lively and amorous, and love the company of ladies and damsels; therefore say, wherever you go, that I gave it to you. I also give you your liberty, free of ransom, and you may go whither you will.[18]

Here and there, amid greed and slaughter, chivalry survived, and the legends of Arthur came close to living history in the pages of Froissart.

III. BLACK DEATH AND OTHER: 1348-49

The Great Plague fell impartially upon an England prosperous with French spoils and a France desolate in defeat. Pestilence was a normal incident in medieval history; it harried Europe during thirty-two years of the fourteenth century, forty-one years of the fifteenth, thirty years of the sixteenth; so nature and human ignorance, those resolute Malthusians, cooperated with war and famine to counteract the reproductive ecstasies of mankind. The Black Death was the worst of these visitations, and probably the most terrible physical calamity in historic times. It came into Provence and France from Italy, and perhaps more directly from the Near East through Oriental rats landing at Marseille. In Narbonne, said a dubious tradition, 30,000 persons died of it; in Paris, 50,000;[14] in Europe, 25,000,000;[15] perhaps, altogether, "one fourth of the population of the civilized world."[16] The medical profession was helpless; it did not know the cause of the disease (Kitazato and Yersin discovered the bacillus of the bubonic plague in 1894), and could only recommend bleedings, purges, cordials, cleanliness of home and person, and fumigation with vapors of vinegar.[17] A few physicians and priests, fearing infection, refused to treat the sick, but the great majority of them faced the ordeal manfully; thousands of doctors and clergymen gave their lives.[18] Of twenty-eight cardinals alive in 1348 nine were dead a year later; of sixty-four archbishops, twenty-five; of 375 bishops, 207.[19]

The epidemic had effects in every sphere of life. As the poor died in greater proportion than the rich, a shortage of labor followed; thousands of acres were left untilled, millions of herring died a natural death. Labor en-

joyed for a while an improved bargaining power; it raised its wages, repudiated many surviving feudal obligations, and staged revolts that kept noble
teeth on edge for half a century; even priests struck for higher pay.[20] Serfs
left farms for cities, industry expanded, the business class made further gains
on the landed aristocracy. Public sanitation was goaded into moderate improvements. The immensity of the suffering and the tragedy weakened many
minds, producing contagious neuroses; whole groups seemed to go mad in
unison, like the Flagellants who in 1349, as they had done in the thirteenth
century, marched through the city streets almost naked, beating themselves
in penitence, preaching the Last Judgment, utopias, and pogroms. People
listened with more than customary eagerness to mind readers, dream interpreters, sorcerers, quacks, and other charlatans. Orthodox faith was weakened; superstition flourished. Strange reasons were given for the plague. Some
ascribed it to an untimely conjunction of Saturn, Jupiter, and Mars; others
to the poisoning of wells by lepers or Jews. Jews were killed in half a hundred
towns from Brussels to Breslau (1348–49). Social order was almost destroyed
by the death of thousands of police, judges, government officials, bishops,
and priests. Even the business of war suffered a passing decline; from the
siege of Calais to the battle of Poitiers (1356) the Hundred Years' War
dallied in reluctant truce, while the decimated ranks of the infantry were
replenished with men too poor to value life at more than a few shillings above
death.

Philip VI consoled himself for plague and defeat by marrying, at fifty-six,
Blanche of Navarre, eighteen, whom he had intended for his son. Seven
months later he died. This son, John II, "the Good" (1350–64), was good
indeed to the nobles; he absolved them from taxes, paid them to defend their
lands against the English, and maintained all the forms and graces of chivalry.
He also debased the currency as an old way to pay war debts, repeatedly
raised taxes on the lower and middle classes, and marched off in splendor to
meet the English at Poitiers. There his 15,000 knights, Scots, and servitors
were routed, slain, or captured by the 7,000 men of the Black Prince; and
King John himself, fighting lustily, leading foolishly, was among the prisoners, along with his son Philip, seventeen earls, and countless barons, knights,
and squires. Most of these were allowed to ransom themselves on the spot,
and many were freed on their promise to bring their ransom to Bordeaux by
Christmas. The Prince treated the King royally, and took him leisurely to
England.

IV. REVOLUTION AND RENEWAL: 1357–80

All France fell into chaos after the disaster at Poitiers. The dishonesty and
incompetence of the government, the depreciation of the currency, the costly

ransoms of King and knights, the desolations of war and plague, and the discouraging taxes laid upon agriculture, industry, and trade, brought the nation to desperate revolt. A States-General of the northern provinces, summoned to Paris by the nineteen-year-old Dauphin,* Charles of Valois, to raise new taxes, undertook to establish a parliamentary government in France. Paris and other cities had long had *parlements*, but these were small appointive bodies, usually of jurists, normally limited to giving legal advice to the local ruler or the king, and registering his decrees as part of French law. This States-General, controlled by a transient coalition of clergy and *bourgeoisie*, demanded of the royal council why the vast sums raised for war had produced only undisciplined troops and shameful defeats; it ordered the arrest of twenty-two governmental agents, and commanded the administrators of the treasury to return the sums they were accused of embezzling; it imposed restrictions on the royal prerogative; it thought even of deposing John the Good, barring his sons from the succession, and giving the throne of France to King Charles the Bad of Navarre, a lineal descendant of Hugh Capet. Appeased by the prudent humility of the Dauphin, it recognized him as regent, and voted him funds for 30,000 men-at-arms; but it bade him dismiss corrupt or ignorant officials, warned him against tampering with the coinage, and appointed a committee of thirty-six men to keep an eye on the operations and expenditures of the government. Judges were condemned for their extravagant equipage, their dilatory idleness, their calendars twenty years behind; hereafter they were to begin their sessions at sunrise, at the same hour when honest citizens went to their shops or their fields. This "Great Ordinance" of 1357 also forbade nobles to leave France or to wage private war, and instructed the local authorities of the towns to arrest any noble violating this edict. In effect the aristocracy was to be subject to the communes, the nobles to the business class; king, prince, and barons were to obey the chosen representatives of the people. France was to have a constitutional government four centuries before the revolution.[21]

The Dauphin signed the ordinance in March, and began to evade it in April. The English were demanding a ruinous ransom for his father, and were threatening an advance upon Paris. The people were slow in paying taxes, on the novel ground that these could properly be levied only by the States-General. Hard pressed for cash, Charles called this body to reassemble on February 1, 1358; meanwhile he further debased the currency to increase

---

* This was apparently at first a proper name, Delphinus (Dolphin), which, often repeated in the ruling families of Vienne and Auvergne, became (*c.* 1250) a title of dignity. In 1285 it was officially conferred upon the eldest son of the Count of Vienne, and Delphinatus or Dauphiné was thenceforth used to designate the county, of which Grenoble is now the principal seat. In 1349 Count Humboldt II of the Viennois sold the Dauphiné, with the title Dauphin, to Charles of Valois, son of King John II. When Charles became king in 1364 he transferred the title to his eldest son; and thereafter the eldest son of a French king was regularly known as the Dauphin of the Viennois.

his funds. On February 2 Étienne Marcel, a rich merchant who, as head of the merchant guilds, had played a leading part in formulating the "Great Ordinance," and had been governing Paris for a year, led an armed band of citizens—all wearing hoods of the city's official colors, blue and red—into the royal palace. He rebuked Charles for disobeying the instructions of the States-General; and when the Prince would not pledge obedience Marcel had his men kill two chamberlains who guarded the Dauphin, so that their blood spurted upon the royal robe.[22]

The new States-General was horrified by this audacious violence; nevertheless it advanced the revolution by decreeing (May 1358) that thereafter only the States-General should enact laws for France, and that in all important matters the king was to act only with the approval of the Estates.[23] Many members of the nobility and clergy fled from Paris; many administrative officials abandoned their posts in fear of their lives. Marcel replaced them with burgesses, and for a time the merchants of Paris attempted to rule France. The Dauphin took refuge with nobles in Picardy, raised an army, and called upon the people of Paris to surrender to him the leaders of the revolt. Marcel organized the capital for defense, ringed it with new walls, and occupied the Louvre, then the seat and symbol of sovereignty.

While revolution captured Paris the peasants of the countryside thought it an opportune time to revenge themselves on their masters. Still mostly serf,[24] taxed to equip their lords, taxed to ransom them, pillaged by soldiers and brigands, tortured to disclose their laborious savings, decimated by plague and starved by war, they rose in uncalculating fury, forced their way into feudal castles, cut all the noble throats their knives could reach, and relieved their hunger and thirst in baronial hoards and cellars. The nobles had traditionally given the typically good-natured peasant the nickname of Jacques Bonhomme—James Goodman; now thousands of such Jacques, their patience spent, plunged into ferocious *jacqueries*, slew their lords, violated the ladies, murdered the heirs, and dressed their own wives in the finery of the dead.[25]

Hoping that this rural revolution would divert the Dauphin from attacking Paris, Marcel sent 800 of his men to aid the peasants. So reinforced, they marched upon Meaux. The Duchesses of Orléans and Normandy, and many other women of lofty pedigree, had sought refuge there; now they saw a mob of serfs and tenants pouring into the town, and gave themselves up as lost in both virtue and life. Then, miraculously, as in some Arthurian romance, a knightly band returning from a crusade galloped into Meaux, fell upon the peasants, killed thousands of them, and flung them by heaps into neighboring streams. The nobles came out of hiding, laid punitive fines upon the villages, and went through the countryside massacring 20,000 rustics, rebel or innocent (June 1358).[26]

The forces of the Dauphin approached Paris, and cut off its food supply.

Despairing of successful resistance by other means, Marcel offered the crown to Charles the Bad and prepared to admit his forces into the city. Rejecting this plan as treason, Marcel's aide and friend, Jean Maillart, made a secret agreement with the Dauphin, and on July 31 Jean and others slew Marcel with an ax. The Dauphin entered Paris at the head of the armed nobility. He behaved with moderation and caution, and set himself to ransom his father and to restore the morale and economy of France. The men who had tried to create a sovereign parliament retreated into obscurity and silence; the grateful nobles rallied around the throne; and the States-General became the obedient instrument of a strengthened monarchy.

In November 1359, Edward III landed with a fresh army at Calais. He avoided Paris, respecting the walls recently raised by Marcel, but he subjected the surrounding country, from Reims to Chartres, to so systematic a destruction of crops that Paris again starved. Charles pleaded for peace on abject terms. France would yield Gascony and Guienne to England, free from all feudal bond to the French king; it would also cede Poitou, Périgord, Quercy, Saintonge, Rouergue, Calais, Ponthieu, Aunis, Angoumois, Agenois, Limousin, and Bigorre; and it would pay 3,000,000 crowns for the return of its king. In return Edward renounced, for himself and his descendants, all claim to the throne of France. This Peace of Brétigny was signed on May 8, 1360, and one third of France fretted and fumed under English rule. Two sons of King John—the Dukes of Anjou and Berry—were sent to England as hostages for French fidelity to the treaty; John returned to Paris amid the ringing of bells and the joy of the noble and the simple. When the Duke of Anjou broke parole and escaped to join his wife, King John returned to England to replace his son as hostage, and in the hope of negotiating a milder peace. Edward received him as a guest, and feted him daily as the flower of chivalry. John died in London in 1364, and was buried in St. Paul's, captive in death. The Dauphin, aged twenty-six, became Charles V of France.

He deserved the name *le Sage*, the Wise, which his people gave him, if only because he knew how to win battles without raising a hand. His right hand was perpetually swollen and his arm was limp, so that he could not lift a lance; it was said that he had been poisoned by Charles the Bad. Half forced to a sedentary life, he gathered about him prudent councilors, reorganized every department of the government, reformed the judiciary, rebuilt the army, encouraged industry, stabilized the currency, supported literature and art, and collected in the Louvre the royal library that provided classic texts and translations for the French Renaissance, and formed the nucleus of the Bibliothèque Nationale. He yielded to the nobles in restoring feudal tolls, but he went over their heads to appoint as constable—commander-in-chief of all French armies—a swarthy, flat-nosed, thick-necked, massive-headed Breton, Bertrand Du Guesclin. Faith in the superiority of this "Eagle of Brittany" to all English generals shared in determining Charles to undertake the redemption of France from English rule. In 1369 he sent Edward III a formal declaration of war.

The Black Prince responded by subduing Limoges and massacring 3,000 men, women, and children; this was his conception of political education. It proved inadequate; every city in his path fortified, garrisoned, and provisioned itself to successful defense, and the Prince was reduced to laying waste the open country, burning the crops, and razing the deserted homes of the peasantry. Du Guesclin refrained from giving battle, but harassed the princely rear, captured foragers, and waited for the English troops to starve. They did, and retreated; Du Guesclin advanced; one by one the ceded provinces were reclaimed; and after two years of remarkable generalship, and the mutual loyalty of commander and King, the English were driven from all of France except Bordeaux, Brest, Cherbourg, and Calais; France for the first time reached to the Pyrenees. Charles and his great constable could die with honors in the same year (1380) on the crest of victory.

V. THE MAD KING: 1380–1422

The gamble of hereditary monarchy now replaced a competent ruler with a lovable idiot. Charles VI was twelve when his father died; his uncles acted as regents till he was twenty, and allowed him to grow up in irresponsible debauchery while half of Europe marched to the brink of revolution. In 1359 the workingmen of Bruges, wearing red hats, stormed the historic *hôtel de ville* in transient revolt. In 1366 the lower classes of Ypres rose in rebellion, preaching a holy war against the rich. In 1378 the Ciompi established in Florence the dictatorship of the proletariat. In 1379 the starving peasants of Languedoc—south-central France—began six years of guerrilla warfare against nobles and priests under a leader who gave orders to "kill all who have soft hands." [27] Workers revolted in Strasbourg in 1380, in London in 1381, in Cologne in 1396. From 1379 to 1382 a revolutionary government ruled Ghent. In Rouen a stout draper was crowned king by an uprising of town laborers; and in Paris the people killed with leaden mallets the tax collectors of the King (1382).

Charles VI took the reins of government in 1388, and for four years reigned so well that he won the name of *Bien-Aimé*, Well-Beloved. But in 1392 he went insane. He could no longer recognize his wife, and begged the strange woman to cease her importunities. Soon only the humblest servants paid any attention to him. For five months he had no change of clothes, and when at last it was decided to bathe him a dozen men were needed to overcome his reluctance. [28] For thirty years the French crown was worn by a pitiful imbecile, while a virile young king prepared to renew the English attack upon France.

On August 11, 1415, Henry V sailed from England with 1,300 vessels and 11,000 men. On the fourteenth they landed near Harfleur, at the mouth of the Seine. Harfleur resisted gallantly and in vain. Jubilant with victory and hurried by dysentery, the English marched toward Calais. The chivalry of France met them at Agincourt, close to Crécy (October 25). The French, having learned nothing from Crécy and Poitiers, still relied on cavalry. Many of their horses were immobilized by mud; those that advanced met the sharp stakes that the English had planted at an angle in the ground around their bowmen. The discouraged horses turned and charged their own army; the English fell upon this chaotic mass with maces, hatchets, and swords; their King Hal led them valiantly, too excited for fear; and their victory was overwhelming. French historians estimate the English loss at 1,600, the French loss at 10,000.

Henry returned to France in 1417, and besieged Rouen. The citizens ate up their food supply, then their horses, their dogs, their cats. To save food, women, children, and old men were thrust forth beyond the city walls; they sought passage through the English lines, were refused, remained foodless and shelterless between their relatives and their enemies, and starved to death; 50,000 French died of starvation in that merciless siege. When the town surrendered, Henry restrained his army from massacring the survivors, but he levied upon them a fine of 300,000 crowns, and kept them in prison till the total was paid. In 1419 he advanced upon a Paris in which nothing remained but corruption, destitution, brutality, and class war. Outdoing the humiliation of 1360, France, by the Treaty of Troyes (1420), surrendered everything, even honor. Charles VI gave his daughter Katherine to Henry V in marriage, promised to bequeath to him the French throne, turned over to him the governance of France, and, to clear up any ambiguity, disowned the Dauphin as his son. Queen Isabelle, for an annuity of 24,000 francs, made no defense against this charge of adultery; and, indeed, in the royal courts of that age it was not easy for a woman to know who was the father of her child. The Dauphin, holding south France, repudiated the treaty, and organized his Gascon and Armagnac bands to carry on the war. But the King of England reigned in the Louvre.

Two years later Henry V died of dysentery; the germs had not signed the treaty. When Charles VI followed him (1422), Henry VI of England was crowned King of France; but as he was not yet a year old, the Duke of Bedford ruled as his regent. The Duke governed severely, but as justly as any Englishman could govern France. He suppressed brigandage by hanging 10,000 bandits in a year; judge therefrom the condition of the land.

Demobilized soldiers—*écorcheurs* (skinners), *coquillards* (shell men)—made the highways perilous, and terrorized even large cities like Paris and Dijon. Over Normandy the ravage of war had passed back and forth like an infernal, murderous tide; even in luckier Languedoc a third of the population had disappeared.[29] Peasants fled to the cities, or hid in caves, or fortified themselves in churches, as armies or feudal factions or robber bands approached. Many peasants never returned to their precarious holdings, but lived by beggary or thievery, or died of starvation or plague. Churches, farms, whole towns, were abandoned and left to decay. In Paris in 1422 there were 24,000 empty houses, 80,000 beggars,[30] in a population of some 300,000.[31] People ate the flesh and entrails of dogs. The cries of hungry children haunted the streets.

VI. LIFE AMONG THE RUINS

Morals were such as any country might expect from so long and tragic a disablement of economy and government. Geoffrey de la Tour-Landry, about 1372, wrote two books to guide his children in the chaos; only that which he addressed to his daughters survives. It is a gentle and tender volume warm with parental love, and disturbed by solicitude for a virginity especially unstable in a time when many women came through generous sins to ungenerous contumely. Against such temptations, the good knight thought, the best protection was frequent prayer.[32] The book reflects an age still clinging to civilized sentiments and moral sense. Seventy years later we come to the gruesome figure of the Maréchal de Rais or Retz, a great and wealthy lord of Brittany. It was his custom to invite children into his castle on pretense of training them for the chapel choir; one by one he killed them and offered them in sacrifice to demons of whom he begged magic powers. But also he killed for pleasure and (we are told) laughed at the cries of his tortured or dying choristers. For fourteen years he followed this routine, until at last the father of a victim dared to indict him; he confessed all these details and was hanged (1440), but only because he had offended the Duke of Brittany; men of his rank could seldom be brought to justice whatever their crimes.[33] Yet the aristocracy to which he belonged produced heroes in abundance, like King John of Bohemia, or the Gaston Phoebus de Foix so loved and lauded by Froissart. The final flowers of chivalry blossomed in this mire.

The morality of the people shared in the common debacle. Cruelty, treachery, and corruption were endemic. Commoner and governor were alike open to bribes. Profanity flourished; Chancellor Gerson complained that the most sacred festivals were passed in card-playing,* gambling, and blasphemy.[35] Sharpers, forgers, thieves, vagabonds, and beggars clogged the streets by day, and gathered at night to enjoy their gleanings, at Paris, in the Cours des Miracles, so called because the mendicants who had posed as cripples during the day appeared there marvelously sound in every limb.[36]

Sodomy was frequent, prostitution was general, adultery was almost universal.[37] A sect of "Adamites" in the fourteenth century advocated nudism, and practiced it in public till the Inquisition suppressed them.[38] Obscene pictures were as widely marketed as now; according to Gerson they were sold even in churches and on holy days.[39] Poets like Deschamps wrote erotic ballads for noble dames.[40] Nicolas de Clémanges, Archdeacon of Bayeux, described the convents of his district as "sanctuaries devoted to the cult of Venus." [41] It was taken as a matter of course that kings and princes should have mistresses, since royal—and many noble—marriages were political matches involving, it was held, no due of love. Highborn ladies continued to hold formal discussions on the casuistry of sexual relations. Philip the Bold of Burgundy established a "court of love" in Paris in 1401.[42] Amid or beneath this moneyed laxity there were presumably some virtuous women and honest men; we catch a fleeting glimpse of them in a strange book written about 1393 by an anonymous sexagenarian known as the *Ménagier*, or householder, of Paris:

> I believe that when two good and honorable people are wed, all loves are put off . . . save only the love of each for the other. And meseems that when they are in each other's presence they look upon each other more than upon the others; they clasp and hold each other; and they do not willingly speak and make signs save to each other. . . . And all their special pleasure, their chief desire and perfect joy, is to do pleasure or obedience one to the other.[43]

Persecutions of Jews (1306, 1384, 1396) and lepers (1321), trials and executions of animals for injuring or copulating with human beings,[44] public hangings that drew immense crowds of eager spectators, entered into the picture of the age. In the cemetery of the Church of the Innocents at Paris so many newly dead sought admission that bodies were exhumed as soon as the flesh might be expected to have fallen from the bones; the bones were indiscriminately piled in charnel houses alongside the cloisters; nevertheless, these cloisters were a popular rendezvous; shops were set up there, and prostitutes invited patronage.[45] On a wall of the cemetery an artist labored for months in 1424 to paint a *Dance of Death*, in which demons, pirouetting with men, women, and children, led them step by merry step to hell. This

---

* Playing cards entered Europe probably in the fourteenth century; the first definite mention of them is in 1379. Apparently they came from the Moslems through Africa, Spain, and the crusaders. The Chinese claim to have used them as early as A.D. 1120.[84]

became a symbolic theme of a desperate age; a play presented it at Bruges in 1449; Dürer, Holbein, and Bosch would illustrate it in their art. Pessimism wrote half the poetry of the period. Deschamps reviled life in almost all its parts; the world seemed to him like a weak, timorous, covetous old man, confused and decayed; "all goes badly," he concluded. Gerson agreed with him: "We lived in the senility of the world," and the Last Judgment was near. An old woman thought that every twitch of pain in her toes announced another soul heaved into hell. Her estimate was moderate; according to popular belief no one had entered paradise in the past thirty years.[46]

What did religion do in this collapse of an assaulted nation? In the first four decades of the Hundred Years' War the popes, immured at Avignon, received the protection and commands of the French kings. Much of the revenues drawn from Europe by the popes of that captivity went to those kings to finance the struggle of life and death against Britain; in eleven years (1345–55) the Church advanced 3,392,000 florins ($84,800,000?) to the monarchy.[47] The popes tried again and again to end the war, but failed. The Church suffered grievously from the century-long devastation of France; hundreds of churches and monasteries were abandoned or destroyed; and the lower clergy shared in the demoralization of the age. Knights and footmen ignored religion until the hour of battle or death, and must have felt some qualms of creed at the maddening indifference of the skies. The people, while breaking all the commandments, clung fearfully to the Church and the faith; they brought their pennies and their griefs to the comforting shrines of the Mother of God; they rose en masse to religious ecstasy at the earnest preaching of Friar Richard or St. Vincent Ferrer. Some houses had statuettes of the Virgin so contrived that a touch would open her abdomen and reveal the Trinity.[48]

The intellectual leaders of the Church in this period were mostly Frenchmen. Pierre d'Ailly was not only one of the most suggestive scientists of the time; he was among the ablest and most incorruptible leaders of the Church; and he was one of the ecclesiastical statesmen who, at the Council of Constance, healed the schism in the papacy. As director of the College of Navarre in Paris he had among his pupils a youth who became the outstanding theologian of his generation. Jean de Gerson visited the Lowlands, and was much impressed by the mysticism of Ruysbroeck and the moderna devotio of the Brethren of the Common Life. When he became chancellor of the University of Paris (1395) he sought to introduce this form of piety into France, even while censuring the egoism and pantheism of the mystic school. His six sisters were overcome by his arguments and example, and we are told that they remained virgins to the end of their lives. Gerson condemned the superstitions of the populace, and the quackeries of astrology, magic, and medicine; but he admitted that charms may have efficacy by working upon the imagination. Our knowledge of the stars, he thought, is too imperfect to allow specific predictions; we cannot even reckon a solar year precisely; we cannot tell the true positions of the stars because their light is refracted, as it passes down to us, through a variety of mediums. Gerson advocated a limited democracy, and the supremacy of the councils, in the Church, but favored a strong monarchy in France; perhaps his inconsistency was justified by the condition of his country, which needed order more than liberty. He was a great man in his fashion and generation; his virtues, as Goethe would have said, were his own attainment, while his delusions were infections from the age. He led the movement to depose rival popes and reform the Church; and he shared in sending John Huss and Jerome of Prague to the stake.

Amid the destitution of their people the upper classes glorified their persons and adorned their homes. Common men wore simple jerkins, blouses, *culottes* or trousers, and high boots; the middle classes, imitating the kings despite sumptuary laws, wore long robes, perhaps dyed in scarlet or edged with fur; noble lords wore doublets and long hose, handsome capes, and feathered hats that swept the earth in courtly bows. Some men wore horns on the toes of their shoes, to correspond with less visible emblems on their heads. Highborn ladies affected conical hats like church steeples, straitened themselves in tight jackets and colorful pantaloons, trailed furry skirts over the floor majestically, and graciously displayed their bosoms while enhancing their faces with veils. Buttons were coming into fashion for fastenings,[49] having before been merely ornaments; we are reversing that movement now. Silks, cloth of gold, brocade, lace, jewelry in the hair, on neck and hands and dress and shoes, made even stout women sparkle; and under this protective brilliance nearly all upper-class women developed a Rubensian amplitude.

The homes of the poor remained as in former centuries, except that glass windows were now general. But the villas and town houses (*hôtels*) of the rich were no longer gloomy donjons; they were commodious and well-furnished mansions, with spacious fountained courts, broad winding stairs, overhanging balconies, and sharply sloping roofs that cut the sky and sloughed the snow; they were equipped with servants' rooms, storerooms, guard room, porter's room, linen room, laundry, wine cellar, and bakery, in addition to the great hall and bedrooms of the master's family. Some châteaux, like those of Pierrefonds (*c.* 1390) and Châteaudun (*c.* 1450), already presaged the regal castles of the Loire. Better preserved than any palace of the time is the house of the great capitalist Jacques Cœur at Bourges, a full block long, with Gothic tower of carved stone, ornate cornices and reliefs, and Renaissance windows, the whole costing, we are told, some $4,000,000 in the money of today.[50] Interiors were now sumptuously furnished: magnificent fireplaces, which could warm at least one side of a room and its occupants; sturdy chairs and tables indefatigably carved; cushioned benches along tapestried walls; gigantic dressers and cupboards displaying gold and silver plate, and far lovelier glass; thick carpets, and floors of polished oak or enameled tiles; and high canopied beds vast enough to hold the lord, his lady, and a child or two. On these recumbent thrones the men and women of the fourteenth and fifteenth centuries slept naked;[51] night-gowns were not yet an indispensable impediment.

VII. LETTERS

Among the ruins men and women continued to write books. The *Postillae perpetuae* (1322–31) of Nicholas of Lyra were major contributions to the textual understanding of the Bible, and prepared the way for Erasmus' New Testament and Luther's German translation. The fiction of the period favored light erotic tales like the *Cent nouvelles nouvelles*—one hundred novel novels—of Antoine de la Salle, or romances of chivalry like *Flore et Blanchefleur*. Almost as fictitious was the book of a Liége physician, Jehan à la Barbe, who called himself Sir John Mandeville, and published (c. 1370) an account of his alleged travels in Egypt, Asia, Russia, and Poland. John claimed to have visited all the places named in the Gospels: "the house where the sweet Virgin went to school," the spot where "the water was warmed with which Our Lord washed the feet of the Apostles," the church in which Mary "hid herself to draw milk from her worthy breasts; in this same church is a marble column against which she leaned, and which is still moist from her milk; and wherever her worthy milk fell the earth is still soft and white."[52] John of the Beard is at his best in describing China, where his eloquence was least cramped by erudition. Now and then he verges on science, as when he tells how a "man traveled ever eastward until he came to his own country again," like Jules Verne's M. Passepartout. He drank twice at the Fountain of Youth, but returned to Europe crippled with arthritis, which perhaps he had caught by never leaving Liége. These *Travels*, translated into a hundred languages, became one of the literary sensations of the later Middle Ages.

By far the most brilliant production of French literature in the fourteenth century was the *Chronicles* of Jean Froissart. Born at Valenciennes in 1338, he lapsed into poetry at an early age; and at twenty-four he crossed to London to lay his verses at the feet of Edward III's wife, Philippa of Hainaut. He became her secretary, met English aristocrats, and admired them too frankly to be impartial in his history. Lust for travel soon uprooted him, and drew him to Scotland, Bordeaux, Savoy, and Italy. Returning to Hainaut, he became a priest and canon of Chimay. Now he decided to rewrite his book in prose, and to extend it at both ends. He traveled again in England and France, sedulously gathering material. Back in Chimay he dedicated himself to finishing "this noble and pleasant history . . . which will be much in request when I am gone . . . to encourage all valorous hearts, and to show them honorable examples." [53] No romance could be more fascinating; he who begins these 1,200 ample pages with intent to leap from peak to peak will find the valleys inviting too, and will move gladly and leisurely to the end. This priest, like Julius II, loved nothing so much as war. He was allured by action, gallantry, aristocracy; commoners enter his pages only as victims of lordly strife. He did not inquire into motives; he relied too trustfully on embellished or prejudiced accounts; he made no pretense of adding philosophy to narrative. He was only a chronicler, but of all chroniclers the best.

Drama marked time. Mysteries, moralities, "miracles," interludes, and farces occupied the stages temporarily erected in the towns. Themes were increasingly secular, and the humor was often scandalous; but religious subjects still predominated, and the people never tired of spectacles representing the Passion of Christ. The most famous theater guild of the time—the Parisian *Confrairie de la Passion de Nôtre Seigneur*—specialized in acting the story of Christ's brief stay in Jerusalem. One such Passion Play, by Arnoul Greban, ran to 35,000 lines.

Poetry, too, had its guilds. Toulouse set up in 1323 a *Consistori de la gaya sciensa*, or Academy of the Gay Science; under its auspices public competitions in poetry sought to revive the art and spirit of the troubadours. Similar literary societies were formed at Amiens, Douai, and Valenciennes, preparing for the French Academy of Richelieu. Kings and great lords had poets as well as minstrels and buffoons attached to their households. The "good René," Duke of Anjou and Lorraine, and titular King of Naples, supported a bevy of poets and artists at his courts in Nancy, Tarascon, and Aix-en-Provence, and so rivaled the best of his rhymers that he received the title of "Last of the Troubadours." Charles V took care of Eustache Deschamps, who sang the beauty of women, married, denounced matrimony in a 12,000-line *Le Miroir de mariage*, and bemoaned the misery and wickedness of his time:

> *Age de plomb, temps pervers, ciel d'airain,*
> *Terre sans fruit, et stérile et prehaigne,*
> *Peuple maudit, de toute douleur plein,*
> *Il est bien droit que de vous tous me plaigne;*
> *Car je ne vois rien au monde qui vienne*
> *Fors tristement et à confusion,*
> *Et qui tout maux en ses faits ne comprenne,*
> *Hui est le temps de tribulation.* * [54]

---

* O age of lead, perverse time, sky of brass,   For I see nothing in tomorrow's world,
Land without fruit, sterile and profitless,   Grievously sad and all disorderly,
People accursed, with every sorrow full!—   Comprising every evil in its deeds.
Is it not right that I should mourn you all?   Today the time of tribulation comes.

Christine de Pisan. reared in Paris as the daughter of Charles V's Italian physician, was left with three children and three relatives to support when her husband died; she did it miraculously by writing exquisite poetry and patriotic history, she deserves a passing obeisance as the first woman in Western Europe to live by her pen. Alain Chartier was more fortunate; his love poems—like *La belle dame sans merci*, which melodiously chided women for hoarding their charms—so captivated the aristocracy that a future queen of France, Margaret of Scotland, was said to have kissed the lips of the poet as he slept on a bench. Étienne Pasquier, a century later, told the legend charmingly:

> When many were astonished at this—for to speak the truth Nature had placed a beautiful spirit in a most ungraceful body—the lady told them they must not be surprised at this mystery, for it was not the man whom she desired to kiss but the lips whence had issued such golden words.[55]

The finest French poet of the age did not have to write poetry, for he was the nephew of Charles VI and the father of Louis XII. But Charles, Duke of Orléans, was taken prisoner at Agincourt, and spent twenty-five years (1415–40) in genteel captivity in England. There, heavy of heart, he consoled himself by writing tender verses about the beauty of women and the tragedy of France. For a time all France sang his song of spring:

> *Le temps a laissié son manteau,*
> *De vent, de froidure, et de pluye,*
> *Et s'est vêtu de brouderie*
> *Du soleil luyant, cler et beau.*
> *Il n'y a beste, ne oyseau*
> *Qu'en son jargon ne chante ou crie:*
> *Le temps a laissié son manteau.** [56]

Even in England there were pretty girls, and Charles forgot his griefs when modest loveliness passed by:

> *Dieu! qu'il fait bon la regarder,*
> *La gracieuse, bonne et belle!*
> *Pour les grands biens qui sont en elle*
> *Chacun est près de la louer.*

---

* The year has changed his mantle cold
   Of wind, of rain, of bitter air;
And he goes clad in cloth of gold,
   Of laughing sun and season fair;
No bird or beast of wood or wold
   But doth with cry or song declare,
The year lays down his mantle cold.[57]

Qui se pourrait d'elle lasser?
Tout jour sa beauté renouvelle.
Dieu! qu'il fait bon la regarder,
La gracieuse, bonne, et belle! * [58]

Allowed at last to return to France, he made his castle at Blois a happy center of literature and art, where Villon was received despite his poverty and his crimes. When old age came, and Charles could no longer join in the revels of his young friends, he made his excuses to them in graceful lines that might have served as his epitaph:

Saluez moi toute la compaignie
Ou a present estes a chière lye,
Et leurs dites que voulentiers seroye
Avecques eulx, mais estre n'y pourroye,
Pour Viellesse qui m'a eu sa baillie.
Au temps passé Jennesse sy jolie
Me gouvernoit; las! or ny suy ge mye.
Amoureus fus, or ne le suy ge mye,
Et en Paris menoye bonne vie.
Adieu, bon temps, ravoir ne vous saroye! ...
Saluez moi toute la compaignie.† [59]

VIII. ART

The artists of France were in this epoch superior to her poets, but they too suffered from her bitter impoverishment. No lavish patronage supported them, of city, Church, or king. The communes, which had expressed the pride of their guilds through majestic temples to an unquestioned faith, had

---

* O God! how good it is to see her,
  Gracious one, so good and fair!
For all choice virtues that are in her
  Each will offer praises rare.
Who then can weary of her beauty,
  Fresh each day beyond compare?
O God! how good it is to see her,
  Gracious one, so good and fair!

† Salute for me all the company
Where now you meet in comradery,
And say how gladly I would be
One of their band if it could be;
Age holds me in captivity.
In time long past Youth joyously
Governed my life; gone now is he.
Lover was I, ne'er more must be;
In Paris led a life so free.
Good-by, good times I ne'er shall see! ...
Salute for me all the company.

been weakened or destroyed by the extension of royal authority, and the enlargement of the economy from a local to a national frame. The French Church could no longer finance or inspire such stupendous structures as had risen in the twelfth and thirteenth centuries from the soil of France. Faith as well as wealth had declined; the hope that in those centuries had undertaken at once the Crusades and the cathedrals—the enterprise and its prayer —had lost its generative ecstasy. It was more than the fourteenth century could do to finish, in architecture, what a more sanguine era had begun. Even so, Jean Ravi completed Notre Dame in Paris (1351), Rouen added a "Lady Chapel" (1302) to a cathedral already dedicated to Our Lady, and Poitiers gave her cathedral its proud west front (1379).

The Rayonnant style of Gothic design was now (1275 f.) gradually yielding to a Geometrical Gothic that stressed Euclidean figures instead of radiating lines. In this manner Bordeaux built her cathedral (1320–25), Caen raised a handsome spire (shattered in the second World War) on the church of St. Pierre (1308), Auxerre gave her cathedral a new nave (1335), Coutances (1371–86) and Amiens (1375) added lovely chapels to their historic shrines, and Rouen enhanced her architectural glory with the noble church of St. Ouen (1318–1545).

In the final quarter of the fourteenth century, when France thought herself victorious, her architects displayed a new Gothic, joyous in spirit, exuberant in carved detail, fancifully intricate in tracery, reveling recklessly in ornament. The ogive, or pointed arch of a continued curve, became now an ogee, or tapered arch of a reversed curve, like the tongue of flame that gave the style its Flamboyant name. Capitals fell into disuse; columns were fluted or spiraled; choir stalls were profusely carved, and were closed with iron screens of delicate lacery; pendentives became stalactites; vaults were a wilderness of intertwined, disappearing, reappearing ribs; the mullions of the windows shunned the old solid geometrical forms, and flowed in charming frailty and incalculable willfulness; spires seemed built of decoration; structure vanished behind ornament. The new style made its debut in the chapel of St. Jean-Baptiste (1375) in the cathedral of Amiens; by 1425 it had captured France; in 1436 it began one of its fragile miracles, the church of St. Maclou at Rouen. Perhaps the revival of French courage and arms by Joan of Arc and Charles VII, the growth of mercantile wealth as instanced by Jacques Cœur, and the inclination of the rising *bourgeoisie* to luxurious ornament helped the Flamboyant style to its triumph in the first half of the fifteenth century. In that feminine form Gothic survived till French kings and nobles brought back from their wars in Italy the classical architectural ideas of the Renaissance.

The growth of civil architecture revealed the rising secularism of the time. Kings and dukes thought there were churches enough, and built themselves palaces to impress the people and house their mistresses; rich burghers spent fortunes on their homes; municipalities announced their wealth through splendid *hôtels-de-ville*, or city halls. Some hospitals, like Beaune's, were designed with a fresh and airy beauty that must have lulled the ill to health. At Avignon the popes and cardinals gathered and nourished a diversity of artists; but the builders, painters, and sculptors of France were now usually grouped about a noble or a king. Charles V built the château of Vincennes (1364–73) and the Bastille (1369), and commissioned the versatile André Beauneveû to carve figures of Philip VI, John II, and Charles himself for the imposing array of royal tombs that crowd the ambulatory and crypt of St. Denis (1364). Louis of Orléans raised the château of Pierrefonds, and John, Duke of Berry, though hard on his peasants, was one of the great art patrons of history.

For him Beauneveû illustrated a Psalter in 1402. It was but one in a series of illuminated manuscripts that stand near the top in what might be called the chamber music of the graphic arts. For the same discriminating lord, Jacquemart de Hesdin painted *Les petites heures*, *Les belles heures*, and *Les grandes heures*, all illustrating books of "hours" for the canonical daily prayers. Again for Duke John the brothers Pol, Jehannequin, and Herman Malouel of Limburg produced *Les tres riches heures* (1416)—sixty-five delicately beautiful miniatures picturing the life and scenery of France: nobles hunting, peasants working, a countryside purified with snow. These *Very Rich Hours*, now hidden even from tourist eyes in the Condé Museum at Chantilly, and the miniatures made for *Le bon roi*, René of Anjou, were almost the last triumphs of illumination; for in the fifteenth century that art was challenged both by wood-block engraving and by the development of thriving schools of mural and easel painting at Fontainebleau, Amiens, Bourges, Tours, Moulins, Avignon, and Dijon, not to speak of the masters who worked for the dukes of Burgundy. Beauneveû and the Van Eycks brought Flemish styles of painting to France; and through Simone Martini and other Italians at Avignon, and the Angevin rule in Naples (1268–1435), Italian art influenced the French long before French arms invaded Italy. By 1450 French painting stood on its own feet, and marked its coming of age with the anonymous *Pietà* of Villeneuve, now in the Louvre.

Jean Fouquet is the first clear personality in French painting. Born at Tours (1416), he studied for seven years in Italy (1440–47), and returned to France with that predilection for classical architectural backgrounds which in the seventeenth century would become a mania with Nicolas Poussin and Claude Lorrain. Nevertheless he painted several portraits that are powerful revelations of character: Archbishop Juvénal des Ursins, Chancellor of France—stout and stern and resolute, and not too pious for statesmanship; Etienne Chevalier, treasurer of the realm—a melancholy man troubled by the impossibility of raising money as fast as a government can spend it; Charles VII himself, after Agnès Sorel had made a man of him; and Agnès in the rosy flesh, transformed by Fouquet into a cold and stately Virgin with downcast eyes and uplifted breast. For Chevalier, Jean illuminated a *Book of Hours*, brightening the tedium of ritual prayer with almost fragrant scenes from the valley of the Loire. An enameled medallion in the Louvre preserves Fouquet as he saw himself—no princely Raphael riding high, but a simple artisan of the brush, dressed for work, eager and diffident, worried and resolved, bearing the mark of a century of poverty on his brow. However, he passed without mishap from one reign to another, and rose at last to be *peintre du roi* for the incalculable Louis XI. After many years of labor comes success, and soon thereafter death.

IX. JOAN OF ARC: 1412–31

In 1422 the repudiated son of Charles VI had himself proclaimed king as Charles VII. In her desolation France looked to him for help, and fell into deeper despair. This timid, listless, heedless youth of twenty hardly credited his own proclamation, and probably shared the doubts of Frenchmen as to the legitimacy of his birth. Fouquet's portrait of him shows a sad and homely face, pockets under the eyes, and an overreaching nose. He was fearfully religious, heard three Masses daily, and allowed no canonical hour to pass without reciting its appointed prayers. In the intervals he attended to a long succession of mistresses, and begot twelve children upon his virtuous wife. He pawned his jewels, and most of the clothes from his back, to finance resistance to England, but he had no stomach for war, and left the struggle to his ministers and his generals. Neither were they enthusiastic or alert; they quarreled jealously among themselves—all but the faithful Jean Dunois, the natural son of Louis, Duke of Orléans. When the English moved south to lay siege to that city (1428), no concerted action was taken to resist them, and disorder was the order of the day. Orléans lay at a bend in the Loire; if it fell, all the south, now hesitantly loyal to Charles VII, would join the north to make France an English colony. North and south alike watched the siege, and prayed for a miracle.

Even the distant village of Domremy, half asleep by the Meuse on the eastern border of France, followed the struggle with patriotic and religious passion. The peasants there were fully medieval in faith and sentiment; they lived from nature but in the supernatural; they were sure that spirits dwelled in the surrounding air, and many women vowed that they had seen and talked with them. Men as well as women there, as generally throughout rural

France, thought of the English as devils who hid their tails in their coattails. Someday, said a prophecy current in the village, God would send a *pucelle*, a virgin maid, to save France from these demons, and end the long Satanic reign of war.[60] The wife of the mayor of Domremy whispered these hopes to her goddaughter Joan.

Joan's father, Jacques d'Arc, was a prosperous farmer, and probably gave no mind to such tales. Joan was noted among these pious people for her piety; she was fond of going to church, confessed regularly and fervently, and busied herself with parochial charities. In her little garden the fowls and the birds ate from her hand. One day, when she had been fasting, she thought she saw a strange light over her head, and that she heard a voice saying, "Jeanne, be a good obedient child. Go often to church." [61] She was then (1424) in her thirteenth year; perhaps some physiological changes mystified her at this most impressionable time. During the next five years her "voices"—as she called the apparitions—spoke many counsels to her, until at last it seemed to her that the Archangel Michael himself commanded her: "Go to the succor of the King of France, and thou shalt restore his kingdom. . . . Go to M. Baudricourt, captain at Vaucouleurs, and he will conduct thee to the King." And at another time the voice said: "Daughter of God, thou shalt lead the Dauphin to Reims that he may there receive worthily his anointing" and coronation. For until Charles should be anointed by the Church, France would doubt his divine right to rule; but if the holy oil should be poured upon his head France would unite behind him and be saved.

After a long and troubled hesitation Joan revealed her visions to her parents. Her father was shocked at the thought of an innocent girl undertaking so fantastic a mission; rather than permit it, he said, he would drown her with his own hands.[62] To further restrain her he persuaded a young villager to announce that she had promised him her hand in marriage. She denied it; and to preserve the virginity that she had pledged to her saints, as well as to obey their command, she fled to an uncle, and prevailed upon him to take her to Vaucouleurs (1429). There Captain Baudricourt advised the uncle to give the seventeen-year-old girl a good spanking, and to restore her to her parents; but when Joan forced her way into his presence, and firmly declared that she had been sent by God to help King Charles save Orléans, the bluff commandant melted, and, even while thinking her charmed by devils, sent to Chinon to ask the King's pleasure. Royal permission came; Baudricourt gave the Maid a sword, the people of Vaucouleurs bought her a horse, and six soldiers agreed to guide her on the long and perilous journey across France to Chinon. Perhaps to discourage male advances, to facilitate riding, and to win acceptance by generals and troops, she donned a masculine and military garb—jerkin, doublet, hose, gaiters, spurs—and cut her hair like a boy's. She rode serene and confident through towns that vacillated between fearing her as a witch and worshiping her as a saint.

After traveling 450 miles in eleven days she came to the King and his council. Though his poor raiment gave no sign of royalty, Joan (we are told—for how could legend keep its hands from her history?) singled him out at once, and greeted him courteously: "God send you long life, gentle Dauphin. . . . My name is Jeanne la Pucelle. The King of Heaven speaks to you through me, and says that you shall be anointed and crowned at Reims, and be lieutenant of the King of Heaven, who is King of France." A priest who now became the Maid's chaplain said later that in private she assured the King of his legitimate birth. Some have thought that from her first meeting with Charles she accepted the clergy as the rightful interpreters of her voices, and followed their lead in her counsel to the King; through her the bishops might displace the generals in forming the royal policies.[63] Still doubtful, Charles sent her to Poitiers to be examined by pundits there. They found no evil in her. They commissioned some women to inquire into her virginity, and on that delicate point too they were satisfied. For, like the Maid, they held that a special privilege belonged to virgins as the instruments and messengers of God.

Dunois, in Orléans, had assured the garrison that God would soon send someone to their aid. Hearing of Joan, he half believed his hopes, and pleaded with the court to send her to him at once. They consented, gave her a black horse, clothed her in white armor, put in her hand a white banner embroidered with the fleur-de-lis of France, and dispatched her to Dunois with a numerous escort bearing provisions for the besieged. It was not hard to find entry to the city (April 29, 1429); the English had not surrounded it entirely, but had divided their two or three thousand men (less than the Orléans garrison) among a dozen forts at strategic points in the environs. The people of Orléans hailed Joan as the Virgin incarnate, followed her trustfully even into dangerous places, accompanied her to church, prayed when she prayed, wept when she wept. At her command the soldiers gave up their mistresses, and struggled to express themselves without profanity; one of their leaders, La Hire, found this impossible, and received from Joan a dispensation to swear by his baton. It was this Gascon *condottiere* who uttered the famous prayer: "Sire God, I beg Thee to do for La Hire what he would do for Thee wert Thou a captain and La Hire were God." [64]

Joan sent a letter to Talbot, the English commander, proposing that both armies should unite as brothers and proceed to Palestine to redeem the Holy Land from the Turks; Talbot thought that this exceeded his commission. Some days later a part of the garrison, without informing Dunois or Joan, issued beyond the walls and attacked one of the British bastions. The English fought well, the French retreated; but Dunois and Joan, having heard the commotion, rode up and bade their men renew the assault; it succeeded, and the English abandoned their position. On the morrow the French attacked two other forts and took them, the Maid being in the thick of the fight. In the second encounter an arrow pierced her shoulder; when the wound had been dressed she returned to the fray. Meanwhile the sturdy cannon of Guillaume Duisy hurled upon the English fortress of Les Tourelles balls weighing 120 pounds each. Joan was spared the sight of the victorious French slaughtering 500 Englishmen when that stronghold fell. Talbot concluded that his forces were inadequate for the siege, and withdrew them to the north (May 8). All France rejoiced, seeing in the "Maid of Orléans" the hand of God; but the English denounced her as a sorceress, and vowed to take her alive or dead.

On the day after her triumph Joan set out to meet the King, who was advancing from Chinon. He greeted her with a kiss, and accepted her plan to march through France to Reims, though this meant passing through hostile terrain. His army encountered English forces at Meung, Beaugency, and Patay, and won decisive victories, tarnished with vengeful massacres that horrified the Maid. Seeing a French soldier slay an English prisoner, she dismounted, held the dying man's head in her hands, comforted him, and sent for a confessor. On July 15 the King entered Reims, and on the seventeenth he was anointed and crowned with awesome ceremonies in the majestic cathedral. Jacques d'Arc, coming up from Domrémy, saw his daughter, still in her male attire, riding in splendor through the religious capital of France. He did not neglect the occasion, but through her intercession secured a remission of taxes for his village. For a passing spell Joan considered her mission accomplished, and thought, "If it would please God that I might go and tend sheep with my sister and brother." [65]

But the fever of battle had entered her blood. Acclaimed as inspired and holy by half of France, she almost forgot now to be a saint, and became a warrior. She was strict with her soldiers, scolded them lovingly, and deprived them of the consolations that all soldiers hold as their due; and when she found two prostitutes accompanying them she drew her sword and struck one so manfully that the blade broke and the woman died. [66] She followed the King and his army in an attack upon Paris, which was still held by the English; she was in the van in clearing the first foss; approaching the second, she was struck in the thigh by an arrow, but remained to cheer on the troops. Their assault failed, they suffered 1,500 casualties, and cursed her for thinking that a prayer could silence a gun; this had not been their experience. Some Frenchwomen, who had jealously waited for her first reverse, censured her for leading an assault on the feast of the Virgin's birth (September 8, 1429). She retired with her detachment to Compiègne. Besieged there by Burgundians allied with the English, she bravely led a sally, which was repulsed; she was the last to retreat, and found the gates of the town closed before she could reach them. She was dragged from her horse, and was taken as a captive to John of Luxembourg (May 24, 1430). Sir John lodged her honorably in his castles at Beaulieu and Beaurevoir.

His good fortune brought him a dangerous dilemma. His sovereign, Duke Philip the Good of Burgundy, demanded the precious prize; the English urged Sir John to surrender her to them, hoping that her ignominious execution would break the charm that had so heartened the French. Pierre Cauchon, Bishop of Beauvais, who had been driven from his diocese for supporting the English, was sent by them to Philip with powers and funds to negotiate the transfer of the Maid to British authority, and was promised the archbishopric of Rouen as the reward of his success. The Duke of Bedford, controlling the University of Paris, induced its pundits to advise Philip to hand over Joan, as a possible sorceress and heretic, to Cauchon as the ecclesiastical head of the region in which she had been captured. When these arguments were rejected, Cauchon offered to Philip and John a bribe of 10,000 gold crowns ($250,000?). This too proving inadequate, the English government laid an embargo on all exports to the Low Countries. Flanders, the richest source of the Duke's revenue, faced bankruptcy. John, over the entreaties of his wife, and Philip, despite his Good name, finally accepted the bribe and surrendered the Maid to Cauchon, who took her to Rouen. There, though formally a prisoner of the Inquisition, she was placed under English guard in the tower of a castle held by the Earl of Warwick as the governor of Rouen. Shackles were put on her feet, and a chain was fastened around her waist and bound to a beam.

Her trial began on February 21, 1431, and continued till May 30. Cauchon presided, one of his canons served as prosecutor, a Dominican monk represented the Inquisition, and some forty men learned in theology and law were added to the panel. The charge was heresy. To check the monstrous regiment of magic-mongers that infested Europe, the Church had made the claim to divine inspiration a heresy punishable with death. Witches were being burned for pretending to supernatural powers; and it was a common opinion, among churchmen and laymen, that those who made such claims might actually have received supernatural powers from the Devil. Some of Joan's jurors seem to have believed this in her case. In their judgment her refusal to acknowledge that the authority of the Church, as the vicar of Christ on earth, could override that of her "voices" proved her a sorceress. This became the opinion of the majority of the court.[67] Nevertheless they were moved by the guileless simplicity of her answers, by her evident piety and chastity; they were men, and seem at times to have felt a great pity for this girl of nineteen, so obviously the prey of English fear. "The king of England," said Warwick, with soldierly candor, "has paid dearly for her;

he would not on any consideration whatever have her die a natural death." [68] Some jurors argued that the matter should be laid before the pope—which would free her and the court from English power. Joan expressed a desire to be sent to him, but drew a firm distinction that ruined her: she would acknowledge his supreme authority in matters of faith, but as concerned what she had done in obedience to her voices she would own no judge but God Himself. The judges agreed that this was heresy. Weakened by months of questioning, she was persuaded to sign a retraction; but when she found that this still left her condemned to lifelong imprisonment within English jurisdiction, she revoked her retraction. English soldiers surrounded the court, and threatened the lives of the judges if the Maid should escape burning. On May 31 a few of the judges convened, and sentenced her to death.

That very morning the faggots were piled high in the market place of Rouen. Two platforms were placed near by—one for Cardinal Winchester of England and his prelates, another for Cauchon and the judges; and 800 British troops stood on guard. The Maid was brought in on a cart, accompanied by an Augustinian monk, Isambart, who befriended her to the last, at peril to his life. She asked for a crucifix; an English soldier handed her one that he had fashioned from two sticks; she accepted it, but called also for a crucifix blessed by the Church; and Isambart prevailed upon the officials to bring her one from the church of Saint Sauveur. The soldiers grumbled at the delay, for it was now noon. "Do you intend us to dine here?" their captain asked. His men snatched her from the hands of the priests, and led her to the stake. Isambart held up a crucifix before her, and a Dominican monk mounted the pyre with her. The faggots were lighted, and the flames rose about her feet. Seeing the Dominican still beside her, she urged him to descend to safety. She invoked her voices, her saints, the Archangel Michael, and Christ, and was consumed in agony. A secretary to the English king anticipated the verdict of history: "We are lost," he cried; "we have burned a saint."

In 1455 Pope Calixtus III, at the behest of Charles VII, ordered a reexamination of the evidence upon which Joan had been condemned; and in 1456 (France being now victorious) the verdict of 1431 was, by the ecclesiastical court of review, declared unjust and void. In 1920 Benedict XV numbered the Maid of Orléans among the saints of the Church.

X. FRANCE SURVIVES: 1431-53

We must not exaggerate the military importance of Joan of Arc; probably Dunois and La Hire would have saved Orléans without her; her tactics of reckless assault won some battles and lost others; and England was feeling the cost of a Hundred Years' War. In 1435 Philip of Burgundy, England's ally, tired of the struggle and made a separate peace with France. His defection weakened the hold of the English on the conquered cities of the south; one by one these expelled their alien garrisons. In 1436 Paris itself, for seventeen years a captive, drove out the British, and Charles VII at last ruled in his capital.

Strange to tell, he who had for so long been a do-nothing shadow of a king, had learned by this time to govern—to choose competent ministers, to reorganize the army, to discipline turbulent barons, to do whatever was needed to make his country free. What had wrought this transformation? The inspiration of Joan had begun it, but how weak he still seemed when he raised not a finger to save her! His remarkable mother-in-law, Yolande of Anjou, had helped him with wise counsel, had encouraged him to receive and support the Maid. Now—if we may trust tradition—she gave her son-in-law the mistress who for ten years ruled the heart of the King.

Agnès Sorel was the daughter of a squire in Touraine. Orphaned in childhood, she had been brought up to good manners by Isabelle, Duchess of Lorraine. Isabelle took her, then twenty-three, to visit the court in Chinon (1432) in the year after Joan's death. Snared in the girl's chestnut tresses, and in love with her laughter, Charles marked her out as his own. Yolande found her tractable, hoped to use her in influencing the King, and persuaded Marie, her daughter, to accept this latest of her husband's mistresses.[69] Agnès remained till death faithful in this infidelity, and a later king, Francis I, after much experience in such matters, praised the "Lady of Beauty" as having served France better than any cloistered nun. Charles "relished wisdom from such lips"; he allowed Agnès to shame him out of indolence and cowardice into industry and resolution. He gathered about him able men like Constable Richemont, who led his armies, and Jacques Cœur, who restored the finances of the state, and Jean Bureau, whose artillery brought recalcitrant nobles to heel and sent the English scurrying to Calais.

Jacques Cœur was a *condottiere* of commerce; a man of no pedigree and little schooling, who, however, could count well; a Frenchman who dared to compete successfully with Venetians, Genoese, and Catalans in trade with the Moslem East. He owned and equipped seven merchant vessels, manned them by hiring convicts and snatching vagrants from the streets, and sailed his ships under the flag of the Mother of God. He amassed the greatest fortune of his time in France, some 27,000,000 francs, when a franc was worth some five dollars in the emaciated currency of our day. In 1436 Charles gave him charge of the mint, soon afterward of the revenues and expenditures of the government. A States-General of 1439, enthusiastically supporting Charles's resolve to drive the English from French soil, empowered the King, by a famous succession of *ordonnances* (1443–47), to take the whole *taille* of France—i.e., all taxes hitherto paid by tenants to their feudal lords; the government's revenue now rose to 1,800,000 crowns ($45,000,000?) a year. From that time onward the French monarchy, unlike the English, was independent of the Estates' "power of the purse," and could resist the growth of a middle-class democracy. This system of national taxation provided the funds for the victory of France over England; but as the King could raise the rate of assessment, it became a major tool of royal oppression, and shared in causing the Revolution of 1789. Jacques Cœur played a leading role in these fiscal developments, earning the admiration of many and the hatred of a powerful few. In 1451 he was arrested on a charge—never proved—of hiring agents to poison Agnès Sorel. He was condemned and banished, and all his property was confiscated to the state—an elegant method of exploitation by proxy. He fled to Rome, where he was made admiral of a papal fleet sent to the relief of Rhodes. He was taken ill at Chios, and died there in 1456, aged sixty-one.

Meanwhile Charles VII, guided by Cœur, had established an honest coinage, rebuilt the shattered villages, promoted industry and commerce, and restored the economic vitality of France. He compelled the disbandment of private companies of soldiers, and gathered these into his service to form the first standing army in Europe (1439). He decreed that in every parish some virile citizen, chosen by his fellows, should be freed from all taxation, should arm himself, practice the use of weapons, and be ready at any moment to join his like in the military service of the King. It was these *francs-tireurs*, or free bowmen, who drove the English from France.

By 1449 Charles was prepared to break the truce that had been signed in 1444. The English were surprised and shocked. They were weakened by internal quarrels, and found their fading empire in France relatively as expensive to maintain in the fifteenth century as India in the twentieth; in 1427 France cost England £68,000, brought her £57,000. The British fought bravely but not wisely; they relied too long on archers and stakes, and the tactics that had stopped the French cavalry at Crécy and Poitiers proved helpless at Formigny (1450) against the cannon of Bureau. In 1449 the English evacuated most of Normandy; in 1451 they abandoned its capital, Rouen. In 1453 the great Talbot himself was defeated and killed at Castillon; Bordeaux surrendered; all Guienne was French again; the English kept only Calais. On October 19, 1453, the two nations signed the peace that ended the Hundred Years' War.

CHAPTER IV

Gallia Phoenix

1453-1515

I. LOUIS XI: 1461-83

THE son of Charles VII was an exceptionally troublesome dauphin. Married against his will at thirteen (1436) to Margaret of Scotland, aged eleven, he revenged himself by ignoring her and cultivating mistresses. Margaret, who lived on poetry, found peace in an early death (1444), saying, as she died, "Fie upon life! Speak to me no more of it."[1] Louis twice rebelled against his father, fled to Flanders after the second attempt, and waited fretfully for power. Charles accommodated him by starving himself to death (1461);[2] and for twenty-two years France was ruled by one of her strangest and greatest kings.

He was now thirty-eight, thin and ungainly, homely and melancholy, with distrustful eyes and far-reaching nose. He looked like a peasant, dressed like an impoverished pilgrim in a rough gray gown and a shabby felt hat, prayed like a saint, and ruled as if he had read *The Prince* before Machiavelli was born. He scorned the pomp of feudalism, laughed at traditions and formalities, questioned his own legitimacy, and shocked all thrones with his simplicity. He lived in the gloomy palace Des Tournelles in Paris, or in the château of Plessis-les-Tours near Tours, usually like a bachelor, though a second time married; penurious though possessing France; keeping only the few attendants he had had in his exile, and eating such food as any peasant might afford. He looked not an iota, but would be every inch, a king.

He subordinated every element of character to his resolve that France should under his hammer be forged out of feudal fragmentation into monarchic unity and monolithic strength, and that this centralized monarchy should lift France out of the ashes of war to new life and power. To his political purpose he gave his thinking day and night, with a mind clear, cunning, inventive, restless, like Caesar counting nothing done if anything remained to do. "As for peace," said Comines, "he could hardly endure the thought of it."[3] However, he was unsuccessful in war, and preferred diplomacy, espionage, and bribery to force; he brought men around to his purposes by persuasion, flattery, or fear, and kept a large staff of spies in his service at home and abroad; he paid regular secret salaries to the ministers of England's Edward IV.[4] He could yield, bear insult, play at humility, wait his chance for victory or revenge. He made major blunders, but recovered from them with unscrupulous and disconcerting ingenuity. He attended to all deails of government, and forgot nothing. Yet he spared time for literature and art, read avidly, collected manuscripts, recognized the revolution that printing presaged, and enjoyed the company of educated men, particularly if they were Bohemians in the Parisian sense. In his Flanders exile he had joined the Count of Charolais in forming an academy of scholars, who salted their pedantry with jolly Boccaccian tales; Antoine de la Salle gathered some of these in the *Cent nouvelles nouvelles*. He was hard on the rich, careless of the poor, hostile to artisan guilds, favorable to the middle class as his strongest support, and in any class ruthless with those who opposed him. After a rebellion in Perpignan he ordered that any banished rebel who dared to return should have his testicles amputated.[5] In his war with the nobles he had some special enemies or traitors imprisoned for years in iron cages eight by eight by seven feet; these were contrived by the bishop of Verdun, who later occupied one for fourteen years.[6] At the same time Louis was much devoted to the Church, needing her aid against nobles and states. He had a rosary nearly always at hand, and repeated paternosters and Ave Marias with the assiduity of a dying nun. In 1472 he inaugurated the Angelus—a midday Ave Maria for the peace of the realm. He visited sacred shrines, conscripted relics, bribed the saints to his service, took the Virgin into partnership in his wars. When he died, he himself was represented as a saint on an abbey portal in Tours.

With the help of his faults he created modern France. He found it a loose association of feudal and ecclesiastical principalities; he made it a nation, the most powerful in Latin Christendom. He brought in silk weavers from Italy, miners from Germany; he improved harbors and transport, protected French shipping, opened new markets to French industry, and allied the government of France with the rising mercantile and financial *bourgeoisie*. He saw that the extension of commerce across local and national frontiers required a strong central administration. Feudalism was no longer needed for the protection and management of agriculture; the peasantry was slowly freeing itself from a stagnant serfdom; the time had passed when the feudal barons could make their own laws, mint their own coins, play sovereign in their domains; by fair means or foul he would bring them, one by one, to submission and order. He restricted their right to trespass on peasant properties in their hunts, established a governmental postal service that ran through their estates (1464), forbade them to wage private wars, and demanded of them all the back dues they had failed to pay to their liege lords, the kings of France.

They did not like him. Representatives of 500 noble families met in Paris and formed the *Ligue du bien public* (1464) to uphold their privileges in the sacred name of the public good. The Count of Charolais, heir to the throne of Burgundy, joined this League, eager to add northeastern France to his duchy. Louis' own brother, Charles, Duke of Berry, decamped to Brittany and headed the revolt. Enemies and armies rose against the King on every side. If they could unite he was lost; his only hope was to defeat them piecemeal. He dashed south across the Allier River and compelled a hostile force to surrender; he rushed back north just in time to prevent a Burgundian army from entering his capital. Each side claimed victory in the battle of Montlhéry; the Burgundians retreated, Louis entered Paris, the Burgundians returned with allies and laid siege to the city. Unwilling to risk rebellion by Parisians too intelligent to starve, Louis yielded by the treaty of Conflans (1465) almost all that his foes demanded—lands, money, offices; brother Charles received Normandy. Nothing was said about the public good; the people had to be taxed to raise the required sums. Louis bided his time.

Charles soon slipped into war with Duke Francis of Brittany, who captured him; Louis marched into Normandy and regained it bloodlessly. But Francis, rightly suspecting that Louis wanted Brittany too, joined with the Count of Charolais—who had now become Duke Charles the Bold of Burgundy—in an offensive alliance against the irrepressible King. Louis strained every nerve of diplomacy, made a separate peace with Francis, and agreed to a conference with Charles at Péronne. There, in effect, Charles took him prisoner, and compelled him to cede Picardy and share in the sack of Liége. Louis returned to Paris at the nadir of his power and repute; even the magpies were taught to mock him (1468). Two years later, in this reciprocation of treachery, Louis took advantage of Charles's preoccupation in Gelderland, and marched his troops into Saint-Quentin, Amiens, and Beauvais. Charles persuaded Edward IV to unite with him against France, but Louis bought Edward off. Knowing Edward's keen appreciation of women, he invited him to come and divert himself with the ladies of Paris; moreover, he would assign to Edward, as royal confessor, the Cardinal of Bourbon, who "would willingly absolve him if he should commit any sin by way of love or gallantry."[7] He maneuvered Charles into war with Switzerland; and when Charles was killed Louis took not only Picardy but Burgundy itself (1477). He soothed the Burgundian nobles with gold, and pleased the people by taking a Burgundian mistress.

Now he felt strong enough to turn upon the barons who had so often fought him, and had so seldom obeyed his summons to come out and fight for France. Many of the lords who had conspired against him in 1465 were dead, or incapacitated by age. Their successors had learned to fear a king who cut off the heads of traitorous aristocrats and confiscated their estates, who had built a strong army of mercenaries, and seemed aiways able to raise immense sums for purchases and bribes. Preferring to spend his subjects' money rather than their lives, Louis bought Cerdagne and Roussillon from Spain. He acquired Rochelle through his brother's death; he took Alençon and Blois by force; he persuaded René to bequeath Provence to the French crown (1481); a year later Anjou and Maine reverted to the monarchy; in 1483 Flanders, seeking the aid of Louis against the Holy Roman Empire, ceded to him the county of Artois, with the thriving cities of Arras and Douai. With the barons subdued, and the municipal *parlements* and communes submitting to the King, Louis accomplished for France that national unification and centralized administration which, a decade later, Henry VII was to achieve for England, Ferdinand and Isabella for Spain, and Alexander VI for the Papal States. Though this substituted one tyranny for many, it was at the time a progressive move, enhancing internal order and external security, standardizing currency and measurements, molding dialects into a language, and furthering the growth of vernacular literature in France. The monarchy was not absolute; the nobles retained large powers, and the consent of the States-General was usually required for new taxes. The nobles, the officials, and the clergy were exempt from taxation: the nobles on the ground that they fought for the people, the officials because they were so poorly paid and bribed, and the clergy because they protected king and country with their prayers. Public opinion and popular customs checked the King; the local *parlements* still claimed that no royal edict could become law in their districts until they had accepted and registered it. Nevertheless the path had been opened to Louis XIV and *L'état c'est moi*.

Amid all these triumphs Louis himself decayed in body and mind. He imprisoned himself at Plessis-les-Tours, fearing assassination, suspicious of all, seeing hardly anyone, punishing faults and defections cruelly, and now and then dressing himself in robes whose magnificence contrasted with the poor garb of his early reign. He became so gaunt and pale that those who saw him could hardly believe that he was not already dead.[8] For years he had suffered agonies from piles,[9] and had had occasional apoplectic strokes. On August 25, 1483, another attack deprived him of speech; and five days later he died.

His subjects rejoiced, for he had made them pay unbearably for his defeats and victories; the people had grown poorer, as France had become greater, under his merciless statesmanship. Nevertheless later ages were to benefit from his subordination of the nobles, his reorganization of finance, administration, and defense, his promotion of industry, commerce, and printing, his formation of a modern unified state. "If," wrote Comines, "all the days of his life were computed in which joys and pleasures outweighed his pains and trouble, they would be found so few that there would be twenty mournful ones to one pleasant." [10] He and his generation paid for the future prosperity and splendor of France.

II. ITALIAN ADVENTURE

Charles VIII was thirteen when his father died. For eight years his sister, Anne de Beaujeu, only ten years his elder, wisely ruled France as regent. She reduced governmental expenditures, forgave the people a quarter of the poll tax, recalled many exiles, freed many prisoners, and successfully resisted the attempt of the barons, in their *Guerre Folle* or Foolish War (1485), to regain the semi-sovereignty that Louis had overthrown. When Brittany joined with Orléans, Lorraine, Angoulême, Orange, and Navarre in a further revolt, her diplomacy and the generalship of Louis de la Trémouille defeated them all, and she ended the turmoil triumphantly by arranging the marriage of Charles to Anne of Brittany, who brought her great duchy as dowry to the crown of France (1491). The Regent then retired from the government, and lived her remaining thirty-one years in peaceful oblivion.

The new queen was quite another Anne. Short, flat, thin, and lame, with a stubby nose over a spacious mouth on a Gothically elongated face, she had a mind of her own, as shrewd and parsimonious as any Bretonne's should be. Though she dressed simply in black gown and hood, she could, on occasions of state, gleam with jewelry and cloth of gold; and it was she, rather than Charles, who favored artists and poets, and commissioned Jean Bourdichon to paint *Les heures d'Anne de Bretagne*. Never forgetting her beloved Brittany and its ways, she hid her pride in modesty, sewed industriously, and struggled to reform the morals of her husband and his court.

Charles, says the gossipy Brantôme, "loved women more than his slight constitution could endure." [11] After his marriage he restricted himself to one mistress. He could not complain of the Queen's looks; he himself was a macrocephalic hunchback, his features homely, his eyes big and colorless and myopic, his underlip thick and drooping, his speech hesitant, his hands twitching spasmodically.[12] However, he was good-natured, kindly, sometimes idealistic. He read chivalric romances, and conceived the notion of reconquering Naples for France, and Jerusalem for Christendom. The house of Anjou had held the Kingdom of Naples (1268–1435) until evicted by Alfonso of Aragon; the claims of the Anjou dukes had been bequeathed to Louis XI; they were now proclaimed by Charles. His council thought him the last person in the world to lead an army in a major war; but they hoped that diplomacy might ease his way, and that a captured Naples would allow French commerce to dominate the Mediterranean. To protect the royal flanks they ceded Artois and Franche-Comté to Maximilian of Austria, and

Cerdagne and Roussillon to Ferdinand of Spain; they thought to get half of Italy for the parings of France. Heavy taxes, pawned gems, and loans from Genoese bankers and Lodovico, Regent of Milan, provided an army of 40,-000 men, one hundred siege guns, eighty-six ships of war.

Charles set out gaily (1494), perhaps not loath to leave two Annes behind. He was welcomed in Milan (which had a score to settle with Naples), and found its ladies irresistible. He left a trail of natural children on his march, but handsomely refused to touch a reluctant maiden who had been conscripted to his pleasure by his *valet-de-chambre;* instead, he sent for her lover, presided over their betrothal, and gave her a dowry of 500 crowns.[13] Naples had no force capable of resisting his; he entered it in easy triumph (1495), enjoyed its scenery, cuisine, women, and forgot Jerusalem. He was apparently one of the lucky Frenchmen who did not contract, in this campaign, the venereal disease that was later called *morbus gallicus* because it spread so rapidly in France after the troops' return. A "Holy Alliance" of Alexander VI, Venice, and Lodovico of Milan (who had changed his mind) forced Charles to evacuate Naples and retreat through a hostile Italy. His reduced army fought an indecisive engagement at Fornovo (1495), and hastened back to France, carrying with it, among other contagions, the Renaissance.

It was at Fornovo that Pierre Terrail, Seigneur de Bayard, then twenty-two, first displayed the courage that earned him half the famous title of *le chevalier sans peur et sans reproche.* Born in the Château Bayard in the Dauphiné, he came of a noble family every head of which, for two centuries past, had died in battle; and in this encounter Pierre seemed bent on continuing the tradition. He had two horses killed under him, captured an enemy standard, and was knighted by his grateful King. In an age of coarseness, promiscuity, and treachery he maintained all the virtues of chivalry—magnanimous without display, loyal without servility, honorable without offensive pride, and carrying through a dozen wars a spirit so kindly and gay that contemporaries called him *le bon chevalier.* We shall meet him again.

Charles survived his Italian journey by three years. Going to watch a game of tennis at Amboise, he struck his head against a loosened door, and died of a cerebral lesion at the age of twenty-eight. As his children had predeceased him, the throne passed to his nephew the Duke of Orléans, who became Louis XII (1498). Born to Charles of Orléans when the poet was seventy, Louis was now thirty-six, and already in feeble health. His morals were abnormally decent for the time, and his manners were so frank and amiable that France learned to love him despite his futile wars. He seemed guilty of discourtesy when, in the year of his accession, he divorced Jeanne de France, daughter of Louis XI; but he had been forced by that pliantly inflexible king to marry the unprepossessing girl when he was but eleven years old. He could never develop affection for her; and now he persuaded Alexander VI—in return for a French bride, county, and pension to the Pope's son, Caesar Borgia—to annul that marriage on grounds of consanguinity, and to sanction his union with the widowed Anne of Brittany, who carried her duchy in her trousseau. They took up their abode at Blois, and gave France a royal model of mutual devotion and loyalty.

Louis XII illustrated the superiority of character to intellect. He had not the shrewd mind of Louis XI, but he had good will and good sense, and wit enough to delegate many of his powers to wisely chosen aides. He left administration, and most policy, to his lifelong friend Georges, Cardinal d'Amboise; and this prudent and kindly prelate managed affairs so well that the whimsical public, when any new task arose, would shrug its shoulders and say, "Let Georges do it." [14] France was astonished to find its taxes reduced, first by a tenth, then by a third. The King, though reared in riches, spent as little as possible on himself and his court, and fattened no favorites. He abolished the sale of offices, forbade the acceptance of gifts by magistrates, opened the governmental postal service to private use, and bound himself to choose, for any administrative vacancy, one of three men nominated by the judiciary, and not to remove any state employee except after open trial and proof of dishonesty or incompetence. Some comedians and courtiers made fun of his economies, but he took their humor in good spirit. "Amongst their ribaldries," he said, "they may sometimes tell us useful truths; let them amuse themselves, provided they respect the honor of women. . . . I had rather make courtiers laugh by my stinginess than make my people weep by my extravagance." [15] The surest means of pleasing him was to show him some new way of benefiting the people.[16] They expressed their gratitude by calling him *Père du Peuple*. Never in its memory had France known such prosperity.

It was a pity that this happy reign tarnished its record with further invasions of Italy. Perhaps Louis and other French kings undertook these sallies to occupy and decimate the quarrelsome nobles who might otherwise have harassed France with civil war, threatening the still unstable monarchy and national unity. After twelve years of victory in Italy, Louis XII had to withdraw his troops from the peninsula, and then lost to the English at Guinegate (1513) an engagement derisively called the Battle of the Spurs because the French cavalry fled from the field in such unwonted haste. Louis made peace, and was content thereafter to be only King of France.

The death of Anne of Brittany (1514) completed the cycle of his woes. She had given him no heir, and it was with little pleasure that he married his daughter Claude to Francis, Count of Angoulême, now next in line for the throne. His aides urged him, at fifty-two, to take a third wife and cheat the ebullient Francis by begetting a son. He accepted Mary Tudor, the sixteen-year-old sister of Henry VIII. She led the ailing King a merry and ex-hausting life, insisting on all the attentions due to beauty and youth. Louis died in the third month of his marriage (1515), leaving to his son-in-law a defeated but prosperous France that remembered with affection the Father of the People.

III. THE RISE OF THE CHÂTEAUX

Every French art but ecclesiastical architecture now felt the influence of the strengthened monarchy and its Italian forays. Church building kept to Flamboyant Gothic, declaring its own decadence through extravagant dec-oration and prodigal detail, but dying like an operatic courtesan with all the fascination of feminine delicacy, adornment, and grace. Even so, some splen-did churches were begun in this age: St. Wulfram at Abbeville, St. Étienne du Mont at Paris, and the perfect little shrine raised at Brou by Margaret of Austria to the memory of her husband Philibert II of Savoy. Old struc-tures received new charms. Rouen Cathedral called its north portal the *Portail des Libraires* from the bookstalls that stood in the court; money con-tributed for indulgences to eat butter in Lent financed the lovely south tower, which French humor therefore named the *Tour de Beurre;* and Car-dinal d'Amboise found funds for the west front in the same Flamboyant style. Beauvais gave its unfinished masterpiece a south transept whose portal and rose window excel most main façades; Senlis, Tours, and Troyes im-proved their fanes; and at Chartres Jean le Texier built a luxuriant northwest steeple and a gorgeous choir screen that showed Renaissance ideas imping-ing upon Gothic lines. At Paris the exquisite Tour St. Jacques is the restored survivor of a church raised in this period to St. James the Greater.

Noble civic buildings redeemed the strife and chaos of the age. Stately city halls rose in Arras, Douai, Saint-Omer, Noyon, Saint-Quentin, Com-piègne, Dreux, Evreux, Orléans, Saumur. Grenoble built a *Palais de Justice* in 1505, Rouen a still more resplendent one in 1493; Robert Ango and Rol-land Leroux designed it in ornate Gothic, the nineteenth century redeco-rated it, the second World War gutted it.

This was the first century of the French châteaux. The Church had been made subject to the state; the enjoyment of this world encroached upon preparation for the next; the kings would themselves be gods, and make for their leisure a Mohammedan paradise along the Loire. Between 1490 and 1530 the *château fort* or castle changed into the *château de plaisance.* Charles VIII, returning from his Neapolitan campaign, demanded of his architects a palace as splendid as those that he had seen in Italy. He brought back with him the architect Fra Giovanni Giocondo, the sculptor and painter Guido

Mazzoni, the woodworker Domenico Bernabei "Boccador," and nineteen other Italian artists, even a landscape architect, Domenico Pacello.[17] He had already restored the old castle at Amboise; now he commissioned these men, aided by French builders and artisans, to transform it "in the style of Italy" into a luxurious *logis du roi*, a royal lodge.[18] The result was superb: a mass of towers, pinnacles, cornices, corbels, dormers, and balconies, rising imperially on a slope overlooking the peaceful river. A new species of architecture had come to birth.

The style offended patriots and purists by wedding Gothic towers to Renaissance palaces, and by replacing Flamboyant decoration with classical forms and details. The walls, the cylindrical towers, the high, sloping roofs, the machicolated battlements, the occasional moats, were still medieval, recalling the time when a man's home had to be his castle and his fort; but the new spirit brought the dwelling out of its massive martial shell, broadened the windows in rectilinear line to let in the sun, beautified them with frames of carved stone, adorned the interior with classical pilasters, moldings, medallions, statues, arabesques, and reliefs, and surrounded the building with gardens, fountains, flowers, and, usually, a hunting wood or a smiling plain. In these amazing homes of luxury, darkness gave place to light, medieval fear and gloom to Renaissance confidence, audacity, and joy. The love of life became an architectural style.

We should credit this first age of the châteaux unduly if we assigned to it either their origin or their full development. Many of them had pre-existed as castles, and were merely modified; the sixteenth and seventeenth centuries perfected the form to an aristocratic elegance, the eighteenth changed the mood and replaced the gay lyric of the châteaux with the grandiose epic of Versailles. Chinon's castle-château was already old when Charles VII received Joan there (1429), and Loches had had a long history as a royal residence and jail when Lodovico il Moro came there as a prisoner (1504) after Louis XII's second capture of Milan. About 1460 Jean Bourré, state minister to Louis XI, restored the thirteenth-century castle of Langeais into a form essentially medieval—though it is still one of the best preserved of the châteaux. At Chaumont, toward 1473, Charles d'Amboise built another château in the medieval manner; and at Gaillon his brother the Cardinal raised an immense castle-château (1497–1510), which the Revolution incontinently destroyed. Dunois, noble "bastard of Orléans," restored the château of Châteaudun (1464), and the Cardinal of Orléans-Longueville gave it a new wing in the Gothic-Renaissance compromise. The château of Blois still contains thirteenth-century portions; Louis XII built for it an east wing in a harmonious union of brick and stone, of Gothic portal and Renaissance windows; but its supreme glory awaited Francis I.

Gothic sculpture made its exit with infinite grace in the exquisitely carved decoration of the tombs and retable in the church at Brou, where the figure of the Sibyl Agrippa is as fair a form as any at Chartres or Reims. But meanwhile Italian artists were remolding French sculpture to Renaissance independence, symmetry, and grace. Intercourse between France and Italy was growing through the visits of ecclesiastics, diplomats, merchants, and travelers; imported Italian objects of art, especially small bronzes, served as envoys of Renaissance and classical forms and taste. With Charles VIII and Georges and Charles d'Amboise the movement became an impetuous stream. It was Italian artists who founded the Italianizing "School of Amboise" at the country capital of the kings. The tombs of French Royalty in the church of St. Denis are a monumental record of the transition from the somber dignity of Gothic sculpture to the smooth elegance and joyous decoration of Renaissance design, proclaiming glory and celebrating beauty even in the triumph of death.

The transition was personified in Michel Colombe. Born about 1431, he was already described in 1467 as "the supreme sculptor of the French realm," long before the French invasion and absorption of Italy. Gallic sculpture had heretofore been nearly all in stone; Colombe imported Genoese marble, and carved it into figures still stern and stiff with Gothic intensity, but set in frames exuberant with classic ornament. For the château of Gaillon he cut a spacious high relief of *St. George and the Dragon*—a lifeless knight on a spirited horse, all enclosed within columns, moldings, and coping of Renaissance design. In *The Virgin of the Pillar*, carved in stone for the church of St. Galmier, Colombe achieved the full delicacy of the Italian style in the modesty and tenderness of the features, the smooth lines of the falling hair. And perhaps it was Colombe who, in old age, chiseled the Easter Sepulcher (1496) in the priory church at Solesmes.*

In painting, France felt the influence of the Netherlands as well as that of Italy. Nicolas Froment began with an almost Dutch realism in *The Resurrection of Lazarus*. But in 1476 he moved from Avignon to Aix-en-Provence, and painted for René of Anjou a triptych, *The Burning Bush*, whose central panel, showing the Virgin enthroned, has Italian qualities in its background, its brunette Madonna, its majestic Moses, its charming angel, its alert hound and trustful sheep; here Italy has won a complete victory. A like evolution of style marked the work of the "Master of Moulins"— probably Jean Perréal. He went to Italy with Charles VIII and again with Louis XII; he returned with half the arts of the Renaissance in his repertoire—miniaturist, muralist, portraitist, sculptor, and architect. At Nantes he designed—and Colombe carved—the imposing tomb of Duke Francis II of Brittany; and at Moulins he commemorated his patrons, Anne and Pierre of Beaujeu, with the handsome portraits that now hang in the Louvre.

The minor arts did not maintain their late-medieval excellence. Whereas the Flemish illuminators had long since passed to secular subjects and earthly scenes, the miniatures of Jean Bourdichon in *Les heures d'Anne de Bretagne* (1508) represented a return to medieval simplicity and piety—the lovely legends of the Virgin and her Child, the tragedy of Golgotha, the triumph of resurrection, the

---

* Reproduced in the Metropolitan Museum of Art in New York.

stories of the saints; the drawing poor, the backgrounds classical, the color rich and pure, all in a serene atmosphere of feminine refinement and sentiment.[19] As if in contrast, the stained glass of the time adopted a Flemish naturalism at first sight unsuited to windows bringing transfigured light to cathedral floors; yet the glass painted in this period for Auch, Rouen, and Beauvais catches some of the thirteenth-century glory. Limoges now rekindled its furnaces, which had been cold for a century, and rivaled Italy and Islam in painting vessels with translucent enamels. The wood carvers had not lost their skill; Ruskin thought the choir stalls of Amiens Cathedral the best in France.[20] Colorful tapestries from the end of the fifteenth century caught the attention of George Sand in the Château de Brissac (1847), and became a treasure of the Musée de Cluny at Paris; and the Musée des Gobelins has a stirring tapestry (c. 1500) of musicians playing in a garden of fleurs-de-lis.

All in all, excepting the châteaux, the fifteenth century was a fallow age in French art. The soil was plowed by soldiers' feet and fertilized with wartime blood; but only toward the end of the period would men have the means and leisure to sow the seeds of the harvest that Francis I would reap. The self-portrait of Fouquet betrays an age of humiliation and distress; the miniatures of his pupil Bourdichon reflect the familial peace of Louis XII's second marriage, and the smiling ease of a recovered land. The worst was over for France; the best was about to come.

IV. FRANÇOIS VILLON: 1431–80

Nevertheless this century of strife and chaos produced a major poet and a major historian. As one result of a national economy and a centralized government, French literature now used the language of Paris, whether the author came from Brittany, Burgundy, or Provence. As if to prove that French had matured, Philippe de Comines chose it, not Latin, for his *Mémoires*. He took his surname from Comines in Flanders, where he was born. He came of favored lineage, for Duke Philip V was his godfather, he was brought up at the Burgundian court, and at seventeen (1464) he was on the staff of the Count of Charolais. When the Count, become Charles the Bold, captured Louis XI at Péronne, Comines resented the behavior of the Duke, perhaps foresaw his fall, and wisely passed to the service of the King. Louis made him chamberlain and enriched him with estates, and Charles VIII sent him on important diplomatic missions. Meanwhile Comines composed two classics of historical literature: *Mémoires, cronique, et hystoire du roy Louis onziesme*, and *Cronique du roi Charles huytiesme*—narratives written in clear and simple French by a man who knew the world and had shared in the events that he described.

These books instance the extraordinary wealth of French literature in memoirs. They have their faults: they spend themselves mostly upon war; they are not as fresh and vivid as Froissart or Villehardouin or Joinville: they make too many curtsies to God while admiring the unscrupulous statecraft of Louis XI; and more often than not the discursive digressions are pits of platitudes. None the less Comines is the first modern philosophical historian: he seeks the relations of cause and effect, analyzes character, motives, and pretenses, judges conduct objectively, and studies events and original documents to illuminate the nature of man and the state. In these regards he anticipates Machiavelli and Guicciardini, and in his pessimistic estimate of mankind:

> Neither natural reason, nor our own knowledge, nor love of our neighbor, nor anything else is always sufficient to restrain us from doing violence to one another, or to withhold us from retaining what we already have, or to deter us from usurping the possessions of others by all possible means. . . . Wicked men grow the worse for their knowledge, but the good improve extremely.[21]

Like Machiavelli, he hopes that his book will teach princes a trick or two:

> Perhaps inferior persons will not give themselves the trouble to read these memoirs, but princes . . . may do it, and find some information to reward their pains. . . . For though neither enemies nor princes are always alike, yet, their affairs being often the same, it is not altogether unprofitable to be informed of what is past. . . . One of the greatest means to make a man wise is to have studied histories . . . and to have learned to frame and proportion our counsels and undertakings according to the model and example of our predecessors. For our life is but of short duration, and insufficient to give us experience of so many things.[22]

The Emperor Charles V, the wisest Christian ruler of his age, agreed with Comines, and called the *Mémoires* his breviary.

The general public preferred romances, farces, and satires. In 1508 appeared the French version of *Amadis de Gaule*. A dozen companies of players continued to present *mistères*, moralities, farces, and *soties*—follies that made fun of everybody, including priests and kings. Pierre Gringore was a master of this form, writing and acting *soties* with verve and success through a generation. The most enduring farce in French literature, *Maistre Pierre Pathelin*, was first played about 1464, and as late as 1872.[23] Pathelin is a poor lawyer starving for cases. He persuades a draper to sell him six ells of cloth, and invites him to dinner that evening to receive payment. When the draper comes, Pathelin is in bed raving with pretended fever, and professes to know nothing about the ells or the dinner. The draper leaves in disgust, meets the shepherd of his flock, accuses him of secretly disposing of several sheep, and hails him before a judge. The shepherd seeks a cheap lawyer and finds Pathelin, who coaches him to play the idiot and to answer all questions with the *baa* (French *bé*) of the sheep. The judge, baffled with baas, and confused by the draper's mingling of complaints against both the shepherd and the lawyer, gives France a famous phrase by begging all parties, *Revenons à ces moutons*—"Let us come back to these sheep"; [24] and finally, in despair of getting any logic out of the fracas, dismisses the case. The triumphant Pathelin asks for his fee, but the shepherd only answers "Baa," and the clever deceiver is rooked by the simpleton. The story is unfolded with all the spirit of a Gallic altercation. Rabelais may have remembered Pathelin when he conceived Panurge, and Molière reincarnated Gringore and the unknown author of this play.

The one unforgettable figure in the French literature of the fifteenth century is François Villon. He lied, stole, cheated, fornicated, and killed like the kings and nobles of his time, but with more rhyme and reason. He was so poor that he could not call even his name his own. Born François de Montcorbier (1431), reared in plague and misery in Paris, and adopted by a kindly priest, Guillaume de Villon, he took his foster-father's name, disgraced it, and gave it immortality. Guillaume put up with the lad's pranks and truancies, financed his studies at the university, and took proud comfort when François received the degree of master of arts (1452). For three years thereafter Guillaume provided him with bed and board in the cloisters of St. Benoît, waiting for the master to mature.

It must have saddened the hearts of Guillaume and François' mother to see him turning from piety to poetry, from theology to burglary. Paris was rich in rakes, trulls, quacks, sneak thieves, beggars, bullies, procurers, and drunks, and the reckless youth made friends in almost every category; for a while he served as a pimp.[25] Perhaps he had received too much religion, and found a cloister cloying; it is especially difficult for a clergyman's son to enjoy the Ten Commandments. On June 5, 1455, a priest, Philippe Chermoye, started a quarrel with him (says François), and cut his lip with a knife, whereupon Villon gashed him so deeply in the groin that within the week Philippe was dead. A hero among his comrades, an outlaw hunted by the police, the poet fled from Paris and for almost a year hid in the countryside.

He returned "shrunk and wan," sharp of features and dry of skin, keeping an eye out for the gendarmes, picking a lock or a pocket now and then, and hungering for food and love. He became enamored of a bourgeois lass, who bore with him till she could find a better cavalier, who beat him; he loved her the more, but commemorated her later as *"ma damoyselle au nez tortu"*— "my lady of the twisted nose." About this time (1456) he composed *Le petit testament*, the shorter of his poetic wills; for he had many debts and injuries to repay, and could never tell when he might close his life with a noose. He scolds his love for the parsimony of her flesh, sends his hose to Robert Vallée, to "clothe his mistress more decently," and bequeaths to Pernet Marchand "three sheaves of straw or hay, upon the naked floor to lay, and so the amorous game to play." He devises to his barber "the ends and clippings of my hair"; and leaves his heart, "piteous, pale, and numb and dead," to her who had "so dourly banished me her sight." [26]

After disposing of all this wealth he seems to have lacked bread. On Christmas Eve, 1456, he joined three others in robbing the College of Navarre of some 500 crowns ($12,500?). Buttressed with his share, François resumed his stay in the country. For a year he disappears from historic sight; then, in the winter of 1457, we find him among the poets entertained at Blois by Charles of Orléans. Villon took part in a poetic tournament there, and must have pleased, for Charles kept him through some weeks as his guest, and replenished the youth's leaking purse. Then some prank or quarrel cooled their friendship, and François returned to the road, versifying an apology. He wandered south to Bourges, exchanged a poem for a present with Duke John II of Bourbon, and rambled as far as Roussillon. We picture him, from his poetry, as living on gifts and loans, on fruit and nuts and hens plucked from roadside farms, talking with peasant girls and tavern tarts, singing or whistling on the highways, dodging the police in the towns. Again we lose track of him; then, suddenly, he reappears, condemned to death in a prison at Orléans (1460).

We do not know what brought him to that pass; we know only that in July of that year Marie of Orléans, daughter of the poet duke, made a formal entry into the city, and that Charles celebrated the occasion with a general amnesty to prisoners. Villon emerged from death to life in an ecstasy of joy. Soon hungry, he stole again, was caught, and—his previous escapades being held against him—was thrown into a dark and dripping dungeon in the village of Meung-sur-Loire, near Orléans. Four months he lived there with rats and toads, biting his scarred lip, and vowing vengeance on a world that punished thieves and let poets starve. But not all the world was unkind. Louis XI, passing through Orléans, declared another amnesty, and Villon, told that he was free, danced a fandango on his prison straw. He rushed back to Paris or its vicinity; and now, old and bald and penniless at thirty, he wrote his greatest poems, which he called simply *Les Lais (The Lays)*; posterity, finding so many of them cast again into the form of ironic bequests, termed them *Le grand testament* (1461–62).

He leaves his spectacles to the hospital for blind paupers, so that they may, if they can, distinguish the good from the bad, the lowly from the great, among the skeletons in the charnel house of the Innocents. So soon in life obsessed with death, he mourns the mortality of beauty, and sings a *Ballade des dames du temps jadis*—of yesterday's belles:

> *Dictes moy ou, n'en quel pays,*
> *Est Flora la belle Romaine,*
> *Archipiades, ne Thaïs,*
> *Qui fut sa cousine germaine,*

Echo parlant quant bruyt on maire,
Dessus rivière ou sus estan,
Que beaulté ot trop plus qu'humaine.
Mais ou sont les neiges d'antan? *

He considers it nature's unforgivable sin to ravish us with loveliness and then dissolve it in our arms. His bitterest poem is *Les regrets de la belle heaulmière*—the lament of the fair helm-maker:

Where is that clear and crystal brow?
　　Those eyebrows arched, and golden hair?
And those bright eyes, where are they now,
　　Wherewith the wisest ravished were?
　　The little nose so straight and fair,
The tiny, tender, perfect ear;
　　Where is the dimpled chin, and where
The pouting lips so red and clear? [28]

The description proceeds from lure to lure, omitting none; and then, in plaintive litany, each charm decays:

The breasts all shriveled up and gone,
The haunches, like the paps, withdrawn,
　　The thighs no longer like to thighs,
Withered and mottled all like brawn—

which here, alas, means sausages *(saulcisses)*.

And so, no longer loving love or life, Villon bequeaths himself to the dust:

Item, my body I ordain
　　Unto the earth, our grandmother;
Thereof the worms will have small gain;
　　Hunger hath worn it many a year.

He leaves his books gratefully to his foster-father; and as a parting gift to his old mother he composes for her a humble ballad to the Virgin. He asks mercy of all but those who imprisoned him: of monks and nuns, mummers and chanters, lackeys and gallants, "wantons who all their charms display . . . brawlers and jugglers and tumblers gay, clowns with their apes and carpets spread . . . gentle and simple, living and dead—I cry folk mercy, one and all." [29] So

---

* Tell me where, in what land of shade,
　Bides fair Flora of Rome, and where
　Are Thaïs and Archipiade,
　Cousins-german of beauty rare,
　And Echo, more than mortal fair,
　That, when one calls by river-flow,
　Or marish, answers out of the air?
　But what is become of last year's snow? [27]

> Here is ended (both great and small)
>   Poor Villon's Testament! When he is dead,
> Come, I pray you, to his funeral,
>   Whilst the bell tinkles overhead . . .
> Prince, that art gentle as a yearling gled,
>   Hear what he did with his latest sigh;
> He drank a long draught of the vine-juice red,
>   Whenas he felt his end draw nigh.[30]

Despite these wills and farewells, he could not so soon turn down the cup of life. In 1462 he went back to Guillaume de Villon and the cloisters, and his mother rejoiced. But the law had not forgotten him. The College of Navarre had him arrested, and consented to his liberation only on condition that he repay it his share of the loot of six years back—forty crowns a year for three years. On the night of his release he had the ill luck to be with two of his old crime mates when they started a drunken brawl in which a priest was stabbed. Apparently Villon had no blame in the matter; he withdrew to his room, and prayed for peace. Nevertheless he was again arrested; he was tortured by having water forced down his throat to the bursting point; and then, to his astonishment, he was condemned to be hanged. For several weeks he lay in close confinement, hoping and despairing. And now, expecting death for himself and his companions, he indited a pitiful farewell to the world.

> Men, brother men, that after us yet live,
>   Let not your hearts too hard against us be;
> For if some pity of us poor men ye give,
>   The sooner God shall take of you pity.
>   Here are we five or six strung up, you see,
> And here the flesh, that all too well was fed,
> Bit by bit eaten and rotten, rent and shred,
>   And we the bones grow dust and ash withal;
> Let no man laugh at us discomforted,
>   But pray to God that He forgive us all . .
>
> The rain has washed and laundered us all five,
>   And the sun dried and blackened; yea, perdie,
> Ravens and pies with beaks that rend and rive
>   Have dug our eyes out, and plucked off for fee
>   Our beards and eyebrows; never we are free,
> Not once, to rest; but here and there still sped,
> Drive at its wild will by the wind's change led,
>   More pecked of birds than fruits on garden wall;
> Men, for God's love, let no gibe here be said,
>   But pray to God that He forgive us all.[31]

Not yet quite hopeless, Villon persuaded his jailer to take a message to his foster-father, and to convey to the court of the *Parlement* an appeal from a sentence so clearly unjust. Guillaume de Villon, who could forgive seventy times seven, once more interceded for the poet, who must have had some virtues to be so undiscourageably loved. On January 3, 1463, the court, say its record, "ordered that . . . the sentence preceding be annulled, and—having regard to the bad character of the said Villon—that he be banished for ten years from the town . . . and viscounty of Paris." [32] François thanked the court in a joyful ballad, and asked for three days' grace to "provide for my journey and bid my folk adieu." It was granted, and presumably he now saw his foster-father and his mother for the last time. He packed his bundle, grasped the bottle of wine and the purse that good Guillaume gave him, received the old man's benediction, and marched out of Paris and history. We hear nothing of him more.

He was a thief, but a melodious thief, and the world has need of melody. He could be brutally coarse, as in the *Ballade de la Grosse Margot*, and he flung obscene epithets at women who fell short of his desires, and he was impishly frank in anatomical details. All this we can forgive for the sins that were committed against his sins, and the ever resurgent tenderness of his spirit, and the wistful music of his verse. He paid the penalty for what ne was, and left us only the reward.

CHAPTER V

England in the Fifteenth Century

1399-1509

I. KINGS

HENRY IV, having reached the throne, found himself challenged by revolt. In Wales Owain Glyn Dwr overthrew the English domination for a moment (1401–08), but the future Henry V, now Prince of Wales, overcame him with dashing strategy; and Owen Glendower, after leading a hunted life for eight years in Welsh fastnesses and crags, died a few hours after receiving full pardon from his gallant conqueror. Synchronizing his rebellion with Glendower's, Henry Percy, Earl of Northumberland, led some nobles of the north into an uprising against a king unable to keep all the promises he had made to them for their aid in deposing Richard II. The Earl's reckless son Harry "Hotspur" (unwarrantably lovable in Shakespeare) led a hesitant and inadequate force against the King at Shrewsbury (1403); there the youth died in foolish heroism, Henry IV fought manfully in the front ranks, and his gay wastrel son, "Prince Hal," displayed the bravery that would win Agincourt and France. These and other troubles left Henry little time or zest for statesmanship; his revenues limped behind his expenditures; he quarreled tactlessly with Parliament, and ended his reign amid fiscal chaos and the personal tribulations of leprosy, prolapse of the rectum, and venereal disease.[1] "He departed to God," says Holinshed, "in the year of his age forty-six . . . in great perplexity and little pleasure."[2]

In tradition and Shakespeare Henry V had lived a free and frolicsome youth, and had even conspired to seize the throne from a father incapacitated by illness but tenacious of power. Contemporary chroniclers merely hint at his revels, but assure us that after his accession "he was changed into another man, studying to be honest, grave, and modest."[3] He who had romped with topers and tarts now dedicated himself to leading a united Christendom against the advancing Turks—adding, however, that he must first conquer France. He accomplished his proximate aim with astonishing speed, and for a precarious moment an English king sat on the throne of France. German princes sent him homage, and thought of making him emperor.[4] He rivaled Caesar briefly in the planning of campaigns, the provisioning of his armies, the affection of his troops, and in exposing himself in all battles and weathers.

Suddenly, still a youth of thirty-five, he died of fever at Bois-de-Vincennes (1422).

His death saved France, and almost ruined England. His popularity might have persuaded the taxpayers to rescue the government from bankruptcy; but his son Henry VI was, at accession, only nine months old, and a disgraceful sequence of corrupt regents and inept generals sank the treasury into irredeemable debt. The new ruler never rose to royal stature; he was a delicate and studious neurasthenic who loved religion and books, and shuddered at the thought of war; the English mourned that they had lost a king and won a saint. In 1452, imitating Charles VI of France, Henry VI went mad. A year later his ministers signed a peace acknowledging England's defeat in the Hundred Years' War.

Richard, Duke of York, governed for two years as Protector; in a cloudylucid interval Henry dismissed him (1454); the angry Duke claimed the throne through descent from Edward III; he branded the Lancastrian kings as usurpers, and joined Salisbury, Warwick, and other barons in those Wars of the Roses—Lancastrian red and Yorkist white—which through thirty-one years (1454–85) pitted noble against noble in the indefatigable suicide of the Anglo-Norman aristocracy, and left England impoverished and desolate. Soldiers demobilized by unwonted peace, and loath to resume the chores of peasantry, enlisted on either side, plundered the villages and towns, and murdered without qualm all who stood in their way. The Duke of York was killed in battle at Goldsmith's Wakefield (1460), but his son Edward, Earl of March, carried on the war remorselessly, slaughtering all captives, with or without pedigree; while Margaret of Anjou, the virile queen of the gentle Henry, led the Lancastrian resistance with unblushing ferocity. March won at Towton (1461), ended the Lancastrian dynasty, and became, as Edward IV, the first Yorkist king.

But the man who really ruled England for the next six years was Richard Neville, Earl of Warwick. Head of a rich and numerous clan, possessed of a dominating and yet engaging personality, as subtle in statesmanship as he was brilliant in war, "Warwick the Kingmaker" had fathered the victory at Towton, and had raised Edward to the throne. The King, resting from strife, dedicated himself to women, while Warwick governed so well that all England south of the Tyne and east of the Severn (for Margaret was still fighting) honored him as in all but name the king. When Edward rebelled against the reality and turned against him, Warwick joined Margaret, drove Edward from England, restored Henry VI to nominal power (1470), and ruled again. But Edward organized an army with Burgundian aid, crossed to Hull, defeated and slew Warwick at Barnet, defeated Margaret at Tewkesbury (1471), had Henry VI murdered in the tower, and lived happily ever afterward.

He was still only thirty-one. Comines describes him as "one of the hand-somest men of his age," who "took no delight in anything but ladies, dancing, entertainment, and the chase."[5] He replenished his treasury by confiscating the estates of the Nevilles, and by accepting from Louis XI, as bribes to peace, 125,000 crowns and a promise of 50,000 more per year.[6] So eased, he could ignore a Parliament whose only use to him would have been to vote him funds. Feeling himself secure, he surrendered himself again to luxury and indolence, wore himself out lovingly, grew fat and jolly, and died at forty-one in the amplitude of his person and his power (1483).

He left two sons: the twelve-year-old Edward V, and Richard, Duke of York, aged nine. Their uncle Richard, Duke of Gloucester, had for the past six years served the state as chief minister, and with such industry, piety, and skill that when he made himself regent England accepted him without pro-test, despite his "ill-featured limbs, crooked back, hard-favored visage, and left shoulder much higher than his right."[7] Whether through the intoxication of power, or a just suspicion of conspiracies to unseat him, Richard im-prisoned several notables, and executed one. On July 6, 1483, he had himself crowned as Richard III, and on July 15 the two young princes were mur-dered in the Tower—no one knows by whom. Once again the nobility rose in revolt, this time led by Henry Tudor, Earl of Richmond. When their modest forces met the King's far larger army on Bosworth Field (1485), most of Richard's soldiers refused to fight; and—lacking both a kingdom and a horse—he died in a desperate charge. The Yorkist dynasty ended; the Earl of Richmond, as Henry VII, began the Tudor line that would close with Elizabeth.

Under the blows of necessity Henry developed the virtues and vices that seemed to him demanded by his place. Holbein pictured him in a Whitehall fresco: tall, slender, beardless, pensive, humane, hardly revealing the subtle, secret calculation, the cold, stern pride, the flexible but patiently obdurate will that brought England from its destitute disintegration under the sixth Henry to its wealth and concentrated power under the eighth. He loved "the felicity of full coffers," says Bacon,[8] because he knew their persuasive-ness in politics. He taxed the nation ingeniously, bled the rich with "benevo-lences" or forced gifts, made avid use of fines to feed his treasury and discourage crime, and winked as judges fitted the fine not to the offense but to the purse. He was the first English king since 1216 who kept his expenses within his income, and his charities and generosities mitigated his parsimony. He devoted himself conscientiously to administration, and skimped his pleas-ures to complete his toil. His life was darkened with perennial suspicion, not without cause; he trusted no one, concealed his purposes, and by fair means or dubious he achieved his ends. He established the Court of Star Chamber to try, in secret sessions, obstreperous nobles too powerful to fear local judges or juries; and year by year he brought the ruined aristocracy and the frightened prelacy into subordination to the monarchy. Strong individuals resented the decline of liberty and the desuetude of Parliament; but peasants forgave much in a king who disciplined their lords, and manufacturers and merchants thanked him for his wise promotion of industry and trade. He had found an England in feudal anarchy, a government too poor and disreputable to win obedience or loyalty; he left to Henry VIII a state respected, orderly, solvent, united, and at peace.

II. THE GROWTH OF ENGLISH WEALTH

Apparently nothing had been gained by the Great Revolt of 1381. Many servile dues were still exacted, and as late as 1537 the House of Lords rejected a bill for the final manumission of all serfs.[9] The enclosure of "commons" was accelerated; thousands of displaced serfs became propertyless proletarians in the towns; the sheep, said Thomas More, were eating up the peasantry.[10] In some ways the movement was good: lands approaching exhaustion were renitrogenated by the grazing sheep, and by 1500 only 1 per cent of the population were serfs. A class of yeomen grew, tilling their own land, and gradually giving to the English commoner the sturdy independent character that would later forge the Commonwealth and build an unwritten constitution of unprecedented liberty.

Feudalism became unprofitable as industry and commerce spread into a national and money economy bound up with foreign trade. When the serf produced for his lord he had scant motive for expansion or enterprise; when the free peasant and the merchant could sell their product in the open market the lust for gain quickened the economic pulse of the nation; the villages sent more food to the towns, the towns produced more goods to pay for it, and the exchange of surpluses overflowed the old municipal limits and guild restrictions to cover England and reach out beyond the sea.

Some guilds became "merchant companies," licensed by the King to sell English products abroad. Whereas in the fourteenth century most English trade had been carried in Italian vessels, the British now built their own ships, and sent them into the North Sea, the coastal Atlantic, and the Mediterranean. The Genoese and Hanseatic merchants resented these newcomers, and fought them with embargoes and piracy; but Henry VII, convinced that the development of England required foreign trade, took English shipping under governmental protection, and arranged with other nations commercial agreements that established maritime order and peace. By 1500 the "merchant adventurers" of England ruled the trade of the North Sea. With an eye to commerce with China and Japan, the farseeing King commissioned the Italian navigator Giovanni Caboto, then living in Bristol as John Cabot, to seek a northern passage across the Atlantic (1497). Cabot had to be content with discovering Newfoundland and, in a second voyage (1498), exploring the coast from Labrador to Delaware; he died in that year, and his son Sebastian passed into the service of Spain. Probably neither the sailor nor his King realized that these expeditions inaugurated British imperialism, and opened to English trade and colonists a region that would in time be England's strength and salvation.

Meanwhile protective tariffs nourished national industry; economic order reduced the rate of interest sometimes to as low as 5 per cent; and governmental decrees rigorously regulated wages and the conditions of labor. A statute of Henry VII (1495) ruled

> that every artificer and labourer be at his work, between the midst of the month of March and the midst of the month of September, before five o'clock in the morning, and that he have but half an hour for his breakfast, and an hour and a half for his [midday] dinner, at such time as he hath season for sleep ... and that he depart not from work ... till between seven and eight of the clock in the evening. ... And that from the midst of September to the midst of March every artificer and labourer be at their work in the springing of the day, and depart not till night ... and that they sleep not by day.[11]

However, the worker rested and drank on Sundays, and on twenty-four additional holidays in the year. "Fair prices" were set by the state for many commodities, and we hear of arrests for exceeding these figures. Real wages, in relation to prices, were apparently higher in the late fifteenth century than in the early nineteenth.[12]

The revolts of English labor in this age stressed political rights as well as economic wrongs. Semi-communistic propaganda continued in almost every year, and workingmen were repeatedly reminded that "you be made of the same mold and metal that the gentles be made of; why then should they sport and play, and you labor and toil?—why should they have so much of the prosperity and treasure of this world, and ye so little?" [13] Riots against enclosures of common lands were numerous, and there were periodic conflicts between merchants and artisans; but we hear too of agitations for municipal democracy, for the representation of labor in Parliament, and for a reduction of taxes.[14]

In June 1450, a large and disciplined force of peasants and town laborers marched upon London and camped at Blackheath. Their leader, Jack Cade, presented their grievances in an orderly document. "All the common people, what for taxes and tallages and other oppressions, might not live by their handiwork and husbandry." [15] The Statute of Labourers should be repealed, and a new ministry should be formed. The government accused Cade of advocating communism.* [16] The troops of Henry VI, and the retainers of certain nobles, met the rebel army at Sevenoaks (June 18, 1450) To the surprise of all, the rebels won, and poured into London. To appease them the King's Council ordered the arrest of Lord Saye and William Crowmer, officials especially hated for their exactions and tyranny. On July 4 they were surrendered to the mob that besieged the Tower; they were tried by the rebels, refused to plead, and were beheaded. According to Holinshed the two heads were raised on pikes and carried through the streets in joyous procession; every now and then their mouths were knocked together in a bloody kiss. [17] The Archbishop of Canterbury and the Bishop of Winchester negotiated a peace, granting some demands and offering amnesty. The rebels agreed and dispersed. Jack Cade, however, attacked the castle of Queensborough in Sheppey; the government outlawed him, and on July 12 he was mortally wounded while resisting arrest. Eight accomplices were condemned to death; the rest were pardoned by the King, "to the great rejoicing of all his subjects." [18]

III. MORALS AND MANNERS

The Venetian ambassador, about 1500, reported to his government:

> The English are for the most part—both men and women, of all ages —handsome and well proportioned.... They are great lovers of themselves, and of everything belonging to them; they think there are no other men than themselves, and no other world but England; and whenever they see a handsome foreigner they say that "he looks like an Englishman," and that it is a great pity that he is not one. [19]

The English might have answered that most of this description, *mutatis mutandis*, would fit all peoples. Assuredly they were a vigorous stock, in body, character, and speech. They swore so heartily that even Joan of Arc regularly called them Goddams. The women too were plainspoken, talking of matters physiological and genetic with a freedom that might shock the sophisticates of today. [20] Humor was as coarse and profane as speech. Manners were rough, even in the aristocracy, and had to be trained and tamed by a rigid code of ceremony. The lusty spirit that would agitate the Elizabethans was already formed, in the fifteenth century, out of a life of danger, violence, and insolence. Every man had to be his own policeman, ready to

---

* Cf. Shakespeare's caricature of Jack Cade: "There shall be in England seven halfpenny loaves sold for a penny.... I will make it a felony to drink small beer; all the realm shall be in common.... And here ... I charge and command that of the city's cost the pissing conduit run nothing but claret wine. ... Henceforth all things shall be in common."—2 *Henry VI*, iv, 2, 6.

meet blow with blow and, at need, kill with a steady stomach. These same powerful animals could be generous, chivalrous, and, on occasion, even tender. Tough warriors wept when Sir John Chandos, the almost "parfit knight," died; and Margaret Paston's letter to her sick husband (1443) shows how timeless and raceless love can be. We should add, however, that this same lady almost broke the head of her daughter for refusing to marry the parental choice.[21]

Girls were brought up in protective demureness and modesty, for men were beasts of prey, and virginity was an economic asset in the marital mart. Marriage was an incident in the transfer of property. Girls could legally marry at twelve, boys at fourteen, even without their parents' consent; but in the upper classes, to accelerate property transactions, betrothals were arranged by the parents soon after the children reached the age of seven. Since love marriages were exceptional, and divorce was forbidden, adultery was popular, especially in the aristocracy. "There reigned abundantly," says Holinshed, "the filthie sin of lechery and fornication, with abominable adulteries, speciallie in the king." [22] Edward IV, after sampling many loves, chose Jane Shore as his favorite concubine. She served him with wanton fidelity, and proved a kind friend at court to many a petitioner. When Edward died, Richard III, possibly to parade his brother's vices and disguise his own, forced her to march through London streets in the white robe of a public penitent. She lived to a destitute old age, despised and rejected by those whom she had helped.[23]

Never in known history had Englishmen (now so law-abiding) been so lawless. A hundred years of war had made men brutal and reckless; nobles returning from France continued to fight in England, and employed demobilized soldiers in their feuds. Aristocrats shared with tradesmen a greed for money that overrode all morality. Petty thefts were innumerable. Merchants sold shoddy goods and used false weights; at one time frauds in the quality and quantity of exports almost ruined England's foreign trade.[24] Commerce on the seas was spiced with piracy. Bribery was almost universal: judges could scarcely judge without "gifts"; juries were paid to be friendly to plaintiff or defendant or both; tax collectors were "greased" to let exemptions slip readily from their palms; recruiting officers, like Shakespeare's Falstaff, could be induced to overlook a town; [25] an English army invading France was bought off by the enemy.[26] Men were as mad for money then as now, and poets like Chaucer, having denounced greed, practiced it. The moral structure of society might have collapsed had not its foundations been mortised in the simple life of common men and women, who, while their betters plotted the wars and mischief of the time, maintained the home and carried on the race.

All classes except merchants and *prolétaires* lived in the country for as much of the year as they might. Castles, being no longer defensible since the development of cannon, were slowly evolving into manor houses. Brick replaced stone, but modest houses were still built of wood and mud. The central hall, once used for all purposes, lost its old size and splendor, and shrank into a vestibule opening into a large living room, some small rooms, and a "drawte chamber" or (with) drawing room for intimate converse. Tapestries hung on rich men's walls, and windows—sometimes of stained glass—brightened the once dark interior. The smoke of the hearth, which formerly had escaped through window, door, and roof, was now gathered into a chimney, and a massive fireplace dignified the living room. Ceilings might be timbered, floors might be tiled; carpets were still rare. If we may trust the literary rather than accurate Erasmus,

> almost all the floors are of clay and rushes from the marshes, so care- lessly renewed that the foundation sometimes remains for twenty years, harboring, there below, spittle and vomit and wine of dogs and men, beer ... remnants of fishes, and other filth unnameable. Hence, with the change of weather, a vapor exhales which in my judgment is far from wholesome.[27]

Beds were sumptuous with carving, flowered coverlet, and canopy. The dining table, in comfortable homes, was a giant masterpiece of carved wal- nut or oak. Near it, or in the hall, stood a cupboard, sideboard, or dresser where table plate was "dressed"—i.e., arranged for display or ornament. The "parler"—a room for talking—was preferred for meals.

To save oil, the main meals were taken in daylight: "dinner" at ten in the morning, "supper" at five in the afternoon. Men wore their hats at table, to keep their long hair from getting into the food. Forks were reserved for special purposes, like serving salad or toasting cheese; their English use in the modern manner first appears in 1463.[28] The knife was supplied by the guest, who carried it in a short sheath attached to his girdle. Etiquette re- quired that food should be brought to the mouth with the fingers. As hand kerchiefs were not in use till the middle of the sixteenth century, men wer requested to blow their noses with the hand that held the knife rather than with that which conveyed the food.[29] Napkins were unknown, and diners were warned not to clean their teeth on the tablecloth.[30] Meals were heavy; the ordinary dinner of a man of rank included fifteen or twenty dishes. Great lords kept great tables, feeding a hundred retainers, visitors, and serv- ants daily; Warwick the Kingmaker used six oxen a day for his table, and sometimes fed 500 guests. Meat was the national food; vegetables were scarce or shunned. Beer and ale were the national drinks; wine was not as plentiful or popular as in France or Italy, but a gallon of beer per day was the usual allowance per person, even for nuns. The English, said Sir John Fortescue

(c. 1470). "drink no water, unless at certain times upon religious score, or by way of doing penance." [31]

Dress was splendid in the aristocracy. Simple men wore a plain gown or hood, or a short tunic convenient for work; moneyed men liked furred and feathered hats, flowered robes, or fancy jackets bulging at the sleeves, and tight high hose which, Chaucer's parson complained, "shewen ... the horrible swollen members, that seemeth . . . hernia, and eke the buttocks . . . as it were the hindre part of a she-ape in the fulle of the moon." Chaucer himself when a page, had a flaming costume with one hose red and the other black The long pointed shoes of the fourteenth century disappeared in the fifteenth, and shoes became rounded or broad at the toe. As for "the outrageous array of wommen, God wot that though the visages of somme of them seem ful chaste and debonaire, yet notifie they," by "the horrible disordinate scantinesse" of their dress, their "likerousnesse" (lecherousness) "and pride." [32] However, the pictures that have come down to us show the alluring sex tightly encased in a plethora of garments from ears to feet.

Amusements ranged from checkers and chess, backgammon and dice, to fishing and hunting, archery and jousts. Playing cards reached England toward the end of the fifteenth century; today they still dress their kings and queens in the fashion of that time. Dancing and music were as popular as gambling; nearly every Englishman took part in choral song; Henry V rivaled John Dunstable among the outstanding composers of the day; and English singers were acclaimed on the Continent. Men played tennis, handball, football, bowls, quoits; they wrestled and boxed, set cocks to fighting, baited bears and bulls. Crowds gathered to see acrobats and ropewalkers perform the feats that amused antiquity and amaze modernity. Kings and nobles kept jugglers, jesters, and buffoons; and a Lord of Misrule, appointed by the king or queen, superintended the sports and revels of Christmastide. Women moved freely among men everywhere: drank in taverns, rode to the hounds, hunted with falcons, and distracted the spectators from the combatants at tournaments; it was they who, led by the queen, judged the jousters and awarded the golden crown.

Travel was still travail, but nobody seemed to stay home—a bad mark for monogamy. Roads were mud or dust, and robbers made no distinction of race, sex, class, or creed. Inns were picturesque and dirty, stocked with roaches, rats, and fleas. Nearly every one of them had a Doll Tearsheet for sale, and virtue could hardly find a bed. The poor went on foot, the well-to-do on horseback, usually in armed companies; the very rich used newfangled horse-drawn coaches—reputedly invented by a fifteenth-century Hungarian in the village of Kocz. Lordly carriages were carved and painted and gilded, cushioned and curtained and carpeted; even so they were less comfortable than camels, and as undulant as a fishing smack. Ships were no better than in antiquity, or worse; that which brought King John from Bordeaux to London in 1357 took twelve days.

Crime flourished. Towns were too poor to have any but unpaid volunteer police; but all males were required to join in the "hue and cry" after a fleeing criminal. Deterrents were sought in severe penalties for the few who were caught; burglary, larceny, arson, and sacrilege, as well as murder and treason, were punished with hanging on any convenient tree, and the corpse was left as a warning to others and a feast for crows. The practice of torture—both on the accused and on witnesses—developed under Edward IV, and continued for 200 years.[33] Lawyers abounded.

Perhaps we judge the age too harshly, forgetting the barbarities of our enlightened century. Sir John Fortescue, Chief Justice under Henry VI, thought more highly of his time, and wrote in its honor two works once renowned. In a dialogue, *De laudibus legum Angliae*, he praised the laws of England, gloried in the right of trial by jury, mourned the use of torture, and, like a thousand philosophers, warned princes to make themselves the law-abiding servants of the people. In *Monarchia, or Governance of England*, he compared France and England patriotically: in France men could be condemned without public trial, the States-General was rarely called, the King levied taxes on necessities like salt and wine. After so exalting his country, Sir John concluded that all governments should be subject to the pope, *usque ad pedum oscula*—"even to kissing his feet." [84]

IV. THE LOLLARDS

Archbishop Arundel, in 1407, reaffirmed the supremacy of canon or ecclesiastical law over all secular legislation, and condemned as a major heresy any rejection of a papal decree.[35] Recovering from Wyclif, the Church grew stronger in fifteenth-century England, and rising wealth overflowed into its coffers. "Chantries" were now a frequent form of contribution: persons expecting death paid for the building of a chapel and for the chanting of Masses to expedite their souls into paradise. As some twenty bishops and twenty-six abbots sat in the House of Lords with only forty-seven laymen, the Church controlled the major chamber of Parliament. To offset this, Henry VII—and later Henry VIII—insisted on the right of the kings to nominate the bishops and abbots of England from the eligible clergy; and this dependence of the hierarchy on the monarchy eased the clerical surrender to Henry VIII's assertion of royal supremacy over the English Church.

Meanwhile Wyclif's Poor Preachers continued to spread their anticlerical ideas. As early as 1382 a monastic chronicler reported, with frightened exaggeration, that "they multiplied exceedingly, like budding plants, and filled the whole realm. . . . You could scarce meet two men on the road but that one of them was a disciple of Wyclif." [36] They found their readiest audience among the industrial workers, especially the weavers of Norfolk. In 1395 the Lollards felt strong enough to present to Parliament a bold statement of their principles. They opposed clerical celibacy, transubstantiation, image worship, pilgrimages, prayers for the dead, the wealth and endowment of the Church, the employment of ecclesiastics in state offices, the necessity of confession to priests, the ceremonies of exorcism, and the worship of the saints. In other pronouncements they recommended that all should read the Bible frequently, and should follow its precepts as superior to the decrees of the Church. They denounced war as unchristian, and luxury as immoral; they called for sumptuary laws that would compel a return to simple foods and dress; they abhorred oaths, and substituted for them such phrases as "I am sure," or "It is sooth"—i.e., truth; already the Puritan mind and view were taking form in Britain.[37] A few preachers mingled socialism with their religion, but most of them refrained from attacking private property, and sought the support of knights and gentry as well as of peasants and *prolétaires*.

Nevertheless the upper classes could not forget their narrow escape from social revolution in 1381, and the Church found in them a new readiness to protect her as a stabilizing force in the community. Richard II threatened with arrest the representatives of the Lollards in Parliament, and reduced them to silence. In 1397 the English bishops petitioned the King for the execution of impenitent heretics "as in other realms subject to the Christian religion," [38] but Richard was loath to go to such lengths. In 1401, however, Henry IV and his Parliament issued the famous statute *De haeretico comburendo*: all persons declared by an ecclesiastical court to be persistent heretics were to be burned, and all heretical books were to be destroyed. In that same year William Sawtrey, a Lollard priest, was burned at the stake. Other Lollards were arrested, recanted, and were treated leniently. In 1406 the Prince of Wales presented to Henry IV a petition alleging that the propaganda of the Lollards, and their attacks on monastic property, threatened the whole existing fabric of society. The King ordered a more vigorous prosecution of the heretics, but the absorption of the bishops in the politics of the Papal Schism temporarily deflected their energy from the hunt. In 1410 John Badby, a Lollard tailor, was condemned by the Church, and was burned in Smithfield Market. Before the faggots were lighted "Prince Hal" pleaded with Badby to recant, and offered him life and money; Badby refused, and mounted the pyre to his death.[39]

The Prince came to the throne in 1413 as Henry V, and gave his full support to the policy of suppression. One of his personal friends was Sir John Oldcastle, Lord Cobham, whom some of Shakespeare's audience later identified with Falstaff.[40] Oldcastle had served the nation well in the field, but he tolerated and protected Lollard preachers on his lands in Herefordshire and Kent. Thrice the bishops summoned him to trial; thrice he refused to come; he yielded, however, to a writ from the King, and appeared before the bishops (1413) in that chapter house of St. Paul's where Wyclif had stood trial thirty-six years before. He affirmed his sincere Christianity, but would not reject the Lollard views on confession or the Eucharist. He was condemned as a heretic, and was confined in the Tower of London; forty days' grace was allowed him in the hope that he would recant; instead he escaped. At the news the Lollards around London rose in revolt, and tried to seize the King (1414). The attempt failed, and some leaders were caught and hanged. Oldcastle hid for three years in the mountains of Herefordshire and Wales; finally he was captured, hanged as a traitor, and then burned as a heretic (1417), state and Church both demanding their due.

As compared with other persecutions, that of Lollardry was almost moderate; the executions for heresy numbered eleven between 1400 and 1485.[41] We hear of several Lollard congregations surviving till 1521; as late as 1518 Thomas Man, who claimed to have converted 700 to Lollardry, suffered death at the stake; and six more were burned in 1521.[42] When Henry VIII divorced England from Rome, and the nation accepted the change without revolution, the Lollards might have claimed that in some measure they had prepared the way.

In 1450 Reginald Pecock, Bishop of Chichester, published a book which he called, in the whimsical fashion of the times, *Repressor of Overmuch Blaming of the Clergy*. It was avowedly a refutation of Lollardry, and assumed a vigorous anticlericalism among the people. It proposed to check these ideas not by imprisonment at the stake, but solely by an appeal to reason. The enthusiastic bishop reasoned so much that he fell in love with reason and in danger of heresy; he found himself refuting by reason some Lollard arguments from Scripture. In a *Treatise on Faith* he definitely placed reason above the Bible as a test of truth—a position that Europe would take 200 years to regain. For good measure the irrepressible Repressor added that the Fathers of the Church were not always to be trusted; that Aristotle was not an unquestionable authority; that the Apostles had had no hand in the Apostles' Creed; and that the Donation of Constantine was a forgery.[43] The English bishops hailed the proud Pecock before their court (1457), and gave him a choice between recanting or burning. He disliked burning, read a public abjuration, was deposed from his see, and was segregated in Thorney Abbey to the end of his days (1460).

V. ENGLISH ART: 1300-1509

Despite anticlericalism and heresy, religion was still sufficiently fervent and opulent to raise English architecture to a minor peak of excellence. The growth of commerce and the spoils of war financed cathedrals, castles, and palaces, and glorified Oxford and Cambridge with the fairest homes ever built for learning. From the marble of Purbeck and the alabaster of Notting-ham to the forests of Sherwood and the brick of any shire, the building mate-rials of England were transformed into noble towers and lordly spires, and wooden ceilings almost as strong and handsome as Gothic stone vaults. The ugly tie beam that had crossed obtrusively from wall to wall was replaced by hammer-beam projections supporting with massive shoulders of oak the soaring arch above; in this manner some of England's finest churches spanned their naves. So Selby Cathedral received an oak ceiling of ribs and bosses rivaling the lierne and fan designs that vaulted the abbey church at Bath, the choir at Ely, and the south transept of Gloucester with complex webs of stone.

Patterns in window tracery, wall paneling, and choir screens gave their names to successive architectural styles, overlapping in time and often min-gled in one edifice. Geometrical Decorated Gothic (*c.* 1250–*c.* 1315) used Euclidean forms, as in Exeter Cathedral. Curvilinear Decorated Gothic (*c.* 1315–*c.* 1380) abandoned definite figures for freely flowing lines that antic-ipated with restraint the Flamboyant style of France, as in the south rose window at Lincoln. Perpendicular Gothic (*c.* 1330–*c.* 1530) stressed hori-zontal and vertical lines within the usual Gothic ogive, as in Henry VII's Chapel at Westminster Abbey. The intense colors of thirteenth-century stained glass were now softened with lighter tints, or with silver stain or pale grisaille; and in these windows the pageant of dying chivalry competed with the legends of Christianity to let Gothic art reach its final splendor and de-cline.

Seldom has England known such an ecstasy of construction. Three cen-turies (1376–1517) labored to build the present nave of Westminster Abbey; in the long gamut of those years we may weakly sense the toil of mind and arm that went to make an unrivaled mausoleum for England's best-behaved geniuses. Only less impressive was the reconstruction of Windsor: there Ed-ward III rebuilt on a massive scale the great Round Tower (1344), and Ed-ward IV began (1473) St. George's Chapel, with its lovely choir stalls, fan vault, and stained glass. Alan de Walsingham designed in Curvilinear Gothic an exquisite Lady Chapel and "lantern" tower for Ely. Gloucester Cathedral received a central tower, a choir vault, a gorgeous east window, and spacious cloisters whose fan vaults are among the wonders of England. Winchester extended its immense nave, and dressed its new front in Perpendicular. Coventry built in that manner the cathedral that saved only its stately spire in the second World War. Peterborough raised its dizzy fan vault; York Minster completed its nave, west towers, and choir screen. Towers were the crowning glory of the age, ennobling Merton and Magdalen colleges at Oxford, Fountains Abbey, Canterbury, Glastonbury, Derby, Taunton, and a hundred other shrines. William of Wykeham used Perpendicular in designing New College, Oxford; William of Waynflete, another nonagenarian, followed suit in the Great Quadrangle at Eton; and Kings College, Cambridge, capped the age with a chapel whose windows, vault, and choir stalls might reconcile Caliban to education, and Timon of Athens to prayer.

There was a secular and matter-of-fact spirit in Perpendicular Gothic that perfectly suited the civic architecture of colleges, castles, fortresses, guild and city halls. It was in this style that the earls of Warwick, in the fourteenth and fifteenth centuries, raised their famous castle near Leamington. The Guildhall of London, fane of the capital's mercantile pride, was built in 1411–35, burned down in 1666, was rebuilt by Christopher Wren, and received in 1866 the new interior that succumbed to bombs in the second World War. Even the town shops took on, in their mullioned windows, a Perpendicular pattern that conspires with carved lintels, cornices, and projecting balconies to bewitch us with the charm of a departing glory.

English sculpture maintained in this age its reputation for mediocrity. The statuary made for church façades, as at Lincoln and Exeter, fell far short of the architecture it was intended to adorn. The great altar screens in Westminster Cathedral and St. Alban's Abbey served as matrices for statues, but these are of too modest merit to add to the burden of our tale. The best sculpture was on funerary monuments. Fine figures were carved, usually in alabaster, of Edward II in Gloucester Cathedral, of Dame Eleanor Percy in Beverly Minster, of Henry IV and Queen Joan at Canterbury, of Richard Beauchamp at Warwick. English sculptors were at their best in representing the flowers and foliage of their verdant land. Good carving was done in wood: the choir stalls of Winchester, Ely, Gloucester, Lincoln, Norwich stop the breath with their laborious beauty.

Painting was still a minor art in England, lagging far behind contemporary work in Flanders and France. Illumination remained a favorite devotion; Edward III paid £66 ($6,600?) for an illuminated volume of romances,[44] and Robert of Ormsby presented to Norwich Cathedral an illuminated psalter which the Bodleian Library ranks as "the finest English manuscript" in its collections. After 1450 the art of the miniature declined with the rise of mural and panel painting, and in the sixteenth century it faded out before the novel miracle of print.

VI. CAXTON AND MALORY

At some unknown date in the fifteenth century a now nameless author produced the most famous of English morality plays. *Everyman* is an allegory whose characters are unprepossessing abstractions: Knowledge, Beauty, Five-Wits, Discretion, Strength, Goods, Good Deeds, Fellowship, Kindred, Confession, Death, Everyman, and God. In the prologue God complains that His commandments are ignored by nine men out of ten six days out of seven, and sends Death to remind the terrestrials that they must soon come to Him and give an account of their doings. In the space of a line Death descends from heaven to earth, finds Everyman meditating earnestly on women and gold, and bids him come into eternity. Everyman pleads unpreparedness, asks for an extension of time, offers a thousand-pound bribe; but Death grants him only one mitigation—to be accompanied into eternity by some chosen friend. Everyman begs Fellowship to join him in the great adventure, but Fellowship excuses himself bravely:

> If thou wilt eat, and drink, and make good cheer,
> Or haunt together women's lusty company,
> I would not forsake you. . . .
> *Everyman:* Then bear me company in my far journey.
> *Fellowship:* Now, in good faith, I will not that way.
> But if thou wilt murder, or any man kill,
> In that I will help thee with a good will.[45]

Everyman appeals to Kindred, his cousin, who rejects the invitation because "I have the cramp in my toe." Everyman calls upon Goods to aid him; but Goods has been so firmly locked away that he cannot be freed to render any help. At last Everyman entreats Good Deeds; she is pleased that he has not quite forgotten her; she introduces him to Knowledge, who leads him to Confession, who shrives him clean. Then Good Deeds descends with Everyman into his grave, and angelic songs welcome the purified sinner into paradise.

The author almost, but not quite, triumphed over an ungainly dramatic form. The personification of a quality can never qualify as a person, for every man is an irritatingly complex contradiction, unique except when part of a crowd; and great art must portray the general through the unique, as through Hamlet or Quixote, Oedipus or Panurge. Experiment and ingenuity would need another century to transform the dull morality play into the living Elizabethan drama of infinitely variable man.

The great literary event in fifteenth-century England was the establishment of its first printing press. Born in Kent, William Caxton migrated to

Bruges as a merchant. In his leisure he translated a collection of French romances. His friends asked for copies, which he made himself; but his hand, he tells us, became "weary and not steadfast with much writing," and his eyes were "dimed with overmuch lokying on the whit paper."[46] On his visits to Cologne, he may have seen the printing press set up there (1466) by Ulrich Zell, who had learned the new technique in Mainz. In 1471 Colard Mansion organized a printing shop in Bruges, and Caxton resorted to it as a means of multiplying copies of his translation. In 1476 he returned to England, and a year later he installed at Westminster the fonts—perhaps the presses—that he had brought from Bruges. He was already fifty-five, and only fifteen years were left him; but in that period he printed ninety-eight books, several of them translated by himself from the Latin or the French. His choice of titles, and the quaint and charming style of his prefaces, laid a lasting mark on English literature. When he died (1491) his Alsatian associate, Wynkyn de Worde, carried on the revolution.

In 1485 Caxton edited and published one of the most lovable masterpieces of English prose—*The Noble Histories of King Arthur and of Certain of His Knights*. Its strange author had died, probably in prison, some sixteen years before. Sir Thomas Malory, in the Hundred Years' War, served in the retinue of Richard de Beauchamp, Earl of Warwick, and represented Warwick in the Parliament of 1445. Lonesome for the license of war, he broke into the home of Hugh Smyth, raped Hugh's wife, extorted a hundred shillings from Margaret Kyng and William Hales, broke again into Hugh Smyth's house, and again raped the wife. He stole seven cows, two calves, and 335 sheep, twice looted the Cistercian Abbey at Coombe, and was twice clapped into jail. It seems incredible that such a man should have written that tender swan song of English chivalry which we now call *Le Morte d'Arthur*; but after a century of dispute it is agreed that these delightful romances were the product of Sir Thomas Malory's incarcerated years.[47]

He took most of the stories from the French forms of the Arthurian legends, arranged them in tolerable sequence, and phrased them in a style of wistful, feminine charm. To an aristocracy losing chivalry in the brutalities and treacheries of war, he appealed for a return to the high standards of Arthur's knights, forgetting their transgressions and his own. Arthur, after outgrowing fornication and incest, settles down with his pretty but venturesome Guinevere, governs England—indeed, all Europe—from his capital a Camelot (Winchester), and requires the 150 knights of his Round Table t pledge themselves

> never to do outrage nor murder . . . by no means to be cruel, but to give mercy unto him that asketh mercy . . . and always to do . . . gentlewomen succour, upon pain of death.[48]

Love and war are the mingled themes of a book resounding with the combats of incomparable chevaliers for dames and damosels beyond compare. Tristram and Lancelot cuckold their kings, but are the soul of honor and bravery. Encountering each other armored, helmeted, and visored, and hence with their identities concealed, they fight for four hours, until their swords are incarnadined and dull.

> Then at last spake Sir Lancelot and said: Knight, thou fightest wonderly well as ever I saw knight, therefore, an it please you, tell me your name. Sir, said Sir Tristram, that is me loath to tell any man my name. Truly, said Sir Lancelot, an I were required, I was never loath to tell my name. It is well said, said Sir Tristram; therefore I require you to tell me your name. Fair knight, he said, my name is Sir Lancelot du Lake. Alas, said Sir Tristram, what have I done? for ye are the man in the world that I love best. Fair knight, said Sir Lancelot, tell me your name. Truly, said he, my name is Sir Tristram de Liones. O Jesu, said Sir Lancelot, what adventure is befallen me! And therewith Sir Lancelot kneeled down and yielded him up his sword. And therewith Sir Tristram kneeled down and yielded him up his sword. . . . Then they both forthwith went to the stone, and set them down upon it, and took off their helms . . . and either kissed other an hundred times.[49]

What a leap it is from this airy realm, in which no one ever worked for a living, and all women were "gentlewomen," to the real matter-of-fact world of the *Paston Letters*, those living missives that bound a scattered family together in affection and finance in the England of the fifteenth century! Here is John Paston, who practices law in London or on circuit while Margaret rears their children and manages his property at Norwich; he is all business, stern, stingy, competent; she is all submission, a humble, able, timid wife, who trembles at the thought that she has offended him;[50] such were the Guineveres of the actual world. And yet here too are delicate sentiments, mutual solicitude, even romance; Margery Brews confesses to Sir John Paston II that she loves him, and mourns that the dowry she can bring him falls far below his state; "but if ye love me, as I trust verily ye do, ye will not leave me therefore"; and he, master of the Paston fortune, marries her despite the complaints of his relatives—and himself dies within two years. There were hearts tender and bruised under the hard surface of that disordered age.

VII. THE ENGLISH HUMANISTS

We must not wonder that the exuberance of classical scholarship in the Italy of Cosimo and Lorenzo de' Medici awoke only a timid echo in an England whose merchants cared little for letters, and whose nobles were not ashamed of illiterate wealth. Sir Thomas More, at the outset of the sixteenth century, reckoned that some 40 per cent of the English people could read.[51] The Church and the universities which she controlled were as yet the sole patrons of scholars. It is to the credit of England that under these circumstances, and amid the waste and violence of war, men like Grocyn, Linacre, Latimer, and Colet were touched by the Italian fire, and brought enough of its heat and light to England to make Erasmus, Europe's *arbiter litterarum*, feel at home when he came to the island in 1499. The humanists, devoted to the study of pagan as well as Christian culture, were denounced by a few ingrown "Trojans," who feared these "Greeks" bringing gifts from Italy; but they were bravely defended and befriended by great churchmen like William of Waynflete, Bishop of Winchester, William Warham, Archbishop of Canterbury, John Fisher, Bishop of Rochester, and, later, Thomas Cardinal Wolsey, Chancellor of England.

From the time when Manuel Chrysoloras visited England (1408), some young English scholars caught a fever whose only cure, they felt, was study or lechery in Italy. Humphrey, Duke of Gloucester, came back from Italy with a passion for manuscripts, and collected a library that afterward enriched the Bodleian. John Tiptoft, Earl of Worcester, studied under Guarino da Verona at Ferrara and John Argyropoulos at Florence, and returned to England with more books than morals. In 1464-67 the monk William Tilley of Selling studied at Padua, Bologna, and Rome, brought back many pagan classics, and taught Greek at Canterbury.

One of his fervent pupils there was Thomas Linacre. When Tilley went again to Italy (1487), Linacre accompanied him, and remained twelve years. He studied under Politian and Chalcondyles in Florence, edited Greek works for Aldus Manutius in Venice, and returned to England so accomplished in diverse fields of learning that Henry VII summoned him to tutor Arthur, Prince of Wales. At Oxford he and Grocyn and Latimer constituted almost an Oxford Movement toward the classic languages and literatures; their lectures inspired John Colet and Thomas More, and attracted Erasmus himself.[52] Linacre was the most universal of the English humanists, at home in Greek and Latin, translating Galen, promoting scientific medicine, founding the Royal College of Physicians and leaving his fortune to endow chairs of medicine at Oxford and Cambridge. Through him, said Erasmus, the new learning was so established in Britain that no Englishman need any longer go to study in Italy.[53]

William Grocyn was already forty when he joined Linacre in Florence. Returning to England in 1492, he hired rooms in Exeter College, Oxford, and lectured daily on Greek, over the protests of conservatives who trembled lest the original text of the New Testament should upset the thousand-year-old authority of Jerome's Vulgate Latin translation. But Grocyn was reassuringly orthodox in doctrine and rigidly upright in his moral life. English humanism never developed, as in some scholars of the Italian Renaissance, even a concealed hostility to Christianity; it treasured the Christian heritage above all intellectual refinements, and its most famous disciple found no embarrassment in being dean of St. Paul's.

John Colet was the eldest son of Sir Henry Colet, a rich merchant who begot twenty-two children and served two terms as mayor of London. At Oxford the youth caught the humanist fervor from Linacre and Grocyn, and "eagerly devoured" Plato, Plotinus, and Cicero. In 1493 he traveled in France and Italy, met Erasmus and Budé in Paris, was strongly moved by Savonarola in Florence, and was shocked by the levity and license of cardinals and Alexander VI in Rome. On his return to England, having inherited his father's wealth, he might have risen to high place in business or politics, but he preferred scholastic life in Oxford. Ignoring the tradition that only a priest might teach theology, he lectured on St. Paul's Epistle to the Romans; he replaced Scholastic dialectic with criticism and elucidation of the Vulgate text; and his large audiences felt refreshed by the novelty of his method, and by his stress on the good life as the best theology. Erasmus, who saw him at Oxford in 1499, described him as a saint perpetually tempted to lust and luxury, but "keeping the flower of his virginity till his death," scorning the easygoing monks of his time, and dedicating his fortune to pious uses and charity.[54]

He was a loyal opposition in the Church, loving her despite her faults. He questioned the literal truth of Genesis, but accepted the divine inspiration of the Bible. He foreshadowed the Reformers in stressing the authority of the Scriptures as against ecclesiastical traditions and forms, in rejecting the Scholastic philosophy as an intellectual dilution of simple Christianity, in doubting the confessional powers of priests and the Real Presence of Christ in the consecrated bread, and in denouncing the worldliness of the clergy:

> If the highest bishop, whom we call the pope ... be a lawful bishop, he of himself does nothing, but God in him. But if he do attempt anything of himself, he is then a breeder of poison. .... This has now indeed been done for many years past, and has by this time so increased as to take powerful hold on all members of the Christian Church, so that unless ... Jesus lay to His hand with all speed, our most disordered Church cannot be far from death. ... Oh, the abominable impiety of those miserable priests, of whom this age contains a great multitude, who fear not to rush from the bosom of some foul harlot into the temple of the Church, to the altars of Christ, to the mysteries of God! On them the vengeance of God will one day fall.[55]

In 1504 Colet was appointed dean of St. Paul's. From that high pulpit he preached against the sale of bishoprics, and the evil of plural benefices held by one man. He aroused an angry opposition, but Archbishop Warham protected him. Linacre, Grocyn, and More were now established in London, free from the conservatism and scholasticism of Oxford, stimulated by the visits of Erasmus, and soon to enjoy the support of the young Henry VIII. Everything seemed prepared for an English Renaissance that would move hand in hand with a peaceful Reformation.

CHAPTER VI

Episode in Burgundy

1363-1515

I. THE ROYAL DUKES

BY its position on the eastern flank of France around Dijon, and by the subtle statesmanship of its dukes, Burgundy emerged with little harm from the Hundred Years' War, and became for half a century the brightest spot in transalpine Christendom. When the Burgundian ducal family of the Capetian line became extinct, and the duchy reverted to the French Crown, John II gave it to his fourth son Philip (1363) as a reward for valor at Poitiers. During his forty-one years as Duke of Burgundy, Philip the Bold (Philippe le Hardi) managed so well, and married so diplomatically, that Hainaut, Flanders, Artois, and Franche-Comté came under his rule; and the duchy of Burgundy, technically a province of France, became in effect an independent state, enriched by Flemish commerce and industry, and graced by the patronage of art.

John the Fearless (*Jean sans Peur*), by a fine web of alliances and intrigues, stretched his power to the bursting point, and France felt challenged to resist. Louis, Duke of Orléans, ruling France for his mad brother Charles VI, allied France with the Holy Roman Empire in a plan to check the unwisely fearless Duke. John's hired assassins killed him; violent strife ensued between the Burgundian party and the Armagnacs—followers of Louis' father-in-law the Count of Armagnac—for the control of French policy; and John in turn died under an assassin s knife (1419). His son Philip the Good renounced all feudal allegiance to France, allied Burgundy with England, and annexed Tournai, Namur, Brabant, Holland, Zeeland, Limburg, and Louvain. When he made his peace with France (1435) he exacted the recognition of his duchy's practical sovereignty, and the cession of Luxembourg, Liége, Cambrai, and Utrecht. Burgundy was now at its zenith, rivaling in wealth and power any kingdom in the West.

Philip might not win from tender minds his title "the Good." He was not above chicanery and cruelty and unmannerly flares of wrath. But he was a devoted son, an excellent administrator, and a fond father even to his sixteen illegitimate offspring. He loved women royally, had twenty-four mistresses, prayed and fasted, gave alms, and made his capitals—Dijon, Bruges, and

Ghent—the art foci of the Western world outside of Italy. His long rule brought to Burgundy and its provinces such affluence that few of his subjects made any fuss about his sins. The Flemish towns fretted under his mastery, and mourned to see their old guild organization and communal liberties yielding to a national economy under a centralized government. Philip and his son Charles suppressed their revolts but allowed them a conciliatory peace, for they knew that from the industry and commerce of these cities came the richest ducal revenues. Before Philip the regions of the lower Rhine had been fragments, as diverse in institutions and policies as in race and speech; he bound them into a unified state, gave them order, and seconded their prosperity.

Burgundian society at Bruges, Ghent, Liége, Louvain, Brussels, and Dijon was now (1420–60) the most polished and amorous in Europe, not excepting the contemporary Florence of Cosimo de' Medici. The dukes preserved all the forms of chivalry; it was Philip the Good who founded the Order of the Golden Fleece (1429); and it was in part from her Burgundian allies that England took the chivalric pomp and glamour that brightened the rough surface of English manners, glorified the campaigns of Henry V, and shone in the pages of Froissart and Malory. The Burgundian nobles, shorn of independent power, lived chiefly as courtiers, and developed all the graces of dress and bearing that could adorn parasitism and adultery.[1] Merchants and manufacturers robed themselves like royalty, and fed and gowned their wives as if preparing the scene for Rubens. Under so loving a duke monogamy would have been *lèse-majesté*. John of Heinsberg, the jolly Bishop of Liége, spawned a dozen bastards; John of Burgundy, Bishop of Cambrai, had thirty-six children and grandchildren begotten out of wedlock; many of the elite, in this eugenic age, were so born.[2] Prostitutes could be found at almost any time and price at the public baths. At Louvain they pretended to be landladies, offering accommodations for students.[3] Festivals were many and extravagant; famous artists were engaged to design the pageants and decorate the floats; and people came over frontiers and seas to view gorgeous spectacles in which nude women played the part of ancient goddesses and nymphs.[4]

II. THE RELIGIOUS SPIRIT

In somber contrast with this effervescent society were the saints and mystics who, under these dukes, gave Holland a high place in religious history. Jan van Ruysbroeck, a Brussels priest, retired at fifty (1343) to an Augustinian monastery at Groenendael, near Waterloo, where he devoted himself to mystical contemplation and compositions. He professed that the

Holy Spirit guided his pen; nevertheless his pantheism verged upon a denial of individual immortality.

> God Himself is swallowed up with all the blessed in an absence of modes . . . an eternal loss of self. . . . The seventh degree is attained when, beyond all knowledge or all knowing, we discover in ourselves a bottomless not-knowing; when, beyond all names given to God or to creatures, we come to expire, and pass over in eternal namelessness, where we lose ourselves . . . and contemplate all these blessed spirits which are essentially sunken away, merged and lost in their super-essence, in an unknown darkness without mode.[5]

The Netherlands * and Rhenish Germany saw in this period a profusion of lay groups—Beghards, Beguines, Brethren of the Free Spirit—whose mystic raptures led often to piety, social service, quietism, and pacifism, sometimes to a rejection of the sacraments as unnecessary, and occasionally to a cheerful acceptance of sin as quite swallowed up in union with God.[6] Gerrit (Geert, Gerard) Groote of Deventer, after receiving a good education at Cologne, Paris, and Prague, spent many days with Ruysbroeck at Groenendael, and was moved to make the love of God the pervading motive of his life. Having received deacon's orders (1379), he began to preach in the towns of Holland, in the vernacular, to audiences so large that the local churches could not hold them; people left their shops and meals to hear him. Scrupulously orthodox in doctrine, and himself a "hammer of heretics," he nevertheless attacked the moral laxity of priests as well as of laymen, and demanded that Christians should live strictly in accord with the ethics of Christ. He was denounced as a heretic, and the bishop of Utrecht withdrew from all deacons the right to preach. One of Groote's followers, Floris Radewijnszoon, drew up a semi-monastic, semi-communistic rule for the "Brethren of the Common Life," who lived in a *Fraterhuis* at Deventer with Groote at their head, and—without taking monastic vows—occupied themselves with manual labor, teaching, religious devotions, and copying manuscripts. Groote died at forty-four (1384) of a pestilence contracted while nursing a friend, but his Brotherhood spread its influence through 200 *Fraterhuizen* in Holland and Germany. The schools of the Brotherhood gave the pagan classics a prominent place in their curriculum, preparing the way for the Jesuit schools that took over their work in the Counter Reformation. The Brethren welcomed printing soon after its appearance, and used it to disseminate their *moderna devotio*. Alexander Hegius at Deventer (1475–98) was a memorable example of the type that fortunate students have known—the saintly teacher who lives only for the instruction and moral

---

* In this volume *Netherlands* and *Lowlands* will be used in their original sense as approximately embracing both modern Belgium and Holland.

guidance of his pupils. He improved the curriculum, centered it around the classics, and won the praise of Erasmus for the purity of his Latin style. When he died he left nothing but his clothes and his books; everything else he had secretly given to the poor.[7] Among the famous pupils of Deventer were Nicholas of Cusa, Erasmus, Rudolf Agricola, Jean de Gerson, and the author of *The Imitation of Christ*.

We are not sure who wrote this exquisite manual of humility. Probably it was Thomas Hamerken of Kempen in Prussia. In the quiet of his cell in the monastery of Mt. St. Agnes near Zwolle, Thomas à Kempis (1380–1471) gathered from the Bible, the Fathers of the Church, and St. Bernard passages expounding the ideal of unworldly piety as conceived by Ruysbroeck and Groote, and rephrased them in simple mellifluous Latin.

> What will it avail thee to be engaged in profound discussions of the Trinity, if thou be void of humility, and art thereby displeasing to the Trinity? Truly, sublime words do not make a man holy and just, but a virtuous life maketh him dear to God. I had rather feel compunction than know how to define it. If thou knewest the whole Bible by heart, and the sayings of all the philosophers, what would it profit thee without the love of God, and without grace? Vanity of vanities, and all is vanity, except to love God, and Him only to serve. This is the highest wisdom, by contempt of the world to tend toward the Kingdom of Heaven. . . . Yet learning is not to be blamed . . . for that is good in itself and ordained by God, but a good conscience and a virtuous life are always to be preferred. . . .
>
> He is truly great who hath great love. He is truly great that is little in his own eyes, and that maketh no account of any height of honor. He is truly wise who casteth aside all earthly things as dung, that he may win Christ. : . .
>
> Fly the tumult of men as much as thou canst, for the treating of worldly affairs is a great hindrance. . . . Truly it is misery to live on the earth. . . . It is a great matter to live in obedience, to be under a superior, and not to be at our own disposing. It is much safer to obey than to govern. . . . The cell, constantly dwelt in, groweth sweet.[8]

There is a gentle eloquence in the Imitation that echoes the profound simplicity of Christ's sermons and parables. It is an ever needed check on the intellectual pride of frail reason and shallow sophistication. When we are weary of facing our responsibilities in life we shall find no better refuge than Thomas à Kempis' Fifth Gospel. But who shall teach us how to be Christians in the stream and storm of the world?

III. SPARKLING BURGUNDY: 1363–1465

Despite such deprecating Thomases, the provinces under Burgundian rule indulged in considerable intellectual activity. The dukes themselves—Philip the Good above the rest—collected libraries and encouraged literature and art. Schools multiplied, and the University of Louvain, founded in 1426, wa soon among the leading educational centers of Europe. Georges Castellain' *Chronique des ducs de Bourgogne* recorded the history of the duchy with rhetorical effulgence and a minimum of philosophy, but in a vigorous French that shared with Froissart and Comines in forming that favorite medium of clear and graceful prose. Private groups organized Chambers of Rhetoric (*Rederijkers*) for contests in oratory and poetry and the performance of plays. The two languages of the realm—the French or Romance of the Walloons in the south and the German dialects of the Flemings and Dutch in the north—rivaled each other in producing poets who repose in the peace of oblivion.

The supreme expression of the duchy was in art. Antwerp began in 1352 its vast, many-aisled cathedral, and finished it in 1518; Louvain raised the beautifully proportioned St. Pierre—another casualty of the second World War. Men and cities were so rich that they could afford mansions or town halls almost as magnificent as the churches that they conceded to God. The bishops who governed Liége housed themselves and their administrative staff in the largest and most elegant palace in the Lowlands. Ghent built its guildhall in 1325, Brussels its town hall in 1410–55, Louvain in 1448–63; Bruges added its *hotel de ville* in 1377–1421, and crowned it with a world-famous belfry (1393–96) that served as a landmark to mariners far out at sea. While these noble Gothic structures expressed the pride of cities and merchants, the dukes and aristocracy of Burgundy financed for their palaces and tombs a brilliant outburst of sculpture, painting, and manuscript illumination. Flemish artists, frightened from France by war, flocked back to their own cities. Philip the Bold gathered a veritable pleiad of geniuses to adorn his summer residence at the Chartreuse de Champmol—a Carthusian monastery in the "gentle field" adjoining Dijon.

In 1386 Philip commissioned Jean de Marville to design for him an elaborate mausoleum in the Chartreuse. When Marville died (1389) Claus Sluter of Holland continued the work; when Sluter died (1406) his pupil Claus de Werve carried on; at last (1411) the tomb was completed, and received the bones of the Duke, now seven years dead. In 1793 a revolutionary assembly at Dijon ordered the dismantling of the great sepulcher, and its components were scattered or destroyed. In 1827 the communal fathers, breathing a reverse political breeze, collected the remaining pieces, and housed them in the Dijon Museum. The Duke and his Duchess, Marguerite of Flanders, lie in handsome alabaster on a massive marble slab; and below them forty *pleurant* figures—sole survivors of the ninety carved—mourn the ducal death in silent and graceful grief. For the portal of the chapel at the Chartreuse, Sluter and his pupils (1391–94) chiseled out five superb figures: the Virgin receiving the homage of Philip and Marguerite, presented to her by John the Baptist and St. Catherine of Alexandria. In the courtyard Sluter set up his master work, the *Puits de Moïse*, Well of Moses: a pedestal bearing statues of Moses, David, Jeremiah, Zachariah, Isaiah, and Daniel, originally surmounted by a "calvary" or crucifixion scene, of which nothing remains but a somber, noble head of Christ crowned with thorns. No sculpture of such masculine power and unique audacity had been seen in Europe since the best days of Roman art.

The painters formed as remarkable a dynasty as the sculptors. The miniaturists still found patrons: Count William of Hainaut paid well for the illumination of *Les tres belles heures de Nôtre Dame* (c. 1414);* and the unknown genius (perhaps Hubert van Eyck) set a model and pace for a thousand Lowland landscape artists by depicting with microscopic zeal a port with ships beached or in full sail, passengers disembarking, sailors and longshoremen at their diverse tasks, waves breaking on a crescent shore, white clouds moving stealthily across the sky—all in the space of a picture card. In 1392 Melchior Broederlam of Ypres brightened the Chartreuse de Champmol with the oldest significant panel extant outside of Italy. But Broederlam and the artists who painted the walls and statuary of the monastery used traditional tempera—mixing their colors with some gelatinous material. Nuances of shading and tint, and translucency of tone, were hardly attainable by these means, and moisture could ruin the finished work. As early as 1329 Jacques Compère of Ghent had experimented with colors mixed in oil. Through a hundred years of trial and error the Flemings developed the new technique; and in the first quarter of the fifteenth century it revolutionized pictorial art. When Hubert van Eyck and his younger brother Jan painted *The Adoration of the Lamb* for the cathedral of St. Bavon at Ghent, they not only established the superiority of oil as a vehicle of color; they produced one of the supreme masterpieces in the history of painting, for whose sake St. Bavon has been a goal of pilgrimage ever since.

In form this greatest of fifteenth-century paintings—this "pivot of the history of the art," Goethe called it [9]—is a folding polyptych of six panels, painted on wood, with twelve pictures on each side; opened, it is eleven feet high, fourteen feet wide. In the center of the lower row is an imaginary countryside, with a city

---

* Also known as *Les heures de Turin*. Some of these miniatures were destroyed in the fire of the Biblioteca Nazionale of Turin in 1904; but photographic reproductions of these remain, and several originals survive in Turin's Museo Civico.

of majestic towers—the Heavenly Jerusalem—rising in the distance beyond the hills; in the foreground a well of the Water of Life; farther back an altar whereon a lamb symbolizing Christ pours out its sacrificial blood, while patriarchs and prophets, Apostles and martyrs, angels and saints, gather around in rapt adoration. In the upper center a throned figure, looking like some benevolent Semitic Charlemagne, is designated as God the Father—a naturally inadequate representation of deity, but a noble conception of a wise ruler and just judge. It is surpassed, in this painting, by only one figure—the Virgin, a soft-featured, blond Teutonic type not so much of beauty as of purity and modesty; the *Sistine Madonna* is less nobly conceived. On Mary's left is a group of angels; at the extreme left a naked Adam, thin and sad, "remembering in misery a happy time." To the right of God the Father is John the Baptist, very sumptuously robed for a shepherd preaching in the wilderness. At the extreme right stands a naked Eve, somber and hardly fair, mourning paradise lost; she for a time, like Adam at the other end, shocked a chilly Flanders unaccustomed to the nude in life or art. Above her, Cain slays his brother as a symbolic prelude to history.

The reverse of the polyptych declines from the exalted type of the inner panels. In the middle row an angel at the left and Mary at the right, separated by a room, picture the Annunciation—the faces stereotyped, the hands remarkably fine, the draperies as lovely as any in Flemish painting. At the bottom is a Latin poem of four lines; some words have been worn out by the centuries; the rest reads: "Hubertus van Eyck, great and skilled beyond any other, began the heavy task, and Johannes, second in art . . . encouraged by the bequest of Jodocus Vyd. This verse on the sixth of May calls you to behold the finished work"; and in the final line certain letters add up in their numerical value to 1432, the year of completion. Vyd and his wife were the donors. How much of the picture was painted by Hubert, how much by Jan, is a problem happily insoluble, so that dissertations thereon may be written till all trace of the painting disappears.*

Perhaps there is in this epochal picture an undue profusion of figures and minutiae: every man, woman, angel, flower, branch, blossom, beast, stone, and gem is reproduced with heroic patience and fidelity—to the amusement of Michelangelo, who saw in Flemish realism a sacrifice of central significance to incidental and irrelevant detail.[11] But nothing in contemporary Italy rivaled this painting in scope, conception, or effect; and in later pictorial art only the Sistine Chapel ceiling of Michelangelo surpasses it, and the Vatican frescoes of Raphael, and probably Leonardo's *Last Supper* before it began its long decay. Even in its own day all literate Europe talked of the *Adoration*. Alfonso the Magnanimous pleaded with Jan van Eyck to come to Naples and paint for him such men and

---

* *The Adoration of the Lamb* has survived many restorations and vicissitudes. It was retouched in 1550, 1663, 1825, 1829, 1859, 1936, 1951. The major portions were removed by the French Revolutionary Army to Paris in 1794, and were returned in 1816. The wings (without Adam and Eve) were sold to an art dealer (1816), were bought by the Berlin Museum (1821), and were restored to Ghent by the Treaty of Versailles (1919). In the second World War the polyptych was removed to France for protection; in 1942 it was taken by the Germans; in 1944 it was hidden in Austrian salt mines; in 1946 it was restored to its chapel in the church of St. Bavon by the Army of the United States.[10]

women, with golden hair, as sang in this picture but were so rare in southern Italy.

Hubert van Eyck moves out of our ken after 1432,* but we can vaguely follow Jan through a prosperous career. Philip the Good made him *varlet de chambre* (then a position of much dignity and affluence), and sent him abroad with embassies as a jewel from the Burgundian crown. Some twenty-four extant paintings are ascribed to him, and nearly every one is a *chef-d'œuvre*. Dresden has a *Virgin and Child* second only to the *Adoration* in the Van Eyck production; Berlin boasts *The Man with the Pink*—a dour face strangely incongruous with the fondled flower; Melbourne has the brilliantly colored "Ince Hall *Madonna*," hardly nine inches by six, yet valued at $250,000; Bruges treasures *The Madonna with Canon van der Paele*—the Virgin lovely from her flowing hair to the hem of her marvelously wrinkled gown, the Canon fat and bald and good-natured, one of the great portraits of the fifteenth century; London shows the newlyweds Giovanni Arnolfini and his spouse in an interior sparkling with mirror and chandelier; the Frick Collection in New York has recently acquired, at unstated but enormous cost, a richly colored *Virgin and Child with Sts. Barbara and Elizabeth;* Washington has an *Annunciation* remarkable for its illusion of spatial depth, and for the splendor of Gabriel's raiment, which steals the scene from Mary; and the Louvre owns *The Madonna with Chancellor Rolin*, with a fascinating landscape of winding river, crowded bridge, towered city, flowered gardens, and a range of hills rising to greet the sun. In all of these, besides their full-bodied colors, there is a resolve to picture the donors as they were and looked, to reveal on a face the life its owner had led, the thoughts and feelings that through the years had formed the features into a confession of character. In such portraits the medieval spirit of idealization is set aside, and a modern naturalism—perhaps reflecting middle-class secularism—is in full swing.

Many other painters reached renown in that fertile land and age: Petrus Christus, Jacques Daret, Robert Campin ("the Master of Flemalle"). We bow to them humbly and pass on to Campin's pupil Roger de la Pasture. By the age of twenty-seven Roger had made such a name for himself in his native Tournai that it gave him twice the three measures or casks of wine that it had voted to Jan van Eyck. Nevertheless he accepted an invitation to be official painter for Brussels, and thenceforth gave his name the Flemish form Rogier van der Weyden. In 1450, aged fifty-one, he went to Rome for the jubilee, met Italian painters, and was feted as a world celebrity; possibly

---

* Uncertainly attributed to him are five paintings: an *Annunciation* (New York); *The Three Maries at the Sepulcher* (Vierhouten, van Beuningen Collection); a small *Madonna* in Frankfurt; and two wings of an altarpiece (New York), representing the Crucifixion and the Last Judgment with almost Boschian *diablerie*.

oil painting in Italy was advanced by his influence. When he died at Brussels in 1464 he was the most widely renowned artist in all Europe.

He is preserved in quantity. He too painted Philip the Good, Rolin—Philip's chancellor for forty years—Charles the Bold, and many other celebrities. Beautiful beyond description is the *Portrait of a Lady* in the Washington National Gallery—embodied pugnacity and piety, modesty and pride. In portraiture Rogier was too romantic to match Jan van Eyck; but in his religious pictures he revealed a tenderness and refinement of sentiment, and an emotional intensity, missing in Jan's masculine and matter-of-fact art; here, it may be, the French or Italian spirit spoke through the Flemish form,[12] and the medieval mood revived.

Like the Italians, Rogier recorded the vital episodes in the moving story of Mary and her Son: Gabriel announcing to a startled girl that she is to be the mother of God; the Infant in the manger; the adoration of the Magi; St. Luke painting the Virgin as she nurses her Babe; the visit of Mary to Elizabeth; the mother happily contemplating her Child; the presentation in the temple; the Crucifixion; the descent from the cross; the Resurrection; the Last Judgment. In this final scene Rogier reached his apogee, in a complex polyptych probably designed, but not quite worthy, to rival *The Adoration of the Lamb*. It was painted for Rolin, and is now in the pretty hospital that the great chancellor founded in Beaune. In the central panel Christ sits in judgment, but more tempered with mercy than in Michelangelo; on either side angels robed in gleaming white carry the instruments of His passion and death; below them Michael the Archangel weighs in a scale the good and the bad; at the left Mary kneels in adoration and supplication; on one side the saved genuflect in grateful prayer, on the other the damned tumble in terror into hell. Almost as famous as this painting is a triptych in Antwerp illustrating the Seven Sacraments with symbolic scenes. And then, lest we think him quite lost in pious ecstasy, Rogier paints a bathing beauty, and two youths peeping at her through a chink in the wall, with that anomalous anatomical curiosity which satisfaction never satisfies.

IV. CHARLES THE BOLD: 1465–77

All this effervescence evaporated under the hot temper of Charles le Téméraire, the Rash, commonly miscalled the Bold. Rogier van der Weyden pictured him as the handsome, serious, black-haired young Count of Charolais, who led his father's armies to bloody victories and champed the bit waiting for him to die. In 1465 Philip the Good, sensing his impatience, yielded the government to him, and relished the youth's ambition and energy.

Charles resented the division of his duchy into northern and southern provinces severed in space and diverse in speech; he resented more the feudal fealty that he owed for some of these provinces to the French King, for others to the German Emperor. He longed to make Greater Burgundy, like the Lotharingia (Lorraine) of the ninth century, a middle kingdom between Germany and France, physically coherent and politically sovereign. Even, at times, he mused that the opportune deaths of a few intervening heirs would hand him the French, English, and Imperial crowns, and raise him to a pinnacle beside the loftiest figures in history.[13] To realize these dreams he organized the best standing army in Europe, taxed his subjects beyond precedent, disciplined himself to every hardship and trial, and gave neither his mind nor his body, neither his friends nor his foes, any respite of ease or peace.

However, Louis XI thought of Burgundy as still an appanage of France, and fought his rich vassal with superior strategy and guile. Charles joined French nobles in war against Louis; he won some further towns, and the lasting enmity of an undiscourageable king. In that struggle Dinant and Liége revolted against Burgundy and declared for France, and some enthusiasts at Dinant labeled a hanged effigy of Charles as the bastard son of a careless priest. Charles shot down the walls of the city, gave it over to three days of pillage by his troops, enslaved all men, expelled all women and children, burned all buildings to the ground, and threw 800 of the rebels, bound hand and foot, into the Meuse (1466). Philip died in the following June, and the Count of Charolais became Charles the Bold. He renewed the war with Louis, and compelled his company and co-operation in the siege of repeatedly rebellious Liége. The starving citizens offered Charles all their goods in return for their lives; he rejected the bargain; the city was plundered down to the last dwelling and chapel; chalices were snatched from the hands of priests celebrating Mass; all captives who could not pay a heavy ransom were drowned (1468).[14]

The world, though long inured to violence, could not forgive Charles his severity, nor his unfeudal imprisonment and humiliation of his King. When he conquered Gelderland, acquired Alsace, and stepped on Imperial toes by interfering in Cologne and besieging Neuss, all his neighbors took steps to check him. Peter van Hagenbach, whom he had appointed to govern Alsace, so provoked the citizens with his insolence, rapacity, and cruelty, that they hanged him; and as Swiss merchants had been among Peter's victims, and French gold was strategically distributed in Switzerland, and the cantons felt their liberties imperiled by the spread of Charles's power, the Swiss Confederation declared war on him to the death (1474). Charles left Neuss, turned south, conquered Lorraine—so for the first time uniting the ends of his duchy—and marched his army over the Jura into Vaud. The Swiss were the doughtiest warriors of the age; they defeated Charles near Granson, and again near Morat (1476); the Burgundians were routed, and Charles neared insanity in his grief. Lorraine saw its chance and rebelled; the Swiss sent men.

Louis sent money, to help the revolt. Charles formed a new army, fought the allies near Nancy, and in that battle met defeat and death (1477). On the morrow his body, stripped naked by ghouls, was found half submerged in a pond, the face frozen fast in the ice. He was forty-four years old. Burgundy was absorbed into France.

V. ART IN THE LOWLANDS: 1465–1515

Southern Flanders declined for a time after Philip the Good. Political disturbances drove many weavers to England; the growth of the British clothing industry took trade and raw materials from the Flemish cities; by 1520 English cloth crowded the markets of Flanders itself. Brussels, Mechlin, and Valenciennes survived through superior lace, carpets, tapestries, and jewelry, Namur by its leather, Louvain through its university and its beer. About 1480 the canal that brought the sea to Bruges began to silt its bed; heroic efforts were made to clear it; wind and sand won; after 1494 seagoing vessels could no longer reach Bruges. Soon its merchants, then its workers, left Bruges for Antwerp, which deep-draught ships could enter by the estuaries of the Scheldt. Antwerp signed agreements with English exporters, and shared with Calais the British trade with the Continent.

Life in Holland existed by grace of the dykes, which had to be repeatedly rebuilt, and might at any time collapse; some gave way in 1470 and drowned 20,000 of the population. The only major industry was the capture and cure of herring. Holland produced many of the famous painters of this period, but was too poor to hold them; all but Geertgen tot Sint Jans migrated to Flanders.

There, even in cities that suffered decline, rich burghers dressed gorgeously, dwelt in sturdy brick houses luxuriously furnished—hung with the tapestries of Arras or Brussels, and gleaming with the brass vessels of Dinant. They built lovely churches like Nôtre Dame du Sablon at Brussels and St. Jacques at Antwerp, raised stone by stone the towering façade of Antwerp Cathedral, and began the proud town hall of Ghent. They financed the painters, sat for portraits, bribed heaven with votive art, and allowed their women to read books. Perhaps it was their earthy mood that led Flemish painting, in its second flowering, to stress realism and landscape even in religious pictures, and to seek new subjects in homes and fields.

Dirk Bouts inaugurated realism with the exaggerations natural to innovators. He came from his native Haarlem to Brussels, studied there under Rogier van der Weyden, settled in Louvain, and painted for its church of St. Pierre a polyptych, *The Last Supper*, with an interesting panel—*Passover in a Jewish Family*—which seemed to suggest that the Last Supper was the celebration of an orthodox Hebrew rite by Jews still faithful to Judaism. For a chapel in the same church Bouts painted *The Martyrdom of St. Erasmus* with a shocking literalness: two executioners turn a windlass that slowly draws the intestines from the naked saint. In *The Martyrdom of St. Hippolytus* four horses, driven in four directions, pull out the arms and legs of the holy victim. In *The Beheading of the Innocent Knight* a cavalier, vengefully accused by an unsuccessfully amorous empress of trying to seduce her, has his head cut off; the bleeding corpse straddles the foreground, the severed head rests comfortably in the widow's lap; Bouts almost redeems his violence with the calm content of the dying and the dead. There are vivid colors in these paintings, now and then a good landscape or perspective; but their mediocre drawing, rigid figures, and lifeless faces suggest that time does not always winnow wisely.

Probably Hugo van der Goes took his surname from Goes in Zeeland, and was another instance of Holland's generating and losing genius. In 1467 he was admitted to the guild of painters at Ghent. It bespeaks the repute of Flemish painting that an Italian merchant in Flanders chose him to paint an immense triptych for the hospital of Santa Maria Nuova in a Florence already teeming with artists. Hugo chose for his theme the phrase *Quem genuit adoravit*—"Whom she bore she adored." The life-size figure of the Virgin, rapt in reverence, is masterly; a shepherd at the left anticipates the magic of Raphael and Titian; the winter landscape is a novel achievement in delicate fidelity to nature. Vigorous realism, original composition, accurate drawing, incisive delineation of character, placed Van der Goes at the top of the Flemish school in the third quarter of the fifteenth century. Whether to find more quiet for his work, or to calm the religious fears that obsessed him, he entered a monastery near Brussels (*c.* 1475), where he continued to paint and (says a brother monk) drink excessively. The notion that God had destined him for eternal damnation darkened his sober moments, and drove him into insanity.[15]

Vespasiano da Bisticci tells us that about 1468 Duke Federigo of Urbino sent to Flanders for a painter to decorate his study, since he "knew of no one in Italy who understood how to paint in oil colors."[16] Joost van Wassenhoeve, a friend of Van der Goes', accepted the call, settled in Urbino, and came to be known as Justus van Ghent. He composed for the learned Duke twenty-eight pictures of philosophers, and for an Urbino fraternity an altarpiece, *The Institution of the Sacrament*. Though these works are Flemish in style, they date a growing exchange of influence between Flanders and Italy: an increased use of oil, and a trend to realism, in Italian painters, and the infiltration of Italian idealism and techniques into Flemish art.

Hans Memling, though we have no record of his visiting Italy, brought into his painting an elegance and delicacy that he may have acquired from the painters of Cologne, or from Rogier van der Weyden, or that may have come up from Venice and along the Rhine to Mainz. Born near Mainz, and probably named from his native Mömlingen, Hans left Germany for Flanders and Bruges about 1465. There, three years later, Sir John Donne, a visiting Englishman, commissioned him to paint a *Virgin Enthroned*. It was conventional in conception and composition, but it already displayed Memling's technical competence, his refinement of feeling, and his professional piety. St. John the Baptist was represented with Flemish realism, St. John the Evangelist with Fra Angelico idealism; and the rising individualism of art betrayed itself in the surreptitious portrait of Memling peering around a pillar.

Like Perugino a generation later, Memling made a hundred Madonnas, tenderly maternal, divinely calm. They hang on museum walls wherever the eye can reach: in Berlin, Munich, Vienna, Florence, Lisbon, Madrid, Paris, London, New York, Washington, Cleveland, Chicago. Two of the best are in the hospital of St. John at Bruges; Mary dominates *The Mystic Marriage of St. Catherine*, where almost every figure is superb; she presides again in *The Adoration of the Child*, but there the Magi—one a veritable Privy Councilor Goethe—capture the scene. In a panoramic painting at Munich Memling pictured all the major episodes in the recorded life of Christ. In another at Turin he told the story of the Passion with such a medley of men and women as even Brueghel would find it hard to outnumber. For the organ case of a monastery at Najera, in Spain, he composed a triptych of *Christ Surrounded by Angels*, rivaling Melozzo da Forlì's *Angeli Musicanti* of a few years before; and the Antwerp Museum did not think itself bilked when it paid 240,000 francs ($1,200,000?) for this picture in 1896.[17] Another multiple altarpiece, *The Last Judgment*, was painted for Iacopo Tani, an agent for Lorenzo de' Medici in Bruges; it was put on a ship bound for Italy, but the vessel was seized by a Hanseatic skipper, who kept the cash and let the picture go to the Marienkirche of Danzig.[18]

In these major works, and in individual panels, Memling painted some admirable portraits: *Martin van Nieuwenhoev* and *A Woman*—stately under her lofty hat and with her many rings—both in the hospital at Bruges; *A Young Man* in the London Gallery; *An Old Man* in New York; *The Man with an Arrow* in Washington. They do not reach the inspiration or penetration of Titian or Raphael or Holbein, but they catch simple surfaces with workmanlike skill. The occasional nudes—*Adam and Eve, Bathsheba at the Bath*—do not allure.

Toward the end of his career Memling decorated for the hospital in Bruges a Gothic shrine designed to receive the relics of St. Ursula. In eight panels he told how the pious maiden, betrothed to Prince Conon, deferred their marriage till she might make a pilgrimage to Rome; how she sailed, with 11,000 virgins, up the Rhine to Basel, led them trippingly over the Alps, basked in the blessings of the Pope, and how, on their return, all 11,001 were martyred by pagan Huns at Cologne. Nine years later (1488) Carpaccio told the same pretty absurdity, with more accurate drawing and finer coloring, for the School of St. Ursula in Venice.

It is unfair to Memling, or any painter, to look at his pictures wholesale; each was meant for a separate time and place, and there conveyed his lyric quality. To view them in the gross is at once to perceive his limitations—his narrowness of range and style, the monotony of his portraits, even of his modest Madonnas with their streaming golden hair. The surface is lovely or true, and shines with smooth, bright hues; but the brush rarely reaches to the soul beneath, to the secret loneliness, wonderment, aspirations, griefs. There is no life in Memling's women; and when he unclothes them we are chagrined to find them all stomach and tiny breasts. Perhaps the fashion in such items was different then than now; even our desires may be indoctrination. Yet we must acknowledge that when Memling died (1495) he was, by the common consent of his patrons and his rivals, the leading painter north of the Alps. If other artists felt his faults more keenly than their own, they could not match the delicacy of his style, the purity of his sentiment, the splendor of his coloring. For a generation his influence was supreme in the Flemish school.

Gerard David continued the mood. Coming from Holland to Bruges about 1483, he felt the spell of Memling's *aria dolce;* his Madonnas are almost identical with Memling's; perhaps they shared a model between them. Sometimes, as in *The Rest on the Flight to Egypt* (Washington), he equaled Memling in the demure beauty of the Virgin, and surpassed him in delineating the Child. In his older years David followed trade and moved to Antwerp. The school of Bruges ended with him, while that of Antwerp was beginning with Quentin Massys.

Son of a Louvain blacksmith, Massys was received into the painters' guild of St. Luke at Antwerp in 1491, aged twenty-five. St. Luke, however, would hardly have approved *The Feast of Herod,* where Herodias prods with a carving knife the severed head of the Baptist, nor *The Entombment of Christ,* where Joseph of Arimathea plucks blood clots from the hair of the bloodless corpse. Having married twice and buried seven children, Massys had some steel in his fiber, some acid in his oils. So he catches a courtesan in the act of cozening an old money-lender out of his coin; and in a gentler mood he shows a banker counting his gold while his wife looks on in mingled appreciation and jealousy. Yet Massys' Madonnas are more human than Memling's; one (in Berlin) kisses and fondles her Child as any mother would; and the bright blue, purple, and red of her garments accentuate her beauty When it came to portraiture Massys could penetrate behind the face to the character more successfully than Memling, as in the remarkable *Study for a Portrait* in the Musée Jacquemart-André in Paris. It was to Massys that Peter Gillis turned when (1517) he wished to send to Thomas More faithful similitudes of Erasmus and himself. Quentin did well with Gillis, but his *Erasmus* had the ill luck to be followed by Holbein's. When Dürer (1520) and Holbein (1526) came to Antwerp it was to Massys that they paid their highest respects as the dean of Flemish art.

Meanwhile, however, there had appeared in Brabant the most original and absurd artist in Flemish history. Here and there in Massys—as in the leering mob in *Christ Shown to the People* (Madrid), or the ugly faces in an *Adoration of the Magi* (New York)—were such gnarled and brutal heads as Leonardo drew in the satirical byplay of his pen. Hieronymus Bosch made a successful business of such grotesqueries. Born, and spending most of his life, in Bois-le-Duc (in northern Brabant, now southern Holland), he came to be known by its Flemish name, 's Hertogenbosch, finally Bosch. For a time he painted the usual religious themes, and in some, like the *Adoration of the Magi* in Madrid, he verged on normality. But his sense of the ridiculous came to dominate his imagination and his art. Perhaps in chilhood he had been frightened by medieval tales of imps and ghosts, of demons starting from behind any rock or sprouting from a tree; now he would caricature those hobgoblins in curative satire, and laugh them out of mind. He resented with an artist's sensitivity the botches of humanity—the bizarre or ugly or deformed—and depicted them with a macabre mixture of wrath and glee. Even in idyllic scenes like *The Nativity* (Cologne) he gave the foreground to the nose of a cow; in *The Adoration of the Magi* (New York) peasants peek through windows and archways at the Virgin and her Child. Yet in this last picture he painted with consummate draftsmanship a majestic St. Peter and a Negro king whose stately dignity puts the other figures in the shade. But as Bosch proceeded with the story of Christ he darkened the pictures with bestial faces, ferocious eyes, enormous noses, grimly protruding and voracious lips. Passing to the legends of the saints, he portrayed a surprisingly tender St. John the Evangelist in an unusual landscape of islands and sea; but in a corner he placed a contemplative devil—with a monkish cowl, rat's tail, and entomological legs—patiently waiting to inherit the earth. In *The Temptation of St. Anthony* he surrounded the desperate anchorite with gay courtesans and weird imaginings—a dwarf with legs rooted in his shoulders, a bird with the legs of a goat, a jug with the legs of a cow, a rat bestridden by a witch, a minstrel capped with a horse's skull. Bosch took the grotesques from the Gothic cathedrals, and made a world of them.

He was anything but a realist. Now and then he drew a scene from life, as in *The Prodigal's Son*, but there too he exaggerated the ugliness, the poverty, and the fear. His *Hay Ride* is no merrymaking in the month of May, but a bitter illustration of "all flesh is grass." [19] Atop the load all is ideal: a youth plays music for a girl who sings; behind them two lovers kiss, and an angel kneels; above them Christ hovers in the clouds. But on the ground a murderer stabs his fallen enemy, a procuress invites a lass to prostitution, a quack sells panaceas, a fat priest receives offerings from nuns, the cart wheels crush some careless celebrants. At the right a company of devils, aided by apes, drag the damned into hell. Philip II, King of Spain and gloom, hung this piece in his Escorial. Near it he placed a companion piece, *The Pleasures of the World*. Around a pool, in which naked men and women bathe, rides a procession of nudes on animals partly zoological, partly phantasmagorical; spikes and thorns enter the picture from every side; in the foreground two nudes clasp each other in a waltz, while a huge bird gazes on them in philosophical amusement. One shutter shows the creation of Eve as the source of all evil; another displays the tortures and contortions of the damned. It is a marvel of composition, of clever drawing, of diseased imagination—veritable Bosch.

Can it be that even in the dawn of modernity there were millions of simple and impressionable Christians who had nightmares like these? Was Bosch one such? Hardly, for in a portrait of him in the library at Arras he is shown in old age, in full vigor of mind and sharpness of eye; he is a man of the world who has survived his satirical rage, and can look upon life with the humor of one who will soon be out of the mess. He could not have painted these ghoulish fancies so skillfully if they had still possessed him. He stood above them, not so much amused as angry that humanity had ever harbored them. That his contemporaries enjoyed his productions as pictorial pranks rather than as theological terrors appears from the wide market found by prints made from engravings of his works. A generation later Pieter Brueghel would exorcise these devils, and transform these hobgoblins into a healthy and jolly multitude; and four centuries later neurotic artists would reflect the neuroses of their time by painting sarcastic fantasies redolent of Hieronymus Bosch.

A more conventional figure closed this chapter in Flemish painting. Born in Maubeuge, and thence also named Mabuse, Jan Gossaert came to Antwerp in 1503, probably after learning his art from David in Bruges. In 1507 he was invited to the court of Duke Philip of Burgundy—one of Philip the Good's erotic by-products. Jan accompanied the Duke to Italy, and returned with some finesse added to his brush, and a flair for nudes and pagan mythologies; his *Adam and Eve* made the unclothed body attractive for the first time in Flemish art. *Mary with the Child and Angels* and *St. Luke Drawing the Madonna* echoed Italy in their fat cherubs and Renaissance architectural backgrounds, and *The Agony in the Garden* may have owed to Italy its brilliant representation of moonlight. But Gossaert's forte was portraiture. No Fleming since Jan van Eyck had turned out such a searching character study as the *Jan Carondelet* in the Louvre; here the artist concentrated on face and hands, and revealed the moneyed ancestry, the stoic administrator, the mind made somber by the burdens of authority. Massys had brought to an end that first line of Flemish painting which had reached nobility in the Van Eycks; Gossaert imported from Italy those novelties of technique, elegances of ornament, graces of line, subtleties of chiaroscuro and portraiture, that would in the sixteenth century (barring Brueghel) turn Flemish painting from its native skill and genius, and leave it in suspended excellence until its culmination under Rubens and Van Dyck.

Charles the Bold left no son, but he had betrothed his daughter Mary to Maximilian of Austria in the hope that the Hapsburgs would protect Burgundy from France. When Louis XI nevertheless appropriated the duchy, Mary fled to Ghent. There, as the price of being accepted as their constitutional sovereign by Flanders, Brabant, Hainaut, and Holland, she signed the *Groote Privilegie* (February 1477), which pledged her to enter into no marriage, levy no taxes, declare no war, without the consent of the "Estates" or assemblies of the signatory provinces. By this and later charters, including the *Joyeuse Entrie*, as Brabant termed its own grant of local liberty, the Netherlands began a century-long struggle for independence. But Mary's marriage to Maximilian (August 1477) brought the powerful Hapsburgs into the Lowlands. When Mary died (1482) Maximilian became regent. When Maximilian was elected emperor (1494) he transmitted the regency to his son Philip. When Philip died (1506) his sister, Margaret of Austria, was appointed governor-general by the Emperor. When Philip's son, the future Charles V, then fifteen, was declared of age (1515), the Netherlands became part of a vast Hapsburg empire under one of the craftiest and most ambitious rulers in history. Thereby would hang a tale.

CHAPTER VII

Middle Europe

1300-1460

I. LAND AND LABOR

SINCE man lives by permission of physical geography, it is his fate to be divided by mountains, rivers, and seas into groups that develop, in semi-isolation, their diverging languages and creeds, their climatically conditioned features, customs, and dress. Driven by insecurity to suspect the strange, he dislikes and condemns the alien, outlandish looks and ways of other groups than his own. All those fascinating varieties of terrain—mountains and valleys, fiords and straits, gulfs and streams—that make Europe a panorama of diverse delight, have broken the population of a minor continent into a score of peoples cherishing their differences, and self-imprisoned in their heritage of hate. There is a charm in this mosaic of originalities, and one would deprecate a world of people confined in identical myths and pantaloons. And yet, above and beneath these dissimilarities of costume, custom, faith, and speech, nature and man's needs have forced upon him an economic uniformity and interdependence that become more visible and compelling as invention and knowledge topple barriers away. From Norway to Sicily, from Russia to Spain, the unprejudiced surveying eye sees men not so much as diversely dressed and phrased, but as engaged in like pursuits molding like characters: tilling and mining the earth, weaving garments, building homes, altars, and schools, rearing the young, trading surpluses, and forging social order as man's strongest organ of defense and survival. For a moment we shall contemplate Middle Europe as such a unity.

In Scandinavia man's prime task was to conquer the cold, in Holland the sea, in Germany the forests, in Austria the mountains; agriculture, the ground of life, hung its fate on these victories. By 1300 the rotation of crops had become general in Europe, multiplying the yield of the soil. But from 1347 to 1381 half the population of Central Europe was wiped out by the Black Death; and the mortality of men arrested the fertility of the earth. In one year Strasbourg lost 14,000 souls, Cracow 20,000, Breslau 30,000.[1] For a century the Harz mines remained without miners.[2] With simple animal patience men resumed the ancient labors, digging and turning the earth. Sweden and Germany intensified their extraction of iron and copper; coal

143

was mined at Aachen and Dortmund, tin in Saxony, lead in the Harz, silver in Sweden and the Tyrol, gold in Carinthia and Transylvania.

The flow of metals fed a growing industry, which fed a spreading trade. Germany, leader in mining, naturally led in metallurgy. The blast furnace appeared there in the fourteenth century; with the hydraulic hammer and the rolling mill it transformed the working of metals. Nuremberg became an ironmongers' capital, famous for its cannon and its bells. The industry and commerce of Nuremberg, Augsburg, Mainz, Speyer, and Cologne made them almost independent city-states. The Rhine, Main, Lech, and Danube gave the South German towns first place in the overland traffic with Italy and the East. Great commercial and financial firms, with far-flung outlets and agencies, rose along these routes, surpassing, in the fifteenth century, the reach and power of the Hanseatic League. The League was still strong in the fourteenth century, dominating trade in the North and Baltic seas; but in 1397 the Scandinavian countries united to break this monopoly, and soon thereafter the English and Dutch began to carry their own goods. Even the herring conspired against the Hanse; about 1417 they decided to spawn in the North Sea rather than the Baltic; Lübeck, a pillar of the League, lost the herring trade and declined; Amsterdam won it and flourished.

Underneath this evolving economy class war seethed—between country and city, lords and serfs, nobles and businessmen, merchant guilds and craft guilds, capitalists and proletarians, clergy and laity, Church and state. In Sweden, Norway, and Switzerland serfdom was going or gone, but elsewhere in Middle Europe it was taking on new life. In Denmark, Prussia, Silesia, Pomerania, and Brandenburg, where peasants had earned their freedom by clearing the wilderness, serfdom was restored in the fifteenth century by a martial aristocracy; we may judge the harshness of these Junkers from a proverb of the Brandenburg peasants, which wished long life to the lord's horses, lest he should take to riding his serfs.[3] In the Baltic lands the barons and the Teutonic knights, at first content to enserf the conquered Slav inhabitants, were induced, by the labor shortages that followed the Black Death and the Polish war of 1409, to impress into bondage any "idlers who roam on the road or in the towns";[4] and treaties were made with neighboring governments for the extradition of fugitive serfs.

The mercantile *bourgeoisie*, favored by the emperors as a foil to the barons, ruled the municipalities so definitely that in many cases the city hall and the merchants' guildhall were one. Craft guilds were reduced to subjection, submitted to municipal regulation of wages, and were prohibited from united action;[5] here, as in England and France, proud craftsmen were turned into defenseless *prolétaires*. Now and then the workers tried revolt. In 1348 the artisans of Nuremberg captured the municipal council and ruled the city for a year, but the Emperor's soldiers restored the patrician merchants to power.[6] In Prussia an ordinance of 1358 condemned any striker to have an ear cut off.[7] Peasant rebellions flared up in Denmark (1340, 1441), Saxony, Silesia, Brandenburg, and the Rhineland (1432), in Norway and Sweden (1434); but they were too laxly organized to achieve more than a passing cathartic violence. Revolutionary ideas circulated through cities and villages. In 1438 an anonymous radical wrote a pamphlet expounding an imaginary "Kaiser Sigismund's Reformation" on socialistic principles.[8] The stage was slowly prepared for the Peasants' War of 1525.

II. THE ORGANIZATION OF ORDER

Order is the mother of civilization and liberty; chaos is the midwife of dictatorship; therefore history may now and then say a good word for kings. Their medieval function was to free the individual in rising measure from local domination, and to centralize in one authority the power to legislate, judge, punish, mint, and make war. The feudal baron mourned the loss of local autonomy, but the simple citizen thought it good that there should be, in his country, one master, one coinage, one law. Men rarely hoped, in those half-illiterate days, that even kings might disappear, and leave no master but the laws and blunders that men had freely made.

Scandinavia had some remarkable monarchs in the fourteenth century. Magnus II of Sweden organized the conflicting laws of his kingdom into a homogeneous national code (1347). In Denmark Eric IV disciplined the barons and strengthened the central power; Christopher II weakened it; Waldemar IV restored it, and made his country one of the major forces in European politics. But the supreme figure in the Scandinavian dynasties of this age was Waldemar's daughter Margaret. Married at ten (1363) to Haakon VI of Norway, who was the son of Magnus II of Sweden, she seemed destined by blood and marriage to unite the kindred thrones. When her father died (1375) she hurried to Copenhagen with her five-year-old son Olaf, and persuaded the baronial and ecclesiastical electors to accept him as king and herself as regent. When her husband died (1380) Olaf inherited the crown of Norway; but as he was still only ten, Margaret, now twenty-seven, there too acted as regent. Her prudence, tact, and courage astonished her contemporaries, who were accustomed to male incompetence or violence; and the feudal lords of Denmark and Norway, after dominating many kings, proudly supported this wise and beneficent queen. When Olaf came of age (1385) her diplomacy won for him the succession to the Swedish throne. Two years later he died, and her patient, far-seeing plans for the unification of Scandinavia seemed frustrated by his death. But the royal council of Denmark, seeing no male heir available who could match "Margrete" in ability to maintain order and peace, overrode Scandinavian laws against a woman ruler, and elected her Regent of the Realm (1387). Proceeding to Oslo, she was chosen Regent of Norway for life (1388), and a year later the Swedish nobles, having deposed an unsatisfactory king, made her their queen. She prevailed upon all three kingdoms to recognize her grandnephew Eric as heir to their thrones. In 1397 she summoned the three councils of state to Kalmar in Sweden; there Sweden, Norway, and Denmark were declared to be forever united, all to be under one ruler, but each to keep its own customs and laws. Eric was crowned king, but as he was only fifteen, Margaret continued to act as regent till her death (1412). No other European ruler of the age had so extensive a realm, or so successful a reign.

Her grandnephew did not inherit her wisdom. Eric allowed the Union to become in effect a Danish Empire, with a council at Copenhagen ruling the three states. In this empire Norway declined, losing the literary leadership that she had held from the tenth to the thirteenth century. In 1434 Engelbrekt Engelbreksson led a revolt of Sweden against the Danish hegemony; he gathered at Arboga (1435) a national diet of nobles, bishops, yeomen, and burghers; and this broad-based assembly became, through a continuity of 500 years, the Swedish Riksdag of today. Engelbreksson and Kark Knutsen were chosen regents. A year later the hero of the revolution was assassinated, and Knutsen ruled Sweden as regent, then intermittently as king, till his death (1470).

Meanwhile Christian I (1448–81) began the Oldenburg dynasty that governed Denmark till 1863 and Norway till 1814. Iceland came under Danish rule during Margaret's regency (1381). The high point of the island's history and literature had passed, but it continued to give chaotic Europe an unheeded lesson in competent and orderly government.

The strongest democracy in the world at this time was in Switzerland. In the history of that invincible country the heroes are the cantons. First were the German-speaking "forest cantons" of Uri, Schwyz, and Unterwalden, which in 1291 united in a Confederation for mutual defense. After the historic victory of the Swiss peasants over the Hapsburg army at Morgarten (1315) the Confederation, while formally acknowledging the sovereignty of the Holy Roman Empire, maintained a virtual independence. New cantons were added: Lucerne (1332), Zurich (1351), Glarus and Zug (1352), Bern (1353); and the name Schwyz was in 1352 extended to the whole. Encouraged to autonomy by geographical barriers, and accepting French, German, or Italian speech and ways according to the slope of its valleys and the course of its streams, each canton made its own laws, through assemblies chosen by the vote of the citizens. The extent of the franchise varied from canton to canton and from time to time, but all cantons pledged themselves to a united foreign policy and to the arbitration of their disputes by a federal diet. Though the cantons sometimes fought one another, nevertheless, the constitution of the Confederation became and remains an inspiring example of federalism—the union of self-governing regions under freely accepted common agencies and laws.

To defend its liberty the Confederation required military training of all males, and military service, at call, from all men between ten and sixty years of age. The Swiss infantry, armed with pikes and sturdy discipline, provided the most feared and expensive legions in Europe. The cantons, to eke out their income, leased their regiments to foreign powers, and for a time "made Swiss valor an article of merchandise." [9] Austrian overlords still claimed feudal rights in Switzerland, and occasionally tried to enforce them; they were repulsed at Sempach (1386) and Näfels (1388) in battles that merit some remembrance in the records of democracy. In 1446 the Treaty of Constance once more confirmed the formal allegiance of Switzerland to the Empire, and its actual liberty.

III. GERMANY CHALLENGES THE CHURCH

Germany too was a federation, but its constituent parts were ruled not by democratic assemblies but by secular or ecclesiastical princes acknowledging only a limited fealty to the head of the Holy Roman Empire. Some of these states—Bavaria, Württemburg, Thuringia, Hesse, Nassau, Meissen, Saxony, Brandenburg, Carinthia, Austria, and the Palatinate—were ruled by dukes, counts, margraves, or other secular lords; some—Magdeburg, Mainz, Halle, Bamberg, Cologne, Bremen, Strasbourg, Salzburg, Trier, Basel, Hildesheim—were politically subject in varying degrees to bishops or archbishops; but nearly a hundred cities had by 1460 won charters of practical freedom from their lay or church superiors. In each principality delegates of the three estates—nobles, clergy, commons—met occasionally in a territorial diet that exercised some restraint, through its power of the purse, on the authority of the prince. Principalities and free cities sent representatives to the Reichstag or Imperial Diet. A special Kurfürstentag, or Diet of Electors, was called to choose a king; normally it was composed of the king of Bohemia, the duke of Saxony, the margrave of Brandenburg, the count palatine, and the archbishops of Mainz, Trier, and Cologne. Their choice created only a king, who became the acknowledged head of the Holy Roman Empire when he was crowned emperor by the pope; hence his precoronation title of "King of the Romans." He made his capital primarily in Nuremberg, often elsewhere, even in Prague. His authority rested on tradition and prestige rather than on possessions or force; he owned no territory beyond his own domain as one feudal prince among many; he was dependent upon the Reichstag or Kurfürstentag for funds to administer his government or to wage war; and this dependence condemned even able men like Charles IV or Sigismund to humiliating failures in foreign affairs. The destruction of the Hohenstaufen dynasty by the powerful popes of the thirteenth century had fatally weakened the Holy Roman Empire founded (A.D. 800) by Pope Leo III and Charlemagne. In 1400 it was a loose association of Germany, Austria, Bohemia, Holland, and Switzerland.

The conflict between Empire and papacy revived when, on the same day in 1314, two rival groups of electors chose Louis of Bavaria and Frederick of Austria as rival kings. John XXII, from his papal seat at Avignon, recognized both as kings, neither as emperor, and argued that since only a pope could crown a king as emperor, he should be accepted as judge of the validity of the election; moreover, said the ambitious pontiff, the administration of the Empire should belong to the papacy between the death of an emperor and the coronation of his successor. Louis and Frederick preferred the arbitrament of war. At Mühldorf (1322) Louis defeated and captured Frederick, and thenceforth assumed full Imperial authority. John ordered him to resign all titles and powers, and to appear before the papal court to receive sentence as a rebel against the Church. Louis refusing, the Pope excommunicated him (1324), bade all Christians in the Empire to resist his rule, and laid an interdict upon any region that recognized him as king. Most of Germany ignored these edicts, for the Germans, like the English, rated the Avignon popes as servants or allies of France. In the progressive weakening of faith and the papacy men were beginning to think of themselves as patriots first and Christians afterward. Catholicism, which is supernational, declined; nationalism, which is Protestant, rose.

At this juncture Louis received aid and comfort from incongruous allies. Pope John's bull *Cum inter nonnulla* (1323) had branded as heresy the notion that Christ and the Apostles refused to own property, and he had directed the Inquisition to summon before its tribunal the "Spiritual Franciscans" who affirmed that view. Many friars retorted the charge of heresy upon the Pope; they expressed holy horror at the wealth of the Church; some of them called the aged pontiff Antichrist; and the general of the Spirituals, Michael Cesena, led a large minority of them into open alliance with Louis of Bavaria (1324). Emboldened by their support, Louis issued at Sachsenhausen a manifesto against "John XXII, who calls himself pope"; denounced him as a man of blood and a friend of injustice, who was resolved to destroy the Empire; and demanded that a general council should try the Pope for heresy.[10]

The King was further encouraged by the appearance, at his court in Nuremberg, of two professors from the University of Paris—Marsilius of Padua and John of Jandun—whose book, *Defensor Pacis*, attacked the Avignon papacy in terms that must have pleased the royal ears: "What do you find there but a swarm of simoniacs from every quarter? What but the clamor of pettifoggers, the . . . abuse of honorable men? There justice to the innocent falls to the ground, unless they can buy it for a price." [11] Echoing the Albigensian and Waldensian preachers of the thirteenth century, and anticipating Luther by two hundred years, the authors argued that Christianity should be based exclusively upon the Bible. A general council of the Church should be summoned not by the pope but by the emperor; the latter's consent should be required for the election of any pontiff; and the pope, like everybody else, should be subject to the emperor.

Delighted to hear this, Louis decided to go to Italy and have himself crowned emperor by the people of Rome. Early in 1327 he set out with a small army, some Franciscans, and the two philosophers whom he employed to compose his public pronouncements. In April the Pope issued new bulls, excommunicating John and Marsilius, and ordering Louis to leave Italy. But Louis was welcomed into Milan by the ruling Visconti, and received the iron crown as the formal sovereign of Lombardy. On January 7, 1328, he entered Rome amid the acclamations of a populace resentful of the papal residence in Avignon. He established himself in the Vatican palace, and summoned a public assembly to meet at the Capitol. To the multitude there he appeared as a candidate for investiture with the Imperial crown. It gave its tumultuous consent; and on January 17 the coveted diadem was placed upon his head by the old syndic Sciarra Colonna—that same unrelenting foe of the papacy who, almost a quarter of a century before, had fought and threatened with death Boniface VIII, and who again symbolized for a moment the challenge of the rising state to the weakened Church.

Pope John, now seventy-eight, never dreamed of accepting defeat. He proclaimed a holy crusade to depose Louis from all authority, and bade the Romans, under pain of interdict, to expel him from their city and return to the papal obedience. Louis replied in terms recalling his excommunicated predecessor Henry IV; he convoked another popular assembly, and in its presence issued an Imperial edict accusing the Pope of heresy and tyranny, deposing him from ecclesiastical office, and sentencing him to punishment by secular powers. A committee of Roman clergy and laity, under his instructions, named Peter of Corvara as a rival pope. Reversing the roles of Leo III and Charlemagne, Louis placed the papal tiara upon Peter's head, and proclaimed him Pope Nicholas V (May 12, 1328). The Christian world marveled, and divided into two camps, almost along the same lines that would divide Europe after the Reformation.

Petty local events changed the situation dramatically. Louis had appointed Marsilius of Padua spiritual administrator of the capital; Marsilius ordered the few priests who remained in Rome to celebrate Mass as usual, despite the interdict; some who refused were tortured; and an Augustinian friar was exposed in a den of lions on the Capitol.[12] Many Romans felt that this was carrying philosophy too far. The Italians had never learned to love Teutons; when some German soldiers took food from the markets without paying for it, riots ensued. To support his troops and retinue Louis needed money; he imposed a tribute of 10,000 florins ($250,000?) upon the laity, and equal sums upon the clergy and the Jews. Resentment mounted so dangerously that Louis thought it time to return to Germany. On August 4, 1328, he began a retreat through Italy. Papal troops took possession of Rome the next day; the palaces of Louis's Roman supporters were destroyed, and their goods were confiscated to the Church. The people made no resistance, but returned to their devotions and their crimes.

Louis was consoled at Pisa by receiving another recruit, the most famous philosopher of the fourteenth century. William of Ockham had fled from a papal prison in Avignon; now he offered his services to the Emperor, saying (according to an unverified tradition), *"Tu me defendas gladio, ego te defendam calamo"*—"Defend me with the sword, and I will defend you with the pen." [13] He wrote vigorously, but he could not save the situation. Louis had alienated all the ruling elements in Italy. His Ghibelline adherents had hoped to rule the peninsula in his name for their own good; they were chagrined to find him assuming all the powers and perquisites of government; moreover, he made them levy unpopular taxes for his exchequer. As his forces were ill proportioned to his pretensions, many Ghibellines, even the Visconti, abandoned him and made what peace they could with the Pope. The Antipope, left to his own resources, submitted to arrest by papal officers, was led before John XXII with a halter around his neck, threw himself at the Pope's feet and begged for pardon (1328). John forgave him, embraced him as a returned prodigal, and imprisoned him for life.

Louis returned to Germany, and sent repeated embassies to Avignon offering recantations and apologies for papal pardon and recognition. John refused, and fought on till his death (1334). Louis recovered some ground when England, beginning the Hundred Years' War, sought his alliance; Edward III recognized Louis as Emperor, and Louis hailed Edward as King of France. Seizing the opportunity provided by this alliance of two major powers against the papacy, an assembly of German princes and prelates at Rense (July 16. 1338) proclaimed that the choice of a German king by the German electors could not be annulled by any other authority; and a diet at Frankfurt-am-Main (August 3, 1338) declared the papal pronouncements against Louis null and void; the Imperial title and power, it ruled, were the gift of the Imperial electors, and needed no confirmation by a pope.[14] Germany and England ignored the protests of Pope Benedict XII, and moved a step toward the Reformation.

Reckless with success, Louis now decided to apply to the full the theories of Marsilius, and to exercise ecclesiastical as well as secular supremacy. He removed papal appointees from church benefices, and put his own candidates in their place; he appropriated the funds that papal collectors were raising for a crusade; he dissolved the marriage of Margaret of Carinthia—heiress to much of Tyrol—and wedded her to his own son, who was related to her by a degree of kinship canonically invalidating marriage. The repudiated husband, his elder brother Charles, and their father, King John of Bohemia, vowed vengeance; and Clement VI, who had become pope in 1342, saw an opportunity to unseat the aging enemy of the Papal See. Skillful diplomacy won elector after elector to the view that peace and order could be restored in the Empire only by deposing Louis and making Charles of Bohemia emperor; and Charles, as the price of papal support, pledged obedience to papal commands. In July 1346, an electoral diet at Rense unanimously declared Charles to be King of Germany. Louis, having failed to secure a hearing at Avignon for his offers of submission, prepared to fight to the death for his throne. Meanwhile, aged sixty, he hunted vigorously, fell from his horse, and was killed (1347).

Charles IV, as King and Emperor, governed well. The Germans disliked him because he made Prague the Imperial capital; but in Germany as well as in his homeland he improved administration, protected commerce and transport, reduced tolls, and maintained an honest currency; and to the whole Empire he gave a generation of comparative peace. In 1356 he acquired equivocal fame in history by issuing a series of regulations known as the Golden Bull—though they were only a few of many documents bearing the Imperial golden seal. Perhaps convinced that his long absence from Germany necessitated such an arrangement, he granted to the seven electors such powers as almost annulled the Imperial authority. The electors were to meet annually to legislate for the realm; the king or emperor was to be merely their president and executive arm. They themselves in their own states were to enjoy full judiciary power, ownership of all minerals and metals in the soil, the right to mint their own coinages, to raise revenue, and, within limits, to make war and peace. The Bull gave its legal sanction to existing facts, and tried to build upon them a co-operative federation of principalities. The electors, however, absorbed themselves in their regional affairs, and so neglected their responsibilities as an Imperial council that Germany remained only a name. This local independence of the electors made possible the protection of Luther by the Elector of Saxony, and the consequent spread of the Protestant faith.

In his old age Charles secured the Imperial succession for his son by wholesale bribery (1378). Wenceslaus IV had some virtues, but he loved alcohol and his native land; the electors resented his tastes, and deposed him (1400) in favor of Rupert III, who left no trace on history. Sigismund of Luxembourg had at the age of nineteen been chosen King of Hungary (1387); in 1411 he was elected King of the Romans, and soon assumed the title of emperor. He was a man of varied accomplishments and personal charm, handsome and vain, generous and amiable, occasionally cruel; he learned several languages and loved literature only next to women and power. His good intentions might have paved a small inferno, but his courage failed him in crisis. He tried honorably to reform the abuses and weaknesses of the German government; he passed some excellent laws, and enforced a few of them; but he was frustrated by the autonomy and inertia of the electors, and their unwillingness to share in the cost of checking the advancing Turks. In his later years he consumed his funds and energies in fighting the Hussites of Bohemia. When he died (1437) Europe mourned that one who for a time had been the voice of European progress had failed in everything but dignity.

He had commended his son-in-law, Albert of Hapsburg, to the electors of Bohemia, Hungary, and Germany. Albert II graced the three crowns, but before his abilities could bear fruit he died of dysentery in a campaign against the Turks (1440). He left no son, but the electors voted the royal and Imperial crowns to another Hapsburg, Frederick of Styria; thereafter their choice fell repeatedly to a Hapsburg prince, and the Imperial power became in effect the hereditary possession of that talented and ambitious family. Frederick III made Austria an archduchy; the Hapsburgs made Vienna their capital; the heir presumptive was regularly the archduke of Austria; and the genial quality of the Austrian and Viennese character entered like a graceful feminine theme to cross with the brusque masculinity of the north in the Teutonic soul.

IV. THE MYSTICS

The fourteenth and fifteenth centuries sowed the seeds of the Reformation: Louis of Bavaria, Wyclif in England, Huss in Bohemia, rehearsed the play for Luther, Henry VIII, Calvin, and Knox. In Scandinavia the rapidly

rising wealth of the clergy, exempt from taxation, became an irritating burden to the people and the state. Critics alleged that the Church owned half
the land of Denmark, holding a fief on Copenhagen itself.[15] Nobles looked
with ominous envy upon possessions protected by only a creed; and even
the orthodox were anticlerical. In Switzerland the proud independence
of the cantons was a prelude to Zwingli and Calvin. In 1433 Magdeburg
expelled her archbishop and clergy; Bamberg revolted against episcopal rule;
Passau besieged her bishop in his citadel.[16] In 1449 a professor in the University of Erfurt (where Luther was to study) addressed to Pope Nicholas
V_a defense of general councils as superior in authority to the popes.[17]
Echoes of the Hussite revolt in neighboring Bohemia spread through Germany; here and there Waldensian congregations furtively preserved old
heresies and semi-communistic aspirations.[18] Piety itself tended toward a
mysticism that hovered near heresy.

In Johannes Eckhart mysticism became a pantheism that by-passed the
Church and almost ignored the defined creed. This Dominican friar was so
learned that the title *Meister* became part of his name. His philosophical
writings were phrased in such scholastic Latin that had these been his sole
works he would never have come to any harm or fame. But in his monastery
at Cologne he preached in epigrammatic German the audacious pantheism
that invited the Inquisition. Following Dionysius the Areopagite and
Johannes Scotus Erigena, he struggled to express his overwhelming sense
of an omnipresent God. This all-bathing ocean of deity Eckhart conceived
as not a person or a spirit, but only "absolute bare unity . . . the abyss, without a mode and without form, of the silent and waste divinity . . . where never
was seen difference, neither Father, Son, nor Holy Ghost, where there is no
one at home, yet where the spark of the soul is more at peace than within
itself." [19] Essentially only this formless divinity exists.

> God is all things, all things are God. The Father begets me, His son,
> without cease. I say more: He begets in me Himself, and in Himself
> me. The eye with which I see God is the same eye with which God
> sees me. . . . My eye and God's eye are one eye.[20]

In each individual there is a fragment of God; through it we can communicate directly with Him, and can identify ourselves with Him. Not through
church ritual, not even through the Bible, but through this cosmic consciousness alone the soul can approach and see God. The more one renounces
individual and worldly aims, the clearer and more farseeing this divine spark
becomes, until at last God and soul are one, and "we are totally transformed
into God." [21] Heaven, purgatory, and hell are not places; they are states of
the soul: separation from God is hell, union with Him is paradise.[22] Some of
these propositions smelled of heresy to the Archbishop of Cologne. He sum-

moned Eckhart to trial (1326); Eckhart affirmed his docile orthodoxy, and proposed that his statements should be viewed as literary hyperboles. The bishop condemned him nevertheless. The friar appealed to Pope John XXII, and then escaped the faggots by a timely death (1327).

His influence was spread by two Dominican pupils who knew how to keep his pantheism within safe bounds. Heinrich Suso tortured himself for sixteen years with ascetic austerities, cut the name of Jesus into his flesh over his heart, claimed to have received into his mouth blood from the wounds of Christ, and wrote his *Little Book of Eternal Wisdom* in German because, he said, it was in German that God had revealed it to him.[28] Johannes Tauler called Eckhart his "most holy Master," and preached at Strasbourg and Basel the doctrine of mystic union with God. It was to Tauler that Luther ascribed a book, *Deutsche Theologie*, which moved him deeply with its simple creed: God, Christ, and immortality.

The Church looked with some concern upon mystics who ignored most of her dogmas, neglected her ritual, and claimed to reach God without the help of priests or sacraments. Here lay in germ the Reformation doctrines of private judgment, and every man a priest, and justification not by good works but by transcendent faith. The Church held that supernatural revelations could come from demons and maniacs as well as from God and the saints, and that some authoritative guidance was needed to keep religion from disintegrating into a chaos of individual visions and theologies. That difference of view still divides honest men.

V. THE ARTS

The Gothic style lingered in Germany long after it had given way, in Italy and France, to the classic influences of the Renaissance. Now it crowned the thriving cities of Central Europe with churches not as overpowering in grandeur as the great shrines of France, yet lifting the spirit with a quiet beauty and unpretentious dignity. Uppsala began its cathedral in 1287, Saxon Freiberg in 1283, Ulm in 1377 (with the highest Gothic tower in the world), Vienna its Stefansdom in 1304, Stralsund its Marienkirche in 1382, Danzig another Marienkirche in 1425. Aachen and Cologne added the choirs of their cathedrals, Strasbourg completed the "frozen music" of its cathedral in 1439; Xanten built a graceful Collegiate Church of St. Victor, which was destroyed in the second World War. Nuremberg gloried in four famous churches that gave piety a schooling in art and taste. The Lorenzkirche (1278–1477) owed to the fourteenth and fifteenth centuries its stately portal and resplendent rose. The Stefansdom, or Cathedral of St. Stephen (1304–1476), was a beloved landmark; its steep roof covered nave and aisles in a single span, and fell to Mars in 1945. About 1309 the Sebalduskirche rebuilt its aisles; in 1361 it raised a new choir; about 1498 it completed its western towers; from 1360 to 1510 it installed magnificent stained glass. The Frauenkirche, or Church of Our Lady (1355–61), with its richly sculptured vestibule, was almost demolished in the second World War, but is already restored; and every day at noon the four manikin electors in the famous clock of the façade bow to Charles IV in untiring acknowledgment of his famous Bull. Sculpture was still crude, but churches in Breslau and Hallgarten, and the Sebalduskirche in Nuremberg, received stone or wood Madonnas of some nobility.

The cities beautified not only their churches but their public buildings, their shops, and their homes. Now rose those gabled and half-timbered houses that give the German towns a wistful medieval charm for idealizing modern eyes. The Rathaus, or Council Hall, was the center of civic life, sometimes also the rendezvous of the greater guilds; its walls might bear frescoes, and its woodwork was usually carved with Teutonic fullness and strength. The Grosse Saal of the Rathaus at Bremen (1410–50) had a ceiling of carved beams, a winding staircase with posts and railing of carved wood, and gaudy chandeliers in the shape of ships. The Rathaus of Cologne (1360–1571), which had seated the first general convocation of the Hanseatic League; of Münster (1335), where the Treaty of Westphalia was signed; of Brunswick, a fourteenth-century gem of civic Gothic; of Frankfurt-am-Main (1405), where the electors dined a newly chosen emperor: all were destroyed in the second World War. In Marienburg the Grand Masters of the Teutonic Order built their massive Deutschordenschloss (1309–80). In Nuremberg the Rathaus confronted the Sebalduskirche; it was built (1340) to hold the fully assembled Reichstag of the Empire; half a dozen restorations have left little of its medieval form. In the market place before the Frauenkirche a Prague sculptor, Heinrich Parler, raised the Schöner Brunnen, or Beautiful Fountain (1361 f.), crowded with statues of pagan, Jewish, and Christian heroes. With its sculptures, churches, and secular architecture Nuremberg, in the three centuries between 1250 and 1550, represented the German spirit at its highest and best. The meandering streets were mostly narrow and unpaved; yet the future Pope Pius II wrote of Nuremberg:

> When one comes from Lower Franconia and perceives this glorious city, its splendor seems truly magnificent. Entering it, one's original impression is confirmed by the beauty of the streets and the fitness of the houses. The churches . . . are worthy of worship as well as of admiration. The imperial castle proudly dominates the town, and the burghers' dwellings seem to have been built for princes. In truth the kings of Scotland would gladly be housed so luxuriously as the common citizen of Nuremberg.[24]

In the German cities the industrial and minor arts—in wood, ivory, copper, bronze, iron, silver, gold—reached now the full ripening of their medieval growth. Artists and weavers composed amazing tapestries; the wood engravers prepared for Dürer and Holbein; the miniaturists illuminated fine manuscripts on the eve of Gutenberg; woodworkers carved gorgeous furniture; and the metal founders cast for the churches, in the fifteenth century, bells whose beauty of tone has never been surpassed. Music was not merely an art; it was half the leisure life of the towns. Nuremberg and other cities staged great carnivals of popular drama and song. The *Volkslied* expressed the pious or amorous sentiments of the people. The middle classes made a mass attack upon the problems of polyphony; the guilds competed in gigantic choruses; butchers, tanners, bell casters, and other mighty men contested the Meistersinger prize in tumultuous vocal tournaments. The first famous school of Meistersinger was established at Mainz in 1311; others rose at Strasbourg, Frankfurt-am-Main, Würzburg, Zurich, Augsburg, Nuremberg, and Prague. Students who passed through the four degrees of *Schüler*, *Schulfreund*, *Dichter*, and *Saenger* (scholar, friend of the school, poet, and singer) earned the title of *Meister*. The romantic and idealistic strain of the minnesingers was brought to earth as the German burghers tied their lusty realism to the wings of song.

Since the business class dominated the cities, all the arts except church architecture took a realistic turn. The climate was cold and often wet, discouraging nudity; the pride and cult of the body did not find a congenial home here as in Renaissance Italy or ancient Greece. When Konrad Witz of Constance painted *Solomon and the Queen of Sheba* he dressed them as if for a winter in the Alps. A dozen cities, however, had schools of painting in the fifteenth century—Ulm, Salzburg, Würzburg, Frankfurt, Augsburg, Munich, Darmstadt, Basel, Aachen, Nuremberg, Hamburg, Colmar, Cologne; and samples survive from all of them. We read in a chronicle of 1380: "There was in Cologne at this time a famous painter named Wilhelm, whose like could not be found in all the land. He portrayed men so cunningly that it seemed they were alive." [25] Meister Wilhelm was one of many "primitives"—Meister Bertram, Meister Francke, The Master of St. Veronica, The Master of the Heisterbacher Altar—who, chiefly under Flemish influence, created a discipline of mural painting in Germany, and suffused the traditional Gospel themes with an emotional piety traceable, it may be, to Eckhart and the other German mystics.

In Stephen Lochner, who died at Cologne in 1451, this preliminary development ends, and we reach the zenith of the early school. His *Adoration of the Magi*, now a prize of the Cologne Cathedral, can bear comparison with most paintings produced before the middle of the fifteenth century: a lovely Virgin at once modest and proud, a delightful Infant, the Wise Men of the East very German but credibly wise, the composition orthodox, the coloring bright with blue and green and gold. In *The Virgin of the Rose Trellis* and *The Madonna of the Violet*, ideal young German mothers, of a soft and pensive beauty, are portrayed with all the technical resources of a medieval art visibly moving toward modernity. Germany was on the threshold of its greatest age.

VI. GUTENBERG

What put an end to the Middle Ages? Many causes, operating through three centuries: the failure of the Crusades; the spreading acquaintance of renascent Europe with Islam; the disillusioning capture of Constantinople; the resurrection of classic pagan culture; the expansion of commerce through the voyages of Henry the Navigator's fleet, and Columbus, and Vasco da Gama; the rise of the business class, which financed the centralization of monarchical government; the development of national states challenging the supernational authority of the popes; the successful revolt of Luther against the papacy; printing.

Before Gutenberg nearly all education had been in the hands of the Church. Books were costly; copying was laborious and sometimes careless. Few authors could reach a wide audience until they were dead; they had to live by pedagogy, or by entering a monastic order, or by pensions from the rich or benefices from the Church. They received little or no payment from those who published their works; and even if one publisher paid them they had no copyright protection, except occasionally by a papal grant. Libraries were numerous but small; monasteries, cathedrals, colleges, and some cities had modest collections, seldom more than 300 volumes; the books were usually kept inside the walls, and some were chained to lecterns or desks. Charles V of France had a library renowned for its size—910 volumes; Humphrey, Duke of Gloucester, had 600; the library of Christ Church Priory at Canterbury was probably as large as any outside of Islam, having some 2,000 volumes in 1300. The best publicized library in England was that of Richard de Bury St. Edmunds, who wrote affectionately of his books in *The Philobiblon* (1345), and made them complain of their maltreatment by "that two-legged beast called woman," who insisted on exchanging them for fine linen or silk.[26]

As schools multiplied and literacy rose, the demand for books increased. The business classes found literacy useful in the operations of industry and trade; women of the middle and upper classes escaped, through reading, into a world of compensatory romance; by 1300 the time had passed when only the clergy could read. It was this rising demand, even more than the increased supply of paper and the development of an oily ink,[27] that led to Gutenberg. Moslems had brought paper manufacture to Spain in the tenth century, to Sicily in the twelfth; it passed into Italy in the thirteenth, into France in the fourteenth; the paper industry was a hundred years old in Europe when printing came. In the fourteenth century, when linen clothing became customary in Europe, castoff linens provided cheap rags for paper; the cost of paper declined, and its readier availability co-operated with the extension of literacy to offer a material and market for printed books.

Printing itself, as imprinting, was older than Christianity. The Babylonians had printed letters or symbols upon bricks, the Romans and many others upon coins, potters upon their wares, weavers upon cloths, bookbinders upon book covers; any ancient or medieval dignitary used printing when he stamped documents with his seal. Similar methods had been employed in the production of maps and playing cards. Block printing—by blocks of wood or metal engraved with words, symbols, or images—goes back in China and Japan to the eighth century, probably beyond; the Chinese in this way printed paper money in or before the tenth century. Block printing appeared in Tabriz in 1294, in Egypt toward 1300; but the Moslems preferred calligraphy to printing, and did not serve in this case, as in so many others, to carry cultural developments from the East to the West.

Typography—printing with separate and movable type for each character or letter—was used in China as early as 1041. In 1314 Wang Chên employed nearly 60,000 movable wooden type characters to print a book on agriculture;[28] he had tried metal type first, but had found that it did not take or hold ink as readily as wood. Movable type, however, offered little advantage or convenience to a language that had no alphabet, but had 40,000 separate characters; consequently block printing remained customary in China till the nineteenth century. In 1403 a Korean emperor printed a large number of volumes from movable metal type; characters were engraved in hard wood, molds of porcelain paste were made from these models, and in these molds metal type were cast.

In Europe printing from movable type may have developed first in Holland; according to Dutch traditions not traceable beyond 1569, Laurens Coster of Haarlem printed a religious manual from movable metal type in 1430; but the evidence is inconclusive.[29] Nothing further is heard of movable type in Holland till 1473, when Germans from Cologne set up a press in Utrecht. But these men had learned the art in Mainz.

Johann Gutenberg was born there of a prosperous family about 1400. His father's name was Gensfleisch—Gooseflesh; Johann preferred his mother's maiden name. He lived most of his first forty years in Strasbourg, and appears to have made experiments there in cutting and casting metal type. Toward 1448 he became a citizen of Mainz. On August 22, 1450, he entered into a contract with Johann Fust, a rich goldsmith, by which he mortgaged his printing press to Fust for a loan of 800 guilders, later raised to 1,600. A letter of indulgence issued by Nicholas V in 1451 was probably printed by Gutenberg; several copies exist, bearing the oldest printed date, 1454.[30] In 1455 Fust sued Gutenberg for repayment; unable to comply, Gutenberg surrendered his press. Fust carried on the establishment with Peter Schöffer, who had been employed by Gutenberg as typesetter. Some believe that it was Schöffer who had by this time developed the new tools and technique of printing: a hard "punch" of engraved steel for each letter, number, and punctuation mark, a metal matrix to receive the punches, and a metal mold to hold the matrix and letters in line.

In 1456 Gutenberg, with borrowed funds, set up another press. From this he issued, in that year or the next, what has been generally considered his first type-printed book, the famous and beautiful "Gutenberg Bible" *—a majestic folio of 1,282 large double-columned pages. In 1462 Mainz was sacked by the troops of Adolf of Nassau; the printers fled, scattering the new art through Germany. By 1463 there were printers in Strasbourg, Cologne, Basel, Augsburg, Nuremberg, and Ulm. Gutenberg, one of the fugitives, settled in Eltville, where he resumed his printing. He struggled painfully through one financial crisis after another, until Adolf gave him (1465) a benefice yielding a protective income. Some three years later he died.

Doubtless his use of movable type would have been developed by others had he never been born; it was an obvious demand of the times; this is true of most inventions. A letter written in 1470 by Guillaume Fichet of Paris suggests how enthusiastically the invention was welcomed: "There has been discovered in Germany a wonderful new method for the production of books, and those who have mastered the art are taking it from Mainz out into the world. . . . The light of this discovery will spread from Germany to all parts of the earth." [31] But not all welcomed it. Copyists protested that printing would destroy their means of livelihood; aristocrats opposed it as a mechanical vulgarization, and feared that it would lower the value of their manuscript libraries; statesmen and clergy distrusted it as a possible vehicle of subversive ideas. It made its triumphant way nevertheless. In 1464 two Germans set up a press in Rome; in or before 1469 two Germans opened a printing shop in Venice; in 1470 three Germans brought the art to Paris; in 1471 it reached Holland, in 1472 Switzerland, in 1473 Hungary, in 1474 Spain, in 1476 England, in 1482 Denmark, in 1483 Sweden, in 1490 Constantinople. Nuremberg with the Koberger family, Paris with the Étiennes, Lyons with Dolet, Venice with Aldus Manutius, Basel with Amerbach and Froben, Zurich with Froschauer, Leiden with the Elzevirs, became humming hives of printing and publishing. Soon half the European population was reading as never before, and a passion for books became one of the effervescent ingredients of the Reformation age. "At this very moment," writes a Basel scholar to a friend, "a whole wagon load of classics, of the best Aldine editions, has arrived from Venice. Do you want any? If you do, tell me at once, and send the money, for no sooner is such a freight landed than thirty buyers rise up for each volume, merely asking the price, and tearing one another's eyes out to get hold of them." [32] The typographical revolution was on.

To describe all its effects would be to chronicle half the history of the

---

* Also known as the "Mazarin Bible," because it was discovered about 1760 in the library left by that cardinal. Forty-six copies survive. The Morgan Library of New York in 1953 paid $75,000 to a Swiss monastery for a "Constance Missal" which it believes was printed by Gutenberg before the Bible, probably in 1452.

modern mind. Erasmus, in the ecstasy of his sales, called printing the greatest of all discoveries, but perhaps he underestimated speech, fire, the wheel, agriculture, writing, law, even the lowly common noun. Printing replaced esoteric manuscripts with inexpensive texts rapidly multiplied, in copies more exact and legible than before, and so uniform that scholars in diverse countries could work with one another by references to specific pages of specific editions. Quality was often sacrificed to quantity, but the earliest printed books were in many cases models of art in typography and binding. Printing published—i.e., made available to the public—cheap manuals of instruction in religion, literature, history, and science; it became the greatest and cheapest of all universities, open to all. It did not produce the Renaissance, but it paved the way for the Enlightenment, for the American and French revolutions, for democracy. It made the Bible a common possession, and prepared the people for Luther's appeal from the popes to the Gospels; later it would permit the rationalist's appeal from the Gospels to reason. It ended the clerical monopoly of learning, the priestly control of education. It encouraged the vernacular literatures, for the large audience it required could not be reached through Latin. It facilitated the international communication and co-operation of scientists. It affected the quality and character of literature by subjecting authors to the purse and taste of the middle classes rather than to aristocratic or ecclesiastical patrons. And, after speech, it provided a readier instrument for the dissemination of nonsense than the world has ever known until our time.

CHAPTER VIII

The Western Slavs

1300-1517

I. BOHEMIA

HERETOFORE the Slavs had been human flotsam, surging westward at times to the Elbe, southward to the Mediterranean, eastward to the Urals, north even to the Arctic Sea; then, in the thirteenth century, repulsed in the west by the Livonian and Teutonic knights, and subjected to Mongol and Tatar domination in the east. In the fourteenth century Bohemia led the Holy Roman Empire and the pre-Lutheran Reformation; and Poland, united with a vast Lithuania, became a major power, with a highly cultured upper class. In the fifteenth century Russia freed herself from the Tatars, and unified her far-flung principalities into a massive state. Like a tidal wave, the Slavs entered history.

In 1306 the death of Wenceslaus III ended the ancient Przemyslid line in Bohemia. After an interlude of minor kings the baronial and ecclesiastical electors brought in John of Luxembourg to found a new dynasty (1310). His gallant adventures made Bohemia for a generation an unwilling citadel of chivalry. He could hardly live without tournaments, and when these proved too innocuous he sallied forth to war in almost every realm of Europe. It became a *bon mot* of the times that "nothing can be done without the help of God and the King of Bohemia."[1] Brescia, besieged by Verona, begged his aid; he promised to come; at the news thereof the Veronese raised the siege. Brescia, Bergamo, Cremona, Parma, Modena, even Milan voluntarily acknowledged him as their feudal sovereign in return for his protection; what Frederick I Barbarossa and Frederick II Wonder of the World had been unable to secure by arms, this King obtained almost by the magic of his name. His dashing wars added terrain to Bohemia but forfeited the affection of the people, who could not forgive him for being so often absent from their country that he neglected its administration and never learned its speech. In 1336, on a crusade in Lithuania, he contracted a disease that left him blind. Nevertheless, when he learned that Edward III of England had landed in Normandy and was moving toward Paris, John and his son Charles, with 500 Bohemian knights, rode across Europe to succor the king of France. Father and son fought in the van at Crécy. When the French retreated, the blind King bade two knights bind their horses on either side to his and lead him against the victorious English, saying, "So will it God, it shall not be said that a king of Bohemia flies from the battlefield." Fifty of his knights were killed around him; he was mortally wounded, and was taken, dying, to the tent of the English King. Edward sent the corpse to Charles with a courtly message: "This day has fallen the crown of chivalry." [2]

Charles IV was a less heroic but much wiser king. He preferred negotiation to war, and was not too cowardly to compromise; yet he extended the boundaries of his kingdom. In the thirty-two years of his reign he kept the Slavs and the Germans in unwonted peace. He reorganized the government, reformed the judiciary, and made Prague one of the handsomest cities in Europe. He built there a royal residence on the style of the Louvre, and the famous castle of Karlstein (Charles's Stone) as a repository for the archives of the state and the jewels of the crown—which were treasured not for vanity and display but as a reserve fund conveniently mobile and immune to debasements of the currency. He brought in Matthew of Arras to design St. Vitus' Cathedral, and Tommaso da Modena to paint frescoes in churches and palaces. He protected the peasantry from oppression, and promoted commerce and industry. He founded the University of Prague (1347), transmitted to his countrymen the cultural interest that he had acquired in France and Italy, and provided the intellectual stimulus that exploded in the Hussite revolt. His court became the center of the Bohemian humanists, led by Bishop John of Stresa, Petrarch's friend. The Italian poet admired Charles beyond any other monarch of the time, visited him in Prague, and begged him to conquer Italy; but Charles had better sense. His reign, despite his Golden Bull, was Bohemia's Golden Age. He survives smiling, in a splendid limestone bust, in the cathedral of Prague.

Wenceslaus IV was a youth of eighteen when his father died (1378). His good nature, his affection for his people, his lenience in taxing them, his skill in administration, won him great favor with all but the nobles, who thought their privileges imperiled by his popularity. His occasional hot temper, and his addiction to drink, gave them a leverage for displacing him. They surprised him at his country seat, threw him into prison (1394), and restored him only on his promise to do nothing of moment without the consent of a council of nobles and bishops. New disputes arose; Sigismund of Hungary was called in; he arrested Wenceslaus, his brother, and took him prisoner to Vienna (1402). Wenceslaus escaped a few years later, made his way back to Bohemia, was received with joy by the people, and regained his throne and powers. The rest of his story mingles with the tragedy of Huss.

II. JOHN HUSS: 1369–1415

Wenceslaus was loved and hated for winking at heresy and scowling at the Germans. A rapid infiltration of Bohemia by German miners, craftsmen, merchants, and students had generated a racial hostility between Teutons and Czechs; Huss would have received less support from people and king had he not symbolized a native resentment of German prominence. Wenceslaus did not forget that the archbishops of Germany had led the movement to depose him from the Imperial throne. His sister Anne had married Richard II of England, and had seen—probably had sympathized with—the attempt of Wyclif to divorce England from the Roman Church. In 1388 Adelbert Ranconis left a sum to enable Bohemian students to go to Paris or Oxford. Some of these in England secured or transcribed works by Wyclif, and took them to Bohemia. Milíč of Kroměříže and Conrad Waldhouser roused Prague with their denunciations of immorality in laity and clergy; Matthias of Janov and Thomas of Stitny continued this preaching; the Emperor, and even Archbishop Ernst, approved; and in 1391 a special church, called the Bethlehem Chapel, was founded in Prague to lead the movement of reform. In 1402 John Huss was appointed to the pulpit of this chapel.

He had begun life in the village of Husinetz, and was known as John of Husinetz, which he later shortened to Hus. Toward 1390 he came as a poor student to Prague, where he earned his way by serving in the churches. He aimed to enter the priesthood; nevertheless, after the custom of the age, he joined in what Paris would later term the gay "Bohemian" ways of university youth. In 1396 he received his degree of master of arts, and began to teach at the university; in 1401 he was chosen dean of the faculty of arts—i.e., of the "humanities." In that year he was ordained priest, and reformed his life to an almost monastic austerity. As head of the Bethlehem Chapel he became the most famous preacher in Prague. Many figures high in the court were among his listeners, and Queen Sophia made him her chaplain. He preached in Czech, and taught his congregation to take an active part in the service by singing hymns.

His accusers later affirmed that in the very first year of his ministry he had echoed Wyclif's doubts as to the disappearance of bread and wine from the consecrated elements in the Eucharist. Unquestionably he had read some of Wyclif's works; he had made copies of them which still exist with his annotations; and at his trial he confessed to having said: "Wyclif, I trust, will be saved; but could I think he would be damned, I would my soul were with his." [3] In 1403 the opinions of Wyclif had won such vogue in the University of Prague that the chapter—the administrative clergy—of the cathedral submitted to the university masters forty-five excerpts from the writings of

Wyclif, and asked should these doctrines be barred from the university. Several masters, including Huss, answered No; but the majority ruled that thereafter no member of the university staff should, either publicly or privately, defend or adhere to any of the forty-five articles.

Huss must have ignored this prohibition, for in 1408 the clergy of Prague petitioned Archbishop Zbynek to reprove him. The Archbishop proceeded cautiously, being then in conflict with the King. But when Huss continued to express sympathy for Wyclif's views Zbynek excommunicated him and several associates (1409); and when they persisted in exercising their priestly functions he placed all Prague under an interdict. He ordered all writings of Wyclif that could be found in Bohemia to be surrendered to him; 200 manuscripts were brought to him; he burned them in the courtyard of his palace. Huss appealed to the newly elected Pope John XXIII. John summoned him to appear before the papal court. He refused to go.

In 1411 the Pope, desiring funds for a crusade against Ladislas, King of Naples, announced a new offering of indulgences. When this was proclaimed in Prague, and the papal agents seemed to the reformers to be selling forgiveness for coin, Huss and his chief supporter, Jerome of Prague, publicly preached against indulgences, questioned the existence of purgatory, and protested against the Church's collecting money to spill Christian blood. Descending to vituperation, Huss called the Pope a money-grubber, even Antichrist.[4] A large section of the public shared Huss's views, and subjected the papal agents to such ridicule and abuse that the King forbade any further preaching or action against the offering of indulgences. Three youths who violated this edict were hailed before the city council; Huss pleaded for them, and admitted that his preaching had aroused them; they were condemned and beheaded. The Pope now launched his own excommunication against Huss; and when Huss ignored it John laid an interdict upon any city where he should stay (1411). On the advice of the King, Huss left Prague, and remained in rural seclusion for two years.

In those years he wrote his major works, some in Latin, some in Czech, nearly all inspired by Wyclif, some perhaps echoing the heresies and anticlericalism that a remnant of the Waldensians had brought with them into Bohemia in the twelfth and thirteenth centuries. He rejected image worship, auricular confession, and the multiplication of ornate religious rites. He gave his movement a popular and nationalistic character by denouncing the Germans and defending the Slavs. In a tract on *Traffic in Holy Things* he attacked the simony of the clergy; in *De sex erroribus* he condemned the taking of fees by priests for baptism, confirmation, Masses, marriages, or burials; he charged some Prague clerics with selling consecrated oil; and he adopted Wyclif's view that a priest guilty of simony could not validly administer a sacrament.[5] His treatise *De ecclesia* became his *apologia* and his ruin; from its pages were drawn the heresies for which he was burned. He followed Wyclif into predestinarianism, and agreed with Wyclif, Marsilius, and Ockham that the Church should have no worldly goods. Like Calvin, he defined the Church neither as the clergy nor as the whole body of Christians, but as the totality, in heaven or on earth, of the saved.[6] Christ, not the pope, is the head of the Church; the Bible, not the pope, should be the Christian's guide. The pope is not infallible, even in faith or morals; the pope himself may be a hardened sinner or heretic. Accepting a legend widely credited at the time (even by Gerson), Huss made much of a supposititious Pope John VIII who (said the legend) had revealed her sex by giving unpremeditated birth to a child on the streets of Rome.[7] A pope, Huss concluded, is to be obeyed only when his commands conform to the law of Christ. "To rebel against an erring pope is to obey Christ." [8]

When a general council met at Constance in 1414 to depose three rival popes and enact a program of ecclesiastical reform, a chance seemed open to reconcile the Hussites with the Church. Emperor Sigismund, heir apparent to the childless Wenceslaus IV, was anxious to restore religious unity and peace in Bohemia. He suggested that Huss should go to Constance and attempt a reconciliation. For this hazardous journey he offered Huss a safe-conduct to Constance, a public hearing before the Council, and a free and safe return to Bohemia in case Huss should reject the judgment of the assembly. Despite the anxious warnings of his associates, Huss set out for Constance (October 1414), escorted by three Czech nobles and several friends. About the same time Stephen of Palecz and other Bohemian opponents of Huss went to Constance to indict him before the Council.

Arrived, he was at first treated courteously, and lived in freedom. But when Palecz laid before the Council a list of Huss's heresies, they summoned and questioned him. Convinced by his replies that he was a major heretic, they ordered him imprisoned. He fell ill, and was for a time near death; Pope John XXIII sent papal physicians to treat him. Sigismund complained that the action of the Council violated the safe-conduct that he had given Huss; it answered that it was not bound by his action; that his authority did not extend to spiritual concerns; that the Church had the right to overrule the state in trying an enemy of the Church. In April Huss was removed to the fortress of Gottlieben on the Rhine; there he was placed in fetters, and was so poorly fed that he again fell gravely ill. Meanwhile his fellow heretic, Jerome of Prague, had rashly entered Constance, and had nailed to the city gates, to the doors of churches, and upon the houses of cardinals, a request that the Emperor and the Council should give him a safe-conduct and a public hearing. At the urging of Huss's friends he left the city and began a return to Bohemia; but on the way he stopped to preach against the Council's treatment of Huss. He was arrested, brought back to Constance, and jailed.

On July 5, after seven months of imprisonment, Huss was led in chains before the Council, and again on the seventh and the eighth. Asked his view of the forty-five articles already condemned in Wyclif's works, he rejected most of them, approved of some. Confronted with extracts from his book, *On the church*, he expressed his willingness to recant such as could be refuted from Scripture (precisely the position taken by Luther at Worms). The Council argued that Scripture must be interpreted not by the free judgment of individuals but by the heads of the Church, and it demanded that Huss should retract all the quoted articles without reservation. Both his friends and his accusers pleaded with him to yield. He refused. He lost the good will of the vacillating Emperor by declaring that a secular as well as a spiritual authority ceases to be a lawful ruler the moment he falls into mortal sin.[9] Sigismund now informed Huss that if the Council condemned him his safe-conduct would be automatically canceled.

After three days of questioning, and vain efforts by the Emperor and cardinals to persuade him to recant, Huss was returned to his prison cell. The Council allowed him and itself four weeks to weigh the matter. It was even more complex to the Council than to Huss. How could a heretic be allowed to live without thereby branding as inhuman crimes all past executions for heresy? This Council had deposed popes; was it to be defied by a simple Bohemian priest? Was not the Church the spiritual, as the state was the physical, arm of society, responsible for a moral order that needed some indisputable authority as its base? To assail that authority seemed to the Council as clearly treason as to take up arms against the king. Opinion would have to develop through another century before Luther would be able to make a similar defiance and live.

Further efforts were made to secure some semblance of retraction from Huss. The Emperor sent special emissaries to plead with him. He gave always the same reply: he would abandon any of his views that could be disproved from Scripture. On July 6, 1415, in the cathedral of Constance, the Council condemned both Wyclif and Huss, ordered Huss's writings to be burned, and delivered him to the secular arm. He was at once unfrocked, and was led out of the city to a place where a pyre of faggots had been prepared. A last appeal was made to him to save himself with a word of retraction; he again refused. The fire consumed him as he chanted hymns.

Jerome, in a forgivable moment of terror, recanted before the Council the teachings of his friend (September 10, 1415). Remanded to prison, he gradually regained his courage. He asked for a hearing, and after a long delay he was led before the assembly (May 23, 1416); but instead of being allowed to state his case he was required first to answer the several charges laid against him. He protested with a passionate eloquence that moved the skeptical but politic Italian humanist, Poggio Bracciolini, who had come to Constance as secretary to Pope John XXIII.

> What iniquity is this, that I, who have been kept in a foul prison for 340 days, without means of preparing my defense, while my adversaries have always had your ears, am now refused an hour to defend myself? Your minds are prejudiced against me as a heretic; you judged me to be wicked before you had any means of knowing what manner of man I was. And yet you are men, not gods; mortals, not eternal; you are liable to error. The more you claim to be held as lights of the world, the more careful you ought to be to prove your justice to all men. I, whose cause you judge, am of no consequence, nor do I speak for myself, for death comes to all; but I would not have so many wise men do an unjust act, which will do more harm by the precedent it gives than by the punishment it inflicts.[10]

The charges were read to him one by one, and he answered each without retraction. When at last he was allowed to speak freely he almost won over the Council by his fervor and sincerity. He reviewed some of the historic cases in which men had been killed for their beliefs; he recalled how Stephen the Apostle had been condemned to death by priests, and held that there could hardly be a greater sin than that priests should wrongly slay a priest. The Council hoped that he would save himself by asking forgiveness; instead he repudiated his earlier recantation, reaffirmed his faith in the doctrines of Wyclif and Huss, and branded the burning of Huss as a crime certain to be punished by God. The Council gave him four days to reconsider. Unrepentant, he was condemned (May 30), and was led out at once to the same spot where Huss had died. When the executioner went behind him to light the pyre, Jerome bade him, "Come in front, and light it before my face; if I had feared death I should never have come here." He sang a hymn till he choked with the smoke.

III. THE BOHEMIAN REVOLUTION: 1415–36

The news of Huss's death, relayed by couriers to Bohemia, aroused a national revolt. An assembly of Bohemian and Moravian nobles sent to the Council of Constance (September 2, 1415) a document signed by 500 leading Czechs; it upheld Huss as a good and upright Catholic, denounced his execution as an insult to his country, and proclaimed that the signatories would fight to the last drop of their blood to defend the doctrines of Christ against man-made decrees. A further declaration pledged the members to obey thereafter only such papal commands as agreed with Scripture; the judges of such agreement were to be the faculty of the University of Prague.

The university itself hailed Huss as a martyr, and praised the imprisoned Jerome. The Council summoned the rebellious nobles to appear before it and answer charges of heresy; none came. It ordered the university closed; the majority of masters and students went on with their work.

About 1412 one of Huss's followers, Jakoubek of Strzibo, had proposed that the early Christian custom of administering the Eucharist in both forms —*sub utraque specie*—wine as well as bread—should be restored throughout Christendom. When the idea captivated the rank and file of his supporters, Huss gave it his approval. The Council forbade it, and defended the abandonment of the primitive custom on the ground that it risked the spilling of Christ's blood. After Huss's death the University of Prague and the nobles, led by Queen Sophia, adopted lay communion in both kinds as a command of Christ, and the chalice became the symbol of the "Utraquist" revolt. The followers of Huss formulated in 1420 the "Four Articles of Prague" as their basic demands: that the Eucharist should be given in wine as well as bread; that ecclesiastical simony should be promptly punished; that the Word of God should be preached without hindrance as the sole standard of religious truth and practice; and that an end should be put to the ownership of extensive material possessions by priests or monks. A radical minority among the rebels rejected the veneration of relics, capital punishment, purgatory, and Masses for the dead. All the elements of the Lutheran Reformation were present in this Hussite revolt.

King Wenceslaus, who had sympathized with the movement, possibly because it promised to transfer church property to the state, now began to fear it as threatening civil as well as ecclesiastical authority. In the "New Town" that he had added to Prague he appointed only anti-Hussites to the council, and these men issued punitive regulations designed to suppress the heresy. On July 30, 1419, a Hussite crowd paraded into New Town, forced its way into the council chamber, and threw the councilors out of the windows into the street, where another crowd finished them off. A popular assembly was organized, which elected Hussite councilors. Wenceslaus confirmed the new council, and then died of a heart attack (1419).

The Bohemian nobles offered to accept Sigismund as their king if he would recognize the Four Articles of Prague. He countered by demanding from all Czechs full obedience to the Church, and burned at the stake a Bohemian who refused to renounce the "lay chalice." The new pope, Martin V, announced a crusade against the Bohemian heretics, and Sigismund advanced with a large force against Prague (1420). Almost overnight the Hussites organized an army; nearly every town in Bohemia and Moravia sent impassioned recruits; Jan Zižka, a sixty-year-old knight with one eye, trained them, and led them to incredible victories. Twice they defeated Sigismund's troops. Sigismund raised another army, but when a false report came that

Žižka's men were approaching, this new host fled in disorder without ever sighting an enemy. Inflated with success, Žižka's Puritans now adopted from their opponents the idea that religious dissent should be suppressed by force; they passed up and down Bohemia, Moravia, and Silesia like a devastating storm, pillaging monasteries, massacring monks, and compelling the population to accept the Four Articles of Prague. The Germans in Bohemia, who wished to remain Catholic, became the favorite victims of Hussite arms. Meanwhile, and for seventeen years (1419–36), Bohemia survived without a king.

Diverse and conflicting elements had united to make the Bohemian revolution. The native Bohemians resented the wealth and arrogance of the German settlers, and hoped to drive them from the country. The nobles coveted ecclesiastical properties, and thought them worth an excommunication. The proletariat aspired to free itself from middle-class masters. The middle classes hoped to raise their modest power, as against the nobility, in the Diet that ruled Prague and gave some government to Bohemia. The serfs, especially on church estates, dreamed of dividing those blessed acres, and, at worst, of freeing themselves from villein bonds. Some of the lower clergy, fleeced by the hierarchy, gave the rebellion their tacit support, and provided for it the religious services interdicted by the Church.

When the arms of the Hussites had won them most of Bohemia, the contradictions in their aims broke them into fratricidal factions. After the nobles had seized most of the property owned by orthodox ecclesiastical groups,[11] they felt that the revolution should subside and invite the sanctifying effects of time. While the serfs who had tilled these lands for the Church clamored for their division among themselves as freemen, the noble appropriators demanded that the peasants should serve the new masters on the same servile basis as before. Žižka supported the peasants, and for a time besieged the now conservative "Calixtine" or chalice Hussites in Prague. Tiring of the struggle, he accepted a truce, withdrew to eastern Bohemia, and founded a "Horeb Brotherhood" dedicated to the Four Articles and to killing Germans. When he died (1424) he bequeathed his skin to be made into a martial drum.[12]

In the town of Tabor another party of Hussites formed, who held that real Christianity required a communistic organization of life. Long before Huss there had been in Bohemia little groups of Waldensians, Beghards, and other irrepressible heretics mingling religious with communistic ideals. They had maintained a salutary quiet until Žižka's troops had overthrown the power of the Church in most of Bohemia; now they came into the open, and captured doctrinal leadership at Tabor. Many of them rejected the Real Presence, purgatory, prayers for the dead, and all sacraments except baptism and communion, and discouraged the veneration of relics, images, and saints, they proposed to restore the simple ritual of the Apostolic Church, and repudiated all ecclesiastical rites and robes that they could not find in early Christianity. They objected to altars, organs, and the splendor of church decoration, and they destroyed such ornaments wherever they could. Like later Protestants, they reduced divine worship to communion, prayer, Scriptural readings, a sermon, and the singing of hymns; and these services were conducted by clergymen indistinguishable from the laity in dress. Most of the Taborites deduced communism from millennarianism: Christ would soon come to establish His Kingdom on earth; in that Kingdom there would be no property, no Church or state, no class distinctions, no human laws, no taxes, no marriage; surely it would please Christ, when he came, to find such a heavenly utopia already established by His worshipers. At Tabor and some other towns these principles were put into practice; there, said a contemporary professor in the University of Prague, "all is held in common, no one owns anything for himself alone; so to own is considered a deadly sin. They hold that all should be equal brothers and sisters." [13]

A Bohemian peasant turned philosopher, Peter Chelčicky, went further, and wrote in vigorous Czech a series of Tolstoian tracts advocating a pacifistic anarchism. He attacked the powerful and the rich, denounced war and capital punishment as murder, and demanded a society without lords or serfs, or laws of any kind. He bade his followers take Christianity literally as they found it in the New Testament: to baptize only adults, to turn their backs upon the world and its ways, upon oaths and learning and class distinctions, upon commerce and city life; and to live in voluntary poverty, preferably tilling the land, and completely ignoring "civilization" and the state. [14] The Taborites found this pacifism unsuited to their temperament. They divided into moderate and advanced radicals (these preached nudism and a communism of women), and the two factions passed from argument to war. In the course of a few years unequal abilities developed inequalities of power and privilege, finally of goods; and the apostles of peace and freedom were replaced by ruthless lawgivers wielding despotic force. [15]

Christendom heard with horror of this supposedly communistic Christianity. The baronial and burgher Hussites in Bohemia began to yearn for the Church of Rome as the only organization strong enough to stop the imminent dissolution of the existing social order. They rejoiced when the Council of Basel invited reconciliation. A delegation from the Council, without papal authorization, came to Bohemia, and signed a series of "Compacts" so worded that complaisant Hussites and Catholics could interpret them as accepting and rejecting the Four Articles of Prague (1433). As the Taborites refused to recognize these Compacts, the conservative Hussites joined with the surviving orthodox groups in Bohemia, attacked and defeated the divided Taborites, and put an end to the communistic experiment (1434). The Bohemian Diet made its peace with Sigismund, and accepted him as king (1436).

But Sigismund, accustomed to crowning his victories with futility, died in the following year. During the chaos that ensued, the orthodox party secured the upper hand in Prague. An able provincial leader, George of Poděbrad, organized .n army of Hussites, captured Prague, restored the Utraquist Jan Rokycana to he archiepiscopal see, and established himself as governor of Bohemia (1451). When Pope Nicholas V refused to recognize Rokycana the Utraquists meditated a transfer of their allegiance to the Greek Orthodox Church, but the fall of Constantinople to the Turks ended the negotiations. In 1458, seeing that Poděbrad's excellent administration had restored order and prosperity, the Diet chose him king.

He turned his energies now to reconstituting religious peace. With the approval of the Diet he sent to Pius II (1462) an embassy requesting papal ratification of the Compacts of Prague. The Pope refused, and forbade the laity anywhere to receive the Eucharist in both kinds. On the advice of Gregor Heimburg, a German jurist, Poděbrad in 1464 invited the monarchs of Europe to form a permanent federation of European states, with its own legislature, executive, and army, and a judiciary empowered to settle current and future international disputes.[16] The kings did not reply; the reinvigorated papacy was too strong to be defied by a League of Nations. Pope Paul II declared Poděbrad a heretic, freed his subjects from their oaths of obedience, and called upon Christian powers to depose him (1466). Matthias Corvinus of Hungary undertook the task, invaded Bohemia, and was crowned king by a group of Catholic nobles (1469). Poděbrad offered the throne to Ladislas, son of King Casimir IV of Poland. Then, worn out with war and dropsy, he died, aged fifty-one (1471). Bohemia, now Czechoslovakia, honors him as, next to Charles IV, her greatest king.

The Diet accepted Ladislas II, and Matthias retired to Hungary. The nobles took advantage of the youthful weakness of the King to consolidate their economic and political power, to reduce the representation of towns and burghers in the Diet, and to debase into serfdom the peasantry that had just dreamed of utopia. Thousands of Bohemians, during this period of revolution and reaction, fled to other lands.* In 1485 the Catholic and Utraquist parties signed the Treaty of Kutna Hora, pledging themselves to peace for thirty years.

In eastern Bohemia and Moravia the followers of Chelčicky formed (1457) a new Christian sect, the Jednota Bratrska, or Church of the Brotherhood, dedi-

---

* The French, confusing the Bohemian exiles with Gypsies who in the fifteenth century were entering Western Europe, supposedly from Bohemia, made *Bohème* their word for Gypsy. The name Gypsy is a corruption of *Egyptian*, and reflects the claim of the tribe to have come from "Little Egypt." Burton traces them to India.[17] In Byzantine lands they took the name *Rom*—i.e., (eastern) Roman; in the Balkans and Central Europe they were called by variants of *Atzigan* (*Czigany, Zigeuner, Zingari*), a word of uncertain origin. In European records they first appear in the early fourteenth century as wandering groups of craftsmen, musicians, dancers, fortunetellers, and—in general belief—thieves. By 1414 they reached Germany, by 1422 Italy, by 1427 France, by 1500 England. Usually they accepted baptism, but they took religion and the Commandments lightly, and soon ran afoul of the Inquisition. They were expelled from Spain (1499), the Holy Roman Empire (1500, 1548), and France (1561). Aside from the gay varicolored dress and ornaments of their more prosperous women, their contribution to civilization lay in dancing and music—whose alternations of sadness and exuberance have inspired some major composers.

cated to a simple agricultural life on the principles of the New Testament. In 1467 it renounced the authority of the Catholic Church, consecrated its own priests, rejected purgatory and the worship of saints, anticipated Luther's doctrine of justification by faith, and became the first modern church to practice Christianity. By 1500 it claimed 100,000 members. These "Moravian Brethren" were almost exterminated in the fury of the Thirty Years' War; they survived through the leadership of John Comenius; they still exist, in scattered congregations in Europe, Africa, and America, astonishing a violent and skeptical world with their religious toleration, their unassuming piety, and their peaceful fidelity to the principles they profess.

IV. POLAND: 1300–1505

The maintenance of peace is difficult even in regions deriving unity and protection from geographical barriers; consider how much more difficult it is in states exposed on one or more borders to neighbors always avid, sometimes tempting, sometimes powerful. Poland in the fourteenth century was half stifled by Teutonic Knights, Lithuanians, Hungarians, Moravians, Bohemians, and Germans pressing upon her frontiers. When Ladislas the Short became grand prince of Lesser—southern—Poland (1306), he faced a multitude of enemies. The Germans in Greater—western—Poland rejected his authority; the Knights seized Danzig and Pomerania; the margrave of Brandenburg plotted to destroy him; and Wenceslaus III of Bohemia claimed the Polish throne. Ladislas fought his way through this sea of troubles by arms, diplomacy, and marriage, united Lesser and Greater Poland into a coherent kingdom, and had himself crowned at Cracow, his new capital (1320). Dying at seventy-three (1333), he bequeathed his uneasy throne to his only son, Casimir the Great.

Some might begrudge Casimir III this title, since he preferred negotiation and compromise to war. Resigning Silesia to Bohemia, and Pomerania to the Knights, he consoled himself by acquiring Galicia, around Lwów, and Mazovia, around Warsaw. He devoted his reign of thirty-seven years to administration, bringing his varied territories under one law, "that the state might not look like a many-headed monster." [18] Under his direction a group of jurists unified the divergent legislation and customs of the provinces into the "Statutes of Casimir"—the first codification of Polish laws, and a model of humanitarian moderation by comparison with contemporary codes. Casimir protected Jewish, Greek Orthodox, and other racial or religious minorities, encouraged education and the arts, established the University of Cracow (1364), and built so extensively that men said he had found a Poland of wood and had rebuilt it in stone. He so wisely promoted all phases of the nation's economy that farmers hailed him as "the peasants' king," merchants throve in the security of peace, and all classes called him Great.

Having no male heir, he left his crown to his nephew Louis the Great of Hungary (1370), hoping to win for his country the protection of a strong monarchy, and a share in the cultural stimulus that the Angevin dynasty had brought from

Italy and France. But Louis was absorbed in Hungary, and neglected Poland. To keep the proud nobles loyal to him in his absence he granted them, by the "Privilege of Kassa" (1374), exemption from most taxes, and a monopoly of high offices. A war of succession followed his death (1382). The Seym or Parliament recognized his daughter Jadwiga, eleven years old, as "king"; but disorder ended only when Jagello, Great Prince of Lithuania, married Jadwiga (1386), uniting his spacious realm with Poland, and bringing a masterful personality to the government.

The growth of Lithuania was a major phenomenon of the fourteenth century Gedymin and his son Olgierd brought under their pagan rule nearly all western Russia: Polotsk, Pinsk, Smolensk, Chernigov, Volhynia, Kiev, Podolia, and the Ukraine; some of these were glad to find, under the Great Princes, a refuge from the Tatar Golden Horde that held eastern Russia in fief. When Jagello succeeded Olgierd (1377) the Lithuanian Empire, governed from Wilno, reached from the Baltic to the Black Sea, and almost to Moscow itself. This was the gift that Jagello brought to Jadwiga, or Poland was the dowry that she brought to him. She was only sixteen at their marriage; she had been reared as a Roman Catholic in the finest culture of the Latin Renaissance; he was thirty-six, illiterate and "heathen"; but he accepted baptism, took the Christian name of Ladislas II, and promised to convert all Lithuania.

It was a timely union, for the eastward advance of the Teutonic Knights was endangering both the wedded states. The "Order of the Cross," originally dedicated to Christianizing the Slavs, had become a band of martial conquerors, taking by the sword whatever terrain they could snatch from pagan or Christian, and establishing a harsh serfdom over lands once tilled by a free peasantry. In 1410 the Grand Master, from his capital at Marienburg, ruled Esthonia, Livonia, Courland, Prussia, and eastern Pomerania, shutting Poland off from the sea. In a ferocious "Northern War" the Grand Master's army and that of Jagello—each, we are told, 100,000 strong—met in battle near Grünewald or Tannenberg (1410). The Knights were defeated and fled, leaving behind them 14,000 prisoners and 18,000 slain—among these the Grand Master himself. From that day the Order of the Cross rapidly declined, until in the Peace of Thorn (1466) it ceded Pomerania and western Prussia to Poland, with the free port of Danzig as a door to the sea.

During the reign of Casimir IV (1447–92) Poland attained the apex of her spread, her power, and her art. Though himself quite illiterate, Casimir ended the knightly scorn of letters by giving his sons a thorough education. Queen Jadwiga, dying, left her jewels to finance the reopening of Cracow University —which, in the next century, would teach Copernicus. Literature, as well as science and philosophy, used the Latin tongue; in Latin Jan Dlugosz wrote his classic *History of Poland* (1478). In 1477 Veit Stoss of Nuremberg was invited to Cracow; he stayed there seventeen years, and raised the city to a high place in the art of the time. For the Church of Our Lady he carved 147 choir stalls, and an enormous altarpiece, forty feet by thirty-three, with a central shrine of the Assumption as impressive as Titian's painting, and with eighteen panels depicting the life of Mary and her Son—panels almost worthy, though in wood, to bear comparison with the bronze doors that Ghiberti had made for the Florentine Baptistery a generation before. For the cathedral of Cracow, Stoss cut in red mottled marble a superb tomb for Casimir IV. With these works Gothic sculpture in Poland reached its crown and end. In the reign of Casimir's son Sigismund I (1506–48) Polish art accepted the style of the Italian Renaissance. Lutheranism seeped in from Germany, and a new age began.

CHAPTER IX

The Ottoman Tide

1300-1516

I. SECOND BLOOMING IN BYZANTIUM: 1261-1373

THE Byzantine Empire, bloodlessly restored under a new Palaeologus dynasty in 1261, survived despite itself for almost two centuries. Its territory was reduced by the advance of the Moslems in Asia and Europe, by the expansion of the Slavs in its rear, and by scattered fragments of its former self retained by the Christian enemies who had sacked Constantinople in 1204—Normans, Venetians, and Genoese. Industry lingered in the towns of the Empire, but its products were carried in Italian vessels that paid no revenue into the treasury. Of the once numerous middle class only a fringe remained. Above it were luxurious nobles and prelates gorgeously garbed, who had learned nothing from history and had forgotten everything but their privileges. Below were turbulent layers of monks who salted piety with politics, and peasant proprietors lapsing into tenancy, and tenant farmers slipping into serfdom, and *prolétaires* dreaming of egalitarian utopias. A revolution at Salonika (1341) expelled the aristocracy, pillaged palaces, and set up a semi-communistic republic that ruled for eight years before it was suppressed by troops from the capital.[1] Constantinople was still a bustling nexus of commerce, but a Moslem traveler in 1330 noted "many destroyed houses, and sown fields within the city walls"; and the Spanish diplomat Ruy González de Clavijo, about 1409, wrote: "Everywhere throughout the capital are great palaces, churches, and monasteries, but most of them are in ruins."[2] The glory had departed from the Queen of the Bosporus.

Amid this political decay the ever-cherished heritage of ancient Greek literature and philosophy combined with the Byzantine-Oriental tradition in architecture and painting to compose the cultural swan song of the Eastern Roman Empire. The schools still expounded Plato, Aristotle, and Zeno the Stoic, though they shunned Epicurus as an atheist; and scholars revised and commented upon classical texts. Maximus Planudes, Byzantine envoy to Venice, edited the *Greek Anthology*, translated Latin classics into Greek, and rebuilt a cultural bridge between Byzantium and Italy. The career of Theodorus Metochites illustrates this Palaeologian Renaissance. Prime minister to Andronicus II, he was at the same time one of the most learned and prolific scholars of his time. Nicephoras Gregoras, himself savant and historian, wrote of him: "From morning to evening he was wholly and eagerly devoted to public affairs, as if scholarship were quite irrelevant to him; but late in the evening, after having left the palace, he became absorbed in studies to as high a degree as if he were a scholar with absolutely no connection with any other interest." [8] Theodorus composed history, poetry, astronomy, and philosophy, of an excellence unmatched by any Greek of that fourteenth century. In the revolution that dethroned his master, he forfeited position, fortune, and home, and was cast into prison; but, falling ill, he was allowed to end his days in the monastery of St. Saviour "in Chora" (i.e., in the fields), whose walls he had ennobled with some of the fairest mosaics in Byzantine history.

In philosophy the old contest between Platonists and Aristotelians recaptured the stage. Emperor John VI Cantacuzene defended Aristotle, while Plato remained the god of Gemistus Pletho. This most renowned of the new Greek Sophists studied philosophy at Brusa in Asia Minor, when that city was already the capital of the Ottoman advance. From a Jewish teacher there he learned the lore of the Zoroastrians; and when he returned to his native Peloponnesus—then renamed Morea—he had probably abandoned the Christian faith. Settling down at Mistra, he became both a judge and a professor. In 1400 he wrote a treatise bearing Plato's title, *The Laws*, in which he proposed the replacement of both Christianity and Mohammedanism by the religion of ancient Greece, merely transforming all the Olympians but Zeus into symbolic personifications of creative processes or ideas; Pletho did not know that religions are born, not made. Nevertheless pupils gathered around him eagerly; one of them, Johannes Bessarion, was destined to become a humanist cardinal in Italy. Both Gemistus and Bessarion accompanied Emperor John VIII to Ferrara and Florence (1438) to attend the council in which the Greek and Roman churches were for a moment reconciled in theology and politics. At Florence Gemistus lectured on Plato to an elite audience, and almost touched off the Italian Renaissance. It was there that he added the cognomen Pletho (complete) to his name, playing upon both *gemistos* (full) and *Platon*. Returning to Mistra he subsided theologically, became an archbishop, and died at ninety-five (1450).

The revival of art was as marked as the rejuvenation of letters. The themes and figures were still ecclesiastical; but now and then a touch of landscape, a breath of naturalism, a new warmth of color and line gave life to the mosaics. Those recently uncovered in the Chora monastery (the Kahriye-Jami Mosque) have so much vitality that Western historians profess to see in them some fresh Italian influence. In the frescoes that increasingly replaced expensive mosaics in the decoration of churches and palaces, the ecclesiastical hold relaxed, and figures of vivid fantasy and secular story appeared beside the legends of the saints. The icon-makers, however, clung to the old hieratic style—forms thinned, faces burning with a puritanic piety strikingly absent from the morals of the time. Byzantine miniature painting suffered now a sharp decline, but the weaving of pictorial designs into silk still produced masterpieces unrivaled in the Western world. The so-called "Dalmatic of Charlemagne" dates from the fourteenth or fifteenth century; on a base of blue-dyed silk an artist designed, a skillful artisan wove in silk threads of silver and gold, scenes from the life of Mary, Christ, and divers saints. Similar splendors of textile painting took form in this age in Salonika, Serbia, Moldavia, and Russia.

Greece was now again a center of great art. As the thirteenth century neared its end the Franks who had dotted the classic sites with picturesque castles made way for the revived Byzantine power. In 1348 the Emperor John VI sent his son Manuel to be *despotes* of the Morea. He established his provincial seat on a hill overlooking the ancient Sparta. To the new capital came nobles, patrons, monks, artists, scholars, and philosophers. Magnificent monasteries were built, and three of them have kept in their churches some of their medieval frescoes: the Metropolis and Peribleptos abbeys from the fourteenth century, the Pantanassa from the early fifteenth. These are the finest murals in the long history of Byzantine art. In their precise draftsmanship, in the flowing grace of their figures, in the depth and glow of their colors, they compare with the best frescoes of the same period in Italy; indeed, they may owe some of their novel grace to Cimabue, Giotto, or Duccio —who all owed so much to Byzantium.

On the eastern coast of Greece, high on the promontory of Mount Athos, monasteries had been raised in the tenth century, and in most centuries since: in the fourteenth the majestic Pantocrator, in the fifteenth St. Paul's. Of the murals in these retreats an eighteenth-century Greek *Guide to Painting* ascribed the best to Manuel Panselinos of Salonika, who "showed such brilliance and skill in his art that he was raised above all painters ancient or modern."[4] But of Manuel's dates or works there is no certainty; he may have belonged to the eleventh or the sixteenth century; and no one can say which of the paintings on Mount Athos are from his hand.

While Byzantine art experienced this final ecstasy, the Byzantine government declined. The army was in disorder, the navy in decay; Genoese or Venetian vessels controlled the Black Sea, and pirates roamed the Greek archipelago. A band of mercenaries from Catalonia—the "Catalan Grand Company"—captured Gallipoli (1306), mulcted the commerce of the Dardanelles, and set up a republic of robbers in Athens (1310); no government succeeded in suppressing them, and they were left to be consumed by their own violence. In 1307 Pope Clement V joined France, Naples, and Venice in a plot to recapture Constantinople. The plot fell apart, but for many years the Byzantine emperors were so fearful of the Christian West that they had no energy or courage to resist the Moslem advance. When that fear subsided the Ottoman Turks were at the door.

Some of the emperors bought their own destruction. In 1342 John VI Cantacuzene, involved in civil war, asked aid of Orkhan, Sultan of the Ottomans; Orkhan sent him ships and helped him take Salonika; the grateful Emperor gave him his daughter Theodora as an extra wife; the Sultan sent him 6,000 additional troops. When John Palaeologus undertook to depose him, John Cantacuzene robbed the churches of Constantinople to pay Orkhan for 20,000 more Turks, and promised the Sultan a fortress in the Thracian Chersonese. In the hour of his apparent victory the people of Constantinople turned against him as a traitor, and revolution transformed him overnight from an emperor into an historian (1355). He retired to a monastery, and wrote the history of his times as a last attempt to overwhelm his enemies.

John V Palaeologus found no ease on the throne. He went to Rome as a suppliant (1369), and offered, in return for help against the Turks, to bring his people into obedience to the papacy. Before the high altar of St. Peter's he abjured the Greek Orthodox Church. Pope Urban V promised aid against the infidels, and gave him letters to the princes of Christendom. But these were busy with other affairs. Instead of receiving assistance, John was held at Venice as a hostage for the payment of Greek debts. His son Manuel brought the money; John returned to Constantinople poorer than before, and was denounced by his people for forswearing the Orthodox creed. Failing in a second attempt to get succor from the West, he recognized Sultan Murad I as his suzerain, agreed to provide military aid to the Ottoman army, and gave his beloved Manuel as hostage for the fulfillment of his pledge.[5] Appeased for the moment, Murad spared Byzantium, and turned to subjugate the Balkans.

II. THE BALKANS MEET THE TURKS: 1300–96

Hitherto the fourteenth century had been for the Balkans a peak in their history. In Wallachia, Bulgaria, Serbia, Bosnia, and Albania hardy Slavs cut the forests, mined and tilled the earth, pastured flocks, and eagerly bred their own replacements. From the Adriatic to the Black Sea, from the Black Sea to the Baltic, Slavs, Italians, Magyars, Bulgars, Greeks, and Jews carried the trade of East and West, and cities sprouted in their path.

The great man of Serbia in this century was Stephen Dushan. His father, Stephen Urosh III, begot him in a brief detour from monogamy, gave him the affectionate name Dusha—i.e., Soul—and had him crowned as heir apparent. When a more legitimate son arrived, and received fond nicknames in his turn, Stephen deposed his father, allowed him to be strangled, and ruled Serbia with a strong hand for a generation. "Of all the men of his time," wrote a contemporary, he was "the tallest, and terrible to look upon." [6] Serbia forgave him everything, for he waged successful war. He trained a large army, led it with masterly generalship, conquered Bosnia, Albania, Epirus, Acarnania, Aetolia, Macedonia, Thessaly. Transferring his capital from Belgrade to Skoplje, he convened there a parliament of nobles, and bade it unify and codify the laws of his diverse states; the resultant *Zabonik Tsara Dushana*, or *Lawbook of Czar Dushan* (1349), revealed a level of legal development and civilized usage not far below that of Western Europe. Financed and perhaps stimulated by this political exaltation, Serbian art in the fourteenth century rivaled the contemporary flourish in Constantinople and the Morea; magnificent churches were built, and their mosaics were freer and livelier than those normally allowed by the more conservative ecclesiasticism of the Greek capital. In 1355 Dushan assembled his armies for the last time. He asked them whether they preferred to be led against Byzantium or Hungary. They answered that they would follow him wherever he chose to lead. "To Constantinople!" he cried. On the way he fell sick and died.

His empire was too heterogeneous to be held together except by a man of alert intelligence and disciplined energy. Bosnia seceded, and attained for a proud moment, under Stephen Trtko, the hegemony of the Balkans. Bulgaria under John Alexander had its last great age. Wallachia, once part of the Byzantine Empire, detached itself (*c.* 1290), and ruled the spreading delta of the Danube. Moldavia threw off its allegiance to Hungary (1349).

Upon these centrifugal statelets the Turkish blight fell even before John V Palaeologus made Byzantium vassal to Murad I. Suleiman, the dashing son of Sultan Orkhan, had led Turkish troops to the aid of John VI Cantacuzene; he received, or took, as his reward the fortress of Tzympe on the European side of the Dardanelles (1353). When an earthquake shattered the walls of near-by Gallipoli, Suleiman moved into the defenseless town. At his invitation Turkish colonists crossed from Anatolia and spread along the northern coast of the Sea of Marmora almost to Constantinople itself. With an expanding Turkish army Suleiman marched into Thrace and captured Adrianople (1361). Five years later Murad made it his European capital. From that center the Turks would for a century aim their blows at the divided Balkans.

Pope Urban V, recognizing the significance of this Turkish infiltration into Europe, called upon all Christendom for another crusade. An army of Serbs, Hungarians, and Wallachians marched gallantly toward Adrianople. At the river Maritsa they celebrated their unresisted advance with a feast.

Amid their cups and revelry they were surprised by a night assault from a relatively small Turkish force. Many were slain before they could arm; many were drowned trying to retreat across the river; the rest fled (1371). In 1385 Sofia capitulated, and half of Bulgaria fell to the Ottomans. In 1386 they took Nish, in 1387 Salonika. All Greece lay open to the Turks.

For one heroic year little Bosnia stemmed the tide. Stephen Trtko joined his forces with the Serbians under Lazar I, and defeated the Turks at Plochnik (1388). A year later Murad marched west with an army that included many Christian contingents. At Kosovo he was met by a coalition of Serbs, Bosnians, Magyars, Vlachs, Bulgars, Albanians, and Poles. A Serb knight, Milosh Kobilich, pretending to be a deserter and informer, made his way into Murad's tent, killed the Sultan, and was hacked to death. Murad's son and heir, Bajazet I, rallied the Turks to angry courage, and led them to victory. King Lazar was captured and beheaded; Serbia became a tribute-paying vassal of the Turks, and its new king, Stephen Lazarevitch, was compelled to send arms and men to Bajazet. In 1392 Wallachia under John Shishman joined the roster of Balkan states tributary to the Ottomans. Only Bulgaria and Byzantium remained capable of defense.

In 1393 Bajazet invaded Bulgaria. After a siege of three months Trnovo, the capital, fell; the churches were desecrated, the palaces were set on fire, the leading nobles were invited to a conference and were massacred. The Pope again appealed to Christendom, and King Sigismund of Hungary summoned Europe to arms. France, though engaged in a life-and-death struggle with England, sent a force of cavaliers under the Count of Nevers; the Count of Hohenzollern and the Grand Master of the Knights of St. John came with their followers; the Elector Palatine brought a company of Bavarian horse; John Shishman renounced his vassalage and came with his troops to fight under the Hungarian King.

The united army, 60,000 strong, marched through Serbia and besieged the Turkish garrison in Nicopolis. Warned that Bajazet, with an army from Asia, was coming to raise the siege, the French knights, gay with wine and women, promised to annihilate it, and boasted that if the sky should fall they would hold it up with their spears. For his part Bajazet vowed that he would stable his horse at the high altar of St. Peter's in Rome.[7] He placed his weakest troops in front, with strategy that should have been obvious. The French knights plunged through them triumphantly, then through 10,000 Janissaries, then through 5,000 Turkish cavalry, then charged recklessly up a hill. Just beyond its summit they found themselves faced by the main body of the Turkish army—40,000 lancers. The nobles fought nobly, were killed or captured or put to flight, and the allied infantry behind them were disordered by their rout. The Hungarians and Germans were nevertheless driving back the Turks when Stephen Lazarevitch of Serbia led 5,000 Christians against the Christian army, and won the crucial battle of Nicopolis for the Sultan (1396).

Maddened by the sight of so many of his men lying dead on the field, and by the claim of the rescued garrison that the Christian besiegers had killed their Turkish prisoners, Bajazet ordered the 10,000 captives to be put to death. The Count of Nevers was allowed to choose twenty-four knights to be saved for the ransom they might bring. Several thousand Christians were slaughtered in a bloody ritual that went on from sunrise to late afternoon, until the Sultan's officers persuaded him to spare the rest.[8] From that day till 1878 Bulgaria was a province of the Ottoman Empire. Bajazet now took most of Greece, and then marched against Constantinople.

III. THE LAST YEARS OF CONSTANTINOPLE: 1373–1453

No other government ever so fully deserved to fall as the Byzantine. Having lost the will to defend itself, and unable to persuade the too sophisticated Greeks that it is sweet and noble to die for one's country, it sent no contingent to the Christian armies at the Maritsa, Kosovo, or Nicopolis. It provided 12,000 soldiers for the Sultan in 1379; and it was Byzantine troops that, on the order of John VII Palaeologus, compelled the Byzantine city of Philadelphia, in Asia Minor, to surrender to the Turks (1390).

When Bajazet resumed the siege of Constantinople (1402), the Byzantine Empire was reduced to its capital: Bajazet commanded both coasts of the Sea of Marmora, controlled the Dardanelles, ruled nearly all of Asia Minor and the Balkans, and passed safely between his Asiatic and European capitals. The final hour seemed to have struck for the beleaguered city. Starving Greeks let themselves down over the walls, and deserted to the Turks in order to eat. Suddenly from the Moslem East an "infidel" savior appeared for the outpost of Christendom. Timur the Lame—Tamerlane the Great—had determined to check the growth and insolence of Ottoman power. As the Tatar hordes rolled west Bajazet abandoned the siege of Constantinople, and hurried to regroup his forces in Anatolia. Turks met Tatars at Ankara (1402); Bajazet was defeated and captured. The Turkish tide ebbed for a generation; God at last seemed to be on the side of the Christians.

Under the wise rule of Manuel II Byzantium recovered most of Greece and parts of Thrace. But Mohammed I reorganized the Turkish army, and Murad II led it, after a major defeat, to major victories. The Moslems still drew inspiration from the belief that to die for Islam was to win paradise; even if there should be no paradise and no houris, they were impartial enough to consider the Greek maidens beautiful. The Christians were not so impartial. Greek Catholics hated Roman Catholics and were hated in turn.

When Venetians hunted and massacred Greek Catholics in Crete for refusing to accept the Roman ritual and papal supremacy, Pope Urban V joined Petrarch in congratulating the doge on his firm protection of the one true Church (*c.* 1350).[9] The populace and lower clergy of Byzantium repudiated all attempts to reunite Greek with Latin Christianity; and a Byzantine noble declared that he would rather see the Turkish turban at Constantinople than the red hat of a Roman cardinal.[10] Most Balkan states hated their neighbors more than the Turks, and some preferred to submit to the Moslems, who taxed no more than the Christian rulers, persecuted heresy less or not at all,[11] and allowed four wives.

In 1422 Murad II renewed the attack upon Constantinople. A revolt in the Balkans compelled him to abandon the siege, and John VIII Palaeologus was allowed to reign in relative peace on condition of paying a heavy annual tribute to the Turks. Murad reconquered Greece, Salonika, and most of Albania. Serbia resisted manfully under George Branković; a combined army of Serbians and Hungarians under Hunyadi János defeated Murad at Kunovitza (1444), and Branković ruled Serbia till his death at the age of ninety (1456). After victories at Varna and in the second battle of Kosovo (1448), Murad signed a peace with the Emperor Constantine XI Palaeologus, and retired to Adrianople to die (1451).

Mohammed II, surnamed the Conqueror, came to the Ottoman throne at twenty-one. He confirmed the treaty with Constantine, and sent his nephew Orkhan to be brought up (possibly as a spy) at the Byzantine court. When other Moslem powers challenged his authority in Western Asia, Mohammed ferried his army across the Straits, and left his European possessions in charge of the Vizier Khalil Pasha, known for friendliness to Byzantium. Constantine had more courage than wit; he informed the Vizier that unless the pension paid for the care of Mohammed's nephew should be doubled, Orkhan would be put forward by Byzantium as a claimant to the Ottoman throne.[12] Apparently Constantine thought that the revolt in Asia offered an opportunity to weaken the Turks in Europe. But he had neglected to secure either his alliances in the west or his communications to the south. Mohammed made peace with his Moslem enemies, and with Venice, Wallachia, Bosnia, and Hungary. Crossing back to Europe, he raised a powerful fortress on the Bosporus above Constantinople, thereby ensuring the unimpeded passage of his troops between the continents, and controlling all commerce entering the Black Sea. For eight months he gathered materials and men. He hired Christian gunsmiths to cast for him the largest cannon yet known, which would hurl stone balls weighing 600 pounds. In June 1452, he declared war, and began the final siege of Constantinople with 140,000 men.[13]

Constantine led the defense with desperate resolution. He equipped his 7,000 soldiers with small cannon, lances, bows and arrows, flaming torches, and crude firearms discharging leaden bullets of a walnut's size. Sleeping only by snatches, he supervised, every night, the repair of the damage done to the walls during the day. Nevertheless the ancient defenses crumbled more and more before the battering rams and superior artillery of the Turks; now ended the medieval fortification of cities by walls. On May 29 the Turks fought their way across a moat filled with the bodies of their own slain, and surged over or through the walls into the terrorized city. The cries of the dying were drowned in the martial music of trumpets and drums. The Greeks at last fought bravely; the young Emperor was everywhere in the heat of the action, and the nobles who were with him died to a man in his defense. Surrounded by Turks, he cried out, "Cannot there be found a Christian to cut off my head?" He threw off his imperial garments, fought as a common soldier, disappeared in the rout of his little army, and was never heard of again.

The victors massacred thousands, till all defense ceased. Then they began that rampant plunder which had so long been the substance of their hopes. Every usable adult among the defeated was taken as a prize; nuns were ravished like other women in an impartial mania of rape; Christian masters and servants, shorn of the garb that marked their state, found themselves suddenly equalized in indiscriminate slavery. Pillage was not quite uncontrolled; when Mohammed II found a Moslem piously destroying the marble pavement of St. Sophia, he smote him with the royal scimitar, and announced that all buildings were to be reserved for orderly rapine by the Sultan. St. Sophia was transformed into a mosque after proper purification; all its Christian insignia were removed, and its mosaics were whitewashed into oblivion for 500 years. On the very day of the city's fall, or on the ensuing Friday, a muezzin mounted the tallest turret of Hagia Sophia and summoned the Moslems to gather in it for prayer to victorious Allah. Mohammed II performed the Moslem ritual in Christendom's most famous shrine.

The capture of Constantinople shook every throne in Europe. The bulwark had fallen that had protected Europe from Asia for over a thousand years. That Moslem power and faith which the Crusaders had hoped to drive back into inner Asia had now made its way over the corpse of Byzantium, and through the Balkans to the very gates of Hungary. The papacy, which had dreamed of all Greek Christianity submitting to the rule of Rome, saw with dismay the rapid conversion of millions of southeastern Europeans to Islam. Routes of commerce once open to Western vessels were now in alien hands, and could be clogged with tolls in peace or closed with guns in war. Byzantine art, exiled from home, found refuge in Russia, while in the West its influence disappeared with its pride. The migration of Greek scholars to Italy and France, which had begun in 1397, was now accelerated, fructifying Italy with the salvage of ancient Greece. In one sense nothing was lost; only the dead had died. Byzantium had finished its role, and yielded its place, in the heroic and sanguinary, noble and ignominious procession of mankind.

IV. HUNYADI JÁNOS: 1387–1456

The population of Hungary, numbering some 700,000 in the fourteenth century, was a fluctuating mixture of Magyars, Pannonians, Slovaks, Bulgars, Khazars, Patzinaks, Cumans, Slavonians, Croats, Russians, Armenians, Wallachians, Bosnians, and Serbs: in summary, a minority of Magyars ruling a majority of Slavs. In the nascent cities a mercantile middle class and an industrial proletariat began to form in the fourteenth century; and as these were mostly immigrants from Germany, Flanders, and Italy, new racial ten-·· sions were added to the ethnic maze.

When Andrew III died, ending the Árpád dynasty (907–1301), a war of succession further divided the nation, and peace returned only when the higher nobility, having made the monarchy elective, conferred the crown of St. Stephen upon Charles Robert of Anjou (1308). Charles brought with him French ideas of feudalism and chivalry, Italian ideas of business and industry. He promoted the development of Hungary's gold mines, encouraged enterprise, stabilized the currency, cleansed the judiciary, and gave the nation a competent administration. Under Charles and his son Louis, Hungary became a Western state, eager to win the help of the West against the proliferating East.

Louis I, wrote Voltaire, "reigned happily in Hungary forty years" (1342–82), and (not so happily) "in Poland twelve years. His people gave him the surname of the Great, which he well deserved; and yet this prince is hardly known in [Western] Europe, because he did not reign over men capable of transmitting his fame and virtues to other nations. How few know that in the fourteenth century there was a Louis the Great in the Carpathian Mountains!" [14] His character mingled urbane culture and chivalrous sentiments with military ardor and capacity. He indulged occasionally in wars—to avenge his murdered brother in Naples, to recover from Venice the Dalmatian ports that had long seemed to Hungary its due outlets to the sea, and to check the aggressive expansion of Serbia and Turkey by bringing Croatia, Bosnia, and northern Bulgaria under Hungarian control. By example and precept he spread the chivalric ideal among the nobility, and raised the level of manners and morals in his people. During his reign and that of his father, Hungarian Gothic achieved its finest embodiments, and Nicholas Kolozsvari and his sons carved such notable statuary as the *St. George* now in Prague. In 1367 Louis founded the University of Pécs; but this, along with much of

Hungary's medieval glory, disappeared in the long and exhausting struggle with the Turks.

Louis's son-in-law, Sigismund I, enjoyed a reign whose length (1387–1437) should have made possible long-term and farsighted policies. But his tasks were greater than his powers. He led a huge army against Bajazet at Nicopolis, and barely escaped from that disaster with his life. He realized that the Turkish advance was now the paramount problem of Europe; he devoted great care and failing funds to fortifying the southern frontier, and built at the junction of the Danube and the Save the great fortress of Belgrade. But his election to the Imperial office compelled him to neglect Hungary during long absences in Germany; and his acquisition of the Bohemian crown widened his responsibilities without enlarging his capacities.

Two years after his death the spreading Turks invaded Hungary. In this crisis the nation produced its most famous hero. Hunyadi János received his surname from the castle of Hunyadi in Transylvania, a stronghold granted to his father for services in war. János—i.e., John—was trained for war almost daily in his youth. He distinguished himself in a victory over the Turks at Semendria, and the new king, Ladislas V, made him commander-in-chief of the armies resisting the Turks. The repulse of the Ottomans became the absorbing devotion of his career. When they entered Transylvania he led against them newly disciplined troops inspired by his patriotism and his generalship. It was in that battle that Simon Kemény, beloved in Hungarian literature, gave his life for his leader. Knowing that the Turks had been instructed to seek out and kill Hunyadi, Simon begged and received permission to exchange costumes with him. He died under concentrated assaults, while Hunyadi directed the army to victory (1442). Murad II dispatched 80,000 new troops to the front; Hunyadi lured them, by feigned retreat, into a narrow pass where only a fraction of them could fight at one time; and again Hunyadi's strategy triumphed. Harassed by revolts in Asia, Murad sued for terms, and agreed to pay a substantial indemnity. At Szeged, King Ladislas and his allies signed with Murad's representatives a truce pledging both sides to peace. Ladislas swore on the Bible, the Turkish ambassadors on the Koran (1442).

But Cardinal Giuliano Cesarini, papal legate at Buda, presently judged the time propitious for an offensive. Murad had moved his army to Asia; an Italian fleet, controlling the Dardanelles, could prevent its return. The Cardinal, who had distinguished himself for probity and ability, argued that a pledge to an infidel could not bind a Christian.[15] Hunyadi advised peace, and the Serbian contingent refused to violate the truce. The envoys of the Western nations agreed with Cesarini, and offered to contribute money and men to a sacred crusade. Ladislas yielded, and in person led an attack upon Turkish positions The promised reinforcements from the West did not come;

the Ottoman army, 60,000 strong, eluded the Italian admiral, and crossed back to Europe. At Varna near the Black Sea—his standard-bearer holding the dishonored treaty aloft on a lance—Murad inflicted an overwhelming defeat upon Ladislas' 20,000 men (1444). Hunyadi counseled retreat, the King ordered advance. Hunyadi begged him to stay in the rear; Ladislas plunged into the van of the fight, and was killed. Cesarini did not quite regain his honor by losing his life.

Four years later Hunyadi tried to redeem the disaster. Forcing his way through a hostile Serbia, he met the Turks at Kosovo in a furious engagement that raged for three days. The Hungarians were routed, and Hunyadi joined them in flight. He hid for days in a marsh; starving, he emerged, and was recognized by the Serbians, who handed him over to the Turks. He was released on promising never to lead an army across Serbian soil again.

In 1456 the Turks laid siege to Belgrade. Mohammed II aimed against the citadel the heavy artillery that had shattered the walls of Constantinople; Europe had never known so violent a bombardment. Hunyadi led the defense with a skill and courage never forgotten in Hungarian poetry.[16] At last, preferring the anesthesia of battle to the agonies of starvation, the besieged rushed from the fortress, fought their way to the Turkish cannon, and so decisively vanquished the enemy that for sixty years thereafter Hungary was spared any Moslem attack. A few days after this historic defense Hunyadi died of a fever in the camp. Hungary honors him as its greatest man.

V. THE TIDE AT FULL: 1453–81

The Turks now resumed the conquest of the Balkans. Serbia finally succumbed in 1459, and remained a Turkish province till 1804. Mohammed II took Corinth by siege, and Athens without raising a lance (1458). The conqueror, like Caesar, gave the Athenians easy terms out of respect for their ancestors, and displayed a cultivated interest in the classical monuments. He could well be genial, having avenged not only the Crusades but Marathon. Bosnia, whose port and capital, Ragusa, had by some veneer of culture received the title of the South Slavonic Athens, accepted Turkish rule in 1463, and adopted the Moslem faith with an ease that startled the West.

The most valiant opponent of the Turks in the second half of the fifteenth century was Scanderbeg of Albania. His real name was George of Castriota, and he was probably of modest Slavonian lineage; but legends precious to his people endow him with royal Epirote blood and an adventurous youth. In his boyhood, we are told, he was given as hostage to Murad II, and was brought up at the Adrianople court of the Ottomans. The Sultan so liked his courage and bearing that he treated him as a son and made him an officer in the Turkish army. Converted to Mohammedanism, George received the mighty name of Iskender Bey—i.e., Alexander the Prince—which busy time shortened to Scanderbeg. After leading the Turks in many battles against the Christians, he repented his apostasy, and plotted escape. He renounced Islam, seized the Albanian capital Kruja from its Turkish governor, and proclaimed revolt (1442). Mohammed II sent army after army to chasten him; Scanderbeg defeated them all by the rapidity of his military movements and the genius of his elusive strategy; finally Mohammed, distracted by larger wars, gave him a ten-year armistice (1461). But the Venetian Senate and Pope Pius II persuaded Scanderbeg to break the truce and renew the war (1463). Mohammed, denouncing the Christians as literally faithless infidels, returned to the siege of Kruja. Scanderbeg defended it so tenaciously that the Sultan again raised the siege; but amid the debris of victory Scanderbeg died (1468). Kruja surrendered in 1479, and Albania became a province of Turkey.

Meanwhile the insatiable Mohammed absorbed the Morea, Trebizond, Lesbos, Negroponte (the old Euboea), and the Crimea. In 1477 one of his armies crossed the Isonzo, ravaged northeastern Italy to within twenty-two miles of Venice, and then, laden with booty, returned into Serbia. Frightened Venice, which had fought long and tenaciously for its possessions in the Aegean and the Adriatic, yielded all claim to Kruja and Scutari, and paid an indemnity of 10,000 ducats. Western Europe, which had failed to help Venice, denounced her for making and keeping peace with the infidel.[17] The Turks had now reached the Adriatic, and only the waters that Caesar had crossed in a rowboat separated them from Italy, Rome, and the Vatican. In 1480 Mohammed sent an army across these waters to attack the Kingdom of Naples. It took Otranto with ease, massacred half the 22,000 inhabitants, enslaved the rest, and cut an archbishop in two.[18] The fate of Christianity and monogamy teetered in the scales. Ferrante of Naples ended his war with Florence, and sent his best forces to recapture Otranto. Mohammed had entangled himself in besieging Rhodes; amid that enterprise he died; Rhodes remained Christian till Suleiman; the Turks left Otranto, and retired into Albania (1481). The Ottoman tide for a moment ceased to flow.

VI. THE HUNGARIAN RENAISSANCE: 1456–90

In the half-century of security that Hunyadi had won for Hungary his son Matthias Corvinus led the nation to its historic culmination. Matthias was only sixteen at his accession, and not entirely royal in form; his legs were too short for his trunk, so that he seemed tall only when on a horse; however, he had the chest and arms, the strength and courage, of a gladiator. Not long after his coronation he challenged to single combat a German knight of massive frame and power, who in a tournament at Buda had felled all competitors; and Matthias threatened to have him executed if he failed to fight with all his vigor and skill. The Hungarian historians assure us that the young King, aided by the horns of this dilemma, decisively vanquished the giant.[19] Matthias matured into a good soldier and general, defeated the Turks wherever he encountered them, absorbed Moravia and Silesia, failed to conquer Bohemia. He fought four wars against the Emperor Frederick III, took Vienna, and annexed Austria (1485); the first Austro-Hungarian Empire was Hungarian.

His victories made the monarchy transiently supreme over the nobility; here, as in Western Europe, centralization of government was the order of the day. At Buda, and in the King's palace at Visegrad, his court equaled any royal grandeur of the age; great noblemen became his servitors; his ambassadors were noted for the splendor of their dress, equipage, and retinue. Matthias' diplomacy was cunning and unscrupulous, amiable and generous; he bought with gold what would have cost twice as much by arms. Meanwhile he found time and zest to restore every department of the government, and to labor in person as a careful administrator and impartial judge. Roaming in disguise among the people, the soldiery, and the courts, he inspected at first hand the behavior of his officials, and corrected incompetence and injustice without favoritism or fear. He did what he could to protect the weak from the strong, the peasants from their rapacious lords. While the Church continued to claim the country as papal property, Matthias appointed and disciplined prelates, and enjoyed the furore when he made a seven-year-old Italian lad the primate of Hungary. The merchants of Ferrara, with rival humor, sent the new archbishop an assortment of toys.[20]

In 1476 Matthias married Beatrice of Aragon, and welcomed to Hungary the gay Neapolitan spirit and refined Italian tastes of the granddaughter of Alfonso the Magnanimous. Intercourse between Hungary and Naples had been encouraged by the Angevin kinship of their kings, and many men at the Buda court had been educated in Italy. Matthias himself resembled the Italian Renaissance "despots" in his cultural proclivities as well as his Machiavellian statecraft. Lorenzo de' Medici sent him two bronze reliefs by Verrocchio, and Lodovico il Moro commissioned Leonardo da Vinci to paint a *Madonna* for the Hungarian King, assuring the artist that "he is able to value a great picture as few men can." [21] Filippino Lippi turned out another *Madonna* for Corvinus, and his pupils adorned with frescoes the royal palace at Esztergom. An Italian sculptor made a pretty bust of Beatrice; [22] probably the famous Milanese goldsmith Caradosso designed the masterly *Calvary* of Esztergom; Benedetto da Maiano carved decorations for the palace at Buda;

and divers Italians built the Renaissance-style tabernacle in the parish church of the Inner City of the capital.[23]

Nobles and prelates joined the King in supporting artists and scholars; even the mining towns of the interior had rich men who sublimated wealth into art. Handsome buildings, civic as well as ecclesiastical, rose not only at Buda but at Visegrad, Tata, Esztergom, Nagyvárad, and Vác. Hundreds of sculptors and painters ornamented these edifices. Giovanni Dalmata made notable statues of Hunyadi János and other Hungarian heroes. At Kassa a veritable school of artists formed. There, for the high altar of the church of St. Elizabeth, "Master Stephen" and others carved (1474–77) an immense and complex reredos, whose central figures are quite Italian in their refinement and grace. In the parish church of Beszterczebánya another group carved in stone a great relief, *Christ in the Garden of Olives*, astonishing in its careful details and dramatic effect. A similar vigor of expression and artistry appears in the Hungarian paintings that survive from this age, as in the *Mary Visiting Elizabeth*, by "Master M.S.," now in the Budapest Museum.[24] Almost all the art of this Hungarian heyday was destroyed or lost in the Ottoman invasions of the sixteenth century. Some of the statues are in Istanbul, to which they were carried by the victorious Turks.

Matthias' interests were literary rather than artistic. Humanists, foreign or native, were welcomed at his court, and received lucrative sinecures in the government. Antonio Bonfini wrote a history of the reign in a Latin modeled on Livy. Janós Vitez, Archbishop of Gran, collected a library of ancient classics, and provided funds to send young scholars to study Greek in Italy. One of these, János Pannonius, spent seven years at Ferrara, won admission to Lorenzo's circle at Florence, and, back in Hungary, astonished the court with his Latin verses and Greek discourses. "When Pannonius spoke Greek," wrote Bonfini, "you would think he must have been born in Athens." [25] Probably in Italy alone could one find, in the last quarter of the fifteenth century, such a galaxy of artists and scholars as received sustenance at Matthias' court. The Sodalitas Litteraria Danubia, founded at Buda in 1497, is among the oldest literary societies in the world.[26]

Like his Medici contemporaries, Corvinus collected art and books. His palace became a museum of statuary and *objets d'art*. Tradition has it that he spent 30,000 florins ($750,000?) yearly on books, which in many cases were costly illuminated manuscripts. Yet he did not, like Federigo da Montefeltro, reject printed works; a press was established at Buda in 1473, three years before printing reached England. The Bibliotheca Corvina, which held 10,000 volumes when Matthias died, was the finest fifteenth-century library outside of Italy. It was housed in his Buda palace in two spacious halls, with windows of stained glass looking on the Danube; the shelves were richly carved, and the books, mostly bound in vellum, were curtained with velvet tapestries.[27] Matthias seems to have read some of the books; at least he used Livy to induce sleep; and he wrote to a humanist: "O scholars, how happy you are! You strive not after blood-stained glory, nor monarchs' crowns, but for the laurels of poetry and virtue. You are even able to compel us to forget the tumult of war." [28]

The centralized power that Matthias had organized only briefly survived his death (1490). The resurgent magnates dominated Ladislas II, and embezzled revenues that should have paid the troops. The army mutinied, the soldiers went home. Freed from taxation, the nobles wasted their income and energies in riotous living, while Islam pressed against the borders and a bitterly exploited peasantry seethed with revolt. In 1514 the Hungarian Diet declared a crusade against the Turks, and called for volunteers. Peasants in great number flocked to the cross, seeing little to choose between life and death. Finding themselves armed, the thought spread among them, Why wait to kill distant Turks, when hated nobles were so near? A soldier of fortune, György Dózsa, led them in a wild *jacquerie;* they overran all Hungary, burning castles and massacring all nobles—men, women, children—who fell into their hands. The nobles called in aid from all directions, armed and paid mercenaries, overwhelmed the disorganized peasants, and punished their leaders with frightful torments. For two weeks Dózsa and his aides were kept without food; then he was tied to a red-hot iron throne, a red-hot crown was placed upon his head, a red-hot scepter forced into his hand; and his starved companions were allowed to tear the roasted flesh from his body while he was still conscious. From barbarism to civilization requires a century; from civilization to barbarism needs but a day.

The peasants were not slaughtered, for they were indispensable; but the Tripartite Code (1514) decreed that "the recent rebellion ... has for all time to come put the stain of faithlessness upon the peasants, and they have thereby forfeited their liberty, and have become subject to their landlords in unconditional and perpetual servitude. . . . Every species of property belongs to the landlords, and the peasant has no right to invoke justice and the law against a noble." [29]

Twelve years later Hungary fell to the Turks.

CHAPTER X

Portugal Inaugurates the Commercial Revolution

1300-1517

THROUGH no natural advantages except a seacoast, but by sheer courage and tenacious enterprise, little Portugal in this period made herself one of the strongest and richest of European states. Founded as a kingdom in 1139, her government, language, and culture reached an established form under her best-beloved ruler, Diniz "the Laborer"—administrator, reformer, builder, educator, patron of the arts, and skilled practitioner of literature and love. His son Affonso IV, after some precautionary murders, matured into a beneficent reign, in which a growing trade with England bound the two countries into a political amity that has endured till our time. To confirm a prudent alliance with rising Castile, Affonso urged his son Pedro to marry Donna Costanza Manuel. Pedro married her, but continued to love the lovely Inés de Castro, herself of royal lineage. After Costanza's death Inés was an obstacle to a second diplomatic marriage for Pedro; Affonso, after due reluctance, had her killed (1355). Camoëns, the Portuguese Milton, recounted this famous romance in his national epic, *The Lusiads:*

> So against Iñez came that murderous crew ...
> The brutes their swords in her white breasts imbrue , . .
> And in mad wrath themselves incarnadine,
> Nor any vengeance yet to come divine.[1]

Pedro supplied the vengeance when, two years later, he inherited the throne. He murdered the murderers, exhumed the corpse of his beloved, crowned her queen, then reburied her in regal style. He ruled with a severity nurtured by this tragedy.

A less exalted romance disordered the reign of his successor. Fernando I lost his head and heart to Leonora, wife of the lord of Pombeiro, repudiated his engagement to a Castilian princess, and married Leonora despite her living husband and a scandalized Church. After Fernando's death (1383), Leonora assumed the regency, made her daughter Beatriz queen, and betrothed her to John I of Castile. The people revolted against the prospect of becoming a Castilian appanage; a Cortes at Coimbra declared the Portuguese throne elective, and chose as king Don João—John—son of Pedro and Inés. Castile undertook to establish Beatriz by force; John improvised an army, borrowed 500 archers from England, and defeated the Castilians at Alju-barrota on August 14, 1385—which is annually celebrated as Portugal's Independence Day.

"John the Great" now opened a reign of forty-eight years, and a dynasty —the house of Aviz—that held the throne for two centuries. Administration was reorganized, law and the judiciary were reformed, the Portuguese language was made official, and its literature began. Scholars here, as in Spain, continued till the eighteenth century to use Latin, but Vasco da Lobeira wrote in the native tongue a chivalric romance, *Amadís da Gaula* (*c.* 1400), which became in translation the most popular secular book in Europe. National art expressed itself proudly in the church of Santa Maria da Victoria, built at Batalha by John I to commemorate "the Battle" of Aljubarrota; here Milan's cathedral is rivaled in size, and Notre Dame of Paris in the intricate splendor of buttresses and pinnacles. In 1436 a chapel of elegant design and decoration was added to receive the remains of the "bastard king."

He was honored in his sons. Duarte—Edward—succeeded him and governed almost as well; Pedro codified the law; Henrique—"Henry the Navigator"—inaugurated the commercial revolution that was to transform the map of the globe. When John I captured Ceuta from the Moors (1415), he left the twenty-one-year-old Henry as governor of that strategic stronghold, just across the Strait from Gibraltar. Excited by Moslem accounts of Timbuktu and Senegal and the gold, ivory, and slaves to be had along the West African coast, the ambitious youth determined to explore that terrain and add it to Portugal. The Senegal River that his informants spoke of might lead eastward to the headwaters of the Nile and to Christian Abyssinia; a water route would be opened across Africa from the Atlantic to the Red Sea —therefore to India; the Italian monopoly of trade with the East would be broken; Portugal would be a major power. The conquered region might be converted to Christianity, and African Islam would be flanked on north and south by Christian states, and the Mediterranean become safe for Christian navigation. Henry does not appear to have thought of a route *around* Africa,[2] but that was the historic result of his work.

About 1420 he set up at Sagres, on the southwestern tip of Portugal and Europe, an informal clearing house of nautical knowledge and enterprise. For forty years he and his aides, including Jewish and Moslem astronomers and map makers, gathered and studied there the accounts of sailors and travelers, and sent out into perilous seas frail vessels powered with sails and oars and thirty to sixty men. One of Henry's captains had already (1418) rediscovered Madeira, which had been seen by Genoese mariners seventy years before and then forgotten; now Portuguese colonists developed its resources; soon its sugar and other products repaid the cost of colonization, and encouraged the Portuguese government to meet Henry's appeals for funds. Noting the Azores marked on an Italian map of 1351, he commissioned Gonzalo Cabral to find them; it was done, and in 1432–44, one after another, these jewels of the sea were added to the Portuguese crown.

But it was Africa that lured Henry most insistently. Catalan and Portuguese navigators had sailed some 900 miles down the west coast as far as Bojador (1341–46). There, however, the enormous westward bulge of the great continent into the Atlantic disheartened mariners seeking the south; they crept back to Europe with self-excusing tales of horrible natives, a sea so thick with salt that no prow would cleave it, and assurances that any Christian who passed Bojador would be transformed into a Negro. With similar apologies Captain Gilianes returned to Sagres in 1433. Henry ordered him forth again, and bade him bring back a clear account of the lands and seas south of the forbidding cape. So prodded, Gilianes reached to 150 miles beyond Bojador (1435), and was astonished to find lush vegetation in equatorial regions where, according to Aristotle and Ptolemy, only deserts could exist under the burning sun. Six years later Nuno Tristão sailed down to Capo Blanco, and brought home some sturdy Negroes, who were at once baptised and enslaved; feudal barons put them to work on Portuguese plantations, and the first major result of Henry's labors was the inauguration of the African slave trade. Fresh financial support now came to the Prince. His ships went out nominally to explore and convert, really to get gold, ivory, and slaves. Captain Lanzarote in 1444 brought back 165 "blackamoors," who were set to tilling the lands of the monastic-military Order of Jesus Christ. A Portuguese contemporary described the capture of these "black Moors":

> Our men, crying out, "Sant' Iago! San Jorge! Portugal!" fell upon them, killing or capturing all they could. There you might have seen mothers catch up their children, husbands their wives, each one escaping as best he could. Some plunged into the sea; others thought to hide themselves in the corners of their hovels; others hid their children under the shrubs . . . where our men found them. And at last our Lord God, Who gives to all a due reward, gave to our men that day a victory over their enemies; and in recompense for all their toil in His service they took 165 men, women, and children, not counting the slain.[3]

By 1448 over 900 African slaves had been brought to Portugal. We should add that the Moslems of North Africa had anticipated the Christians in developing a slave trade, and African Negro chieftains themselves bought

Negro slaves from the Portuguese with ivory and gold.[4] Man was a commodity to human beasts of prey.

In 1445 Diniz Dias reached the fertile promontory named Cape Verde; in 1446 Lanzarote explored the mouth of the Senegal; in 1456 Ca Da Mosto found the Cape Verde Islands. In that year Prince Henry died, but the enterprise continued with the impetus that he had given it and the economic gains that now financed it. João da Santarem crossed the equator (1471), Diogo Cão reached the Congo River (1484); finally, half a century after Henry's first expedition, Bartholomeu Dias, fighting his way through tempest and shipwreck, rounded the southernmost point of Africa (1486). He rejoiced to find that he could now sail eastward; India lay straight ahead, and seemed almost in his grasp; but his weary men forced him to turn back. Mourning the rough seas that had broken the spirit of his men, he named the southern tip of the continent Cabo Tormentoso; but King John II, seeing India around the bend, renamed the point the Cape of Good Hope.

Neither Dias nor the King lived to see fulfilled the dream that now stirred all Portugal—an all-water route to India. In 1497 King Manuel, jealous of the honors and wealth that Columbus was bringing to Spain, commissioned Vasco da Gama to sail around Africa to India. Forced by storms to take a circuitous route, the twenty-eight-year-old captain voyaged some 5,000 miles through 137 days to the Cape of Good Hope, then, through a hundred perils and tribulations, 178 days and 4,500 miles more to Calicut, a main nexus of east-west and north-south trade in Asia; there he anchored on May 20, 1498, ten months and twelve days after leaving Lisbon. Landing, he was at once arrested as a pirate, and narrowly escaped execution. With remarkable courage and address he overcame Indian suspicions and Moslem jealousies, won permission for the Portuguese to trade, took on a rich cargo of pepper, ginger, cinnamon, cloves, nutmeg, and jewelry, and left Calicut August 29 for an arduous year-long return to Lisbon. The Portuguese had finally found a route to India free from the costly transshipments and tolls suffered by the sea-and-land routes from Italy through Egypt or Arabia or Persia. The economic results were to be, for a century, more vital to Europe than those that flowed from the discovery of America.

Proud of having reached the real India while the Spanish navigators were floundering in the supposed Indies of the Caribbean, the Portuguese till 1500 hardly thought of trying a passage west. But in that year Pedro Cabral, driven from the course that he had set for India via Africa, stumbled upon Brazil; and again in that year Gaspar Corte-Real rediscovered Labrador. In 1503 Amerigo Vespucci, sailing under the Portuguese flag, explored the Rio Plata and Paraguay; and in 1506 Tristão da Cunha found the South Atlantic island that bears his name. Portuguese statesmen, however, saw little profit in Brazil, whereas every cargo from India fattened the royal treasury and the purses of merchants and mariners.

The Portuguese government kept full control of the new trade, since the commerce required unremitting military protection. Moslem merchants had long since been established in Indian posts; some Indian potentates joined them in resisting the Portuguese invasion; trade and war, money and blood, now mingled in the far-flung commercial revolution. In 1509 Affonso de Albuquerque became the first governor of Portuguese India. Waging campaign after campaign against Moslems and Hindus, he captured and fortified Aden and Hormuz on the Arabian coast, Goa in India, and Malacca in the Malay Peninsula; and from Malacca he brought home a million ducats' worth of booty. So armed, Portugal became for 150 years the master of European trade with India and the East Indies. Portuguese merchants established themselves as far east as the Moluccas (1512), and rejoiced to find the nutmegs, mace, and cloves of these "Spice Islands" tastier and cheaper than India's. Still insatiate, Albuquerque sailed with twenty vessels into the Red Sea, and proposed to the Christian king of Abyssinia that they join forces in digging a canal from the Upper Nile to the Red Sea, so diverting the river and turning all Moslem Egypt into a desert. Trouble summoned Albuquerque back to Goa, where he died in 1515. In the following year Duarte Coelho opened Cochin China and Siam to Portuguese trade; and in 1517 Fernão Peres de Andrade established commercial relations with Canton and Peking.

The Portuguese Empire—the first modern imperialism—was now the most extensive in the world, rivaled only by the empire that was being built for Spain in the Americas. Lisbon became a thriving emporium, whose waters harbored ships from romantically distant lands. There, rather than in Venice or Genoa, the merchants of northern Europe now found the lowest prices for Asiatic goods. Italy mourned her lost monopoly of the Oriental trade. Slowly the Italian Renaissance, mortally stricken by Columbus, Vasco da Gama, and Luther in one generation, faded away, while Portugal and Spain, commanders of the open sea, led the flowering of the Atlantic states.

Literature and art basked in the new glory. Fernão Lopes, writing for twenty years (1434-54) his voluminous *Cronacas*, told the story of Portugal with a vivacity of narrative and a power of characterization rivaling Froissart. Gil Vicente inaugurated the Portuguese drama with little plays for the court and *autos*—acts—for public festivals (*c.* 1500). A Portuguese school of painting developed, taking a lead from Flanders but achieving its own temper and qualities. Nuno Gonçalves (*fl.* 1450-72) rivaled Mantegna, and almost the Van Eycks, in the somber polyptych that he painted for the convent of St. Vincent: the six panels primitive in perspective and modeling, but the fifty-five portraits—the best of them Henry the Navigator—individualized with realistic power. To commemorate the victorious voyage of Vasco da Gama, King Manuel "the Fortunate" commissioned the architect João de Castilho to build near Lisbon, in Flamboyant Gothic, the magnificent monastery of Belem (*c.* 1500). Portugal had entered her golden age.

CHAPTER XI

Spain

1300-1517

I. THE SPANISH SCENE: 1300-1469

SPAIN'S mountains were her protection and tragedy: they gave her comparative security from external attack, but hindered her economic advance, her political unity, and her participation in European thought. In a little corner of the northwest a half-nomad population of Basques led their sheep from plains to hills and down again with the diastole and systole of the seasons. Though many Basques were serfs, all claimed nobility, and their three provinces governed themselves under the loose sovereignty of Castile or Navarre. Navarre remained a separate kingdom until Ferdinand the Catholic absorbed its southern part into Castile (1515), while the rest became a kingly appanage of France. Sardinia was appropriated by Aragon in 1326; the Baleares followed in 1354, Sicily in 1409. Aragon itself was enriched by the industry and commerce of Valencia, Tarragona, Saragossa, and Barcelona—capital of the province of Catalonia within the kingdom of Aragon. Castile was the strongest and most extensive of the Spanish monarchies; it ruled the populous cities of Oviedo, León, Burgos, Valladolid, Salamanca, Córdova, Seville, and Toledo, its capital; its kings played to the largest audience, and for the greatest stakes, in Spain.

Alfonso XI (r. 1312–50) improved the laws and courts of Castile, deflected the pugnacity of the nobles into wars against the Moors, supported literature and art, and rewarded himself with a fertile mistress. His wife bore him one legitimate son, who grew up in obscurity, neglect, and resentment, and became Pedro el Cruel. Peter's accession at fifteen (1350) so visibly disappointed the nine bastards of Alfonso that they were all banished, and Leonora de Guzmán, their mother, was put to death. When Peter's royal bride, Blanche of Bourbon, arrived unsolicited from France, he married her, spent two nights with her, had her poisoned on a charge of conspiracy (1361), and married his paramour Maria de Padilla, whose beauty, legend assures us, was so intoxicating that the cavaliers of the court drank with ecstasy the water in which she had bathed. Pedro was popular with the lower classes, which supported him to the very bitter end; but the repeated attempts of his half-brothers to depose him drove him to such a series of treacheries, murders, and sacrileges as would clog and incarnadine any tale. Finally Henry of Trastamara, Leonora's eldest son, organized a successful revolt, slew Peter with his own hand, and became Henry II of Castile (1369).

But we do nations injustice when we judge them from their kings, who agreed with Machiavelli that morals are not made for sovereigns. While the rulers played with murder, individual or nationalized, the people, numbering some 10,000,000 in 1450, created the civilization of Spain. Proud of their pure blood, they were an unstable mixture of Celts, Phoenicians, Carthaginians, Romans, Visigoths, Vandals, Arabs, Berbers, and Jews. At the social bottom were a few slaves, and a peasantry that remained serf till 1471; above them were the artisans, manufacturers, and merchants of the towns; above these, in rising layers of dignity, were the knights *(caballeros)*, the nobles dependent upon the king *(hidalgos)*, and the independent nobles *(proceres)*; and alongside these laymen were grades of clergy mounting from parish priests through bishops and abbots to archbishops and cardinals. Every town had its *conseijo* or council, and sent delegates to join nobles and prelates in provincial and national *cortes;* in theory the edicts of the kings required the consent of these "courts" to become laws. Wages, labor conditions, prices, and interest rates were regulated by municipal councils or the guilds. Trade was hampered by royal monopolies, by state or local tolls on imports and exports, by diverse weights and measures, by debased currencies, highway brigands, Mediterranean pirates, ecclesiastical condemnation of interest, and the persecution of Moslems—who manned most industry and commerce—and Jews, who managed finance. A state bank was opened in Barcelona (1401) with governmental guarantee of bank deposits; bills of exchange were issued; and marine insurance was established by 1435.[1]

As the Spaniards mingled anti-Semitism with Semitic ancestry, so they retained the heat of Africa in their blood, and were inclined, like the Berbers, to rarity and violence of action and speech. They were sharp and curious of mind, yet eagerly credulous and fearfully superstitious. They sustained a proud independence of spirit, and dignity of carriage, even in misfortune and poverty. They were acquisitive and had to be, but they did not look down upon the poor, or lick the boots of the rich. They despised and deferred labor, but they bore hardship stoically; they were lazy, but they conquered half the New World. They thirsted for adventure, grandeur, and romance. They relished danger, if only by proxy; the bullfight, a relic of Crete and Rome, was already the national game, formal, stately, colorful, exacting, and teaching bravery, artistry, and an agile intelligence. But the Spaniards, like the modern (unlike the Elizabethan) English, took their pleasures sadly; the aridity of the soil and the shadows of the mountain slopes were reflected in a dry somberness of mood. Manners were grave and perfect, much better than hygiene; every Spaniard was a gentleman, but few were knights of the bath. Chivalric forms and tourneys flourished amid the squalor of the populace; the "point of honor" became a religion; women in Spain were goddesses and prisoners. In the upper classes, dress, sober on weekdays, burst into splendor on Sundays and festive occasions, flaunting silks and ruffs and puffs and lace and gold. The men affected perfume and high heels, and the women, not content with their natural sorcery, bewitched the men with color, lace, and mystic veils. In a thousand forms and disguises the sexual chase went on; solemn ecclesiastical terrors, lethal laws, and the *punto de onor* struggled to check the mad pursuit, but Venus triumphed over all, and the fertility of women outran the bounty of the soil.

The Church in Spain was an inseparable ally of the state. It took small account of the Roman pope; it made frequent demands for the reform of the papacy, even while contributing to it the unreformable Alexander VI; in 1513 Cardinal Ximenes forbade the promulgation in Spain of the indulgence offered by Julius II for rebuilding St. Peter's.[2] In effect the king was accepted as the head of the Spanish Church; in this matter Ferdinand did not wait for Henry VIII to instruct him; no Reformation was needed in Spain to make state and Church, nationalism and religion, one. As part of the unwritten bargain the Spanish Church enjoyed substantial prerogatives under a government consciously dependent upon it for maintaining moral order, social stability, and popular docility. Its personnel, even in minor orders, were subject only to ecclesiastical courts. It owned great tracts of land, tilled by tenants; it received a tenth of the produce of other holdings, but paid a third of this tithe to the exchequer; otherwise it was exempt from taxation.[3] It was probably richer, in comparison with the state, than in any other country except Italy.[4] Clerical morals and monastic discipline were apparently above the medieval average; but, as elsewhere, clerical concubinage was widespread and condoned.[5] Asceticism continued in Spain while declining north of the Pyrenees; even lovers scourged themselves to melt the resistance of tender, timid *señoritas*, or to achieve some masochistic ecstasy.

The people were fiercely loyal to Church and king, because they had to be in order to fight with courage and success their immemorable enemies the Moors; the struggle for Granada was presented as a war for the Holy Faith, *Santa Fé*. On holy days men, women, and children, rich and poor, paraded the streets in solemn procession, somberly silent or chanting, behind great dolls *(pasos)* representing the Virgin or a saint. They believed intensely in the spiritual world as their real environment and eternal home; beside it earthly life was an evil and transitory dream. They hated heretics as traitors to the national unity and cause, and had no objection to burning them; this was the least they could do for their outraged God. The lower classes had hardly any schooling, and this was nearly all religious. Stout Cortes, finding among the pagan Mexicans a rite resembling the Christian Eucharist, complained that Satan had taught it to them just to confuse the conquerors.[6]

The intensity of Catholicism in Spain was enhanced by economic competition with Moslems and Jews, who together made up almost a tenth of the population of Christian Spain. It was bad enough that the Moors held fertile Granada; but more closely irritating were the Mudejares—the unconverted Moors who lived among the Spanish Christians, and whose skill in business, crafts, and agriculture was the envy of a people mostly bound in primitive drudgery to the soil. Even more unforgivable were the Spanish Jews. Christian Spain had persecuted them through a thousand years: had subjected them to discriminatory taxation, forced loans, confiscations, assassinations, compulsory baptism; had compelled them to listen to Christian sermons, sometimes in their own synagogues, urging their conversion, while the law made it a capital crime for a Christian to accept Judaism. They were invited or conscripted into debates with Christian theologians, where they had to choose between a shameful defeat or a perilous victory. They and the Mudejares had been repeatedly ordered to wear a distinctive badge, usually a red circle on the shoulder of their garments. Jews were forbidden to hire a Christian servant; their physicians were not allowed to prescribe for Christian patients; their men, for cohabiting with a Christian woman, were to be put to death.

In 1328 the sermons of a Franciscan friar goaded the Christians of Estella, in Navarre, to massacre 5,000 Jews and burn down their houses.[7] In 1391 the sermons of Fernán Martínez aroused the populace in every major center of Spain to massacre all available Jews who refused conversion. In 1410 Valladolid, and then other cities, moved by the eloquence of the saintly and fanatical Vicente Ferrer, ordered the confinement of Jews and Moors within specified quarters—*Juderia* or *alhama*—whose gates were to be closed from sunset to sunrise; this segregation, however, was probably for their protection.[8]

Patient, laborious, shrewd, taking advantage of every opportunity for development, the Jews multiplied and prospered even under these disabilities. Some kings of Castile, like Alfonso XI and Pedro el Cruel, favored them and raised brilliant Jews to high places in the government. Alfonso made Don Joseph of Écija his minister of finance, and another Jew, Samuel ibn-Wakar, his physician; they abused their position, were convicted of intrigue, and died in prison.[9] Samuel Abulafia repeated the sequence; he became state treasurer under Pedro, amassed a large fortune, and was put to death by the King.[10] Three years earlier (1357) Samuel had built at Toledo a classically simple and elegant synagogue, which was changed under Ferdinand into the Christian church of El Transito, and is now preserved by the government as a monument of Hebraeo-Moorish art in Spain. Pedro's protection of the

Jews was their misfortune: when Henry of Trastamara deposed him 1,200 Jews were massacred by the victorious soldiers (Toledo, 1355); and worse slaughters ensued when Henry brought into Spain the "Free Companions" recruited by Du Guesclin from the rabble of France.

Thousands of Spanish Jews preferred baptism to the terror of abuse and pogroms. Being legally Christians, these *Conversos* made their way up the economic and political ladder, in the professions, even in the Church; some became high ecclesiastics, some were counselors to kings. Their talents in finance earned them invidious prominence in the collection and management of the national revenue. Some surrounded themselves with aristocratic comforts, some made their prosperity offensively conspicuous. Angry Catholics fastened upon the *Conversos* the brutal name of *Marranos*—swine.[11] Nevertheless Christian families with more pedigree than cash, or with a prudent respect for ability, accepted them in marriage. In this way the Spanish people, especially the upper classes, received a substantial infusion of Jewish blood. Ferdinand the Catholic and Torquemada the Inquisitor had Jews in their ancestry.[12] Pope Paul IV, at war with Philip II, called him and the Spanish the "worthless seed of the Jews and Moors." [13]

II. GRANADA: 1300–1492

Ibn-Batuta described the situation of Granada as "unequaled by any city in the world. . . . Around it on every side are orchards, gardens, flowering meadows, vineyards"; and in it "noble buildings." [14] Its Arabic name was *Karnattah*—of uncertain meaning; its Spanish conquerors christened it *Granada*—"full of seeds"—probably from the neighboring abundance of the pomegranate tree. The name covered not only the city but a province that included Xeres, Jaén, Almería, Málaga, and other towns, with a total population of some four millions. The capital, with a tenth of these, rose "like a watchtower" to a summit commanding a magnificent valley, which rewarded careful irrigation and scientific tillage with two crops a year. A wall with a thousand towers guarded the city from its encompassing foes. Mansions of spacious and elegant design sheltered the aristocracy; in the public squares fountains cooled the ardor of the sun; and in the fabulous halls of the Alhambra the emir or sultan or caliph held his court.

A seventh of all agricultural produce was taken by the government, and probably as much by the ruling class as a fee for economic management and military leadership. Rulers and nobles distributed some of their revenue to artists, poets, scholars, scientists, historians, and philosophers, and financed a university where learned Christians and Jews were allowed to hold chairs and occasional rectorships. On the college portals five lines were inscribed:

"The world is supported by four things: the learning of the wise, the justice of the great, the prayers of the good, and the valor of the brave." [15] Women shared freely in the cultural life; we know the names of feminine savants of Moorish Granada. Education, however, did not prevent the ladies from stirring their men not only to swelling passions but to chivalric devotion and displays. Said a gallant of the time: "The women are distinguished for the symmetry of their figures, the gracefulness of their bodies, the length and waviness of their hair, the whiteness of their teeth, the pleasing lightness of their movements . . . the charm of their conversation, and the perfume of their breath." [16] Personal cleanliness and public sanitation were more advanced than in contemporary Christendom. Dress and manners were splendid, and tournaments or pageants brightened festive days. Morals were easy, violence was not rare, but Moorish generosity and honor won Christian praise. "The reputation of the citizens" of Granada "for trustworthiness," said a Spanish historian, "was such that their bare word was more relied on than a written contract is among ourselves." [17] Amid these high developments the growth of luxury sapped the vigor of the nation, and internal discord invited external attack.

Christian Spain, slowly consolidating its kingdoms and increasing its wealth, looked with envious hostility upon this prosperous enclave, whose religion taunted Christianity as an infidel polytheism, and whose ports offered dangerous openings to an infidel power; moreover, those fertile Andalusian fields might atone for many a barren acre in the north. Only because Catholic Spain was divided among factions and kings did Granada retain its liberty. Even so the proud principality agreed (1457) to send annual tribute to Castile. When a reckless emir, Ali abu-al-Hasan, refused to continue this bribe to peace (1466), Henry IV was too busy with debauchery to compel obedience. But Ferdinand and Isabella, soon after their accession to the throne of Castile, sent envoys to demand resumption of the tribute. With fatal audacity Ali replied: "Tell your sovereigns that the kings of Granada who paid tribute are dead. Our mint now coins nothing but sword blades!" [18] Unaware that Ferdinand had more iron in him than was in the Moorish mint, and claiming provocation by Christian border raids, abu-al-Hasan took by assault the Christian frontier town of Zahara, and drove all its inhabitants into Granada to be sold as slaves (1481). The Marquis of Cádiz retaliated by sacking the Moorish stronghold of Alama (1482). The conquest of Granada had begun.

Love complicated war. Abu-al-Hasan developed such an infatuation for one of his slaves that his wife, the Sultana Ayesha, roused the populace to depose him and crown her son abu-'Abdallāh, known to the West as Boabdil (1482). Abu-al-Hasan fled to Málaga. A Spanish army marched to besiege Málaga; it was almost annihilated in the mountain passes of the Ajarquia range by troops still loyal to the fallen emir. Jealous of his father's martial exploits, Boabdil led an army out from Granada to attack a Christian force near Lucena. He fought bravely, but was defeated and taken prisoner. He obtained his release by promising to aid the Christians against his father, and to pay the Spanish government 12,000 ducats a year. In the meantime his uncle Abu-Abd-Allahi, known as Az-Zaghral (the Valiant), had made himself emir of Granada. A three-cornered civil war ensued among uncle, father, and son for the Granadine throne. The father died, the son seized the Alhambra, the uncle retired to Guadix, whence he emerged repeatedly to attack Spaniards wherever he could find them. Stirred to imitation, Boabdil repudiated pledge and tribute, and prepared his capital to resist inevitable assault.

Ferdinand and Isabella deployed 30,000 men to devastate the plains that grew Granada's food. Mills, granaries, farm houses, vineyards, olive and orange groves were destroyed. Málaga was besieged to prevent its receiving or sending supplies for Granada; it held out until its population had consumed all available horses, dogs, and cats, and were dying by hundreds of starvation or disease. Ferdinand forced its unconditional surrender, condemned the 12,000 survivors to slavery, but allowed the rich to ransom themselves by yielding up all their possessions. Az-Zaghral submitted. The entire province of Granada outside its capital was now in Christian hands.

The Catholic sovereigns built around the beleaguered citadel a veritable city for their armies, called it Santa Fé, and waited for starvation to deliver the "pride of Andalusia" to their mercy. Moorish cavaliers rode out from Granada and dared Spanish knights to single battle; the knights responded with equal gallantry; but Ferdinand, finding that his best warriors were being killed one by one on this chivalric plan, put an end to the game. Boabdil led out his troops in a forlorn sally, but they were beaten back. Appeals for help were sent to the sultans of Turkey and Egypt, but no help came; Islam was as divided as Christendom.

On November 25, 1491, Boabdil signed terms of capitulation that did rare honor to the conquerors. The people of Granada were to keep their property, language, dress, religion, ritual; they were to be judged by their own laws and magistrates; no taxes were to be imposed till after three years, and then only such as Moslem rulers had levied. The city was to be occupied by the Spanish, but all Moors who wished to leave it might do so, and transportation would be provided for those who wished to cross to Moslem Africa.

Nevertheless the Granadines protested Boabdil's surrender. Insurrection so threatened him that he turned the keys of the city over to Ferdinand (January 2, 1492), and rode through the Christian lines, with his relatives and fifty horsemen, to the little mountain principality which he was to rule as a vassal of Castile. From the crag over which he passed he turned to take a last look at the wonderful city that he had lost; that summit is still called El Ultimo Sospiro del Moro—the Last Sigh of the Moor. His mother reproved him for his tears: "You do well to weep like a woman for what you could not defend as a man." [19]

Meanwhile the Spanish army marched into Granada. Cardinal Mendoza raised a great silver cross over the Alhambra, and Ferdinand and Isabella knelt in the city square to give thanks to the God who after 781 years had evicted Islam from Spain.

III. FERDINAND AND ISABELLA

The century between the death of Henry of Trastamara (1379) and the accession of Ferdinand to the throne of Aragon was a fallow time for Spain. A series of weak rulers allowed the nobles to disorder the land with their strife; government was negligent and corrupt; private vengeance was uncurbed; civil war was so frequent that the roads were unsafe for commerce, and the fields were so often despoiled by armies that the peasants left them untilled. The long reign of John II (1406–54) of Castile, who loved music and poetry too much to care for the chores of state, was followed by the disastrous tenure of Henry IV, who by his administrative incompetence, his demoralization of the currency, and his squandering of revenue on favored parasites, earned the title of Enrique el Impotente. He willed his throne to Juana, whom he called his daughter; the scornful nobles denied his parentage and potency, and forced him to name his sister Isabella as his successor. But at his death (1474) he reaffirmed Juana's legitimacy and her right to rule. It was out of this paralyzing confusion that Ferdinand and Isabella forged the order and government that made Spain for a century the strongest state in Europe.

The diplomats prepared the achievement by persuading Isabella, eighteen, to marry her cousin Ferdinand, seventeen (1469). Bride and bridegroom were both descended from Henry of Trastamara. Ferdinand was already King of Sicily; on the death of his father he would be also King of Aragon; the marriage, therefore, wed three states into a powerful kingdom. Paul II withheld the papal bull needed to legalize the marriage of cousins; the requisite document was forged by Ferdinand, his father, and the archbishop of Barcelona;[20] after the *fait* had been *accompli* a genuine bull was obtained from Pope Sixtus IV. A more substantial difficulty lay in the poverty of the bride, whose brother refused to recognize the marriage, and of the bridegroom, whose father, immersed in war, could not afford a royal ceremony. A Jewish lawyer smoothed the course of true politics with a loan of 20,000

Fig. 25—HANS HOLBEIN THE YOUNGER: *Edward VI, aged six*. The Metropolitan Museum of Art, New York

PAGE 844

Fig. 26—HANS HOLBEIN THE YOUNGER: *Family of the Artist*. Museum, Basel

PAGE 840

Fig. 27—LUCAS CRANACH: *Self-Portrait*. Uffizi Gallery, Florence

PAGE 837

Fig. 28—TITIAN: *Paul III and His Nephews.* National Museum, Naples

PAGE 921

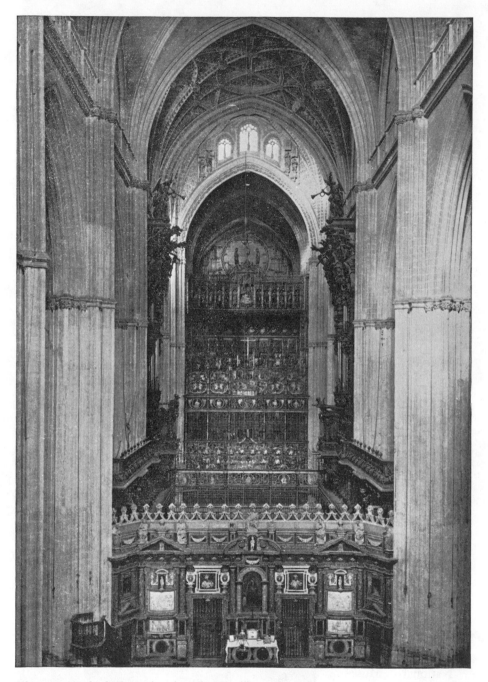

Fig. 29—*Cathedral* (main chapel), Seville

Fig. 30—*Cathedral*, Seville

Fig. 31—Hans Holbein the Younger: *Henry VIII*. Corsini Gallery, Rome

PAGE 573

Fig. 32—After Holbein: *Thomas More and His Family*. National Portrait Gallery, London

PAGE 842

Fig. 33—PIETER BRUEGHEL THE ELDER: *Hunters in the Snow*. Kunsthistorisches Museum, Vienna

PAGE 834

Fig. 34—HANS HOLBEIN THE YOUNGER: *Portrait of Bonifacius Amerbach*. Museum, Basel

PAGE 841

Fig. 35—ANONYMOUS PAINTER OF THE SIXTEENTH CENTURY: *Rabelais*. Bibliothèque Publique et Universitaire, Geneva

PAGE 795

Fig. 36—TITLE PAGE OF VESALIUS' *De humani corporis fabrica*

PAGE 871

sueldos, which Isabella repaid when she became Queen of Castile (1474).*

Her right to the throne was challenged by Affonso V of Portugal, who had married Juana. War decided the issue at Toro, where Ferdinand led the Castilians to victory (1476). Three years later he inherited Aragon; all Spain except Granada and Navarre was now under one government. Isabella remained only Queen of Castile; Ferdinand ruled Aragon, Sardinia, and Sicily, and shared in ruling Castile. The internal administration of Castile was reserved to Isabella, but royal charters and decrees had to be signed by both sovereigns, and the new coinage bore both the regal heads. Their complementary qualities made Ferdinand and Isabella the most effective royal couple in history.

Isabella was incomparably beautiful, said her courtiers—that is, moderately fair; of medium stature, blue eyes, hair of chestnut brown verging on red. She had more schooling than Ferdinand, with a less acute and less merciless intelligence. She could patronize poets and converse with cautious philosophers, but she preferred the company of priests. She chose the sternest moralists for her confessors and guides. Wedded to an unfaithful husband, she seems to have sustained full marital fidelity to the end; living in an age as morally fluid as our own, she was a model of sexual modesty. Amid corrupt officials and devious diplomats, she herself remained frank, direct, and incorruptible. Her mother had reared her in strict orthodoxy and piety; Isabella developed this to the edge of asceticism, and was as harsh and cruel in suppressing heresy as she was kind and gracious in everything else. She was the soul of tenderness to her children, and a pillar of loyalty to her friends. She gave abundantly to churches, monasteries, and hospitals. Her orthodoxy did not deter her from condemning the immorality of some Renaissance popes.[22] She excelled in both physical and moral bravery; she withstood, subdued, and disciplined powerful nobles, bore quietly the most desolating bereavements, and faced with contagious courage the hardships and dangers of war. She thought it wise to maintain a queenly dignity in public, and pushed royal display to costly extravagance in robes and gems; in private she dressed simply, ate frugally, and amused her leisure by making delicate embroideries for the churches she loved. She labored conscientiously in the tasks of government, took the initiative in wholesome reforms, administered justice with perhaps undue severity; but she was resolved to raise her realm from lawless disorder to a law-abiding peace. Foreign contemporaries like Paolo Giovio, Guicciardini, and the Chevalier Bayard ranked her among the ablest sover-

---

* The unit of Castilian currency in the fifteenth century was the copper *maravedi;* 18.7 of these equaled an Aragonese *sueldo;* 34 made a silver *real;* 374 made a gold *escudo* or ducat. The fluctuations of currencies make it especially hazardous to suggest modern equivalents for these coins. But as the wage of a day laborer in fifteenth-century Spain was some six *maravedis* per day, we shall hardly exaggerate if we equate the *maravedi* with $.067 in the United States currency of 1954, the *sueldo* with $1.20, the *real* with $2.28, and the *escudo* with $25.00.[21]

eigns of the age, and likened her to the stately heroines of antiquity. Her sub-jects worshiped her, while they bore impatiently with the King.

The Castilians could not forgive Ferdinand for being a foreigner—i.e., an Aragonese; and they found many faults in him even while they gloried in his successes as statesman, diplomat, and warrior. They contrasted his cold and reserved temperament with the warm kindliness of the Queen, his calculated indirectness with her straightforward candor, his parsimony with her generosity, his illiberal treatment of his aides with her openhanded rewards for services, his extramarital gallantries with her quiet continence. Probably they did not resent his establishment of the Inquisition, nor his use of their religious feelings as a weapon of war; they applauded the campaign against heresy, the conquest of Granada, the expulsion of unconverted Jews and Moors; they loved most in him what posterity would least admire. We hear of no protest against the severity of his laws—cutting out the tongue for blasphemy, burning alive for sodomy.[23] They noted that he could be just, even lenient, when it did not hinder personal advantage or national policy; that he could lead his army dauntlessly and cleverly, though he preferred to match minds in negotiation rather than men in battle; and that his parsimony financed not personal luxuries but expensive undertakings for the aggrandizement of Spain. They must have approved of his abstemious habits, his constancy in adversity, his moderation in prosperity, his discerning choice of aides, his tireless devotion to government, his pursuit of farseen ends with flexible tenacity and cautious means. They forgave his duplicity as a diplomat, his frequent faithlessness to his word; were not all other rulers trying by like methods to cozen him and swindle Spain? "The King of France," he said grimly, "complains that I have twice deceived him. He lies, the fool; I have deceived him ten times, and more."[24] Machiavelli carefully studied Ferdinand's career, relished his cunning, praised "his deeds . . . all great and some extraordinary," and called him "the foremost king in Christendom."[25] And Guicciardini wrote: "What a wide difference there was between the sayings and doings of this prince, and how deeply and secretly he laid his measures!"[26] Some accounted Ferdinand lucky, but in truth his good fortune lay in careful preparation for events and prompt seizure of opportunities. When the balance was struck between his virtues and his crimes, it appeared that by fair means and foul he had raised Spain from a motley of impotent fragments to a unity and power that in the next generation made her the dictator of Europe.

He co-operated with Isabella in restoring security of life and property in Castile; in reviving the Santa Hermandad, or Holy Brotherhood, as a local militia to maintain order; in ending robbery on the highways and sexual intrigues at the court; in reorganizing the judiciary and codifying the laws; in reclaiming state lands recklessly ceded to favorites by previous kings; and in exacting from the nobles full obedience to the crown; here too, as in France and England, feudal freedom and chaos had to give way to the centralized order of absolute monarchy. The municipal communes likewise surrendered their privileges; the provincial *cortes* rarely met, and then chiefly to vote funds to the government; a weak-rooted democracy languished and died under an adamantine king. Even the Spanish Church, so precious to *los reyes católicos*,* was shorn of some of its wealth and all of its civil jurisdiction; the morals of the clergy were rigorously reformed by Isabella; Pope Sixtus IV was compelled to yield to the government the right to appoint the higher dignitaries of the Church in Spain; and able ecclesiastics like Pedro Gonzáles de Mendoza and Ximenes de Cisneros were promoted to be at once arch-bishops of Toledo and prime ministers of the state.

Cardinal Ximenes was as positive and powerful a character as the King. Born of a family noble but poor, he was dedicated in childhood to the Church. At the University of Salamanca he earned by the age of twenty the doctoral degrees in both civil and canon law. For some years he served as vicar and administrator for Mendoza in the diocese of Sigüenza. Successful but unhappy, caring little for honors or possessions, he entered the strictest monastic order in Spain—the Observantine Franciscans. Only asceticism delighted him: he slept on the ground or a hard floor, fasted frequently, flogged himself, and wore a hair shirt next to his skin. In 1492 the pious Isabella chose this emaciated cenobite as her chaplain and confessor. He accepted on condition that he might continue to live in his monastery and conform to the rigid Franciscan rule. The order made him its provincial head, and at his bidding submitted to arduous reforms. When Isabella nominated him archbishop of Toledo (1495) he refused to accept, but after six months of resistance he yielded to a papal bull commanding him to serve. He was now nearly sixty, and seems to have sincerely wished to live as a monk. As primate of Spain and chief of the royal council he continued his austerities; under the splendid robes required by his office he wore the coarse Franciscan gown, and under this the hair shirt as before.[27] Against the opposition of high ecclesiastics, but supported by the Queen, he applied to all monastic orders the reforms that he had exacted from his own. It was as if St. Francis, shorn of his humility, had suddenly been endowed with the powers and capacities of Bernard and Dominic.

It could not have pleased this somber saint to find two unconverted Jews high in favor at the court. One of Isabella's most trusted counselors was Abraham Senior; he and Isaac Abrabanel collected the revenue for Ferdinand, and organized the financing of the Granada war. The King and Queen were at this time especially concerned about the *Conversos*. They had hoped

---

* "The Catholic Sovereigns"—a title conferred upon Ferdinand and Isabella by Pope Alexander VI in 1404.

that time would make these converts sincere Christians; Isabella had had a catechism specially prepared for their instruction; yet many of them secretly maintained their ancient faith, and transmitted it to their children. Catholic dislike of the unbaptized Jews subsided for a time, while resentment against the "New Christians" rose. Riots against them broke out in Toledo (1467), Valladolid (1470), Córdova (1472), and Segovia (1474). The religious problem had become also racial; and the young King and Queen pondered means of reducing the disorderly medley and conflict of peoples, languages, and creeds to homogeneous unity and social peace. They thought that no better means were available for these ends than to restore the Inquisition in Spain.

IV. THE METHODS OF THE INQUISITION

We are today so uncertain and diverse in our opinions as to the origin and destiny of the world and man that we have ceased, in most countries, to punish people for differing from us in their religious beliefs. Our present intolerance is rather for those who question our economic or political principles, and we explain our frightened dogmatism on the ground that any doubt thrown upon these cherished assumptions endangers our national solidarity and survival. Until the middle of the seventeenth century Christians, Jews, and Moslems were more acutely concerned with religion than we are today; their theologies were their most prized and confident possessions; and they looked upon those who rejected these creeds as attacking the foundations of social order and the very significance of human life. Each group was hardened by certainty into intolerance, and branded the others as infidels.

The Inquisition developed most readily among persons whose religious tenets had been least affected by education and travel, and whose reason was most subject to custom and imagination. Nearly all medieval Christians, through childhood schooling and surroundings, believed that the Bible had been dictated in every word by God, and that the Son of God had directly established the Christian Church. It seemed to follow, from these premises, that God wished all nations to be Christian, and that the practice of non-Christian—certainly of anti-Christian—religions must be a crass insult to the Deity. Moreover, since any substantial heresy must merit eternal punishment, its prosecutors could believe (and many seem to have sincerely believed) that in snuffing out a heretic they were saving his potential converts, and perhaps himself, from everlasting hell.

Probably Isabella, who lived in the very odor of theologians, shared these views. Ferdinand, being a hardened man of the world, may have doubted some of them; but he was apparently convinced that uniformity of religious belief would make Spain easier to rule, and stronger to strike its enemies. At his request and Isabella's, Pope Sixtus IV issued a bull (November 1, 1478) authorizing them to appoint six priests, holding degrees in theology and canon law, as an inquisitorial board to investigate and punish heresy. The remarkable feature of this bull was its empowerment of the Spanish sovereigns to nominate the inquisitorial personnel, who in earlier forms of the Inquisition had been chosen by the provincial heads of the Dominican or Franciscan orders. Here for three generations, as in Protestant Germany and England in the next century, religion became subject to the state. Technically, however, the inquisitors were only nominated by the sovereigns, and were then appointed by the pope; the authority of the inquisitors derived from this papal sanction; the institution remained ecclesiastical, an organ of the Church, which was an organ of the state. The government was to pay the expenses, and receive the net income, of the Inquisition. The sovereigns kept detailed watch over its operations, and appeal could be made to them from its decisions. Of all Ferdinand's instruments of rule, this became his favorite. His motives were not primarily financial; he profited from the confiscated property of the condemned, but he refused tempting bribes from rich victims to overrule the inquisitors. The aim was to unify Spain.

The inquisitors were authorized to employ ecclesiastical and secular aides as investigators and executive officers. After 1483 the entire organization was put under a governmental agency, the Concejo de la Suprema y General Inquisicion, usually termed the Suprema. The jurisdiction of the Inquisition extended to all Christians in Spain; it did not touch unconverted Jews or Moors; its terrors were directed at converts suspected of relapsing into Judaism or Mohammedanism, and at Christians charged with heresy; till 1492 the unchristened Jew was safer than the baptized. Priests, monks, and friars claimed exemption from the Inquisition, but their claim was denied; the Jesuits resisted its jurisdiction for half a century, but they too were overcome. The only limit to the power of the Suprema was the authority of the sovereigns; and in later centuries even this was ignored. The Inquisition demanded, and usually received, co-operation from all secular officials.

The Inquisition made its own laws and procedural code. Before setting up its tribunal in a town, it issued to the people, through the parish pulpits, an "Edict of Faith" requiring all who knew of any heresy to reveal it to the inquisitors. Everyone was encouraged to be a delator, to inform against his neighbors, his friends, his relatives. (In the sixteenth century, however, the accusation of near relatives was not allowed.) Informants were promised full secrecy and protection; a solemn anathema—i.e., excommunication and curse —was laid upon all who knew and concealed a heretic. If a baptized Jew still harbored hopes of a Messiah to come; if he kept the dietary laws of the Mosaic code; if he observed the Sabbath as a day of worship and rest, or changed his linen for that day; if he celebrated in any way any Jewish holy day; if he circumcised any of his children, or gave any of them a Hebrew name, or blessed them without making the sign of the cross; if he prayed with motions of the head, or repeated a Biblical psalm without adding a Gloria; if he turned his face to the wall when dying: these and the like were described by the inquisitors as signs of secret heresy, to be reported at once to the tribunal.[28] Within a "Term of Grace" any person who felt guilty of heresy might come and confess it; he would be fined or assigned a penance, but would be forgiven, on condition that he should reveal any knowledge he might have of other heretics.

The inquisitors seem to have sifted with care the evidence collected by informers and investigators. When the tribunal was unanimously convinced of a person's guilt it issued a warrant for his arrest. The accused was kept incommunicado; no one but agents of the Inquisition was allowed to speak with him; no relative might visit him. Usually he was chained.[29] He was required to bring his own bed and clothing, and to pay all the expenses of his incarceration and sustenance. If he did not offer sufficient cash for this purpose, enough of his property was sold at auction to meet the costs. The remainder of his goods was sequestrated by Inquisition officers lest it be hidden or disposed of to escape confiscation. In most cases some of it was sold to maintain such of the victim's family as could not work.

When the arrested person was brought to trial the tribunal, having already judged him guilty, laid upon him the burden of proving his innocence. The trial was secret and private, and the defendant had to swear never to reveal any facts about it in case he should be released. No witnesses were adduced against him, none was named to him; the inquisitors excused this procedure as necessary to protect their informants. The accused was not at first told what charges had been brought against him; he was merely invited to confess his own derelictions from orthodox belief and worship, and to betray all persons whom he suspected of heresy. If his confession satisfied the tribunal, he might receive any punishment short of death. If he refused to confess he was permitted to choose advocates to defend him; meanwhile he was kept in solitary confinement. In many instances he was tortured to elicit a confession. Usually the case was allowed to drag on for months, and the solitary confinement in chains often sufficed to secure any confession desired.

Torture was applied only after a majority of the tribunal had voted for it on the ground that guilt had been made probable, though not certain, by the evidence. Often the torture so decreed was postponed in the hope that dread of it would induce confession. The inquisitors appear to have sincerely believed that torture was a favor to a defendant already accounted guilty, since it might earn him, by confession, a slighter penalty than otherwise; even if he should, after confession, be condemned to death, he could enjoy priestly absolution to save him from hell. However, confession of guilt was not enough, torture might also be applied to compel a confessing defendant to name his associates in heresy or crime. Contradictory witnesses might be tortured to find out which was telling the truth; slaves might be tortured to bring out testimony against their masters. No limits of age could save the victims; girls of thirteen and women of eighty were subjected to the rack; but the rules of the Spanish Inquisition usually forbade the torture of nursing women, or persons with weak hearts, or those accused of minor heresies, such as sharing the widespread opinion that fornication was only a venial sin. Torture was to be kept short of permanently maiming the victim, and was to be stopped whenever the attendant physician so ordered. It was to be administered only in the presence of the inquisitors in charge of the case, and a notary, a recording secretary, and a representative of the local bishop. Methods varied with time and place. The victim might have his hands tied behind his back and be suspended by them; he might be bound into immobility and then have water trickle down his throat till he nearly choked; he might have cords tied around his arms and legs and tightened till they cut through the flesh to the bone. We are told that the tortures used by the Spanish Inquisition were milder than those employed by the earlier papal Inquisition, or by the secular courts of the age.[30] The main torture was prolonged imprisonment.

The Inquisition tribunal was not only prosecutor, judge, and jury; it also issued decrees on faith and morals, and established a gradation of penalties. In many cases it was merciful, excusing part of the punishment because of the penitent's age, ignorance, poverty, intoxication, or generally good reputation. The mildest penalty was a reprimand. More grievous was compulsion to make a public abjuration of heresy—which left even the innocent branded to the end of his days. Usually the convicted penitent was required to attend Mass regularly, wearing the "sanbenito"—a garment marked with a flaming cross. He might be paraded through the streets stripped to the waist and bearing the insignia of his offense. He and his descendants might be barred from public office forever. He might be banished from his city, rarely from Spain. He might be scourged with one or two hundred lashes to "the limit of safety"; this was applied to women as well as men. He might be imprisoned, or condemned to the galleys—which Ferdinand recommended as more useful to the state. He might pay a substantial fine, or have his property confiscated. In several instances dead men were accused of heresy, were tried post-mortem, and were condemned to confiscation, in which case the heirs forfeited his bequests. Informers against dead heretics were offered 30 to 50 per cent of the proceeds. Families fearful of such retroactive judgments sometimes paid "compositions" to the inquisitors as insurance against confiscation of their legacies. Wealth became a peril to its owner, a temptation to informers, inquisitors, and the government. As money flowed into the coffers of the

Inquisition its officials became less zealous to preserve the orthodox faith than to acquire gold, and corruption flourished piously.[81]

The ultimate punishment was burning at the stake. This was reserved for persons who, judged guilty of serious heresy, failed to confess before judgment was pronounced, and for those who, having confessed in time, and having been "reconciled" or forgiven, had relapsed into heresy. The Inquisition itself professed that it never killed, but merely surrendered the condemned person to the secular authorities; however, it knew that the criminal law made burning at the stake mandatory in all convictions for major and impenitent heresy. The official presence of ecclesiastics at the auto-da-fé frankly revealed the responsibility of the Church. The "act of faith" was not merely the burning, it was the whole impressive and terrible ceremony of sentence and execution. Its purpose was not only to terrify potential offenders, but to edify the people as with a foretaste of the Last Judgment.

At first the procedure was simple: those condemned to death were marched to the public plaza, they were bound in tiers on a pyre, the inquisitors sat in state on a platform facing it, a last appeal for confessions was made, the sentences were read, the fires were lit, the agony was consummated. But as burnings became more frequent and suffered some loss in their psychological power, the ceremony was made more complex and awesome, and was staged with all the care and cost of a major theatrical performance. When possible it was timed to celebrate the accession, marriage, or visit of a Spanish king, queen, or prince. Municipal and state officials, Inquisition personnel, local priests and monks, were invited—in effect required—to attend. On the eve of the execution these dignitaries joined in a somber procession through the main streets of the city to deposit the green cross of the Inquisition upon the altar of the cathedral or principal church. A final effort was made to secure confessions from the condemned; many then yielded, and had their sentences commuted to imprisonment for a term or for life. On the following morning the prisoners were led through dense crowds to a city square: impostors, blasphemers, bigamists, heretics, relapsed converts; in later days, Protestants; sometimes the procession included effigies of absent condemnees, or boxes carrying the bones of persons condemned after death. In the square, on one or several elevated stages, sat the inquisitors, the secular and monastic clergy, and the officials of town and state; now and then the King himself presided. A sermon was preached, after which all present were commanded to recite an oath of obedience to the Holy Office of the Inquisition, and a pledge to denounce and prosecute heresy in all its forms and everywhere. Then, one by one, the prisoners were led before the tribunal, and their sentences were read. We must not imagine any brave defiances; probably, at this stage, every prisoner was near to spiritual exhaustion and physical collapse. Even now he might save his life by confession; in that case the Inquisition usually contented itself with scourging him, confiscating his goods, and imprisoning him for life. If the confession was withheld till after sentence had been pronounced, the prisoner earned the mercy of being strangled before being burned; and as such last-minute confessions were frequent, burning alive was relatively rare. Those who were judged guilty of major heresy, but denied it to the end, were (till 1725) refused the last sacraments of the Church, and were, by the intention of the Inquisition, abandoned to everlasting hell. The "reconciled" were now taken back to prison; the impenitent were "relaxed" to the secular arm, with a pious caution that no blood should be shed. These were led out from the city between throngs that had gathered from leagues around for this holiday spectacle. Arrived at the place prepared for execution, the confessed were strangled, then burned; the recalcitrant were burned alive. The fires were fed till nothing remained of the dead but ashes, which were scattered over fields and streams. The priests and spectators returned to their altars and their homes, convinced that a propitiatory offering had been made to a God insulted by heresy. Human sacrifice had been restored.

V. PROGRESS OF THE INQUISITION: 1480–1516

The first inquisitors were appointed by Ferdinand and Isabella in September 1480, for the district of Seville. Many Sevillian *Conversos* fled to the countryside, and sought sanctuary with feudal lords. These were inclined to protect them, but the inquisitors threatened the barons with excommunication and confiscation, and the refugees were surrendered. In the city itself some *Conversos* planned armed resistance; the plot was betrayed; the implicated persons were arrested; soon the dungeons were full. Trials followed with angry haste, and the first auto-da-fé of the Spanish Inquisition was celebrated on February 6, 1481, with the burning of six men and women. By November 4 of that year 298 had been burned; seventy-nine had been imprisoned for life.

In 1483, at the nomination and request of Ferdinand and Isabella, Pope Sixtus IV appointed a Dominican friar, Tomás de Torquemada, inquisitor-general for all of Spain. He was a sincere and incorruptible fanatic, scorning luxury, working feverishly, rejoicing in his opportunity to serve Christ by hounding heresy. He reproved inquisitors for lenience, reversed many acquittals, and demanded that the rabbis of Toledo, on pain of death, should inform on all Judaizing *Conversos*. Pope Alexander VI, who had at first praised his devotion to his tasks, became alarmed at his severity, and ordered him (1494) to share his powers with two other "inquisitors general." Torquemada overrode these colleagues, maintained a resolute leadership, and made the Inquisition an *imperium in imperio*, rivaling the power of the sovereigns. Under his prodding the Inquisition at Ciudad Real in two years (1483–84) burned fifty-two persons, confiscated the property of 220 fugitives, and punished 183 penitents. Transferring their headquarters to Toledo, the inquisitors within a year arrested 750 baptized Jews, confiscated a fifth of their goods, and sentenced them to march in penitential processions on six Fridays, flogging themselves with hempen cords. Two further autos-da-fé in that year (1486) at Toledo disciplined 1,650 penitents. Like labors were performed in Valladolid, Guadalupe, and other cities of Castile.

Aragon resisted the Inquisition with forlorn courage. At Teruel the magistrates closed the gates in the face of the inquisitors. These laid an interdict upon the city; Ferdinand stopped the municipal salaries, and sent an army to enforce obedience; the environing peasants, always hostile to the city, ran to the support of the Inquisition, which promised them release from all rents and debts due to persons convicted of heresy. Teruel yielded, and Ferdinand authorized the inquisitors to banish anyone whom they suspected of having aided the opposition. In Saragossa many "Old Christians" joined the "New Christians" in protesting against the entry of the Inquisition; when, nevertheless, it set up its tribunal there, some *Conversos* assassinated an inquisitor (1485). It was a mortal blunder, for the shocked citizens thronged the streets crying "Burn the *Conversos!*" The archbishop calmed the mob with a promise of speedy justice. Nearly all the conspirators were caught and executed; one leaped to his death from the tower in which he was confined; another broke a glass lamp, swallowed the fragments, and was found dead in his cell. In Valencia the Cortes refused to allow the inquisitors to function; Ferdinand ordered his agents to arrest all obstructors; Valencia gave way. In support of the Inquisition the King violated one after another of the traditional liberties of Aragon; the combination of Church and monarchy, of excommunications and royal armies, proved too strong for any single city or province to resist. In 1488 there were 983 condemnations for heresy in Valencia alone, and a hundred men were burned.

How did the popes view this use of the Inquisition as an instrument of the state? Doubtless resenting such secular control, moved, presumably, by humane sentiment, and not insensitive to the heavy fees paid for dispensations from Inquisition sentences, several popes tried to check its excesses, and gave occasional protection to its victims. In 1482 Sixtus IV issued a bull which, if implemented, would have ended the Inquisition in Aragon. He complained that the inquisitors were showing more lust for gold than zeal for religion; that they had imprisoned, tortured, and burned faithful Christians on the dubious evidence of enemies or slaves. He commanded that in future no inquisitor should act without the presence and concurrence of some representative of the local bishop; that the names and allegations of the accusers should be made known to the accused; that the prisoners of the Inquisition should be lodged only in episcopal jails; that those complaining of injustice should be allowed to appeal to the Holy See, and all further action in the case should be suspended until judgment should be rendered on the appeal; that all persons convicted of heresy should receive absolution if they confessed and repented, and thereafter should be free from prosecution or molestation on that charge. All past proceedings contrary to these provisions were declared null and void, and all future violators of them were to incur excommunication. It was an enlightened decree, and its thoroughness suggests its sincerity. Yet we must note that it was confined to Aragon, whose *Conversos* had paid for it liberally.[32] When Ferdinand defied it, arrested the agent who had procured it, and bade the inquisitors go on as before, Sixtus took no further action in the matter, except that five months later he suspended the operation of the bull.[33]

The desperate *Conversos* poured money into Rome, appealing for dispensations and absolutions from the summons or sentences of the Inquisition. The money was accepted, the dispensations were given, the Spanish inquisitors, protected by Ferdinand, ignored them; and the popes, needing the friendship of Ferdinand and the annates of Spain, did not insist. Pardons were paid for, issued, and then revoked. Occasionally the popes asserted their authority, citing inquisitors to Rome to answer charges of misconduct. Alexander VI tried to moderate the severity of the tribunal. Julius II ordered the trial of the inquisitor Lucero for malfeasance, and excommunicated the inquisitors of Toledo. The gentle and scholarly Leo, however, denounced as a reprehensible heresy the notion that a heretic should not be burned.[34]

How did the people of Spain react to the Inquisition? The upper classes and the educated minority faintly opposed it; the Christian populace usually approved it.[35] The crowds that gathered at the autos-da-fé showed little sympathy, often active hostility, to the victims; in some places they tried to kill them lest confession should let them escape the pyre. Christians flocked to buy at auction the confiscated goods of the condemned.

How numerous were the victims? Llorente * estimated them, from 1480 to 1488, at 8,800 burned, 96,494 punished; from 1480 to 1808, at 31,912 burned, 291,450 heavily penanced. These figures were mostly guesses, and are now generally rejected by Protestant historians as extreme exaggerations.[36] A Catholic historian reckons 2,000 burnings between 1480 and 1504, and 2,000 more to 1758.[37] Isabella's secretary, Hernando de Pulgar, calculated the burnings at 2,000 before 1490. Zurita, a secretary of the Inquisi-

* Juan Antonio Llorente, a Spanish priest, was general secretary of the Inquisition from 1789 to 1801. In 1809 he was commissioned by Joseph Bonaparte to examine the archives of the Inquisition and write its history. He left Spain with the retreating French, and published his history of the Inquisition in Paris in 1817.

tion, boasted that it had burned 4,000 in Seville alone. There were victims, of course, in most Spanish cities, even in Spanish dependencies like the Baleares, Sardinia, Sicily, the Netherlands, America. The rate of burnings diminished after 1500. But no statistics can convey the terror in which the Spanish mind lived in those days and nights. Men and women, even in the secrecy of their families, had to watch every word they uttered, lest some stray criticism should lead them to an Inquisition jail. It was a mental oppression unparalleled in history.

Did the Inquisition succeed? Yes, in attaining its declared purpose—to rid Spain of open heresy. The idea that the persecution of beliefs is always ineffective is a delusion; it crushed the Albigensians and Huguenots in France, the Catholics in Elizabethan England, the Christians in Japan. It stamped out in the sixteenth century the small groups that favored Protestantism in Spain. On the other hand, it probably strengthened Protestantism in Germany, Scandinavia, and England by arousing in their peoples a vivid fear of what might happen to them if Catholicism were restored.

It is difficult to say what share the Inquisition had in ending the brilliant period of Spanish history from Columbus to Velásquez (1492–1660). The peak of that epoch came with Cervantes (1547–1616) and Lope de Vega (1562–1635), after the Inquisition had flourished in Spain for a hundred years. The Inquisition was an effect, as well as a cause, of the intense and exclusive Catholicism of the Spanish people; and that religious mood had grown during centuries of struggle against "infidel" Moors. The exhaustion of Spain by the wars of Charles V and Philip II, and the weakening of the Spanish economy by the victories of Britain on the sea and the mercantile policies of the Spanish government, may have had more to do with the decline of Spain than the terrors of the Inquisition. The executions for witchcraft, in northern Europe and New England, showed in Protestant peoples a spirit akin to that of the Spanish Inquisition—which, strange to say, sensibly treated witchcraft as a delusion to be pitied and cured rather than punished. Both the Inquisition and the witch-burning were expressions of an age afflicted with homicidal certainty in theology, as the patriotic massacres of our era may be due in part to homicidal certainty in ethnic or political theory. We must try to understand such movements in terms of their time, but they seem to us now the most unforgivable of historic crimes. A supreme and unchallengeable faith is a deadly enemy to the human mind.

VI. *IN EXITU ISRAEL*[88]

The Inquisition was intended to frighten all Christians, new or old, into at least external orthodoxy, in the hope that heresy would be blighted in the bud, and that the second or third generation of baptized Jews would forget the Judaism of their ancestors. There was no intent to let baptized Jews leave Spain; when they tried to emigrate, Ferdinand and the Inquisition forbade it. But what of the unbaptized Jews? Some 235,000 of them remained in Christian Spain. How could the religious unity of the nation be effected if these were allowed to practice and profess their faith? Torquemada thought it impossible, and recommended their compulsory conversion or their banishment.

Ferdinand hesitated. He knew the economic value of Hebrew ability in commerce and finance. But he was told that the Jews taunted the *Conversos* and sought to win them back to Judaism, if only secretly. His physician, Ribas Altas, a baptized Jew, was accused of wearing on a pendant from his neck a golden ball containing a representation of himself in the act of desecrating a crucifix; the charge seems incredible, but the physician was burned (1488).[39] Letters were forged in which a Jewish leader in Constantinople advised the head of the Jewish community in Spain to rob and poison Christians as often as possible.[40] A *Converso* was arrested on the charge of having a consecrated wafer in his knapsack; he was tortured again and again until he signed a statement that six *Conversos* and six Jews had killed a Christian child to use its heart in a magic ceremony designed to cause the death of all Christians and the total destruction of Christianity. The confessions of the tortured man contradicted one another, and no child was reported missing; however, four Jews were burned, two of them after having their flesh torn away with red-hot pincers.[41] These and similar accusations may have influenced Ferdinand; in any case they prepared public opinion for the expulsion of all unbaptized Jews from Spain. When Granada surrendered (November 5, 1491), and the industrial and commercial activities of the Moors accrued to Christian Spain, the economic contribution of the unconverted Jews no longer seemed vital. Meanwhile popular fanaticism, inflamed by autos-da-fé and the preaching of the friars, was making social peace impossible unless the government either protected or expelled the Jews.

On March 30, 1492—so crowded a year in Spanish history—Ferdinand and Isabella signed the edict of exile. All unbaptized Jews, of whatever age or condition, were to leave Spain by July 31, and were never to return, on penalty of death. In this brief period they might dispose of their property at whatever price they could obtain. They might take with them movable goods and bills of exchange, but no currency, silver, or gold. Abraham Senior and Isaac Abrabanel offered the sovereigns a large sum to withdraw the edict, but Ferdinand and Isabella refused. No royal accusation was made against the Jews, except their tendency to lure *Conversos* back to Judaism. A supplementary edict required that taxes to the end of the year should be paid on all Jewish property and sales. Debts due from Christians or Moors were to be collected only at maturity, through such agents as the banished creditors might find, or these claims could be sold at a discount to Christian purchasers. In this enforced precipitancy the property of the Jews passed into Christian hands at a small fraction of its value. A house was sold for an ass, a vineyard for a piece of cloth. Some Jews, in despair, burned down their homes (to collect insurance?); others gave them to the municipality. Synagogues were appropriated by Christians and transformed into churches. Jewish cemeteries were turned into pasturage. In a few months the largest part of the riches of the Spanish Jews, accumulated through centuries, melted away. Approximately 50,000 Jews accepted conversion, and were permitted to remain; over 100,000 left Spain in a prolonged and melancholy exodus.

Before departing they married all their children who were over twelve years of age. The young helped the old, the rich succored the poor. The pilgrimage moved on horses or asses, in carts or on foot. At every turn good Christians—clergy and laity—appealed to the exiles to submit to baptism. The rabbis countered by assuring their followers that God would lead them to the promised land by opening a passage through the sea, as He had done for their fathers of old.[42] The emigrants who gathered in Cádiz waited hopefully for the waters to part and let them march dryshod to Africa. Disillusioned, they paid high prices for transport by ship. Storms scattered their fleet of twenty-five vessels; sixteen of these were driven back to Spain, where many desperate Jews accepted baptism as no worse than seasickness. Fifty Jews, shipwrecked near Seville, were imprisoned for two years and then sold as slaves.[43] The thousands who sailed from Gibraltar, Málaga, Valencia, or Barcelona found that in all Christendom only Italy was willing to receive them with humanity.

The most convenient goal of the pilgrims was Portugal. A large population of Jews already existed there, and some had risen to wealth and political position under friendly kings. But John II was frightened by the number of Spanish Jews—perhaps 80,000—who poured in. He granted them a stay of eight months, after which they were to leave. Pestilence broke out among them, and spread to the Christians, who demanded their immediate expulsion. John facilitated the departure of the immigrant Jews by providing ships at low cost; but those who confided themselves to these vessels were subjected to robbery and rape; many were cast upon desolate shores and left to die of starvation or to be captured and enslaved by Moors.[44] One shipload of 250 Jews, being refused at port after port because pestilence still raged among them, wandered at sea for four months. Biscayan pirates seized one vessel, pillaged the passengers, then drove the ships into Málaga, where the priests and magistrates gave the Jews a choice of baptism or starvation.

After fifty of them had died, the authorities provided the survivors with bread and water, and bade them sail for Africa.[45]

When the eight months of grace had expired, John II sold into slavery those Jewish immigrants who still remained in Portugal. Children under fifteen were taken from their parents, and were sent to the St. Thomas Islands to be reared as Christians. As no appeals could move the executors of the decree, some mothers drowned themselves and their children rather than suffer their separation.[46] John's successor, Manuel, gave the Jews a breathing spell: he freed those whom John had enslaved, forbade the preachers to incite the populace against the Jews, and ordered his courts to dismiss as malicious tales all allegations of the murder of Christian children by Jews.[47] But meanwhile Manuel courted Isabella, daughter and heiress of Isabella and Ferdinand, and dreamed of uniting both thrones under one bed. The Catholic sovereigns agreed, on condition that Manuel expel from Portugal all unbaptized Jews, native or immigrant. Loving honors above honor, Manuel consented, and ordered all Jews and Moors in his realm to accept baptism or banishment (1496). Finding that only a few preferred baptism, and loath to disrupt the trades and crafts in which the Jews excelled, he ordered all Jewish children under fifteen to be separated from their parents and forcibly baptized. The Catholic clergy opposed this measure, but it was carried out. "I have seen," reported a bishop, "many children dragged to the font by the hair."[48] Some Jews killed their children, and then themselves, in protest. Manuel grew ferocious; he hindered the departure of Jews, then ordered them to be baptized by force. They were dragged to the churches by the beards of the men and the hair of the women, and many killed themselves on the way. The Portuguese *Conversos* sent a dispatch to Pope Alexander VI begging his intercession; his reply is unknown; it was probably favorable, for Manuel now (May 1497) granted to all forcibly baptized Jews a moratorium of twenty years, during which they were not to be brought before any tribunal on a charge of adhering to Judaism. But the Christians of Portugal resented the economic competition of the Jews, baptized or not; when one Jew questioned a miracle alleged to have occurred in a Lisbon church, the populace tore him to pieces (1506); for three days massacre ran free; 2,000 Jews were killed; hundreds of them were buried alive. Catholic prelates denounced the outrage, and two Dominican friars who had incited the riot were put to death.[49] Otherwise, for a generation, there was almost peace.

From Spain the terrible exodus was complete. But religious unity was not yet achieved: the Moors remained. Granada had been taken, but its Mohammedan population had been guaranteed religious liberty. Archbishop Hernando de Talavera, commissioned to govern Granada, scrupulously observed this compact, and sought to make converts by kindness and justice. Ximenes did not approve such Christianity. He persuaded the Queen that faith need not be kept with infidels, and induced her to decree (1499) that the Moors must become Christians or leave Spain. Going himself to Granada, he overruled Talavera, closed the mosques, made public bonfires of all the Arabic books and manuscripts he could lay his hands on,[50] and supervised wholesale compulsory christenings. The Moors washed the holy water from their children as soon as they were out of the priests' sight. Revolts broke out in the city and the province; they were crushed. By a royal edict of February 12, 1502, all Moslems in Castile and León were given till April 30 to choose between Christianity and exile. The Moors protested that when their forefathers had ruled much of Spain they had given religious liberty, with rare exceptions, to the Christians under their sway,[51] but the sovereigns were not moved. Boys under fourteen and girls under twelve were forbidden to leave Spain with their parents, and feudal barons were allowed to retain their Moorish slaves provided these were kept in fetters.[52] Thousands departed; the rest accepted baptism more philosophically than the Jews; and as "Moriscos" they took the place of the baptized Jews in suffering the penalties of the Inquisition for relapses into their former faith. During the sixteenth century 3,000,000 superficially converted Moslems left Spain.[53] Cardinal Richelieu called the edict of 1502 "the most barbarous in history";[54] but the friar Bleda thought it "the most glorious event in Spain since the time of the Apostles. Now," he added, "religious unity is secured, and an era of prosperity is certainly about to dawn."[55]

Spain lost an incalculable treasure by the exodus of Jewish and Moslem merchants, craftsmen, scholars, physicians, and scientists, and the nations that received them benefited economically and intellectually. Knowing henceforth only one religion, the Spanish people submitted completely to their clergy, and surrendered all right to think except within the limits of the traditional faith. For good or ill, Spain chose to remain medieval, while Europe, by the commercial, typographical, intellectual, and Protestant revolutions, rushed into modernity.

VII. SPANISH ART

Spanish architecture, persistently Gothic, powerfully expressed this enduring medieval mood. The people did not grudge the maravedis that helped royal and noble conscience money, or religious policy, to build immense cathedrals, and to lavish costly ornaments and awesome sculpture and painting upon their favorite saints and the passionately worshiped Mother of God. Barcelona's cathedral rose slowly between 1298 and 1448: amid the chaos of minor streets it lifts its towering columns, an undistinguished portal, a majestic nave, while its many-fountained cloisters still give refuge from the strife of the day. Valencia, Toledo, Burgos, Lérida, Tarragona, Saragossa, León, extended or embellished their pre-existing temples, while new ones rose at Huesca and Pamplona—whose cloisters of white marble, elegantly carved, are as fair as the Alhambra's patios. In 1401 the cathedral chapter at Seville resolved to erect a church "so great and so beautiful that those who in coming ages shall look upon it will think us lunatics for attempting it." [56] The architects removed the decayed mosque that stood on the chosen site, but kept its foundations, its ground plan, and its noble Giralda minaret. All through the fifteenth century stone rose upon stone until Seville had raised the largest Gothic edifice in the world,* so that, said Théophile Gautier, "Notre Dame de Paris might walk erect in the nave." [57] However, Notre Dame is perfect; Seville Cathedral is vast. Sixty-seven sculptors and thirty-eight painters from Murillo to Goya toiled to adorn this mammoth cave of the gods.

About 1410 the architect Guillermo Boffi proposed to the cathedral chapter of Gerona to remove the columns and arches that divided the interior into nave and aisles, and to unite the walls by a single vault seventy-three feet wide. It was done, and the nave of Gerona Cathedral has now the broadest Gothic vault in Christendom. It was a triumph for engineering, a defeat for art. Shrines not so stupendous rose in the fifteenth century at Perpignan, Manresa, Astorga, and Valladolid. Segovia crowned itself with a fortresslike cathedral in 1472; Sigüenza finished its famous cloisters in 1507; Salamanca began its new fane in 1513. In almost every major city of Spain, barring Madrid, a cathedral rises in overwhelming majesty of external mass, with interiors darkly deprecating the sun and terrifying the soul into piety, yet brilliant with the high colors of Spanish painting, and painted statuary, and the gleam of jewelry, silver, and gold. These are the homes of the Spanish spirit, fearfully subdued and fiercely proud.

Nevertheless the kings, nobles, and cities found funds for costly palaces. Peter the Cruel, Ferdinand and Isabella, and Charles V remodeled the Alcazar that a Moorish architect had designed at Seville in 1181; most of the reconstruction was done by Moors from Granada, so that the edifice is a weak sister of the Alhambra. In like Saracenic style Don Pedro Enríquez built for the dukes of Alcalá at Seville (1500 f.) a lordly palace, the Casa de Pilatos, supposedly duplicating the house from whose portico Pilate was believed to have surrendered Christ to crucifixion. Valencia's Audiencia, or Hall of Audience (1500), provided for the local Cortes a Salon Dorado whose splendor challenged the Sala del Maggior Consiglio in the Palace of the Doges at Venice.

Sculpture was still a servant of architecture and the faith, crowding Spanish

---

* Covering 125,000 square feet. St. Peter's covers 230,000; the Mosque of Córdoba 160,000.

churches with Virgins in marble, metal, stone, or wood; here piety was petrified into forms of religious intensity or ascetic severity, enhanced with color, and made more awe-inspiring by the profound gloom of the naves. Retables—carved and painted screens raised behind the altar table—were a special pride of Spanish art; great sums, usually bequeathed in terror of death, were spent to gather and maintain the most skillful workers—designers, carvers, *doradores* who gilded or damascened the surfaces, *estofadores* who painted the garments and ornaments, *encarnadores* who colored the parts representing flesh; all labored together or by turns on the propitiatory shrine. Behind the central altar of Seville Cathedral a retable of forty-five compartments (1483–1519) pictured beloved legends in painted or gilded statuary of late Gothic style; while another in the Chapel of St. James in Toledo Cathedral displayed in gilt larchwood and stern realism the career of Spain's most honored saint.

Princes and prelates might be represented in sculpture, but only on their tombs, which were placed in churches or monasteries conceived as the antechambers of paradise. So Doña Mencia Enríquez, Duchess of Albuquerque, was buried in a finely chiseled sepulcher now in the Hispanic Society Museum in New York; and Pablo Ortiz carved for the cathedral of Toledo sumptuous sarcophagi for Don Alvaro de Luna and his wife. In the Carthusian monastery of Miraflores, near Burgos, Gil de Siloé designed in Italian style a superb mausoleum for the parents and brothers of the Queen. Isabella was so pleased with these famous *Sepulcros de los Reyes* that when her favorite page, Juan de Padilla (so recklessly brave that she called him *mi loco,* "my fool") was shot through the head at the siege of Granada, she commissioned De Siloé to carve a tomb of royal quality to harbor his corpse; and Gil again rivaled the best Italian sculpture of his time.

No art is more distinctive than the Spanish, yet none has more devoutly submitted to foreign influence. First, of course, to the Moorish influence, long domiciled in the Peninsula, but having its roots in Mesopotamia and Persia, and bringing into the Iberian style a delicacy of workmanship, and a passion for ornament, hardly equaled in any other Christian land. In the minor arts, where decoration was most in place, Spain imitated, and never surpassed, her Saracenic preceptors. Pottery was left almost entirely to the Mudejares, whose lustered ware was rivaled only by the Chinese, and whose colored tiles—above all, the blue *azulejos*—glorified the floors, altars, fountains, walls, and roofs of Christian Spain. The same Moorish skill made Spanish textiles—velvets, silks, and lace— the finest in Christendom. It appears again in Spanish leather, in the arabesques of the metal screens, in the religious monstrances, in the wood carving of the retables, choir stalls, and vaults. Later influences seeped in from Byzantine painting, then from France, Burgundy, the Netherlands, Germany From the Dutch and the Germans, Spanish sculpture and painting derived their startling realism— emaciated Virgins graphically old enough to be the mother of the Crucified, despite Michelangelo's dictum about virginity embalming youth. In the sixteenth century all these influences receded before the continent-wide triumph of the Italian style.

Spanish painting followed a similar evolution, but developed tardily, perhaps because the Moors gave here no help or lead. The Catalan frescoes of the twelfth and thirteenth centuries are inferior in design to the Altamira cave paintings of prehistoric Spain. Yet by 1300 painting had become a craze in the Peninsula; a thousand artists painted immense murals, huge altarpieces; some of these, from as early as 1345, have survived much longer than they deserved. In 1428 Jan van Eyck visited Spain, importing a powerful Flemish influence. Three years later the King of Aragon sent Luis Dalmau to study in Bruges; returning, Luis painted an all-too-Flemish *Virgin of the Councilors*. Thereafter Spanish painters, though still preferring tempera, more and more mixed their colors in oil.

The age of the Primitives in Spanish painting culminated in Bartolomé Bermejo (d. 1498). As early as 1447 he made a name for himself with the *Santo Domingo* that hangs in the Prado. The *Santa Engracia* bought by the Gardner Museum of Boston, and the gleaming *St. Michael* of Lady Ludlow's collection are almost worthy of Raphael, who came a generation later. But best of all is the *Pietà* (1490) in the Barcelona Cathedral: a bald, bespectacled Jerome; a dark and Spanish Mary holding her limp, haggard, lifeless Son; in the background the towers of Jerusalem under a lowering sky; and on the right a ruthless portrait of the donor, Canon Despla, uncombed and unshaved, resembling a bandit penitent but condemned, and suggesting Bermejo's "dour conception of humanity."[58] Here Italian grace is transformed into Spanish force, and realism celebrates its triumph in Spanish art.

The Flemish influence continued in Fernando Gallegos, and it produced a startling masterpiece in *A Knight of the Order of Calatrava*, by Miguel Sithium, a Fleming in the service of Isabella; this is one of the finest portraits in the National Gallery in Washington. But then again the Italian influence rose when Pedro Berruguete returned to Spain after a long experience in Italy. There he studied with Piero della Francesca and Melozzo da Forlì, and absorbed their quiet Umbrian style. When Federigo of Urbino sought painters to adorn his palace he chose Justus von Ghent and "Pietro Spagnolo." After the Duke's death (1582) Pedro brought the Umbrian art to Spain, and painted famous altarpieces at Toledo and Ávila. The pictures ascribed to him in the Louvre, the Brera, the Prado, and the Cleveland Museum hardly support his present *réclame* as the Velásquez of the Catholic sovereigns, but in drawing and composition they seem superior to anything produced in Spain before him.

Slowly the foreign stimuli were blending with the native genius to prepare for the maturer works of Alonso Coello and El Greco under Philip II, and the triumphs of Velásquez, Zurbarán, and Murillo in the Golden Age of Spain's seventeenth century. Genius is an individual endowment of force and will, but it is also a social heredity of discipline and skills formed in time and absorbed in growth. Genius is born *and* made.

VIII. SPANISH LITERATURE

In letters the Italian ascendancy had to wait while Spain exchanged influences with medieval France. It was probably from Moslem and Christian Spain that the troubadours of Provence had taken their poetic forms and conceits; nevertheless John I of Aragon sent an embassy to Charles VI of France (1388), asking for troubadours from Toulouse to come to Barcelona and organize there a branch of their fraternity, the *Gay Saber* or Joyful Wisdom. It was done. At Barcelona and Tortosa poetic contests were held in Provençal fashion, and the composition and recitation of verses became a passion among the literate minority in Aragon and Castile. Lyrics of love or faith or war were sung by wandering *juglares* to a simple accompaniment of strings.

In the next generation John II of Castile supported Italian models of poetry. Through Naples and Sicily, where Spaniards ruled, and through the University of Bologna, where Spanish youths like the Borgias studied, Italian moods and meters of verse swept into the Peninsula, and Dante and Petrarch found eager emulators in the Castilian tongue. Periodically the lyrics of the Spanish poets were collected in *cancioneros*, books of ballads chivalric in sentiment, Petrarchan in style. The Marqués de Santillana—statesman, scholar, patron, poet—imported the sonnet form from Italy, and compiled so soon a history of Spanish literature. Juan de Mena candidly imitated Dante in an epic poem, *The Labyrinth*, which did almost as much to establish Castilian as a literary language as *The Divine Comedy* had done for the Tuscan speech. Meanwhile Don Juan Manuel anticipated Boccaccio by writing dramatic tales, from one of which Shakespeare drew the quite incredible legend of Petruchio's taming of a shrew.

Romance continued to entrance all classes of readers. *Amadís da Gaula* was translated into Spanish (*c.* 1500) by García Ordóñez, who assured his readers that he had vastly improved upon the Portuguese original; and as this is lost we cannot gainsay him. Amadis, illegitimate son of an imaginary British princess, is exposed by her mother on the sea. He is rescued by a Scottish knight, and becomes a page to the queen of Scotland. Lisuarte, King of England, leaves his ten-year-old daughter Oriana at the Scottish court while he suppresses a usurper in his realm. The queen assigns the twelve-year-old Amadis as a page to Oriana, saying, "This is a child who shall serve you."

> And she answered that it pleased her. And the child kept this word in his heart, in such wise that it never afterwards left it . . . and he was never, in all the days of his life, wearied with serving her. And this their love lasted as long as they lasted; but Amadis, who knew not at all how she loved him, held himself to be very bold in that he had placed his thoughts on her, considering both her greatness and her beauty, and never so much as dared to speak a word concerning it. And she too, though she loved him in her heart, took heed that she should not speak with him more than with another; but her eyes took

great solace in showing to her heart what thing in the world she most
loved.[59]

It is a comfort to know that their love was triumphantly consummated, after
tribulations as numerous before marriage in fiction as after it in life. There are
many moments of tenderness, and some of nobility, in the long story; and Cervantes, vowing to destroy all such romances, spared this one as the best.

Romance provided one source of the drama, which slowly evolved out of the
mystery and morality plays, the popular farces, and the court masques. The oldest
date in the history of the Spanish drama is 1492, when the dramatic dialogues of
Juan del Encina were put upon the stage. Fernando de Rojas, a *Converso*, took
a further step toward drama in *La Celestina* (1499), a story told throughout in
dialogue, and divided into twenty-two acts; it was too long to be staged, but its
vivid characterizations and sprightly dialogue prepared for the classic comedies
of Spain.

Scholarship was both hampered and fostered by the Church. While the Inquisition policed thought, leading ecclesiastics did much for learning and education.
Italians like Pietro Martire d'Anghiera, coming to Spain in 1487, brought the
news of the humanist movement, and Spaniards educated in Italy returned with
the enthusiastic infection. At the Queen's request Peter Martyr opened at her
court, as Alcuin had done for Charlemagne seven centuries before, a school of
classical languages and literatures; Princess Juana studied Latin dutifully on the
way to insanity. Peter himself wrote the first history of the discoveries in America,
under the title *De rebus oceanis et novo orbe* (1504 f.); the last two words shared
with Vespucci's earlier (1502?) use of the term to name the "New World."

Cardinal Ximenes, whose faith was as firm and sharp as steel, joined
actively in the classical movement. In 1499 he founded the College of San
Ildefonso, and in 1508 the University of Alcalá. There, in 1502, nine lin-
guists under his supervision began one of the major achievements of Renaissance scholarship, the *Biblia Polyglotta Compluti*, or Complutensian
Polyglot Bible,* the first complete edition of the Christian Scriptures in the
original languages. To the Masoretic Hebrew text of the Old Testament
and the Greek of the New the editors added, in parallel or subjoined columns,
the Septuagint Greek translation, the Latin "Vulgate" version by Jerome,
and a Syraic paraphrase of the Pentateuch. Leo X opened up for Ximenes'
staff the manuscripts of the Vatican Library; and three baptized Jews contributed their Hebraic learning. The work of editing was completed in 1517,
but the six volumes were not printed till 1522. Ximenes, anticipating death,
urged on his savants. "Lose no time in the prosecution of our glorious task,
lest, in the casualties of life, you lose your patron, or I have to lament the
loss of those whose services are of greater price in my eyes than the wealth
and honors of the world." [60] A few months before he died the final volume

---

* Complutum (fruitful) was the old Latin name of Alcalá.

was presented to him with the compliments of his friends. Of all the acts of his administration, he told them, there was none better entitled than this to their congratulations. He projected an edition of Aristotle on the same scale, with a new Latin translation, but the brevity of his long life defeated him.

IX. SOVEREIGN DEATH

Isabella had preceded her energetic minister in the culminating adventure. With all her severity she was a woman of deep sensitivity, who bore bereavements more heavily than wars. In 1496 she buried her mother. Of her ten children five were stillborn or died in infancy, and two others died in early youth. In 1497 she lost her only son, her sole hope for an orderly succession, and in 1498 her best-beloved daughter, the Queen of Portugal, who might have united the Peninsula in peace. Amid these blows she suffered the daily tragedy of seeing her daughter Juana, now heiress-apparent to the throne, slowly going insane.

Juana had married Philip the Handsome, Duke of Burgundy and son of the Emperor Maximilian I (1496). By him she bore two future emperors, Charles V and Ferdinand I. Whether because of a fickle temperament, or because Juana was already incompetent, Philip neglected her, and carried on a liaison with a lady of her court at Brussels. Juana had the charmer's hair cut off, whereupon Philip swore he would never cohabit with his wife again. Hearing of all this, Isabella fell ill. On October 12, 1504, she wrote her will, directing that she should receive the plainest funeral, that the money so saved should be given to the poor, and that she should be buried in a Franciscan monastery within the Alhambra; "but," she added, "should the King my Lord prefer his sepulcher in some other place, then my will is that my body should be transported and laid by his side, that the union which we have enjoyed in this world, and, through the mercy of God, may hope again for our souls in heaven, may be represented by our bodies in the earth." [61] She died November 24, 1504, and was buried as she had directed; but after Ferdinand's death her remains were placed beside his in the cathedral of Granada. "The world," wrote Peter Martyr, "has lost its noblest ornament. . . . I know none of her sex, in ancient or modern times, who in my judgment is at all worthy to be named with this incomparable woman." [62] (Margaret of Sweden had been too remote from Peter's ken, and Elizabeth of England was still to be.)

Isabella's will had named Ferdinand as regent in Castile for a Philip absorbed in the Netherlands and a Juana moving ever more deeply into a consoling lunacy. Hoping to keep the Spanish throne from falling to the Hapsburgs in the person of Philip's son Charles, the fifty-three-year-old

Ferdinand hurriedly married (1505) Germaine de Foix, the seventeen-year-old niece of Louis XII; but the marriage increased the distaste of the Castilian nobles for their Aragonese master, and its only offspring died in infancy. Philip now claimed the crown of Castile, arrived in Spain, and was welcomed by the nobility (1506), while Ferdinand retired to his role as King of Aragon. Three months later Philip died, and Ferdinand resumed the regency of Castile in the name of his mad daughter. Juana la Loca remained technically Queen; she lived till 1555, but never, after 1507, left her royal palace at Tordesillas; she refused to wash or be dressed; and day after day she gazed through a window at the cemetery that held the remains of the unfaithful husband whom she had never ceased to love.

Ferdinand ruled more absolutely as regent than before as king. Freed from the tempering influence of Isabella, the hard and vindictive elements in his character came to sharp dominance. He had already recovered Roussillon and Cerdagne (1493), and Gonzalo de Córdoba had conquered Naples for him in 1503. This violated an agreement signed by Philip with Louis XII at Lyons for the division of the Kingdom of Naples between Spain and France; Ferdinand assured the world that Philip had exceeded his instructions. He sailed to Naples, and took personal possession of the Neapolitan throne (1506). He suspected that Gonzalo wanted this seat for himself; when he returned to Spain (1507) he brought the *Gran Capitan* with him, and consigned him to a retirement that most of Spain considered an unmerited humiliation.

Ferdinand had mastered everything but time. Gradually the wells of will and energy in him sank. His hours of rest grew longer, fatigue came sooner; he neglected the government; he became impatient and restless, morbidly suspicious of his most loyal servitors. Dropsy and asthma weakened him; he could hardly breathe in cities. In January 1516, he fled south to Andalusia, where he hoped to spend the winter in the open country. He fell ill on the way, and was at last persuaded to prepare for death. He named Ximenes regent for Castile, and his own illegitimate son, the Archbishop of Saragossa, regent for Aragon. He died January 23, 1516, in the sixty-fourth year of his life, the forty-second of his reign.

No wonder Machiavelli admired him: here was a king who acted *The Prince* before its author thought of writing it. Ferdinand made religion a tool of national and military policy, filled his documents with pious phrases, but never allowed considerations of morality to overcome motives of expediency or gain. No one could doubt his ability, his competent supervision of the government, his discerning choice of ministers and generals, his invariable success in diplomacy, persecution, and war. Personally he was neither greedy nor extravagant; his appetite was for power rather than for luxury, and his greed was for his country, to make it one and strong. He had no belief in democracy; under him local liberties languished and died; he was readily convinced that the old communal institutions could not be expanded to govern successfully a nation of so many states, faiths, and tongues. His achievement, and Isabella's, was to replace anarchy with monarchy, weakness with strength. He paved the way for Charles V to maintain the royal supremacy despite long absences, and for Philip II to concentrate all the government in one inadequate head. To accomplish this he was guilty of what to our time seems barbarous intolerance and inhuman cruelty, but seemed to his contemporaries a glorious victory for Christ.

Ximenes as regent zealously preserved the absolutism of the throne, perhaps as an alternative to a relapse into feudal fragmentation. Though now eighty years old, he ruled Castile with inflexible will, and defeated every effort of the feudality or the municipalities to regain their former powers. When some nobles asked by what right he curbed their privileges, he pointed not to the insignia of office on his person but to the artillery in the courtyard of the palace. Yet his will to power was subordinated to his sense of duty, for he repeatedly urged the young King Charles to leave Flanders and come to Spain to assume the royal authority. When Charles came (September 17, 1517), Ximenes hurried north to meet him. But Charles's Flemish counselors had seconded the Castilian nobles in giving him so unfavorable a report of the Cardinal's administration and character that the King, still an immature youth of seventeen, dispatched a letter to Ximenes thanking him for his services, deferring an interview, and bidding him retire to his see at Toledo for a merited rest. Another letter, dismissing the old zealot from all political office, reached him too late to deepen his humiliation; he had died on November 8, 1517, aged eighty-one. People wondered how, though apparently incorruptible, he had amassed the great personal fortune that his will left to the University of Alcalá.

He ended for Spain an age rich in honors, horrors, and forceful men. The aftermath suggests that the victory of the crown over Cortes and communes removed the medium through which the Spanish character might have expressed and maintained independence and variety; that the unification of faith was secured at the cost of riveting upon Spain a machine for the suppression of original thought on first and last things; that the expulsion of unconverted Jews and Moors undermanned Spanish commerce and industry just when the opening of the New World called for economic expansion and improvement; that the progressive involvement of Spain in the politics and wars of France and Italy (later of Flanders, Germany, and England), instead of turning policy and enterprise toward the development of the Americas, laid unbearable burdens upon the nation's resources in money and men. This, however, is hindsight, and judges the Spain of Ferdinand and Isabella in terms that no European people of their time would have understood. All religious groups except for a few Moslems and Anabaptists persecuted religious dissent; all governments—Catholic France and Italy, Protestant Germany and England—used force to unify religious faith; all countries hungered for the gold of the "Indies," East or West; all used war and diplomatic deceit to ensure their survival, extend their boundaries, or increase their wealth. To all Christian governments Christianity was not a rule of means but a means of rule; Christ was for the people, Machiavelli was preferred by the kings. The state in some measure had civilized man, but who would civilize the state?

CHAPTER XII

The Growth of Knowledge

1300-1517

I. THE MAGICIANS

THE two centuries whose European history has been so hastily sketched in the preceding chapters were still part of what tradition calls the Middle Ages—which we may loosely define as the life of Europe between Constantine and Columbus, 325 to 1492 A.D. As we summarize now the science, pedagogy, and philosophy of Western Europe in the fourteenth and fifteenth centuries, we must remind ourselves that rational studies had to fight for soil and air in a jungle of superstition, intolerance, and fear. Amid famines, plagues, and wars, in the chaos of a fugitive or divided papacy, men and women sought in occult forces some explanation for the unintelligible miseries of mankind, some magical power to control events, some mystical escape from a harsh reality; and the life of reason moved precariously in a milieu of sorcery, witchcraft, necromancy, palmistry, phrenology, numerology, divination, portents, prophecies, dream interpretations, fateful stellar conjunctions, chemical transmutations, miraculous cures, and occult powers in animals, minerals, and plants. All these marvels remain deathless with us today, and one or another wins from almost every one of us some open or secret allegiance; but their present influence in Europe falls far short of their medieval sway.

The stars were studied not only to guide navigation and date religious festivals, but also to forecast terrestrial occurrences and personal destinies. The pervasive influences of climate and season, the relation of tides to the moon, the lunar periodicity of women, and the dependence of agriculture upon the modes and moods of the sky, seemed to justify the claims of astrology that the heavens of today forecast the events of tomorrow. Such predictions were regularly published (as now), and reached a wide and avid audience. Princes dared not begin a campaign, a battle, a journey, or a building without assurance from the astrologers that the stars were in a propitious configuration. Henry V of England kept his own astrolabe to chart the sky, and when his queen was lying-in he cast his own horoscope of the child.[1] Astrologers were as welcome as humanists at Matthias Corvinus's enlightened court.

The stars, men believed, were guided by angels, and the air was congested with invisible spirits, some from heaven, some from hell. Demons lurked everywhere, especially in one's bed; to them some men ascribed their night losses, some women their untimely pregnancies; and theologians agreed that such infernal concubines were real.[2] At every turn, at any moment, the credulous individual could step out of the sense world into a realm of magic beings and powers. Every natural object had supernatural qualities. Books of magic were among the "best sellers" of the day. The bishop of Cahors was tortured, scourged, and burned at the stake (1317) after confessing that he had burned a wax image of Pope John XXII in the hope that the original, as the magic art promised, would suffer like the effigy.[3] People believed that a wafer consecrated by a priest would, if pricked, bleed with the blood of Christ.

The repute of the alchemists had declined, but their honest research and glittering chicanery went on. While royal and papal edicts denounced them, they persuaded some kings that alchemy might replenish exhausted treasuries, and simple people swallowed "potable gold"[4] guaranteed to cure anything but gullibility. (Gold is still taken by patients and physicians in treating arthritis.)

The science of medicine contended at every step with astrology, theology, and quackery. Nearly all physicians related the prognosis of a disease to the constellation under which the sufferer had been born or taken ill; so the great surgeon Guy de Chauliac could write (1363), "If anyone is wounded in the neck while the moon is in Taurus, the affliction will be dangerous."[5] One of the earliest printed documents was a calendar published at Mainz (1462) indicating the astrologically best times for bloodletting. Epidemics were widely ascribed to unlucky associations of the stars. Probably through disillusionment with medicine, millions of Christians turned to faith healing. Thousands came to the kings of France or England to be cured of scrofula by a touch of the royal hand. Apparently the custom had begun with Louis IX, whose saintliness led to the belief that he could work miracles. His power was supposed to have gone down to his successors, and, through Isabella of Valois, mother of Edward III, to the rulers of England. More thousands made pilgrimages to curative shrines, and turned some saints into medical specialists; so a chapel of St. Vitus was frequented by sufferers from chorea, since that saint was believed to be a specific for this disease. The tomb of Pierre de Luxembourg, a cardinal who at eighteen died of ascetic austerities, became a favorite goal, where, within fifteen months after his death, 1,964 cures were ascribed to the magic efficacy of his bones.[6] Quacks flourished, but the law began to hamper them. In 1382 Roger Clerk, who had pretended to cure disease by applying charms, was condemned to ride through London with urinals hanging from his neck.[7]

Most Europeans believed in sorcery—i.e., the power of persons to control evil spirits and secure their help. The Dark Ages had been comparatively enlightened in this respect: Saints Boniface and Agobard denounced the belief in sorcery as sinful and ridiculous; Charlemagne made it a capital crime to execute anyone on a charge of witchcraft; and Pope Gregory VII Hildebrand forbade inquisition to be made for sorcerers as the cause of storms or plagues.[8] But the emphasis laid by preachers upon the reality of hell and the wiles of Satan strengthened popular belief in the ubiquitous and iniquitous presence of himself or one of his company; and many a diseased mind or desperate soul harbored the idea of summoning such devils to its aid. Accusations of sorcery were made against a great variety of people, including Pope Boniface VIII. In 1315 the aristocrat Enguerrand de Marigny was hanged for sorcery, and in 1317 Pope John XXII ordered the execution of various obscure persons for plotting to kill him by invoking the assistance of demons. John repeatedly denounced the appeal to demons, ordered prosecutions for it, and prescribed penalties; but his edicts were interpreted by the people as confirming their belief in the existence and availability of demonic powers. After 1320 the indictments for sorcery multiplied, and many of the accused were hanged or burned at the stake. It was a common opinion in France that Charles VI had been made insane by magic means; two sorcerers were engaged who promised to restore his wits; when they failed they were beheaded (1397). In 1398 the theological faculty of the University of Paris issued twenty-eight articles condemning sorcery, but assuming its occasional efficacy. Chancellor Gerson pronounced it a heresy to question the existence or activity of demons.[9]

Witchcraft was the practice of sorcery by persons who were alleged to worship Satan, in nocturnal assemblies or "Sabbaths," as the master of the demons whom they affected to employ. According to popular belief the witches, usually women, secured supernatural powers at the price of this devil-worship. So commissioned, they were supposed to override natural laws, and to bring misfortune or death to whom they wished. Scholars like Erasmus and Thomas More accepted the reality of witchcraft; some priests in Cologne doubted it; the University of Cologne affirmed it.[10] Most churchmen claimed—and lay historians in some measure agree—that the secret gatherings by night were excuses for promiscuous sexual relations, and for initiating young people into the arts of debauchery.[11] Whether through insane delusion, or to secure release from torture, many witches allegedly confessed to one or another of the evil practices charged to them. It may be that these "witches' Sabbaths" served as a moratorium on a burdensome Christianity, and as a partly playful, partly rebellious worship of Satan as the powerful enemy of a God who condemned so many pleasures to repression and so many souls to hell; or these clandestine rites may have recalled and reaffirmed pagan cults and feasts of the deities of earth and field and forest, of procreation and fertility, of Bacchus, Priapus, Ceres, and Flora.

Secular and episcopal courts joined in efforts to suppress what seemed to them the most blasphemous depravity. Several popes—in 1374, 1409, 1437, 1451, and especially Innocent VIII in 1484—commissioned agents of the Inquisition to deal with witches as abandoned heretics, whose sins and machinations blighted the fruit of fields and wombs, and whose pretensions might seduce whole communities into demonolatry. The popes took literally a passage in Exodus (22:18): "Thou shalt not suffer a witch to live." Nevertheless the ecclesiastical courts, before 1446, contented themselves with mild penalties, unless a pardoned offender relapsed. In 1446 the Inquisition burned several witches at Heidelberg; in 1460 it burned twelve men and women at Arras; and the name *Vaudois* given them, as generally to heretics (Waldenses) and witches in France, survived an Atlantic voyage to generate the word *Voodooism* for Negro sorcery in the French colonies of America.[12] In 1487 the Dominican inquisitor Jacob Sprenger, honestly frightened by the apparent spread of sorcery, published an official guide for the detection of witches, *Malleus maleficarum (Hammer of Witches)*. Maximilian I, then King of the Romans, prefaced with a letter of warm recommendation this "most portentous monument of superstition which the world has produced."[13] These maleficent women, said Sprenger, by stirring up some devilish brew in a caldron, or by other means, can summon swarms of locusts and caterpillars to devour a harvest; they can make men impotent and women barren; they can dry up a woman's milk, or bring abortion; by a look alone they can cause love or hatred, sickness or death. Some of them kidnap children, roast them, and eat them. They can see things at a distance, and foresee the weather; they can transform themselves, and others, into beasts.[14] Sprenger wondered why there were more female than male witches, and concluded that it was because women were more lightheaded and sensual than men; besides, he added, they had always been favorite instruments of Satan.[15] He burned forty-eight of them in five years. From his time onward the ecclesiastical attack upon witchcraft was intensified until it reached its full fury in the sixteenth century, under Catholic and Protestant auspices alike; in this type of fearful ferocity the Middle Ages were outdone by modern times. In 1554 an officer of the Inquisition boasted that in the preceding 150 years the Holy Office had burned at least 30,000 witches, who, if they had been left unpunished, would have brought the whole world to destruction.[16]

Many books were written in this age against superstition, and all contained superstitions.[17] Agostino Trionfo addressed to Pope Clement V a treatise advising him to outlaw occult practices, but Trionfo held it unpardonable in a physician to perform a phlebotomy during certain phases of the moon.[18] Pope John XXII issued powerful blasts against alchemy (1317) and magic (1327); he mourned what he thought was the increasing prevalence of sacrifices to demons, pacts with the Devil, and the making of images, rings, and potions for magical purposes; he pronounced *ipso facto* excommunication upon all practitioners of such arts; but even he implied a belief in their possible efficacy.[19]

The great antagonist of astrology in this age was Nicole Oresme, who died as bishop of Lisieux in 1382. He laughed at astrologers who could not predict the sex of an unborn child but, after its birth, professed to foretell its earthly fate; such horoscopes, said Oresme, are old wives' tales. Repeating the title and effort of Cicero fourteen centuries back, he wrote *De divinatione* against the claims of soothsayers, dream interpreters, and the like. Amid his general skepticism of the occult he admitted that some events could be explained as the work of demons or angels. He accepted the notion of the "evil eye"; he thought that a criminal would darken a mirror by looking into it, and that the glance of a lynx could penetrate a wall. He acknowledged the miracles of the Bible, but he repudiated supernatural explanations where natural causes sufficed. Many people, said Nicole, are credulous of magic because they lack acquaintance with natural causes and processes. They accept on hearsay what they have not seen, and so legend—as of a magician climbing a rope thrown into the air—may become a popular belief.[20] (This is the oldest-known mention of the rope-climbing myth.) Consequently, Oresme argued, the wide prevalence of a belief is no proof of its truth. Even if many persons claim to have witnessed an event contrary to our ordinary experience of nature, we should hesitate to believe them. Moreover, the senses are so easily deceived! The color, shape, and sound of objects vary with distance, light, and the condition of the sensory organs; an object at rest may seem to be moving, and one in motion may seem at rest; a coin at the bottom of a vase filled with water appears more remote than one so placed in an empty vase. Sensations must be interpreted by judgment, and this too may err. These deceptions of senses and judgment, says Oresme, explain many of the marvels ascribed to supernatural or magical powers.[21]

Despite such brave advances toward a scientific spirit, the old superstitions survived, or merely changed their form. Nor were they confined to the populace. Edward III of England paid a great sum for a phial which, he was assured, had belonged to St. Peter. Charles V of France was shown, in Sainte Chapelle, a phial allegedly containing some of Christ's blood; he asked his savants and theologians whether this could be true; they answered cautiously in the affirmative.[22] It was in this atmosphere that education, science, medicine, and philosophy struggled to grow.

II. THE TEACHERS

The rise of commerce and industry put a new premium on education. Literacy had been a costly luxury in an agricultural regime; it was a necessity in an urban commercial world. Law tardily recognized the change. In England (1391) the feudal landowners petitioned Richard II to enforce the old rule that forbade a serf to send his son to school without his lord's consent and reimbursement for the loss of a farm hand. Richard refused, and in the next reign a statute decreed that any parent might send any of his children to school.[23]

Under this education-emancipation act elementary schools multiplied. In the countryside monastic schools survived; in the cities grade schools were provided by churches, hospitals, chantries, and guilds. Attendance was voluntary but general, even in villages. Usually the teachers were priests, but the proportion of lay instructors rose in the fourteenth century. The curriculum stressed the catechism, the Creed, the basic prayers, reading, writing, arithmetic, singing, and flogging. Even in secondary schools flogging was the staff of instruction. A divine explained that "the boys' spirits must be subdued";[24] the parents agreed with him; and perhaps 'tis so. Agnes Paston urged the tutor of her unstudious son to "belash him" if he did not amend, "for I had lever he were fairly buried than lost by default."[25]

Secondary schools continued the religious training, and added *grammatica*, which included not merely grammar and composition, but the language and expurgated literature of classic Rome; the students—boys of the middle class —learned to read and write Latin, however indifferently, as a necessity in foreign trade as well as in a church career. The best secondary schools of the time were those established in the Lowlands and Germany by the Brethren of the Common Life; the one at Deventer drew 2,000 pupils. The wealthy and energetic Bishop of Winchester, William of Wykeham, set a precedent by founding there (1372) the first of England's "public" schools— institutions endowed, by private or public philanthropy, to provide college preparatory training for a limited selection of boys. The example was followed by Henry VI, who established (1440) and richly endowed Eton School to prepare students for King's College, Cambridge.

Above the elementary level the education of women, with some highborn exceptions, was confined to the home. Many women of the middle class, like Margaret Paston, learned to write fair English, and a sprinkling of women acquired some acquaintance with literature and philosophy. The sons of the aristocracy received an education quite different from that of the schools. Till the age of seven they were taught by the women of the house; then they were sent to serve, as pages, a related or neighboring noble. Safe there from the excesses of affection, they learned reading, writing, religion, and manners from the ladies and the local priest. At fourteen they became squires—i.e., adult servitors of their lord. Now they learned to ride, shoot, hunt, joust, and wage war. Book learning they left to their inferiors.

These were meanwhile developing one of the noblest legacies of the Middle Ages—the universities. While the ecstasy of ecclesiastical architecture cooled, the zeal for founding colleges mounted. In this period Oxford saw the establishment of Exeter, Oriel, Queen's, New, Lincoln, All Souls, Magdalen, Brasenose, and Corpus Christi colleges, and the Divinity School. They were not yet colleges in the modern sense; they were "halls," places of residence for selected students; hardly a tenth of the pupils at Oxford lived in them. Most university instruction was given by clergymen in schoolrooms or auditoriums scattered about the town. Benedictine monks, Franciscan, Dominican, and other friars maintained their own colleges at Oxford; and from these monastic academies came some of the most brilliant men of the fourteenth century; among them were Duns Scotus and William of Ockham, both of whom did some damage to orthodox theology. Students of law received their training in London, at the Inns of Court.

In Oxford no love was wasted between town and gown—citizens and scholars. In 1355 the hostile camps rushed into open war, and so many heroes were killed that the year was known as that of the Great Slaughter. Despite the introduction of flogging into the universities of England (c. 1350), the students were a troublesome lot. Forbidden to engage in intramural athletics, they spent their energy in profanity, tippling, and venery; taverns and brothels throve on their patronage. Attendance at Oxford fell from its thirteenth-century peak to as low as a thousand; and after the expulsion of Wyclif academic freedom was rigorously curtailed by episcopal control.

Cambridge profited from the Wyclif controversy and the Lollard scare; cautious conservatives kept their sons from Oxford and sent them to the younger university, so that by the end of the fifteenth century the rival institutions had a fairly equal registration. New "halls" were founded along the Cam: Michaelhouse, University or Clare, Pembroke, Gonville and Caius, Trinity, Corpus Christi, King's, Queen's, St. Catherine's, Jesus', Christ's, and St. John's. Like the residence halls at Oxford, these became colleges in our sense during the fifteenth century as more and more teachers chose them as the places where their lectures would draw the largest attendance. Classes began at six in the morning, and continued till five in the afternoon. Meanwhile Scotland and Ireland, out of their poverty, founded the universities of St. Andrews, Glasgow, and Aberdeen, and Trinity College, Dublin—four institutions destined to pour genius, generation after generation, into the intellectual life of the British Isles.

In France, education, like almost everything else, suffered from the Hundred Years' War. Nevertheless the rising demand for lawyers and physicians, added to the traditional attractions of an ecclesiastical career, encouraged the establishment of new universities at Avignon, Orléans, Cahors, Grenoble, Orange, Aix-en-Provence, Poitiers, Caen, Bordeaux, Valence, Nantes, and Bourges. The University of Paris, perhaps because the monarchy was near collapse, became in the fourteenth century a national power, challenging the *Parlement*, advising the king, serving as a court of appeals in French theology, and recognized by most continental educators as *universitas universitatum*. The rise of provincial and foreign universities reduced registration at Paris; even so the faculty of arts alone was reputed to have a thousand teachers and ten thousand pupils in 1406; [26] and in 1490 the entire university had nearly twenty thousand.[27] Some fifty "colleges" helped to house them. Discipline was laxer than at Oxford, and the morals of the students complimented their virility rather than their religion. Courses in Greek, Arabic, Chaldaic, and Hebrew were added to the curriculum.

Spain had founded its leading universities in the thirteenth century—at Palencia, Salamanca, and Lérida; others now rose at Perpignan, Huesca, Valladolid, Barcelona, Saragossa, Palma, Sigüenza, Valencia, Alcalá, and Seville. In these institutions ecclesiastical control was complete, and theology predominated; however, at Alcalá, fourteen chairs were given to grammar, literature, and rhetoric, twelve to divinity and canon law. Alcalá became for a time the greatest educational center in Spain; in 1525 it had an enrollment of seven thousand. Scholarships were provided for needy students. The salary of a professor was regulated by the number of his pupils; and every professor was required to resign quadrennially, being eligible for reappointment if he had proved satisfactory. At Lisbon King Diniz had founded a university in 1300, but the turbulence of the students led him to remove it to Coimbra, whose pride it is today.

Mental activity was in this period more vigorous in Central Europe than in France or Spain. In 1347 Charles IV founded the University of Prague, which soon became the intellectual head and voice of the Bohemian people. Other universities appeared at Cracow, Vienna, Pécs, Geneva, Erfurt, Heidelberg, Cologne, Buda, Würzburg, Leipzig, Rostock, Louvain, Trier, Freiburg-im-Breisgau, Greifswald, Basel, Ingolstadt, Pressburg, Mainz, Tübingen, Copenhagen, Uppsala, Frankfurt-an-Oder, and Wittenberg. In the second half of the fifteenth century these institutions seethed with students and debates. Cracow alone had 18,338 pupils at one time.[28] The Church provided most of the funds, and naturally called the tune of thought; but princes, nobles, cities, and businessmen shared in endowing colleges and scholarships. The Elector Frederick of Saxony financed the University of Wittenberg partly from money that came from the sale of indulgences, but which he refused to remit to Rome.[29] Scholasticism sat in the chairs of philosophy, while humanism grew outside the university walls. Hence most of the universities of Germany adhered to the Church during the Reformation, with two significant exceptions: Erfurt, where Luther studied, and Wittenberg, where he taught.

III. THE SCIENTISTS

The scientific mood was hardly more popular with the pundits than with the people. The spirit of the age inclined to the "humanities"; even the revival of Greek studies ignored Greek science. In mathematics the Roman numerals obstructed progress; they seemed inseparable from Latin culture; the Hindu-Arabic numerals seemed heretically Mohammedan, and were coldly received, especially north of the Alps; the Cour des Comptes—the French Bureau of Audit—used the clumsy Roman figures till the eighteenth century. Nevertheless Thomas Bradwardine, who died of the plague (d 349) a month after being consecrated archbishop of Canterbury, introduced into England several Arabic theorems in trigonometry. His pupil, Richard Wallingford, Abbot of St. Albans, was the leading mathematician of the fourteenth century; his *Quadripartitum de sinibus demonstratis* was the first major work on trigonometry in Western Europe. He died of leprosy at forty-three, mourning the time he had taken from theology for science.

Nicole Oresme led an active ecclesiastical career, and yet invaded a dozen sciences successfully. He paved the way for analytical geometry by developing the systematic use of co-ordinates, and by employing graphs to show the growth of a function. He played with the idea of a fourth dimension, but rejected it. Like several of his contemporaries he adumbrated Galileo's law that the speed of a falling body increases regularly with the duration of its fall.[30] In a commentary on Aristotle's *De caelo et mundo* he wrote: "We cannot prove by any experiment that the heavens undergo a daily movement and the earth does not"; there are "good reasons indicating that the earth, and not the sky, undergoes a daily motion."[31] Oresme fell back upon the Ptolemaic system, but he had helped to prepare for Copernicus.

When we consider that no telescope or camera existed as yet to watch or record the sky, it is encouraging to note the energy and intelligence of medieval astronomers, Moslem, Jewish, and Christian. Jean de Liniers, after years of personal observations, described the positions of forty-eight stars with an accuracy then rivaled only by Moslems; and he calculated the obliquity of the ecliptic to within seven seconds of the most modern estimate. Jean de Meurs and Firmin de Beauval (1344) proposed to reform the Julian calendar—which was outstripping the sun—by omitting the quadrennial February 29 for the next forty years (which would have erred by excess); the reform had to wait till 1582, and still awaits international and interfaith

understandings. William Merle of Oxford rescued meteorology from astrology by keeping record of the weather through 2,556 days. Unknown ob-
servers or navigators discovered in the fifteenth century the declination of
the magnetic needle: the needle does not point due north, but inclines toward
the astronomic meridian at a small but important angle, which, as Columbus
noted, varies from place to place.

The peak figure in the mathematics and astronomy of this epoch was
Johann Müller, known to history as Regiomontanus from his birth (1436)
near Königsberg in Lower Franconia. At fourteen he entered the University
of Vienna, where Georg von Purbach was introducing humanism and the
latest Italian advances in mathematics and astronomy. Both men matured
early and died soon: Purbach at thirty-eight, Müller at forty. Resolved to
learn Greek in order to read Ptolemy's *Almagest* in the original, Müller
went to Italy, studied Greek with Guarino da Verona, and devoured all
available texts, Greek or Latin, on astronomy and mathematics. Returning
to Vienna, he taught these sciences there, and with such success that he
was called to Buda by Matthias Corvinus, and then to Nuremberg, where
a rich burgher built for him the first European observatory. Müller equipped
it with instruments built or improved by himself. We feel the pure breeze
of science in a letter that he wrote to a fellow mathematician in 1464: "I do
not know whither my pen will run; it will use up all my paper if I don't stop
it. One problem after another occurs to me, and there are so many beautiful
ones that I hesitate as to which I should submit to you." [32] In 1475 Sixtus IV
summoned him to Rome to reform the calendar. There, a year later, Regiomontanus died.

The short span of his life limited his achievement. He had planned treatises
on mathematics, physics, astrology, and astronomy, and had hoped to edit the
classics in those sciences; only fragments of these works found form and
survival. He completed Purbach's *Epitome* of the *Almagest*. He composed
an essay *De triangulis*—the first book devoted solely to trigonometry. He was
apparently the first to suggest the use of tangents in astronomic calculations,
and his tables of sines and tangents facilitated the calculations of Copernicus.
He formulated astronomical tables more accurate than any drawn up before.
His method of calculating latitude and longitude proved a boon to mariners.
Under the title of *Ephemerides* he issued (1474) an almanac showing the
daily position of the planets for the next thirty-two years; from this book
Columbus would predict the lunar eclipse that would fill the stomachs of his
starving men on February 29, 1504. The observations made of Halley's
comet by Regiomontanus laid the bases of modern cometary astronomy. But
his personal and living influence was greater than that of his books. His
popular lectures in science helped to raise an intellectual exhilaration in
Nuremberg in Dürer's youth; and he made the city famous for its nautical

instruments and maps. One of his pupils, Martin Behaim, drew in color on vellum the oldest known terrestrial globe (1492), still preserved in the Germanisches Museum in Nuremberg.

Modern geography was created not by geographers but by sailors, merchants, missionaries, envoys, soldiers, and pilgrims. Catalonian skippers made or used excellent maps; their *portolani*—pilot guides to Mediterranean ports—were in the fourteenth century almost as accurate as the navigation charts of our time.[33] Old trade routes to the East having fallen into Turkish hands, European importers developed new overland routes through Mongol territory. The Franciscan friar Oderic of Pordenone, after spending three years in Peking (*c.* 1323–26), wrote an illuminating record of his trip to China via India and Sumatra, and of his return via Tibet and Persia. Clavijo, as we shall see, gave a fascinating account of his embassy to Timur. Johann Schnittberger of Bavaria, captured by the Turks at Nicopolis (1396), wandered for thirty years in Turkey, Armenia, Georgia, Russia, and Siberia, and wrote in his *Reisebuch* the first West-European description of Siberia. In 1500 Juan de la Cosa, one of Columbus' pilots, issued an extensive map of the world, showing for the first time in cartography the explorations of his master, of Vasco da Gama, and others. Geography was a moving drama in the fifteenth century.

In one particular the most influential medieval treatise on geography was the *Imago mundi* (1410) of Cardinal Pierre d'Ailly, which encouraged Columbus by describing the Atlantic as traversable "in a very few days if the wind be fair."[34] It was but one of half a dozen works that this alert ecclesiastic wrote on astronomy, geography, meteorology, mathematics, logic, metaphysics, psychology, and the reform of the calendar and the Church. Reproached for giving so much time to secular studies, he replied that a theologian should keep abreast of science.[35] He saw some science even in astrology; and on astrological grounds he predicted a great change in Christianity within a hundred years, and world-shaking events in 1789.[36]

The best scientific thought of the fourteenth century was in physics. Dietrich of Freiburg (d. 1311) gave essentially our modern explanation of the rainbow as due to two refractions, and one reflection, of the sun's rays in drops of water. Jean Buridan did excellent work in theoretical physics; it is a pity that he is famous only for his ass, which may not have been his.* Born near Arras before 1300, Buridan studied and taught at the University of Paris. He not only argued for the daily rotation of the earth, but he

---

* The tale of "Buridan's ass" is not found in his extant works, but is a tradition of respectable age; it may have occurred in one of his lectures. Jean had argued that the will, on fronting alternatives, is compelled to choose whichever the intellect judges the more advantageous. Consequently, some wit concluded, a hungry ass placed at equal distances from two equally attractive bales of hay would have no reason for preferring either, and—other food lacking—would starve to death.

eliminated from astronomy the angelic intelligences to which Aristotle and Aquinas had ascribed the guidance and motion of the heavenly bodies. Nothing more is needed to explain their movements, said Buridan, than a start originally given them by God, and the law of impetus—that a body in motion continues its motion except as hindered by some existing force; here Buridan anticipated Galileo, Descartes, and Newton. The motions of planets and stars, he added, are governed by the same mechanical laws that operate on earth.[37] These propositions, now so trite, were deeply damaging to the medieval world view. They almost date the beginning of astronomical physics.

Buridan's ideas were taken to Germany and Italy by his pupils, and influenced Leonardo, Copernicus, Bruno, and Galileo.[38] Albert of Saxony carried them to the university that he founded at Vienna (1364), Marsilius von Inghen to the university that he founded at Heidelberg (1386). Albert was one of the first to reject the Aristotelian notion that a vacuum is impossible; he developed the idea of a center of gravity in every body; he anticipated Galileo's principles of static equilibrium and the uniform acceleration of falling bodies; and he held that the erosion of mountains by water, and the gradual or volcanic elevation of the land, are compensating forces in geology[39]—an idea that fascinated Leonardo.

Practical mechanics made some modest advances. Complicated windmills were used to pump water, drain soil, grind grain, and do other chores. Water power was employed in smelting and sawing, in driving furnace bellows, tilt hammers, silk-spinning machines. Cannon were cast and bored. Steel was made in sizable quantities; large blast furnaces were set up in northern Europe in the fourteenth century. Well boring is mentioned in 1373; wiredrawing was practiced at Nuremberg in the fifteenth century; a pump composed of buckets on an endless chain is pictured in a manuscript of 1438.[40] In a drawing by the Hussite engineer Conrad Keyser (c. 1405) occurs the earliest known representation of reciprocating motion converted into rotary motion: two arms, moving in alternation, revolve a shaft precisely as the pistons turn the crankshaft of an automobile.[41]

Better mechanisms for measuring time were demanded as commerce and industry grew. Monks and farmers had divided the daylight into the same number of periods in all seasons, making the periods longer in summer than in winter. City life required more uniform divisions of time, and in the thirteenth and fourteenth centuries clocks and watches were made that divided the day into equal parts throughout the year. In some places the hours were numbered from one to twenty-four, as in the military chronometry of our time; and as late as 1370 some clocks, like that of San Gotardo in Milan, struck the full number. This proved to be a noisy extravagance. By 1375 the day was regularly divided into two halves of twelve hours each.

The essential principle of the mechanical clock was a weight slowly turning a wheel, whose revolution was checked by an escapement tooth sufficiently resistant to allow the wheel to turn by only one cog in a given interval of time. Such a timepiece had been described about 1271. The first mechanical clocks were set up in church towers or belfries visible through large areas of a town. One of the earliest was installed (1326–35) in the abbey of St. Albans by Richard Wallingford; it showed not only the hours and minutes of the day but the ebb and flow of the tide, and the motions of the sun and moon. Later clocks added a medley of gadgets. The clock (1352) in Strasbourg Cathedral showed a crowing cock, the three Magi, and a human figure on which were indicated, for each part of the body, the proper time for bloodletting. The cathedral clock at Wells used a moving image of the sun to point the hour, and a small star, moving on an inner circle, to indicate the minute; a third circle gave the day of the month; and on a platform above the dial four horsemen emerged and charged as each hour struck. On a fifteenth-century clock at Jena a buffoon's head opened its monstrous mouth to receive a golden apple from a pilgrim, only to have the apple snatched away as his mouth began to close upon it; this comedy was performed every hour of every day for hundreds of years; and the clock still exists. A similar clock at Nuremberg, set up in 1506 and rudely interrupted by the second World War, resumed its theatrical performances in 1953.

To make watches a spiral spring was substituted (c. 1450) for the hanging weight: a band of fine steel, rolled up into a small circle or drum, produced, by its gradual unwinding, the effect of the weight on the retarded wheel. By the end of the fifteenth century watches were numerous, some as large as a hand, some as small as an almond, many ovoid like the "Nuremberg eggs" made by Peter Hele (1510). The principle of weight, escapement, and wheel was applied to other purposes, so that the mechanical clock became the parent of a myriad diverse machines.

While physics thus foreshadowed the Industrial Revolution, alchemy slowly grew into chemistry. By the close of this age the alchemists had discovered and described zinc, bismuth, liver of sulfur, regulus of antimony, volatile fluorine of alkali, and many other substances. They distilled alcohol, volatilized mercury, and made sulfuric acid by the sublimation of sulfur. They prepared ether and aqua regia, and a scarlet dye superior to those now used.[42] They bequeathed to chemistry the experimental method that would prove the greatest gift of medieval science to the modern mind.

Botany was still mostly confined to manuals of husbandry or to herbals describing medicinal plants. Henry of Hesse (1325–97) suggested that new species, especially among plants, might evolve naturally from old ones;[43] this 500 years before Darwin. Royal or papal menageries, animal breeding, veterinary medicine, treatises on hunting or fishing or the culture of bees or silkworms, bestiaries that told animal stories to insinuate morality, and books on falconry, like the *Miroir de Phoebus* (1387) of Gaston III Count of Foix, half unwittingly gathered material for a science of zoology.

Anatomy and physiology had for the most part to depend upon the dissection of animals, the wounds of soldiers, and occasional cases where the law required post-mortem autopsy. Honest Christians felt reasonable objections to the dissection of human bodies which, however dead, were supposed to rise intact from the grave at the Last Judgment. All through the fourteenth century it was difficult to get cadavers for anatomical study; north of the Alps very few physicians, before 1450, had ever seen a dissected human corpse. Nevertheless, about 1360, Guy de Chauliac persuaded the authorities at Avignon (then ruled by the papal court) to turn over to medical schools, for dissection, the bodies of executed criminals.[44] Dissections were performed before medical students at Venice in 1368, Montpelier in 1377, Florence in 1388, Lérida in 1391, Vienna in 1404; and in 1445 the University of Padua built the first known anatomical theater. The results for medicine were endless.

IV. THE HEALERS

In the science and practice of medicine, as in literature and art, northern Europe was half a century or more behind Italy; and even Italy had by 1300 barely regained the medical knowledge reached by Galen and Soranus a thousand years before. But the medical schools at Montpelier, Paris, and Oxford were making good progress, and the greatest surgeons of this age were French. The profession was now well organized, and defended its privileges lustily; but as the demand for health always exceeded the supply, herbalists, apothecaries, midwives, wandering leeches, and barber surgeons—not to mention quacks—everywhere competed with trained practitioners. The public, inviting disease by wrong living, and then seeking infallible diagnoses and cheap overnight cures, made the usual complaints about mercenary or murderous doctors. Froissart considered it "the object of all medical men to gain large salaries" [45]—as if this were not a disease endemic to all civilization.

The most interesting medical men of the age were the surgeons. They had not yet persuaded the physicians to recognize them as equals; indeed, the University of Paris would admit no student to its school of medicine in the fourteenth century except on his oath never to perform a surgical operation. Even bloodletting, which had already become a panacea, was forbidden to physicians, and had to be left to their underlings. Barbers were still used by the people for many operations; but the barber surgeons were now abandoning tonsorial practice, and were specializing in surgery; in 1365 there were forty such barber surgeons in Paris; in England they continued till 1540.

An ordinance of 1372 restricted them in France to the treatment of "wounds not of a character likely to cause death"; and thereafter major operations could be legally performed only by "master surgeons" dedicated to their specialty. A Royal College of Surgeons was chartered at Edinburgh in 1505.

The great names in surgery, in the first half of the fourteenth century, were Henri de Mondeville and Guy de Chauliac. Froissart might have noted that Mondeville, though always in great demand, remained poor to the end of his days, and carried on his work despite his own asthma and tuberculosis. His *Chirurgia* (1306–20), the first work on surgery by a Frenchman, covered the whole field with a thoroughness and competence that earned a new standing for surgeons. His distinctive contribution was the application and development of a method which he had learned from Theodoric Borgognoni at Bologna for treating wounds by complete cleansing, prevention of suppuration, exclusion of air, and dressings with wine. He defended his innovations by warning against a supine acceptance of Galen or other classic authorities. "Modern authors," he wrote, using a favorite medieval adjective, "are to the ancient like a dwarf placed upon the shoulders of a giant; he sees all that the giant sees, and farther still." [46]

The generation after him produced the most famous of medieval surgeons. Born of peasant stock in the French village that gave him its name, Guy de Chauliac so impressed the lords of the manor that they paid his tuition at Toulouse, Montpelier, Bologna, and Paris. In 1342 he became papal physician at Avignon, and held that difficult position for twenty-eight years. When the Black Death struck Avignon he stayed at his post, ministered to the victims, contracted the pestilence, and barely survived. Like any man, he committed serious errors: he blamed the plague now on an unfortunate con-junction of planets, now on Jews aiming to poison all Christendom; and he retarded the surgery of wounds by rejecting Mondeville's simple cleansing method and returning to the use of plasters and salves. But for the most part he lived up to the finest traditions of his great profession. His *Chirurgia magna* (1363) was the most thorough, systematic, and learned treatise on surgery produced before the sixteenth century.

Social and individual hygiene hardly kept pace with the advances of medi-cine. Personal cleanliness was not a fetish; even the King of England bathed only once a week, and sometimes skipped. The Germans had public baths—large vats in which the bathers stood or sat naked, sometimes both sexes to-gether; [47] Ulm alone had 168 such *Badestuben* in 1489. In all Europe—not always excepting the aristocracy—the same article of clothing was worn for months, or years, or generations. Many cities had a water supply, but it reached only a few homes; most families had to fetch water from the nearest fountain, well, or spring. The air of London was befouled by the odor of slaughtered cattle, till such carnage was forbidden in 1371. The smell of latrines detracted from the idyllic fantasies of rural life. London tenements had but one latrine for all occupants; many houses had none at all, and emptied their ordure into the yards or streets. Thousands of privies poured into the Thames; a city ordinance of 1357 denounced this, but the practice continued. In 1388, prodded by several returns of the plague, Parliament passed the first Sanitary Act for all England:

> For that so much dung and filth of the garbage and entrails, as well of beasts killed as of other corruptions, be cast and put in ditches, rivers, and other waters . . . that the air is greatly corrupt and infect, and many maladies and other intolerable diseases do daily happen, as well to inhabitants . . . as to others repairing or traveling thither . . . it is accorded and assented, That proclamation be made . . . throughout the realm of England . . . that all they which do cast and lay all such annoyances . . . shall cause them utterly to be removed . . . upon pain to lose and forfeit to our Lord the King.[48]

Similar ordinances were promulgated in France about this time. In 1383 Marseille, following the example of Ragusa (1377), ordered the isolation of plague-stricken persons for forty days—a *quarantine*. Epidemics continued to occur—the sweating sickness in England (1486, 1508), diphtheria and smallpox in Germany (1492)—but with diminished virulence and mortality. Though sanitation was lax, hospitals were relatively abundant; in 1500 England had 460, York alone had sixteen.[49]

The treatment of the insane gradually passed from superstitious reverence or barbaric cruelty to semi-scientific care. In 1300 the corpse of a girl who had claimed to be the Holy Ghost was dug up and burned by ecclesiastical order, and two women who expressed belief in her claim perished at the stake.[50] In 1359 the Archbishop of Toledo commissioned the civil authorities to burn alive a Spaniard who professed to be a brother of the Archangel Michael, and to visit heaven and hell daily.[51] Matters improved in the fifteenth century. A monk named Jean Joffre, filled with compassion for lunatics who were being hooted through the streets of Valladolid by a mob, established there an asylum for the insane (1409); and his example was followed in other cities. The hospital of St. Mary of Bethlehem, founded in London in 1247, was transformed into an insane asylum in 1402, and the word Bethlehem, corrupted into Bedlam, became a synonym for a place of insanity.

Confirmed lepers were still outcast from society, but leprosy almost disappeared from Western Europe in the fifteenth century. Syphilis took its place. Possibly a development of the *gros vérole* previously known in France, possibly an importation from America,* it appeared definitely in Spain in

---

* Cf. *The Renaissance*, pp. 534-7.

1493, in Italy in 1495; it spread so widely in France that it came to be called *morbus gallicus*; and some cities in Germany were so ravaged by it that they begged exemption from taxation.[52] As early as the end of the fifteenth century we hear of mercury being used in treating it. The progress of medicine ran a brave race then as now with the inventiveness of disease.

V. THE PHILOSOPHERS

Though the age of the system-makers had passed, philosophy was still vigorous; indeed in the fourteenth century it shook the whole dogmatic structure of Christendom. A change of emphasis ended the sway of the theologians in philosophy: the leading thinkers now took a major interest in science, like Buridan, or in economics, like Oresme, or in Church organization, like Nicholas of Cusa, or in politics, like Pierre Dubois and Marsilius of Padua. Intellectually these men were quite the equal of Albertus Magnus, Thomas Aquinas, Siger de Brabant, Bonaventura, and Duns Scotus.

Scholasticism—both as a method of argument and exposition and as an attempt to show the consistency of reason with faith—continued to dominate the northern universities. Aquinas was canonized in 1323; thereafter his fellow Dominicans, especially at Louvain and Cologne, felt it a point of honor to maintain his doctrine against all challenges. The Franciscans, as a loyal opposition, preferred to follow Augustine and Duns Scotus. One unmoored Dominican, William Durand of Saint-Pourçain, shocked his order by going over to the Scotists. At thirty-eight (*c.* 1308) he began a vast commentary, which he finished in old age. As he progressed he abandoned Aristotle and Aquinas, and proposed to put reason above the authority of "any doctor, however famous or solemn"—here was a philosopher with some sense of humor.[53] While remaining overtly orthodox in theology, he prepared for the uncompromising nominalism of Ockham by restoring the conceptualism of Abélard: only individual things exist; all abstract or general ideas are merely the useful shorthand concepts of the mind. William's friends called him *Doctor Resolutissimus*; his opponents called him *Durus Durandus*—Durand the Hard—and warmed themselves with the hope that the fires of hell would soften him at last.

William of Ockham was much harder, but did not wait till death to burn; his whole life was one of hot controversy, cooled only by occasional imprisonment, and the compulsion of the times to phrase his heat in Scholastic form. He admitted in philosophy no authority but experience and reason. He took his theorems passionately, and set half of Europe by the ears in defending his views. His life, adventures, and aims prefigure Voltaire's, and perhaps his effect was as great.

We cannot say precisely where or when he was born; probably at Ockham in Surrey, toward the end of the thirteenth century. While yet young he entered the Franciscan order, and about the age of twelve he was sent to Oxford as a bright lad who would surely be a shining light in the Church. At Oxford, and perhaps at Paris, he felt the influence of another subtle Franciscan, Duns Scotus; for though he opposed the "realism" of Scotus, he carried his predecessor's rationalist critique of philosophy and theology many steps further to a skepticism that would dissolve alike religious dogmas and scientific laws. He taught for six years at Oxford, and may have taught at Paris. Apparently before 1324—while still a tyro in his twenties—he wrote commentaries on Aristotle and Peter Lombard, and his most influential book, *Summa totius logicae*—a summary of all logic.

It seems at first sampling to be a dreary desert of logic-chopping and technical terminology, a lifeless procession of definitions, divisions, subdivisions, distinctions, classifications, and subtleties. Ockham knew all about "semantics"; he deplored the inaccuracy of the terms used in philosophy, and spent half his time trying to make them more precise. He resented the Gothic edifice of abstractions—one mounted upon the other like arches in super-imposed tiers—that medieval thought had raised. We cannot find in his extant works precisely the famous formula that tradition called "Ockham's razor": *entia non sunt multiplicanda praeter necessitatem*—entities are not to be multiplied beyond need. But he expressed the principle in other terms again and again: *pluralitas non est ponenda sine necessitate*—a plurality (of entities or causes or factors) is not to be posited (or assumed) without necessity; [54] and *frustra fit per plura quod potest fieri per pauciora*—it is vain to seek to accomplish or explain by assuming several entities or causes what can be explained by fewer.[55] The principle was not new; Aquinas had accepted it, Scotus had used it.[56] But in Ockham's hands it became a deadly weapon, cutting away a hundred occult fancies and grandiose abstractions.

Applying the principle to epistemology, Ockham judged it needless to assume, as the source and material of knowledge, anything more than sensations. From these arise memory (sensation revived), perception (sensation interpreted through memory), imagination (memories combined), anticipation (memory projected), thought (memories compared), and experience (memories interpreted through thought). "Nothing can be an object of the interior sense" (thought) "without having been an object of the exterior sense" (sensation); [57] here is Locke's empiricism 300 years before Locke. All that we ever perceive outside ourselves is individual entities—specific persons, places, things, actions, shapes, colors, tastes, odors, pressures, temperatures, sounds; and the words by which we denote these are "words of first intention" or primary intent, directly referring to what we interpret as external realities. By noting and abstracting the common features of similar entities so perceived, we may arrive at general or abstract ideas—man, virtue, height, sweetness, heat, music, eloquence; and the words by which we denote such abstractions are "words of second intention," referring to conceptions derived from perceptions. These "universals" are never experienced in sensation; they are *termini, signa, nomina*—terms, signs, names—for generalizations extremely useful (and dangerous) in thought or reason, in science, philosophy, and theology; they are not objects existing outside the mind. "Everything outside the mind is singular, numerically one." [58] Reason is magnificent, but its conclusions have meaning only in so far as they refer to experience—i.e., to the perception of individual entities, or the performance of individual acts; otherwise its conclusions are vain and perhaps deceptive abstractions. How much nonsense is talked or written by mistaking ideas for things, abstractions for realities! Abstract thought fulfills its function only when it leads to specific statements about specific things.

From this "nominalism" Ockham moved with devastating recklessness into every field of philosophy and theology. Both metaphysics and science, he announced, are precarious generalizations, since our experience is only of individual entities in a narrowly restricted area and time; it is mere arrogance on our part to assume the universal and eternal validity of the general propositions and "natural laws" that we derive from this tiny sector of reality. Our knowledge is molded and limited by our means and ways of perceiving things (this is Kant before Kant); it is locked un in the prison of our minds, and it must not pretend to be the objective or ultimate truth about anything. [59]

As for the soul, it too is an abstraction. It never appears in our sensations or perceptions, external or internal; all that we perceive is will, the ego asserting itself in every action and thought. Reason itself and all the glory of intellect are tools of the will; the intellect is merely the will thinking, seeking its ends by thought. [60] (This is Schopenhauer.)

God Himself seems to fall before this razor philosophy. Ockham (like Kant) found no conclusive force in any of the arguments used to prove the existence of deity. He rejected Aristotle's notion that the chain of motions or causes compels us to assume a Prime Mover or First Cause; an "infinite regress" of motions or causes is no more inconceivable than the unmoved Mover or uncaused Cause of Aristotle's theology. [61] Since nothing can be known save through direct perception, we can never have any clear knowledge that God exists—*non potest sciri evidenter quod Deus est*. [62] That God is omnipotent or infinite, omniscient or benevolent or personal, cannot be shown by reason; much less can reason prove that there are three persons in one God, or that God became man to atone for Adam and Eve's disobedience, or that the Son of God is present in the consecrated Host. [63] Nor is monotheism more rational than polytheism; there may be more worlds than one, and more gods to govern them.[64]

What then remained of the majestic edifice of Christian faith, its lovely myths and songs and art, its God-given morality, its fortifying hope? Ockham recoiled before the ruin of theology by reason, and in a desperate effort to save a social order based on a moral code based on religious belief, he proposed at last to sacrifice reason on the altar of faith. Though it cannot be proved, it is probable that God exists, and that He has endowed each of us with an immortal soul.[65] We must distinguish (as Averroës and Duns Scotus had advised) between theological truth and philosophical truth, and humbly accept in faith what proud reason doubts.

It was too much to expect that this caudal appendage in honor of "practical reason" would be accepted by the Church as atoning for Ockham's critique of pure reason. Pope John XXII ordered an ecclesiastical inquiry into the "abominable heresies" of the young friar, and summoned him to appear at the papal court in Avignon. Ockham came, for we find him, in 1328, in a papal prison there, with two other Franciscans. The three escaped, and fled to Aiguesmortes; they embarked in a small boat, and were picked up by a galley that took them to Louis of Bavaria at Pisa. The Pope excommunicated them, the Emperor protected them. William accompanied Louis to Munich, joined Marsilius of Padua there, lived in an anti-papal Franciscan monastery, and issued from it a torrent of books and pamphlets against the power and heresies of the popes in general, and of John XXII in particular.

As he had in his metaphysics outdone the skepticism of Scotus, so now in his practical theory Ockham carried to daring conclusions the anticlericalism of Marsilius of Padua. He applied his "razor" to the dogmas and rites that the Church had added to early Christianity, and demanded a return to the simpler creed and worship of the New Testament. In a pugnacious *Centiloquium theologicum* he brought before the tribunal of his reason a hundred dogmas of the Church, and argued that many of them led logically to intolerable absurdities. If, for example, Mary is the Mother of God, and God is father of us all, Mary is the mother of her father.[66] Ockham questioned the Apostolic Succession of the popes, and their infallibility; on the contrary, he urged, many of them had-been heretics, and some had been criminals.[67] He advocated a lenient treatment of heresy, proposing that all expression of opinion be left free except for the dissemination of conscious falsehood.[68] What Christianity needed, he thought, was a return from the Church to Christ, from wealth and power to simplicity of life and humility of rule. The Church should be defined not as the clergy alone but as the whole Christian community. This entire fellowship, including the women, should choose representatives, including women, to a general council, and this council should choose and govern the pope. Church and state should be under one head.[69]

The state itself should be subject to the will of the people, for in them is vested all final sovereignty on the earth. They delegate their right of legislation and administration to a king or emperor on the understanding that he will enact laws for the welfare of all. If the common good requires it, private property may be abolished.[70] If the ruler commits a great crime, or is guilty of negligence so extreme that it threatens the survival of the state, the people may justly depose him.

We know little of Ockham's fate. The beer of Munich could not console him for the lost wine of Paris. He compared himself to John the Evangelist on Patmos, but he dared not leave the protective orbit of the Emperor. According to a Franciscan chronicler the rebel in his final years signed a recantation of his heresies. Perhaps the reconciliation of Louis with the Church made this advisable; and William may have come to feel that to question the truth of a religion's dogmas is jejune. He died of the Black Death in 1349 or 1350, still in the prime of life.[71]

Long before his death he was recognized as the most forceful thinker of his age, and the universities shook with disputes over his philosophy. Many theologians accepted his view that the basic tenets of the Christian religion could not be proved by reason;[72] and the distinction between philosophical truth and religious truth was as widely spread in the fourteenth century as is today the tacit truce between scientific inquiry and religious ministrations. At Oxford a school of Ockhamists took form, called itself the *via moderna* (as Abélard had called his conceptualism 300 years before), and smiled at the metaphysical realism of Scotus and Aquinas.[73] The modernists were especially victorious in the universities of Central Europe; Huss at Prague and Luther at Erfurt were taught nominalism, and may have been conditioned by it for their revolt. At Paris the university authorities forbade (1339-40) the teaching of Ockham's views, but many of the students, and some masters, acclaimed him as the standard-bearer of free thought, and more than once the opposed factions, as in our times, fought with words and fists in the cafés or the streets.[74] It was probably in reaction against Ockhamism that Thomas à Kempis condemned philosophy in *The Imitation of Christ*.

Ockham played a part, if only as a voice, in the uprising of the nationalist state against the universalist Church. His propaganda for ecclesiastical poverty influenced Wyclif, and his assaults upon the papacy, as well as his constant appeal from the Church to the Bible and early Christianity, prepared for Luther, who ranked Ockham as the "chiefest and most ingenious of Scholastic doctors."[75] His voluntarism and individualism expressed in advance the heady spirit of the Renaissance. His skepticism passed down to Ramus and Montaigne, perhaps to Erasmus; his subjectivist limitation of knowledge to ideas foreshadowed Berkeley; his attempt to rescue faith through "practical reason" anticipated Kant. Though philosophically an idealist, his emphasis on sensation as the sole source of knowledge gave him a place in the procession of empirical English philosophy from Roger and Francis Bacon through Hobbes, Locke, Hume, Mill, and Spencer to Bertrand Russell. His occasional sallies into physical science—his perception of a law of inertia, his doctrine of action at a distance—stimulated thinkers from Jean Buridan to Isaac Newton.[76] The general effect of his work, like that of Duns Scotus, was to undermine the basic assumption of Scholasticism—that medieval Christian dogma could be proved by reason. Scholasticism maintained till the seventeenth century a pallid post-mortem existence, but it never recovered from these blows.

VI. THE REFORMERS

While ibn-Khaldun was founding sociology in Islam, Pierre Dubois, Nicole Oresme, Marsilius of Padua, and Nicholas of Cusa were developing kindred studies, less systematically, in Christendom. Dubois served Philip IV of France as Ockham and Marsilius served Louis of Bavaria, by aiming intellectual broadsides against the papacy, and singing doxologies to the state. In a *Supplication du peuple de France au roi contre le pape Boniface* (1308), and in a treatise *De recuperatione terre sancte* (*On the Recapture of the Holy Land*, 1305), the ardent lawyer recommended that the papacy should shed all its temporal possessions and powers, that the rulers of Europe should repudiate the papal authority in their realms, and that the French Church should divorce itself from Rome and submit to secular authority and law. Moreover, proceeded Dubois, all Europe should be united under the French king as emperor, with his capital at Constantinople as a bastion against Islam. An international court should be established to adjudicate the quarrels of nations, and an economic boycott should be declared against any Christian nation that should open war against another. Women should have the same educational opportunities and political rights as men.

No one seemed to pay much attention to these proposals, but they entered into the intellectual currents that undermined the papacy. Two centuries after Dubois, Henry VIII, who doubtless had never heard of him, followed his program, and Wyclif's, in religion; and in the early nineteenth century Napoleon set up for a moment a united Europe under French leadership, with the pope a captive of the state. Dubois belonged to that rising legal profession which aspired to replace the clergy in administering the government. He won his battle; we live in the heyday of his victory.

Oresme, who stirred so many pools, wrote toward 1355 one of the clearest and most straightforward essays in all economic literature—*On the Origin, Nature, Law, and Alterations of Money*. The money of a country, he argued, belongs to the community, not to the king; it is a social utility, not a royal perquisite; the ruler or government may regulate its issue, but should make no profit from minting it, and should maintain its metallic quality undebased. A king who dilutes the coinage is a thief.[77] Moreover, bad money (as "Gresham's Law" would say two centuries later) drives good money out of circulation; people will secrete or export good coin, and the dishonest government will receive in its revenues only its depreciated currency. These ideas of Oresme were not merely ideals; he taught them, as tutor, to the son of John II. When his pupil became Charles V, the young King, after one desperate devaluation, profited from his teacher's instruction by restoring the shattered finances of war-ridden France to a sound and honest basis.

Marsilius of Padua was of more volatile temperament than Oresme: an uncompromising individualist proud of his intellect and courage, and making his political philosophy an inextricable part of his hectic life. Son of a notary in Padua, he studied medicine at the university; probably he owed some of his anticlerical radicalism to the atmosphere of Averroistic skepticism that Petrarch found and denounced there in the same generation. Passing to Paris, he became for a year rector of the university. In 1324, with the minor collaboration of John of Jandun, he composed the most remarkable and influential political treatise of the Middle Ages—*Defensor pacis (The Defender of Peace)*. Knowing that the book must be condemned by the Church, the authors fled to Nuremberg and placed themselves under the wing of the Emperor Louis of Bavaria, then at war with the pope.

They could not have expected so lusty a fighter as John XXII to take calmly their bellicose defense of peace. The book argued that the peace of Europe was being destroyed by strife between state and Church, and that peace could be restored and best maintained by bringing the Church, with all her property and personnel, under the same Imperial or royal authority as other groups and goods. It was (ran the argument) a mistake for the Church ever to have acquired property; nothing in Scripture justified such acquisition.

Like Ockham, the authors defined the Church as the whole body of Christians. As the Roman people, in Roman law, was the real sovereign, and merely delegated its authority to consuls, senate, or emperors, so the Christian community should delegate, but should never surrender, its powers to its representatives, the clergy; and these should be held responsible to the people whom they represent. The derivation of the papal supremacy from the Apostle Peter is, in Marsilius's view, an historical error; Peter had no more authority than the other Apostles, and the bishops of Rome, in their first three centuries, had no more authority than the bishops of several other ancient capitals. Not the pope but the emperor or his delegates presided over the first general councils. A general council, freely elected by the people of Christendom, should interpret the Scriptures, define the Catholic faith, and choose the cardinals, who should choose the pope.[78] In all temporal matters the clergy, including the pope, should be subject to civil jurisdiction and law. The state should appoint and remunerate the clergy, fix the number of churches and priests, remove such priests as it finds unworthy, take control of ecclesiastical endowments, schools, and income, and relieve the poor out of the surplus revenues of the Church.[79]

Here again was the strident voice of the upsurging national state. Having, through the support of the rising middle classes, subdued the barons and the communes, the kings now felt strong enough to repudiate the claims of the Church to sovereignty over the civil power. Seizing the opportunity presented by the deterioration of the Church's international and intellectual authority, the secular rulers now dreamed of mastering every phase of life in their realms, including religion and the Church. This was the basic issue that would be fought out in the Reformation; and the triumph of the state over the Church would mark one terminus of the Middle Ages. (In 1535 Henry VIII, at the height of his revolt against the Church, had the *Defensor pacis* translated and published at governmental expense.)

Marsilius, like Ockham and Luther, after proposing to replace the authority of the Church with that of the people, was compelled, both for social order and for his own security, to replace it with the authority of the state. But he did not raise the kings into ogres of omnipotence. He looked beyond the triumph of the state to the day when the people might actually exercise the sovereignty that legal theorists had long affected to vest in them. In ecclesiastical reform he advocated democracy: each Christian community should choose its representative to church councils, each parish should choose its own priests, control them, dismiss them if need should be; and no member of the parish should be excommunicated without its consent. Marsilius applied similar principles to civil government, but with hesitant modifications:

> We declare, according to truth and the opinion of Aristotle, that the legislator—the prime and proper effective cause of law—should be the people, the whole body of citizens, or its weightier part (*valentiorem partem*), commanding or deciding by its own choice or will, expressed verbally in a general assembly of the citizens. . . . I say weightier part, taking into consideration both the number of persons, and their quality, in the community for which the law is enacted. The whole body of citizens, or its weightier part, either makes law directly or commits this duty to some one or a few; but the latter do not, and cannot, constitute the legislator in the strict sense of the term; they act only in such matters, and for such periods, as are covered by the

authorization from the primary legislator. . . . I call citizen him who participates in the civil community with either deliberative or judicial authority, according to his rank. By this definition boys, slaves, aliens, and women are distinguished from citizens. . . . Only out of the deliberation and will of the whole multitude is the best law produced. . . . A majority, more readily than any of its parts, can discern the defects in a law proposed for enactment, for an entire body is greater in power and worth than any of its separate parts.[80]

This is a remarkable statement for its time (1324), and the conditions of the age justify its hesitations. Even Marsilius would not advocate equal suffrage for all adults in a Europe where hardly one person in ten could read, communication was difficult, and class divisions were mortised in the cement of time. Indeed, he rejected complete democracy, wherein policy and legislation would be determined by a count of noses (*egenorum multitudo*—"a multitude of needy people"); and to correct this "corruption of a republic" he was willing that individuals should have political power commensurate with their value to the community—though he did not say how or by whom this was to be judged. He left room for monarchy, but added that "a ruler who is elected is greatly to be preferred to rulers who are hereditary." [81] The king is to be a delegate and servant of the public; and if he seriously misbehaves it may rightly depose him.[82]

These ideas had a medieval, even an ancient, origin: the Roman lawyers and the Scholastic philosophers had regularly endowed the people with a theoretical sovereignty; the papacy itself was an elective monarchy; the pope called himself *servus servorum Dei*—"servant of the servants of God"; and Thomas Aquinas had agreed with John of Salisbury on the right of the people to overthrow a lawless king. But rarely in Christendom had these ideas been extended to so explicit a formulation of representative government. Here in one man, in the fourteenth century, were the ideas of both the Protestant Reformation and the French Revolution.

Marsilius was too far ahead of his time to be comfortable. He rose rapidly with Louis of Bavaria, and fell rapidly with his fall. When Louis made peace with the popes he was required to dismiss Marsilius as a heretic. We do not know the sequel. Apparently Marsilius died in 1343, an outcast alike from the Church that he had fought and from the state that he had labored to exalt.

His temporary success would have been impossible had not the rising legal profession given to the state an authority rivaling that of the Church. Over the ruins of feudal and communal law, beside and often against the canon law of the Church, the lawyers raised the "positive law" of the state; and year by year this royal or secular law extended its reach over the affairs of men. The law schools of Montpelier, Orléans, and Paris turned out bold and subtle legists who used Roman law to build up, as against papal claims, a theory of divine right and absolute power for their royal masters. These ideas were strongest in France, where they evolved into *L'état c'est moi* and *Le roi soleil;* they prevailed also in Spain, preparing the absolutism of Ferdinand, Charles V, and Philip II; and even in parliamentary England Wyclif expounded the unlimited authority of the divine king. Lords and commons opposed the theory, and Sir John Fortescue insisted that the English king could not issue laws without the consent of Parliament, and that English judges were bound, by their oath, to judge by the law of the land, whatever the king might desire; but under Henry VII, Henry VIII, and Elizabeth, England too would kneel to absolute rulers. Between the rival absolutisms of popes and kings some idealistic spirits clung to the notion of a "natural law," a divine justice implanted in the human conscience, phrased in the Gospels, and superior to any law of man. Neither the state nor the Church paid more than lip service to this conception; it remained in the background, professed and ignored, but ever faintly alive. In the eighteenth century it would father the American Declaration of Independence and the French Declaration of the Rights of Man, and would play a minor but eloquent role in a revolution that for a time upset both the absolutisms that had ruled mankind.

Nicholas of Cusa fought, and then resigned himself to, the absolutism of the papacy. In his varied career he showed the best face of organized Christianity to a Germany always suspicious of the Church. Philosopher and administrator, theologian and legist, mystic and scientist, he combined in one powerful personality the best constituents of those Middle Ages that were closing with his life. Born at Cues, near Trier (1401), he learned a medley of scholarship and devotion in the school of the Brethren of the Common Life at Deventer. In a year at Heidelberg he felt the influence of Ockham's nominalism; at Padua he was touched for a time with the skepticism of Averroës; at Cologne he absorbed the orthodox tradition of Albertus Magnus and Thomas Aquinas; all the elements were mixed in him that would make him the most complete Christian of his time.

He never quite abandoned the mystical mood that had reached him from Meister Eckhart; he wrote a classic of mysticism in *De visione Dei;* and in a philosophic defense of such visions *(Apologia doctae ignorantiae)* he coined a famous phrase—"learned ignorance." He rejected the Scholastic rationalism that sought to prove theology by reason; all human knowledge, he felt, is relative and uncertain; truth is hidden in God.[83] Generally he rejected astrology; but, succumbing to the delusions of his epoch, he indulged in some astrological calculations, and reckoned that the end of the world would come in 1734.[84] Amid a life crowded with ecclesiastical activity he kept abreast of scientific thought. He urged more experiment and more accurate measurements; he suggested timing the fall of different bodies from different heights; he taught that the earth "cannot be fixed, but moves like other stars"; [85] every star, however fixed it may seem, moves; no orbit is precisely circular; the earth is not the center of the universe, except in so far as any point may be taken as the center of an infinite universe.[86] These were sometimes judicious borrowings, sometimes brilliant *aperçus*.

In 1433 Nicholas went to Basel to present to the ecclesiastical council there the claims of a friend to the archiepiscopal see of Cologne. His plea failed, but he took the opportunity of presenting to the council—then at odds with the pope—a work of some moment in the history of philosophy. He called it *De concordantia Catholica,* and its general purpose was to find terms of accord between the councils and the popes. In an elaborate analogy with a living organism, he pictured the Church as an organic unity, incapable of successful functioning except through the harmonious co-operation of its parts. Instead of concluding, as the popes might have done, that the parts should be guided by the head, Nicholas argued that only a general council could represent, express, and unify the interdependent elements of the Church. He repeated Aquinas and Marsilius, and almost plagiarized Rousseau and Jefferson, in an idealistic passage:

> Every law depends upon the law of nature; and if it contradicts this it cannot be a valid law.... Since by nature all men are free, then every government ... exists solely by the agreement and consent of the subjects.... The binding power of any law consists in this tacit or explicit agreement and consent.[87]

The sovereign people delegates its powers to small groups equipped by education or experience to make or administer laws; but these groups derive their just powers from the consent of the governed. When the Christian community delegates its powers to a general council of the Church, that council, and not the pope, represents the sovereign authority in religion. Nor can the pope rest his claim to legislative absolutism on the supposed Donation of Constantine, for that Donation is a forgery and a myth.[88] A pope has a right to summon a general council, but such a council, if it judges him unfit, may rightly depose him. And the same principles hold for secular princes. An elective monarchy is probably the best government available to mankind in its present depraved condition; but the secular ruler, like the pope, should periodically convene a representative assembly, and should submit to its decrees.

Nicholas' later life was a model for prelates. Made a cardinal (1448), he became in person a Catholic Reformation. In a strenuous tour through the Netherlands and Germany, he held provincial synods, revived ecclesiastical discipline, reformed the monasteries and nunneries, attacked priestly concubinage, furthered the education of the clergy, and raised, at least for a time, the level of clerical and popular morality. "Nicholas of Cusa," wrote the learned Abbot Trithemius, "appeared in Germany as an angel of light and peace amid darkness and confusion. He restored the unity of the Church, strengthened the authority of her Supreme Head, and sowed a precious seed of new life." [89]

To his other titles Nicholas could have added that of humanist. He loved the ancient classics, encouraged their study, and planned to print for wide circulation the Greek manuscripts that he himself had brought from Constantinople. He had the true scholar's tolerance. In a *Dialogue on Peace*, composed in the very year when Constantinople fell to the Turks, he pleaded for mutual understanding among the religions as diverse rays of one eternal truth.[90] And in the dawn of modern thought, when the rising freedom of the intellect was an intoxication, he wrote sound and noble words:

> To know and to think, to see the truth with the eye of the mind, is always a joy. The older a man grows, the greater is the pleasure that this affords him. . . . As love is the life of the heart, so is the endeavor after knowledge and truth the life of the mind. Amid the movements of time, the daily labor, perplexities, and contradictions of life, we should lift our gaze fearlessly to the clear vault of heaven, and seek ever to obtain a firmer grasp of . . . the origin of all goodness and beauty, the capacities of our own hearts and minds, the intellectual fruits of mankind throughout the centuries, and the wonderful works of Nature around us; but remembering always that in humility alone lies true greatness, and that knowledge and wisdom are profitable only in so far as our lives are governed by them.[91]

Had there been more such Nicholases there might have been no Luther.

CHAPTER XIII

The Conquest of the Sea

1492-1517

I. COLUMBUS

IT was "manifest destiny" that someone in this age would dare the perils of the Atlantic to find India or "Cathay." For two thousand years legend had told of an Atlantis across the sea; and later myths had placed beyond the Atlantic a fountain whose waters conferred eternal youth. The failure of the Crusades compelled the discovery of America; the domination of the eastern Mediterranean by the Turks, the closing or obstruction of land routes by the Ottomans at Constantinople and by anti-Christian dynasties in Persia and Turkestan, made the old avenues of East-West trade costly and dangerous. Italy and even France might cling to the remnants of that trade over every discouragement of tolls and war, but Portugal and Spain were too far west to make such arrangements profitably; their problem was to find another route. Portugal found one around Africa; nothing was left for Spain but to try a passage west.

The growth of knowledge had long since established the sphericity of the earth. The very errors of science encouraged audacity by underestimating the width of the Atlantic, and picturing Asia as lying ready for conquest and exploitation on the farther side. Scandinavian mariners had reached Labrador in 986 and 1000, and had brought back news of an immense continent. In 1477, if we may believe his own account, Christopher Columbus visited Iceland,[1] and presumably heard proud traditions of Leif Ericsson's voyage to "Vinland." All that was needed now, for the great adventure, was money. Bravery abounded.

Columbus himself, in the *Mayorazzo* or will that he made before setting out on his third voyage across the Atlantic, named Genoa as his birthplace. It is true that in his extant writings he always calls himself by the Spanish name Cristóbal Colón, never by the Italian name Cristoforo Colombo; but this was presumably because he was writing in Spanish, living in Spain, or sailing for a Spanish sovereign, not because he had been born in Spain. Possibly his forebears had been Spanish Christianized Jews who had migrated to Italy; the evidence of Hebraic blood and sentiment in Columbus is almost convincing.[2] His father was a weaver, and Christoforo appears to have followed that craft for a time in Genoa and Savona. The biography written by his son Ferdinand credits him with studying astronomy, geometry, and cosmography at the University of Pavia, but the university records do not list him, and he himself tells us that he became a sailor at fourteen.[3] For in Genoa every road leads down to the sea.

In 1476 a ship on which he was heading for Lisbon was attacked by pirates; the vessel foundered; Columbus relates that with the support of some wreckage he swam six miles to the shore; but the great admiral had high powers of imagination. A few months later (he says) he sailed for England as seaman or captain, thence to Iceland, thence to Lisbon. There he married, and settled down as a maker of maps and charts. His father-in-law was a mariner who had served Prince Henry the Navigator; doubtless Columbus heard from him some glowing tales of the Guinea coast. In 1482, probably as an officer, he joined a Portuguese fleet that sailed that coast to Elmina. He read with interest, and many annotations, Pope Pius II's *Historia rerum gestarum*, which suggested the circumnavigability of Africa.[4]

But his studies more and more inclined him to the west. He knew that Strabo, in the first century of our era, had told of an attempt to circle the globe. He was familiar with Seneca's lines: "An age will come in after years when Ocean will loose the bonds of things, and an immense land will appear, and the prophet Tiphys will reveal new worlds, and Thule [Iceland?] will no longer be the end of the earth."[5] He had read *The Book of Ser Marco Polo*, which glorified the riches of China and placed Japan 1,500 miles east of the mainland of Asia. He made over a thousand notes in his copy of Pierre d'Ailly's *Imago mundi*. He accepted the prevailing estimate of the earth's circumference as 18,000 to 20,000 miles; and combining this with Polo's displacement of Japan, he reckoned that the nearest Asiatic islands would be some 5,000 miles west of Lisbon. He had heard of a letter (1474) in which the Florentine physician Paolo Toscanelli had advised King Affonso V of Portugal that a shorter way to India than that around Africa could be found by sailing 5,000 miles west. Columbus wrote to Toscanelli, and received an encouraging reply. His purpose matured, and seethed in his brain.

About 1484 he proposed to John II of Portugal that the King should equip three vessels for a year of exploration across the Atlantic and back; that Columbus should be appointed "Great Admiral of the Ocean" and perpetual governor of whatever lands he might discover; and that he should receive a tenth of all revenues and precious metals thereafter derived from those lands by Portugal.[6] (Obviously the idea of spreading Christianity was secondary to material considerations.) The King submitted the proposal to a committee of savants; they rejected it on the ground that Columbus's estimate of the distance across the Atlantic as merely 2,400 miles was far too small. (It was approximately correct from the Canary Islands to the West Indies.)

In 1485 two Portuguese navigators proposed a similar project to King John, but agreed to finance it themselves; John gave them at least his blessing; they sailed (1487), followed too northern a route, encountered rough westerly winds, and turned back in despair. Columbus renewed his appeal (1488); the King invited him to an audience; Columbus came just in time to witness the triumphant return of Bartholomeu Dias from a successful rounding of Africa. Absorbed in prospects of an African route to India, the Portuguese government abandoned consideration of a passage across the Atlantic. Columbus turned to Genoa and Venice, but they too gave him no encouragement, for they had a vested interest in the eastward route to the East. He commissioned his brother to sound out Henry VII of England, who invited Columbus to a conference. When the invitation reached him he had already committed himself to Spain.

He was now (1488) some forty-two years old; tall and thin, with long face, ruddy complexion, eagle nose, blue eyes, freckles, bright red hair already turning gray, and soon to be white. His son and his friends described him as modest, grave, affable, discreet, temperate in eating and drinking, fervently pious. Others alleged that he was vain, that he paraded and inflated the titles he received, that he ennobled his ancestry in his imagination and his writings, and that he bargained avidly for his share in the New World's gold; however, he was worth more than he asked. He deviated occasionally from the Ten Commandments, for at Córdoba, after his wife's death, Beatriz Enríquez bore him an illegitimate son (1488). Columbus did not marry her, but he provided well for her in his life and his will; and as most dignitaries in those agile times had such by-products, no one seems to have been put out by the accident.

Meanwhile he had laid his petition before Isabella of Castile (May 1, 1486). She referred it to a group of advisers presided over by the saintly Archbishop Talavera. After long delay they reported the plan to be impracticable, arguing that Asia must be much farther west than Columbus supposed. Nevertheless Ferdinand and Isabella gave him an annuity of 12,000 *maravedis* ($840?), and in 1489 they furnished him with a letter ordering all Spanish municipalities to provide him with food and lodging; perhaps they wished to keep an option on his project lest by some chance it should bestow a continent on a rival king. But when the Talavera committee, after reconsidering the scheme, again rejected it, Columbus resolved to submit it to Charles VIII of France. Fray Juan Pérez, head of the monastery of La Rabida, dissuaded him by arranging another audience with Isabella. She sent him 20,000 *maravedis* to finance his trip to her headquarters at the siege city of Santa Fé. He went; she heard his plea kindly enough, but her advisers once more discountenanced the idea. He resumed his preparations for going to France (January 1492).

At this critical juncture a baptized Jew prodded the march of history. Luis de Santander, finance minister to Ferdinand, reproached Isabella for lack of imagination and enterprise, tempted her with the prospect of converting Asia to Christianity, and proposed to finance the expedition himself with the aid of his friends. Several other Jews—Don Isaac Abrabanel, Juan Cabrero, Abraham Senior—supported his plea.[7] Isabella was moved, and offered to pledge her jewels to raise the needed sum. Santander judged this unnecessary; he borrowed 1,400,000 *maravedis* from the fraternity of which he was treasurer; he added 350,000 out of his own pocket; and Columbus somehow got together 250,000 more.* On April 17, 1492, the King signed the requisite papers. Then or later he gave Columbus a letter to the Khan of Cathay; it was China, not India, that Columbus hoped to reach, and which to the end of his life he thought he had found. On August 3 the *Santa María* (his flagship), the *Pinta*, and the *Niña* sailed from Palos with eighty-eight men, and provisions for a year.

II. AMERICA

They headed south to the Canary Islands, seeking winds from the east before they faced into the west. After a long stay at the islands they ventured forth (September 6) along the twenty-eighth parallel of latitude—not quite far enough south to get the full boon of the trade winds; we know now that a still more southerly crossing would have shortened the distance and tribulation to America. The weather was kindly, "like April in Andalusia," Columbus noted in his log; "the only thing wanting was to hear nightingales." Thirty-three days passed anxiously. Columbus understated to his men the nautical mileage of each day; but as he overestimated his speed, his statements were unwillingly correct. The calms persisting, he changed his course, whereupon, even more than before, the crew felt lost in the aimless wastes of the sea. On October 9 the captains of the *Pinta* and the *Niña* boarded the flagship and pleaded for an immediate turnabout back to Spain. Columbus promised that unless land were sighted in three days he would do as they wished. On October 10 his own crew mutinied, but he appeased them with the same pledge. On October 11 they drew from the ocean a green branch bearing flowers; their trust in the Admiral returned. At two o'clock the next morning, under a nearly full moon, Rodrigo de Triana, the lookout on the *Niña*, shouted *Tierra! tierra!* It was land at last.

When dawn came they saw naked natives on the beach, "all of good

---

* All these private contributions were later repaid by the government. Santander was summoned before the Inquisition July 17, 1491, on charges unknown; he was "reconciled," but apparently relapsed into heresy or Judaism, for all his property was confiscated; Ferdinand, however, restored it to his children.[8]

stature." The three captains were rowed to the shore by armed men; they knelt, kissed the ground, and thanked God. Columbus christened the island San Salvador—Holy Saviour—and took possession of it in the name of Ferdinand, Isabella, and Christ. The savages received their future enslavers with civilized courtesies. The Admiral wrote:

> In order that we might win good friendship—because I knew that they were a people who could better be freed and converted to our Holy Father by love than by force, I gave to some of them red caps, and to some glass beads . . . and many other things of slight value, in which they took much pleasure. They remained so much our friends that it was a marvel; and later they came swimming to the ships' boats, and brought us parrots and cotton thread . . . and many other things, and in exchange we gave them little glass beads. . . . Finally they exchanged with us everything they had, with good will.[9]

The report of the "friendly and flowing savage" which was to bewitch Rousseau, Chateaubriand, and Whitman may have begun then and there. But among the first things that Columbus learned on the island was that these natives were subject to slave raids by other native groups, and that they themselves, or their ancestors, had conquered earlier indigenes. Two days after landing, the Admiral struck an ominous note in his journal: "These people are very unskilled in arms. . . . With fifty men they could all be subjected and made to do all that one wished." [10]

But alas, there was no gold in San Salvador. On October 14 the little fleet sailed again, seeking Cipango—Japan—and gold. On October 28 a landing was made on Cuba. There too the natives were well disposed; they tried to join their visitors in singing the Ave Maria, and did their best to make the sign of the cross. When Columbus showed them gold they seemed to indicate that he would find some at a point in the interior which they called Cubanacam—i.e., mid-Cuba. Mistaking this for *El gran can*—the Great Khan of China—he sent two Spaniards, with full diplomatic credentials, to find that elusive potentate. They returned without locating the Khan, but with a pleasant account of the courtesies with which they had been everywhere received. They brought also the first report, by Europeans, of American tobacco: they had seen male and female natives smoking *tabaco* herbs rolled into a cigar, which was inserted into the nose. Disappointed, Columbus left Cuba (December 4), taking with him, by force, five native youths to serve as interpreters, and seven women to comfort them. All died en route to Spain.

Meanwhile Columbus's senior captain, Martín Alonso Pinzón, had deserted with his ship to hunt gold on his own. On December 5 Columbus reached Haiti. There he remained four weeks, welcomed and feasted by the natives. He found some gold, and felt himself a bit closer to the Khan; but his flagship grounded on a reef, and was smashed to pieces by waves and rocks, on the eve of the Christmas that he had planned to celebrate as the happiest of his life. Luckily the *Niña* was near by to rescue the crew, and the kindly natives ventured out in their canoes to help salvage most of the cargo before the vessel sank. Their chieftain consoled Columbus with hospitality and gold, and assurances that there was plenty of the murderous metal in Haiti. The Admiral thanked God for the gold, forgave Him for the shipwreck, and wrote in his journal that Ferdinand and Isabella would now have funds sufficient to conquer the Holy Land. He was so impressed with the good manners of the natives that he left part of his crew as a settlement to explore the island while he returned to Spain to report his discoveries. On January 6, 1493, Pinzón rejoined him with the *Pinta;* his apologies were accepted, for Columbus was loath to sail back with only one ship. On January 16 they began the journey home.

It was a long and miserable voyage. All through January the winds were hostile, and on February 12 a violent storm buffeted the tiny ships, which were not much more than seventy feet long.[11] As they approached the Azores, Pinzón deserted again, hoping to be the first to reach Spain with the great news that Asia had been found. The *Niña* anchored off Santa Maria in the Azores (February 17); half the crew went ashore, partly to make a pilgrimage to a shrine of the Virgin; they were arrested by the Portuguese authorities and were kept in jail for four days while Columbus fretted offshore. They were released, and the *Niña* sailed again; but another storm drove it from its course, split its sails, and so depressed the sailors that they vowed to spend their first day on land fasting on bread and water and observing the Ten Commandments. On March 3 they sighted Portugal, and though Columbus knew that he was risking a diplomatic mess, he decided to debark at Lisbon rather than attempt the remaining 225 miles to Palos with one sail. John II received him with courtesy; the *Niña* was repaired; and on March 15 it reached Palos after "infinite toil and terror" (said Columbus), 193 days after leaving that port. Martín Pinzón had landed on northwestern Spain several days before, and had sent a message to Ferdinand and Isabella, but they refused to see him or his messenger. The *Pinta* sailed into Palos a day after the *Niña*. Pinzón fled in fear and disgrace to his home, took to his bed, and died.

III. THE WATERS OF BITTERNESS

Columbus was welcomed by King and Queen at Barcelona, lived six months at the court, and received the title *Almirante del Mar Oceano*—"Admiral of the Ocean Sea"—by which was meant the Atlantic west of the

Azores. He was made governor of the New World, or, as he described him-self, "Vice-King and General Governor of the Islands and Terra Firma of Asia and India." [12] As John II was rumored to be fitting out a fleet to cross the Atlantic, Ferdinand appealed to Alexander VI to define the rights of Spain in the "Ocean Sea." The Spanish Pope, in a series of bulls (1493), al-lotted to Spain all non-Christian lands west, and to Portugal all those east, of an imaginary line drawn north and south 270 miles west of the Azores and the Cape Verde Islands. The Portuguese refused to accept this line of de-marcation, and war was imminent when the rival governments, by the Treaty of Tordesillas (June 7, 1494), agreed that the line should run along a meridian of longitude 250 leagues west of the Cape Verde Islands for dis-coveries before that date, but 370 leagues west for later discoveries. (The eastern corner of Brazil lies east of this second line.) The papal bulls termed the new terrain "Indies"; scholars like Pietro Martire d' Anghiera accepted Columbus's notion that he had reached Asia; and this delusion persisted till Magellan circumnavigated the globe.

Hoping for gold, Ferdinand and Isabella provided Columbus with a new fleet of seventeen vessels, equipped with 1,200 seamen, animals to start flocks and herds in the "Indies," and five ecclesiastics to shrive the Spaniards and convert the "Indians." The second voyage sailed from Seville on September 25, 1493. Thirty-nine days later (as against seventy days for the first voy-age), the watch sighted an island which Columbus, because the day was Sunday, named Dominica. No landing was made there; the Admiral scented bigger prey. He passed through the westernmost group of the Lesser An-tilles, and was so impressed by their number that he named them Once Mil Virgenes—"Eleven Thousand Virgins"; they are still the Virgin Islands. Sailing on, he discovered Puerto Rico; he dallied there briefly, then hurried on to see what had happened to the Spanish settlement that he had left in Haiti ten months before. Hardly a man remained of it. The Europeans had roamed the island robbing the natives of gold and women; they had estab-lished a tropical paradise with five women to each man; they had quarreled and murdered one another, and nearly all the rest had been killed by the out-raged Indians.

The fleet sailed eastward along the Haitian coast. On January 2, 1494, the Admiral landed men and cargo to found a new settlement, which he called Isabella. After supervising the construction of a town and the repair of his ships, he left to explore Cuba. Unable to circumnavigate it, he concluded that it was the mainland of Asia, perhaps the Malay Peninsula. He thought of rounding it and circling the globe, but his ships were not equipped for it. He turned back toward Haiti (October 29, 1494), wondering how his new settlement had fared. He was shocked to find that it had behaved like its predecessor; that the Spaniards had raped native women, stolen native stores of food, and kidnaped native boys to serve as slaves; and that the natives had killed many Spaniards in revenge. The missionaries had made little attempt to Christianize the Indians. One friar had joined a group of malcontents who had sailed back to Spain to give the sovereigns a discouraging report of Haiti's reputed resources. Columbus himself now became a slave dealer. He sent out expeditions to capture 1,500 natives; 400 of these he gave to the settlers, 500 he dispatched to Spain. Two hundred of these died on the voyage; the survivors were sold at Seville, but died in a few years, unable to adjust themselves to the colder climate, or perhaps to the savagery of civilization.

Leaving orders with his brother Bartolomé to transfer the settlement from Isabella to a better site at Santo Domingo (now Ciudad Trujillo), Columbus sailed for Spain (March 10, 1496), and reached Cádiz after an unhappy voyage of ninety-three days. He presented his sovereigns with Indians and gold nuggets; it was not much, but it modified the doubts that had formed at court about the wisdom of pouring more money into the Atlantic. The Admiral was uncomfortable on land; the salt of the sea was in his blood; he begged for at least eight ships for another trial of fortune. The sovereigns consented; and in May 1498, Columbus sailed again.

This third voyage moved southwest to the tenth meridian of latitude, then followed this due west. On July 31 the crew sighted the great island which the pious commander named Trinidad; and on August 31 he saw the mainland of South America, perhaps a year before, perhaps a year after, Vespucci. After exploring the Gulf of Paria he sailed northwest, and reached Santo Domingo August 31. This third settlement had survived, but one of every four of the five hundred Spaniards that he had left there in 1496 was suffering from syphilis, and the settlers had divided into two hostile groups that were now on the verge of war. To appease the discontent, Columbus allowed each man to appropriate a large tract of land, and to enslave the natives dwelling on it; this became the rule in the Spanish settlements. Worn now with hardships, disappointments, arthritis, and a disease of the eyes, Columbus almost broke down under these problems. His mind clouded occasionally, he became irritable, querulous, dictatorial, avaricious, and ruthless in his punishments; so at least many of the Spaniards claimed, and they fretted under an Italian's rule. He recognized that the problems of managing the settlement were alien to his training and temperament. In October 1499, he sent two caravels to Spain with a request that Ferdinand and Isabella should appoint a royal commissioner to help him govern the island.

The sovereigns took him at his word, and appointed Francisco de Bobadilla; but, going beyond the Admiral's request, they gave their commissioner full authority, even over Columbus. Bobadilla reached Santo Domingo while Columbus was away, and heard many complaints of the manner in which Cristoforo and his brothers Bartolomé and Diego had ruled what was now called Hispaniola. When Columbus returned, Bobadilla had him cast into jail, with manacles on his arms and fetters on his feet. After a further inquest the commissioner sent the three brothers, in chains, to Spain (October 1, 1500). Arriving at Cádiz, Columbus wrote a pitiful letter to friends at court:

> It is now seventeen years since I came to serve these princes with the Enterprise of the Indies. They made me pass eight of them in discussion, and at the end rejected it as a thing of jest. Nonetheless I persisted therein. . . . Over there I have placed under their sovereignty more land than there is in Africa and Europe, and more than 1,700 islands. . . . In seven years I, by the divine will, made that conquest. At a time when I was entitled to expect rewards and retirement, I was incontinently arrested and sent home loaded with chains. . . . The accusation was brought out of malice on the basis of charges made by civilians who had revolted and wished to take possession of the land. . . .
>
> I beg your graces, with the zeal of faithful Christians in whom their Highnesses have confidence, to read all my papers, and to consider how I, who came from so far to serve these princes . . . now at the end of my days have been despoiled of my honor and my property without cause, wherein is neither justice nor mercy.[18]

Ferdinand was busy dividing the Kingdom of Naples with Louis XII; six weeks went by before he ordered Columbus and his brothers released, and summoned them to court. King and Queen received them in the Alhambra, consoled them, and restored them to affluence, but not to their former authority in the New World. By the Capitulations or agreement that they had signed in 1492, the sovereigns were bound to leave Columbus full authority in the lands he had discovered, but they felt that he was no longer fit to exercise it. They named Don Nicolás de Ovando as new governor of the Indies; however, they allowed the Admiral to collect all his property rights at Santo Domingo, and all that was hitherto due him of the gold diggings and trade. Columbus lived the rest of his life a rich man.

But he was not content. He importuned the King and Queen for one more fleet; and though they were not yet clear that the "Enterprise of the Indies" would bring them a net gain, they felt that they owed him another trial. On May 9, 1502, from Cádiz, Columbus began his fourth voyage, with four ships and 140 men, including his brother Bartolomé and his son Fernando. On June 15 he sighted Martinique. On June 29, feeling a storm in the air and in his joints, he anchored off a sheltered spot of the Haitian shore near Santo Domingo. A fleet of thirty ships was in the main harbor, about to sail for Spain. Columbus sent word to the governor that a hurricane was brewing, and advised him to detain the vessels for a while. Ovando rejected the warnings and dispatched the fleet. The hurricane arrived; the Admiral's ships survived it with minor damage; of the governor's fleet all vessels but one were wrecked; 500 lives were lost, including Bobadilla's; and a rich cargo of gold was surrendered to the sea.

Columbus now began, unsuspectingly, the most arduous and tragic months in his troubled career. Continuing westward, he reached Honduras, and explored the coast of Nicaragua and Costa Rica in the hope of finding a strait that would let him circumnavigate the earth. On December 5, 1502, a tempest of wind and rain arose, whose mad force is vividly described in Columbus's journal:

> For nine days I was as one lost, without any hope of life. Eyes never beheld the sea so high, angry, and covered with foam. The wind not only prevented our progress, but offered no opportunity to run behind any headland for shelter; hence we were forced to keep out in this bloody ocean, seething like a pot on a hot fire. Never did the sky look more terrible; for one whole day and night it blazed like a furnace, and the lightning broke forth with such violence that each time I wondered if it had carried off my spars and sails; the flashes came with such fury and frightfulness that we all thought that the ships would be blasted. All this time the water never ceased to fall from the sky; I do not say it rained, for it was like another deluge. The men were so worn out that they longed for death to end their dreadful suffering.[14]

To add to the terror of wind, water, lightning, and rocky reefs near by, a waterspout—a spray-spreading "twister" in the sea—appeared, perilously close to the ships, and shooting water "up to the clouds." Columbus took out his Bible, and read from it how Christ had stilled the storm at Capernaum; then he exorcized the waterspout by tracing with his sword a cross in the sky, whereupon, we are told, the tower of water collapsed. After twelve awful days the fury passed, and the fleet rested in a harbor near the present eastern end of the Panama Canal. There Columbus and his men celebrated sadly the Christmas of 1502 and the New Year's Day of 1503, not knowing that the Pacific was only forty miles away.

Further misfortunes came. Thirteen sailors, rowing the flagship's boat up a river to find fresh water, were attacked by Indians; all but one of the Spaniards were killed, and the boat was lost. Two vessels had to be abandoned as too worm-eaten to be seaworthy; the other two leaked so badly that the pumps had to be worked night and day. Finally the worms proved stronger than the men, and these surviving ships had to be beached on a shore of Jamaica (June 25, 1503). There the hapless crew remained a year and five days, depending for food on the precarious friendship of the natives, who themselves had little to spare. Diego Mendez, whose calm courage in all this adversity kept Columbus from complete despair, volunteered to lead six

Christians and ten Indians in a dugout canoe 455 miles—eighty of them out of sight of land—to Santo Domingo to solicit aid. On that venture their water ran out, and several Indians died. Mendez reached his goal, but Ovando would not or could not spare a vessel till May 1504, to go to the Admiral's relief. By February the Jamaica Indians had reduced their gifts of food to the stranded crew to the point where the Spaniards began to starve. Columbus had with him Regiomontanus's *Ephemerides*, which calculated a lunar eclipse for February 29. He called in the native chiefs, and warned them that God, in His anger at their letting his men starve, was about to blot out the moon. They scoffed, but when the eclipse began they hurriedly brought food to the ships. Columbus reassured them, saying that he had prayed to God to restore the moon, and had promised Him that the Indians would properly feed the Christians thereafter. The moon reappeared.

Four more months passed before help came; even then the ship that Ovando sent leaked so badly that it was barely able to return to Santo Domingo. Columbus, with his brother and son, sailed in a stouter vessel to Spain, arriving November 7 after a long and stormy voyage. The King and Queen were disappointed that he had not found more gold, or a strait to the Indian Ocean; and neither Ferdinand nor Isabella, who was dying, had time to receive the white-haired sailor finally home from the sea. His "tenths" from Haiti were still paid to him; he suffered from arthritis, but not from poverty. When at last Ferdinand consented to see him Columbus, older than his fifty-eight years, could hardly bear the long journey to the court at Segovia. He demanded all the titles, rights, and revenues promised him in 1492. The King demurred, and offered him a rich estate in Castile; Columbus refused. He followed the court to Salamanca and Valladolid; and there, broken in body and heart, he died, May 20, 1506. No man had ever so remade the map of the earth.

IV. THE NEW PERSPECTIVE

Now that he had shown the way, a hundred other mariners rushed to the New World. That name was apparently first used by a Florentine merchant whose own name now describes the Americas. Amerigo Vespucci was sent to Spain by the Medici to straighten out the affairs of a Florentine banker. In 1495 he won a contract to fit out twelve vessels for Ferdinand. He caught the exploration fever, and in letters later (1503–04) written to friends in Florence, he claimed that he had made four voyages to what he termed *novo mondo*, and that on one of these, on June 16, 1497, he had touched the mainland of South America. As John Cabot reached Cape Breton Island, in the Gulf of St. Lawrence, on June 24, 1497, and Columbus sighted Venezuela in

1498, Vespucci's account would give him the credit of being the first European to reach the mainland of the Western Hemisphere since Leif Ericsson (*c.* 1000). Confusion and inaccuracies in Vespucci's reports have cast doubt on his claims; but it is noteworthy that in 1505 Columbus, who by that time should have been able to judge Vespucci's reliability, entrusted him with a letter to the Admiral's son Diego.[15] In 1508 Vespucci was made *piloto mayor* —chief of all the pilots—of Spain, and held that position till his death.

A Latin version of one of his letters was printed at Saint-Dié (Lorraine) in April 1507. Martin Waldseemüller, professor of cosmography in the University of Saint-Dié, quoted the letter in his *Cosmographiae introductio*, which he published there in that year; he accepted Vespucci's account as trustworthy, and suggested that the name *Amerige* or *America* should be given to what we now term South America. In 1538 Gerhardus Mercator applied *America*, on one of his famous maps, to all the Western Hemisphere. It is agreed that in 1499, if not in 1497, Vespucci, sailing with Alonso de Ojeda, explored the coast of Venezuela. In 1500, shortly after Cabral's accidental discovery of Brazil, Vicente Pinzón, who had commanded the *Niña* on Columbus's first voyage, explored the Brazilian coast and discovered the Amazon. In 1513 Vasco Núñez de Balboa sighted the Pacific, and Ponce de Leon, dreaming of a fountain of youth, discovered Florida.

The discoveries begun by Henry the Navigator, advanced by Vasco da Gama, culminating in Columbus, and rounded out by Magellan effected the greatest commercial revolution in history before the coming of the airplane. The opening of the western and southern seas to navigation and trade ended the Mediterranean epoch in the history of civilization, and began the Atlantic era. As more and more of America's gold came to Spain, economic decline progressed in the Mediterranean states, and even in those South German cities which, like Augsburg and Nuremberg, had been commercially tied with Italy. The Atlantic nations found in the New World an outlet for their surplus population, their reserve energy, and their criminals, and developed there avid markets for European goods. Industry was stimulated in Western Europe, and demanded the mechanical inventions, and better forms of power, that made the Industrial Revolution. New plants came from America to enrich European agriculture—the potato, tomato, artichoke, squash, maize. The influx of gold and silver raised prices, encouraged manufacturers, harassed workers, creditors, and feudal lords, and generated and ruined Spain's dream of dominating the world.

The moral and mental effects of the explorations rivaled the economic and political results. Christianity was spread over a vast hemisphere, so that the Roman Catholic Church gained more adherents in the New World than the Reformation took from her in the Old. The Spanish and Portuguese languages were given to Latin America, and produced there vigorous independent literatures. European morals were not improved by the discoveries; the lawless brutality of the colonists flowed back to Europe with returning seamen and settlers, and brought an intensification of violence and sexual irregularity. The European intellect was powerfully moved by the revelation of so many peoples, customs, and cults; the dogmas of the great religions suffered by mutual attrition; and even while Protestants and Catholics raised their hostile certainties to ruinous wars, those certitudes were melting away into the doubts and consequent tolerance of the Enlightenment.

Above all, a pride of achievement inspired the human mind just when Copernicus was about to reduce the cosmic importance of the earth and its inhabitants. Men felt that the world of matter had been conquered by the courage of the human mind. The medieval motto for Gibraltar—*ne plus ultra* —was denied by abbreviation; it became now *plus ultra*—more beyond. All limits were removed; all the world was open; everything seemed possible. Now, with a bold and optimistic surge, modern history began

CHAPTER XIV

Erasmus the Forerunner

1469-1517

I. THE EDUCATION OF A HUMANIST

THE greatest of the humanists was born in or near Rotterdam in 1466 or 1469, the second and natural son of Gerard, a clerk in minor orders, and of Margaret, the widowed daughter of a physician. Apparently the father became a priest shortly after this *contretemps*. We do not know how the boy came by the fond name of Desiderius Erasmus, meaning the desired beloved. His first teachers taught him to read and write Dutch, but when he went to study with the Brethren of the Common Life at Deventer he was fined for speaking his native tongue; there Latin was the *pièce de résistance*, and piety was as rigorous as discipline. Nevertheless the Brethren encouraged the study of selected pagan classics, and Erasmus began at Deventer to acquire his astonishing command of the Latin language and literature.

About 1484 both his parents died. The father left a modest estate to his two sons, but their guardians absorbed most of it, and steered the youths into a monastic career as one requiring no patrimony at all. They protested, wishing to go to a university; finally they were persuaded—Erasmus, we are told, by the promise of access to many books. The older son accepted his fate, and rose to be (Erasmus reported) *strenuus compotor nec scortator ignavus*—"a mighty toper and no mean fornicator." [1] Desiderius took vows as an Augustinian canon in the priory of Emmaus at Steyn. He tried hard to like monastic life, even wrote an essay *De contemptu mundi* to convince himself that a monastery was just the place for a lad of avid spirit and queasy stomach. But his stomach complained of fasts and turned at the smell of fish; the vow of obedience proved yet more irksome than that of chastity; and perhaps the monastic library ran short on classics. The kindly prior took pity on him, and lent him as secretary to Henry of Bergen, Bishop of Cambrai. Erasmus now (1492) accepted ordination as a priest.

But wherever he was he had one foot elsewhere. [2] He envied the young men who had gone on from their local schooling to universities. Paris exuded an aroma of learning and lust that could intoxicate keen senses across great distances. After some years of able service, Desiderius induced the Bishop to send him to the University of Paris, armed with just enough money to survive. He listened impatiently to lectures, but consumed the libraries. He attended plays and parties, and occasionally explored feminine charms;[8] he remarks, in one of his *Colloquies*, that the most pleasant way of learning French was from the *filles de joie*.[4] Nevertheless his strongest passion was for literature, the musical magic of words opening the door to a world of imagination and delight. He taught himself Greek; in time the Athens of Plato and Euripides, Zeno and Epicurus became as familiar to him as the Rome of Cicero, Horace, and Seneca; and both cities were almost as real to him as the left bank of the Seine. Seneca seemed to him as good a Christian as St. Paul, and a much better stylist (a point on which, perhaps, his taste was not quite sound). Wandering at will through the centuries, he discovered Lorenzo Valla, the Neapolitan Voltaire; he relished the elegant Latin and reckless audacity with which Valla had flayed the forgery of the "Donation of Constantine," had noted serious errors in the Vulgate, and had debated whether epicureanism might not be the wisest *modus vivendi*; Erasmus himself would later startle theologians, and comfort some cardinals, by seeking to reconcile Epicurus and Christ.[5] Echoes of Duns Scotus and Ockham still resounded in Paris; nominalism was in the ascendant, and threatened such basic doctrines as transubstantiation and the Trinity. These escapades of thought damaged the young priest's orthodoxy, leaving him not much more than a profound admiration for the ethics of Christ.

His addiction to books was almost as expensive as a vice. To add to his allowance he gave private instruction to younger students, and went to live with one of them. Even so he had not enough to be comfortable. He importuned the Bishop of Cambrai: "My skin and my purse both need filling—the one with flesh, the other with coins. Act with your usual kindness";[6] to which the Bishop responded with his usual moderation. One pupil, the Lord of Vere, invited him to his castle at Tournehem in Flanders; Erasmus was charmed to find in Lady Anne of Vere a patroness of genius; she recognized this condition in him, and helped him with a gift, which was soon consumed. Another rich pupil, Mountjoy, took him to England (1499). There, in the great country houses of the aristocracy, the harassed scholar found a realm of refined pleasure that turned his monastic past into a shuddering memory. He reported his progress to a friend in Paris, in one of those innumerable, inimitable letters that are now his most living monument:

> We are getting on. If you are wise you too will fly over here. . . . If you only knew the blessings of Britain! . . . To take one attraction out of many: there are nymphs here with divine features, so gentle and kind. . . . Moreover, there is a fashion that cannot be commended enough. Wherever you go you are received on all hands with kisses; when you leave you are dismissed with kisses; if you go back your salutes are returned to you. . . . Wherever a meeting takes place there

are salutes in abundance; wherever you turn you are never without them. O Faustus! if you had once tasted how soft and fragrant those lips are, you would wish to be a traveler, not for ten years, like Solon, but for your whole life in England.[7]

At Mountjoy's house in Greenwich Erasmus met Thomas More, then only twenty-two, yet distinguished enough to secure the scholar an introduction to the future Henry VIII. At Oxford he was almost as charmed by the informal companionship of students and faculty as he had been by the embraces of country-house divinities. There he learned to love John Colet, who, though "assertor and champion of the old theology," astonished his time by practicing Christianity. Erasmus was impressed by the progress of humanism in England:

> When I hear my Colet I seem to be listening to Plato himself. In Grocyn who does not marvel at such a perfect world of learning? What can be more acute, profound, and delicate than the judgment of Linacre? What has nature ever created more gentle, sweet, and happy than the genius of Thomas More? [8]

These men influenced Erasmus profoundly for his betterment. From a vain and flighty youth, drunk with the wine of the classics and the ambrosia of women, he was transformed into an earnest and painstaking scholar, anxious not merely for shillings and renown, but for some lasting and beneficent achievement. When he left England (January 1500) he had formed his resolve to study and edit the Greek text of the New Testament as the distilled essence of that real Christianity which, in the judgment of reformers and humanists alike, had been overlaid and concealed by the dogmas and accretions of centuries.

His pleasant memory of this first visit to England was darkened by the final hour. At Dover, passing through the customs, the money that his English friends had given him, amounting to some £20 ($2,000?), was confiscated by the authorities, as the English law forbade the export of gold or silver. More, not yet a great lawyer, had mistakenly advised him that the prohibition applied only to English currency; and Erasmus had changed the pounds into French coins. Neither his stumbling English nor his prancing Latin availed to deflect the avid orthodoxy of the law; and Erasmus embarked for France practically penniless. "I suffered shipwreck," he said, "before I went to sea." [9]

II. THE PERIPATETIC

Stationing himself for a few months in Paris, he published his first significant work, *Collectanea adagiorum*, a collection of 818 adages or quotations,

mostly from classical authors. The revival of learning—i.e., of ancient literature—had set a fashion of adorning one's opinions with a snatch from some
Greek or Latin author; we see the custom in extreme form in Montaigne's
Essays and Burton's *Anatomy of Melancholy*; it lingered into the eighteenth
century in the forensic oratory of England. Erasmus accompanied each
adage with a brief comment, usually pointed to current interest and salted
with satiric wit; so, he observed, "priests are said in Scripture to devour the
sins of the people; and they find sins so hard to digest that they must have
the best wine to wash them down." [10] The book was a boon to writers and
speakers; it sold so well that for a year Erasmus could feed himself unaided.
Moreover, Archbishop Warham, relishing the book despite its barbs, sent
the author a gift of money and offered him a benefice in England; Erasmus,
however, was not prepared to abandon the Continent for an island. In the
next eight years he published several revisions of the *Adagia*, expanding it to
3,260 entries. Sixty editions appeared in his lifetime; translations were issued
from the original Latin into English, French, Italian, German, and Dutch;
altogether it was among the "best sellers" of its time.

Even so the proceeds were meager; and food was not enough. Pinched
for pounds, Erasmus wrote (December 12, 1500) to his friend James Batt,
who was tutoring a son of the Lady Anne of Vere, asking him to

> point out to her how much more credit I shall do her by my learning
> than the other divines whom she maintains. They preach ordinary
> sermons; I write what will live forever. They, with their silly rub-
> bish, are heard in one or two churches; my works will be read by all
> who know Latin and Greek in every country in the world. Such
> unlearned ecclesiastics abound everywhere; men like me are scarcely
> found in many centuries. Repeat all this to her unless you are too
> superstitious to tell a few fibs for a friend.[11]

When this approach failed, he wrote again in January, suggesting that Batt
tell the lady that Erasmus was losing his eyesight, and adding: "Send me four
or five gold pieces of your own, which you will recover out of the Lady's
money." [12] As Batt did not enter this trap, Erasmus wrote directly to the
lady, comparing her with the noblest heroines of history and the fairest concubines of Solomon, and predicting for her an eternity of fame.[13] To this
ultimate vanity she succumbed; Erasmus received a substantial gift, and recovered his eyesight. The custom of the time forgave a writer for begging
aid from patrons, since publishers were not yet equipped to sustain even
widely read authors. Erasmus could have had benefices, episcopacies, even,
later, a cardinal's hat; he refused such offers time and again in order to remain a "free lance," intellectually fetterless. He preferred to beg in freedom
rather than decay in bonds.

In 1502, fleeing plague, Erasmus moved to Louvain. Adrian of Utrecht, head of the university, offered him a professorship; Erasmus declined. Returning to Paris, he settled down to earn his living by his pen—one of the earliest modern attempts at that reckless enterprise. He translated Cicero's *Offices*, Euripides' *Hecuba*, and Lucian's *Dialogues*. Doubtless this jolly skeptic shared in forming Erasmus' mind and style. In 1504 Erasmus wrote to a friend:

> Good heavens! with what humor, with what rapidity does Lucian deal his blows, turning everything to ridicule, and letting nothing pass without a touch of mockery. His hardest strokes are aimed at the philosophers . . . on account of their supernatural assumptions, and at the Stoics for their intolerable arrogance. . . . He uses no less liberty in deriding the gods, whence the surname of atheist was bestowed upon him—an honorable distinction coming from the impious and superstitious.[14]

On a second visit to England (1505–06) he joined Colet in a pilgrimage to the shrine of St. Thomas à Becket at Canterbury. Describing this trip under fictitious names in one of his *Colloquies*, he told how "Gratian" (Colet) offended their monastic guide by suggesting that some of the wealth that adorned the cathedral might be used to alleviate poverty in Canterbury; how the monk showed them milk that had really come from the Virgin's breast, and "an amazing quantity of bones," all of which had to be kissed reverently; how Gratian balked at kissing an old shoe that Becket was said to have worn; and how, as a climactic favor and a sacred souvenir the guide offered Gratian a cloth allegedly used by the saint to wipe his brow and blow his nose, and still showing evidences thereof, whereat Gratian grimaced and rebelled. The two humanists, mourning for humanity, returned to London.[15]

Good fortune came to Erasmus there. Henry VII's physician was sending two sons to Italy; Erasmus was engaged to accompany them as "general guide and supervisor." He stayed with the lads at Bologna for a year, devouring the libraries, and adding daily to his fame for learning, Latinity, and wit. Till this time he had worn the garb of an Augustinian canon—black robe, mantle, and cowl, and a white hood usually carried on the arm; now (1506) he discarded these for the less conspicuous dress of a secular priest, and claimed to have received permission for this change from Pope Julius II, then in Bologna as a military conqueror. For reasons unknown to us he returned to England in 1506, and lectured on Greek at Cambridge. But in 1508 we find him again in Italy—preparing an enlarged edition of his *Adagia* for the press of Aldus Manutius in Venice. Passing on to Rome (1509), he was charmed by the easy life, fine manners, and intellectual cultivation of the cardinals. He was amused—as Luther, in Rome the year before, had been shocked—by the inroads that pagan themes and ways had made in the capital of Christendom. What offended Erasmus more was the martial policy, ardor, and pursuits of Julius II; there he agreed with Luther; but he agreed also with the cardinals, who warmly approved the frequent absences of the pugnacious Pope. They welcomed Erasmus to their social gatherings, and offered him some ecclesiastical sinecure if he would settle in Rome.

Just as he was learning to love the Eternal City, Mountjoy sent him word that Henry VII had died, that the friend of the humanists had become Henry VIII, and that all doors and preferments would now be open to Erasmus if he would come back to England. And along with Mountjoy's letter came one from Henry VIII himself:

> Our acquaintance began when I was a boy. The regard which I then learned to feel for you has been increased by the honorable mention you have made of me in your writings, and by the use to which you have applied your talents in the advancement of Christian truth. So far you have borne your burden alone; give me now the pleasure of assisting and protecting you so far as my power extends. . . . Your welfare is precious to us all. . . . I propose therefore that you abandon all thought of settling elsewhere. Come to England, and assure yourself of a hearty welcome. You shall name your own terms; they shall be as liberal and honorable as you please. I recollect that you once said that when you were tired of wandering you would make this country the home of your old age. I beseech you, by all that is holy and good, carry out this promise of yours. We have not now to learn the value of either your acquirements or your advice. We shall regard your presence among us as the most precious possession that we have. . . . You require your leisure for yourself; we shall ask nothing of you save to make our realm your home. . . . Come to me, therefore, my dear Erasmus, and let your presence be your answer to my invitation.[16]

How could so courteous and generous an invitation be refused? Even if Rome made him a cardinal, Erasmus' tongue would be tied; in England, surrounded by influential friends and protected by a powerful king, he might write more freely and yet be safe. Half reluctantly he bade farewell to the humanists of Rome, to the great palaces and libraries, to the cardinals who had favored him. He made his way again over the Alps, and to Paris, and to England.

III. THE SATIRIST

He stayed there five years, and in all that time he received from the King nothing more than an occasional salutation. Was Henry too busy with foreign relations or domestic relatives? Erasmus waited and fretted. Mountjoy came to the rescue with a gift; Warham dowered him with the revenues of a parish in Kent; and John Fisher, Bishop of Rochester and Chancellor of Cambridge University, appointed him professor of Greek at £13 ($1,300) a year. To raise this income to the maintenance of a servant and a horse, Erasmus dedicated his publications to his friends, who responded ever inadequately.

In the first year of this third sojourn in England, and in the home of Thomas More, Erasmus wrote in seven days his most famous book, *The Praise of Folly*. Its Latinized Greek title, *Encomium Moriae*, was a pun on More's name, but *moros* was Greek for fool, and *moria* for folly. Erasmus kept the work in manuscript for two years, then went briefly to Paris to have it printed (1511). Forty editions were published in his lifetime; there were a dozen translations; Rabelais devoured it; as late as 1632 Milton found it "in everyone's hand" at Cambridge.

Moria in Erasmus' use meant not only folly, absurdity, ignorance, and stupidity, but impulse, instinct, emotion, and unlettered simplicity, as against wisdom, reason, calculation, intellect. The whole human race, we are reminded, owes its existence to folly, for what is so absurd as the male's polymorphous pursuit of the female, his feverish idealization of her flesh, his goatish passion for copulation? What man in his senses would pay for such detumescence with the lifelong bondage of monogamy? What woman in her senses would pay for it with the pains and tribulations of motherhood? Is it not ridiculous that humanity should be the accidental by-product of this mutual attrition? If men and women paused to reason, all would be lost.[17]

This illustrates the necessity of folly, and the foolishness of wisdom. Would bravery exist if reason ruled?[18] Would happiness be possible?—or was Ecclesiastes right in believing that "he that increaseth knowledge increaseth sorrow, and in much wisdom is much grief"? Who would be happy if he knew the future? Fortunately science and philosophy are failures, are ignored by the people, and do no great damage to the vital ignorance of the race. The astronomers "will give you to a hair's breadth the dimensions of the sun, moon, and stars, as easily as they would do that of a flagon or a pipkin," but "nature laughs at their puny conjectures."[19] The philosophers confound the confused and darken the obscure; they lavish time and wit upon logical and metaphysical subtleties with no result but wind; we should send them, rather than our soldiers, against the Turks, who would retreat in terror before such bewildering verbosity.[20] The physicians are no better; "their whole art as now practiced is one incorporated compound of imposture and craft."[21] As for the theologians, they

> will tell you to a tittle all the successive proceedings of Omnipotence in the creation of the universe; they will explain the precise manner of original sin being derived from our first parents; they will satisfy you as to how . . . our Saviour was conceived in the Virgin's womb,

and will demonstrate, in the consecrated wafer, how accidents may subsist without a subject . . . how one body can be in several places at the same time, and how Christ's body in heaven differs from His body on the cross or in the sacrament.[22]

Think also of the nonsense purveyed as miracles and prodigies—apparitions, curative shrines, evocations of Satan, and "such like bugbears of superstition."

> These absurdities . . . are a good trade, and procure a comfortable income to such priests and friars as by this craft get their gain. . . . What shall I say of such as cry up and maintain the cheat of pardons and indulgences?—that by these compute the time of each soul's residence in purgatory, and assign them a longer or shorter continuance according as they purchase more or fewer of these paltry pardons and saleable exemptions? Or what can be said bad enough of others who pretend that by the force of such magical charms, or by the fumbling over their beads in the rehearsal of such and such petitions (which some religious impostors invented, either for diversion, or, what is more likely, for advantage), they shall procure riches, honors, pleasure, long life, and lusty old age, nay, after death, a seat at the right hand of the Saviour? [23]

The satire runs on at the expense of monks, friars, inquisitors, cardinals, popes. Monks pester the people with begging, and think to take heaven by a siege of soporific psalmodies. The secular clergy hunger and thirst after money; "they are most subtle in the craft of getting . . . tithes, offerings, perquisites, etc." [24] All ranks and varieties of the clergy agree in putting witches to death. The popes have lost any resemblance to the Apostles in "their riches, honors, jurisdictions, offices, dispensations, licenses, indulgences . . . ceremonies and tithes, excommunications and interdicts," their lust for legacies, their worldly diplomacy and bloody wars.[25] How could such a Church survive except through the folly, the gullible simplicity of mankind?[26]

The Praise of Folly stirred the theologians to an understandable fury. "You should know," wrote Martin Dropsius to Erasmus, "that your *Moria* has excited a great disturbance even among those who were formerly your most devoted admirers." [27] But the satire in this gay devastation was mild compared to that which marked Erasmus' next outburst. The third and final year of his teaching at Cambridge (1513) was the year of Pope Julius II's death. In 1514 there appeared in Paris a skit or dialogue called *Iulius exclusus.* Erasmus made every effort, short of explicit denial, to conceal his authorship, but the manuscript had circulated among his friends, and More unguardedly listed it among Erasmus' works.[28] It may stand here as perhaps an extreme sample of Erasmus the satirist. The dead warrior-pope finds the gates of heaven closed against him by an obstinate St. Peter.

> *Julius*: Enough of this. I am Julius the Ligurian, P.M. . . .
>
> *Peter*: P.M! What is that? *Pestis maxima?*
>
> *J*: *Pontifex Maximus*, you rascal.
>
> *P*: If you are three times *Maximus* . . . you can't get in here unless you are *Optimus* also.
>
> *J*: Impertinence! You, who have been no more than *Sanctus* all these ages—and I *Sanctissimus, Sanctissimus Dominus, Sanctitas,* Holiness itself, with bulls to show it.
>
> *P*: Is there no difference between being holy and being called Holy? . . . Let me look a little closer. Hum! Signs of impiety aplenty. . . . Priest's cassock, but bloody armor beneath it; eyes savage, mouth insolent, forehead brazen, body scarred with sins all over, breath loaded with wine, health broken with debauchery. Ay, threaten as you will, I will tell you what you are. . . . You are Julius the Emperor come back from hell. . . .
>
> *J*: Make an end, or I will excommunicate you. . . .
>
> *P*: Excommunicate me? By what right, I would know?
>
> *J*: The best of rights. You are only a priest, perhaps not that—you cannot consecrate. Open, I say!
>
> *P*: You must show your merits first. . . .
>
> *J*: What do you mean by merits?
>
> *P*: Have you taught true doctrine?
>
> *J*: Not I. I have been too busy fighting. There are monks to look after doctrine, if that is of any consequence.
>
> *P*: Have you gained souls to Christ by pure example?
>
> *J*: I have sent a good many to Tartarus.
>
> *P*: Have you worked any miracles?
>
> *J*: Pshaw! Miracles are out of date.
>
> *P*: Have you been diligent in your prayers?
>
> *J*: The invincible Julius ought not to answer a beggarly fisherman. However, you shall know who and what I am. First, I am a Ligurian, and not a Jew like you. My mother was a sister of the great Pope Sixtus IV. The pope made me a rich man out of Church property. I became a cardinal. I had my misfortunes. I had the French pox. I was banished, hunted out of my country, but I knew all along that I should come to be pope. . . . It came true, partly with French help, partly with money which I borrowed at interest, partly with promises. Croesus could not have produced all the money that was wanted. The bankers will tell you about that. But I succeeded. . . . And I have done more for the Church and Christ than any pope before me.
>
> *P*: What did you do?
>
> *J*: I raised the revenue. I invented new offices and sold them. . . . I

recoined the currency and made a great sum that way. Nothing can be done without money. Then I annexed Bologna to the Holy See.... I set all the princes of Europe by the ears. I tore up treaties, and kept great armies in the field. I covered Rome with palaces, and left five millions in the treasury behind me. . . .

P: Why did you take Bologna?

J: Because I wanted the revenue. . . .

P: And how about Ferrara?

J: The duke was an ungrateful wretch. He accused me of simony, called me a pederast. . . . I wanted the duchy of Ferrara for a son of my own, who could be depended upon to be true to the Church, and who had just poniarded the Cardinal of Pavia.

P: What? Popes with wives and children?

J: Wives? No, not wives, but why not children? . . .

P: Were you guilty of the crimes of which they accused you?

J: That is nothing to the purpose. . . .

P: Is there no way of removing a wicked pope?

J: Absurd! Who can remove the highest authority of all? . . . A pope can be corrected only by a general council, but no general council can be held without the pope's consent. . . . Thus he cannot be deposed for any crime whatsoever.

P: Not for murder?

J: No, not even if it were parricide.

P: Not for fornication?

J: Not for incest.

P: Not for simony?

J: Not for 600 acts of simony.

P: Not for poisoning?

J: No, nor for sacrilege.

P: Not for all these crimes gathered in a single person?

J: Add 600 more to them, there is no power that can depose the pope.

P: A novel privilege for my successors—to be the wickedest of men, yet be safe from punishment. So much the unhappier the Church that cannot shake such a monster off its shoulders. . . . The people ought to rise with paving stones and dash such a wretch's brains out. . . . If Satan needed a vicar he could find none fitter than you. What sign have you ever shown of an apostle?

J: Is it not apostolic to increase Christ's Church? . . .

P: How have you increased the Church? . . .

J: I filled Rome with palaces . . . troops of servants, armies, offices. . . .

P: The Church had nothing of this when it was founded by Christ. . . .

J: You are thinking of the old affair when you starved as pope, with a handful of poor hunted bishops about you. Time has changed all that. . . . Look now at our gorgeous churches . . . bishops like kings . . . cardinals gloriously attended, horses and mules checked with gold and jewels and shod with gold and silver. Beyond all, myself, Supreme Pontiff, borne on soldiers' shoulders in a golden chair, and waving my hand majestically to adoring crowds. Hearken to the roar of the cannon, the bugle notes, the boom of the drums. Observe the military engines, the shouting populace, torches blazing in street and square, and the kings of the earth scarce admitted to kiss my Holiness's foot. . . . Look at all this, and tell me, is it not magnificent? . . . You perceive what a poor wretch of a bishop you are, compared to me.

P: Insolent wretch! Fraud, usury, and cunning made you pope. . . . I brought heathen Rome to acknowledge Christ; you have made it heathen again. Paul did not talk of the cities he had stormed, the legions he had slaughtered . . . he talked of shipwrecks, bonds, disgraces, stripes; these were his apostolic triumphs, these were the glories of a Christian general. When he boasted it was of the souls he had recovered from Satan, not of his piles of ducats. . . .

J: All this is news to me.

P: Very likely. With your treaties and your protocols, your armies and your victories, you had no time to read the Gospels. . . . You pretend to be a Christian, you are no better than a Turk; you think like a Turk, you are as licentious as a Turk. If there is any difference you are worse. . . .

J: Then you won't open the gates?

P: Sooner to anyone else than to such as you. . . .

J: If you don't give in I will take your place by storm. They are making fine havoc below just now; I shall soon have 60,000 ghosts behind me.

P: O wretched man! O miserable Church! . . . I am not surprised that so few now apply here for admission, when the Church has such rulers. Yet there must be good in the world, too, when such a sink of iniquity can be honored merely because he bears the name of pope.[29]

This, of course, is outrageously one-sided. No such unredeemed rascal as was here represented could have freed Italy from her invaders, replaced the old St. Peter's with the new, discovered, directed, and developed Michelangelo and Raphael, united Christian and classic civilization in the *Stanze* of the Vatican, and offered to Raphael's skill that visage of profound thought and exhausting care pictured in the incomparable portrait of Julius in the Uffizi Gallery. And poor Erasmus, calling all priests to apostolic poverty while himself importuning his friends for coin! That a priest should pen so savage an indictment of a pope reveals the rebellious mood of the time. In 1518—year 2 of Luther—Peter Gillis wrote to Erasmus from Antwerp: "The

Iulius exciusus is for sale everywhere here. Everyone is buying it, everyone is talking of it." [30] No wonder the Reformers later reproached Erasmus for having sounded the tocsin of revolt and then himself fled.

In 1514 another product of Erasmus' pen startled the intellectual world of Western Europe. From 1497 onward he had composed informal dialogues, professedly to teach Latin style and conversation, but incidentally discussing a rich variety of lively topics guaranteed to rouse schoolboys from their daily slumbers. His friend Beatus Rhenanus, with his permission, published a series of these as *Familiarium colloquiorum formulae*—"Forms of Familiar Conversations, by Erasmus of Rotterdam, useful not only for polishing a boy's speech but for building his character." Later editions added more colloquies, so that they became Erasmus' most substantial composition.

They are a strange concoction—serious discussions of marriage and morals, exhortations to piety, exposés of absurdities and abuses in human conduct and belief, with a sprinkling of pungent or risqué jokes—all in a chatty and idiomatic Latin which must have been harder to write than the formal language of learned discourse. An English translator in 1724 judged "no book fitter to read which does, in so delightful and instructing a manner, utterly overthrow almost all the Popish Opinions and Superstitions." [31] This slightly overstates the point, but certainly Erasmus, in his gay way, used his "textbook of Latin style" to attack again the shortcomings of the clergy. He condemned relic-mongering, the misuse of excommunication, the acquisitiveness of prelates and priests, the false miracles foisted upon the credulous, the cult of saints for worldly ends, the excesses of fasting, the shocking contrasts between the Christianity of the Church and the Christianity of Christ. [32] He made a prostitute praise monks as her most faithful clients. [33] He warned a young lady who wished to keep her virginity that she should avoid "those brawny, swill-bellied monks. . . . Chastity is more endangered in the cloister than out of it." [34] He deplored the exaltation of virginity, and sang a paean to married love as superior to celibacy. He mourned that men so carefully mated good horses with good, but, in marriages of financial convenience, wed healthy maids to sickly men; and he proposed to forbid marriage to syphilitics or persons with any other serious disability or disease. [35] Mingled with these sober reflections were passages of broad humor. Boys were advised to salute people when they sneezed, but not when they "broke wind backward"; [36] and a pregnant woman was hailed with a unique blessing: "Heaven grant that this burden that you carry . . . may have as easy an exit as it had an entrance." [37] Circumcision was recommended, "for it moderates the itch of coition." A long dialogue between "The Young Man and the Harlot" ended reassuringly with the lady's reform.

Critics complained that these colloquies were a very reckless way of teaching Latin style. One alleged that all the youth of Freiburg were being corrupted by them.[38] Charles V made their use in school a crime punishable with death. Luther here agreed with the Emperor: "On my deathbed I shall forbid my sons to read Erasmus' *Colloquies*." The furore assured the book's success; 24,000 copies were sold soon after publication; till 1550 only the Bible outsold it. Meanwhile Erasmus had almost made the Bible his own.

IV. THE SCHOLAR

He left England in July 1514, and made his way through fog and customs to Calais. There he received from the prior of his forgotten monastery at Steyn a letter suggesting that his leave of absence had long since expired, and that he had better return to spend his remaining years in repentant piety. He was alarmed, for in canon law the prior might call upon secular power to drag him back to his cell. Erasmus excused himself, and the prior did not press the matter; but to avoid a recurrence of the embarrassment the wandering scholar asked his influential English friends to secure for him, from Leo X, a dispensation from his obligations as a monk.

While these negotiations were proceeding, Erasmus made his way up the Rhine to Basel, and offered to Froben the printer the manuscript of his most important production—a critical revision of the Greek text of the New Testament, with a new Latin translation and a commentary. It was a labor of love, pride, and risk for author and publisher alike: the preparation had taken years, the printing and editing would be laborious and expensive, the presumption to improve upon Jerome's Latin version, long sanctified as the "Vulgate," might be condemned by the Church, and the sales would probably fail to meet the costs. Erasmus reduced one hazard by dedicating the work to Leo X. In February 1516, Froben at last brought out *Novum Instrumentum omne, diligenter ab Erasmo Rot. recognitum et emendatum*. A later edition (1518) changed *Instrumentum* to *Testamentum*. In parallel columns Erasmus presented the Greek text as revised by him, and his Latin translation. His knowledge of Greek was imperfect, and he shared with the typesetters the responsibility for many errors; from the standpoint of scholarship this first edition of the Greek New Testament to be published in print was inferior to that which a corps of scholars had completed and printed for Cardinal Ximenes in 1514, but which was not given to the public till 1522. These two works marked the application of humanistic learning to the early literature of Christianity, and the beginning of that Biblical criticism which in the nineteenth century restored the Bible to human authorship and fallibility.

Erasmus' notes were published in a separate volume. They were written in clear and idiomatic Latin, intelligible to all college graduates at the time, and were widely read. Though generally orthodox, they anticipated many findings of later research. In his first edition he omitted the famous Comma Johanneum (I John 5:7), which affirmed the Trinity but is rejected by the Standard Revised Version today as a fourth-century interpolation. He printed, but marked as probably spurious, the story of the woman taken in adultery (John 7:53; 8:11), and the last twelve verses of the Gospel of Mark. He repeatedly signalized the difference between primitive and current Christianity. So on Matthew 23:27, he commented:

> What would Jerome say could he see the Virgin's milk exhibited for money, with as much honor paid to it as to the consecrated body of Christ; the miraculous oils; the portions of the true cross, enough, if collected, to freight a large ship? Here we have the hood of St. Francis, there our Lady's petticoat, or St. Anne's comb ... not presented as innocent aids to religion, but as the substance of religion itself—and all through the avarice of priests and the hypocrisy of monks playing upon the credulity of the people.

Noting that Matthew 19:12 ("Some have made themselves eunuchs for the kingdom of heaven's sake") was alleged to counsel monastic celibacy, Erasmus wrote:

> In this class we include those who by fraud or intimidation have been thrust into that life of celibacy where they were allowed to fornicate but not to marry; so that if they openly keep a concubine they are Christian priests, but if they take a wife they are burned. In my opinion parents who intend their children for celibate priesthood would be much kinder to castrate them in infancy, rather than to expose them whole against their will to this temptation to lust.[39]

And on I Timothy 3:2:

> There are priests now in vast numbers, enormous herds of them, seculars and regulars, and it is notorious that very few of them are chaste. The great proportion fall into lust and incest and open profligacy. It would surely be better if those who cannot be continent should be allowed lawful wives of their own, and so escape this foul and miserable pollution.[40]

Finally, in a note on Matthew 11:30, Erasmus sounded the basic note of the Reformers—the return from the Church to Christ:

> Truly the yoke of Christ would be sweet, and his burden light, if petty human institutions added nothing to what he himself imposed. He commanded us nothing save love for one another, and there is nothing so bitter that affection does not soften and sweeten it. Everything according to nature is easily borne, and nothing accords better

with the nature of man than the philosophy of Christ, of which the sole end is to give back to fallen nature its innocence and integrity. . . . The Church added to it many things, of which some can be omitted without prejudice to the faith . . . as, for example, all those philosophic doctrines on . . . the nature of—and the distinction of persons in—the Deity. . . . What rules, what superstitions, we have about vestments! . . . How many fasts are instituted! . . . What shall we say about vows . . . about the authority of the pope, the abuse of absolutions and dispensations? . . . Would that men were content to let Christ rule by the laws of the Gospel, and that they would no longer seek to strengthen their obscurant tyranny by human decrees! [41]

It was probably the notes that carried the book to a success that must have surprised author and publisher alike. The first edition was disposed of in three years; new and revised editions were issued in sixty-nine printings before Erasmus died. Criticism of the work was vehement; many errors were pointed out; and Dr. Johann Eck, professor at Ingolstadt and proto-antagonist of Luther, branded as scandalous Erasmus' statement that the Greek of the New Testament was inferior to that of Demosthenes. Leo X, however, approved the work, and Pope Adrian VI asked Erasmus to do for the Old Testament what he had done for the New; but the Council of Trent condemned Erasmus' translation, and pronounced Jerome's Vulgate the only authentic Latin version of the Bible. Erasmus' New Testament was soon superseded as scholarship, but as an event in the history of thought its influence was immense. It facilitated and welcomed the vernacular translations that were soon to follow. Said a fervent passage in the preface:

> I would have the weakest woman read the Gospels and the Epistles of St. Paul. . . . I would have those words translated into all languages, so that not only Scots and Irishmen, but Turks and Saracens might read them. I long for the plowboy to sing them to himself as he follows the plow, the weaver to hum them to the tune of his shuttle, the traveler to beguile with them the dullness of his journey. . . . Other studies we may regret having undertaken, but happy is the man upon whom death comes when he is engaged in these. These sacred words give you the very image of Christ speaking, healing, dying, rising again, and make him so present, that were he before your very eyes you would not more truly see him.

Rejoicing in the competence of Froben's press and staff, Erasmus issued (November 1516) a critical edition of Jerome, and followed it with similarly revised classical and patristic texts, correcting 4,000 errors in the received text of Seneca; these were substantial services to scholarship. He retold the story of the New Testament in *Paraphrases* (1517). Such tasks required frequent stays in Basel, but a new attachment fixed his residence near the royal court at Brussels. Charles was at this time only King of Castile and ruler of the Netherlands, not yet Emperor Charles V. He was only fifteen, but his keen mind already ranged over diverse interests, and he was readily persuaded that his court might enhance its luster if he included the outstanding writer of the age among his privy councilors. It was so ordered; and on returning from Basel (1516) Erasmus accepted the honorary position at a modest salary. He was offered a canonry at Courtrai, with the promise of a bishopric; he refused it, remarking to a friend, "There's a dream to amuse you." [42] He received and rejected invitations to teach at the universities of Leipzig and Ingolstadt. Francis I tried to detach him from Charles with a flattering request that he join the court of France; Erasmus said no with flowered courtesy.

Meanwhile Leo X had sent to London the solicited dispensations. In March 1517, Erasmus crossed to London, and received the papal letters freeing him from his monastic obligations and the disabilities of bastardy. To the formal documents Leo added a personal note:

> Beloved son, health and apostolic benediction. The good favor of your life and character, your rare erudition and high merits, witnessed not only by the monuments of your studies, which are everywhere celebrated, but also by the general vote of the most learned men, and commended to us finally by the letters of two most illustrious princes, the King of England and the Catholic King [of France], give us reason to distinguish you with special and singular favor. We have therefore willingly granted your request, being ready to declare more abundantly our affection for you when you shall either yourself minister occasion, or accident shall furnish it, deeming it right that your holy industry, assiduously exerted for the public advantage, should be encouraged to higher endeavors by adequate rewards. [43]

Perhaps it was a judicious bribe to good behavior, perhaps an honest gesture from a tolerant and humanist court; in any case Erasmus never forgot this papal courtesy, and would always find it hard to break from a Church that had so patiently borne the sting of his critique.

V. THE PHILOSOPHER

Returning to Brussels, he found himself further seduced to caution by cordial welcome at the royal court. He took his privy councilorship seriously, forgetting that brilliant authors are rarely equipped for statesmanship. In the busy year 1516 he composed in haste an *Institutio principis Christiani (Education of a Christian Prince)*, rich in pre-Machiavellian platitudes of how a king should behave. In the dedication to Charles he wrote with bold directness: "You owe it to Providence that your realm has been acquired without injury to any; your wisdom will be best shown if you can keep it in peace and tranquillity." [44] Like most philosophers, Erasmus reckoned monarchy the least evil form of government; he feared the people as a "fickle, many-headed monster," deprecated the popular discussion of laws and politics, and judged the chaos of revolution worse than the tyranny of kings. [45] But he counseled his Christian prince to guard against the concentration of wealth. Taxes should fall only upon luxuries. There should be fewer monasteries, more schools. Above all, there should be no war among Christian states—nor even against the Turks. "We shall better overcome the Turks by the piety of our lives than by arms; the empire of Christianity will thus be defended by the same means by which it was originally established." [46] "What does war beget except war?—but civility invites civility, justice invites justice." [47]

As Charles and Francis edged toward hostilities, Erasmus made appeal after appeal for peace. He complimented the French King on a passing mood of conciliation, and asked how anyone could think of waging war with France, "the purest and most flourishing part of Christendom." [48] In *Querela pacis (The Complaint of Peace,* 1517) he reached his peak of passionate eloquence:

> I pass silently over the tragedies of ancient wars. I will stress only those which have taken place in the course of these last years. Where is the land or sea where people have not fought in the most cruel manner? Where is the river that has not been dyed with human blood . . . with Christian blood? O supreme shame! They behave more cruelly in battle than non-Christians, more savagely than wild beasts. . . . All [these wars] were undertaken at the caprice of princes, to the great detriment of the people, whom these conflicts in no way concerned. . . . Bishops, cardinals, popes who are vicars of Christ—none among them is ashamed to start the war that Jesus so execrated. What is there in common between the helmet and the miter? . . . Bishops, how dare you, who hold the place of the Apostles, teach people things that touch on war at the same time that you teach the precepts of the Apostles? . . . *There is no peace, even unjust, which is not preferable to the most just of wars.* [49]

Princes and generals may profit from war, but the masses bear the tragedies and the costs. [50] It may sometimes be necessary to fight a war of self-defense, but even in such cases it may be wiser to buy off the enemy than to wage war. [51] Let the kings submit their disputes to the pope. This would have been impracticable under Julius II, himself a warrior; but Leo X, "a learned, honest, and pious pontiff," might arbitrate with justice, and preside effectively over an international court. [52] Erasmus called nationalism a curse to humanity, and challenged statesmen to forge a universal state. "I wish," he said, "to be called a citizen of the world." [53] He forgave Budé for loving France, but "in my opinion it is more philosophical to put our relations with things and men on such a footing as to treat the world as the common country of us all." [54] Erasmus was the least national spirit in the rising nationalism of the Reformation age. "The most sublime thing," he wrote, "is to deserve well of the human race." [55]

We must not look to Erasmus for any realistic conception of human nature, or of the causes of war, or of the behavior of states. He never faced the problem that Machiavelli was dealing with in those same years—whether a state can survive if it practices the morality that it preaches to its citizens. The function of Erasmus was to cut dead branches from the tree of life rather than to construct a positive and consistent philosophy. He was not even sure that he was a Christian. He frequently professed to accept the Apostles' Creed; yet he must have doubted hell, for he wrote that "they are not as impious who deny the existence of God as are those who picture Him as inexorable." [56] He could hardly have believed in the divine authorship of the Old Testament, for he averred his willingness to "see the whole Old Testament abolished" if that would quiet the furore raised over Reuchlin. [57] He smiled at the traditions that Minos and Numa persuaded their peoples to obey uncongenial legislation by fathering it upon the gods, [58] and probably suspected Moses of similar statesmanship. He expressed surprise that More was satisfied with the arguments for personal immortality. [59] He thought of the Eucharist as a symbol rather than a miracle; [60] he obviously doubted the Trinity, the Incarnation, and the Virgin Birth; and More had to defend him from a correspondent who declared that Erasmus had privately confessed his unbelief. [61] He called in question one after another of the Christian usages of his time—indulgences, fasting, pilgrimages, auricular confession, monasticism, clerical celibacy, relic worship, prayers to the saints, the burning of heretics. He gave allegorical or rational explanations of many Biblical passages; he compared the story of Adam and Eve with that of Prometheus, and advised "the least literal" interpretation of the Scriptures. [62] He resolved the pains of hell into "the perpetual anguish of mind that accompanies habitual sin." [63] He did not broadcast his doubts among the people, for he had no comforting or deterrent myths to offer in place of the old ones. "Piety," he wrote, "requires that we should sometimes conceal truth, that we should take care not to show it always, as if it did not matter when, where, or to whom we show it. . . . Perhaps we must admit with Plato that lies are useful to the people." [64]

Despite this strong bent toward rationalism, Erasmus remained externally orthodox. He never lost his affection for Christ, for the Gospels, and for the symbolic ceremonies with which the Church promoted piety. He made a character in the *Colloquies* say: "If anything is in common use with Christians that is not repugnant to the Holy Scriptures, I observe it for this reason, that I may not offend other people." [65] He dreamed of replacing theology with "the philosophy of Christ," and strove to harmonize this with the thought of the greater pagans. He applied to Plato, Cicero, and Seneca the phrase, "divinely inspired"; [66] he would not admit that such men were excluded from salvation; and he could "scarce forbear" praying to "Saint Socrates." He asked the Church to reduce the essential dogmas of Christianity to as "few as possible, leaving opinion free on the rest." [67] He did not advocate the full tolerance of all opinions (who does?), but he favored a lenient attitude toward religious heresy. His ideal of religion was the imitation of Christ; we must admit, however, that his own practice was less than evangelical.

VI. THE MAN

How, actually, did he live? At this time (1517) he resided for the most part in Flanders—at Brussels, Antwerp, and Louvain. He dwelt in celibate privacy with one servant, but often accepted the hospitality of the prosperous, who courted his company as a social distinction and an intellectual feast. His tastes were fastidious; his nerves and feelings were refined to the point of frequent suffering from the vigorous vulgarities of life. He drank wine abundantly, and prided himself on his ability to carry it steadily. It may have been part cause of the gout and stones that galled him, but he thought it relieved his pain by dilating his arteries. In 1514, aged forty-five or forty-eight, he described himself as "a gray-headed invalid . . . who must drink nothing but wine," and must "be nice in what he eats." [68] Fasting disagreed with him, and he fumed against fish; perhaps his bile colored his theology. He slept poorly, like most people whose busy brains recognize no curfew. He consoled himself with friends and books. "I seem deprived of myself when I am shut out from my usual habits of study. . . . My home is where I have my library." [69]

It was partly to buy books that he solicited money with all the assiduity of a parish priest. He received regular pensions from Mountjoy and Warham, substantial gifts like the 300 florins ($7,500?) from Jean le Sauvage, Chancellor of Burgundy, and royalties exceeding those earned by any other author of his time. He disclaimed any love of money; he sought it because, as a man without moorings, he feared the insecurity of a lonely old age. Meanwhile he continued to refuse lucrative posts that would have extended his income at the cost of his freedom.

His appearance was at first unimpressive. He was short, thin, pale, weak in voice and constitution. He impressed by his sensitive hands, his long, sharp nose, his blue-gray eyes flashing with wit, and his speech—the conversation of the richest and quickest mind of that brilliant age. The greatest artists among his northern contemporaries were eager to paint his portrait, and he consented to sit for them because such portraits were welcomed as gifts by his friends. Quentin Massys pictured him in 1517—absorbed in writing, bundled in a heavy coat as protection against the chilly rooms of those centuries; this was presented to More. Dürer made a charcoal drawing of Erasmus in 1520, and a remarkable engraving in 1526; here the German touch gave the "good European" a thoroughly Dutch physiognomy; "if I look like that," said the sitter, "I am a great knave." [70] Holbein surpassed all these efforts in the many portraits that he made of Erasmus. One is in Turin, another in England, a third in Basel, the best in the Louvre—all masterly performances by the greatest portrait painter in the north. Here the scholar has become a philosopher, quiet, meditative, somewhat melancholy, reluctantly resigned to the careless neutrality of nature and the mortality of genius. "What our lot brings must be borne," he wrote in 1517, "and I have composed my mind for every event" [71]—a Stoic *ataraxia* that he never really achieved. "He loves glory," he said of an ambitious youth, "but he does not know what a weight glory is"; [72] yet Erasmus, like many a noble soul, labored night and day to win that incubus.

His faults leaped to the eye; his virtues were secrets known only to his intimates. He could beg shamelessly, but he could also give, and many a rising spirit expanded in the warmth of his praise. When Reuchlin was assailed by Pfefferkorn, Erasmus wrote to his friends among the cardinals at Rome, and helped to win protection for the harassed Hebraist. He lacked modesty and gratitude, which came hard to one courted by popes and kings. He was impatient and resentful of criticism, [73] and sometimes answered it in the abusive manner of that polemic age. He shared the anti-Semitism of even the scholars of the Renaissance. His interests were as narrow as they were intense: he loved literature when it clothed philosophy, and philosophy when it left logic for life, but he almost ignored science, scenery, music, and art. He smiled at the systems of astronomy that then strutted the stage, and the stars smiled with him. In all his multitudinous correspondence there is no appreciation of the Alps, or the architecture of Oxford and Cambridge, or the painting of Raphael or the sculpture of Michelangelo, who were working for Julius II when Erasmus was in Rome (1509); and the lusty singing of the Reformed congregations would later offend his educated ears. His sense of humor was usually subtle and refined, occasionally Rabelaisian, often sarcastic, once inhuman, as when he wrote to a friend, on hearing that some heretics had been burned, "I would pity them the less if they raise the price of fuel now that winter is coming on." [74] He had not only the natural egoism or selfishness of all men, but also that secret and cherished egotism, or self-conceit, without which the writer or artist would be crushed in the ruthless rush of an indifferent world. He loved flattery, and agreed with it despite frequent disclaimers. "Good judges," he told a friend, "say that I write better than any other man living." [75]

It was true, though only in Latin. He wrote bad French, spoke a little Dutch and English, "tasted Hebrew only with the tip of the tongue," [76] and knew Greek imperfectly; but he mastered Latin thoroughly, and handled it as a living tongue applicable to the most un-Latin nuances and trivia of his time. A century newly enamored of the classics forgave most of his faults for the lively brilliance of his style, the novel charm of his understatements, the bright dagger of his irony. His letters rival Cicero's in elegance and urbanity, surpass them in vivacity and wit. Moreover, his Latin was his own, not imitatively Ciceronian; it was a living, forceful, flexible speech, not an echo 1,500 years old. His letters, like Petrarch's, were coveted by scholars and princes only next to the stimulus of his conversation. He tells us, perhaps with some literary license, that he received twenty letters a day and wrote forty.[77] Several volumes of them were published in his lifetime, carefully edited by their author so conscious of posterity. Leo X, Adrian VI, Queen Marguerite of Navarre, King Sigismund I of Poland, Henry VIII, More, Colet, Pirkheimer, were among his correspondents. The modest More wrote: "I cannot get rid of a prurient feeling of vanity . . . when it occurs to my mind that I shall be commended to a distant posterity by the friendship of Erasmus." [78]

No other contemporary writer equaled his fame, unless we think of Luther as a writer. One Oxford bookseller reported in 1520 that a third of all his sales were of works by Erasmus. He had many enemies, especially among the theologians of Louvain, but he had disciples in a dozen universities, and humanists throughout Europe hailed him as their exemplar and chief. In the field of literature he was the Renaissance and humanism embodied—their cult of the classics and a polished Latin style, their gentlemen's agreement not to break with the Church, and not to disturb the inevitable mythology of the masses, provided the Church winked at the intellectual freedom of the educated classes and permitted an orderly, internal reform of ecclesiastical abuses and absurdities. Erasmus, like all humanists, was heartened by the elevation of Leo X to the papacy; their dream had come true—a humanist, a scholar, and a gentleman, the living unification of the Renaissance and Christianity, had mounted the greatest of thrones. Surely now a peaceful cleansing of the Church would come; education would spread; the people would keep their lovely ritual and consolatory faith, but the human mind would be free.[79]

Almost to the brink of Luther Erasmus kept that hope. But on September 9, 1517, he wrote from Antwerp to Thomas, Cardinal of York, an ominous line: "In this part of the world I am afraid a great revolution is impending." [80] In less than two months it came.

CHAPTER XV

Germany on the Eve of Luther

1453-1517

I. THE AGE OF THE FUGGERS

IN the final half-century before the Reformation all classes in Germany prospered except the knights. Probably it was the rising status of the peasants that sharpened their resentment against surviving disabilities. A few were bondsmen, a minority were proprietors, the great majority were tenant farmers paying rent to feudal lords in produce, services, or money. The tenants complained of the lord's exactions; of the twelve—in some cases sixty— days of labor which custom required them to give him yearly; of his withdrawal of land from the *Allgemeine* or commons in which tradition had allowed them to fish, cut timber, and pasture their animals; of the damage done to crops by the lord's huntsmen and hounds; of biased administration of justice in the local courts which the landlords controlled; and of the death tax laid upon the tenant family when the passing of its head interrupted the care of the land. Peasant proprietors raged at the usurious rates they had to pay for loans to move their crops, and at the quick foreclosure of farms by clever money lenders who had made loans to owners obviously unable to repay. All classes of tillers grudged the annual tithe levied by the Church on their harvests and broods.

These discontents ignited agrarian revolts sporadically throughout the fifteenth century. In 1431 the peasants around Worms rose in futile rebellion. They chose as their standard a farmer's shoe—actually a boot laced from ankle to knee; they stuck it on poles or painted its likeness on flags; and *Bundschuh*—the Bond of the Shoe—became the favorite title of rebel rural bands in the age of Luther. In 1476 a cowherd, Hans Böhm, announced that the Mother of God had revealed to him that the Kingdom of Heaven on earth was at hand. There should be no more emperors, popes, princes, or feudal lords; all men were to be brothers, all women sisters; all were to share alike in the fruits of the earth; lands, woods, waters, pastures, were to be common and free. Thousands of peasants came to hear Hans; a priest joined him; the bishop of Würzburg smiled tolerantly. But when Hans told his followers to bring to the next meeting all the weapons they could muster, the bishop had him arrested; the bishop's soldiers fired into the crowd that tried to save him; and the movement collapsed.

In 1491 the peasants on the domain of the abbot of Kempten in Alsace attacked his monastery, alleging that they were being forced into serfdom by forged documents; the Emperor Frederick III effected a compromise. Two years later the feudatories of the bishop of Strasbourg proclaimed a *Bundschuh;* they demanded an end to feudal dues and ecclesiastical tithes, the abolition of all debts, and the death of all Jews. They planned to seize the town of Schlettstadt, whence they hoped to spread their power through Alsace. The authorities got wind of the plot, seized the leaders, tortured and hanged them, and frightened the rest into temporary submission. In 1502 the peasants of the bishop of Speyer formed a *Bundschuh* of 7,000 men pledged to end feudalism, to "hunt out and kill all priests and monks," and to restore what they believed to have been the communism of their ancestors. A peasant revealed the scheme in the confessional; ecclesiastics and nobles joined in circumventing it; the main conspirators were tortured and hanged.[1]

In 1512 Joss Fritz secretly organized a similar movement near Freiburg-im-Breisgau; God, the pope, and the emperor were to be spared, but all feudal ownership and dues were to be abolished. A peasant who had been constrained to join this *Bund* exposed it to his confessor; the authorities arrested and tortured the leaders; the revolt aborted, but Joss Fritz lived to join in the Peasants' Revolt of 1525. In 1517 a league of 90,000 peasants in Styria and Carinthia undertook to end feudalism there: for three months their bands attacked castles and slew lords; finally Emperor Maximilian, who sympathized with their cause but rebuked their violence, sent against them a small force of soldiery, which subdued them into sullen peace. But the stage was set for the Peasants' War, and the Anabaptist communism, of Reformation Germany.

Meanwhile a more matter-of-fact revolution was proceeding in German industry and commerce. Most industry was still handicraft, but it was increasingly controlled by entrepreneurs who provided material and capital, and bought and sold the finished product. The mining industry was making rapid progress; great profits were drawn from mining silver, copper, and gold; gold and silver bullion now became a favorite means of storing wealth; and the royalties paid for mining rights to territorial princes—especially to the elector of Saxony who protected Luther[2]—enabled some of them to resist both pope and emperor. Reliable silver coins were minted, currency multiplied, the passage to a money economy was almost complete. Silver plate became a common possession in the middle and upper classes; some families displayed tables or chairs of solid silver; monstrances, chalices, reliquaries, even statues, of silver or gold accumulated in the German churches, and inclined princes to a religious reform that allowed them to confiscate ecclesiastical wealth. Aeneas Sylvius, in 1458, marveled to see German inn-keepers regularly serving drinks in silver cups, and asked: "What woman, not only among the nobility but among the plebeians, does not glitter with gold?—and shall I make mention of horse bridles embossed with the purest gold, of . . . armor and helmets sparkling with gold?" [3]

The financiers were now a major political power. The Jewish money-lenders of Germany were displaced by the Christian family-firms of the Welsers, the Hochstetters, and the Fuggers—all of Augsburg, which, at the end of the fifteenth century, was the financial capital of Christendom. Jo-hannes Fugger, a weaver's son, became a textile merchant, and left at his death (1409) a small fortune of 3,000 florins ($75,000?). His son Jakob ex-panded the business; when he died (1469) his wealth ranked seventh in Augsburg. Jakob's sons Ulrich, Georg, and Jakob II raised the firm to supremacy by advancing money to the princes of Germany, Austria, and Hungary in return for the revenue of mines, lands, or cities. From these speculative investments the Fuggers derived immense profits, so that by 1500 they were the richest family in Europe.

Jakob II was the culminating genius of the family, enterprising, ruthless, and industrious. He trained himself stoically by studying every phase of the business, every advance in bookkeeeping, manufacturing, merchandising, and finance. He demanded the sacrifice of everything but the family itself to the business, and the subordination of every individual Fugger to the family interest; he established the principle that none but a Fugger should have power in the concern; and he never allowed his political friendships to influence his loans. He formed cartels with other firms to control the price and sale of various products; so in 1498 he and his brothers entered into an agreement with Augsburg merchants to "corner" the Venetian market in copper and uphold the price.[4] In 1488 the family lent 150,000 florins to Archduke Sigismund of Austria, and as security it received the entire yield of the Schwarz silver mines until the debt should be repaid. In 1492 the Fuggers intermarried with the Thurzos of Cracow in a cartel to work the silver and copper mines of Hungary, and to maintain the "highest possible prices" for the products.[5] By 1501 the Fuggers were operating vast mining enterprises in Germany, Austria, Hungary, Bohemia, and Spain. In ad-dition they imported and manufactured textiles; they traded in silks, velvets, furs, spices, citrus fruits, munitions, jewelry; they organized express trans-portation and a private postal service. By 1511, when Jakob II became sole head of the firm, its assets reached 196,791 guilders; by 1527 (two years after his death) its capital was reckoned at 2,021,202 guilders ($50,000,000?)—a profit of 50 per cent per year through sixteen years.[6]

Part of this profit came from the Fuggers' relations with emperors and popes. Ulrich Fugger made loans to Frederick III; Jakob II became chief broker to Maximilian I and Charles V; the vast extension of the Hapsburg power in the sixteenth century was made possible by Fugger loans. Though Jakob rejected the ecclesiastical limitations on interest, and the attempts of churchmen to fix a "just price" for consumers' goods, he remained a Catholic, made loans to clergymen to pay their promotion fees, and, with Ulrich, obtained (1494) the management of papal finances in Germany, Scandinavia, Bohemia, and Hungary.

In his final years Jakob Fugger was the most honored and unpopular citizen in Germany. Some Catholics attacked him as a usurer; some nobles for outbribing them in the pursuit of office or power; some merchants for his enviable monopolies; many workers for overriding medieval regulations of trade and finance; most Protestants for managing the export of German money to the popes. But emperors and kings, princes and prelates, sent envoys to him as to a ruler; Dürer, Burgkmair, and the elder Holbein painted his portrait as a stern and simple realist; and Maximilian gave him the title of Count of the Empire. Jakob tried to atone for his wealth by building 106 houses for the poor but Catholic of Augsburg.* For his bones he raised a pretty chapel in the church of St. Anna. He died in the odor of sanctity, leaving millions of guilders and no children; the greatest gift of all had been denied him.

From him we may date the capitalist era in Germany, the growth of private monopolies, the dominance of businessmen controlling money over feudal lords owning land. German mining and textiles were already organized on capitalist lines—i.e., controlled by providers of capital—by the end of the fifteenth century, following the lead of Flanders and Italy in textiles a hundred years before. The Middle Ages had thought of private property as in some measure a public trust: the rights of the owner were limited by the necessities of the group whose organization gave him opportunities, facilities, and protection. Perhaps under the influence of Roman law—which now overshadowed German jurisprudence—the property owner began to think of his ownership as absolute; he felt that he had a right to do what he liked with his own. It did not seem wrong to the Fuggers, the Hochstetters, and the other "merchant princes" to "corner" a product and then force up its price, or to form cartels for the limitation of output and the control of trade, or to manipulate investments so as to cheat small stockholders.[7] In many instances a merchant placed his agents at the city gates with orders to buy for him all specified incoming goods, so that he might resell them at his own price in the town.[8] Ambrose Hochstetter bought up all available quicksilver, then raised the retail price 75 per cent.[9] A German company bought 600,000 guilders' worth of pepper from the king of Portugal at higher than

---

* This settlement, the "Fuggerei," still exists. It charges forty-two pfennigs (eighty-six cents) per family per year.

the usual price, on condition that the king would charge a still higher price to all other importers of pepper from Portugal into Germany.[10] Partly through such agreements and monopolies, partly through growing wealth and an increase in the demand for goods, partly through a rising supply of precious metals from Central Europe and America, prices mounted between 1480 and 1520 with a celerity rivaled only in our century. "In a short time, because of usury and avarice," Luther complained, "he that could formerly live on a hundred guilders cannot do so now on two hundred." [11] It is more than a twice-told tale.

The Middle Ages had seen great inequalities of political power; the new age of the Fuggers added such economic disparities as Europe had not known since the millionaires and slaves of Imperial Rome. Some merchant capitalists of Augsburg or Nuremberg were worth 5,000,000 francs each ($25,000,000?). Many bought their way into the landed aristocracy, sported coats of arms, and repaid highborn contempt with "conspicuous consumption." Joachim Hochstetter and Franz Baumgartner spent 5,000 florins ($125,000?) on a single banquet, or gambled with 10,000 florins in one game.[12] The luxuriously furnished and artistically decorated homes of rich businessmen aroused the resentment of nobility, clergy, and proletariat alike. Preachers, writers, revolutionaries, and legislators joined in fulminating against monopolists. Geiler von Kaisersberg demanded that they "should be driven out like wolves, since they fear neither God nor man, and breed famine, thirst, and poverty." [13] Ulrich von Hutten distinguished four classes of robbers: merchants, jurists, priests, and knights, and judged the merchants to be the greatest robbers of them all.[14] The Cologne Reichstag of 1512 called upon all civic authorities to proceed "with diligence and severity . . . against the usurious, forestalling, capitalistic companies." [15] Such decrees were repeated by other diets, but to no effect; some legislators themselves had investments in the great merchant firms, agents of the law were pacified with shares of stock,[16] and many cities prospered from the growth of unimpeded trade.

Strasbourg, Colmar, Metz, Augsburg, Nuremberg, Ulm, Vienna, Ratisbon (Regensburg), Mainz, Speyer, Worms, Cologne, Trier, Bremen, Dortmund, Hamburg, Magdeburg, Lübeck, Breslau, were thriving hubs of industry, commerce, letters, and arts. They and seventy-seven others were "free cities"—i.e., they made their own laws, sent representatives to the provincial and Imperial diets, and acknowledged no political obedience except to the emperor, who was too indebted to them for financial or military aid to attack their liberties. Though these cities were ruled by guilds dominated by businessmen, nearly every one of them was a paternalistic "welfare state" to the extent that it regulated production and distribution, wages and prices and the quality of goods, with a view to protecting the weak from the strong, and to ensure the necessaries of life to all.[17] We should now call them towns rather than cities, since none of them exceeded 52,000 population; nevertheless they were as populous as at any time before the middle of the nineteenth century,[18] and more prosperous than at any time before Goethe. Aeneas Sylvius, a proud Italian, wrote of them enthusiastically in 1458:

> Never has Germany been richer, more resplendent, than today. . . . Without exaggeration it may be said that no country in Europe has better or more beautiful cities. They look as fresh and new as if they had been built yesterday; and in no other cities is so much freedom to be found. . . . Nothing more magnificent . . . can be found in all Europe than Cologne, with its wonderful churches, city hall, towers, and palaces, its dignified burghers, its noble streams, its fertile cornfields. . . . Nor is Augsburg surpassed in wealth by any city in the world. Vienna has palaces and churches that even Italy may envy.[19]

Augsburg was not only the financial center of Germany, it was the main commercial link with then flourishing Italy. It was chiefly Augsburg merchants who built and managed that Fondaco Tedesco, in Venice, whose walls were frescoed by Giorgione and Titian. So bound to Italy, Augsburg echoed the Italian Renaissance; its merchants supported scholars and artists, and some of its capitalists became models of manners and culture, if not of morals. So Konrad Peutinger, syndic or mayor in 1493, was diplomat, merchant, scholar, jurist, Latinist, Hellenist, and antiquarian as well as businessman.

Nuremberg was a center of arts and crafts rather than of large-scale industry or finance. Its streets were still medievally tortuous, and shaded by overhanging upper stories or balconies; its red-tiled roofs, high-peaked gables, and oriel windows made a picturesque confusion against its rural background and the Pegnitz' turgid stream. The people were not as affluent here as in Augsburg, but they were joyous, *gemütlich*, and loved to disport themselves in such festivities as their annual carnival of mask, costume, and dance. Here Hans Sachs and the Meistersingers sang their lusty airs; here Albrecht Dürer raised German painting and engraving to their zenith; here the best goldsmiths and silversmiths north of the Alps made costly vases, church vessels, statuettes; here the metal workers fashioned a thousand plant, animal, and human forms in bronze, or wrought iron into handsome railings or screens; here the woodcutters were so numerous that we wonder how they could all make a living. The churches of the cities became repositories and museums of art, for every guild or corporation or prosperous family commissioned some work of beauty for the shrine of a patron saint. Regiomontanus chose Nuremberg as his home "because I find there without difficulty all the peculiar instruments necessary for astronomy; and there it is easiest for me to keep in touch with the learned of all countries, for Nuremberg, thanks to the perpetual journeyings of her merchants, may be counted the center of Europe." [20] It was characteristic of Nuremberg that the most famous of her merchants, Willibald Pirkheimer, was also an enthusiastic humanist, a patron of the arts, and a devoted friend of Dürer's. Erasmus called Pirkheimer "the chief glory of Germany." [21]

The voyages of Da Gama and Columbus, the Turkish control of the Aegean, and Maximilian's wars with Venice disturbed the trade between Germany and Italy. More and more German exports and imports moved along the great rivers to the North Sea, the Baltic, and the Atlantic; wealth and power passed from Augsburg and Nuremberg to Cologne, Hamburg, Bremen, and, above all, Antwerp. The Fuggers and Welsers furthered this trend by making Antwerp a chief center of their operations. The northward movement of German money and trade divorced northern Germany from the Italian economy, and made it strong enough to protect Luther from emperor and pope. South Germany, perhaps for opposite reasons, remained Catholic.

II. THE STATE

How was Germany governed in this critical and formative age?

The knights or lower nobility, who in former years had ruled the countryside as vassals of feudal seigneurs, were losing their miltary, economic, and political position. Mercenary troops hired by princes or cities, and equipped with firearms and artillery, were mowing down knightly cavalry helplessly brandishing swords; commercial wealth was raising prices and costs, and was outstripping landed property as a source of power; cities were establishing their independence, and princes were centralizing authority and law. The knights took some revenge by waylaying the commerce that passed their way; and when merchants and municipalities protested, the knights asserted their right to wage private wars. Comines described the Germany of this time as prickly with castles from which at any time "robber barons" and their armed retainers might pour forth to plunder merchant, traveler, and peasant alike.[22] Some knights made it their custom to cut off the right hands of the merchants they robbed. Götz von Berlichingen, though he himself had lost his right hand in the service of his prince, substituted an iron hand, and led knightly bands to attack not only merchants but cities— Nuremberg, Darmstadt, Metz, and Mainz (1512). His friend Franz von Sickingen laid claims against the city of Worms, ravaged its environs, seized its councilors, tortured its burgomaster, resisted all attempts of Imperial troops to capture him, and was transiently subdued only by receiving an annual subsidy to serve the emperor. Twenty-two cities of Swabia—chiefly

Augsburg, Ulm, Freiburg, and Constance—joined with some of the higher nobility to re-form the Swabian League (1488); these and other combinations checked the robber knights, and succeeded in having private war declared illegal; but Germany on the eve of Luther was a scene of social and political disorder, "a universal reign of force." [23]

The secular and ecclesiastical princes who presided over the chaos contributed to it by their venality, their diverse coinages and customs dues, their confused competition for wealth and place, their distortion of Roman Law to give themselves almost absolute authority at the expense of the people, the knights, and the emperor. Great families like the Hohenzollerns in Brandenburg, the Wettins in Saxony, the Wittelsbachers in the Palatinate, the dukes of Württemberg, not to speak of the Hapsburgs of Austria, behaved like irresponsible sovereigns. If the power of the Catholic emperor over the German princes had been greater the Reformation might have been defeated or postponed. And the rejection of Rome by many of the princes was a further move toward financial and political independence.

The character of the emperors in this period accentuated the weakness of the central government. Frederick III (r. 1440–93) was an astrologer and alchemist who so loved the studious tranquillity of his gardens at Graz that he allowed Schleswig-Holstein, Bohemia, Austria, and Hungary to detach themselves from the Empire. But toward the end of his fifty-three-year reign he played a saving stroke by betrothing his son Maximilian to Mary, heiress to Charles the Bold of Burgundy. When Charles fought himself into an icy grave in 1477, the Hapsburgs inherited the Netherlands.

Maximilian I (r. 1493–1519), emperor-elect but never crowned, began his reign with every omen of success. All the Empire rejoiced in his good looks and good nature, his unassuming sensibility, his effervescent cheerfulness, his generosity and chivalry, his courage and skill in joust and hunt; it was as if an Italian of the High Renaissance had mounted a German throne. Even Machiavelli was impressed, calling him "a wise, prudent, God-fearing prince, a just ruler, a great general, brave in peril, bearing fatigue like the most hardened soldier . . . a pattern of many princely virtues." [24] But "Max" was not a great general, and he lacked the cynical intellect required for Machiavelli's model prince. He dreamed of restoring the grandeur of the Holy Roman Empire by recapturing its former possessions and influence in Italy; he invaded the peninsula time and again in futile wars which the more practical Diet refused to finance; he allowed himself to think of deposing the doughty Julius II and making himself pope as well as emperor; [25] and (like his contemporary, Charles VIII of France) he excused his territorial ambitions as necessary preludes to an overwhelming assault upon the Turks. But he was constitutionally and financially incapable of sustained enterprise; he was unable to will the means as well as to wish the ends; and at times he was so poor that he lacked funds to pay for his dinner. He labored to reform the administration of the Empire, but he violated his own reforms, and they died with him. He thought too much in terms of the Hapsburg power. After many disappointments in war he returned to his father's policy of diplomatic marriages. So for his son Philip he accepted Ferdinand's offer of Juana's hand; she was a bit off-color mentally, but she brought Spain as her dowry. In 1515 he betrothed his granddaughter Mary and his grandson Ferdinand to Louis and Anne, son and daughter of Ladislas, King of Bohemia and Hungary; Louis was killed at Mohacs (1526), Ferdinand became King of Bohemia and (so far as the Turks would permit) of Hungary, and the Hapsburg power reached its widest range.

The most amiable facet of Maximilian was his love and encouragement of music, learning, literature, and art. He applied himself zealously to the study of history, mathematics, and languages; we are assured that he could speak German, Latin, Italian, French, Spanish, Walloon, Flemish, and English, and that on one campaign he talked with seven alien commanders in their seven different tongues. Partly through his example and exertions, the dialects of South and North Germany merged into a *gemeines Deutsch* which became the language of German government, of Luther's Bible, and of German literature. Between wars he tried to be an author, and left compositions on heraldry, artillery, architecture, hunting, and his own career. He planned an extensive collection of *monumenta*—relics and inscriptions—from the German past, but again funds ran out. He proposed to the popes a calendar reform which they effected eighty years later. He reorganized the University of Vienna, established new professorships of law, mathematics, poetry, and rhetoric, and made Vienna for a time the most active seat of learning in Europe. He invited Italian humanists to Vienna, and empowered Conradus Celtes to open there an academy of poetry and mathematics. He favored humanists like Peutinger and Pirkheimer, and made the harassed Reuchlin a Count Palatine of the Empire. He gave commissions to Peter Vischer, Veit Stoss, Burgkmair, Dürer, and the other artists who flourished in his reign. He ordered at Innsbruck an ornate tomb to cherish his remains; it was left incomplete at his death, but it gave occasion for Peter Vischer's fine statues of Theodoric and Arthur. If Maximilian had been as great as his plans he would have rivaled Alexander and Charlemagne.

In the Emperor's last year Dürer painted an honest portrait of him—worn out and disillusioned, defeated by the maddening stinginess of time. "Earth possesses no joy for me," said this once joyous soul, and he mourned, "Alas, poor land of Germany!" [26] But he exaggerated his failure. He left Germany and the Empire (if only through economic developments) far stronger than he had found them. Population had risen, education had spread; Vienna was becoming another Florence; and soon his grandson, inheriting half of Western Europe, would become the most powerful ruler in Christendom.

III. THE GERMANS: 1300–1517

They were probably at this time the healthiest, strongest, most vital and exuberant people in Europe. As we see them in Wolgemut and Dürer, in Cranach and Holbein, the men were stout, thick-necked, massive-headed, lion-hearted animals ready to consume the world and wash it down with beer. They were coarse but jolly, and tempered their piety with sensuality. They could be cruel, as witness the awful instruments of torture that they used on criminals, but they could be merciful and generous, too, and rarely displayed their theological ferocity in physical ways; in Germany the Inquisition was bravely resisted and usually subdued. Their robust spirits made for bibulous humor rather than dry wit, dulled their sense of logic and beauty, and denied them the grace and subtlety of the French or Italian mind. Their meager Renaissance foundered in bibliolatry; but there was a steady persistence, a disciplined industry, a brute courage, in German thought that enabled them to break the power of Rome, and already gave promise of making them the greatest scholars in history.

By comparison with other nations they were clean. Bathing was a national passion. Every well-arranged house, even in rural districts, had its bathroom. As in ancient Rome, the numerous public bathhouses provided much more than baths; men could be shaved there, women could have their hair dressed, diverse forms of massage were offered, drinking and gambling were allowed, and relief could be found from monogamy. Usually the two sexes bathed together, chastely clothed; but there were no laws against flirtations, and an Italian scholar, visiting Baden-Baden in 1417, remarked that "no baths in the world are more fit for the fecundity of women." [27]

The Germans of that age could not be accused of puritanism. Their conversation, correspondence, literature, and humor were sometimes coarse by our standards, but that went with their vigor of body and soul. They drank too much at all ages, and imbibed sexual experience lavishly in their youth; Erfurt in 1501 seemed to the pious Luther "nothing better than a brothel and beerhouse." [28] German rulers, ecclesiastical as well as secular, agreed with St. Augustine and St. Thomas Aquinas that prostitution must be permitted if women are to be safe from seduction or assault. Houses of prostitution were licensed and taxed. We read of the bishops of Strasbourg and Mainz receiving revenues from brothels; and the bishop of Würzburg gave the municipal brothel to Graf von Hennenberg as a revenue-producing fief. [29] Hospitality to valued guests included placing at their disposal the *Frauen-*

haüser, or houses of women; King Sigismund was honored with this privilege at Bern (1414) and Ulm (1434), so heartily to his satisfaction that he publicly thanked his hosts for it.[30] Unlicensed women sometimes set up *Winkelhaüser*—irregular houses; in 1492 the licensed prostitutes of Nuremberg complained to the burgomaster of this unfair competition; in 1508 they received permission to storm the *Winkelhaus;* they did. In the actual moral code of Europe in the later Middle Ages resort to a prostitute was condoned as a venial but normal sin. Perhaps the spread of syphilis after 1492 made it a mortal affair.

Marriage, as elsewhere, was a union of properties. Love was considered a normal result, not a reasonable cause, of marriage. Betrothal was as binding as matrimony. Weddings were ceremonious and luxurious in all classes; festivities might last for a week or two; the purchase of a husband was as expensive as the upkeep of a wife. The authority of the male was theoretically absolute, but was more real in deeds than in words; we note that Frau Dürer had much to say to her husband. The women of Nuremberg were undaunted enough to pull the half-naked Emperor Maximilian from bed, throw a wrap around him, and lead him in a merry nocturnal dance in the street.[31] According to a hoary legend, some men of the upper classes in fourteenth-century Germany, when leaving for extended absences from home, locked an iron "chastity belt" around the waist and thighs of their wives, and took the key with them.[32] Traces of the custom are found in medieval Venice and sixteenth-century France; but in the rare cases that seem authentic the belt was voluntarily donned by wife or mistress, and the key was given to husband or lover, as a guarantee of fidelity in marriage or sin.[33]

Family life flourished. An Erfurt chronicle reckons eight or ten offspring per couple as normal; households of fifteen children were not uncommon. These numbers included bastards, for illegitimate children, who abounded, were usually taken into the father's home after his marriage. Family names came into use in the fifteenth century, often indicating ancestral occupation or place of origin, but now and then congealing a moment's jest into the rigor of time. Discipline was firm at home and school; even the future Emperor Max received many a spanking, and no harm seems to have come from it except to parent or teacher. German homes were now (*c.* 1500) the most comfortable in Europe, with wide staircases, sturdy balustrades, massive furniture, cushioned seats, carved chests, windows of colored glass, canopied beds, tapestried walls, carpeted floors, bulging stoves, shelves crowded with books or flowers or musical instruments or silver plate, and kitchens gleaming with all the utensils for a German feast.

Externally the houses were mostly of wood, and fires were frequent. Overhanging eaves and windowed balconies shaded the streets. Only a few avenues in the larger towns were paved. Street lighting was unknown except on festival evenings; life was unsafe outdoors at night. Petty criminals were as numerous as the pigs and cows that strayed in the street. There was no organized police; severe punishments were relied upon to deter crime. The penalty for robbery was death, or, in mild theft, cutting off the ears. Blasphemers had their tongues torn out; exiles illegally returning to Nuremberg had their eyes gouged out. Women who had murdered their husbands were buried alive, or were tortured with red-hot tongs and then hanged.[34] Among the mechanisms of torture formerly exhibited in the Schloss or Castle of Nuremberg were chests filled with sharp stones, against which the victim was crushed; racks for stretching his limbs; braziers to apply fire to the soles of his feet; sharp iron frames to dissuade him from sitting, lying, or sleeping; and *die verflüchte Jungfer*, or Cursed Maiden of iron, who received the condemned with arms of steel, enclosed him in a spiked embrace, and then, relaxing, let him fall, pierced and bloody and broken, to a slow death in a pit of revolving knives and pointed bars.[35]

Political morality accorded with the general moral laxity. Bribery was widespread, and worst at the top. Adulteration of goods was common, despite the live burial of two men at Nuremberg for adulterating wine (1456). Commercialism—the sacrifice of morals to money—was as intense as in any age; money, not man, was the measure of all things. Yet these same hustling burghers gave large sums to charity. "In papal times," Luther wrote, "men gave with both hands, joyfully and with great devotion. It snowed alms, foundations, and legacies. Our forefathers, lords and kings, princes and other folk, gave richly and compassionately—yes, to overflowing—to churches, parishes, burses [scholarships], hospitals."[36] It was a sign of a secularizing age that many charitable bequests were left not to ecclesiastical bodies but to town councils, for distribution to the poor.

Manners became coarser—in France and England as well as in Germany—when the plutocracy of money superseded the aristocracy of birth in controlling the economy. Drunkenness was the national vice; both Luther and Hutten denounced it, though Hutten preferred it to "the deceit of the Italians, the thievery of the Spaniards, the pride of the French."[37] Some of the drinking may have been due to the sharp spices used in preparing meals. Table manners were rough and ready. Forks had come to Germany in the fourteenth century, but men and women still liked to eat with their fingers; even in the sixteenth century a preacher condemned forks as contrary to the will of God, Who "would not have given us fingers if He had wanted us to use forks."[38]

Dress was grandiose. Workmen were content with cap or felt hat, short blouse, and trousers overlapping—or tucked into—boots or high shoes. The middle classes added a vest, and an open coat lined and/or bordered with fur. But the possessors of pedigree competed feverishly with the collectors of guilders in the glory of their garb. In both these classes the hats of the men were spacious involutions of costly cloth, sometimes trimmed with feathers, ribbons, pearls, or gold. Shirts were often of silk. Outer garments, brightly colored, were lined with fur, and might be threaded with silver. Rich women wore crowns of gold, or gold-embroidered hoods, and braided gold thread into their hair; but modest maidens covered their heads with muslin handkerchiefs tied under the chin. Geiler von Kaisersberg alleged that smart women had wardrobes costing as much as 4,000 florins ($100,-000?).[39] Men wore their chins shaved but their hair long; male curls were carefully fostered; note Dürer's proud ringlets, and Maximilian's fancy locks. Finger rings were a sign or pretense of class, as now. Conradus Celtes remarked that fashions in clothing changed more rapidly in Germany than elsewhere, and as often for men as for women. On festive occasions the men might outshine the women in magnificence.

Festivals were numerous, continuing the medieval spirit of make-believe and gay display, with a happy moratorium on labor and the Commandments. Christmas was still Christian, despite its pagan vestiges; the Christmas tree was to be a seventeenth-century innovation. Every town celebrated a *Kermis* (Dutch *kerk*, church, and *mis*, Mass) or feast of its patron saint; men and women would then dance together in the streets, merriment would be *de rigueur*, and no saint or preacher could abate the revel's rough hilarity. Dancing sometimes became an epidemic mania, as in Metz, Cologne, and Aix in 1374, or at Strasbourg in 1412. In some such cases sufferers from St. Vitus's dance would seek relief from what they thought to be demoniacal possession, by dancing themselves to exhaustion, as some young maniacs do today. Men found other outlets for their instincts in hunting, or in the dying sport of the joust. Thousands of men and women traveled, often using a distant shrine as an excuse. They moved in painful delight on horses or mules or in coaches or sedan chairs, bearing the discomforts of unpaved roads and unwashed inns. Sensible persons, when they could, journeyed by boat along the Rhine, the Danube, or the other majestic streams of Central Europe. By 1500 a postal service, open to all, united the major towns.

All in all the picture is one of a people too vigorous and prosperous to tolerate any longer the manacles of feudalism or the exactions of Rome. A proud sense of German nationality survived all political fragmentation, and checked supernational emperors as well as supernatural popes; the Reformation would defeat the Holy Roman Empire as well as the papacy. In the 1,500-year war between Teuton and Roman victory was once more, as in the fifth century, inclining toward Germany.

IV. THE MATURING OF GERMAN ART

This coming of age first manifested itself in art. We may find it hard to believe, but it is true, that at the very height of the Italian Renaissance—from the birth of Leonardo (1452) to the death of Raphael (1520)—German artists were in demand throughout Europe for their excellence in every craft in wood, iron, copper, bronze, silver, gold, engraving, painting, sculpture, architecture. Perhaps with more patriotism than impartiality, Felig Fabri of Ulm wrote in 1484: "When anyone wishes to have a first-rate piece of workmanship in bronze, stone, or wood, he employs a German craftsman. I have seen German jewelers, goldsmiths, stonecutters, and carriage makers do wonderful things among the Saracens; they surpassed even the Greeks and Italians in art." [40] Some fifty years later an Italian found this still true: "The Germans," wrote Paolo Giovio, "are carrying everything before them in art, and we, sluggish Italians, must needs send to Germany for good workmen." [41] German architects were engaged by Florence, Assisi, Orvieto, Siena, Barcelona, and Burgos, and were called upon to complete the *duomo* at Milan. Veit Stoss captivated Cracow, Dürer received honors in Venice, and Holbein the Younger took England by storm.

In ecclesiastical architecture, of course, the zenith had passed with the thirteenth and fourteenth centuries. None the less a single generation of Munich citizens raised in Late Gothic their Frauenkirche (1468–88) or Church of Our Lady, and the Altes Rathaus (1470–88) or Old Town Hall; in the first two decades of the sixteenth century Freiburg in Saxony completed its choir, Augsburg built the Fugger Chapel, Strasbourg Cathedral finished its Lawrence Chapel, and a lovely Chörlein, or oriel window, was added to the parsonage of the Sebalduskirche in Nuremberg. Domestic architecture in this period built charming cottages, with red tiled roofs, timbered upper stories, flower-decked balconies, and spacious eaves to protect the windows from sun or snow; so in Mittenwald's arduous climate the undiscourageable Germans countered the sublimity of the Bavarian Alps with the simple and cherished beauty of their homes.

Sculpture was the glory of the age. Minor carvers abounded who would have shone as major stars in a less brilliant galaxy: Nicolaus Gerhart, Simon Leinberger, Tilman Riemenschneider, Hans Backoffen.... Nuremberg alone in one generation produced a trio of masters hardly surpassed in equal time by any town in Italy. The career of Veit Stoss was a tale of two cities Nurtured in Nuremberg, and acquiring fame as engineer, bridge-builder, architect, engraver, sculptor, and painter, he went to Cracow at thirty, and did his best work there in a flamboyant Late Gothic style that well expressed both the piety and the excitability of the Poles. He returned to Nuremberg

(1496) with sufficient funds to buy a new house and marry a second wife, who bore him five children to add to her predecessor's eight. At the height of his abundance Veit was arrested for having shared, perhaps unwittingly, in a forgery; he was branded by burning through both cheeks, and was forbidden ever to leave Nuremberg again. The Emperor Maximilian pardoned him and restored his civic rights (1506), but Stoss remained an outcast to the end of his painfully long life. In 1517 he carved a large group representing the Annunciation or Angelical Salutation; he enclosed the two figures—among the most nearly perfect in all the range of wood sculpture— in a garland of roses, surrounded this with a rosary, attached seven medallions picturing the joys of the Virgin, and crowned the whole—all in linden wood—with an unprepossessing portrayal of God the Father. The fragile composition was suspended from the vault of the choir in the Lorenzkirche, where it still hangs as a treasured relic of the great city's halcyon days. For the Sebalduskirche, Stoss carved in wood a *Crucifixion* never surpassed in its kind (1520). In that year his son Andreas, as prior of the Nuremberg Carmelites, procured for Stoss a commission to design an altar for a church in Bamberg. While the artist labored on this assignment the Reformation captured Nuremberg; Andreas was replaced as prior because he remained a Catholic; Veit himself clung to the colorful faith that had inspired his art; payments on the altar commission were stopped, and the work remained incomplete. Stoss spent his final ten years in blindness, solitude, and desolation, predeceased by his wives, abandoned by his children, and rejected by an age too absorbed in theology to recognize that it was losing, at ninety-three (1533), the greatest wood carver in history.[42]

A bronze worker equally supreme in his line lived in the same city and time, but led a quieter and happier life. Peter Vischer the Elder portrayed himself in a niche of his most famous product as an earnest, simple laborer, short, stocky, full-bearded, with a leather apron around his waist, and hammer and chisel in his hands. He and his five sons gave eleven years (1508–19) to their *chef-d'œuvre*, the Sebaldusgrab or Tomb of Sebald, Nuremberg's patron saint. The enterprise was costly; funds ran out, and the work lay unfinished when Anton Tucher roused the citizens to contribute the 800 guilders ($20,000?) still required. This masterpiece is not impressive at first sight; it does not seem to rival Orcagna's Tabernacle (1348) at Florence; and the snails and dolphins on whose backs the structure rests are not the likeliest carriers of so immense a weight. But a closer inspection reveals an astonishing perfection in the parts. The central sarcophagus of silver is adorned with four reliefs representing the miracles of the saint. Around it rise the bronze pillars of a Gothic canopy, delicately carved with Renaissance ornament, and joined in lovely metal lacery at the top. On the pillars, around the base, in the socles, in the niches of the crowning baldachin, the artists deposited a veritable population of pagan, Hebrew, or Christian figures—Tritons, Centaurs, Nereids, Sirens, Muses, Fauns, Hercules, Theseus, Samson, the Prophets, Jesus, the Apostles, and angels playing music or sporting with lions or dogs. Some of these effigies are still crude, many are finished with the precision of a Donatello or a Ghiberti; all contribute vividly to a varied realization of life. The statues of Peter, Paul, Matthew, and John rival the *Four Apostles* that Dürer painted some seven years later in this same Nuremberg.

No prince or potentate, we are told, came to Nuremberg in these first decades of the sixteenth century without visiting Peter Vischer's foundry, and many solicited his art. A score of churches displayed his products, from the great brass candelabra in the Lorenzkirche to the tomb of Maximilian I at Innsbruck. His five sons followed him in sculpture, but two preceded him in death. Hermann Vischer the Younger, who died at thirty-one (1517), cast a handsome bronze relief for the tomb of Cardinal Casimir in the cathedral of Cracow.

As the Vischers excelled in bronze, and Veit Stoss in wood, so Adam Kraft led all his contemporaries in the sculpture of stone. German chroniclers pictured him, and Peter Vischer the Elder, and Sebastian Lindenast (who designed the obsequious electors on the Frauenkirche clock) as devoted artists and friends. "They were like brothers. Every Friday, even in their old age, they met and studied together like apprentices, as the designs that they executed at their meetings prove. Then they separated, having quite forgotten to eat or drink." [43] Born probably in the same year as Peter (1460?), Adam resembled him in simplicity, honesty, piety, and fondness for self-portraiture. In 1492 he carved for the Sebalduskirche the tomb of Sebaldus Schreyer, with reliefs of the Passion and Resurrection. Moved by their excellence, Hans Imhoff, a merchant prince, commissioned Kraft to design a ciborium to hold the bread and wine of the Eucharist in the Lorenzkirche. Adam made this *Sakramenthaus* a tall and slender tabernacle in Late Gothic style, a miracle of stone filigree rising stage by stage to a height of sixty-four feet, and tapering to a graceful crosier-head curve; the pillars alive with saints, the doors of the "House" guarded by angels, the square surfaces cut in relief with scenes from the life of Christ, and the whole airy edifice resting anomalously on three crouching figures—Adam Kraft and two of his aides. There are no compliments in the self-portrait: the clothes are worn and torn with toil, the hands are rough, the beard is unkempt, the broad, uplifted face is intent upon the conception and execution of the work. When this absorbing masterpiece was finished Kraft returned to his favorite subject by carving seven sandstone pillars with scenes from the Passion; six of these are now in the Germanisches Museum; one of them, *The Entomb-*

ment, is typical of Teutonic art—a courageous realism that does not need idealization to convey a sincere piety and faith.

The minor arts continued the same medieval moods and themes. Miniaturists were still in sufficient demand to maintain prosperous guilds. Major artists like Dürer and Holbein drew designs for stained glass; this art, declining in France and England, now reached its apex in Germany; the Lorenzkirche, the cathedrals of Ulm and Cologne, received world-famous windows in this period. Not only churches but guildhalls, castles, even private homes had some windows of stained glass. Cities like Nuremberg, Augsburg, Regensburg, Cologne, and Mainz were proud of their craftsmen-artists: metalworkers who glorified torches, chandeliers, basins, ewers, locks, trays; goldsmiths whose products, from spoons to altars, were treasured throughout Europe; textile workers who wove fine carpets, tapestries, ecclesiastical vestments, and the ornate garb of the patrician class; devout women who wore out their fingers and eyes to cover altars and priests with embroideries and silk. Woodcutters were never better. Michael Wolgemut, besides painting two magnificent windows for the Lorenzkirche, cut in wood a dozen altar-masterpieces, and then taught Dürer to surpass him.

Engraving by cutting a design into wood or copper developed in the fifteenth century into a mature art, respected on a par with painting. The greatest painters cultivated it. Martin Schongauer carried it to completion; some of his engravings —*The Scourging of Christ, Carrying the Cross, St. John on Patmos, The Temptation of St. Anthony*—are among the greatest of all time.[44] Book illustration by engravings became convenient and popular, and rapidly replaced illumination. The most famous paintings of the period were multiplied in engravings that sold readily at book stalls, fairs, and festivals. Lucas van Leyden showed an astonishing precocity in this field, engraving his *Mohammed* at fourteen, his *Ecce Homo* at sixteen (1510), and nearing perfection in his copper engraving of Maximilian.[45] Dry point engraving, by a pointed instrument throwing up a burr or ridge of excised metal along the lines of the design, was used by the anonymous "Master of the House Book" toward 1480. Etching by covering a metal surface with wax, cutting a design in the wax, and letting an acid eat (German *ätzen*) into the exposed lines, grew from the decoration of armor into the incision of metal plates from which etchings could be printed; Daniel Hopfer, an armorer, seems to have made the first recorded etching in 1504. Burgkmair and Dürer practiced the new art imperfectly; Lucas van Leyden probably learned it from Dürer, but soon went beyond him to mastery.

In painting this was Germany's greatest age. Influenced by both Dutch and Italian schools, and by their own expatriated Memling, German painters in the second half of the fifteenth century graduated from Gothic intensity and ungainliness into a more graceful line, and figures that moved with ease in natural scenes reflecting the domestic life of the triumphant *bourgeoisie*. Subjects remained predominantly sacred, but secular topics advanced; altarpieces gave way to panel pictures, and rich donors, no longer satisfied to kneel in the corner of a religious group, demanded portraits in which they would be all in all. Painters themselves emerged from medieval anonymity into distinct individualities, signing their work with their names as a grasp at immortality. Still anonymous is the "Master of the *Life of the Virgin*," who worked at Cologne toward 1470, and left a *Virgin and St. Bernard* with a very German Virgin squeezing milk from her breast for the Child, before a devout monk who hardly suggests the hound of heaven that pursued Abélard. Michael Pacher is one of the first who transmitted his name as well as his work. The Parish Church of St. Wolfgang in Salzkammergut still shows the massive altarpiece, thirty-six feet long, that he carved and painted for it in 1479-81; the study of perspective in these panels shared in the education of German art. Martin Schongauer brought into his painting the finesse of an accomplished engraver, and the delicate sentiment of Rogier van der Weyden. Born at Augsburg (*c.* 1445), Schongauer settled in Colmar, and developed there a school of engraving and painting that played a major role in bringing the arts to fulfillment in Dürer and Holbein.

Year by year the thriving cities of the south stole the leadership of German art from Cologne and the north. At Augsburg, the center of the trade with Italy, Hans Burgkmair brought Italian decorative touches into his pictures, and Hans Holbein the Elder combined Italian ornament with the high seriousness of the Gothic style. Hans passed his art down to his sons Ambrose and Hans, whom he fondly portrayed in his paintings. Ambrose faded from history, but Hans Jr. became one of the glories of Germany, Switzerland, and England.

The greatest of Dürer's predecessors was Matthias Gothardt Neihardt, who by a scholar's error became known to posterity as Matthias Grünewald. In the immemorial social heredity of art he learned the painter's magic from Schongauer at Colmar, added his own hunger for fame and perfection, practiced patiently at Ghent, Speyer, and Frankfurt, and chose Strasbourg as his home (1479). Probably there he painted his first master product, a double portrait of Philip II of Hanau-Lichtenberg and his wife; Dürer himself would never excel this in depth of penetration and grace of execution.[46] Wandering anew, Grünewald worked for a while with Dürer at Basel—where he painted the *Portrait of a Man* now in New York—and again with Dürer making woodcuts in Nuremberg. In 1503 he settled at Seligenstadt, and there finally he developed his own mature and characteristic style—the graphic rendering of Biblical scenes with passionate feeling and tragic power. Archbishop Albrecht made him court painter at Mainz (1509), but dismissed him when Grünewald persisted in applauding Luther (1526). H married unfortunately, and withdrew into a melancholy solitude that may have lent some dark shades to the *chiaroscuro* of his art.

His masterpiece—probably the greatest German painting—is the complex polyptych made for a monastery at Isen in 1513. The central panel shows the Virgin and her Child in an almost Turneresque glow of golden color against a background of distant seas. But the outstanding and unforgettable panel is a gruesome *Crucifixion:* Christ in His final agony, the body covered with wounds and bloody sweat, the limbs distorted with pain; Mary swooning in the arms of St. John; Magdalen hysterical with angry and incredulous grief. Still other panels could be major paintings by themselves: a concert of angels in a Gothic architectural setting of brilliant reds and browns; a macabre *Temptation of St. Anthony;* the same saint and a fellow anchorite in a weird forest of decaying trees; and a Boschian nightmare apparently symbolizing Anthony's dreams. In the predominance of color, light, and feeling over line, form, and representation this almost theatrical outburst of pictorial power is the culmination of German Gothic painting on the eve of the triumph of line and logic in a Dürer who, rooted in the mysticism of medieval Germany, stretched out hands of longing to the humanism and art of the Italian Renaissance.

V. ALBRECHT DÜRER: 1471–1528

No other nation has so unanimously chosen one of its sons as its representative in art as Germany—Protestant and Catholic, North and South— has chosen Dürer. On April 6, 1928, the four-hundredth anniversary of his death, the Reichstag in Berlin and the city council in Nuremberg put aside politics and dogmas to honor the artist whom Germany loves best. Meanwhile connoisseurs vainly offered $1,000,000 for a painting—*The Feast of the Rose Garlands*—for which Dürer himself received 110 guilders ($2,-750?).[47]

His Hungarian father was a goldsmith settled in Nuremberg. Albrecht was the third of eighteen children, most of whom died in infancy. In the parental studio the boy learned to draw with pencil, charcoal, and pen, and to engrave with the burin; he taught himself to observe microscopically, and to represent objects and subjects in indefatigable detail, so that in some of his portraits almost every hair seems to have received its individual stroke of the brush. The father had hoped that his son would be another goldsmith, but he yielded to the youth's desire to widen his art, and sent him as an apprentice to Wolgemut (1486). Albrecht developed slowly; his genius lay in ambition, perseverance, patience. "God lent me industry," he said, "so that I learned well; but I had to put up with a great deal of annoyance from his assistants." [48] Having little opportunity to study the nude, he frequented the public baths, and drew such Apollos as he could find there. He himself was something of an Apollo in those years. A friend described him fondly:

> A body remarkable in build and stature, and not unworthy of the noble mind it contained . . . face intelligent, eyes flashing . . . a long

neck, broad chest, narrow waist, powerful thighs, steady legs. As to his hands, you would have said that you had never seen anything more elegant. And of his speech the sweetness was so great that one wished it would never end.[49]

Attracted by Schongauer's engravings, he made his way to Colmar (1492), only to find that that master was dead. He learned what he could from Schongauer's brothers, then passed on to Basel, where he absorbed from Grünewald the secret of intensely religious art. He was already a skilled draftsman; an edition of St. Jerome's letters, printed at Basel in 1492, bore on its title page a portrait of the saint by Dürer; and this was so acclaimed that several publishers competed for his future work. However, his father urged him to come home and marry; a wife had been chosen for him in his absence. He returned to Nuremberg, and settled down to wedded life with Agnes Frey (1494).

A year earlier he had painted himself as a youth garbed and coiffured almost like a woman, proud yet diffident, distrusting and defying the world. In 1498, still vain of his features, and now also of his beard, he painted his portrait as a young patrician richly dressed, with tasseled cap and long brown curls; this is one of the great self-portraits of all time. In 1500 he pictured himself again, more simply costumed, the face elongated between masses of hair falling to the shoulders, the penetrating eyes mystically intent; Dürer seems here to have deliberately presented himself in an imagined likeness of Christ, not in impious bravado, but presumably in his oft-voiced opinion that a great artist is an inspired mouthpiece of God.[50] Vanity was the prop of his industry. He not only multiplied self-portraits, but found room for himself in many of his pictures. At times he could be modest, and sadly conscious of his limitations. "When we are praised," he told Pirkheimer, "we turn up our noses and believe it all; but perhaps a master mocker is laughing at us behind our backs." [51] For the rest he was good-natured, pious, loyal, generous, and as happy as circumstances would permit.

He could not have been infatuated with his wife, for he set out for Italy shortly after his marriage, leaving her behind. He had heard of what he called the "regrowth" of the arts in Italy "after they had been in hiding for a millennium"; [52] and though he never intimately shared in that resurrection of classic literature, philosophy, and art which accompanied the Renaissance, he was anxious to see at first hand what it was that had given the Italians their excellence in painting and sculpture, in prose and poetry. He stayed chiefly in Venice, where the Renaissance had not yet reached full bloom; but when he came back to Nuremberg (1495) he had somehow received the stimulus that sparked the rapid productivity of his next ten years. In 1507, with a loan of a hundred florins ($2,500?) from Pirkheimer, he went again to

Italy, and this time he stayed for a year and a half. He studied the works of Mantegna and Squarcione at Padua, copied drawings humbly, and was soon recognized by the Bellini and other Venetians as an accomplished draftsman. *The Feast of the Rose Garlands*, which he painted for a German church in Venice, won praise even from the Italians, who still considered most Germans to be barbarians. The Venetian Signory offered him a permanent post if he would take up his residence there, but his wife and friends were importuning him to come back to Nuremberg. He noted that artists had won a much higher social standing in Italy than in Germany, and resolved to demand a similar status on his return. "Here," he wrote, "I am a fine gentleman; at home I am a parasite"—i.e., unproductive of material goods.[53]

He was delighted by the excitement of art in Italy, the number and conflicts of artists, the learned and passionate discussions of art theories. When Jacopo de' Barbari expounded to him the principles of Piero della Francesca and other Italians on the mathematical proportions of a perfect human body, Dürer remarked that he "would rather have had this explained to him than to have received a new kingdom." [54] In Italy he became accustomed to the nude in art, if only by studying classic statuary. While his own work remained thoroughly Teutonic and Christian, he adopted with enthusiasm the Italian admiration for pagan art, and in a long sequence of writings he strove to teach his countrymen the Italian secrets of perspective, proportion, and coloring. With these two trips of Dürer to Italy the Gothic style came to an end in German painting, and the same German generation that rejected Rome in religion accepted Italy in art.

Dürer himself remained in a creative but confusing tension between the Middle Ages and the Renaissance, between German mysticism and Italian worldliness; and the joy of life that he had seen in Italy never quite overcame in his soul the medieval meditation on death. Except for his portraits, his subjects remained almost wholly religious, and many mystical. Nevertheless his real religion was art. He worshiped a perfect line more than the imitation of Christ. Even in his religious productions he showed the artist's driving interest in all the objects of even the most common daily experience. Like Leonardo, he drew nearly everything that he saw—rocks, streams, trees, horses, dogs, pigs, ugly faces and figures, and imaginary beings of marvelous or horrible form. He drew his left leg as seen in diverse positions, and punched a pillow into seven different shapes to be studied by his indefatigable pen. He crowded his work with a veritable menagerie of animals, and sometimes he drew a whole city as a background for a picture. He illustrated with relish and humor the life and doings of country folk. He loved the Germans, painted their enormous heads and rubicund features without protest, and introduced them into the unlikeliest environments, always richly robed like prosperous burghers, and wrapped and muffled, even in Rome or

Palestine, against the German cold. His drawings are an ethnography of Nuremberg. His chief patrons were its merchant princes, whom he rescued from death with his portraits, but he received commissions also from dukes and Imperial electors, and at last from Maximilian himself. As Titian loved best to portray the nobility and royalty, Dürer was most at home in the middle class, and his woodcut of the Emperor made him look like what Louis XII had called him—the "burgomaster of Augsburg." Once only Dürer achieved nobility in a portrait—an imaginary rendering of Charlemagne.

The thirty-six portraits are his most readily enjoyable works, for they are simple, sensual, earthy, swelling with character. Behold Hieronymus Holzschuher, the Nuremberg senator: a powerful head, stern face, thinning hair on a massive forehead, a beard trimmed to immaculate symmetry, sharp eyes as if watching politicians, yet with the beginning of a twinkle in them; here is a man with a good heart, good humor, good appetite. Or consider Dürer's dearest friend, Willibald Pirkheimer: the head of a bull concealing the soul of a scholar, and suggesting the gastric needs of Gargantua. And who would guess, behind the creased and flattened features of the immense Frederick the Wise of Saxony, the Elector who defied a pope to protect Luther? Nearly all the portraits are fascinating: Oswolt Krell, whose earnest concentration shows even in the veins of his hands; or Bernhard von Resten, with the delicate blue blouse, the majestic overspreading hat, the meditative eyes of an absorbed artist; or Jakob Muffel, burgomaster of Nuremberg, a brown study of earnest devotion, shedding some light on the greatness and prosperity of the city; or the two portraits of Dürer's father, weary with toil in 1490, quite worn out in 1497; or the *Portrait of a Gentleman* in the Prado—virility incarnate, tarnished with cruelty and greed; or Elizabeth Tucher, holding her wedding ring and gazing diffidently into marriage; or the *Portrait of a Venetian Lady*—Dürer had to go to Italy to find beauty as well as strength. There is seldom refinement in his male portraits, no elegance, only force of character. "What is not useful in a man," he said, "is not beautiful." [55] He was interested in reality and its faithful transcription, rather than in beauty of features or form. He pointed out that an artist can draw or paint a beautiful picture of an ugly object or disagreeable subject. He was a Teuton, all industry, duty, fidelity; he left beauty and grace to the ladies, and concentrated on power.

Painting was not his forte, nor much to his taste. But his visits to Italy stirred him to seek color as well as line. For Frederick of Saxony and his Castle Church in Wittenberg he painted a triptych later known as the Dresden Altarpiece; here Italian modes of proportion and perspective framed figures resolutely German: a *Frau* as the Virgin, a professor as St. Anthony, a German acolyte as St. Sebastian; the result is not irresistible. Finer is the Paumgärtner Altarpiece in Munich: a splendid St. Joseph and a *Mädchen* Mary against an architectural

background of Roman ruins; but the foreground is littered with absurd mani-
kins *The Adoration of the Magi*, in the Uffizi, is a triumph of color in the Virgin's blue robe and the gorgeous vestments of the Oriental kings. *Christ among
the Doctors* shows a pretty Jesus with girlish curls surrounded by bearded and
wrinkled pundits—one a horrible caricature all nose and teeth. *The Feast of the
Rose Garlands* rivaled the greatest Italian pictures of the time in its skillfully ordered composition, the loveliness of both Mother and Child, the general splendor
of the color; this is Dürer's greatest painting, but one must now venture all the
way to Prague to see it. Vienna and Berlin have attractive Dürer Madonnas, and
the New York *Madonna and Child with St. Anne* presents a tender German
maiden as the Virgin, and a dark-skinned Semite as her mother. Excellent are the
Prado panels of Adam and Eve; here for a moment a German artist has rendered
the beauty of a healthy female nude.

Discouraged by inadequate remuneration for the labor of painting, and
perhaps by the compulsion to repeat old religious themes, Dürer turned increasingly to the more gainful and original work of woodcutting and engraving; for there one plate could make a thousand copies easily carried to every
market in Europe, and could provide the same illustration for a thousand
printed volumes. Line was Dürer's forte, drawing was his realm, wherein
no man then alive surpassed him; there even the proud Italians marveled at
his finesse. Erasmus compared him, as a draftsman, with an ancient master
of line:

> Apelles was aided by color. . . . But Dürer, though admirable also
> in other respects—what does he not express in monochrome . . . pro-
> portions, harmonies? Nay, he even depicts that which cannot be
> depicted—fire, rays of light, thunder . . . lightning . . . all the sensa-
> tions and emotions, in fine, the whole mind of man as it reflects itself
> in the behavior of the body, and almost the voice itself. These things
> he places before the eyes in the most pertinent lines—black ones, yet
> so that if you should spread pigments on them you would injure the
> work. And is it not more wonderful to accomplish without the
> blandishments of color what Apelles accomplished with their aid? [56]

Dürer returned the compliment by engraving a portrait of Erasmus (1526),
not from the living sitter but from the painting by Massys. It did not rival
that portrait, much less Holbein's; even so it is a masterpiece of drawing in
the folds and shadows of the cloak, the wrinkles of face and hands, the
ruffled leaves of the open book.

Dürer has left us over a thousand drawings, most of them miracles of realistic
or pious or impishly fanciful design. Some are obvious caricatures; one is age
and wisdom drawn to a hair.[57] Occasionally the subject is inanimate, as in *The
Wire-drawing Mill.* or just plain vegetation, like *A Piece of Turf*, or an animal,
like the *Head of a Walrus.* Usually plants and beasts crowd around living per-

sons, as in the complex *Madonna with a Multitude of Animals.* The religious subjects are the least successful, but we must except and honor the remarkable *Hands of a Praying Apostle.* And lastly there are fine studies of classic mythology, like the *Apollo* or the *Orpheus.*

Dürer transformed some 250 of his drawings into woodcuts, and a hundred into engravings; these two groups are the most distinctive portions of his legacy. Until the turn of the century he incised the designs himself; later he delegated the woodcutting to others—only by this collaboration could he have delineated so vast an area of life. He began by illustrating books like *Der Ritter von Turn* and Sebastian Brant's *Narrenschiff;* twenty years afterward he drew fascinating border figures for the Prayer Book of Maximilian. He tried his pen at nudes, and succeeded handsomely in *The Men's Bath,* not so well in *The Women's Bath;* in both he served as a revolutionary force in a German art that had shunned the nude as a scandal or a disillusionment. Famous were the woodcuts that portrayed the life of the Virgin and the Passion of Christ. Devout women could now contemplate, by their own hearths, a print showing the betrothal of Joseph and Mary; and practical Germans were pleased to find, in *The Sojourn of the Holy Family in Egypt,* all the cozy details of Teutonic domesticity and industry— Mary sewing, Joseph working at his bench, and angelic children bringing in firewood without being asked. Thirty-seven small woodcuts—the "Little Passion"—and eleven larger ones—the "Great Passion"—brought the story of the sufferings and death of Christ into thousands of homes, and whetted the public appetite for Luther's translation of the New Testament. Another series illustrated the Book of Revelation; some of these woodcuts, like *The Four Horsemen of the Apocalypse* and *St. Michael Fighting the Dragon,* were so vivid that for centuries the German mind thought of the Apocalypse in terms of Dürer's prints.

From woodcuts he passed to the more painstaking art of engraving. Now and then he tried dry point etching, as in the chiaroscuro *Holy Family;* usually he worked with the burin. *The Fall of Man* is sculpture on copper, in forms worthy of the Greeks, in proportion and symmetry worthy of the Italians, with Dürer's customary profusion of fauna and flora, where nearly every item held for him and his generation a symbolical significance. Nude females of an excellence unprecedented in German art emerged from the metal in *The Sea Monster* and *The Combat of Virtue and Pleasure,* with background landscapes beautifully drawn. The sixteen engravings constituting the "Engraved Passion" are less impressive than the woodcut Passions. But the *St. Eustace* is a cornucopia of vivid designs: five dogs, a horse, a forest, a swarm of birds, a congeries of castles on a hill, a stag bearing a crucifix between his antlers, and persuading the handsome hunter to leave off killing and become a saint.

In 1513–14 Dürer reached his summit as a draftsman in three *Meisterstiche,* Master Engravings. *The Knight, Death, and the Devil* is a powerful version of a somber medieval theme: a stern-faced rider in full armor on a Verrocchian steed, hemmed in by ugly figures of death and Satan, but moving forward resolutely to the triumph of virtue over all; it seems incredible that such plenitude and delicacy of detail could be cut into metal. *St. Jerome in His Study* shows a quieter phase of the Christian victory: the old bald saint bent over his manuscript, writing apparently by the light of his halo, a lion and a dog lying peacefully on the floor, a skull sitting in silent eloquence on a window sill, and what looks for all the world like his wife's hat hanging on the wall—the whole room drawn in the most careful perspective, with all shadows and sun rays meticulously drawn. Finally the engraving that Dürer entitled *Melancholia I* reveals an angel seated amid the chaos of an unfinished building, with a medley of mechanical tools and scientific instruments at her feet; a purse and keys attached to her girdle as emblems of wealth and power; her head resting pensively on one hand, her eyes gazing half in wonder, half in terror, about her. Is she asking to what end all this labor, this building and demolition and building, this pursuit of wealth and power and the mirage called truth, this glory of science and Babel of intellect vainly fighting inevitable death? Can it be that Dürer, at the very outset of the modern age, understood the problem faced by triumphant science, of progressive means abused by unchanging ends?*

So, drawing by drawing, painting by painting, with an arduous industry and patience so different from Leonardo's procrastination and Raphael's ease, Dürer passed into the age of Luther. About 1508 he bought the house that made Nuremberg famous; the second World War destroyed it; the tourist trade rebuilt it as a copy of the original. Its two lower stories were of stone, the third and fourth of pink stucco and half timber; and over a projecting eave two further stories crouched under the gabled roof. Here for nineteen years Dürer lived in moderate misery with his childless wife. Agnes was a simple *Hausfrau* who wondered why Albrecht spent so much time on unremunerative studies or with bibulous friends. He moved in circles beyond her mental reach, neglected her socially, traveled most often without her, and when he took her to the Netherlands, dined with celebrities or with his host, while leaving his wife to eat "in the upper kitchen" with their maid.[58] In 1504 his widowed mother joined Dürer's household; she persisted ten years more; his portrait of her moves our sympathy for the wife—who was not too charming herself. His friends considered Agnes a shrew incapable of sharing Dürer's rapt intellectual life.

In his later years the Nuremberg master enjoyed a European fame as the leader and glory of German art. In 1515 the Emperor allotted him a modest pension of a hundred florins a year ($2,500?). This was irregularly paid, for Maximilian's income never caught up with his plans. When Max died the pension stopped, and Dürer decided to visit the Netherlands and solicit its renewal from Charles V. He took with him a large assortment of drawings

---

* For other dubious interpretations cf. Panofsky, *Dürer*, I, 156-71.

and paintings to sell or exchange in Holland or Flanders, and managed thereby to pay nearly all the cost of the trip. The journal that he kept of his tour (July 1520–July 1521) is almost—not quite—as intimate as those that Boswell would write two centuries later. It records his expenses, sales, purchases, visits, and honors; it reveals the burgher's care with financial details, and the artist's forgivable delight in the recognition of his genius. After chasing Charles through a dozen cities, Dürer obtained the renewal of his pension, and could give the rest of his journey to viewing the sights and heroes of the Lowlands. He was astonished by the wealth and beauty of Ghent, Brussels, and Bruges; by the great polyptych of the Van Eycks in St. Bavon's, and by the Antwerp Cathedral, "the like of which I have never seen in German lands." [59] He met Erasmus, Lucas van Leyden, Bernaert van Orley, and other Netherlands worthies, and was feted in the cities by the artists' guilds. In the mosquito swamps of Zeeland he contracted the malaria that ruined the health of his remaining years.

One entry in his journal reads: "I have bought Luther's tract for five white-pennies, and have given one for the *Condemnation* of that mighty man." [60] At Antwerp (May 1521) a rumor reached him that Luther had been "treacherously seized" on leaving the Diet of Worms. Dürer did not know that this abduction had been arranged to protect the Reformer; and fearing that Luther had been killed, he wrote in his journal a passionate defense of the rebel, and an appeal to Erasmus to come to the aid of his party:

> So this man, enlightened by the Holy Ghost to be the continuer of the true faith, has disappeared. . . . If he has suffered it is for the Christian truth against the unchristian papacy, which works against the freedom of Christ, exacting from us our blood and sweat therewith to nourish itself in idleness while the peoples famish. O God! never were men so cruelly put down under human laws as under those of the Roman See. . . . Everyone sees how clear is the doctrine announced in Luther's books, and how it conforms to the Holy Gospel. We must preserve these books from being burned; rather let us throw into the fire the books written to oppose him. . . . All you pious Christians, deplore with me the loss of this man, and pray the Lord that he will send another guide. O Erasmus of Rotterdam, where wilt thou remain? Wilt thou see the injustice and blind tyranny of the powers now ruling? Hear me, knight of Christ, ride by the side of Our Lord XS; old as thou art . . . thou too mayst win the martyr's crown. . . . Make thy voice heard! . . . O Erasmus, may God thy Judge be glorified in thee! [61]

When Dürer returned to Nuremberg he devoted himself almost wholly to religious art, and with new emphasis on the Gospels. In 1526 he completed his greatest group of paintings—*The Four Apostles*—improperly named, since Mark the Evangelist was not one of the Twelve; but perhaps that very error pointed to the Protestant idea of returning from the Church to the Gospels. The two panels are among the proudest possessions of that *Haus der Kunst* in which war-wounded Munich has regathered her famous collections of art. One panel pictures John and Peter, the other Mark and Paul—all four in gorgeously colored robes hardly befitting fishermen communist saints; in these vestments Dürer bowed to Italian idealization, while in the broad and massive heads he asserted his German environment. Probably these majestic figures had been intended to form the wings of a triptych for a Catholic church. But in 1525 the municipal council of Nuremberg declared for the Reformation. Abandoning the plan for an altarpiece, Dürer presented the panels to the city, and affixed to each panel inscriptions strongly stressing the importance of the Gospels. Despite the keys in Peter's hand—usually taken as representing the divine establishment and powers of the Church—these paintings could be interpreted as Dürer's Protestant testament.

He had now only two more years to live. Periodic attacks of malarial fever broke both his health and his spirit. Even in 1522 he had drawn his final self-portrait as the Man of Sorrows, naked, disheveled, haggard, sickly, in pain, holding in his hands the scourge and whip of the Passion of Christ. Nevertheless he worked to the end. When he died (April 6, 1528), aged fifty-seven, he left enough drawings, woodcuts, and engravings—besides 6,000 florins—to support his widow in somber comfort for the remainder of her life. Pirkheimer, who mourned him as "the best friend I have had in my life," wrote a simple epitaph for the tomb:

QUICQUID ALBERTI DURERI MORTALE
FUIT SUB HOC CONDITUR TUMULO

—"Whatever was mortal of Albrecht Dürer lies under this mound."

He missed supreme stature as an artist by sacrificing the greatest task o art to a lesser one: he was so charmed to see the passing shapes of persons, places, and things take lasting life under his hands that he absorbed himself chiefly in representing the real—lovely or ugly, significant or meaningless— and only occasionally fused the scattered elements of sense perception to form in creative imagination, and then in line or color, ideal beauties to give us goals to aim at, or revealing visions to offer understanding or peace. But he rose to the call of his time. He cut into wood or copper a biography of his expectant and generative generation; his pen or pencil, burin or brush evoked the hidden souls of the forceful men who trod the stage of the age; he made that epoch live for us, across four centuries, in all its enthusiasms, devotions, fears, superstitions, protests, dreams, and wonderment. He was Germany.

VI. THE GERMAN HUMANISTS

It was a lusty Germany in letters as well as in life and art. Literacy was spreading. Books were pouring forth from sixteen publishers in Basel, twenty in Augsburg, twenty-one in Cologne, twenty-four in Nuremberg; there Anton Koberger alone employed twenty-four presses and a hundred men. The trade in books was a major line in the busy commerce of the fairs at Frankfurt, Salzburg, Nördlingen, and Ulm. "Everybody nowadays wants to read and write," said a contemporary German; and another reported: "There is no end to the new books that are written." [62] Schools multiplied in the towns; every city provided bursaries or scholarships for poor but able students; nine new universities were founded in this half-century; and those at Vienna, Heidelberg, and Erfurt opened their doors to the New Learning. Literary academies arose in Strasbourg, Augsburg, Basel, Vienna, Nuremberg, and Mainz. Rich burghers like Peutinger and Pirkheimer, and the Emperor Maximilian himself, opened their libraries, art collections, and purses to eager scholars; and great ecclesiastics like Johann von Dahlberg, Bishop of Worms, and Albrecht of Brandenburg, Archbishop of Mainz, were enlightened patrons of scholarship, poetry, and art. The Church in Germany, following the lead of the popes, welcomed the Renaissance, but emphasized linguistic studies of Biblical and patristic texts. The Latin Vulgate Bible was printed in twenty-six editions in Germany between 1453 and 1500; there were twenty German translations of the Bible before Luther's; [63] the spread of the New Testament among the people prepared them for Luther's challenging contrast between the Gospels and the Church; and the reading of the Old Testament shared in the Protestant re-Judaizing of Christianity.

The humanist movement in Germany was at first—and after its flirtation with Luther—more orthodox in theology than its Italian counterpart. Germany had no classical past like Italy's; she had not had the privilege of being conquered and educated by Imperial Rome; she had no direct bond with non-Christian antiquity. Her memory hardly went beyond her Christian centuries; her scholarship, in this age, hardly ventured beyond the Christian fathers; her Renaissance was a revival of early Christianity rather than of classic letters and philosophy. In Germany the Renaissance was engulfed in the Reformation.

Nevertheless German humanism took its lead from Italy. Poggio Bracciolini, Aeneas Sylvius, and other humanists, visiting Germany, brought the seed; German students, pilgrims, ecclesiastics, merchants, and diplomats, visiting Italy, came back bearing on them, even unwittingly, the pollen of the Renaissance. Rodolphus Agricola, son of a Dutch parish priest, received plentiful schooling at Erfurt, Cologne, and Louvain; gave seven years to further studies of Latin and Greek in Italy; and returned to teach at Groningen, Heidelberg, and Worms. The age marveled at his unpopular virtues —modesty, simplicity, honesty, piety, chastity. He wrote in a Latin almost worthy of Cicero; he predicted that Germany would soon "appear no less Latin than Latium"; [64] and indeed, in the next generation, Agricola's Holland produced in Erasmus a Latinist who would have been quite at home in the Rome of Tacitus and Quintilian. It was on a trip to Rome that Agricola contracted the fever from which he died at Heidelberg at the age of forty-two (1485).

He was rivaled in influence—hardly in amiability—by Jakob Wimpheling, whose temper was as harsh as his Latin was smooth. Resolved to lift Germany to Italy's level in education and letters, this "Schoolmaster of Germany" drew up plans for a system of public schools, established learned societies, and yet foresaw how dangerous intellectual advance would be without moral development. "What profits all our learning," he asked, "if our characters be not correspondingly noble, or all our industry without piety, or all our knowledge without love of our neighbor, or all our wisdom without humility?" [65]

The last of these orthodox humanists was Johannes Trithemius, Abbot of Sponheim, who nevertheless wrote in 1496: "The days of building monasteries are past; the days of their destruction are coming." [66] A less devout humanist, Celtes, described Trithemius as "abstemious in drink, disdaining animal food, living on vegetables, eggs, and milk, as did our ancestors when . . . no doctors had begun to brew their gout-and-fever-breeding concoctions." * [67] In his brief life he became a very *summa* of learning: skilled in Latin, Greek, Hebrew, and their literatures, and carrying on a correspondence with Erasmus, Maximilian, Imperial electors, and other celebrities. The common people of the time could only explain his attainments on the theory that he possessed secret supernatural powers. However, he died at fifty-four (1516).

Conradus Celtes was the most zealous and effective of the German humanists. Passing like some hurried diplomat of letters from city to city, studying in Italy, Poland, and Hungary, teaching in Cologne, Heidelberg, Cracow, Prague, Mainz, Vienna, Ingolstadt, Padua, Nuremberg, he un-

---

* Our animal ancestors seem to have been vegetarians when they could not get lice; but our human ancestors were apparently hunters, and therefore meat-eaters, for 50,000 years before the discovery of agriculture. Dietetic arguments from history are treacherous.

earthed precious forgotten manuscripts like the plays of Hrotswitha, and ancient maps like that which he gave to Peutinger, whose name it came to bear. Wherever he went he gathered students about him, and inspired them with his passion for poetry, classical literature, and German antiquities. In 1447, at Nuremberg, the Emperor Frederick III crowned him poet laureate of Germany. At Mainz Celtes founded (1491) the influential Rhenish Literary Society, which included scientists, theologians, philosophers, physicians, historians, poets, such lawyers as the distinguished jurist Ulrich Zasius, and such scholars as Pirkheimer, Trithemius, Reuchlin, and Wimpheling. At Vienna, with funds provided by Maximilian, he organized (1501) an Academy of Poetry which became an honored part of the university, and in which teachers and pupils lived together in the same house and enterprise. In the course of his studies Celtes apparently lost his religious faith; he raised such questions as "Will the soul live after death?" and "Is there, really, a God?" In his travels he took many samples of femininity, but none to the altar; and he concluded lightheartedly that "there is nothing sweeter under the sun, to banish care, than a pretty maid in a man's arms." [68]

This skeptical amoralism grew in fashion among the German humanists in the final decades before Luther. Eoban Hesse wrote in good Latin *Heroides Christianae* (1514), which imitated Ovid even more in scandal than in form; he included love letters from Magdalen to Jesus, and from the Virgin Mary to God the Father. To suit the deed to the word, he lived as loosely as Cellini, outdrank all rivals, and thought nothing of emptying a bucket of ale at one draught.

Conradus Mutianus Rufus, however, achieved an amiable reconciliation of skepticism with religion. After studying at Deventer, at Erfurt, and in Italy, he contented himself with a modest canonry at Gotha, put over his door the motto *Beata tranquillitas*, collected admiring students, and taught them to "esteem the decrees of philosophers above those of priests"; [69] but, he warned them, they must conceal their doubts of Christian dogma from the multitude by a gentlemanly adherence to ecclesiastical ceremonies and forms.[70] "By faith," he said, "we mean not the conformity of what we say with fact, but an opinion about divine things founded upon credulity and profit-seeking persuasion." [71] He objected to Masses for the dead as useless, to fasts as unpleasant, and to auricular confession as embarrassing.[72] The Bible, he thought, contains many fables, like those of Jonah and Job; probably Christ had not really died on the cross; the Greeks and the Romans, so far as they lived honorably, were Christians without knowing it, and doubtless went to paradise.[73] Creeds and ceremonies are to be judged not on their literal claims but by their moral effects; if they promote social order and private virtue they should be accepted without public questioning. Mutianus demanded a clean life from his disciples; and in his later years he vowed, "I will turn my studies to piety, and will learn nothing from poets, philoso-phers, or historians save what can promote a Christian life." [74] Having lived with all the consolations of philosophy, he died with all the blessings of the Church (1526).

The natural resentment aroused among the orthodox by the skepticism of the later humanists fell in accumulation upon the mildest and kindliest scholar of the time. Johannes Reuchlin observed the medieval tradition of gathering education from a dozen centers, through the ubiquity of Latin as the language of instruction in Western Europe. In the grammar school of his native Pforzheim, in the universities of Freiburg, Paris, Basel, Orléans, and Poitiers, in Linz, Milan, Florence, and Rome, he pursued with almost fanatical ardor the study of Latin, Greek, Hebrew, and law. Following the custom of the German humanists, he changed his name—which he derived from *rauchen*, to smoke—to Capnio—*kapnos* being Greek for smoke. At twenty he compiled a Latin dictionary, which went through several editions. At Rome Johannes Argyropoulos gave him a difficult passage in Thucydides to translate; Reuchlin responded so readily that the old Greek exclaimed: "Greece has now fled beyond the Alps." [75] The avid student let no rabbi pass without learning some Hebrew from him; Mutianus claimed to have heard of Reuchlin giving a Jewish scholar ten gold pieces for explaining one Hebrew phrase [76]—but this may have been a humanist's dream. Pico della Mirandola persuaded Reuchlin to seek wisdom in the Cabala. Comparing Jerome's translation of the Old Testament with the original Hebrew text, "Capnio" pointed out many errors in what theologians habitually quoted as an infallible document. At thirty-eight (1493) he was appointed professor of Hebrew in the University of Heidelberg. The Hebrew dictionary and grammar that he composed put the study of Hebrew and of the Old Testa-ment on a scientific basis, and contributed to the powerful influence of the Hebrew Scriptures on Protestant thought. Gradually his admiration for Hebrew eclipsed his devotion to the classics. "The Hebrew language," he wrote, "is unadulterated, concise, and brief. It is the language in which God spoke to man, and in which man conversed with the angels face to face." [77] Through all his studies he retained the orthodox faith. He muddied it a bit with mysticism, but he devoutly submitted all his writings and teachings to the authority of the Church.

A strange medley of circumstances made him the hero of the German Renaissance. In 1508 Johannes Pfefferkorn, a rabbi turned priest, issued a book, *Judenspiegel* (*Mirror of the Jews*), condemning persecution of the Jews, and clearing them from legendary crimes popularly laid to their charge, but urging them to give up moneylending and the Talmud, and accept Christianity. Supported by the Dominicans of Cologne, he submitted to the Emperor a recommendation that all Hebrew books except the Old

Testament should be suppressed. Maximilian ordered that all Jewish literature critical of Christianity should be surrendered to Pfefferkorn, and that
it should be examined by the universities of Cologne, Erfurt, Mainz, and
Heidelberg, by Jakob van Hoogstraeten, head of the Inquisition at Cologne,
and by Reuchlin because of his fame for Hebrew learning. All but Reuchlin
advised that the books should be confiscated and burned. Reuchlin's minority opinion proved a landmark in the history of religious toleration. He
divided Jewish books into seven classes; one group, consisting of works ex-
pressly mocking Christianity, should be burned; all the rest, including the
Talmud, should be preserved, if only because they contained much of value
to Christian scholarship. Moreover, he argued, the Jews had a right to
freedom of conscience, both as citizens of the Empire and as having undertaken no obligations to Christianity.[78] In private correspondence Reuchlin
spoke of Pfefferkorn as an "ass" who had no real understanding of the books
he proposed to destroy.

Pfefferkorn responded to these courtesies in a *Handspiegel* (*Hand
Mirror*) that attacked Reuchlin as a bribed tool of the Jews. Reuchlin retorted in the same vituperative vein in an *Augenspiegel* (*Eyeglass*) that
aroused a storm among the orthodox. The theological faculty at Cologne
complained to Reuchlin that his book was making the Jews too happy, and
they urged him to withdraw it from circulation. Maximilian forbade its sale.
Reuchlin appealed to Leo X; the Pope turned the matter over to various
counselors, who reported that the book was harmless. Leo suspended action,
but assured the humanists around him that no harm should come to Reuchlin.
Meanwhile Pfefferkorn and his Dominican supporters accused Reuchlin, before the tribunal of the Inquisition at Cologne, as an unbeliever and a traitor
to Christianity. The archbishop interposed, and remitted the case to Rome,
which passed it on to the episcopal court of Speyer, which acquitted Reuchlin. The Dominicans in their turn appealed to Rome; and the university
faculties of Cologne, Erfurt, Mainz, Louvain, and Paris ordered Reuchlin's
books to be burned.

It is remarkable—and eloquent of Germany's cultural vitality in this age—
how many notables now came to Reuchlin's defense: Erasmus, Pirkheimer,
Peutinger, Oecolampadius of Basel, Bishop Fisher of Rochester, Ulrich von
Hutten, Mutianus, Eoban Hesse, Luther, Melanchthon, even some of the
higher clergy, who, as in Italy, favored the humanists. Imperial electors,
princes, and fifty-three cities proclaimed their support of Reuchlin. Letters
from his defenders were collected and published (1514) as *Clarorum virorum epistolae ad Johannem Reuchlin*. In 1515 the humanists sent forth a
more devastating book, *Epistolae obscurorum virorum ad venerabilem
virum magistrum Ortuinum Gratium* (*Letters of Obscure Men to the Venerable Master Ortuinus Gratius*, professor of literature ·· ^ologne). This is

one of the major satires in literary history. It succeeded so well that an enlarged edition was issued in 1516, and a continuation a year later. The authors pretended to be pious monks, admirers of Gratius and enemies of Reuchlin, and concealed themselves under grotesque pseudonyms—Nicolaus Caprimulgius (goat-milker), Johannes Pellifex (skin-maker), Simon Wurst (sausage), Conradus Unckebunck. In Latin made deliberately bad to imitate the monastic style, the writers complained of the ridicule heaped upon them by the "poets" (as the German humanists were called); they inquired eagerly about the prosecution of Reuchlin; meanwhile they exposed their absurd ignorance, the grossness of their morals and their minds; they argued ridiculous questions in solemn Scholastic form, quoted Scripture in extenuation of obscenities, and unwittingly made fun of auricular confession, the sale of indulgences, the worship of relics, the authority of the pope—the very themes of the Reformation. All literate Germany puzzled over the authorship of the volumes; only later was it admitted that Crotus Rubianus of Erfurt, a disciple of Mutianus, had written most of the first edition, and Hutten most of the continuation. Roused to anger, Leo X forbade the reading or possession of the book, condemned Reuchlin, but let him off with the costs of the Speyer trial (1520). Reuchlin, sixty-five and exhausted, retired into obscurity, peacefully lost in the glare of the Reform.

The German humanist movement too disappeared in that conflagration. On one side it was fought by most of the universities; on the other, the Reformers, engaged in a struggle for life, strengthened their cause with a religious faith that centered on personal salvation in the other world and left little time for studies of classical civilization, or of human amelioration here below. The German humanists themselves invited defeat by failing to advance from Greek literature to Greek philosophy, by wandering into coarse polemics or a mysticism far less mature than Eckhart's. They left no major works; the grammars and dictionaries that Reuchlin hoped would be his "monument more lasting than brass" were soon superseded and forgotten. And yet who knows if Luther would have dared sling his David's shots at Tetzel and the popes if the mind of Germany had not been in a measure freed from ultramontane terrors by the humanists? The followers of Reuchlin and Mutianus were a vigorous minority at Erfurt, where Luther studied for four years. And the greatest German poet of the age, nurtured in humanism, became the ardent herald of the Reformation.

VII. ULRICH VON HUTTEN

There were no giants in the German literature of this age before Luther; there was only an amazing effervescence and fertility. Poetry was written to be read aloud, and was therefore welcomed in cottage and palace. Mystery and Passion plays continued to be acted, overlaying a rough piety with a strong interest in dramatic art. By 1450 the German popular drama was largely secularized. It included, even in the course of religious plays, crude and sometimes scandalous farces.[79] Humor frolicked in the literature; now the vicissitudes and drolleries of Till Eulenspiegel, that wandering trickster (literally, owlglass), romped through Germany, his merry pranks sparing neither layman nor priest; and in 1515 his adventures took printed form. Time and again the literature, as well as the art, showed monks and priests being dragged down to hell.[80] Satire flourished in every literary form.

The most effective satire of the time was the *Narrenschiff* (1494), or *Ship of Fools*, of Sebastian Brant; no one could have expected so lively a performance from a professor of law and classical literature at Basel. Brant imagined a fleet (he forgot it *en voyage* and later called it a ship) manned by fools and trying to navigate the sea of life. One fool after another struts the scene; one class after another bears the whip of the jurist's angry doggerel—peasant, mechanic, beggar, gambler, miser, usurer, astrologer, lawyer, pedant, fop, philosopher, priest; the vanity of ambitious men, the idleness of students, the venality of tradesmen, the dishonesty of journeymen—all get their share of the blows, and Brant reserves his respect only for the pious and orthodox Catholic who ordains his life so as to gain paradise. Beautifully printed, and adorned with woodcuts that pointed each barb of the tale, the book sailed to triumph everywhere in Western Europe, through a dozen translations; next to the Bible it was the most widely read book of the time.

Brant laid his lash tenderly upon the clergy, but Thomas Murner, a Franciscan friar, attacked monks and priests, bishops and nuns with satires at once sharper, coarser, and wittier than Brant's. The priest, said Murner, is interested in money more than in religion; he coaxes every possible penny from his parishioners, then pays part of his gleanings to his bishop for permission to keep a concubine. Nuns make love clandestinely, and the one who has the most children is chosen abbess.[81] Murner, however, agreed with Brant in fidelity to the Church; he denounced Luther as one more fool; and in a touching poem *Von dem Untergang des christlichen Glaubens* he mourned the decline of Christian belief and the deepening chaos of the religious world.

If the immense popularity of these satires revealed the scorn in which even loyal Catholics held their clergy, the still more passionate satires of Ulrich von Hutten abandoned all hope for the self-reform of the Church, and called for open revolt. Born of a knightly family in Franconia, Ulrich was sent at eleven to the monastery of Fulda with the expectation that he would become a monk. After six years of probation he fled (1505), and led the life of a wandering student, composing and reciting poetry, begging his way and often shelterless, but finding means to make love to a lass who left her signature in his blood.[82] His small body was almost consumed with fever; his left leg was often made useless by ulcers and swellings; his temper took on the irritability of an invalid, but Eoban Hesse found him "altogether lovable." [83] A kindly bishop took him to Vienna, where the humanists welcomed him, but he quarreled with them and moved on to Italy. He studied at Pavia and Bologna, shot poisoned epigrams at Pope Julius II, joined an invading German army in order to eat, and then, always in pain, made his way back to Germany.

At Mainz fortune gave him a passing smile: he wrote a panegyric on young Archbishop Albrecht, and received 200 guilders ($5,000?) in acknowledgment. Albrecht's court was now a very hive of humanists, many of them irreverent freethinkers.[84] There Hutten began his contribution to the *Epistolae obscurorum virorum;* there he met Erasmus, and was captivated by the great scholar's learning, wit, and charm. With Albrecht's guilders and aid from his relenting father, he again sought the sun of Italy, blasting at every stop the "hypocritical, corrupt race of theologians and monks." [85] From the papal capital he sent a warning to Crotus Rubianus:

> Renounce your desire to see Rome, my friend; what you seek there is not to be found there any longer. . . . You may live from plunder, commit murder and sacrilege . . . you may revel in lust and deny God in heaven; but if you do but bring money to Rome you are a most respectable person. Virtue and heavenly blessings are sold here; you may even buy the privilege of sinning in future. You would then be crazy to be good; sensible folk will be wicked.[86]

With gay irony he dedicated to Leo X (1517) a new edition of Valla's devastating treatise on the fictitious "Donation of Constantine," and assured the Pope that most of his papal predecessors had been tyrants, robbers, and extortioners, who had turned the punishments of the next world into revenue for themselves.[87] This work came into Luther's hands, and warmed his ire against the papacy.

Despite the vituperative violence in many of Hutten's poems, they won him a scattered fame in Germany. Repatriating himself in 1517, he was entertained at Nuremberg by Konrad Peutinger; and at this rich scholar's suggestion Maximilian crowned Hutten poet laureate. Albrecht now took him into his diplomatic service, and sent him on important missions as far afield as Paris. When Hutten returned to Mainz (1518) he found Germany agitated by Luther's theses on indulgences; and he must have smiled to see his own easygoing Archbishop uncomfortably involved. Luther was being summoned to Augsburg to face Cardinal Cajetan and a charge of heresy.

Hutten hesitated; he was attached to the Archbishop emotionally and financially, but he felt in his blood the call to war. He mounted his horse and rode off to Augsburg.

VIII. THE GERMAN CHURCH

What actually was the condition of the German Church in the youth of Luther? One indication appeared in the readiness of high ecclesiastics to accept the criticism and critics of the Church. There were some scattered atheists whose names are lost in the censorship of time; and Erasmus mentions "men amongst us who think, like Epicurus, that the soul dies with the body." [88] There were skeptics among the humanists. There were mystics who denied the necessity of Church or priest as intermediaries between man and God, and emphasized inward religious experience as against ceremonies and sacraments. Here and there were little pockets of Waldensians who denied the distinction between priests and laymen; and in eastern Germany were some Hussites who called the pope Antichrist. In Eger two brothers, John and Lewin of Augsburg, denounced indulgences as a hoax (1466).[89] Johan von Wesel, an Erfurt professor, preached predestination and election by divine grace, rejected indulgences, sacraments, and prayers to the saints, and declared: "I despise the pope, the Church, and the councils, and I worship only Christ"; he was condemned by the Inquisition, recanted, and died in prison (1481).[90] Wessel Gansfort, wrongly known as Johann Wessel, questioned confession, absolution, indulgences, and purgatory, made the Bible the sole rule of faith, and made faith the sole source of salvation; here was Luther in a sentence. "If I had read his works before," said Luther in 1522, "my enemies might have thought that Luther had borrowed everything from Wessel, so great is the agreement between our spirits." [91]

Nevertheless, by and large, religion was flourishing in Germany, and the overwhelming majority of the people were orthodox and—between their sins and their cups—pious. The German family was almost a church in itself, where the mother served as catechist and the father as priest; prayer was frequent, and books of family devotions were in every home. For those who could not read there were picture books, *Biblia pauperum*, illustrating the stories of Christ, Mary, and the saints. Pictures of the Virgin were as numerous as those of Jesus; the rosary was recited with hopeful frequency; Jakob Sprenger, the inquisitor, founded a fraternity for its repetition; and one German prayer was addressed to the only really popular Trinity: "Glory be to the Virgin, the Father, and the Son." [92]

Some of the clergy were as religious as the people. There must have been—though their names were rarely heard above the din made by wickedness—

faithful ministers of the faith to produce or sustain such widespread piety among the people. The parish priest, as like as not, had a concubine or a common-law wife; [93] but the lion-loined Germans seem to have condoned this as an improvement upon promiscuity; and had not the popes themselves, in this lusty period, rebelled against celibacy? As for the "regular" clergy—those subject to a monastic *regula* or rule—many of their orders were now engaged in earnest self-reform. The Benedictines had settled into a half-conventual, half-worldly ease, and the Teutonic Knights continued their loose morals, martial cruelties, and territorial greed; but the Dominican, Franciscan, and Augustinian friars returned to the observance of their rules, and performed many works of practical benevolence. [94] Most zealous in this reform were the Augustinian Eremites, originally anchorites or hermit monks, but later gathered into communities. They kept with apparent fidelity their monastic vows of poverty, chastity, and obedience, and were learned enough to fill many chairs in German universities. It was this order that Luther chose when he decided to become a monk.

The complaints against the German clergy were chiefly against the prelates, and on the score of their wealth and worldliness. Some bishops and abbots had to organize the economy and administration of great areas that had come into the possession of the Church; they were mitered or tonsured feudal seigneurs, and not always the most lenient. [95] These ecclesiastics behaved like men of the world rather than men of God; and it was alleged that several of them rode to provincial or federal diets with their concubines in their trains. [96] A learned Catholic prelate and historian, Johannes Janssen, has summed up perhaps too severely the abuses of the German Church on the eve of the Reformation:

> The contrast of pious love and worldly greed, of godly renunciation and godless self-seeking, made itself apparent in the ranks of the clergy as well as in other classes of society. By too many among the ministers of God and religion preaching and the care of souls were altogether neglected. Avarice, the besetting sin of the age, showed itself among the clergy of all orders and degrees, in their anxiety to increase to the utmost extent all clerical rents and incomes, taxes and perquisites. The German Church was the richest in Christendom. It was reckoned that nearly a third of the whole landed property of the country was in the hands of the Church—which made it all the more reprehensible in the ecclesiastical authorities to be always seeking to augment their possessions. In many towns the church buildings and institutions covered the greater part of the ground.
>
> Within the sacerdotal body itself there were also the most marked contrasts in respect of income. The lower orders of parochial clergy, whose merely nominal stipends were derived from the many precari-

ous tithes, were often compelled by poverty—if not tempted by avarice—to work at some trade which was quite inconsistent with their position, and which exposed them to the contempt of their parishioners. The higher ecclesiastical orders, on the other hand, enjoyed abundant and superfluous wealth, which many of them had no scruples in parading in such an offensive manner as to provoke the indignation of the people, the jealousy of the upper classes, and the scorn of all serious minds. . . . In many places complaints were loud against the mercenary abuse of sacred things . . . against the large and frequent sums of money sent to Rome, of annates and hush money. A bitter feeling of hatred against the Italians . . . began gradually to gain ground, even amongst men who, like Archbishop Berthold von Henneberg, were true sons of the Holy Church. "The Italians," he wrote on September 9, 1496, "ought to reward the Germans for their services, and not drain the sacerdotal body with frequent extortions of gold.[97]

Germany might have forgiven the worldliness of its bishops if it could have been spared the pretensions and exactions of the popes. The rising spirit of nationalism resented the claims of the papacy to hold no emperor legitimate till papally confirmed, and to depose emperors and kings at will. Conflicts between secular and ecclesiastical authorities persisted in appointments to benefices, in the overlapping jurisdiction of civil and episcopal courts, in the immunity of the clergy from nearly all civil legislation. German nobles looked with fretting concupiscence upon the rich possessions of the Church, and businessmen grieved that monasteries claiming exemption from taxation were competing with them in manufacturing and trade.[98] The quarrel at this stage was over material concerns rather than over theological differences. Says another Catholic historian:

> It was the general opinion in Germany that in the matter of taxation the Roman Curia put on the pressure to an unbearable degree. . . . Again and again was the complaint made that chancery dues, annates . . . and consecration fees were unduly raised or unlawfully extended; that numerous new indulgences were published without the consent of the bishops of the country, and tithe after tithe raised for a crusade and diverted to another object. Even men devoted to the Church and the Holy See . . . often declared that the German grievances against Rome were, from a financial point of view, for the most part only too well founded.[99]

In 1457 Martin Meyer, Chancellor to Archbishop Dietrich of Mainz, addressed to Cardinal Piccolomini an angry recapitulation of the wrongs that Germany suffered from the Roman Curia:

The election of prelates is frequently postponed without cause, and benefices and dignities of all kinds are reserved for the cardinals and papal secretaries; Cardinal Piccolomini himself has been granted a general reservation in an unusual and unheard-of form in three German provinces. Expectancies * without number are conferred, annates and other taxes are collected harshly, and no delay is granted, and it is also known that more has been exacted than the sums due. Bishoprics have been bestowed not on the most worthy but on the highest bidder. For the sake of amassing money, new indulgences have daily been published, and war tithes imposed, without consulting the German prelates. Lawsuits that ought to have been dealt with at home have been hastily transferred to the Apostolic tribunal. The Germans have been treated as if they were rich and stupid barbarians, and drained of their money by a thousand cunning devices. . . . For many years Germany has lain in the dust, bemoaning her poverty and her sad fate. *But now her nobles have awakened as from sleep; now they have resolved to shake off the yoke, and to win back their ancient freedom.*[100]

When Cardinal Piccolomini became Pius II (1458) he defied this challenge; from Diether von Isenburg he demanded 20,500 guilders before confirming him as the next archbishop of Mainz (1459). Diether refused to pay, charging that the sum exceeded every precedent; Pius excommunicated him; Diether ignored the ban, and several German princes supported him. Diether engaged a Nuremberg jurist, Gregor Heimburg, to arouse public sentiment for giving councils supremacy over the popes; Heimburg went to France to arrange concerted action against the papacy; for a time it seemed that the northern nations would throw off allegiance to Rome. But papal agents detached from the movement one after another of Diether's allies, and Pius appointed Adolf of Nassau to replace him. The armies of the two archbishops fought a bloody war; Diether was defeated; he addressed to the German leaders a warning that unless they stood together they would be repeatedly oppressed; and this manifesto was one of the first documents printed by Gutenberg.[101]

German discontent was not quieted by this victory of the popes. After a large sum of money had gone from Germany to Rome in the jubilee of 1500, a diet at Augsburg demanded that part of the money should be returned to Germany.[102] The Emperor Maximilian grumbled that the pope drew a hundred times more revenue from Germany than he himself could collect. In 1510, being at war with Pope Julius II, he directed the humanist Wim-

---

* An expectancy was a promise of appointment to a benefice in anticipation of the incumbent's death or removal. The postponement of appointments was often due to the rule that between the death of one bishop and the selection of his successor the revenues of the see went to the Roman Curia.

pheling to draw up a list of Germany's grievances against the papacy; for a time he thought of proposing the separation of the German Church from Rome, but Wimpheling dissuaded him on the ground that he could not expect persistent support from the princes. Nevertheless all the economic developments of this age prepared for Luther. A basic diversity of material interests finally opposed the German Reformation—demanding an end to the flow of German money into Italy—to an Italian Renaissance that financed poetry and art with transalpine gold.

Among the people anticlericalism went hand in hand with piety. "A revolutionary spirit of hatred for the Church and the clergy," writes the honest Pastor, "had taken hold of the masses in various parts of Germany. . . . The cry of 'Death to the priests!' which had long been whispered in secret, was now the watchword of the day." [103] So keen was this popular hostility that the Inquisition, then rising in Spain, hardly dared condemn anyone in Germany. Violent pamphlets rained assaults not so much upon the German Church as upon the Roman See. Some monks and priests joined in the attack, and stirred up their congregations against the luxury of the higher clergy. Pilgrims returning from the jubilee of 1500 brought to Germany lurid—often exaggerated—stories of immoral popes, papal poisonings, cardinals' roisterings, and of a general paganism and venality. Many Germans vowed that as their ancestors had broken the power of Rome in 476, they or their children would crush that tyranny again; others recalled the humiliation of the Emperor Henry IV by Pope Gregory VII at Canossa, and thought the time had come for revenge. In 1521 the papal nuncio Aleander, warning Leo X of an imminent uprising against the Church, said that five years earlier he had heard from many Germans that they were only waiting for "some fool" to open his mouth against Rome.[104]

A thousand factors and influences—ecclesiastical, intellectual, emotional, economic, political, moral—were coming together, after centuries of obstruction and suppression, in a whirlwind that would throw Europe into the greatest upheaval since the barbarian conquest of Rome. The weakening of the papacy by the Avignon exile and the Papal Schism; the breakdown of monastic discipline and clerical celibacy; the luxury of prelates, the corruption of the Curia, the worldly activities of the popes; the morals of Alexander VI, the wars of Julius II, the careless gaiety of Leo X; the relic-mongering and peddling of indulgences; the triumph of Islam over Christendom in the Crusades and the Turkish wars; the spreading acquaintance with non-Christian faiths; the influx of Arabic science and philosophy; the collapse of Scholasticism in the irrationalism of Scotus and the skepticism of Ockham; the failure of the conciliar movement to effect reform; the discovery of pagan antiquity and of America; the invention of printing; the extension of literacy and education; the translation and reading of the Bible; the newly realized contrast between the poverty and simplicity of the Apostles and the ceremonious opulence of the Church; the rising wealth and economic independence of Germany and England; the growth of a middle class resentful of ecclesiastical restrictions and claims; the protests against the flow of money to Rome; the secularization of law and government; the intensification of nationalism and the strengthening of monarchies; the nationalistic influence of vernacular languages and literatures; the fermenting legacies of the Waldenses, Wyclif, and Huss; the mystic demand for a less ritualistic, more personal and inward and direct religion: all these were now uniting in a torrent of forces that would crack the crust of medieval custom, loosen all standards and bonds, shatter Europe into nations and sects, sweep away more and more of the supports and comforts of traditional beliefs. and perhaps mark the beginning of the end for the dominance of Christianity in the mental life of European man.

BOOK II

THE RELIGIOUS REVOLUTION

1517–64

CHAPTER XVI

Luther: The Reformation in Germany

1517-24

I. TETZEL

ON March 15, 1517, Pope Leo X promulgated the most famous of all indulgences. It was a pity, yet just, that the Reformation should strike during a pontificate that gathered into Rome so many of the fruits, and so much of the spirit, of the Renaissance. Leo, son of Lorenzo the Magnificent, was now head of the Medici family, which had nourished the Renaissance in Florence; he was a scholar, a poet, and a gentleman, kindly and generous, in love with classical literature and delicate art. His morals were good in an immoral milieu; his nature inclined to a gaiety pleasant and legitimate, which set an example of happiness for a city that a century before had been destitute and desolate. All his faults were superficial except his superficiality. He made too little distinction between the good of his family and that of the Church, and wasted the funds of the papacy on questionable poets and wars. He was normally tolerant, enjoyed the satire directed against ecclesiastics in Erasmus' *Praise of Folly*, and practiced, with occasional lapses, the unwritten agreement by which the Renaissance Church accorded considerable freedom to philosophers, poets, and scholars who addressed themselves—usually in Latin—to the educated minority, but who left the irreplaceable faith of the masses undisturbed.

The son of a banker, Leo was accustomed to spending money readily, and chiefly on others. He inherited full papal coffers from Julius II, and emptied them before he died. Perhaps he did not care much for the massive basilica that Julius had planned and begun, but the old St. Peter's was beyond repair, immense sums had been poured into the new one, and it would be a disgrace to the Church to let that majestic enterprise abort. Possibly with some reluctance he offered the indulgence of 1517 to all who would contribute to the cost of completing the great shrine. The rulers of England, Germany, France, and Spain protested that their countries were being drained of wealth, their national economies were being disturbed, by repeated campaigns for luring money to Rome. Where kings were powerful Leo was considerate: he agreed that Henry VIII should keep a fourth of the proceeds in England; he advanced a loan of 175,000 ducats to King Charles I (the later Emperor Charles V) against expected collections in Spain; and Francis I was to retain part of the sum raised in France. Germany received less favored treatment, having no strong monarchy to bargain with the Pope; however, the Emperor Maximilian was allotted a modest 3,000 florins from the receipts, and the Fuggers were to take from the collections the 20,000 florins that they had loaned to Albrecht of Brandenburg to pay the Pope for his confirmation as Archbishop of Mainz. Unfortunately that city had lost three archbishops in ten years (1504–14), and had twice paid heavy confirmation fees; to spare it from paying a third time Albrecht borrowed. Now Leo agreed that the young prelate should manage the distribution of the indulgence in Magdeburg and Halberstadt as well as in Mainz. An agent of the Fuggers accompanied each of Albrecht's preachers, checked expenses and receipts, and kept one of the keys to the strongbox that held the funds.[1]

Albrecht's principal agent was Johann Tetzel, a Dominican friar who had acquired skill and reputation as a money-raiser. Since 1500 his main occupation had been in disposing of indulgences. Usually, on these missions, he received the aid of the local clergy: when he entered a town a procession of priests, magistrates, and pious laity welcomed him with banners, candles, and song, and bore the bull of indulgence aloft on a velvet or golden cushion, while church bells pealed and organs played.[2] So propped, Tetzel offered, in an impressive formula, a plenary indulgence to those who would penitently confess their sins and contribute according to their means to the building of a new St. Peter's:

> May our Lord Jesus Christ have mercy on thee, and absolve thee by the merits of His most holy Passion. And I, by His authority, that of his blessed Apostles Peter and Paul, and of the most holy Pope, granted and committed to me in these parts, do absolve thee, first from all ecclesiastical censures, in whatever manner they may have been incurred, and then from all thy sins, transgressions, and excesses, how enormous soever they may be, even from such as are reserved for the cognizance of the Holy See; and as far as the keys of the Holy Church extend, I remit to you all punishment which you deserve in purgatory on their account, and I restore you to the holy sacraments of the Church . . . and to that innocence and purity which you possessed at baptism; so that when you die the gates of punishment shall be shut, and the gates of the paradise of delight shall be opened; and if you shall not die at present, this grace shall remain in full force when you are at the point of death. In the name of the Father, and of the Son, and of the Holy Ghost.[3]

This splendid bargain for a believer was in harmony with the official con-ception of indulgences for the living. Tetzel was again within the letter of his archiepiscopal instructions when he dispensed with preliminary confes-sion if the contributor applied the indulgence to a soul in purgatory. Says a Catholic historian:

> There is no doubt that Tetzel did, according to what he consid-ered his authoritative instructions, proclaim as Christian doctrine that nothing but an offering of money was required to gain the indulgence for the dead, without there being any question of contrition or con-fession. He also taught, in accordance with the *opinion* then held, that an indulgence could be applied to any given soul with unfailing effect. Starting from this assumption, there is no doubt that his doc-trine was virtually that of the drastic proverb: "As soon as the money in the coffer rings, the soul from purgatory's fire springs." The papal bull of indulgence gave no sanction whatever to this proposi-tion. It was a vague Scholastic opinion . . . not any doctrine of the Church.[4]

Myconius, a Franciscan friar perhaps hostile to the Dominicans, heard Tetzel perform, and reported, for this year 1517: "It is incredible what this ignorant monk said and preached. He gave sealed letters stating that even the sins which a man was intending to commit would be forgiven. The pope, he said, had more power than all the Apostles, all the angels and saints, more even than the Virgin Mary herself; for these were all subject to Christ, but the pope was equal to Christ." This is probably an exaggeration, but that such a description could be given by an eyewitness suggests the antipathy that Tetzel aroused. A like hostility appears in the rumor mentioned skepti-cally by Luther,[5] which quoted Tetzel as having said at Halle that even if, *per impossibile*, a man had violated the Mother of God the indulgence would wipe away his sin. Tetzel obtained certificates from civil and ecclesiastical authorities at Halle that they had never heard the story.[6] He was an enthusi-astic salesman, but not quite conscienceless.

He would have escaped history had he not approached too closely to the lands of Frederick the Wise, Elector of Saxony.* Frederick was a pious and provident ruler. He had no theoretical objection to indulgences; he had gathered 19,000 saintly relics into his Castle Church at Wittenberg,[7] and had arranged to have an indulgence attached to their veneration; he had procured another indulgence for contributors to the building of a bridge at

---

* In 1485 the domains of the house of Wettin were divided into two regions. The smaller but richer part, containing Leipzig and Dresden, was given to the younger son, Duke Albert, and became known as Ducal or Albertine Saxony. The larger but less populous portion, in-cluding Wittenberg and Weimar, was assigned to the elder brother, the Imperial Elector Ernest, and came to be known as Electoral or Ernestine Saxony. This division proved of some moment in the Reformation.

Torgau, and had engaged Tetzel to advertise the benefits of that pontifical indulgence.[8] However, he had withheld from Pope Alexander VI (1501) the sum raised in Electoral Saxony by an indulgence for donations to a crusade against the Turks; he would release the money, he said, when the crusade materialized. It did not; Frederick the Wise kept the funds, and applied them to the University of Wittenberg.[9] Now, moved by reluctance to let coin of Saxony emigrate, and perhaps by reports of Tetzel's hyperboles, he forbade the preaching of the 1517 indulgence in his territory. But Tetzel came so close to the frontiers that people in Wittenberg crossed the border to obtain the indulgence. Several purchasers brought these "papal letters" to Martin Luther, professor of theology in the university, and asked him to attest their efficacy. He refused. The refusal came to Tetzel's ears; he denounced Luther, and became immortal.

He had underestimated the pugnacity of the professor. Luther quickly composed in Latin ninety-five theses, which he entitled *Disputatio pro declaratione virtutis indulgentiarum (Disputation for Clarification of the Power of Indulgences)*. He did not consider his propositions heretical, nor were they indubitably so. He was still a fervent Catholic who had no thought of upsetting the Church; his purpose was to refute the extravagant claims made for indulgences, and to correct the abuses that had developed in their distribution. He felt that the facile issuance and mercenary dissemination of indulgences had weakened the contrition that sin should arouse, had indeed made sin a trivial matter to be amicably adjusted over a bargain counter with a peddler of pardons. He did not yet deny the papal "power of the keys" to forgive sins; he conceded the authority of the pope to absolve the confessing penitent from the terrestrial penalties imposed by churchmen; but in Luther's view the power of the pope to free souls from purgatory, or to lessen their term of punishment there, depended not on the power of the keys—which did not reach beyond the grave—but on the intercessory influence of papal prayers, which might or might not be heard. (Theses 20–22.) Moreover, Luther argued, all Christians shared automatically in the treasury of merits earned by Christ and the saints, even without the grant of such a share by a papal letter of indulgence. He exonerated the popes from responsibility for the excesses of the preachers, but slyly added: "This unbridled preaching of pardons makes it no easy matter, even for learned men, to rescue the reverence due the pope from . . . the shrewd questionings of the laity, to wit: 'Why does not the pope empty purgatory for the sake of holy love and of the dire need of the souls that are there, if he redeems a . . . number of souls for the sake of miserable money with which to build a church?'" (Theses 81–82.)

At noon on October 31, 1517, Luther affixed his theses to the main door of the Castle Church of Wittenberg. Annually, on November 1—All Saints'

Day—the relics collected by the Elector were displayed there, and a large crowd could be expected. The practice of publicly announcing theses, which the proponent offered to defend against all challengers, was an old custom in medieval universities, and the door that Luther used for his proclamation had been regularly employed as an academic bulletin board. To the theses he prefixed an amiable invitation:

> Out of love for the faith and the desire to bring it to light, the following propositions will be discussed at Wittenberg under the chairmanship of the Reverend Father Martin Luther, Master of Arts and Sacred Theology, and Lecturer in Ordinary on the same at that place. Wherefore he requests that those who are unable to be present and debate orally with us may do so by letter.

To make sure that the theses would be widely understood, Luther had a German translation circulated among the people. With characteristic audacity he sent a copy of the theses to Archbishop Albrecht of Mainz. Courteously, piously, unwittingly, the Reformation had begun.

II. THE GENESIS OF LUTHER

What circumstances of heredity and environment had molded an obscure monk, in a town of three thousand souls, into the David of the religious revolution?

His father Hans was a stern, rugged, irascible anticlerical; his mother was a timid, modest woman much given to prayer; both were frugal and industrious. Hans was a peasant at Möhra, then a miner at Mansfeld; but Martin was born at Eisleben on November 10, 1483. Six other children followed. Hans and Grethe believed in the rod as a magic wand for producing righteousness; once, says Martin, his father beat him so assiduously that for a long time they were open enemies; on another occasion, for stealing a nut, his mother thrashed him till the blood flowed; Martin later thought that "the severe and harsh life I led with them was the reason that I afterward took refuge in the cloister and became a monk." [10] The picture of deity which his parents transmitted to him reflected their own mood: a hard father and strict judge, exacting a joyless virtue, demanding constant propitiation, and finally damning most of mankind to everlasting hell. Both parents believed in witches, elves, angels, and demons of many kinds and specialties; and Martin carried most of these superstitions with him to the end. A religion of terror in a home of rigorous discipline shared in forming Luther's youth and creed.

At school in Mansfeld there were more rods and much catechism; Martin was flogged fifteen times in one day for misdeclining a noun. At thirteen he was advanced to a secondary school kept by a religious brotherhood at Magdeburg. At fourteen he was transferred to the school of St. George at Eisenach, and had three relatively happy years lodging in the comfortable home of Frau Cotta. Luther never forgot her remark that there was nothing on earth more precious to a man than the love of a good woman. It was a boon that he took forty-two years to win. In this healthier atmosphere he developed the natural charm of youth—healthy, cheerful, sociable, frank. He sang well, and played the lute.

In 1501 his prospering father sent him to the university at Erfurt. The curriculum centered around theology and philosophy, which was still Scholastic; but Ockham's nominalism had triumphed there, and presumably Luther noted Ockham's doctrine that popes and councils could err. He found Scholasticism in any form so disagreeable that he complimented a friend on "not having to learn the dung that was offered" as philosophy.[11] There were some mild humanists at Erfurt; he was very slightly influenced by them; they did not care for him when they found him in earnest about the other world. He learned a little Greek and less Hebrew, but he read the major Latin classics. In 1505 he received the degree of master of arts. His proud father sent him, as a graduation present, an expensive edition of the *Corpus iuris*, and rejoiced when his son entered upon the study of law. Suddenly, after two months of such study, and to his father's dismay, the youth of twenty-two decided to become a monk.

The decision expressed the contradiction in his character. Vigorous to the point of sensuality, visibly framed for a life of normal instincts, and yet infused by home and school with the conviction that man is by nature sinful, and that sin is an offense against an omnipotent and punishing God, he had never in thought or conduct reconciled his natural impulses with his acquired beliefs. Passing presumably through the usual erotic experiments and fantasies of adolescence, he could not take these as stages of development, but viewed them as the operations of a Satan dedicated to snaring souls into irrevocable damnation. The conception of God that had been given him contained hardly any element of tenderness; the consoling figure of Mary had little place in that theology of fear, and Jesus was not the loving son who could refuse nothing to His mother; He was the Jesus of the Last Judgment so often pictured in the churches, the Christ who had threatened sinners with everlasting fire. The recurrent thought of hell darkened a mind too intensely religious to forget it in the zest and current of life. One day, as he was returning from his father's house to Erfurt (July 1505), he encountered a frightful storm. Lightning flashed about him, and struck a near-by tree. It seemed to Luther a warning from God that unless he gave his thoughts to salvation, death would surprise him unshriven and damned.

Where could he live a life of saving devotion? Only where four walls would exclude, or ascetic discipline would overcome, the world, the flesh, and the devil: only in a monastery. He made a vow to St. Anne that if he survived that storm he would become a monk.

There were twenty cloisters in Erfurt. He chose one known for faithful observance of monastic rules—that of the Augustinian Eremites. He called his friends together, drank and sang with them for what he told them was the last time, and on the morrow he was received as a novice in a monastery cell. He performed the lowliest duties with a proud humility. He recited prayers in self-hypnotizing repetition, he froze in an unheated cubicle, he fasted and scourged himself, in the hope of exorcizing devils from his body. "I was a pious monk, and so strictly observed the rules of my order that . . . if ever a monk got into heaven by monkery, so should I also have gotten there. . . . If it had lasted longer I should have tortured myself to death with watching, praying, reading, and other work." [12] On one occasion, when he had not been seen for several days, friends broke into his cell and found him lying senseless on the ground. They had brought a lute; one played it; he revived, and thanked them. In September 1506, he took the irrevocable vows of poverty, chastity, and obedience; and in May 1507, he was ordained a priest.

His fellow friars gave him friendly counsel. One assured him that the Passion of Christ had atoned for the sinful nature of man, and had opened to redeemed man the gates of paradise. Luther's reading of the German mystics, especially of Tauler, gave him hope of bridging the awful gap between a naturally sinful soul and a righteous, omnipotent God. Then a treatise by John Huss fell into his hands, and doctrinal doubts were added to his spiritual turmoil; he wondered why "a man who could write so Christianly and so powerfully had been burned. . . . I shut the book and turned away with a wounded heart." [13] Johann von Staupitz, provincial vicar of the Augustinian Eremites, took a fatherly interest in the troubled friar, and bade him replace asceticism with careful reading of the Bible and St. Augustine. The monks expressed their solicitude by giving him a Latin Bible—then a rare possession for an individual.

One day in 1508 or 1509 he was struck by a sentence in St. Paul's Epistle to the Romans (1:17): "The just shall live by faith." Slowly these words led him to the doctrine that man can be "justified"—i.e., made just and therefore saved from hell—not by good works, which could never suffice to atone for sins against an infinite deity, but only by complete faith in Christ and in his atonement for mankind. In Augustine Luther found another idea that perhaps renewed his terror—predestination—that God, even before the creation, had forever destined some souls to salvation, the rest to hell; and that the elect had been chosen by God's free will to be saved by the divine sacrifice of Christ. From that consistent absurdity he fled back again to his basic hope of salvation by faith.

In 1508, by the recommendation of Staupitz, he was transferred to an Augustinian monastery at Wittenberg, and to the post of instructor in logic and physics, then professor of theology, in the university. Wittenberg was the northern capital—seldom the residence—of Frederick the Wise. A contemporary pronounced it "a poor, insignificant town, with little, old, ugly wooden houses." Luther described the inhabitants as "beyond measure drunken, rude, and given to reveling"; they had the reputation of being the amplest drinkers in Saxony, which was rated the most drunken province of Germany. One mile to the east, said Luther, civilization ended and barbarism began. Here, for the most part, he remained to the close of his days.

He must have become by this time an exemplary monk, for in October 1510, he and a fellow friar were sent to Rome on some obscure mission for the Augustinian Eremites. His first reaction on sighting the city was one of pious awe; he prostrated himself, raised his hands, and cried: "Hail to thee, O holy Rome!" He went through all the devotions of a pilgrim, bowed reverently before saintly relics, climbed the Scala Santa on his knees, visited a score of churches, and earned so many indulgences that he almost wished his parents were dead, so that he might deliver them from purgatory. He explored the Roman Forum, but was apparently unmoved by the Renaissance art with which Raphael, Michelangelo, and a hundred others were beginning to adorn the capital. For many years after this trip he made no extant comment on the worldliness of the Roman clergy or the immorality then popular in the holy city. Ten years later, however, and still more in the sometimes imaginative reminiscences of his Table Talk in old age, he described the Rome of 1510 as "an abomination," the popes as worse than pagan emperors, and the papal court as being "served at supper by twelve naked girls." [14] Very probably he had no entry to the higher ecclesiastical circles, and had no direct knowledge of their unquestionably easy morality.

After his return to Wittenberg (February 1511) he was rapidly advanced in the pedagogical scale, and was made provincial vicar-general of his order. He gave courses in the Bible, preached regularly in the parish church, and carried on the work of his office with industry and devotion. Says a distinguished Catholic scholar:

> His official letters breathe a deep solicitude for the wavering, a gentle sympathy for the fallen; they show profound touches of religious feeling and rare practical sense, though not unmarred with counsels that have unorthodox tendencies. The plague which afflicted Wittenberg in 1516 found him courageously at his post, which spite of the concern of his friends, he would not abandon. [15]

Slowly, during these years (1512-17), his religious ideas moved away from the official doctrines of the Church. He began to speak of "our theology," in contrast with that which was taught at Erfurt. In 1515 he ascribed the corruption of the world to the clergy, who delivered to the people too many maxims and fables of human invention, and not the Scriptural world of God. In 1516 he discovered an anonymous German manuscript, whose mystic piety so supported his own view of the utter dependence of the soul, for salvation, on divine grace that he edited and published it as *Theologia Germanica* or *Deutsche Theologie*. He blamed the preachers of indulgences for taking advantage of the simplicity of the poor. In private correspondence he began to identify the Antichrist of John's First Epistle with the pope.[16] In July 1517, invited by Duke George of Albertine Saxony to preach in Dresden, he argued that the mere acceptance of the merits of Christ assured the believer's salvation. The Duke complained that such stress on faith rather than virtue "would only make the people presumptuous and mutinous." [17] Three months later the reckless friar challenged the world to debate the ninety-five theses that he had posted on Wittenberg Church.

III. THE REVOLUTION TAKES FORM

Cranach's woodcut of 1520 may reasonably suggest the Luther of 1517: a tonsured monk of middle stature, temporarily slender, with large eyes of serious intent, larger nose, and resolute chin, a face not pugnaciously but quietly announcing courage and character. Yet it was honest anger, rather than jejune audacity, that wrote the theses. The local bishop saw nothing heretical in them, but mildly advised Luther to write no more on the subject for a while. The author himself was at first dismayed by the furor he had aroused. In May 1518, he told Staupitz that his real ambition was to lead a life of quiet retirement. He deceived himself; he relished battle.

The theses became the talk of literate Germany. Thousands had waited for such a protest, and the pent-up anticlericalism of generations thrilled at having found a voice. The sale of indulgences declined. But many champions rose to meet the challenge. Tetzel himself, with some professional aid, replied in *One Hundred and Six Anti-Theses* (December 1517). He made no concessions or apologies, but "gave at times an uncompromising, even dogmatic, sanction to mere theological opinions that were hardly consonant with the most accurate scholarship." [18] When this publication reached Wittenberg a hawker offering it for sale was mobbed by university students, and his stock of 800 copies was burned in the market square—a proceeding of which Luther joyously disapproved. He answered Tetzel in "A Sermon on Indulgences and Grace," concluding with a characteristic defiance: "If

I am called a heretic by those whose purses will suffer from my truths. I care not much for their brawling; for only those say this whose dark understanding has never known the Bible." [19] Jakob van Hoogstraeten of Cologne thundered invectives against Luther, and suggested burning him at the stake. Johann Eck, Vice-Chancellor of the University of Ingolstadt, issued a pamphlet, *Obelisci* (March 1518), which charged Luther with disseminating "Bohemian poison" (the heresies of Huss), and subverting all ecclesiastical order. In Rome Sylvester Prierias, papal censor of literature, published a *Dialogue* "maintaining the absolute supremacy of the pope in terms not altogether free from exaggeration, especially stretching his theory to an unwarrantable point in dealing with indulgences." [20]

Luther countered in a Latin brochure *Resolutiones* (April 1518), copies of which he sent to his local bishop and to the Pope—in both cases with assurances of orthodoxy and submission. The text spoke quite handsomely of Leo X:

> Although there are in the Church both very learned and very holy men, it is nevertheless the infelicity of our age that even they . . . cannot succor the Church. . . . Now at last we have a most excellent Pontiff, Leo X, whose integrity and learning are a delight to all good men's ears. But what can that most benign of men do alone, in so great a confusion of affairs, worthy as he is to reign in better times? . . . In this age we are worthy only of such popes as Julius II and Alexander VI. . . . Rome herself, yea, Rome most of all, now laughs at good men; in what part of the Christian world do men more freely make a mock of the best bishops than in Rome, the true Babylon?

To Leo directly he professed an unwonted humility:

> Most blessed Father, I offer myself prostrate at the feet of your Holiness, with all that I am and have. Quicken, slay, call, recall, approve, reprove, as may seem to you good. I will acknowledge your voice as the voice of Christ, residing and speaking in you. If I have deserved death I will not refuse to die.[21]

However, as Leo's advisers noted, the *Resolutiones* affirmed the superiority of an ecumenical council to the pope, spoke slightingly of relics and pilgrimages, denied the surplus merits of the saints, and rejected all additions made by the popes in the last three centuries to the theory and practice of indulgences. As these were a prime source of papal revenue, and Leo was at his wits' end to finance his philanthropies, amusements, and wars, as well as the administration and building program of the Church, the harassed Pontiff, who had at first brushed the dispute aside as a passing fracas among monks, now took the matter in hand, and summoned Luther to Rome (July 7, 1518).

Luther faced a critical decision. Even if the most genial of popes should treat him leniently, he might find himself politely silenced and buried in a Roman monastery, to be soon forgotten by those who now applauded him. He wrote to Georg Spalatin, chaplain to Elector Frederick, suggesting that German princes should protect their citizens from compulsory extradition to Italy. The Elector agreed. He had a high regard for Luther, who had made the University of Wittenberg prosper; and besides, Emperor Max, seeing in Luther a possible card to play in diplomatic contests with Rome, advised the Elector to "take good care of that monk." [22]

At this very time the Emperor had summoned an Imperial Diet to meet at Augsburg to consider the Pope's request that it should tax Germany to help finance a new crusade against the Turks. The clergy (Leo proposed) should pay a tenth, the laity a twelfth, of their income, and every fifty householders should furnish one man. The Diet refused; on the contrary, it firmly restated the grievances that were providing the background of Luther's success. It pointed out to the papal legate that Germany had often taxed herself for crusades, only to see the funds used for other papal purposes; that the people would vigorously oppose any further remission of money to Italy; that the annates, confirmation fees, and costs of canonical litigation referred to Rome were already an intolerable burden; and that German benefices were given as plums to Italian priests. So bold a rejection of papal requests, said one delegate, had never been known in German history.[23] Noting the spirit of rebellion among the princes, Maximilian wrote to Rome advising caution in the treatment of Luther, but promising cooperation in suppressing heresy.

Leo was disposed or compelled to lenience; indeed, a Protestant historian has ascribed the triumph of the Reformation to the moderation of the Pope.[24] He put aside the order for Luther's appearance in Rome; instead he bade him present himself at Augsburg before Cardinal Cajetan, and answer charges of indiscipline and heresy. He instructed his legate to offer Luther full pardon, and future dignities, if he would recant and submit; otherwise the secular authorities should be asked to send him to Rome.[25] About the same time Leo announced his intention of presenting to Frederick an honor that the pious Elector had long coveted—that "Golden Rose" which the popes bestowed upon secular rulers whom they wished to signalize with their highest favor. Probably Leo now offered to support Frederick as successor to the Imperial crown.[26]

Armed with an Imperial safe-conduct, Luther met Cajetan at Augsburg (October 12–14, 1518). The Cardinal was a man of great theological learning and exemplary life, but he misread his function to be that of judge, not diplomat. As he saw the matter, it was primarily a question of ecclesiastical discipline and order: should a monk be allowed to criticize publicly his superiors—to whom he had vowed obedience—and to advocate views condemned

by the Church? Refusing to discuss the right or wrong of Luther's statements, he demanded a retraction and a pledge never again to disturb the peace
of the Church. Each lost patience with the other. Luther returned impenitent to Wittenberg; Cajetan asked Frederick to send him to Rome;
Frederick refused. Luther wrote a spirited account of the interviews, which
was circulated throughout Germany. In forwarding it to his friend Wenzel
Link, he added: "I send you my trifling work that you may see whether I
am not right in supposing that, according to Paul, the real Antichrist holds
sway over the Roman court. I think he is worse than any Turk." [27] In a
milder letter to Duke George he asked that "a common *reformation* should
be undertaken of the spiritual and temporal estates" [28]—his first known use
of the word that was to give his rebellion its historic name.

Leo continued his efforts for conciliation. By a bull of November 9, 1518,
he repudiated many of the extreme claims for indulgences; these forgave
neither sins nor guilt, but only those earthly penalties that the Church—not
secular rulers—had imposed; as to releasing souls from purgatory, the power
of the pope was limited to his prayers, beseeching God to apply to a dead
soul the surplus merits of Christ and the saints. On November 28 Luther
issued an appeal from the judgment of the pope to that of a general council.
In that same month Leo commissioned Karl von Miltitz, a young Saxon
nobleman in minor orders in Rome, to take the Golden Rose to Frederick,
and also to make a quiet effort to bring Luther, that "child of Satan," back
to obedience. [29]

On reaching Germany, Miltitz was astonished to find half the country
openly hostile to the Roman See. Among his own friends in Augsburg and
Nuremberg three out of five were for Luther. In Saxony anti-papal feeling
ran so strong that he divested himself of all indications that he was a papal
commissioner. When he met Luther at Altenburg (January 3, 1519), he
found him more open to reason than to fear. Probably at this stage Luther
was sincerely anxious to preserve the unity of Western Christendom. He
made generous concessions: to observe silence if his opponents would do
likewise; to write a letter of submission to the Pope; to acknowledge publicly
the propriety of prayers to the saints, the reality of purgatory, and the usefulness of indulgences in remitting canonical penances; and to recommend
to the people a peaceful allegiance to the Church; meanwhile the details of
the controversy were to be submitted for adjudication to some German
bishop acceptable to both parties. [30] Well pleased, Miltitz went to Leipzig,
summoned Tetzel, reproved him for excesses, accused him of mendacity
and embezzlement, and dismissed him. Tetzel retired to his monastery, and
died soon afterward (August 11, 1519). On his deathbed he received a kindly
letter from Luther, assuring him that the indulgence sale was only an occasion, not a cause, of the disturbance, "that the affair had not been begun

on that account, but that the child had quite another father." [31] On March 3 Luther wrote to the Pope a letter of complete submission. Leo replied in a friendly spirit (March 29), inviting him to come to Rome to make his confession, and offering him money for the journey.[32] However, with consistent inconsistency, Luther had written to Spalatin on March 13: "I am at a loss to know whether the Pope is Antichrist or his apostle." [33] Under the circumstances he thought it safer to stay in Wittenberg.

There the faculty, students, and citizens were predominantly friendly to his cause. He was especially happy to receive the support of a brilliant young humanist and theologian whom the Elector had appointed in 1518, at the age of twenty-one, to teach Greek at the university. Philipp Schwarzert (Black Earth) had had his name Hellenized as Melanchthon by his great-uncle Reuchlin. A man of small stature, frail physique, halting gait, homely features, lofty brow, and timid eyes, this intellectual of the Reformation became so loved in Wittenberg that five or six hundred students crowded his lecture room, and Luther himself, who described him as having "almost every virtue known to man," [34] humbly sat among his pupils. "Melanchthon," said Erasmus, "is a man of gentle nature; even his enemies speak well of him." [35] Luther enjoyed combat; Melanchthon longed for peace and conciliation. Luther sometimes chided him as immoderately moderate; but Luther's noblest and mildest side showed in his uninterrupted affection for one so opposed to him in temperament and policy.

> I have been born to war, and fight with factions and devils; therefore my books are stormy and warlike. I must root out the stumps and stocks, cut away the thorns and hedges, fill up the ditches, and am the rough forester to break a path and make things ready. But Master Philip walks softly and silently, tills and plants, sows and waters with pleasure, as God has gifted him richly.[36]

Another Wittenberg professor shone with a fiercer light than Melanchthon's. Andreas Bodenstein, known from his birthplace as Carlstadt, had joined the university staff at the age of twenty-four (1504); at thirty he received the chair of Thomistic philosophy and theology. On April 13, 1517, he anticipated Luther's historic protest by publishing 152 theses against indulgences. At first opposed to Luther, he soon turned into an ardent supporter, "hotter in the matter than I," said the great rebel.[37] When Eck's *Obelisci* challenged Luther's theses Carlstadt defended them in 406 propositions; one of these contained the first definite declaration, in the German Reformation, of the Bible's paramount authority over the decretals and traditions of the Church. Eck replied with a challenge to a public debate; Carlstadt readily agreed, and Luther made the arrangements. Eck then published a prospectus listing thirteen theses which he offered to prove in the debate. One ran: "We deny that the Roman Church was not superior to other churches before the time of Sylvester; we have always recognized the possessor of Peter's chair as his successor and as the vicar of Christ." But it was not Carlstadt, it was Luther who, in the *Resolutiones,* had raised the point that in the first centuries of Christianity the Roman See had no more authority than several other bishops of the Church. Luther felt himself challenged, and claimed that Eck's thesis freed him from his vow of silence. He determined to join Carlstadt in the theological tournament.

In June 1519, the two warriors rode off to Leipzig, accompanied by Melanchthon and six other professors, and escorted in country carts by 200 Wittenberg students armed and armored as if for battle; and in truth they were entering territory hostile to Luther. In the great tapestried hall of Pleissenburg Castle, packed with excited spectators, and under the presidency of the orthodox Duke George of Albertine Saxony, Eck and Carlstadt began the joust between the old and the new (June 27). Hardly anyone in Leipzig cared that on the morrow a new emperor was to be elected at Frankfurt-am-Main. After Carlstadt had for days suffered under Eck's superior argumentative skill, Luther took the stand for Wittenberg. He was brilliant and powerful in debate, but recklessly candid. He denied emphatically the primacy of the bishop of Rome in the early days of Christianity, and reminded his mostly antipathetic audience that the widespread Greek Orthodox Church still rejected the supremacy of Rome. When Eck charged that Luther's view echoed that of Huss, which the Council of Constance had condemned, Luther replied that even ecumenical councils could err, and that many doctrines of Huss were sound. When this debate ended (July 8), Eck had accomplished his real purpose—to have Luther commit himself to a definite heresy. The Reformation now advanced from a minor dispute about indulgences to a major challenge of papal authority over Christendom.

Eck passed on to Rome, presented to the Curia a report of the disputation, and recommended the excommunication of Luther. Leo was not so precipitate; he still hoped for some peaceable solution, and he was too distant from Germany to realize how far the revolt had gone. Prominent and respected citizens like Johan Holzschuher, Lazarus Spengler, and Willibald Pirkheimer spoke up for Luther; Dürer prayed for his success; the humanists were sending forth a cloud of pamphlets satirizing the papacy with all the exuberant vituperation characteristic of the age. Ulrich von Hutten, on reaching Augsburg in 1518, turned his rhymes against Leo's call for crusading funds, and expressed the hope that the collectors would go home with empty bags. When news came of the Leipzig debate he hailed Luther as the liberator of Germany, and from that time his pen was a sword for the Reform. He enlisted among Franz von Sickingen's knights—who were itching for revolution—and induced him to offer Luther all the support and protection that his armed band could provide. Luther replied in warm appreciation, but was not ready to use force in defense of his person.

In March 1520, Hutten published an old German manuscript written in the time of the Emperor Henry IV (r. 1056–1106), and supporting Henry in his struggle against Pope Gregory VII. He dedicated the book to the young Emperor Charles V, as a hint that Germany expected him to avenge Henry's humiliation and defeat. To free Germany from Rome, said Hutten, was of greater urgency than to repel the Turks. "While our forefathers thought it unworthy of them to submit to the Romans when these were the most martial nation in the world, we not only submit to these effeminate slaves of lust and luxury, but suffer ourselves to be plundered to minister to their sensuality." [38] In April 1520, Hutten issued the first of two series of *Gespräche*, verse dialogues that played a role second only to Luther's works in voicing and stimulating the national desire for independence from Rome. He described Rome as a "gigantic bloodsucking worm," and declared that "the Pope is a bandit chief, and his gang bears the name of the Church. . . . Rome is a sea of impurity, a mire of filth, a bottomless sink of iniquity. Should we not flock from all quarters to compass the destruction of this common curse of humanity?" [39] Erasmus pleaded with Hutten to temper his style, and gave him a friendly warning that he was in danger of arrest. Hutten hid himself in one after another of Sickingen's castles, but continued his campaign. To Elector Frederick he recommended the secular appropriation of all monastic wealth, and described the excellent uses to which Germany could put the money that was annually sent to Rome.[40]

But the center of the war remained in little Wittenberg. In the spring of 1520 Luther published, with furious notes, an *Epitome* in which he quoted the most recent and still uncompromising claims made by orthodox theologians for the primacy and powers of the popes. Luther met extremes with extremes:

> If Rome thus believes and teaches with the knowledge of popes and cardinals (which I hope is not the case), then in these writings I freely declare that the true Antichrist is sitting in the temple of God and is reigning in Rome—that empurpled Babylon—and that the Roman Curia is the Synagogue of Satan. . . . If the fury of the Romanists thus goes on, there will be no remedy left except that the emperors, kings, and princes, girt about with force and arms, should attack these pests of the world, and settle the matter no longer by words but by the sword. . . . If we strike thieves with the gallows, robbers with the sword, heretics with fire, why do we not much more attack in arms these masters of perdition, these cardinals, these popes, and all this sink of the Roman Sodom which has without end corrupted the Church of God, and wash our hands in their blood? [41]

Later in the same year Carlstadt issued a "little book"—*De canonicis scripturis libellus*—exalting the Bible over popes, councils, and traditions, and the Gospels over the Epistles; if Luther had followed this last line, Protestantism might have been less Pauline, Augustinian, and predestinarian. The *libellus* was ahead of its time in doubting the Mosaic authorship of the Pentateuch, and the full authenticity of the Gospels. But it was weak in its central argument: it decided the authenticity of Biblical books by the traditions of the early centuries, and then rejected tradition in favor of the books so certified.

Heartened by the support of Melanchthon and Carlstadt, Hutten and Sickingen, Luther wrote to Spalatin (June 11, 1520):

> I have cast the die. I now despise the rage of the Romans as much as I do their favor. I will not reconcile myself to them for all eternity. . . . Let them condemn and burn all that belongs to me; in return I will do as much for them. . . . Now I no longer fear, and I am publishing a book in the German tongue about Christian reform, directed against the pope, in language as violent as if I were addressing Antichrist.[42]

IV. BULLS AND BLASTS

On June 15, 1520, Leo X issued a bull, *Exsurge Domine*, which condemned forty-one statements by Luther, ordered the public burning of the writings in which these had appeared, and exhorted Luther to abjure his errors and return to the fold. After sixty days of further refusal to come to Rome and make a public recantation, he was to be cut off from Christendom by excommunication, he was to be shunned as a heretic by all the faithful, all places where he stayed were to suspend religious services, and all secular authorities were to banish him from their dominions or deliver him to Rome.

Luther marked the end of his period of grace by publishing the first of three little books that constituted a program of religious revolution. Hitherto he had written in Latin for the intellectual classes; now he wrote in German—and as a German patriot—*An Open Letter to the Christian Nobility of the German Nation Concerning the Reform of the Christian Estate*. He included in his appeal the "noble youth" who, a year before, had been chosen emperor as Charles V, and whom "God has given us to be our head, thereby awakening great hopes of good in many hearts."[43] Luther attacked the "three walls" that the papacy had built around itself: the distinction between the clergy and the laity, the right of the pope to decide the interpretation of Scripture, and his exclusive right to summon a general council of the Church. All these defensive assumptions, said Luther, must be overthrown.

First. there is no real difference between clergy and laity; every Christian is made a priest by baptism. Secular rulers, therefore, should exercise their powers "without let or hindrance, regardless whether it be pope, bishop or priest whom they affect. . . . All that the canon law has said to the contrary is sheer invention of Roman presumption." [44] Second, since every Christian is a priest, he has the right to interpret the Scriptures according to his own light. [45] Third, Scripture should be our final authority for doctrine or practice, and Scripture offers no warrant for the exclusive right of the pope to call a council. If he seeks by excommunication or interdict to prevent a council, "we should despise his conduct as that of a madman, and, relying on God, hurl back the ban on him, and coerce him as best we can." [46] A council should be called very soon; it should examine the "horrible" anomaly that the head of Christendom lives in more worldly splendor than any king; it should end the appropriation of German benefices by Italian clergymen; it should reduce to a hundredth the "swarm of vermin" holding ecclesiastical sinecures in Rome and living chiefly on money from Germany.

> Some have estimated that every year more than 300,000 gulden find their way from Germany to Italy. . . . *We here come to the heart of the matter.* . . . How comes it that we Germans must put up with such robbery and such extortion of our property at the hands of the pope? . . . If we justly hang thieves and behead robbers, why should we let Roman avarice go free? For he is the greatest thief and robber that has come or can come into the world, and all in the holy name of Christ and St. Peter! Who can longer endure it or keep silence? [47]

Why should the German Church pay this perpetual tribute to a foreign power? Let the German clergy throw off their subjection to Rome, and establish a national church under the leadership of the Archbishop of Mainz. Mendicant orders should be reduced, priests should be allowed to marry, no binding monastic vows should be taken before the age of thirty; interdicts, pilgrimages, Masses for the dead, and holydays (except Sundays) should be abolished. The German Church should be reconciled with the Hussites of Bohemia; Huss was burned in flagrant violation of the safe-conduct given him by the emperor; and in any case "we should vanquish heretics with books, not with burning." [48] All canon law should be discarded; there should be only one law, for clergy and laity alike.

> Above all, we should drive out from German lands the papal legates with their "powers"—which they sell us for large sums of money— to legalize unjust gains, dissolve oaths, vows, and agreements, saying that the pope has authority to do this—though it is sheer knavery. . . . If there were no other evil wiles to prove that the pope is the true Antichrist, this one thing would be enough to prove it. Hearest thou this, O pope, not most holy of men but most sinful? Oh, that

God from heaven would soon destroy thy throne, and sink it in the abyss of hell! . . O Christ my Lord, look down, let the day of thy judgment break, and destroy the Devil's nest at Rome! [49]

This headlong assault of one man against a power that pervaded all Western Europe became the sensation of Germany. Cautious men considered it intemperate and rash; many reckoned it among the most heroic deeds in German history. The first edition of the *Open Letter* was soon exhausted, and the presses of Wittenberg were kept busy with new printings. Germany, like England, was ripe for an appeal to nationalism; there was as yet no Germany on the map, but there were Germans, newly conscious of themselves as a people. As Huss had stressed his Bohemian patriotism, as Henry VIII would reject not Catholic doctrine but papal power over England, so Luther now planted his standard of revolt not in theological deserts, but in the rich soil of the German national spirit. Wherever Protestantism won, nationalism carried the flag.

In September 1520, Eck and Jerome Aleander promulgated the bull of excommunication in Germany. Luther fought back with a second manifesto, *The Babylonian Captivity of the Church* (October 6). Addressed to theologians and scholars, it reverted to Latin, but it was soon translated, and had almost as much influence on Christian doctrine as the *Open Letter* had on ecclesiastical and political history. As the Jews had suffered a long captivity in Babylonia, so the Church as established by Christ, and as described in the New Testament, had undergone over a thousand years of captivity under the papacy in Rome. During that period the religion of Christ had been corrupted in faith, morals, and ritual. Since Christ had given his Apostles wine as well as bread at the Last Supper, the Hussites were right: the Eucharist should be administered in both forms wherever the people so desired. The priest does not change the bread and wine into the body and blood of Christ; no priest has such mystical potency; but to the fervent communicant Christ comes spiritually and substantially, not through any miraculous transformation by a priest, but by His own will and power; He is present in the Eucharist *along with* bread and wine, by consubstantiation, not by transubstantiation. [50] Luther rejected with horror the notion that in the Mass the priest offers up Christ to His Father as a sacrifice in atonement for man's sins—though he found nothing horrible in the idea that God had allowed man to crucify God as a sacrifice to God in atonement for man's sins.

To these theological subtleties he added some ethical novelties. Marriage is not a sacrament, for Christ made no promise to infuse it with divine grace. "The marriages of the ancients were no less sacred than ours, nor are those of unbelievers less true." [51] Consequently there should be no prohibition of marriage between Christians and non-Christians. "Just as I may eat, drink, sleep, walk . . . and do business with a heathen, a Jew, a Turk, or a heretic, so also I may marry any of them. Do not give heed to the fool's law which forbids this. . . . A heathen is just as much a man or a woman created by God as St. Peter, St. Paul, or St. Lucy." [52] A woman married to an impotent husband should be allowed, if he consents, to have intercourse with another man in order to have a child, and should be permitted to pass the child off as her husband's. If the husband refuses consent she may justly divorce him. Yet divorce is an endless tragedy; perhaps bigamy would be better.[53] Then, adding defiance to heresy, Luther concluded: "I hear a rumor of new bulls and papal maledictions sent out against me, in which I am urged to recant. . . . If that is true, I desire this book to be a portion of the recantation I shall make." [54]

Such a taunt should have deflected Miltitz from still dreaming of a reconciliation. Nevertheless he again sought out Luther (October 11, 1520), and persuaded him to send to Pope Leo a letter disclaiming any intent to attack him personally, and presenting temperately the case for reform. For his part Miltitz would try to secure a revocation of the bull. Luther, the thirty-seven-year-old "peasant, son of a peasant" (as he proudly called himself), wrote a letter not of apology but of almost paternal counsel to the forty-five-year-old heir of St. Peter and the Medici. He expressed his respect for the Pope as an individual, but condemned without compromise the corruption of the papacy in the past, and of the papal Curia in the present:

> Thy reputation, and the fame of thy blameless life . . . are too well known and too high to be assailed. . . . But thy See, which is called the Roman Curia, and of which neither thou nor any man can deny that it is more corrupt than any Babylon or Sodom ever was, and which is, as far as I can see, characterized by a totally depraved, hopeless, and notorious wickedness—that See I have truly despised. . . . The Roman Church has become the most licentious den of thieves, the most shameless of all brothels, the kingdom of sin, death, and hell. . . . I have always grieved, most excellent Leo, that thou hast been made pope in these times, for thou wert worthy of better days. . . .
> Do not listen, therefore, my dear Leo, to those sirens who make thee out to be no mere man but a demigod, so that thou mayest command . . . what thou wilt. . . . Thou art a servant of servants, and beyond all other men in a most pitiable and dangerous position. Be not deceived by those who pretend that thou art lord of the world . . . who prate that thou hast power over heaven, hell, and purgatory. . . . They err who exalt thee above a council and above the Church universal. They err who ascribe to thee the right of interpreting Scripture, for under cover of thy name they seek to set up their own

wickedness in the Church, and, alas, through them Satan has already made much headway under thy predecessors. In short, believe none who exalt thee, believe those who humble thee.[55]

Along with this letter Luther sent to Leo the third of his manifestoes. He called it *A Treatise on Christian Liberty* (November 1520), and felt that "unless I am deceived, it is the whole of Christian living in a brief form."[56] Here he expressed with uncongenial moderation his basic doctrine—that faith alone, not good works, makes the true Christian and saves him from hell. For it is faith in Christ that makes a man good; his good works follow from that faith. "The tree bears fruit, the fruit does not bear the tree."[57] A man firm in his faith in the divinity and redeeming sacrifice of Christ enjoys not freedom of will, but the profoundest freedom of all: freedom from his own carnal nature, from all evil powers, from damnation, even from law; for the man whose virtue flows spontaneously from his faith needs no commands to righteousness.[58] Yet this free man must be servant to all men, for he will not be happy if he fails to do all in his power to save others as well as himself. He is united to God by faith, to his neighbor by love. Every believing Christian is a ministering priest.

While Luther was writing these historic treatises, Eck and Aleander were encountering the religious revolution at first hand. In Meissen, Merseburg, and Brandenburg they were successful in proclaiming the bull of excommunication; at Nuremberg they elicited apologies from Pirkheimer and Spengler; at Mainz Archbishop Albrecht, after flirting a while with the Reformation, excluded Hutten from his court and imprisoned the printers of Hutten's books; at Ingolstadt Luther's books were confiscated, and in Mainz, Louvain, and Cologne they were burned. But at Leipzig, Torgau, and Döbeln the posted bull was pelted with dirt and torn down; at Erfurt many professors and clergymen joined in a general refusal to recognize the bull, and students threw all available copies into the river; finally Eck fled from the scenes of his triumphs a year before.[59]

Luther denounced the ban in a series of bitter pamphlets, in one of which he fully approved the doctrines of Huss. About August 31, 1520, as "a single flea daring to address the king of kings," he appealed to the Emperor for protection; and on November 17 he published a formal appeal from the Pope to a free council of the Church. When he learned that the papal envoys were burning his books, he decided to reply in kind. He issued an invitation to the "pious and studious youths" of Wittenberg to assemble outside the Elster gate of the city on the morning of December 10. There, with his own hands, he cast the papal bull into a fire, along with some canonical decretals and volumes of Scholastic theology; in one act he symbolized his rejection of canon law, of Aquinas's philosophy, and of any coercive authority of the Church. The students joyfully collected other books of the kind, and with them kept the fire burning till late afternoon.

On December 11 Luther proclaimed that no man could be saved unless he renounced the rule of the papacy.[60] The monk had excommunicated the pope.

V. THE DIET OF WORMS: 1521

A third actor now mounted the stage, and from this moment played through thirty years a major role in the conflict of theologies and states. In a dozen chapters he will impinge upon our narrative.

The future Emperor Charles V began with a royal but tarnished heredity. His paternal grandparents were the Emperor Maximilian and Mary of Burgundy, daughter of Charles the Bold; his maternal grandparents were Ferdinand and Isabella; his father was Philip the Handsome, King of Castile at twenty-six, dead at twenty-eight; his mother was Juana la Loca, who went insane when Charles was six, and survived till he was fifty-five. He was born in Ghent (February 24, 1500), was brought up in Brussels, and remained Flemish in speech and character till his final retirement in Spain; neither Spain nor Germany forgave him. But in time he learned to speak German, Spanish, Italian, and French, and could be silent in five languages. Adrian of Utrecht tried to teach him philosophy, with inconsiderable success. From this good bishop he received a strong infusion of religious orthodoxy, yet he probably imbibed, in middle age, a secret skepticism from his Flemish advisers and courtiers, among whom an Erasmian indifference to dogma was smilingly popular. Some priests complained of the freedom allowed to religious opinion in Charles's entourage.[61] He made a point of piety, but studied carefully the art of war. He read Comines, and learned almost in childhood the tricks of diplomacy and the unmorality of states.

On his father's death (1506) he inherited Flanders, Holland, Franche-Comté, and a claim to Burgundy. At fifteen he assumed the government, and devoted himself to administration. At sixteen he became Charles I, King of Spain, Sicily, Sardinia, Naples, and Spanish America. At nineteen he aspired to be emperor. Francis I of France sought the same honor at the same time, and the Imperial Electors were pleased with his *douceurs;* but Charles spent 850,000 florins on the contest, and won (1519). To assemble this heavy *Trinkgelt* he borrowed 543,000 florins from the Fuggers;[62] from that time Charles was for the Fuggers and the Fuggers were for Charles. When he dallied in repaying the loan, Jakob Fugger II sent him a sharp reminder:

> It is well known that your Majesty without me might not have acquired the Imperial honor, as I can attest with the written statements of all the delegates. . . . And in all this I have looked not to my

own profit. . . . My respectful request is that you will graciously . . . order that the money which I have paid out, together with the interest on it, shall be returned without further delay.[68]

Charles met part of his obligation by giving the Fuggers a lien on the port duties of Antwerp.[64] When the Fuggers were almost ruined by Turkish conquests in Hungary, he came to their rescue by turning over to them control of Spanish mines.[65] Henceforth the key to much political history would be *Cherchez le banquier*.

The youth who at nineteen found himself titular head of all Central and Western Europe except England, France, Portugal, and the Papal States was already marked by the feeble health that was to multiply his vicissitudes. Pale, short, homely, with aquiline nose and sharp, challenging chin, feeble in voice and grave of mien, he was kindly and affable by nature, but he soon learned that a ruler must maintain distance and bearing, that silence is half of diplomacy, and that an open sense of humor dims the aura of royalty. Aleander, meeting him in 1520, reported to Leo X: "This prince seems to me well endowed with . . . prudence beyond his years, and to have much more at the back of his head than he carries on his face."[66] He was not mentally keen, except in judging men—which is half the battle; he barely rose to the crises that confronted him—but that was much indeed. A conserving indolence of body and mind kept him inert until the situation demanded decision; then he met it with sudden resolution and resourceful pertinacity. Wisdom came to him not by nature but by trials.

On October 23, 1520, Charles V, no older than the century, went to Charlemagne's Aachen to be crowned. Elector Frederick started out to attend the ceremony, but was stopped at Cologne by gout. There Aleander presented to him another plea for the arrest of Luther. Frederick called in Erasmus and asked his advice. Erasmus defended Luther, pointed out that there were crying abuses in the Church, and argued that efforts to remedy them should not be suppressed. When Frederick asked him what were Luther's chief errors, he replied: "Two: he attacked the pope in his crown and the monks in their bellies."[67] He questioned the authenticity of the papal bull; it seemed to him irreconcilable with the known gentleness of Leo X.[68] Frederick informed the nuncio that Luther had lodged an appeal, and that until its results were known, Luther should remain free.

The Emperor gave the same answer; he had promised the electors, as a condition of his election, that no German would be condemned without a fair trial in Germany. However, his position made orthodoxy imperative. He was more firmly established as King of Spain than as Emperor in a Germany that resented centralized government; and the clergy of Spain would not long bear with a monarch lenient to heretics. Besides, war loomed with

France; it would be fought over Milan as the prize; there the support of the pope would be worth an army. The Holy Roman Empire was tied to the papacy in a hundred ways; the fall of one would profoundly injure the other; how could the Emperor rule his scattered and diverse realm without the aid of the Church in moral discipline and political administration? Even now his chief ministers were clergymen. And he needed ecclesiastical funds and influence to protect Hungary from the Turks.

It was with these varied problems in mind, rather than the question of a refractory monk, that Charles summoned an Imperial Diet to meet at Worms. But when the leading nobles and clergy, and representatives of the free cities, assembled there (January 27, 1521), Luther was the chief topic of conversation. The forces that through centuries had been preparing the Reformation came now to a head in one of the most dramatic scenes in European history. "The great body of the German nobles," says a Catholic historian, "applauded and seconded Luther's attempts." [69] Aleander himself reported:

All Germany is up in arms against Rome. All the world is clamoring for a council that shall meet on German soil. Papal bulls of excommunication are laughed at. Numbers of people have ceased to receive the sacrament of penance. . . . Martin is pictured with a halo above his head. The people kiss these pictures. Such a quantity has been sold that I am unable to obtain one. . . . I cannot go out in the streets but the Germans put their hands to their swords and gnash their teeth at me. I hope the Pope will give me a plenary indulgence and look after my brothers and sisters if anything happens to me. [70]

The excitement was fanned by a whirlwind of antipapal pamphlets; a wagon, mourned Aleander, would not hold all these scurrilous tracts. From Sickingen's castle of Ebernburg, a few miles from Worms, Hutten issued a frantic attack on the German clergy:

Begone, ye unclean swine! Depart from the sanctuary, ye infamous traffickers! Touch not the altars with your desecrated hands! . . . How dare you spend the money intended for pious uses in luxury, dissipation, and pomp, while honest men are suffering hunger? The cup is full. See ye not that the breath of liberty is stirring? [71]

So strong was the sentiment for Luther that the Emperor's confessor, the Franciscan monk Jean Glapion, privately approached Frederick's chaplain, Georg Spalatin, in an attempt at conciliation. He professed considerable sympathy for Luther's early writings, but the *Babylonian Captivity* had made him feel "as if he had been scourged and pummeled from head to foot." He pointed out that no system of religious belief could be securely based upon Scripture, for "the Bible is like soft wax, which every man can twist

and stretch according to his pleasure." He admitted urgent need for ecclesiastical reform; indeed, he had warned his Imperial penitent that "God
will punish him and all princes if they do not free the Church from such
overweening abuses"; and he promised that Charles would accomplish the
major reforms within five years. Even now, after those terrible Lutheran
blasts, he thought peace possible if Luther would recant.[72] Luther, apprised
of this at Wittenberg, refused.

On March 3 Aleander presented to the Diet a proposal for the immediate
condemnation of Luther. The Diet protested that the monk should not
be condemned without a hearing. Charles thereupon invited Luther to come
to Worms and testify concerning his teaching and his books. "You need fear
no violence or molestation," he wrote, "for you have our safe-conduct." [73]
Luther's friends begged him not to go, and reminded him of the safe-conduct
that the Emperor Sigismund had given Huss. Adrian of Utrecht, now Cardinal of Tortosa, soon to be pope, sent a plea to his former pupil, the Emperor, to ignore the safe-conduct, arrest Luther, and send him to Rome. On
April 2 Luther left Wittenberg. At Erfurt a large crowd, including forty
professors from the university, hailed him as a hero. When he approached
Worms Spalatin rushed a warning to him not to enter, but rather to hurry
back to Wittenberg. Luther answered: "Though there were as many devils
in Worms as there are tiles on the roofs, I will go there." [74] A band of knights
rode out to meet him and escort him into the city (April 16). The streets
filled at news of his arrival; 2,000 people gathered around his carriage; all
the world came to see him, said Aleander, and even Charles was cast into
the shade.

On April 17 Luther, in his monastic garb, appeared before the Diet: the
Emperor, six electors, an awesome court of princes, nobles, prelates, and
burghers, and Jerome Aleander armed with papal authority, formal documents, and forensic eloquence. On a table near Luther stood a collection of
his books. Johann Eck—not he of the Leipzig debate but an official of the
archbishop of Trier—asked him were these his compositions, and would he
retract all heresies contained in them? For a moment, standing before the
assembled dignity of the Empire and the delegated power and majesty of the
Church, Luther's courage failed him. He replied in a low and diffident voice
that the books were his, but as to the second question he begged time to
consider. Charles granted him a day. Back in his lodging he received a message from Hutten beseeching him to stand fast; and several members of the
Diet came privately to encourage him. Many seemed to feel that his final
answer would mark a turning point in history.

On April 18 he faced the Diet with fuller confidence. Now the chamber
was so crowded that even the electors found it difficult to reach their seats,
and most of those present stood. Eck asked him would he repudiate, in whole

or in part, the works that he had written. He replied that those portions that dealt with ecclesiastical abuses were by common consent just. The Emperor interrupted him with an explosive "No!"—but Luther went on, and hit at Charles himself: "Should I recant at this point, I would open the door to more tyranny and impiety, and it will be all the worse should it appear that I had done so at the instance of the Holy Roman Empire." As to the doctrinal passages in his books, he agreed to retract any that should be proved contrary to Scripture. To this Eck, in Latin, made an objection that well expressed the view of the Church:

> Martin, your plea to be heard from Scripture is the one always made by heretics. You do nothing but renew the errors of Wyclif and Huss. . . . How can you assume that you are the only one to understand the sense of Scripture? Would you put your judgment above that of so many famous men and claim that you know more than all of them? You have no right to call into question the most holy orthodox faith, instituted by Christ the perfect Lawgiver, proclaimed throughout the world by the Apostles, sealed by the red blood of martyrs, confirmed by the sacred councils, and defined by the Church . . . and which we are forbidden by the Pope and the Emperor to discuss, lest there be no end to debate. I ask you, Martin —answer candidly and without distinctions—do you or do you not repudiate your books and the errors which they contain? [75]

Luther made his historic response *in German:*

> Since your Majesty and your lordships desire a simple reply, I will answer without distinctions. . . . Unless I am convicted by the testimony of Sacred Scripture or by evident reason (I do not accept the authority of popes and councils, for they have contradicted each other), my conscience is captive to the Word of God. I cannot and I will not recant anything, for to go against my conscience is neither right nor safe. God help me. Amen.* [76]

Eck countered that no error could be proved in the doctrinal decrees of the councils; Luther answered that he was prepared to prove such errors, but the Emperor intervened peremptorily: "It is enough; since he has denied councils, we wish to hear no more." [78] Luther returned to his lodging weary with the strife, but confident that he had borne good testimony in what Carlyle was to call "the greatest moment in the modern history of man." [79]

The Emperor was as shaken as the monk. Born to the purple, and already

---

* We cannot fully authenticate the famous words engraved on the majestic Luther *Denkmal* or Memorial at Worms: *Hier stehe Ich, Ich kann nicht anders*—"Here I stand, I can do no other." The words do not occur in the transcript of Luther's reply as given in the records of the Diet; they make their first appearance in the earliest printed version of his speech.[77]

accustomed to authority, he thought it self-evident that the right of each individual to interpret Scripture, and to accept or reject civil or ecclesiastical decrees according to private judgment and conscience, would soon erode the very foundations of social order, for this seemed to him based on a moral code that in turn derived its strength from the supernatural sanctions of religious belief. On April 19 he called the leading princes to a conference in his own chambers, and presented to them a declaration of faith and intent, written in French, and apparently by himself:

> I am descended from a long line of Christian emperors of this noble German nation, of the Catholic kings of Spain, the archdukes of Austria, and the dukes of Burgundy. They were all faithful to the death to the Church of Rome, and they defended the Catholic faith and the honor of God. I have resolved to follow in their steps. A single friar who goes counter to all Christianity for a thousand years must be wrong. Therefore I am resolved to stake my lands, my friends, my body, my blood, my life, and my soul. . . . After having heard yesterday the obstinate defense of Luther, I regret that I have so long delayed in proceeding against him and his false teaching. I will have no more to do with him. He may return under his safe-conduct, but without preaching or making any tumult. I will proceed against him as a notorious heretic, and I ask you to declare yourselves as you promised me.[80]

Four electors agreed to this procedure; Frederick of Saxony and Ludwig of the Palatinate abstained. That night—April 19—anonymous persons posted upon the door of the town hall, and elsewhere in Worms, placards bearing the German symbol of social revolution, the peasant's shoe. Some ecclesiastics were frightened, and privately solicited Luther to make his peace with the Church, but he stood by his statement to the Diet. On April 26 he began his return journey to Wittenberg. Leo X sent orders that the safe-conduct should be respected.[81] Nevertheless the Elector Frederick, fearful that Imperial police might attempt to arrest Luther after the expiration of the safe-conduct on May 6, arranged, with Luther's reluctant consent, to have him ambushed en route homeward as if by highwaymen, and taken for concealment to the castle of Wartburg.

On May 6 the Emperor presented to the Diet—now thinned by many departures—the draft that Aleander had prepared of the "Edict of Worms." It charged that Luther

> has sullied marriage, disparaged confession, and denied the body and blood of Our Lord. He makes the sacraments depend upon the faith of the recipient. He is pagan in his denial of free will. This devil in the habit of a monk has brought together ancient errors into one stinking puddle, and has invented new ones. He denies the power of

the keys, and encourages the laity to wash their hands in the blood of the clergy. His teaching makes for rebellion, division, war, murder, robbery, arson, and the collapse of Christendom. He lives the life of a beast. He has burned the decretals. He despises alike the ban and the sword. He does more harm to the civil than to the ecclesiastical power. We have labored with him, but he recognizes only the authority of Scripture, which he interprets in his own sense. We have given him twenty-one days, dating from April 15. . . . When the time is up, no one is to harbor him. His followers also are to be condemned. His books are to be eradicated from the memory of man.[82]

Two days after the presentation of this edict Leo X transferred his political support from Francis I to Charles V. The rump Diet agreed to the edict, and on May 26 Charles promulgated it formally. Aleander praised God, and ordered that the books of Luther should be burned wherever found.

VI. THE RADICALS

The Wartburg was in itself a somber punishment. The ancient castle, perched on a mountaintop a mile from Eisenach, was hidden from the world as well as from the Emperor. For almost ten months (May 4, 1521, to February 29, 1522) Luther dwelt there in a gloomy chamber equipped with bed, table, stove, and a stump as a stool. A few soldiers guarded the fortress, a warden tended the grounds, two boys served Luther as pages. For convenience, and perhaps as a local disguise, he shed his monastic robe, donned knightly garb, and grew a beard; he was now Junker George. He went out hunting, but he did not relish killing rabbits when there were so many Antichrists still unslain. Idleness and insomnia, and too much food and beer, made him ill and stout. He fretted and cursed like a Junker. "I had rather burn on live coals," he wrote, "than rot here. . . . I want to be in the fray." [83] But Frederick's minister advised him to stay in hiding for a year while Charles's fervor cooled. Charles, however, made no effort to find or arrest him.

In Luther's intellectual solitude doubts and hallucinations plagued him. Could it be, he wondered, that he was right and so many pundits wrong? Was it wise to break down the authority of the established creed? Did the principle of private judgment portend the rise of revolution and the death of law? If we may believe the story that he told in his anecdotage, he was disturbed, in the castle, by strange noises that he could explain only as the activity of demons. He professed to have seen Satan on several occasions; once, he vouched, the Devil pelted him with nuts; [84] once, says a famous legend, Luther flung an ink bottle at him, but missed his aim.[85] He solaced himself by writing vivid letters to his friends and his enemies, by composing theological treatises, and by translating the New Testament into German. Once he made a flying trip to Wittenberg to harness a revolution.

His defiance at Worms, and his survival, had given his followers a heady elation. At Erfurt students, artisans, and peasants attacked and demolished forty parish houses, destroyed libraries and rent rolls, and killed a humanist (June 1521). In the fall of that exciting year the Augustinian friars of Erfurt abandoned their monastery, preached the Lutheran creed, and denounced the Church as "mother of dogma, pride, avarice, luxury, faithlessness, and hypocrisy."[86] At Wittenberg, while Melanchthon composed his *Loci communes rerum theologicarum* (1521)—the first systematic exposition of Protestant theology—his fellow professor Carlstadt, now archdeacon of the Castle Church, demanded that Mass should be said (if at all) in the vernacular, that the Eucharist should be given in wine and bread without preliminary confession or fasting, that religious images should be removed from churches, and that the clergy—monks as well as secular priests—should marry and procreate. Carlstadt set a pace by marrying, at forty, a girl of fifteen (January 19, 1522).

Luther approved of this marriage, but "Good Heavens!" he wrote, "will our Wittenbergers give wives to monks?"[87] Nevertheless he found something attractive in the idea, for he sent to Spalatin (November 21, 1521) a treatise *On Monastic Vows*, defending their repudiation. Spalatin delayed its publication, for it was unconventionally frank. It accepted the sexual instinct as natural and irrepressible, and declared that monastic vows were lures of Satan, multiplying sins. Four years would elapse before Luther himself would marry; his belated appreciation of woman apparently played no part in inaugurating the Reformation.

The revolution proceeded. On September 22, 1521, Melanchthon administered communion in both kinds; here the Utraquists of Bohemia won a delayed victory. On October 23 the Mass ceased to be said in Luther's monastery. On November 12 thirteen of the monks walked out of the cloister and headed for marriage; soon a similar exodus would empty half the monasteries of Germany. On December 3 some students and townsfolk, armed with knives, entered the parish church of Wittenberg, drove the priests from the altars, and stoned some worshipers who were praying before a statue of the Virgin. On December 4 forty students demolished the altars of the Franciscan monastery in Wittenberg. On that same day Luther, still disguised as a Junker, clandestinely visited the city, approved the marriage of the monks, but warned clergy and laity against violence. "Constraint," he said, "is not all ruled out, but it must be exercised by the constituted authorities."[88] On the morrow he returned to the Wartburg.

Shortly thereafter he sent to Spalatin, for publication, an *Earnest Exhortation for All Christians, Warning Them against Insurrection and Rebellion.* He feared that if the religious revolution went too fast, or became a social revolution, it would alienate the nobility and destroy itself. But its opening pages were themselves criticized as an incitation to violence:

> It seems probable that there is danger of an uprising, and that priests, monks, bishops, and the entire spiritual estate may be murdered or driven into exile, unless they seriously and thoroughly reform themselves. For the common man has been brooding over the injury he has suffered in property, in body, and in soul, and has become provoked. They have tried him too far, and have most unscrupulously burdened him beyond measure. He is neither able nor willing to endure it longer, and could indeed have good reason to lay about him with flails and cudgels, as the peasants are threatening to do. Now I am not at all displeased to hear that the clergy are brought to such a state of fear and anxiety. Perhaps they will come to their senses and moderate their mad tyranny. . . . I will go further. If I had ten bodies, and could acquire so much favor with God that he would chasten them [the clergy] by the gentle means [*Fuchsschwanz*—the fox's fluffy tail] of bodily death or insurrection, I would most gladly give all my ten bodies to death in behalf of the poor peasants.[89]

Nevertheless, he went on, it is inadvisable for private individuals to use force; vengeance is God's.

> Insurrection is unreasoning, and generally hurts the innocent more than the guilty. Hence no insurrection is ever right, no matter how good the cause in whose interest it is made. The harm resulting from it always exceeds the amount of reformation accomplished. . . . When Sir Mob [*Herr Omnes*—Mister Everybody] breaks loose he cannot tell the wicked from the godly; he strikes at random, and then horrible injustice is inevitable. . . . My sympathies are and always will be with those against whom insurrection is made.[90]

Revolution, more or less peaceful, continued. On Christmas Day 1521, Carlstadt celebrated Mass in German, in civilian dress, and invited all to receive communion by taking the bread in their hands and drinking from the chalice. About this time Gabriel Zwilling, a leader of the Augustinian Congregation, invited his hearers to burn religious pictures and demolish altars wherever found. On December 27 oil was poured upon the fire by "prophets" arriving from Zwickau. That town was one of the most industrial in Germany, having a large population of weavers under a municipal government of merchant employers. A socialist movement among the workers was encouraged by echoes and memories of the suppressed Taborite experiment that had agitated near-by Bohemia. Thomas Münzer, pastor of the weavers' church of St. Catherine, became the mouthpiece of their aspirations, and at the same time an enthusiastic supporter of the Reformation. Realizing that Luther's exaltation of the Bible as the sole rule of faith opened the question who should interpret the text, Münzer and two associates—Nicholas Storch the weaver and Marcus Stübner the scholar—announced that they were singularly qualified as interpreters, for they felt themselves directly inspired by the Holy Ghost. This divine spirit, they declared, bade them defer baptism till maturity; for the sacrament could have effect only through faith, which was not to be expected of babies. The world, they predicted, was soon to suffer a general devastation, in which all ungodly men—including especially all orthodox priests—would perish; thereafter the communistic Kingdom of God would begin on earth.[91] In 1521 an insurrection of the weavers was put down, and the three "Zwickau Apostles" were banished. Münzer went to Prague, was expelled, and took a pastorate in Allstedt in Saxony. Storch and Stübner went to Wittenberg, and in the absence of Luther they made a favorable impression on Melanchthon and Carlstadt.

On January 6, 1522, the Augustinian Congregation at Wittenberg completely disbanded. On January 22 Carlstadt's adherents were strong enough in the municipal council to carry a decree ordering all images to be removed from Wittenberg churches, and prohibiting Mass except in Carlstadt's simplified form. Carlstadt included the crucifix among forbidden images, and, like the early Christians, banned music from religious services. "The lascivious notes of the organ," he said, "awaken thoughts of the world. When we should be meditating on the sufferings of Christ we are reminded of Pyramus and Thisbe. . . . Relegate organs, trumpets, and flutes to the theater."[92] When the agents of the council proved dilatory in removing images, Carlstadt led his followers into the churches; pictures and crucifixes were torn from the walls, and resisting priests were pelted with stones.[93] Accepting the view of the Zwickau Prophets—that God speaks directly to men as well as through the Scriptures, and speaks rather to the simple in mind and heart than to the learned in languages and books—Carlstadt, himself erudite, proclaimed that schools and studies were deterrents to piety, and that real Christians would shun all letters and learning, and would become illiterate peasants or artisans. One of his followers, George Mohr, dismissed the school that he taught, and exhorted the parents to keep their children innocent of letters. Several students left the university and went home to learn a handicraft, saying that there was no further need for study.

Hearing of all this, Luther feared that his conservative critics would soon be justified in their frequent predictions that his repudiation of ecclesiastical authority would loosen all bonds of social discipline. Defying the Emperor's ban, and waiving all protection by the Elector should Charles seek to arrest him, Luther left his castle, resumed his monastic robe and tonsure, and hurried back to Wittenberg. On March 9, 1522, he began a series of eight sermons that sternly called the university, the churches, and the citizens to order. He now rejected all appeals to force; had he not freed millions of men from ecclesiastical oppression without lifting more than a pen? "Follow me," he said. "I was the first whom God entrusted with this matter; I was the one to whom He first revealed how His Word should be preached to you. Therefore you have done wrong in starting such a piece of work without . . . having first consulted me. . . .[94] Give me time. . . . Do not suppose that abuses are eliminated by destroying the object which is abused. Men can go wrong with wine and women; shall we then prohibit wine and abolish women? The sun, the moon, the stars, have been worshiped; shall we then pluck them out of the sky?" [95] Those who wished to keep pictures, statuary, crucifixes, music, or the Mass should not be interfered with; he himself approved of religious images.[96] He arranged that in one Wittenberg church the Mass should be performed according to the traditional rite; in another, communion was administered in bread alone at the high altar, but in bread and wine at a side altar. The form, said Luther, made little difference; what counted was the spirit in which the Eucharist was received.

He was at his best and most Christian in those eight sermons in eight days. He risked all on being able to win Wittenberg back to moderation, and he succeeded. The Zwickau Prophets sought to convert him to their views, and offered, as proof of their divine inspiration, to read his thoughts. He accepted the challenge; they answered that he was feeling a secret sympathy for their ideas; he attributed their clairvoyance to the Devil, and ordered them to leave Wittenberg. Carlstadt, dismissed from his posts by a reconstructed town council, took a pastorate in Orlamünde, from whose pulpit he denounced Luther as a "gluttonous ecclesiastic . . . the new Wittenberg pope." [97] Anticipating the Quakers, Carlstadt abandoned all clerical garb, donned a plain gray coat, dispensed with titles, asked to be called "Brother Andreas," refused payment for his ministry, earned his living at the plow, renounced all use of drugs, preferred prayer to medicine, advocated polygamy as Biblical, and adopted a merely symbolical view of the Eucharist. At the Elector's request Luther went to Orlamünde to preach against him, but was pelted out of the town with stones and mud.[98] When the Peasants' Revolt collapsed, Carlstadt, fearing arrest as an instigator, sought and received refuge with Luther. After much wandering, the tired radical found port as a professor in Basel, and there, in 1541, he achieved a peaceful scholastic death.

VII. THE FOUNDATIONS OF FAITH

Luther resumed the uneven tenor of his ways as priest to his congregation and professor in the university. The Elector paid him 200 guilders ($5,000?) a year, to which each student added a slight honorarium for attending his lectures. Luther and another monk, now both in layman's garb, lived in the Augustinian monastery with a student servant. "My bed was not made up for a whole year, and became foul with sweat. But I worked all day, and was so tired at night that I fell into bed without knowing that anything was amiss." [99] Hard work made his appetite forgivable. "I eat like a Bohemian and drink like a German, thank God, Amen." [100] He preached often, but with humane brevity, and in simple, vigorous language that held his rough auditors in hand. His only recreations were chess and the flute; but he seems to have enjoyed more the hours that he spent in attacking "papists." He was the most powerful and uninhibited controversialist in history. Nearly all his writings were warfare, salted with humor and peppered with vituperation. He let his opponents elaborate superior Latin to be read by a few scholars; he too wrote Latin when he wished to address all Christendom; but most of his diatribes were composed in German, or were at once translated into German, for his was a nationalist revolution. No other German author has equaled him in clarity or force of style, in directness and pungency of phrase, in happy—sometimes hilarious—similes, in a vocabulary rooted in the speech of the people, and congenial to the national mind.

Printing fell in with his purposes as a seemingly providential innovation, which he used with inexhaustible skill; he was the first to make it an engine of propaganda and war. There were no newspapers yet, nor magazines; battles were fought with books, pamphlets, and private letters intended for publication. Under the stimulus of Luther's revolt the number of books printed in Germany rose from 150 in 1518 to 990 in 1524. Four fifths of these favored the Reformation. Books defending orthodoxy were hard to sell, while Luther's were the most widely purchased of the age. They were sold not only in bookstores but by peddlers and traveling students; 1,400 copies were bought at one Frankfurt fair; even in Paris, in 1520, they outsold everything else. As early as 1519 they were exported to France, Italy, Spain, the Netherlands, England. "Luther's books are everywhere and in every language," wrote Erasmus in 1521; "no one would believe how widely he has moved men." [101] The literary fertility of the Reformers transferred the preponderance of publications from southern to northern Europe, where it has remained ever since. Printing was the Reformation; Gutenberg made Luther possible.

Luther's supreme achievement as a writer was his translation of the Bible into German. Eighteen such translations had already been made, but they were based on Jerome's Vulgate, were crowded with errors, and were awkwardly phrased. The difficulties of translating from the original were appalling; there were as yet no dictionaries from Hebrew or Greek into German; every page of text evoked a hundred problems of interpretation; and the German language itself was still crude and but half formed. For the New Testament Luther used the Greek text that Erasmus had edited with a Latin version in 1516. This part of the task was completed in 1521, and published in 1522. After twelve more years of labor, amid constant theological strife, but aided by Melanchthon and several Jewish scholars, Luther published the Old Testament in German. Despite their imperfect scholarship, these translations were epochal events. They inaugurated German literature, and established *Neuhochdeutsch*—the New High German of Upper Saxony—as the literary language of Germany. Yet the translations were deliberately unliterary, couched in the speech of the populace. In his usual vivid way Luther explained his method: "We must not, as asses do, ask the Latin letters how we should speak German, but we must ask the mothers in their houses, the children in the streets, the common people in the market place . . . we must be guided by them in translating; then they will understand us, and will know that we are speaking German to them." [102] Hence his translation had the same effect and prestige in Germany as the King James version in England a century later: it had endless and beneficent influence on the national speech, and is still the greatest prose work in the national literature. In Wittenberg, and during Luther's lifetime, 100,000 copies of his New Testament were printed; a dozen unauthorized editions appeared elsewhere; and despite edicts forbidding its circulation in Brandenburg, Bavaria, and Austria, it became and remained the best-selling book in Germany. The translations of the Bible shared, as both effect and contributory cause, in that displacement of Latin by vernacular languages and literatures which accompanied the nationalist movement, and which corresponded to the defeat of the universal Church in lands that had not received and transformed the Latin tongue.

Laboring so long on the Bible, and inheriting the medieval view of its divine authorship, Luther fondly made it the all-sufficient source and norm of his religious faith. Though he accepted some traditions not based on Scripture—like infant baptism and the Sunday Sabbath—he rejected the right of the Church to add to Christianity elements resting not on the Bible but on her own customs and authority, like purgatory, indulgences, and the worship of Mary and the saints. Valla's revelation of the "Donation of Constantine" (the supposed bequest of Western Europe to the popes) as a hoary hoax of history had shaken the faith of thousands of Christians in the reliability of Church traditions and the compulsive validity of Church decrees; and in 1537 Luther himself translated Valla's treatise into German. Tradition was human and fallible, but the Bible was accepted by nearly all Europe as the infallible word of God.

Reason, too, seemed a weak instrument when compared with faith in a divine revelation. "We poor, wretched people . . . presumptuously seek to understand the incomprehensible majesty of the incomprehensible light of God's wonders. . . . We look with blind eyes, like a mole, on the glory of God." [103] You cannot, said Luther, accept both the Bible and reason; one or the other must go.

> All the articles of our Christian faith, which God has revealed to us in His Word, are in presence of reason sheerly impossible, absurd, and false. What (thinks that cunning little fool) can be more absurd and impossible than that Christ should give us in the Last Supper His body and blood to eat and drink? . . . or that the dead should rise again at the last day?—or that Christ the Son of God should be conceived, borne in the womb of the Virgin Mary, become man, suffer, and die a shameful death on the cross? [104] . . . Reason is the greatest enemy that faith has.[105] . . . She is the Devil's greatest whore . . . a whore eaten by scab and leprosy, who ought to be trodden underfoot and destroyed, she and her wisdom. . . . Throw dung in her face . . . drown her in baptism.[106]

Luther condemned the Scholastic philosophers for making so many concessions to reason, for trying to prove Christian dogmas rationally, for trying to harmonize Christianity with the philosophy of that "cursed, conceited, wily heathen" Aristotle. [107]

Nevertheless Luther took two steps in the direction of reason: he made the sermon, not ceremony, the center of religious ritual; and in the early days of his rebellion he proclaimed the right of every individual to interpret the Scriptures for himself. He drew up his own canon of authenticity for the books of the Bible: how far did they agree with the teaching of Christ? "Whatever does not preach Christ is not Apostolic, even though it be written by St. Peter or St. Paul. . . . Whatever does preach Christ would be Apostolic even if it proceeded from Judas, Pilate, or Herod." [108] He rejected the Epistle of James, and called it an "epistle of straw," because he could not reconcile it with Paul's doctrine of justification by faith; he questioned the Epistle to the Hebrews because it seemed to deny the validity of repentance after baptism (thereby upholding the Anabaptists); and at first he rated the Apocalypse as an unintelligible farrago of promises and threats "neither Apostolic nor Prophetic." [109] "The Third Book of Esdras I throw into the Elbe." [110] Though based on whorish reason, most of his judgments on the canon of Scripture were accepted by later Biblical critics as intelligent and sound. "The discourses of the Prophets," he said, "were none of them regularly committed to writing at the time; their disciples and hearers collected them subsequently. . . . Solomon's Proverbs were not the work of Solomon." But Catholic opponents contended that his tests of authenticity and inspiration were subjective and arbitrary, and they predicted that after his example other critics would reject, according to their own tastes and views, other Scriptural books, until nothing would be left of the Bible as a basis for religious faith.

With the exceptions indicated, Luther defended the Bible as absolutely and literally true. He admitted that if the story of Jonah and the whale were not in Scripture he would laugh at it as a fable; so too with the tales of Eden and the serpent, of Joshua and the sun; but, he argued, once we accept the divine authorship of the Bible we must take these stories along with the rest as in every sense factual. He rejected as a form of atheism the attempts of Erasmus and others to harmonize Scripture and reason by allegorical interpretations.[111] Having himself won mental peace not through philosophy but through faith in Christ as presented in the Gospels, he clung to the Bible as the last refuge of the soul. As against the humanists and their worship of the pagan classics, he offered the Bible as no mere product of man's intellect but as a divine gift and consolation. "It teaches us to see, feel, grasp, and comprehend faith, hope, and charity far otherwise than mere human reason can; and when evil oppresses us it teaches how these virtues throw light upon the darkness, and how, after this poor, miserable existence of ours on earth, there is another and eternal life." [112] Asked on what basis he rested the divine inspiration of the Bible, he answered, simply, on its own teaching: none but God-inspired men could have formed so profound and solacing a faith.

VIII. LUTHER'S THEOLOGY

Though his theology was founded with trusting literalness on the Scriptures, his interpretation unconsciously retained late medieval traditions. His nationalism made him a modern, his theology belonged to the Age of Faith. His rebellion was far more against Catholic organization and ritual than against Catholic doctrine; most of this remained with him to the end. Even in his rebellion he followed Wyclif and Huss rather than any new scheme: like theirs his revolt lay in rejecting the papacy, the councils, the hierarchy, and any other guide to faith than the Bible; like them he called the pope Antichrist; and like them he found protection in the state. The line from Wyclif to Huss to Luther is the main thread of religious development from the fourteenth to the sixteenth century. Theologically the line was anchored on Augustine's notions of predestination and grace, which in turn were rooted in the Epistles of Paul, who had never known Christ. Nearly all the pagan elements in Christianity fell away as Protestantism took form; the

Judaic contribution triumphed over the Greek; the Prophets won against the Aristotle of the Scholastics and the Plato of the humanists; Paul—in the line of the Prophets rather than that of the Apostles—transformed Jesus into an atonement for Adam; the Old Testament overshadowed the New; Yahweh darkened the face of Christ.

Luther's conception of God was Judaic. He could speak with eloquence of the divine mercy and grace, but more basic in him was the old picture of God as the avenger, and therefore of Christ as the final judge. He believed, without recorded protest, that God had drowned nearly all mankind in a flood, had set fire to Sodom, and had destroyed lands, peoples, and empires with a breath of His wrath and a wave of His hand. Luther reckoned that "few are saved, infinitely many are damned." [113] The mitigating myth of Mary as intercessor dropped out of the story, and left the Last Judgment in all its stark terror for naturally sinful men. Meanwhile God had appointed wild beasts, vermin, and wicked women to punish men for their sins. Occasionally Luther reminded himself that we know nothing about God except that a cosmic intelligence exists. When one troublesome young theologian asked him where God had been before the world was created, he answered, in his blunt Johnsonian way: "He was building hell for such presumptuous, fluttering, and inquisitive spirits as you." [114]

He took heaven and hell for granted, and believed in an early end of the world. [115] He described a heaven of many delights, including pet dogs "with golden hair shining like precious stones"—a genial concession to his children, who had expressed concern over the damnation of their pets. [116] He spoke as confidently as Aquinas about angels as bodiless and beneficent spirits. Sometimes he represented man as an endless bone of contention between good and bad angels, to whose differing dispositions and efforts were to be ascribed all the circumstances of man's fate—a Zoroastrian intrusion into his theology. He accepted fully the medieval conception of devils wandering about the earth, bringing temptation, sin, and misfortune to men, and easing man's way into hell. "Many devils are in woods, in waters, in wilderness, and in dark, pooly places, ready to hurt . . . people; some are also in the thick black clouds." [117] Some of this may have been conscious pedagogical invention of helpful supernatural terrors; but Luther spoke so familiarly of devils that he seems to have believed all he said of them. "I know Satan very well," he said, and detailed their conversations with each other. [118] Sometimes he charmed the Devil by playing the flute; [119] sometimes he frightened the poor Devil away by calling him filthy names. [120] He became so accustomed to ascribing to the Devil the eerie sounds of walls contracting in the cold of the night that when he was awakened by such noises, and could confidently conclude that they were made by Satan rambling about, he could resume his sleep in peace. [121] He attributed to diabolical agency various unpleasant phenomena

—hail, thunder, war, plague—and to divine action all beneficent events; [122] he could hardly conceive of what we call natural law. All the Teutonic folklore about the poltergeist, or noise-making spirit, was apparently credited by Luther at its face value. Snakes and monkeys were favorite incarnations of the Devil.[123] The old notion that devils could lie with women and beget children seemed plausible to him; in one such case he recommended that the resultant child should be drowned.[124] He accepted magic and witchcraft as realities, and thought it a simple Christian duty to burn witches at the stake.[125] Most of these ideas were shared by his contemporaries, Catholic or Protestant. The belief in the power and ubiquity of devils attained in the sixteenth century an intensity not recorded in any other age; and this preoccupation with Satan bedeviled much of Protestant theology.

Luther's philosophy was further darkened by the conviction that man is by nature wicked and prone to sin.* As punishment for the disobedience of Adam and Eve the divine image was torn from the human heart, leaving only natural inclinations. "No one is by nature Christian or pious . . . the world and the masses are and always will be unchristian. . . . The wicked always outnumber the good." [126] Even in the good man evil actions outnumber the good, for he cannot escape from his nature; as Paul said, "There is none righteous, no, not one." "We are the children of wrath," Luther felt, "and all our works, intentions, and thoughts are nothing at all in the balance against our sins." [127] So far as good works go, every one of us would merit damnation. By "good works" Luther meant especially those forms of ritual piety recommended by the Church—fasting, pilgrimages, prayers to the saints, Masses for the dead, indulgences, processions, gifts to the Church; but he also included all "works, whatever their character." [128] He did not question the need of charity and love for a healthy social life, but he felt that even a life blessed with such virtues could not earn an eternity of bliss. "The Gospel preaches nothing of the merit of works; † he that says the Gospel requires works for salvation, I say flat and plain he is a liar." [129] No amount of good works could atone for the sins—each an insult to an infinite deity—committed by the best of men. Only the redeeming sacrifice of Christ—the suffering and death of the Son of God—could atone for man's sins; and only belief in that divine atonement can save us from hell. As Paul said to the Romans, "If thou shalt confess with thy mouth the Lord Jesus, and shalt believe in thine heart that God hath raised him from the dead, thou shalt be saved." [130] It is this faith that "justifies"—makes a man just despite his sins, and eligible for salvation. Christ Himself said: "He that believeth and is baptized shall be saved, but he that believeth not shall be damned." [131] "Wherefore," rea-

---

* Or, as we should now say, man is born with instincts fitted for the hunting stage but requiring persistent restraint in civilization.
† Cf. the Beatitudes, Matt. 5 : 3-1.

soned Luther, "it ought to be the first concern of every Christian to lay aside all trust in works, and more and more strengthen faith alone." [182] And he proceeded, in a passage that disturbed some theologians but comforted many sinners:

> Jesus Christ stoops and lets the sinner jump on His back, and so saves him from death. . . . What a consolation for pious souls to put Him on like this and wrap Him in my sins, your sins, the sins of the whole universe, and consider Him thus bearing all our sins! . . . When you see that your sins cleave to Him, then you will be safe from sin, death, and hell. Christianity is nothing but a continual exercise in feeling that you have no sin although you sin, but that your sins are thrown on Christ. It is enough to know the Lamb that bears the sins of the world; sin cannot detach us from Him, were we to commit a thousand fornications a day, or as many murders. Is not that good news if, when some one is full of sins, the Gospel comes and tells him: Have confidence and believe, and henceforth your sins are remitted? Once this stop is pulled out, the sins are forgiven; there is nothing more to work for.[138]

This may have been intended to comfort and revive some sensitive souls who were taking their sins too much to heart; Luther could recall how he too had once magnified the majestic unforgivability of his sins. But to some it sounded very much like Tetzel's alleged "drop the coin in the box and all your sins fly away"; faith was now to do all the wonders formerly claimed for confession, absolution, contribution, and indulgence. Still more arresting was a passage in which the hearty and ebullient Luther found a good word to say for sin itself. When the Devil tempts us with annoying persistency, he said, it may be wise to yield him a sin or two.

> Seek out the society of your boon companions, drink, play, talk bawdy, and amuse yourself. One must sometimes commit a sin out of hate and contempt for the Devil, so as not to give him the chance to make one scrupulous over mere nothings; if one is too frightened of sinning, one is lost. . . . Oh, if I could find some really good sin that would give the Devil a toss! [134]

Such lusty and humorous *obiter dicta* invited misconstruction. Some of Luther's followers interpreted him as condoning fornication, adultery, murder. A Lutheran professor had to caution Lutheran preachers to say as little as possible about justification by faith alone.[135] However, by faith Luther meant no merely intellectual assent to a proposition, but vital, personal self-committal to a practical belief; and he was confident that complete belief in God's grace given because of Christ's redeeming death would make a man so basically good that an occasional frolic with the flesh would do no lasting harm; faith would soon bring the sinner back to spiritual health. He heartily approved of good works; [186] what he denied was their efficacy for salvation. "Good works," he said, "do not make a good man, but a good man does good works." [187] And what makes a man good? Faith in God and Christ.

How does a man come to such saving faith? Not through his merits, but as a divine gift granted, regardless of merits, to those whom God has chosen to save. As St. Paul put it, remembering the case of Pharaoh, "God has mercy on whom He will have mercy; and whom He wills He hardens." [138] By divine predestination the elect are chosen for eternal happiness, the rest are left graceless and damned to everlasting hell.[139]

> This is the acme of faith, to believe that God, Who saves so few and condemns so many, is merciful; that He is just Who has made us necessarily doomed to damnation, so that . . . . . . He seems to delight in the tortures of the wretched, and to be more deserving of hatred than of love. If by any effort of reason I could conceive how God, Who shows so much anger and iniquity, could be merciful and just, there would be no need of faith.[140]

So Luther, in his medieval reaction against a paganizing Renaissance Church, went back not only to Augustine but to Tertullian: *Credo quia incredibile;* it seemed to him a merit to believe in predestination because it was, to reason, unbelievable. Yet it was, he thought, by hard logic that he was driven to this incredibility. The theologian who had written so eloquently about the "freedom of a Christian man" now (1525), in a treatise *De servo arbitrio,* argued that if God is omnipotent He must be the sole cause of all actions, including man's; that if God is omniscient He foresees everything, and everything must happen as He has foreseen it; that therefore all events, through all time, have been predetermined in His mind, and are forever fated to be. Luther concluded, like Spinoza, that man is as "unfree as a block of wood, a rock, a lump of clay, or a pillar of salt." [141] More strangely still, the same divine foresight deprives the angels, nay, God Himself, of freedom; He too must act as He has foreseen; His foresight is His fate. A lunatic fringe interpreted this doctrine *ad libitum:* a youth beheaded his brother and attributed the act to God, of Whom he was merely the helpless agent; and another logician stamped his wife to death with his heels, crying, "Now is the Father's will accomplished." [142]

Most of these conclusions lay annoyingly implicit in medieval theology, and were deduced by Luther from Paul and Augustine with irrefutable consistency. He seemed willing to accept medieval theology if he might disown the Renaissance Church; he could tolerate the predestination of the multitudinous damned more easily than the authority of scandalous tax-gathering popes. He rejected the ecclesiastical definition of the Church as the prelacy; he defined it as the community of believers in the divinity and redeeming passion of Christ; but he echoed papal doctrine when he wrote: "All people who seek and labor to come to God through any other means than only through Christ (as Jews, Turks, Papists, false saints, heretics, etc.) walk in horrible darkness and error, and so at last must die and be lost in their sins." [143] Here, reborn in Wittenberg, was the teaching of Boniface VIII and the Council of Rome (1302) that *extra ecclesiam nulla salus*—"no salvation outside the Church."

The most revolutionary item in Luther's theology was his dethronement of the priest. He allowed for priests not as indispensable dispensers of the sacraments, nor as privileged mediators with God, but only as servants chosen by each congregation to minister to its spiritual wants. By marrying and raising a family these ministers would shed the aura of sanctity that had made the priesthood awesomely powerful; they would be "first among equals," but any man might at need perform their functions, even to absolving a penitent from sin. Monks should abandon their selfish and often idle isolation, should marry and labor with the rest; the man at the plow, the woman in the kitchen, serve God better than the monk mumbling in stupefying repetition unintelligible prayers. And prayers should be the direct communion of the soul with God, not appeals to half-legendary saints. The adoration of the saints, in Luther's judgment, was not a friendly and consoling intercourse of the lonely living with the holy dead; it was a relapse into primitive polytheistic idolatry. [144]

As for the sacraments, viewed as priestly ceremonies conferring divine grace, Luther severely reduced their role. They involve no miraculous powers, and their efficacy depends, not on their forms and formulas, but on the faith of the recipient. Confirmation, matrimony, episcopal ordination of priests, and extreme unction of the dying are rites to which no special promise of divine grace is attached in Scripture; the new religion could dispense with them. Baptism has the warrant of St. John the Baptist's example. Auricular confession may be retained as a sacrament, despite some doubt as to its Scriptural basis.* The supreme sacrament is the Lord's Supper, or Eucharist. The notion that a priest, by the incantation of his words, can change bread into Christ seemed to Luther absurd and blasphemous; nevertheless, he argued, Christ of His own will comes down from heaven to be present consubstantially with the bread and wine of the sacrament. The Eucharist is no priestly magic, but a divine and perpetual miracle. [145]

Luther's doctrine of the sacraments, his replacement of the Mass by the Lord's Supper, and his theory of salvation by faith rather than by good

---

* It has been replaced in Lutheran practice by collective confession of sinfulness, followed by a general absolution.

works, undermined the authority of the clergy in northern Germany. Furthering this process, Luther rejected episcopal courts and canon law. In Lutheran Europe civil courts became the only courts, secular power the only legal power. Secular rulers appointed Church personnel, appropriated Church property, took over Church schools and monastic charities. Theoretically Church and state remained independent; actually the Church became subject to the state. The Lutheran movement, which thought to submit all life to theology, unwittingly, unwillingly, advanced that pervasive secularization which is a basic theme of modern life.

IX. THE REVOLUTIONIST

When some bishops sought to silence Luther and his followers, he emitted an angry roar that was almost a tocsin of revolution. In a pamphlet "Against the Falsely Called Spiritual Order of the Pope and the Bishops" (July 1522), he branded the prelates as the "biggest wolves" of all, and called upon all good Germans to drive them out by force.

> It were better that every bishop were murdered, every foundation or cloister rooted out, than that one soul should be destroyed, let alone that all souls should be lost for the sake of their worthless trumpery and idolatry. Of what use are they who thus live in lust, nourished by the sweat and labor of others? . . . If they accepted God's Word, and sought the life of the soul, God would be with them. . . . But if they will not hear God's Word, but rage and rave with bannings and burnings, killings and every evil, what do they better deserve than a strong uprising which will sweep them from the earth? And we would smile did it happen. All who contribute body, goods, and honor that the rule of the bishops may be destroyed are God's dear children and true Chirstians.[146]

He was at this time almost as critical of the state as of the Church. Stung by the prohibition of the sale or possession of his New Testament in regions under orthodox rulers, he wrote, in the fall of 1522, a treatise *On Secular Authority: To What Extent It Should Be Obeyed*. He began amiably enough by approving St. Paul's doctrine of civil obedience and the divine origin of the state. This apparently contradicted his own teaching as to the perfect freedom of the Christian man. Luther explained that though true Christians do not need law, and will not use law or force on one another, they must obey the law as good examples to the majority, who are not true Christians, for without law the sinful nature of man would tear a society to pieces. Nevertheless the authority of the state should end where the realm of the spirit begins. Who are these princes that assume to dictate what people shall read or believe?

> You must know that from the beginning of the world a wise prince is a rare bird indeed; still more so a pious prince. They are usually the greatest fools or the worst knaves on earth. They are God's jailers and hangmen, and His divine wrath needs them to punish the wicked and preserve outward peace. . . . I would, however, in all fidelity advise those blinded folk to take heed to the short saying in Psalm CVII: "He poureth contempt upon princes." I swear to you by God that if through your fault this little text becomes effective against you, you are lost, though every one of you be as mighty as the Turk; and your snorting and raving will help you nothing. A large part has already come true. For . . . the common man is learning to think, and . . . contempt of princes is gathering forces among the multitude and the common people. . . . Men ought not, men cannot, men will not suffer your tyranny and presumption much longer. Dear princes and lords, be wise and guide yourselves accordingly. God will no longer tolerate you. The world is no longer what it was when you hunted and drove people like so much game.[147]

A Bavarian chancellor charged that this was a treasonable call to revolution. Duke George denounced it as scandalous, and urged Elector Frederick to suppress the publication. Frederick let it pass with his usual equanimity. What would the princes have said had they read Luther's letter to Wenzel Link (March 19, 1522)?—"We are triumphing over the papal tyranny, which formerly crushed kings and princes; how much more easily, then, shall we not overcome and trample down the princes themselves!" [148] Or if they had seen his definition of the Church?—"I believe that there is on earth, wise as the world, but one holy, common Christian Church, which is no other than the community of the saints. . . . I believe that in this community or Christendom all things are in common, and each man's goods are the other's, and nothing is simply a man's own." [149]

These were casual ebullitions, and should not have been taken too literally. Actually Luther was a conservative, even a reactionary, in politics and religion, in the sense that he wished to return to early medieval beliefs and ways. He considered himself a restorer, not an innovator. He would have been content to preserve and perpetuate the agricultural society that he had known in his childhood, with some humane improvements. He agreed with the medieval Church in condemning interest, merely adding, in his jovial way, that interest was an invention of Satan. He regretted the growth of foreign trade, called commerce a "nasty business," [150] and despised those who lived by buying cheap and selling dear. He denounced as "manifest robbers" the monopolists who were conspiring to raise prices; "the authorities would do right if they took from such people everything they have, and drove them out of the country." [151] He thought it was high time to "put a bit in the mouth of the Fuggers." [152] And he concluded ominously, in a blast *On Trade and Usury* (1524):

> Kings and princes ought to look into these things and forbid them by strict laws, but I hear that they have an interest in them, and the saying of Isaiah is fulfilled, "Thy princes have become companions of thieves." They hang thieves who have stolen a gulden or half a gulden, but trade with those who rob the whole world. . . . Big thieves hang the little ones; and as the Roman senator Cato said, "Simple thieves lie in prisons and in stocks; public thieves walk abroad in gold and silk." But what will God say to this at last? He will do as he says by Ezekiel: princes and merchants, one thief with another, He will melt them together like lead and brass, as when a city burns, so that there shall be neither princes nor merchants any more. That time, I fear, is already at the door.[153]

It was.

CHAPTER XVII

The Social Revolution

1522-36

I. THE MOUNTING REVOLT: 1522–24

THE famished knights had waited impatiently for a chance to rise against princes, prelates, and financiers. In 1522 Charles V was far away in Spain; Sickingen's troops were fretfully idle; rich Church lands lay open to easy seizure. Hutten was calling for action. Luther had invited the German people to sweep their oppressors from the earth.

On August 13 a number of knights signed at Landau a pledge of united action. Sickingen besieged Trier, and shot letters into it inviting the people to join him in overthrowing the ruling archbishop; they remained quiet. The archbishop gathered troops, played general, and beat back five assaults. Sickingen raised the siege and retired to his castle at Landstuhl. The archbishop, with help from neighboring princes, stormed the castle; Sickingen was mortally wounded in its defense; on May 6, 1523, he surrendered; on May 7 he died. The knights submitted to the princes, disbanded their private armies, and clung with desperate severity to the peasant feudal dues that were their main support.

Foreseeing this debacle, Luther had dissociated himself, none too soon (December 19, 1522), from the revolt. Otherwise his star continued to ascend. "The cause of Luther," wrote Archduke Ferdinand to his brother the Emperor (1522), "is so deeply rooted in the whole Empire that not one person in a thousand is free from it." [1] Monks and priests were flocking to the new altar of matrimony. At Nuremberg the Lorenzkirche and the Sebalduskirche resounded with "God's Word"--the Reformers' phrase for a faith based solely on the Bible. "Evangelical" preachers moved freely through northern Germany, capturing old pulpits and setting up new ones; and they denounced not only popes and bishops as "servants of Lucifer," but secular lords as "iniquitous oppressors." [2] However, secular lords were themselves converts: Philip of Hesse, Casimir of Brandenburg, Ulrich of Württemberg, Ernest of Lüneberg, John of Saxony. Even the Emperor's sister Isabella was a Lutheran.

Charles's old teacher had now become Pope Adrian VI (1521). To a

Diet at Nuremberg (1522) he sent a demand for Luther's arrest, and a candid confession of ecclesiastical faults:

> We know well that for many years things deserving of abhorrence have gathered round the Holy See. Sacred things have been misused, ordinances transgressed, so that in everything there has been a change for the worse. Thus it is not surprising that the malady has crept down from the head to the members, from the popes to the hierarchy. We all, prelates and clergy, have gone astray from the right way, and for long there is no one that has done good, no, not one. ... Therefore ... we shall use all diligence to reform before all else the Roman Curia, whence perhaps all these evils have had their origin. ... The whole world is longing for such reform.[3]

The assembly agreed to ask Elector Frederick to check Luther, but it asked why Luther should be condemned for pointing out clerical abuses now so authoritatively confirmed. Finding the Pope's confession insufficiently detailed, it sent him its own list of one hundred *gravamina* of Germany against the Church, and proposed that these grievances should be considered and remedied by a national council to be held in Germany under the presidency of the Emperor.

The same Diet, dominated by the nobility, gave a sympathetic hearing to charges that monopolists were enriching themselves at the expense of the people. A committee wrote to the major cities of Germany asking their advice as to whether the monopolies were harmful, and should they be regulated or destroyed. Ulm replied that they were an evil, and that business firms should be limited to a father, his son, and his son-in-law. Augsburg, home of the Fuggers, submitted a classic defense of "big business," *laissez faire*, and widows and orphans:

> Christendom (or shall we say the whole world?) is rich because of business. The more business a country does, the more prosperous are its people. ... Where there are many merchants there is plenty of work. ... It is impossible to limit the size of the companies. ... The bigger and more numerous they are, the better for everybody. If a merchant is not perfectly free to do business in Germany he will go elsewhere, to Germany's loss. ... If he cannot do business above a certain amount, what is he to do with his surplus money? ... It would be well to let the merchant alone, and put no restrictions on his ability or capital. Some people talk of limiting the earning capacity of investments. This would ... work great injustice and harm by taking away the livelihood of widows, orphans, and other sufferers ... who derive their income from investments in these companies.[4]

The Diet legislated that companies should not be capitalized above 50,000 guilders; that profits must be distributed every two years, and public accounting made; that money should not be loaned at usurious rates; that no merchant should buy more than a stated maximum of any commodity in any quarter-year; and that prices should be fixed by law. The merchants appealed to Charles V; he supported them for reasons that have been stated; and as many city magistrates shared in the profits of the monopolies, the edicts of Nuremberg soon became a dead letter.

To a later session of the Diet (January 1524) a new pope, Clement VII, sent Cardinal Lorenzo Campeggio with fresh demands for the arrest of Luther. Crowds jeered the nuncio in Augsburg; he had to enter Nuremberg secretly to avoid hostile demonstrations; and he had the humiliation of seeing 3,000 persons, including the Emperor's sister, receive the Eucharist in both kinds from a Lutheran pastor. He warned the Diet that the religious revolt, if not soon suppressed, would soon undermine civil authority and order; but the Diet replied that any attempt to put down Lutheranism by force would result in "riot, disobedience, slaughter . . . and a general ruin." [5] While the deliberations proceeded the social revolution began.

II. THE PEASANTS' WAR: 1524-26

The religious revolt offered the tillers of the fields a captivating ideology in which to phrase their demands for a larger share in Germany's growing prosperity. The hardships that had already spurred a dozen rural outbreaks still agitated the peasant mind, and indeed with feverish intensity now that Luther had defied the Church, berated the princes, broken the dams of discipline and awe, made every man a priest, and proclaimed the freedom of the Christian man. In the Germany of that age Church and state were so closely meshed—clergymen played so large a role in social order and civil administration—that the collapse of ecclesiastical prestige and power removed a main barrier to revolution. The Waldensians, Beghards, Brethren of the Common Life, had continued an old tradition of basing radical proposals upon Biblical texts. The circulation of the New Testament in print was a blow to political as well as to religious orthodoxy. It exposed the compromises that the secular clergy had made with the nature of man and the ways of the world; it revealed the communism of the Apostles, the sympathy of Christ for the poor and oppressed; in these respects the New Testament was for the radicals of this age a veritable *Communist Manifesto*. Peasant and proletarian alike found in it a divine warrant for dreaming of a utopia where private property would be abolished, and the poor would inherit the earth.

In 1521 a pamphlet circulated in Germany under the title of "Karsthans" —i.e., Pitchfork John. This "Man with the Hoe" and a pen pledged peasant protection to Luther; and a continuation published in the same year advocated a rural insurrection against the Catholic clergy.[6] Another pamphlet of 1521, by Johannes Eberlin, demanded universal male suffrage, the subordination of every ruler and official to popularly elected councils, the abolition of all capitalist organizations, a return to medieval price-fixing for bread and wine, and the education of all children in Latin, Greek, Hebrew, astronomy, and medicine.[7] In 1522 a pamphlet entitled "The Needs of the German Nation" (*Teutscher Nation Notturft*), and falsely ascribed to the dead Emperor Frederick III, called for the removal of "all tolls, duties, passports, and fines," the abolition of Roman and canon law, the limitation of business organizations to a capital of 10,000 guilders, the exclusion of the clergy from civil government, the confiscation of monastic wealth, and the distribution of the proceeds among the poor.[8] Otto Brunfels proclaimed (1524) that the payment of tithes to the clergy was contrary to the New Testament. Preachers mingled Protestant evangelism with utopian aspirations. One revealed that heaven was open to peasants but closed to nobles and clergymen; another counseled the peasants to give no more money to priests or monks; Münzer, Carlstadt, and Hubmaier advised their hearers that "farmers, miners, and cornthreshers understand the Gospel better, and can teach it better, than a whole village . . . of abbots and priests . . . or doctors of divinity"; Carlstadt added, "and better than Luther." [9] Almanacs and astrologers, as if giving a cue to action, predicted an uprising for 1524. A Catholic humanist, Johannes Cochlaeus, warned Luther (1523) that "the populace in the towns, and the peasants in the provinces, will inevitably rise in rebellion. . . . They are poisoned by the innumerable abusive pamphlets and speeches that are printed and declaimed among them against both papal and secular authority." [10] Luther, the preachers, and the pamphleteers were not the cause of the revolt; the causes were the just grievances of the peasantry. But it could be argued that the gospel of Luther and his more radical followers "poured oil on the flames," [11] and turned the resentment of the oppressed into utopian delusions, uncalculated violence, and passionate revenge.

Thomas Münzer's career caught all the excitement of the time. Appointed preacher at Allstedt (1522), he demanded the extermination of the "godless"—i.e., the orthodox or the conservative—by the sword; "the godless have no right to live except in so far as they are permitted to do so by the elect." [12] He proposed to the princes that they should lead the people in a communistic revolt against the clergy and the capitalists. When the princes did not rise to the opportunity, he called upon the people to overthrow the princes too, and "to establish a refined society such as was contemplated by Plato . . . and Apuleius of *The Golden Ass*." [13] "All things are in common," he wrote, "and should be distributed as occasion requires, according to the several necessities of all. Any prince, count, or baron who, after being earnestly reminded of this truth, shall be unwilling to accept it, is to be beheaded or hanged." [14] Elector Frederick tolerated this gospel humorously, but his brother Duke John and his cousin Duke George joined with Luther in having Münzer expelled from his pastorate (1524). The irate apostle wandered from town to town, announcing the deliverance of "Israel," and the imminent Kingdom of Heaven on earth.[15]

He found a congenial political climate in the free city of Mühlhausen in Thuringia, where the textile industry had gathered a numerous proletariat. Heinrich Pfeiffer, an ex-monk, had already begun there, with the support of the lower middle class, a movement to capture the municipal council from the patrician oligarchy. Münzer preached his radical program to the workingmen of the town and to the neighboring peasantry. On March 17, 1525, the armed followers of Pfeiffer and Münzer deposed the patricians and set up an "Eternal Council" to rule Mühlhausen. According to Melanchthon the victorious radicals drove out the monks, and appropriated all the property of the Church; [16] however, no theologian in this age could be trusted to report impartially the activities or views of his opponents. No communist commonwealth was established; Pfeiffer proved abler in practice than Münzer, and tamed the revolt to the needs of the middle class. Anticipating attack by Imperial troops, Münzer organized workers and peasants into an army, and had heavy artillery cast for it in the monastery of the Barefoot Friars. "Forward!" was his call to his men; "forward while the fire is hot! Let your swords be ever warm with blood!" [17]

About the same time peasant uprisings were convulsing South Germany. Perhaps a ruinous hailstorm (1524), which destroyed all hopes for a harvest in Stühlingen, served as the trigger of revolt. This district, near Schaffhausen, was not too far from Switzerland to feel the example of the sturdy peasants who had there freed themselves from all but the formalities of feudal power. On August 24, 1524, Hans Müller, acting on a suggestion from Münzer, gathered about him some Stühlingen peasants, and bound them into an "Evangelical Brotherhood" pledged to emancipate farmers throughout Germany. Soon they were joined by the discontented tenants of the abbot of Reichenau, the bishop of Constance, the counts of Werdenburg, Montfort, Lupfen, and Sulz. By the end of 1524 there were some 30,000 peasants in arms in South Germany refusing to pay state taxes, church tithes, or feudal dues, and sworn to emancipation or death. At Memmingen their delegates, under the guidance or influence of Zwinglian Protestants from Zurich, formulated (March 1525) the "Twelve Articles" that set half of Germany on fire.

> To the Christian reader peace, and the grace of God through Christ.

There are many anti-Christians who have lately taken occasion of the assembly of the peasants to cast scorn upon the Gospel, saying, Is this the fruit of the new evangel? Is no one to be obedient, but all are to rebel . . . to overthrow, or perhaps to slay, the spiritual and temporal lords? To all these godless and wicked critics the following articles make answer, in order, first, to remove this reproach from the Word of God, and second, to justify in a Christian way the disobedience, nay the rebellion, of the peasants.

First, It is our humble petition and request, as also the will and intention of all of us, that in the future we should have authority and power so that a whole community should choose and appoint a pastor, and also have the right to depose him. . . .

Second, Since the tithe is appointed in the Old Testament and fulfilled in the New, we will . . . pay the just tithe of grain, but in a proper way. . . . We will that for the future this be gathered and received by our church provost, whom the community appoints; that out of it there shall be given to the pastor . . . a modest, sufficient maintenance for him and his . . . that the remainder shall be distributed to the poor and needy who are in the same village. . . . The small tithe we will not give at all, for God created cattle for the free use of men. . . .

Third, It has been the custom hitherto for men to hold us as their own property, and this is pitiable, seeing that Christ has redeemed and bought us all with the precious shedding of His blood, the lowly as well as the great. . . . Therefore it agrees with Scripture that we be free, and will be so. . . . To our chosen and appointed rulers (appointed for us by God) we are willingly obedient in all proper a d Christian matters, and have no doubt that, as true and real Christians, they will gladly release us from serfdom, or show us in the Gospel that we are serfs. . . .

Sixth, We have a heavy grievance because of the services which are increased from day to day. . . .

Eighth, We are greatly aggrieved, as many of us have holdings th t will not support the rents we pay, and the peasants suffer loss and ruin. Let the lords have honorable men inspect said holdings, and fix fair rent . . . for every laborer is worthy of his hire. . . .

Tenth, We are aggrieved because some have appropriated to themselves meadows out of the common fields, which once belonged to the community. . . .

Eleventh, We would have the death dues entirely abolished. We will not suffer it, nor allow widows and orphans to be so shamefully robbed. . . .

Twelfth, If one or more of the articles here set forth . . . can be shown to us by the Word of God to be improper, we will recede from it if this is explained to us with arguments from Scripture.[18]

The peasant leaders, encouraged by Luther's semi-revolutionary pronouncements, sent him a copy of the Articles, and asked for his support. He
replied with a pamphlet printed in April 1525: *Ermahung zum Frieden*
(*Admonition to Peace*). He applauded the peasants' offer to submit to correction by Scripture. He noted the charges, now rising, that his speeches
and writings had stirred revolt; he denied his responsibility, and referred to
his inculcation of civil obedience. But he did not withdraw his criticism of
the master class:

> We have no one on earth to thank for this mischievous rebellion
> except you, princes and lords, and especially you blind bishops and
> mad priests and monks, whose hearts are hardened against the Holy
> Gospel, though you know that it is true and that you cannot refute
> it. Besides, in your temporal government, you do nothing but flay
> and rob your subjects, in order that you may lead a life of splendor
> and pride, until the poor common people can bear it no longer. . . .
> Well, then, since you are the cause of this wrath of God, it will
> undoubtedly come upon you, if you do not mend your ways in time.
> . . . The peasants are mustering, and this must result in the ruin,
> destruction, and desolation of Germany by cruel murder and blood-
> shed, unless God shall be moved by our repentance to prevent it.[19]

He counseled the princes and lords to recognize the justice of many of the
Articles, and urged a policy of kindly consideration. To the peasants he addressed a frank admission of their wrongs, but pleaded with them to refrain
from violence and revenge; a resort to violence, he predicted, would leave
the peasants worse off than before. He foresaw that a violent revolt would
bring discredit upon the movement for religious reform, and that he would
be blamed for everything. He objected to the appropriation of tithes by
each congregation. The authorities should be obeyed, and had a right to tax
the people to pay the expenses of government. The "freedom of the Christian man" was to be understood as a spiritual liberty, consistent with serfdom, even with slavery.

> Did not Abraham and other patriarchs and prophets use slaves?
> Read what St. Paul teaches about servants, who at that time were all
> slaves. Therefore your third article is dead against the Gospel. . . .
> This article would make all men equal . . . and that is impossible. For
> a worldly kingdom cannot stand unless there is in it an inequality of
> persons, so that some are free, some imprisoned, some lords, some
> subjects.[20]

His final advice, had it been followed, would have spared Germany much
bloodshed and devastation:

> Choose among the nobles certain counts and lords, and from the cities certain councilmen, and have these matters dealt with and settled in a friendly way. You lords, let down your stubbornness ... and give up a little of your tyranny and oppression, so that poor people get air and room to live. The peasants for their part should let themselves be instructed, and give over and let go some of the Articles that grasp too far and too high.[21]

The peasant leaders, however, felt that it was now too late to retrace their steps; in any conciliation they would sooner or later be punished. They mourned Luther as a traitor, and went on with the revolt. Some of them took quite literally the dream of equality: the nobles were to dismantle their castles, and live like peasants and burghers; they were no longer to ride on horseback, for that raised them above their fellow men. Pastors were to be informed that they were henceforth servants, not masters, of their congregations, and would be expelled if they did not adhere strictly and only to the Scriptures.[22] Corresponding demands came from the workmen of the towns. They denounced the monopoly of city offices by the rich, the embezzlement of public funds by corrupt officials, the perpetually rising prices while wages stood almost still. "It would be better for the salvation of the soul," said one radical, "if the lord prelates were not so rich and luxurious, and if their possessions were divided among the poor." [23] Wendel Hipler and Friedrich Weigant proposed that all Church property should be confiscated to secular needs; that all transport tolls and tariff duties should be removed; that there should be throughout the Empire one coinage and one system of weights and measures.[24]

The movement had a colorful assortment of leaders: the innkeepers George Metzler and Metern Feuerbacher, the jolly roisterer Jäcklein Rohrbach, some ex-soldiers and priests, and two knights from Sickingen's defeated band—Florian Geyer and Götz von Berlichingen "of the Iron Hand"; Hauptmann and Goethe would later choose these two as heroes for vivid plays. Each leader was sovereign over his own group, and rarely concerted his action with the others. Nevertheless, in the spring of 1525, the revolt flared up in a dozen scattered localities about the same time. At Heilbronn, Rothenburg, and Würzburg a commune of labor representatives captured the municipal administration. At Frankfurt-am-Main the victorious commune announced that it would thereafter be council, burgomaster, pope, and emperor all in one. At Rothenburg the priests were driven from the cathedral, religious images were demolished, a chapel was smashed to the ground (March 27, 1525), and clerical wine cellars were emptied with triumphant gaiety.[25] Towns subject to feudal lords renounced their fealty; episcopal towns called for an end to clerical privileges, and agitated for the secularization of ecclesiastical property. Nearly the whole duchy of Franconia joined the revolt. Many lords and bishops, unprepared to resist, swore to accept the reforms demanded of them; so the bishops of Speyer and Bamberg, and the abbots of Kempten and Herzfeld. Count William of Henneberg freed his serfs. Counts George and Albrecht of Hohenlohe were summoned before peasant leaders and were initiated into the new order: "Brother George and brother Albrecht, come hither and swear to the peasants to be as brothers to them, for you are now no longer lords but peasants." [26] Most of the towns received the rural rebels with a hearty welcome. Many of the lower clergy, hostile to the hierarchy, supported the revolt.

The first serious encounter took place at Leipheim on the Danube near Ulm (April 4, 1525). Under an energetic priest, Jakob Wehe, 3,000 peasants captured the town, drank all discoverable wine, pillaged the church, smashed the organ, made themselves leggings from sacerdotal vestments, and paid mock homage to one of their number seated on the altar and robed as a priest.[27] An army of mercenaries hired by the Swabian League and led by an able general, Georg von Truchsess, laid siege to Leipheim, and frightened the undisciplined peasants into surrender. Wehe and four other leaders were beheaded, the rest were spared, but the League's troops burned many peasant cottages.

On Good Friday, April 15, 1525, three rebel contingents under Metzler, Geyer, and Rohrbach laid siege to the town of Weinsberg (near Heilbronn), whose ruling Count Ludwig von Helfenstein was especially hated for his severities. A delegation of peasants approached the walls and asked for a parley; the Count and his knights made a sudden sortie and massacred the delegation. On Easter Sunday the attackers, helped by some citizens of the town, broke through the walls, and cut down the forty men-at-arms who cared to resist. The Count, his wife (a daughter of the late Emperor Maximilian), and sixteen knights were taken prisoner. Rohrbach, without consulting Metzler or Geyer, ordered the seventeen men to run the gantlet between rows of peasants armed with pikes. The Count offered all his fortune in ransom; it was refused as a temporizing expedient. The Countess, prostrate and delirious, begged for her husband's life; Rohrbach bade two men hold her up so that she could witness the orgy of revenge. As the Count walked to his death amid a volley of daggers and pikes, the peasants recalled to him his own brutalities. "You thrust my brother into a dungeon," one cried, "because he did not bare his head as you passed by." "You harnessed us like oxen to the yoke," shouted others; "you caused the hands of my father to be cut off because he killed a hare on his own field. . . . Your horses, dogs, and huntsmen have trodden down my crops. . . . You have wrung the last penny out of us." During the next half-hour the sixteen knights were similarly laid to rest. The Countess was allowed to retire to a convent.[28]

In nearly every section of Germany peasant bands were running riot.

Monasteries were sacked, or were compelled to pay high ransoms. "No-where," says a letter of April 7, 1525, "do the insurgents make a secret of . . . their intention to kill all clerics who will not break with the Church, to destroy all cloisters and episcopal palaces, and to root the Catholic religion utterly out of the land." [29] This is probably an exaggeration, but we may note that in Bavaria, Austria, and Tirol, where Protestantism had apparently been suppressed, the rebels captured many towns, and compelled Archduke Ferdinand to agree that all preaching should henceforth be according to Scripture—a characteristic Protestant demand. At Mainz Archbishop Albrecht fled before the storm, but his deputy saved the see by signing the Twelve Articles and paying a ransom of 15,000 guilders. On April 11 the townsfolk of Bamberg renounced the bishop's feudal sovereignty, pillaged and burned his castle, and plundered the houses of the orthodox. In Alsace the revolt spread so rapidly that by April's end every Catholic or rich landlord in the province was in terror of his life. On April 28 an army of 20,000 peasants attacked Zabern, seat of the bishop of Strasbourg, and despoiled his monastery; on May 13 they took the town, forced every fourth man to join them, renounced all payment of tithes, and demanded that thereafter all officials except the emperor should be elected by popular suffrage, and be subject to recall.[30] At Brixen in Tirol a former episcopal secretary, Michael Gasmaier, organized a revolt that attacked all orthodox clergymen, sacked the local monastery (May 12), and remained rampant and unsubdued for a year. In all the valleys of the Inn and Etsch rivers, says an unsympathetic chronicler of the time, "there was such a concourse, cry, and tumult that hardly might a good man walk in the streets. Robbing and plundering . . . became so common that even pious men were tempted thereto." [31] At Freiburg-im-Breisgau the peasants looted castles and monasteries, and forced the city to join the "Evangelical Brotherhood" (May 24). In that same month a peasant band drove the bishop of Würzburg out of his palace, and feasted on his stores. In June the powerful and warlike Archbishop Matthias Lang was chased from his palace in Salzburg into his castle fortress overlooking the city. In Neustadt in the Palatinate Elector Ludwig, surrounded by 8,000 armed peasants, invited their leaders to dinner, and cheerfully complied with their demands. "There," said a contemporary, "one saw villeins and their lord sit together, eat and drink together. He had, as it seemed, one heart to them, and they to him." [32]

Amid this torrent of events Luther issued from the press of Wittenberg, toward the middle of May 1525, a pamphlet "Against the Robbing and Murdering Hordes of Peasants." Its vehemence startled prince and peasant, prelate and humanist, alike. Shocked by the excesses of the infuriated rebels, dreading a possible overturn of all law and government in Germany, and stung by charges that his own teachings had loosed the flood, he now ranged himself unreservedly on the side of the imperiled lords.

> In the former book I did not venture to judge the peasants, since they had offered to be set right and be instructed. . . . But before I look around they, forgetting their offer, betake themselves to violence, and rob and rage and act like mad dogs. . . . It is the Devil's work they are at, and in particular it is the work of the archdevil [Münzer] who rules at Mülhausen. . . . I must begin by setting their sins before them. . . . Then I must instruct the rulers how they are to conduct themselves in these circumstances. . . .
>
> Any man against whom sedition can be proved is outside the law of God and the Empire, so that the first who can slay him is doing right and well. . . . For rebellion brings with it a land full of murder and bloodshed, makes widows and orphans, and turns everything upside down. . . . Therefore let everyone who can, smite, slay, and stab, secretly or openly, remembering that nothing can be more poisonous, hurtful, or devilish than a rebel. It is just when one must kill a mad dog; if you do not strike him he will strike you, and a whole land with you. . . .

He rejected the supposed Scriptural warrant for communism:

> The Gospel does not make goods common, except in the case of those who do of their own free will what the Apostles and disciples did in Acts iv. They did not demand, as do our insane peasants in their raging, that the goods of others—of a Pilate or a Herod—should be common, but only their own goods. Our peasants, however, would have other men's goods common, and keep their own goods for themselves. Fine Christians these! I think there is not a devil left in hell; they have all gone into the peasants.

To Catholic rulers he offered his forgiveness if they smote the rebels without trial. To Protestant rulers he recommended prayer, contrition, and negotiation; but if the peasants remain obdurate,

> then swiftly grasp the sword. For a prince or lord must remember in this case that he is God's minister and the servant of His wrath (Romans, xiii), to whom the sword is committed for use upon such fellows. . . . If he can punish and does not—even though the punishment consist in the taking of life and the shedding of blood—then he is guilty of all the murder and all the evil which these fellows commit. . . . The rulers, then, should go on unconcerned, and with a good conscience lay about them as long as their hearts still beat. . . . If anyone think this too hard, let him remember that rebellion is intolerable, and that the destruction of the world is to be expected every hour.[88]

It was Luther's misfortune that this outburst reached its readers just about the time that the forces of the propertied classes were beginning to subdue the revolt; and the Reformer received undue credit for the terrorism of the suppression. It is unlikely that the endangered masters were influenced by the pamphlet; it was in their temper to handle the insurgents with a severity that would serve as a deterrent in unforgettable memory. For a time they had bemused the simple peasants with parleys and promises, and had thereby persuaded many of the bands to disperse; meanwhile the masters organized and armed their levies.

At the height of the turmoil Elector Frederick died (May 5, 1525), himself calm and at peace, admitting that he and other princes had wronged the peasant, refusing to join in extreme measures of retaliation, and leaving to his successor, Duke John, urgent counsels of moderation. But the new Elector felt that his brother's policy had been unwisely lenient. He joined his forces with those of Duke Henry of Brunswick and Philip Landgrave of Hesse, and together they moved against Münzer's encampment outside Mühlhausen. The opposed armies were matched only in number—each some 8,000 strong; but the ducal troops were mostly trained soldiers, while the peasants, despite Münzer's home-made artillery, were indifferently armed, poorly disciplined, and disordered with natural frigh⁻ Münzer relied on his eloquence to restore morale, and led the peasants in   ayer and hymns. The first barrage of the princely cannon slaughtered hur_dreds, and the terrified rebels fled into the town of Frankenhausen (May 15, 1525). The victors followed, and massacred 5,000. Three hundred prisoners were condemned to death; their women pleaded mercy for them; it was granted, on condition that the women should beat out the brains of two priests who had encouraged the revolt; it was so done, while the triumphant dukes looked on.[84] Münzer hid, was captured, was tortured into confessing the error of his ways, and was beheaded before the headquarters of the princes. Pfeiffer and his 1,200 soldiers defended Mühlhausen; they were overcome; Pfeiffer and other leaders were put to death, but the citizens were spared on paying a total ransom of 40,000 guilders ($1,000,000?).

Meanwhile Truchsess took the town of Böblingen by negotiation, and from within its walls turned his guns upon a rebel camp outside (May 12). Those of the peasants who survived this cannonade were cut down by his cavalry; this ended the revolt in Württemberg. Turning next to Weinsberg, Truchsess burned it to the ground, and slowly roasted Jäcklein Rohrbach, who had directed the "Massacre of Weinsberg." Truchsess marched on to rout peasant forces at Königshofen and Ingolstadt, recaptured Würzburg, and beheaded eighty-one chosen rebels as a memento for the rest (June 5). Florian Geyer escaped from Würzburg into obscurity, and remained a cherished legend. Götz von Berlichingen surrendered in apt time, lived to fight for Charles V against the Turks, and died in his own bed and castle at eighty-two (1562). Rothenberg was taken on June 20, Memmingen soon afterward. The revolt in Alsace was crushed by the slaughter of from 2,000 to 6,000 men at Lipstein and Zabern (May 17–18). By May 27 some 20,000 peasants had been killed in Alsace alone, in many cases after surrender; the air of the towns was fetid with the stench of the dead.[35] Markgraf Casimir had some of his surrendering peasants beheaded, some hanged; in milder cases he chopped off hands or gouged out eyes.[36] Saner princes finally intervened to reduce the barbarism of the retaliation, and at the end of August the Diet of Augsburg issued a rescript urging moderation in punishments and fines. "If all the rebels are killed," one philosophic noble asked, "where shall we get peasants to provide for us?" [37]

In Austria the revolt continued for a year. In January 1526, Michael Gasmaier proclaimed throughout Tirol the most radical of the revolutionary programs. All "godless" (i.e., non-Protestants) who persecuted the true Word of God, or who oppressed the common man, were to be put to death. All pictures and shrines were to be removed from the churches, and no Masses were to be said. Town walls, towers, and fortresses were to be demolished; there should now be only villages, and all men were to be equal. Officials and judges were to be chosen by universal adult male suffrage. Feudal rents and dues were to end at once; tithes were to be collected, but were to be given to the Reformed Church and the poor. Monasteries were to be converted into hospitals or schools. Mines were to be nationalized. Prices were to be fixed by the government.[38] For a time Gasmaier, with clever strategy, defeated the troops sent against him, but he was finally outwitted, and fled to Italy. The Archduke Ferdinand set a price on his head, and two Spanish cutthroats earned the sum by assassinating him in his room in Padua (1528).

The losses of German life and property in the Peasants' Revolt were to be exceeded only in the Thirty Years' War. Of peasants alone some 130,000 died in battle or in expiation. There were 10,000 executions under the jurisdiction of the Swabian League; Truchsess' executioner boasted that he had killed 1,200 condemned men with his own practiced hand. The peasants themselves had destroyed hundreds of castles and monasteries. Hundreds of villages and towns had been depopulated or ruined, or impoverished by huge indemnities. Over 50,000 homeless peasants roamed the highways or hid in the woods. Widows and orphans were legion, but charity was heartless or penniless. The rebels had in many instances burned the charters that recorded their feudal dues; new charters were now drawn up, renewing the obligations, sometimes more leniently, sometimes more rigorously, than before. Concessions were made to the peasants in Austria, Baden, and Hesse; elsewhere serfdom was strengthened, and would continue, east of the Elbe, till the nineteenth century. Democratic beginnings were aborted. Intellectual developments were stunted; censorship of publications increased, under Catholic and Protestant authorities alike. Humanism wilted in the fire; the Renaissance joy in life and literature and love gave way to theology, pietism, and meditations on death.

The Reformation itself almost perished in the Peasants' War. Despite Luther's disclaimers and denunciations, the rebellion had flaunted Protestant colors and ideas: economic aspirations were dressed in phrases that Luther had sanctified; communism was to be merely a return to the Gospel. Charles V interpreted the uprising as "a Lutheran movement." [39] Conservatives classed the expropriation of ecclesiastical property by Protestants as revolutionary actions on a par with the sacking of monasteries by peasants. In the south the frightened princes and lords renewed their fealty to the Roman Church. In several places, as at Bamberg and Würzburg, men even of the propertied class were executed for having accepted Lutheranism. [40] The peasants themselves turned against the Reformation as a lure and a betrayal; some called Luther *Dr. Lügner*—"Dr. Liar"—and "toady of the princes." [41] For years after the revolt he was so unpopular that he seldom dared leave Wittenberg, even to attend his father's deathbed (1530). "All is forgotten that God has done for the world through me," he wrote (June 15, 1525); "now lords, priests, and peasants are all against me, and threaten my death." [42]

It was not in his character to yield ground or apologize. On May 30, 1525, he wrote to Nicholas Amsdorf: "My opinion is that it is better that all peasants be killed than that the princes and magistrates perish, because the rustics took the sword without divine authority." [43] In July 1525, he published *An Open Letter Concerning the Hard Book against the Peasants*. His critics, he said, deserved no answer; their criticisms showed them to be rebels at heart, like the peasants, and no more deserving of mercy; "the rulers ought to seize these people by the cap and make them hold their tongues." [44]

> If they think this answer is too hard, and that this is talking violence and only shutting men's mouths, I reply that this is right. A rebel is not worth answering with arguments, for he does not accept them. The answer for such mouth is a fist that brings blood from the nose. The peasants would not listen . . . their ears must be unbuttoned with bullets, till their heads jump off their shoulders. Such pupils need such a rod. He who will not hear God's Word when it is spoken with kindness must listen to the headsman when he comes with his axe. . . . Of mercy I will neither hear nor know anything, but give heed to God's will in His Word. . . . If He will have wrath and not mercy, what have you to do with mercy? Did not Saul sin by showing mercy upon Amalek when he failed to execute God's wrath as he had been commanded? . . . You who are praising mercy so highly because the

peasants are beaten, why did you not praise it when the peasants were raging, smiting, robbing, burning, and plundering, until they were terrible to men's eyes and ears? Why were they not merciful to the princes and lords, whom they wanted to wipe out entirely?

Mercy, Luther argued, is the duty of Christians in their private capacity; as officers of the state, however, they must normally follow justice rather than mercy, for since Adam and Eve's sin man has been so wicked that government, laws, and penalties are needed to control him. We owe more consideration to the community endangered by crime than to criminals endangering the community.

> If the intentions of the peasants had been carried out, no honest man would have been safe from them, but whoever had a pfennig more than another would have had to suffer for it. They had already begun that, and they would not have stopped there; women and children would have been put to shame; they would have taken to killing one another too, and there would have been no peace or safety anywhere. Has anything been heard of more unrestrained than a mob of peasants when they are fed full and have gotten power? . . . The ass will have blows, and the people will be ruled by force.[45]

Luther's extreme statements about the Peasants' War shock us today because social order has been so well established that we presume on its continuance, and can treat with lenience those few who would violently disturb it. But Luther faced the harsh reality of peasant bands transforming their just grievances into indiscriminate pillage, and threatening the complete overturn of law, government, production, and distribution in Germany. Events justified his premonition that the religious revolution for which he had risked his life would be gravely imperiled by the conservative reaction that was bound to follow an unsuccessful revolt. He may have felt some personal debt to the princes and nobles who had protected him in Wittenberg and Worms and the Wartburg, and he might well wonder who would save him against Charles V and Clement VII if princely power ceased to shield the Reformation. The one freedom that seemed to him worth fighting for was the freedom to worship God, to seek salvation according to one's conscience. What difference did it make whether, in this brief *Vorspiel* to eternal life, one was a prince or a slave? We should accept our state here without complaint, bound in body and duty, but free in soul and the grace of God.

And yet the peasants had a case against him. He had not only predicted social revolution, he had said he would not be displeased by it, he would greet it with a smile, even if men washed their hands in episcopal blood. He too had made a revolution, had endangered social order, had flouted authority not less divine than the state's. He had made no protest against the secular appropriation of ecclesiastical property. How otherwise than by force could peasants better their lot when ballots were forbidden them, and their oppressors daily wielded force? The peasants felt that the new religion had sanctified their cause, had aroused them to hope and action, and had deserted them in the hour of decision. Some of them, in angry despair, became cynical atheists.[46] Many of them, or their children, shepherded by Jesuits, returned to the Catholic fold. Some of them followed the radicals whom Luther had condemned, and heard in the New Testament a summons to communism.

III. THE ANABAPTISTS TRY COMMUNISM: 1534-36

Only by observing with what devout enthusiasm some of our contemporaries adopt economic heresies can we understand the fervor with which pious rebellious minorities followed, even to the stake, one or another turn of the religious revolution in the sixteenth century.

The most radical of the new sects took the name of Anabaptists (*Wieder-täufer*, Again- Baptizers) from its insistence that baptism, if given in infancy, should be repeated in maturity, and that still better it should be deferred, as by John the Baptist, till the mature recipient could knowingly and voluntarily make his profession of the Christian faith. There were sects within this sect. Those who followed Hans Denck and Ludwig Hätzer denied the divinity of Christ: He was only the most godly of men, Who had redeemed us not by His agony on the cross but by the example of His life.[47] Denck exalted the individual conscience above the Church, the state, and the Bible itself. Most Anabaptists adopted a Puritan severity of morals and simplicity of manners and dress. Developing with rash logic Luther's idea of Christian liberty, they condemned all government by force, and all resistance to it by force. They rejected military service on the ground that it is invariably sinful to take human life. Like the early Christians, they refused to swear oaths, not excepting oaths of allegiance to prince or emperor. Their usual salutation was "The peace of the Lord be with you"—an echo of the Jewish and Moslem greeting, and a forerunner of the Quaker mode. While Luther, Zwingli, Calvin, and Knox agreed with the popes on the absurdity of religious toleration, the Anabaptists preached and practiced it; one of them, Balthasar Hübmaier, wrote the first clear defense of it (1524).[48] They shunned public office and all resort to litigation. They were Tolstoyan anarchists three centuries before Tolstoy, and a century after Peter Chelčicky, from whom they may have derived their creed. Consciously or unwittingly inheriting the doctrine of the Bohemian Taborites or the Moravian Brethren, some Anabaptists proclaimed a community of goods; [49] a few, if we may credit hostile chroniclers, proposed a community of wives.[50] In general, however, the sect rejected any compulsory sharing of goods, advocated voluntary mutual aid, and held that in the Kingdom of Heaven communism would be automatic and universal.[51] All the Anabaptist groups were inspired by the Apocalypse and the confident expectation of Christ's early return to the earth; many believers professed to know the day and hour of His coming. Then all the ungodly—in this case all but Anabaptists—would be swept away by the sword of the Lord, and the elect would live in glory in a terrestrial paradise without laws or marriage, and abounding in all good things.[52] So hopeful men steeled themselves against toil and monogamy.

The Anabaptists appeared first in Switzerland. Perhaps a pacifistic Christianity had seeped in from the Waldenses of southern France and the Beghards of the Netherlands. Here and there, as in Basel, a few intellectuals sponsored the idea of a communistic society. Communistic passages in More's *Utopia* may have stirred the scholars who gathered around Erasmus there. Three members of that circle became Anabaptist leaders: Conrad Grebel and Felix Manz of Zurich, and Balthasar Hübmaier of Waldshut—just across the border in Austria. In 1524 Münzer visited Waldshut, Carlstadt came to Zurich, and an Anabaptist sect formed in Zurich under the name of "Spirituals" or "Brethren." It preached adult baptism and the coming of Christ, rejected Church and state, and proposed an end to interest charges, taxes, military service, tithes, and oaths.

At this time Ulrich Zwingli was winning the Great Council of Zurich to his Protestant views, which included the control of religion by the secular authorities. He pleaded with the "Brethren" to relax their antipathy to the state, and to practice infant baptism; they refused. The Council summoned them to a public disputation (January 17, 1525); failing to convert them, it decreed that the parents of unbaptized children must leave the town. The Anabaptists denounced the Council, called Zwingli an old dragon, and paraded the streets crying, "Woe to Zurich!"[53] Their leaders were arrested and banished, which enabled them to spread their doctrines. Saint-Gall and Appenzell took up the movement; Bern and Basel were stirred by it; Hübmaier won nearly all Waldshut to his views. In Appenzell 1,200 men and women, accepting literally the words of Christ—"Take no thought what ye shall eat"—sat down and waited for God to come and feed them.[54]

The apparent success of the Peasants' War in the spring of 1525 promoted these conversions, but its failure encouraged the propertied classes in the Swiss cities to repressive measures. The Council of Zurich arrested Manz (July), then Grebel, then Hübmaier, and ordered that all obstinate Anabaptists "should be laid in the tower," kept on bread and water, and "left to die and rot."[55] Grebel did; Manz was drowned; Hübmaier recanted. was freed, recanted his recantation, and undertook to convert Augsburg and Moravia; Hätzer was beheaded at Constance for Anabaptism and adultery. Protestant and Catholic cantons showed equal energy in subduing the sect, and by 1530 nothing remained of it in Switzerland except some secret and negligible bands.

Meanwhile the movement had spread like a rumor through South Germany. A zeal for evangelistic propaganda caught the converts, and turned them into ardent missionaries for the new creed. In Augsburg Denck and Hübmaier made rapid headway among the textile workers and the lower middle class. In Tirol many miners, contrasting their poverty with the wealth of the Fuggers and Hochstetters who owned the mines, took up Anabaptism when the Peasants' Revolt collapsed. In Strasbourg the struggle between Catholics and Protestants allowed the sect to multiply unnoticed for a time. But a pamphlet of 1528 warned the authorities that "he who teaches that all things are" to be "in common has naught else in mind than to excite the poor against the rich, the subjects against the rulers ordained by God." [56] In that year Charles V issued a mandate making rebaptism a capital crime. The Diet of Speyer (1529) ratified the Emperor's edict, and ordered that Anabaptists everywhere were to be killed like wild beasts as soon as taken, without judge or trial. An Anabaptist chronicler, perhaps exaggerating, reported the result in the mood of early Christian hagiographers:

> Some were racked and drawn asunder; others were burnt to ashes and dust; some were roasted on pillars or torn with red-hot pincers. ... Others were hanged on trees, beheaded with the sword, or thrown into the water. . . . Some starved or rotted in darksome prisons. . . . Some who were deemed too young for execution were whipped with rods, and many lay for years in dungeons. . . . Numbers had holes burnt into their cheeks. . . . The rest were hunted from one country and place to another. Like owls and ravens, which durst not fly by day, they were often compelled to hide and live in rocks and clefts, in wild forests, or in caves and pits. [57]

By 1530, says the contemporary Sebastian Franck, 2,000 Anabaptists had been put to death. In one Alsatian city, Ensisheim, 600 were executed. In Salzburg those who recanted were allowed to have their heads cut off before being placed upon the pyre; the unrepentant were roasted to death over a slow fire (1528). [58] Anabaptists composed touching hymns to commemorate these martyrdoms; and most of the hymn writers became martyrs in their turn.

Despite these killings the sect increased, and moved into northern Germany. In Prussia and Württemberg some nobles welcomed the Anabaptists as peaceful and industrious farmers. In Saxony, says an early Lutheran historian, the valley of the Werra was filled with them, and in Erfurt they claimed to have sent forth 300 missionaries to convert the dying world. In Lübeck, Jürgen Wullenwever, who was accused of Anabaptism, briefly captured control of the city (1533–34). In Moravia, Hübmaier made progress with his moderate doctrine, which explained communism not as "common property," but as holding that "one should feed the hungry, give drink to the thirsty, and clothe the naked, for in truth we are not masters of our possessions, but stewards or dispensers only." [59] Hans Hut, fired by the teachings of Münzer, won the Anabaptists of Moravia away from Hübmaier by preaching a full community of goods. Hübmaier retired to Vienna, where he was burned at the stake, and his wife was thrown bound into the Danube (1528).

Hut and his followers established a communist center at Austerlitz, where, as if foreseeing Napoleon, they renounced all military service, and denounced every kind of war. Confining themselves to tillage and petty industry, these Anabaptists maintained their communism for almost a century. The nobles who owned the land protected them as enriching the estates by their conscientious toil. Farming was communal among them; materials for agriculture and handicraft were bought and allotted by communal officers; part of the proceeds was paid to the landlord as rent, the rest was distributed according to need. The social unit was not the family but the *Haushabe*, or household, containing some 400 to 2,000 persons, with a common kitchen, a common laundry, a school, a hospital, and a brewery. Children, after weaning, were brought up in common, but monogamy remained. In the Thirty Years' War, by an Imperial edict of 1622, this communistic society was suppressed; its members accepted Catholicism or were banished. Some of the exiles went to Russia, some to Hungary. We shall hear of them again.

In the Netherlands Melchior Hofmann, a Swabian tanner, preached the Anabaptist gospel with exciting success. At Leyden his pupil Jan Matthys rose to the conclusion that the advent of the New Jerusalem could no longer be patiently awaited, but must be achieved at once, and, if necessary, by force. He sent out through Holland twelve apostles to announce the glad tidings. The ablest of them was a young tailor, Jan Beuckelszoon, known to history as John of Leyden, and to Meyerbeer's opera as *Le Prophète*. Without formal education, he had a keen mind, a vivid imagination, a handsome presence, a ready tongue, a resolute will. He wrote and staged plays, and composed poetry. Coming upon the writings of Thomas Münzer, he felt that all other forms of Christianity than that which had gained and lost Mühlhausen were halfhearted and insincere. He heard Jan Matthys and was won to Anabaptism (1533). He was then twenty-four. In that year he accepted a fatal invitation to come and preach in Münster, the rich and populous capital of Westphalia.

Named from the monastery around which it had grown, Münster was feudally subject to its bishop and cathedral chapter. Nevertheless the growth of industry and commerce had generated a degree of democracy. The assembled citizens, representing seventeen guilds, annually chose ten electors, who chose the city council. But the well-to-do minority provided most of the political ability, and naturally dominated the council. In 1525, enthusiastic over the peasants' uprisings, the lower classes presented thirty-six "demands" to the council. A few of these were granted, the rest were humored with procrastination. A Lutheran preacher, Bernard Rottman, made himself the mouthpiece of discontent, and asked Jan Matthys to send some Dutch Anabaptists to his aid. John of Leyden came (January 13, 1534), and soon Jan Matthys himself. Fearing insurrection, the "party of order" arranged to have Bishop Franz von Waldeck enter the town with his 2,000 troops. The populace, led by Matthys, Rottman, and John of Leyden, fought them in the streets, drove them out, and took martial control of Münster (February 10, 1534). New elections were held; the Anabaptists won the council; two of their number, Knipperdollingk and Kippenbroick, were chosen burgomasters; the exciting experiment began.

Münster found itself at once in a state of war, besieged by the Bishop and his reinforced army, and fearful that soon all the powers of order and custom in Germany would unite against it. To protect itself against internal opposition, the new council decreed that all non-Anabaptists must accept rebaptism or leave the city. It was a cruel measure, for it meant that old men, women carrying infants, and barefoot children had to ride or trudge from the town at the height of a German winter. During the siege both sides executed without mercy any persons found working for the enemy. Under the stress of war the council was superseded by a popular assembly and an executive Committee of Public Safety, in both of which the religious leaders were supreme. Matthys died fighting in an abortive sortie (April 5, 1534), and thereafter John of Leyden ruled the city as its king.

The "communism" that was now set up was a war economy, as perhaps all strict communism must be; for men are by nature unequal, and can be induced to share their goods and fortunes only by a vital and common danger; internal liberty varies with external security, and communism breaks under the tensions of peace. In peril of their lives if they fell short of unity, inspired by religious faith and inescapable eloquence, the besieged accepted a "socialist theocracy" [60] in the desperate hope that they were realizing the New Jerusalem visioned in the Apocalypse. The members of the Committee of Public Safety were called "the elders of the twelve tribes of Israel," and John of Leyden became "King of Israel." Perhaps to give, in the minds of the simple, some helpful dignity to his precarious office, John, along with his aides, clothed himself in the splendid garments left behind by wealthy exiles. Enemies further accused the radical chiefs of eating abundantly while the besieged population neared starvation; the evidence is inconclusive, and leaders always feel an urgent obligation to keep well. Most of the confiscated luxuries were distributed among the people; "the poorest among us," wrote one of them, "now go about sumptuously attired"; [61] they hungered in magnificence.

Otherwise the communism of Münster was limited and tentative. The rulers, according to a hostile witness, decreed that "all possessions should be in common," [62] but in truth private property continued in practically everything except jewels, precious metals, and the booty of war. Meals were taken in common, but only by those engaged in defense of the town. At these meals a chapter was read from the Bible, and sacred songs were sung. Three "deacons" were appointed to supply the necessities of the poor; and to secure materials for these charities the remaining well-to-do were persuaded or compelled to yield up their superfluity. Land available for cultivation within the city was assigned to each household according to its size. One edict confirmed the traditional dominion of the husband over the wife. [63]

Public morals were regulated by strict laws. Dances, games, and religious plays were encouraged, under supervision, but drunkenness and gambling were severely punished, prostitution was banned, fornication and adultery were made capital crimes. An excess of women, caused by the flight of many men, moved the leaders to decree, on the basis of Biblical precedents, that unattached women should become "companions of wives"—in effect, concubines. [64] The newly attached women seem to have accepted the situation as preferable to solitary barrenness. Some conservatives in the city protested, organized a revolt, and imprisoned the King; but their soldiers, soon besotted with wine, were slaughtered by the resurgent Anabaptist soldiery; and in this victory of the New Jerusalem the women played a virile role. John, released and re-enthroned, took several wives and (say the hostile chroniclers) governed with violence and tyranny. [65] He must have had some genial qualities, for thousands gladly bore his rule, and offered their lives in his service. When he called for volunteers to follow him in a sortie against the Bishop's camp, more women enlisted than he thought it wise to use. When he asked for "apostles" to venture forth and seek aid from other Anabaptist groups, twelve men tried to get through the enemy's lines, were all caught, and all killed. One fervent woman, inspired by the story of Judith, sallied out to assassinate the Bishop; she was intercepted and put to death.

Though many Anabaptists in Germany and Holland repudiated the resort of their Münster brethren to force, many more applauded the revolution. Cologne, Trier, Amsterdam, and Leyden murmured with Anabaptist prayers for its success. From Amsterdam fifty vessels sailed (March 22 and 25, 1535) to carry reinforcements to the beleaguered city, but all were dispersed by the Dutch authorities. On March 28, echoing the Münster uprising, an Anabaptist band captured and fortified a monastery in West Friesland; it was overcome with a loss of 800 lives.

Confronted with this spreading revolt, the conservative forces of the Empire, Protestant as well as Catholic, mobilized to suppress Anabaptism everywhere. Luther, who in 1528 had counseled lenience with the new heretics, advised in 1530 "the use of the sword" against them as "not only blasphemous but highly seditious"; [66] and Melanchthon concurred. City after city sent money or men to the Bishop; a diet at Worms (April 4, 1535) ordered a tax on all Germany to finance the siege. The Bishop was now able to surround the town and effectively shut off all its supplies.

Facing famine and deteriorating morale. King John announced that all who wished might leave the city. Many women and children, and some men, seized the opportunity. The men were imprisoned or killed by the Bishop's soldiers, who spared the women for divers services. One of the émigrés saved his life by offering to show the besiegers an undefended part of the walls. Under his guidance a force of Landsknechts scaled them and opened a gate (June 24); soon several thousand troops poured into the town. Starvation had so far done its work that only 800 of the besieged could still bear arms. They barricaded themselves in the market place; then they surrendered on a promise of a safe-conduct to leave Münster; when they had yielded up their arms they were massacred en masse. Houses were searched, and 400 hidden survivors were slain. John of Leyden and two of his aides were bound to stakes; every part of their bodies was clawed with red-hot pincers, until "nearly all who were standing in the market place were sickened by the stench"; their tongues were pulled from their mouths; at last daggers were driven into their hearts. [67]

The Bishop regained his city and augmented his former power; henceforth all actions of the civil authorities were to be subject to episcopal veto. Catholicism was triumphantly restored. Throughout the Empire the Anabaptists, fearing for their lives, repudiated every member guilty of using force. Nevertheless many of these pacifist heretics were executed. Melanchthon and Luther advised Philip of Hesse to put to death all adherents of the sect. [68] The conservative leaders felt that so serious a threat to the established economic and political order should be punished with an unforgettable severity.

The Anabaptists accepted the lesson, postponed communism to the millennium, and resigned themselves to the practice of such of their principles—of sober, simple, pious, peaceful living—as did not offend the state. Menno Simons, a Catholic priest converted to Anabaptism (1531), gave to his Dutch and German followers such skillful guidance that the "Mennonites" survived all tribulations, and formed successful agricultural communities in Holland, Russia, and America. There is no clear filiation between the Continental Anabaptists and the English Quakers and the American Baptists; but the

Quaker rejection of war and oaths, and the Baptist insistence on adult baptism probably stem from the same traditions of creed and conduct that in Switzerland, Germany, and Holland took Anabaptist forms.[69] One quality nearly all these groups had in common—their willingness to bear peaceably with faiths other than their own. The theology that supported them through hardship, poverty, and martyrdom hardly accords with our transient philosophy; but they, too, in their sincerity, devotion, and friendliness, enriched our heritage, and redeemed our tarnished humanity.*

---

* A branch of the Anabaptists migrated (1719) from Germany to Pennsylvania, and settled in or near Germantown, Philadelphia; these "Dunkers" now number some 200,000. In 1874 many Anabaptists of Moravian descent left Russia and settled in South Dakota and Alberta. In eastern Pennsylvania the "Amish" Mennonites—named from a seventeenth-century leader, Jakob Amen—still officially reject razors, buttons, railroads, automobiles, motion pictures, newspapers, even tractors, but their farms are among the tidiest and most prosperous in America. The world total of Mennonites in 1949 was 400,000.[70]

CHAPTER XVIII

Zwingli: The Reformation in Switzerland

1477-1531

I. MULTUM IN PARVO

THE success of the Swiss cantons in repelling the assault of Charles the Bold (1477) strengthened their Confederation, fired their pride of nationality, and steeled them to withstand the attempt of Maximilian to subject them in fact as well as in theory to the Holy Roman Empire. Disputes over the division of the spoils after the defeat of Burgundy brought the cantons close to civil war; but at the Diet of Stans (1481) a hermit philosopher, Nikolaus von der Flüe—Bruder Klaus in Swiss memory—persuaded them to peace.

Canton by canton the sturdy Confederation grew. Fribourg and Solothurn were admitted in 1481, Basel and Schaffhausen in 1501, Appenzell in 1513; now they were thirteen, all speaking German dialects, except that French too was spoken in Fribourg and Bern. They formed a federal republic: each canton regulated its internal affairs, but was governed in its external relations by a common legislature. The single chamber of this federal diet was composed of an equal number of deputies from each canton. Democracy was not complete; several cantons appropriated minor communities as voteless vassals. Nor was Switzerland as yet a model lover of peace. In 1500-12 the cantons took advantage of Italian disruption to seize Bellinzona, Locarno, Lugano, and other regions south of the Alps; and they continued to lease Swiss legions—with their consent—to foreign powers. But after the defeat of the Swiss pikemen at Marignano (1515) the Confederation renounced territorial expansion, adopted a policy of neutrality, and directed its virile peasantry, its skillful artisans, and its resourceful merchants in developing one of the most civilized civilizations in history.

The Church was as genial and corrupt in Switzerland as in Italy. She gave patronage and considerable freedom to the humanists who gathered around Froben and Erasmus at Basel. It was part of the moral tolerance of the age that most Swiss priests enjoyed the services of concubines.[1] One Swiss bishop charged his clergy four guilders for every child born to them, and in one year garnered 1522 guilders from this source.[2] He complained that many priests gambled, frequented taverns, and got drunk[3]—apparently without paying an episcopal fee. Several cantons—Zurich in particular—set up civic supervision of churchmen and taxed monastic properties. The bishop of Constance claimed all Zurich as his feudal fief, and demanded of it obedience and tithes; but the papacy was too enmeshed in Italian politics to support his claims effectively. In 1510 Pope Julius II, in return for some Genevese legions, agreed that the town council of Geneva should regulate the monasteries, convents, and public morals within its domain.[4] So, seven years before Luther's theses, the essence of the Reformation was achieved in Zurich and Geneva—the supremacy of secular over ecclesiastical authority. The path was cleared for Zwingli and Calvin to establish their diverse mergers of Church and state.

II. ZWINGLI

A visit to the birthplace of Huldreich or Ulrich Zwingli suggests the not invariable rule that great men are born in small houses. The most rational and unsuccessful of the Reformers began life (January 1, 1484) in a tiny cottage in the mountain valley village of Wildhaus, fifty miles southeast of Zurich, in the present canton of Saint-Gall. A low gable roof, walls of heavy boards, little mullioned windows, floors of massive planks, low ceilings, dark rooms, creaking stairs, sturdy beds of oak, a table, a chair, a shelf for books: this historic home bespeaks an environment in which natural selection was rigorous, and supernatural selection seemed an indispensable hope. Ulrich's father was chief magistrate in that hidden hamlet, and his mother was the proud sister of a priest. He was the third of eight sons, who competed for the admiration of two sisters. From his boyhood he was destined for the priesthood.

His uncle, dean of the church at near-by Wesen, shared with his parents in his education, and gave Zwingli a humanistic bent and breadth that sharply distinguished him from Luther and Calvin. At ten the boy was sent to a Latin school at Basel; at fourteen he entered at Bern a college headed by an outstanding native classicist; from sixteen to eighteen he studied in the University of Vienna in its humanist heyday under Conrad Celtes. He lightened his labors by playing on the lute, harp, violin, flute, and dulcimer. At eighteen he returned to Basel, and took theology under Thomas Wyttenbach, who, as early as 1508, attacked indulgences, clerical celibacy, and the Mass. At twenty-two (1506) Zwingli received his master's degree, and was ordained priest. He celebrated his first Mass at Wildhaus amid joyful relatives, and, with a hundred guilders raised for him, bought appointment[5] to a pastorate in Glarus, twenty miles away.

There, while zealously performing his duties, he continued his studies. He taught himself Greek to read the New Testament in the original. He read with enthusiasm Homer, Pindar, Democritus, Plutarch, Cicero, Caesar, Livy, Seneca, Pliny the Younger, Tacitus, and wrote a commentary on the skeptical humorist Lucian. He corresponded with Pico della Mirandola and Erasmus, called Erasmus "the greatest philosopher and theologian," visited him reverently (1515), and read him every night as a prelude to sleep. Like Erasmus, he grew a sharp nose for ecclesiastical corruption, a genial scorn for doctrinal bigotry, and an ardent refusal to think of the classical philosophers and poets as burning in hell. He vowed that he "would rather share the eternal lot of a Socrates or a Seneca than that of a pope." [6] He did not let his sacerdotal vows exclude him from the pleasures of the flesh; he had some affairs with generous women, and continued so to indulge himself until his marriage (1514). His congregation did not seem to mind, and the popes paid him, till 1520, an annual pension of fifty florins for supporting them against the pro-French party in Glarus. In 1513 and 1515 he accompanied the Glarus contingent of Swiss mercenaries to Italy as their chaplain, and did his best to keep them faithful to the papal cause; but his contact with war at the battles of Navarro and Marignano turned him strongly against any further sale of Swiss valor to foreign governments.

In 1516 the French faction in Glarus won the upper hand, and Zwingli moved to a pastorate at Einsiedeln in the canton of Schwyz. His preaching there took a Protestant tinge even before Luther's rebellion. In 1517 he called for a religion based exclusively on the Bible, and he told his archbishop, Cardinal Matthäus Schinner, that there was scant warrant in Scripture for the papacy. In August 1518, he attacked abuses in the sale of indulgences, and persuaded Benedictine monks to remove, from their lucrative shrine of the Virgin, an inscription promising pilgrims "full remission of all sins in guilt and punishment alike." [7] Some pilgrims from Zurich brought to their pastors an enthusiastic report of his preaching. On December 10, 1518, he accepted a call to be vicar or "people's priest" at the Grossmünster, or Great Minster, of Zurich, the most enterprising city in Switzerland.

He was now approaching maturity in morals and mind. He undertook a series of sermons expounding, from the Greek text, all the New Testament except the Apocalypse, which he disliked; he had little in him of the mysticism that shared in forming Luther. We have no portrait of him from life, but his contemporaries described him as a handsome, ruddy-faced, full-blooded man, with a melodious voice that captured his congregation. He did not rival Luther in eloquence or exegesis; yet his sermons were so convincing in sincerity and clarity that soon all Zurich responded to his influence. His ecclesiastical superiors supported him when he resumed his campaign against the sale of indulgences. Bernhardin Samson, a Franciscan friar from Milan, had crossed the Saint Gotthard Pass in August 1518, to become the Tetzel of Switzerland. He offered Pope Leo's indulgence to the rich on parchment for a crown, to the poor on paper for a few pennies; and with a wave of his hand he absolved from the pains of purgatory all souls that had died in Bern. Zwingli protested; the bishop of Constance seconded him; and Leo X, learning something from events in Germany, recalled his lavish apostle.

In 1519 plague struck Zurich, taking a third of the population in half a year. Zwingli stayed at his post, toiled night and day in the care of the sick, caught the infection himself, and came close to death. When he recovered he was the most popular figure in Zurich. Distant dignitaries like Pirkheimer and Dürer sent him felicitations. In 1521 he was made head priest of the Grossmünster. He was now strong enough to proclaim openly the Reformation in Switzerland.

III. THE ZWINGLIAN REFORMATION

Almost unconsciously, but as a natural result of his unusual education, he had changed the character of the pastorate in his church. Before him the sermon had counted for little; Mass and communion had been nearly all the service; Zwingli made the sermon dominate the ritual. He became teacher as well as preacher; and as his confidence grew he drove home ever more forcefully his conviction that Christianity should be restored to its early simplicity of organization and worship. He was deeply stirred by Luther's revolt and writings, and by Huss's treatise *On the Church*. By 1520 he was publicly attacking monasticism, purgatory, and the invocation of saints; furthermore, he argued that the payment of tithes to the Church should be purely voluntary, as in Scripture. His bishop begged him to withdraw these statements; he persisted; and the cantonal council supported him by ordering all priests within its jurisdiction to preach only what they found in the Bible. In 1521 Zwingli persuaded the council to forbid the enlistment of Swiss soldiery by the French; a year later the prohibition was extended to all foreign powers; and when Cardinal Schinner continued to recruit Swiss troops for the pope, Zwingli pointed out to his congregation that the Cardinal wore a red hat not without reason, for "if it were wrung you would see the blood of your nearest kindred drip from its folds." [8] Finding no text in the Testament for the avoidance of meat in Lent, he allowed his parishioners to ignore the Church's rules for Lenten fasts. The bishop of Constance protested; Zwingli answered him in a book, *Archeteles* (beginning and end), which predicted a universal rebellion against the Church, and advised the prelates to imitate Caesar, fold their garments about them, and die with grace and dignity. With ten other priests he petitioned the bishop to end clerical immorality by allowing sacerdotal marriage (1522). He was at this time keeping Anna Reinhard as his mistress or secret wife. In 1524 he publicly married her, a year before Luther's marriage to Catherine von Bora.

This definite rupture with the Church was preceded by two disputations that recalled the Leipzig debate of Luther and Eck, and distantly echoed the Scholastic disputations of the medieval universities. As a semi-democratic republic, Switzerland was not shocked by Zwingli's suggestion that the differences between his views and those of his conservative opponents should receive an open and impartial hearing. The Great Council of Zurich, blithely assuming theological jurisdiction, invited the bishops to send representatives. They came in force, and altogether some 600 persons gathered for the exciting contest in the city hall (January 25, 1523).

Zwingli offered to defend sixty-seven theses.

1. All who say that the Gospel is nothing without the approbation of the Church err. . . .

15. In the Gospel the whole truth is clearly contained. . . .

17. Christ is the one eternal high priest. Those who pretend to be high priests resist, yea, set aside, the honor and dignity of Christ.

18. Christ, Who offered Himself once on the cross, is the sufficient and perpetual sacrifice for the sins of all believers. Therefore the Mass is no sacrifice, but a commemoration of the one sacrifice of the cross. . . .

24. Christians are not bound to any works which Christ has not commanded. They may eat at all times all kinds of food. . . .

28. Whatsoever God permits and has not forbidden is right. Therefore marriage is becoming to all men. . . .

34. The spiritual power so called [the Church] has no foundation in the Holy Scriptures and the teaching of Christ.

35. But the secular power is confirmed by the teaching and example of Christ (Luke, ii, 5; Matt., xxii, 21). . . .

49. I know of no greater scandal than the prohibition of lawful marriage to priests, while they are permitted, on payment of a fine, to have concubines. Shame! *(Pfui der Schande!)* . . .

57. The Holy Scripture knows nothing of a purgatory. . . .

66. All spiritual superiors should repent without delay, and set up the cross of Christ alone, or they will perish. The axe is laid to the root.[9]

Johann Faber, Vicar-General of the diocese of Constance, refused to discuss these propositions in detail, claiming that they should be laid before great universities or a general council of the Church. Zwingli thought this unnecessary; now that the New Testament was available in the vernaculars, all could have the Word of God to decide these issues; that was enough. The Council agreed; it declared Zwingli guiltless of heresy, and bade all

Zurich clergymen to preach only what they could establish by Scripture. Here, as in Lutheran Germany, the state took over the Church.

Most priests—their salaries being now guaranteed by the state—accepted the Council's order. Many of them married, baptized in the vernacular, neglected the Mass, and abandoned the veneration of images. A band of enthusiasts began indiscriminately to destroy pictures and statues in the churches of Zurich. Disturbed by the spread of violence, Zwingli arranged a second disputation (October 26, 1523), which was attended by 550 laymen and 350 clergymen. The outcome was an order of the Council that a committee including Zwingli should prepare a booklet of doctrinal instruction for the people, and that meanwhile all violence should cease. Zwingli rapidly composed *Eine kurze Christliche Einleitung*, which was sent to all the clergy of the canton. The Catholic hierarchy protested, and the Diet of the Confederation, meeting at Lucerne (January 26, 1524), seconded the protest, at the same time pledging itself to ecclesiastical reform. The Council ignored the protests.

Zwingli formulated his doctrine more amply in two Latin treatises: *De vera et falsa religione* (1525) and *Ratio fidei* (1530). He accepted the basic theology of the Church—a triune God, the Fall of Adam and Eve, the Incarnation, Virgin Birth, and Atonement; but he interpreted "original sin" not as a taint of guilt inherited from our "first parents," but as an unsocial tendency inherent in the nature of man.[10] He agreed with Luther that man can never earn salvation by good works, but must believe in the redeeming efficacy of Christ's sacrificial death. He agreed with Luther and Calvin on predestination: every event, and therefore every individual's eternal fate, has been foreseen by God, and must occur as so foreseen. But God has fated for damnation only those who reject the Gospel offered them. All children (of Christian parents) who die in infancy are saved, even if unbaptized, for they were too young to sin. Hell is real, but purgatory is "a figment . . . a lucrative business for its authors"; Scripture knows nothing of it.[11] The sacraments are not miraculous vehicles, but useful symbols, of divine grace. Auricular confession is unnecessary; no priest—only God—can forgive sin; but it is often beneficial to confide our spiritual troubles to a priest.[12] The Lord's Supper is no actual eating of the body of Christ, but a symbol of the union of the soul with God, and of the individual with the Christian community.

Zwingli kept the Eucharist as part of the Reformed service, and administered it in both bread and wine, but he offered it only four times a year. In that occasional celebration much of the Mass was retained, but it was recited in Swiss German by congregation and priest. During the remainder of the year the Mass was replaced by the sermon; the appeal of ritual to the senses and the imagination was subordinated to the appeal of discourse to the mind—a rash gamble on popular intelligence and the stability of ideas. Since an infallible Bible had now to substitute for an infallible Church as a guide to doctrine and conduct, Luther's German translation of the New Testament was adapted to the Swiss German dialect, and a corps of scholars and divines, led by the saintly Leo Jud, was commissioned to prepare a German version of the entire Bible. This was published by Christian Froschauer at Zurich in 1534, four years before Luther's better version appeared.

In faithful obedience to the Second Commandment, and signalizing the return of Protestant Christianity to its early Jewish traditions, the Zurich Council ordered the removal of all religious images, relics, and ornaments from the churches of the city; even the organs were banished, and the immense interior of the Grossmünster was left dismally bare, as it is today. Some of the images were absurd enough, some lent themselves so readily to superstition as to merit destruction; but some were sufficiently beautiful to make Zwingli's successor, Heinrich Bullinger, mourn their loss. Zwingli himself had a tolerant attitude toward images that were not worshiped as wonder-working idols,[13] but he condoned the demolition as a reproof to idolatry.[14] Village churches in the canton were allowed to keep their images if a majority of the congregation so desired. Catholics retained some civic rights, but were ineligible to public office. Attendance at Mass was punishable by a fine; eating fish instead of meat on Friday was forbidden by law.[15] Monasteries and nunneries (with one exception) were closed or turned into hospitals or schools; monks and nuns emerged from the cloister into marriage. Saints' days were abolished, and pilgrimages, holy water, and Masses for the dead disappeared. Though not all these changes were consummated by 1524, yet the Reformation was by that time far more advanced in Zwingli and Zurich than in Luther and Wittenberg; Luther then was still a celibate monk, and still said Mass.

In November 1524, Zurich formed a Privy Council (Heimliche Rath) of six members to prepare settlements of urgent or delicate problems of government. Between Zwingli and this Council a working compromise took form: he surrendered to it the regulation of ecclesiastical as well as secular affairs, and in both fields it followed his lead. Church and state in Zurich became one organization, of which Zwingli was unofficial head, and in which the Bible was accepted (like the Koran in Islam) as the first source and final test of law. In Zwingli, as later in Calvin, the Old Testament ideal of the prophet guiding the state was realized.

So quickly and completely successful in Zurich, Zwingli turned an acquisitive eye upon the Catholic cantons, and wondered whether all Switzerland might not be won to the new form of the old faith.

IV. ONWARD, CHRISTIAN SOLDIERS

The Reformation had split the Confederation, and seemed destined to destroy it. Bern, Basel, Schaffhausen, Appenzell, and the Grisons favored Zurich; the other cantons were hostile. Five cantons—Lucerne, Uri, Schwyz, Unterwalden, and Zug—formed a Catholic League to suppress all Hussite, Lutheran, and Zwinglian movements (1524). Archduke Ferdinand of Austria urged all Catholic states to united action, promised his aid, and doubtless hoped to restore the Hapsburg power in Switzerland. On July 16 all the cantons except Schaffhausen and Appenzell agreed to exclude Zurich from future federal diets. Zurich and Zwingli responded by sending missionaries into the Thorgau district to proclaim the Reformation. One of these was arrested; friends rescued him, and led a wild crowd that sacked and burned a monastery, and destroyed images in several churches (July 1524). Three of the leaders were executed, and a martial spirit rose on both sides. Erasmus, timid in Basel, was alarmed to see pious worshipers, aroused by their preachers, come out of church "like men possessed, with anger and rage painted on their faces . . . like warriors animated by their general to some mighty attack." [16] Six cantons threatened to leave the Confederation if Zurich were not chastised.

Zwingli, enjoying his new role of war leader, advised Zurich to increase its army and arsenal, to seek alliance with France, to build a fire behind Ferdinand by fomenting revolution in Tirol, and to promise Thorgau and Saint-Gall the properties of their monasteries in return for their support. To the Catholic League he offered peace on three conditions: that it yield to Zurich the famous abbey of St. Gall; that it renounce the Austrian alliance; and that it surrender to Zurich the Lucerne satirist Thomas Murner, who had written too pungently of the Reformers. The League scorned these terms. Zurich ordered its representatives in Saint-Gall to seize the abbey; they obeyed (January 28, 1529). In February the tension was raised by events in Basel.

The Protestant leader in that "Athens of Switzerland" was Johannes Hausschein, who had Hellenized his name, meaning house lamp, into Oecolampadius. He wrote Latin poetry at twelve, mastered Greek soon afterward, and rose to rank second only to Reuchlin as a Hebraist. In his pulpit at St. Martin's Church and in his chair of theology at the university, he made a name for himself as a reformer and moralist, humane in everything but religion. By 1521 he was attacking the abuses of the confessional, the doctrine of transubstantiation, the idolatry of the Virgin. In 1523 Luther acclaimed him. In 1525 he adopted the Zwinglian program, including the prosecution of Anabaptists. But he rejected predestination; *salus nostra ex Deo,* he taught, *perditio nostra ex nobis*—"Our salvation comes from God, our damnation from ourselves." [17] When the Basel Council, now predominantly Protestant, proclaimed freedom of worship (1528), Oecolampadius protested, and demanded the suppression of the Mass.

On February 8, 1529, 800 men, assembled in the church of the Franciscans, sent to the Council a demand that the Mass should be forbidden, that all Catholics should be dismissed from office, and that a more democratic constitution should be put in force. The Council deliberated. On the following day the petitioners came in arms to the market place. When by noon the Council had still reached no decision, the crowd moved into the churches with hammers and axes, and destroyed all discoverable religious images.[18] Erasmus described the affair in a letter to Pirkheimer:

> The smiths and workmen removed the pictures from the churches, and heaped such insults upon the images of the saints and the crucifix itself, that it is quite surprising there was no miracle, seeing how many always used to occur whenever the saints were even slightly offended. Not a statue was left either in the churches, or the vestibules, or the porches, or the monasteries. The frescoes were obliterated by means of a coating of lime. Whatever would burn was thrown into the fire, and the rest was pounded into fragments. Nothing was spared for love or money.[19]

The Council took the hint, and voted full abolition of the Mass. Erasmus, Beatus Rhenanus, and nearly all professors in the university left Basel. Oecolampadius, triumphant, survived the outbreak by only two years, dying soon after Zwingli's death.

In May 1529, a Protestant missionary from Zurich, attempting to preach in the city of Schwyz, was burned at the stake. Zwingli persuaded the Zurich Council to declare war. He drew up the plan of campaign, and led the canton's troops in person. At Kappel, ten miles south of Zurich, they were stopped by one man, Landemann Aebli of Glarus, who begged an hour's truce while he negotiated with the League. Zwingli suspected treachery, and favored immediate advance; he was overruled by his Bernese allies, and by his soldiers, who readily fraternized, across the cantonal and theological border, with the soldiers of the enemy. For sixteen days negotiations continued; finally the good sense of the Swiss prevailed, and the First Peace of Kappel was signed (June 24, 1529). The terms were a victory for Zwingli: the Catholic cantons agreed to pay an indemnity to Zurich, and to end their alliance with Austria; neither party was to attack the other because of religious differences; and in the "common lands" subject to two or more cantons the people were to decide, by a majority vote, the regulation of their religious life. Zwingli, however, was dissatisfied: he had demanded, and not received, freedom for Protestant preaching in Catholic cantons. He predicted an early rupture of the peace.

It lasted twenty-eight months. In the interim an effort was made to unite the Protestants of Switzerland and Germany. Charles V had patched up his quarrel with Clement VII; both were now free to join forces against the Protestants. But these were already a powerful political force. Half of Germany was Lutheran; many German cities—Ulm, Augsburg, Württemberg, Mainz, Frankfurt-am-Main, Strasbourg—had strong Zwinglian sympathies; and in Switzerland, though the rural districts were Catholic, most of the towns were Protestant. Obviously self-protection against the Empire and the papacy required Protestant unity. Only theology stood in the way.

Philip, Landgrave of Hesse, took the initiative by inviting Luther, Melanchthon, and other German Protestants to meet Zwingli, Oecolampadius, and other Swiss Protestants in his castle at Marburg, north of Frankfurt. On September 29, 1529, the rival factions met. Zwingli made generous concessions; he dispelled Luther's suspicion that he doubted the divinity of Christ; he accepted the Nicene Creed, and the dogma of original sin. But he would not withdraw his view of the Eucharist as a symbol and commemoration rather than a miracle. Luther chalked on the conference table the words ascribed to Christ—"This is my body"—and would admit none but a literal interpretation. On fourteen articles the parties signed an agreement; on the Eucharist they parted (October 3), and not amicably. Luther refused Zwingli's proffered hand, saying, "Your spirit is not our spirit"; he drew up a theological profession in seventeen articles, including "consubstantiation," and persuaded the Lutheran princes to reject alliance with any group that would not sign all seventeen.[20] Melanchthon agreed with his master. "We told the Zwinglians," he wrote, "that we wondered how their consciences would allow them to call us brethren when they held that our doctrine was erroneous";[21] here in one sentence is the spirit of the age. In 1532 Luther admonished Duke Albrecht of Prussia not to allow any Zwinglian in his territory, on pain of everlasting damnation. It was too much to ask of Luther that he should pass at one step from the Middle Ages into modernity; he had received too profound an impress of medieval religion to bear patiently with any repudiation of its fundamentals; he felt, like a good Catholic, that his world of thought would collapse, the whole meaning of life would fade away, if he lost any basic element of the faith in which he had been formed. Luther was the most medieval of modern men.

Crushed with this failure, Zwingli returned to a Zurich that was becoming restless under his dictatorship. Strict sumptuary laws were resented; trade was hampered by the religious differences among the cantons; artisans were dissatisfied with their still small voice in the government; and Zwingli's sermons, cluttered with politics, had lost their inspiration and charm. He felt the change so keenly that he asked the Council's leave to seek a pastorate elsewhere. He was prevailed upon to stay.

He gave much of his time now to writing. In 1530 he sent his *Ratio fidei* to Charles V, who gave no sign of receiving it. In 1531 he addressed to Francis I a *Christianae fidei brevis et clara expositio*. In this "brief and clear exposition of the Christian faith" he expressed his Erasmian conviction that a Christian, on reaching paradise, would find there many noble Jews and pagans: not only Adam, Abraham, Isaac, Moses, Isaiah . . . but Hercules, Theseus, Socrates, Aristides, Numa, Camillus, the Catos, the Scipios; "in short, there has not been any good man, nor any holy mind, nor any faithful soul, from the very beginning of the world even to its end, whom you will not see there with God. What could be imagined more joyful, pleasing, and noble, than this sight?" [22] This passage so shocked Luther that he concluded that Zwingli must have been a "heathen"; [23] and Bishop Bossuet, agreeing for once with Luther, quoted it to prove that Zwingli had been a hopeless infidel.[24]

On May 15, 1531, an assembly of Zurich and her allies voted to compel the Catholic cantons to allow freedom of preaching in their territory. When the cantons refused, Zwingli proposed war, but his allies preferred an economic blockade. The Catholic cantons, denied all imports, declared war. Again rival armies marched; again Zwingli led the way and carried the standard; again the armies met at Kappel (October 11, 1531)—the Catholics with 8,000 men, the Protestants with 1,500. This time they fought. The Catholics won, and Zwingli, aged forty-seven, was among the 500 Zurichers slain. His body was quartered and then burned on a pyre of dung.[25] Luther, hearing of Zwingli's death, pronounced it the judgment of heaven on a heathen,[26] and "a triumph for us." [27] "I wish from my heart," he is reported to have said, "that Zwingli could be saved, but I fear for the contrary, for Christ has said that those who deny Him shall be damned." [28]

Zwingli was succeeded in Zurich by Heinrich Bullinger, and at Basel Oswald Myconius carried on after Oecolampadius' death. Bullinger avoided politics, superintended the city's schools, sheltered fugitive Protestants, and dispensed charity to the needy of any creed. He approved the execution of Servetus, but, barring that, he approached a theory of general religious freedom. He joined with Myconius and Leo Jud in formulating the First Helvetic Confession (1536), which for a generation was the authoritative expression of Zwinglian views; and with Calvin he drew up the *Consensus Tigurinus* (1549), which brought the Zurich and Genevan Protestants into one "Reformed Church."

Despite that protective accord, Catholicism regained in later years much of its lost ground in Switzerland, partly through its victory at Kappel; theologies are proved or disproved in history by competitive slaughter or fertility. Seven cantons adhered to Catholicism—Lucerne, Uri, Schwyz, Zug, Unterwalden, Fribourg, and Solothurn; four were definitely Protestant—Zurich, Basel, Bern, and Schaffhausen; the rest remained poised between the two faiths, uncertain of their certainties. Zwingli's successor at Glarus, Valentin Tschudi, compromised by saying Mass in the morning for Catholics, and preaching an evangelical—purely Scriptural—sermon in the evening for the Protestants; he argued for mutual toleration, and was tolerated; he wrote a *Chronicle* so impartial that no one could tell from it which faith he favored. Even in that age there were Christians.

CHAPTER XIX

Luther and Erasmus

1517-36

I. LUTHER

HAVING summarized the economic, political, religious, moral, and intellectual conditions that cradled the Reformation, we must still count it among the wonders of history that in Germany one man should have unwittingly gathered these influences into a rebellion transforming a continent. We need not exaggerate the role of the hero here; the forces of change would have found another embodiment had Luther continued in his obedience. Yet the sight of this rough monk, standing in doubt and terror and immovable resolution against the most entrenched institutions and most hallowed customs of Europe, stirs the blood, and points again the distance that man has come from the slime or the ape.

What was he like, this lusty voice of his time, this peak of German history? In 1526, as pictured at forty-three by Lucas Cranach,[1] he was in transition from slender to stout; very serious, with only a hint of his robust humor; hair curly and still black; nose immense; eyes black and brilliant—his enemies said that demons shone in them. A frank and open countenance made him unfit for diplomacy. A later portrait (1532), also by Cranach, showed Luther cheerfully obese, with a broad, full face; this man enjoyed living. In 1524 he abandoned the monastic garb and dressed like a layman, sometimes in the robes of a teacher, sometimes in ordinary jacket and trousers. He was not above mending these himself; his wife complained that the great man had cut a piece out of his son's pantaloons to patch his own.

He had slipped into marriage by inadvertence. He agreed with St. Paul that it is better to marry than to burn, and proclaimed sex to be as natural and necessary as eating.[2] He retained the medieval notion that copulation is sinful even in marriage, but "God covers the sin."[3] He condemned virginity as a violation of the divine precept to increase and multiply. If "a preacher of the Gospel . . . cannot live chastely unmarried, let him take a wife; God has made that plaster for that sore."[4] He considered the human method of reproduction a bit absurd, at least in retrospect, and suggested that "had God consulted me in the matter, I should have advised Him to continue the generation of the species by fashioning human beings out of clay, as Adam was made." [5] He had the traditional and German conception of woman as divinely designed for childbearing, cooking, praying, and not much else. "Take women from their housewifery, and they are good for nothing." [6] "If women get tired and die of bearing, there is no harm in that; let them die as long as they bear; they are made for that." [7] The wife should give her husband love, honor, and obedience; he is to rule her, though with kindness; she must keep to her sphere, the home; but there she can do more with the children with one finger than the man with two fists. [8] Between man and wife "there should be no question of mine and thine"; all their possessions should be in common. [9]

Luther had the male's usual dislike for an educated woman. "I wish," he said of his wife, "that women would repeat the Lord's Prayer before opening their mouths." [10] But he despised writers who composed satires on women. "What defects women have we must check them for in private, gently . . . for woman is a frail vessel." [11] Despite his rough candor about sex and marriage he was not insensible to esthetic considerations. "The hair is the finest ornament women have. Of old, virgins used to wear it loose, except when they were in mourning. I like women to let their hair fall down their back; it is a most agreeable sight." [12] (This should have made him more lenient with Pope Alexander VI, who fell in love with Giulia Farnese's loosened hair.)

Apparently it was for no physical need that Luther married. In a burst of humor he said that he had married to please his father and spite the Devil and the pope. But he took a long time to make up his mind, and then it was made up for him. When, on his recommendation, some nuns left their convent, he undertook to find them husbands. Finally only one remained unmatched, Catherine von Bora, a woman of good birth and character, but hardly designed to arouse precipitate passion. She had set her sights on a young Wittenberg student of patrician stock; she failed to get him, and entered domestic service to keep alive. Luther suggested a Dr. Glatz as a husband; she replied that Glatz was unacceptable, but that Herr Amsdorf or Dr. Luther would do. Luther was forty-two, Catherine twenty-six; he thought the discrepancy prohibitive, but his father urged him to transmit the family name. On June 27, 1525, the ex-monk and the ex-nun became man and wife.

The Elector gave them the Augustinian monastery as a home, and raised Luther's salary to 300 guilders ($7,500) a year; later this was increased to 400, then to 500. Luther bought a farm, which Katie managed and loved. She bore him six children, and cared faithfully for them, for all Martin's domestic needs, for a home brewery, a fish pond, a vegetable garden, chickens, and pigs. He called her "my lord Katie," and implied that she could put him in his place when he forgot the biological subordination of man to woman; but she had much to bear from his occasional storms and his trustful improvidence; for he cared nothing for money, and was recklessly generous. He took no royalties for his books, though they made a fortune for his publisher. His letters to or about Catherine reveal his growing affection for her, and a generally happy marriage. He repeated in his own way what had been told him in his youth: "The greatest gift of God to man is a pious, kindly, God-fearing, home-loving wife." [13]

He was a good father, knowing as if by instinct the right mixture of discipline and love. "Punish if you must, but let the sugar-plum go with the rod." [14] He composed songs for his children, and sang these songs with them while he played the lute. His letters to his children are among the jewels of German literature. His sturdy spirit, which could face an emperor in war, was almost broken by the death of his favorite daughter Magdalena at the age of fourteen. "God," he said, "has given no bishop so great a gift in a thousand years as He has given me in her." [15] He prayed night and day for her recovery. "I love her very much, but, dear God, if it is Thy holy will to take her, I would gladly leave her with Thee." [16] And he said to her: "Lena dear, my little daughter, thou wouldst love to remain here with thy father; art thou willing to go to that other Father?" "Yes, dear father," Lena answered, "just as God wills." When she died he wept long and bitterly. As she was laid in the earth he spoke to her as to a living soul: "*Du liebes Lenichen*, you will rise and shine like the stars and the sun. How strange it is to know that she is at peace and all is well, and yet be so sorrowful!" [17]

Not content with six children, he took into his many-chambered monastery-home eleven orphaned nephews and nieces, brought them up, sat with them at table, and discoursed with them tirelessly; Catherine mourned their monopoly of him. Some of them made uncensored notes of his table talk; the resulting mass of 6,596 entries rivals Boswell's *Johnson* and Napoleon's recorded conversations in weight, wit, and wisdom. In judging Luther we should remember that he never edited these *Tischreden;* few men have been so completely exposed to the eavesdropping of mankind. Here, rather than in the controversies of the theological battlefield, is Luther *chez lui, en pantoufles*, at home, himself.

We perceive, first of all, that he was a man, not an inkwell; he lived as well as wrote. No healthy person will resent Luther's relish for good food and beer, or his fruitful enjoyment of all the comforts that Catherine Bora could give him. He might have been more prudently reticent on these points, but reticence came with the Puritans, and was unknown to Renaissance Italians as well as to Reformation Germans; even the delicate Erasmus shocks us with his candid physiological speech. Luther ate too much, but he could punish himself with long fasts. He drank too much, and deplored drinking as a national vice; but beer was the water of life to the Germans, as wine to the Italians and the French; water could literally be poison in those careless days. Yet we never hear of his overstepping exuberance into intoxication. "If God can forgive me for having crucified Him with Masses twenty years running, he can also bear with me for occasionally taking a good drink to honor Him." [18]

His faults leaped to the eye and the ear. Proud amid his constant expressions of humility, dogmatic against dogma, intemperate in zeal, giving no quarter of courtesy to his opponents, clinging to superstitions while laughing at superstition, denouncing intolerance and practicing it—here was no paragon of consistency or Grandison of virtue, but a man as contrary as life and scorched with the powder of war. "I have not been slow to bite my adversaries," he confessed, "but what is the good of salt if it does not bite?" [19] He spoke of papal decrees as *Dreck*, dung; [20] of the pope as "the Devil's sow" or lieutenant, and as Antichrist; of bishops as "larvae," unbelieving hypocrites, "ignorant apes"; of sacerdotal ordination as marking a man with "the sign of the beast in the Apocalypse"; of monks as worse than hangmen or murderers, or, at best, "fleas on God Almighty's fur coat"; [21] we may surmise how his audiences enjoyed this hilarity. "The only portion of the human anatomy which the pope has had to leave uncontrolled is the hind end." [22] Of the Catholic clergy he wrote: "The Rhine is scarcely big enough to drown the whole accursed gang of Roman extortioners . . . cardinals, archbishops, bishops, and abbots"; [23] or, water failing, "may it please God to send down upon them the rain of fire and sulphur that consumed Sodom and Gomorrha." [24] One is reminded of the Emperor Julian's comment: "There is no wild beast like an angry theologian." [25] But Luther, like Clive, marveled at his own moderation.

> Many think I am too fierce against popery; on the contrary I complain that I am, alas, too mild; I wish I could breathe out lightning against pope and popedom, and that every wind were a thunderbolt.[26]. . . I will curse and scold the scoundrels until I go to my grave, and never shall they have a civil word from me. . . . For I am unable to pray without at the same time cursing. If I am prompted to say, "Hallowed be Thy name," I must add, "Cursed, damned, outraged be the name of papists." If I am prompted to say, "Thy Kingdom come," I must perforce add, "Cursed, damned, destroyed must be the papacy." Indeed, I pray thus orally every day and in my heart, without intermission.[27] . . . I never work better than when I am inspired by anger. When I am angry I can write, pray, and preach well, for then my whole temperament is quickened, my understanding sharpened.[28]

Such rhetorical passion was in the temper of the times. "Some of the preachers and pamphlet writers on the orthodox side," confesses the learned Cardinal Gasquet, "were Luther's match in this respect." [29] Vituperation was expected of intellectual gladiators, and was relished by their audiences; po-

liteness was suspected of cowardice. When Luther's wife reproached him
—"Dear husband, you are too rude"—he answered, "A twig can be cut with
a bread knife, but an oak calls for an axe"; [30] a soft answer could turn away
wrath, but could not overturn the papacy. A man mollified to refined speech
would have shrunk from so mortal a combat. It took a thick skin—thicker
than Erasmus'—to slough off papal excommunications and Imperial bans.

And it took a strong will. This was Luther's bedrock; hence his self-con-
fidence, dogmatism, courage, and intolerance. But he had some gentle virtues
too. In his middle years he was the height of sociability and cheerfulness, and
a pillar of strength to all who needed consolation or aid. He put on no airs,
assumed no elegances, never forgot that he was a peasant's son. He deprecated the publication of his collected works, begging his readers to study the
Bible instead. He protested against applying the name Lutheran to the
churches that followed his lead. When he preached he turned his speech to
the vocabulary and understanding of his hearers. His humor was rural—
rough, rollicking, Rabelaisian. "My enemies examine all that I do," he complained; "if I break wind in Wittenberg they smell it in Rome." [31] "Women
wear veils because of the angels; I wear trousers because of the girls." [32]
Many of us have committed such quips, but have not had such merciless
reporters. The same man who uttered them loved music this side of idolatry,
composed tender or thundering hymns, and set them—theological prejudice
for a moment stilled—to polyphonic strains already used in the Roman
Church. "I would not give up my humble musical gift for anything, however
great. . . . I am quite of the opinion that . . . next to theology, there is no art
which can be compared to music; for it alone, after theology, gives us . . .
rest and joy of heart." [33]

His theology led him to a lenient ethic, for it told him that good works
could not win salvation without faith in redemption by Christ, nor could
sin forfeit salvation if such faith survived. A little sin now and then, he
thought, might cheer us up on the straight and narrow path. Tired of seeing
Melanchthon wear himself thin with gloomy scruples about minor lapses
from sanctity, he told him, with full-blooded humor, *Pecca fortiter*—"Sin
powerfully; God can forgive only a hearty sinner," but scorns the anemic
casuist; [34] yet it would be absurd to rear an indictment of Luther on this
incidental raillery. One thing is clear: Luther was no puritan. "Our loving
God wills that we eat, drink, and be merry." [35] "I seek and accept joy wherever I can find it. We now know, thank God, that we can be happy with a
good conscience." [36] He advised his followers to feast and dance on Sunday.
He approved of amusements, played a good game of chess, called card-playing a harmless diversion for immature minds,[37] and said a wise word for
dancing: "Dances are instituted that courtesy may be learned in company,
and that friendship and acquaintance may be contracted between young men

and girls; here their intercourse may be watched, and occasion of honorable meeting given. I myself would attend them sometimes, but the youth would whirl less giddily if I did." [38] Some Protestant preachers wished to prohibit plays, but Luther was more tolerant: "Christians must not altogether shun plays because there are sometimes coarseness and adulteries therein; for such reasons they would have to give up the Bible too." [39] All in all, Luther's conception of life was remarkably healthy and cheerful for one who thought that "all natural inclinations are either without God or against Him," [40] and that nine of every ten souls were divinely predestined to everlasting hell.[41] The man was immeasurably better than his theology.

His intellect was powerful, but it was too clouded with the miasmas of his youth, too incarnadined with war, to work out a rational philosophy. Like his contemporaries, he believed in goblins, witches, demons, the curative value of live toads,[42] and the impish *incubi* who sought out maidens in their baths or beds and startled them into motherhood.[43] He ridiculed astrology but sometimes talked in its terms. He praised mathematics as "relying upon demonstrations and sure proofs"; [44] he admired the bold reach of astronomy into the stars, but, like nearly all his contemporaries, he rejected the Copernican system as contradicting Scripture. He insisted that reason should stay within the limits laid down by religious faith.

Doubtless he was right in his judgment that feeling, rather than thought, is the lever of history. The men who mold religions move the world; the philosophers clothe in new phrases, generation after generation, the sublime ignorance of the part pontificating about the whole. So Luther prayed while Erasmus reasoned; and while Erasmus courted princes Luther spoke to God —now imperiously, as one who had fought strenuously in the battles of the Lord and had a right to be heard, now humbly as a child lost in infinite space. Confident that God was on his side, he faced insuperable obstacles, and won. "I bear upon me the malice of the whole world, the hatred of the Emperor, of the Pope, and of all their retinue. Well, onward, in God's name!" [45] He had the courage to defy his enemies because he did not have the intellect to doubt his truth. He was what he had to be to do what he had to do.

II. THE INTOLERANT HERETICS

It is instructive to observe how Luther moved from tolerance to dogma as his power and certainty grew. Among the "errors" that Leo X, in the bull *Exsurge Domine*, denounced in Luther was that "to burn heretics is against the will of the Holy Spirit." In the *Open Letter to the Christian Nobility* (1520) Luther ordained "every man a priest," with the right to interpret the Bible according to his private judgment and individual light; [46] and added,

"We should vanquish heretics with books, not with burning."[47] In the essay
On Secular Authority (1522) he wrote:

> Over the soul God can and will let no one rule but Himself. . . .
> We desire to make this so clear that everyone shall grasp it, and that
> our *Junkers*, the princes and bishops, may see what fools they are
> when they seek to coerce the people . . . into believing one thing or
> another. . . . Since belief or unbelief is a matter of everyone's con-
> science . . . the secular power should be content to attend to its own
> affairs, and permit men to believe one thing or another as they are
> able and willing, and constrain no one by force. For faith is a free
> work, to which no one can be compelled. . . . Faith and heresy are
> never so strong as when men oppose them by sheer force, without
> God's word.[48]

 n a letter to Elector Frederick (April 21, 1524) Luther asked toleration
for Münzer and other of his own enemies. "You should not prevent them
from speaking. There must be sects, and the Word of God must face battle. . . . Let us leave in His hands the combat and free encounter of minds."
In 1528, when others were advocating the death penalty for Anabaptists, he
advised that unless they were guilty of sedition they should be merely banished.[49] Likewise, in 1530, he recommended that the death penalty for blasphemy should be softened to exile. It is true that even in these liberal years
he talked as if he wished his followers or God to drown or otherwise eliminate
all "papists"; but this was "campaign oratory," not seriously meant. In January 1521, he wrote: "I would not have the Gospel defended by violence or
murder"; and in June of that year he reproved the Erfurt students for attacking priests; however, he did not object to "frightening them" a bit to improve
their theology.[50] In May 1529, he condemned plans for the forcible conversion of Catholic parishes to Protestantism. As late as 1531 he taught that "we
neither can nor should force anyone into the faith."[51]

But it was difficult for a man of Luther's forceful and positive character
to advocate tolerance after his position had been made relatively secure. A
man who was sure that he had God's Word could not tolerate its contradiction. The transition to intolerance was easiest concerning the Jews. Till 1537
Luther argued that they were to be forgiven for keeping their own creed,
"since our fools, the popes, bishops, sophists, and monks, those coarse ass-
heads, dealt with the Jews in such a manner that any Christian would have
preferred to be a Jew. Indeed, had I been a Jew, and had seen such idiots and
dunderheads expound Christianity, I should rather have become a hog than
a Christian. . . . I would advise and beg everybody to deal kindly with the
Jews, and to instruct them in the Scripture; in such case we could expect
them to come over to us."[52] Luther may have realized that Protestantism was

in some aspects a return to Judaism, in its rejection of monasticism and clerical celibacy, its emphasis on the Old Testament, the Prophets, and the Psalms,
and its adoption (Luther himself excepted) of a sterner sexual ethic than that
of Catholicism. He was disappointed when the Jews made no corresponding
move toward Protestantism; and his hostility to the charging of interest
helped to turn him against Jewish moneylenders, then against Jews in general.
When Elector John expelled the Jews from Saxony (1537) Luther rejected
a Jewish appeal for his intercession. In his Table Talk he united "Jews and
papists" as "ungodly wretches . . . two stockings made of one piece of
cloth."[53] In his declining years he fell into a fury of anti-Semitism, denounced
the Jews as "a stiff-necked, unbelieving, proud, wicked, abominable nation,"
and demanded that their schools and synagogues should be razed with fire.

> And let whosoever can, throw brimstone and pitch upon them;
> if one could hurl hell-fire at them, so much the better. . . . And this
> must be done for the honor of Our Lord and of Christianity, so that
> God may see that we are indeed Christians. Let their houses also be
> shattered and destroyed. . . . Let their prayer books and Talmuds be
> taken from them, and their whole Bible too; let their rabbis be for-
> bidden, on pain of death, to teach henceforth any more. Let the streets
> and highways be closed against them. Let them be forbidden to prac-
> tice usury, and let all their money, and all their treasures of silver and
> gold be taken from them and put away in safety. And if all this be not
> enough, let them be driven like mad dogs out of the land.[54]

Luther should never have grown old. Already in 1522 he was outpapaling
the popes. "I do not admit," he wrote, "that my doctrine can be judged by
anyone, even by the angels. He who does not receive my doctrine cannot
be saved."[55] By 1529 he was drawing some delicate distinctions:

> No one is to be compelled to profess the faith, but no one must be
> allowed to injure it. Let our opponents give their objections and hear
> our answers. If they are thus converted, well and good; if not, let them
> hold their tongues and believe what they please. . . . In order to avoid
> trouble we should not, if possible, suffer contrary teachings in the
> same state. Even unbelievers should be forced to obey the Ten Com-
> mandments, attend church, and outwardly conform.[56]

Luther now agreed with the Catholic Church that "Christians require certainty, definite dogmas, and sure Word of God which they can trust to live
and die by."[57] As the Church in the early centuries of Christianity, divided
and weakened by a growing multiplicity of ferocious sects, had felt compelled to define her creed and expel all dissidents, so now Luther, dismayed
by the variety of quarrelsome sects that had sprouted from the seed of private judgment, passed step by step from toleration to dogmatism. "All men

now presume to criticize the Gospel," he complained; "almost every old doting fool or prating sophist must, forsooth, be a doctor of divinity." [58] Stung by Catholic taunts that he had let loose a dissolvent anarchy of creeds and morals, he concluded, with the Church, that social order required some cloture to debate, some recognized authority to serve as "an anchor of faith." What should that authority be? The Church answered, the Church, for only a living organism could adjust itself and its Scriptures to inescapable change. No, said Luther; the sole and final authority should be the Bible itself, since all acknowledge it to be the Word of God.

In the thirteenth chapter of Deuteronomy, in this infallible book, he found an explicit command, allegedly from the mouth of God, to put heretics to death: "Neither shalt thine eye pity him, neither shalt thou conceal him," even though it be "thy brother, or thy son, or the wife of thy bosom . . . but thou shalt surely kill him, thy hand shall be the first upon him to put him to death." On that awful warrant the Church had acted in annihilating the Albigensians in the thirteenth century; that divine imprecation had been made a certificate of authority for the burnings of the Inquisition. Despite the violence of Luther's speech he never rivaled the severity of the Church in dealing with dissent; but he proceeded, within the area and limits of his power, to silence it as peaceably as he could. In 1525 he invoked the aid of existing censorship regulations in Saxony and Brandenburg to stamp out the "pernicious doctrines" of the Anabaptists and the Zwinglians. [59] In 1530, in his commentary on the Eighty-second Psalm, he advised governments to put to death all heretics who preached sedition or against private property, and "those who teach against a manifest article of the faith . . . like the articles children learn in the creed, as, for example, if anyone should teach that Christ was not God but a mere man." [60] Sebastian Franck thought there was more freedom of speech and belief among the Turks than in the Lutheran states, and Leo Jud, the Zwinglian, joined Carlstadt in calling Luther another pope. We should note, however, that toward the end of his life Luther returned to his early feeling for toleration. In his last sermon he advised abandonment of all attempts to destroy heresy by force; Catholics and Anabaptists must be borne with patiently till the Last Judgment, when Christ will take care of them. [61]

Other reformers rivaled or surpassed Luther in hounding heresy. Bucer of Strasbourg urged the civil authorities in Protestant states to extirpate all who professed a "false" religion; such men, he said, are worse than murderers; even their wives and children and cattle should be destroyed. [62] The comparatively gentle Melanchthon accepted the chairmanship of the secular inquisition that suppressed the Anabaptists of Germany with imprisonment or death. "Why should we pity such men more than God does?" he asked, for he was convinced that God had destined all Anabaptists to hell. [63] He recommended that the rejection of infant baptism, or of original sin, or of the Real Presence of Christ in the Eucharist, should be punished as capital crimes.[64] He insisted on the death penalty for a sectarian who thought that heathens might be saved, or for another who doubted that belief in Christ as the Redeemer could change a naturally sinful into a righteous man.[65] He applauded, as we shall see, the execution of Servetus. He asked the state to compel all the people to attend Protestant religious services regularly.[66] He demanded the suppression of all books that opposed or hindered Lutheran teaching; so the writings of Zwingli and his followers were formally placed on the index of prohibited books in Wittenberg.[67] Whereas Luther was content with the expulsion of Catholics from regions governed by Lutheran princes, Melanchthon favored corporal penalties. Both agreed that the civil power was in duty bound to promulgate and uphold "the law of God"—i.e., Lutheranism.[68] Luther, however, counseled that where two sects existed in a state the minority should yield to the majority: in a predominantly Catholic principality the Protestants should yield and emigrate; in a prevailingly Protestant province the Catholics should give way and depart; if they resisted, they should be effectively chastised.[69]

The Protestant authorities, following Catholic precedents, accepted the obligation of maintaining religious conformity. At Augsburg (January 18, 1537) the town council issued a decree forbidding the Catholic worship, and banishing, after eight days, all who would not accept the new faith. At the expiration of the period of grace the council sent soldiers to take possession of all churches and monasteries; altars and statues were removed, and priests, monks, and nuns were banished.[70] Frankfurt-am-Main promulgated a similar ordinance; and the seizure of Catholic church properties, and the suppression of Catholic services, spread through the states controlled by Protestants.[71] Censorship of the press, already established in Catholic areas, was adopted by the Protestants; so Elector John of Saxony, at the request of Luther and Melanchthon, promulgated (1528) an edict that prohibited the publication, sale, or reading of Zwinglian or Anabaptist literature, or the preaching or teaching of their doctrines; "and anyone who is aware of such being done by anybody, whether a stranger or an acquaintance, must give information to the ... magistrates of the place, in order that the offender may be taken up in due time and punished. ... Those who are aware of such breeches of the orders ... and do not give information, shall be punished by loss of life or property."[72]

Excommunication, like censorship, was adopted by the Protestants from the Catholics. The Augsburg Confession of 1530 proclaimed the right of the Lutheran Church to excommunicate any member who should reject a fundamental Lutheran doctrine.[73] Luther explained that "although excommunication in popedom has been and is shamefully abused, and made a mere torment, yet we must not suffer it to fall, but make right use of it, as Christ commanded." [74]

III. THE HUMANISTS AND THE REFORMATION

The intolerant dogmatism of the Reformers, their violence of speech, their sectarian fragmentation and animosities, their destruction of religious art, their predestinarian theology, their indifference to secular learning, their renewed emphasis on demons and hell, their concentration on personal salvation in a life beyond the grave—all these shared in alienating the humanists from the Reformation. Humanism was a pagan reversion to classical culture; Protestantism was a pious return to gloomy Augustine, to early Christianity, even to Old Testament Judaism; the long contest between Hellenism and Hebraism was renewed. The humanists had made remarkable headway within the Catholic fold; in Nicholas V and Leo X they had captured the papacy; popes had not only tolerated but protected them, and had helped them to recover lost treasures of classic literature and art—all on the tacit understanding that their writings would be addressed, presumably in Latin, to the educated classes, and would not upset the orthodoxy of the people. Disturbed now in this cozy entente, the humanists found that Teutonic Europe cared less for them and their aristocratic culture than for the soul-warming talk of the new vernacular preachers about God and hell and individual salvation. They laughed at the passionate debates of Luther and Eck, Luther and Carlstadt, Luther and Zwingli, as battles over issues that they had thought long dead or courteously forgotten. They had no taste for theology; heaven and hell had become myths to them, less real than the mythology of Greece and Rome. Protestantism, as they saw it, was treason to the Renaissance, was restoring all the supernaturalism, irrationalism, and diabolism that had darkened the medieval mind; this, they felt, was not progress but reaction; it was the resubjection of the emancipated mind to the primitive myths of the populace. They resented Luther's vituperation of reason, his exaltation of a faith that was now to be dogmatically defined by Protestant popelets or potentates. And what remained of that human dignity which Pico della Mirandola had so nobly described, if everything that happened on the earth —every heroism, every sacrifice, every advance in human decency and worth —was merely the mechanical fulfillment, by helpless and meaningless men, of God's foreknowledge and inescapable decrees?

Humanists who had criticized, but never left, the Church—Wimpheling, Beatus Rhenanus, Thomas Murner, Sebastian Brant—now hastened to confirm their loyalty. Many humanists who had applauded Luther's initial rebellion as the wholesome correction of a shameful abuse drew away from him as Protestant theology and polemics took form. Willibald Pirkheimer, Hellenist and statesman, who had so openly supported Luther that he had been excommunicated in the first draft of the bull *Exsurge Domine*, was shocked by Luther's violence of speech, and dissociated himself from the revolt. In 1529, while still critical of the Church, he wrote:

> I do not deny that at the beginning all Luther's acts did not seem to be vain, since no good man could be pleased with all those errors and impostures that had accumulated gradually in Christianity. So, with others, I hoped that some remedy might be applied to such great evils; but I was cruelly deceived. For, before the former errors had been extirpated, far more intolerable ones crept in, compared with which the others seemed child's play. . . . Things have come to a pass that the popish scoundrels are made to appear virtuous by the Evangelical ones. . . . Luther, with his shameless, ungovernable tongue, must have lapsed into insanity, or been inspired by the Evil Spirit.[75]

Mutianus agreed. He had hailed Luther as the "morning star of Wittenberg"; soon he was complaining that Luther "had all the fury of a maniac." [76] Crotus Rubianus, who had opened a path for Luther by the *Letters of Obscure Men*, fled back to the Church in 1521. Reuchlin sent Luther a courteous letter, and prevented Eck from burning Luther's books in Ingolstadt; but he scolded his nephew Melanchthon for adopting the Lutheran theology, and he died in the arms of the Church. Johannes Dobenek Cochlaeus, at first for Luther, turned against him in 1522, and addressed to him a letter of reproach:

> Do you suppose that we wish to excuse or defend the sins and wickedness of the clergy? God save us!—we would far rather help you to root them out, as far as it can be done legitimately. . . . But Christ does not teach such methods as you are carrying on so offensively with "Antichrist," "brothels," "Devil's nests," "cesspools," and other unheard-of terms of abuse, not to speak of your threatenings of sword, bloodshed, and murder. O Luther, you were never taught this method of working by Christ! [77]

The humanists of Germany had perhaps forgotten the scurrility of their Italian predecessors—Filelfo, Poggio, and many more—which had set a pace for Luther's contumelious pen. But the style of Luther's warfare was only the surface of their indictment. They noted—as Luther noted—a deterioration of morals and manners in Germany, and ascribed it to the disruption of ecclesiastical authority, and the Lutheran discounting of "good works" as a merit for salvation. They were hurt by the Protestant derogation of learning, Carlstadt's equating of pundit and peasant, Luther's slighting of scholarship and erudition. Erasmus voiced the general view of the humanists—and here Melanchthon sadly concurred [78]—that wherever Lutheranism triumphed, letters (i.e., education and literature) declined.[79] The Protestants retorted that this was merely because learning, to the humanist, meant chiefly the study of pagan classics and history. For a generation the books and pamphlets of religious polemics so absorbed the mind and presses of Germany and Switzerland that nearly every other form of literature (except the satire) lost its audience. Publishing firms like Froben's in Basel and the Atlansee in Vienna found so few purchasers for the learned works that they had issued at great cost that they verged on bankruptcy.[80] Rival fanaticisms stifled the young German Renaissance, and the trend of Renaissance Christianity toward reconciliation with paganism came to an end.

Some humanists, like Eoban Hess and Ulrich von Hutten, remained faithful to the Reformation. Hess wandered from post to post, returned to Erfurt to find the university deserted (1533), and died professing poetry at Marburg (1540). Hutten, after the fall of Sickingen, fled to Switzerland, robbing for his food on the way.[81] Destitute and diseased, he sought out Erasmus at Basel (1522), though he had publicly branded the humanist as a coward for not joining the Reformers.[82] Erasmus refused to see him, alleging the inadequacy of his stove to warm Hutten's bones. The poet now composed *An Expostulation* denouncing Erasmus as a chicken-hearted renegade; he offered to withhold it from publication if Erasmus would pay him; Erasmus balked, and urged upon Hutten the wisdom of settling their differences peaceably. But Hutten had allowed the manuscript of his lampoon to circulate privately; it came to Erasmus' knowledge, and moved him to join the clergy of Basel in urging the city council to banish the irascible satirist. Hutten sent the *Expostulation* to the press, and moved to Mulhouse. There a mob gathered to attack his refuge; he fled again, and was taken in by Zwingli at Zurich (June 1533). "Behold," said the Reformer, here more humane than the humanist, "behold this destroyer, the terrible Hutten, whom we see so fond of the people and of children! This mouth, which blew storms upon the pope, breathes nothing but gentleness and goodness."[83] Meanwhile Erasmus replied to the *Expostulation* in a hastily written *Spongia Erasmi adversus aspergines Hutteni (Erasmus' Sponge on Hutten's Aspersions)*; and he wrote to the town council of Zurich protesting against the "lies" Hutten had told of him, and recommending the poet's banishment.[84] But Hutten was now dying; the war of ideas and the ravages of syphilis had exhausted him. He breathed his last (August 29, 1523) on an island in the Lake of Zurich, being thirty-five years old, and possessing nothing but his clothes and a pen.

IV. ERASMUS APPENDIX: 1517–36

The reaction of Erasmus to the Reformation provides a living debate among historians and philosophers. Which method was the better for mankind—Luther's direct attack upon the Church, or Erasmus' policy of peaceful compromise and piecemeal reform? The answers almost define two types of personality: "tough-minded" warriors of action and will, "tender-minded" compromisers given to feeling and thought. Luther was basically a man of action; his thoughts were decisions, his books were deeds. His thinking was early medieval in content, early modern in result; his courage and decisiveness, rather than his theology, co-operated with nationalism to establish the modern age. Luther spoke in masculinely vigorous German to the German people, and aroused a nation to overthrow an international power; Erasmus wrote in femininely graceful Latin for an international audience, a cosmopolitan elite of university graduates. He was too sensitive to be a man of action; he praised and longed for peace while Luther waged and relished war. He was a master of moderation, deprecating intemperance and extravagance. He fled from action into thought, from rash certainties into cautious doubt. He knew too much to see truth or error all on one side; he saw both sides, tried to bring them together, and was crushed in between.

He applauded Luther's Theses. In March 1518, he sent copies of them to Colet and More, and wrote to Colet: "The Roman Curia has cast aside all shame. What is more impudent than these indulgences?" [85] In October he wrote to another friend:

> I hear that Luther is approved by all good men, but it is said that his writings are unequal. I think his Theses will please all, except a few about purgatory, which they who make their living from it don't want taken from them. . . . I perceive that the monarchy of the Roman high priest (as that see now is) is the plague of Christendom, though it is praised through thick and thin by shameless preachers. Yet I hardly know whether it is expedient to touch this open sore, for that is the duty of princes; but I fear that they conspire with the pontiff for part of the spoils.[86]

For the most part Erasmus lived now in Louvain. He shared in founding at the university the *Collegium Trilingue*, with professorships in Latin, Greek, and Hebrew. In 1519 Charles V gave him a pension. Erasmus made it a condition of acceptance that he was to keep his independence of body and mind; but if he was human this pension, added to those that he was receiving from Archbishop Warham and Lord Mountjoy, must have played some part in molding his attitude toward the Reformation.

As Luther's revolt passed from criticism of indulgences to rejection of papacy and councils, Erasmus hesitated. He had hoped that Church reform could be advanced by appealing to the good will of the humanist pope. He still revered the Church as (it seemed to him) an irreplaceable foundation of social order and individual morality; and though he believed that the orthodox theology was shot through with nonsense, he had no trust in the wisdom of private or popular judgment to develop a more beneficent ritual or creed; the progress of reason could come only through the percolation of enlightenment from the instructed few to the emulous many. He acknowledged his share in opening a path for Luther; his own *Praise of Folly* was at that moment circulating by the thousands throughout Europe, pointing scorn at monks and theologians, and giving sharp point to Luther's blunt tirades. When the monks and theologians charged him with laying the egg that Luther hatched, he answered, wryly: "Yes, but the egg I laid was a hen, whereas Luther has hatched a gamecock." [87] Luther himself had read the *Praise of Folly*, and nearly everything else published by Erasmus, and he told his friends that he was merely giving more direct form to what the famous humanist had said or hinted for many years past. On March 18, 1519, he wrote to Erasmus humbly and reverently, soliciting his friendship and, by implication, his support.

Erasmus had now to make one of the pivotal decisions of his life, and either horn of the dilemma seemed fatal. If he renounced Luther he would be called a coward. If he associated himself with Luther in rejecting the Roman Church he would not merely forfeit three pensions and the protection that Leo X had given him against obscurantist theologians; he would have to abandon his own plan and strategy of Church reform through the improvement of minds and morals in influential men. Already he had (he thought) made real progress on this line with the Pope, Archbishop Warham, Bishop Fisher, Dean Colet, Thomas More, Francis I, Charles V. These men, of course, would never consent to renounce the Church; they would shrink from disrupting an institution which in their view was inextricably allied with princely government in maintaining social stability; but they could be enlisted in a campaign to reduce the superstitions and horrors in the prevailing cult, to cleanse and educate the clergy, to control and subordinate the monks, and to protect intellectual freedom for the progress of the mind. To exchange that program for a violent division of Christendom into warring halves, and for a theology of predestination and the unimportance of good works, would seem to these men, and seemed to Erasmus, the way to madness.

He hoped that peace might still be restored if all parties would lower their voices. In February 1519, he advised Froben to publish no more of Luther's works, as being too inflammatory.[88] In April he wrote to Elector Frederick encouraging him to protect Luther as more sinned against than sinning.[89] Finally (May 30) he answered Luther:

> Dearest brother in Christ, your epistle, showing the keenness of your mind and breathing a Christian spirit, was most pleasant to me.

I cannot tell you what a commotion your books are raising here. These men cannot by any means be disabused of the suspicion that your works are written by my aid, and that I am, as they call it, the standard-bearer of your party.... I have testified to them that you are entirely unknown to me, that I have not read your books, and neither approve nor disapprove of your writings, but that *they* should read them before they speak so loudly. I suggested, too, that the subjects on which you have written are not of a sort to be declaimed from pulpits, and that as your character was admitted to be spotless, denouncing and cursing were not precisely in place. It was of no use; they are as mad as ever.... I am myself the chief object of animosity. The bishops generally are on my side. . . .

For yourself, you have good friends in England, even among the greatest persons there. You have friends here too—me in particular. As to me, my business is with literature. I confine myself to it as far as I can, and keep aloof from other quarrels; but generally I think courtesy to opponents is more effective than violence. . . . It might be wiser of you to denounce those who misuse the Pope's authority than to censure the Pope himself. So also with kings and princes. Old institutions cannot be rooted up in an instant. Quiet argument may do more than wholesale condemnation. Avoid all appearance of sedition. Keep cool. Do not get angry. Do not hate anybody. Do not be excited over the noise you have made. I have looked into your *Commentary on the Psalms*, and am much pleased with it. . . . Christ give you His spirit, for His own glory and the world's good.[90]

Despite this cautious ambivalence the theologians of Louvain continued to attack Erasmus as the fountainhead of the Lutheran flood. On October 8, 1520, Aleander arrived, posted the papal bull excommunicating Luther, and scored Erasmus as a secret fomenter of the revolt. The pundits accepted Aleander's lead, and expelled Erasmus from the Louvain faculty (October 9, 1520). He moved to Cologne, and there, as we have seen, defended Luther in conference with Frederick of Saxony (November 5). On December 5 he sent to the Elector a statement known as the *Axiomata Erasmi*, to the effect that Luther's request to be tried by impartial judges was reasonable; that good men and lovers of the Gospel were those who had taken least offense at Luther; that the world was thirsting for evangelical truth (i.e., truth based solely on the Gospel); and that such a mood, so widely spread, could not be suppressed.[91] With the Dominican Johann Faber he composed a memorial to Charles V, recommending that Charles, Henry VIII, and Louis II of Hungary should appoint an impartial tribunal to try Luther's case. In a letter to Cardinal Campeggio (December 6) he urged justice for Luther:

I perceived that the better a man was, the less he was Luther's enemy. . . . A few persons only were clamoring at him in alarm for their own pockets. . . . No one has yet answered him or pointed out his faults. . . . How, while there are persons calling themselves bishops . . . whose moral character is abominable, can it be right to persecute a man of unblemished life, in whose writings distinguished and excellent persons have found so much to admire? The object has been simply to destroy him and his books out of mind and memory, and it can only be done when he is proved wrong. . . .

If we want truth, every man ought to be free to say what he thinks without fear. If the advocates of one side are to be rewarded with miters, and the advocates on the other with rope or stake, truth will not be heard. . . . Nothing could have been more invidious or unwise than the Pope's bull. It was unlike Leo X, and those who were sent to publish it only made things worse. It is dangerous, however, for secular princes to oppose the papacy, and I am not likely to be braver than princes, especially when I can do nothing. The corruption of the Roman court may require reform extensive and immediate, but I and the like of me are not called on to take a work like that upon themselves. I would rather see things left as they are than see a revolution that may lead to one knows not what. . . . You may assure yourself that Erasmus has been, and always will be, a faithful subject of the Roman See. But I think, and many will think with me, that there would be a better chance of a settlement if there were less ferocity, if the management should be placed in the hands of men of weight and learning, if the Pope would follow his own disposition and would not let himself be influenced by others.[92]

Luther made it more and more difficult for Erasmus to intercede for him, since with each month the violence of his speech increased, until in July 1520, he invited his readers to wash their hands in the blood of bishops and cardinals. When news came that Luther had publicly burned Leo's bull of excommunication, Erasmus confessed himself shocked. On January 15, 1521, the Pope sent him a letter expressing pleasure in his loyalty; at the same time Leo sent instructions to Aleander to treat the humanist with every courtesy. As the Diet of Worms approached, a German prince asked Erasmus to come to Luther's help, but he replied that it was too late. He regretted Luther's refusal to submit; such submission, he thought, would have furthered the movement for reform; now he feared civil war. In February 1521, he wrote to a friend:

Everyone confessed that the Church suffered under the tyranny of certain men, and many were taking counsel to remedy this state of affairs. Now this man has arisen to treat the matter in such a way . . . that no one dares to defend even what he has said well. Six months ago I warned him to beware of hatred. *The Babylonian Captivity* has alienated many from him, and he daily puts forth more atrocious things.[93]

Luther now abandoned hope of Erasmus' support, and put him aside as a cowardly pacifist who "thinks that all can be accomplished with civility and benevolence." [94] At the same time, and despite Leo's instructions, Aleander and the Louvain theologians continued to attack Erasmus as a secret Lutheran. Disgusted, he moved to Basel (November 15, 1521), where he hoped to forget the young Reformation in the old Renaissance. Basel was the citadel of Swiss humanism. Here labored Beatus Rhenanus, who edited Tacitus and Pliny the Younger, discovered Velleius Paterculus, and superintended the printing of Erasmus' New Testament. Here were printers and publishers who were also scholars, like Hans Amerbach and that saint among publishers, Johann Froben(ius), who wore himself out over his presses and texts, and (said Erasmus) "left his family more honor than fortune." [95] Here Dürer lived for years; here Holbein made breath-taking portraits of Froben and Bonifacius Amerbach—who gathered the art collection now in the Basel Museum. Seven years before, on an earlier visit, Erasmus had described the circle with fond exaggeration:

> I seem to be living in some charming sanctuary of the Muses, where a multitude of learned persons . . . appears as a matter of course. No one is ignorant of Latin, none of Greek; most of them know Hebrew. This one excels in the study of history, that one is deeply versed in theology, one is skilled in mathematics, another is a student of antiquity, another is learned in the law. Certainly up to this time it has never been my good fortune to live in such an accomplished society. . . . What a sincere friendship prevails among them all, what cheerfulness, what concord! [96]

Living with Froben, Erasmus acted as literary adviser, wrote prefaces, edited the Fathers. Holbein made famous portraits of him at Basel (1523–24). One is still there; another was sent to Archbishop Warham, and is now in the Earl of Radnor's collection; the third, in the Louvre, is Holbein's masterpiece. Standing at a table writing, wrapped in a heavy fur-trimmed coat, hooded with a beret covering half of each ear, the greatest of the humanists betrays in his premature age (he was now fifty-seven) the toll taken by ill health, a peripatetic life of controversy, and the spiritual loneliness and grief brought on by his attempt to be fair to both sides in the dogmatic conflicts of his time. Disheveled strays of white hair emerge from the beret. Grim, thin lips; features refined but strong; a sharp, ferreting nose; heavy eyelids almost closed on tired eyes; here, in one of the greatest of all portraits, is the Renaissance slain by the Reformation.

On December 1, 1522, the new pope, Adrian VI, wrote to Erasmus in terms suggestive of the extraordinary influence with which both sides credited him:

> It lies with you, God helping, to recover those who have been seduced by Luther from the right road, and to hold up those who still stand. . . . I need not tell you with what joy I shall receive back these heretics without need to smite them with the rod of the Imperial law. You know how far are such rough methods from my own nature. I am still as you knew me when we were students together. Come to me in Rome. You will find here the books which you will need. You will have myself and other learned men to consult with; and if you will do what I ask you shall have no cause for regret.[97]

After a preliminary exchange of letters pledging each other to secrecy, Erasmus opened his heart to the Pope:

> Your Holiness requires my advice, and you wish to see me. I would go to you with pleasure if my health allowed. . . . As to writing against Luther, I have not learning enough. You think my words will have authority. Alas, my popularity, such as I had, is turned to hatred. Once I was Prince of Letters, Star of Germany . . . High Priest of Learning, Champion of a Purer Theology. The note is altered now. One party says I agree with Luther because I do not oppose him; the other finds fault with me because I oppose him. . . . At Rome and in Brabant I am called heretic, heresiarch, schismatic. I entirely disagree with Luther. They quote this and that to show we are alike. I could find a hundred passages where St. Paul seems to teach the doctrines which they condemn in Luther. . . .
>
> Those counsel you best who advise gentle measures. The monks —Atlases they call themselves of a tottering Church—estrange those who would be its supporters. . . . Some think there is no remedy but force. That is not my opinion . . . there would be frightful bloodshed. The question is not what heresy deserves, but how to deal with it wisely. . . . For myself, I should say, discover the roots of the disease. Clean out those to begin with. Punish no one. Let what has taken place be regarded as a chastisement sent by Providence, and grant a general amnesty. If God forgives my sins, God's vicar may forgive. The magistrates may prevent revolutionary violence. If possible, there should be a check on the printing presses. Then let the world know and see that you mean in earnest to reform the abuses which are justly cried out against. If your Holiness desires to know what are the roots to which I refer, send persons whom you can trust to every part of Latin Christendom. Let them consult the wisest men they can find in the different countries; and you will soon know.[98]

Poor Adrian, whose good intentions outran his powers, died broken-hearted in 1523. His successor, Clement VII. continued to urge Erasmus to enter the lists against Luther. When finally the scholar yielded, it was with no personal attack on Luther, no general indictment of the Reformation, but by an objective and mannerly discussion of free will (*De libero arbitrio*, 1524). He admitted that he could not fathom the mystery of moral freedom, nor reconcile it with divine omniscience and omnipotence. But no humanist could accept the doctrines of predestination and determinism without sacrificing the dignity and value of man or of human life: here was another basic cleavage between the Reformation and the Renaissance. To Erasmus it seemed obvious that a God who punished sins that His creatures as made by Him could not help committing, was an immoral monster unworthy of worship or praise; and to ascribe such conduct to Christ's "Father in heaven" would be the direst blasphemy. On Luther's assumptions the worst criminal would be an innocent martyr, fated to sin by an act of God, and then condemned by divine vengeance to eternal suffering. How could a believer in predestination make any creative effort, or labor to improve the condition of mankind? Erasmus confessed that a man's moral choice is fettered by a thousand circumstances over which he has had no control; yet man's consciousness persists in affirming some measure of freedom, without which he would be a meaningless automaton. In any case, Erasmus concluded, let us admit our ignorance, our incapacity to reconcile moral freedom with divine prescience or omnipresent causality; let us postpone the solution to the Last Judgment; but meanwhile let us shun any hypothesis that makes man a puppet, and God a tyrant crueler than any in history.

Clement VII sent Erasmus 200 florins ($5,000?) on receiving the treatise. Most Catholics were disappointed by the conciliatory and philosophical tone of the book; they had hoped for an exhilarating declaration of war. Melanchthon, who had expressed predestinarian views in his *Loci communes*, was favorably impressed by Erasmus' argument, and omitted the doctrine in later editions; [99] he, too, still hoped for peace. But Luther, in a delayed response entitled *De servo arbitrio* (1525), defended predestination uncompromisingly:

> The human will is like a beast of burden. If God mounts it, it wishes and goes as God wills; if Satan mounts it, it wishes and goes as Satan wills. Nor can it choose its rider. . . . The riders contend for its possession. . . . God foresees, foreordains, and accomplishes all things by an unchanging, eternal, and efficacious will. By this thunderbolt free will sinks shattered in the dust.[100]

It is significant of the sixteenth-century mood that Luther rejected free will not, as some eighteenth-century thinkers would do, because it ran counter to a universal reign of law and causality, nor, as many in the nineteenth century would do, because heredity, environment, and circumstance seemed to determine, like another trinity, the desires that seem to determine the will. He rejected free will on the ground that God's omnipotence makes Him the real cause of all events and all actions, and that consequently it is He, and not our virtue or our sins, Who decides our salvation or damnation. Luther faces the bitterness of his logic manfully:

> Common sense and natural reason are highly offended that God by His mere will deserts, hardens, and damns, as if He delighted in sin and in such eternal torments, He Who is said to be of such mercy and goodness. Such a concept of God seems wicked, cruel, and intolerable, and by it many men have been revolted in all ages. I myself was once offended to the very depth of the abyss of desperation, so that I wished that I had never been created. There is no use trying to get away from this by ingenious distinctions. Natural reason, however much it is offended, must admit the consequences of the omniscience and omnipotence of God. . . . If it is difficult to believe in God's mercy and goodness when He damns those who do not deserve it, we must recall that if God's justice could be recognized as just by human comprehension, it would not be divine.[101]

Typical again of the age was the wide sale that this treatise *On the Slave Will* had in the seven Latin and two vernacular editions that were called for within a year. In the sequel this proved the great source book of Protestant theology; here Calvin found the doctrine of predestination, election, and reprobation which he transmitted to France, Holland, Scotland, England, and America. Erasmus answered Luther in two minor tracts, *Hyperaspistes (The Defender)* I and II (1526–27), but contemporary opinion gave the Reformer the better of the argument.

Even at this stage Erasmus continued his efforts for peace. To his correspondents he recommended tolerance and courtesy. He thought that the Church should permit clerical marriage and communion in both kinds; that she should yield some of her vast properties to lay authorities and uses; and that such divisive questions as predestination, free will, and the Real Presence should be left undefined, open to diverse interpretations.[102] He advised Duke George of Saxony to treat the Anabaptists humanely; "it is not just to punish with fire any error whatever, unless there be joined to it sedition or some other crime such as the laws punish with death." [103] This was in 1524; in 1533, however, moved by friendship or senility, he defended the imprisonment of heretics by Thomas More.[104] In Spain, where some humanists had become Erasmians, the monks of the Inquisition began a systematic scrutiny of Erasmus' works, with a view to having him condemned as a heretic (1527). Nevertheless he continued his criticism of monastic immorality and theological dogmatism as main provocatives of the Reformation. In 1528 he repeated the charge that "many convents, both of men and women, are public brothels," and "in many monasteries the last virtue to be found is chastity." [105] In 1532 he condemned the monks as importunate beggars, seducers of women, hounders of heretics, hunters of legacies, forgers of testimonials.[106] He was all for reforming the Church while deprecating the Reformation. He could not bring himself to leave the Church, or to see her torn in half. "I endure the Church till the day I shall see a better one." [107]

He was dismayed when he heard of the sack of Rome by Protestant and Catholic troops in the service of the Emperor (1527); he had hoped that Charles would encourage Clement to compromise with Luther; now Pope and Emperor were at each other's throats. A closer shock came when, in a pious riot, the reformers at Basel destroyed the images in the churches (1529). Only a year before, he himself had denounced the worship of images: "the people should be taught that these are no more than signs; it would be better if there were none at all, and prayer were addressed only to Christ. But in all things let there be moderation" [108]: this was precisely, on this point, the position of Luther. But the incensed and senseless denudation of churches seemed to him an illiberal and barbarous reaction. He left Basel and moved to Freiburg-im-Breisgau, in Catholic Austrian territory. The city authorities received him with honors, and gave him the unfinished palace of Maximilian I for a residence. When the Imperial pension came too irregularly the Fuggers sent him whatever funds he needed. But the monks and theologians of Freiburg attacked him as a secret skeptic, and as the real cause of the turmoil in Germany. In 1535 he returned to Basel. A delegation of university professors went out to welcome him, and Jerome Froben, son of Johann, gave him rooms in his home.

He was now sixty-nine, thin, with features drawn taut with age. He suffered from ulcers, diarrhea, pancreatitis, gout, stone, and frequent colds; note the swollen hands in Dürer's drawing. In his final year he was confined to his rooms, often to his bed. Harassed with pain, and hearing almost daily of fresh attacks made upon him by Protestants and Catholics, he lost the habitual good cheer that had endeared him to his friends, and became morose. Yet, almost daily, letters of homage came to him from kings, prelates, statesmen, scholars, or financiers, and his dwelling was a goal of literary pilgrimage. On June 6, 1536, he was stricken with acute dysentery. He knew himself to be dying, but he did not ask for a priest or confessor, and passed away (June 12) without the sacraments of the Church, repeatedly invoking the names of Mary and Christ. Basel gave him a princely funeral and a tomb in the cathedral. The humanists, the printers, and the bishop of the city joined in erecting over his remains a stone slab, still in place, commemorating his "incomparable erudition in every branch of learning " His will left no legacy for religious purposes, but assigned sums for the care of the sick or the old, for providing dowries for poor girls, and for the education of promising youths.

His standing with posterity fluctuated with the prestige of the Renaissance. Almost all parties, in the fever of religious revolution, called him a trimmer and a coward. The Reformers charged him with having led them to the brink, inspired them to jump, and then taken to his heels. At the Council of Trent he was branded as an impious heretic, and his works were forbidden to Catholic readers. As late as 1758 Horace Walpole termed him "a begging parasite, who had parts enough to discover the truth, and not courage enough to profess it." [109] Late in the nineteenth century, as the smoke of battle cleared, a learned and judicious Protestant historian mourned that the Erasmian conception of reform, "a scholar's conception . . . was soon interrupted and set aside by ruder and more drastic methods. Yet it may be questioned whether, after all, the slow way is not in the long run the surest, and whether any other agent of human progress can permanently be substituted for culture. The Reformation of the sixteenth century was Luther's work; but if any fresh Reformation is . . . coming, it can only be based on the principles of Erasmus." [110] And a Catholic historian adds an almost rationalistic appreciation: "Erasmus belonged, intellectually, to a later and more scientific and rational age. The work which he had initiated, and which was interrupted by the Reformation troubles, was resumed at a more acceptable time by the scholarship of the seventeenth century." [111] Luther had to be; but when his work was done, and passion cooled, men would try again to catch the spirit of Erasmus and the Renaissance, and renew in patience and mutual tolerance the long, slow labor of enlightenment.

CHAPTER XX

The Faiths at War

1525-60

I. THE PROTESTANT ADVANCE: 1525-30

WHAT combination of forces and circumstances enabled nascent Protestantism to survive the hostility of both papacy and Empire? Mystical piety, Biblical studies, religious reform, intellectual development, Luther's audacity, were not enough; they might have been diverted or controlled. Probably the economic factors were decisive: the desire to keep German wealth in Germany, to free Germany from papal or Italian domination, to transfer ecclesiastical property to secular uses, to repel Imperial encroachments upon the territorial, judicial, and financial authority of the German princes, cities, and states. Add certain political conditions that *permitted* the Protestant success. The Ottoman Empire, after conquering Constantinople and Egypt, was expanding dangerously in the Balkans and Africa, absorbing half of Hungary, besieging Vienna, and threatening to close the Mediterranean to Christian trade; Charles V and Archduke Ferdinand required a united Germany and Austria—Protestant as well as Catholic money and men—to resist this Moslem avalanche. The Emperor was usually engrossed in the affairs of Spain or Flanders or Italy, or in mortal conflict with Francis I of France; he had no time or funds for civil war in Germany. He agreed with his pensioner Erasmus that the Church badly needed reform; he was intermittently at odds with Clement VII and Paul III, even to allowing his army to sack Rome; only when Emperor and Pope were friends could they effectually combat the religious revolution.

But by 1527 the Lutheran "heresy" had become orthodoxy in half of Germany. The cities found Protestantism profitable; "they do not care in the least about religion," mourned Melanchthon; "they are only anxious to get dominion into their hands, to be free from the control of the bishops"; [1] for a slight alteration in their theological garb they escaped from episcopal taxes and courts, and could appropriate pleasant parcels of ecclesiastical property.[2] Yet an honest desire for a simpler and sincerer religion seems to have moved many citizens. At Magdeburg the members of St. Ulrich's parish met in the churchyard and chose eight men who were to select the preacher and manage the affairs of the church (1524); soon all churches in the city were administering the Lord's Supper in the Lutheran mode. Augsburg was so fervently Protestant that when Campeggio came there as papal legate the populace dubbed him Antichrist (1524). Most of Strasbourg accepted the new theology from Wolfgang Fabricius Capito (1523), and Martin Bucer, who succeeded him there, also converted Ulm. In Nuremberg great business leaders like Lazarus Spengler and Hieronymus Baumgärtner won the city council to the Lutheran creed (1526); the Sebalduskirche and the Lorenzkirche transformed their ritual accordingly, while keeping their Catholic art. In Brunswick the writings of Luther were widely circulated; his hymns were publicly sung; his version of the New Testament was so earnestly studied that when a priest misquoted it he was corrected by the congregation; finally the city council ordered all clergymen to preach only what could be found in the Scriptures, to baptize in German, and to serve the sacrament in both forms (1528). By 1530 the new faith had won Hamburg, Bremen, Rostock, Lübeck, Stralsund, Danzig, Dorpat, Riga, Reval, and almost all the Imperial cities of Swabia. Iconoclastic riots broke out in Augsburg, Hamburg, Brunswick, Stralsund. Probably some of this violence was a reaction against the ecclesiastical use of statues and paintings to inculcate ridiculous and lucrative legends.

The princes, gladly adopting Roman law—which made the secular ruler omnipotent as delegate of the "sovereign people"—saw in Protestantism a religion that not only exalted the state but obeyed it; now they could be spiritual as well as temporal lords, and all the wealth of the Church could be theirs to administer or enjoy. John the Steadfast, who succeeded Frederick the Wise as Elector of Saxony (1525), definitely accepted the Lutheran faith, which Frederick had never done; and when John died (1532) his son John Frederick kept Electoral Saxony firmly Protestant. Philip the Magnanimous, Landgrave of Hesse, formed with John the League of Gotha and Torgau (1526) to protect and extend Lutheranism. Other princes fell in line: Ernest of Lüneburg, Otto and Francis of Brunswick-Lüneburg, Henry of Mecklenburg, Ulrich of Württemberg. Albert of Prussia, Grand Master of the Teutonic Knights, following Luther's advice, abandoned his monastic vows, married, secularized the lands of his order, and made himself Duke of Prussia (1525). Luther saw himself, apparently by the mere force of his personality and eloquence, winning half of Germany.

Since many monks and nuns now left their convents, and the public seemed unwilling to support the remainder, the Lutheran princes suppressed all monasteries in their territory except a few whose inmates had embraced the Protestant faith. The princes agreed to share the confiscated properties and revenues with the nobles, the cities, and some universities, but this pledge was very laxly redeemed. Luther inveighed against the application of ecclesiastical wealth to any but religious or educational purposes, and condemned the precipitate seizure of church buildings and lands by the nobility. A modest part of the spoils was yielded to schools and poor relief; the princes and nobles kept the rest. "Under cover of the Gospel," wrote Melanchthon (1530), "the princes were only intent on the plunder of the churches." [8]

For good or evil, for spiritual or material ends, the great transformation progressed. Whole provinces—East Friesland, Silesia, Schleswig, Holstein— went over almost unanimously to Protestantism; nothing could better show how moribund Catholicism had there become. Where priests survived, they continued their support of concubines,[4] and clamored for permission to marry legally as the Lutheran clergy were doing.[5] Archduke Ferdinand reported to the Pope that the desire for marriage was almost universal among the Catholic secular clergy, that out of a hundred pastors scarcely one was not openly or secretly married; and Catholic princes pleaded with the papacy that the abolition of celibacy had become a moral necessity.[6] A loyal Catholic complained (1524) that the bishops, with revolution on their door-steps, went on with their Lucullan feasts; [7] and a Catholic historian, speaking of Albrecht, Archbishop of Mainz, describes "the luxuriously furnished apartments which this unholy prince of the Church used for secret inter-course with his mistress." [8] "Everybody," says the same historian, "had be-come so hostile to priests that these were mocked and annoyed wherever they went." [9] "The people everywhere," wrote Erasmus (January 31, 1530), "are for the new doctrines." [10] This was true, however, only in north-ern Germany; and even there Duke George of Saxony and Elector Joachim of Brandenburg were resolutely Catholic. Southern and western Germany —which had been part of the ancient Roman Empire, and had received some Latin culture—remained for the most part loyal to the Church; the *gemütlich* South preferred the gaily colorful and sexually lenient ways of Catholicism to the predestinarian stoicism of the North. The powerful elector-arch-bishops of Mainz, Trier, and (till 1543) Cologne kept their regions predom-inantly Catholic; and Pope Adrian VI saved Bavaria by granting its dukes, for their secular uses, a fifth of ecclesiastical income in their state. A similar grant of Church revenues appeased Ferdinand in Austria.

Hungary entered vitally into the drama. The premature accession of Louis II at the age of ten (1516), and his premature death, were formative elements in the Hungarian tragedy. Even his birth was premature; the medicos of his time barely saved the frail infant by enclosing it in the warm carcasses of animals slaughtered to give it heat. Louis grew into a handsome youth, kindly and generous, but given to extravagance and festivities on meager resources amid a corrupt and incompetent court. When Sultan Suleiman sent an ambassador to Buda the nobles refused to receive him, dragged him around the country, cut off his nose and ears, and turned him back to his master.[11] The infuriated Sultan invaded Hungary, and seized two of its most vital strongholds—Szabacs and Belgrade (1521). After long delays, and amid the treason or cowardice of his nobles, Louis raised an army of 25,000 men, and marched out with mad heroism to face 100,000 Turks on a field near Mohács (August 30, 1526). The Hungarians were slaughtered almost to a man, and Louis himself was drowned in stumbling flight. Suleiman entered Buda in triumph; his army sacked and burned the handsome capital, destroyed all its major buildings except the royal palace, and gave to the flames most of Matthias Corvinus's precious library. The victorious host spread over the eastern half of Hungary, burning and pillaging, and Suleiman drove 100,000 Christian captives before him to Constantinople.

The surviving magnates divided into hostile factions. One group, judging resistance impossible, chose John Zápolya as king, and authorized him to sign a submissive peace; Suleiman allowed him to reign in Buda as his vassal, but the eastern half of Hungary remained in effect under Turkish domination till 1686. Another faction united with the nobles of Bohemia to give the crown of both Hungary and Bohemia to Ferdinand, in the hope of securing the aid of the Holy Roman Empire and the powerful Hapsburg family. When Suleiman returned to the attack (1529), marching 135 miles from Buda along the Danube to the gates of Vienna, Ferdinand successfully defended his capital. But during those critical years Charles V had been forced to humor the Protestants lest all Europe should fall to Islam. The westward advance of the Turks so obviously protected Protestantism that Philip of Hesse rejoiced at Turkish victories. When Suleiman, balked at Vienna, returned to Constantinople, Catholics and Protestants were free to renew their struggle for the soul of Germany.

II. THE DIETS DISAGREE: 1526-41

As internal liberty varies (other things equal) with external security, Protestantism, during its safe period, indulged in the sectarian fragmentation that seemed inherent in the principles of private judgment and the supremacy of conscience. Already in 1525 Luther wrote: "There are nowadays almost as many sects and creeds as there are heads." [12] Melanchthon was kept grievously busy moderating his master and finding ambiguous formulas for reconciling contradictory certitudes. Catholics pointed gleefully to the mutually recriminating Protestant factions, and predicted that freedom of interpretation and belief would lead to religious anarchy, moral disintegration, and a skepticism abominable to Protestants as well as Catholics.[13] In 1525 three artists were banished from Protestant Nuremberg for questioning the divine authorship of the Bible, the Real Presence in the Eucharist, and the divinity of Christ.

While Suleiman was preparing the campaign that cut Hungary in half, a Diet of German princes, prelates, and burghers met at Speyer (June 1526) to consider the demands of the Catholics that the Edict of Worms should be enforced, and the counterproposal of the Protestants that religion be left free until a general council under German auspices should adjudicate the disputes. The Protestants prevailed, and the concluding decree of this Diet ruled that—pending such a council—each German state, in religion, "should so live, rule, and bear itself as it thought it could answer to God and the Emperor"; that no one should be punished for past offenses against the Edict of Worms; and that the Word of God should be preached by all parties, none interfering with the others. The Protestants interpreted this "Recess of Speyer" * as sanctioning the establishment of Lutheran churches, the religious autonomy of each territorial prince, and the prohibition of the Mass in Lutheran areas. The Catholics rejected these assumptions, but the Emperor, embroiled with the Pope, accepted them for the time being; and Ferdinand was soon too busy with affairs in Hungary to make any effectual resistance.

Having made his peace with Clement, Charles returned to the natural conservatism of a king, and ordered the Diet of Speyer to reconvene on February 1, 1529. Under the influence of the presiding Archduke and the absent Emperor the new assembly repealed the "Recess" of 1526, and passed a decree permitting Lutheran services—but requiring the toleration of Catholic services—in Lutheran states, completely forbidding Lutheran preaching or ritual in Catholic states, enforcing the Edict of Worms, and outlawing Zwinglian and Anabaptist sects everywhere. On April 25, 1529, the Lutheran minority published a "Protest" declaring that conscience forbade their acceptance of this decree; they appealed to the Emperor for a general council; meanwhile they would adhere to the original Recess of Speyer at whatever cost. The term *Protestant* was applied by the Catholics to the signers of this Protest, and gradually came into use to designate the German rebels from Rome.

Still needing German unity against the Turks, Charles called another diet, which met at Augsburg (June 20, 1530) under his presidency. During this conference he stayed with Anton Fugger, now head of the firm that had made him emperor. According to an old story, the banker pleased the ruler by lighting a fire with an Imperial certificate of indebtedness.[14] As the Fuggers were financially allied with the popes, the gesture may have moved

---

* *Recess* is the accepted mistranslation of *Abschied*, which, like the better rendering, *decision*, meant a cutting off—a concluding decree to govern conduct between the adjournment and reconvening of a conference.

Charles a step nearer to the papacy. Luther did not attend, for he was still under the Imperial ban, and might at any moment be arrested; but he went to Coburg, on the Saxon border, and kept in touch, through messengers, with the Protestant delegation. He compared the assembly to a congregation of jackdaws that chattered and maneuvered before his windows, and he complained that "each bishop brought as many devils" or voters to the Diet "as there are fleas on a dog on St. John's Day." [15] It was apparently at this time that he composed the greatest of his hymns—"*Ein feste Burg ist unser Gott*" —"A mighty fortress is our God."

On June 24 Cardinal Campeggio appealed to the Diet for the utter suppression of the Protestant sects. On the twenty-fifth Christian Bayer read to the Emperor and a portion of the assembly the famous Augsburg Confession, which Melanchthon had prepared, and which, with some modifications, was to become the official creed of the Lutheran churches. Partly because he feared a war of the combined Imperial and papal forces against the divided Protestants, partly because he was by temperament inclined to compromise and peace, Melanchthon gave the statement (says a Catholic scholar) "a dignified, moderate, and pacific tone," [16] and strove to minimize the differences between the Catholic and Lutheran views. He expatiated on the heresies that the Evangelicals (as the Lutherans called themselves from their sole reliance on the Gospels or the New Testament) and the Roman Catholics alike condemned; he dissociated the Lutheran from the Zwinglian reform, and left the latter to shift for itself. He softened the doctrines of predestination, "consubstantiation," and justification by faith; he spoke temperately of the ecclesiastical abuses that Protestantism had abated; he defended with courtesy the administration of the sacrament in both forms, the abolition of monastic vows, the marriage of the clergy; and he appealed to Cardinal Campeggio to accept this Confession in the conciliatory spirit in which it had been composed. Luther regretted some of the concessions, but gave the document his indispensable approval. Zwingli sent his own *Ratio fidei* to the Emperor, frankly stating his disbelief in the Real Presence. Strasbourg, Constance, Lindau, and Memmingen presented a separate Confession, the *Tetrapolitana*, in which Capito and Bucer struggled to bridge the gaps among the Lutheran, Zwinglian, and Catholic creeds.

The extreme faction of the Catholics, led by Eck, retorted with a Confutation so intransigeant that the assembly refused to submit it to the Emperor until it had been twice toned down. So revised, it insisted on transubstantiation, seven sacraments, the invocation of saints, clerical celibacy, communion in bread alone, and the Latin Mass. Charles approved this Confutation, and declared that the Protestants must accept it or face war. A milder party of Catholics entered into negotiation with Melanchthon, and offered to permit communion in bread and wine. Melanchthon in return agreed to recognize auricular confession, fasts, episcopal jurisdiction, even, with some provisos, the authority of the popes. But other Protestant leaders refused to go so far; Luther protested that the restoration of episcopal jurisdiction would subject the new ministers to the Roman hierarchy, and would soon liquidate the Reformation. Seeing agreement impossible, several Protestant princes left for their homes.

On November 19 the diminished Diet issued its final Recess or decree. All phases of Protestantism were condemned; the Edict of Worms was to be enforced; the Imperial Chamber of Justice (*Reichskammergericht*) was to start legal actions against all appropriators of ecclesiastical property; the Protestants were to have until April 15, 1531 to accept the Confutation peaceably. Charles's signature made this "Recess of Augsburg" an Imperial decree. To the Emperor it must have seemed the height of reasonableness to give the rebels six months to adjust themselves to the will of the Diet. Within that period he offered them immunity from the Edict of Worms. Thereafter, if other duties would allow, he might have to submit the rival theologies to the supreme court of war.

While the Diet was yet in session several states formed a Catholic League for the defense and restoration of the traditional faith. Interpreting this as a martial gesture, Protestant princes and cities organized (March 1531) the Schmalkaldic League, which took its name from its birthplace near Erfurt. When the period of grace ran out, Ferdinand, now "King of the Romans," proposed to Charles to begin war. But Charles was not yet ready. Suleiman was planning another attack upon Vienna; Suleiman's confederate, Barbarossa, was raiding Christian commerce in the Mediterranean; and Suleiman's ally, Francis of France, was waiting to pounce upon Milan the moment Charles became involved in a German civil war. In April 1531, instead of enforcing the Augsburg decree, he suspended it, and asked for Protestant aid against the Turks. Luther and the princes responded loyally; Lutherans and Catholics signed the Peace of Nuremberg (July 23, 1532), pledging united aid to Ferdinand, and mutual religious toleration until a general council should be convened. So numerous an army of Protestant and Catholic Germans, of Spanish and Italian Catholics, gathered under the Emperor's standard at Vienna that Suleiman found the omens unfavorable and turned back to Constantinople, while the Christian army, drunk with its bloodless victory, plundered Christian towns and homes, "spreading greater disaster," said eyewitness Thomas Cranmer of England, "than the Turks themselves." [17]

The patriotism of the Protestants gave their movement new dignity and impetus. When Aleander, again papal emissary, offered the Lutheran leaders a hearing at a general council if they would promise submission to the council's final decisions, they rejected the proposal. A year later (1534) Philip of Hesse, disregarding Luther's condemnation of any offensive policy, accepted French aid in restoring the Protestant Duke Ulrich to power in Württemberg. Ferdinand's rule there was ended; the churches were pillaged, the monasteries were closed, and their property was taken by the state.[18] Circumstances again favored the Protestants: Ferdinand was absorbed in the east, Charles in the west; the Anabaptists were apparently consolidating a communistic revolution in Münster; Jürgen Wullenwever's radicals captured Lübeck (1535); the Catholic princes now needed Lutheran aid against internal revolt as much as against the Ottomans. Moreover, Scandinavia and England had by this time renounced Rome, and Catholic France was seeking the alliance of Lutheran Germany against Charles V.

Elated with this growing strength, the Schmalkaldic League voted to raise an army of 12,000 men. When the new pope, Paul III, asked on what terms the League would accept a general council, it replied that it would recognize only a council held independently of the pope, composed of the secular as well as the ecclesiastical leaders of Germany, and receiving the Protestants not as heretics but as equal participants.[19] It repudiated the Imperial Chamber of Justice, and notified the Emperor's vice-chancellor that it would not admit the right of Catholics to retain Church property, or to carry on their worship, in the territories of Protestant princes.[20] The Catholic states renewed their League, and demanded of Charles full enforcement of the powers given to the *Reichskammergericht*. He replied with gracious words, but fear of Francis I at his back kept him at bay.

The Protestant tide continued to flow. Says a Catholic historian:

> On the 9th of September, 1538, Aleander wrote to the Pope from Linz that the religious condition of Germany was well-nigh ruinous; divine worship and the administration of the sacraments had for the most part ceased; the secular princes, with the exception of Ferdinand I, were either entirely Lutheran, or full of hatred of the priesthood, and greedy of church property. The prelates lived just as extravagantly as before. . . . The religious orders had dwindled down to handfuls; the secular clergy were not much more numerous, and so immoral and ignorant that the few Catholics shunned them.[21]

When the Catholic Duke George of Albertine Saxony died he was succeeded by his brother Henry, a Lutheran; Henry in turn was succeeded by Maurice, who was to be the military savior of Protestantism in Germany. In 1539 Joachim II, Elector of Brandenburg, set up in his capital at Berlin a Protestant Church proudly independent of both Rome and Wittenberg. In 1542 the duchy of Cleves, the bishopric of Naumburg, even Albrecht's see of Halle, were added to the Protestant roster by timely mixtures of politics and war; and in 1543 Count Hermann von Wied, Archbishop-Elector of Cologne, shocked Rome by transforming himself into a Lutheran. The Protestant leaders were so confident that in January 1540, Luther, Melanchthon, and others issued a declaration to the effect that peace could be had only through the renunciation, by the Emperor and the Catholic clergy, of their "idolatry and error," and by their adoption of the "pure doctrine" of the Augsburg Confession. And the document proceeded: "Even if the Pope were to concede to us our doctrines and ceremonies, we should still be obliged to treat him as a persecutor and an outcast, since in other kingdoms he would not renounce his errors." "It is all up with the Pope," said Luther, "as it is with his god, the Devil." [22]

Charles almost agreed, for in April 1540, he took the religious initiative from the Pope, and invited the Catholic and Protestant leaders of Germany to meet in "Christian colloquy" to seek again a peaceful settlement of their differences. "Unless the Pope intervenes decisively," wrote a papal nuncio, "the whole of Germany will fall a prey to Protestantism." At a preliminary conference in Worms a long debate between Eck and Melanchthon resulted in the tentative acceptance, by the previously intransigeant Catholic, of the mild positions formulated in the Augsburg Confession.[23] Encouraged, Charles summoned the two groups to Ratisbon (Regensburg). There, under his leadership (April 5–May 22, 1541), they made their closest approach to a settlement. Paul III was disposed to peace, and his chief delegate, Cardinal Gasparo Contarini, was a man of good will and high moral character. The Emperor, harassed by threats from France and appeals from Ferdinand for help against the returning Turks, was so anxious for an agreement that many Catholic leaders suspected him of Protestant leanings. The conference concurred in permitting marriage of the clergy and communion in both kinds; but no legerdemain could find a formula at once affirming and denying the religious supremacy of the popes, and transubstantiation in the Eucharist; and Contarini was not amused by a Protestant query whether a mouse that nibbled at a fallen consecrated Host was eating bread or God.[24] The conference failed, but Charles, hurrying off to war, gave an interim pledge to the Protestants that there would be no proceedings against them for holding the doctrines of the Augsburg Confession, or for retaining confiscated Church property.

During these years of controversy and growth the new faith had created a new Church. At Luther's suggestion it called itself Evangelical. He had originally advocated an ecclesiastical democracy, in which each congregation would select its own minister and determine its own ritual and creed; but his increasing dependence on the princes compelled him to surrender these prerogatives to commissions appointed by, and responsible to, the state. In 1525 Elector John of Saxony ordered all churches in his duchy to adopt an Evangelical service as formulated by Melanchthon with Luther's approval; priests who refused to obey lost their benefices, and obstinate lay-men, after a period of grace, were exiled.[25] Other Lutheran princes followed a similar procedure. As a doctrinal guide for the new churches Luther drew up a five-page *Kleiner Katechismus* (1529), consisting of the Ten Com-mandments, the Apostles' Creed, and brief interpretations of each article. It would have been considered quite orthodox in the first four centuries of Christianity.

The new ministers were generally men of good morals, learned in Scrip-ture, careless of humanistic erudition, and devoted to the tasks of their pastorates. Sunday was observed as the Sabbath; here Luther accepted tra-dition rather than the Bible. "Divine service" retained much of the Catholic ritual—altar, cross, candles, vestments, and parts of the Mass in German; but a larger role was given to the sermon, and there were no prayers to the Virgin or the saints. Religious paintings and statues were discarded. Church architecture was transformed to bring the worshipers within easier hearing of the preacher; hence galleries became a regular feature of Protestant churches. The most pleasant innovation was the active participation of the congregation in the music of the ceremony. Even the noteless long to sing, and now every voice could fondly hear itself in the protective anonymity of the crowd. Luther became overnight a poet, and wrote didactic, polem-ical, and inspirational hymns of a rough and masculine power typical of his character. Not only did the worshipers sing these and other Protestant hymns; they were called together during the week to rehearse them; and many families sang them in the home. A worried Jesuit reckoned that "the hymns of Luther killed [converted] more souls than his sermons." [26] The Protestant music of the Reformation rose to rival the Catholic painting of the Renaissance.

III. THE LION OF WITTENBERG: 1536–46

Luther took no direct part in the pacific conferences of these his declin-ing years; the princes rather than the theologians were now the Protestant leaders, for the issues concerned property and power far more than dogma and ritual. Luther was not made for negotiation, and he was getting too old to fight with weapons other than the pen. A papal envoy described him in 1535 as still vigorous and heartily humorous ("the first question he asked me was whether I had heard the report, current in Italy, that he was a Ger-man sot" [27]); but his expanding frame harbored a dozen diseases—indigestion, insomnia, dizziness, colic, stones in the kidneys, abscesses in the ears, ulcers, gout, rheumatism, sciatica, and palpitation of the heart. He used alcoholic drinks to dull his pain and bring him sleep; he sampled the drugs that the doctors prescribed for him; and he tried impatient prayer; the diseases progressed. In 1537 he thought he would die of the stone, and he issued an ultimatum to the Deity: "If this pain lasts longer I shall go mad and fail to recognize Thy goodness." [28] His deteriorating temper was in part an expression of his suffering. His friends increasingly avoided him, for "hardly one of us," said a saddened votary, "can escape his anger and his public scourging"; and the patient Melanchthon winced under frequent humiliations by his rough-hewn idol. As for "Oecolampadius, Calvin . . . and the other heretics," said Luther, "they have in-deviled, through-deviled, over-deviled, corrupt hearts and lying mouths." [29]

He tried hard to be reasonable in his treatise *On the Councils and the Churches* (1539). He compared the various papal promises and postponements of a general council to teasing a hungry animal by offering food and snatching it away. With considerable learning he reviewed conciliar history, and noted that several ecclesiastical councils had been called and presided over by emperors—a hint to Charles. He doubted if any council called by a pope would reform the Curia. Before sanctioning Protestant attendance at a Church council "we must first condemn the bishop of Rome as a tyrant, and burn all his bulls and decretals." [30]

His political opinions in his later years suggest that silence is trebly golden after sixty. He had always been politically conservative, even when appearing to encourage social revolution. His religious revolt was against practice rather than theory; he objected to the high cost of indulgences, and later to papal domination, but he accepted to the end of his life the most difficult doctrines of orthodox Christianity—Trinity, Virgin Birth, Atonement, Real Presence, hell—and made some of these more indigestible than before. He despised the common people, and would have corrected Lincoln's famous error on that spawn of carelessness. *Herr Omnes*—Mr. Crowd—needs strong government, "lest the world become wild, peace vanish, and commerce . . . be destroyed. . . . No one need think that the world can be ruled without blood. . . . The world cannot be ruled with a rosary." [31] But when government by rosaries lost its power, government by the sword had to take its place. So Luther had to transfer to the state most of the authority that had been held by the Church; therefore he defended the divine right of kings. "The hand that wields the secular sword is not a human hand but the hand of God. It is God, not man, Who hangs, and breaks on the wheel, and decapitates, and flogs; it is God who wages war." [32] In this exaltation of the state as now the sole source of order lay the seeds of the absolutist philosophies of Hobbes and Hegel, and a premonition of Imperial Germany. In Luther Henry IV brought Hildebrand to Canossa.

As he aged Luther became more conservative than the princes. He approved the exaction of forced labor and heavy feudal dues from the peasant; and when one baron had twitches of conscience Luther reassured him on the ground that if such burdens were not imposed upon them commoners would become overbearing.[33] He quoted the Old Testament as justifying slavery. "Sheep, cattle, men-servants, and maid-servants were all possessions to be sold as it pleased their masters. It were a good thing were it still so. For else no man may compel nor tame the servile folk." [34] Every man should stay patiently in the task and walk of life to which God has assigned him. "To serve God is for everyone to remain in his vocation and calling, be it ever so mean and simple." This conception of vocation became a pillar of conservatism in Protestant lands.

A prince who had been a loyal supporter of the Protestant cause brought Luther an uncomfortable problem in 1539. Philip of Hesse was at once warlike, amorous, and conscientious. His wife, Christine of Savoy, was a faithful and fertile eyesore; Philip hesitated to divorce one so deserving, but he powerfully desired Margaret of Saale, whom he had met while convalescing from syphilis.[35] After practicing adultery for some time he decided that he was in a state of sin, and must abstain from the Lord's Supper. This proving inconvenient, he suggested to Luther that the new religion, so indebted to the Old Testament, should, like it, allow bigamy—for which, however, the prevailing legal penalty was death. After all, was this not more seemly than Francis I's succession of mistresses, and more humane than Henry VIII's executive husbandry? So anxious was Philip for his Biblical solution that he intimated his defection to the Imperial, even the papal, camp, if the Wittenberg theologians could not see the Scriptural light. Luther was ready; indeed, in *The Babylonian Captivity* he had preferred bigamy to divorce; he had recommended bigamy as the best solution for Henry VIII; [36] and many theologians of the sixteenth century had an open mind on the matter.[37] Melanchthon was reluctant; he finally agreed with Luther that their consent should be given, but that it should be withheld from the public. Christine consented too, on condition that Philip "was to fulfill his marital duties toward her more than ever before." [38] On March 4, 1540, Philip formally but privately married Margaret as an additional wife, in the presence of Melanchthon and Bucer. The grateful Landgrave sent Luther a cartload of wine as a *pourboire*.[39] When news of the marriage leaked out Luther denied giving consent; "the secret Yea," he wrote, "must for the sake of Christ's Church remain a public Nay." [40] Melanchthon fell seriously ill, apparently with remorse and shame, and refused to eat until Luther threatened to excommunicate him.[41] Melanchthon, wrote Luther, "is terribly grieved about this scandal, but I am a tough Saxon and a sturdy peasant, and my skin has grown thick enough to bear such things." [42] Most Evangelicals, however, were scandalized. Catholics were amused and delighted, not knowing that

Pope Clement VII had himself thought of allowing bigamy to Henry VIII.[43] Ferdinand of Austria announced that though he had had some inclination toward the new faith, he now abhorred it. Charles V, as the price of not prosecuting Philip, exacted from him a pledge of support in all future political divisions.

Luther's temper became hot lava as he neared the grave. In 1545 he attacked the Zwinglian "Sacramentarians" with such violence that Melanchthon mourned the widened chasm between the Protestants of the South and the North. Asked by Elector John to restate the case against participation in a papally directed council, Luther sent forth a tirade *Against the Papacy at Rome Founded by the Devil* (1545), in which his flair for vituperation surpassed itself. All his friends were shocked except the painter Lucas Cranach, who illustrated the book with woodcuts of unrestrained satire. One showed the Pope riding on a hog and blessing a heap of dung; another chained him and three cardinals to gibbets; and the frontispiece pictured the Pontiff on his throne surrounded by devils and crowned with a scavenger's bucket. The word *devil* peppered the text; the Pope was "the most hellish father," "this Roman hermaphrodite" and "Sodomite pope"; the cardinals were "desperately lost children of the Devil . . . ignorant asses. . . . One would like to curse them so that thunder and lightning might smite them, hell-fire burn them, the plague, syphilis, epilepsy, scurvy, leprosy, carbuncles, and all diseases attack them." [44] He repudiated again the notion that the Holy Roman Empire was a gift of the popes; on the contrary, he thought, the time had come for the Empire to absorb the Papal States.

> Fall to, now, Emperor, King, princes, lords, and whoever will fall to along with you; God brings no luck to idle hands. And first of all, take from the pope Rome, the Romagna, Urbino, Bologna, and all that he has as a pope, for he got these by lies and tricks; with blasphemies and idolatry he has shamefully filched and stolen them from the Empire, has trampled them under foot, and therefore has led countless souls to their reward in the eternal fire of hell. . . . Therefore ought he, the pope, his cardinals, and all the rabble of his idolatry and papal holiness, to be taken and, as blasphemers, have their tongues torn out by the backs of their necks, and nailed in rows on the gallows.[45]

Perhaps his mind had begun to fail when he wrote this clarion call to violence. The gradual poisoning of the internal organs by time and food and drink may have reached and injured the brain. In his last years Luther became uncomfortably stout, with hanging jowls and convoluted chin. He had been a volcano of energy, a restless Leviathan, saying *Rast Ich, so rost Ich*—"If I rest I rust." [46] But now spells of weariness came upon him; he described himself (January 17, 1546) as "old, decrepit, sluggish, weary, cold, with but one good eye." [47] "I am tired of the world, and it is tired of me," he wrote; [48] and when the Electress Dowager of Saxony wished him forty more years of life, he answered, "Madam, rather than live forty years more, I would give up my chance of paradise." [49] "I pray the Lord will come forthwith and carry me hence. Let Him come, above all, with His Last Judgment; I will stretch out my neck, the thunder will burst forth, and I shall be at rest." [50] To the end he continued to have visions of the Devil; and, now and then, doubts of his mission. "The Devil assaults me by objecting that out of my mouth great offenses and much evil have proceeded; and with this he many times vehemently perplexes me." [51] Sometimes he despaired of the future of Protestantism: "godly servants of the Most High become rarer and rarer"; [52] sects and factions grow in number and bitterness; and "after Melanchthon's death there will be a sad falling off" in the new faith.[53] But then his courage returned. "I have set Christ and the pope together by the ears, so I trouble myself no further. Though I get between the door and the hinges and be squeezed, it is no matter; Christ will go through with it." [54]

His will began in full character: "I am well known in heaven, on earth, and in hell." It told how he, "a damnable and miserable sinner," had received from God the grace to spread the Gospel of His Son, and how he had won recognition as "a doctor of truth, spurning the ban of pope, emperor, kings, princes, and priests, and the hatred of all the demons." And it concluded: "Wherefore, for the disposition of my meager estate let the present witness of my hand suffice; and let it be said: 'Dr. Martin Luther, notary of God and the witness of His Gospel, wrote this.' " [55] He did not doubt that God was waiting to welcome him.

In January 1546, he went through wintry weather to Eisleben, the place of his birth, to arbitrate a dispute. During his absence he sent charming letters to his wife—as on February 1:

> I wish you peace and grace in Christ, and send you my poor, old, infirm love. Dear Katie, I was weak on the road to Eisleben, but that was my own fault. . . . Such a cold wind blew from behind through my cap upon my head that it was like to turn my brain to ice. This may have helped my vertigo, but now, thank God, I am so well that I am sore tempted by fair women, and care not how gallant I am. . . . God bless you.[56]

He dined merrily on February 17. Early the next morning he fell ill with violent stomach pains. He weakened rapidly, and the friends who gathered by his bedside made it clear that he was dying. One of them asked him, "Reverend father, will you stand steadfast by Christ and the doctrine you have preached?" He answered, "Yes." Then an apoplectic stroke deprived him of speech, and in its course he died (February 18, 1546). The body was taken back to Wittenberg, and was buried in the Castle Church on whose door he had pinned his Theses twenty-nine years before.

Those years were among the most momentous in history, and Luther had been their strident and dominant voice. His faults were many. He lacked appreciation of the historic role that the Church had played in civilizing northern Europe, lacked understanding of mankind's hunger for symbolic and consolatory myths, lacked the charity to deal justly with his Catholic or Protestant foes. He freed his followers from an infallible pope, but subjected them to an infallible book; and it has been easier to change the popes than the book. He retained the most cruel and incredible dogmas of medieval religion, while allowing almost all its beauty to be stamped out in its legends and its art, and bequeathed to Germany a Christianity no truer than the old one, far less joyous and comforting, only more honest in its teaching and personnel. He became almost as intolerant as the Inquisition, but his words were harsher than his deeds. He was guilty of the most vituperative writing in the history of literature. He taught Germany the theological hatred that incarnadined its soil until a hundred years after his death.

And yet his faults were his success. He was a man of war because the situation seemed to demand war, because the problems he attacked had for centuries resisted all the methods of peace. His whole life was a battle—against the sense of guilt, against the Devil, the Pope, the Emperor, Zwingli, even against the friends who would have compromised his revolt into a gentlemanly protest politely heard and carefully forgotten. What could a milder man have done against such handicaps and powers? No man of philosophic breadth, no scientific mind restricting belief to the evidence, no genial nature making generous allowances for the enemy, would have flung down so world-shaking a challenge, or would have marched so resolutely, as if in blinders, to his goal. If his predestinarian theology was as repugnant to reason and human kindness as any myth or miracle in the medieval faith, it was by this passionate irrationality that it moved the hearts of men. It is hope and terror that make men pray, not the evidence of things seen.

It remains that with the blows of his rude fist he smashed the cake of custom, the shell of authority, that had blocked the movement of the European mind. If we judge greatness by influence—which is the least subjective test that we can use—we may rank Luther with Copernicus, Voltaire, and Darwin as the most powerful personalities in the modern world. More has been written about him than about any other modern man except Shakespeare and Napoleon. His influence on philosophy was tardy and indirect; it moved the fideism of Kant, the nationalism of Fichte, the voluntarism of Schopenhauer, the Hegelian surrender of the soul to the state. His influence on German literature and speech was as decisive and pervasive as that of the

King James Bible on language and letters in England. No other German is so frequently or so fondly quoted. Along with Carlstadt and others, he affected the moral life and institutions of Western man by breaking away from clerical celibacy, and pouring into secular life the energies that had been diverted to monastic asceticism, idleness, or piety. His influence lessened as it spread; it was immense in Scandinavia, transitory in France, superseded by Calvin's in Scotland, England, and America. But in Germany it was supreme; no other thinker or writer cut so deep a mark into the German mind and character. He was the most powerful figure in German history, and his countrymen love him not less because he was the most German German of them all.

IV. THE TRIUMPH OF PROTESTANTISM: 1542-55

He died just a year before a disaster that seemed fatal to Protestantism in Germany.

In 1545 Charles V, helped by Lutheran troops, compelled Francis I to sign the Peace of Crépy. Suleiman, at war with Persia, gave the West a five-year truce. Pope Paul III promised the Emperor 1,100,000 ducats, 12,000 infantry, 500 horse, if he would turn his full force against the heretics. Charles felt that at last he might effect what all along had been his hope and policy: to crush Protestantism, and give to his realm a unified Catholic faith that would, he thought, strengthen and facilitate his government. How could he be a real emperor in Germany if Protestant princes continued to flout his authority, and to dictate the terms on which they would accept him? He had not taken Protestantism seriously as a religion; the disputes between Luther and the Catholic theologians meant little or nothing to him; but Protestantism as the theology of princes leagued in arms against him, as a political power capable of determining the next Imperial election, as the faith of pamphleteers who lampooned him, of artists who caricatured him, of preachers who called him Son of Satan [57]—this he could bear in somber silence when he had to; but now for a fleeting season he was free to fight back, and to mold his chaotic realm into one faith and force. He decided for war.

In May 1546, he mobilized his Spanish, Italian, German, and Lowland troops, and summoned to his side the Duke of Alva, his ablest general. When the Protestant princes dispatched delegates to him at Ratisbon to ask the meaning of his moves, he answered that he intended to restore Germany to Imperial obedience. During that conference he won to his support the most competent military leader in Germany, the young and ambitious Duke Maurice of Albertine Saxony. The Fuggers promised financial aid, and the

Pope issued a bull excommunicating all who should resist Charles, and offering liberal indulgences to all who should aid him, in this holy war. Charles
proclaimed the Imperial ban against Duke John of Ernestine Saxony and
Landgrave Philip of Hesse; he absolved their subjects from allegiance to
them, and vowed to confiscate their lands and goods. To divide the opposition he announced that he would not interfere with Protestantism where it
was definitely established; his brother Ferdinand made a like pledge to
Bohemia; and Maurice was tied to the cause by a promise that he would
replace John as Elector of Saxony. Hopeful or fearful, the electors of
Cologne and Brandenburg, the count Palatine, and Protestant Nuremberg
remained neutral. Realizing that not only their theology but their goods and
persons were at stake, John of Saxony, Philip of Hesse, the princes of Anhalt,
the cities of Augsburg, Strasbourg, and Ulm mobilized all their forces, and
put into the field 57,000 men.

But when John and Philip marched south to challenge Charles, Ferdinand
moved north and west to seize John's duchy; and Maurice, to have a finger
in the pie, joined him in invading Ernestine Saxony. Appraised of this, John
hurried north to defend his duchy. He did it brilliantly; but meanwhile
Philip's troops began to desert for lack of pay, and the Protestant cities,
lured by promises of fair play, sued for peace with Charles, who let them
off with heavy fines that broke the financial backbone of their freedom.
Charles was now as superior in arms as in diplomacy. The only force favoring the Protestants was the Pope. Paul III had begun to fear too great a
success for the Emperor; if no Protestant princes should survive to check
the Imperial power, it would establish itself as supreme in northern as well
as southern Italy, would surround or absorb the Papal States, and would
irresistibly dominate the papacy. Suddenly (January 1547) Paul ordered
the papal troops who were with Charles to leave him and return to Italy.
They gladly obeyed. The Pope found himself heretically rejoicing over the
victories of Elector John in Saxony.

But Charles was determined to bring the campaign to a decision. March-
ing north, he met the depleted forces of the Elector at Mühlberg on the
Meissen, routed them completely (April 24, 1547), and took John captive.
Ferdinand demanded the execution of the doughty prince; canny Charles
agreed to commute the sentence to life imprisonment if Wittenberg would
open its gates to him; it did, and the capital of German Protestantism fell into
Catholic hands while Luther slept peacefully under a slab in the Castle
Church. Maurice of Saxony and Joachim of Brandenburg persuaded Philip
of Hesse to surrender on their promise that he would soon be freed. Charles
had made no such pledge; the extent of his geniality was to promise Philip
release after fifteen years. No one seemed left to challenge the victorious

Emperor. Henry VIII had died on January 28, Francis I on March 31. Never since Charlemagne had the Imperial power been so great.

But the winds of fortune veered again. German princes, assembled in another diet at Augsburg (September 1547), resisted the efforts of Charles to consolidate his military victory into a legal autocracy. Paul III accused him of conniving at the murder of Pierluigi Farnese, the Pope's natural son; and Bavaria, ever loyal to the Church, turned against the Emperor. A Protestant majority re-formed among the princes, and wrung from Charles his temporary consent to clerical marriage, the double administration of the sacrament, and the Protestant retention of Church property (1548). The Pope fumed at the Emperor's assumption of power to rule on such ecclesiastical matters, and Catholics murmured that Charles was more interested in extending his Empire and entrenching the Hapsburgs than in restoring the one true faith. Maurice, now Elector of Saxony at Wittenberg, found himself, Protestant and victorious, dangerously unpopular amid a population Protestant and conquered; his treachery had poisoned the power it had won. His appeals to Charles to free the Landgrave were ignored. He began to wonder had he chosen the better part. Secretly he joined the Protestant princes in the Treaty of Chambord (January 1552), by which Henry II of France promised aid in expelling Charles from Germany. While Henry invaded Lorraine and seized Metz, Toul, and Verdun, Maurice and his Protestant allies marched south with 30,000 men. Charles, resting on his laurels at Innsbruck, had carelessly disbanded his troops; he had now no defense except diplomacy, and even at that shifty game Maurice proved his match. Ferdinand proposed an armistice; Maurice prolonged the negotiations courteously, meanwhile advancing on Innsbruck. On May 9, accompanied only by a few attendants, Charles moved painfully, by litter, through rain and snow and the night, over the Brenner Pass to Villach in Carinthia. One throw of fortune's dice had transformed the master of Europe into a gouty fugitive shivering in the Alps.

On May 26 Maurice and the triumphant Protestants met with Ferdinand and some Catholic leaders at Passau. Charles, after a long interlude of self-deflation, consented to have Ferdinand sign a treaty (August 2, 1552) by which Philip was to be released, the Protestant armies were to disband, both Protestants and Catholics were to enjoy freedom of worship till a new diet could meet, and if that diet failed to reach an acceptable settlement, this freedom of worship should continue forever—a favorite word in treaties. Maurice had begun with treachery, and had risen to victorious statesmanship; soon (1553) he would die for his country at the age of thirty in battle against Albrecht Alcibiades, who had turned half of Germany into an anarchy perilous to all.

Charles, despairing of a solution for his problems in Germany, turned west to renew his struggle with France. Ferdinand presided with patience over the historic Diet of Augsburg (February 5–September 25, 1555), which at last, for half a century, gave Germany peace. He saw that the territorial principle of ducal freedom was too strong to allow such a central and absolute sovereignty as the kings had won in France. The Catholic representatives were a majority in the Diet, but the Protestants, superior in military power, bound themselves to stand by every article of the Augsburg Confession of 1530; the Elector Augustus, who had succeeded Maurice in Saxony, adhered to the Protestant view; and the Catholics perceived that they must yield or renew the war. Charles, in the senility of his diplomacy, urged the electors to name his son Philip as his successor to the Imperial title; even the Catholics dreaded the prospect of that dour Spaniard ruling them; and Ferdinand, aspiring to the same throne, could not hope to win without Protestant support in the electoral college.

Arms and circumstances so favored the Protestants that they demanded everything: they were to be free in the practice of their faith in all German territory; Catholic worship was to be forbidden in Lutheran territory; present and future confiscations of Church property were to be held valid and irrevocable.[58] Ferdinand and Augustus worked out a compromise that in four famous words—*cuius regio eius religio*—embodied the spiritual infirmity of the nation and the age. In order to permit peace among and within the states each prince was to choose between Roman Catholicism and Lutheranism; all his subjects were to accept "his religion whose realm" it was; and those who did not like it were to emigrate. There was no pretense on either side to toleration; the principle which the Reformation had upheld in the youth of its rebellion—the right of private judgment—was as completely rejected by the Protestant leaders as by the Catholics. That principle had led to such a variety and clash of sects that the princes felt justified in restoring doctrinal authority, even if it had to be fractured into as many parts as there were states. The Protestants now agreed with Charles and the popes that unity of religious belief was indispensable to social order and peace; and we cannot judge them fairly unless we visualize the hatred and strife that were consuming Germany. The results were bad and good: toleration was now definitely less after the Reformation than before it;[59] but the princes banished dissenters instead of burning them—a rite reserved for witches; and the resultant multiplication of infallibilities weakened them all.

The real victor was not freedom of worship but the freedom of the princes. Each became, like Henry VIII of England, the supreme head of the Church in his territory, with the exclusive right to appoint the clergy and the men who should define the obligatory faith. The "Erastian" principle—

that the state should rule the Church—was definitely established.* As it was the princes, not the theologians, who had led Protestantism to its triumph, they naturally assumed the fruits of victory—their territorial supremacy over the emperor, their ecclesiastical supremacy over the Church. Protestantism was nationalism extended to religion. But the nationalism was not that of Germany; it was the patriotism of each principality; German unity was not furthered, it was hindered, by the religious revolution; but it is not certain that unity would have been a blessing. When Ferdinand was chosen emperor (1558) his Imperial powers were less than those that even the harassed and hampered Charles had possessed. In effect the Holy Roman Empire died not in 1806 but in 1555.

The German cities, like the Empire, lost in the triumph of the princes. The Imperial communes had been wards of the emperor, protected by him against domination by the territorial rulers; now that the emperor was crippled the princes were free to interfere in municipal affairs, and communal independence waned. Meanwhile the growing vigor of Holland absorbed most of the trade that poured German products into the North Sea through the mouths of the Rhine; and the southern cities languished with the relative commercial decline of Venice and the Mediterranean. Commercial and political enfeeblement brought cultural decay; not for two centuries to come would the German towns show again the vitality of trade and thought that had preceded and supported the Reformation.

Melanchthon, surviving the Peace of Augsburg by five years, was not sure that he wanted the reprieve. He had outlived his leadership, not only in negotiations with the Catholics but in the determination of Protestant theology. He had so far liberated himself from Luther as to reject complete predestination and the bodily presence of Christ in the Eucharist,[60] and he struggled to maintain the importance of good works while insisting with Luther that they could not earn salvation. A bitter controversy arose between "Philippists"—Melanchthon and his followers—and the orthodox Lutherans, who fulminated chiefly from Jena; these called Melanchthon "an apostate Mameluke" and "servant of Satan"; he described them as idolatrous sophistical blockheads.[61] Professors were engaged or dismissed, imprisoned or released, as the tides of theological lava ebbed or flowed. The two parties agreed in proclaiming the right of the state to suppress heresy by force. Melanchthon followed Luther in sanctioning serfdom and upholding the divine right of kings;[62] but he wished that the Lutheran movement, instead of allying itself with the princes, had sought rather the protection of municipal burgher aristocracies, as in Zurich, Strasbourg, Nuremberg, and Ge-

* The principle is named after the Swiss theologian Thomas Erastus (1524-83), but cannot be found explicitly in his works.

neva. In his most characteristic moments he spoke like the Erasmian that he had hoped to be: "Let us speak only of the Gospel, of human weakness and divine mercy, of the organization of the Church, and the true worship. To reassure souls and give them a rule of right action—is this not the essence of Christianity? The rest is scholastic debate, sectarian disputes." [63] When death came to him he welcomed it as a benign liberation from the "fury of theologians" and the "barbarity" of "this sophistical age." [64] History had miscast as a general in a revolutionary war a spirit that nature had made for scholarship, friendliness, and peace.

CHAPTER XXI

John Calvin

1509-64

I. YOUTH

HE was born at Noyon, France, July 10, 1509. It was an ecclesiastical city, dominated by its cathedral and its bishop; here at the outset he had an example of theocracy—the rule of a society by clergymen in the name of God. His father, Gérard Chauvin, was secretary to the bishop, proctor in the cathedral chapter, and fiscal procurator of the county. Jean's mother died while he was still young; the father married again, and perhaps Calvin owed to stern step-rearing part of his somber spirit. Gérard destined three of his sons for the priesthood, confident that he could place them well. He found benefices for two, but one of these became a heretic and died refusing the sacraments. Gérard himself was excommunicated after a financial dispute with the cathedral chapter, and had some trouble getting buried in holy ground.

Jean was sent to the Collège de la Marche at the University of Paris. He registered as Johannes Calvinus, and learned to write excellent Latin. He passed later to the Collège de Montaigu, where he must have heard echoes of its famous pupil Erasmus; and he remained there till 1528, when his Catholic counterpart, Ignatius Loyola, entered. "The stories told at one time of Calvin's ill-regulated youth," says a Catholic authority, "have no foundation." [1] On the contrary, the available evidence indicates an assiduous student, shy, taciturn, pious, and already "a severe censor of his comrades' morals"; [2] yet loved by his friends, now as later, with an unshakable fidelity. In the hot pursuit of esoteric knowledge or fascinating theory he read far into the night; even in those student years he developed some of the many ailments that plagued his mature life and helped to form his mood.

Unexpectedly, late in 1528, a directive came from his father to go to Orléans and study law, presumably, said the son, "because he judged that the science of laws commonly enriched those who followed it." [3] Calvin took readily enough to the new study; law, not philosophy or literature, seemed to him the outstanding intellectual achievement of mankind, the molding of man's anarchic impulses to order and peace. He carried into theology and ethics the logic, precision, and severity of Justinian's *Institutes*, and gave his own masterpiece a similar name. He became above all a lawgiver, the Numa and Lycurgus of Geneva.

Having taken his degree as Licentiate or Bachelor of Laws (1531), he returned to Paris and entered upon a voracious study of classical literature. Feeling the common urge to see himself in print, he published (1532) a Latin essay on Seneca's *De clementia;* the sternest of religious legislators began his public career with a salute to mercy. He sent a copy to Erasmus, hailing him as the "second glory" (after Cicero) and "first delight of letters." He seemed dedicated to humanism when some sermons of Luther reached him and stirred him with their audacity. Alert circles in Paris were discussing the new movement, and there must have been much talk about the reckless monk who had burned the bull of a pope and defied the ban of an emperor; indeed, Protestantism had already had martyrs in France. Some men who were urging Church reform were among Calvin's friends; one of them, Gérard Roussel, was a favorite of the King's sister, Marguerite of Navarre; another, Nicholas Cop, was chosen rector of the university, and Calvin probably had a hand in preparing Cop's fateful inaugural address (November 1, 1533). It began with an Erasmian plea for a purified Christianity, proceeded to a Lutheran theory of salvation through faith and grace, and ended with an appeal for a tolerant hearing of the new religious ideas. The speech created a furore; the Sorbonne erupted in anger; the *Parlement* began proceedings against Cop for heresy. He fled; a reward of 300 crowns was offered for his capture alive or dead, but he managed to reach Basel, which was now Protestant.

Calvin was warned by friends that he and Roussel were scheduled for arrest. Marguerite seems to have interceded for him. He left Paris (January 1534) and found refuge in Angoulême; and there, probably in the rich library of Louis de Tillet, he began to write his *Institutes.* In May he ventured back to Noyon, and surrendered the benefices whose income had been supporting him. He was arrested there, was freed, was rearrested and again freed. He returned clandestinely to Paris, talked with Protestant leaders, and met Servetus, whom he was to burn. When some Protestant extremists posted abusive placards at various points in Paris, Francis I retaliated with a furious persecution. Calvin fled just in time (December 1534), and joined Cop in Basel. There, a lad of twenty-six, he completed the most eloquent, fervent, lucid, logical, influential, and terrible work in all the literature of the religious revolution.

II. THE THEOLOGIAN

He published the book in Latin (1536) as *Christianae religionis institutio* (*The Principles of the Christian Religion*). Within a year the issue was sold

Fig. 37—SANCHEZ COELLO: *Ignatius Loyola*

PAGE 970

Fig. 38—*Cathedral*, Segovia

PAGE 846

Fig. 39—SULTAN MUHAMMAD NUR: *Khusrau Sees Shirin Bathing.* From Basil
Gray, *Persian Painting* (Courtesy Oxford University Press)

Fig. 40—BIHZAD: *The Herdsman and King Dara*. From Basil Gray, *Persian Painting* (Courtesy Oxford University Press)

Fig. 41—ISLAMIC CAL-
LIGRAPHY (about
1460). De Motte
Collection

PAGE 701

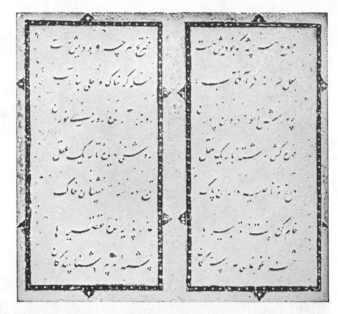

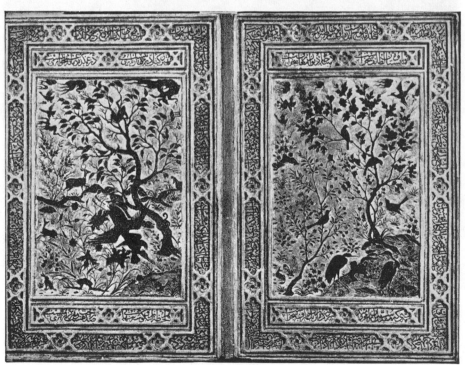

Fig. 42—PERSIAN BOOK COVER (about 1560)   PAGE 701

Fig. 43–CORONATION CARPET (used for the coronation of Edward VII in 1901). Los Angeles County Museum

Fig. 44—*Tomb of Hafiz*, Shiraz, Persia

PAGE 669

Fig. 45—*Blue Mosque* (Sultan Ahmet Mosque), Constantinople   PAGE 686

Fig. 46—*Mosque of Suleiman*, Constantinople   PAGE 716

Fig. 47—*Shrine of Imam Riza*, Mashhad   PAGE 715

Fig. 48—GENTILE BELLINI: *Medallion of Mohammed II*. National Gallery, London

out and a new edition was invited. Calvin responded with a much enlarged version (1539), again in Latin; in 1541 he translated this into French; and this form of the work is one of the most impressive productions in the gamut of French prose. The *Parlement* of Paris proscribed the book in both languages, and copies of it were publicly burned in the capital. Calvin continued throughout his life to expand and republish it; in its final form it ran to 1,118 pages.

The first edition opened with a passionate but dignified "Preface to the Most Christian King of France." Two events gave occasion for addressing Francis: the royal edict of January 1535 against the French Protestants, and the almost simultaneous invitation of Francis to Melanchthon and Bucer to come to France and arrange an alliance between the French monarch and the Lutheran princes against Charles V. Calvin hoped to reinforce political expediency with theological arguments, and help incline the King, like his sister, toward the Protestant cause. He was anxious to dissociate this from the Anabaptist movement then verging on communism in Münster. He described the French reformers as patriots, devoted to the King and averse from all economic or political disturbance. The beginning and end of this famous Preface reveal the majesty of Calvin's thought and style.

> When I began this work, Sire, nothing was further from my thoughts than writing a book which would afterwards be presented to your Majesty. My intention was only to lay down some elementary principles, by which inquirers on the subject of religion might be instructed in the nature of true piety.... But when I perceived that the fury of certain wicked men in your kingdom had grown to such a height as to leave no room in the land for sound doctrine, I thought I should be usefully employed if in the same work ... I exhibited my confession to you, that you may know the nature of that doctrine which is the object of such unbounded rage in those madmen who are now disturbing the country with fire and sword. For I shall not be afraid to acknowledge that this treatise contains a summary of that very doctrine, which, according to their clamors, deserves to be punished with imprisonment, banishment, proscription, and flames, and to be exterminated from the face of the earth. I well know with what atrocious insinuations your ears have been filled by them, in order to render our cause most odious in your esteem; but your clemency should lead you to consider that if accusation be accounted sufficient evidence of guilt, there will be an end to all innocence in words and actions. . . .
>
> You yourself, Sire, can bear witness of the false calumnies with which you hear it [our cause] daily traduced: that its only tendency is to wrest the scepters of kings out of their hands, to overturn all the tribunals . . . to subvert all order and government, to disturb the peace

and tranquillity of the people, to abrogate all laws, to scatter all properties and possessions, and, in a word, to involve everything in total
confusion. . . .

Wherefore I beseech you, Sire—and surely it is not an unreasonable request—to take upon yourself the entire cognizance of this
cause, which has hitherto been confusedly and carelessly agitated,
without any order of law, and with outrageous passion rather than
judicial gravity. Think not that I am now meditating my own individual defense in order to effect a safe return to my native country;
for though I feel the affection which every man ought to feel for it,
yet, under the existing circumstances, I regret not my removal from
it. But I plead the cause of all the godly, and consequently of Christ
Himself. . . .

Is it probable that we are meditating the subversion of kingdoms?
—we who were never heard to utter a factious word, whose lives were
ever known to be peaceable and honest while we lived under your
government, and who, even now in our exile, cease not to pray for
all prosperity to attend yourself and your kingdom! . . . Nor have we,
by Divine Grace, profited so little in the Gospel, but that our life may
be an example to our detractors of chastity, liberality, mercy, temperance, patience, modesty, and every other virtue. . . .

Though you are now averse and alienated from us, and even inflamed against us, we despair not of regaining your favor, if you will
only read with calmness and composure this our confession, which
we intend as our defense before your Majesty. But, on the contrary,
if your ears are so preoccupied with the whispers of the malevolent
as to leave no opportunity for the accused to speak for themselves,
and if those outrageous furies, with your connivance, continue to
persecute with imprisonments, scourges, tortures, confiscations,
and flames, we shall indeed, like sheep destined for the slaughter,
be reduced to the greatest extremities. Yet shall we in patience possess our souls, and wait for the mighty hand of the Lord . . . for the
deliverance of the poor from their affliction, and for the punishment
of their despisers, who now exult in such perfect security. May the
Lord, the King of Kings, establish your throne with righteousness
and your kingdom with equity.[4]

It is difficult for us, in an age when theology has given place to politics as
the center of human interest and conflict, to recapture the mood in which
Calvin composed the *Institutes*. He, much more than Spinoza, was a God-intoxicated man. He was overwhelmed by a sense of man's littleness and God's
immensity. How absurd it would be to suppose that the frail reason of so
infinitesimal a mite as man could understand the Mind behind these innumerable, obedient stars? In pity of man's reason God has revealed Himself

to us in the Bible. That this Holy Book is His Word (says Calvin) is proved by the unrivaled impression that it makes on the human spirit.

> Read Demosthenes or Cicero, read Plato, Aristotle, or any others of that class; I grant you that you will be attracted, delighted, moved, and enraptured by them in a surprising manner; but if, after reading them, you turn to the perusal of the sacred volume, whether you are willing or unwilling, it will affect you so powerfully, it will so penetrate your heart, and impress itself so strongly on your mind, that, compared with its energetic influence, the beauties of rhetoricians and philosophers will almost entirely disappear; so that it is easy to perceive something divine in the sacred Scriptures, which far surpasses the highest attainments and ornaments of human industry.[5]

Consequently this revealed Word must be our final authority, not only in religion and morals but in history, politics, everything. We must accept the story of Adam and Eve; for by their disobedience to God we explain man's evil nature and his loss of free will.

> The mind of man is so completely alienated from the righteousness of God that it conceives, desires, and undertakes everything that is impious, perverse, base, impure, and flagitious. His heart is so thoroughly infected by the poison of sin that it cannot produce anything but what is corrupt; and if at any time men do anything apparently good, yet the mind always remains involved in hypocrisy and deceit, and the heart enslaved by its inward perversity.[6]

How could so depraved a being ever deserve eternal happiness in paradise? Not one of us could ever earn it by any amount of good works. Good works are good, but only the sacrificial death of the Son of God could avail to earn salvation for men. Not for all men, for God's justice demands the damnation of most men. But His mercy has chosen some of us to be saved; and to these he has given an upholding faith in their redemption by Christ. For St. Paul said: "God the Father hath chosen us in Him before the foundation of the world, that we should be holy and without blame before Him in love; having predestinated us unto the adoption of children by Jesus Christ to Himself, according to the good pleasure of His will."[7] Calvin, like Luther, interpreted this to mean that God, by a free choice quite independent of our virtues and vices, determined, long before the creation, just who is to be saved and who is to be damned.[8] To the question why God should choose men for salvation or damnation without regard to their merits, Calvin answers again in the words of Paul: "For He saith to Moses, I will have mercy on whom I will have mercy, and I will have compassion on whom I will have compassion."[9] Calvin concludes:

> In conformity, therefore, to the clear doctrine of Scripture, we assert that by an eternal and immutable counsel God has once for all determined both whom He would admit to salvation, and whom He would condemn to destruction. We affirm that this counsel, as far as concerns the elect, is founded on His gratuitous mercy, totally irrespective of human merit; but that to those whom He devotes to condemnation, the gate of life is closed by a just and irreprehensible, but incomprehensible, judgment.[10]

Even the fall of Adam and Eve, with all its consequences, in the Pauline theory, to the human race, "was ordained by the admirable counsel of God." [11]

Calvin admits that predestination is repulsive to reason, but he replies, "It is unreasonable that man should scrutinize with impunity those things which the Lord has determined to be hidden in Himself." [12] Yet he professes to know why God so arbitrarily determines the eternal fate of billions of souls: it is "to promote our admiration of His glory" by the display of His power.[13] He agrees that this is "a horrible decree" (*decretum horribile*), "but no one can deny that God foreknew the future final fate of man before He created him, and that He foreknew it because it was appointed by His own decree." [14] Others might argue, like Luther, that the future is determined because God has foreseen it and His foresight cannot be falsified; Calvin reverses the matter, and considers that God foresees the future *because* He has willed and determined it. And the decree of damnation is absolute; there is no purgatory in Calvin's theology, no halfway house where one might, by a few million years of burning, wipe out his "reprobation." And therefore there is no room for prayers for the dead.

We might suppose that on Calvin's assumptions there would be no sense in any kind of prayer; all being fixed by divine decree, not an ocean of orisons could wash away one jot of the inexorable destiny. However, Calvin is more human than his theology: let us pray with humility and faith, he tells us, and our prayers will be answered; the prayer and the answer were also decreed. Let us worship God in humble religious services, but we must reject the Mass as a sacrilegious pretense of priests to transform earthly materials into the body and blood of Christ. Christ is present in the Eucharist only spiritually, not physically; and the adoration of the consecrated wafer as literally Christ is sheer idolatry. The use of graven images of the Deity, in clear violation of the Second Commandment, encourages idolatry. All religious pictures and statuary, even the crucifix, should be removed from the churches.

The true Church is the invisible congregation of the elect, dead, living, or to be born. The visible Church is composed of "all those who, by a confession of faith, an exemplary life, and participation in the sacraments of

baptism and the Lord's Supper" (Calvin rejects the other sacraments), "profess the same God and Christ with ourselves." [15] Outside of this Church there
is no salvation.[16] Church and state are both divine, and are designed by God
to work in harmony as the soul and body of one Christian society: the
Church should regulate all details of faith, worship, and morals; the state,
as the physical arm of the Church, should enforce these regulations.[17] The
secular authorities must also see to it that "idolatry" (largely synonymous
with Catholicism in Protestant usage) and "other scandals to religion be not
publicly set forth and broadcast among the people," and that only the pure
Word of God should be taught and received.[18] The ideal government will
be a theocracy, and the Reformed Church should be recognized as the voice
of God. All the claims of the popes for the supremacy of the Church over
the state were renewed by Calvin for his Church.

It is remarkable how much of Roman Catholic tradition and theory survived in Calvin's theology. He owed something to Stoicism, especially to
Seneca, and something to his studies of law; but his chief reliance was on St.
Augustine, who drew predestinarianism out of St. Paul, who did not know
Christ. Calvin sternly ignored Christ's conception of God as a loving and
merciful father, and calmly passed by a multitude of Biblical passages that
assumed man's freedom to mold his own destiny (2 Pet. 3:9; 1 Tim. 2:4; 1
John 2:2; 4:14, etc.). Calvin's genius lay not in conceiving new ideas but
in developing the thought of his predecessors to ruinously logical conclusions, expressing these with an eloquence equaled only by Augustine, and
formulating their practical implications in a system of ecclesiastical legislation. He took from Luther the doctrine of justification or election by faith;
from Zwingli the spiritual interpretation of the Eucharist; and from Bucer
the contradictory notions of the divine will as the cause of all events, and
the requirement of a strenuous practical piety as the test and witness of
election. Most of these Protestant doctrines had come down, in milder form,
in Catholic tradition; Calvin gave them stark emphasis, and neglected the
compensatory mitigating elements in the medieval faith. He was more medieval than any thinker between Augustine and Dante. He completely rejected the humanist concern with earthly excellence, and turned men's
thoughts again, more somberly than before, to the after world. In Calvinism
the Reformation again repudiated the Renaissance.

That so unprepossessing a theology should have won the assent of hundreds
of millions of men in Switzerland, France, Scotland, England, and North
America is at first sight a mystery, then an illumination. Why should Calvinists, Huguenots, and Puritans have fought so valiantly in defense of their
own helplessness? And why has this theory of human impotence shared in
producing some of the strongest characters in history? Is it because these
believers gained more strength from believing themselves the few elect than

they lost by admitting that their conduct contributed nothing to their fate? Calvin himself, at once shy and resolute, was confident that he belonged to the elect, and this so comforted him that he found the "horrible decree" of predestination "productive of the most delightful benefit." [19] Did some of the self-elect take pleasure in considering how few were to be saved, and how many were to be damned? The belief that they were chosen of God gave many souls the courage to face the vicissitudes and apparent aimlessness of life, as a similar faith enabled the Jewish people to preserve itself amid difficulties that might otherwise have sapped the will to live; indeed, the Calvinist idea of being divinely chosen may have been indebted to the Jewish form of the belief, as Protestantism in general owed so much to the Old Testament. The confidence in divine election must have been a tower of courage to Huguenots suffering war and massacre, and to Pilgrims uprooting themselves perilously to seek new homes on hostile shores. If a reformed sinner could catch this confidence, and could believe that his reform had been ordained by God, he could stand unshaken to the end. Calvin enhanced this feeling of pride in election by making the elect, penniless or not, an hereditary aristocracy: the children of the elect were automatically elect by the will of God.[20] So, by a simple act of faith in one's self, one could, if only in imagination, possess and transmit paradise. For such immortal boons a confession of helplessness was a bargain price.

Calvin's followers needed such consolation, for he taught them the medieval view that earthly life is a vale of misery and tears. He cheerfully granted "the correctness of their opinion who considered it as the greatest boon not to be born, and, as the next greatest, to die immediately; nor was there anything irrational in the conduct of those who mourned and wept at the birth of their relations, and solemnly rejoiced at their funerals"; he merely regretted that these wise pessimists, being mostly pagans ignorant of Christ, were doomed to everlasting hell.[21] Only one thing could make life bearable-- the hope of uninterrupted happiness after death. "If heaven is our country, what is the earth but a place of exile?—and if the departure out of this world is an entrance into life, what is the world but a sepulcher?" [22] Unlike his poetical counterpart, Calvin gives his most eloquent pages not to the phantasmagoria of hell but to the loveliness of heaven. The pious elect will suffer without a murmur all the pains and griefs of life. "For they will keep in view that day when the Lord will receive His faithful servants into His peaceful kingdom, will wipe every tear from their eyes, invest them with robes of joy, adorn them with crowns of glory, entertain them with ineffable delights, and exalt them to a fellowship with His majesty, and . . . a participation in His happiness." [23] For the poor or unfortunate, who cover the earth, it may have been an indispensable belief.

III. GENEVA AND STRASBOURG: 1536-41

While the *Institutes* was in the press (March 1536), Calvin, according to a tradition generally but not unanimously accepted,[24] made a hurried trip across the Alps to Ferrara, probably to ask help for the persecuted Protestants of France from the Protestant Duchess Renée, wife of Duke Ercole II and daughter of the late Louis XII. Moved by the fervor of his religious convictions, she made him her spiritual guide through reverent correspondence till his death. Returning to Basel in May, Calvin ventured to Noyon to sell some property; then, with a brother and a sister, he started for Strasbourg. War barring the road, they stopped for a time at Geneva (July 1536).

The capital of French Switzerland was older than history. In prehistoric times it was a congeries of lake dwellings, built upon piles, some of which can still be seen. In Caesar's day it was a busy crossing of trade routes at the bridge where the Rhone rushes out of Lake Leman to wander through France in search of the Mediterranean. In the Middle Ages Geneva fell under the secular as well as spiritual rule of its bishop. Normally the bishop was chosen by the cathedral chapter, which thereby became a power in the city; this was essentially the government that Calvin later restored in Protestant form. In the fifteenth century the dukes of Savoy, which lay just beyond the Alps, secured control of the chapter, and raised to the episcopate men subservient to Savoy and given to the pleasures of this world for fear there might not be a next. The once excellent episcopal government, and the morals of the clergy under it, deteriorated. A priest, bidden to dismiss his concubine, agreed to do so as soon as his fellow clergymen would be equally ungallant; gallantry prevailed.[25]

Within this ecclesiastical-ducal rule the leading families of Geneva organized a Council of Sixty for municipal ordinances, and the Council chose four syndics as executive officers. Usually the Council met in the bishop's cathedral of St. Peter; and religious and civil jurisdiction were so mingled that while the bishop minted the coinage and led the army, the Council regulated morals, issued excommunications, and licensed prostitutes. As in Trier, Mainz, and Cologne, the bishop was also a prince of the Holy Roman Empire, and naturally assumed functions from which bishops are now free. Some civic leaders, led by François de Bonnivard, sought to liberate the city from both the episcopal and the ducal authority. To strengthen this movement these *Patriotes* effected an alliance with Catholic Fribourg and Protestant Bern. Adherents of the alliance were called by the German term for confederates—*Eidgenossen*, oath comrades; the French corrupted this into *Huguenots*. By 1520 the Genevese leaders were mostly businessmen, for Geneva, unlike Wittenberg, was a commercial city, mediating in trade be-

^{nr}een Switzerland on the north, Italy on the south, and France on the west. The Genevese burghers set up (1526) a Great Council of Two Hundred, and this chose a Small Council of Twenty-Five, which became the real ruler of the municipality, frequently flouting the authority of bishop and duke alike. The bishop declared the city in rebellion, and summoned ducal troops to his aid. These seized Bonnivard, and imprisoned him in the castle of Chillon. The Bernese army came to the aid of beleaguered Geneva; the duke's forces were defeated and dispersed; the bishop fled to Annecy; Byron's hero was freed from his dungeon. The Great Council, angered by the clergy's support of Savoy, declared for the Reformed faith, and assumed ecclesiastical as well as civil jurisdiction throughout the city (1536), two months before Calvin arrived.

The doctrinal hero of this revolution was William Farel. Like Luther, he was passionately pious in youth. At Paris he came under the influence of Jacques Lefèvre d'Etaples, whose translation and explanation of the Bible upset Farel's orthodoxy; for in the Scriptures he could find no trace of popes, bishops, indulgences, purgatory, seven sacraments, the Mass, the celibacy of the clergy, the worship of Mary or the saints. Disdaining ordination, he set out as an independent preacher, wandering from town to town in France and Switzerland. Small of stature, weak of frame, strong of voice and spirit, his pale face brightened by fiery eyes and a beard of flaming red, he denounced the pope as Antichrist, the Mass as sacrilege, the church icons as idola that must be destroyed. In 1532 he began to preach in Geneva. He was arrested by the bishop's agents, who proposed to throw the "Lutheran dog" into the Rhone; the syndics intervened, and Farel escaped with a few bruises on his head and some spittle on his coat. He won the Council of Twenty-Five to his views, and, with the aid of Peter Viret and Antoine Froment, aroused so much popular support that nearly all the Catholic clergy departed. On May 21, 1536, the Small Council decreed the abolition of the Mass, and the removal of all images and relics from the churches. Ecclesiastical properties were converted to Protestant uses for religion, charity, and education; education was made compulsory and free of charge; and a strict moral discipline was made law. The citizens were called upon to swear allegiance to the Gospel, and those who refused to attend Reformed services were banished.[26] This was the Geneva to which Calvin came.

Farel was now forty-seven; and though he was destined to outlive Calvin by a year, he saw in the stern and eloquent youth, twenty years his junior, just the man needed to consolidate and advance the Reform. Calvin was reluctant; he had planned a life of scholarship and writing; he was more at ease with God than with men. But Farel, with the mien of some thundering Biblical prophet, threatened to lay a holy curse upon him if he should prefer his private studies to the arduous and dangerous preaching of the undiluted

Word. Calvin yielded; Council and presbytery approved; and—with no other ordination—he began his ministry (September 5, 1536) by giving in the church of St. Peter the first of several addresses on the Epistles of St. Paul. Everywhere in Protestantism, except among the socially radical sects, the influence of Paul overshadowed that of Peter, the reputed founder of the Roman See.

In October Calvin accompanied Farel and Viret to Lausanne, and took a minor part in the famous disputation that won that city to the Protestant camp. Returning to Geneva, the senior and junior pastors of St. Peter's set about to rededicate the Genevese to God. Sincerely accepting the Bible as the literal Word of God, they felt an inescapable obligation to enforce its moral code. They were shocked to find many of the people given to singing, dancing, and similar gaieties; moreover, some gambled, or drank to intoxication, or committed adultery. An entire district of the city was occupied by prostitutes, under the rule of their own *Reine du bordel*, the Brothel Queen. To the fiery Farel and the conscientious Calvin a genial acceptance of this situation was treason to God.

To restore the religious basis of an effective morality, Farel issued a *Confession of Faith and Discipline*, and Calvin a popular *Catechism*, which the Great Council approved (November 1536). Citizens persistently transgressing the moral code were to be excommunicated and exiled. In July 1537, the Council ordered all citizens to go to the church of St. Peter and swear allegiance to Farel's *Confession*. Any manifestation of Catholicism—such as carrying a rosary, cherishing a sacred relic, or observing a saint's day as holy—was subject to punishment. Women were imprisoned for wearing improper hats. Bonnivard, too joyous in his liberty, was warned to end his licentious ways. Gamblers were put into the stocks. Adulterers were driven through the streets into banishment.

Accustomed to ecclesiastical rule, but to the lenient moral discipline of a Catholicism softened by southern climes, the Genevese resisted the new dispensation. The *Patriotes*, who had freed the city from bishop and duke, reorganized to free it from its zealous ministers. Another party, demanding liberty of conscience and worship, and therefore called *Libertins* or Liberals,* joined with the *Patriotes* and the secret Catholics; and this coalition, in the election of February 3, 1538, captured a majority in the Great Council. The new Council told the ministers to keep out of politics. Farel and Calvin denounced the Council, and refused to serve the Lord's Supper until the rebellious city conformed to the sworn discipline. The Council deposed the two ministers (April 23), and ordered them to leave the city within three days. The people celebrated the dismissal with public rejoicings.[27] Farel ac-

---

* Calvin, by charging them with moral laxity, gave the word *libertine* its new connotation.

cepted a call to Neuchâtel; there he preached to the end of his days (1565), and there a public monument honors his memory.

Calvin went to Strasbourg, then a free city subject only to the emperor, and ministered to *L'Église des Étrangers*, a congregation of Protestants chiefly from France. To eke out the fifty-two guilders ($1,300?) annually paid him by the church, he sold his library and took students as boarders. Finding bachelorhood inconvenient in this situation, he asked Farel and Bucer to search out a wife for him, and listed specifications: "I am none of those insane lovers who, when once smitten with the fine figure of a woman, embrace also her faults. This only is the beauty which allures me—that she be chaste, obliging, not fastidious, economical, patient, and careful for my health." [28] After two false starts he married (1540) Idelette de Bure, a poor widow with several children. She bore him one child, who died in infancy. When she passed away (1549) he wrote of her with the private tenderness that underlay his public severity. He lived in domestic loneliness the remaining fifteen years of his life.

While he labored in Strasbourg events moved on at Geneva. Encouraged by the expulsion of Farel and Calvin, the exiled bishop planned a triumphant return to his cathedral. As a preliminary step he persuaded Iacopo Sadoleto to write an *Epistle to the Genevese*, urging them to resume their Catholic worship and faith (1539). Sadoleto was a gentleman of exceptional virtue for a cardinal and a humanist; he had already advised the papacy to handle Protestant dissent gently, and he later received under his protection at Carpentras heretical Waldenses fleeing from massacre (1545). In a fine Latin learned under the impeccable Bembo, he addressed "to his dearly beloved Brethren, the Magistrates, Senate, and citizens of Geneva," twenty pages of diplomatic courtesies and theological exhortation. He noted the rapid division of Protestantism into warring sects, led, he alleged, by crafty men avid for power; he compared this with the centuries-long unity of the Roman Church, and asked whether it was more likely that truth lay with those contradictory factions than with a Catholic doctrine formed by the experience of ages and the assembled intelligence of ecclesiastical councils. He concluded by offering to Geneva whatever service it was in his power to give.

The Council thanked him for his compliments, and promised him a further response. But no one could be found in Geneva who would undertake to cross swords, or Latin, with the polished humanist. Meanwhile a number of citizens asked to be released from their oath to support the *Confession of Faith and Discipline*, and for a time it seemed that the city would return to Catholicism. Calvin learned of the situation, and in a reply to the Cardinal he rose with all the power of his mind and pen to the defense of the Reformation. He countered courtesy with courtesy, eloquence with eloquence, but he would not yield an inch of his theology. He protested against the implication that he had rebelled through personal ambition; he could have risen to far greater comfort had he remained orthodox. He admitted the divine foundation of the Catholic Church, but he charged that the vices of the Renaissance popes proved the capture of the papacy by Antichrist. To the wisdom of Church councils he opposed the wisdom of the Bible, which Sadoleto had almost ignored. He regretted that the corruption of the Church had necessitated secession and division, but only so could the evils be cured. If Catholics and Protestants would now co-operate to cleanse the doctrine, ritual, and personnel of all the Christian churches, they would be rewarded with a final unity in heaven with Christ. It was a powerful letter, perhaps unappreciative of the incidental virtues of the Renaissance popes, but otherwise phrased with a comity and dignity rare in the controversies of the time. Luther, reading it in Wittenberg, hailed it as quite annihilating the Cardinal; "I rejoice," he cried, "that God raises up men who will . . . finish the war against Antichrist which I began." [29] The Council of Geneva was so impressed that it ordered the two letters printed at the city's expense (1540). It began to wonder whether, in banishing Calvin, it had lost the ablest man in the Swiss Reform.

Other factors nourished the doubt. The ministers who had replaced Farel and Calvin proved incompetent both in preaching and in discipline. The public lost respect for them, and returned to the easy morality of unreformed days. Gambling, drunkenness, street brawls, adultery, flourished; lewd songs were publicly sung, persons romped naked through the streets.[30] Of the four syndics who had led the movement to expel Farel and Calvin, one had to be condemned to death for murder, another for forgery, a third for treason, and the fourth died while trying to escape arrest. The businessmen who controlled the Council must have frowned upon this disorder as impeding trade. The Council itself had no taste for being replaced and perhaps excommunicated by a restored bishop. Gradually a majority of the members came to the idea of recalling Calvin. On May 1, 1541, the Council annulled the sentence of banishment, and pronounced Farel and Calvin to be honorable men. Deputation after deputation was sent to Strasbourg to persuade Calvin to resume his pastorate at Geneva. Farel forgave the city for not extending him a similar invitation, and with noble generosity joined the deputations in urging Calvin to return. But Calvin had made many friends in Strasbourg, felt obligations there, and saw nothing but strife in store for him at Geneva; "there is no place in the world that I fear more." He agreed only to pay the city a visit. When he arrived (September 13, 1541) he received so many honors, so many apologies, so many promises of co-operation in re-establishing order and the Gospel, that he had not the heart to refuse. On September 16 he wrote to Farel: "Your wish is granted. I am held fast here. May God give His blessing." [31]

IV. THE CITY OF GOD

Calvin behaved, in the early years of his recall, with a moderation and modesty that won all but a small minority to his support. Eight assistant pastors were appointed, under him, to serve St. Peter's and the other churches of the city. He labored twelve to eighteen hours a day as preacher, administrator, professor of theology, superintendent of churches and schools, adviser to municipal councils, and regulator of public morals and church liturgy; meanwhile he kept enlarging the *Institutes*, wrote commentaries on the Bible, and maintained a correspondence second in extent only to that of Erasmus, and surpassing it in influence. He slept little, ate little, fasted frequently. His successor and biographer, Théodore de Bèze, marveled that one little man *(unicus homunculus)* could carry so heavy and varied a burden.

His first task was the reorganization of the Reformed Church. At his request the Small Council, soon after his return, appointed a commission of five clergymen and six councilors, with Calvin at their head, to formulate a new ecclesiastical code. On January 2, 1542, the Great Council ratified the resultant *Ordonnances ecclésiastiques*, whose essential features are still accepted by the Reformed and Presbyterian churches of Europe and America. The ministry was divided into pastors, teachers, lay elders, and deacons. The pastors of Geneva constituted "The Venerable Company," which governed the Church and trained candidates for the ministry. No one henceforth was to preach in Geneva without authorization by the Company; the consent of the city council and the congregation was also required, but episcopal ordinations—and bishops—were taboo. The new clergy, while never claiming the miraculous powers of the Catholic priests, and though decreeing themselves ineligible for civil office, became under Calvin more powerful than any priesthood since ancient Israel. The real law of a Christian state, said Calvin, must be the Bible; the clergy are the proper interpreters of that law; civil governments are subject to that law, and must enforce it as so interpreted. The practical men in the councils may have had some doubts on these points, but they appear to have felt that social order was so profitable to the economy that some ecclesiastical assumptions might for the time being go unchallenged. Through an astonishing quarter of a century a theocracy of clergymen seemed to dominate an oligarchy of merchants and men of affairs.

The authority of the clergy over Genevese life was exercised through a Consistory or Presbytery composed of five pastors and twelve lay elders, all chosen by the Council. As the pastors held tenure throughout their ministry, and the elders for only a year, the Consistory, in matters not vitally affecting business, was ruled by its ecclesiastical members. It took the right to ordain the religious worship and moral conduct of every inhabitant; it sent a minister and an elder to visit every house and family annually; it could summon any person before it for examination; it could publicly reprove or excommunicate offenders, and could rely on the Council to banish from the city those whom the Consistory banned from the Church. Calvin held power as the head of this Consistory; from 1541 till his death in 1564 his voice was the most influential in Geneva. His dictatorship was one not of law or force but of will and character. The intensity of his belief in his mission, and the completeness of his devotion to his tasks, gave him a strength that no one could successfully resist. Hildebrand, revived, could have rejoiced over this apparent triumph of the Church over the state.

So empowered, the clergy first regulated religious worship. "The whole household shall attend the sermons on Sunday, except when someone shall be left at home to tend the children or the cattle. If there is preaching on weekdays all who can must come." (Calvin preached three or four times a week.) "Should anyone come after the sermon has begun, let him be warned. If he does not amend, let him pay a fine of three sous." [32] No one was to be excused from Protestant services on the plea of having a different or private religious creed; Calvin was as thorough as any pope in rejecting individualism of belief; this greatest legislator of Protestantism completely repudiated that principle of private judgment with which the new religion had begun. He had seen the fragmentation of the Reformation into a hundred sects, and foresaw more; in Geneva he would have none of them. There a body of learned divines would formulate an authoritative creed; those Genevans who could not accept it would have to seek other habitats. Persistent absence from Protestant services, or continued refusal to take the Eucharist, was a punishable offense. Heresy again became an insult to God and treason to the state, and was to be punished with death. Catholicism, which had preached this view of heresy, became heresy in its turn. Between 1542 and 1564 fifty-eight persons were put to death, and seventy-six were banished, for violating the new code. Here, as elsewhere, witchcraft was a capital crime; in one year, on the advice of the Consistory, fourteen alleged witches were sent to the stake on the charge that they had persuaded Satan to afflict Geneva with plague.[33]

The Consistory made little distinction between religion and morality. Conduct was to be guided as carefully as belief, for good conduct was the goal of right belief. Calvin himself, austere and severe, dreamed of a community so well regulated that its virtue would prove his theology, and would shame the Catholicism that had produced or tolerated the luxury and laxity of Rome. Discipline should be the backbone of personality, enabling it to rise out of the baseness of human nature to the erect stature of the self-conquered man. The clergy must lead by example as well as precept; they may marry and beget, but they must abstain from hunting, gambling, feasting, commerce, and secular amusements, and accept annual visitation and moral scrutiny by their ecclesiastical superiors.

To regulate lay conduct a system of domiciliary visits was established: one or another of the elders visited, yearly, each house in the quarter assigned to him, and questioned the occupants on all phases of their lives. Consistory and Council joined in the prohibition of gambling, card-playing, profanity, drunkenness, the frequenting of taverns, dancing (which was then enhanced by kisses and embraces), indecent or irreligious songs, excess in entertainment, extravagance in living, immodesty in dress. The allowable color and quantity of clothing, and the number of dishes permissible at a meal, were specified by law. Jewelry and lace were frowned upon. A woman was jailed for arranging her hair to an immoral height.[34] Theatrical performances were limited to religious plays, and then these too were forbidden. Children were to be named not after saints in the Catholic calendar but preferably after Old Testament characters; an obstinate father served four days in prison for insisting on naming his son Claude instead of Abraham.[35] Censorship of the press was taken over from Catholic and secular precedents, and enlarged (1560): books of erroneous religious doctrine, or of immoral tendency, were banned; Montaigne's *Essays* and Rousseau's *Émile* were later to fall under this proscription. To speak disrespectfully of Calvin or the clergy was a crime.[36] A first violation of these ordinances was punished with a reprimand, further violation with fines, persistent violation with imprisonment or banishment. Fornication was to be punished with exile or drowning; adultery, blasphemy, or idolatry, with death. In one extraordinary instance a child was beheaded for striking its parents.[37] In the years 1558–59 there were 414 prosecutions for moral offenses; between 1542 and 1564 there were seventy-six banishments and fifty-eight executions; the total population of Geneva was then about 20,000.[38] As everywhere in the sixteenth century, torture was often used to obtain confessions or evidence.

Regulation was extended to education, society, and the economic life. Calvin established schools and an academy, searched through Western Europe for good teachers of Latin, Greek, Hebrew, and theology, and trained young ministers who carried his gospel into France, Holland, Scotland, and England with all the ardor and devotion of Jesuit missionaries in Asia; in eleven years (1555–66) Geneva sent 161 such envoys into France, many of whom sang Huguenot psalms as they suffered martyrdom. Calvin considered class divisions natural, and his legislation protected rank and dignity by prescribing the quality of dress, and the limits of activity for each class.[39] Every person was expected to accept his place in society, and to perform its duties without envy of his betters or complaint of his lot. Begging was banned, and indiscriminate charity was replaced by careful communal administration of poor relief.

Calvinism gave to hard work, sobriety, diligence, frugality, and thrift a religious sanction and laurel that may have shared in developing the industrious temper of the modern Protestant businessman; but this relationship has been overstressed.[40] Capitalism was more highly developed in Catholic Florence and Flanders before the Reformation than in Calvin's Geneva. Calvin rejected individualism in economics as well as in religion and morals. The unit of society, in his view, was not the free individual (with whom Luther had begun his revolt) but the city-state community, whose members were bound to it in rigorous law and discipline. "No member of the Christian community," he wrote, "holds his gifts to himself, or for his private use, but shares them among his fellow members; nor does he derive benefit save from those things which proceed from the common profit of the body as a whole." [41] He had no sympathy with acquisitive speculation or ruthless accumulation.[42] Like some late-medieval Catholic theorists, he permitted interest on loans, but in theory he limited it to 5 per cent, and urged loans without interest to necessitous individuals or the state.[43] With his approval the Consistory punished engrossers, monopolists, and lenders who charged excessive interest; it fixed prices for food and clothes and surgical operations; it censured or fined merchants who defrauded their clients, dealers who skimped their measures, clothiers who cut their cloth too short.[44] Sometimes the regime moved toward state socialism: the Venerable Company established a bank, and conducted some industries.[45]

If we bear these limiting factors in mind, we may admit a quiet and growing entente between Calvinism and business. Calvin could not long have kept his leadership had he obstructed the commercial development of a city whose commerce was its life. He adjusted himself to the situation, allowed interest charges of 10 per cent, and recommended state loans to finance the introduction or expansion of private industry, as in the manufacture of clothing or the production of silk. Commercial centers like Antwerp, Amsterdam, and London took readily to the first modern religion that accepted the modern economy. Calvinism took the middle classes into its fold, and grew with their growth.

What were the results of Calvin's rule? The difficulties of enforcement must have been extreme, for never in history had such strict virtue been required of a city. A considerable party opposed the regimen, even to the point of open revolt, but a substantial number of influential citizens must have supported it, if only on the general theory of morals—that others need them. The influx of French Huguenots and other Protestants must have strengthened Calvin's hand; and the limitation of the experiment to Geneva and its hinterland raised the chances of success. The recurrent fear of invasion and absorption by hostile states (Savoy, Italy, France, the Empire) compelled political stability and civic obedience; external danger promoted internal discipline. In any case we have an enthusiastic description of the results from the pen of an eyewitness, Bernardino Ochino, an Italian Protestant who had found refuge in Geneva:

> Cursing and swearing, unchastity, sacrilege, adultery, and impure living, such as prevail in many places where I have lived, are here unknown. There are no pimps and harlots. The people do not know what rouge is, and they are all clad in seemly fashion. Games of chance are not customary. Benevolence is so great that the poor need not beg. The people admonish one another in brotherly fashion, as Christ prescribes. Lawsuits are banished from the city, nor is there any simony, murder, or party spirit, but only peace and charity. On the other hand, there are no organs here, no voice of bells, no showy songs, no burning candles or lamps [in the churches], no relics, pictures, statues, canopies, or splendid robes, no farces or cold ceremonies. The churches are quite free from idolatry.[46]

The extant records of the Council for this period do not quite agree with this report: they reveal a high percentage of illegitimate children, abandoned infants, forced marriages, and sentences of death;[47] Calvin's son-in-law and his stepdaughter were among those condemned for adultery.[48] But then again, as late as 1610, we find Valentin Andreae, a Lutheran minister from Württemberg, praising Geneva enviously:

> When I was in Geneva I observed something great which I shall remember and desire as long as I live. There is in that city not only the perfect institute of a perfect republic, but, as a special ornament, a moral discipline which makes weekly investigations into the conduct, and even the smallest transgressions, of the citizens. . . . All cursing and swearing, gambling, luxury, strife, hatred, fraud, etc., are forbidden, while greater sins are hardly heard of. What a glorious ornament of the Christian religion is such a purity of morals! We must lament with tears that it is wanting with us [Germans], and almost totally neglected. If it were not for the difference of religion, I would have been chained to Geneva forever.[49]

V. THE CONFLICTS OF CALVIN

Calvin's character harmonized with his theology. The oil painting in the University Library at Geneva pictures him as a severe and somber mystic; dark but bloodless complexion, scanty black beard, high forehead, penetrating, ruthless eyes. He was short and thin and physically frail, hardly fit to carry a city in his hands. But behind the weak frame burned a mind sharp, narrow, devoted, and intense, and a firm, indomitable will, perhaps a will to power. His intellect was a citadel of order, making him almost the Aquinas of Protestant theology. His memory was crowded and yet precise. He was ahead of his time in doubting astrology, abreast of it in rejecting Copernicus, a bit behind it (like Luther) in ascribing many terrestrial occurrences to the Devil. His timidity concealed his courage, his shyness disguised an inner pride, his humility before God became at times a commanding arrogance before men. He was painfully sensitive to criticism, and could not bear opposition with the patience of one who can conceive the possibility that he may be wrong. Racked with illness, bent with work, he often lost his temper and broke out into fits of angry eloquence; he confessed to Bucer that he found it difficult to tame "the wild beast of his wrath." [50] His virtues did not include humor, which might have softened his certainties, nor a sense of beauty, which might have spared ecclesiastical art. Yet he was no unmitigated kill-joy; he bade his followers be cheerful, play harmless games like bowling or quoits, and enjoy wine in moderation. He could be a kind and tender friend, and an unforgiving enemy, capable of hard judgments and stern revenge. Those who served him feared him,[51] but those loved him most who knew him best. Sexually his life showed no fault. He lived simply, ate sparingly, fasted unostentatiously, slept only six hours a day, never took a holiday, used himself up without stint in what he thought was the service of God. He refused increases in salary, but labored to raise funds for the relief of the poor. "The strength of that heretic," said Pope Pius IV, "consisted in this, that money never had the slightest charm for him. If I had such servants my dominion would extend from sea to sea." [52]

A man of such mettle must raise many enemies. He fought them with vigor, and in the controversial language of the time. He described his opponents as riffraff, idiots, dogs, asses, pigs, and stinking beasts [53]—epithets less becoming to his elegant Latinity than to Luther's gladiatorial style. But he had provocations. One day Jerome Bolsec, an ex-monk from France, interrupted Calvin's sermon at St. Peter's to denounce the predestinarian doctrine as an insult to God; Calvin answered him by citing Scripture; the police arrested Bolsec; the Consistory charged him with heresy; the Council was inclined to put him to death. But when the opinions of theologians in Zurich, Basel, and Bern were solicited, they proved disconcerting: Bern recommended caution in dealing with problems beyond human ken—a new note in the literature of the age; and Bullinger warned Calvin that "many are displeased with what you say in your *Institutes* about predestination, and draw the same conclusions as Bolsec." [54] The Council compromised on banishment (1551). Bolsec returned to France and Catholicism.

More important in result was Calvin's controversy with Joachim Westphal. This Lutheran minister of Hamburg denounced as "Satanic blasphe-mies" the view of Zwingli and Calvin that Christ was only spiritually present in the Eucharist, and thought the Swiss Reformers should be refuted not by the pens of theologians but by the rods of magistrates (1552). Calvin an-swered him in terms so severe that his fellow Reformers at Zurich, Basel, and Bern refused to sign his remonstrance. He issued it nevertheless; Westphal and other Lutherans returned to the attack; Calvin branded them as "apes of Luther," and argued so effectively that several regions hitherto Lutheran— Brandenburg, the Palatinate, and parts of Hesse, Bremen, Anhalt, and Baden —were won to the Swiss view and the Reformed Church; only the silence of Melanchthon (who secretly agreed with Calvin), and the post-mortem echo of Luther's thunderbolts saved the rest of northern Germany for the Lutheran creed.

Turning from these assaults on the right, Calvin faced on the left a group of radicals recently arrived in Switzerland from Counter Reformation Italy. Caelius Secundus Curio, teaching in Lausanne and Basel, shocked Calvin by announcing that the saved—including many heathen—would far outnumber the damned. Laelius Socinus, son of a leading Italian jurist, settled in Zurich, studied Greek, Arabic, and Hebrew in order to understand the Bible better, learned too much, and lost his faith in the Trinity, predestination, original sin, and the atonement. He expressed his skepticism to Calvin, who answered as well as possible. Socinus agreed to refrain from public utterance of his doubts; but later he spoke out against the execution of Servetus, and was among the few who, in that fevered age, stood up for religious toleration.

In a state where religion and government were fused in an intoxicating mixture, it was natural that Calvin's most persistent conflicts should be with the *Patriotes* and *Libertins* who had once expelled him and now deplored his return. The Patriots resented his French origin and supporters, abhorred his theology, nicknamed him Cain and called their dogs Calvin; they insulted him in the streets, and probably it was they who one night fired fifty shots outside his home. The *Libertins* preached a pantheistic creed without devils, angels, Eden, atonement, Bible, or pope. Queen Margaret of Navarre re-ceived and supported them at her court in Nérac, and reproved Calvin for his severity with them.

On June 27, 1547, Calvin found attached to his pulpit a placard reading:

> Gross hypocrite! You and your companions will gain little by your pains. If you do not save yourselves by flight, nobody shall prevent your overthrow, and you will curse the hour when you left your monkery.... After people have suffered long they avenge themselves. ... Take care that you are not served like M. Verle [who had been killed].... We will not have so many masters....[55]

Jacques Gruet, a leading *Libertin*, was arrested on suspicion of having written the placard; no proof was adduced. It was claimed that he had, some days
previously, uttered threats against Calvin. In his room were found papers,
allegedly in his handwriting, calling Calvin a haughty and ambitious hypocrite, and ridiculing the inspiration of the Scriptures and the immortality of
the soul. He was tortured twice daily for thirty days until he confessed—we
do not know how truthfully—that he had affixed the placard and conspired
with French agents against Calvin and Geneva. On July 26, half dead, he
was tied to a stake, his feet were nailed to it, and his head was cut off.[56]

Tension mounted until, on December 16, 1547, the *Patriotes* and *Libertins*
came armed to a meeting of the Great Council, and demanded an end to the
power of the Consistory over the citizens. At the height of a violent tumult
Calvin entered the room, faced the hostile leaders, and said, striking his
breast: "If you want blood, there are still a few drops here; strike, then!"
Swords were drawn, but no one ventured to be the first assassin. Calvin
addressed the gathering with rare moderation, and finally persuaded all parties to a truce. Nevertheless his confidence in himself was shaken. On December 17 he wrote to Viret: "I hardly hope that the Church can be upheld
much longer, at least by my ministry. Believe me, my power is broken, unless God stretch forth His hand." But the opposition divided into factions,
and subsided till the trial of Servetus offered another opportunity.

VI. MICHAEL SERVETUS: 1511–53

Miguel Serveto was born at Villanova (some sixty miles north of Saragossa), son of a notary of good family. He grew up at a time when the
writings of Erasmus were enjoying a transitory tolerance in Spain. He was in
some measure influenced by the literature of the Jews and the Moslems; he
read the Koran, made his way through rabbinical commentaries, and was
impressed by the Semitic criticism of Christianity (with its prayers to a
Trinity, to Mary, and to saints) as polytheistic. Luther called him "the
Moor." At Toulouse, where he studied law, he saw for the first time a complete Bible, vowed to read it "a thousand times," and was deeply moved by
the visions of the Apocalypse. He won the patronage of Juan de Quintana,
confessor to Charles V, and was taken by Juan to Bologna and Augsburg
(1530). Michael discovered Protestantism, and liked it; he visited Oecolampadius at Basel, and Capito and Bucer at Strasbourg; soon he was too
heretical for their taste, and was invited to graze in other fields.

In 1531 and 1532 he published the first and second edition of his basic
work, *De Trinitatis erroribus*. It was rather confused, and in a crude Latin
that must have made Calvin smile if ever; but in wealth of Biblical erudition

it was an astonishing performance for a lad of twenty. Jesus, in Servetus's view, was a man into whom God the Father had breathed the Logos, the Divine Wisdom; in this sense Jesus *became* the Son of God; but he was not equal or co-eternal with the Father, Who might communicate the same spirit of wisdom to other men; "the Son was sent from the Father in no other way than as one of the Prophets." [57] This was pretty close to Mohammed's conception of Christ. Servetus proceeded to take the Semitic view of Trinitarianism. "All those who believe in a Trinity in the essence of God are tritheists"; and, he added, they are "true atheists" as deniers of the One God.[58] This was youthfully extreme, but Servetus tried to soften his heresy by inditing rhapsodies on Christ as the Light of the World; most of his readers, however, felt that he had extinguished the light. As if to leave no stone unhurled, he concurred with the Anabaptists that baptism should be given only to adults. Oecolampadius and Bucer repudiated him, and Servetus, reversing Calvin's itinerary, fled from Switzerland to France (1532).

On July 17 the Inquisition at Toulouse issued a warrant for his arrest. He thought of going to America, but found Paris more agreeable. There, disguising himself as Michel de Villeneuve (the family name), he studied mathematics, geography, astronomy, and medicine, and flirted with astrology. The great Vesalius was his fellow student in dissection, and their teachers praised them equally. He quarreled with the dean of the medical faculty, and seems in general to have given offense by his impetuosity, passion, and pride. He challenged Calvin to a debate, but did not appear at the appointed place and time (1534). In the furore over Cop's address and the heretical placards, Servetus, like Calvin, left Paris. At Lyons he edited a scholarly edition of Ptolemy's *Geography*. In 1540 he moved to Vienne (sixteen miles south of Lyons), and there he lived till his last year, practicing medicine and scholarship. Out of so many scholars available to the Lyons publishers-printers, he was chosen to edit a Latin translation of the Bible by Santes Pagnini. The work took him three years, and ran to six volumes. In a note on Isaiah 7:14, which Jerome had rendered "a virgin shall conceive," Servetus explained that the Hebrew word meant not virgin but young woman, and he suggested that it referred not prophetically to Mary but simply to Hezekiah's wife. In the same spirit he indicated that other seemingly prophetic passages in the Old Testament referred only to contemporary figures or events. This proved disconcerting to Protestants and Catholics alike.

We do not know when Servetus discovered the pulmonary circulation of the blood—the passage of the blood from the right chamber of the heart along the pulmonary artery to and through the lungs, its purification there by aeration, and its return via the pulmonary vein to the left chamber of the heart. So far as is now known, he did not publish his finding till 1553, when

he included it in his final work, *The Restitution of Christianity*. He brought
the theory into a theological treatise because he thought of the blood as the
vital spirit in man, and therefore—more probably than the heart or the brain
—the real seat of the soul. Deferring for a while the problem of Servetus's
priority in this discovery, we merely note that he had apparently completed
the *Christianismi restitutio* by 1546, for in that year he sent the manuscript
to Calvin.

The very title was a challenge to the man who had written the *Christianae
religionis institutio;* but further, the book sharply rejected, as blasphemy, the
notion that God had predestined souls to hell regardless of their merits or
guilt. God, said Servetus, condemns no one who does not condemn himself.
Faith is good, but love is better, and God Himself is love. Calvin thought it
sufficient refutation of all this to send Servetus a copy of the *Institutes*.
Servetus returned it with insulting annotations,[59] and followed up with a
series of letters so contemptuous that Calvin wrote to Farel (February 13,
1546): "Servetus has just sent me a long volume of his ravings. If I consent
he will come here, but I will not give my word, for should he come, if my
authority is of any avail, I will not suffer him to get out alive." [60] Servetus,
angry at Calvin's refusal to continue the correspondence, wrote to Abel
Poupin, one of the Genevese ministers (1547):

> Your gospel is without God, without true faith, without good
> works. Instead of a God you have a three-headed Cerberus [the
> predestinating Trinity?]. For faith you have a deterministic dream.
> . . . Man is with you an inert trunk, and God is a chimera of the en-
> slaved will. . . . You close the Kingdom of Heaven before men. . . .
> Woe! woe! woe! This is the third letter that I have written to warn
> you, that you may know better. I will not warn you again. In this
> fight of Michael I know that I shall certainly die . . . but I do not
> falter. . . . Christ will come. He will not tarry.[61]

Obviously Servetus was a bit more insane than the average of his time. He
announced that the end of the world was at hand, that the Archangel Michael
would lead a holy war against both the papal and the Genevese Antichrists,
and that he, who had been named after the Archangel, would fight and die
in that war.[62] The *Restitutio* was a call to that war. No wonder it had difficulty finding a publisher. The Basel printers shied away from it. Finally
(January 3, 1553) it was clandestinely printed in Vienne by Balthasar Ar-
nouillet and Guillaume Guéroult. Their names, and the place of publication,
were omitted, and the author signed himself only as MSV. He paid all the
expenses, corrected the proofs, and then destroyed the manuscript. The
volume ran to 734 pages, for it included a revised form of *De Trinitatis
erroribus*, and Servetus's thirty letters to Calvin.

Of the thousand copies printed some were sent to a bookseller in Geneva. There one came into the hands of Guillaume Trie, a friend of Calvin's. The thirty letters made plain to Calvin that MSV stood for Michael Servetus of Villanova. On February 26, 1553, Trie wrote to a Catholic cousin in Lyons, Antoine Arneys, expressing surprise that Cardinal François de Tournon should allow such a book to be printed in his diocese. How did Trie know the place of publication? Calvin knew that Servetus was living in Lyons or Vienne.

Arneys brought the matter to Matthias Ory, inquisitor at Lyons. Ory notified the Cardinal, who ordered Maugiron, Lieutenant-Governor of Vienne, to investigate. On March 16 Servetus was summoned to Maugiron's house. Before obeying he destroyed all papers that might incriminate him. He denied having written the book. Arneys dispatched to Trie a request for more evidence of Servetus's authorship. Trie obtained from Calvin some of Servetus's letters, and sent them to Lyons. They tallied with several letters in the book. On April 4 Servetus was arrested. Three days later he escaped by leaping over a garden wall. On June 17 the civil court of Vienne condemned him, if found, to be burned alive by a slow fire.

Servetus wandered about France for three months. He decided to seek refuge in Naples, and to go via Geneva. For reasons unknown he remained in Geneva a month, under an assumed name; and meanwhile he arranged for transportation to Zurich. On Sunday, August 13, he attended church, perhaps to avoid investigation by the authorities. He was recognized. Calvin was informed, and ordered his arrest. Calvin explained this action in a later letter (September 9, 1553): "When the papists are so harsh and violent in defense of their superstitions that they rage cruelly to shed innocent blood, are not Christian magistrates shamed to show themselves less ardent in defense of the sure truth?" The Small Council followed Calvin's lead, and outran his ferocity. Since Servetus was only a transient, and not a citizen subject to the laws of Geneva, the Council could not legally do more than banish him.

He was confined in the former episcopal palace, now a prison. He was not tortured, except by the lice that infested his cell. He was allowed paper and ink, and whatever books he cared to buy, and Calvin lent him several volumes of the early Fathers. The trial was carefully conducted, lasting over two months. The indictment was drawn up by Calvin in thirty-eight articles, supported by quotations from the writings of Servetus. One charge was that he had accepted Strabo's description of Judea as a barren country, whereas the Bible called it a land flowing with milk and honey.[63] The basic accusations were that Servetus had rejected the Trinity and infant baptism; he was also accused of having, "in the person of M. Calvin, defamed the doctrines of the Gospel of the Church of Geneva." [64] On August 17 and 21 Calvin appeared in person as the accuser. Servetus defended his views boldly, even to pantheism. By an unusual co-operation of hostile faiths, the Protestant Council of Geneva asked the Catholic judges at Vienne for particulars of the charges that had been brought against Servetus there. One new count was sexual immorality; Servetus replied that rupture had long since made him impotent, and had kept him from marriage. [65] He was further accused of having attended Mass at Vienne; he pleaded fear of death as exculpation. He challenged the jurisdiction of a civil court over cases of heresy; he assured the court that he had engaged in no sedition, and had not violated the laws of Geneva; and he asked for an attorney, better acquainted than himself with these laws, to help him in his defense. These pleas were refused. The French Inquisition sent an agent to Geneva to demand that Servetus be sent back to France for the execution of the sentence that had been pronounced against him; Servetus, in tears, begged the Council to reject this demand; it did; but the demand may have stimulated the Council to equal the Inquisition in severity.

On September 1 two enemies of Calvin—Ami Perrin and Philibert Berthelier—were allowed to join the judges in the trial. They engaged Calvin in disputes, to no result; but they persuaded the Council to consult the other churches of Protestant Switzerland on how Servetus should be treated. On September 2 Calvin's leadership in the city was again challenged in the Council by *Patriotes* and *Libertins;* he survived the storm, but the evident desire of the opposition to rescue Servetus may have hardened Calvin to pursue the heretic to the death. However, we should note that the chief prosecutor in the trial was Claude Rigot, a *Libertin.*[66]

On September 3 Servetus presented to the Council a written reply to the thirty-eight charges adduced by Calvin. He met each point with keen argument and Scriptural or patristic citations; he questioned Calvin's right to interfere in the trial, and called him a disciple of Simon Magus, a criminal, and a homicide.[67] Calvin answered in twenty-three pages; these were submitted to Servetus, who returned them to the Council with such marginal comments as "liar," "impostor," "hypocrite," "miserable wretch"; [68] probably the strain of a month's imprisonment and mental torment had broken Servetus's self-control. Calvin's reports of the trial are themselves in the manner of the time; he writes of Servetus that "the dirty dog wiped his snout"; "the perfidious scamp" soils each page with "impious ravings." [69] Servetus petitioned the Council to indict Calvin as a "repressor of the truth of Jesus Christ," to "exterminate" him, confiscate his goods, and, with the proceeds, reimburse Servetus for the losses he had sustained by Calvin's actions. The suggestion was not favorably received.

On October 18 the replies came in from the Swiss churches whose counsel had been asked; all advised the condemnation of Servetus, none his execution.

On October 25 Perrin made a last effort to save him by moving for a retrial before the Council of Two Hundred; he was overruled. On the twenty-sixth the Small Council, with no member dissenting, passed sentence of death on two counts of heresy—Unitarianism and the rejection of infant baptism. When Servetus heard the sentence, says Calvin, "he moaned like a madman, and ... beat his breast, and bellowed in Spanish, *Misericordia! Misericordia!*" He asked to talk with Calvin; he pleaded with him for mercy; Calvin offered no more than to give him the final consolations of the true religion if he would retract his heresies. Servetus would not. He asked to be beheaded rather than burned; Calvin was inclined to support this plea, but the aged Farel, in at the death, reproved him for such tolerance; and the Council voted that Servetus should be burned alive.[70]

The sentence was carried out the next morning, October 27, 1553, on the hill of Champel, just south of Geneva. On the way Farel importuned Servetus to earn divine mercy by confessing the crime of heresy; according to Farel the condemned man replied, "I am not guilty, I have not merited death"; and he besought God to pardon his accusers.[71] He was fastened to a stake by iron chains, and his last book was bound to his side. When the flames reached his face he shrieked with agony. After half an hour of burning he died.*

VII. AN APPEAL FOR TOLERATION

Catholics and Protestants united in approving the sentence. The Inquisition at Vienne, cheated of its living prey, burned Servetus in effigy. Melanchthon, in a letter to Calvin and Bullinger, gave "thanks to the Son of God" for the "punishment of this blasphemous man," and called the burning "a pious and memorable example to all posterity."[73] Bucer declared from his pulpit in Strasbourg that Servetus had deserved to be disemboweled and torn to pieces.[74] Bullinger, generally humane, agreed that civil magistrates must punish blasphemy with death.[75]

Yet even in Calvin's day some voices spoke for Servetus. A Sicilian wrote a long poem, *De iniusto Serveti incendio*. David Joris of Basel, an Anabaptist, published a protest against the execution, but under a pseudonymn; after his death his authorship was discovered; his body was exhumed and publicly burned (1566). The political opponents of Calvin naturally condemned his treatment of Servetus, and some of his friends deprecated the severity of the sentence as encouraging the Catholics of France to apply the death penalty to Huguenots. Such criticism must have been widespread, for in February 1554, Calvin issued a *Defensio orthodoxae fidei de sacra Trinitate*

* In 1903 a monument was raised to Servetus at Champel. First on the list of contributors to the cost was the Consistory of the Reformed Church of Geneva.[72]

contra prodigiosos errores Michaelis Serveti. If, he argued, we believe in the inspiration of the Bible, then we know the truth, and all who oppose it are enemies and blasphemers of God. Since their offense is immeasurably greater than any other crime, the civil authority must punish heretics as worse than murderers; for murder merely kills the body, while heresy accepted damns the soul to everlasting hell. (This was precisely the Catholic position.) Moreover, God Himself has explicitly instructed us to kill heretics, to smite with the sword any city that abandons the worship of the true faith revealed by Him. Calvin quoted the ferocious decrees of Deut. 13:5-15, 17:2-5; Exodus 22:20; and Lev. 24:16, and argued from them with truly burning eloquence:

> Whoever shall maintain that wrong is done to heretics and blasphemers in punishing them makes himself an accomplice in their crime.... There is no question here of man's authority; it is God Who speaks, and it is clear what law He would have kept in the Church even to the end of the world. Wherefore does He demand of us so extreme severity if not to show us that due honor is not paid Him so long as we set not His service above every human consideration, so that we spare not kin nor blood of any, and forget all humanity when the matter is to combat for His glory? [76]

Calvin moderated his conclusions by counseling mercy to those whose heresies were not fundamental, or were clearly due to ignorance or feebleness of mind. But whereas in general he accepted St. Paul as his guide, he refused to use the Pauline expedient of declaring the old law superseded by the new. In truth the theocracy that he had apparently established would have crumbled into disorder if differences of creed had been allowed public voice.

What, meanwhile, had become of the Erasmian spirit of tolerance? Erasmus had been tolerant because he had not been certain; Luther and Melanchthon had abandoned tolerance as they progressed in certainty; Calvin, with lethal precocity, had been certain almost from his twentieth year. A few humanists who had studied classic thought, and had not been frightened back into the Roman fold by distaste for the violence of theological strife, remained to suggest, diffidently, that certainty in religion and philosophy is unattainable, and that therefore theologians and philosophers should not kill.

The humanist who most clearly spoke for tolerance amid the clash of certainties had been for a time one of Calvin's closest friends. Sebastian Castellio, born in the French Jura in 1515, became an adept in Latin, Greek, and Hebrew, taught Greek at Lyons, lived with Calvin in Strasbourg, was appointed by him rector of the Latin School at Geneva (1541), and began there a translation of the entire Bible into Ciceronian Latin. While he admired Calvin as a man, he abominated the doctrine of predestination, and fretted under the new discipline of body and mind. In 1544 he charged the Genevese ministers with intolerance, impurity, and drunkenness. Calvin complained to the Council; Castellio was found guilty of calumny, and was banished (1544). For nine years he lived in great poverty, supporting a large family, and working at night on his version of the Scriptures. He finished this in 1551; then, lonesome for the placid drudgery of scholarship, he began again at Genesis 1:1, and translated the Bible into French. Finally (1553) he obtained a professorship of Greek at the University of Basel. He sympathized with the Unitarians, longed to help Servetus, and was shocked by Calvin's defense of the execution. Under assumed names he and Caelius Curio published (March 1554) the first modern classic on toleration: *De haereticis an sint persequendi (Should Heretics Be Persecuted?)*

The main body of the work was an anthology, compiled by Curio, of Christian pleas for tolerance, from Lactantius and Jerome to Erasmus, the early Luther, and Calvin himself. Castellio contributed the argument in preface and epilogue. For hundreds of years, he pointed out, men had debated free will, predestination, heaven and hell, Christ and the Trinity, and other difficult matters; no agreement had been reached; probably none would ever be reached. But none is necessary, said Castellio; such disputes do not make men better; all that we need is to carry the spirit of Christ into our daily lives, to feed the poor, help the sick, and love even our enemies. It seemed to him ridiculous that all the new sects, as well as the old Church, should pretend to absolute truth and make their creeds obligatory on those over whom they had physical power; as a result a man would be orthodox in one city and become a heretic by entering another; he would have to change his religion, like his money, at each frontier. Can we imagine Christ ordering a man to be burned alive for advocating adult baptism? The Mosaic laws calling for the death of a heretic were superseded by the law of Christ, which is one of mercy, not of despotism and terror. If a man denies life after death, and rejects all law, he may (said Castellio) be justly silenced by the magistrates, but he should not be killed. Moreover (he thought), persecution of beliefs is futile; martyrdom for an idea spreads the idea far more rapidly than the martyr could have done had he been allowed to live. What a tragedy (he concluded) that those who had so lately freed themselves from the terrible Inquisition should so soon imitate its tyranny, should so soon force men back into Cimmerian darkness after so promising a dawn![77]

Knowing Castellio's sentiments, Calvin at once recognized his hand in the *De haereticis*. He delegated the task of answering it to his most brilliant disciple, Théodore de Besze, or Bèze, or Beza. Born in Vézelay of aristocratic lineage, Théodore studied law at Orléans and Bourges, practiced it successfully in Paris, wrote Latin poetry, charmed some women by his wit, more by his prosperity, lived a gay life, married, fell dangerously ill, experienced a sickbed conversion reverse to Loyola's, adopted Protestantism, fled to Geneva, presented himself to Calvin, and was made professor of Greek at the University of Lausanne. It is remarkable that a Protestant refugee from a Huguenot-persecuting France should have undertaken to defend persecution. He did it with the skill of a lawyer and the devotion of a friend. In September 1554, he issued his *De haereticis a civili magistratu puniendis libellus (A Little Book on the Duty of Civil Magistrates to Punish Heretics)*. He pointed out again that religious toleration was impossible to one who accepted the divine inspiration of the Scriptures. But if we reject the Bible as God's Word, on what shall we build the religious faith that is so clearly indispensable—considering the natural wickedness of men—to moral restraint, social order, and civilization? Nothing would then be left but chaotic doubts disintegrating Christianity. To a sincere believer in the Bible there could be only one religion; all others must be false or incomplete. Yes, the New Testament preaches a law of love, but this does not excuse us from punishing thieves and murderers; how then does it warrant us in sparing heretics?

Castellio returned to the contest in a tract *Contra libellum Calvini*, but it lay unpublished for half a century. In another manuscript, *De arte dubitandi*, he anticipated Descartes by making the "art of doubting" the first step in the pursuit of truth. In *Four Dialogues* (1578) he defended free will and the possibility of universal salvation. In 1562, in *Conseil à la France désolée*, he appealed in vain to Catholics and Protestants to end the civil wars that were devastating France, and to allow every believer in Christ "to serve God according not to other men's faith but to his own." [78] Hardly anyone heard a voice so out of tune with the time. Castellio died in poverty at the age of forty-eight (1563). Calvin pronounced his early death a just judgment of a just God.

VIII. CALVIN TO THE END: 1554–64

Perhaps Calvin knew Castellio's secret leaning toward Unitarianism—belief in a God not triune, therefore a rejection of Christ's divinity; and he can be forgiven for seeing in this basic doubt the beginning of the end for Christianity. He feared this heresy all the more because he found it in Geneva itself, above all among the Protestant fugitives from Italy. These men saw no sense in replacing incredible transubstantiation with incredible predestination; their rebellion attacked the fundamental assumption of Christianity, that Christ was the Son of God. Matteo Gribaldi, professor of jurisprudence at Padua, had a summer home near Geneva. During the trial of Servetus he spoke openly against civil punishment for religious opinions, and advocated freedom of worship for all. Hailed before the Council, he was banished on suspicion of Unitarianism (1559). He secured appointment as professor of law in the University of Tübingen; Calvin sent word there of Gribaldi's doubts; the university pressed him to sign a Trinitarian confession; instead he fled to Bern, where he died of the plague in 1564. Giorgio Blandrata, an Italian physician domiciled in Geneva, was summoned before the Council on a charge of questioning the divinity of Christ; he fled to Poland, where he found some tolerance for his heresy. Valentino Gentile, from Calabria, openly expressed Unitarian views in Geneva, was thrown into prison, was sentenced to death (1557), recanted, was released, went to Lyons, was arrested by the Catholic authorities, but was freed on his assurance that his chief interest lay in refuting Calvin. He joined Blandrata in Poland, returned to Switzerland, was seized by the Bernese magistrates, was convicted of perjury and heresy, and was beheaded (1566).

Amid these battles for the Lord, Calvin continued to live simply, and to rule Geneva by the power of a personality armed with the delusions of his followers. His position became stronger as years gave it roots. His only weakness was physical; headaches, asthma, dyspepsia, stone, gout, and fever racked and thinned his frame, and formed his face to taut severity and gloom. A long illness in 1558–59 left him lame and feeble, with repeated hemorrhages of the lungs. Thereafter he had to keep to his bed most of the time, though he continued to study, direct, and preach, even when he had to be borne to the sanctuary in a chair. On April 25, 1564, he made his will, full of confidence in his election to everlasting glory. On the twenty-sixth the syndics and the Council came to his bedside; he asked their pardon for his outbreaks of anger, and begged them to hold steadfastly to the pure doctrine of the Reformed Church. Farel, now in his eightieth year, came from Neuchâtel to bid him au revoir. After many days of prayer and suffering Calvin found peace (May 27, 1564).

His influence was even greater than Luther's, but he walked in a path that Luther had cleared. Luther had protected his new church by rallying German nationalism to its support; the move was necessary, but it tied Lutheranism too narrowly to Teutonic stocks. Calvin loved France, and labored to promote the Huguenot cause, but he was no nationalist; religion was his country; and so his doctrine, however modified, inspired the Protestantism of Switzerland, France, Scotland, and America, and captured large sectors of Protestantism in Hungary, Poland, Germany, Holland, and England. Calvin gave to Protestantism in many lands an organization, confidence, and pride that enabled it to survive a thousand trials.

A year before his death his pupil Olevianus joined with Melanchthon's pupil Ursinus in preparing the Heidelberg Catechism, which became the accepted expression of the Reformed faith in Germany and Holland. Bèze and Bullinger reconciled the creeds of Calvin and Zwingli in the Second Helvetic Confession (1566), which became authoritative for the Reformed churches in Switzerland and France. In Geneva itself Calvin's work was ably continued by Bèze. But year by year the business leaders who controlled the Councils resisted more and more successfully the attempts of the Consistory and the Venerable Company to place moral checks upon economic operations. After Bèze's death (1608) the merchant princes consolidated their supremacy, and the Genevan Church lost the directive privileges that Calvin had won for it in nonreligious affairs. In the eighteenth century the influence of Voltaire moderated the Calvinist tradition, and ended the sway of a puritan ethic among the people. Catholicism patiently struggled to recapture a place in the city; it offered a Christianity without gloom and an ethic without severity; in 1954 the population was 42 per cent Catholic, 47 per cent Protestant.[79] But the most impressive man-made structure in Geneva is the noble "Reformation Monument" which, running majestically along a park wall, celebrates the victories of Protestantism, and raises at its center the powerful figures of Farel, Calvin, Bèze, and Knox.

Meanwhile the hard theocracy of Calvin was sprouting democratic buds. The efforts of the Calvinist leaders to give schooling to all, and their inculcation of disciplined character, helped the sturdy burghers of Holland to oust the alien dictatorship of Spain, and supported the revolt of nobles and clergy in Scotland against a fascinating but imperious queen. The stoicism of a hard creed made the strong souls of the Scottish Covenanters, the English and Dutch Puritans, the Pilgrims of New England. It steadied the heart of Cromwell, guided the pen of blind Milton, and broke the power of the backward-facing Stuarts. It encouraged brave and ruthless men to win a continent and spread the base of education and self-government until all men could be free. Men who chose their own pastors soon claimed to choose their governors, and the self-ruled congregation became the self-governed municipality. The myth of divine election justified itself in the making of America.

When this function had been performed, the theory of predestination fell into the backwaters of Protestant belief. As social order returned in Europe after the Thirty Years' War, in England after the revolutions of 1642 and 1689, in America after 1793, the pride of divine election changed into the pride of work and accomplishment; men felt stronger and more secure; fear lessened, and the frightened cruelty that had generated Calvin's God gave way to a more humane vision that compelled a reconception of deity. Decade by decade the churches that had taken their lead from Calvin discarded the harsher elements of his creed. Theologians dared to believe that all who died in infancy were saved, and one respected divine announced, without causing a commotion, that "the number of the finally lost . . . will be very inconsiderable." [80] We are grateful to be so reassured, and we will agree that even error lives because it serves some vital need. But we shall always find it hard to love the man who darkened the human soul with the most absurd and blasphemous conception of God in all the long and honored history of nonsense.

CHAPTER XXII

Francis I and the Reformation in France

1515-59

I. *LE ROI GRAND NEZ*

HE was born under a tree in Cognac on September 12, 1494. His grandfather was Charles of Orléans, the poet; perhaps song and the love of beauty were in his blood. His father was Charles of Valois and Orléans, Count of Angoulême, who died, after many adulteries, in the third year of Francis' life. His mother was Louise of Savoy, a woman of beauty, ability, and ambition, with a taste for wealth and power. Widowed at seventeen, she refused the hand of Henry VII of England, and devoted herself—barring some liaisons—to making her son king of France. She did not mourn when Anne of Brittany, second wife of Louis XII, had a stillborn son, leaving Francis heir to the throne. Louis sadly made Francis Duke of Valois, and appointed tutors to instruct him in the art of royalty. Louise and his sister Marguerite mothered him to idolatry, and prepared him to be a ladies' king. Louise called him *Mon roi, mon seigneur, mon César*, fed him chivalric romances, gloried in his gallantries, and swooned at the blows he received in the jousts that he loved. He was handsome, gay, courteous, brave; he met dangers like a Roland or an Amadis; when a wild boar, escaping from its cage, sought to frolic in his princely court, it was Francis who, while others fled, faced the beast and slew it splendidly.

At the age of twelve (1506) he was betrothed to Claude of France, the seven-year-old daughter of Louis XII. She had been promised to the boy who was to become the Emperor Charles V; the engagement had been broken to avoid yoking France to Spain; this was one item in a hundred irritations that urged Hapsburg and Valois into conflict from youth to death. At fourteen Francis was bidden leave his mother and join Louis at Chinon. At twenty he married Claude. She was stout and dull, lame and fertile and good; she gave him children in 1515, 1516, 1518, 1520, 1522, 1523, and died in 1524.

Meanwhile he became king (January 1, 1515). Everybody was happy, above all his mother, to whom he gave the duchies of Angoulême and Anjou, the counties of Maine and Beaufort, the barony of Amboise. But he was generous to others too—to nobles, artists, poets, pages, mistresses. His pleasant voice, his cordiality and good temper, his vivacity and charm, his living synthesis of chivalry and the Renaissance, endeared him to his country, even to his court. France rejoiced, and placed high hopes in him, as England in those years in Henry VIII, and the Empire in Charles V; the world seemed young again, so freshened with royal youth. And Francis, even more than Leo X, was resolved to enjoy his throne.

What was he really, this Arthur plus Lancelot? Physically he would have been magnificent, had not his nose been more so; irreverent contemporaries called him *le roi grand nez.* He was six feet tall, broad-shouldered, agile, strong; he could run, jump, wrestle, fence with the best; he could wield a two-handed sword or a heavy lance. His thin beard and mustache did not disguise his youth; he was twenty-one when crowned. His narrow eyes suggested alertness and humor, but not subtlety or depth. If his nose betokened virility it conformed to his reputation. Brantôme, whose *Dames Galantes* cannot be taken as history, wrote therein that "King Francis loved greatly and too much; for being young and free, he embraced now one, now another, with indifference . . . from which he took the *grande vérole* that shortened his days." [1] The King's mother was reported to have said that he was punished where he had sinned.* Perhaps history has exaggerated the variety of his amours. Whatever their number, he remained outwardly faithful first to Françoise de Foix, Comtesse de Chateaubriand, then, from 1526 to his death, to Anne de Pisselieu, whom he made Duchesse d'Étampes. Gossip spread a hundred romantic tales about him—that he besieged Milan not for Milan but for a pair of unforgettable eyes that he had seen there,[3] or that a siren in Pavia lured him to his central tragedy.[4] In any case we may have some sympathy for so sensitive a king. He was capable of tenderness as well as infatuation: when he proposed to divorce his son from the persistently barren Catherine de Médicis, her tears dissuaded him.[5] "Nothing can be imagined more humane than Francis," said Erasmus;[6] and if that was the pathos of distance, Budé, France's own humanist, described him as "gentle and accessible."[7]

He was vain even for a man. He rivaled Henry VIII in the splendor of his royal robes, and in the furry insouciance of his beret. He took the salamander as his symbol, betokening persistent resurrection from every conflagration, but life scorched him none the less. He loved honors, distinctions, adulation, and could not bear criticism. He had an actor whipped for satirizing the court; Louis XII, bitten by the same wit, had merely smiled.[8] He could be ungrateful, as to Anne de Montmorency, unfair, as to Charles of Bourbon,

---

* Almost certainly legendary is the story of the lawyer who, when his wife, *La Belle Ferronière* (The Pretty Ironmonger), was conscripted to the royal bed, deliberately infected himself and gave her syphilis that she might give it to the king.[2]

cruel, as to Semblançay; but by and large he was forgiving and generous; Italians marveled at his liberality.[9] No ruler in history was kinder to artists. He loved beauty intensely and intelligently, and spent almost as readily on art as on war; he was half the purse of the French Renaissance.

His intellectual ability did not equal his charm of character. He had little Latin and no Greek, but astonished many men by the variety and accuracy of his knowledge in agriculture, hunting, geography, military science, litera- ture, and art; and he enjoyed philosophy when it did not interfere with love or war. He was too reckless and impetuous to be a great commander, too lighthearted and fond of pleasure to be a great statesman, too fascinated by appearances to get to essences, too amiably influenced by favorites and mistresses to choose the best available generals and ministers, too open and frank to be a competent diplomat. His sister Marguerite grieved over his incapacity for government, and foresaw that the subtle but inflexible Em- peror would unhorse him in their lifelong joust. Louis XII, who admired him as "a fine young gallant," saw with foreboding the lavish hedonism of his successor. "All our work is useless," he said; "this great boy will spoil everything." [10]

II. FRANCE IN 1515

France was now enjoying the prosperity engendered by a bountiful soil, a skillful and thrifty people, and a beneficent reign. The population was some 16,000,000, compared with 3,000,000 in England and 7,000,000 in Spain. Paris, with 300,000, was the largest city in Europe after Constanti- nople. The social structure was semi-feudal: nearly all the peasants owned the land they tilled, but usually they held it in fief—and owed dues or serv- ices—to seigneurs and chevaliers whose function was to organize agriculture and provide military protection to their locality and the nation. Inflation, caused by the repeated debasement of coinages and the mining or import of precious metals, eased the traditional money dues, and enabled peasants to buy land cheaply from the land-rich, money-poor nobility; hence a rural prosperity that kept the French peasant merry and Catholic while the Ger- man *Bauer* was making economic and religious revolution. Stimulated by ownership, French energy drew from the soil the best corn and wine in Eu- rope; cattle grew fat and multiplied; milk, butter, and cheese were on every table; chickens or other fowl were in almost every yard; and the peasant accepted the odor of his pigsty as one of the blessed fragrances of life.

The town worker—still chiefly a craftsman in his own shop—did not share proportionately in this prosperity. Inflation raised prices faster than wages, and protective tariffs and royal monopolies, as of salt, helped to keep the cost of living high. Discontented workers went on strike, but were nearly always defeated; and the law forbade workingmen to unite for economic purposes. Commerce moved leisurely along the bountiful rivers, but painfully along the poor roads, paying each lord a toll to pass through his domain. Lyons, where the trade of the Mediterranean, ascending the Rhone, met the flow of goods from Switzerland and Germany, was second only to Paris in French industry, and only to Antwerp as a bourse or center of investment and finance. From Marseilles French commerce roamed the Mediterranean, and profited from the friendly relations that Francis dared to maintain with Suleiman and the Turks.

From this economy Francis, after the fashion of governments, drew revenues to the limit of tolerance. The *taille* (cut) fell as a personal or property tax upon all but nobles and clergy; the clergy paid the King ecclesiastical tithes and grants, the nobles supplied and equipped the cavalry that was still the flamboyant mainstay of French arms. Taking a lesson from the popes, Francis sold—and created to sell—noble titles and political offices; in this way the *nouveaux riches* slowly formed (as in England) a new aristocracy, ınd the lawyers, buying offices, established a powerful bureaucracy that—sometimes over the head of the King—administered the government of France.

The King's pleasures did not allow him much time for government. He delegated its tasks, even the formation of its policies, to men like Admiral Bonnivet, Anne de Montmorency, Cardinals Duprat and de Tournon, and the Vicomte de Lautrec. Three councils aided and advised these men and the King: a Privy Council of Nobles, a more intimate Council of Affairs, and a Grand Council that handled appeals to the King. Except for this, the *Parlement* of Paris, composed of some 200 secular or ecclesiastical members appointed for life by the King, served as a supreme court. It had the right to remonstrate with him when it thought that his edicts contravened the fundamental institutions of France; and his decrees lacked the full prestige of law until "registered"—in effect ratified—by this ancient corps. Dominated by lawyers and old men, the *Parlement* of Paris became the national political organ of the middle classes, and—next to the Sorbonne—the most conservative organization in France. Local *parlements*, and governors appointed by the King, administered the provinces. The States-General was for the time being ignored; the collection of taxes replaced grants-in-aid, and the role of the nobility in government declined.

The function of the nobles was twofold: to organize the army, and to serve the King at court. The court, consisting of the administrative heads, the leading nobles, their wives, and the family and favorites of the King, now became the head and front of France, the mirror of fashion, the mobile perpetual festival of royalty. At the summit of this whirl was the Master of the King's Household, who organized the whole and patrolled the protocol;

then the Chamberlain, who had charge of the royal bedchamber; then four Gentlemen of the Bedchamber or First Lords in Waiting, who were always at the King's elbow to wait on his desires; these men were changed every three months, to give other notables a turn at this exhilarating intimacy; lest anyone be overlooked, there were twenty to fifty-four Lords of the Bedchamber to serve the highest four; add twelve Pages of the Bedchamber a.1d four Ushers of the Bedchamber, and the King's sleeping quarters were adequately cared for. Twenty lords served as stewards of the King's cuisine, managing a staff of forty-five men and twenty-five cupbearers. Some thirty *enfants d'honneur*—boys of awesome pedigree—functioned as royal pages, shining in silvered livery; and a host of secretaries multiplied the hand and memory of the King. A cardinal was Grand Chaplain of the royal chapel; a bishop was Master of the Oratory or prayer service; and fifty diocesan bishops were allowed to grace the court and so augment their fame. Honorary positions as "grooms of the chamber," with pensions of 240 livres, were awarded for divers accomplishments, as to scholars like Budé and poets like Marot. We must not forget seven physicians, seven surgeons four barbers, seven choristers, eight craftsmen, eight clerks of the kitchen, eight ushers for the audience chamber. Each of the King's sons had his own attendants—stewards, chancellors, tutors, pages, and servants. Each of the two queens at court—Claude and Marguerite—had her retinue of fifteen or ten ladies in waiting, sixteen or eight maids of honor—*filles demoiselles*. It was the most characteristic distinction of Francis that he raised women to high place at his court, winked expertly at their liaisons, encouraged and enjoyed their parade of finery and soft charms. "A court without ladies," he said, "is a garden without flowers"; [11] and probably it was the women—dowered with the ageless beauty of art—who gave the court of Francis I a graceful splendor and gay stimulus unequaled even in the palaces of Imperial Rome. All the potentates of Europe taxed their peoples to provide some minor mirroring of this Parisian fantasy.

Beneath the polished surface was an immense base of servantry: four chefs, six assistant chefs, cooks specializing in soups or sauces or pastries or roasts, and a countless personnel to supply and serve the King's table, the *cuisine commune* of the court, and the needs and comforts of ladies and gentlemen. There were court musicians, led by the most notable singers, composers, and instrumentalists in Europe outside of Rome. A Master of the Horse, twenty-five noble equerries, and a swarm of coachmen and grooms attended the royal stables. There were Masters of the Hunt, a hundred dogs, and 300 falcons—trained and cared for by a hundred falconers under a Grand Falconer. Four hundred archers formed the King's bodyguard, and brightened the court with their colorful costumes.

For court banquets, balls, marriages, and diplomatic receptions no one building in Paris sufficed. The Louvre was then a gloomy fortress; Francis abandoned it for the assorted palaces known as Les Tournelles (The Little Towers) near the Bastille, or for the spacious palace where the *Parlement* had been wont to sit; better still, loving to hunt, he moved out to Fontaine-bleau, or down to his châteaux along the Loire at Blois, Chambord, Amboise, or Tours—dragging half the court and wealth of France with him. Cellini, with his wonted hyperbole, described his royal patron as traveling with a retinue of 18,000 persons and 12,000 horses.[12] Foreign ambassadors protested the cost and weariness of catching or keeping up with the King; and when they found him he was, as like as not, in bed till noon, recovering from the pleasures of the night before, or busy preparing a hunt or a tournament. The cost of all this perambulating glory was enormous. The treasury was always near bankruptcy, taxes were forever mounting, the bankers of Lyons were dragooned into risky royal loans. In 1523, perceiving that his expenditures were losing sight of his revenues, the King promised to put a limit on his personal indulgences, "not including, however, the ordinary run of our little necessities and pleasures." [13] He excused his extravagance as needed to impress envoys, overwhelm ambitious nobles, and please the populace; the Parisians, he thought, hungered for spectacles, and admired rather than resented the splendor of their King.

Now the government of France became bisexual. Francis ruled in apparent omnipotence, but he was so fond of women that he readily yielded to his mother, his sister, his mistress, even his wife. He must have loved Claude somewhat, to keep her so constantly pregnant. He had married her for reasons of state; he felt entitled to appreciate other women more artistically designed. The court followed the lead of the King in making a mannerly art of adultery. The clergy adjusted themselves after making the requisite objections. The people made no objections, but gratefully imitated the easy code of the court—except one girl, who, we are told, deliberately marred her beauty to deflect the royal lechery (1524).[14]

The most influential woman at the court was the King's mother. "Address yourself to me," said Louise of Savoy to a papal legate; "and we shall go our way. If the King complains we'll just let him talk." [15] Very often her advice was good, and when she served as his regent the country fared better than at his own lax hands. But her covetousness drove the Duke of Bourbon to treason, and let a French army starve in Italy. Her son forgave her everything, grateful that she had made him a god.

III. MARGUERITE OF NAVARRE

Probably he loved his sister only next to his mother, and above his mistresses—whose ministrations gave him something less lasting and profound than her selfless adoration. Love was her life—love of her mother, of her brother, of her husbands, Platonic love, mystical religious love. A pretty story said "she was born smiling, and held out her little hand to each comer." [16] She called her mother, her brother, and herself *Nôtre Trinité*, and was content to be "the smallest angle" of that "perfect triangle." [17] By her birth she was Marguerite of Angoulême, Orléans, and Valois. Two years older than Francis, she shared in bringing him up, and in their childhood games "she was his mother, his mistress, and his little wife." [18] She watched over him as fondly as if he had been some saving divinity become man; and when she found that he was also a satyr she accepted that disposition as the right of a Greek god, though she herself seems to have taken no taint from her environment. She far outstripped Francis in studies, but she never equaled his connoisseur's appreciation of art. She learned Spanish, Italian, Latin, Greek, and some Hebrew; she surrounded herself avidly with scholars, poets, theologians, and philosophers. Nevertheless she grew into an attractive woman, not physically beautiful (she too had the long Valois nose), but exercising a strong fascination by her charms of character and intellect. She was *sympatica*, agreeable, generous, kind, with a frequent dash of sprightly humor. She herself was one of the best poets of the time, and her court at Nérac or Pau was the most brilliant literary center in Europe. Everyone loved her and wished to be near her. That romantic but cynical age called her *la perle des Valois*—for *margarita* was Latin for pearl; and a pretty legend grew that Louise of Savoy had conceived her by swallowing a pearl.

Her letters to her brother are among the fairest and tenderest in literature. There must have been much good in him to draw out such devotion. Her other loves flowed or ebbed, burned or cooled; this pure passion was constant through fifty years, and always intense. The breath of that love almost clears the air of that perfumed time.

Gaston de Foix, nephew of Louis XII, aroused her first romance, then went off to Italy to conquer and die at Ravenna (1512). Guillaume de Bonnivet fell deeply in love with her, but found her heart still full of Gaston; he married one of her ladies in waiting to be near her. At seventeen (1509) she was wed to Charles, Duke of Alençon, also of royal pedigree; Francis had requested the marriage to cement an alliance of troublesomely rival families; but Marguerite found it hard to love the youth. Bonnivet offered her the consolations of adultery; she disfigured her face with a sharp stone to break th~ spell of her charm on him. Both Alençon and Bonnivet went to fight for Francis in Italy; Bonnivet died a hero at Pavia; Alençon was reported to have fled at the crisis of the battle. He returned to Lyons to find himself universally scorned; Louise of Savoy berated him as a coward; he fell ill of pleurisy; Marguerite forgave him and nursed him tenderly, but he died (1525).

After two years of widowhood Marguerite, now thirty-five, married Henri d'Albret, titular King of Navarre, a youth of twenty-four. Kept out of his principality by the claims of Ferdinand II and Charles V to Navarre, Henri was made governor of Guienne by Francis, and established a minor court at Nérac, sometimes at Pau, in southwest France. He treated Marguerite as a mother, almost as a mother-in-law; he did not imitate her fidelity to the marriage vows, and she had to console herself by playing hostess and protectress to writers, philosophers, and Protestant refugees. In 1528 she bore Henri a daughter, Jeanne d'Albret, destined to fame as the mother of Henry IV. Two years later she gave birth to a son, who died in infancy; thereafter she wore nothing but black. Francis wrote her a letter of such tender piety as we might rather have expected from her pen. Soon, however, he commanded her and Henri to surrender Jeanne to him to be brought up near the royal court; he feared that Henri would betroth her to Philip II of Spain, or that she would be reared as a Protestant. This separation was the profoundest of Marguerite's many griefs before the death of the King, but it did not interrupt her devotion to him. It is sad but necessary to relate that when Francis bade Jeanne marry the Duke of Cleves, and Jeanne refused, Marguerite supported the King to the point of instructing Jeanne's governess to thrash her till she consented. Several beatings were administered, but plucky Jeanne—a girl of twelve—issued a signed document to the effect that if she were forced into the marriage she would hold it null. The wedding was arranged nevertheless, on the theory that the needs of the state were the supreme law; Jeanne resisted to the last, and had to be carried into the church. As soon as the ceremony was over she fled, and went to live with her parents at Pau, where her extravagance in dress, retinue, and charities almost ruined them.

Marguerite herself was the embodiment of charity. She walked unescorted in the streets of Pau, "like a simple demoiselle," allowed anyone to approach her, and heard at first hand the sorrows of her people. "No one ought to go away sad or disappointed from the presence of a prince," she said, "for kings are the ministers of the poor . . . and the poor are the members of God." [19] She called herself the "Prime Minister of the Poor." She visited them in their homes, and sent them physicians from her court. Henri co-operated fully in this, for he was as excellent a ruler as he was a negligent husband, and the public works directed by him served as a model to France. Together he and Marguerite financed the education of a large number of poor students, among them the Amyot who later translated Plutarch. Marguerite gave shelter and safety to Marot, Rabelais, Desperiers, Lefèvre d'Étaples, Calvin, and so many others that one of her protégés compared her to "a hen carefully calling together her chicks, and covering them with her wings." [20]

Aside from her charities three interests dominated her life at Nérac and Pau: literature, Platonic love, and a mystic theology that found room for Catholicism and Protestantism alike, and tolerance even for free thought. It was her custom to have poets read to her as she embroidered; and she herself composed verses of some worth, in which human and divine love mingled in one obscure ecstasy. She published in her lifetime several volumes of poetry and drama; they are not as fine as her letters, which were not printed till 1841. All the world knows of her *Heptameron*, because of its reputed indecency; but patrons of pornography will be disappointed in it. These stories were in the manner of the time, which found its chief humor in the pranks, anomalies, and vicissitudes of love, and in the deviations of monks from their vows; the stories themselves are told with restraint. They are the tales related by the men and women of Marguerite's court, or that of Francis; they were written down by or for her (1544–48), but were never published by her; they appeared in print ten years after her death. She had intended them to form another *Decameron*, but as the book stopped short with the seventh day of the storytelling, the editor called it *Heptameron*. Many of the narratives seem to be authentic histories, disguised with changed names. Brantôme tells us that his mother was one of the storytellers, and that she had a key to the real persons concealed by pseudonyms in the tales; he assures us, for example, that the fourth tale of the fifth day is an account of Bonnivet's attempts upon Marguerite herself.[21]

It must be admitted that the professed taste of our day would feel obliged to blush at these stories of seduction, told by French ladies and gentlemen who thus beguiled their days of waiting for a flood to abate and let them return from the baths of Cauterets. Some of the incidental remarks are startling: "You mean to say, then, that all is lawful to those who love, provided no one knows?" "Yes, in truth; 'tis only fools who are found out." [22] The general philosophy of the book finds expression in a pregnant sentence of the fifth story: "Unhappy the lady who does not carefully preserve the treasure which does her so much honor when well kept, and so much dishonor when she continues to keep it." [23] The stories are lightened by many a jolly quip: so we hear of a pious pharmacist of Pau "who never had anything to do with his wife except in Holy Week by way of penance." [24] Half the humor, as in Boccaccio, turns on monastic gamboling. "These good fathers," says a character in the fifth story, "preach chastity to us, and want to foul our wives." An outraged husband agrees: "They dare not touch money, but they are ready to handle women's thighs, which are much more dangerous." It should be added that the merry storytellers hear Mass every morning, and fumigate every second page with arias of piety.

That Marguerite should have enjoyed or collected these tales points the mood of the age, and cautions us not to picture her as a saint until her declining years. While she herself seems to have been sedulously pure, she tolerated much laxity in others, made no recorded objections to the King's distribution of his powers, and kept on terms of intimate friendship with his successive mistresses. Apparently the men, and most of the women, thought of love between the sexes in unashamedly sexual terms. It was a charming custom of French women, in that lighthearted reign, to make presents of their garters to imaginative men.[25] Marguerite considered physical desire as quite permissible, but she herself made room in her heart for Platonic and religious love. The cult of Platonic love had come down from medieval "courts of love," reinforced by such Italian strains as Bembo's paean at the end of Castiglione's *Courtier*. It was good, Marguerite felt, that women should accept, in addition to the usual sexual passion, the devotion of men who were to be rewarded only with a tender friendship and some harmless intimacies; this association would train esthetic sensitivity in the male, refine his manners, and teach him moral restraint; so woman would civilize man. But in Marguerite's philosophy there was a higher love than either the sexual or the Platonic—the love of goodness, beauty, or any perfection, and therefore, above all, the love of God. But "to love God one must first love a human creature perfectly." [26]

Her religion was as complex and confused as her conception of love. Just as the selfishness of her brother could not dim her devotion to him, so the tragedies and brutalities of life left her religious faith pure and fervent, however unorthodox. She had skeptical moments; in *Le miroir de l'âme pécheresse* she confessed that at times she had doubted both Scripture and God; she charged God with cruelty, and wondered had He really written the Bible.[27] In 1533 the Sorbonne summoned her to answer an accusation of heresy; she ignored the summons; a monk told his congregation that she deserved to be sewn in a sack and thrown into the Seine; [28] but the King told the Sorbonne and the monks to let his sister alone. He could not credit the charges against her; "she loves me so much," he said, "that she will believe only what I believe." [29] He was too happy and confident to dream of being a Huguenot. But Marguerite could; she had a sense of sin, and made mountain peaks out of her peccadilloes. She despised the religious orders as idling, wenching wastrels; reform, she felt, was long overdue. She read some of the Lutheran literature, and approved its attacks upon ecclesiastical immorality and greed. Francis was amazed to find her, once, praying with Farel [30]—the John the Baptist of Calvin. At Nérac and Pau. while continuing to pray to the Virgin with trustful piety, she spread her protective skirts over fugitive Protestants, including Calvin himself. However, Calvin was much offended to find at her court freethinkers like Etienne Dolet and Bonaventure Desperiers; he reproved her for her tolerance, but she continued it. She would gladly have composed the Edict of Nantes for her grandson. In Marguerite the Renaissance and the Reformation were for a moment one.[31]

Her influence radiated through France. Every free spirit looked up to her as protectress and ideal. Rabelais dedicated *Gargantua* to her. Ronsard and Joachim du Bellay followed, now and then, her Platonizing, Plotinizing mysticism. Marot's translations of the Psalms breathed her half-Huguenot spirit. In the eighteenth century Bayle sang an ode to her in his *Dictionnaire*. In the nineteenth century the Protestant Michelet, in that magnificent, interminable, unwearying rhapsody called *Histoire de France*, offered her his gratitude: "Let us always remember this tender Queen of Navarre, in whose arms our people, fleeing from prison or the pyre, found safety, honor, and friendship. Our gratitude to you, lovable Mother of our Renaissance! Your hearth was that of our saints, your heart was the nest of our freedom." [32]

IV. THE FRENCH PROTESTANTS

No one questioned the need of religious reform. The same ecclesiastical good and evil appeared here as elsewhere: faithful priests, devout monks, saintly nuns, here and there a bishop dedicated to religion rather than politics; and ignorant or lackadaisical priests, idle and lecherous monks, money-grubbing friars pretending poverty, weak sisters in the convents, bishops who took the earthly cash and let the celestial credit go. As education rose, faith fell; and as the clergy had most of the education, they showed in their conduct that they no longer took to heart the once terrifying eschatology of their official creed. Some bishops appropriated to themselves a luxurious multiplicity of benefices and sees; so Jean of Lorraine held—and enjoyed revenues from—the bishoprics of Metz, Toul, and Verdun, the archbishoprics of Reims, Lyons, Narbonne, Albi, Macon, Agen, and Nantes, and the abbeys of Gorze, Fécamp, Cluny, Marmoutiers, Saint-Ouen, Saint-de-Laon, Saint-Germer, Saint-Médard of Soissons, and Saint-Mansuy of Toul.[33] It was not enough for his needs; he complained of poverty.[34] Monks denounced the worldliness of the bishops; priests denounced the monks; Brantôme quotes a phrase then popular in France: "Avaricious or lecherous as a priest or a monk." [35] The first sentence of the *Heptameron* describes the Bishop of Sées as itching to seduce a married woman; and a dozen stories in the book retail the similar enterprises of various monks. "I have such a horror of the very sight of a monk," says one character, "that I could not even confess to them, believing them to be worse than all other men." [36] "There are some good men among them," admits Oisille—which is Margaret's name, in the *Heptameron*, for her mother—but this same Louise of Savoy wrote in her journal: "In the year 1522 . . . my son and I, by the grace of the Holy Spirit, began to know the hypocrites, white, black, gray, smoky, and of all colors, from whom God in His infinite mercy and goodness preserve and defend us; for if Jesus Christ is not a liar, there is not among all mankind a more dangerous generation." [37]

Yet the acquisitiveness of Louise, the polygyny of her son, the anarchic morals of the court, gave no inspiring example to the clergy, who were so largely subject to the King. In 1516 Francis secured from Leo X a Concordat empowering him to appoint the bishops and abbots of France; but since he used these appointments largely as rewards for political services, the worldly character of the prelacy was confirmed. The Concordat in effect made the Gallican Church independent of the papacy and dependent upon the state. In this way Francis, a year before Luther's Theses, achieved in fact, though graciously not in form, what the German princes and Henry VIII would win by war or revolution—the nationalization of Christianity. What more could French Protestants offer the French King?

The first of them antedated Luther. In 1512 Jacques Lefèvre, born at Étaples in Picardy but then teaching at the University of Paris, published a Latin translation of Paul's Epistles, with a commentary expounding, among other heresies, two that ten years later would be basic with Luther: that men can be saved not by good works but only by faith in the grace of God earned by the redeeming sacrifice of Christ; and that Christ is present in the Eucharist by His own operation and good will, not through any priestly transubstantiation of bread and wine. Lefèvre, like Luther, demanded a return to the Gospel; and, like Erasmus, he sought to restore and clarify the authentic text of the New Testament as a means of cleansing Christianity from medieval legends and sacerdotal accretions. In 1523 he issued a French translation of the Testament, and, a year later, of the Psalms. "How shameful it is," said one of his comments, "to see a bishop soliciting people to drink with him, caring for naught but gambling . . . constantly hunting . . . frequenting bad houses!" [38] The Sorbonne condemned him as a heretic; he fled to Strasbourg (1525); Marguerite interceded for him; Francis recalled him and made him royal librarian at Blois and tutor to his children. In 1531, when Protestant excesses had angered the King, Lefèvre took refuge with Marguerite in southern France, and lived there till his death at the age of eighty-seven (1537).

His pupil Guillaume Briçonnet, appointed Bishop of Meaux (1516), set himself to reform that diocese in the spirit of his master. After four years of zealous work he felt strong enough to venture upon theological innovations. He appointed to benefices such known reformers as Lefèvre, Farel, Louis de

Berquin, Gérard Roussel, and François Vatable, and encouraged them to preach a "return to the Gospel." Marguerite applauded him, and made him her spiritual director. But when the Sorbonne—the school of theology that now dominated the University of Paris—proclaimed its condemnation of Luther (1521), Briçonnet bade his cohorts make their peace with the Church. The unity of the Church seemed to him, as to Erasmus and Marguerite, more important than reform.

The Sorbonne could not stop the flow of Lutheran ideas across the Rhine. Students and merchants brought Luther's writings from Germany as the most exciting news of the day; Froben sent copies from Basel to be sold in France. Discontented workingmen took up the New Testament as a revolutionary document, and listened gladly to preachers who drew from the Gospels a utopia of social equality. In 1523, when Bishop Briçonnet published on his cathedral doors a bull of indulgences, Jean Leclerc, a woolcarder of Meaux, tore it down and replaced it with a placard calling the pope Antichrist. He was arrested, and by order of the *Parlement* of Paris was branded on the forehead (1525). He moved to Metz, where he smashed the religious images before which a procession was planning to offer incense. His right hand was cut off, his nose was torn away, his nipples were plucked out with pincers, his head was bound with a band of red-hot iron, and he was burned alive (1526).[39] Several other radicals were sent to the stake in Paris for "blasphemy," or for denying the intercessory power of the Virgin and the saints (1526–27).

The people of France generally approved of these executions;[40] it cherished its religious faith as God's own revelation and covenant, and abominated heretics as robbing the poor of their greatest consolation. No Luther appeared in France to rouse the middle class against papal tyranny and exactions; the Concordat precluded such an appeal; and Calvin had not as yet reached the Genevan eminence from which he could send his stern summons to reform. The rebels found some support among the aristocracy, but the lords and ladies were too lighthearted to take the new ideas to the point of unsettling the faith of the people or the comforts of the court. Francis himself tolerated the Lutheran propaganda so long as it offered no threat of social or political disturbance. He too had his doubts—about the powers of the pope, the sale of indulgences, the existence of purgatory;[41] and possibly he thought to use his toleration of Protestantism as a weapon over a pope too inclined to favor Charles V. He admired Erasmus, sought him for the new Collège Royale, and believed with him in the encouragement of education and ecclesiastical reform—but by steps that would not divide the people into warring halves, or weaken the services of the Church to private morality and social order.[42] "The King and Madame" (Louise of Savoy), wrote Marguerite to Briçonnet in 1521, "are more than ever well-disposed toward the reformation of the Church."[43] When the Sorbonne arrested Louis de Berquin for translating some of Luther's works (1523), he was freed by Marguerite's intercession with the King. But Francis was frightened by the Peasants' Revolt in Germany, which seemed to have grown out of Protestant propaganda; and before leaving for his debacle at Pavia he bade the prelates stamp out the Lutheran movement in France. While the King was a captive in Madrid, Berquin was again imprisoned, but Marguerite again secured an order for his release. When Francis himself was freed he indulged in a jubilee of liberalism, perhaps in gratitude to the sister who had so labored for his liberation. He recalled Lefèvre and Roussel from exile, and Marguerite felt that the movement for reform had won the day.

Two events drove the King back to orthodoxy. He needed money to ransom the two sons whom he had surrendered to Charles in exchange for his own freedom; the clergy voted him 1,300,000 livres, but accompanied the grant with a request for a firmer stand against heresy; and he agreed (December 16, 1527). On May 31, 1528, he was dismayed to learn that both the heads on a statue of the Virgin and Child outside a church in the parish of Saint-Germain had been smashed during the night. The people cried out for vengeance. Francis offered a thousand crowns for the discovery of the vandals, and led a somber procession of prelates, state officials, nobles, and populace to repair the broken statues with silver heads. The Sorbonne took advantage of the reaction to imprison Berquin once more; and while Francis was absent at Blois the impenitent Lutheran was burned at the stake (April 17, 1529), to the joy of the attendant multitude.[44]

The mood of the King varied with the shifts of his diplomacy. In 1532, angry at the collaboration of Clement VII with Charles V, he made overtures to the Lutheran princes of Germany, and allowed Marguerite to install Roussel as preacher to large gatherings in the Louvre; and when the Sorbonne protested he banished its leaders from Paris. In October 1533, he was on good terms with Clement, and promised active measures against the French Protestants. On November 1 Nicholas Cop delivered his pro-Lutheran address at the university; the Sorbonne rose in wrath, and Francis ordered a new persecution. But then his quarrel with the Emperor sharpened, and he sent Guillaume du Bellay, favorable to reform, to Wittenberg with a request that Melanchthon should formulate a possible reconciliation between the old faith and the new ideas (1534), and thereby make possible an alliance of Protestant Germany and Catholic France. Melanchthon complied, and matters were moving fast, when an extreme faction among the French reformers posted in the streets of Paris, Orléans, and other cities, and even on the doors of the King's bedchamber at Amboise, placards denouncing the Mass as idolatry, and the Pope and the Catholic clergy as "a brood of vermin . . . apostates, wolves . . . liars, blasphemers, murderers of souls"

(October 18, 1534).[45] Enraged, Francis ordered an indiscriminate imprisonment of all suspects; soon the jails were full. Many printers were arrested, and for a time all printing was prohibited. Marguerite, Marot, and many moderate Protestants joined in condemning the placards. The King, his sons, ambassadors, nobles, and clergy marched in solemn silence, bearing lighted candles, to hear an expiatory Mass in Notre Dame (January 21, 1535). Francis declared that he would behead his own children if he found them harboring these blasphemous heresies. That evening six Protestants were burned to death in Paris by a method judged fit to appease the Deity: they were suspended over a fire, and were repeatedly lowered into it and raised from it so that their agony might be prolonged.[46] Between November 10, 1534, and May 5, 1535, twenty-four Protestants were burned alive in Paris. Pope Paul III reproved the King for needless severity, and ordered him to end the persecution.[47]

Before the year was out Francis was again wooing the German Protestants. He himself wrote to Melanchthon (July 23, 1535), inviting him to come and "confer with some of our most distinguished doctors as to the means of re-establishing in the Church that sublime harmony which is the chief of all my desires." [48] Melanchthon did not come. Perhaps he suspected Francis of using him as a thorn in the Emperor's side; or he was dissuaded by Luther or the Elector of Saxony, who said, "The French are not Evangelicals, they are Erasmians." [49] This was true of Marguerite, Briçonnet, Lefèvre, Roussel; not true of the placardists, or of the Calvinistic Huguenots who were beginning to multiply in southern France. After making peace with Charles (1538), Francis abandoned all efforts to conciliate his own Protestants.

The darkest disgrace of his reign was only partly his fault. The Vaudois or Waldenses, who still cherished the semi-Protestant ideas of Peter Waldo, their twelfth-century founder, had been allowed, under royal protection, to maintain their Quakerlike existence in some thirty villages along the Durance River in Provence. In 1530 they entered into correspondence with reformers in Germany and Switzerland, and two years later they drew up a profession of faith based on the views of Bucer and Oecolampadius. A papal legate set up the Inquisition among them; they appealed to Francis; he bade the prosecution cease (1533). But Cardinal de Tournon, alleging that the Waldenses were in a treasonable conspiracy against the government, persuaded the ailing, vacillating King to sign a decree (January 1, 1545) that all Waldenses found guilty of heresy should be put to death. The officers of the *Parlement* at Aix-en-Provence interpreted the order to mean mass extermination. The soldiers at first refused to obey the command; they were, however, induced to kill a few; the heat of murder inflamed them, and they passed into massacre. Within a week (April 12–18) several villages were burned to the ground; in one of them 800 men, women, and children were slaughtered; in two months 3,000 were killed, twenty-two villages were razed, 700 men were sent to the galleys. Twenty-five terrified women, seeking refuge in a cavern, were asphyxiated by a fire built at its mouth. Protestant Switzerland and Germany raised horrified protests; Spain sent Francis congratulations.[50] A year later a small Lutheran group was found meeting at Meaux under the leadership of Pierre Leclerc, brother of branded Jean; fourteen of the group were tortured and burned, eight after having their tongues torn out (October 7, 1546).

These persecutions were the supreme failure of Francis' reign. The courage of the martyrs gave dignity and splendor to their cause; thousands of onlookers must have been impressed and disturbed, who, without these spectacular executions, might never have bothered to change their inherited faith. Despite the recurrent terror, clandestine "swarms" of Protestants existed in 1530 in Lyons, Bordeaux, Orléans, Reims, Amiens, Poitiers, Bourges, Nîmes, La Rochelle, Châlons, Dijon, Toulouse. Huguenot legions sprang almost out of the ground. Francis, dying, must have known that he had left his son not only the encompassing hostility of England, Germany, and Switzerland, but a heritage of hate in France herself.

V. HAPSBURG AND VALOIS: 1515–26

It was not to be expected that so volatile a monarch would be content to surrender all the hopes that had agitated his predecessors for adding Milan, and if possible Naples, as brilliants in the French crown. Louis XII had accepted the natural limits of France—had recognized, so to speak, the sovereignty of the Alps. Francis withdrew the recognition, and challenged the right of Duke Maximilian Sforza to Milan. During several months of negotiations he collected and equipped an immense force. In August 1515, he led it by a new and perilous path—blasting his way across rocky cliffs—over the Alps and down into Italy. At Marignano, nine miles from Milan, the French knights and infantry met Sforza's Swiss mercenaries in two days (September 13–14, 1515) of such killing as Italy had not known since the barbarian invasions; 10,000 men were left dead on the ground. Time and again the French seemed defeated, when the King himself charged to the front and rallied his troops by the example of his daring. It was customary for a ruler victorious in battle to reward special bravery by creating new knights on the field; but before doing this Francis, in an unprecedented but characteristic gesture, knelt before Pierre, Seigneur de Bayard, and asked to be knighted by the hand of the famous Chevalier *sans peur et sans reproche*. Bayard protested that the King was ex officio the knight of knights and needed no dubbing, but the young sovereign, still only twenty-one, insisted. Bayard went through the traditional motions magnificently, and then put away his sword, saying: "Assuredly, my good sword, thou shalt be well guarded as a relic, and honored above all others, for having this day conferred upon so handsome and puissant a king the order of chivalry; and never will I wear thee more except against Turks, Moors, and Saracens!"[51] Francis entered Milan as its master, sent its deposed Duke to France with a comfortable pension, took also Parma and Piacenza, and signed with Leo X, in splendid ceremonies at Bologna, a treaty and Concordat that allowed both Pope and King to claim a diplomatic victory.

Francis returned to France the idol of his countrymen, and almost of Europe. He had charmed his soldiers by sharing their hardships and outbraving their bravery; and though in his triumph he had indulged his vanity, he tempered it by giving credit to others, softening all egos with words of praise and grace. In the intoxication of fame he made his greatest mistake: he entered his candidacy for the Imperial crown. He was legitimately disturbed by the prospect of having Charles I, King of Spain and Naples and Count of Flanders and Holland, become also head of the Holy Roman Empire—with all those claims to Lombardy, and therefore Milan, for which Maximilian had so repeatedly invaded Italy; within such a new Empire France would be surrounded by apparently invincible enemies. Francis bribed and lost; Charles bribed more, and won (1519). The bitter rivalry began that kept Western Europe in turmoil till within three years of the King's death.

Charles and Francis never ran out of reasons for hostility. Even before becoming Emperor, Charles had claimed Burgundy through his grandmother Mary, daughter of Charles the Bold, and had refused to recognize the reunion of Burgundy with the French crown. Milan was formally a fief of the Empire. Charles continued the Spanish occupation of Navarre; Francis insisted that it should be returned to his vassal, Henri d'Albret. And above all these *casus belli* lay the question of questions: Who was to be master of Europe—Charles or Francis? The Turks answered, Suleiman.

Francis struck the first blow. Noting that Charles had on his hands a political revolution in Spain and a religious revolution in Germany, he sent an army across the Pyrenees to recapture Navarre; it was defeated in a campaign whose most important incident was the wounding of Ignatius Loyola (1521). Another army went south to defend Milan; the troops mutinied for lack of pay; they were routed at La Bicocca by Imperial mercenaries, and Milan fell to Charles V (1522). To cap these mishaps the constable of the French armies went over to the Emperor.

Charles, Duke of Bourbon, was head of the powerful family that would rule France from 1589 to 1792. He was the richest man in the country after the King; 500 nobles were among his retainers; he was the last of the great barons who could defy the monarch of the now centralized state. He served Francis well in war, fighting bravely at Marignano; less well in government, alienating the Milanese by his harsh rule. Ill supplied there with funds from the King, he laid out 100,000 livres of his own, expecting to be repaid; he was not. Francis looked with jealous misgiving upon this almost royal vassal. He recalled him from Milan, and offered him thoughtless or intentional affronts that left Bourbon his brooding enemy. The Duke had married Suzanne of Bourbon, whose extensive estates were by her mother's will to revert to the Crown if Suzanne should die without issue. Suzanne so died (1521), but after making a will that left all her property to her husband. Francis and his mother claimed the property as the most direct descendants of the previous duke of Bourbon; Charles fought the claim; the *Parlement* of Paris decided against him. Francis proposed a compromise that would let the Duke enjoy the income of the property till his death; he rejected the proposal. Louise, fifty-one, offered herself as a bride to the thirty-one-year-old Duke, with a clear title to the property as her dowry; he refused. Charles V made a rival offer: the hand of his sister Eleonora in marriage, and full support, by Imperial troops, of the Duke's claims. The Duke accepted, fled by night across the frontier, and was made lieutenant-general of the Imperial army in Italy (1523).

Francis sent Bonnivet against him. Marguerite's lover proved incompetent; his army was overwhelmed at Romagnano by the Duke; and in the retreat the Chevalier de Bayard, commanding the dangerous rear guard, was fatally wounded by a shot from a harquebus (April 30, 1524). The victorious Bourbon found him dying under a tree, and offered him some consolatory compliments. "My lord," answered Bayard, "there is pity for me; I die having done my duty; but I have pity for you, to see you serving against your King, your country, and your oath." [52] The Duke was moved, but had burned all bridges behind him. He entered into an agreement with Charles V and Henry VIII by which all three were to invade France simultaneously, overwhelm all French forces, and divide the land among them. As his part of the bargain the Duke entered Provence, took Aix, and laid siege to Marseille; but his campaign was poorly provisioned, met unexpectedly strong resistance, and collapsed. He retreated into Italy (September 1524).

Francis thought it wise to pursue him and recapture Milan. Bonnivet, foolish to the end, advised him to take Pavia first, and then come upon Milan from the south; the King agreed, and laid siege (August 26, 1524). But here too the defense was superior to the offense; for four months the French host was held at bay, while Bourbon, Charles of Lannoy (Viceroy of Naples), and the Marquis of Pescara (husband of Vittoria Colonna) gathered a new army of 27,000 men. Suddenly this force appeared behind the

French; on the same day (February 24, 1525) Francis found his men assaulted on one side by this unexpected multitude, and on the other by a sortie from Pavia. As usual, he fought in the van of the melee, and killed so many of the enemy with his own sword that he thought victory assured. But his generalship was sacrificed to his courage; his forces were poorly deployed; his infantry moved in between his artillery and the foe, making the superior French guns useless. The French faltered; the Duke of Alençon fled, taking the rear guard with him. Francis challenged his disordered army to follow him back into the battle; only the most gallant of his nobles accompanied him, and a slaughter of French chivalry ensued. Francis received wounds in the face, on the arms and legs, but struck out tirelessly; his horse collapsed under him; still he fought. His loyal knights fell one by one till he was left alone. He was surrounded by enemy soldiers, and was about to be slain when an officer recognized him, saved him, and led him to Lannoy, who with low bows of respect accepted his sword.

The fallen King was confined in the fortress of Pizzighettone near Cremona, whence he was allowed to send his oft quoted, oft misquoted letter to his mother, who was ruling France in his absence:

> TO THE REGENT OF FRANCE: Madame, that you may know how stands the rest of my misfortune: there is nothing in the world left to me but honor and my life, which is saved (*de toute chose ne m'est demeuré que l'honneur et la vie, qui est sauvée*). And in order that in your adversity this news might bring you some little comfort, I prayed for permission to write you this letter . . . entreating you, in the exercise of your accustomed prudence, to do nothing rash, for I have hope, after all, that God will not forsake me. . . .[53]

He sent a similar note to Marguerite, who answered both:

> MY LORD: The joy we are still feeling at the kind letters which you were pleased to write yesterday to me and your mother, makes us so happy with the assurance of your health, on which our life depends, that it seems to me that we ought to think of nothing but of praising God and desiring a continuance of your good news, which is the best meat we can have to live on. And inasmuch as the Creator has given us grace that our *trinity* should be always united, *the other two* do entreat you that this letter, presented to you who are *the third*, may be accepted with the same affection with which it is cordially offered you by your most humble and obedient servants, your mother and sister,
>
> LOUISE, MARGUERITE [54]

To the Emperor at Madrid Francis wrote a very humble letter telling him that "if it please you to have so much honorable pity as to answer for the safety which a captive king of France deserves to find . . . you may be sure of obtaining an acquisition instead of a useless prisoner, and of making a king of France your slave forever." [55] Francis had not been trained to misfortune.

Charles received the news of his victory calmly, and refused to celebrate it, as many suggested, with a splendid festival. He retired into his bedroom (we are told), and knelt in prayer. To Francis and Louise he sent what seemed to him moderate terms for peace and the liberation of the King. (1) France must give up Burgundy and all claims to Flanders, Artois, and Italy. (2) All lands and dignities claimed by the Duke of Bourbon must be surrendered to him. (3) Provence and Dauphiné should be made an independent state. (4) France must restore to England all French territory formerly held by Britain—i.e., Normandy, Anjou, Gascony, and Guienne. (5) Francis must sign an alliance with the Emperor, and join him in a campaign against the Turks. Louise answered that France would not yield an inch of territory, and was prepared to defend itself to the last man. The Regent acted now with an energy, resolution, and intelligence that made the French people forgive her headstrong faults. She arranged at once for the organization and equipment of new armies, and set them to guard all points of possible invasion. To keep the Emperor's mind off France, she urged Suleiman of Turkey to defer his attack on Persia and undertake instead a westward campaign; we do not know what part her plea played in the Sultan's decision, but in 1526 he marched into Hungary, and inflicted so disastrous a defeat upon the Christian army at Mohács that any invasion of France by Charles would have been deemed treason to Christendom. Meanwhile Louise pointed out to Henry VIII and Clement VII how both England and the papacy would be reduced to bondage if the Emperor were allowed all the territory that he demanded. Henry wavered; Louise persisted, and offered him an "indemnity" of 2,000,000 crowns; he signed a defensive and offensive alliance with France (August 30, 1525). This female diplomacy opened male eyes, and shattered Charles's confidence.

By agreement among Louise, Lannoy, and the Emperor, the captive King was transported to Spain. When Francis reached Valencia (July 2, 1525), Charles sent him a courteous letter, but his treatment of his prisoner went no further toward chivalry. Francis was assigned a narrow room in an old castle in Madrid, under rigorous vigilance; the sole freedom allowed him was to ride on a mule near the castle, under watch of armed and mounted guards. He asked Charles for an interview; Charles put it off, and allowed two weeks of fretting confinement to incline Francis toward paying a heavy price for liberty. Louise offered to meet the Emperor and negotiate, but he thought it better to play upon his prisoner than have a woman charm him into lenience. She informed him that her daughter Marguerite, now a widow, "would be happy if she could be agreeable to his Imperial Majesty," but he preferred Isabella of Portugal, who, with a dowry of 900,000 crowns, could provide him at once with bed and board. After two months of anxious imprisonment, Francis fell dangerously ill. The Spanish people, regretting the Emperor's severity, went to their churches to pray for the French King. Charles prayed too, for a dead ruler would be worthless as a political pawn. He visited Francis briefly, promised him an early release, and sent permission to Marguerite to come and comfort her brother.

Marguerite sailed from Aiguesmortes (August 27, 1525) to Barcelona, and thence was carried by slow and tortuous litter through half the length of Spain to Madrid. She consoled herself with writing poetry, and sending characteristically fervent messages to the King. "Whatever may be required of me, though it be to fling to the winds the ashes of my bones to do you service, nought will be strange or difficult or painful to me, but will be solace, ease of mind, honor." [56] When at last she reached the bedside of her brother she found him apparently recovering; but on September 25 he had a relapse, fell into a coma, and seemed to be dying. Marguerite and the household knelt and prayed, and a priest administered the sacrament. A tedious convalescence followed. Marguerite stayed with Francis a month, then went to Toledo to appeal to the Emperor. He received her pleas coldly; he had learned of Henry's league with France, and longed to punish the duplicity of his late ally, and the audacity of Louise.

Francis had one card left to play, though it would almost certainly mean his lifelong imprisonment. Having warned his sister to leave Spain as quickly as possible, he signed (November 1525) a formal letter of abdication in favor of his eldest son; and since this second Francis was a boy of only eight years, he named Louise—and, in case of her death, Marguerite—as regent of France. Charles saw at once that a king without a kingdom, with nothing to surrender, would be useless. But Francis had more physical than moral courage. On January 14, 1526, he signed with Charles the Treaty of Madrid. Its terms were essentially those that the Emperor had proposed to Louise; they were even more severe, for they required that the two oldest sons of the King should be handed over to Charles as hostages for the faithful execution of the agreement. Francis further consented to marry the Emperor's sister Eleonora, Queen-Dowager of Portugal; and he swore that if he should fail to carry out the terms of the treaty he would return to Spain to resume imprisonment.[57] However, on August 22, 1525, he had deposited with his aides a paper nullifying in advance "all pacts, conventions, renunciations, quittances, revocations, derogations, and oaths that he might have to make contrary to his honor and the good of his crown"; and on the eve of signing the treaty he repeated this statement to his French negotiators, and declared that "it was through force and constraint, confinement, and length of imprisonment that he was signing; and that all that was contained in it was and should remain null and of no effect." [58]

On March 17, 1526, Viceroy Lannoy delivered Francis to Marshal Lautrec on a barge in the Bidassoa River, which separates Spanish Irún from French Hendaye; and in return Lannoy received Princes Francis and Henry. Their father gave them a blessing and a tear, and hurried on to French soil. There he leaped upon a horse, cried joyfully, "I am a king again!" and rode on to Bayonne, where Louise and Marguerite awaited him. At Bordeaux and Cognac he spent three months in sports to recover his health, and indulged in a little love; had he not been a monk for a year? Louise, who had quarreled with the Comtesse de Chateaubriand, had brought with her a pretty, blonde-haired maid of honor, eighteen years old, Anne de Heilly de Pisselieu, who, as planned, struck the King's famished eye. He wooed her in haste, and soon won her as his mistress; and from that moment till death parted them the new favorite shared with Louise and Marguerite the heart of the King. She put up patiently with his marriage to Eleonora, and with his incidental liaisons. To save appearances he gave her a husband, Jean de Brosse, made him Duc, and her Duchesse, d'Étampes, and smiled appreciatively when Jean retired to a distant estate in Britanny.

VI. WAR AND PEACE: 1526–47

When the terms of the Treaty of Madrid became generally known they aroused almost universal hostility to Charles. The German Protestants trembled at the prospect of facing so strengthened an enemy. Italy resented his claim to suzerainty in Lombardy. Clement VII absolved Francis from the oath he had sworn at Madrid, and joined France, Milan, Genoa, Florence, and Venice in forming the League of Cognac for common defense (May 22, 1526). Charles called Francis "no gentleman," bade him return to his Spanish prison, ordered a harsher confinement for the King's sons, and gave free rein to his generals to discipline the Pope.

An Imperial army collected in Germany and Spain poured down through Italy, scaled the walls of Rome (the Duke of Bourbon dying in the process), sacked the city more thoroughly than any Goths or Vandals had ever done, killed 4,000 Romans, and imprisoned Clement in Sant' Angelo. The Emperor, who had remained in Spain, assured a scandalized Europe that his starving army had exceeded his instructions; nevertheless his representatives in Rome kept the Pope shut up in Sant' Angelo from May 6 to December 7, 1527, and exacted from an almost bankrupt papacy an indemnity of 368,000 crowns. Clement appealed to Francis and Henry for aid. Francis dispatched

Lautrec to Italy with an army that sacked Pavia in reckless revenge for its resistance two years before, and Italy wondered whether French friends were any better than German enemies. Lautrec by-passed Rome and besieged Naples, and the city began to starve. But meanwhile Francis had offended Andrea Doria, head of the Genoese navy. Doria called his fleet from the siege of Naples, went over to the side of the Emperor, and provisioned the besieged. Lautrec's army starved in turn; Lautrec himself died, and his army melted away (1528).

The comedy of the rulers hardly relieved the tragedy of the people. When the emissaries of Francis and Henry appeared at Burgos to make a formal declaration of war, Charles retorted to the French envoy: "The King of France is not in a position to address to me such a declaration; he is my prisoner. . . . Your master acted like a dastard and a scoundrel in not keeping his word that he gave me touching the Treaty of Madrid; if he likes to say the contrary I will maintain my words against him with my body to his." [59] This challenge to a duel was readily accepted by Francis, who sent a herald to tell Charles, "You have lied in your throat." Charles responded grandly, naming a place for the encounter and asking Francis to name the time; but French nobles intercepted the messenger, and judicious delays put off the match to the Greek kalends. Nations had grown so large that their differences of economic or political interest could not be settled by private combat, or by the small mercenary armies that had been playing the game of war in Renaissance Italy. The modern method of decision by competitive destruction took form in this Hapsburg-Valois debate.*

It took two women to teach the potentates the art and wisdom of peace. Louise of Savoy communicated with Margaret of Austria, Regent of the Netherlands, and suggested that Francis, anxious for the return of his sons, would abandon all claim to Flanders, Artois, and Italy, and would pay a ransom of 2,000,000 gold crowns for his children, but would never cede Burgundy. Margaret persuaded her nephew to defer his claim to Burgundy, and to forget the claims of the Duke of Bourbon, now conveniently dead. On August 3, 1529, the two women and their diplomatic aides signed *La Paix des Dames*—the "Ladies Peace" of Cambrai. The ransom was raised out of the commerce, industry, and blood of France, and the royal princes, after four years of captivity, returned to freedom with stories of cruel treatment that enraged Francis and France. While the two able women found

---

* The duel had existed in the Middle Ages as an appeal, under royal or judicial sanction and control, to the judgment of God. In the sixteenth century it became a private and individual defense of slighted honor; it developed its own strict laws outside the laws of the state; and it shared in some measure in developing the rules of gentlemanly courtesy and discreet restraint. It was not legally permitted in France after 1547, but public opinion continued to sanction it. In England it fell into disuse under Elizabeth; trial by combat, however, remained legal there till 1817.

lasting peace—Margaret in 1530, Louise in 1531—the kings prepared to re-new their war.

Francis turned everywhere for help. To Henry VIII he sent a money ap-peasement for having almost ignored him in the Cambrai settlement; and Henry, furious at Charles for opposing his "divorce," pledged his support to France. Within a year or so Francis negotiated alliances with the Protes-tant princes of Germany, with the Turks, and with the Pope. The vacillating Pontiff, however, soon made peace with Charles, and crowned him emperor (1530)—the last coronation of a Holy Roman Emperor by a pope. Then, frightened by a monarch who had in effect made Italy a province of his realm, Clement sought a new bond with France by offering his niece Cather-ine de Médicis in marriage to Francis' son Henry, Duke of Orléans. King and Pope met at Marseille (October 28, 1533), and the marriage, pregnant with history, was performed by the Pope himself. A year later Clement died, not yet having made up his mind about anything.

The Emperor, already old at thirty-five, shouldered his self-imposed bur-dens with weary fortitude. He was shocked to learn—on the word of the Sultan's vizier to Ferdinand of Austria—that the Turkish siege of Vienna in 1529 had been undertaken in response to an appeal from Francis, Louise, and Clement VII for help against the encompassing Empire.[60] Moreover, Francis had allied himself with the Tunisian chieftain Khair ed-Din Barbarossa, who was harassing Christian commerce in the western Mediterranean, raiding coastal towns, and carrying captive Christians into slavery. Charles collected another army and navy, crossed to Tunis (1535), captured it, freed 10,000 Christian slaves, and rewarded his unpaid troops by letting them loot the city and massacre the Moslem population. Leaving garrisons in Bona and La Gol-eta, Charles returned to Rome (April 5, 1536) as the triumphant defender of Christendom against Islam and the King of France. Francis had meanwhile renewed his claim to Milan, and in March 1536, he had conquered the duchy of Savoy to clear his road into Italy. Charles was furious. In a passionate ad-dress before the new pope, Paul III, and the full consistory of cardinals, he recounted his efforts for peace, the French King's violations of the treaties of Madrid and Cambrai, and the alliances of his "Most Christian Majesty" (as Francis was called) with the enemies of the Church in Germany, and of Christianity in Turkey and Africa; and he ended by again challenging Francis to a duel: "Let us not continue wantonly to shed the blood of our innocent subjects; let us decide the quarrel man to man, with what arms he pleases to choose . . . and after that let the united forces of Germany, Spain, and France be employed to humble the power of the Turk, and to exter-minate heresy out of Christendom."

It was a subtle speech, for it compelled the Pope to align himself with the Emperor; but no one took seriously its proposal for a duel; fighting by proxy was much safer. Charles invaded Provence (July 25, 1536) with 50,000 men, hoping to flank or divert the French in Savoy by moving up the Rhone. But Constable Anne de Montmorency ordered the weak French forces to burn in their retreat everything that could supply the Imperial troops; soon Charles, always lacking money, and unable to feed his men, abandoned the campaign. Paul III, anxious to free Charles for an attack on the Turks or the Lutherans, persuaded the crippled Titans to meet with him—in jealously separate rooms—at Nice, and to sign a ten-year truce (June 17, 1538). A month later Eleonora, wife to one, sister to the other, brought King and Emperor together in a personal meeting at Aiguesmortes. There they ceased to be royal, and became human; Charles knelt to embrace the King's youngest children; Francis gave him a costly diamond set in a ring which was inscribed *Dilectionis testis et exemplum*—"a witness and token of love"; and Charles transferred from his own neck to the King's the collar of the Golden Fleece. They went together to hear Mass, and the townspeople, rejoicing in peace, cried, "The Emperor! The King!"

When Ghent rebelled against Charles (1539) and joined Bruges and Ypres in offering themselves to Francis, the King resisted the temptation; and when Charles, in Spain, found the seaways closed by rebel vessels or *mal de mer*, Francis granted his request for passage through France. His councilors advised the King to force the Emperor, en route, to sign the cession of Milan to the Duke of Orléans, but Francis refused. "When you do a generous thing," he said, "you must do it completely and boldly." He found his court fool writing in a "Fool's Diary" the name of Charles V; for, said Tribouillet, "he's a bigger fool than I am if he comes through France." "And what will you say if I let him pass?" asked the King. "I will rub out his name and put yours in his place." [61] Francis let Charles pass unhindered, and ordered every town on the way to receive the Emperor with royal honors and feasts.

This precarious friendship was ended when Spanish soldiers near Pavia captured French emissaries bearing new offers of alliance from Francis to Suleiman (July 1541). At this time Barbarossa was again raiding the coastal towns of Italy. Charles sailed from Mallorca with another armada to destroy him, but storms so buffeted the fleet that it was compelled to return empty-handed to Spain. The Emperor's fortunes were ebbing. His young wife, whom he had learned to love, had died (1539), and his own health was worsening. In 1542 Francis declared war on him over Milan; the King's allies now included Sweden, Denmark, Gelderland, Cleves, Scotland, the Turks, and the Pope; only Henry VIII supported Charles, for a price; and the Spanish Cortes refused additional subsidies for the war. A Turkish fleet combined with a French fleet to besiege Nice, which was now Imperial territory (1543); the siege failed, but Barbarossa and his Moslem troops were allowed to winter at Toulon, where they openly sold Christian slaves.[62] The Emperor patiently retrieved the situation. He found means of pacifying the Pope; he won Philip of Hesse to his side by winking at his bigamy; he attacked and vanquished the Duke of Cleves; he effected a junction with his English allies, and faced France with so strong a force that Francis retreated and yielded him the honors of the campaign (October 1543). Again too poor to further provision his army, Charles welcomed an offer of peace, and signed with Francis the Treaty of Crépy (September 18, 1544). The King withdrew his claims to Flanders, Artois, and Naples; Charles no longer demanded Burgundy; a Hapsburg princess would marry a French prince, and bring him Milan as her dowry. (Most of this could have been peaceably arranged in 1525.) Charles was now free to overwhelm the Protestants at Mühlberg; Titian pictured him there without the arthritis, proud and triumphant, worn and weary after a thousand vicissitudes, a hundred turns of fortune's ironic wheel.

As for Francis, he was finished, and France nearly so. In one sense he had lost nothing but honor; he had preserved his country by scuttling the ideals of chivalry. Yet the Turks would have come without his call, and their coming helped Francis to check an Emperor who, unresisted, might have spread the Spanish Inquisition into Flanders, Holland, Switzerland, Germany, and Italy. Francis had found France peaceful and prosperous; he left it bankrupt and on the brink of another war. A month before his death, while swearing friendship with Charles, he sent 200,000 crowns to the Protestants of Germany to support them against the Emperor.[63] He—and in slightly less degree Charles—agreed with Machiavelli that statesmen, whose task is to preserve their countries, may violate the moral code which they require from their citizens, whose task is only to preserve their lives. The French people might have forgiven him his wars, but they lost relish for the splendor of his ways and his court when they perceived the cost. He was already unpopular in 1535.

He consoled himself with beauty living and dead. In his later years he made Fontainebleau his favorite residence, rebuilt it, and rejoiced in the graceful feminine art with which the Italians were adorning it. He surrounded himself with a *Petite Bande* of young women who pleased him with their good looks and gaiety. In 1538 a disease injured his uvula, and thereafter he stammered shamefully. He tried to cure what was probably his syphilis with mercury pills recommended by Barbarossa, but they had no success.[64] A persistent and ill-smelling abscess broke his spirit, gave a dull and plaintive look to his once keen eyes, and moved him to an uncongenial piety. He had to watch his food, for he suspected that some courtiers who expected to rise under his successor were seeking to poison him. He noted sadly that the court now pivoted around his son, who was already distributing offices and impatiently awaiting his turn at the resources of France. To his deathbed at Rambouillet he called his sole heir and warned him not to be dominated by a woman—for Henry was already devoted to Diane de Poitiers. The King confessed his sins in hurried summary, and, breathing painfully, welcomed death. Francis, Duke of Guise, at the door, whispered to those in the next room, *Le vieux gallant s'en va*—"The old gallant is going." [65] He went, whispering the name of Jesus. He was fifty-three, and had reigned thirty-two years. France felt that it was too much; but when it had recovered from him it forgave him everything, because he had sinned gracefully, he had loved beauty, he had been incarnate France.

In that same year Henry VIII died, and two years later, Marguerite. She had been too long away from Francis, and too far, to realize that death was stalking him. When word came to her, in a convent at Angoulême, that he was seriously ill, she almost lost her reason. "Whosoever shall come to my door," she said, "and announce to me the recovery of the King my brother, such a courier, should he be tired and worn out, muddy and dirty, I will go and kiss and embrace as if he were the sprucest prince and gentleman in France; and should he be in want of a bed ... I would give him mine, and I would gladly lie on the ground for the good news he brought me." [66] She sent couriers to Paris; they returned and lied to her; the King, they assured her, was quite well; but the furtive tears of a nun betrayed the truth. Marguerite stayed in the convent for forty days, acting as abbess, and singing the old sacred chants with the nuns.

Back in Pau or Nérac she resigned herself to austerities, to her husband's infidelities, and to her daughter's wandering willfulness. She found comfort, after all her brave, half-Protestant years, in the color and incense and hypnotic music of Catholic ritual; the Calvinism that was capturing southern France chilled her, and frightened her back to her childhood piety. In December 1549, while watching a comet in the skies, she caught a fever that proved strong enough to break a frame and spirit already weakened by life's inclemencies. Years before she had written lines as if half in love with the anesthesia of death:

Seigneur, quand viendra le jour,	Lord, when will come the day,
Tant désirée,	Wished ardently,
Que je serai par amour	That I shall be by love
A vous tiré? ...	Drawn close to Thee? ...
Essuyez les tristes yeux	Still then my parting sighs,
Le long gemir,	Let me not weep;
Et me donnez pour le mieux	Give the best gift of all,
Un doux dormir.	Sweet boon of sleep.

VII. DIANE DE POITIERS

The "old gallant" had had seven children, all by Claude. The eldest son, Francis, was like his father, handsome, charming, gay. Henry, born in 1519, was quiet, shy, a bit neglected; he matched his brother only in misfortune. Their four years of hardship and humiliation in Spain had marked them indelibly. Francis died six years after liberation. Henry grew more taciturn than before, turned within himself, shunned the frolics of the court; he had companions, but they rarely saw him smile. Men said that he had become Spanish in Spain.

It was not his choice to marry Catherine de Médicis, nor hers to marry him. She too had had tribulations. Both her parents had died of syphilis within twenty-two days of her birth (1519); and from that time till her marriage she was shifted from place to place, helpless and unasked. When Florence expelled its Medici rulers (1527) it kept Caterina as a hostage for their good behavior, and when these exiles returned to besiege the city she was threatened with death to deter them. Clement VII used her as a pawn to win France to papal policies; she went obediently to Marseille, a girl of fourteen, and married a boy of fourteen who hardly spoke to her during all the festival. When they arrived in Paris she met a cold reception because she brought too many Italians with her; she became to the Parisians "the Florentine"; and though she tried hard to charm them, neither they nor her husband ever warmed to her. Despite many efforts she remained barren for ten years, and the doctors suspected some evil inheritance from her infected parents. Losing hope of offspring, Catherine de Médicis, as she was called in France, went to Francis weeping, and offered to submit to a divorce and retire to a convent. The King graciously refused the sacrifice. At last the gates of motherhood burst, and children came in almost annual succession. Ten in all, they were chiefly Francis II, who would marry Mary Stuart; Elizabeth, who would marry Philip II; Charles IX, who would give the order for the Massacre of St. Bartholomew; Edward, who became the tragic Henry III; and Marguerite of Valois, who would marry and harry Henry of Navarre. Through all but the first four of these barren or fertile years her husband, while begetting children on her body, gave his love to Diane de Poitiers.

Diane was unique among the royal mistresses who played so leading a role in French history. She was not beautiful. When Henry, seventeen, fell in love with her (1536), she was already thirty-seven, her hair was turning gray, and wrinkles were beginning to score the years on her brow. Her only physical charms were grace, and a complexion kept fresh by washing with cold water at all seasons. She was not a courtesan; apparently she was faithful to her husband, Louis de Brézé, till his death; and though, like Henry, she indulged in two or three asides during her royal liaison, these were venial incidents, mere grace notes in her song of love. She was not romantic; rather she was too practical, making hay while her sun shone; France condemned not her morals but her money. She was not like Francis' *mignons*—pretty heads but empty, prancing on gay feet till motherhood surprised them. Diane had good education, good sense, good manners, good wit; here was a mistress who charmed with her mind.

She came of high lineage, and was brought up at the art-loving court of the Bourbons at Moulins. Her father, Jean de Poitiers, Comte de Saint-Val-lier, shared the Duke of Bourbon's treason after trying to prevent it; he was captured and sentenced to death (1523); Diane's husband, in favor with Francis, secured her father's pardon.* Louis de Brézé was grandson of Charles VII by Agnès Sorel; he had ability or influence, for he became Grant' Sénéschal and Governor of Normandy. He was fifty-six when Diane, sixteen, became his wife (1515). When he died (1531) she raised to his memory at Rouen a magnificent tomb with an inscription vowing eternal fidelity. She never married again, and wore, thereafter, only black and white.

She met Henry when, a lad of seven, he was being handed over at Bayonne as a hostage for his father. The bewildered boy wept; Diane, then twenty-seven, mothered and comforted him, whose own mother Claude was two years dead; and perhaps the memory of those pitying embraces revived in him when he met her again eleven years later. Though then four years a husband, he was still mentally immature, as well as abnormally melancholy and diffident; he wanted a mother more than a wife; and here again Diane appeared, quiet, tender, comforting. He came to her first as a son, and their relations for some time were apparently chaste. Her affection and counsel gave him confidence; under her tutelage he ceased to be a misanthrope, and prepared to be a king. Popular opinion credited them with having one child, Diane de France, whom she brought up with her two daughters by Brézé; she also adopted the daughter borne to Henry in 1538 by a Piedmontese maiden who paid for her royal moment by a lifetime as a nun. Another illegitimate child resulted from Henry's later affair with Mary Fleming, governess of Mary Stuart. Despite these experiments, his devotion was increasingly to Diane de Poitiers. He wrote to her poems of real excellence; he showered her with jewelry and estates. He did not entirely neglect Catherine; usually he dined and spent the evenings with her; and she, grateful for the parings of his love, accepted in silent sorrow the fact that another woman was the real dauphiness of France. She must have felt it as an added wound that Diane occasionally prodded Henry into sleeping with his wife.[68]

His accession to the throne did not lower Diane's state. He wrote to her

---

* There is no truth in the story, spread by Hugo in *Le roi s'amuse*, that Diane bought the pardon by giving herself to the King.[67]

the most abject letters, entreating her to let him be her servant for life. His infatuation made her almost as rich as the Queen. He guaranteed to Diane a fixed percentage of all receipts from the sale of appointments to office, and nearly all appointments were in her power. He gave her the crown jewels that the Duchesse d'Étampes had worn; when the Duchess protested, Diane threatened to accuse her of Protestantism, and was bought off only by a gift of property. Henry allowed her to keep for her use 400,000 thalers that Francis had bequeathed for the secret support of the Protestant princes in Germany.[69] So dowered, Diane rebuilt, on a design by Philibert Delorme, the old Brézé mansion of Anet into an extensive château that became not only a second home for the King but also a museum of art, and a handsome rendezvous for poets, artists, diplomats, dukes, generals, cardinals, mistresses, and philosophers. Here in effect sat the Privy Council of the state, and Diane was prime ministress, passionless and intelligent. Everywhere—at Anet, Chenonceaux, Amboise, the Louvre—dishes, coats of arms, works of art, choir stalls, bore the bold symbol of the royal romance, two Ds placed back to back, with a dash between them forming the letter H. There is something touching and beautiful about this unique friendship, built on love and money, but enduring till death.

In the struggle of the Church against heresy, Diane put all her influence behind orthodoxy and suppression. She had abundant reasons for piety: her daughter was married to a son of Francis, Duke of Guise; and Francis, with his brother Charles, Cardinal of Lorraine, both favorites at Anet, were the leaders of the Catholic party in France. As for Henry, his childhood piety had been intensified by his years in Spain; his love letters confused God and Diane as rivals for his heart. The Church was helpful; it gave him 3,000,000 golden crowns for canceling his father's decree restricting the power of ecclesiastical courts.[70]

Nevertheless Protestantism was growing in France. Calvin and others were sending in missionaries whose success was alarming. Several towns—Caen, Poitiers, La Rochelle, and many in Provence—were predominantly Huguenot by 1559; a priest reckoned the French Protestants in that year at nearly a quarter of the population.[71] Says a Catholic historian: "The source of the apostasy from Rome—ecclesiastical corruption—had not been removed, nay, had only been strengthened, by the . . . Concordat" between Leo X and Francis I.[72] In the middle and lower classes Protestantism was in part a protest against a Catholic government that curbed municipal autonomy, taxed unbearably, and wasted revenues and lives in war. The nobility, shorn of its former political power by the kings, looked with envy at Lutheran princes victorious over Charles V; perhaps a similar feudalism could be restored in France by using widespread popular resentment against abuses in Church and state. Prominent nobles like Gaspard de Coligny, his younger brother François d'Andelot, Prince Louis de Condé, and his brother Antoine de Bourbon, took active part in organizing the Protestant revolt.

For its theology Gallic Protestantism adopted Calvin's *Institutes;* its author and language were French, and its logic appealed to the French mind. After 1550 Luther was almost forgotten in France; the very name Huguenot came from Zurich through Geneva to Provence. In May 1559, the Protestants felt strong enough to send deputies to their first general synod, held secretly in Paris. By 1561 there were 2,000 "Reformed" or Calvinistic churches in France.[73]

Henry II set himself to crush out the heresy. By his instructions the *Parlement* of Paris organized a special commission (1549) to prosecute dissent; those condemned were sent to the stake, and the new court came to be called *le chambre ardente,* "the burning room." By the Edict of Chateaubriand (1551) the printing, sale, or possession of heretical literature was made a major crime, and persistence in Protestant ideas was to be punished with death. Informers were to receive a third of the goods of the condemned. They were to report to the *Parlement* any judge who treated heretics leniently, and no man could be a magistrate unless his orthodoxy was beyond doubt. In three years the *chambre ardente* sent sixty Protestants to a flaming death. Henry proposed to Pope Paul IV that the Inquisition should be established in France on the new Roman model, but the *Parlement* objected to allowing its authority to be superseded. One of its members, Anne du Bourg, boldly suggested that all pursuit of heresy should cease until the Council of Trent should complete its definitions of orthodox dogma. Henry had him arrested, and vowed to see him burned, but fate cheated the King of this spectacle.

For meanwhile he had been lured into renewing the war against the Emperor. He could never forgive the long imprisonment of his father, his brother, and himself; he hated Charles with the same intensity with which he loved Diane. When the Lutheran princes made their decisive stand against the Emperor for Christ and feudalism, they sought alliance with Henry, and invited him to seize Lorraine. So he agreed in the Treaty of Chambord (1552). In a rapid and well-directed campaign he took with little trouble Toul, Nancy, Metz, and Verdun. Charles, readier to yield victory to Protestantism in Germany than to the Valois in France, signed a humble peace with the princes at Passau, and hurried to besiege the French in Metz. Francis, Duke of Guise, made his reputation there by the skill and pertinacity of his defense. From October 19 to December 26, 1552, the siege continued; then Charles, pale, haggard, white-bearded, crippled, withdrew his disheartened troops. "I see very well," he said, "that fortune resembles a woman; she prefers a young king to an old emperor." [74] "Before three years are up," he added, "I shall turn Cordelier"—i.e., a Franciscan friar.[75]

In 1555–56 he resigned his power in the Netherlands and Spain to his son, signed the Truce of Vaucelles with France, and left for Spain (September 17, 1556). He thought he was bequeathing to Philip a realm at peace, but Henry felt that the situation called for another sally into Italy. Philip had no reputation as a general; he was unexpectedly plunged into war with Pope Paul IV; to Henry the opportunity seemed golden. He sent Guise to take Milan and Naples, and himself prepared to meet Philip on the ancient battle-fields of northeastern France. Philip rose to the occasion. He borrowed a million ducats from Anton Fugger, and charmed Queen Mary of England into the war. At Saint-Quentin (August 10, 1557) Duke Emmanuel Philibert of Savoy led Philip's combined armies to an overwhelming victory, took Coligny and Montmorency prisoners, and prepared to march upon Paris. The city was in panic; defense seemed impossible. Henry recalled Guise and his troops from Italy; the Duke crossed France, and by remarkable celerity of movement surprised and captured Calais (1558), which England had held since 1348. Philip, hating war and anxious to return to Spain, was readily persuaded to sign the Treaty of Cateau-Cambrésis (April 2, 1559): Henry agreed to stay north of the Alps, and Philip consented to let him keep Lorraine and—over Mary's tears—Calais. Suddenly the two kings became friends; Henry gave his daughter Elizabeth in marriage to Philip, and his sister Marguerite of Berry was pledged to Emmanuel Philibert, who now recovered Savoy; and a stately festival of jousts, banquets, and weddings was arranged.

So, while cautious Philip remained in Flanders, French, Flemish, and Spanish notables gathered around the royal palace of Les Tournelles in Paris; lists were fenced off in the Rue St.-Antoine, with gaily decorated stands and balconies; and all went merry as a wedding bell. On June 22 the Duke of Alva, as proxy for Philip, received Elizabeth as new Queen of Spain. Henry, now forty, insisted on entering the tournament. In such jousts victory was adjudged to the rider who, without being unhorsed, broke three lances against the armor of his foe. Henry accomplished this upon the Dukes of Guise and Savoy, who knew their proper roles in the play. But a third opponent, Montgomery, after breaking a lance against the King, awkwardly allowed the sharp-pointed stump of the weapon to pass under Henry's visor; it pierced the King's eye and reached the brain. For nine days he lay unconscious. On July 9 the marriage of Philibert and Marguerite was celebrated. On July 10 the King died. Diane de Poitiers retired to Anet, and survived seven years. Catherine de Médicis, who had hungered for his love, wore mourning all the rest of her life.

CHAPTER XXIII

Henry VIII and Cardinal Wolsey

1509-29

I. A PROMISING KING: 1509–11

NO one, beholding the youth who mounted the throne of England in 1509, would have foreseen that he was to be both the hero and the villain of the most dramatic reign in English history. Still a lad of eighteen, his fine complexion and regular features made him almost girlishly attractive; but his athletic figure and prowess soon canceled any appearance of femininity. Foreign ambassadors vied with native eulogists in praising his auburn hair, his golden beard, his "extremely fine calf." "He is extremely fond of tennis," reported Giustiniani to the Venetian Senate; "it is the prettiest thing in the world to see him play, his fair skin glowing through a shirt of finest texture." [1] In archery and wrestling he equaled the best in his kingdom; at the hunt he never seemed to tire; two days a week he gave to jousts—and there only the Duke of Suffolk could match him. But he was also an accomplished musician, "sang and played all kinds of instruments with rare talent" (wrote the papal nuncio), and composed two Masses, which are still preserved. He loved dancing and masquerades, pageantry and fine dress. He liked to drape himself in ermine or purple robes, and the law gave him alone the right to wear purple, or gold brocade. He ate with gusto, and sometimes prolonged state dinners to seven hours, but in the first twenty years of his reign his vanity curbed his appetite. Everybody liked him, and marveled at his genial ease of manners and access, his humor, tolerance, and clemency. His accession was hailed as the dawn of a golden age.

The intellectual classes rejoiced too, for in those halcyon days Henry aspired to be a scholar as well as an athlete, a musician, and a king. Originally destined for an ecclesiastical career, he became something of a theologian, and could quote Scripture to any purpose. He had good taste in art, collected with discrimination, and wisely chose Holbein to immortalize his paunch. He took an active part in works of engineering, shipbuilding, fortification, and artillery. Sir Thomas More said of him that he "has more learning than any English monarch ever possessed before him" [2]—no high praise. "What may we not expect," More continued, "from a king who has been nourished by philosophy and the nine Muses?" [3] Mountjoy wrote ecstatically to Erasmus, then in Rome:

> What may you not promise yourself from a prince with whose extraordinary talent and almost divine character you are well ac- quainted? But when you know what a hero he now shows himself, how wisely he behaves, what a lover he is of justice and goodness, what affection he bears to the learned, I venture to swear that you will need no wings to make you fly to behold this new and auspicious star. Oh, my Erasmus, if you could see how all the world here is re- joicing in the possession of so great a prince, how his life is all their desire, you would not contain your tears for joy. The heavens laugh, the earth exults. [4]

Erasmus came, and for a moment shared the delirium. "Heretofore," he wrote, "the heart of learning was among such as professed religion. Now, while these for the most part give themselves up to the belly, luxury, and money,* the love of learning is gone from them to secular princes, the court, and the nobility. . . . The King admits not only such men as More to his court, but he invites them—forces them—to watch all that he does, to share his duties and his pleasures. He prefers the companionship of men like More to that of silly youths or girls or the rich." [5] More was one of the King's Council, Linacre was the King's physician, Colet was the King's preacher at St. Paul's.

In the year of Henry's accession Colet, inheriting his father's fortune, used much of it to establish St. Paul's School. Some 150 boys were chosen to study, there, classical literature and Christian theology and ethics. Colet violated tradition by staffing the school with lay teachers; it was the first non- clerical school in Europe. The "Trojans," who at Oxford inveighed against the teaching of the classics on the ground that it led to religious doubt, op- posed Colet's program, but the King overruled them and gave Colet full encouragement. Though Colet was himself orthodox and a model of piety, his enemies charged him with heresy. Archbishop Warham silenced them, and Henry concurred. When Colet saw Henry bent on war with France, he publicly condemned the policy, and declared, like Erasmus, that an un- just peace was to be preferred to the justest war. Even with the King sitting in the congregation Colet denounced war as flying in the face of the precepts of Christ. Henry privately begged him not to disrupt the morale of the army, but when the King was urged to depose Colet he answered: "Let everyone have his own doctor . . . this man is the doctor for me." [6] Colet continued

---

* But Erasmus' ecclesiastical friends, Dean Colet, Bishop Fisher of Rochester, and Arch- bishop Warham of Canterbury, were generous and devoted friends of learning.

to take Christianity seriously. To Erasmus he wrote (1517) in the spirit of Thomas à Kempis:

> Ah, Erasmus, of books of knowledge there is no end; but there is nothing better for this short term of ours than that we should live a pure and holy life, and daily do our best to be cleansed and enlightened . . . by the ardent love and imitation of Jesus. Wherefore it is my most earnest wish that, leaving all indirect courses, we may proceed by a short method to the Truth. Farewell.[7]

In 1518 he prepared his own simple tomb, with only *Johannes Coletus* inscribed on it. A year later he was buried in it, and many felt that a saint had passed away.

II. WOLSEY

Henry, who was to become the incarnation of Machiavelli's *Prince*, was as yet an innocent novice in international politics. He recognized his need for guidance, and sampled the men around him. More was brilliant, but only thirty-one, and inclined to sanctity. Thomas Wolsey was a mere three years older, and was a priest, but his whole turn was for statesmanship, and religion was for him a part of politics. Born at Ipswich, "of low extraction and despicable blood" (so the proud Guicciardini described him),[8] Thomas had covered the baccalaureate course at Oxford by the age of fifteen; at twenty-three he was bursar of Magdalen College, and showed his quality by applying adequate funds, beyond his authority, for the completion of that hall's most majestic tower. He knew how to get along. Displaying a flair for management and negotiation, he rose through a succession of chaplainships to serve Henry VII in that capacity and in diplomacy. Henry VIII, on accession, made him almoner—director of charities. Soon the priest was a member of the Privy Council, and shocked Archbishop Warham by advocating a military alliance with Spain against France. Louis XII was invading Italy, and might again make the papacy a dependency of France; in any case France must not become too strong. Henry yielded in this matter to Wolsey and his own father-in-law, Ferdinand of Spain; he himself was at this time inclined to peace. "I content myself with my own," he told Giustiniani; "I wish to command only my own subjects; but on the other hand I do not choose that anyone shall have it in his power to command me";[9] this almost sums up Henry's political career. He had inherited the claim of the English kings to the crown of France, but he knew that this was an empty pretense. The war petered out quickly in the Battle of the Spurs (1513). Wolsey arranged the peace, and persuaded Louis XII to marry Henry's sister Mary. Leo X, pleased with being rescued, made Wolsey Archbishop of York

(1514) and Cardinal (1515); Henry, triumphant, made him Chancellor (1515). The King prided himself on having protected the papacy; and when a later pope refused him a marriage easement he deemed it gross ingratitude.

The first five years of Wolsey's chancellorship were among the most successful in the record of English diplomacy. His aim was to organize the peace of Europe by using England as a makeweight to preserve a balance of power between the Holy Roman Empire and France; presumably it also entered into his purview that he would thus become the arbiter of Europe, and that peace on the Continent would favor England's vital trade with the Netherlands. As a first step, he negotiated an alliance between France and England (1518), and betrothed Henry's two-year-old daughter Mary (later queen) to the seven-month-old son of Francis I. Wolsey's taste for lavish entertainment revealed itself when French emissaries came to London to sign the agreements; he feted them in his Westminster palace with a dinner "the like of which," reported Giustiniani, "was never given by Cleopatra or Caligula, the whole banqueting hall being decorated with huge vases of gold and silver." [10] But the worldly Cardinal could be forgiven; he was playing for high stakes, and he won. He insisted that the alliance should be open to Emperor Maximilian I, King Charles I of Spain, and Pope Leo X; they were invited to join; they accepted; and Erasmus, More, and Colet thrilled with the hope that an era of peace had dawned for all Western Christendom. Even Wolsey's enemies congratulated him. He took the opportunity to bribe [11] English agents in Rome to secure his appointment as papal legate *a latere* in Britain; the phrase meant "on the side," confidential, and was the highest designation of a papal emissary. Wolsey was now supreme head of the English Church, and—with strategic obeisances to Henry—ruler of England.

The peace was clouded a year later by the rivalry of Francis I and Charles I for the Imperial throne; even Henry thought of flinging his beret into the ring, but he had no Fugger. The winner, as now Charles V, briefly visited England (May 1520), paid his respects to his aunt Catherine of Aragon, Henry's Queen, and offered to marry Princess Mary (already betrothed to the Dauphin) if England would promise to support Charles in any future conflict with France; so unnatural is peace. Wolsey refused, but accepted a pension of 7,000 ducats from the Emperor, and drew from him a pledge to help him in becoming pope.

The brilliant Cardinal achieved his most spectacular triumph in the meeting of the French and English sovereigns on the Field of the Cloth of Gold (June 1520). Here, in an open space between Guînes and Ardres near Calais, medieval art and chivalry displayed themselves in sunset magnificence. Four thousand English noblemen, chosen and placed by the Cardinal and dressed in the silks, flounces, and lace of late medieval costume, accompanied Henry as the young red-bearded King rode on a white palfrey to meet Francis I; and not last or least came Wolsey himself, clad in crimson satin robes rivaling the splendor of the Kings. An impromptu palace had been built to receive their Majesties, their ladies, and their staffs; a pavilion covered with gold-threaded cloth and hung with costly tapestries shaded the conference and the feasts; a fountain ran wine; and space was cleared for a royal tournament. The political and marital alliance of the two nations was confirmed. The happy monarchs jousted, even wrestled; and Francis risked the peace of Europe by throwing the English King. With characteristic French grace he repaired his *faux pas* by going, early one morning, unarmed and with a few unarmed attendants, to visit Henry in the English camp. It was a gesture of friendly trust which Henry understood. The monarchs exchanged precious gifts and solemn vows.

In truth neither could trust the other, for it is a lesson of history that men lie most when they govern states. From seventeen days of festivities with Francis, Henry went to three days of conference with Charles at Calais (July 1520). There King and Emperor, chaperoned by Wolsey, swore eternal friendship, and agreed to proceed no further with their plans to marry into the royal family of France. These separate alliances were a more precarious basis for European peace than the multilateral entente that Wolsey had arranged before Maximilian's death, but it still left England in the position of mediator and, in effect, arbiter—a position far loftier than any that could be based on English wealth or power. Henry was satisfied. To reward his Chancellor he ordered the monks of St. Albans to elect Wolsey as their abbot and dower him with their net revenue, for "my Lord Cardinal has sustained many charges in this his voyage." The monks obeyed, and Wolsey's income neared his needs.

He was, on a grander scale than most of us, a fluid compound of virtues and faults. "He is very handsome," wrote Giustiniani, "extremely eloquent, of vast ability, and indefatigable." [12] His morals were imperfect. Twice he slipped into illegitimate parentage; these were peccadilloes readily overlooked in that lusty age; but, if we may believe a bishop, the Cardinal suffered from the "pox." [13] He accepted what might or might not be called bribes— large gifts of money from both Francis and Charles; he kept them bidding against each other with the pensions and benefices that they offered him; these were courtesies of the time; and the expensive Cardinal, who felt that his policies were serving all Europe, felt that all Europe should serve him. Beyond doubt he loved money and luxury, pomp and power. A large part of his income went to maintain an establishment whose surface extravagance may have been a tool of diplomacy, designed to give foreign ambassadors an exaggerated notion of English resources. Henry paid Wolsey no salary, so that the Chancellor had to live and entertain on his ecclesiastical revenues and his pensions from abroad. Even so we may marvel that he should have required all the income that came to him as holder of two rectories, six prebends, one provostship, as Abbot of St. Albans, Bishop of Bath and Wells, Archbishop of York, administrator of the diocese of Winchester, and a partner of the absentee Italian bishops of Worcester and Salisbury.[14] He disposed of nearly all the major ecclesiastical and political patronage of the realm, and presumably each appointment yielded him a gratuity. A Catholic historian has estimated that Wolsey at his zenith received a third of all the ecclesiastical revenues of England.[15] He was the richest and most powerful subject in the nation; "seven times more powerful than the pope," thought Giustiniani;[16] he is, said Erasmus, "the second king." Only one step more remained to be taken—the papacy. Twice Wolsey tried for it, but in that game the wily Charles, ignoring promises, outplayed him.

The Cardinal believed that ceremony is the cement of power; force can gain power, but only public habituation can cheaply and peaceably sustain it; and people judge a man's altitude by the ceremony that hedges him in. So in his public and official appearances Wolsey dressed in the formal splendor that seemed to him advisable in the supreme representative of both pope and king. Red hat of a cardinal, red gloves, robes of scarlet or crimson taffeta, shoes of silver or gilt inlaid with pearls and precious stones—here were Innocent III, Benjamin Disraeli, and Beau Brummel all in one. He was the first clergyman in England who wore silk.[17] When he said Mass (which was seldom) he had bishops and abbots as his acolytes; and on some occasions dukes and earls poured out the water with which he washed his consecrating hands. He allowed his attendants to kneel in waiting upon him at table. Five hundred persons, many of high lineage, served him in his office and his home.[18] Hampton Court that he built as his residence was so luxurious that he presented it to the King (1525) to avert the evil eye of royal jealousy.

Sometimes, however, he forgot that Henry was king. "On my first arrival in England," Giustiniani wrote to the Venetian Senate, "the Cardinal used to say to me, 'His Majesty will do so and so.' Subsequently, by degrees, he forgot himself, and commenced saying, 'We shall do so and so.' At present he ... says, 'I shall do so and so.' "[19] And again the ambassador wrote: "If it were necessary to neglect either King or Cardinal, it would be better to pass over the King; the Cardinal might resent precedence conceded to the King."[20] Peers and diplomats seldom obtained audience with the Chancellor until their third request. With each passing year the Cardinal ruled more and more openly as a dictator; he called Parliament only once during his ascendancy; he paid little attention to constitutional forms; he met opposition with resentment and criticism with rebuke. The historian Polydore Vergil wrote that these methods would bring Wolsey's fall; Vergil was sent to the Tower;

and only repeated intercession by Leo X secured his release. Opposition grew.

Perhaps those whom Wolsey superseded or disciplined secured the ear of history, and transmitted his sins unabsolved. But no one questioned his ability, or his assiduous devotion to his many tasks. "He transacts as much business," Giustiniani told the proud Venetian Senate, "as that which occupies all the magistracies, offices, and councils of Venice, both civil and criminal; and all state affairs are likewise managed by him, let their nature be what they may." [21] He was loved by the poor and hated by the powerful for his impartial administration of justice; almost beyond any precedent in English history after Alfred, he opened his court to all who complained of oppression, and he fearlessly punished the guilty, however exalted.[22] He was generous to scholars and artists, and began a religious reform by replacing several monasteries with colleges. He was on the way to a stimulating improvement of English education when all the enemies he had made in the haste of his labors and the myopia of his pride conspired with a royal romance to engineer his fall.

III. WOLSEY AND THE CHURCH

He recognized and largely exemplified the abuses that still survived in the ecclesiastical life of England: absentee bishops, worldly clergymen, idle monks, and priests snared into parentage. The state, which had so often called for a reform of the Church, was now part cause of the evils, for the bishops were appointed by the kings. Some bishops, like Morton and Warham and Fisher, were men of high character and caliber; many others were too absorbed in the comforts of prelacy to train their clergy in spiritual fitness as well as financial assiduity. The sexual morality of the curates was probably better than in Germany, but among the 8,000 parishes of England there were inevitably cases of sacerdotal concubinage, adultery, drunkenness, and crime —enough to make Archbishop Morton say (1486) that "the scandal of their lives imperiled the stability of their order." [23] Richard Foxe, toward 1519, informed Wolsey that the clergy in the diocese of Winchester were "so depraved by license and corruption" that he despaired of any reformation in his lifetime.[24] The parish priests, suspecting that their promotion depended on their collections, were more than ever exacting of tithes; some took a tenth, each year, of the peasant's chickens, eggs, milk, cheese, and fruit, even of all wages paid to his help; and any man whose will left no legacy to the Church ran high risk of being denied Christian burial, with prospective results too horrible to contemplate. In short the clergy, to finance their services, taxed almost as sedulously as the modern state. By 1500 the Church owned, on a conservative Catholic estimate, about a fifth of all property in

England.[25] The nobility, here as in Germany, envied this ecclesiastical wealth, and itched to recover lands and revenues alienated to God by their pious or fearful ancestors.

The condition of the secular clergy in England was summed up with obvious exaggeration by Dean Colet in an address to an assembly of churchmen in 1512:

> I wish that at length, mindful of your name and profession, you would consider the reformation of ecclesiastical affairs; for never was it more necessary. . . . For the Church—the spouse of Christ—which He wished to be without spot or wrinkle, is become foul and deformed. As saith Isaiah, "The faithful city is become a harlot"; and as Jeremiah speaks, "She hath committed fornication with many lovers," whereby she hath conceived many seeds of iniquity, and daily bringeth forth the foulest of offspring. . . . Nothing has so disfigured the face of the Church as the secular and worldly living on the part of the clergy. . . . What eagerness and hunger after honor and dignity are found in these days among ecclesiastical persons! What a breathless race from benefice to benefice, from a less to a greater one! . . .
>
> As to lust of the flesh, has not this vice inundated the Church with a flood . . . so that nothing is more carefully sought after . . . by the most part of priests, than that which ministers to sensual pleasure? They give themselves to feasting and banqueting . . . devote themselves to hunting and hawking, are drowned in the delights of this world. . . .
>
> Covetousness also . . . has so taken possession of the hearts of all priests . . . that nowadays we are blind to everything but that alone which seems able to bring us gain. . . . We are troubled in these days by heretics—men mad with strange folly; but this heresy of theirs is not so pestilential and pernicious to us and the people as the vicious and depraved lives of the clergy. . . . Reformation must begin with you.[26]

And again the angry Dean cried:

> O priests! O priesthood! . . . Oh, the abominable impiety of those miserable priests, of whom this age of ours contains a great multitude, who fear not to rush from the bosom of some foul harlot into the temple of the Church, to the altar of Christ, to the mysteries of God! [27]

The regular or monastic clergy incurred even severer censure. Archbishop Morton in 1489 charged Abbot William of St. Albans with "simony, usury, embezzlement, and living publicly and continuously with harlots and mistresses within the precincts of the monastery and without"; he accused the monks of "a life of lasciviousness . . . nay, of defiling the holy places, even the very churches of God, by infamous intercourse with nuns," making a neighboring priory "a public brothel." [28] The records of episcopal visitations paint a less lurid picture. Of forty-two monasteries visited between 1517 and 1530 fifteen were found without serious fault, and in most of the others the offenses were against discipline rather than chastity.[29] Some monasteries still faithfully practiced the medieval regimen of prayer, scholarship, hospitality, charity, and education of the young. Some exploited the credulity—and gathered the coins—of the commons by bogus relics to which they ascribed miraculous cures; bishops complained of the "stinking boots, mucky combs . . . rotten girdles . . . locks of hair, and filthy rags . . . set forth and commended unto the ignorant people" as authentic relics of holy women or men.[30] All in all, in the estimate of the latest Catholic historian, the 600 monasteries of England, in the first quarter of the sixteenth century, showed widespread misconduct, wasteful idleness, and a costly negligence in the care of ecclesiastical property.[31]

In 1520 there were some 130 nunneries in England. Only four had over thirty inmates.[32] Eight were suppressed by the bishops, in one case, said the bishop, because of "the dissolute disposition and incontinence of the religious women of the house, by reason of the vicinity of Cambridge University." [33] In thirty-three visitations of twenty-one nunneries in the diocese of Lincoln, sixteen reports were favorable; fourteen noted lack of discipline or devotion; two told of prioresses living in adultery, and one found a nun pregnant by a priest.[34] Such deviations from arduous rules were natural in the moral climate of the times, and may have been outweighed by kindly services in education and charity.

The clergy were not popular. Eustace Chapuys, Catholic ambassador of Charles V to England, wrote to his master in 1529: "Nearly all the people hate the priests." [35] Many men fully orthodox in creed denounced the severity of ecclesiastical taxation, the extravagance of the prelates, the wealth and idleness of the monks. When the chancellor of the bishop of London was accused of murdering a heretic (1514), the bishop begged Wolsey to prevent trial by a civil jury, "for assured I am, if my chancellor be tried by any twelve men in London, they be so maliciously set in favor of heretical pravity that they will cast and condemn my clerk though he were as innocent as Abel." [36]

Heresy was rising again. In 1506 forty-five men were charged with heresy before the bishop of Lincoln; forty-three recanted, two were burned. In 1510 the bishop of London tried forty heretics, burned two; in 1521 he tried forty-five and burned five. The records list 342 such trials in fifteen years.[37] Among the heresies were contentions that the consecrated Host remains merely bread; that priests have no more power than other men to consecrate or absolve; that the sacraments are not necessary to salvation; that pilgrimages to holy shrines, and prayer for the dead, are worthless; that prayers should be addressed only to God; that man can be saved by faith alone, regardless of good works; that the faithful Christian is above all laws but that of Christ; that the Bible, not the Church, should be the sole rule of faith; that all men should marry, and that monks and nuns should repudiate their vows of chastity. Some of these heresies were echoes of Lollardry, some were reverberations of Luther's trumpet blasts. As early as 1521 young rebels in Oxford eagerly imported news of the religious revolution in Germany. Cambridge in 1521–25 harbored a dozen future heresiarchs: William Tyndale, Miles Coverdale, Hugh Latimer, Thomas Bilney, Edward Fox, Nicholas Ridley, Thomas Cranmer. . . . Several of them, anticipating persecution, migrated to the Continent, printed anti-Catholic tracts, and sent them clandestinely into England.

Possibly as a deterrent to this movement, and perhaps to display his theological erudition, Henry VIII issued in 1521 his famous *Assertion of the Seven Sacraments against Martin Luther*. Many thought Wolsey the secret author, and Wolsey may have suggested the book and its leading ideas as part of his diplomacy at Rome; but Erasmus claimed that the King had actually thought out and composed the treatise, and opinion now inclines to that view. The book has the ring of a tyro; it hardly attempts a rational refutation, but relies on Biblical quotations, Church traditions, and vigorous abuse. "What serpent so venomous," wrote the future rebel against the papacy, "as he who calls the pope's authority tyrannous? . . . What a great limb of the Devil he is, endeavoring to tear the Christian members of Christ from their head!" No punishment could be too great for one who "will not obey the Chief Priest and Supreme Judge on earth," for "the whole Church is subject not only to Christ but . . . to Christ's only vicar, the pope of Rome." [38] Henry envied the honorific titles given by the Church to the king of France as "Most Christian," and to Ferdinand and Isabella as "the Catholic Sovereigns"; now his agent, presenting the book to Leo X, asked him to confer on Henry and his successors the title *Defensor Fidei*—Defender of the Faith. Leo consented; and the inaugurator of the English Reformation placed the words upon his coins.

Luther took his time answering. In 1525 he replied characteristically to that "lubberly ass," that "frantic madman . . . that King of Lies, King Heinz, by God's disgrace King of England. . . . Since with malice aforethought that damnable and rotten worm has lied against my King in heaven it is right for me to bespatter this English monarch with his own filth." [39] Henry, unaccustomed to such sprinkling, complained to the Elector of Saxony, who was too polite to tell him not to meddle with lions. The King never forgave

Luther, despite the latter's later apology; and even when in full rebellion against the papacy he repudiated the German Protestants.

Luther's most effective answer was his influence in England. In that same year 1525 we hear of a London "Association of Christian Brothers," whose paid agents went about distributing Lutheran and other heretical tracts, and English Bibles in part or whole. In 1408 Archbishop Arundel, disturbed by the circulation of Wyclif's version of the Scriptures, had forbidden any vernacular translation without episcopal approval, on the ground that an unauthorized version might misconstrue difficult passages, or color the rendering to support a heresy. Many clergymen had discouraged the reading of the Bible in any form, arguing that special knowledge was necessary to a right interpretation, and that Scriptural excerpts were being used to foment sedition.[40] The Church had raised no official objection to pre-Wyclif translations, but this tacit permission had been of no moment, since all English versions before 1526 were manuscript.[41]

Hence the epochal importance of the English New Testament printed by Tyndale in 1525–26. Early in his student days he had planned to translate the Bible, not from the Latin Vulgate as Wyclif had done, but from the original Hebrew and Greek. When an ardent Catholic reproved him, saying, "It would be better to be without God's law"—i.e., the Bible—"than without the pope's," Tyndale answered: "If God spare me life, ere many years I will cause the boy that driveth the plow to know more of the Scripture than you do."[42] A London alderman gave him bed and board for six months, while the youth labored on the task. In 1524 Tyndale went to Wittenberg, and continued the work under Luther's guidance. At Cologne he began to print his version of the New Testament from the Greek text as edited by Erasmus. An English agent roused the authorities against him; Tyndale fled from Catholic Cologne to Protestant Worms, and there printed 6,000 copies, to each of which he added a separate volume of notes and aggressive prefaces based on those of Erasmus and Luther. All these copies were smuggled into England, and served as fuel to the incipient Protestant fire. Cuthbert Tunstall, Bishop of London, alleging serious errors in the translation, prejudice in the notes, and heresies in the prefaces, tried to suppress the edition by buying all discoverable copies and publicly burning them at St. Paul's Cross; but new copies kept coming from the Continent, and More commented that Tunstall was financing Tyndale's press. More himself wrote a lengthy *Dialogue* (1528) criticizing the new version; Tyndale replied; More replied to the reply in a *Confutation* of 578 folio pages. The King thought to quiet the disturbance by forbidding the reading or circulation of the Bible in English until an authoritative translation could be made (1530). Meanwhile all printing, sale, importation, or possession of heretical works was banned by the government.

Wolsey sent orders to arrest Tyndale, but Philip, Landgrave of Hesse, protected the author, and he proceeded, at Marburg, with his translation of the Pentateuch (1530). Slowly, by his own labor or under his supervision, most of the Old Testament was rendered into English. But in a careless moment he fell into the hands of Imperial officials; he was imprisoned for sixteen months at Vilvorde (near Brussels), and was burned at the stake (1536) despite the intercession of Thomas Cromwell, minister to Henry VIII. Tradition reports his last words as "Lord, ope the King of England's eyes." [43] He had lived long enough to accomplish his mission; the plowboy could now hear the Evangelists tell in firm, clear, pithy English the inspiring story of Christ. When the historic Authorized Version appeared (1611), 90 per cent of the greatest and most influential classic in English literature was unaltered Tyndale. [44]

Wolsey's attitude toward this nascent English Reformation was as lenient as could be expected of a man who headed both Church and state. He hired secret police to spy out heresy, to examine suspicious literature, and to arrest heretics. But he sought to persuade these to silence rather than to punish them, and no heretic was ever sent to the stake by his orders. In 1528 three Oxford students were jailed for heresy; the bishop of London allowed one to die in confinement; one recanted and was released; the third was taken in charge by Wolsey, and was allowed to escape. [45] When Hugh Latimer, the most eloquent of the early Reformers in sixteenth-century England, denounced the deterioration of the clergy, and the bishop of Ely asked Wolsey to suppress him, Wolsey gave Latimer license to preach in any church in the land.

The Cardinal had an intelligent plan for Church reform. "He despised the clergy," according to Bishop Burnet, "and in particular . . . the monks, that did neither the Church nor state any service, but were through their scandalous lives a reproach to the Church and a burden to the state. Therefore he resolved to suppress a great number of them, and to change them to another institution." [46] To close a malfunctioning monastery was not unheard of; it had been done by ecclesiastical order in many instances before Wolsey. He began (1519) by issuing statutes for the reform of the canons regular of St. Augustine; if these rules were followed the canons became quite exemplary. He commissioned his secretary, Thomas Cromwell, to visit the monasteries in person or through agents, and to report the conditions found; these visitations made Cromwell a practiced hand in later executing Henry's orders for a severer scrutiny of England's conventual life. Complaints were heard of the harshness of these agents, of their receiving or exacting "gifts," and of their sharing these with Cromwell and the Cardinal. [47] In 1524 Wolsey obtained permission from Pope Clement VII to close such monasteries as had less than seven inmates, and to apply the revenues of these properties to establishing colleges. He was happy when these funds enabled him to open a college in his native Ipswich and another at Oxford. He hoped to continue this process, to close more monasteries year by year and replace them with colleges.[48] But his good intentions were lost in the confusion of politics, and the chief result of his monastic reforms was to provide Henry with a respectable precedent for a more extensive and lucrative scheme.

Meanwhile the Cardinal's foreign policy had come to grief. Perhaps because he sought the Emperor's support for election to the papacy (1521, 1523), he allowed England to join Charles in war with France (1522). The English campaigns were unsuccessful and expensive in money and lives. To finance fresh efforts Wolsey summoned (1523) the first Parliament in seven years, and shocked it by asking an unprecedented subsidy of £800,000—a fifth of every layman's property. The Commons protested, then voted a seventh; the clergy protested, but yielded half a year's revenue from every benefice. When news came that Charles's army had overwhelmed the French at Pavia (1525) and taken Francis prisoner, Henry and Wolsey thought it advisable to share in the impending dismemberment of France. A new invasion was planned; more money was needed; Wolsey risked the last shreds of his popularity by asking all Englishmen with over £50 ($5,000?) income to contribute a sixth of their goods to an "Amicable Grant" for the prosecution of the war to a glorious end; let us amicably grant that the purpose may have been to prevent Charles from swallowing all France. The demand was so widely resisted that Wolsey had to veer to a program of peace. A treaty of mutual defense was signed with France as another effort to restore the balance of power. But in 1527 Imperial troops captured Rome and the Pope; Charles seemed now the invincible master of the Continent; Wolsey's policy of check and balance was ruined. In January 1528, England joined France in war against Charles.

Now Charles was the nephew of Catherine of Aragon, from whom Henry earnestly desired a divorce; and Clement VII, who could grant it for reasons of state, was in person and policy a captive of Charles.

IV. THE KING'S "DIVORCE"

Catherine of Aragon, daughter of Ferdinand and Isabella, came to England in 1501, aged sixteen, and married (November 14) Arthur, aged fifteen, oldest son of Henry VII. Arthur died on April 2, 1502. It was generally assumed that the marriage had been consummated; the Spanish ambassador dutifully sent "proofs" thereof to Ferdinand; and Arthur's title, Prince of Wales, was not officially transferred to his younger brother Henry till two months after Arthur's death.[49] But Catherine denied the consummation. She had brought with her a dowry of 200,000 ducats ($5,000,000?). Loath to let Catherine go back to Spain with these ducats, and anxious to renew a marital alliance with the powerful Ferdinand, Henry VII proposed that Catherine should marry Prince Henry, though she was the lad's elder by six years. A Biblical passage (Lev. 20:21) forbade such a marriage: "If a man shall take his brother's wife it is an unclean thing . . . they shall be childless." Another passage, however, ruled quite the contrary: "If brethren dwell together, and one of them die, and have no child . . . her husband's brother . . . shall take her to him to wife" (Deut. 25:5). Archbishop Warham condemned the proposed union; Bishop Fox of Winchester defended it if a papal dispensation could be obtained from the impediment of affinity. Henry VII applied for the dispensation; Pope Julius II granted it (1503). Some canonists questioned, some affirmed, the papal power to dispense from a Biblical precept,[50] and Julius himself had some doubts.[51] The betrothal—in effect a legal marriage—was made formal (1503), but as the bridegroom was still only twelve, cohabitation was postponed. In 1505 Prince Henry asked to have the marriage annulled as having been forced upon him by his father,[52] but he was prevailed upon to confirm the union as in the interest of England; and in 1509, six weeks after his accession, the marriage was publicly celebrated.

Seven months later (January 31, 1510) Catherine bore her first child, which died at birth. A year thereafter she bore a son; Henry rejoiced in a male heir who would continue the Tudor line; but in a few weeks the infant died. A second and third son succumbed soon after birth (1513, 1514). Henry began to think of a divorce—or, more precisely, an annulment of his marriage as invalid. Poor Catherine tried again, and in 1516 she gave birth to the future Queen Mary. Henry relented; "if it was a daughter this time," he told himself, "by the grace of God the sons will follow."[53] In 1518 Catherine was delivered of another stillborn child. The disappointment of King and country was sharpened by the fact that Mary, aged two, had already been betrothed to the dauphin of France; if no son came to Henry, Mary would inherit the English throne, and her husband, becoming King of France, would in effect be King of England too, making Britain a province of France. The dukes of Norfolk, Suffolk, and Buckingham had hopes of displacing Mary and securing the crown; Buckingham talked too much, was accused of treason, and was beheaded (1521). Henry expressed fear that his sonlessness was a divine punishment for having used a papal dispensation from a Biblical command.[54] He took a vow that if the Queen would bear him a son he would lead a crusade against the Turks. But Catherine had no further pregnancies. By 1525 all hope of additional offspring by her was abandoned.

Henry had long since lost taste for her as a woman. He was now thirty-four, in the prime of lusty manhood; she was forty, and looked older than her years. She had never been alluring, but her frequent illnesses and misfortunes had deformed her body and darkened her spirit. She excelled in culture and refinement, but husbands have seldom found erudition charming in a wife. She was a good and faithful spouse, loving her husband only next to Spain. She thought of herself as—for a time she was—Spanish envoy, and she argued that England should always side with Ferdinand or Charles. About 1518 Henry took his first-known post-marriage mistress, Elizabeth Blount, sister of Erasmus' friend Mountjoy. She gave him a son in 1519; Henry made the boy Duke of Richmond and Somerset, and thought of entailing the succession to him. About 1524 he took another mistress, Mary Boleyn; [55] indeed, Sir George Throckmorton accused him to his face of adultery with Mary's mother, too.[56] It was an unwritten law of the times that royalty, if married for reasons of state rather than choice, might seek outside of marriage the romance that had missed the legal bed.

In or before 1527 Henry turned his charm upon Mary's sister Anne. Their father was Sir Thomas Boleyn, a merchant and diplomat long favored by the King; their mother was a Howard, daughter of the Duke of Norfolk. Anne was sent to Paris as a finishing school; there she was made a lady-in-waiting to Queen Claude, then to Marguerite of Navarre, from whom she may have imbibed some Protestant leanings. Henry could have seen her as a vivacious girl of thirteen at the Field of the Cloth of Gold. Returning to England at fifteen (1522), she became lady-in-waiting to Queen Catherine. She was not strikingly beautiful; she was short, with dark complexion, broad mouth, and long neck; but Henry and others were lured by her flashing black eyes, her flowing brown hair, her grace and wit and gaiety. She had some ardent lovers, including Thomas Wyatt the poet, and Henry Percy, future Earl of Northumberland; her enemies later charged that she had been clandestinely married to Percy before she set her sights on the King; the evidence is inconclusive.[57] We do not know when Henry began to court her; the earliest of his extant love letters to her is conjecturally assigned to July 1527.

What was the relation of this romance to Henry's petition for the annulment of his marriage? Unquestionably he had thought of this as far back as 1514, when Anne was a girl of seven. He seems to have put the notion aside till 1524, when, according to his own account, he ceased to have conjugal relations with Catherine.[58] The earliest recorded proceedings for an annulment were taken in March 1527, long after Henry's acquaintance with Anne, and about the time that she replaced her sister in the bosom of the King. Wolsey was apparently unaware of any royal intention to marry Anne when, in July 1527, he went to France partly to arrange a union between Henry and Renée, that daughter of Louis XII who was soon to make a Protestant stir in Italy. The first known reference to Henry's intention is in a letter sent on August 16, 1527, by the Spanish ambassador informing Charles

V of a general belief in London that if the King obtained a "divorce" he would marry "a daughter of Sir Thomas Boleyn"; [59] this could hardly have meant Mary Boleyn, for by the end of 1527 Henry and Anne were living in neighboring apartments under the same roof in Greenwich.[60] We may conclude that Henry's suit for annulment was accelerated, though hardly caused, by his infatuation with Anne. The basic cause was his desire for a son, to whom he might transmit the throne with some confidence in a peaceful succession. Practically all England shared that hope. The people remembered with horror the many years (1454–85) of war between the houses of York and Lancaster for the crown. The Tudor dynasty was but forty-two years old in 1527; its title to the throne was dubious; only a legitimate and direct male heir to the King could continue the dynasty unchallenged. If Henry had never met Anne Boleyn he would still have desired and deserved a divorce and an adequately fertile wife.

Wolsey agreed with the King on this point, and assured him that a papal annulment could be readily obtained; the papal power to grant such separations was generally accepted as a wise provision for precisely such national needs, and many precedents could be adduced. But the busy Cardinal had reckoned without two disagreeable developments: Henry wanted not Renée but Anne, and the annulment would have to come from a pope who, when the problem reached him, was a prisoner of an emperor who had plentiful cause for hostility to Henry. Probably Charles would have opposed the annulment as long as his aunt resisted it, and all the more if a new marriage, such as Wolsey planned, would ally England firmly with France. The proximate cause of the English Reformation was not the climbing beauty of Anne Boleyn but the obstinate refusal of Catherine and Charles to see the justice of Henry's desire for a son; the Catholic Queen and the Catholic Emperor collaborated with the captive Pope to divorce England from the Church. But the ultimate cause of the English Reformation was not Henry's suit for annulment so much as the rise of the English monarchy to such strength that it could repudiate the authority of the pope over English affairs and revenues.

Henry affirmed that his active desire for an annulment was occasioned by Gabriel de Grammont, who came to England in February 1527, to discuss the proposed marriage of Princess Mary with French royalty. Grammont, according to Henry, raised a question as to Mary's legitimacy, on the ground that Henry's marriage with Catherine might have been invalid as violating a Scriptural ban irremovable by a pope. Some have thought that Henry invented the story,[61] but Wolsey repeated it, it was reported to the French government (1528), it was not (so far as is known) denied by Grammont, and Grammont labored to persuade Clement that Henry's suit for annulment was just. Charles informed his ambassador in England (July 29, 1527) that he was advising Clement to deny Henry's plea.

While he was in France Wolsey was definitely informed that Henry wished to marry not Renée but Anne. He continued to work for the annulment, but he did not hide his chagrin over Henry's choice. By-passing his Chancellor, the King, in the fall of 1527, sent his secretary, William Knight, to present two requests to the captive Pope. The first was that Clement, recognizing the doubtful validity of Henry's marriage, its lack of male issue, and Catherine's unwillingness to be divorced, should allow Henry to have two wives. A last-minute order from Henry deterred Knight from presenting this proposal; Henry's audacity had abated; and he must have marveled when, three years later, he received from Giovanni Casale, one of his agents in Rome, a letter dated September 18, 1530, saying, "A few days ago the Pope secretly proposed to me that your Majesty might be allowed two wives." [62] Henry's second request was quite as strange: that the Pope should grant him a dispensation to marry a woman with whose sister the King had had sexual relations. [63] The Pope agreed to this on condition that the marriage with Catherine should be annulled; but as to this annulment he was not yet ready to decide. Clement was not only fearful of Charles; he was reluctant to rule that a previous pope had made a serious error in validating the marriage. At the end of 1527 he received a third request—that he should appoint Wolsey and another papal legate to sit as a court in England, to hear evidence, and to pass judgment on the validity of Henry's marriage with Catherine. Clement complied (April 13, 1528), named Cardinal Campeggio to sit with Wolsey in London, and promised—in a bull to be shown only to Wolsey and Henry —to confirm whatever decision the legates should render. [64] Probably the fact that Henry had joined Francis (January 1528) in declaring war on Charles and pledging themselves to liberate the Pope affected Clement's compliance.

Charles protested, and sent to Clement a copy of a document which he claimed had been found in Spanish archives, and in which Julius II confirmed as valid the dispensation that Henry and Wolsey proposed to void. At his wits' end the Pope, still a prisoner of Charles, rushed instructions to Campeggio "not to pronounce sentence without express commission hence. . . . If so great an injury be done to the Emperor, all hope is lost of universal peace, and the Church cannot escape utter ruin, as it is entirely in the power of the Emperor's servants. . . . Delay as much as possible." [65]

On Campeggio's arrival in England (October 1528) he tried to secure Catherine's consent to retire to a nunnery. She agreed, on condition that Henry should take monastic vows. But nothing could be further from Henry's mind than poverty, obedience, and chastity; however, he suggested that he would take these vows if the Pope would promise to release him from them on demand. Campeggio refused to transmit this proposal to the Pope. Instead he reported (February 1529) the King's determination to marry Anne. "This passion," he wrote, "is a most extraordinary thing. He sees nothing, he thinks of nothing, but his Anne; he cannot be without her for an hour. It moves me to pity to see how the King's life, the stability and downfall of the whole country hang upon this one question." [66]

Changes in the military situation turned the Pope more and more against Henry's proposal. The French army that Henry had helped to finance failed in its Italian campaign, leaving the Pope completely dependent upon the Emperor. Florence expelled its ruling Medici—and Clement was as devoted to that family as Charles to the Hapsburgs. Venice took advantage of the Pope's impotence to snatch Ravenna from the Papal States. Who now could rescue the papacy except its captor? "I have quite made up my mind," said Clement (June 7, 1529), "to become an Imperialist, and to live and die as such." [67] On June 29 he signed the Treaty of Barcelona, by which Charles promised to restore Florence to the Medici, Ravenna to the papacy, and liberty to Clement; but one condition was that Clement would never agree to the annulment of Catherine's marriage without Catherine's free consent. On August 5 Francis I signed the Treaty of Cambrai, which in effect surrendered Italy and the Pope to the Emperor.

On May 31 Campeggio, having delayed as long as possible, opened with Wolsey the legatine court to hear Henry's suit. Catherine, having appealed to Rome, refused to acknowledge the competence of the court. On June 21, however, both King and Queen attended. Catherine threw herself on her knees before him, and made a moving plea for the continuance of their marriage. She reminded him of their many labors, her complete fidelity, her patience with his extramural sports; she took God to witness that she had been a maid when Henry married her; and she asked, in what had she offended him? [68] Henry raised her up, and assured her that he wished nothing so earnestly as that their marriage had been successful; he explained that his reasons for separation were not personal but dynastic and national, and he rejected her appeal to Rome on the ground that the Emperor controlled the Pope. She withdrew in tears, and refused to take further part in the proceedings. Bishop Fisher spoke in her defense, thereby earning the enmity of the King. Henry demanded a clear decision from the court. Campeggio procrastinated skillfully, and finally (July 23, 1529) adjourned the court for the summer vacation. To make indecision more decisive Clement "revoked" the case to Rome.

Henry raged. Feeling that Catherine had been unreasonably obstinate, he refused to have anything more to do with her, and spent his pleasure hours openly with Anne. Probably to this period belong most of the seventeen love letters that Cardinal Campeggio spirited away from England,[69] and which the Vatican Library preserves among its literary treasures. Anne, wise in the ways of men and kings, had apparently given him as yet only encouragement and titillation; now she complained that her youth was passing while cardinals, who could not understand the desire of a maid for a well-to-do man, dallied over Henry's right to adorn desire with a marriage tie. She blamed Wolsey for not pressing Henry's appeal with more resolution and dispatch; and the King shared her resentment.

Wolsey had done his best, though his heart was not in the matter. He had sent money to Rome to bribe the cardinals,[70] but Charles had sent money too, and an army to boot. The Cardinal had even connived at the idea of bigamy,[71] as Luther would do a few years afterward. Yet Wolsey knew that Anne and her influential relatives were maneuvering for his fall. He tried to appease her with dainty viands and costly gifts, but her hostility grew as the annul-ment issue dragged on. He spoke of her as "the enemy that never slept, both studied and continually imagined, both sleeping and waking, his utter de-struction."[72] He foresaw that if the annulment should be granted Anne would be queen and would ruin him; and that if it were not granted Henry would dismiss him as a failure, and would demand an account of his steward-ship, in painful financial detail.

The King had many reasons for dissatisfaction with his Chancellor. The foreign policy had collapsed, and the turn from friendship with Charles to alliance with France had proved disastrous. Hardly a man in England now had a good word to say for the once omnicompetent Cardinal. The clergy hated him for his absolute rule; the monks feared more dissolution of monas-teries; the commons hated him for taking their sons and money to fight futile wars; the merchants hated him because the war with Charles obstructed their trade with Flanders; the nobles hated him for his exactions, his upstart pride, his proliferating wealth. Some nobles, reported the French ambassador (October 17, 1529), "intend, when Wolsey is dead or destroyed, to get rid of the Church, and spoil the goods of the Church and Wolsey both."[73] Kentish clothiers suggested that the Cardinal should be installed in a leaking boat and set adrift in the sea.[74]

Henry was subtler. On October 9, 1529, one of his attorneys issued a writ summoning Wolsey to answer, before the King's judges, a charge that his acts as legate had violated the Statute of Praemunire (1392), which imposed forfeiture of goods upon any Englishman who brought papal bulls into England. It made no difference that Wolsey had secured the legatine author-ity at the King's request,[75] and had used it chiefly in the King's behalf. Wol-sey knew that the King's judges would convict him. He sent in to Henry a humble submission, confessing his failures, but begging him to remember also his services and his loyalty. Then he left London by a barge on the Thames. At Putney he received a kindly message from the King. In abject gratitude he knelt in the mud and thanked God. Henry appropriated the rich contents of the Cardinal's palace at Whitehall, but allowed him to retain the archbishopric of York, and enough personal goods to require 160 horses and 72 carts to haul them to his episcopal seat.[76] The Duke of Norfolk succeeded Wolsey as prime minister; Thomas More succeeded him as chancellor (November 1529).

For almost a year the fallen Cardinal served as a pious and exemplary archbishop, visiting his parishes regularly, arranging the repair of churches, and acting as a trusted court of arbitration. "Who was less loved in the north than my Lord the Cardinal before he was amongst them?" asked a Yorkshireman, "and who better beloved after he had been there awhile?" [77] But ambition reawoke in him as the fear of death subsided. He wrote letters to Eustace Chapuys, the Imperial ambassador to England; they are lost, but a report from Chapuys to Charles reads: "I have a letter from the Cardinal's physician, in which he tells me that his master . . . thought the Pope should proceed to weightier censures, and should call in the secular arm" [78]—i.e., excommunication, invasion, and civil war. Norfolk got wind of these exchanges, arrested Wolsey's physician, and drew from him, by means uncertain, a confession that the Cardinal had advised the Pope to excommunicate the King. We do not know if the Ambassador or the Duke honestly reported the physician, or if the physician truthfully reported the Cardinal. In any case Henry, or the Duke, ordered Wolsey's arrest.

He submitted peaceably (November 4, 1530), bade farewell to his household, and set out for London. At Sheffield Park a severe dysentery confined him to bed. There the King's soldiers came with orders to conduct him to the Tower. He resumed the journey, but after two more days of riding he was so weak that his escort allowed him to take to bed in Leicester Abbey. To the King's officer, Sir William Kingston, he uttered the words reported by Cavendish and adapted by Shakespeare: "If I had served my God as diligently as I have done my King, He would not have given me over in my gray hairs." [79] In Leicester Abbey, November 29, 1530, Wolsey, aged fifty-five, died.

CHAPTER XXIV

Henry VIII and Thomas More

1529-35

I. THE REFORMATION PARLIAMENT

IN the Parliament that assembled at Westminster on November 3, 1529, the controlling groups—the nobles in the Upper House, the merchants in the Commons—agreed on three policies: the reduction of ecclesiastical wealth and power, the maintenance of trade with Flanders, and support of the King in his campaign for a male heir. This did not carry with it approval of Anne Boleyn, who was generally condemned as an adventuress, nor did it prevent an almost universal sympathy with Catherine.[1] The lower classes, politically impotent, were as yet unfavorable to the divorce, and the northern provinces, intensely Catholic, sided wholeheartedly with the Pope.[2] Henry kept this oppisition temporarily quiet by remaining orthodox in everything but the right of the popes to govern the English Church. On that point the national spirit, even stronger in England than in Germany, upheld the hand of the King; and the clergy, though horrified at the thought of making Henry their master, were not averse to independence from a papacy so obviously subject to a foreign power.

About 1528 one Simon Fish published a six-page pamphlet which Henry read without known protest, and many read with frank delight. It was called "The Supplication of the Beggars," and asked the King to confiscate, in whole or part, the wealth of the English Church:

> In the times of your noble predecessors past, [there] craftily crept into your realm ... holy and idle beggars and vagabonds ... bishops, abbots, deacons, archdeacons, suffragans, priests, monks, canons, friars, pardoners, and summoners. And who is able to number this idle, ruinous sort, which (setting all labor aside) have begged so importunately that they have gotten into their hands more than a third part of all your Realm? The goodliest lordships, manors, lands, and territories are theirs. Besides this, they had the tenth part of all corn, meadow, pasture, grass, wool, colts, calves, lambs, pigs, geese, and chickens. ... Yea, and they look so narrowly upon their profits that the poor wives must be countable to them of every tenth egg, or else she getteth not her rights at Easter. ... Who is she that will set

543

her hand to work to get 3d. a day, and may have at least 20d. a day to sleep an hour with a friar, a monk, or a priest? [8]

The nobles and merchants might have admitted some exaggeration in the indictment, but they thought it led to a charming conclusion—the secularization of Church property. "These lords," wrote the French ambassador Jean du Bellay, "intend . . . to impeach . . . the Church and take all its goods; which it is hardly needful for me to write in cipher, for they proclaim it openly. . . . I expect the priests will never have the Great Seal"—i.e., never head the government—"again, and that in this Parliament they will have terrible alarms." [4] Wolsey had held off this attack on Church property, but his fall left the clergy powerless except through the (declining) faith of the people; and the papal authority that might have protected them by its prestige, its interdicts, or its allies, was now the main object of royal wrath, and the football of Imperial politics. Custom required that legislation affecting the Church in England should be passed, or require confirmation, by the Convocation of the clergy under the archbishops of Canterbury and York. Could this assembly assuage the anger of the King and check the anticlericalism of Parliament?

The battle was opened by the Commons. It drew up an address to the King, professing doctrinal orthodoxy, but strongly criticizing the clergy. This famous "Act of Accusation" charged that Convocation made laws without the consent of King or Parliament, seriously limiting the liberty of laymen, and subjecting them to heavy censures or fines; that the clergy exacted payment for the administration of the sacraments; that the bishops gave benefices to "certain young folks, calling them their nephews," and despite the youth or ignorance of such appointees; that the episcopal courts greedily exploited their right to levy fees and fines; that these courts arrested persons, and imprisoned them, without stating the charges against them; that they indicted and severely punished laymen upon suspicion of the slightest heresy; and the document concluded by begging the King for the "reformation" of these ills. [5] Henry, who may have been privy to the composition of this address, submitted its main points to the Convocation, and asked for an answer. The bishops admitted some abuses, which they attributed to occasional individuals; they affirmed the justice of their courts; and they looked to the pious King, who had so nobly rebuked Luther, to aid them in suppressing heresy. Then, grievously mistaking the royal temper, they added warlike words:

> Forasmuch as we repute and take our authority of making the laws to be grounded upon the Scriptures of God and the determination of Holy Church . . . we may not submit the execution of our charges and duty, certainly prescribed to us by God, to your Highness' as-

sent. . . . With all humility we therefore beseech your Grace . . . to maintain and defend such laws and ordinances as we . . . by the authority of God, shall for His honor make to the edification of virtue and the maintaining of Christ's faith.[6]

The issue was joined. Henry did not meet it at once. His first interest was to get Parliament's approval for a strange request—that he be excused from repaying the loans that had been made to him by his subjects.* The Commons protested and consented. Three other bills were introduced, which aimed to check the authority of the clergy over the probate of wills, their exaction of death taxes, and their holding of plural benefices. These bills were passed by the Commons; they were passionately opposed by the bishops and abbots sitting in the Upper House; they were amended, but in essence they were made law. Parliament adjourned on December 17.

During the summer of 1530 the King received some costly encouragement. Thomas Cranmer, a doctor of divinity at Cambridge, suggested to Henry that the major universities of Europe should be polled on the question whether a pope could permit a man to marry his brother's widow. A merry game of rival bribery ensued: Henry's agents scattered money to induce negative judgments; Charles's agents used money or threats to secure affirmative replies.[7] The Italian answers were divided; the Lutheran universities refused any comfort to the Defender of the Faith; but the University of Paris, under pressure by Francis,[8] gave the answer so doubly dear to the King. Oxford and Cambridge, after receiving stern letters from the government, approved Henry's right to have his marriage annulled.

So strengthened, he issued through his attorney general (December 1530) a notice that the government intended to prosecute, as violators of the Praemunire Statute, all clergymen who had recognized Wolsey's legatine power. When Parliament and Convocation reassembled (January 16, 1531), the King's agents happily announced to the clergy that the prosecution would be withdrawn if they would confess their guilt and pay a fine of £118,000 ($11,800,000?).[9] They protested that they had never wanted Wolsey to have such power, and had recognized him as legate only because the King had done so in the trial of his suit before Wolsey and Campeggio. They were quite right, of course, but Henry sorely needed money. They mournfully agreed to raise the sum from their congregations. Feeling his oats, the King now demanded that the clergy should acknowledge him as "the protector and only supreme head of the Church and clergy of England"—i.e., that they should end their allegiance to the Pope. They offered a dozen compromises, tried a dozen ambiguous phrases; Henry was merciless, and insisted on Yes or No. Finally (February 10, 1531) Archbishop War-

---

* Depreciation of the currency now exempts governments from such honest burglary.

ham, now eighty-one, reluctantly proposed the King's formula, with a saving clause—"so far as the law of Christ permits." The Convocation remained silent; the silence was taken as consent; the formula became law. Mollified, the King now allowed the bishops to prosecute heretics.

Parliament and Convocation adjourned again (March 30, 1531). In July Henry left Catherine at Windsor, never to see her again. Soon thereafter she was removed to Ampthill, while Princess Mary was lodged at Richmond. The jewels that Catherine had worn as Queen were required of her by Henry, who gave them to Anne Boleyn.[10] Charles V protested to Clement, who addressed a brief to the King (January 25, 1532) rebuking him for adultery, and exhorting him to dismiss Anne and keep Catherine as his lawful queen until decision should be given on his application for annulment. Henry ignored the rebuke, and pursued his romance. About this time he wrote one of his tender missives to Anne:

> Myne awne Sweetheart, this shall be to advertise you of the great ellingness [loneliness] that I find here since your departing; for, I ensure you, me thinketh the Tyme longer since your departing now last than I was wont to do a whole Fortnight; I think your Kindness and my Fervence of love causeth it. . . . But now that I am coming toward you, me thinketh my Pains by half released . . . in wishing my self (especially an evening) in my Sweethearts Armes whose pretty Duckys [breasts] I trust shortly to kysse. Writne with the Hand of him that was, is, and shall be yours by his will, H.R.[11]

When Parliament and Convocation reconvened (January 15, 1532) Henry secured from all four houses further anticlerical legislation: that clerics under the degree of subdeacon, when charged with felony, should be tried by civil courts; that fees and fines in ecclesiastical courts should be reduced; that ecclesiastical death dues and probate fees should be lowered or abolished; that the annates (the first year's revenues of a newly appointed prelate) should no longer be paid to the Pope; and that the transfer of English funds to Rome for dispensations, indulgences, and other papal services should cease. A sly hint was sent to the Curia that the annates would be restored to the Pope if the marriage with Catherine should be annulled.

By this time a majority of the bishops had been won over to the view that they would not lose in authority or revenue if the English Church were independent of Rome. In March 1532, the Convocation announced its readiness to separate from the papacy: "May it please your Grace to cause the said unjust exactions to cease. . . . And in case the Pope will make process against this realm for the attaining these annates . . . may it please your Highness to ordain in the present Parliament that the obedience of your Highness and of the people be withdrawn from the See of Rome." [12] And on

May 15 the Convocation presented to the King a pledge to submit all its subsequent legislation to a committee—half laymen, half clergymen—empowered to veto any ordinances which it should judge injurious to the realm. So, in this epochal "Reformation Parliament" and Convocation the Church of England was born, and became an arm and subject of the state.

On May 16 Thomas More, having failed to stem the anticlerical tide, resigned as chancellor, and retired to his home. In August Archbishop Warham died, after dictating a deathbed repudiation of the Convocation's submission to the King. Henry replaced More with Thomas Audley, and Warham with Thomas Cranmer. The revolution proceeded. In February 1533, Parliament enacted a "Statute of Appeals," by which all litigation that had formerly been sent for judgment to Rome was henceforth to be decided "in the spiritual and temporal courts within the Realm, without regard to any . . . foreign . . . inhibition, excommunication, or interdict." [13]

On January 15, 1533, Henry married Anne, who was already four months pregnant.[14] The King had now urgent reasons for the annulment of his union with Catherine. Having made, without result, another appeal to the Pope, he secured from Convocation an approval of his "divorce" (April 1533); on May 23 Cranmer, as Archbishop of Canterbury, declared the marriage with Catherine unlawful and void; and on May 28 he pronounced Anne to be Henry's lawful wife. Three days later Anne, in brocade and jewels, rode to her coronation as Queen of England in a stately pageant designed by tradition and Hans Holbein the Younger. Amid the exaltation she noticed the disapproving silence of the crowd, and she may have wondered how long her uneasy head would wear the crown. Pope Clement pronounced the new marriage null, and its future offspring illegitimate, and excommunicated the King (July 11, 1533). On September 7 Elizabeth was born. Charles's ambassador reported to him that the King's mistress had given birth to a bastard.[15]

Parliament, which had adjourned on May 4, resumed its sittings on January 15, 1534. Annates and other papal revenues were now definitely appropriated to the Crown, and the appointment of bishops became in law, as already in practice, a prerogative of the King. Indictments for heresy were removed from clerical to civil jurisdiction.

In 1533 Elizabeth Barton, a nun of Kent, announced that she had received orders from God to condemn the King's remarriage, and had been allowed to see the place that was being prepared for Henry in hell. The royal court put her through a severe examination, and drew from her a confession that her divine revelations were impostures, and that she had permitted others to use them in a conspiracy to overthrow the King.[16] She and six "accomplices" were tried by the House of Lords, were judged guilty, and were executed (May 5, 1534). Bishop Fisher was accused of having known of the conspiracy and of having failed to warn the government; it was also charged that he and Catherine had been privy to a plan, conceived by Chapuys and discouraged by Charles, for an invasion of England to coincide with an insurrection of Catherine's supporters.[17] Fisher denied the charges, but remained under suspicion of treason.

Henry's most aggressive agent in these affairs was Thomas Cromwell. Born in 1485, the son of a Putney blacksmith, he grew up in poverty and hardship, and wandered for years, as practically a vagabond, through France and Italy. Back in England, he entered the textile business, became a moneylender, and made a fortune. He served Wolsey faithfully for five years, defended him in adversity, and earned Henry's respect for his industry and loyalty. He was made successively chancellor of the exchequer, master of the rolls, and (May 1534), secretary to the King. From 1531 to 1540 he was the chief administrator of the government as an obedient executor of the royal will. His aristocratic enemies, who despised him as a parvenu symbol of their rising rivals, the businessmen, accused him of practicing the principles of Machiavelli's *Prince*, of accepting bribes, of selling offices, of inordinately loving wealth and power. His aim, which he hardly sought to disguise, was to make the King supreme over every phase of English life, and to finance an absolute monarchy with the confiscated wealth of the Church. In pursuing his purposes he showed consummate and unscrupulous ability, multiplied his fortune, and won every battle except the last.

It was probably at his suggestion and through his manipulation that Henry, disturbed by increasing hostility among the people, persuaded Parliament to pass an Act of Succession (March 30, 1534) which declared the marriage with Catherine invalid, transformed Mary into a bastard, named Elizabeth heiress to the throne unless Anne should have a son, and made it a capital crime for any person to question the validity of Anne's marriage to Henry, or the legitimacy of their offspring. All Englishmen and women were by the Act required to take an oath of loyalty to the King. Royal commissioners, supported by soldiery, rode through the country, entered homes, castles, monasteries, and convents, and exacted the oath. Only a few refused it; among these were Bishop Fisher and Thomas More. They offered to swear to the succession, but not to the other contents of the Act. They were committed to the Tower. Finally the Parliament voted the decisive Statute of Supremacy (November 11, 1534); this reaffirmed the King's sovereignty over Church and state in England, christened the new national Church *Ecclesia Anglicana*, and gave the King all those powers over morals, organization, heresy, creed, and ecclesiastical reform which had heretofore belonged to the Church. The Act made it treason to speak or write of the King as a usurper, tyrant, schismatic, heretic, or infidel. A new oath was required of all bishops, that they would accept the civil and ecclesiastical supremacy of the King without the reservation "So far as the law of Christ allows," and would never in the future consent to any resumption of papal authority in England.

All the forces of the government were deployed to paralyze the opposition to these unprecedented decrees. The secular clergy generally pretended to submit. Many monks and friars, owning a direct allegiance to the Pope, shied away from the oaths, and their resistance shared in the King's later decision to close the monastries. Henry and Cromwell were especially incensed by the obstinacy of the friars in the Charterhouse, a Carthusian monastery in London. Three Carthusian priors came to Cromwell to explain their reluctance to acknowledge any layman as head of the Church in England; Cromwell sent them to the Tower. On April 26, 1535, they, with another friar and a secular priest, were tried by the King's judges, who were for pardoning them; but Cromwell, fearing that lenience would encourage wider resistance, demanded a verdict of guilty, and the judges yielded. On May 3 all five men, still refusing to accept the Act of Supremacy, were dragged on hurdles to Tyburn, and one after another was hanged, cut down alive, disemboweled, and dismembered.[18] One severed arm was hung over the entrance arch of the Charterhouse to instruct the remaining friars, but none withdrew his refusal. Three were put in the Tower; they were fastened to uprights by irons around their necks and feet, and were forced to stand in that position for seventeen days, fed, but never loosed for any natural need. The remaining Carthusians, still obdurate, were dispersed among other monasteries, with the exception of ten who were imprisoned in Newgate; nine of these died of "prison fever and filth."[19]

Henry was now the sole judge of what, in religion and politics, the English people were to believe. Since his theology was still Catholic in every respect except the papal power, he made it a principle to persecute impartially Protestant critics of Catholic dogma, and Catholic critics of his ecclesiastical supremacy. Indeed, the prosecution of heresy had continued, and would continue, all through his reign. In 1531, by order of Chancellor More, Thomas Bilney was burned for speaking against religious images, pilgrimages, and prayers for the dead. James Bainham was arrested for holding that Christ was only spiritually present in the Eucharist; he was tortured to draw from him the names of other heretics; he held fast, and was burned at Smithfield in April 1532. Two others were burned in that year, and the Bishop of Lincoln offered an indulgence of forty days to good Christians who would carry a faggot to feed the fire.[20]

This reign of terror reached its apex in the prosecution of Fisher and More. Erasmus had described the Bishop of Rochester as "a person loaded with every virtue."[21] But Fisher had himself been guilty of persecution, and he had joined the Spanish ambassador in urging Charles to invade England

and depose Henry.[22] In law he had committed treason to the state, which could not excuse him on the plea that he had been loyal to the Church. The new pontiff, Paul III, made the mistake of naming the imprisoned Bishop a cardinal. Though Fisher declared that he had not sought the honor, Henry interpreted the appointment as a challenge. On June 17, 1535, the Bishop, now in his eightieth year, was given a final trial, and again refused to sign the oath acknowledging Henry as head of the English Church. On June 22 he was led to a block on Tower Hill; "a long, lean body," an eyewitness described him, "nothing in a manner but skin and bones, so that the most part that there saw him marveled to see any man, bearing life, to be so far consumed." [23] On the scaffold he received an offer of pardon if he would take the oath; he refused. His severed head was hung upon London Bridge; it might now, if it could, said Henry, go to Rome and get its cardinal's hat.[24]

But a more troublesome recusant remained.

II. THE UTOPIAN

The father of Thomas More was a successful lawyer and prominent judge. Thomas received his education at St. Anthony's School in London; was farmed out as a page to Archbishop Morton, and was by him confirmed in orthodoxy, integrity, and a cheerful piety. Morton predicted, we are told, that "this child here waiting at table . . . will prove a marvelous man." [25] At fifteen the youth went to Oxford, and was soon so fascinated with classical literature that his father, to save the youth from becoming an impecunious scholar, pulled him out of the university and sent him to study law in London. Oxford and Cambridge still aimed at preparing students for an ecclesiastical career; New Inn and Lincoln's Inn trained the men who were now taking over from the clergy the government of England. Only eight members of the House of Commons in the Reform Parliament of 1529–37 had received a university education, while a rising proportion were lawyers and businessmen.

In 1499, aged twenty-one, More met Erasmus, and was charmed into humanism. Their friendship is one of the fragrant essences of the time. They were both given to a measured merriment, and salted their studies with laughing satire. They shared a distaste for Scholastic philosophy, whose subtleties, said More, were as profitable as milking a he-goat into a sieve.[26] They both hoped for a reform of the Church from within, avoiding a violent disruption of religious unity and historical continuity. More was not the peer of Erasmus in learning or tolerance; indeed, his customary gentleness and generosity were sometimes interrupted by strong passions, even by bigotry; in controversy he stooped now and then, like nearly all his contemporaries, to fierce invective and bitter vituperation.[27] But he was the superior of Erasmus in courage, sense of honor, and devotion to a cause. The letters that they exchanged are a precious testimony to the graces of an ungracious age. "Farewell," ends one of More's, "sweetest Erasmus, dearer to me than my eyes!" [28]

He was one of the most religious men of the century, shaming with his laic piety the wordliness of ecclesiastics like Wolsey. At twenty-three, when he was already advanced in the study of law, he thought of becoming a priest. He gave public lectures (1501) on Augustine's *City of God*, and such older pundits as Grocyn sat in his audience. Though he criticized the monks for shirking their rule, he fervently admired the sincere monastic state, and sometimes regretted that he had not chosen it. For a long time he wore a horsehair shirt next to his skin; now and then it drew enough blood to visibly stain his clothing. He believed in miracles and saintly legends, therapeutic relics, religious images, and pilgrimages,[29] and wrote devotional works to the medieval tune that life is a prison, and that the aim of religion and philosophy should be to prepare us for death. He married twice, and brought up several children in a Christian discipline at once sober and cheerful, with frequent prayer, mutual love, and complete trust in Providence. The "Manor House" in Chelsea, to which he moved in 1523, was famous for its library and gallery, and its gardens extending for a hundred yards down to the Thames.

At twenty-six (1504) he was chosen a burgess delegate to Parliament. There he argued so successfully against a measure proposed by Henry VII that the King briefly imprisoned and heavily fined the senior More as a devious means of teaching the young orator the comforts of conformity. At the close of that Parliament More returned to private life, and prospered in the practice of law. In 1509 he was persuaded to take the office of under-sheriff in the City—i.e., ancient London north of the Thames. His functions, suiting his temperament, were judicial rather than adventurous. His judgments earned him wide renown for wisdom and impartiality, and his polite refusal of presents from litigants violated time-dishonored precedents that were still vigorous in Francis Bacon's day. Soon he was back in Parliament; and by 1515 he was Speaker of the House of Commons.

In a famous letter to Hutten (July 23, 1517) Erasmus described More as of medium height, pale complexion, auburn hair, careless of dress or formality, abstemious in food and drink, cheerful with quick humor and ready smile, inclined to jokes and pranks, and keeping in his house a jester, a monkey, and many minor animal pets; "all the birds in Chelsea came to him to be fed." A faithful husband, a loving and idolized father, a persuasive orator, a judicious counselor, a man alert with charity and friendly offices—"in short," concluded this fond sketch, "what did Nature ever create milder, sweeter, and happier than the genius of Thomas More?" [30]

He found time to write books. He began a *History of Richard III*, but as its tenor was sharply against autocracy, and autocracy was on the throne, he thought it discreet to avoid the fatality of print. It was published after his death; Shakespeare based a play on it; and the biography, broadcast by the drama, may bear some responsibility for the character that Richard bears. In 1516, as if in a playful aside, More tossed off, in Latin, one of the most famous of all books, creating a word, setting a precedent and pace for modern utopias, anticipating half of socialism, and voicing such criticism of English economy, society, and government that again he put valor behind discretion, and had the volume published abroad in six Latin editions before allowing it to be printed, still in Latin, in England. He professed to have written it for amusement, with no intention to make it public; but he thanked Erasmus for seeing it through the press at Louvain.[31] It was translated into German, Italian, and French before the first English version appeared (1551), sixteen years after the author's death. By 1520 it was the talk of the Continent.

More had called it *Nusquama*, Nowhere; we do not know who had the happy thought of changing this, amid the printing, to the Greek equivalent *Utopia*.[32] The *mise-en-scène* of the tale was so ingenious that many readers took it as authentic history, and a missionary was said to have planned to go and convert the Utopians to Christianity.[33] More had been sent by Henry VIII on an embassy to Bruges (1515); thence he had passed to Antwerp with a letter of introduction from Erasmus to Peter Giles, the city clerk. The prelude pretended that Giles had introduced More to a bearded, weather-worn Portuguese mariner, Raphael Hythlodaye (Greek for "skilled in nonsense"), who had sailed with Amerigo Vespucci in 1504, had made his way round the globe (six years before Magellan's voyage), and had visited, in the New World, a happy island whose inhabitants had solved most of the problems plaguing Europe at that time. The Louvain edition made the hoax more plausible by prefixing a woodcut of the isle, and a specimen of the Utopian language. Only one slip gave the plot away: Hythlodaye digresses to praise Archbishop Morton,[34] in terms more natural to More's gratitude than to the mariner's experience.

The imaginary Magellan describes the communism of the islanders:

> Among the Utopians . . . all things being common, every man hath abundance of everything. . . . I compare with them so many nations . . . where every man calleth that, which he hath gotten, his own proper and private goods. . . . I hold well with Plato . . . that all men should have and enjoy equal portions of wealth and commodities. . . . For where every man, under certain titles and pretenses, draweth and plucketh to himself as much as he can, so that a few divide among

themselves all the whole riches . . . there to the residue is left lack and poverty.[35]

In Utopia each man takes his product to the common store, and receives from it according to his needs. None asks more than enough, for security from want forestalls greed. Meals are eaten in common, but if a man wishes he may eat at home. There is no money in Utopia, no buying cheap and selling dear; the evils of cheating, stealing, and quarreling over property are unknown. Gold is used not as currency but to make useful things, like chamber pots. No famines or lean years come, for the communal storehouses maintain a reserve against emergencies. Every family engages in both agriculture and industry, men and women alike. In order to ensure adequate production, six hours of work per day are required of each adult, and choice of occupation is limited by collective needs. The Utopians are free in the sense of freedom from hunger and fear, but they are not free to live on the labor of others. There are laws in Utopia, but they are simple and few; therefore every man is expected to plead his own case, and no lawyers are allowed. Those who violate the laws are condemned for a time to serve the community as bondmen; they do the more disagreeable tasks; but after finishing their turn they are restored to full equality with their fellow men. Those who repeatedly and seriously offend are put to death. The supply of bondmen is raised by ransoming prisoners condemned to death in other lands.

The unit of society in Utopia is the patriarchal family. "The wives be ministers to their husbands, the children to their parents."[36] Monogamy is the only form of sexual union permitted. Before marriage the betrothed are advised to view each other naked, so that physical defects may be revealed in time; and if they are serious the contract may be annulled. The wife after marriage goes to live with her husband in his father's household. Divorce is allowed for adultery and by free mutual consent, conditional on the consent of the communal council. Annually every thirty families choose a phylarch to govern them; every ten phylarchs choose a chief phylarch to administer a district of 300 households. The 200 phylarchs serve as a national council, which elects for life the prince or king.

A basic obligation of the phylarchs is to preserve the health of the community by providing clean water, public sanitation, medical and hospital care; for health is the chief of all earthly boons. The rulers organize education for children and for adults; they stress vocational training, support science, and discourage astrology, fortunetelling, and superstition. They may make war on other peoples if they judge that the good of the community so requires. "They count this the most just cause of war, when any people holdeth a piece of ground void and vacant to no good nor profitable use, keeping other from the use or possession of it, who . . . by the law of nature ought thereby to be nourished and relieved." [37] (Was this a defense of the colonization of America?) But the Utopians do not glorify war; "they hate it as plainly brutal . . . and, contrary to the sentiment of nearly every other nation, they regard nothing more inglorious than glory derived from war." [38]

Religion in Utopia is almost, not quite, free. Tolerance is given to any creed except atheism and the denial of human immortality. The Utopian may, if he wishes, worship the sun or the moon. But those who use violence of action or speech against any recognized religion are arrested and punished, for the laws seek to prevent religious strife.[39] Deniers of immortality are not punished, but they are excluded from office, and are forbidden to voice their views to any but priests and "men of gravity." Otherwise "it should be lawful for every man to favor and follow what religion he would . . . and might do his best to bring other to his opinion, so that he did it peaceably . . . and soberly, without haste and contentious rebuking and inveighing against other." [40] So in Utopia there are various religions, but "the most and wisest part . . . believe that there is a certain godly power unknown, everlasting, incomprehensible, inexplicable, far above the reach and capacity of man's wit, dispersed through the world." [41] Monasticism is permitted, provided the monks will busy themselves with works of charity and communal utility, such as repairing roads and bridges, cleaning ditches, cutting timber, and acting as servants, even as bondmen; and they may marry if they so desire. There are priests, but they too marry. The state keeps as religious feasts the first and last of every month and year, but in the religious exercises of these holydays "no image of any god is seen in the church," and "no prayers be used but such as every man may boldly pronounce without the offending of any sect." [42] On each of these holydays wives and children prostrate themselves before their husbands or parents, and ask forgiveness for any offense committed, or any duty omitted; and no one is to come to church until he has made peace with his enemy.—It is a Christian touch, but More's youthful humanism appears in his partial acceptance of the Greek view of suicide: if a man suffers from a painful and incurable disease he is permitted and encouraged to end his life. In other cases, More believes, suicide is cowardice, and the corpse is to be "cast unburied into some stinking marsh." [43]

We do not know how much of this represented More's considered conclusions, how much was Erasmus, how much was half-playful imagination. However, the young statesman carefully dissociated himself from the socialism of his Utopians: "I am of opinion," he represents himself as saying to Hythlodaye, ". . . that men shall never live wealthily where all things are in common. For how can there be abundance of goods . . . where the regard of his own gains driveth not to work, but the hope that he hath in other men's travails maketh him slothful. . . . It is not possible for all things to be well unless all men were good—which I think will not be yet these good many years." [44] Yet some sympathy with radical yearnings must have inspired so extensive a picture of the communist ideal. Other pages of the *Utopia* criticize with angry severity the exploitation of the poor by the rich. Enclosures of once common lands by English lords are condemned with such detail and spirit as seem unlikely in a foreigner. Says Hythlodaye to More:

> The unreasonable covetousness of a few hath turned to the utter undoing of your island. . . . Suffer not these rich men to buy up all, to engross and forestall, and with their monopoly to keep the market alone as pleases them.[45] . . . When I consider and weigh in my mind all these commonwealths which now anywhere flourish, I can perceive nothing—so God help me—but a certain conspiracy of rich men promoting their own commodities under the name and title of the commonwealth. They invent and devise all means and crafts . . . how to hire and abuse . . . the labor of the poor for as little money as may be. . . . These devices be then made laws.[46]

It is almost the voice of Karl Marx moving the world from a foot of space in the British Museum. Certainly *Utopia* is one of the most powerful, as well as one of the first, indictments of the economic system that continued in modern Europe until the twentieth century; and it remains as contemporary as a planned economy and the welfare state.

III. THE MARTYR

How did it come about that a man with such ideas seething in his head should have been appointed to Henry VIII's council in the year after the publication of *Utopia?* Probably the King, despite his reputation for learning, could not bear to read the book in Latin, and died before it was Englished. More kept his radical fancies for his friends. Henry knew him as a rare synthesis of ability and integrity, valued him as a tie with the House of Commons, knighted him, made him Under-Treasurer (1521), and entrusted him with delicate tasks of diplomacy. More opposed the foreign policy by which Wolsey led England into war with Charles V; the Emperor, in More's view, was not only dangerously resourceful, he was also the heroic defender of Christendom against the Turks. When Wolsey fell More so far forgot his manners as to review, in Parliament, the faults and errors that had caused the fall. As leader of the opposition he was the logical successor of the Cardinal, and for thirty-one months he served as Chancellor of England.

But the real successor to Wolsey was the King. Henry had discovered his own power and capacity, and was resolved, he said, to free himself from an unfriendly and obstructive papacy, and to legitimate his union with the woman whom he loved, and who could give him an heir to the throne. More found himself no guide of policy, but a servant of aims that ran counter to his deepest loyalties. He consoled himself by writing books against Protestant theology, and prosecuting Protestant leaders. In *A Dialogue Concerning Heresies* (1528), and in later works, he agreed with Ferdinand II, Calvin, and the Lutheran princes on the necessity of religious unity for national strength and peace. He feared the division of Englishmen into a dozen or a hundred religious sects. He who had defended Erasmus' Latin translation of the New Testament protested against Tyndale's English version as distorting the text to prove Lutheran points; translations of the Bible, he felt, should not be turned into weapons for tavern philosophers. In any case, he held, the Church was too precious a vehicle of discipline, consolation, and inspiration to be torn to pieces by the hasty reasoning of vain disputants.

From this mood he passed to the burning of Protestants at the stake. The charge that in his own house he had a man flogged for heresy [47] is disputed; More's account of the offender seems far removed from theology: "If he spied any woman kneeling" in prayer, and "if her head hung anything low in her meditations, then would he steal behind her, and . . . would labor to lift up all her clothes and cast them quite over her head." [48] It may be that in the three death sentences pronounced in his diocese during his chancellorship he was obeying the law that required the state to serve as the secular arm of ecclesiastical courts; [49] but there is no doubt that he approved of the burnings.[50] He admitted no inconsistency between his conduct and the large toleration of religious differences in his *Utopia;* for even there he had refused toleration to atheists, deniers of immortality, and those heretics who resorted to violence or vituperation. Yet he himself was guilty of vituperation in arguing against the English Protestants.*

The time came when More thought Henry the most dangerous heretic of all. He refused to approve the marriage with Anne Boleyn, and he saw in the anticlerical legislation of 1529–32 a ruinous assault upon a Church that to his mind stood as an indispensable base of social order. When he retired from office to the privacy of his Chelsea home (1532), he was still in his prime at fifty-four, but he suspected that he had not much longer to live.

---

* "Howbeit, there be swine that receive no learning but to defile it; and there be dogs that rend all good learning with their teeth. . . . To such dogs men may not only preach, but must with whips and bats beat them well and keep them from tearing of good learning with their teeth . . . till they lie still and hearken what is said unto them. And by such means be both swine kept from doing harm, and dogs fall sometimes so well to learning, that . . . they learn to dance after their master's pipe, such an effectual thing is punishment, whereas bare teaching will not suffice. And who be now more properly such dogs than be those heretics that bark against the blessed sacraments? . . . And who be more properly such hogs than these heretics of our days, of such a filthy kind as never came before, which in such wise defile all holy vowed chastity . . . into an unclean shameful liberty of friars to wed nuns." [51]

He tried to prepare his family for tragedy by talking (so reports his son-in-law William Roper)

> of the lives of holy martyrs, and of . . . their marvelous patience, and of their passions [sufferings] and deaths, that they suffered rather than they would offend God, and what an happy and a blessed thing it was, for the love of God, to suffer loss of goods, imprisonment, loss of lands, and life also. He would further say unto them that upon his faith, if he might perceive his children would encourage him to die in a good cause, it should so comfort him that for the very joy thereof it would make him merrily to run to death.[52]

His expectations were fulfilled. Early in 1534 he was indicted on a charge of having been privy to the conspiracy connected with the Nun of Kent. He admitted having met her, and having believed her to be inspired, but he denied any knowledge of conspiracy. Cromwell recommended, Henry granted, forgiveness. But on April 17 More was committed to the Tower for refusing to take oath to the Act of Succession, which, as presented to him, involved a repudiation of papal supremacy over the Church in England. His favorite daughter Margaret wrote to him begging him to take the oath; he replied that her plea gave him more pain than his imprisonment. His (second) wife visited him in the Tower, and (according to Roper) berated him for obstinacy:

> What the good year, Mr. More, I marvel that you, that have always been hitherunto taken for a wise man, will now so play the fool to lie here in this close, filthy prison, and be content to be shut up among mice and rats, when you might be abroad at your liberty, and with the favor and good will of the King and his Council, if you would but do as all the bishops and best learned of this realm have done. And seeing you have at Chelsea a right fair house, your library, your books, your gallery, your garden, your orchards, and all other necessaries so handsomely about you, where you might, in the company of me, your wife, your children, and your household, be merry, I muse what a God's name you mean here still thus fondly to tarry.[53]

Other efforts were made to move him, but he smilingly resisted them all.

On July 1, 1535, he was given a final trial. He defended himself well, but he was pronounced guilty of treason. While he was returning from Westminster to the Tower his daughter Margaret twice broke through the guard, embraced him, and received his last blessing. On the day before his execution he sent his hairshirt to Margaret, with a message that "tomorrow were a day very meet" to "go to God. . . . Farewell, my dear child; pray for me, and I shall pray for you and all your friends, that we may merrily meet in heaven." [54] When he mounted the scaffold (July 7), and found it so weak that it threatened to collapse, he said to an attendant, "I pray you, Mr. Lieutenant, see me safe up, and for my coming down let me shift for myself." [55] The executioner asked his forgiveness; More embraced him. Henry had given directions that only a few words should be allowed the prisoner. More begged the spectators to pray for him, and to "bear witness that he . . . suffered death in and for the faith of the Holy Catholic Church." He then asked them to pray for the King, that God might give him good counsel; and he protested that he died being the King's good servant, but God's first.[56] He repeated the Fifty-first Psalm. Then he laid his head upon the block, carefully arranging his long gray beard that it should take no harm; "pity that should be cut," he said, "that hath not committed treason." [57] His head was affixed to London Bridge.

A wave of terror passed through an England that now realized the resolute mercilessness of the King, and a shudder of horror ran through Europe. Erasmus felt that he himself had died, for "we had but one soul between us"; [58] he said that he had now no further wish to live, and a year later he too was dead. Charles V, apprised of the event, told the English ambassador: "If I had been master of such a servant, of whose doing I myself have had these many years no small experience, I would rather have lost the best city in my dominions than lose such a worthy councilor." [59] Pope Paul III formulated a bull of excommunication outlawing Henry from the fellowship of Christendom, interdicting all religious services in England, forbidding all trade with it, absolving all British subjects from their oaths of allegiance to the King, and commanding them, and all Christian princes, to depose him forthwith. As neither Charles nor Francis would consent to such measures, the Pope withheld issuance of the bull till 1538. When he did promulgate it Charles and Francis forbade its publication in their realms, unwilling to sanction papal claims to power over kings. The failure of the bull signalized again the decline of papal authority and the rise of the sovereign national state.

Dean Swift thought More the man "of the greatest virtue"—perhaps using this word in its old sense of courage—"this kingdom ever produced." [60] On the four hundredth anniversary of their execution the Church of Rome enrolled Thomas More and John Fisher among her saints.

IV. A TALE OF THREE QUEENS

Within some thirty months of More's death Henry lost three of his six queens. Catherine of Aragon wasted away in her northern retreat, still claiming to be Henry's only lawfully wedded wife and England's rightful queen. Her faithful maids continued to give her that title. In 1535 she was removed to Kimbalton Castle, near Huntingdon, and there she confined herself to one room, leaving it only to hear Mass. She received visitors, and "used them very obligingly." [61] Mary, now nineteen, was kept at Hatfield, only twenty miles away; but mother and daughter were not allowed to see each other, and were forbidden to communicate. They did nevertheless, and Catherine's letters are among the most touching in all literature. Henry offered them better quarters if they would acknowledge his new queen; they would not. Anne Boleyn had her aunt made governess to Mary, and bade her keep "the bastard" in place by "a box on the ears now and then." [62] In December 1535, Catherine sickened, made her will, wrote to the Emperor asking him to protect her daughter, and addressed a moving farewell to her "most dear lord and husband" the King:

> The hour of my death now approaching, I cannot choose but, out of the love I bear you, advise you of your soul's health, which you ought to prefer above all considerations of the world or flesh whatsoever; for which yet you have cast me into many calamities, and yourself into many troubles. But I forgive you all, and pray God to do likewise. For the rest I commend unto you Mary our daughter, beseeching you to be a good father to her.... Lastly I make this vow, that my eyes desire you above all things. Farewell.[63]

Henry wept on receiving the letter; and when Catherine died (January 7, 1536), aged fifty, he ordered the court to go into mourning. Anne refused.[64]

Anne could not know that within five months she too would be dead; but she knew that she had already lost the King. Her hot temper, her imperious tantrums, her importunate demands, wearied Henry, who contrasted her railing tongue with Catherine's gentleness.[65] On the day of Catherine's burial Anne was delivered of a dead child; and Henry, who still yearned for a son, began to think of another divorce—or, as he would put it, an annulment; his second marriage, he was quoted as saying, had been induced by witchcraft, and was therefore void.[66] From October 1535 he began to pay special attention to one of Anne's maids, Jane Seymour. When Anne reproached him he bade her bear with him patiently, as her betters had done.[67] Perhaps following ancient tactics, he accused her of infidelity. It seems incredible that even a flighty woman should have risked her throne for a moment's dalliance, but the King appears to have sincerely believed in her guilt. He referred the rumors of her amours to his Council; it investigated, and reported to the King that she had committed adultery with five members of the court— Sir William Brereton, Sir Henry Norris, Sir Francis Weston, Mark Smeton, and her brother Lord Rochford. The five men were sent to the Tower, and on May 2, 1536, Anne followed them.

Henry wrote to her holding out hopes of forgiveness or lenience if she would be honest with him. She replied that she had nothing to confess. Her attendants in prison alleged that she had admitted receiving proposals of love from Norris and Weston, but that she claimed to have repulsed them. On May 11 the grand jury of Middlesex, having been asked to make local inquiries into offenses allegedly committed by the Queen in that county, reported that it found her guilty of adultery with all five of the accused men, and gave specific names and dates.[68] On May 12 four of the men were tried at Westminster by a jury including Anne's father, the Earl of Wiltshire. Smeton confessed himself guilty as charged; the others pleaded not guilty; all four were convicted. On May 15 Anne and her brother were tried by a panel of twenty-six peers under the presidency of the Duke of Norfolk, her uncle but political enemy. Sister and brother affirmed their innocence, but each member of the panel announced himself convinced of their guilt, and they were sentenced to be "burned or beheaded, as shall please the King." On May 17 Smeton was hanged; the other four men were beheaded as befitted their rank. On that day Archbishop Cranmer was required by royal commissioners to declare the marriage with Anne invalid, and Elizabeth a bastard; he complied. The grounds for this judgment are not known, but presumably Anne's alleged prior marriage with Lord Northumberland was now pronounced real.

On the eve of her death Anne knelt before Lady Kingston, wife of the warden, and asked a last favor: that she should go and kneel before Mary and beseech her, in Anne's name, to forgive the wrongs that had come to her through the pride and thoughtlessness of a miserable woman.[69] On May 19 she begged that her execution should take place soon. She appeared to derive some comfort from the thought that "the executioner I have heard to be very good, and I have a little neck"—whereupon she laughed. That noon she was led to the scaffold. She asked the spectators to pray for the King, "for a gentler and more merciful prince was there never; and to me he was ever a good, a gentle, and sovereign lord." [70] No one could be sure of her guilt, but few regretted her fall.

On the day of her death Cranmer gave the King a dispensation to marry again in renewed quest for a son; on the morrow Henry and Jane Seymour were secretly betrothed; on May 30, 1536, they were married; and on June 4 she was proclaimed queen. She was of royal lineage, being descended from Edward III; she was related to Henry in the third or fourth degree of consanguinity, which called for another dispensation from the obedient Cranmer. She was of no special beauty, but she impressed all with her intelligence, kindness, even modesty; Cardinal Pole, Henry's most thoroughgoing enemy, described her as "full of goodness." She discouraged the King's advances while Anne lived, refused his gifts, returned his letters unopened, and asked him never to speak to her except in the presence of others.[71]

One of her first acts after marriage was to effect a reconciliation between Henry and Mary. He did it in his own way. He had Cromwell send her a paper entitled "The Confession of the Lady Mary": it acknowledged the King as supreme head of the Church in England, repudiated "the Bishop of Rome's pretended authority," and recognized the marriage of Henry with Catherine as "incestuous and unlawful." Mary was required to sign her name to each clause. She did, and never forgave herself. Three weeks later the King and Queen came to see her, and gave her presents and 1,000 crowns. She was again called Princess; and at Christmas, 1536, she was received at court. There must have been something good in Henry—and in "Bloody Mary"—for in his later years she almost learned to love him.

When Parliament met again (June 8, 1536) it drew up at the King's request a new Act of Succession, by which both Elizabeth and Mary were declared illegitimate, and the crown was settled on the prospective issue of Jane Seymour. In July Henry's bastard son, the Duke of Richmond, died; now all the hopes of the King lay in Jane's pregnancy. England rejoiced with him when (October 12, 1537) she was delivered of a boy, the future Edward VI. But poor Jane, to whom the King was now as deeply attached as his self-centered spirit allowed, died twelve days after her son's birth. Henry was for some time a broken man. Though he married thrice again, he asked, at his death, to be buried beside the woman who had given her life in bearing his son.

What were the reactions of the English people to the events of this world-shaking reign? It is difficult to say; the testimony is prejudiced, ambiguous, and sparse. Chapuys reported in 1533 that, in the opinion of many Englishmen, "the last King Richard was never so much hated by his people as this King." [72] Generally the people sympathized with Henry's desire for a son, condemned his severity to Catherine and Mary, shed no tears over Anne, but were deeply shocked by the execution of Fisher and More. The nation was still overwhelmingly Catholic,[73] and the clergy—now that the government had appropriated the annates—were hoping for reconciliation with Rome. But hardly any man dared raise his voice in criticism of the King. Criticism he received, and from an Englishman, but one with the Channel between him and the King's practiced arm.

Reginald Pole was the son of Margaret Plantagenet, Countess of Salisbury, herself the niece of Edward IV and Richard III. He was educated at Henry's expense, received a royal pension of 500 crowns a year, and was apparently destined for the highest offices in the English Church. He studied in Paris and Padua, and returned to England in high favor with the King. But when Henry insisted on hearing his opinion of the divorce, Reginald frankly replied that he could not approve of it unless it should be sanctioned by the Pope. Henry continued the youth's pension, and permitted him to return to the Continent. There Pole remained twenty-two years, rose in papal esteem as scholar and theologian, and was made a cardinal at the age of thirty-six (1536). In that year he composed in Latin a passionate attack upon Henry—*Pro ecclesiasticae unitatis defensione* (*In Defense of Church Unity*). He argued that Henry's assumption of ecclesiastical supremacy in England invited the division of the Christian religion into national varieties, and that the resultant clash of creeds would bring social and political chaos to Europe. He charged Henry with egomania and autocracy. He scored the English bishops for yielding to the enslavement of the Church by the state. He denounced the marriage with Anne as adultery, and predicted (not too wisely) that the English nobility would forever rank Elizabeth as "a harlot's bastard." [74] He called upon Charles V to waste no ammunition on the Turks, but to turn the Imperial forces against England's impious King. It was a powerful invective, spoiled by youthful pride in eloquence. Cardinal Contarini advised the author not to publish it, but Pole insisted, and sent a copy to England. When Paul III made Pole a cardinal Henry took it as an act of war. The King abandoned all thought of compromise, and agreed with Cromwell that the monasteries of England should be dissolved, and their property added to the Crown.

CHAPTER XXV

Henry VIII and the Monasteries

1535-47

I. THE TECHNIQUE OF DISSOLUTION

IN 1535 Henry, too busy with love and war to play pope in retail as well as gross, appointed the agnostic[1] Cromwell "viceregent of the King in all his ecclesiastical jurisdiction." Cromwell now guided foreign policy, domestic legislation, the higher judiciary, the Privy Council, the intelligence service, the Star Chamber, and the Church of England; Wolsey at apogee had never had so many long and grasping fingers in so many juicy pies. He kept an eye, too, on all printing and publication; he persuaded the King to forbid the printing, sale, or importation of books except after approval by agents of the Crown; and he had anti-papal literature published at the government's expense. Cromwell's innumerable spies kept him informed on all movements or expressions of opposition to Henry or himself. A remark of pity for Fisher or More, a jest about the King, could bring a secret trial and long imprisonment;[2] and to predict the date of the King's death was to incur one's own.[3] In special cases, to make conclusions certain, Cromwell acted as prosecutor, jury, and judge. Nearly everyone in England feared and hated him.

His chief difficulty was that Henry, though omnipotent, was bankrupt. The King was anxious to enlarge the navy, to increase or improve his harbors and ports; his court and personal expenses were extravagant; and Cromwell's system of government required a broad stream of funds. How to raise money? Taxes were already high to the point where resistance made further collection more costly than lucrative; the bishops had drained their parishes to appease the King; and no gold poured in from America such as daily succored England's enemy, the Emperor. Yet one institution in England was wealthy, suspect, decrepit, and defenseless: the monasteries. They were suspect because their ultimate allegiance was to the pope, and their subscription to the Act of Supremacy was considered insincere and incomplete; they were, in the eyes of the government, a foreign body in the nation, bound to support any Catholic movement against the King. They were decrepit because they had in many cases ceased to perform their traditional functions of education, hospitality, and charity. They were defenseless because the bishops resented their exemption from episcopal control; because the nobility, impoverished by civil war, coveted their wealth; because the business classes looked upon monks and friars as idling wasters of natural resources; and because a large section of the commonalty, including many good Catholics, no longer believed in the efficacy of the relics that the monks displayed, or in the Masses that the monks, if paid, offered for the dead. And there were excellent precedents for closing monasteries; Zwingli had done it in Zurich, the Lutheran princes in Germany, Wolsey in England. Parliament had already (1533) voted authority to the government to visit the monasteries and compel their reform.

In the summer of 1535 Cromwell sent out a trio of "visitors," each with a numerous staff, to examine and report on the physical, moral, and financial condition of the monasteries and nunneries of England, and, for good measure, the universities and episcopal sees as well. These "visitors" were "young, impetuous men, likely to execute their work rather thoroughly than delicately"; [4] they were not immune to "presents"; [5] "the object of their mission was to get up a case for the Crown, and they probably used every means in their power to induce the monks and the nuns to incriminate themselves." [6] It was not difficult to find, among the 600 monasteries of England, an impressive number that showed sexual—sometimes homosexual—deviations,[7] loose discipline, acquisitive exploitation of false relics, sale of sacred vessels or jewelry to add to monastic wealth and comforts,[8] neglect of ritual, hospitality, or charity.[9] But the reports usually failed to state the proportion of offending to meritorious monks, and to discriminate clearly between gossip and evidence.[10]

To the Parliament that met on February 4, 1536, Cromwell submitted a "Black Book," now lost, revealing the faults of the monasteries, and recommending, with strategic moderation, that monasteries and convents having an income of £200 ($20,000?) or less per year should be closed. The Parliament, whose members had been largely chosen by Cromwell's aides,[11] consented. A Court of Augmentations was appointed by the King to receive for the royal treasury the property and revenues of these 376 "lesser monasteries." Two thousand monks were released to other houses or to the world —in the latter case with a small sum or pension to tide them over till they found work. Of the 130 nunneries only eighteen had an income over £200, but only half were now closed.

The drama of dissolution was interrupted by a triple rebellion in the north. Just as Christianity had been born in the cities and had reached the villagers —pagani—last, so, in Switzerland, Germany, and England the Reformation rose in the towns and was long resisted in the countryside. Protestantism in England and Scotland decreased as distance from London or Edinburgh increased; it reached Wales and northern England tardily, and found scant welcome in Ireland. In the northern shires of England the spoliation of the lesser monasteries kindled a fire of resentment that had long been prepared by mounting taxation, the royal dictatorship over the clergy, and clandestine priestly exhortations. Dispossessed monks who found it hard to collect their pensions or to get work joined the already numerous and plaintive unemployed; dispossessed nuns, wandering from shelter to shelter, stirred public anger against the government; and the aides of Cromwell's visitors fed the fury by decking themselves in the spoils of the monastic chapels, making copes into doublets, priestly tunics into saddlecloths, and relic cases into dagger sheaths.[12]

On October 2, 1536, a visitor who had just closed a convent in Legbourne was attacked by a crowd in neighboring Louth; his records and credentials were seized and burned, and, with a sword at his breast, he was compelled to swear loyalty to the commons. All in the crowd took an oath to be faithful to the King and the Roman Catholic Church. On the morrow a rebel army gathered at Caistor, a few miles away; priests and homeless monks exhorted them; the local gentry were forced—some were willing—to join. On the same day a larger muster of villagers took place at Horncastle, another town in Lincolnshire. The chancellor of the bishop of Lincoln was accused of being an agent of Cromwell; he was taken from his bed and beaten to death with staves. The rebels designed a banner picturing a plow, a chalice, a horn, and the five "last words" of Christ, and they drew up demands which were dispatched to the King: the monasteries should be restored, taxes should be remitted or eased, the clergy should no more pay tithes or annates to the Crown, "villein blood" (namely, Cromwell) should be removed from the Privy Council, and heretic bishops—chiefly Cranmer and Latimer—should be deposed and punished. Recruits for the rebellion came in from the northern and eastern counties. Some 60,000 men assembled at Lincoln, and awaited the answer of the King.

His answer was furious and uncompromising. He charged the rebels with ingratitude to a gracious ruler; insisted that the closing of the lesser monasteries was the will of the nation expressed through Parliament; and bade the insurgents surrender their leaders and disperse to their homes on pain of death and confiscation of goods. At the same time Henry ordered his military aides to collect their forces and march under the Earl of Suffolk to the assistance of Lord Shrewsbury, who had already organized his retainers to withstand attack; and he wrote privately to the few nobles who had joined the revolt. These, now perceiving that the King could not be awed, and that the poorly armed insurgents would soon be overwhelmed, persuaded so many of them to return to their villages that the rebel army, over the protests of the priests, rapidly melted away. Louth gave up fifteen leaders; a hundred more were captured, and a royal pardon was declared for the rest.

The captives were taken to London and the Tower; thirty-three, including seven priests and fourteen monks, were hanged; the rest were leisurely freed.[13]

Meanwhile a still more serious uprising had developed in Yorkshire. A young barrister, Richard Aske, found himself caught, physically and emotionally, in the movement; another lawyer, William Stapleton, was frightened into the captaincy of a rebel division at Beverley; Lord Darcy of Templehurst, an ardent Catholic, lent the revolt his secret support; two Percys joined, and most of the northern nobility followed suit. On October 15, 1536, the main army of some 9,000 men, under Aske, laid siege to York. The citizens of the city compelled the mayor to open the gates. Aske kept his men from pillage, and in general maintained remarkable order in his untrained host. He proclaimed the reopening of the monasteries; the monks joyfully returned to them, and gladdened the hearts of the pious with the new ardor of their chants. Aske advanced and captured Pomfret, and Stapleton took Hull, without shedding blood. To the demands presented by the Lincolnshire men others were added and sent to the King: to suppress all heretics and their literature, to resume ecclesiastical ties with Rome, to legitimize Mary, to dismiss and punish Cromwell's visitors, and to annul all enclosures of common lands since 1489.

This was the most critical point in Henry's reign. Half the country was in arms against his policies; Ireland was in revolt; and Paul III and Cardinal Pole were urging Francis I and Charles V to invade England and depose the King. With a last burst of his declining energy, he sent out orders in all directions for the mustering of loyal troops, and meanwhile instructed the Duke of Norfolk to bemuse the rebellious leaders with negotiations. The Duke arranged a conference with Aske and several nobles, and won them over by a promise of pardon to all. Henry invited Aske to a personal conference, and gave him a safe-conduct. He came to the King, was charmed by the aura of royalty, and returned meek and unharmed to Yorkshire (January 1537); there, however, he was arrested, and was sent to London as a prisoner. Shorn of its captains, the insurgent host fell into angry divisions and wild disorder; defections multiplied; and as the united levies of the King approached, the rebel army disappeared like a vanishing mirage (February 1537).

When Henry was assured that the revolt and invasion had both collapsed, he repudiated Norfolk's promise of a general pardon, ordered the arrest of such disaffected leaders as could be found, and had several of them, including Aske, put to death. To the Duke he wrote:

> Our pleasure is that before you close up our banner again you shall cause such dreadful execution to be done upon a good number of the

inhabitants of every town, village, and hamlet that have offended, as they may be a fearful spectacle to all others hereafter that would practice any like matter. . . . Forasmuch as all these troubles have ensued by the solicitation and traitorous conspiracies of the monks and canons of these parts, we desire you, at such places as have conspired and kept their houses with force . . . you shall, without pity or circumstance, cause all the monks and canons that be in any wise faulty to be tied up without further delay or ceremony.[14]

With the opposition so sternly terrified, Cromwell proceeded to close the remaining religious houses in England. All the monasteries and nunneries that had joined the revolt were dissolved forthwith, and their property was confiscated to the state. Visitations were extended, and yielded reports of indiscipline, immorality, treason, and decay. Many monks, anticipating closure, sold relics and valuables from their houses to the highest bidder; a finger of St. Andrew fetched £40.[15] The monks at Walsingham were convicted of faking miracles, and their lucrative image of the Virgin was cast into the fire. The historic tomb of St. Thomas à Becket at Canterbury was demolished; Henry VIII proclaimed the victor over Henry II to have been no real saint; the relics that had offended Colet and amused Erasmus were burned; the precious objects donated by the piety of pilgrims during 250 years were carted away to the royal treasury (1538); and thereafter Henry wore on his thumb a great ruby taken from the shrine. Some monasteries sought to fool fate by sending Cromwell money or gifts; Cromwell accepted everything and closed all. By 1540 all monasteries, and all monastic property except cathedral abbey churches, had passed to the King.

All in all 578 monasteries were closed, some 130 convents; 6,521 monks or friars were dispersed, 1,560 nuns. Among these some fifty monks and two nuns willingly abandoned the religious habit; but many more pleaded to be allowed to continue somewhere their conventual life.[16] Some 12,000 persons formerly employed by, or dependent upon, the religious houses lost their places or alms. The confiscated lands and buildings had enjoyed an annual revenue of some £200,000 ($20,000,000?), but quick sales reduced the annual income of the properties after nationalization to some £37,000. To this should be added £85,000 in confiscated precious metal, so that the total spoils in goods and income accruing to Henry during his life may have been some £1,423,500.[17]

The King was generous with these spoils. Some of the properties he gave —most of them he sold at bargain prices—to minor nobles or major burgesses —merchants or lawyers—who had supported or administered his policies. Cromwell received or bought six abbeys, with an annual revenue of £2,293; his nephew Sir Richard Cromwell received seven, with an income of £2,-552;[18] this was the origin of the fortune that made Richard's great-grandson

Oliver a man of substance and influence in the next century. Some of the spoils went to build ships, forts, and ports; some helped to finance war; some went into the royal palaces at Westminster, Chelsea, and Hampton Court; some the King lost at dice.[19] Six monasteries were returned to the Anglican Church as episcopal sees; and a small sum was assigned to continue the most urgent of the charities formerly provided by the monks and nuns. The new aristocracy created by Henry's gifts and sales became a powerful support to the Tudor throne, and a bulwark of economic interest against any Catholic restoration. The old feudal aristocracy had decimated itself; the new one, rooted in commerce and industry, changed the nature of the English nobility from static conservatism to dynamic enterprise, and poured fresh blood and energy into the upper classes of England. This—and the spoils—may have been one source of the Elizabethan exuberance.

The effects of the dissolution were complex and interminable. The liberated monks may have shared modestly or not in the increase of England's population from about 2,500,000 in 1485 to some 4,000,000 in 1547.[20] A temporary increase in the unemployed helped to depress the earnings of the lower classes for a generation, and the new landlords proved more grasping than the old.[21] Politically the effect was to augment still further the power of the monarchy; the Church lost the last stronghold of resistance. Morally the results were a growth of crime, pauperism, and beggary, and a diminished provision of charity.[22] Over a hundred monastic hospitals were closed; a few were rehabilitated by municipal authorities. The sums that fearful or reverent souls had bequeathed to priests as insurance against infernal or purgatorial fire were confiscated in expectation that no harm would come to the dead; 2,374 chantries, with their endowments for Masses, were appropriated by the King.[23] The severest effects were in education. The convents had provided schools for girls, the monasteries and the chantry priests had maintained schools and ninety colleges for boys; all these institutions were dissolved.

Having stated the facts as impartially as unconscious prejudice allowed, the historian may be permitted to add a confessedly hypothetical comment. Henry's greed and Cromwell's ruthlessness merely advanced by a generation an inevitable lessening in the number and influence of English monasteries. These had once done admirable work in education, charity, and hospital care, but the secularization of such functions was proceeding throughout Western Europe, even where Catholicism prevailed. The decline in religious fervor and other-worldliness was rapidly narrowing the flow of novices into conventual establishments; and many of these were reduced to so small a number as seemed out of proportion to the splendor of their buildings and the income of their lands. It is a pity that the situation was met by the brusque haste of Cromwell rather than by Wolsey's humane and sounder plan of transforming more and more monasteries into colleges. Henry's procedure here, as in his quest for a son, was worse than his aim. It was good that an end should be put, in some measure, to the exploitation of simple piety by pious fraud. Our chief regrets go to the nuns who for the most part labored dutifully in prayer, schooling, and benevolence; and even one who cannot share their trustful faith must be grateful that their like again minister, with lifelong devotion, to the needs of the sick and the poor.

II. THE OBSTINATE IRISH: 1300–1558

The English kings justified their domination of Ireland on the ground that a hostile Continental power might at any moment use that verdant island for a flank attack upon England; and this consideration, seconding the love of power, became more active when Protestant England failed to win Ireland from the Roman Church. The Irish people, heroic and anarchic, virile and violent, poetically gifted and politically immature, resisted, every day, their subjection to an alien blood and speech.

The evils of the English occupation mounted. Under Edward III many Anglo-Irish landowners returned to England to live there in ease on Irish rents; and though the English Parliament repeatedly denounced this practice, "absentee landlordism" rose through three centuries to be a leading spur to Irish revolts. Englishmen who remained in Ireland tended to marry Irish girls, and were gradually absorbed into Irish blood and ways. Anxious to dam this racial drain, the Irish Parliament, dominated by English residents and influence, passed the famous Statute of Kilkenny (1366), which, along with some wise and generous provisions, forbade intermarriage, fosterage, or other intimate relations between the English and the Irish in Ireland, and any use, by the English, of Irish speech, customs, or dress, on pain of imprisonment and forfeiture of property. No Irishman was henceforth to be received into any English religious organization; and no Irish bards or storytellers were to enter English homes.[24] These prohibitions failed; the roses in Irish cheeks outshone the majesty of the law, and racial fusion went on in that narrow March, Border, or Pale where alone the English in Ireland dared to dwell.*

During the Wars of the Roses Ireland might have expelled the English had the Irish chiefs united, but they preferred fraternal strife, sometimes encouraged thereto by English gold. Henry VII re-established English authority in the Pale, and his lord deputy, Sir Edward Poynings, pushed through the Irish Parliament the humiliating "Peynings' Law" (1494)—that in future no Irish Parliament should be convened until all bills to be presented to it had been approved by the king and privy council of England. So emasculated, the English government in Ireland became the most incompetent, ruthless, and corrupt

---

* In 1500 the Pale was confined to half the counties of Dublin, Meath, and Louth, and a portion of Kildare.

in Christendom. Its favorite device was to appoint one of the sixty Irish chieftains as deputy to the viceroy, and commission him to buy or subdue the rest. Gerald, eighth Earl of Kildare, so appointed, made some progress in this direction, and mitigated the intertribal lawlessness that helped English exactions to keep Ireland weak and poor. On his death (1513) his son Gerald Fitzgerald was named to succeed him as deputy. This ninth Earl of Kildare had a career typical of the Irish lords. Accused of conspiring with the Earl of Desmond to let a French force land in Ireland, he was summoned to England and committed to the Tower. On his promise faithfully to aid the English cause, Henry VIII released him and reappointed him deputy. Soon he was charged with maladministration. He was again brought to England, and again sent to the Tower, where he died within the year (1534). His devoted son, "Silken Thomas" Fitzgerald, at once declared war on the English; he fought bravely and recklessly for fourteen months, was overcome, and was hanged (1537).

By this time Henry VIII had completed his divorce from the Roman Church. With characteristic audacity he bade the Irish Parliament acknowledge him head of the Church in Ireland as well as in England. It did. An oath accepting his ecclesiastical supremacy was required of all governmental officials in Ireland, and all church tithes were henceforth to be paid to the King. Reformers entered the churches in the Pale, and demolished religious relics and images. All monasteries but a remote few were closed, their property was taken by the government, their monks were dismissed with pensions if they made no fuss. Some of the spoils were distributed among the Irish chieftains; so oiled, most of them accepted titles of nobility from the English King, acknowledged his religious supremacy, and abjured the pope (1539).[25] The clan system was abolished, and Ireland was declared a kingdom, with Henry as king (1541).

Henry was victorious, but mortal; he died within five years of his triumph. Catholicism in Ireland survived. The chieftains took their apostasy as a passing incident in politics; they continued to be Catholics (as Henry did) except for ignoring the pope; and the priests whose ministrations they supported and received remained quietly orthodox. The faith of the people underwent no change; or rather it took on new vigor because it maintained the pride of nationality against a schismatic king and, later, a Protestant queen. The struggle for freedom became more intense than before, since now it spoke for body and soul.

III. EVERY OUNCE A KING

Henry in 1540 was the most absolute monarch that England had ever known. The old Norman nobility, whose ancestors had checked even William the Conqueror, were now timidly obedient, and almost forgot the Magna Charta of their prerogatives. The new nobility, enriched by commerce and endowed by the King, served as a barrier to aristocratic or religious revolts. The House of Commons, once the jealous protector of English liberties but now hand-picked by agents of the King, yielded to him almost unprecedented powers: the right to confiscate property, to name anyone his successor, to determine orthodoxy and heresy, to send men to death after only a mock trial, and to issue proclamations that were to have the authority of acts of Parliament. "In Henry's reign the English spirit of independence burned low in its socket, and love of freedom grew cold." [26] The English people accepted this absolutism partly through fear, partly because it seemed the alternative to another War of the Roses. Order was more important than liberty.

The same alternatives persuaded Englishmen to suffer Henry's ecclesiastical supremacy. With Catholics and Protestants ready to fly at each other's throats, with Catholic citizens, ambassadors, and potentates conspiring against him almost to invasion, Henry believed that order could be secured in the religious life of England only by royal determination of faith and ritual; implicitly he accepted the case that the Church had made for authority in religion. He tried to dictate who should read the Bible. When the bishops suppressed Tyndale's translation he bade them prepare a better one; when they dallied too long he allowed Cromwell to commission a new translation by Miles Coverdale. This first complete British version appeared in Zurich in 1535. In 1539 a revised edition was printed, and Cromwell ordered this "Great Bible" placed in every English church. Henry, "of the royal liberality and goodness," granted the citizens the privilege of reading the Bible in their homes; and soon it became a daily influence in nearly every English family. But it was a fountain of discord as well as of inspiration; every village sprouted amateur exegetes who proved anything or its opposite by Scripture; fanatics wrangled over it in churches, and came to blows over it in taverns. [27] Some ambitious men gave their wives writs of divorce, or kept two wives at once, on the plea that this was sound Biblical practice. [28] The King regretted the liberty of reading that he had allowed, and reverted to the Catholic stand. In 1543 he induced Parliament to rule that only nobles and property owners might legally possess the Bible, and only priests might preach on it, or discuss it publicly. [29]

It was difficult for the people—even for the King—to know the King's mind. Catholics continued to go to the stake or the block for denying his ecclesiastical supremacy, Protestants for questioning Catholic theology. Prior Forest of the Observant Franciscans at Greenwich, who refused to disown the pope, was suspended in chains over a fire, and was slowly roasted to death (May 31, 1537). [30] John Lambert, a Protestant, was arrested for denying the Real Presence of Christ in the Eucharist; he was tried by Henry himself, was by Henry condemned to die, and was burned at Smithfield (November 16, 1538). Under the growing influence of Stephen Gardiner, Bishop of Winchester, Henry veered more and more toward orthodoxy.

In 1539 King, Parliament, and Convocation, by the "Act of the Six Articles," proclaimed the Roman Catholic position on the Real Presence, clerical celibacy, monastic vows, Masses for the dead, the necessity of auricular confession to a priest, and the sufficiency of communion in one kind. Whoever, by spoken or written word, denied the Real Presence should suffer death by burning, without opportunity to abjure, confess, and be absolved; whoever denied any of the other articles should for the first offense forfeit his property, for the second his life. All marriages hitherto contracted by priests were declared void, and for a priest thereafter to retain his wife was to be a felony.[31] The people, still orthodox, generally approved these Articles, but Cromwell did his best to moderate them in practice; and in 1540 the King, tacking again, ordered prosecution under the Act to cease. Nevertheless Bishops Latimer and Shaxton, who disapproved of the Articles, were deposed and jailed. On July 30, 1540, three Protestants and three Catholic priests suffered death at Smithfield in unwilling unison, the Protestants for questioning some Catholic doctrines, the Catholics for rejecting the ecclesiastical sovereignty of the King.[32]

Henry was as forceful in administration as in theology. Though he maintained an extravagant court, and spent much time in eating, he toiled heavily in the tasks of government. He chose competent aides as ruthless as himself. He reorganized the army, equipped it with new weapons, and studied the latest fashions in tactics and strategy. He built the first permanent royal navy, which cleared the coasts and Channel of pirates and prepared for the naval victories of Elizabeth. But he taxed his people to the limit of tolerance, repeatedly debased the currency, confiscated private property on flimsy pretexts, demanded "contributions," repudiated his debts, borrowed from the Fuggers, and promoted the English economy in the hope that it would yield him added revenue.

Agriculture was in depression. Serfdom was still widespread. Enclosures for sheep pasturage continued; and the new landlords, unhindered by feudal traditions, doubled or quadrupled the rents of their tenants on the ground of rising prices, and refused to renew expiring leases. "Thousands of dispossessed tenants made their way to London, and clamored at the doors of the courts of law for redress which they could not obtain." [33] Catholic More drew a pitiful picture of the beggared peasantry,[34] and Protestant Latimer denounced the "rent-raiser steplords," and, like Luther, idealized a Catholic past when "men were full of pity and compassion." [35] Parliament laid ferocious penalties upon vagabondage and beggary. By an act of 1530–31 any able-bodied mendicant, whether man or woman, was to be "tied to the end of a cart naked, and be beaten with whips throughout the town till his body be bloody"; for a second offense an ear was to be cut off; for a third, another ear; in 1536, however, the third offense incurred death.[36] Gradually the displaced peasants found work in the cities, and poor relief mildly mitigated pauperism. In the end the productivity of the land was raised by large-scale farming, but the inability of the government to ease the transition was a criminal and heartless failure of statesmanship.

The same government protected industry with tariffs, and manufacturers profited from the cheap labor made available by the migration of peasants to the towns. Capitalistic methods reorganized the textile industry, and raised a new class of wealthy men to stand beside the merchants in support of the King; cloth now replaced wool as England's chief export. Most exports were of necessaries produced by the lower classes; most imports were of luxuries available only to the rich.[37] Commerce and industry were benefited by a law of 1536 legalizing interest rates of 10 per cent; and the rapid rise of prices favored enterprise while it penalized workers, peasants, and old-style feudal lords. Rents rose 1,000 per cent between 1500 and 1576;[38] food prices rose 250 to 300 per cent; wages rose 150 per cent.[39] "Such poverty reigneth now," wrote Thomas Starkey about 1537, "that in no case may stand with a very true and flourishing common weal." [40] Guild members found some relief in the insurance and mutual aid provided them against poverty and fire; but in 1545 Henry confiscated the property of the guilds.[41]

IV. THE DRAGON RETIRES

What sort of a man was this ogre of a king? Holbein the Younger, coming to England about 1536, painted portraits of Henry and Jane Seymour. The gorgeous costume almost conceals the royal corpulence; the gems and ermine, the hand on the jeweled sword, reveal the pride of authority, the vanity of the uncontradicted male; the broad fat face bespeaks a hearty sensualism; the nose is a pillar of strength; the tight lips and stern eyes warn of a despot quick to anger and cold to cruelty. Henry was now forty-six, at the top of his political curve, but entering physical decline. He was destined to marry thrice again, and yet to have no further progeny. From all his six wives he had but three children who outlived infancy. One of these three— Edward VI—was sickly and died at fifteen; Mary remained desolately barren in marriage; Elizabeth never dared marry, probably through consciousness of some physical impediment. The curse of semi-sterility or bodily defect lay upon the proudest dynasty in English history.

Henry's mind was keen, his judgment of men was penetrating, his courage and will power were immense. His manners were coarse, and his scruples disappeared with his youth. To his friends, however, he remained kind and generous, jovially amiable, and capable of winning affection and devotion. Born to royalty, he was surrounded from birth with obeisance and flattery;

only a few men dared withstand him, and they were buried without their heads. "Surely," wrote More from the Tower, "it is a great pity that any Christian prince should by a flexible [knee-bending] council ready to follow his affections [desires], and by a weak clergy . . . be with flattery so shamefully abused." [42] This was the external source of Henry's retrogression in character—that the absence of resistance to his will, after the death of More, made him as flabby in moral sense as in physique. He was not more lax in sex than Francis I, and after the passing of Anne Boleyn he seems to have been more monogamous, seriatim, than Charles V; sexual looseness was not his worst failing. He was greedy for money as well as for power, and seldom allowed considerations of humanity to halt his appropriations. His ungrateful readiness to kill women whom he had loved, or men who, like More and Cromwell, had served him loyally for many years, is despicable; yet in result he was not one tenth as murderous as the well-meaning Charles IX sanctioning the Massacre of St. Bartholomew, or Charles V condoning the sack of Rome, or German princes fighting through thirty years for their right to determine the religious beliefs of their subjects.

- The inner source of his deterioration was the repeated frustration of his will in love and parentage. Long disappointed in his hope for a son, dishonestly checked in his reasonable request for an annulment of his first marriage, deceived (he believed) by the wife for whom he had risked his throne, bereaved so soon of the only wife who gave him an heir, tricked into marriage by a woman utterly alien to him in language and temperament, cuckolded (he thought) by the wife who seemed to promise him at last the happiness of a home—here was a king possessing all England but denied the domestic joys of the simplest husband in his realm. Suffering intermittent agony from an ulcer in his leg, buffeted with revolts and crises throughout his reign, forced at almost every moment to arm against invasion, betrayal, and assassination—how could such a man develop normally, or avoid degeneration into suspicion, craft, and cruelty? And how shall we, who fret at the pinpricks of private tribulation, understand a man who bore in his mind and person the storm and stress of the English Reformation, weaned his people by perilous steps from a deeply rooted loyalty, and yet must have felt in his divided soul an erosive wonder—had he freed a nation or shattered Christendom?

Danger, as well as power, was the medium in which he lived. He could never tell how far his enemies would go, or when they would succeed. In 1538 he ordered the arrest of Sir Geoffrey Pole, brother to Reginald. Fearing torture, Geoffrey confessed that he, another brother, Lord Montague, Sir Edward Neville, and the Marquis and Marchioness of Exeter had had treasonable correspondence with the Cardinal. Geoffrey was pardoned; Exeter, Montague, and several others were hanged and quartered (1538–

39); Lady Exeter was imprisoned; and the Countess of Salisbury, mother of the Poles, was placed under guard. When the Cardinal visited Charles V in Toledo (1539), bearing a futile request from Paul III that the Emperor would join with Francis in outlawing all commerce with England,[48] Henry retaliated by arresting the Countess, who was now seventy years old; perhaps he hoped that by keeping her in the Tower he could check the Cardinal's enthusiasm for invasion. All was fair in the game of life and death.

Having remained for two years unmarried, Henry bade Cromwell seek for him a marital alliance that would strengthen his hand against Charles. Cromwell recommended Anne, sister-in-law of the Elector of Saxony, and sister of the Duke of Cleves, who was then at odds with the Emperor. Cromwell set his heart on the marriage, by which he hoped ultimately to form a league of Protestant states, and thereby compel Henry to repeal the anti-Lutheran Six Articles. Henry dispatched Holbein to paint a likeness of the lady; possibly Cromwell added some instructions to the artist; the picture came, and Henry judged the Princess bearable. She looks discouragingly sad in the Holbein portrait that hangs in the Louvre, but not less plain of feature than the Jane Seymour who had for a moment softened the heart of the King. When Anne came in body, and Henry laid eyes on her (January 1, 1540), love died at first sight. He shut his eyes, married her, and prayed again for a son to strengthen the Tudor succession now that Prince Edward was revealing his physical frailty. But he never forgave Cromwell.

Four months later, alleging malfeasance and corruption, he ordered the arrest of his most profitable minister. Hardly anyone objected; Cromwell was the most unpopular subject in England—for his origin, his methods, his venality, his wealth. In the Tower he was required to sign statements impugning the validity of the new marriage. Henry announced that he had not given his "inward consent" to the union, and had never consummated it. Anne, confessing that she was still a maid, agreed to an annulment in return for a comfortable pension. Loath to face her brother, she chose a lonely life in England; and it was small comfort to her that when she died (1557) she was buried in Westminster Abbey. Cromwell was beheaded on July 28, 1540.

On the same day Henry married Catherine Howard, twenty years old, of a strictly Catholic house; the Catholic party was gaining. The King ceased to flirt with Continental Protestants, and made his peace with the Emperor. Feeling himself at last safe in that quarter, he turned his fancy northward in the hope of annexing Scotland and thereby rounding out the geographical boundaries and security of Britain. He was distracted by another rebellion in the north of England. Before leaving to suppress it, and to discourage conspiracy at his back, he ordered all the political prisoners in the Tower, including the Countess of Salisbury, to be put to death (1541). The rebellion collapsed, and Henry, distraught with cares, returned to Hampton Court to seek solace from his new Queen.

The second Catherine was the fairest of his mates. More dependent than before on wifely ministrations, the King learned almost to love her, and he gave thanks to God for "the good life he was leading and hoped to lead" under her supervision. But on the day after this Te Deum (November 2, 1541), Archbishop Cranmer handed him documents indicating that Catherine had had premarital relations with three successive suitors. Two of these confessed; so did the Queen. Henry "took such grief," the French ambassador reported, "that it was thought he had gone mad"; [44] the fear haunted him that God had cursed all his marriages. He was inclined to pardon Catherine, but evidence was given him that she had, since her royal marriage, committed adultery with her cousin. She admitted having received her cousin in her private apartment late at night, but only in the presence of Lady Rochford; she denied any misdeed then or at any time since her marriage; and Lady Rochford testified to the truth of these statements so far as her own knowledge went. [45] But the royal court pronounced the Queen guilty; and on February 13, 1542, she was beheaded on the same spot where Anne Boleyn's head had fallen six years before. Her paramours were sentenced to life imprisonment.

The King was now a broken man. His ulcer baffled the medical science of his time, and syphilis, never quite cured, was spreading its ravages through his frame. [46] Losing the zest of life, he had allowed himself to become an unwieldly mass of flesh, his cheeks overlapping his jaws, his narrowed eyes half lost in the convolutions of his face. He could not walk from one room to another without support. Realizing that he had not many years to live, he issued (1543) a new decree fixing the succession to his throne: first on Edward, then on Mary, then on Elizabeth; he went no further, for next in line was Mary Stuart of Scotland. In a final effort to beget a healthy son, and after repeated urging from his Council, he married a sixth wife (July 12, 1543). Catherine Parr had survived two previous husbands, but the King no longer insisted on virgins. She was a woman of culture and tact; she nursed her royal invalid patiently, reconciled him with his long-neglected daughter Elizabeth, and tried to soften his theology and his persecuting zeal.

Theological bonfires continued to the end of the reign: twenty-six persons were burned for heresy in its final eight years. In 1543 spies reported to Bishop Gardiner that Henry Filmer had said, "If God is really present [in the consecrated Host], then in my lifetime I have eaten twenty gods"; that Robert Testwood, at the elevation of the Host, had jocularly warned the priest not to let God fall; and that Anthony Pierson had called any priest a thief who preached anything but "the Word of God"—i.e., the Scriptures. All these men, by the Anglican Bishop's orders, were burned in a meadow before the royal palace at Windsor. The King was disturbed to find that the evidence given by a witness in these cases was perjury; the culprit was sent to the Tower.[47] In 1546 Gardiner condemned four more to the stake for denying the Real Presence. One was a young woman, Anne Askew, who kept to her heresy through five hours of questioning. "That which you call your God," she said at her trial, "is a piece of bread; for proof thereof let it lie in a box three months, and it will be moldy." She was tortured till nearly dead to elicit from her the names of other heretics; she remained silent in her agony, and went to her death, she said, "as merry as one that is bound toward heaven." [48] The King was not active in these persecutions, but the victims appealed to him without result.

In 1543 he fell into war with Scotland and his "beloved brother" Francis I, and soon found himself allied with his old enemy Charles V. To finance his campaigns he demanded new "loans" from his subjects, repudiated payment on the loans of 1542, and confiscated the endowments of the universities.[49] He was carried to the war in person, and supervised the siege and capture of Boulogne. His armies invaded Scotland and wrecked the abbeys of Melrose and Dryburgh, and five other monasteries, but were routed at Ancrum Moor (1545). A profitable accord was signed with France (1546), and the King could die in peace.

He was now so weak that noble families openly contended as to which should have the regency for young Edward. A poet, the Earl of Surrey, was so confident that his father, the Duke of York, would be regent that he adopted a coat of arms suitable only to an heir-apparent to the throne. Henry arrested both; they confessed their guilt; the poet was beheaded on January 9, 1547, and the Duke was scheduled for execution soon after the twenty-seventh. But on the twenty-eighth the King died. He was fifty-five years old, but he had lived a dozen lives in one. He left a large sum to pay for Masses for the repose of his soul.

The thirty-seven years of his reign transformed England more deeply than perhaps he imagined or desired. He thought to replace the pope while leaving unchanged the old faith that had habituated the people to moral restraints and obedience to law; but his successful defiance of the papacy, his swift dispersal of monks and relics, his repeated humiliation of the clergy, his appropriation of Church property, and his secularization of the government so weakened ecclesiastical prestige and authority as to invite the theological changes that followed in the reigns of Edward and Elizabeth. The English Reformation was less doctrinal than the German, but one outstanding result was the same—the victory of the state over the Church. The people escaped from an infallible pope into the arms of an absolute king.

In a material sense they had not benefited. They paid church tithes as before, but the net surplus went to the government. Many peasants now tilled their tenancies for "steplords" more ruthless than the abbots whom Carlyle was to idealize in *Past and Present*. William Cobbett thought that "viewed merely in its social aspect, the English Reformation was in reality the rising of the rich against the poor." [50] Records of prices and wages indicate that the agricultural and town workers were better off at Henry's accession than at his death.[51]

The moral aspects of the reign were bad. The King gave the nation a demoralizing example in his sexual indulgence, his callous passing in a few days from the execution of one wife to the bed of the next, his calm cruelty, fiscal dishonesty, and material greed. The upper classes disordered the court and government with corrupt intrigues; the gentry emulated Henry in grasping at the wealth of the Church; the industrialists mulcted their workers and were mulcted by the King. The decay of charity did not complete the picture, for there remained the debasing subserviency of a terrified people to a selfish autocrat. Only the courage of the Protestant and Catholic martyrs redeemed the scene, and Fisher and More, the noblest of them, had persecuted in their turn.

In a large perspective even those bitter years bore some good fruit. The Reformation had to be; we must repeatedly remind ourselves of this while we record the deviltry of the century that gave it birth. The break with the past was violent and painful, but only a brutal blow could shake its grip on the minds of men. When that incubus was removed, the spirit of nationalism, which at first permitted despotism, became a popular enthusiasm and a creative force. The elimination of the papacy from English affairs left the people for a time at the mercy of the state; but in the long run it compelled them to rely on themselves in checking their rulers and claiming, decade after decade, a measure of freedom commensurate with their intelligence. The government would not always be as powerful as under Henry the Terrible; it would be weak under a sickly son and an embittered daughter; then, under a vacillating but triumphant queen, the nation would rise in a burst of liberated energy, and lift itself to the leadership of the European mind. Perhaps Elizabeth and Shakespeare could not have been had not England been set free by her worst and strongest king.

CHAPTER XXVI

Edward VI and Mary Tudor

1547-58

I. THE SOMERSET PROTECTORATE: 1547–49

THE ten-year-old boy who succeeded to the throne of England as Edward VI had been painted by Holbein four years before in one of the most appealing of all portraits: feathered beret, red hair, ermine-collared robe, and a face of such gentleness and wistful delicacy that we should imagine him to be all Jane Seymour, nothing of Henry VIII. Perhaps he inherited the physical frailty that had made her life his ransom; he never gained the strength to rule. Yet he took in noble earnest the obligations falling to him as prince or king: zealously studied languages, geography, government, and war; kept close watch on all affairs of state that were allowed to come under his ken; and showed to all except nonconforming Catholics so much kindness and good will that England thought it had buried an ogre to crown a saint. Educated by Cranmer, he had become an ardent Protestant. He discouraged any severe punishment for heresy, but was unwilling to let his Catholic half-sister Mary hear Mass, for he sincerely believed the Mass to be the most blasphemous idolatry. He accepted gladly the decision of the Royal Council that chose as regent for him his uncle Edward Seymour—soon made Duke of Somerset—who favored a Protestant policy.

Somerset was a man of intelligence, courage, and integrity imperfect but, in his time, outstanding. Handsome, courteous, generous, he shamed by his life the cowardly and self-seeking aristocracy that could forgive him everything but his sympathy for the poor. Though almost absolute in power, he ended the absolutism established by Henry VII and VIII, allowed much greater freedom of speech, reduced the number of actions previously classed as treason or felony, required sounder evidence for conviction, returned their dowries to the widows of condemned men, and repealed the more oppressive laws of the preceding reign concerning religion. The King remained head of the English Church, and to speak irreverently of the Eucharist was still a punishable offense; but the same statute ordered the sacrament to be administered in both kinds, prescribed English as the language of the service, and repudiated purgatory and Masses for the dead. English Protestants who had fled from England returned with the pollen of Luther, Zwingli, and Calvin on them; and foreign reformers, scenting the new freedom, brought their diverse gospels to the troubled isle. Peter Martyr Vermigli and Martin Bucer came from Strasbourg, Bernardino Ochino from Augsburg, Jan Laski from Emden. Anabaptists and Unitarians crossed the Channel to preach in England heresies that shocked Protestants as much as Catholics. Iconoclast crowds in London removed crucifixes, paintings, and statues from the churches; Nicholas Ridley, Principal of Pembroke College, Cambridge, preached powerfully against religious images and holy water; and, to cap it all, Archbishop Cranmer "did eat meat openly in Lent, the like of which was never seen since England was a Christian country."[1] The Royal Council thought this was going too far, but Somerset overruled it, and gave Reform its head. Under his lead Parliament (1547) ordered that every picture on church wall or window, commemorating a Prophet, Apostle, or saint, should be extirpated "so that there should remain no memory of the same." Most of the stained glass in the churches was destroyed; most of the statues were crushed; crucifixes were replaced with the royal arms; whitewashed walls and stainless windows took the color out of the religion of England. There was a general scramble in each locality for church silver and gold; and in 1551 the government appropriated what remained. The magnificent medieval cathedrals barely remained.

The leading spirit in these changes was Archbishop Cranmer; their leading opponents were Edmund Bonner, Bishop of London, and Stephen Gardiner, Bishop of Winchester; Cranmer had them sent to the Fleet.* Meanwhile the Archbishop had been working for years on an attempt to provide in one book a substitute for both the missal and the breviary of the defeated Church. Peter Martyr and other scholars helped him; but this First Book of Common Prayer (1548) was essentially Cranmer's personal product, in which zeal for the new faith merged with a fine sense for solemn beauty in feeling and phrase; even his translations from the Latin had the spell of genius on them. The Book was not quite revolutionary; it followed some Lutheran leads, as in rejecting the sacrificial character of the Mass, but it neither denied nor affirmed transubstantiation; it retained much Catholic ritual, and could be accepted by not too precise a Romanist. Cranmer submitted it not to Convocation but to Parliament, and that laic body had no qualms of jurisdiction in prescribing religious ritual and belief. The Book was made law of the realm, and every church in England was ordered to adopt it. Bonner and Gardiner, who were released from jail in a general amnesty (1549), were reimprisoned when they rejected the right of Parlia-

---

* A London jail so named from its proximity to the Fleet Stream, an estuary (now covered) of the Thames.

ment to legislate on religion. Princess Mary was allowed to hear Mass in the privacy of her chambers.

A dangerous international situation quieted for a time the violent debate between Catholics and Protestants. Henry II of France demanded the evacuation of Boulogne; refused, he prepared to besiege it; and at any moment Mary Stuart, Queen of Scots, then a girl of five in France, might bring Scotland into the war. Learning that the Scots were arming and were stirring up rebellion in Ireland, Somerset led a force across the border, and defeated them at Pinkie Cleugh (September 10, 1547). The terms that he offered to the Scots were remarkably generous and farseeing: the Scots were not to suffer any forfeiture of liberty or property; Scotland and England were to be merged into one "Empire of Great Britain"; each nation was to have self-government under its own laws, but both were to be ruled, after the current reign, by the offspring of the Queen of Scots. This was precisely the union effected in 1603, except that it would have facilitated a restoration of Catholicism in England, and its continuance in Scotland. The Catholics of Scotland rejected the plan for fear that English Protestantism would infect their own land; besides, Scottish nobles were receiving pensions from the French government, and thought a livre in the hand worth two pounds in the bush.

Frustrated in seeking peace, facing war with France, struggling to establish a compromise among uncompromising faiths at home, and hearing renewed noises of agrarian revolt in England, Somerset drank the cup of power to the dregs when his own brother plotted to overthrow him. Thomas Seymour was not content to be Lord High Admiral and a member of the Privy Council; he would be king. He wooed Princess Mary, then Princess Elizabeth, but in vain. He received money stolen from the mint, and spoils from the pirates whom he allowed in the Channel; and so financed he gathered secret stores of arms and ammunition. His conspiracy was discovered; he was accused by the Earls of Warwick and Southampton; he was almost unanimously condemned by both houses of Parliament; and on March 20, 1549, he was put to death. Somerset tried to protect him, but failed; and the Protector's prestige fell with his brother's head.

Somerset's ruin was completed by Ket's rebellion. That uprising illustrated the apparent anomaly that whereas in Germany peasant revolt was Protestant, in England it was Catholic; in each case religion was a front for economic discontent, and in England the front was Catholic because the government was now Protestant. "In the experience of the agricultural poor," wrote the Protestant Froude, "an increase of personal suffering was the chief result of the Reformation."[2] It is to the credit of Protestant divines in this reign—Cranmer, Latimer, Lever, Crowley—that they condemned the sharpened exploitation of the peasantry; and Somerset with hot indignation denounced the merciless exactions of new landowners "sprung from the dunghill" of city wealth.[8] Parliament could think of no wiser remedies than to pass ferocious laws against beggary, and instruct the churches to take up weekly a collection for the poor. Somerset sent out a commission to get the facts about enclosures and high rents; it met with subtle or open resistance from the landlords; tenants were terrified into concealing their wrongs; and the modest recommendations of the commission were rejected by the Parliament, in which the agricultural districts were represented by landowning gentry. Somerset opened a private court in his own house to hear the complaints of the poor. More and more nobles, led by John Dudley, Earl of Warwick, joined in a movement to depose him.

But now the peasants, furious with accumulated wrongs and frustrated suits for redress, burst into revolt from one end of England to the other. Somersetshire rose first, then Wilts and Gloucestershire, Dorset and Hampshire, Berks and Oxford and Buckingham, in the west Cornwall and Devon, in the east Norfolk and Kent. At Norwich a minor landlord, Robert Ket, organized the rebels, seized the municipal government, and set up a peasant commune that for a month ruled the town and its hinterland. On Mousehold Hill, north of the city, Ket encamped 16,000 men, and there, under an oak tree, he sat daily in judgment upon offending landlords arrested by the peasants. He was not bloodthirsty; those whom he condemned were imprisoned and fed. But of property rights and title deeds he made small account. He bade his men scour the surrounding country, force entry into the manor houses, confiscate all weapons, and corral for the commune all cattle and provisions wherever found. Sheep—chief rivals of the peasants for the use of the soil—were rounded up to the number of 20,000, and were incontinently consumed, along with "infinite beeves," swans, hinds, ducks, venison, and pigs. Amid this feasting Ket nevertheless maintained remarkable order, even allowing preachers to exhort the men to abandon the revolt. Somerset felt much sympathy with the rebels, but agreed with Warwick that they must be dispersed lest the whole economic structure of English life should be overturned. Warwick was sent against them with an army recently raised to fight in France. He offered the rebels a general pardon if they would return to their homes. Ket favored acceptance, but hotter heads were for judgment by battle, and Ket yielded to them. On August 17, 1549, the issue was decided; Warwick's superior tactics won; 3,500 of the rebels were cut down; but when the remnant surrendered Warwick contented himself with nine hangings, and sent Ket and a brother to prison in London. News of the defeat took the heart out of the other rebel groups; one after another laid down its arms on promise of amnesty. Somerset used his influence to have most of the leaders released, and the Ket brothers for a while survived.

The Protector was accused of having encouraged the revolt by his outspoken sympathy with the poor. He was branded also with failure in foreign affairs, for France was now besieging Boulogne. He was justly accused of allowing corruption among governmental personnel, of debasing the currency, of augmenting his own fortune, of building his sumptuous Somerset House amid the near-bankruptcy of the nation. Warwick and Southampton led a move to unseat him. The majority of the nobles, who could pardon his wealth but not his tenderness for their peasants, seized the opportunity for revenge. On October 12, 1549, the Duke of Somerset was paraded as a prisoner through the streets of London, and was shut up in the Tower.

II. THE WARWICK PROTECTORATE: 1549–53

By the standards of the time Somerset's enemies were lenient. He was deprived of such property as he had acquired during his regency; on February 6, 1550, he was released; in May he was restored to membership in the Royal Council. But Warwick was now Protector of the Realm.

He was a frank Machiavellian. Himself inclined to Catholicism, he adopted a Protestant line because his rival Southampton was the accepted leader of the Catholics, and the majority of the nobles were financially wedded to the new creed. He had learned well the art of war, but he knew that with a bankrupt government and an impoverished people he could not hold Boulogne against a France having twice the resources of England. He surrendered the town to Henry II, and signed an ignominious, inescapable peace (1550).

Under the domination of landlords noble or common, Parliament (1549) passed legislation fearfully punishing the rebellion of the peasants. Enclosures were sanctified by express law; the taxes that Somerset had imposed on sheep and wool to discourage enclosures were repealed. Severe penalties were prescribed for workers who combined to raise their wages.[4] Assemblies gathering to discuss a lowering of rents or prices were declared illegal; persons attending them were to forfeit their property. Robert Ket and his brother were hanged. Poverty increased, but the almshouses that had been swept away by the religious revolution were not replaced. Sickness became endemic, but hospitals were abandoned. The people were famished, but the currency was again debased, and prices soared. The once sturdy yeomanry of England were perishing, and the poorest of the poor were sinking into savagery.[5]

Religious chaos rivaled economic anarchy. The majority of the people remained Catholic,[6] but the victory of Warwick over Southampton left them leaderless, and they felt the weakness of those who stand for the past.

The collapse of the spiritual and moral authority of the priesthood, together with the instability and corruption of the government, allowed not only a growth of immorality but a bedlam of heresies that frightened Catholics and Protestants alike. John Clement (1556) described "the wonderful sort of sects swarming everywhere, not only of papists . . . but also of Arians, Anabaptists, and all other kind of heretics . . . some denying the Holy Ghost to be God, some denying original sin, some denying predestination . . . innumerable such like, too long to be recited." [7] Roger Hutchinson (c. 1550) wrote of "Sadducees and Libertines" (freethinkers), who say "that the Devil . . . is nothing but . . . a filthy affection of the flesh . . . that there is neither place of rest nor pain after this life, that hell is nothing but a tormenting and desperate conscience, and that a joyful, quiet, and merry conscience is heaven." [8] And John Hooper, Protestant Bishop of Gloucester, reported that "there are some who say that the soul of man is no better than the soul of a beast, and is mortal and perishable. There are wretches who dare, in their conventicles, not only to deny that Christ is our Saviour, but to call that blessed Child a mischief-maker and deceiver." [9]

Utilizing the liberty that had been granted by Somerset, a reckless fringe among the Protestants satirized the old religion heartlessly. Oxford students parodied the Mass in their farces, chopped missals to pieces, snatched consecrated bread from the altar and trampled it under foot. London preachers called priests "imps of the whore of Babylon"—i.e., the pope. [10] Businessmen met for conferences in St. Paul's; young gallants gathered there, fought, and slew. The new protectorate was now definitely Protestant. Reformers were named to bishoprics, usually on condition that they transfer part of the episcopal manor to the courtiers responsible for their appointment. [11] Parliament (1550) ruled that all paintings and statues were to be removed from any church in England except "the monumental figures of kings or nobles who had never been taken for saints"; and all prayer books except that of Cranmer were to be destroyed. [12] Vestments, copes, and altar textiles were confiscated, sold, or given away, and soon graced the homes of the nobility. [13] An order of Council confiscated to the Treasury all plate remaining in the churches after 1550; later Parliament appropriated for the government the coins in the poor boxes of the churches. [14] Further funds were found for the government or its personnel by canceling scholarships for poor students, and suppressing the regius (state-supported) professorships established at the universities by Henry VIII. [15] The Parliament of 1552 recommended celibacy to the clergy, but permitted them to marry if chastity proved irksome.

Religious persecution, so long of heretics by Catholics, was now in England, as in Switzerland and Lutheran Germany, of heretics and Catholics by Protestants. Cranmer drew up a list of heresies which, if not abjured, were to be punished with death; they included *affirmation* of the Real Presence in the Eucharist, or the ecclesiastical supremacy of the pope, and denial of the inspiration of the Old Testament, or the two natures in Christ, or justification by faith.[16] Joan Bocher of Kent went to the stake for questioning the Incarnation (1550). To Ridley, Protestant Bishop of London, who begged her to recant, she said: "Not long ago you burnt Anne Askew for a piece of bread [for denying transubstantiation], yet came yourselves to believe the doctrine for which you burnt her; and now you will burn me for a piece of flesh [referring to the phrase in the Fourth Gospel—"The Word was made flesh"], and in the end you will believe this also." [17] Only two heretics were burned in Edward's reign; however, many Catholics were imprisoned for hearing Mass, or openly criticizing the currently orthodox creed.[18] Obstinately Catholic priests were deposed from their posts, and some were sent to the Tower.[19] Gardiner, still there, was offered freedom if he would consent to preach the Reformed faith; refusing, he was removed "to a meaner lodging" in the Tower, and was deprived of paper, pen, and books. In 1552 Cranmer issued his Second Book of Common Prayer, which denied the Real Presence, rejected the sacrament of extreme unction, and otherwise revised the First Book in a Protestant direction. Parliament now passed a Second Act of Uniformity, which required all persons to attend regularly, and only, religious services conducted according to this Book of Common Prayer; three violations of this Act were to be punished with death. In 1553 the Royal Council promulgated forty-two "Articles of Religion" drawn up by Cranmer, and made them obligatory on all Englishmen.

While virtue and orthodoxy became law, the Warwick protectorate was distinguishing itself, in a corrupt age, by its corruption. This did not prevent the malleable young Edward from making Warwick Duke of Northumberland (October 4, 1551). A few days later the Duke atoned for an act of political decency—the release of Somerset—by charging his predecessor with an attempt to re-establish himself in power. Somerset was arrested, tried, and convicted, chiefly on evidence given by Sir Thomas Palmer; an order of the King was forged to call for Somerset's execution; and on January 22, 1552, he met his death with courage and dignity. Northumberland, when he in turn faced execution, confessed that through his means Somerset had been falsely accused; and Palmer, before his death, confessed that the evidence he had sworn to had been invented by Northumberland.[20]

Rarely in English history had an administration been so unpopular. Protestant clergymen, who had praised the new Protector in gratitude for his support, turned against him as his crimes increased. King Edward was sinking toward death; Mary Tudor, by an act of Parliament, had been named heiress to the throne if Edward remained childless; and Mary, made queen, would soon revenge herself on those who had led England from the old faith. Northumberland felt that his life was in jeopardy. His one comfort was that his agents had formed Edward to his obedience. He induced the dying King to settle the crown upon Lady Jane Grey, daughter of the Duke of Suffolk and granddaughter of Henry VIII's sister; moreover, Jane had recently married Northumberland's son. Edward had not, like his father, received Parliamentary authority to name his successor; nearly all England took Princess Mary's accession as inevitable and just; and Jane protested that she did not want to be queen. She was a woman of unusual education: she wrote Greek, studied Hebrew, and corresponded with Bullinger in Latin as good as his own. She was no saint; she could be sharply critical of Catholics, and laughed at transubstantiation; but she was far more sinned against than sinning. At first she took her father-in-law's scheme as a jest. When her mother-in-law insisted, Jane resisted. Finally her husband commanded her to accept the throne, and she—"not choosing," she said, "to be disobedient to her husband"—obeyed. Northumberland now prepared to arrest Mary's leading supporters, and to lodge the Princess herself in the Tower, where she might be taught resignation.

Early in July the King neared his end. He coughed and spat blood, his legs swelled painfully, eruptions broke out over his body, his hair fell out, then his nails. No one could say what this strange disease was; many suspected that Northumberland had poisoned him. At last, after long suffering, Edward died (July 6, 1553), still but fifteen, too young to share the guilt of his reign.

The next morning Northumberland rode out toward Hunsdon to seize the Princess. But Mary, warned, escaped to Catholic friends in Suffolk, and Northumberland returned to London without his prey. By promises, threats, or bribes, he persuaded the Privy Council to join him in proclaiming Jane Grey queen. She fainted. Recovering, she still protested that she was unfit for the perilous honor forced upon her. Her relatives pleaded with her, arguing that their lives depended upon her acceptance. On July 9 she reluctantly acknowledged herself to be Queen of England.

But on July 10 news reached London that Mary had proclaimed herself queen, that the northern nobles were flocking to her support, and that their forces were marching upon the capital. Northumberland hurriedly gathered what troops he could, and led them out to the issue of battle. At Bury his soldiers told him that they would not take another step against their lawful sovereign. Crowning his crimes, Northumberland sent his brother, with gold and jewels and the promise of Calais and Guines, to bribe Henry II of France to invade England. The Privy Council got wind of the mission, intercepted it, and announced allegiance to Mary. The Duke of Suffolk went to Jane's room, and informed her that her ten-day reign was over. She welcomed the news, and asked innocently might she now go home; but the

Council, which had sworn to serve her, ordered her confined in the Tower. There, soon, Northumberland too was a prisoner, praying for pardon but expecting death. The Council sent out heralds to proclaim Mary Tudor queen. England received the tidings with wild rejoicing. All through that summer night bells caroled and bonfires blazed. The people brought out tables and food, and picnicked and danced in the streets.

The nation seemed to regret the Reformation, and to look with longing upon a past that could now be idealized since it could not return. And truly the Reformation had as yet shown only its bitterest side to England: not a liberation from dogma, inquisition and tyranny, but their intensification; not a spread of enlightenment but a spoliation of universities and the closing of hundreds of schools; no enlargement of kindness but almost an end to charity and carte blanche to greed; no mitigation of poverty but such merciless grinding of the poor as England had not known for centuries—perhaps had never known.[21] Almost any change would be welcome that would eliminate Northumberland and his crew. And poor Princess Mary, who had won the secret love of England by her patience in twenty-two years of humiliation—surely this chastened woman would make a gentle queen.

III. THE GENTLE QUEEN: 1553-54

To understand her we should have had to live with her the tragic youth during which she had hardly ever tasted happiness. She was scarcely two (1518) when her father took to mistresses and neglected her grieving mother; eight when he asked for an annulment of his marriage; fifteen when her parents parted, and mother and daughter went into a separate exile. Even when the mother was dying the daughter was forbidden to go to her.[22] After the birth of Elizabeth (1533) Mary was declared a bastard, and was shorn of her title of princess. The Imperial ambassador feared that Anne Boleyn would seek the death of her daughter's rival for the throne. When Elizabeth was moved to Hatfield Mary was compelled to go and serve her there, and to live in "the worst room of the house." [23] Her servants were taken from her, and were replaced by others subject to Miss Shelton of Hatfield, who, reminding her that she was a bastard, said, "If I were in the King's place I would kick you out of the King's house for your disobedience," and told her that Henry had expressed his intention to have her beheaded.[24] All that first winter at Hatfield (1534) Mary was ill, her nerves shattered with contumely and fear, her body and soul not unwillingly near death. Then the King relented and spared her some casual affection, and for the remainder of the reign her position eased. But as the price of this hard graciousness she was required to sign an acknowledgment of Henry's ecclesiastical supremacy, her mother's "incestuous marriage," and her own illegitimate birth.[25]

Her nervous system was permanently affected by these experiences; "she was subject to a heart complaint," [26] and she remained in frail health till the end of her life. Her courage returned when, under the Somerset protectorate, Parliament declared her heiress-apparent to the throne. Since her Catholic faith, bred into her childhood with Spanish fervor, and strengthened by her mother's living and dying exhortations, had been a precious support in her griefs, she refused to abandon it when she hovered on the edge of power; and when the King's Council bade her cease hearing Mass in her rooms (1549) she would not obey. Somerset connived at her resistance; but Somerset fell, her brother the King approved the order, and three of her servants, for ignoring it, were sent to the Tower (1551). The chaplain who had said Mass for her was taken from her, and she finally agreed to forgo the beloved ritual. Her spirit broken, she begged the Imperial ambassador to arrange her escape to the Continent. The cautious Emperor refused to sanction the plan, and it fell through.

Her moment of triumph came at last when Northumberland could find no man to fight against her, and those who came in arms to uphold her cause asked no pay, but brought their own supplies and offered their personal fortunes to finance the campaign. When she entered London as queen (August 3, 1553) even that half-Protestant city rose almost unanimously to welcome her. Princess Elizabeth came diffidently to meet her at the city gates, wondering whether Mary would hold against her the indignities suffered in Elizabeth's name; but Mary greeted her with a warm embrace, and kissed all the ladies in her half-sister's train. England was as happy as when Henry VIII, young and handsome and generous, had mounted the throne.

Mary was now thirty-seven, and heartless time had already crossed her face with omens of decay. She had seldom known an adult year without a serious illness. She was troubled with dropsy, indigestion, and racking headaches; she was treated with repeated bloodlettings, which left her nervous and pale. Her recurrent amenorrhea plunged her at times into hysterical grief with fear that she would never bear a child.[27] Now her body was thin and frail, her forehead was wrinkled, her reddish hair was streaked with gray, her eyes were so weak that she could read only with the page held close to her face. Her features were plain, almost masculine; her voice was as deep as a man's; life had given her all the frailties, none of the charms, of womanhood. She had some womanly accomplishments—she knitted patiently, embroidered skillfully, and played the lute; to which she added a knowledge of Spanish, Latin, Italian, and French. She would have made a good woman had she not been cursed with theological certainty and royal power. She was honest to the point of simplicity, incapable of diplomacy, and pitifully anxious to love and be loved. She had bursts of temper and shrewish speech.

She was obstinate, but not proud; she recognized her mental limitations, and listened humbly to advice. She was inflexible only where her faith was concerned; otherwise she was clement and compassionate, liberal to the unfortunate, and eager to redress the wrongs of the law. Frequently she visited incognito the homes of the poor, sat and talked with the housewives, made note of needs and grievances, and gave whatever help she could.[28] She restored to the universities the endowments filched from them by her predecessors.

The best side of her character showed in the relative tolerance of her early reign. She not only released Gardiner, Bonner, and others who had been imprisoned for refusing to accept Protestantism, but she pardoned almost all those who had tried to keep her from the throne. Some of these, however, like the Duke of Suffolk, she compelled to pay heavy fines into the treasury; then, the revenue being so aided, she reduced taxes substantially. Peter Martyr and other alien Protestants were allowed safe-conducts to leave the country. The Queen's Council gave a hasty trial to Northumberland and six others who had conspired to arrest Mary and crown Jane Grey; all seven were condemned to die. Mary wished to pardon even Northumberland, but Simon Renard, now Imperial ambassador, dissuaded her. All the unforgiven three made a last-minute profession of the Roman Catholic faith. Jane Grey called the sentence just, and the confessions cowardly.[29] Mary proposed to release her, but yielded so far to her councilors as to order her to be kept in loose confinement within the Tower grounds.[30]

On August 13 the Queen issued an official declaration that she would not "compel or constrain consciences" in the matter of religious belief;[31] this was one of the first proclamations of religious tolerance by a modern government. Innocently hopeful of converting Protestants by argument, she arranged a public debate between opposed theologians, but it evaporated in bitter and inconclusive dispute. Shortly thereafter Bishop Bonner's chaplain had a dagger thrown at him from a crowd that resented his Catholic preaching; he was rescued from death by two Protestant divines.[32] Frightened out of her tolerance, Mary ordered (August 18, 1553) that until Parliament could meet and consider the problems raised by the conflict of faiths, no doctrinal sermons should be preached except in the universities. Cranmer, still Archbishop, was bidden keep to his Lambeth palace; he retorted with a blast against the Mass as an "abominable blasphemy"; he and Latimer were committed to the Tower (September 1553). Bishop Ridley of London, who had branded both Mary and Elizabeth as bastards, had gone to the Tower two months before. All in all, Mary's conduct in these early months of her reign excelled, in lenience and tolerance, that of the other major rulers of her time.

The problems she faced might have overwhelmed one far superior to her in intelligence and tact. She was shocked by the confusion and corruption prevalent in the administration. She ordered the corruption to stop; it hid its head and continued. She gave a good example by reducing the expenses of the royal household, pledging a stable currency, and leaving parliamentary elections free from royal influence; the new elections were "the fairest which had taken place for many years." [33] But her reduction of taxes left government income lower than outgo; to make up the difference she levied an export duty on cloth and an import duty on French wines; these measures, which were expected to help the poor, caused a commercial recession. She tried to arrest the growth of capitalism by limiting to one or two the looms that any individual might own. She denounced "rich clothiers" for paying low wages, and forbade the payment of wages in kind.[34] But she could not find in her entourage men of the force and integrity required to implement her good will; and economic laws overrode her aims.

Even in religion she met with severe economic obstacles. There was hardly an influential family in England that did not hold property taken from the Church; [35] such families, of course, opposed any return to the Roman faith. The Protestants, numerically a minority, financially powerful, might at any moment provide the sinews for a revolt that would place Protestant Elizabeth on the throne. Mary was anxious to restore the right of Catholics to worship according to their own ritual; yet the Emperor, who had been fighting Protestantism for thirty-two years, cautioned her to move slowly, and to be content with having Mass said privately for herself and her immediate circle. But she felt her religion too deeply to be politic with it. The skeptical generation that had grown up in London marveled at the frequency and fervor of her prayers, and the Spanish ambassador probably thought it a nuisance when she asked him to kneel beside her to ask divine guidance. She felt that she had a sacred mission to restore the faith that had become so dear to her because she had suffered for it. She sent a messenger to the Pope begging him to remove the interdict on religious services in England; but when Cardinal Pole wished to come to England as papal legate, she agreed with Charles that the time was not ripe for so bold a move.

The Parliament that met on October 5, 1553, was by no means subservient. It agreed to repeal all the legislation of Edward's reign concerning religion; it reduced to their earlier proportions the severe penalties prescribed in the laws of Henry VIII and Edward VI; and it graciously informed the Queen that "the illegitimation of your most noble person" was now annulled, and she had ceased to be a bastard. But it refused even to consider the restoration of ecclesiastical property, it resisted any hint that papal sovereignty should be acknowledged, and it left Mary the unwilling head of the English Church. By this authority she replaced Protestant bishops with the Catholic prelates that had been expelled; Bonner was again Bishop of London; Gardiner was again Bishop of Winchester, and a close adviser of the Crown. Married priests were dismissed from their parishes. The Mass was again allowed, then encouraged; and (says a Protestant historian) "the eagerness with which the country generally availed itself of the permission to restore the Catholic ritual proved beyond a doubt that except in London and a few large towns, the popular feeling was with the Queen." [36] By an edict of March 4, 1554, the Catholic worship was completely reinstated, Protestantism and other "heresies" were made illegal, and all Protestant preaching or publication was prohibited.

The nation was much less disturbed by this return of the theological pendulum than by Mary's marriage plans. She was constitutionally fearful of marriage, but she faced the trial in the hope of having an heir who would prevent the accession of Protestant Elizabeth. Mary claimed to be a virgin, and probably was; perhaps if she had sinned a bit she would have been less somber, tense, and certain. Her Council recommended to her Edward Courtenay, great-grandson of Edward IV, but his debauched ways were not to Mary's taste. Rejected, he schemed to marry Elizabeth, depose Mary, enthrone Elizabeth, and rule England through her—never dreaming how little chance he had of dominating that virile lady. Charles V offered Mary his son Philip, to whom he was about to bequeath all but the Imperial title; and he pledged the Netherlands as a gift to any male issue of the marriage. Mary thrilled at the thought of having as her husband the ruler of Spain, Flanders, Holland, Naples, and the Americas; and her half-Spanish blood warmed at the prospect of a political and religious union of England with Spain. She modestly suggested that her greater age—ten years above Philip's—was a barrier; she feared that her faded charms would not suffice his youthful vigor or imagination; she was not even sure that she would know how to make love. [37] For his part Philip was reluctant; his English agents reported that Mary was "a perfect saint," who "dressed badly"; [38] could not something more alluring be found among the royal families of Europe? Charles persuaded him by pointing out that the marriage would give Spain a strong ally against France, and precious support in the Netherlands, which were bound to England commercially; perhaps Protestantism in Germany could be suppressed by the united action of Spain, France, and England as Catholic states; and the union of the Hapsburgs and the Tudors would constitute a power capable of giving Western Europe a generation of compulsory peace.

The Queen's Council and the English people recognized the force of these considerations, but they feared that the marriage would make England an appendage of Spain, and would involve England in recurrent wars against France. Charles countered by offering, in his son's name, a marriage contract by which Philip should bear the title King of England only so long as Mary lived; she was to retain sole and full royal authority over English affairs;

she was to share all of Philip's titles; and if Don Carlos (Philip's son by an earlier marriage) died without issue, Mary or her son was to inherit the Spanish Empire; moreover, added the astute Emperor, Mary was to receive £60,000 a year for life from the Imperial revenues. All this seemed generous enough, and with a few minor provisions the English Council sanctioned the marriage. Mary herself, despite her modest timidity, looked forward to it eagerly. How long she had waited for a lover!

But the people of England resented her choice. The Protestant minority, which was bearing up under suppression in the hope that Elizabeth would soon succeed a fragile and barren Mary, feared for its life if the power of Spain should stand beside Mary in enforcing the Catholic restoration. Nobles rich in ecclesiastical property shivered at the thought of disgorging. Even Catholic Englishmen objected to putting upon the throne a dour foreigner who would doubtless use England for his own alien purposes. Protests were voiced everywhere in the land. The city of Plymouth, in panic, asked the King of France to take it under his protection. Four nobles laid plans for an uprising to begin on March 18, 1554. The Duke of Suffolk (pardoned father of Jane Grey) was to raise Warwickshire, Sir James Croft was to lead his Welsh tenants, Sir Peter Carew would rouse Devonshire, and Sir Thomas Wyatt the Younger would lead the revolt in Kent. The elder Wyatt—the poet—had secured a mass of Church lands, which his son was loath to surrender. The conspirators made the mistake of confiding their plans to Courtenay, whose task was to secure Elizabeth's co-operation. Bishop Gardiner, who had kept watch on Courtenay as a rejected and per- haps vengeful suitor for Mary's hand, had him arrested, and Courtenay, presumably under torture, betrayed the plot.

The conspirators, preferring to die in battle rather than on the block, rose hurriedly to arms, and revolt flared up in four counties at once (Febru- ary 1554). Wyatt led an army of 7,000 men toward London, and sent out an appeal to all citizens to prevent England from becoming an appanage of Spain. The Protestant part of the London populace set in motion a plan to open the gates to Wyatt. The Queen's Council hesitated to commit itself, and raised not one soldier in her defense. Mary herself could not understand why the country that had so welcomed her accession should refuse her the happiness and fulfillment that she had dreamed of through so many years of misery. If now she had not taken matters into her own hands with un- wonted resolution, her reign and her life would have soon ended. But she went in person to the Guildhall, and faced an excited assemblage that was debating which side to take. She told it that she was quite ready to abandon the Spanish marriage if the Commons so wished, and indeed "to abstain from marriage while I live"; but meanwhile she would not let that issue be made "a Spanish cloak" for a political revolution. "I cannot tell," she said, "how naturally the mother loveth her child, for I was never the mother of any; but certainly if a queen may as naturally and earnestly love her subjects as the mother doth her child, then assure yourselves that I, being your lady and mistress, do as earnestly and tenderly love and favor you." [39] Her words and spirit were warmly applauded, and the assembly pledged her its support. Agents of the government were able, almost in a day, to muster 25,000 armed men. Suffolk was arrested, Croft and Carew fled into hiding. Wyatt. so abandoned, led his small force to battle in the streets of London, and made his way almost to the Queen's palace at Whitehall. Mary's guards begged her to flee; she would not. Finally Wyatt's men were overcome; he yielded in exhaustion of body and soul, and was taken to the Tower. Mary breathed safely again, but she was never more the gentle Queen.

IV. "BLOODY MARY": 1554–58

Her advisers had often condemned her policy of pardon. The Emperor and his ambassador had censured her for allowing life, even liberty, to persons who had conspired against her and would be free to do so again. How, she was asked, could Philip trust himself in a land where his enemies were left unhindered to plot his assassination? Bishop Gardiner argued that mercy to the nation required that traitors should be put to death. The Queen, in a panic of fright, veered to the views of her counselors. She ordered the execution of Lady Jane Grey, who had never wanted to be queen, and of Jane's husband, who had so wanted to be king. Jane, still but seventeen, went to her death stoically, without protest or tears (February 12, 1554). Suffolk, her father, was beheaded, and a hundred lesser rebels were hanged. Some conspirators were spared for a while in the hope of eliciting useful confessions. Wyatt at first incriminated Elizabeth as privy to the plan, but on the scaffold (April 11, 1554) he exonerated her of all cognizance. Courtenay, after a year's imprisonment, was let off with banishment. Charles advised Mary to put Courtenay and Elizabeth to death as perpetual threats to her life. Mary sent for Elizabeth, kept her in the palace of St. James for a month, then for two months imprisoned her in the Tower. Renard urged her immediate execution, but Mary objected that Elizabeth's complicity had not been proved.[40] During these fateful months Elizabeth's life hung in the balance, and this terror helped to form her character to suspicion and insecurity, and was echoed in the severity of her later reign, when she had the same worry about Mary Stuart that Mary Tudor now had about Elizabeth. On May 18 the future queen was moved to Woodstock, where she lived in loose confinement but under watch. Fear that another plot might raise Elizabeth to the throne urged Mary on to marriage in the hope of motherhood.

Philip was not so eager. Through a proxy in England he married Mary on March 6, 1554, but he did not reach England till July 20. The English were pleasantly surprised to find him physically and socially tolerable: a rather strange triangular face sloping from broad forehead to narrow chin, adorned with yellow hair and beard; but also a gracious manner, a ready wit, gifts for all, and no hint that he and his retinue considered the English to be barbarians. Even for Elizabeth he had a kind word, perhaps foreseeing that Mary might prove childless, that Elizabeth would someday be queen, and that this would be a lesser evil than the accession of Mary Queen of Scots— long since bound to France—to the throne of England. Mary, though so much older than Philip, looked up to him with girlish admiration. Starved for affection through so many years, she rejoiced now to have won so charming and mighty a prince, and she gave herself to him with such unquestioning devotion that her court wondered whether England was not already subject to Spain. To Charles V she wrote humbly that she was now "happier than I can say, as I daily discover in the King my husband so many virtues and perfections that I constantly pray God to grant me grace to please him." [41]

Her desire to give Philip a son and England an heir was so absorbing that she soon conceived herself pregnant. Her amenorrhea was now welcomed as a royal sign, and hope silenced the thought that that condition had often come to her before. Digestive disturbances were accepted as additional proofs of motherhood, and the Venetian ambassador reported that the Queen's "paps" had swollen and given milk. For a long time Mary rejoiced in the thought that she too, like the poorest woman in her realm, could bear a child; and we cannot imagine her desolation when her doctors finally convinced her that her swelling was dropsy. Meanwhile the rumor of her pregnancy had swept through England; prayers and processions were arranged for her happy delivery; soon gossip said that she had borne a boy. Shops closed for a holiday, men and women feasted in the streets, church bells rang, and a clergyman announced that the child was "fair and beautiful" as became a prince. [42] Broken with frustration and shame, Mary hid herself for months from the public view.

She was in a measure consoled by the return of Cardinal Pole to England. Charles had detained him at Brussels because Pole had opposed the Spanish marriage; but now that this had been consummated the Imperial objections subsided; the Cardinal, as papal legate, crossed the Channel (November 20, 1554) to the land he had left twenty-two years before; and the warm welcome given him by officials, clergy, and people attested the general satisfaction over renewal of relations with the papacy. He greeted Mary with almost the choicest phrase in his vocabulary: *Ave Maria, gratia plena, Dominus tecum, benedicta tu in mulieribus,* and he trusted that he might soon add, "Blessed is the fruit of thy womb." [43] When Parliament learned that Pole brought papal consent to the retention of confiscated Church property by the present holders, all went merry as a wedding should. Parliament, on its knees, expressed repentance for its offenses against the Church, and Bishop Gardiner, having confessed his own vacillation, gave the penitents absolution. The ecclesiastical supremacy of the pope was acknowledged, his right to annates and "first fruits" was reaffirmed, episcopal courts were re-established, and parish tithes were restored to the clergy. The old statutes against Lollardry were renewed, and censorship of publications was returned from state to Church authorities. After the turmoil of twenty years everything seemed as before.

Philip stayed with Mary thirteen months, hoping with her for a child; when no sure sign of it appeared he begged her to let him go to Brussels, where the planned abdication of his father required his presence. She consented sadly, went with him to the barge that was to take him down the Thames, and watched from a window till the barge disappeared (August 28, 1555). Philip felt that he had done his duty through an arduous year of making love to a sick woman, and he rewarded himself with the full-blooded ladies of Brussels.

Pole was now the most influential man in England. He busied himself with the reorganization and reform of the English Church. With Mary's help he restored some monasteries and a nunnery. Mary was happy to see the old religious customs live again, to see crucifixes and holy pictures again in the churches, to join in pious processions of priests, children, or guilds, to sit or kneel through long Masses for the quick and the dead. On Maundy Thursday, 1556, she washed and kissed the feet of forty-one old women, shuffling from one to the next on her knees, and gave alms to all. [44] Now that hope of motherhood had gone, religion was her sustaining solace.

But she could not quite resurrect the past. The new ideas had aroused an exciting ferment in city minds; there were still a dozen sects clandestinely publishing their literature and their creeds. Mary was pained to hear of groups that denied the divinity of Christ, the existence of the Holy Ghost, the transmission of original sin. To her simple faith these heresies seemed mortal crimes, far worse than treason. Could the heretics know better than her beloved Cardinal how to deal with the human soul? Word came to her that one preacher had prayed aloud, before his congregation, that God would either convert her or soon remove her from the earth. [45] One day a dead dog with a monastically tonsured head, and a rope around its neck, was thrown through a window into the Queen's chamber. [46] In Kent a priest had his nose cut off. [47] It seemed unreasonable to Mary that the Protestant *émigrés*, to whom she had allowed safe departure from England, should be sending back pamphlets attacking her as a reactionary fool, and speaking of the "lousy Latin service" of an "idolatrous Mass." [48] Some pamphlets urged their readers to rise in revolt and depose the Queen.[49] A meeting of 17,000 persons at Aldgate (March 14, 1554) heard a call to put Elizabeth on the throne.[50] Insurrections in England were planned by English Protestants abroad.

Mary was by nature and habit merciful—till 1555. What transformed her into the most hated of English queens? Partly the provocation of attacks that showed no respect for her person, her faith, or her feelings; partly the fear that heresy was a cover for political revolt; partly the sufferings and disappointments that had embittered her spirit and darkened her judgment; partly the firm belief of her most trusted advisers—Philip, Gardiner, Pole—that religious unity was indispensable to national solidarity and survival. Philip was soon to illustrate his principles in the Netherlands. Bishop Gardiner had already (in the spring of 1554) vowed to burn the three Protestant bishops— Hooper, Ridley, Latimer—unless they recanted.[51] Cardinal Pole, like Mary, was of a kindly disposition, but inflexible in dogma; he loved the Church so much that he shuddered at any questioning of her doctrines or authority. He did not take any direct or personal lead in the Marian persecution; he counseled moderation, and once freed twenty persons whom Bishop Bonner had sentenced to the stake.[52] Nevertheless he instructed the clergy that if all peaceful methods of suasion failed, major heretics should be "removed from life and cut off as rotten members from the body." [53] Mary's own view was expressed hesitantly. "Touching the punishment of heretics, we think it ought to be done without rashness, not leaving meanwhile to do justice to such as by learning would seek to deceive the simple." [54] Her responsibility was at first merely permissive, but it was real. When (1558) the war with France proved disastrous to her and England, she ascribed the failure to God's anger at her lenience with heresy, and thereafter she positively promoted the persecution.

Gardiner opened the reign of terror by summoning to his episcopal court (January 22, 1555) six clergymen who had refused to accept the re-established creed.* One recanted; four, including John Hooper, deposed Bishop of Gloucester and Worcester, were burned (February 4-8, 1555). Gardiner

---

* The chief source for the Marian persecution is John Foxe's *Rerum in ecclesia gestarum commentarii* (1559), translated into English as *Acts and Monuments* (1563), and familiarly known as *The Book of Martyrs*. This vivid description of the trials and deaths of the Protestants became, next to the Bible, a cherished household possession among the Puritans; and though the Jesuit Father Parsons published (1603) five volumes assailing its accuracy, it had a powerful influence in forming the mood of Oliver Cromwell's England. Many Protestant churchmen have criticized it for exaggeration, misquotation, prejudice, and carelessness with details; [55] a Catholic historian compares it, in reliability, with medieval legends of the saints, but concludes that, though many details are dubious, "no one doubts that these events did so happen." [56]

seems to have had a revulsion of feeling after these executions; he took no further part in the persecution; his health broke down, and he died in November of this year. Bishop Bonner took charge of the slaughter. Philip, still in England, advised moderation; when Bonner condemned six more to the stake the Imperial ambassador, Renard, objected to "this barbarous precipitancy"; [57] and Philip's confessor, a Spanish friar, preaching before the court, denounced the convictions as contrary to the mild and forgiving spirit inculcated by Christ.[58] Bonner suspended the sentences for five weeks, then ordered them carried out. He thought himself lenient, and indeed was once reprimanded by the Queen's Council for insufficient zeal in prosecuting heresy.[59] To each heretic he offered full pardon for recantation, and often added a promise of financial aid or some comfortable employment; [60] but when such inducements failed he passed sentence grimly. Usually a bag of gunpowder was placed between the legs of the condemned, so that the flames would cause a speedy death; but in Hooper's case the wood burned too slowly, the powder failed to explode, and the former bishop suffered agonies for almost an hour.

Most of the martyrs were simple workingmen who had learned to read the Bible, and had been encouraged in the Protestant interpretation of it during the previous reign. Perhaps the persecutors thought it justice that the ecclesiastics who had done most to inculcate the Protestant faith should be called upon to testify to it by martyrdom. In September 1555, Cranmer, sixty-six, Ridley, sixty-five, and Latimer, eighty, were brought from the Tower to stand trial at Oxford. Latimer had tarnished his eloquent career by approving the burning of Anabaptists and obstinate Franciscans under Henry VIII. Ridley had actively supported Jane Grey's usurpation, had called Mary a bastard, and had assisted in deposing Bonner and Gardiner from their sees. Cranmer had been the intellectual head of the English Reformation: had dissolved the marriage of Henry and Catherine, had married Henry to Anne Boleyn, had replaced the Mass with the Book of Common Prayer, had prosecuted Frith, Lambert, and other Catholics, had signed Edward's devise of the crown to Jane Grey, and had denounced the Mass as a blasphemy. All these men had now been in the Tower for two years, daily expecting death.

Cranmer was tried at Oxford on September 7. His examiners made every effort to elicit a recantation. He stood his ground firmly, and was judged guilty; but as he was an archbishop his sentence was reserved to the Pope, and he was returned to the Tower. On September 30 Ridley was tried, and stood his ground. On the same day Latimer was led before the ecclesiastical court: a man now quite careless of life, dressed in an old threadbare gown, his white head covered with a cap upon a nightcap over a handkerchief, his spectacles hanging from his neck, a New Testament attached to his belt. He too denied transubstantiation. On October 1 they were condemned; on October 6 they were burned. Before the pyre they knelt and prayed together. They were bound with chains to an iron post, a bag of powder was hung around each man's neck, the faggots were lit. "Be of good cheer, Master Ridley," said Latimer, "play the man; we shall this day light such a candle, by God's grace, in England, as I trust shall never be put out." [61]

On December 4 Pope Paul IV confirmed the sentence against Cranmer. For a time the first Protestant archbishop of Canterbury gave way to forgivable fear; no man who could write such sensitive English as the Book of Common Prayer could face these ordeals without exceptional suffering of body and mind. Moved perhaps by Pole's fervent appeal, Cranmer repeatedly "renounced and abhorred and detested all manner of heresies and errors of Luther and Zwingli," and professed belief in the seven sacraments, in transubstantiation, purgatory, and all other teachings of the Roman church. By every precedent such recantations should have commuted his sentence to imprisonment, but (according to Foxe) Mary rejected the retractions as insincere, and ordered Cranmer's execution. [62]

In St. Mary's Church, Oxford, on the morning of his death (March 21, 1556), he read his seventh and last recantation. Then, to the astonishment of all present, he added:

> And now I come to the great thing, which so much troubleth my conscience more than anything that ever I did or said in my whole life, and that is the setting abroad of a writing contrary to the truth; which now here I renounce and refuse ... as written for fear of death ... and that is, all such bills and papers which I have written or signed with my hand since my degradation. ... And forasmuch as my hand offended, writing contrary to my heart, my hand shall first be punished therefor, for ... it shall be first burned. And as for the pope, I refuse him as Christ's enemy and Antichrist. [63]

On the pyre, as the flames neared his body, he stretched out his hand into them, and held it there, says Foxe, "steadfast and immovable ... that all men might see his hand burned before his body was touched. And using often the words of Stephen, 'Lord, receive my spirit,' in the greatness of the flame he gave up the ghost." [64]

His death marked the zenith of the persecution. Some 300 persons died in its course, 273 of them in the last four years of the reign. As the holocaust advanced it became clear that it had been a mistake. Protestantism drew strength from its martyrs as early Christianity had done, and many Catholics were disturbed in their faith, and shamed in their Queen, by the sufferings and fortitude of the victims. Bishop Bonner, though he did not enjoy the work, came to be called "Bloody Bonner" because his diocese saw most of the executions; one woman called him "the common cutthroat and general slaughter-slave to all the bishops in England." [65] Hundreds of English Protestants found refuge in Catholic France, and labored there to bring the sorry reign to an end. Henry II, while persecuting French Protestants, encouraged English plots against Catholic Mary, whose marriage with the King of Spain left France surrounded by hostile powers. In April 1556, British agents discovered a conspiracy, led by Sir Henry Dudley, to depose Mary and enthrone Elizabeth. Several arrests were made, including two members of Elizabeth's household; one confession implicated Elizabeth herself, and the French King. The movement was suppressed, but it left Mary in constant fear of assassination.

One group of fugitives encountered tribulations that reveal the dogmatic temper of the times. Jan Laski, a Polish Calvinist, had come to London in 1548, and had founded there the first Presbyterian church in England. A month after Mary's accession Laski and part of his congregation left London in two Danish vessels. At Copenhagen they were denied entry unless they signed the official Lutheran confession of faith. As firm Calvinists, they declined. Refused permission to land, they sailed to Wismar, Lübeck, and Hamburg, and in each case met with the same demand and repulse. [66] The Lutherans of Germany shed no tears over Mary's victims, but denounced them as detestable heretics and "Devil's martyrs" for denying the Real Presence of Christ in the Eucharist. [67] Calvin condemned the merciless sectarianism of the Lutherans, and in that year (1553) burned Servetus at the stake. After buffeting the North Sea through most of the winter, the refugees at last found entry and humanity at Emden.

Mary moved with somber fatality to her end. Her pious husband, now anomalously at war with the papacy as well as with France, came to England (March 20, 1557) and urged the Queen to bring Britain into the war as his ally. To make his mission less hateful to the English, he persuaded Mary to moderate the persecution. [68] But he could not so easily win public support; on the contrary, a month after his arrival, Thomas Stafford, a nephew of Cardinal Pole, fomented a rebellion with a view to freeing England from both Mary and Philip. He was defeated and hanged (May 28, 1557). To fill the Queen's cup of misery the Pope in that month repudiated Pole as papal legate, and accused him of heresy. On June 7 Mary, anxious to please Philip, and convinced that Henry II had supported Stafford's plot, declared war against France. Having accomplished his purpose, Philip left England in July. Mary suspected that she would never see him again. "I will live the rest of my days without the company of men," she said. [69] In this unwanted war England lost Calais (January 6, 1558), which it had held for 211 years; and the thousands of Englishmen and women who had lived there, and now fled as penniless fugitives to Britain, spread the bitter charge that Mary's government had been criminally negligent in defending England's last possession on the Continent. Philip made a peace favorable to himself, without requiring the restoration of Calais. It was an old phrase that that precious port was "the brightest jewel in the English crown." Mary added another *mot* to the tale: "When I am dead and opened you will find Calais lying in my heart." [70]

Early in 1558 the Queen again thought herself pregnant. She made her will in expectation of a dangerous delivery, and dispatched a message to Philip beseeching his presence at the happy event. He sent his congratulations, but he did not have to come; Mary was mistaken. She was now quite forlorn, perhaps in some measure insane. She sat for hours on the floor with knees drawn up to her chin; she wandered like a ghost through the palace galleries; she wrote tear-blotted letters to a King who, anticipating her death, ordered his agents in England to incline the heart of Elizabeth toward marriage with some Spanish grandee, or with Philip himself.

In Mary's final summers a plague of ague fever moved through England. In September 1558, it struck the Queen. Combined with dropsy and "a superfluity of black bile," it so weakened her that her will to live fell away. On November 6 she sent the crown jewels to Elizabeth. It was a gracious act, in which love of the Church yielded to her desire to give England an orderly succession. She suffered long periods of unconsciousness; from one of these she awoke to tell how she had happily dreamed of children playing and singing before her. [71] On November 17 she heard Mass early, and uttered the responses ardently. Before dawn she died.

On the same day died Cardinal Pole, as profoundly defeated as his Queen. In estimating him we must record the bitter fact that at the beginning of his last month he had condemned three men and two women to be burned for heresy. It is true that all parties except the Anabaptists, in those years of mad certainty, agreed that religious unity had to be preserved, even, if necessary, by punishing dissent with death. But nowhere in contemporary Christendom —not even in Spain—were so many men and women burned for their opinions as during Reginald Pole's primacy of the English Church.

For Mary we may speak a more lenient word. Grief, illness, and many suffered wrongs had warped her mind. Her clemency passed into cruelty only after conspiracies had sought to deprive her of her crown on her head. She listened too trustingly to ecclesiastics who, having themselves been persecuted, sought revenge. Till the end she thought she was fulfilling by murder her obligations to the faith which she loved as the vital medium of her life. She does not quite deserve the name of "Bloody Mary," unless we are to spread that adjective over all her time; it simplifies pitilessly a character in which there had been much to love. It is her strange distinction that she carried on the work of her father in alienating England from Rome. She showed to an England still Catholic the worst side of the Church she served. When she died England was readier than before to accept the new faith that she had labored to destroy.

CHAPTER XXVII

From Robert Bruce to John Knox

1300-1561

I. THE INDOMITABLE SCOTS

THE warm and genial south generates civilization; the cold and hardy north repeatedly conquers the lax and lazy south, and absorbs and transforms civilization. The extreme north—Scotland, Norway, Sweden, Finland—fights the almost Arctic elements to provide some welcome to civilization, and to contribute to it in the face of a thousand obstacles.

In Scotland the sterile, roadless Highlands encouraged feudalism and discouraged culture, while the green and fertile Lowlands invited invasion after invasion by Englishmen who could not understand why Scotland should not receive their overflow and their kings. The Scots, anciently Celtic, medievally mingled with Irish, Norse, Angles, Saxons, and Normans, had by 1500 merged into a people narrow as their peninsula in feelings and ideas, deep as their mists in superstition and mythology, proud as their promontories, rough as their terrain, impetuous as their torrents; at once ferocious and tender, cruel and brave, and always invincible. Poverty seemed rooted in geography, and manners in poverty; so parsimony grew out of the grudging soil. The peasants were too burdened with toil to have time for letters, and the nobles who kept them in bondage prided themselves on illiteracy, finding no use for the alphabet in their feuds or wars. The mountains and clans divided the sparse population into passionate jealousies that gave no quarter in war, no security in peace. The nobles, having nearly all the military power in their private bands, dominated the Parliament and the kings; the Douglases alone had 5,000 retainers, and revenues rivaling the Crown's.

Before 1500 industry was primitive and domestic, commerce was precarious, cities were few and small. All Scotland had then some 600,000 inhabitants—half of Glasgow's number today. Glasgow was a minor fishing town; Perth was, till 1452, the capital; Edinburgh had 16,000 souls. The individual, local, and national spirit of independence expressed itself in village and township institutions of self-government within the framework of feudalism and monarchy. The burghers—the enfranchised citizens of the towns—were allowed representatives in the Parliament or Assembly of Estates, but they had to sit, not in their own Commons as in England, but amid the feudal landowners, and their voice and vote were lost in the noble majority. Unable to buttress their power against the nobles by an alliance, as in France, with rich merchants and populous cities, the kings sought support in the affluence and influence of the Church. The nobles, always at odds with the kings, learned to hate the Church and love her property, and joined in the universal cry that national wealth was being siphoned to Rome. In Scotland it was the nobles—not, as in England, the kings and merchants— who made the Reformation, i.e., freed secular from ecclesiastical power.[1]

Through its hold on the piety of the people the Scottish Church achieved opulence amid dulling poverty and transmundane hopes. A papal envoy, toward the end of the fifteenth century, reported to the pope that ecclesiastical income in Scotland equaled all other income combined.[2] The preachers and the burghers almost monopolized literacy. The Scottish clergy were already in the sixteenth century noted for scholarship, and it was the Church, of course, that founded and maintained the universities of St. Andrews and Aberdeen. After 1487 the bishops and abbots were "nominated"—in effect appointed—by the kings, who used these offices as rewards for political services or as sinecures for their illegitimate sons. James V endowed three of his bastards with the ecclesiastical revenues of Kelso, Melrose, Holyrood, and St. Andrews. The worldly tastes of these royal appointees were in a measure responsible for the deterioration of the clergy in the sixteenth century.

But the general laxity of morals and discipline that marked the Church in the later Middle Ages was evident in Scotland long before the royal nomination of the prelacy. "The corruption of the Church, bad everywhere throughout Europe in the fifteenth century," writes the strongly Catholic Hilaire Belloc, "had in Scotland reached a degree hardly known elsewhere";[3] hence, in part, the indifference with which the common people, though orthodox in creed, would look upon the replacement of Catholic with Protestant clergymen. In 1425 King James I complained of monastic dissoluteness and sloth; in 1455 a chaplain at Linlithgow, before receiving his appointment, had to give bond that he would not pawn the property of his church, and would not keep a "continual concubine."[4] Cardinal Beaton had eight bastards, and slept with Marion Ogilvy on the night before he went to meet his Maker;[5] John, Archbishop Hamilton, obtained from divers sessions of the Scottish Parliament letters of legitimation for his increasing brood. The pre-Reformation poets of Scotland spared no words in satirizing the clergy; and the clergy themselves, in the Catholic provincial synod of 1549, ascribed the degradation of the Church in Scotland to "corruption in morals and profane lewdness of life in churchmen of almost all ranks."[6] We should add, however, that the morals of the clergy merely reflected those of the laity—above all, of the nobles and the kings.

II. ROYAL CHRONICLE: 1314–1554

The basic fact in the history of the Scottish state is fear of England. English kings, for England's safety from rear attack, time and again tried to annex Scotland to the English crown. Scotland, to protect itself, accepted alliance with England's perennial enemy, France. Thereby hangs this chronicle.

With bows and arrows and battle-axes the Scots won freedom from England at Bannockburn (1314). Robert Bruce, having there led them to victory, ruled them till his death by leprosy (1329). His son David II, like Scottish kings from time beyond memory, was crowned on the sacred "Stone of Destiny" in the abbey of Scone. When Edward III of England began the Hundred Years' War with France he thought it wise first to secure his northern front; he defeated the Scots at Halidon Hill, and set up Edward Balliol as his puppet on the Scottish throne (1333). David II regained the crown only by paying the English a ransom of 100,000 marks ($6,667,000?). As he left no direct heir at his death (1371), the kingdom passed to his nephew Robert Stuart, with whom the fateful Stuart dynasty began.

The war of Britain's two halves against the whole was soon resumed. The French sent an army to Scotland; Scots and French ravaged the border counties of England, took Durham, and put to death all its inhabitants—men, women, children, nuns, monks, priests. Playing the next move in this royal chess, the English invaded Scotland, burned Perth and Dundee, and destroyed Melrose Abbey (1385). Robert III carried on; but when the English captured his son James (1406) he died of grief. England kept the boy king in genteel imprisonment until the Scots signed the "Perpetual Peace" (1423), renouncing all further co-operation with France.

James I had picked up, in captivity, considerable education, and an English bride. In honor of this "milk-white dove" he composed, in the Scots tongue, *The King's Quair* (i.e., book), an allegorical poem of surprising merit for a king. Indeed James was remarkable in a dozen ways. He was one of the best wrestlers, runners, riders, archers, spearmen, craftsmen, and musicians in Scotland, and he was a competent and beneficent ruler. He imposed penalties upon dishonest commerce and negligent husbandry, built hospitals, required taverns to close at nine, turned the energies of youth from football to martial exercises, and demanded a reform of ecclesiastical discipline and monastic life. When his active reign began (1424) he pledged himself to put down chaos and crime in Scotland, and to end the private wars of the nobles and their feudal despotism; "if God gives me but a dog's life I will make the key keep the castle and the bracken keep the cow"—i.e., end robbery of homes and cattle—"through all Scotland."[7] A Highland thief robbed a woman of two cows; she vowed that she would ne'er wear shoon till she had walked to the King to denounce the weakness of the law. "You lie," said the thief; "I will have you shod"; and he nailed horseshoes to her naked feet. She found her way to the King nevertheless. He had the robber hunted down, had him led about Perth with a canvas picture of the crime, and saw to it that the brute was safely hanged. Meanwhile he quarreled opportunely with obstructive barons, brought a few to the scaffold, confiscated excess holdings, taxed the lords as well as the burgesses, and gave the government the funds it needed to replace many tyrannies with one. He called to the Parliament the lairds—proprietors of the lesser estates—and made them and the middle class an offset to the nobles and the clergy. In 1437 a band of nobles killed him.

The sons of the nobles whom he had cut down in life or property continued against James II their struggle against the centralizing monarchy. While the new king was still a lad of seven his ministers invited the young Earl of Douglas, and a younger brother, to be the King's guests; they came, were given a mock trial, and were beheaded (1440). Twelve years later James II himself invited William, Earl of Douglas, to his court at Stirling, gave him a safe-conduct, entertained him royally, and slew him on the charge that he had had treasonable correspondence with England. The King captured all English strongholds in Scotland but one, and was blown to bits by the accidental explosion of his own cannon. James III paid the penalty of his father's lawlessness; after many ferocious encounters he was captured by nobles and summarily killed (1488). James IV married Margaret Tudor, sister of Henry VIII; through that marriage Mary Queen of Scots would later claim the English throne. Nevertheless, when Henry joined Spain, Austria, Venice, and the papacy in attacking France (1511), James felt bound to help Scotland's old ally, now so imperiled, by invading England. On Flodden Field he fought with mad courage while many of his men turned and fled; and in that disaster he died (1513).

James V was then but a year old. An involved struggle ensued for the regency. David Beaton—an ecclesiastic distinguished by ability, courage, and appreciation of women—secured the prize, was made Archbishop of St. Andrews, then Cardinal, and trained the young King in fervent allegiance to the Church. In 1538 James married Mary of Lorraine, sister of Francis, Duke of Guise, the leader of the Catholic party in dogma-divided France. The Scottish nobility, increasingly anticlerical, looked with interest at the current divorce of England from the papacy, envied English lords appropriating or receiving church property, and took "wages" from Henry VIII to oppose their King's alliance with France. When James V waged war on England the nobles refused to support him. Defeated at Solway Moss (1542), he fled in shame to Falkland, and died there on December 14. On December

8 his wife had given birth to Mary, who, six days old, became Queen of Scots.

Beaton produced a will in which the late King had named him regent for the infant Queen. The nobles questioned the authenticity of the document, imprisoned the Cardinal, and chose as regent James, Earl of Arran; but Arran released Beaton and made him chancellor. When Beaton renewed the alliance with France, Henry VIII resolved on merciless war. To his army in the north he sent orders to burn and destroy everything in its path, "putting nan, woman, and child to fire and sword without exception where any resistance shall be made," and particularly "sparing no creature alive" in Beaton's St. Andrews.[8] The army did its best; "abbey and grange, castle and hamlet, were buried in a common ruin";[9] for two days Edinburgh was sacked and burned; farm villages for seven miles around were pillaged and razed; 10,000 horned cattle, 12,000 sheep, 1,300 horses, were led away to England (1544). Sir James Kirkcaldy, Norman Leslie, and other Scottish gentlemen offered to help the English "burn places belonging to the extreme party in the Church, to arrest and imprison the principal opponents of the English alliance, and to 'apprehend and slay' the Cardinal himself."[10] Henry welcomed the offer, and promised a thousand pounds toward expenses. The plan fell through for a time, but was carried out on May 29, 1546. Two Kirkcaldies, two Leslies, and a numerous band of nobles and cutthroats forced entry into the Cardinal's palace, and slew him almost *in fragrante delicto*, "for," said Knox, "he had been busy at his accounts with Mistress Ogilvy that night."[11] "Now, because the weather was hot," Knox added, "it was thought best, to keep him from stinking, to give him great salt enough, a cope of lead . . . to await what exequies his brethren the bishops could prepare for him. These things we write merrily."[12] The assassins retired to the castle of St. Andrews on the coast, and awaited aid from England by sea.

Arran resumed charge of the government. To assure French help he promised the infant Queen Mary Stuart to the French dauphin; and to prevent her seizure by the English she was clandestinely sent to France (August 13, 1548). The accession of Mary Tudor in England ended for a time the danger of further English invasions; Catholicism now ruled on both sides of the border. French influences prevailed upon Arran to resign the regency (1554) to Mary of Lorraine, mother of the absent Queen. She was a woman of intelligence, patience, and courage, who yielded only to the overwhelming spirit of the age. Dowered with the culture of the French Renaissance, she smiled tolerantly at the rival religious dogmas that raged around her. She ordered the release of several imprisoned Protestants, and allowed such freedom of preaching and worship to "heretics" that many English Protestants, fleeing from Mary Tudor, found refuge, and were allowed to form congregations, under Mary of Lorraine. She was the most humane and civilized ruler that Scotland had known for centuries.

III. JOHN KNOX: 1505–59

The propaganda of reform was already a hundred years old in Scotland. In 1433 Paul Crawar was accused of importing the doctrines of Wyclif and Huss; he was convicted by the Church and burned by the state. In 1494 thirty "Lollards of Kyle" were summoned before the Bishop of Glasgow on charges of repudiating religious relics and images, auricular confession, priestly ordination and powers, transubstantiation, purgatory, indulgerces, Masses for the dead, clerical celibacy, and papal authority; [13] here was almost a summary of the Reformation twenty-three years before Luther's Theses. Apparently the accused men recanted.

Soon after 1523 the writings of Luther entered Scotland. A Scots translation of Wyclif's New Testament circulated in manuscript, and a cry arose for a Christianity based exclusively on the Bible. Patrick Hamilton went to Paris and Louvain, studied Erasmus and Greek philosophy, went on to Wittenberg, returned to Scotland swelling with the new dogmas, preached justification by faith, was invited by James (uncle of David) Beaton, then Archbishop of St. Andrews, to come and explain himself, came, stood his ground, and was burned (1528). Two other "professors," as the early Scottish reformers called themselves, were burned in 1534. Four men were hanged, and one woman was drowned, in 1544; according to the not always reliable Knox, she went to her death with a sucking babe at her breast.[14]

These murders had been too scattered in time and place to arouse any powerful public reaction; but the hanging of George Wishart touched the souls of many, and was the first effective event of the Scottish Reformation. About 1543 Wishart translated the First Helvetic Confession; unfortunately this Protestant declaration ordered secular powers to punish heretics.[15] From that time the Swiss forms of Protestantism—at first humanely Zwinglian, then rigorously Calvinist—more and more displaced Lutheranism in the Scottish movement. Wishart preached in Montrose and Dundee, bravely tended the sick in a plague, and expounded the new faith in Edinburgh at a time when David Beaton was holding a convocation of Scottish clergy there. The Cardinal had him arrested and tried for heresy; he was convicted, strangled, and burned (1546).

Among his converts was one of the most powerful and influential figures in history. John Knox was born between 1505 and 1515 near Haddington. His peasant parents destined him for the priesthood; he studied at Glasgow, was ordained (c. 1532), and became known for his learning in both civil and canon law. His autobiographical *History of the Reformation of Religion within the Realm of Scotland* says nothing of his youth, but suddenly introduces him (1546) as the ardent disciple and fearless bodyguard of George

Wishart, bearing a heavy two-handed sword. After Wishart's arrest Knox wandered from one hiding place to another; then, at Easter of 1547, in the castle of St. Andrews, he joined the band that had killed Cardinal Beaton.

Feeling a need for religion, the hunted men asked Knox to be their preacher. He protested his unfitness, and consented, and they soon agreed that they had never heard such fiery preaching before. He called the Roman Church "the Synagogue of Satan," and identified her with the awful beast described in the Apocalypse. He adopted the Lutheran doctrine that man is saved "only by faith that the blood of Jesus Christ purges us from all sins." [16] In July a French fleet sailed up and bombarded the castle. For four weeks the besieged held out; finally they were overpowered, and for nineteen months Knox and the others labored as galley slaves. We have few details of their treatment, except that they were importuned to hear Mass, and (Knox tells us) stoutly refused. Perhaps those bitter days, and the cut of the overseer's lash, shared in sharpening Knox's spirit to hatred and his tongue and pen to violence.

When the captives were freed (February 1549), Knox took service as a Protestant clergyman in England, on a salary from the Somerset government. He preached every day in the week, "if the wicked carcass would permit." We of today, who do not often enjoy sermons, can but faintly imagine the hunger that the sixteenth century felt for them. The parish priests had left preaching to the bishops, who had left it to the friars, who were occasional. In Protestantism the preachers became journals of news and opinion; they told their congregation the events of the week or day; and religion was then so interwoven with life that nearly every occurrence touched the faith or its ministers. They denounced the vices and errors of their parishioners, and instructed the government as to its duties and faults. In 1551 Knox, preaching before Edward VI and Northumberland, asked how it was that the most pious princes had so often the most ungodly councilors. The Duke tried to silence him with a bishopric, but failed.

Mary Tudor was more dangerous, and after some cautious dallying Knox fled to Dieppe and Geneva (1554). Calvin recommended him to an English-speaking congregation at Frankfurt, but his code and countenance proved too severe for his hearers, and he was asked to leave. He returned to Geneva (1555), and we may judge the force of Calvin's character from the influence that he now exerted upon a personality as positive and powerful as his own. Knox described Geneva under Calvin as "the most perfect school of Christ that ever was on earth since the days of the Apostles." [17] Calvinism suited his temper because that faith was sure of itself, sure of being inspired by God, sure of its divine obligation to compel the individual in conduct and creed, sure of its right to direct the state. All this sank into Knox's spirit, and through him into Scottish history. Anticipating with horror the rule of Catholic Mary Stuart in Scotland, he asked Calvin and Bullinger whether a people might righteously refuse to obey "a magistrate who enforces idolatry and condemns true religion." They would not commit themselves, but John Knox knew his own mind.

In the fall of 1555, now presumably fifty years old, he showed the tender side of a rough character by returning to Mary Tudor's England, going to Berwick, and marrying Margaret Bowes because he loved her mother. Mrs. Elizabeth Bowes had five sons, ten daughters, and a Catholic husband. She was won to Protestantism by Knox's preaching; she confided her domestic troubles to him; he found pleasure in advising her, and comfort in her friendship, and apparently the relationship remained spiritual to the end. When Margaret married Knox, Mrs. Bowes left her husband and went to live with her daughter and her confessor. The wife died after five years of marriage. Knox married again, but Mrs. Bowes remained with him. Rarely in history has a mother-in-law been so loving and so loved.

The strange trio went on to Scotland, where Mary of Lorraine still found tolerance useful in winning the support of the Protestant faction in the nobility. He praised the Regent as "a princess honorable, endowed with wisdom and graces singularly." [18] He organized Protestant congregations in Edinburgh and elsewhere, and made such influential converts as William Maitland, Laird of Lethington, and Mary Stuart's illegitimate brother, James Stuart, destined to be regent as Earl of Murray or Moray. An ecclesiastical court, disliking this development, summoned Knox to give an account of his doings. He chose discretion, and slipped out of Scotland with his wife and her mother (July 1556). In his absence the ecclesiastical court burned him in effigy. This painless martyrdom ennobled him in the eyes of the Scottish Protestants, and from that moment, wherever he was, he was accepted as the leader of the Scottish Reform.

In Geneva, as pastor of an English congregation, he developed the full Calvinist program of ministerial supervision over the morals and manners of his parishioners. At the same time he invited Mrs. Anne Locke, whom he had converted in London, to leave her husband and come with her daughter to live near him in Geneva. He wrote her irresistible letters:

> Dearest sister, if I could express the thirst and languor which I have for your presence, I shall appear to pass measure. Yea, I weep and rejoice in remembrance of you; but that would evanish by the comfort of your presence, which I assure you is so dear to me that if the charge of this little flock here, gathered in Christ's name, did not impede me, my presence should anticipate my letter. . . . Were it not that partly ye be impeded by your head [husband] . . . in my heart I would have wished, yea, and cannot cease to wish, that it would please God to guide you to this place. [19]

Over the opposition of her "head" Mrs. Locke left London and arrived in Geneva (1557) with a son, a daughter, and a maid. The daughter died a few days later, but Mrs. Locke remained near Knox, and helped the aging and now less comforting Mrs. Bowes to minister to the preacher's needs. We have no evidence of sexual relations, and we hear of no complaint from Mrs. Knox; we hardly hear of her at all. The old home-breaker would be mothered, and had his way in Christ's name.

He had his way in almost everything. Like so many great men, he was physically small, but his broad shoulders warned of strength, and his stern visage announced certitude and demanded authority. Black hair, narrow forehead, dense eyebrows, penetrating eyes, intrusive nose, full cheeks, large mouth, thick lips, long beard, long fingers—here were incarnate devotion and will to power. A man of fanatical energy, who liked to preach two or three times a week for two or three hours at a time, and, in addition, governed public affairs and private lives—no wonder that "in twenty-four hours I have not four free to natural rest." [20] His courage was tempered with timely timidity; he had the good sense to flee from imminent death; he was accused of urging Protestants to perilous revolution in England and Scotland while himself remaining at Geneva or Dieppe; yet he faced a hundred dangers, denounced the corrupt Northumberland to his face, and would later proclaim democracy to a queen. No money could buy him. He thought or claimed that his voice was the voice of God. Many accepted his claim, and hailed him as a divine oracle; hence when he spoke, said an English ambassador, "he put more life in us than 500 trumpets blustering in our ears." [21]

The Calvinist creed was one source of his strength. God had divided all men into the elect and the damned; Knox and his supporters were of the elect, and were therefore divinely destined to victory; their opponents were reprobates, and sooner or later hell would be their home. "We are persuaded," he wrote, "that all which our adversaries do is diabolical." [22] For such God-damned opponents no Christian love was due, for they were sons of Satan, not of God; there was no good in them whatever, and it would be well to exterminate them completely from the earth. He rejoiced in that "perfect hatred which the Holy Ghost engendereth in the hearts of God's elect against the contemners of His holy statutes." [23] In conflict with the reprobate all methods were justified—lies, treachery,[24] flexible contradictions of policy.[25] The cause hallowed the means.

Yet Knox's moral philosophy, on its surface, was precisely the opposite of Machiavelli's. He did not admit that statesmen should be freed from the moral code required of citizens; he demanded that governors and governed alike should obey the precepts of the Bible. But the Bible to him meant chiefly the Old Testament; the thundering prophets of Judea were more to his purpose than the man on the cross. He would bend the nation to his will or burn it with flaming prophecies. He claimed prophetic power, and correctly predicted Mary Tudor's early death and Mary Stuart's fall—or were these wishes luckily fulfilled? He was an undeceivable judge of other men's characters, sometimes of his own. "Of nature I am churlish," he handsomely confessed; [26] and he attributed his flight from Scotland to human weakness and "wickedness." [27] There was a rough humor behind his growl, and he could be gentle as well as violent. He gave himself in full-blooded sincerity to his task, which was to set up the sway of a cleansed and learned priesthood over mankind, beginning with the Scots. He argued that a virtuous priesthood would be inspired by God, so that in a society so administered God and Christ would be the king. He believed in a theocracy, but did more for democracy than any other man of his time.

His writings were no literary exercises; they were political thunderclaps. They rivaled Luther's in vigor of vituperation. The Roman Church was to him, as to Luther, a "harlot . . . altogether polluted with all kinds of spiritual fornication." [28] Catholics were "pestilent papists" and "Mass-mongers," [29] and their priests were "bloody wolves." [30] No man of that eloquent age was more eloquent. When Mary Tudor married Philip II, Knox burst out in *A Faithful Admonition to the Professors of God's Truth in England* (1554): Has not Mary shown herself

> to be an open traitress to the Imperial Crown of England . . . to bring
> in a stranger and make a proud Spaniard King, to the shame, dishonor,
> and destruction of the nobility; to the spoil from them and theirs of
> their honors, lands, possessions, chief offices, and promotions; to the
> utter decay of the treasures, commodities, navy, and fortifications of
> the Realm; to the abasing of the yeomanry, to the slavery of the com-
> monalty, to the overthrow of Christianity and God's true religion;
> and finally to the utter subversion of the whole public estate and com-
> monwealth of England? . . . God, for His great mercy's sake, stir up
> some Phinehas, Elijah, or Jehu, that the blood of abominable idolators
> may pacify God's wrath that it consume not the whole multitude! [31]

But now and then, though more rarely, he wrote passages of tenderness and beauty worthy of St. Paul, who inspired them, as in *A Letter . . . to His Brethren in Scotland*:

> I will use no threatenings, for my good hope is that ye shall walk
> as the sons of light in the midst of this wicked generation; that ye
> shall be as stars in the night season, who yet are not changed in the
> darkness; that ye shall be as wheat amongst the cockle . . . that ye shall
> be of the number of the prudent virgins, daily renewing your lamps
> with oil, as they that patiently do abide the glorious apparition and
> coming of the Lord Jesus, whose omnipotent spirit rule and instruct,

illuminate and comfort your hearts and minds in all assaults now and ever.[32]

More characteristic was the *First Blast of the Trumpet against the Monstrous Regiment of Women*, written at Dieppe in 1558 against what seemed to Knox a plague of women rulers in Europe—Mary Tudor, Mary of Lorraine, Mary Stuart, and Catherine de Médicis. We can understand his horror at Mary Tudor's application of his principles. But even if Mary had not persecuted, Knox would have considered her a monster, a political freak, violating the normal rule that men should govern states. He began:

> Wonder it is that amongst so many pregnant wits as the Isle of Great Britain hath produced, so many godly and zealous preachers as England did sometime nourish, and amongst so many learned, and men of grave judgment, as this day by Jezebel [Mary Tudor] are exiled, none is found so stout of courage, so faithful to God . . . that they dare admonish the inhabitants of that Isle how abominable before God is the Empire or Rule of a wicked woman, yea, of a traitorous and bastard; and what may a people or nation left destitute of a lawful head do by authority of God's Word in electing and appointing common rulers and magistrates. . . . We hear the blood of our brethren, the members of Christ Jesus, most cruelly to be shed, and the monstrous empire of a cruel woman . . . we know to be the only occasion of all those miseries. . . .
>
> To promote a woman to bear rule, superiority, dominion, or empire above any realm, nation, or city is repugnant to Nature, contumely to God, a thing most contrarious to His revealed will and approved ordinance; and finally it is the subversion of good order, of all equity and justice. . . . For who can deny but it is repugnant to Nature that the blind shall be appointed to lead and conduct such as do see? That the weak, sick, and impotent persons shall nourish and keep the whole strong? And finally that the foolish, mad, and phrenetic shall govern the discreet, and give counsel to such as be of sober mind? And such be all women, compared unto men in bearing of authority. . . . Woman in her greatest perfection was made to serve and obey man, not to rule and command him.[33]

For this Knox quoted indisputable Scriptural authority; but when he passed to history, and sought for examples of states ruined by women rulers, he was evidently perplexed to find their record much better than that of the kings. Nevertheless he concluded with confident damnation:

> Cursed Jezebel of England, with the pestilent and detestable generation of papists, make no little bragging and boast that they have triumphed not only against Wyatt, but also against all such as have enterprised anything against them. . . . I fear not to say that the day of

vengeance, which shall apprehend that horrible monster Jezebel of England . . . is already appointed in the council of the Eternal. . . . Let all men be advertised, for the Trumpet has once blown.[34]

Knox took the manuscript of his *Blast* to Geneva, had it printed secretly and without his name, and sent copies to England. Mary banned the book as an incitation to rebellion, and made its possession a capital crime.

Knox returned to the attack in *An Appellation to the Nobility and Estates of Scotland* (July 1558):

> None provoking the people to idolatry * ought to be exempted from the punishment of death. . . . The same ought to be done where-soever Christ Jesus and His Evangel is so received . . . that the magistrates and people have solemnly avowed and promised to defend the same; as under King Edward of late days was done in England. In such place, I say, it is not only lawful to punish to the death such as labor to subvert the true religion, but the magistrates and people are bound to do so unless they will provoke the wrath of God against themselves. . . . I fear not to affirm that it had been the duty of the nobility, judges, rulers, and people of England not only to have resisted and againstanded Mary, that Jezebel . . . but also to have punished her to the death.[36]

Knox urged the people of Scotland to apply this doctrine of legitimate rebellion to Mary of Lorraine. He complained that the Regent had surrounded herself with French courtiers and soldiers who were eating the spare substance of the Scots:

> While strangers are brought in to suppress us, our commonwealth, and posterity; while idolatry is maintained, and Christ Jesus His true religion despised, while idle bellies and bloody tyrants, the bishops, are maintained and Christ's true messengers persecuted; while, finally, virtue is contemned and vice extolled . . . what godly man can be offended that we shall seek reformation of these enormities (yes, even by force of arms, seeing that otherwise it is denied us)? . . . The punishment of such crimes as are idolatry, blasphemy, and others that touch the majesty of God, doth not appertain to kings and chief rulers only, but also to the whole body of that people, and to every member of the same, according to that possibility and occasion which God doth minister to revenge the injury done against His glory.[37]

There is a strange mixture of revolution and reaction in Knox's appeals. Many thinkers, including French Huguenots like Hotman and Jesuits like

---

* "By idolatry," Knox wrote in 1560, "we understand the Mass, invocation of saints, adoration of images, and the keeping and retaining of the same, and all honoring of God not contained in His Holy Word." [35]

Mariana, were to agree with him on the occasional justification of tyran-nicide. Yet his conviction that those who were sure of their theology should suppress—if necessary, kill—their opponents harked back to the darkest practices of the Inquisition. Knox took the thirteenth chapter of Deuteron-omy as still in force, and interpreted it literally. Every heretic was to be put to death, and cities predominantly heretical were to be smitten with the sword and utterly destroyed, even to the cattle therein, and every house in them should be burned down. Knox confesses that at times these merciless commandments appalled him:

> To the carnal man this may appear a rigorous and severe judgment, yea, it may rather seem to be pronounced in rage than in wisdom. For what city was ever yet in which . . . were not to be found many innocent persons, as infants, children, and some simple and ignorant souls who neither did nor could consent to . . . impiety? And yet we find no exception, but all are appointed to the cruel death. But in such cases God wills that all creatures stoop, cover their faces, and desist from reasoning when commandment is given to execute His judg-ments.[38]

We must not try Knox by our own frail standards of tolerance; he voiced with hard consistency the almost universal spirit of the time. His years in Geneva, where Servetus had just been burned, confirmed his own tendency toward stern literalism and proud certainty; and if he read Castellio's plea for toleration, he was presumably reassured by Bèze's answer to it. Yet an obscure Anabaptist in those same years penned a criticism of Calvinism, under the title of *Careless by Necessity*; Scottish Protestants sent it to Knox to be confuted, and for a moment the voice of reason whispered amid the war of faiths. The author wondered how the Calvinists, after knowing Christ's conception of a loving Father, could believe that God had created men whose eternal damnation he had foreseen and willed. God, said the Anabaptist, had given men a natural inclination to love their offspring; if man was made in the image of God how could God be more cruel than man? Calvinists, the author continued, did more harm than atheists, for "they are less injurious to God who believe that He is not, than they which say that He is unmerciful, cruel, and an oppressor." Knox replied that there are mysteries beyond human reason. "The pride of those shall be punished who, not content with the will of God revealed, delight to mount and fly above the skies, there to ask the secret will of God." "Nature and reason," he wrote elsewhere, "do lead men from the true God. For what impudence is it to prefer corrupt nature and blind reason to God's Scriptures?"[39]

Unconvinced by reason, and believing himself faithful to the spirit of

Christ, Knox in 1559, when England was under a Protestant queen, sent to its people *A Brief Exhortation* advising them to atone for the Marian persecution by making the Calvinist creed and its moral discipline compulsory throughout the land. England rejected the advice. In that year Knox returned to Scotland to preside over the ideology of its revolution.

IV. THE CONGREGATION OF JESUS CHRIST: 1557–60

His appeals to the Scots to throw off the yoke of Rome had combined with the preaching of other reformers, the influx of Protestants from England, the infiltration of Bibles and pamphlets from England and the Continent, the land-hunger of Scottish nobles, and their irritating displacement by powdered Frenchmen at the court, to raise the temperature of revolt to the bursting point. The populace of Edinburgh, firmly Catholic in 1543, bore most directly and resentfully the influx of supercilious Gauls during the regency of Mary of Lorraine. Everything was done to make life miserable for the intruders. Feeling rose on both sides, and as the clergy supported the French, the spirit of nationalism took on anti-Catholic overtones. Religious processions—in which effigies of the Virgin and the saints were carried and apparently worshiped, and relics were reverently displayed and kissed—aroused increasing ridicule and doubt. In September 1557, a group of enthusiastic skeptics seized the image of St. Giles, in the "Mother Kirk" of that name in Edinburgh, doused it in a pond, and later burned it to ashes. According to Knox similar iconoclastic sallies occurred in all parts of the country.

On December 3, 1557, a "Common Band" of anticlerical nobles—Argyll, Glencairn, Morton, Lorne, and Erskine—met at Edinburgh (which had become the capital in 1542), and signed the "First Scottish Covenant." They called themselves "Lords of the Congregation of Jesus Christ," as opposed to the "Congregation of Satan"—i.e., the Church. They pledged themselves to maintain "the most blessed Word of God," called for a "reformation in religion and government," and demanded from the Regent the liberty to "use ourselves in matters of religion and conscience as we must answer to God." They resolved to establish reformed churches throughout Scotland, and announced that the Book of Common Prayer, prescribed for England under Edward VI, was to be adopted by all their congregations. The Catholic bishops protested against this bold schism, and urged Archbishop Hamilton to suppress it. Reluctantly he ordered the burning (April 28, 1558) of Walter Milne—an aged priest who had unfrocked himself, married, and taken to preaching the Reformed faith among the poor. The people had high respect for the old man; they voiced their horror at this last burning of a Scottish Protestant for heresy, and raised a cairn of stones over the site of his death. When another preacher was summoned to trial his defenders took up arms, forced their way into the Regent's presence, and warned her that they would allow no further persecution of religious belief. The Lords of the Congregation notified the Regent (November 1558) that unless liberty of worship were granted they would not be responsible "if it shall chance that abuses be violently reformed." [40] In that month they sent word to Knox that they would protect him if he returned.

He took his time, but on May 2, 1559, he reached Edinburgh. On May 3 he preached at Perth the sermon that let loose the revolution. It was a sermon, he tells us, "vehement against idolatry"; it explained "what idolatry and what abomination was in the Mass," and "what commandment God had given for the destruction of the monuments thereof." [41] The "rascal multitude," as he describes it, got out of hand. When a priest in a neighboring church tried to celebrate Mass a youth cried out: "This is intolerable, that when God by His Word hath plainly damned idolatry, we shall stand to see it used in despite." The priest, in Knox's account, "gave the child a great blow, who in anger took up a stone, and casting at the priest, did hit the tabernacle and broke down an image; and immediately the whole multitude that were about cast stones, and put hands to the said tabernacle, and to all other monuments of idolatry." [42] The crowd poured into three monasteries, pillaged them, smashed the images, but allowed the friars to carry away whatever their shoulders could bear. "Within two days these three great places . . . were so destroyed that the walls only did remain." [43]

The Regent was between fires. Her brother, the Cardinal of Lorraine, advised her to imitate Mary Tudor and cut down the leading Protestants; while in and around Perth the victorious rebels were threatening to kill any priest who dared to say Mass. [44] And on May 22 the Lords of the Congregation, now backed by their armed retainers, sent her an ominous ultimatum:

> To the Queen's Grace Regent, all humble duty and obedience premised: As heretofore, with jeopardy of our lives, and yet with willing hearts, we have served the authority of Scotland and your Grace . . . so now with most dolorous minds we are constrained, by unjust tyranny proposed against us, to declare unto your Grace, that except this cruelty be stayed by your wisdom, we will be compelled to take the sword of just defense against all that shall pursue us for the matter of religion. . . . This cruel, unjust, and most tyrannical murder intended against towns and multitudes was, and is, the only cause of our revolt against our accustomed obedience, which, in God's presence, we faithfully promise to our Sovereign Mistress [Mary Queen of Scots], to her husband, and unto your Grace Regent; provided that our consciences may live in that peace and liberty which Christ

Jesus hath purchased unto us by His blood. . . . Your Grace's obedient subjects in all things not repugnant to God.—*The Faithful Congregation of Jesus Christ in Scotland.*[45]

At the same time the Congregation dispatched an appeal to the nobles to support the revolt; and another public letter warned "the generation of Antichrist, the pestilent prelates and their shavelings . . . that if ye proceed in this your malicious cruelty ye shall be treated, wheresoever ye shall be apprehended, as murderers and open enemies of God. . . . Contract of peace shall never be made until ye desist from your open idolatry and cruel persecution of God's children." [46]

Regent Mary entered Perth with what troops she could muster. But the friends of the Congregation gathered in armed array, and Mary, perceiving that she could not overcome them, signed a truce (May 29, 1559). Knox retired to St. Andrews, and, over archiepiscopal prohibitions, preached in the parish church against idolatry (June 11–14). Moved by his fervor, his hearers removed "all monuments of idolatry" from the churches of the city, and burned these images before the eyes of the Catholic clergy.[47] The archbishop fled to Perth; but the forces of the Congregation, claiming that Mary had violated the truce by using French funds to pay her Scottish troops, attacked and captured that citadel (June 25). On the twenty-eighth they sacked and burned the abbey of Scone. If we may believe the sometimes imaginative Knox, a "poor aged matron," watching the conflagration, said: "Now I see and understand that God's judgments are just. Since my remembrance this place hath been nothing else but a den of whoremongers. It is incredible . . . how many wives have been adulterated, and virgins deflowered, by the filthy beasts that have been fostered in this den, but especially by that wicked man . . . the bishop." [48]

Mary of Lorraine, now so seriously ill that she momentarily expected death, fled to Leith, and tried to delay the victorious Protestants with negotiations until aid might come from France. The Congregation outplayed her by winning support from Elizabeth of England. Knox wrote the Queen a letter assuring her that she had not been included in his trumpet blast against female sovereigns. William Cecil, Elizabeth's first minister, advised her to help the Scottish revolution as a move toward bringing Scotland into political dependence upon England; this, he felt, was a legitimate protection against Mary Stuart, who, on becoming Queen of France (1559), had claimed also the throne of England on the ground that Elizabeth was a bastard usurper. Soon an English fleet in the Firth of Forth blocked any landing of French aid for the Regent, and an English army joined the Congregation's forces in attacking Leith. Mary of Lorraine retired to the castle of Edinburgh, and—having kissed her retinue one by one—died (June 10,

1560). She was a good woman cast for the wrong part in an inescapable tragedy.

Her last defenders, blockaded and starving, surrendered. On July 6, 1560, the representatives of the Congregation, of Mary Stuart, France, and England, signed the Treaty of Edinburgh, whose articles were to enter deeply into the later conflict between Mary and Elizabeth. All foreign troops except 120 French were to leave Scotland; Mary Stuart and Francis II relinquished claim to the English crown; Mary was acknowledged Queen of Scotland, but she was never to make war or peace without the consent of the Estates; these were to name five of the twelve men in her privy council; no foreigner or clergyman was to hold high office; and a general amnesty was to be declared, with exceptions to be specified by the Estates. It was a humiliating peace for the absent Queen, and a remarkable and almost bloodless triumph for the Congregation.

The Parliament that met on August 1, 1560, accepted, with only eight dissenting votes, a Confession of Faith drawn up by Knox and his aides and softened in some clauses by Maitland of Lethington. As still the official creed of the Presbyterian Church of Scotland, some major articles should be commemorated:

I. We confess and acknowledge one only God . . . in three persons.

II. We confess and acknowledge this our God to have created man (to wit, our first father Adam), of whom also God formed the woman in His own image . . . so that in the whole nature of man could be noted no imperfection. From which honor and perfection man and woman did both fall, the woman being deceived by the serpent, and man obeying to the voice of the woman. . . .

III. By which transgression, commonly called Original Sin, was the image of God utterly defiled in man; and he and his posterity of nature became enemies to God, slaves to Satan, and servants to sin; in samekill that death everlasting has had, and shall have, power and dominion over all that has not been, are not, or shall not be regenerate from above; which regeneration is wrought by the Holy Ghost, working in the hearts of the elect of God an assured faith in the promise of God . . . by which faith they apprehend Christ Jesus. . . .

VIII. That same eternal God and Father . . . of mere mercy elected us in Christ Jesus . . . before the foundation of the world. . . .

XVI. We most earnestly believe that from the beginning there has been, now is, and to the end of the world shall be, a Church, that is to say, a company and multitude of men chosen by God, who rightly worship and embrace Him by true faith in Christ Jesus . . . out of which Church there is neither life nor eternal felicity. And therefore we utterly abhor the blasphemy of those that affirm that men which live accordingly to equity and justice shall be saved, what religion soever they have professed. . . .

XXI. . . . We acknowledge . . . two chief sacraments only . . . Baptism and the Supper. . . . Not that we imagine any transubstantiation of bread into God's natural body . . . but, by the operation of the Holy Ghost . . . we believe that the Faithful, in the right use of the Lord's Table, so do eat the body, and drink the blood, of the Lord Jesus. . . .

XXIV. We confess and acknowledge empires, kingdoms, dominions, and cities to be . . . ordained by God. . . . To kings, princes, and magistrates . . . chiefly and most principally the conservation and purgation of the Religion appertains; so that not only are they appointed for civil policy, but also for maintenance of the true Religion, and for suppressing of idolatry and superstition whatsoever. . . .[49]

Pursuant to this Confession the Scottish Reformation Parliament repudiated the jurisdiction of the pope, made the Reformed creed and ritual compulsory, and forbade celebration of the Mass on pain of corporal punishment and confiscation of goods for the first offense, exile for the second, death for the third. But as the nobles who controlled the Parliament wanted land rather than blood, and did not take the Calvinist theology literally, the persecution of those Scots who still remained Catholic was kept comparatively mild, and never came to corporal punishment. Now that the nobles were allowed to reject purgatory as a myth, they claimed to have been cheated in some part of their patrimony by ancestral donations of land or money to pay priests to say Masses for the dead, who, on the new theology, were irrevocably saved or damned before the creation of the world. So the appropriation of ecclesiastical property could be pleasantly phrased as the restoration of stolen goods. Most of the Scottish monasteries were closed, and their wealth was taken by the nobles. At first no provision was made by the government for the Calvinist ministers; these had been used as ideological aides in the revolution, but the nobles had now lost interest in theology. Knox and his fellow preachers, who had risked and sacrificed so much for the new order, had expected the property of the Church to be applied to the support of the Kirk and its clergy. They petitioned Parliament for such an arrangement; they received no reply, but were finally allotted a sixth of the spoils. Finding this inadequate, they turned against the grasping aristocracy, and began the historic alliance of Scottish Presbyterianism with democracy.

Of all the Reformations, the Scottish shed the least blood, and was the most permanent. The Catholics suffered silently; their bishops fled; mos parish priests accepted the change as no worse than episcopal exactions and visitations. Rural districts lost their wayside crosses, ancient shrines of pilgrimage were deserted, the saints no longer provided easeful holydays.

Many spirits must have mourned and idealized the past, many must have waited hopefully for the coming of their young queen from France. Much had been lost that had been gay and beautiful, much that had been brutal and merciless and insincere; much was to come that would be hard and dour. But the change had to be. When the recriminations died down, and men adjusted themselves to the new order, it would be a boon that some likeness of faith joined with converging lines of royalty to end the bitter wars between Scots and Englishmen. Soon the weaker nation would give the stronger land a king, and Britain would be one.

CHAPTER XXVIII

The Migrations of Reform

1517-60

I. THE SCANDINAVIAN SCENE: 1470–1523

THE piety of the people had by 1500 made the Church the economic master of Scandinavia. In Denmark half the soil was owned by the Church, and was tilled by tenants verging on serfdom.[1] Copenhagen itself was an ecclesiastical fief. Clergy and nobility were exempt from land taxes: the nobles because they served at their own expense in war, the clergy because they organized worship, morals, education, and charity. The universities at Copenhagen and Uppsala were of course in ecclesiastical hands. The Church required a tenth, annually, of all nonecclesiastical produce or income; it exacted a small fee for every building raised, every child born, every couple married, every corpse interred; it claimed a day of gratis labor from every peasant yearly; and no one could inherit property without making a contribution to the Church as the probate court of wills.[2] These imposts were defended as financing the ministrations of the Church, but complaints rose that too much of the proceeds went to maintain bishops in regal splendor. The merchants of Denmark, harassed by Hanseatic dominance in the North and Baltic seas, chafed at the additional competition of nobles and clergy who directly exported, often in their own ships, the surplus product of their estates. In Scandinavia, as elsewhere, nobles hankered after ecclesiastical lands. And there, as elsewhere, nationalism conflicted with the supernational Church.

In all three countries the Church supported the Scandinavian Union of Calmar, which Christian I of Denmark had renewed (1457). But in Sweden a National party of burghers and peasants rejected the Union as in effect a Danish supremacy, and proclaimed Sten Sture the Younger regent of an independent nation (1512). Archbishop Gustav Trolle of Uppsala—then the capital of Sweden—defended the Union; Sten Sture the Younger deposed him; Pope Leo X ordered him reinstated; Sture refused; Leo interdicted religious services in Sweden, and commissioned Christian II of Denmark to invade Sweden and punish the Regent. Christian's first attempt failed; he had to sign a truce; but he carried back with him to Copenhagen (January 18, 1520) several hostages as pledges for Swedish adherence to the truce; one of these hostages was Gustavus Vasa. In a second expedition Christian won a decisive victory, and Sture died of wounds received in battle. His widow improvised an army, which held Stockholm for five months against Danish siege; finally she surrendered on the promise, by Christian's general, of a general amnesty. On November 4 Christian was crowned King of Sweden by the restored and triumphant Trolle.

On November 7 the leading Swedes who had supported Sture were summoned to the presence of the King in the citadel of Stockholm. A representative of Trolle accused them of major crimes in having deposed the Archbishop and having destroyed his castle, and he called upon the King to revenge these wrongs. Despite the amnesty seventy leading Swedes were condemned to death. On November 8 they were beheaded in the Grand Square; on November 9 several others were arrested and executed; some spectators who expressed sympathy were added to the slaughter; and the property of the dead was confiscated to the King. All Sweden cried out with horror. The Union of Calmar, men said, was drowned in this "Stockholm Bath of Blood," and the Church suffered severely in public esteem for having initiated the massacre. Christian had thought to make his rule secure by destroying the brains of the National party. In reality he had cleared a way to the throne for the young hostage who was to make Sweden free.

His name was Gustavus Eriksson, but posterity called him also Vasa, from the bundle (Swedish *vasa*, Latin *fascis*) of sticks that appeared in his family's coat of arms. At thirteen he was sent to study at Uppsala; at twenty he was called to the court of Sture the Younger, who had married a half-sister of Gustavus's mother; and there he received further instruction from the prime minister, Bishop Hemming Gad. In 1519 he escaped from surveillance in Denmark, made his way to Lübeck, persuaded its senate (always hostile to Denmark) to lend him money and a ship, and regained his native shores (May 31, 1520). For months he wandered in disguise, or hid in obscure villages. In November news reached him that nearly a hundred Swedish patriots, including his father, had been slaughtered in Stockholm. He mounted the swiftest horse he could find, and rode north to his own province of Dalecarlia, resolved to organize there, from the hardy yeomanry, the beginnings of an army that might free Sweden from the Danes.

His life was now an epic worthy of Homeric song. Traveling icy roads, he sought rest at the home of a former schoolmate. This friend gave him every hospitality, and then went off to notify the pro-Danish police that the escaped hostage could now be caught; but the wife warned Gustavus to flee. Riding onward twenty miles, he found asylum with a priest, who hid him for a week. Moving thirty miles farther, he tried to rouse the town of Rättvik to revolt; but its people had not yet heard, and would not believe, the story of the Bath of Blood. Vasa rode over frozen meadows twenty-five miles north to Mora, and again pleaded for a revolutionary uprising, but the peasants listened in skeptical apathy. Friendless and for a moment hopeless, Gustavus turned his horse to the west, resigned to seeking asylum in Norway. Before he reached the frontier a messenger from Mora overtook him, and begged him to come back, pledging that now he would be heard with a spirit as hot as his own. The peasants had at last heard of the horror in Stockholm; moreover, it was rumored that the King was planning to journey through Sweden, and had ordered gallows to be set up in every major town. New taxes were to be imposed upon a people already struggling for life against the greed of masters and the tyranny of the elements. When Gustavus spoke again to the citizens of Mora they gave him a bodyguard of sixteen highlanders, and vowed to arm themselves, discipline themselves, and follow wherever he led them against the Danes.

They knew no weapons yet but bows and arrows and axes. Vasa taught them to make javelins and pikes with iron heads. He trained them with all the ardor of a youth inspired by love of country and power. So inspired, they captured Vesteres, then Uppsala; once more Archbishop Trolle fled. Patiently, resolutely, the growing army won province after province from the Danish garrisons. Christian II could not come to lead his forces in person, for in his own country he was confronted by civil strife, but his navy repeatedly raided Swedish shores. Gustavus dispatched emissaries to Lübeck to ask for ships of war. For a large promised sum the merchant city equipped ten vessels, which diverted the energies of the Danish fleet. On June 7, 1523, the victorious revolutionaries, in a new Riksraad, named their leader King Gustavus I; on June 20 Stockholm surrendered to him, and thereafter Vasa made it his capital. Meanwhile Christian II had been deposed in Denmark, and Frederick I, his successor, renounced all Danish claims to sovereignty over Sweden. The Union of Calmar (1397-1523) came to an end; the Vasa dynasty began.

II. THE SWEDISH REFORMATION

Gustavus was still a youth of twenty-seven. He was not as tall as we expect men of the north to be, but he had a Viking's vigor of body, his round face was ruddy with health, and his long yellow beard gave him a dignity befitting his royalty rather than his age. His morals were excellent for a king, and even the Church that he was soon to reject could not impugn his piety. He devoted himself to the tasks of government with an impatient energy that sometimes slipped into violence or tyranny, but the condition of Sweden at his accession almost justified his temper and autocracy. In the chaos of war thousands of peasants had left their farms unsown, miners had abandoned their pits, the cities were devastated with conflict, the currency was debased, the national treasury was bankrupt, the executive brains of the country had been spilled out in the "Bath." The surviving feudal barons considered Gustavus an upstart, and looked down their noses at his assumption of power. Conspiracies were formed to depose him; he put them down with a strong arm. Finland, which had been part of Sweden, was still in Danish hands, and Sören Norby, the Danish admiral, held the strategic island of Gotland. Lübeck clamored for the repayment of its loans.

The first need of a government is money paid, or promised, to the armed forces that protect it, then to the officials that administer it. But in Vasa's Sweden taxes cost almost as much to collect as they brought in, for those who alone could pay them were strong enough to resist. Gustavus stooped to the desperate expediency of again debasing the coinage, but the bad coins soon fell to their actual value, and the state's finances were worse than before. Only one group in Sweden was still rich—the clergy. Gustavus turned to them for aid, thinking it just that the wealth of the Church should alleviate the poverty of the people and the government. In 1523 he wrote to Bishop Hans Brask of Linköping for a donation of 5,000 guilders to the state. The Bishop protested and yielded. To the churches and monasteries of Sweden Vasa sent an urgent request that all money and precious metal not indispensable to the continuance of their services should be remitted to the government as a loan; and he published a list of the amounts he expected from each source. The response was not what he had hoped for, and he began to wonder whether it would not be wise to do as the Lutheran princes of Germany were doing—confiscate the wealth of the Church to the needs of the state. He had not forgotten that most of the higher clergy had opposed the revolution, and had buttressed the rule of Christian II in Sweden.

In 1519 Olaus Petri, son of a Swedish ironmaster, returned from several years of study in Wittenberg. As deacon of the cathedral school at Strängnärs he permitted himself some heresies—that purgatory was a myth, that prayers should be addressed, and confession should be made, only to God, and that the preaching of the Gospel was better than the ritual of the Mass. The writings of Luther began to circulate in Sweden. Brask importuned Vasa to forbid their sale; the King replied that "Luther's teachings have not been found by impartial judges to be false."[3] Perhaps he thought it politic to keep a heretic in reserve as a bargaining point with the Church.

Matters grew livelier when Pope Adrian VI refused to confirm his own legate, Johannes Magnus, as Archbishop of Uppsala, and proposed to restore Gustav Trolle, enemy of the revolution. Vasa sent to the Curia a letter that would then (1523) have shocked, and would later have delighted, Henry VIII:

> If our Most Holy Father has any care for the peace of our country, we shall be pleased to have him confirm the election of his legate . . .

and we shall comply with the Pope's wishes as to a reformation of the Church and religion. But if His Holiness, against our honor and the peace of our subjects, sides with the crime-stained partisans of Archbishop Trolle, we shall allow his legate to return to Rome, and shall govern the Church in this country with the authority which we have as king.

Adrian's death, and the absorption of Clement VII with Luther, Charles V, and Francis I left Vasa free to advance the Swedish Reformation. He appointed Olaus Petri to the church of St. Nicholas at Stockholm; he made Olaus's brother Laurentius professor of theology at Uppsala, and raised a third reformer, Laurentius Andreae, to be archdeacon of the cathedral. In the chapter house of the cathedral, under the presidency of the King, Olaus Petri defended Lutheranism in debate with Peter Galle (December 27, 1524). Vasa judged Olaus victor, and was not disturbed when Olaus, four months before Luther's marriage, took a wife (1525). Bishop Brask, however, was shocked by this violation of clerical celibacy, and demanded that the King should place Petri under the ban. Gustavus replied that Olaus should be punished if he had done wrong, but "it would seem surprising if that should be the effect of marriage (a ceremony not forbidden by God), and yet for debauchery, and other sins that are forbidden, one should not fall under the ban." [4] Instead of outlawing Petri he commissioned him and his brother to translate the Bible into Swedish. As in many other countries the vernacular version helped to form the national language, and to transform the national religion.

Gustavus, like most rulers, considered any measure moral that strengthened his country or his throne. He saw to it that bishops pliable to his plans should be promoted to Swedish sees. He found irresistible reasons for appropriating, *gradatim*, monastic lands; and as he shared the spoils with the nobles, he explained that he was merely returning to laymen what their ancestors had been wheedled into giving to the Church. Pope Clement VII complained that Swedish priests married, gave communion in bread and wine, neglected the sacrament of extreme unction, and altered the ritual of the Mass; and he appealed to the King to remain faithful to the Church. But Gustavus had gone too far to come back; orthodoxy would have ruined his treasury. At the Diet of Vesteres (1527) he openly declared for the Reformation.

It was an historic meeting in both its constitution and its results. Four bishops, four canons, fifteen members of the Riksraad, 129 nobles, thirty-two burgesses, fourteen deputies of the miners, 104 representatives of the peasantry—this was one of the broadest-based national assemblies of the sixteenth century. The King's chancellor laid a revolutionary proposal before the Diet: the state, he said, was so impoverished that it could not function for the good of the people; the Swedish Church was so rich that it could transfer much of its wealth to the government and yet have enough left to fulfill all its tasks. Bishop Brask, fighting to the last for his own ideals and realty, declared that the Pope had commanded the clergy to defend their property. The Diet voted in favor of obeying the Pope. Gustavus, staking everything on one throw, announced that if this was the sentiment of the Diet and the nation he would resign and leave Sweden. For three days the assembly debated. The burghers and the deputies of the peasants came over to the side of the King; the nobles had good cause for moving in the same direction; finally the Diet, convinced that Vasa was more valuable to Sweden than any pope, agreed to the royal wishes. In the Recess or conclusions of Vesterås the monasteries were made fiefs of the King, though the monks were allowed to use them; all property granted by nobles to the Church since 1454 was to be returned to the donors' heirs; the bishops were to surrender their castles to the Crown; no bishop was to seek papal confirmation; the clergy were to yield to the state all income not needed for their services; auricular confession was ended, and all sermons were to be based exclusively on the Bible. In Sweden, even more decisively than elsewhere, the Reformation was the nationalization of religion, the triumph of the state over the Church.

Vasa survived this crisis for thirty-three years, and remained to the end a forceful but beneficent autocrat. He was convinced that only a centralized authority could reorganize Sweden into order and prosperity, that in so complex a task he could not stop at every step to consult a deliberative assembly. Under his encouragement and regulation the mines of the north poured their iron into the sinews of Sweden; industry expanded; commercial treaties with England, France, Denmark, and Russia found markets for Swedish goods, brought into Sweden the products of a dozen lands, and gave new refinement and confidence to a civilization that before him had been arrested in rural and illiterate simplicity. Sweden flourished now as never before.

Gustavus engaged in several wars, suppressed four rebellions, and took in succession three wives. The first bore him the future Eric XIV; the second gave him five sons and five daughters; the third, who was sixteen when he, fifty-six, married her, outlived him by sixty years. He induced the Rigsraad to accept his sons as heirs to the throne, and to establish hereditary succession in the male line as a rule for Swedish royalty. Sweden forgave his dictatorship, because it understood that order is the parent, not the child, of liberty. When he died (September 29, 1560), after a reign of thirty-seven years, he was buried in Uppsala Cathedral with fond and lavish ceremony. He had not given his people the personal freedom for which they seem so peculiarly fitted, but he had given them collective freedom from foreign domination in religion or government; and he had created the conditions under which his nation could mature in economy, literature, and art. He was the father of modern Sweden.

III. THE DANISH REFORMATION

Christian II of Denmark (r. 1513–23) was as colorful a character as the Gustavus Vasa who defeated him in Sweden. Forced by the barons to sign humiliating "capitulations" as the price of his election, he surrounded himself with middle-class advisers, ignored the Rigsraad of highborn magnates, and took as his chief counselor the mother of his beautiful Dutch mistress. This privy council must have had some ability and spirit, for Christian's domestic policy was as constructive as his foreign adventures were futile. He labored assiduously in administration, reformed the government of the cities, revised the laws, put down piracy, improved the roads, began a public postal system, abolished the worst evils of serfdom, ended the death penalty for witchcraft, organized poor relief, opened schools for the poor, made education compulsory, and developed the University of Copenhagen into a light and haven of learning. He incurred the enmity of Lübeck by restricting the power of the Hanse; he encouraged and protected Danish trade; and he put an end to the barbarous custom by which maritime villagers had been privileged to plunder all ships wrecked on their shores.

In 1517 Leo X sent Giovanni Arcimboldo to Denmark to offer indulgences. Paul Helgesen, a Carmelite monk, denounced what seemed to him the sale of these indulgences; and in this he anticipated Luther's Theses.[5] Legate and King quarreled over the division of the proceeds; Arcimboldo decamped to Lübeck with a part, Christian confiscated the rest. Finding excellent reasons for Protestantism in the real abuses and available wealth of the Church, Christian brought Helgesen to a post in the University of Copenhagen, where, for a time, this eloquent Danish Erasmus led the movement for reform. When Helgesen turned cautious, Christian asked Elector Frederick the Wise of Saxony to send him Luther himself, or·at least some theologian of Luther's school. Carlstadt came, but did not stay long. Christian issued some reform legislation: no one was to be ordained without having studied sufficiently to expound the Gospel in Danish; the clergy could not legally own property or receive bequests unless they married; bishops were bidden to moderate their luxury; ecclesiastical courts lost jurisdiction where property was involved; and a supreme court appointed by the King was to have final authority over ecclesiastical as well as civil affairs. However, when the Diet of Worms placed Luther under the Imperial ban Christian suspended his reforms, and Helgesen advised reconciliation with the Church.

While these domestic policies were exciting his people, Christian lost the reins by his failures in foreign affairs. His cruelty in Sweden turned many Danes against him. Lübeck declared war on him for his attacks upon Hanseatic shipping. Nobles and clergy, alienated by high taxation and hostile legislation, ignored his summons to a national assembly, and proclaimed his uncle, Duke Frederick of Schleswig-Holstein, as the new king of Denmark. Christian fled to Flanders with his queen, the Protestant sister of Charles V; he made his peace with the Church, hoping to get a kingdom for a Mass; he was captured in a futile attempt to regain his throne, and for twenty-seven years he lived in the dungeons of Sönderborg with no companion but a half-wit Norwegian dwarf. The paths of glory led him with leisurely ignominy to the grave (1559).

Frederick I found no happiness under his challenged crown. Nobles and clergy had accepted him on many conditions, one of which was that he would never allow a heretic to preach in Denmark. Helgesen, while continuing to criticize the shortcomings of the Church, now turned most of his passionate polemics against the Protestants, urging that gradual reform was better than turbulent revolution. But he could not stem the tide. Frederick's son, Duke Christian, was already a Lutheran, and the King's daughter, with his consent, had married Albrecht of Brandenburg, the Lutheran ex-head of the Teutonic Knights. In 1526 Frederick veered with the wind, and appointed as his chaplain Hans Tausen, who had studied under Luther. Tausen left his monastery, married, and openly advocated Lutheran ideas. Frederick found it convenient to order that episcopal confirmation fees should be paid to him, not to the pope. Lutheran preachers took courage and multiplied; the bishops asked for their expulsion; Frederick answered that he had no lordship over men's souls, and was resolved to leave faith free—a most unusual proceeding. In 1524 a Danish translation of the New Testament appeared; in 1529 a much better version was published by Christian Pedersen, which immensely advanced the Protestant development. The people, eager to end tithe payments to the clergy, readily accepted the new theology; by 1530 the Lutherans dominated Copenhagen and Viborg. In that year, at the Diet of Copenhagen, a public debate was held between Catholic and Protestant leaders; both King and people gave the victory to the Protestants; and the Confession of Faith presented there by Hans Tausen remained for a decade the official creed of the Danish Lutherans.

Frederick's death (1533) ushered in the final act of the Danish Reformation. The merchant princes of Denmark joined with their old enemies in Lübeck in an attempt to restore Christian II; Count Christopher of Oldenburg led the Lübeck forces and gave his name to the "Count's War"; Copenhagen fell to him, and Lübeck dreamed of ruling all Denmark. But the burghers and peasants rallied to the standard of Frederick's son Christian; their army defeated Oldenburg, and captured Copenhagen after a year's siege (July 1536). All bishops were arrested, and were released only on promising to abide by the Protestant regime. The national assembly, in October 1536, formally established the Lutheran State Church, with Christian III as its supreme head. All episcopal and monastic properties were confiscated to the King, and the bishops lost all voice in the government. Norway and Iceland accepted Christian III and his legislation, and the triumph of Lutheranism in Scandinavia was complete (1554).

IV. PROTESTANTISM IN EASTERN EUROPE

Poland had her Golden Age under Sigismund I (1506–48) and his son Sigismund II (1548–72). Both were men of culture and spirit, discerning patrons of literature and art, and both gave to religious thought and worship a freedom which, though imperfect, made most other nations of Europe seem medieval by comparison. Sigismund I married the gay and talented Bona Sforza (1518), daughter of Duke Giangaleazzo of Milan; she brought to Cracow a retinue of Italian courtiers and scholars, and the King, instead of resenting them, welcomed them as a bridge to the Renaissance. A taste for luxury in ornate dress and rich furnishings took hold of the aristocracy, language and manners became more refined, letters and arts flourished, and Erasmus wrote (1523): "I congratulate this nation . . . which now, in sciences, jurisprudence, morals, and religion, and in all that separates us from barbarism, is so flourishing that it can rival the first and most glorious of nations." [6] Dominating her husband by her beauty, grace, and craft, Bona became queen in fact as well as in fashion. Her son Sigismund II was a humanist, linguist, orator, and transvestite.[7] Wars marred these brilliant reigns, for Poland was involved with Sweden, Denmark, and Russia in a contest for control of the Baltic Sea and its ports. Poland lost Prussia, but she absorbed Mazovia, including Warsaw (1529), and Livonia, including Riga (1561). Poland was in this age a major European state.

Meanwhile the Reformation filtered in from Germany and Switzerland. The freedom of worship guaranteed by the Polish Crown to its Greek Catholic subjects had habituated the nation to religious tolerance, and the century-long rebellion of Hussites and Utraquists in neighboring Bohemia had made Poland somewhat careless of distant papal authority. The bishops, nominated by the Kings, were cultured patriots, favoring Church reform with Erasmian caution, and generously supporting the humanist movement. This, however, did not allay the envy with which nobles and townsmen looked upon their property and revenues. Complaints grew of national wealth being drained off to Rome, of indulgences expensively absurd, of ecclesiastical simony, of costly litigation in episcopal courts. The szlachta, or lesser nobility, took particular offense at the exemption of the clergy from taxation, and the clerical collection of tithes from the nobles themselves. Probably for economic reasons some influential barons listened with sympathy to Lutheran criticism of the Church; and the semi-sovereignty of the individual feudal lords provided protection to local Protestant movements, much as the independence of the German princes made possible the revolt and shielding of Luther. In Danzig a monk championed Luther's Theses, called for ecclesiastical reforms, and married an heiress (1518); another preacher followed the Lutheran vein so effectively that several congregations removed all religious images from their churches (1522); the city council released monks and nuns from their vows, and closed the monasteries (1525); by 1540 all Danzig pulpits were in Protestant hands. When some clergymen in Polish-Prussian Braunsberg introduced the Lutheran ritual, and the cathedral canons complained to their bishop, he replied that Luther based his views on the Bible, and that whoever felt able to refute them might undertake the task (1520).[8] Sigismund I was prevailed upon to censor the press and forbid the importation of Lutheran literature; but his own secretary and Bona's Franciscan confessor were secretly won to the forbidden creed; and in 1539 Calvin dedicated his *Commentary on the Mass* to the Crown Prince.

When the Prince became Sigismund II both Lutheranism and Calvinism advanced rapidly. The Bible was translated into Polish, and the vernacular began to replace Latin in religious services. Prominent priests like Jan Laski announced their conversion to Protestantism. In 1548 the Bohemian Brethren, exiled from their own country, moved into Poland, and soon there were thirty conventicles of their sect in the land. The attempt of the Catholic clergy to indict some members of the *szlachta* for heresy, and to confiscate their property, led many minor nobles to rebel against the Church (1552). The national Diet of 1555 voted religious freedom for all faiths based on "the pure Word of God," and legalized clerical marriage and communion in bread and wine. The Reform in Poland was now at its crest.

The situation was complicated by the development, in Poland, of the strongest Unitarian movement in sixteenth-century Europe. As early as 1546 the anti-trinitarian tentatives of Servetus were discussed in this Far East of Latin Christianity. Laelius Socinus visited Poland in 1551, and left a ferment of radical ideas; Giorgio Blandrata continued the campaign; and in 1561 the new group issued its confession of faith. Continuing the confusion of Servetus's theology, they restricted full divinity to God the Father, but professed belief in the supernatural birth of Christ, His divine inspiration, miracles, resurrection, and ascension. They rejected the ideas of original sin and Christ's atonement; they admitted baptism and communion as symbols only; and they taught that salvation depended above all upon a conscientious practice of Christ's teachings. When the Calvinist synod of Cracow (1563) condemned these doctrines, the Unitarians formed their own separate church. The full flourishing of the sect came only with Laelius's nephew Faustus Socinus, who reached Poland in 1579.

The Catholic Church fought these developments with persecution, literature, and diplomacy. In 1539 the bishop of Cracow sent to the stake an eighty-year-old woman on the charge that she refused to worship the consecrated Host.[9] Stanislaus Hosius, Bishop of Kulm in Prussia, later Cardinal, carried on the counteroffensive with ability and zeal. He labored for ecclesiastical reform, but had no sympathy with Protestant theology or ritual. At his suggestion Lodovico Lippomano, Bishop of Verona, was sent to Poland as papal legate, and Giovanni Commendone, Bishop of Zante, was made papal nuncio at Cracow. They won Sigismund II to active support of the Church by stressing the divisions among the Protestants, and magnifying the difficulty of organizing the moral life of the nation on such inimical and fluctuating creeds. In 1564 Hosius and Commendone brought the Jesuits into Poland. These trained and devoted men secured strategic places in the educational system, caught the ear of pivotal personalities, and turned the Polish people back to the traditional faith.

The Bohemians had been Protestants before Luther, and found little to terrify them in his ideas. A large German element on the border readily accepted the Reform; the Bohemian Brethren, numbering some 10 per cent of the 400,000 population, were more Protestant than Luther; 60 per cent were Utraquists—Catholics who took the Eucharist in wine as well as bread, and ignored the protests of the popes.[10] By 1560 Bohemia was two thirds Protestant; but in 1561 Ferdinand introduced the Jesuits, and the tide turned back to the orthodox Catholic creed.

The Reformation came to Hungary through German immigrants bearing the news of Luther—that one could defy the Church and the Empire and yet live. Hungarian peasants oppressed by a Church-supported feudalism viewed with some favor a Protestantism that might end ecclesiastical tithes and dues; feudal barons looked with grasping eyes upon vast Church properties whose products competed with their own; town laborers, infected with Utopia, saw in the Church the chief obstacle to their dream, and indulged in image-breaking ecstasies. The Church co-operated by persuading the government to make Protestantism a capital crime. In western Hungary King Ferdinand labored for a compromise, and wished to allow clerical marriage and communion in both forms. In eastern Hungary Protestantism spread freely under a Turkish rule scornfully indifferent to varieties of Christian belief. By 1550 it seemed that all Hungary would become Protestant. But Calvinism began then to compete with Lutheranism in Hungary; the Magyars, constitutionally anti-German, supported the Swiss style of Reform; and by 1558 the Calvinists were numerous enough to hold an impressive synod at Czenger. The rival focuses of reform tore the movement in two. Many officials or converts, seeking social stability or mental peace, returned to Catholicism; and in the seventeenth century the Jesuits, led by the son of a Calvinist, restored Hungary to the Catholic fold.

V. CHARLES V AND THE NETHERLANDS

In the Flanders of Charles's maturity a thriving commerce was more than making up for sporadic industrial decline. Bruges and Ghent were depressed, but Brussels survived by being the Flemish capital, Louvain was brewing theology and beer, and Antwerp was becoming—would be by 1550—the richest, busiest city in Europe. To that hectic port on the broad and navigable Scheldt international trade and finance were drawn by low import and export dues, by the political connection with Spain, and by a bourse dedicated, its inscription said, *ad usum mercatorum cuiusque gentis ac linguae*—"to the use of merchants of every land and tongue." [11] Business enterprise was here free from the guild restrictions and municipal protectionism that had kept medieval industry happily unprogressive. Here Italian bankers opened agencies, English "merchant adventurers" established a depot, the Fuggers centered their commercial activities, the Hanse built its lordly House of the Easterlings (1564). The harbor saw 500 ships enter or leave on any day, and 5,000 traders trafficked on the exchange. A bill on Antwerp was now the commonest form of international currency. In this period Antwerp gradually replaced Lisbon as the chief European port for the spice trade; cargoes sailing into Lisbon were bought afloat by Flemish agents there, and were sailed directly to Antwerp for distribution through northern Europe. "I was sad at the sight of Antwerp," wrote a Venetian ambassador, "for I saw Venice surpassed"; [12] he was witnessing the historic transfer of commercial hegemony from the Mediterranean to the North Atlantic. Spurred on by this commerce, Flemish industry revived, even in Ghent; and the Lowlands provided Charles V with 1,500,000 livres ($37,500,000?) a year, half his total revenue.[13]

He responded by giving Flanders and Holland reasonably good government except in religious liberty—a boon hardly conceived by his friends or his foes. His authority was constitutionally limited by his sworn pledge to observe the charters and local laws of the cities and provinces; by personal and domiciliary rights stoutly maintained by the burghers; by councils of state and finance, and a court of appeal, established as part of the central administration. Generally Charles ruled the Netherlands by indirection, through regents acceptable to the citizens: first his aunt, nurse, and tutor, Margaret of Austria, then his sister Mary, ex-queen of Hungary, both women of competence, humanity, and tact. But Charles became more imperious with more Empire. He stationed Spanish garrisons in the proud cities, and suppressed with severity any serious contravention of his international policies. When Ghent refused to vote the military funds demanded by him and granted by the other cities, Charles put down the revolt by a show of indisputable force, exacted the subsidy and an indemnity, abolished the traditional liberties of the municipality, and substituted Imperial appointees for the locally chosen government (1540).[14] But this was hardly typical. Despite such occasional harshness Charles remained popular with his Lowland subjects; he received credit for the political stability and social order that supported the economic prosperity; and when he announced his abdication nearly all citizens mourned.[15]

Accepting the current theory that national peace and strength required unity of religious belief, and fearing that Protestantism in the Netherlands would endanger his flank in his strife with France and Lutheran Germany, Charles fully supported the Church in prosecuting heresy in Flanders and Holland. The reform movement there was mild before Luther; after 1517 it entered as Lutheranism and Anabaptism from Germany, as Zwinglianism and Calvinism from Switzerland, Alsace, and France. Luther's writings were soon translated into Dutch, and were expounded by ardent preachers in Antwerp, Ghent, Dordrecht, Utrecht, Zwolle, and The Hague. Dominican friars led a vivacious rebuttal; one said he wished he could fasten his teeth on Luther's throat, and would not hesitate to go to the Lord's Supper with that blood on his mouth.[16] The Emperor, still young, thought to stop the agitation by publishing (1521), at the Pope's request, a "placard" forbidding the printing or reading of Luther's works. In the same year he ordered the secular courts to enforce throughout the Netherlands the Edict of Worms against all proponents of Lutheran ideas. On July 1, 1523, Henry Voes and Johann Eck, two Augustinian friars, were sent to the stake at Brussels as the first Protestant martyrs in the Lowlands. Henry of Zutphen, friend and pupil of Luther's, and prior of the Augustinian monastery at Antwerp, was imprisoned, escaped, was caught in Holstein, and was there burned (1524). These executions advertised the Reformers' ideas.

Despite censorship Luther's translation of the New Testament was widely circulated, more fervently in Holland than in rich Flanders. A longing for the restoration of Christianity to its pristine simplicity generated a millenarian hope for the early return of Christ and the establishment of a New Jerusalem in which there would be no government, no marriage, and no property; and with these notions were mingled communistic theories of equality, mutual aid, and even "free love." [17] Anabaptist groups formed at Antwerp, Maastricht, and Amsterdam. Melchior Hofmann came from Emden to Amsterdam in 1531, and in 1534 John of Leyden returned the visit by carrying the Anabaptist creed from Haarlem to Münster. In some Dutch towns it was estimated that two thirds of the population were Anabaptists; in Deventer even the burgomaster was converted to the cause. Fanned by famine, the movement became a social revolt. "In these provinces," wrote a friend to Erasmus in 1534, "we are made extremely anxious by the Anabaptist conflagration, for it is mounting up like flames. There is hardly a spot or town where the torch of insurrection does not secretly glow." [18] Mary of Hungary, then Regent, warned the Emperor that the rebels planned to plunder all forms of property among the nobility, clergy, and mercantile aristocracy, and to distribute the spoils to every man according to his need.[19] In 1535 John of Leyden sent emissaries to arrange a simultaneous uprising of Anabaptists at several Dutch centers. The rebels made heroic efforts; one group captured and fortified a monastery in West Friesland; the governor besieged them with heavy artillery; 800 died in a hopeless defense (1535). On May 11 some armed Anabaptists stormed and captured the city hall of Amsterdam; the burghers dislodged them, and wreaked upon the leaders the frightful vengeance of frightened men: tongues and hearts were torn from living bodies and flung into the faces of the dying or dead.[20]

Thinking the whole social structure challenged by a communistic revolution, Charles imported the Inquisition into the Netherlands, and gave its officials power to stamp out the movement, and all other heresies, at whatever cost to local liberties. Between 1521 and 1555 he issued placard after placard against social or religious dissent. The most violent of these (September 25, 1550) revealed the deterioration of the Emperor, and laid the foundations for the revolt of the Netherlands against his son.

No one shall print, write, copy, keep, conceal, sell, buy, or give, in churches, streets, or other places, any book or writing made by Martin Luther, John Oecolampadius, Ulrich Zwingli, Martin Bucer, John Calvin, or other heretics reprobated by the Holy Church . . . nor break or otherwise injure the images of the Holy Virgin or canonized saints . . . nor hold conventicles, or illegal gatherings, or be present at any such in which the adherents of the above-mentioned heretics teach, baptize, and form conspiracies against the Holy Church and the general welfare. . . . We forbid all lay persons to converse or dispute concerning the Holy Scriptures, openly or secretly . . . or to read, teach, or expound the Scriptures, unless they have duly studied theology, or have been approved by some renowned university . . . or to entertain any of the opinions of the above-mentioned heretics . . . on pain of being . . . punished as follows . . . the men [to be beheaded] with the sword, and the women to be buried alive, if they do not persist in their errors; if they persist in them they are to be executed with fire; all their property in both cases to be confiscated to the Crown. . . .

We forbid all persons to lodge, entertain, furnish with food, fire, or clothing, or otherwise to favor, anyone holden or notoriously suspected of being a heretic; and anyone failing to denounce any such we ordain shall be liable to the above-mentioned punishments. . . . All who know of any person tainted with heresy are required to denounce and give them up. . . . The informer, in case of conviction, shall be entitled to one half the property of the accused. . . . To the end that the judges and officers may have no reason—under pretext that the penalties are too great and heavy and only devised to terrify delinquents—to punish them less severely than they deserve, [we ordain] that the culprits really be punished by the penalties above declared; we forbid all judges to alter or moderate the penalties in any manner; we forbid anyone, of whatever condition, to ask of us, or of anyone having authority, to grant pardon to, or to present any petition in favor of, such heretics, exiles, or fugitives, on penalty of being declared forever incapable of civil or military office, and of being arbitrarily punished.[21]

In addition, any person entering the Low Countries was required to sign a pledge of loyalty to the full orthodox creed.[22]

Through these desperate edicts the Netherlands were made a major battleground between the old and the new forms of Christianity. The Venetian ambassador at Charles's court estimated in 1546 that 30,000 persons, nearly all Anabaptists, perished in this prolonged Imperial pogrom;[23] a less excited estimate reduced the victims to 1,000.[24] So far as the Dutch Anabaptists were concerned, the Caroline Inquisition succeeded; a remnant survived in Holland by adopting non-resistance; some fled to England, where they became active supporters of Protestantism under Edward VI and Elizabeth. The communistic movement in the Netherlands collapsed, frightened by prosecution and stifled by prosperity.

But as the Anabaptists wave subsided, a stream of hunted Huguenots poured into the Lowlands from France, bringing the gospel of Calvin. The stern and theocratic fervor of the new heresy appealed to those who inherited the traditions of the mystics and the Brethren of the Common Life; and the Calvinist acceptance of work as a dignity instead of a curse, of wealth as a blessing instead of a crime, of republican institutions as more responsive than monarchy to the political ambitions of the business class, contained ingredients diversely welcome to many elements in the population. By 1555 there were Calvinist congregations in Ypres, Tournai, Valenciennes, Bruges, Ghent, and Antwerp, and the movement was spreading into Holland. It was with Calvinism, not Lutheranism or Anabaptism, that Charles's son would be locked, through a bitter generation, in the conflict that would break the Netherlands in two, liberate Holland from the Spanish domination, and make her one of the major homes and havens of the modern mind.

In 1555 Charles V put aside all dreams except that of dying in sanctity. He relinquished his hope of either suppressing Protestantism in Germany and the Netherlands, or reconciling it with Catholicism at the Council of Trent. He abandoned his aspiration to lead Protestants and Catholics, Germans and French, in a magnificent march against Suleiman, Constantinople, and the Turkish threat to Christendom. His excesses in eating, drinking, and sex, his exhausting campaigns, the burdens of an office that bore the brunt of revolutionary change, had ruined his body, dulled his statesmanship, and broken his will. Suffering from ulcers at thirty-three, old at thirty-five, afflicted at forty-five with gout, asthma, indigestion, and stammering, he was now half his waking time in pain, and found it hard to sleep; often his difficulty in breathing kept him sitting upright all the night through. His fingers were so distorted with arthritis that he could hardly grasp the pen with which he signed the Peace of Crépy. When Coligny presented a letter from Henry II, Charles could hardly open it. "What think you of me, Sir Admiral?" he asked. "Am I not a fine knight to charge and break a lance, I who can only open a letter after so much trouble?" [25] Perhaps his occasional cruelty, and something of the savagery with which he attacked Protestantism in the Netherlands, came from the exhaustion of his patience by his pains. He ordered the amputation of the feet of captured German mercenaries who had fought for France, though his son, the future inexorable Philip II, begged mercy for them. [26] He had mourned long and bitterly the death of his beloved wife Isabella (1539); but in time he allowed helpless maidens to be brought to his bed. [27]

In the fall of 1555 he called a meeting of the States-General of the Netherlands for October 25, and summoned Philip to it from England. In the great tapestried hall of the dukes of Brabant at Brussels, where the Knights of the Golden Fleece were wont to hold their assemblies, the deputies, nobles, and magistrates of the seventeen provinces gathered within a guard of armed soldiery. Charles entered leaning on the shoulder of his son's future enemy, William of Orange. Philip followed with the Regent Mary of Hungary; then Emmanuel Philibert of Savoy, and the Emperor's councilors, and the Knights of the Fleece, and many other notables around whom the world once turned before forgetting them. When all had been seated Philibert rose and explained, too lengthily and vividly for Charles's enjoyment, the medical, mental, and political reasons why the Emperor wished to abdicate his rule in the Netherlands to his son. Then Charles himself stood up, leaning again on the tall and handsome Prince of Orange, and spoke simply and to the point. He summarized his rise to successively wider powers, and the absorption of his life in government. He recalled that he had visited Germany nine times, Spain six, Italy seven, France four, England and Africa twice, and had made eleven voyages by sea. He continued:

> This is the fourth time that I am setting out hence for Spain. . . . Nothing that I have ever experienced has given me so much pain . . . as that which I feel in parting from you today without leaving behind me that peace and quiet which I so much desired. . . . But I am no longer able to attend to my affairs without great bodily fatigue and consequent detriment to the state. . . . The cares which so great a responsibility involves, the extreme dejection which it causes, my health already ruined—all these leave me no longer the vigor necessary for governing. . . . In my present state I should have to render a serious account to God and man if I did not lay aside authority. . . . My son, King Philip, is of an age sufficiently advanced to be able to govern you, and he will be, I hope, a good prince to all my beloved subjects. . . . [28]

When Charles sank painfully into his chair the audience forgot his sins, his persecutions, and his defeats in pity for a man who for forty years had labored according to his lights under the heaviest obligations of the time. Many auditors wept. Philip was formally installed as ruler of the Netherlands, and took a solemn oath (as he would be later reminded) to observe all the laws and traditional rights of the provinces. Early in 1556 Charles surrendered to him the crown of Spain, with all its possessions in the Old World and the New. Charles reserved the Imperial title, hoping to transmit that too to his son; but Ferdinand protested, and in 1558 the Emperor resigned it to his brother. On September 17, 1556, Charles sailed from Flushing to Spain.

VI. SPAIN: 1516-58

1. The Revolt of the Comuneros: 1520-22

It was a questionable boon for Spain that her King Charles I (1516-56) became the Emperor Charles V (1519-58). Born and reared in Flanders, he acquired Flemish ways and tastes, until in his final years the spirit of Spain conquered him. The King could be only a small part of the Emperor who had his hands full with the Reformation, the papacy, Suleiman, Barbarossa, and Francis I; the Spaniards complained that he gave them so little of his time and spent so much of their human and material resources on campaigns apparently foreign to Spanish interests. And how could an emperor sympathize with the communal institutions that had made Spain half a democracy before the coming of Ferdinand the Catholic, and that she so longed to restore?

Charles's first visit to his kingdom (1517) earned him no love. Though king for twenty months past, he still knew no Spanish. His curt dismissal of the devoted Ximenes shocked Spanish courtesy. He came surrounded by Flemings who thought Spain a barbarous country waiting to be milked; and the seventeen-year-old monarch appointed these leeches to the highest posts. The various provincial Cortes, dominated by the hidalgos or lower nobility, did not conceal their reluctance to accept so alien a king. The Cortes of Castile refused him the title, then grudgingly recognized him as co-ruler with his demented mother Juana; and it let him understand that he must learn Spanish, live in Spain, and name no more foreigners to office. Other Cortes laid down similar demands. Amid these humiliations Charles received the news that he had been elected emperor, and that Germany was summoning him to show himself and be crowned. When he asked the Cortes at Valladolid (then the capital) to finance the trip, he was rebuffed, and a public tumult threatened his life. Finally he secured the money from the Cortes of Corunna, and hurried off to Flanders. To make matters trebly perilous ¹ e sent *corregidores* to protect his interests in the cities, and left his former tutor, Cardinal Adrian of Utrecht, as regent of Spain.

Now one after another of the Spanish municipalities rose in the "Revolt of the *Comuneros*" or commune members. They expelled the *corregidores*, murdered a few of the delegates who had voted funds to Charles, and leagued themselves in a *Santa Comunidad* pledged to control the King. Nobles, ecclesiastics, and burghers alike joined the movement, and organized at Ávila (August 1520) the *Santa Junta*, or Holy Union, as a central government. They demanded that the Cortes should share with the royal council in choosing the regent, that no war should be made without the consent of the Cortes, and that the town should be ruled not by *corregidores* but by *alcaldes* or mayors chosen by the citizens.[29] Antonio de Acuña, Bishop of Zamora, openly advocated a republic, turned his clergy into revolutionary warriors, and gave the resources of his diocese to the revolt. Juan de Padilla, a Toledo noble, was made commander of the rebel forces. He led them to the capture of Tordesillas, took Juana la Loca as a hostage, and urged her to sign a document deposing Charles and naming herself queen. Wise in her madness, she refused.

Adrian, having no soldiery strong enough to suppress the uprising, appealed to Charles to return, and frankly blamed the revolt on the King's arbitrary and absentee government. Charles did not come, but either he or his councilors found a way to divide and conquer. The nobles were warned that the rebellion was a threat to the propertied classes as well as to the Crown. And indeed the working classes, long oppressed with fixed wages, forced labor, and prohibition of unions, had already seized power in several towns. In Valencia and its neighborhood a *Germania* or Brotherhood of guildsmen took the reins, and ruled the committees of workingmen. This proletarian dictatorship was unusually pious; it imposed upon the thousands of Moors who still remained in the province the choice of baptism or death; hundreds of the obstinate were killed.[30] In Majorca the commons, whose masters had treated them as slaves, rose in arms, deposed the royal governor, and slew every noble who could not elude them. Many towns renounced their feudal ties and dues. In Madrid, Sigüenza, and Guadalajara the new municipal administration excluded all nobles and gentry from office; here and there aristocrats were slain; and the *Junta* assessed for taxation noble properties formerly exempt. Pillage became general; commoners burned the palaces of nobles, nobles massacred commoners. Class war spread through Spain.

The revolt destroyed itself by extending its aims beyond its powers. The nobles turned against it, raised their own forces, co-operated with those of the King, captured Valencia, and overthrew the proletarian government after days of mutual slaughter (1521). At the height of the crisis the rebel army divided into rival groups under Padilla and Don Pedro Girón; the *Junta* also split into hostile factions; and each province carried on its revolution without co-ordination with the rest. Girón went over to the royalists, who recaptured Tordesillas and Juana. Padilla's dwindling army was routed at Villalar, and he was put to death. When Charles returned to Spain (July 1522) with 4,000 German troops, victory had already been won by the nobles, and nobles and commoners had so weakened each other that he was able to subdue the municipalities and the guilds, tame the Cortes, and establish an almost absolute monarchy. The democratic movement was so completely suppressed that the Spanish commons remained cowed and obedient till the nineteenth century. Charles tempered his power with courtesy, surrounded himself with grandees, and learned to talk good Spanish; Spain was pleased when he remarked that Italian was the proper language to use to women, German to enemies, French to friends, Spanish to God.[31]

2. The Spanish Protestants

Only one power could now challenge Charles in Spain—the Church. He was pro-Catholic but anti-papal. Like Ferdinand the Catholic he sought to make the Spanish Church independent of the popes, and he so far succeeded that during his rule ecclesiastical appointments and revenues were in his control, and were used to promote governmental policies. In Spain, as in France, no Reformation was needed to subordinate the Church to the state. Nonetheless, during the half of his reign that Charles spent in his kingdom, the fervor of Spanish orthodoxy so worked upon him that in his later years nothing (except the power of the Hapsburgs) seemed more important to him than the suppression of heresy. While the popes tried to moderate the Inquisition, Charles supported it till his death. He was convinced that heresy in the Netherlands was leading to chaos and civil war, and was resolved to circumvent such a development in Spain.

The Spanish Inquisition abated its fury, but extended its jurisdiction, un-'er Charles. It undertook the censorship of literature, had every bookstore ·arched, and ordered bonfires of books charged with heresy.[32] It investiated and punished sexual perversions. It instituted rules of *limpieza* (purity of blood), which closed all avenues of distinction to descendants of *Conversos* and to all who had ever been penanced by the tribunal. It looked upon mystics with a stern eye, for some of these claimed that their direct intercourse with God exempted them from attending church, and others gave their mystical ecstasies a suspiciously sexual flavor. The lay preacher Pedro Ruiz de Alcaraz announced that coitus was really union with God; and Friar Francisco Ortiz explained that when he lay with a pretty fellow mystic

—even when he embraced her naked body—it was not a carnal sin but a spiritual delight.[33] The Inquisition dealt leniently with these *Alumbrados* (Enlightened Ones), and kept its severest measures for the Protestants of Spain.

As in northern Europe, an Erasmian skirmish preceded the Protestant battle. A few liberal churchmen applauded the humanist's strictures on the faults of the clergy; but Ximenes and others had already reformed the more palpable abuses before the coming of Charles. Perhaps Lutheranism had seeped into Spain with Germans and Flemings in the royal entourage. A German was condemned by the Inquisition at Valencia in 1524 for avowing Lutheran sympathies; a Flemish painter was sentenced to life imprisonment in 1528 for questioning purgatory and indulgences. Francisco de San Roman, the first-known Spanish Lutheran, was burned at the stake in 1542, while fervent onlookers pierced him with their swords. Juan Díaz of Cuenca imbibed Calvinism at Geneva; his brother Alfonso rushed up from Italy to reconvert him to orthodoxy; failing, Alfonso had him killed (1546).[34] At Seville a learned canon of the cathedral, Juan Gil or Egidio, was imprisoned for a year for preaching against image worship, prayer to the saints, and the efficacy of good works in earning salvation; after his death his bones were exhumed and burned. His fellow canon, Constantino Ponce de la Fuente, continued his propaganda, and died in the dungeons of the Inquisition. Fourteen of Constantino's followers were burned, including four friars and three women; a large number were sentenced to diverse penalties; and the house in which they had met was razed to the ground.

Another semi-Protestant group developed in Valladolid; and here influential nobles and high ecclesiastics were involved. They were betrayed to the Inquisition; nearly all were arrested and condemned; some, trying to leave Spain, were caught and brought back. Charles V, then in retirement at Yuste, recommended that no mercy be shown them, that the repentant should be beheaded, and the unrepentant burned. On Trinity Sunday, May 21, 1559, fourteen of the condemned were executed before a cheering crowd.[35] All but one recanted, and were let off with beheading; Antonio de Herrezuelo, impenitent, was burned alive. His twenty-three-year-old wife, Leonor de Cisneros, repentant, was allowed life imprisonment. After ten years of confinement she retracted her recantation, proclaimed her heresy, and asked to be burned alive like her husband; her request was granted.[36] Twenty-six more of the accused were displayed in an auto-da-fé on October 8, 1559, before a crowd of 200,000, presided over by Philip II. Two victims were burned alive, ten were strangled.

The most famous prey of the Inquisition in this period was Bartolomé de Carranza, Archbishop of Toledo and Primate of Spain. As a Dominican friar he was active for many years in hounding heretics. Charles appointed him envoy to the Council of Trent, and sent him to England to attend the marriage of Philip and Queen Mary. When he was elected archbishop (1557) only his own vote kept the choice from being unanimous. But some of the "Protestants" arrested at Valladolid testified that Carranza had secretly sympathized with their views; he was found to have corresponded with the Spanish Italian reformer Juan de Valdés; and the influential theologian Melchior Cano accused him of upholding the Lutheran doctrine of justification by faith. He was arrested only two years after his elevation to the highest ecclesiastical dignity in Spain; we may judge from this the power of the Spanish Inquisition. For seventeen years he was kept in one prison or another while his life and writings were subjected to scrutiny at Toledo and Rome. Gregory XIII proclaimed him "vehemently suspected" of heresy, ordered him to abjure sixteen propositions, and suspended him for five years from the exercise of his office. Carranza accepted the sentence humbly, and tried to perform the penances assigned to him; but within five weeks, exhausted by imprisonment and humiliation, he died (1576).

With him ended all danger of Protestantism in Spain. Between 1551 and 1600 there were some 200 executions there for Protestant heresies—i.e., four per year. The temper of the people, formed by centuries of hatred for Moors and Jews, had congealed into an unshakable orthodoxy; Catholicism and patriotism had merged; and the Inquisition found it a simple matter to stamp out in a generation or two the passing Spanish adventure with independent thought.

3. The Emperor Passes: 1556–58

On September 28, 1556, Charles V made his final entry into Spain. At Burgos he dismissed with rewards most of those who had attended him, and took leave of his sisters, Mary of Hungary and Eleonora, widow of Francis I. They wished to share his monastic retreat, but the rules forbade it, and they took up their residence not too far from this brother whom they alone now seemed to love. After suffering many ceremonies en route, he reached the village of Juandilla in the valley of Plasencia, some 120 miles west of Madrid. There he tarried several months while workmen completed and furnished the accommodations that he had ordered in the monastery of Yuste (St. Justus), six miles away. When he made the last stage of his journey (February 3, 1557) it was not to a monastic cell but to a mansion spacious enough to house the more intimate of his fifty servitors. The monks rejoiced to have so distinguished a guest, but were chagrined to find that he had no intention of sharing their regimen. He ate and drank as abundantly as before—i.e., excessively. Sardine omelets, Estremadura sausages, eel pies, pickled partridges, fat capons, and rivers of wine and beer disappeared into the Imperial paunch; and his physicians were obliged to prescribe large quantities of senna and rhubarb to carry off the surplusage.

Instead of reciting rosaries, litanies, and psalms, Charles read or dictated dispatches from or to his son, and offered him advice on every aspect of war, theology, and government. In his final year he became a merciless bigot; he recommended ferocious penalties to "cut out the root" of heresy, and he regretted that he had allowed Luther to escape him at Worms. He ordered that a hundred lashes should be laid upon any woman who should approach within two bowshots of the monastery walls.[37] He revised his will to provide that 30,000 Masses should be said for the repose of his soul. We should not judge him from those senile days; some taint of insanity may have come down to him with his mother's blood.

In August 1558, his gout developed into a burning fever. This returned intermittently, and with rising intensity. For a month he was racked with all the pains of death before he was allowed to die (September 21, 1558). In 1574 Philip had the remains removed to the Escorial, where they lie under a stately monument.

Charles V was the most impressive failure of his age, and even his virtues were sometimes unfortunate for mankind. He gave peace to Italy, but only after a decade of devastation, and by subjecting it and the papacy to Spain; and the Italian Renaissance withered under that somber mastery. He defeated and captured Francis, but he lost at Madrid a royal opportunity to make with him a treaty that could have saved all faces and a hundred thousand lives. He helped to turn back Suleiman at Vienna, and checked Barbarossa in the Mediterranean. He strengthened the Hapsburgs but weakened the Empire; he lost Lorraine and surrendered Burgundy. The princes of Germany frustrated his attempt to centralize authority there, and from his time the Holy Roman Empire was a decaying tissue waiting for Napoleon to pronounce it dead. He failed in his efforts to crush Protestantism in Germany, and his method of repressing it in the Netherlands left a tragic legacy to his son. He had found the German cities flourishing and free; he left them ailing under a reactionary feudalism. When he came to Germany it was alive with ideas and energy beyond any other nation in Europe; when he abdicated it was spiritually and intellectually exhausted, and would lie fallow for two centuries. In Germany and Italy his policies were a minor cause of decline, but in Spain it was chiefly his action that crushed municipal liberty and vigor. He might have saved England for the Church by persuading Catherine to yield to Henry's need for an heir; instead he forced Clement into a ruinous vacillation.

And yet it is our hindsight that sees his mistakes and their enormity; our historical sense can condone them as rooted in the limitations of his mental

environment and in the harsh delusions of the age. He was the ablest statesman among his contemporaries, but only in the sense that he dealt coura-
geously with the profoundest issues in their widest range. He was a great
man dwarfed and shattered by the problems of his time.

Two fundamental movements pervaded his long reign. The most fundamental was the growth of nationalism under centralized monarchies; in
this he did not share. The most dramatic was a religious revolution rising
out of national and territorial divisions and interests. Northern Germany
and Scandinavia accepted Lutheranism; southern Germany, Switzerland,
and the Lowlands divided into Protestant and Catholic sections; Scotland
became Calvinist Presbyterian, England became Anglican Catholic or Calvinist Puritan. Ireland, France, Italy, Spain, and Portugal remained loyal to
a distant or chastened papacy. Yet amid that double fragmentation a subtle
integration grew: the proudly independent states found themselves interdependent as never before, increasingly bound in one economic web, and
forming a vast theater of interrelated politics, wars, law, literature, and art.
The Europe that our youth knew was taking form.

BOOK III

THE STRANGERS IN THE GATE

1300–1566

CHAPTER XXIX

The Unification of Russia

1300-1584

I. THE PEOPLE

IN 1300 Russia did not exist. The north belonged for the most part to three self-governed city-states: Novgorod, Viatka, Pskov. The western and southern provinces were dependencies of Lithuania. In the east the principalities of Moscow, Ryazan, Suzday, Nijni Novgorod, and Tver all claimed individual sovereignty, and were united only in common subjection to the Golden Horde.

The Horde took its noun from Turkish *ordu*, camp, and its adjective from the domed tent, covered with cloth of gold, that had served as headquarters for Batu the Splendid, grandson of Ghengis Khan. Having conquered southern Russia and western Asia, these marauding Asiatics built their capital at Sarai on a branch of the lower Volga, and there received annual tribute from the Russian princes. The Horde was partly agricultural, partly nomad pastoral. The ruling families were Mongol, the rest were mostly Turks. The name Tatar came to the Horde from the Ta-ta tribes of the Gobi, who in the ninth century had started the Mongol avalanche toward the West. The chief results from the long subjection of Russia to the Horde were social: the autocracy of the Moscow dukes, the servile loyalty of the people to their princes, the low status of woman, the military, financial, and judicial organization of the Muscovite government on Tatar lines. The Tatar domination deferred for two centuries the attempt of Russia to become a European Occidental state.

The Russian people faced the most arduous conditions with silent stoicism, except that amid their tribulations they found the courage to sing. Their enemies called them coarse, cruel, dishonest, cunning, and violent;[1] doubtless toil and trouble and a trying climate toughened them; but their patience, good humor, friendliness, and hospitality redeemed them—so much so that they were inclined to believe themselves, *more humano*, the salt of the earth. They were beaten into civilization by barbarous laws and frightful penalties; so, we are told, a wife who murdered her husband was buried alive up to the neck, sorcerers were burned alive in an iron cage, and counterfeiters had liquid metal poured down their throats.[2] Like any people fighting cold, the

Russians drank alcohol abundantly, sometimes to drunken stupor; even their food was seasoned to warm them. They enjoyed hot baths, and bathed more frequently than most Europeans. Religion bade women hide their tempting forms and hair, and branded them as Satan's chosen instrument; yet they were equal with men before the law, and often joined in public pastimes or the dance—which was forbidden as a sin. The Russian Church preached a strict morality, and prohibited conjugal relations during Lent; presumably the severity of the code was a counterpoise to the tendency of the people to indulge excessively in almost the only pleasure left to them. Marriages were arranged by the parents, and came early; girls of twelve, boys of fourteen, were considered nubile. Wedding ceremonies were complex, with ancient symbolism and festivities; through all these the bride was required to keep a modest silence; her revenge was deferred. On the morrow she was expected to show to her husband's mother the evidence that he had married a virgin. Usually the women of the household remained in an upper apartment or *terem*, away from the men; and the authority of the father was as absolute in the family as that of the czar in the state.

Piety sublimated poverty into a preparation for paradise. Every house of any size had a room decorated with icons as a place of frequent prayer. A proper visitor, before saluting his hosts, saluted the icons first. Good women carried rosaries wherever they went. Prayers were recited as magic incantations; so, said the *Domostroi*—a famous manual of the sixteenth century— a certain prayer repeated 600 times a day for three years would cause the incarnation, in the re-petitioner, of the Father, the Son, and the Holy Ghost.[3] But there were many beautiful features in this superstitious religion. On Easter morning people greeted one another with the joyful words, "Christ is risen." In this hope death was in some measure eased; facing it, a decent man would pay his debts, relieve his debtors, free one or more of his bondmen, leave alms to the poor and the Church, and breathe his last in confident expectation of eternal life.

The Russian Church stimulated this piety with architecture, murals, icons, powerful sermons, hypnotic ceremonies, and massive choral song that seemed to rise from the most mystical depths of the soul or the stomach. The Church was a vital organ of the state, and her services in teaching letters and morality, disciplining character, and buttressing social order were lavishly rewarded. Monasteries were numerous and immense. The Troitsa-Sergievskaya Lavra—the Monastery of the Trinity founded by St. Sergius in 1335 —had amassed by 1600 such extensive lands that over 100,000 peasants were needed for their cultivation. In return the monasteries distributed charity on a Russian scale; some fed 400 people daily; in a famine year the monastery at Volokolamsk fed 7,000 in one day. Monks took a vow of chastity, but priests were obliged to marry. These "papas" were mostly illiterate, but that was not held against them by the people. The metropolitans of Moscow were in many cases the ablest, as well as the most learned, men of their generation, risking their silver to preserve the state, and guiding the princes toward national unity. St. Alexis was the virtual ruler of Russia during his tenure of the Muscovite see (1354–70). With all her faults—which may have been dictated by her tasks—the Russian Church in this formative age served as the supreme civilizing agent among a people brutalized by the hardships of life and the predatory nature of man.

In 1448 the Russian Church, repudiating the merger of Greek with Roman Christianity at the Council of Florence, declared her independence of the Byzantine patriarch; and when, five years later, Constantinople fell to the Turks, Moscow became the metropolis of the Orthodox faith. "Know now," wrote a fervent monk to a Grand Prince of Moscow about 1505, "that the sovereignty of all Christendom has been united in thine own. For the two Romes have fallen, but the third doth endure. A fourth there shall never be, for thy Christian empire shall last forever." [4]

The Church was almost the sole patron of letters and the arts, and therefore their dictator. The best literature was unwritten. The songs of the people, passing from mouth to mouth, from generation to generation, celebrated their loves, weddings, sorrows, seasons, holydays, or deaths; and there were popular lays of cherished saints, ancient heroes, and legendary exploits, like those of Sadko the merchant of Novgorod. Blind men or cripples went from village to village singing such songs and lays and sacred chants. Written literature was nearly all monastic, and served religion.

It was the monks who now brought icon painting to a finished art. Upon a small panel of wood, sometimes covered with cloth, they applied a glutinous coat; on this they drew their design; within this they laid their colors in tempera; they covered the painting with varnish, and enclosed it in a metal frame. The subjects were determined by ecclesiastical authority; the figures and features were derived from Byzantine models, and went back in continuous evolution through the mosaics of Constantinople to the paintings of Hellenistic Alexandria. The best icons from this age are the anonymous *Christ Enthroned* in the Cathedral of the Assumption in Moscow; the *Entry of Christ into Jerusalem*, from the school of Novgorod; and *The Holy Trinity* of the monk Andrei Rubliov in the Monastery of the Trinity. Rubliov and his teacher, Theophanes the Greek, painted frescoes, half Byzantine and half Byzantine El Greco, in Vladimir, Moscow, and Novgorod, but time has had its way with them.

Every ruler signalized his splendor, and eased his conscience, by building or endowing a church or a monastery. Forms and motives from Armenia, Persia, India, Tibet, Mongolia, Italy, and Scandinavia joined with the predominant Byzantine heritage to mold Russian church architecture, with its picturesque multiplicity of units, its central gilded dome, its bulbous cupolas admirably designed to shed rain and snow. After the fall of Constantinople and the expulsion of the Tatars the dependence of Russia upon Byzantine and Oriental art subsided, and influences from the West entered to modify the Slavic style. In 1472 Ivan III, hoping thereby to inherit the rights and titles of the Byzantine emperors, married Zoë Palaeologus, niece of the last ruler of the Eastern Empire. She had been brought up in Rome, and had imbibed something of the early Renaissance. She brought Greek scholars with her, and acquainted Ivan with Italian art. It may have been at her suggestion that he sent the first Russian mission to the West (1474), with instructions to secure Italian artists for Moscow. Ridolfo Fieravante of Bologna, called Aristotle because of the range of his abilities, accepted the invitation; and further Russian forays netted Pietro Solario, Alevisio Novi, and several other artists. It was these Italians who, with Russian aides and labor, rebuilt the Kremlin.

Yuri Dolgoruki had founded Moscow (1156) by raising a wall around his villa, which was strategically situated at the confluence of two rivers; this fortress *(kreml)* was the first form of the Kremlin. In time the enclosure was enlarged, and churches and palaces rose within a massive wall of oak. Ivan III set himself to transform the entire ensemble. It was apparently Fieravante who (1475–79) reconstructed, in the Kremlin, the old Cathedral of the Assumption (Uspenskiy Sobor), where future czars were to be crowned; the design remained Byzantine, with Italian decoration. Architects from Pskov added, in the enclosure, the little Cathedral of the Annunciation (Blagovyeschenskiy Sobor, 1484–89); and, again in the Kremlin, Alevisio raised the Cathedral of the Archangel (1505–09). Solario and others rewalled the circuit in pink brick (1485–1508), in the style of the Castello Sforzesco at Milan.[5] It was from this many-templed center of Russia, this overpowering union and concentration of secular and ecclesiastical authority, that the grand princes and the metropolitans of Moscow spread their rule over nobles, merchants, and peasants, and laid in blood and bones and piety the foundations of one of the mightiest empires in history.

II. THE PRINCES OF MOSCOW

Moscow remained an obscure village until Daniel Alexandrovitch, toward the end of the thirteenth century, extended its hinterland and made it a minor principality. Historical hindsight [6] attributes Moscow's growth to its position on the navigable Moscow River, which was connected by short overland portage with the Volga on the east and the Oka, Don, and Dnieper on the south and west. Yuri Danielovitch—son of Daniel—Prince of Moscow, coveted the neighboring principality of Suzdal, with its relatively rich capital, Vladimir; Michael, Prince of Tver, coveted the same; Moscow and Tver fought for the prize; Moscow won; Michael was killed and canonized; Moscow grew. Yuri's brother and successor, Ivan I, took the double title of Grand Prince of Moscow and Grand Duke of Vladimir.

As collector of Russian tribute for the Tatar khan, Ivan I exacted more than he remitted, and prospered wickedly. His rapacity won him the nickname Kalita, Moneybag, but he gave the principalities thirteen years' respite from Tatar raids. He died as a tonsured monk, censered with the odor of sanctity (1341). His son Simeon the Proud inherited his flair for taxgathering. Claiming authority over every province, he called himself Grand Prince of All the Russias, which did not prevent his dying of the plague (1353). Ivan II was a gentle and peaceable ruler, under whom Russia fell into fratricidal war. His son Dmitri had all requisite martial qualities; he defeated every rival, and defied the khan. In 1380 Khan Mamai assembled a horde of Tatars, Genoese mercenaries, and other flotsam, and advanced toward Moscow. Dmitri and his Russian allies met the horde at Kulikovo, near the Don, defeated it (1380), and won the cognomen Donskoi. Two years later the Tatars attacked again, with 100,000 men. The Russians, deceived and exhausted by victory, failed to raise a comparable force; the Tatars captured Moscow, massacred 24,000 of the population, and burned the city to the ground. Dmitri's son Vasili I made peace with the Tatars, annexed Nijni Novgorod, and compelled Novgorod and Viatka to accept him as their overlord.

The Grand Princes of Moscow adopted the Tatar technique of despotism, perhaps as the alternative to an illiterate chaos. Under an autocracy of violence and craft a bureaucracy on Byzantine lines administered the government, subject to a Council of Boyars advising and serving the prince. The boyars were at once the leaders of the army, the governing lords of their localities, the organizers, protectors, and exploiters of the semifree peasants who tilled the land. Adventurous colonists migrated to unsettled regions, drained the swamps, fertilized the soil by burning the woods and brush, exhausted it with improvident tillage, and moved on again, until they reached the White Sea and the Urals, and seeped into Siberia. In the endless plains towns were many but small; houses were of wood and mud, calculated to burn down within twenty years at most. Roads were unpaved, and were least agonizing in winter, when they were covered with snow packed by sleds and patient boots. Merchants preferred rivers to roads, and by water or ice carried on a plodding trade between north and south, with Byzantium, Islam, and the Hanse. Probably it was this spreading commerce that overcame the individualism of the princes and compelled the unification of Russia. Vasili II (1425–62), called Tëmny, the Blind, because his foes gouged out his eyes (1446), brought all rebels to obedience with torture, mutilation, and the knout, and left to his son a Russia sufficiently strong to end the ignominy of Tatar rule.

Ivan III became "the Great" because he accomplished this task, and made Russia one. He was built to need: unscrupulous, subtle, calculating, tenacious, cruel, guiding his armies to distant victories from his seat in the Kremlin; punishing disobedience or incompetence savagely, whipping, torturing, mutilating even the boyars, beheading a doctor for failing to cure his son, and so sternly dominating his entourage that women fainted at his glance. Russia called him the Terrible until it met his grandson.

The easiest of his conquests was Novgorod. He looked with hungry anticipation upon that thriving taxable mart, and the merchants of Moscow urged him to destroy their competitors in the north.[7] The Grand Prince controlled the plains between Moscow and Novgorod; there the mercantile republic bought its food and sold its goods; Ivan had only to close that granary and market to Novgorod's trade, and the city-state must go bankrupt or yield. After eight years of alternating war and truce, the republic surrendered its autonomy (1478). Seven thousand of its leading inhabitants were transplanted to Suzdal, the Hanse was expelled, the merchants of Moscow inherited the markets, their Prince the revenues, of Novgorod.

Absorbing the colonies of the dead republic, Ivan extended his rule to Finland, the Arctic, and the Urals. Pskov submitted in time to preserve its republican forms under the sovereignty of the Grand Prince. Tver sought preservation by allying itself with Lithuania; Ivan marched in person against the city, and took it without a blow. Rostov and Iaroslavl followed. When Ivan's brothers died he refused to let their appanages descend to their heirs; he added their territories to his own. One brother, Andrei, flirted with Lithuania; Ivan captured and imprisoned him; Andrei died in jail; Ivan wept, but confiscated Andrei's lands. *La politique n'a pas d'entrailles.*

Liberation from the Tatars seemed impossible and proved easy. The remnants of the Mongol-Turkish invaders had settled down in three rival groups centering at Sarai, Kazan, and in the Crimea. Ivan played one against another until he was assured that they would not unite against him. In 1480 he refused tribute. Khan Akhmet led a great army up the Volga to the banks of the Oka and Ugra south of Moscow; Ivan led 150,000 men to the opposite banks. For months the hostile hosts faced each other without giving battle; Ivan hesitated to risk his throne and life on one throw, the Tatars feared his improved artillery. When the rivers froze and no longer protected the armies from each other, Ivan ordered a retreat. Instead of pursuing, the Tatars too retreated, all the way to Sarai (1480). It was an immense and ridiculous victory. From that time no tribute was paid by Moscow to the Horde; the Grand Prince called himself autocrat (Samoderzhets). meaning that he paid tribute to none. The rival khans were maneuvered into mutual war; Akhmet was defeated and slain; the Golden Horde of Sarai melted away.

Lithuania remained. Neither the Grand Prince nor the metropolitan of Moscow could suffer peace so long as the Ukraine and Kiev and western Russia were under a power perpetually threatening Moscow, and inviting Orthodox Christians into Latin Christianity. An alleged Polish plot to assassinate Ivan gave him a *casus belli* and let loose a holy war for the redemption of the seduced provinces (1492). Many Lithuanian princes, uneasy under the Polish-Roman-Catholic union, opened their gates to Ivan's troops. Alexander, Great Prince of Lithuania, made a stand at Vedrosha, and lost (1500). Pope Alexander VI arranged a six-year truce; meanwhile Moscow kept the region it had won—west to the river Sozh, including Chernigov and reaching almost to Smolensk. Ivan III, now sixty-three, left the redemption of the remainder to his heirs.

His reign of forty-three years was as important as any in the history of Russia before the twentieth century. Whether inspired by lust for wealth and power, or by a conviction that the security and prosperity of the Russians required the unification of Russia, Ivan III achieved for his country what Louis XI was doing for France, Henry VII for England, Ferdinand and Isabella for Spain, Alexander VI for the Papal States; the simultaneity of these events revealed the progress of nationalism and monarchy, dooming the supernational power of the papacy. The boyars lost their independence, the principalities sent tribute to Moscow, Ivan took the title "Sovereign of All the Russias." Possibly at the behest of his Greek wife he assumed also the Roman-Greek title of czar (Caesar), adopted the Imperial double eagle as the national emblem, and claimed inheritance to all the political and religious authority of defunct Byzantium. Byzantine theories and ceremonies of government, and of the Church as an organ of the state, followed Byzantine Christianity, the Byzantine Greek alphabet, and Byzantine art forms, into Russia; and so far as Byzantium had been Orientalized by its proximity to Asia, so Russia, already oriented by Tatar rule, became in many ways an Oriental monarchy, alien and unintelligible to the West.

III. IVAN THE TERRIBLE: 1533–84

Vasili III Ivanovitch (1505–33) continued the integration of Russia. He brought Smolensk within his realm, and compelled the principalities of Ryazan and Novgorod-Severski to acknowledge his sovereignty. "Only the infants at the breast," said a Russian annalist, "could refrain from tears" when the once proud republic of Pskov submitted to Vasili's rule (1510).

Russia was now a major European power; Vasili corresponded on equal terms with Maximilian I, Charles V, Suleiman the Magnificent, and Leo X. When some boyars tried to limit his autocracy he checked them with a contemptuous word—"Peasants!"—and had one noble head cut off. Getting no children from his wife, he divorced her and married the accomplished and masterful Helena Glinski. After his death she took the regency for her three-year-old son Ivan IV Vasilievitch. The boyars resumed their turbulence when she died; their rival factions controlled the government in turn; they disordered the cities with their violence, and spilled the blood of their helpless muzhiks in civil war.

Amid these struggles the young Sovereign of All the Russias was almost ignored, even at times left destitute. Seeing brutality everywhere around him, he took it as an accepted mode of behavior, adopted the most cruel sports, and grew into a moody and suspicious youth. Suddenly, while still a boy of thirteen (1544), he threw to his dogs Andrei Shuiski, leader of a boyar faction, and seized command of the state. Three years later he had himself crowned czar by the metropolitan of Moscow. Then he ordered a selection of noble virgins to be sent to him from divers parts of his realm; from them he chose and married Anastasia Romanovna, whose family name would soon designate a dynasty.

In 1550 he summoned the first national assembly (Zemski Sobor) of all Russia. He confessed to it the errors of his youth, and promised a just and merciful government. Perhaps influenced by the Reformation in Germany and Scandinavia, the assembly considered a motion to confiscate ecclesiastical wealth for the support of the state. The proposal was rejected, but a related motion was passed by which all alodial lands—those free from liens—deeded to the Church were to be restored, all gifts made to the Church during Ivan's minority were canceled, and monasteries were no longer to acquire certain kinds of property without the czar's consent. The clergy were partly appeased when Ivan took the priest Sylvester as his spiritual director and made him and Alexis Adashef his chief ministers. Supported by these able aides, Ivan at twenty-one was master of a realm reaching from Smolensk to the Urals, and from the Arctic Ocean almost to the Caspian Sea.

His first care was to strengthen the army, and to balance the forces provided by the unfriendly nobles with two organizations responsible directly to himself: Cossack cavalry and Strieltsi infantry armed with harquebuses—matchlock firearms invented in the fifteenth century.* The Cossacks originated in that century as peasants whose position in South Russia, between Moslems and Muscovites, obliged them to be ready to fight at short notice, but gave them irresistible opportunities to rob the caravans that carried trade

---

* Strieltsi from *strielati*, to fire; Cossack (Russian *Kazak*) probably from Turki *quzzag*, adventurer.

between north and south. The main Cossack "hosts"—the Don Cossacks in southeast Russia and the Zaporogue Cossacks in the southwest—were semi-independent republics, strangely democratic; male householders chose a hetman (German *Hauptmann*, head man) as executive officer of a popularly elected assembly. All land was owned in common, but was leased to individual families for temporary use; and all classes were equal before the law.[8] Famous for their dashing courage, the Cossack horsemen became the main support of Ivan IV at home and in war.

His foreign policy was simple: he wanted Russia to connect the Baltic Sea with the Caspian. The Tatars still held Kazan, Astrakhan, and the Crimea, and still demanded tribute from Moscow, though in vain. Ivan was sure that Russia's security and unity required its possession of these khanates, and control of the Volga to its outlet. In 1552 the young Czar led 150,000 men against the gates of Kazan in a siege that lasted fifty days. The 30,000 Moslems resisted with religious pertinacity; they sallied out in repeated sorties; and when some of them were captured and hanged on gibbets before the walls, the defenders shot them with arrows, saying that "it was better for these captives to receive death from the clean hands of their countrymen than to perish by the impure hands of Christians."[9] When the besiegers lost heart after a month of failure, Ivan sent to Moscow for a miraculous cross; this, displayed to them, reanimated his men; on both sides God was conscripted into military service. A German engineer mined the walls; they collapsed; the Russians poured into the city, crying "God with us!"—and massacred all who could not be sold as slaves. Ivan, we are told, wept with pity for the defeated; "they are not Christians," he said, "but they are men." He repeopled the ruins with Christians. Russia acclaimed him as the first Slav to take a Tatar stronghold, and celebrated the victory as France had hailed the check of the Moslems at Tours (732). In 1554 Ivan took Astrakhan, and the Volga became a completely Russian stream. The Crimea remained Moslem till 1774, but the Cossacks of the Don now bowed to Moscow's rule.

Having cleared his frontier in the east, Ivan looked longingly toward the west. He dreamed of Russian commerce flowing west and north along great rivers into the Baltic. He envied the industrial and commercial expansion of Western Europe, and looked for any opening by which the Russian economy might attach itself to that development. In 1553 Sir Hugh Willoughby and Richard Chancellor were commissioned by London merchants to find an Arctic route around Scandinavia to China. They sailed from Harwich in three vessels; two crews perished in a Lapland winter, but Chancellor reached the site of Arkhangelsk—which the British so named after the archangel Michael. Chancellor made his way through a hundred perils and hardships to Moscow. With him, and later with Anthony Jenkinson, Ivan signed treaties giving "The London and Muscovite Company" special trading privileges in Russia.

But to Ivan these treaties were knotholes, not a door or window, into the West. He tried to import German technicians; 123 were gathered for him at Lübeck, but Charles V refused to let them go. A great river, the Southern Dvina, flowed from the heart of Russia into the Baltic near Riga, but through hostile Livonia. The headwaters of the Dvina and the Volga were not far apart; the two rivers could be connected by canals; here, by "manifest destiny," was the water route that might atone for the disproportion of Russia's enormous land mass to her coasts and ports; so the Baltic would mingle with the Caspian and the Black Sea, East and West would meet, and amid the interchange of goods and ideas the West could repay some of its ancient cultural debt to the East.

So in 1557 Ivan invented a *casus belli*—usually a case of the belly—with Livonia. He sent against it an army under Shah-Ali, lately Tatar Khan of Kazan; it ravaged the country brutally, burning houses and crops, enslaving men, raping women till they died. In 1558 another Russian army captured Narva, only eight miles from the Baltic. Desperate Livonia appealed to Poland. Denmark, Sweden, Germany, all Central Europe trembled at the prospect of a Slav inundation reaching westward, as in the sixth century, to the Elbe. Stephen Báthory roused the Poles, and led them to victory over the Russians at Polotsk (1582). Ivan, defeated, yielded Livonia to Poland.

Long before this decisive setback the failure of his campaigns had led to revolt at home. The merchants whom Ivan had thought to enrich with new avenues of trade lost stomach for the costly and disruptive war. The nobles had opposed it as bound to unite the Baltic powers, with their superior armament, against a Russia still feudal in political and military organization. During and before the war Ivan had suspected the boyars of conspiracies against his throne. In a nearly fatal illness (1553) he learned that a powerful group of nobles was planning, when he died, to repudiate his son Dmitri and crown Prince Vladimir, whose mother was disbursing large gifts to the army. His closest advisers, Sylvester and Adashef, were flirting with treasonable boyars. For seven years after suspecting them Ivan kept these officials in power; then (1560) he dismissed them, but without violence; Sylvester died in a monastery, Adashef in one of the Livonian campaigns. Several of the boyars deserted to Poland and took up arms against Russia; in 1564 Ivan's bosom friend and leading general, Prince Andrei Kurbski, joined this flight, alleging that the Czar was planning to kill him. From Poland Kurbski sent to Ivan what amounted to a declaration of war, denouncing him as a leprous criminal. Tradition claims that Ivan, when this letter was read to him, nailed a foot of the bearer to the floor with a blow of the royal staff. But the Czar condescended to reply to Kurbski in a rebuttal sixty-two pages long, eloquent and chaotic, passionate and Biblical, recounting the intrigues of the boyars to depose him. Believing that they had poisoned Anastasia, he asked, "Why did you divide me from my wife? Had you not taken from me my young heifer, never had there been the slayings of the boyars. . . . In vain I have looked for some man to have pity on me, but I have found none." [10] Kurbski, in the evening of his life, wrote a relentlessly hostile *History of Ivan*, which is our chief source for Ivan's *terribilità*.

These plots and desertions illuminate the most famous and peculiar event of the reign. On December 13, 1564, Ivan left Moscow with his family, his icons, his treasury, and a small force of soldiery, withdrew to his summer home at Alexandrovsk, and sent to Moscow two proclamations. One alleged that the boyars, the bureaucracy, and the Church had conspired against him and the state; therefore "with great sorrow" he now resigned his throne, and would henceforth live in retirement. The other assured the people of Moscow that he loved them, and that they might rest assured of his lasting good will. In fact he had consistently favored the commons and merchants against the aristocracy, and the present action of the middle and lower classes attested it. They broke out in threatening cries against the nobility and the clergy, and demanded that a deputation of bishops and boyars should go to the Czar and beg him to resume his throne. It was done, and Ivan agreed to "take unto him his state anew," on conditions that he would later specify.

He returned to Moscow (February 1565), and summoned the national assembly of clergy and boyars. He announced that he would execute the leaders of the opposition, and confiscate their property; he would henceforth assume full power, without consulting the nobles or assembly, and he would banish all who should disobey his edicts. The assembly, fearing a revolt of the masses, yielded and dissolved. Ivan decreed that in the future Russia should be divided into two parts: one, the *Zemstchina* or assemblage of provinces, was to remain under the government of the boyars and their duma; it was to be taxable in gross by the Czar, and be subject to him in military and foreign affairs, but would otherwise be self-governed and free; the other part, the *Oprichnina*, or "separate estate," was to be ruled by him, and was to be composed of lands assigned by him to the *oprichniki* or separate class, chosen by the Czar to police and administer this half-realm, to guard it from sedition, and to give him personal protection and special military service. The new officials—at first a thousand, ultimately six thousand —were selected chiefly from the younger sons of the nobility, who, being landless, were ready to support Ivan in return for the estates now conferred upon them. These lands were taken partly from the possessions of the Crown, largely from the confiscated properties of rebellious boyars. By the end of the reign the *Oprichnina* included nearly half of Russia, much of Moscow, and the most important trade routes. The revolution was akin to that which

Peter the Great attempted 150 years later—the elevation of a new class to political power, and the promotion of Russian commerce and industry. In a century when practically all the military power was held by the aristocracy, the enterprise required a wild courage in a Czar armed only with his personal soldiery and the unreliable support of the merchants and the populace. Some contemporaries assure us that in this critical period Ivan, then thirty-five, aged twenty years.[11]

Ivan now made Alexandrovsk his regular residence, and transformed it into a fortified citadel. The strain of his revolt against the boyars, added to the failure of the long war against Livonia, may have disordered a never quite balanced mind. He clothed his guardsmen like monks in black cassocks and skull caps, called himself their abbot, sang in their choir, attended Mass with them daily, and so fervently prostrated himself before the altar that his forehead was repeatedly bruised. This added to the awe that he inspired; Russia began to mingle reverence with the fear it felt for him; and even the armed *oprichniki* were so abject before him that they came to be called his *dvor* or court.

Ivan's revolution, like others, had its terror. Those who opposed it and were caught were executed without mercy. A monastic chronicle, presumably hostile to him, reckoned the casualties of his wrath in those years (1560–70) at 3,470; often, it reports, the victim was executed "with his wife," or "with his wife and children," and, in one case, "with ten men who came to his help." [12] Prince Vladimir and his mother were put to death, but his children were spared and provided for. The Czar, we are told, asked the monks to pray for the repose of his victims' souls. He defended the executions as the usual punishment for treason, especially in time of war; an agent of Poland conceded the argument; and an Englishman who witnessed some of the butchery prayed, "Would to God our own stiff-necked rebels could be taught their duty to their prince after the same fashion!" [13]

The climax of the terror came in Novgorod. Ivan had recently given its archbishop a large sum to repair churches, and thought himself popular with at least the clergy there. But he was informed that a document—not indisputably genuine—had been found behind a picture of the Virgin in a Novgorod monastery, pledging the co-operation of Novgorod and Pskov with Poland in an attempt to overthrow the Czar. On January 2, 1570, a strong military force led by *oprichniki* pounced upon Novgorod, sacked its monasteries, and arrested 500 monks and priests. Arriving in person on January 6, Ivan ordered those clerics who could not pay fifty rubles' ransom to be flogged to death. The archbishop was unfrocked and jailed. According to the *Third Chronicle of Novgorod* a massacre of the population ensued for five weeks; sometimes 500 persons were slain in a day; the official records number 2,770 dead; Ivan protested they were only 1,505. Since many merchants, eager for the reopening of trade with the West, were believed to have shared in the conspiracy, the soldiers of the Czar burned all the shops in the city, and the homes of the merchants in the suburbs; even the farmhouses in the environs were destroyed. Unless unfriendly monastic chroniclers have exaggerated the carnage, we must go back to the punishment of rebellious Liége by Charles the Bold (1468), or the Sack of Rome by the troops of Charles V (1527) to find analogies for Ivan's savage revenge. Novgorod never recovered its old prominence in the commercial life of Russia. Ivan passed on to Pskov, where he restricted his soldiers to pillage. Then he returned to Moscow and celebrated with a royal masquerade ball his escape from a dangerous conspiracy.

So turbulent a reign hardly favored economic progress or cultural pursuits. Commerce was favored in peace and wounded in war. In the lands allotted to the *oprichniki*, and then on other lands as well, the peasant was legally attached to the soil as a means of promoting continuous cultivation (1581); serfdom, rare in Russia before 1500, became by 1600 the law of the land. Taxation was predatory, inflation was precipitous. The ruble in 1500 was worth ninety-four, in 1600 twenty-four, times the ruble of 1910;[14] we need not follow the decline further, except to note, as one of the lessons of history, that money is the last thing that a man should save.

The improvident fertility of families and exhaustion of soils compelled a restless migration to fresh terrain. When this passed the Urals it found a Tatar khanate established over a population of Bashkirs and Ostyaks, around a capital known by the Cossack word *Sibir*. In 1581 Semën Stroganov enlisted 600 Cossacks and sent them under Ermak Timofeevitch to conquer these tribes. It was done; western Siberia became part of the swelling Russian realm; and Ermak, who had been a brigand chief, was canonized by the Orthodox Church.

The Church remained the real ruler of Russia, for the fear of God was everywhere, while Ivan's reach was limited. Strict rules of ritual, if not of morality, bound even the Czar; the priests saw to it that he washed his hands after giving audience to ambassadors from outside the Orthodox pale. No Roman Catholic worship was allowed, but Protestants were tolerated as fellow foes of the Roman pope. Ivan IV, like Henry VIII, prided himself on his knowledge of theology. He indulged in a public debate in the Kremlin with a Bohemian Lutheran divine, and it must be admitted that the most violent of the Czars conducted the discussion with more courtesy than appeared in the religious disputes of contemporary Germany.[15] He did not come off so well with another theologian. At a Sunday service in the Cathedral of the Assumption (1568) Philip, Metropolitan of Moscow, conspicuously refused the blessing that Ivan solicited. Thrice the Czar asked for it in vain. When his attendants demanded reason for the refusal, Philip began to list Ivan's crimes and debaucheries. "Hold thy peace," cried the Czar, "and give me thy blessing!" "My silence," answered the prelate, "lays a sin upon thy soul, and calls down thy death." Ivan departed unblessed, and for a wondering month Philip remained unhurt. Then a servitor of the Czar entered the cathedral, seized the Metropolitan, and dragged him to a prison in Tver. His fate is debated; the account accepted by the Russian Church is that he was burned alive. In 1652 he was canonized, and his relics remained till 1917 an object of reverence in the Uspenskiy Sobor.

The Church still produced most of the literature and art of Russia. Printing arrived about 1491, but the only books printed during this reign were manuals of prayer. The leading scholar was the metropolitan Macarius; in 1529, aided by secretaries, he began to compile the surviving literature of his country in twelve huge volumes, which again were almost entirely religious, mostly monkish, chronicles. Ivan's confessor Sylvester composed a famous *Domostroi*, or *Household Book*, as a guide to domestic economy, manners, and eternal salvation; we note in it the admonition to the husband to beat his wife lovingly, and precise instructions for spitting and for blowing the nose.[16] Ivan himself, in his letters, was not the least vigorous writer of his time.

The most brilliant product of Russian art under his rule was the Church of Basil the Blessed (Khram Vasilia Blajennoi), which still stands aloof from the Kremlin at one end of the Red Square. On returning from his triumphant campaigns against Kazan and Astrakhan (1554) Ivan began what he called Pokrovski Sobor—the Cathedral of the Intercession of the Virgin, to whom he judiciously ascribed his victories. Around this central shrine of stone there later rose seven chapels in wood, dedicated to saints on whose festivals Ivan had overcome his foes. Each chapel was crowned with a graceful painted cupola, each bulbous but varying from the others in ornament. The final chapel, raised to St. Basil in 1588, gave its name in time to the whole charming ensemble. Inevitable legend credited the architecture to an Italian, and told how Ivan had gouged out his eyes lest he should ever rival this masterpiece; but it was two Russians, Barma and Postnikov, who designed it, merely adopting some Renaissance motives in its decoration.[17] Every year, on Palm Sunday, as part of the wisdom of government, the lords and clergy of Moscow walked in awesome procession to this cathedral; the metropolitan rode sideways on a horse equipped with artificial ears to simulate the ass on which Christ was described as entering Jerusalem; and the Czar, on foot, humbly led the horse by the bridle; banners, crosses, icons, and censers flourished, and children raised hosannas of praise and gratitude to inclement skies for the blessings of Russian life.

By 1580 Ivan seemed to have triumphed over all his enemies. He had survived several wives, was married to a sixth, and thought of adding another in friendly bigamy.[18] He had four children: the first died in infancy, the third, Feodor, was a half-wit; the fourth, Dmitri, was alleged to have epileptic fits. One day in November 1580, the Czar, seeing the wife of his second son, Ivan, in what seemed to him immodest attire, reproved and struck her; she miscarried; the Czarevitch reproached his father; the Czar, in unpremeditated rage, struck him on the head with the imperial staff; the son died from the blow. The Czar went insane with remorse; he spent his days and nights crying aloud with grief; each morning he offered his resignation; but even the boyars now preferred him to his sons. He survived three years more. Then a strange disease attacked him, which made his body swell and emit an unbearable stench. On March 18, 1584, he died while playing chess with Boris Godunov. Gossip accused Boris of poisoning him, and the stage was set for grand opera in the history of the czars.

We must not think of Ivan IV as merely an ogre of brutality. Tall and strong, he would have been handsome but for a broad flat nose that overlay a spreading mustache and a heavy auburn beard. The appellation *Groznyi* is mistranslated Terrible; it meant, rather, awesome, like the *Augustus* that was applied to the Caesars; Ivan III had also received the name. To our minds, and even to his cruel contemporaries, he was repulsively cruel and vengeful, and he was a merciless judge. He lived in the age of the Spanish Inquisition, the burning of Servetus, the decapitating habits of Henry VIII, the Marian persecution, the Massacre of St. Bartholomew; when he heard of this holocaust (which a pope welcomed with praise) he denounced the barbarism of the West.[19] He had some provocations, which set on fire a readily combustible temper made violent by heredity or environment; sometimes, says a witness, a small annoyance made him "foam at the mouth like a horse."[20] He confessed and at times exaggerated his sins and crimes, so that his enemies could only plagiarize him in their accusations. He studied zealously, and made himself the best-educated layman of his land and time. He had a sense of humor, and could roar with Jovian laughter, but a sinister cunning showed often in his smile. He paved his hell with wonderful intentions: he would protect the poor and the weak against the rich and the strong; he would favor commerce and the middle classes as checks on the feudal and quarrelsome aristocracy; he would open a door of trade in goods and ideas to the West; he would give Russia a new administrative class not bound, like the boyars, to ancient and stagnant ways; he would free Russia from the Tatars, and raise her out of chaos into unity. He was a barbarian barbarously struggling to be civilized.

He failed because he never matured to self-mastery. The reforms that he had planned were half forgotten in the excitement of revolution. He left the peasants more bitterly subject to the landlords than before; he clogged the avenues of trade with war; he drove able men into the arms of the enemy;

he divided Russia into hostile halves, and guided her into anarchy. He gave his people a demoralizing example of pious cruelty and uncontrolled passion. He killed his ablest son, and bequeathed his throne to a weakling whose incapacity invited civil war. He was one of the many men of his time of whom it might be said that it would have been better for their country and humanity if they had never been born.

CHAPTER XXX

The Genius of Islam

1258-1520

THE Moslem world had sustained, from 1095 to 1291, a series of assaults as violent and religious as those by which it later subdued the Balkans and changed a thousand churches into mosques. Eight Crusades, inspired by a dozen popes, had hurled the royalty, chivalry, and rabble of Europe against Mohammedan citadels in Asia Minor, Syria, Palestine, Egypt, and Tunisia; and though these attacks had finally failed, they had gravely weakened the order and resources of the Moslem states. In Spain the Crusades had succeeded; there Islam had been beaten back while its survivors were crowded into a Granada whose doom was leisurely delayed. Sicily had been taken from Islam by the virile Normans. But what were these wounds and amputations compared with the wild and ruinous descent of the Mongols (1219–58) into Transoxiana, Persia, and Iraq? City after city that had been a haven of Moslem civilization was subjected to pillage, massacre, and fire—Bokhara, Samarkand, Balkh, Merv, Nishapur, Rayy, Herat, Baghdad. . . . Provincial and municipal governments were shattered; canals, neglected, succumbed to the swirling sand; commerce was put to flight; schools and libraries were destroyed; scholars and scientists were scattered, slaughtered, or enslaved. The spirit of Islam was broken for almost a century. It slowly revived; and then Timur's Tatars swept across western Asia in a fresh desolation, and the Ottoman Turks cut their way through Asia Minor to the Bosporus. No other civilization in history has known disasters so numerous, so widespread, and so complete.

And yet the Mongols, Tatars, and Turks brought their new blood to replace the human rivers they had shed. Islam had grown luxurious and supine; Baghdad, like Constantinople, had lost the will to live by its own arms; men there were so in love with easeful life that they half invited death; that picturesque civilization, too, as well as the Byzantine, was ripe to die. But so rich had it been that—like ancient Greece and Renaissance Italy—it was able, by its salvaged fragments and memories, to civilize its conquerors. Persia under the Mongol Il-Khans developed an enlightened government, produced good literature and majestic art, and graced history with a noble scholar, Rashidu'd-Din. In Transoxiana Timur built almost as impressively as he had destroyed; and amid his ravages he paused to honor Hafiz. In Anatolia the

Turks were already civilized, and poets among them were as plentiful as concubines. In Egypt the Mamluks continued to build like giants; and in West Africa Islam fathered a philosopher-historian beside whom the greatest pundits of contemporary Christendom were midges snared and starved in the cobwebs of Scholasticism. And meanwhile Islam was spreading through India to the farthest reaches of the East.

I. THE IL-KHANS OF PERSIA: 1265–1337

When Marco Polo set out across Persia (1271) to see the China of Kublai Khan, he found himself within the Mongol Empire almost all the way. History had never before recorded so vast a realm. On the west it touched the Dnieper in Russia; in the south it included the Crimea, Iraq, Persia, Tibet, and India to the Ganges; in the east it embraced Indochina, China, and Korea; in the north lay its original home, Mongolia. Throughout these states the Mongol rulers maintained roads, promoted commerce, protected travelers, and permitted freedom of worship to diverse faiths.

Hulagu, grandson of Genghis Khan, after destroying Baghdad (1258), established a new capital at Maragha in northwest Persia. When he died (1265) his son Abaqa became khan or prince of Persia, loosely subject to the distant Kublai Khan; so began the Il-Khan dynasty that ruled Persia and Iraq till 1337. Greatest of the line was Ghazan Khan. He was almost the shortest man among his troops, but his will was stronger than their arms. He broke off allegiance to the Great Khan in Mongolia or China, and made his state an independent kingdom, with its capital at Tabriz. Envoys came to him from China, India, Egypt, England, Spain. . . . He reformed administration, stabilized the currency, protected the peasants from landlords and robbers, and promoted such prosperity as recalled Baghdad in its proudest days. At Tabriz he built a mosque, two colleges, a philosophical academy, an observatory, a library, a hospital. He set aside the revenues of certain lands in perpetuity to support these institutions, and secured for them the leading scholars, physicians, and scientists of the age. He was himself a man of wide culture and many languages, apparently including Latin.[1] For himself he raised a mausoleum so majestic and immense that his death (1304) seemed a triumphal entry into a nobler home.

Marco Polo described Tabriz as "a great and glorious city." Fra Oderic (1320) pronounced it "the finest city in the world for trade. Every article is found here in abundance. . . . The Christians here say that the revenue the city pays to its ruler is greater than that which all of France pays to its king."[2] Clavijo (1404) called it "a mighty city abounding in riches and goods," with "many fine buildings," magnificent mosques, and "the most splendid bathhouses in the world." [3] He calculated the population at a million souls.

Uljaitu continued the enlightened policies of his brother Ghazan. His reign saw some of the noblest architecture and illumination in Persian history. The career of his chancellor, Rashidu'd-Din Fadlu'llah, illustrates the prosperity of education, scholarship, and literature at this time. Rashidu'd-Din was born in 1247 at Hamadan, perhaps of Jewish parentage; so his enemies held, citing his remarkable knowledge of Mosaic Law. He served Abaqa as physician, Ghazan as premier, Uljaitu as treasurer. In an eastern suburb of Tabriz he established the Rab'-i-Rashidi, or Rashidi Foundation, a spacious university center. One of his letters, preserved in the Library of Cambridge University, describes it:

> In it we have built twenty-four caravanserais [inns] touching the sky, 1,500 shops surpassing pyramids in steadfastness, and 30,000 fascinating houses. Salubrious baths, pleasant gardens, stores, mills, factories for cloth weaving and paper-making . . . have been constructed. . . . People from every city and border have been removed to the said Rab'. Among them are 200 reciters of the Koran. . . . We have given dwellings to 400 other scholars, theologians, jurists, and traditionalists [*Hadith* scholars] in the street which is named "The Street of the Scholars"; daily payments, pensions, yearly clothing allowances, soap money and sweets money have been granted for them all. We have established 1,000 other students . . . and have given orders for their pensions and daily pay . . . in order that they may be comfortably and peacefully occupied in acquiring knowledge and profiting people by it. We have prescribed, too, which and how many students should study with which professor and teacher; and after ascertaining each knowledge-seeker's aptness of mind and capability of learning a particular branch of the sciences . . . we have ordered him to learn that science. . . .
>
> Fifty skilled physicians who have come from the cities of Hindustan, China, Misr [Egypt], and Sha'm [Syria] have all been granted our particular attention and favor in a thousand ways; we have ordered that they should frequent our "House of Healing" [hospital] every day, and that every one should take ten students capable of learning medicine under his care, and train them in the practice of this noble art. To each of the opticians and surgeons and bonesetters who work in . . . our hospital we have ordered that five of the sons of our servitors should be entrusted so as to be instructed in the oculist's art, in surgery and bonesetting. For all these men . . . we have founded a quarter behind our hospital . . . their street is called "The Street of the Healers." Other craftsmen and industrialists too, whom we have transferred from various countries, have been established, each group in a particular street. [4]

We must marvel at the industry of a man who, while actively sharing in the administration of a kingdom, found time and knowledge to write five books on theology, four on medicine and government, and a voluminous history of the world. Moreover, an admiring Moslem assures us, Rashidu'd-Din could give to his writing only the time between morning prayer and sunrise; however, there are cloudy days even in Azerbaijan. He labored seven years on his *Jami'ut-Tawarikh*, or *Compendium of Histories;* he published it in two tremendous volumes, which in English would make seven. Here were substantial accounts of the Mongols from Genghis Khan to Ghazan; of the various Mohammedan states and dynasties in Eastern and Western Islam; of Persia and Judea before and after Mohammed; of China and India, with a full study of Buddha and Buddhism; and a chasteningly brief report on the doings and ideas of European kings, popes, and philosophers. Those who have read these volumes—not yet translated into a European tongue— pronounce them the most valuable and scholarly work in all the prose literature of Persia. Not only did Rashidu'd-Din use the archives of his own government; he engaged Chinese scholars to secure for him Chinese treaties and other documents, and he appears to have read these—and Arabic, Hebrew, Turkish, and Mongolian authorities—in their original languages.[5]

To transmit this *Compendium* to posterity despite time and war, Rashidu'd-Din sent copies to scattered libraries, had it translated and disseminated in Arabic, and assigned revenues for making two copies every year, one in Arabic, one in Persian, to be presented to some city of the Moslem world. Nevertheless much of it has been lost, along with his other works, and perhaps as the result of his political disaster. In 1312 Uljaitu associated with him Ali-Shah as co-chancellor of the exchequer. Under Uljaitu's successor, Abu Sa'id, Ali-Shah spread divers charges against his colleague, and persuaded the Khan that Rashidu'd-Din and his son Ibrahim had poisoned Uljaitu. The historian was dismissed, and soon thereafter was put to death (1318), at the age of seventy, along with one of his sons. His properties were confiscated, his foundations were deprived of their endowments, and the suburb Rab'-i-Rashidi was plundered and destroyed.

Abu Sa'id made belated amends by appointing another son of the historian his vizier. Ghiyathu'd-Din governed wisely and justly. After Abu Sa'id's death a period of anarchy brought the dynasty of the Il-Khans to an end, and their realm was divided into petty states ravaged by war and redeemed by poetry.

II. HAFIZ: 1320-89

For in Persia every other man wrote verses, and kings honored poets only next to mistresses, calligraphers, and generals. In Hafiz's time a score of

Persian poets won renown from the Mediterranean to the Ganges and from Yemen to Samarkand. All of them, however, bowed to Shamsu'd-Din Muhammad Hafiz, and assured him that he had surpassed the melodius Sa'di himself. He agreed with this estimate, and addressed himself reverently:

> I have never seen any poetry sweeter than thine, O Hafiz,
> I swear it by that Koran which thou keepest in thy bosom.[6]

Hafiz means rememberer; it was a title given to anyone who, like our poet, had memorized the whole Koran. Born at Shiraz at a date and of ancestry unknown, he soon fell into verse. His first patron was Abu Ishaq, who had been appointed shah of Fars (southeastern Persia) by Ghazan Khan. Abu Ishaq so loved poetry that he neglected government. When warned that hostile forces were preparing to attack his capital, Shiraz, he remarked what a fool a man must be to waste so fair a spring on war. An insensitive general, Ibn-Muzaffar, captured Shiraz, killed Abu Ishaq (1352), forbade the drinking of wine, and closed every tavern in the town. Hafiz wrote a mournful elegy:

> Though wine gives delight, and the wind distills the perfume
>   of the rose,
> Drink not the wine to the strains of the harp, for the constable
>   is alert.
> Hide the goblet in the sleeve of the patchwork cloak,
> For the time, like the eye of the decanter, pours forth blood.
> Wash the wine stain from your dervish cloak with tears,
> For it is the season of piety, and the time of abstinence.[7]

Muzaffar's successor, finding prohibition impracticable, or having discovered that wine-bibbers can be more easily ruled than puritans, reopened the taverns, and Hafiz gave him immortality.

He followed Persian conventions in spending so many verses on wine; at times he reckoned a glass of wine as "worth more than a virgin's kiss." [8] But even the grape grows dry after a thousand couplets, and soon Hafiz found love, virginal or practiced, indispensable to poetry:

> Knowest thou what fortune is? 'Tis beauty's sight obtaining;
> 'Tis asking in her lane for alms, and royal pomp disdaining.[9]

No freedom now seemed so sweet as love's slavery.

> Our stay is brief, but since we may attain
> The glory that is love, do not disdain
>   To hearken to the pleadings of the heart;
> Beyond the mind life's secret will remain.

> Leave then your work and kiss your dear one now,
> With this rich counsel I the world endow;
>   When spring buds lure, the wind deserts his mill
> And gently glides to kiss the leafy bough. . . .
>
> Belle of Shiraz, grant me but love's demand,
> And for your mole—that clinging grain of sand
>   Upon a cheek of pearl—Hafiz would give
> All of Bokhara, all of Samarkand. . . .
>
> If I with Fate but once might throw the dice,
> I'd try a throw, no matter what the price,
>   To have my breath, O Love, be one with yours;
> What need would I have then for paradise? . . .
>
> He who of gold and silk your tresses spun,
> Who made the red rose and the white rose one,
>   And gave your cheek to them for honeymoon—
> Can He not patience give to me, His son? [10]

He seems at last to have cooled into marriage; if we interpret his subtle verses rightly, he found a wife, and had several children, before he could quite make up his mind between woman and wine. In some verses he seems to mourn her death:

> My lady, that did change this house of mine
> Into a heaven when that she dwelt therein,
> From head to foot an angel's grace divine
> Enwrapped her; pure she was, spotless of sin;
> Fair as the moon her countenance, and wise;
> Lords of the kind and tender glance, her eyes
> With an abounding loveliness did shine.
>
> Then said my heart: Here will I take my rest!
> This city breathes her love in every part.
> But to a distant bourne was she addressed,
> Alas! he knew it not, alas, poor heart!
> The influence of some cold malignant star
> Has loosed my hand that held her; lone and far
> She journeyeth that lay upon my breast. [11]

In any case he became domesticated, cultivated a quiet privacy, and seldom stirred abroad; he would, he said, let his poems travel for him. He was invited to many a royal court, and was moved for a moment to accept Sultan Ahmad's offer of a home in the royal palace at Baghdad. [12] But his love for Shiraz kept him prisoner; he doubted if paradise itself had streams as lovely, or roses as red. He indited a laud, now and then, to the Persian kinglets of his time, in hopes of a gift to ease his poverty; for there were no publishers in Persia to launch one's ink upon public seas, and art had to wait, hat in hand, in the antechambers of nobles or kings. Once, indeed, Hafiz almost went abroad: an Indian shah sent him not only an invitation but money for the trip; he set out, and reached Hormuz on the Persian Gulf; he was about to board a ship when a tempest upset his imagination and enamored him of stability. He returned to Shiraz, and sent the shah a poem in lieu of himself.

The *divan* or collected poetry of Hafiz contains 693 poems. Most are odes, some are quatrains, some are unintelligible fragments. They are more difficult than Dante to translate, for they jingle with multiple rhymes which in English would make doggerel, and they teem with recondite allusions that tickled the wits of the time but now lie heavy on the wings of song. Often he can be better rendered in prose:

> The night was about to fade when, drawn by the perfume of the roses, I went down into the garden to seek, like the nightingale, balm for my fever. In the shadow there gleamed a rose, a rose red as a veiled lamp, and I gazed upon its countenance. . . .
> The rose is lovely only because the face of my beloved is lovely. . . . What were the fragrance of the greensward and the breeze that blows in the garden were it not for the cheek of my beloved, which is like a tulip? . . .
> In the darkness of the night I sought to unloose my heart from the bonds of thy tresses, but I felt the touch of thy cheek, and drank of thy lips. I pressed thee to my breast, and thy hair enveloped me like a flame. I pressed my lips to thine, and yielded up my heart and soul to thee as in ransom.[18]

Hafiz was one of those blessed and harassed souls who, through art, poetry, imitation, and half-unconscious desire, have become so sensitive to beauty that they wish to worship—with eyes and speech and fingertips—every fair form in stone or paint or flesh or flower, and suffer in stifled silence as beauty passes by; but who find, in each day's fresh revelation of loveliness or grace, some forgiveness for the brevity of beauty and the sovereignty of death. So Hafiz mingled blasphemies with his adoration, and fell into angry heresies even while praising the Eternal One as the source from which all earthly beauty flows.

Many have sought to make him respectable by interpreting his wine as Spiritual Ecstasy, his taverns as monasteries, his flames as the Divine Fire. It is true that he became a Sufi and a sheik, assumed the dervish robe, and wrote poems of misty mysticism; but his real gods were wine, woman, and song. A movement was begun to try him for unbelief, but he escaped by pleading that the heretical verses were meant to express the views of a Christian, not his own. And yet he wrote:

O zealot! think not that you are sheltered from the sin of pride,
For the difference between the mosque and the infidel church is
    but vanity,[14]

where *infidel*, of course, means Christian. Sometimes it seemed to Hafiz that
God was but a figment of man's hope:

And He who draws us in these flashing days,
Whom we adore, though we know whom He slays,
    He well may sorrow, for when we are gone,
He too will vanish in that selfsame blaze.[15]

When he died his orthodoxy was so doubtful, and his hedonism so voluminous, that some objected to giving him a religious funeral; but his friends
saved the day by allegorizing his poetry. A later generation enshrined his
bones in a garden—the Hafiziyya—flaming with the roses of Shiraz, and the
poet's prediction was fulfilled—that his grave would become "a place of
pilgrimage for the freedom-lovers of all the world." On the alabaster tombstone was engraved one of the master's poems, profoundly religious at last:

Where are the tidings of union? that I may arise—
Forth from the dust I will rise up to welcome thee!
My soul, like a homing bird, yearning for paradise,
Shall arise and soar, from the snares of the world set free.
When the voice of thy love shall call me to be thy slave,
I shall rise to a greater far than the mastery
Of life and the living, time and the mortal span.
Pour down, O Lord! from the clouds of thy guiding grace,
The rain of a mercy that quickeneth on my grave,
Before, like dust that the wind bears from place to place,
I arise and flee beyond the knowledge of man.

When to my grave thou turnest thy blessed feet,
Wine and the lute thou shalt bring in thine hand to me;
Thy voice shall ring through the folds of my winding-sheet,
And I will arise and dance to thy minstrelsy.
Though I be old, clasp me one night to thy breast,
And I, when the dawn shall come to awaken me,
With the flush of youth on my cheek from thy bosom will rise.

Rise up! let mine eyes delight in thy stately grace!
Thou art the goal to which all men's endeavor has pressed,
And thou the idol of Hafiz's worship; thy face
From the world and life shall bid him come forth and arise! [16]

III. TIMUR: 1336–1405

We first hear of the Tatars as a nomad people of Central Asia, kin and neighbors to the Mongols, and joining these in European raids. A Chinese writer of the thirteenth century describes the common run of them much as Jordanes had pictured the Huns a thousand years before: short of stature, hideous of visage to those unfamiliar with them, innocent of letters, skilled in war, aiming their arrows unerringly from a speeding horse, and continuing their race by an assiduous polygamy. In trek and campaigns they took with them bed and board—wives and children, camels, horses, sheep, and dogs; pastured the animals between battles, fed on their milk and flesh, clothed themselves with their skins. They ate gluttonously when supplies were plentiful, but they could bear hunger and thirst, heat and cold, "more patiently than any people in the world."[17] Armed with arrows—sometimes tipped with flaming naphtha—and cannon and all the medieval mechanisms of siege, they were a fit and ready instrument for a man who dreamed of empire with his mother's milk.

When Genghis Khan died (1227) he divided his dominions among his four sons. To Jagatai he gave the region around Samarkand, and the name of this son came to be applied to the Mongol or Tatar tribes under his rule. Timur (i.e., iron) was born at Kesh in Transoxiana to the emir of one such tribe. According to Clavijo the new "Scourge of God" assumed this function precociously: he organized bands of young thieves to steal sheep or cattle from near-by herds.[18] In one of these enterprises he lost the third and fourth fingers of his right hand; in another he was wounded in the heel, and so limped the rest of his life.[19] His enemies called him Timur-i-Lang, Timur the Lame, which careless Occidentals like Marlowe made into Tamburlane or Tamerlane. He found time for a little schooling; he read poetry, and knew the difference between art and degeneration. When he was sixteen his father bequeathed to him the leadership of the tribe and retired to a monastery, for the world, the old man said, is "no better than a golden vase filled with serpents and scorpions." * The father, we are told, advised his son always to support religion. Timur followed the precept even to turning men into minarets.

In 1361 the khan of Mongolia appointed Khoja Ilias governor of Transoxiana, and made Timur one of Khoja's councilors. But the energetic youth was not ripe for statesmanship; he quarreled violently with other members of Khoja's staff, and was forced to flee from Samarkand into the desert. He gathered some youthful warriors about him, and joined his band with that

---

* This, however, is from Timur's *Memoirs* (v, 1), supposedly dictated by him in last years, but of doubtful authenticity.

of his brother Amir Husein, who was in like straits. Wandering from one hiding place to another, they were hardened in body and soul by danger, homelessness, and poverty, until they were raised to moderate fortune by being employed to suppress a revolt in Sistan. So ripened, they declared war on Khoja, deposed and slew him, and became joint rulers, at Samarkand, over the Jagatai tribes (1365). Five years later Timur connived at the assassination of Amir Husein, and became sole sultan.

"In 769," (1367) reads his dubious autobiography, "I entered my thirty-third year; and being of restless disposition, I was much inclined to invade some of the neighboring countries."[20] Resting at Samarkand during the winters, he marched forth almost every spring in a new campaign. He taught the towns and tribes of Transoxiana to accept his rule docilely; he conquered Khurasan and Sistan, and subdued the rich cities of Herat and Kabul; he discouraged resistance and revolt by savage punishments. When the city of Sabzawar surrendered after a costly siege, he took 2,000 captives, "piled them alive one upon another, compacted them with bricks and clay, and erected them into a minaret, so that men, being apprised of the majesty of his wrath, might not be seduced by the demon of arrogance"; so the matter is reported by a contemporary panegyrist.[21] The town of Zirih missed the point and resisted; the heads of its citizens made more minarets. Timur overran Azerbaijan, took Luristan and Tabriz, and sent their artists to Samarkand. In 1387 Isfahan yielded, and accepted a Tatar garrison, but when Timur had gone the population rose and slew the garrison. He returned with his army, stormed the city, and ordered each of his troops to bring him the head of a Persian. Seventy thousand Isfahan heads, we are told, were set on the walls, or were made into towers to adorn the streets.[22] Appeased, Timur reduced the taxes that the city had been paying to its governor. The remaining towns of Persia paid ransom quietly.

At Shiraz in 1387, says a tradition too pretty to be trusted, Timur summoned to his presence the town's most famous citizen, and angrily quoted to him the lines which had offered all Bokhara and Samarkand for the mole on a lady's cheek. "With the blows of my lustrous sword," Timur is said to have complained, "I have subjugated most of the habitable globe . . . to embellish Samarkand and Bokhara, the seats of my government; and you, miserable wretch, would sell them both for the black mole of a Turk of Shiraz!" Hafiz, we are assured, bowed low and said: "Alas, O Prince, it is this prodigality which is the cause of the misery in which you find me." Timur so relished the reply that he spared the poet and gave him a handsome gift. It is regrettable that no early biographer of Timur mentions this charming incident.[23]

While Timur was in south Persia word was brought to him that Tuqatmish, Khan of the Golden Horde, had taken advantage of his absence to invade Transoxiana, and even to sack that picturesque Bokhara which Hafiz had valued at half a mole. Timur marched a thousand miles north (consider the commissary problems involved in such a march), and drove Tuqatmish back to the Volga. Turning south and west, he raided Iraq, Georgia, and Armenia, slaughtering en route the heretical Sayyids, whom he branded as "misguided communists." [24] He took Baghdad (1393) at the request of its inhabitants, who could no longer put up with the cruelty of their Sultan Ahmed ibn Uways. Finding the old capital in decay, he bade his aides rebuild it; meanwhile he added some choice wives to his harem, and a celebrated musician to his court. Ahmed found asylum in Brusa with the Ottoman Sultan Bajazet I; Timur demanded Ahmed's extradition; Bajazet replied that this would violate Turkish canons of hospitality.

Timur would have advanced at once upon Brusa, but Tuqatmish had again invaded Transoxiana. The angry Tatar swept across south Russia, and, while Tuqatmish hid in the wilderness, he sacked the Golden Horde's cities of Sarai and Astrakhan. Unresisted, Timur marched his army westward from the Volga to the Don, and perhaps planned to add all Russia to his realm. Russians of all provinces prayed feverishly, and the Virgin of Vladimir was borne to Moscow between lines of kneeling suppliants who cried out, "Mother of God, save Russia!" The poverty of the steppes helped to save it. Finding little to plunder, Timur turned back at the Don, and led his weary and hungry soldiers back to Samarkand (1395-96).

In India, said all reports, there was wealth enough to buy a hundred Russias. Proclaiming that Moslem rulers in north India were too tolerant of Hindu idolatry, and that all Hindus must be converted to Mohammedanism, Timur, aged sixty-three, set out for India at the head of 92,000 men (1398). Near Delhi he met the army of its Sultan Mahmud, defeated him, slaughtered 100,000 (?) prisoners, pillaged the capital, and brought back to Samarkand all that his troops and beasts could carry of the fabled riches of India.

In 1399, still remembering Ahmed and Bajazet, he marched forth again. He crossed Persia to Azerbaijan, deposed his wastrel son as governor there, hanged the poets and ministers who had seduced the youth into revelry, and redevastated Georgia. Entering Asia Minor, he besieged Sivas, resented its long resistance, and, when it fell, had 4,000 Christian soldiers buried alive— or were such stories war propaganda? Wishing to protect his flank while attacking the Ottomans, he sent an envoy to Egypt proposing a nonaggression pact. The Sultan al-Malik imprisoned the envoy and hired an assassin to kill Timur. The plot failed. After reducing Aleppo, Hims, Baalbek, and Damascus, the Tatar moved on to Baghdad, which had expelled his appointees. He took it at great cost, and ordered each of his 20,000 soldiers to bring him a head. It was done—or so we are told: rich and poor, male and female, old and young, paid this head tax, and their skulls were piled in ghastly pyramids before the city's gates (1401). Moslem mosques, monasteries, and nunneries were spared; everything else was sacked and destroyed, so thoroughly that the once brilliant capital recovered only in our time, by the grace of oil.

Feeling now reasonably sure on left and right, Timur sent Bajazet a final invitation to submit. The Turk, made too confident by his triumph at Nicopolis (1396), retorted that he would annihilate the Tatar army, and would make Timur's chief wife his slave.[25] The two ablest generals of the age joined battle at Ankara (1402). Timur's strategy compelled the Turks to fight when exhausted by a long march. They were routed. Bajazet was taken prisoner, Constantinople rejoiced, Christendom was for half a century saved by the Tatars from the Turks. Timur continued Europeward to Brusa, burned it, and carried away its Byzantine library and silver gates. He marched to the Mediterranean, captured Smyrna from the Knights of Rhodes, butchered the inhabitants, and rested at Ephesus. Christendom trembled again. The Genoese, who still held Chios, Phocaea, and Mitylene, sent in their submission and tribute. The Sultan of Egypt released the Tatar envoy, and entered the distinguished company of Timur's vassals. The conqueror returned to Samarkand as the most powerful monarch of his time, ruling from Central Asia to the Nile, from the Bosporus to India. Henry IV of England sent him felicitations, France sent him a bishop with gifts, Henry III of Castile dispatched to him a famous embassy under Ruy González de Clavijo.

It is to Clavijo's detailed memoirs that we owe most of our knowledge of Timur's court. He left Cádiz on May 22, 1403, traveled via Constantinople, Trebizond, Erzerum, Tabriz, Tehran (here first mentioned by a European), Nishapur, and Mashhad, and reached Samarkand on August 31, 1404. He had with some reason expected to find there only a horde of hideous butchers. He was astonished at the size and prosperity of Timur's capital, the splendor of the mosques and palaces, the excellent manners of the upper class, the wealth and luxury of the court, the concourse of artists and poets celebrating Timur. The city itself, then over 2,000 years old, had some 150,000 inhabitants, and "most noble and beautiful houses," and many palaces "embowered among trees"; altogether, and not including the extensive suburbs, Clavijo reckoned Samarkand to be "rather larger than Seville." Water was piped into the houses from a river that ran by the city, and irrigation canals greened the hinterland. There the air was fragrant with orchards and vineyards; sheep grazed, cattle ranged, lush crops grew. In the town were factories that made artillery, armor, bows, arrows, glass, porcelain, tiles, and textiles of unsurpassed brilliance, including the *kirimze* or red dye that gave its name to crimson. Working in shops or fields, dwelling in houses of brick or clay or wood, or taking their ease urbanely on the riverside promenade, were Tatars, Turks, Arabs, Persians, Iraqi, Afghans, Georgians, Greeks, Armenians

Catholics, Nestorians, Hindus, all freely practicing their rites and preaching their contradictory creeds. The principal streets were bordered with trees, shops, mosques, academies, libraries, and an observatory; a great avenue ran in a straight line from one end of the city to the other, and the main section of this thoroughfare was covered with glass.[26]

Clavijo was received by the Tatar emperor on September 8. He passed through a spacious park "wherein were pitched many tents of silk," and pavilions hung with silk embroideries. The tent was the usual abode of the Tatar; Timur himself, in this park, had a tent 300 feet in circumference. But there were palaces there too, with floors of marble or tile, and sturdy furniture inset with precious stones or sometimes altogether made of silver or gold. Clavijo found the monarch seated cross-legged on silken cushions "under the portal of a most beautiful palace," facing a fountain that threw up a column of water which fell into a basin wherein apples bobbed incessantly. Timur was dressed in a cloak of silk, and wore a high, wide hat studded with rubies and pearls. He had once been tall, vigorous, and alert; now, aged sixty-eight, he was bent, weak, ailing, almost blind; he could barely raise his eyelids to see the ambassador.

He had acquired as much culture as a man of action could bear; he read history, collected art and artists, befriended poets and scholars, and could on occasion assume elegant manners. His vanity equaled his ability, which no one exceeded in that time. Contradicting Caesar, he reckoned cruelty a necessary part of strategy; yet, if we may believe his victims, he seems to have been often guilty of cruelty as mere revenge. Even in civil government he conferred death lavishly—as to a mayor who had oppressed a city, or a butcher who had charged too much for meat.[27] He excused his harshness as needed in ruling a people not yet reconciled to law, and he justified his massacres as means of forcing disorderly tribes into the order and security of a united and powerful state. But, like all conquerors, he loved power for its own sake, and spoils for the grandeur they could finance.

In 1405 he set out to conquer Mongolia and China, dreaming of a half-world state that would wed the Mediterranean to the China Sea. His army was 200,000 strong; but at Otrar, on the northern border of his realm, he died. His last orders were that his troops should march on without him; and for a while his white horse, saddled and riderless, paced the host. But his soldiers well knew that his mind and will had been half their might; soon they turned back, mourning and relieved, to their homes. His children built for him at Samarkand the majestic Gur-i-Mir, or Mausoleum of the Emir, a tower crowned with a massive bulbous dome, and faced with bricks enameled in lovely turquoise blue.

His empire crumbled with his brain. The western provinces almost at once fell away, and his progeny had to content themselves with the Middle

East. The wisest of this Timurid line was Shah Rukh, who allowed his son Ulug to govern Transoxiana from Samarkand, while he himself ruled Khurasan from Herat. Under these descendants of Timur the two capitals became rival centers of a Tatar prosperity and culture equal to any in Europe at the time (1405–49). Shah Rukh was a competent general who loved peace, favored letters and art, and founded a famous library at Herat. "Herat," wrote a Timurid prince, "is the garden of the world." [28] Ulug Beg cherished scientists, and raised at Samarkand the greatest observatory of the age. He was, says a florid Moslem biographer,

> learned, just, masterful, and energetic, and attained to a high degree in astronomy, while in rhetoric he could split hairs. In his reign the status of men of learning reached its zenith. . . . In geometry he expounded subtleties, and on questions of cosmography he elucidated Ptolemy's *Almagest*. . . . Until now no monarch like him has ever sat on a throne. He recorded observations of the stars with the co-operation of the foremost scientists. . . . He constructed in Samarkand a college the like of which, in beauty, rank, and worth, is not to be found in the seven climes.[29]

This paragon of patronage was murdered in 1449 by his bastard son; but the high culture of the Timurid dynasty continued under the sultans Abu Sa'id and Husein ibn-Baiqara at Herat till the end of the fifteenth century. In 1501 the Uzbeg Mongols captured Samarkand and Bokhara; in 1510 Shah Ismail, of the new Safavid dynasty, took Herat. Babur, last of the Timurid rulers, fled to India, and founded there a Mogul (Mongol) dynasty which made Moslem Delhi as brilliant a capital as Medicean Rome.

IV. THE MAMLUKS: 1340–1517

While Islam in Asia suffered repeated invasions and revolutions, Egypt was exploited with relative stability by the Mamluk sultans (1250–1517). The Black Death destroyed Egyptian prosperity for a time, but through such vicissitudes the Mamluks continued to reconcile competent administration and artistic interests with embezzlement and atrocity. In 1381, however, with Sultan Malik al-Nasir Barquq, the Burji Mamluks began a dynasty of luxury, intrigue, violence, and social decay. They debased the coinage even beyond the custom of governments, taxed the necessaries of life, abused the state monopoly of sugar and pepper, and laid such heavy dues at Alexandria on European trade with India that Occidental merchants were provoked into finding a route to India around Africa. Within a generation after Vasco da Gama's voyage (1498) Egypt lost much of its once rich share of the commerce between East and West; and this economic disaster reduced the country to such destitution that it offered only feeble resistance when Selim I ended the Mamluk rule and made Egypt a province of the Ottoman Empire.

Cairo remained from 1258 to 1453 the richest, fairest, and most populous city in Islam. Ibn-Batuta described it glowingly in 1326; and Ibn-Khaldun, visiting it in 1383, called it "the metropolis of the universe, the garden of the world, the ant heap of the human species, the throne of royalty; a city adorned with palaces and châteaux, convents, monasteries, and colleges, and illumined by the stars of erudition; a paradise so bounteously watered by the Nile that the earth seems here to offer its fruits to men as gifts and salutations" [30]—to which the toilsome fellaheen might have demurred.

The Egyptian mosques of this age reflected the severity of the government rather than the colors of the sky. Here were no "ivans" or portals of glazed brick and tinted tile as in Islamic Asia, but massive stone walls that made the mosque a fortress rather than a house of prayer. The mosque (1356–63) of Sultan Hassan was the wonder of its age, and is still the stateliest monument of Mamluk art. The historian al-Maqrizi thought that "it surpassed all other mosques ever built," [31] but he was a Cairene patriot. An uncertain tradition tells how the Sultan collected renowned architects from many lands, asked them to name the tallest edifice on earth, and bade them erect a loftier one. They named the palace of Khosru I at Ctesiphon, whose surviving arch rises 105 feet from the ground. Stealing stones from crumbling pyramids, their workmen built the walls of the new mosque up to 100 feet, added a cornice for thirteen feet more, and raised at one corner a minaret to 280 feet. The gloomy towering mass impresses, but hardly pleases, the Western eye; the Cairotes, however, were so proud of it that they invented or borrowed a legend in which the Sultan cut off the right hand of the architect lest he should ever design an equal masterpiece—as if an architect designed with his hand. More attractive, despite their function, were the funerary mosques that the Mamluk sultans built outside Cairo's walls to embalm their bones. Sultan Barquq al-Zahir, who began life as a Circassian slave, ended in mute glory in the most splendid of these tombs.

The greatest builder among the Burji Mamluks was Qa'it Bey. Though harassed by war with the Turks, he managed to finance costly edifices in Mecca, Medina, and Jerusalem; restored in Cairo the Citadel of Saladin and the university mosque of el-Azhar; built a hotel famous for its arabesques of stone; raised within the capital a mosque with ornate ornament; and crowned his demise with a memorial mosque, in granite and marble, whose superb decoration, lofty balconied minaret, and geometrically carved dome make it one of the lesser victories of Moslem art.

All the minor arts flourished under the Mamluks. Carvers in ivory, bone, and wood made a thousand handsome products, from pen boxes to pulpits, conceived with taste and executed with unremitting industry and skill; witness the pulpit from Qa'it Bey's extramural mosque, in the Victoria and Albert Museum. Gold and silver inlay reached its peak during these bloody dynasties. And Egyptian pottery, which had invented a thousand novelties in its immemorial millenniums, now gave the world enameled glass: mosque lamps, beakers, vases.

painted with figures or formal ornament in colored enamel, sometimes enhanced with gold. In these and numberless other ways the Moslem artists, giving beauty a lasting form, atoned for the barbarities of their kings.

V. THE OTTOMANS: 1288–1517

History begins after origins have disappeared. No one knows where the "Turks" arose; some have guessed that they were a Finno-Ugric tribe of the Huns, and that their name meant a helmet, which is *durko* in one Turkish dialect. They formed their languages from Mongolian and Chinese, and later imported Persian or Arabic words; these "Turkish" dialects are the sole means of classifying their speakers as Turks. One such clan took its name from its leader Seljuq; it grew from victory to victory, until its multiplied descendants, in the thirteenth century, ruled Persia, Iraq, Syria, and Asia Minor. A kindred clan under Ortoghrul fled in that century from Khurasan to avoid drowning in the Mongol inundation. It found military employment with the Seljuq emir of Konya (Iconium) in Asia Minor, and received a tract of land to pasture its herds.

When Ortoghrul died (1288?) his son Othman or Osman, then thirty years old, was chosen to succeed him; from him the Ottomans or Osmanlis received their name. They did not, before the nineteenth century, call themselves Turks; they applied that name to semi-barbarous peoples in Turkestan and Khurasan. In 1290, seeing that the Seljuqs were too weak to prevent him, Othman made himself the independent emir of a little state in northwestern Asia Minor; and in 1299 he advanced his headquarters westward to Yeni-Sheir. He was not a great general, but he was patiently persistent; his army was small, but it was composed of men more at home on horse than on foot, and willing to risk a weary life or limb for land, gold, women, or power. Between them and the Sea of Marmora lay drowsy Byzantine cities ill governed and poorly defended. Othman laid siege to one such town, Brusa; failing at first, he returned again and again to the attempt; finally it surrendered to his son Orkhan, while Othman himself lay dying at Yeni-Sheir (1326).

Orkhan made Brusa, sanctified with his father's bones, the new capital of the Ottomans. "Manifest destiny"—i.e., desire plus power—drew Orkhan toward the Mediterranean, ancient circlet of commerce, wealth, and civilization. In the very year of Brusa's fall he seized Nicomedia, which became Izmid; in 1330 Nicaea, which became Iznik; in 1336 Pergamum, which became Bergama. These cities, reeking with history, were centers of crafts and trade; they depended for food and markets upon environing agricultural communities already held by the Ottomans; they had to live with this hinterland or die. They did not resist long; they had been oppressed by their Byzantine governors, and heard that Orkhan taxed lightly and allowed religious liberty; and many of these Near Eastern Christians were harassed heretics—Nestorians or Monophysites. Soon a large part of the conquered terrain accepted the Moslem creed; so war solves theological problems before which reason stands in hesitant impotence. Having thus extended his realm, Orkhan took the title Sultan of the Ottomans. The Byzantine emperors made their peace with him, hired his soldiers, and allowed his son Suleiman to establish Ottoman strongholds on European soil. Orkhan died in 1359, aged seventy-one, firmly placed in the memory of his people.

His successors formed a dynasty hardly equaled in history for a merger of martial vigor and skill, administrative ability, barbarous cruelty, and cultured devotion to letters, science, and art. Murad (Amurath) I was the least attractive of the line. Illiterate, he signed his name by pressing his inked fingers upon documents, in the fashion of less distinguished homicides. When his son Saondji led a criminally unsuccessful revolt against him Murad tore out the youth's eyes, cut off his head, and compelled the fathers of the rebels to behead their sons.[32] He trained an almost invincible army, conquered most of the Balkans, and eased their submission by giving them a more efficient government than they had known under Christian domination.

Bajazet I inherited his father's crown on the field of Kosova (1389). After leading the army to victory, he ordered the execution of his brother Yakub, who had fought valiantly throughout that crucial day. Such fratricide became a regular aftermath of an Ottoman accession, on the principle that sedition against the government is so disruptive that all potential claimants to the throne should be disposed of at the earliest convenience. Bajazet earned the title of Yilderim—the Thunderbolt—by the speed of his military strategy, but he lacked the statesmanship of his father, and wasted some of his wild energy in sexual enterprise. Stephen Lazarevitch, vassal ruler of Serbia, contributed a sister to Bajazet's harem; this Lady Despoina became his favorite wife, taught him to love wine and sumptuous banquets, and perhaps unwittingly weakened him as a man. His pride flourished till his fall. After deflowering Europe's chivalry at Nicopolis he released the Count of Nevers with a characteristic challenge, as reported or improved by Froissart:

> John, I know well thou art a great lord in thy country, and son to a great lord. Thou art young, and peradventure thou shalt bear some blame or shame that this adventure hath fallen to thee in thy first chivalry; and to excuse thyself of this blame, and to recover thine honor, peradventure thou wilt assemble a puissance of men, and come to make war against me. If I were in doubt or fear thereof, ere thou departed I should cause thee to swear by thy law and faith that never thou, nor none of thy company, should bear arms . . . against me. But I will neither make thee nor none of thy company to make any such oath or promise, but I will that when thou art returned and art at thy pleasure, thou shalt raise what puissance thou wilt, and spare not, but come against me; thou shalt find me always ready to receive thee and thy company. . . . And this that I say, show it to whom thou list, for I am able to do deeds of arms, and every ready to conquer further into Christendom.[33]

When Timur captured Bajazet at Ankara he treated him with all respect despite the year of insulting correspondence that had passed between them. He ordered the Sultan's bonds removed, seated him at his side, assured him that his life would be spared, and directed that three splendid tents should be fitted out for his suite. But when Bajazet tried to escape he was confined to a room with barred windows, which legend magnified into an iron cage. Bajazet fell ill; Timur summoned the best physicians to treat him, and sent the Lady Despoina to attend and console him. These ministrations failed to revive the vital forces of the broken Sultan, and Bajazet died a prisoner, a year after his defeat.

His son Mohammed I reorganized the Ottoman government and power. Though he blinded one pretender and killed another, he acquired the cognomen "Gentleman" by his courtly manners, his just rule, and the ten years of peace that he allowed to Christendom. Murad II had like tastes, and preferred poetry to war; but when Constantinople set up a rival to depose him, and Hungary violated its pledge of peace, he proved himself, at Varna (1444), as good a general as any. Then he retired to Magnesia in Asia Minor, where twice a week he held reunions of poets and pundits, read verse, and talked science and philosophy. A revolt at Adrianople called him back to Europe; he suppressed it, and overcame Hunyadi János in a second battle of Kosovo. When he died (1451), after thirty years of rule, Christian historians ranked him among the greatest monarchs of his time. His will directed that he should be buried at Brusa in a modest chapel without a roof, "so that the mercy and blessing of God might come unto him with the shining of the sun and moon, and the falling of the rain and dew upon his grave." [34]

Mohammed II equaled his father in culture and conquests, political acumen, and length of reign, but not in justice or nobility. Bettering Christian instruction, he broke solemn treaties, and tarnished his victories with superfluous slaughter. He was Orientally subtle in negotiation and strategy. Asked what his plans were, he answered, "If a hair in my beard knew, I would pluck it out." [35] He spoke five languages, was well read in several literatures, excelled in mathematics and engineering, cultivated the arts, gave pensions to thirty Ottoman poets, and sent royal gifts to poets in Persia and India. His grand vizier, Mahmud Pasha, seconded him as a patron of letters and art; he and his master supported so many colleges and pious foundations that the Sultan received the name "Father of Good Works." Mohammed was also "Sire of Victory"; to him and his cannon Constantinople fell; under the guns of his navy the Black Sea became a Turkish pond; before his legions and diplomacy the Balkans crumbled into servitude. But this irresistible conqueror could not conquer himself. By the age of fifty he had worn himself out by every form of sexual excess; aphrodisiacs failed to implement his lust; finally his harem classed him with his eunuchs. He died (1481), aged fifty-one, just when his army seemed on the verge of conquering Italy for Islam.

A contest among his sons gave the throne to Bajazet II. The new sultan was not inclined to war, but when Venice took Cyprus, and challenged Turkish control of the eastern Mediterranean, he roused himself, deceived his deceivers with a pledge of peace, built an armada of 270 vessels, and destroyed a Venetian fleet off the coasts of Greece. A Turkish army raided northern Italy as far west as Vicenza (1502); Venice sued for peace; Bajazet gave her lenient terms, and retired to poetry and philosophy. His son Selim deposed him, and mounted the throne (1512); presently—some said of poison—Bajazet died.

History is in some aspects an alternation of contrasting themes: the moods and forms of one age are repudiated by the next, which tires of tradition and lusts for novelty; classicism begets romanticism, which begets realism, which begets impressionism; a period of war calls for a decade of peace, and peace prolonged invites aggressive war. Selim I despised his father's pacific policy. Vigorous in frame and will, indifferent to pleasures and amenities, loving the chase and the camp, he won the nickname of "the Grim" by having nine relatives strangled to contracept revolt, and waging war after war of conquest. It did not displease him that Shah Isma'il of Persia raided the Turkish frontier. He registered a vow that if Allah would grant him victory over the Persians, he would build three mighty mosques—in Jerusalem, Buda, and Rome.[36] Having heated the religious predilections of his people to the fighting point, he marched against Isma'il, captured Tabriz, and made northern Mesopotamia an Ottoman province. In 1515 he turned his artillery and Janissaries against the Mamluks, and added Syria, Arabia, and Egypt to his realm (1517). He carried to Constantinople, as an honored captive, the Cairene "caliph"—rather the high priest—of orthodox Mohammedanism; and thereafter the Ottoman sultans, like Henry VIII, became the masters of the church as well as of the state.

In the full glory of his powers Selim prepared to conquer Rhodes and Christendom. When all his preparations were complete he caught the plague and died (1520). Leo X, who had trembled more at Selim's advance than at Luther's rebellion, ordered all Christian churches to chant a litany of gratitude to God.

VI. ISLAMIC LITERATURE: 1400–1520

Even Selim the Grim threaded verses on rhyme, and bequeathed to Suleiman the Magnificent a royal *divan* of his collected poems as well as an empire ranging from the Euphrates to the Danube and the Nile. Twelve sultans and many princes—including that Prince Djem whom his brother Bajazet II paid Christian kings and popes to keep in refined confinement—appear among the 2,200 Ottoman poets who have won fame in the last six centuries.[37] Most of these bards took their forms and ideas, sometimes the language, of their verse from the Persians; they continued to celebrate, in endless rivulets of rhyme, the greatness of Allah, the wisdom of the shah or sultan, and the trembling envy of the cypress trees seeing the white slenderness of the beloved's legs. We of the West are now too familiar with these charms to thrill to such lofty similes; but the "terrible Turks," whose women were alluringly robed from nose to toes, were stirred to the roots by these poetic revelations; and the poetry that in its denatured translation leaves us unmoved could inspire them to piety, polygamy, and war.

From a thousand dead immortals we cull with untutored fancy three names still unfamiliar to the provincial Occident. Ahmedi of Sives (d. 1413), taking his cue from the Persian master Nizami, wrote an *Iskander-nama*, or *Book of Alexander*, an immense epic in strong, crude style, which gave not only the story of Alexander's conquest *by* Persia, but as well the history, religion, science, and philosophy of the Near East from the earliest times to Bajazet I. We must forgo quotation, for the English version is such stuff as nightmares are made of. The poetry of Ahmad Pasha (d. 1496) so delighted Mohammed II that the Sultan made him vizier; the poet fell in love with a pretty page in the conqueror's retinue; Mohammed, having the same predilection, ordered the poet's death; Ahmad sent his master so melting a lyric that Mohammed gave him the boy, but banished both to Brusa.[38] There Ahmad took into his home a younger poet, soon destined to surpass him. Nejati (d. 1508), whose real name was Isa (Jesus), wrote an ode in praise of Mohammed II, and fastened it to the turban of the Sultan's favorite partner in chess. Mohammed's curiosity fell for the lure; he read the scroll, sent for the author, and made him an official of the royal palace. Bajazet II kept him in favor and affluence, and Nejati, triumphing heroically over prosperity, wrote in those two reigns some of the most lauded lyrics in Ottoman literature.

Even so the great masters of Moslem poetry were still the Persians. The court of Husein Baiqara at Herat so teemed with nightingales that his vizier, Mir Ali Shir Nawa'i, complained, "If you stretch out your feet you kick the backside of a poet"; to which a bard replied, "And so do you if you pull up yours." [39] For Mir Ali Shir (d. 1501), besides helping to rule Khurasan, supporting literature and art, and winning renown as a miniaturist and a composer, was also a major poet—at once the Maecenas and Horace of his time. It was his enlightened patronage that gave aid and comfort to the painters Bihzad and Shah Muzaffar, and the musicians Qul-Muhammad, Shayki Na'i, and Husein Udi, and the supreme Moslem poet of the fifteenth century—Mulla Nuru'd-Din Abd-er-Rahman Jami (d. 1492).

In a long and uneventful life Jami found time to achieve fame as a scholar and mystic as well as a poet. As a Sufi he expounded in graceful prose the old mystic theme, that the joyous union of the soul with the Beloved—i.e., God—comes only when the soul realizes that self is a delusion, and that the things of this world are a maya of transitory phantoms melting in a mist of mortality. Most of Jami's poetry is mysticism in verse, spiced with some attractive sensuality. *Salaman wa Absal* tells a pretty tale to point the superiority of divine to earthly love. Salaman is the son of the shah of Yun (i.e., Ionia); born without a mother (which is much more difficult than parthenogenesis), he is brought up by the fair princess Absal, who becomes enamored of him when he reaches fourteen. She conquers him with cosmetics:

> The darkness of her eyes she darkened round
> With surma, to benight him in midday,
> And over them adorned and arched the bows

> To wound him there when lost; her musky locks
> Into so many snaky ringlets curled,
> In which Temptation nestled o'er her cheek,
> Whose rose she kindled with vermilion dew,
> And then one subtle grain of musk laid there,
> The bird of that belovéd heart to snare.
> Sometimes, in passing, with a laugh would break
> The pearl-enclosing ruby of her lips. . . .
> Or, rising as in haste, her golden anklets
> Clash, at whose sudden summons to bring down
> Under her silver feet the golden crown [40]

of the heir-apparent Prince. He yields without effort to these lures, and for a time boy and lady enjoy a lyric love. The King reproaches the youth for such dalliance, and bids him steel himself for war and government. Instead Salaman elopes with Absal on a camel, "like sweet twin almonds in a single shell." Reaching the sea, they make a boat, sail it "for a moon," and come to a verdant isle rich in fragrant flowers, singing birds, and fruit falling profusely at their feet. But in this Eden conscience stabs the Prince with thoughts of the royal tasks he has shunned. He persuades Absal to return with him to Yun; he tries to train himself for kingship, but is so torn between duty and beauty that at last, half mad, he joins Absal in suicide: they build a pyre and leap hand in hand into its flames. Absal is consumed, but Salaman emerges incombustible. Now, his soul cleansed, he inherits and graces the throne— It is all an allegory, Jami explains: the King is God, Salaman is the soul of man, Absal is sensual delight; the happy isle is a Satanic Eden in which the soul is seduced from its divine destiny; the pyre is the fire of life's experience, in which sensual desire is burned away; the throne that the purified soul attains is that of God Himself. It is hard to believe that a poet who could so sensitively picture a woman's charms would seriously ask us to shun them, except occasionally.

With an audacity redeemed by the result, Jami dared to rhyme again the favorite themes of a dozen poets before him: *Yusuf u Zulaikha*, and *Laila wa Majnun*. In an eloquent exordium he restates the Sufi theory of heavenly and earthly beauty:

> In the Primal Solitude, while yet Existence gave no sign of being, and the universe lay hid in the negation of itself, Something was. . . . It was beauty absolute, showing Herself to Herself alone, and by Her own light. As of a most beautiful lady in the bridal chamber of mystery was Her robe, pure of all stain of imperfection. No mirror had Her face reflected, nor had the comb passed through Her tresses, nor the breeze with balmy breath stirred even a single hair, nor any nightingale come nestling to her Rose. . . . But beauty cannot bear to be unknown; behold the Tulip on the mountain top, piercing the rock with its shoot at the first smile of spring. . . . So Beauty Eternal came forth from the Holy Places of Mystery to beam on all horizons

and all souls; and a single ray, darting from Her, struck Earth and its Heavens; and so She was revealed in the mirror of created things. ... And all atoms of the universe became as mirrors casting back each one an aspect of the Eternal Glory. Something of Her brightness fell upon the rose, and the nightingale was crazed with helpless love. Fire caught Her ardor, and a thousand moths came to perish in the flame. ... And She it was who gave the Moon of Canaan that sweet brightness which made Zulaikha mad.[41]

From these celestial heights Jami descends to describe the Princess Zulaikha's loveliness with fervent repetition and detail, even to her "chaste fortress and forbidden place."

> Her breasts were orbs of a light most pure,
> Twin bubbles new-risen from fount Kafur,
> Two young pomegranates grown on one spray,
> Where bold hope never a finger might lay.[42]

She sees Joseph in a dream, and falls in love with him at first seeming; but her father marries her to Potiphar, his vizier. Then she sees Joseph in the flesh, exposed in the market as a slave. She buys him, tempts him, he refuses her advances, she wastes away. The vizier dies; Joseph displaces him and marries Zulaikha; soon both waste away, at last to death. Only the love of God is truth and life. —It is an old tale; but who could sleep over such sermons?

VII. ART IN ASIATIC ISLAM

Through all the reach of Islam, from Granada to Delhi and Samarkand, kings and nobles used geniuses and slaves to raise mosques and mausoleums, to paint and fire tiles, to weave and dye silks and rugs, to beat metal and carve wood and ivory, to illuminate manuscripts with liquid color and line. The Il-Khans, the Timurids, the Ottomans, the Mamluks, even the petty dynasties that ruled the frailer fragments of Islam, maintained the Oriental tradition of tempering pillage with poetry, and assassination with art. In rural villages and urban palaces wealth graduated into beauty, and a fortunate few enjoyed the nearness of things tempting to the touch or fair to see.

The mosque was still the collective shrine of Moslem arts. There brick and tile composed the lyric of the minaret; portals of faïence broke into flashing colors the ardor of the sun; the pulpit displayed the carved contours or inlaid intricacies of its wood; the splendor of the mihrab pointed the worshiper to Mecca; grilles and chandeliers offered their metal lacery as homage to Allah; rugs softened tiled floors and cushioned praying knees; precious silks enveloped illuminated Korans. At Tabriz Clavijo marveled at "beautiful mosques adorned with tiles in blue and gold"; [43] and at Isfahan one of Uljaitu's viziers set up in the Friday Mosque a mihrab in which prosaic stucco became a lure of arabesques and lettering. Uljaitu himself raised at Sultaniya a sumptuous mausoleum (1313), planning to bring to it the remains of Ali and Husein, the founder saints of the Shi'a sect; the plan miscarried graciously, and the Khan's own bones were housed in this imposing ceno- taph. Immense and majestic are the ruins of the mosque at Varamin (1326).

Timur loved to build, and stole architectural ideas, as well as silver and gold, from the victims of his arms. Like a conqueror, he favored mass, as symbolizing his empire and his will; like a *nouveau riche* he loved color, and carried decoration to extravagance. Charmed by the glazed blue tiles of Herat, he drew Persian potters to Samarkand to face with gleaming slabs the mosques and palaces of his capital; soon the city shone and sparkled with glorified clay. At Damascus he noted a bulbous dome swelling out above the base and then tapering upward to a point; he bade his engineers take its plan and measurements before it fell in the general conflagration; he topped Samarkand with such domes, and spread the style between India and Russia, so that it ranges now from the Taj Mahal to the Red Square. When he re- turned from India he brought back so many artists and artisans that they raised for him in three months a gigantic mosque—the "Church of the King" —with a portal 100 feet high and a ceiling upheld by 480 pillars of stone. For his sister Tchouchouk Bika he built the funerary mosque that became the architectural masterpiece of his reign.[44] When he ordered a mosque to honor the memory of his chief wife, Bibi Khanun, he supervised the construction himself, threw meat to the workers in the excavations and coins to assiduous artisans, and inspired or compelled all to work *con furia* until winter halted building and cooled his architectural fire.

His descendants achieved a maturer art. At Mashhad, on the way from Tehran to Samarkand, Shah Rukh's enterprising wife, Gawhar Shad, en- gaged the architect Qavam ad-Din to build the mosque that bears her name (1418). It is the most gorgeous and colorful production of Moslem Persian architecture.[45] Minarets carrying exquisite "lanterns" guard the shrine. Four lordly arches lead into a central court, each faced with faïence tiles "never equaled before or since"[46]—a splendor of time-defying color in a hundred forms of arabesque and geometrical patterns and floral motives and stately Kufic script, all made more brilliant by the Persian sun. Over the southwest "Portico of the Sanctuary" a dome of blue tiles rivals the sky; and on the portal, in large white letters on a blue ground, is the proud and pious dedica- tion of the Queen:

> Her Highness, the Noble in Greatness, the Sun of the Heaven of Chastity and Continence . . . Gawhar Shad—may her greatness be eternal, and may her chastity endure! . . . from her private property,

and for the benefit of her future state, and for the day on which the
works of everyone will be judged, with zeal for Allah and with
thankfulness . . . built this great Masjid-i-Jami, the Holy House, in
the reign of the Great Sultan, the Lord of Rulers, the Father of Victory, Shah Rukh. . . . May Allah make eternal his Kingdom and Empire! And may He increase on the inhabitants of the world His
Goodness, His Justice, and His Generosity! [47]

The mosque of Gawhar Shad was but one of a complex of buildings that
made Mashhad the Rome of the Shi'a sect. There the worshipers of Imam
Riza, in the course of thirty generations, have accumulated an architectural
ensemble of arresting splendor: graceful minarets, dominating domes, archways faced with luminous tiles or with plates of silver or gold, spacious
courts whose blue and white mosaic or faïence return the greeting of the
sun: here, in an overwhelming panorama of color and form, Persian art has
wielded all its magic to honor a saint and awe the pilgrim into piety.

From Azerbaijan to Afghanistan a thousand mosques rose in this age out
of the soil of Islam, for the poetry of faith is as precious to man as the fruits
of the earth. To us of the West, imprisoned in the provinces of the mind,
these shrines are but empty names, and even to honor them with these curt
obeisances may weary us. What does it mean to us that Gawhar Shad received for her chaste bones a lovely mausoleum at Herat; that Shiraz rebuilt
its Masjid-i-Jami in the fourteenth century; that Yazd and Isfahan added
resplendent mihrabs to their Friday Mosques? We are too far away in
space and years and thought to feel these grandeurs, and those who worship
in them have little taste for our Gothic audacities or the sensual images of
our Renaissance. Yet even we must be moved when, standing before the
ruins of the Blue Mosque at Tabriz (1437–67), we recall its once famed
glory of blue faïence and golden arabesques; and we are not unmindful that
Mohammed II and Bajazet II raised at Constantinople (1463, 1497) mosques
almost rivaling St. Sophia's majesty. The Ottomans took Byzantine plans,
Persian portals, Armenian domes, and Chinese decorative themes to form
their mosques at Brusa, Nicaea, Nicomedia, and Konia. In architecture, at
least, Moslem art was still in apogee.

Only one art—a David before Goliath—dared stand up to architecture in
Islam. Perhaps even more honored than the makers of mosques were the
masters of calligraphy and the patient miniaturists who illuminated books
with the infinitesimal calculus of the brush or pen. Murals were painted,
but from this period none survives. Portraits were painted, and a few remain.
The Ottomans publicly obeyed the Biblical and Koranic prohibition of
graven images, but Mohammed II imported Gentile Bellini from Venice to
Constantinople (1480) to make the likeness of him that now hangs in the
London National Gallery. Copies exist of alleged portraits of Timur. In

general the Mongol converts to Islam preferred the traditions of Chinese art to the taboos of the Mohammedan faith. From China they brought into Persian illumination dragons, phoenixes, cloud forms, saintly halos, and moonlike faces, and mated them creatively with Persian styles of limpid color and pure line. The mingling modes were closely kin. Chinese and Persian miniaturists alike painted for aristocrats of perhaps too refined a taste, and sought rather to please the imagination and the sense than to represent objective forms.

The great centers of Islamic illumination in this age were Tabriz, Shiraz, and Herat. Probably from the Tabriz of the Il-Khans come the fifty-five leaves of the "De Motte" *Shah-nama*—Firdausi's *Book of Kings*—painted by divers artists in the fourteenth century. But it was at Herat, under the Timurid rulers, that Persian miniature painting touched its zenith. Shah Rukh engaged a large staff of artists, and his son Baisunkur Mirza founded an academy devoted to calligraphy and illumination. From this school of Herat came the *Shah-nama* (1429)—a miracle of glowing color and flowing grace—now so carefully hidden and religiously handled in the Gulistan Palace Library at Tehran. To view it for the first time is like discovering the odes of Keats.

The real Keats of illumination—the "Raphael of the East"—was Kamal al-Dim Bihzad. He knew in life, and reflected in art, the terrors and vicissitudes of war. Born at Herat about 1440, he studied at Tabriz, then returned to Herat to paint for Sultan Husein ibn-Baiqara and his versatile vizier Mir Ali Shir Nawa'i. When Herat became the center of Uzbeg and Safavid campaigns Bihzad moved again to Tabriz. He was among the first Persian painters to sign their works, yet his art remains are literally few and far between. Two miniatures in the Royal Egyptian Library at Cairo, illustrating Sa'di's *Bustan*, show some theologians debating their mysteries in a mosque; the manuscript bears the date 1489, and the colophon reads: "Painted by the slave, the sinner, Bihzad." The Freer Gallery in Washington has a *Portrait of a Young Man Painting*, copied from Gentile Bellini and signed "Bihzad"; the fine hands reveal the two artists—portrayer and portrayed. Less certainly his are the miniatures in a British Museum copy of Nizami's *Khamza*, and in the same treasury a manuscript of a *Zafar-nama*, or *Book of the Victories* of Timur.

These relics hardly explain Bihzad's unrivaled reputation. They reveal a sensitive perception of persons and things, an ardor and range of color, a vivacity of action caught in a delicate accuracy of line; but they can hardly compare with the miniatures painted for the Duke of Berry almost a century before. Yet Bihzad's contemporaries felt that he had revolutionized illumination by his original patterns of composition, his vivid landscapes, his carefully individualized figures almost leaping into life. The Persian historian

Khwandamir, who was near fifty when Bihzad died (*c.* 1523), said of him, perhaps with the prejudice of friendship: "His draughtsmanship has caused the memory of all other painters in the world to be obliterated; his fingers, endowed with miraculous qualities, have erased the pictures of all other artists among the sons of Adam."[48] It should chasten our certitudes to reflect that this was written after Leonardo had painted *The Last Supper*, Michelangelo the Sistine Chapel ceiling, and Raphael the *Stanze* of the Vatican, and that Khwandamir had probably never heard their names.

The art of the potter declined in this epoch from its finesse in Seljuq Rayy and Kashan. Rayy had been laid in ruins by earthquakes and Mongol raids, and Kashan devoted most of its kilns to tiles. New ceramic centers, however, rose at Sultaniya, Yazd, Tabriz, Herat, Isfahan, Shiraz, and Samarkand. Mosaic faïence was now a favored product: small slabs of earthenware, each painted in one metallic color, and glazed to a brilliance that only needed care for permanence. When patrons were opulent, Persian builders used such faïence not only for mihrabs and decoration, but even to cover large surfaces of mosque portals or walls; there is an arresting example in a mihrab—from the mosque of Baba Kasin (*c.* 1354)—in the Metropolitan Museum of Art in New York.

The metalworkers of Islam maintained their skill. They made bronze doors and chandeliers for mosques from Bokhara to Marraqesh, though none quite matched Ghiberti's "gates to paradise" (1401-52) in the Baptistery of Florence. They forged the best armor of the age—helmets conically shaped to deflect descending blows, shields of shining iron encrusted with silver or gold, swords inlaid with golden lettering or flowers. They made handsome coins, and such medallions as that which preserves the pudgy profile of Mohammed the Conqueror, and great brass candlesticks engraved with stately Kufic script or delicate floral forms; they cast and adorned incense burners, writing cases, mirrors, caskets, braziers, flasks, ewers, basins, trays; even scissors and compasses were artistically chased. A like superiority was conceded to the Moslem artist-artisans who cut gems, or worked with precious metals, or carved or inlaid ivory or wood. The textile remains are fragmentary, but the miniatures of the time picture a vast variety of beautiful fabrics, from the fine linens of Cairo to the silken tents of Samarkand; indeed it was the illuminators who designed the complex yet logical patterns for Mongol and Timurid brocades, velvets, and silks, and even for those Persian and Turkish rugs that were soon to be the envy of Europe. In the so-called minor arts Islam still led the world.

VIII. ISLAMIC THOUGHT

In science and philosophy the glory had gone. Religion had won its war against them, just when it was giving ground in the adolescent West. The highest honors now went to theologians, dervishes, fakirs, saints; and scientists aimed rather to absorb the findings of their predecessors than to look nature freshly in the face. At Samarkand Moslem astronomy had its last fling when the stargazers in the observatory of Uleg Beg formulated (1437) astronomic tables that enjoyed high esteem in Europe till the eighteenth century. Armed with tables and an Arab map, an Arab navigator piloted Vasco da Gama from Africa to India on the historic voyage that ended the economic ascendancy of Islam.[49]

In geography the Moslems produced a major figure in this age. Born at Tangier in 1304, Muhammad Abu Abdallah ibn-Batuta wandered through Daru'l-Islam —the Mohammedan world—for twenty-four years, and returned to Morocco to die in Fez. His itinerary suggests the immense spread of Mohammed's creed: he claims to have traveled 75,000 miles (more than any other man before the age of steam); to have seen Granada, North Africa, Timbuktu, Egypt, the Near and Middle East, Russia, India, Ceylon, and China, and to have visited every Moslem ruler of the time. In each city he paid his respects first to the scholars and divines, only then to the potentates. We see our own provincialism mirrored in him when he lists "the seven mighty kings of the world," all Moslems except one Chinese.[50] He describes not only persons and places, but the fauna, flora, minerals, food, drinks, and prices in the various countries, the climate and physiography, the manners and morals, the religious rituals and beliefs. He speaks reverently of Jesus and Mary, but takes some satisfaction in noting that "every pilgrim who visits the church [of the Resurrection in Jerusalem] pays a fee to Moslems." [51] When he returned to Fez and related his experiences, most of his hearers put him down as a romancer, but the vizier ordered a secretary to record Batuta's dictated memoirs. The book was lost and almost forgotten until it was discovered in the modern French occupation of Algiers.

Between 1250 and 1350 the most prolific writers on "natural history" were Moslems. Mohammed ad-Damiri of Cairo wrote a 1,500-page book on zoology. Medicine was still a Semitic forte; hospitals were numerous in Islam; a physician of Damascus, Ala'al-din ibn-al-Nafis, expounded the pulmonary circulation of the blood 270 years (c. 1260) before Servetus;[52] and a Granada physician, Ibn-al-Khatib, ascribed the Black Death to contagion—and advised quarantine for the infected—in the face of a theology that attributed it to divine vengeance on man's sins. His treatise On Plague (c. 1360) contained a notable heresy: "It must be a principle that a proof taken from the Traditions" of the companions of Mohammed "has to undergo modification when in manifest contradiction with the evidence of the senses." [53]

Scholars and historians were as numerous as poets. Always they wrote in Arabic, the Esperanto of Islam; and in many cases they combined study and writing with political activity and administration. Abu-l-Fida of Damascus took part in a dozen military campaigns, served al-Nasir as minister at Cairo, returned to Syria as governor of Hamah, collected an extensive library, and wrote some books that in their day stood at the head of their class. His treatise on geography (*Taqwin al-Buldan*) outranged in scope any European work of the kind and time; it calculated that three quarters of the globe were covered with water, and noted that a traveler gained or lost a day in going westward or eastward around the world. His famous *Abridgement of the History of the Human Race* was the chief Moslem history known to the West.

But the great name in the historiography of the fourteenth century is Abd-er-Rahman ibn-Khaldun. Here is a man of substance, even to Western eyes: solid with experience, travel, and practical statesmanship, yet familiar with the art and literature, science and philosophy of his age, and embracing almost every Moslem phase of it in a *Universal History*. That such a man was born in Tunis (1332) and raised there suggests that the culture of North Africa was no mere echo of Asiatic Islam, but had a character and vitality of its own. "From my childhood," says Ibn-Khaldun's autobiography, "I showed myself avid of knowledge, and devoted myself with great zeal to schools and their courses of instruction." The Black Death took his parents and many teachers, but he continued his studies until "I found at last that I knew something"[54]—a characteristic delusion of youth. At twenty he was secretary to the sultan at Tunis; at twenty-four, to the sultan at Fez; at twenty-five he was in jail. He moved to Granada, and was sent as its ambassador to Peter the Cruel at Seville. Returning to Africa, he became chief minister to Prince Abu Abdallah at Bougie; but he had to flee for his life when his master was deposed and slain. In 1370 he was sent by the city of Tlemcen as envoy to Granada; he was arrested on the way by a Moorish prince, served him four years, and then retired to a castle near Oran. There (1377) he wrote the *Muqaddama al-Alamat*, literally *Introduction to the Universe*. Needing more books than Oran could supply, he returned to Tunis, but he made influential enemies there, and removed to Cairo (1384). His fame as a scholar was already international; when he lectured in the mosque of el-Azhar students crowded around him, and Sultan Barquq gave him a pension, "as was his wont with savants."[55] He was appointed *qadi malekite*, or royal judge; took the laws too seriously, closed the cabarets, was lampooned out of office, again retired to private life. Restored as chief *qadi*, he accompanied Sultan Nasir ad-Din Faraj in a campaign against Timur; the Egyptian forces were defeated; Ibn-Khaldun sought refuge in Damascus; Timur besieged it; the historian, now an old man, led a delegation to ask lenient terms of the invincible Tatar. Like any other author, he brought a manuscript of his history with him; he read to Timur the section on Timur, and invited corrections; perhaps he had revised the pages *ad hoc*.

The plan worked; Timur freed him; soon he was once more chief judge at Cairo; and he died in office at the age of seventy-four (1406).

Amid this hectic career he composed an epitome of Averroes' philosophy, treatises on logic and mathematics, the *Muqaddama*, a *History of the Berbers*, and *The Peoples of the East*. Only the last three survive; together they constitute the *Universal History*. The *Muqaddama* or *Prolegomena* is one of the high lights in Islamic literature and in the philosophy of history, an amazingly "modern" product for a medieval mind. Ibn-Khaldun conceives history as "an important branch of philosophy," [56] and takes a broad view of the historian's task:

> History has for its true object to make us understand the social state of man, i.e., his civilization; to reveal to us the phenomena that naturally accompany primitive life, and then the refinement of manners ... the diverse superiorities that peoples acquire, and which beget empires and dynasties; the diverse occupations, professions, sciences, and arts; and lastly all the changes that the nature of things can effect in the nature of society.[57]

Believing himself the first to write history in this fashion, he asks pardon for inevitable errors:

> I confess that of all men I am the least able to traverse so vast a field. ... I pray that men of ability and learning will examine my work with good will, and when they find faults will indulgently correct them. That which I offer to the public will have little value in the eyes of scholars ... but one should always be able to count on the courtesy of his colleagues.[58]

He hopes that his work will help in the dark days that he foresees:

> When the world experiences a complete overturn it seems to change its nature in order to permit new creation and a new organization. Hence there is need today of an historian who can describe the state of the world, of its countries and peoples, and indicate the changes in customs and beliefs.[59]

He devotes some proud pages to pointing out the errors of some historians. They lost themselves, he feels, in the mere chronicling of events, and rarely rose to the elucidation of causes and effects. They accepted fable almost as readily as fact, gave exaggerated statistics, and explained too many things by supernatural agency. As for himself, he proposes to rely entirely on natural factors in explaining events. He will judge the statements of historians by the present experience of mankind, and will reject any alleged occurrence that would now be accounted impossible. Experience must judge tradition.[60] His own method, in the *Muqaddama*, is first to deal with the philosophy of history; then with professions, occupations, and crafts; then with the history of science and art. In succeeding volumes he gives the political history of the various nations, taking them one by one, deliberately sacrificing the unity of time to that of place. The true subject of history, says Ibn-Khaldun, is civilization: how it arises, how it is maintained, how it develops letters, sciences, and arts, and why it decays.[61] Empires, like individuals, have a life and trajectory which are their own. They grow, they mature, they decline.[62] What are the causes of this sequence?

The basic conditions of the sequence are geographical. Climate exercises a general but basic influence. The cold north eventually produces, even in peoples of southern origin, a white skin, light hair, blue eyes, and a serious disposition; the tropics produce in time a dark skin, black hair, "dilatation of the animal spirits," lightness of mind, gaiety, quick transports of pleasure, leading to song and dance.[63] Food affects character: a heavy diet of meats, condiments, and grains begets heaviness of body and mind, and quick succumbing to famine or infection; a light diet, such as desert peoples eat, makes for agile and healthy bodies, clearness of mind, and resistance to disease.[64] There is no inherent inequality of potential ability among the peoples of the earth; their advancement or retardation is determined by geographical conditions, and can be altered by a change in those conditions, or by migration to a different habitat.[65]

Economic conditions are only less powerful than the geographical. Ibn-Khaldun divides all societies into nomad or sedentary according to their means of getting food, and ascribes most wars to the desire for a better food supply. Nomad tribes sooner or later conquer settled communities because nomads are compelled by the conditions of their life to maintain the martial qualities of courage, endurance, and solidarity. Nomads may destroy a civilization, but they never make one; they are absorbed, in blood and culture, by the conquered, and the nomad Arabs are no exception. Since a people is never long content with its food supply, war is natural. It is war that generates and renews political authority. Hence monarchy is the usual form of government, and has prevailed through nearly all history.[66] The fiscal policy of a government may make or break a society; excessive taxation, or the entry of a government into production and distribution, can stifle incentive, enterprise, and competition, and kill the goose that lays the revenues.[67] On the other hand, an excessive concentration of wealth may tear a society to pieces by promoting revolution.[68]

There are moral forces in history. Empires are sustained by the solidarity of the people, and this can be best secured through the inculcation and practice of the same religion; Ibn-Khaldun agrees with the popes, the Inquisition, and the Protestant Reformers on the value of unanimity in faith.

> To conquer, one must rely upon the allegiance of a group animated with one corporate spirit and end. Such a union of hearts and wills can operate only through divine power and religious support. . . . When men give their hearts and passions to a desire for worldly goods, they become jealous of one another, and fall into discord. . . . If, however, they reject the world and its vanities for the love of God . . . jealousies disappear, discord is stilled, men help one another devotedly; their union makes them stronger; the good cause makes rapid progress, and culminates in the formation of a great and powerful empire.[69]

Religion is not only an aid in war, it is likewise a boon to order in a society and to peace of mind in the individual. These can be secured only by a religious faith adopted without questioning. The philosophers concoct a hundred systems, but none has found a substitute for religion as a guide and inspiration for human life. "Since men can never understand the world, it is better to accept the faith transmitted by an inspired legislator, who knows better than we do what is better for us, and has prescribed for us what we should believe and do." [70] After this orthodox prelude our philosopher-historian proceeds to a naturalistic interpretation of history.

Every empire passes through successive phases. (1) A victorious nomad tribe settles down to enjoy its conquest of a terrain or state. "The least civilized peoples make the most extensive conquests." [71] (2) As social relations become more complex, a more concentrated authority is required for the maintenance of order; the tribal chieftain becomes king. (3) In this settled order wealth grows, cities multiply, education and literature develop, the arts find patrons, science and philosophy lift their heads. Advanced urbanization and comfortable wealth mark the beginning of decay. (4) The enriched society comes to prefer pleasure, luxury, and ease to enterprise, risk, or war; religion loses its hold on human imagination or belief; morals deteriorate, pederasty grows; the martial virtues and pursuits decline; mercenaries are hired to defend the society; these lack the ardor of patriotism or religious faith; the poorly defended wealth invites attack by the hungry, seething millions beyond the frontiers. (5) External attack, or internal intrigue, or both together, overthrow the state.[72] Such was the cycle of Rome, of the Almoravids and Almohads in Spain, of Islam in Egypt, Syria, Iraq, Persia; and "it is always so." [73]

These are a few of the thousands of ideas that make the *Muqaddama* the most remarkable philosophical product of its century. Ibn-Khaldun has his own notions on almost everything but theology, where he thinks it unwise to be original. While writing a major work of philosophy he pronounces philosophy dangerous, and advises his readers to let it alone; [74] probably he meant metaphysics and theology rather than philosophy in its wider sense as an attempt to see human affairs in a large perspective. At times he talks like the simplest old woman in the market place; he accepts miracles, magic, the "evil eye," the occult properties of the alphabet, divination through dreams, entrails, or the flight of birds. [75] Yet he admires science, admits the superiority of the Greeks to the Moslems in that field, and mourns the decline of scientific studies in Islam.[76] He rejects alchemy, but acknowledges some faith in astrology.[77]

Certain other discounts must be made. Though Ibn-Khaldun is as broad as Islam, he shares many of its limitations. In the three volumes of the *Muqaddama* he finds room for but seven pages on Christianity. He makes only casual mention of Greece, Rome, and medieval Europe. When he has written the history of North Africa, Moslem Egypt, and the Near and Middle East, he believes that he has narrated "the history of all peoples." [78] Sometimes he is culpably ignorant: he thinks Aristotle taught from a porch, and Socrates from a tub.[79] His actual writing of history falls far short of his theoretical introduction; the volumes on the Berbers and the Orient are a dreary record of dynastic genealogies, palace intrigues, and petty wars. Apparently he intended these volumes to be political history only, and offered the *Muqaddama* as a history—though it is rather a general consideration—of culture.

To recover our respect for Ibn-Khaldun we need only ask what Christian work of philosophy in the fourteenth century can stand beside the *Prolegomena*. Perhaps some ancient authors had covered part of the ground that he charted; and among his own people al-Masudi (d. 956), in a work now lost, had discussed the influence of religion, economics, morals, and environment on the character and laws of a people, and the causes of political decline.[80] Ibn-Khaldun, however, felt, and with some reason, that he had created the science of sociology. Nowhere in literature before the eighteenth century can we find a philosophy of history, or a system of sociology, comparable in power, scope, and keen analysis with Ibn-Khaldun's. Our leading contemporary philosopher of history has judged the *Muqaddama* to be "undoubtedly the greatest work of its kind that has ever yet been created by any mind in any time or place." [81] Herbert Spencer's *Principles of Sociology* (1876–96) may compare favorably with it, but Spencer had many aides. In any case we may agree with a distinguished historian of science, that "the most important historical work of the Middle Ages" [82] was the *Muqaddama* of Ibn-Khaldun.

CHAPTER XXXI

Suleiman the Magnificent

1520-66

I. AFRICAN ISLAM: 1200–1566

IT is hard for us, pigeonholed in Christendom, to realize that from the eighth to the thirteenth century Islam was culturally, politically, and militarily superior to Europe. Even in its decline in the sixteenth century it prevailed from Delhi and beyond to Casablanca, from Adrianople to Aden, from Tunis to Timbuktu. Visiting the Sudan in 1353, Ibn-Batuta found there a creditable civilization under Moslem leadership; and a Negro Mohammedan, Abd-er-Rahman Sa'di, would later write a revealing and intelligent history, *Tarik-es-Sudan* (*c.* 1650), describing private libraries of 1,600 volumes in Timbuktu, and massive mosques whose ruins attest a departed glory.

The Marini dynasty (1195–1270) made Morocco independent, and developed Fez and Marraqesh into major cities, each with august gateways, imposing mosques, learned libraries, colleges squatting amid shady colonnades, and wordy bazarres where one could buy anything at half the price. In the thirteenth century Fez had some 125,000 inhabitants, probably more than any city in Europe except Constantinople, Rome, and Paris. In its Karouine Mosque, seat of Morocco's oldest university, religion and science lived in concord, taking eager students from all African Islam, and—in arduous courses of three to twelve years—training teachers, lawyers, theologians, and statesmen. Emir Yaqub II (r. 1269–86), ruling Morocco from Fez or Marraqesh, was one of the most enlightened princes of a progressive century, a just governor, a wise philanthropist, tempering theology with philosophy, shunning bigotry, and encouraging friendly intercourse with Europeans. The two cities received many refugees from Spain, and these brought a new stimulus to science, art, and industry. Ibn-Batuta, who had seen nearly all of vast Islam, called Morocco the earthly paradise.

On the way from Fez to Oran the modern traveler is surprised to find at Tlemcen the modest remnant of what in the thirteenth century was a city of 125,000 souls Three of its once sixty-four mosques—the Jama-el-Kebir (1136), the mosque of Abul Hassan (1298), and that of El-Halawi (1353)— are among the finest in the Mohammedan world; marble columns, complex mosaics, brilliant mihrabs, arcaded courts, carved wood, and towering minarets survive to tell of a splendor gone and almost forgotten. Here the Abd-el-Wahid dynasty (1248–1337, 1359–1553) maintained for three centuries a relatively enlightened rule, protecting Christians and Jews in religious freedom, and providing patronage to letters and arts. After the Turks captured the city (1553) it lost its importance as a center of trade, and declined into the shadows of history.

Farther east, Algiers flourished through a mixture of commerce and piracy. Half-hidden in a rock-bound semicircular bay, this picturesque port, rising in tier upon tier of white tenements and palaces from the Mediterranean to the Casbah, provided a favorite lair for "privateers"; even from Pompey's days the corsairs of that coast had preyed upon defenseless shipping. After 1492 Algiers became a refuge for Moors fleeing from Spain; many of them joined the pirate crews, and turned with vengeful fury upon what Christian shipping they could waylay. Growing in number and audacity, the pirates manned fleets as strong as national navies, and raided the North Mediterranean coasts. Spain retaliated with protective expeditions that captured Oran, Algiers, and Tripoli (1509–10).

In 1516 a colorful buccaneer entered the picture. The Italians called him Barbarossa from his red beard; his actual name was Khair ed-Din Khizr; he was a Greek of Lesbos, who came with his brother Horush to join the pirate crew. While Khair ed-Din raised himself to command of the fleet, Horush led an army against Algiers, expelled the Spanish garrison, made himself governor of the city, and died in battle (1518). Khair ed-Din, succeeding to his brother's power, ruled with energy and skill. To consolidate his position he went to Constantinople, and offered Selim I sovereignty over Tripoli, Tunisia, and Algeria in return for a Turkish force adequate to maintain his own authority as vassal governor of these regions. Selim agreed, and Suleiman confirmed the arrangement. In 1533 Khair ed-Din became the hero of Western Islam by ferrying 70,000 Moors from inhospitable Spain to Africa. Appointed first admiral of the entire Turkish fleet, Barbarossa, with eighty-four vessels at his command, raided town after town on the coasts of Sicily and Italy, and took thousands of Christians to be sold as slaves. Landing near Naples, he almost succeeded in capturing Giulia Gonzaga Colonna, reputed the loveliest woman in Italy. She escaped half clad, rode off with one knight as her escort, and, on reaching her destination, ordered his death for reasons which she left to be inferred.

But Barbarossa aimed at less perishable booty than a beautiful woman. Landing his Janissaries at Bizerte, he marched against Tunis (1534). The Nefsid dynasty had ruled that city reasonably well since 1336; arts and letters had flourished under their patronage; but Muley Hassan, the current prince, had alienated the people by his cruelties. He fled as Barbarossa approached; Tunis was taken bloodlessly; Tunisia was added to the Ottoman realm, and Barbarossa was master of the Mediterranean.

It was another crisis for Christendom, for the unchallenged Turkish fleet could at any moment secure a foothold for Islam in the Italian boot. Strangely enough, Francis I was at this time allied with the Turks, and Pope Clement VII was allied with France. Fortunately, Clement died (September 25, 1534); Pope Paul III pledged funds to Charles V for an attack on Barbarossa, and Andrea Doria offered the full co-operation of the Genoese fleet. In the spring of 1535 Charles assembled at Cagliari, in Sardinia, 400 vessels and 30,000 troops. Crossing the Mediterranean, he laid siege to La Goletta, a fort commanding the Gulf of Tunis. After a month's fighting, La Goletta fell, and the Imperial army marched on to Tunis. Barbarossa tried to stop the advance; he was defeated and fled. Christian slaves in Tunis broke their chains and opened the gates, and Charles entered the city unresisted. For two days he surrendered it to pillage by his soldiers, who would otherwise have mutinied; thousands of Moslems were massacred; the art of centuries was shattered in a day or two. The Christian slaves were joyously freed, and the surviving Mohammedan population was enslaved. Charles reinstated Muley Hassan as his tributary vassal, left garrisons in Bona and La Goletta, and returned to Europe.

Barbarossa escaped to Constantinople, and there, with Suleiman's funds, built a new fleet of 200 ships. In July 1537, this force effected a landing at Taranto, and Christendom was again besieged. A new "Holy League" of Venice, the papacy, and the Empire took form, and gathered 200 vessels off Corfu. On September 27 the rival armadas, at the entrance to the Ambracian Gulf, fought an engagement almost in the same waters where Antony and Cleopatra had met Octavian at Actium. Barbarossa won, and again ruled the seas. Sailing east, he took one after another of the Venetian possessions in the Aegean and Greece, and forced Venice to a separate peace.

Charles tried to win Barbarossa to his service by gifts and an offer to make him vassal king of North Africa, but Khair ed-Din preferred Islamic bait. In October 1541, Charles and Doria led an expedition against Algiers; it was defeated on land by Barbarossa's army, and at sea by a storm. Barbarossa returned the call by ravaging Calabria and landing, unhindered, at Ostia, the port of Rome. The great capital shivered in its shrines, but Paul III was at that time on good terms with Francis, and Barbarossa, allegedly out of courtesy to his ally, paid in cash for all that he took at Ostia, and departed peacefully.[1] He sailed up to Toulon, where his fleet was welcomed by the matter-of-fact French; he asked that the church bells should suspend their ringing while Allah's vessels were in the harbor, for the bells disturbed his sleep, and his request was law. He joined a French fleet in taking Nice and

Villefranche from the Emperor. Then, seventy-seven, the triumphant corsair retired with full honors to die in bed at eighty (1546).

Bona, La Goletta, and Tripoli fell back to Islam, and the Ottoman Empire reached from Algiers to Baghdad. Only one Moslem power dared to challenge its predominance in Islam.

II. SAFAVID PERSIA: 1502–76

Persia, which had enjoyed so many periods of cultural fertility, was now entering another epoch of political vitality and artistic creation. When Shah Ismail I founded the Safavid dynasty (1502–1736) Persia was a chaos of kinglets: Iraq, Yazd, Samnan, Firuzkuh, Diyarbekir, Kashan, Khurasan, Qandahar, Balkh, Kirman, and Azerbaijan were independent states. In a succession of ruthless campaigns Ismail of Azerbaijan conquered most of these principalities, captured Herat and Baghdad, and made Tabriz again the capital of a powerful kingdom. The people welcomed this native dynasty, gloried in the unity and power it gave their country, and expressed their spirit in a new outburst of Persian art.

Ismail's rise to royalty is an incredible tale. He was three years old when his father died (1490), thirteen when he set out to win himself a throne, still thirteen when he had himself crowned Shah of Persia. Contemporaries described him as "brave like a young gamecock" and "lively as a faun," stout, broad-shouldered, with furious mustaches and flaming red hair; he wielded a mighty sword with his left hand, and with the bow he was another Odysseus, shooting down seven apples in a row of ten.[2] We are told that he was "amiable as a girl," but he killed his own mother (or stepmother), ordered the execution of 300 courtesans at Tabriz, and massacred thousands of enemies.[3] He was so popular that "the name of God is forgotten" in Persia, said an Italian traveler, "and only that of Ismail is remembered."[4]

Religion and audacity were the secrets of his success. Religion in Persia was Shi'a—i.e., "the party" of Ali, son-in-law of Mohammed. The Shi'a recognized no rightful caliphs but Ali and his twelve lineal descendants— "imams" or holy kings; and since religion and government were not distinct in Islam, each such descendant had, in this doctrine, a divine right to rule both church and state. As Christians believed that Christ would return to establish His kingdom on earth, so the Shi'ites believed that the twelfth imam—Muhammad ibn-Hasan—had never died, but would someday reappear and set up his blessed rule over the earth. And as Protestants condemned Catholics for accepting tradition, along with the Bible, as a guide to right belief, so the Shi'ites denounced the Sunnites—the orthodox Mohammedan majority—who found the *sunna* or "path" of righteousness not only in the

Koran but also in the practice of Mohammed as handed down in the traditions of his companions and followers. And as Protestants gave up praying to the saints and closed the monasteries, so the Shi'ites discountenanced the Sufi mystics and closed the cloisters of the dervishes, which, like the monasteries of Europe in their prime, had been centers of hospitality and charity. As Protestants called their faith the "true religion," so the Shi'ites took the name *al-Ma-minum*, "true believers." [5] No faithful Shi'ite would eat with a Sunnite; and if a Christian's shadow passed over a Shi'ite's meal, the food was to be discarded as unclean. [6]

Ismail claimed descent from the seventh imam, Safi-al-Din ("Purity of the Faith"), from whom the new dynasty was named. By proclaiming Shi'a as the national and official religion of Iran, and as the sacred standard under which he fought, Ismail united his people in pious devotion against the Sunnite Moslems who hemmed Persia in—the Uzbeks and Afghans on the east, the Arabs, Turks, and Egyptians on the west. His strategy succeeded; despite his cruelties he was worshiped as a saint, and his subjects so trusted in his divine power to protect them that some refused to wear armor in battle. [7]

Having won this fervent support, Ismail felt strong enough to challenge his neighbors. The Uzbeks who ruled Transoxiana had spread their power into Khurasan; Ismail took Herat from them, and drove them out of Persia. Secure in the east, he turned west against the Ottomans. Each faith now persecuted the other with holy intensity. Sultan Selim, we are unreliably told, had 40,000 Shi'ites in his dominions killed or imprisoned before going forth to war (1514), and Shah Ismail hanged some of the Sunnites who formed a majority in Tabriz, and compelled the rest to utter daily a prayer cursing the first three caliphs as usurpers of Ali's rights. Nevertheless, in battle at Chaldiran, the Persians found Shi'a helpless before the artillery and Janissaries of Selim the Grim; the Sultan took Tabriz, and subdued all northern Mesopotamia (1516). But his army mutinied, he retreated, and Ismail returned to his capital with all the glory that shrouds a martial king. Letters declined during his hectic reign, but art prospered under his patronage; he protected the painter Bihzad, and rated him as worth half of Persia. [8] After twenty-four years of rule Ismail died at thirty-eight, leaving the throne to his ten-year-old son (1524).

Shah Tamasp I was a faithless coward, a melancholy sybarite, an incompetent king, a harsh judge, a patron and practitioner of art, a pious Shi'ite, and the idol of his people. Perhaps he had some secret virtues which he hid from history. The continuing emphasis on religion disturbed as well as strengthened the government, for it sanctioned a dozen wars, and kept the Islam of the Near and Middle East divided from 1508 to 1638. Christendom benefited, for Suleiman interrupted his assaults upon the West by campaigns against Persia; "only the Persian stands between us and ruin," wrote Ferdinand's ambassador in Constantinople.[9] In 1533 the Grand Vizier Ibrahim Pasha led a Turkish army into Azerbaijan, took fortress after fortress by bribing Persian generals, and finally captured Tabriz and Baghdad without striking a blow (1534). Fourteen years later, during an armistice with Ferdinand, Suleiman led another army against "the rascally Red-heads" (the Turkish name for the Persians), took thirty-one towns, and then resumed his attacks upon Christendom. Between 1525 and 1545 Charles repeatedly negotiated with Persia, presumably to co-ordinate Christian and Persian resistance to Suleiman. The West rejoiced when Persia assumed the offensive and captured Erzerum; but in 1554 Suleiman returned, devastated great stretches of Persia, and forced Tamasp to a peace in which Baghdad and Lower Mesopotamia fell permanently under Turkish rule.

More interesting than these dismal conflicts were the venturesome journeys that Anthony Jenkinson made into Transoxiana and Persia in search of an overland trade route to India and "Cathay." In this matter Ivan the Terrible proved amiable; he welcomed Jenkinson in Moscow, sent him as his ambassador to the Uzbek rulers at Bokhara, and agreed to let English goods enter Russia duty free and pass down the Volga and across the Caspian. After surviving a violent storm on that sea, Jenkinson continued into Persia and reached Qasvin (1561). There he delivered to Tamasp letters of salutation from a distant queen who seemed to the Persians a minor ruler over a barbarous people. They were inclined to sign a trade agreement, but when Jenkinson confessed himself a Christian they bade him depart; "we have no need of friendship with infidels," they told him; and as he left the Shah a servant spread purifying sand to cover the Christian footprints that had polluted the Shi'a court.[10]

The death of Tamasp (1576) concluded the longest but one of all Mohammedan reigns, and one of the most disastrous. It was not distinguished by any literature lovingly cherished in Persian memory, unless we include the fascinating memoirs of the expatriated Babur. But Safavid art, though its zenith would come later, already in these two reigns began to pour forth works of that grandeur, brilliance, and refinement which for twenty-two centuries have marked the products of Persia. In Isfahan the mausoleum of Harun-i-Vilaya displayed all the finesse of classic Persian design, and the best color and cutting of mosaic faïence; and a complex half-dome crowned the portal of the great Friday Mosque. Another Masjid-i-Jami rose in this age at Shiraz, but time has swallowed it.

In many instances the delicate work of the illuminators and calligraphers has outlasted the architectural monuments, and has justified the care that made the book, in Islam, almost an idol of loving reverence. The Arabs, proud of everything, were forgivably enamored of their alphabet, which lent itself to lines of sinuous grace. The Persians above all made that script an art in adorning the mihrabs and portals of their mosques, the metal of their weapons, the clay of their pottery, the texture of their rugs, and in transmitting their Scriptures and their poets in manuscripts that many generations would cherish as delights to eye and soul. The Nastaliq or sloping script, which had flourished under the Timurids at Tabriz, Herat, and Samarkand, returned to Tabriz under the Safavids, and went with them to Isfahan. As the mosque brought together a dozen arts, so the book employed poet, calligrapher, miniaturist, and binder into a collaboration quite as dedicated and devout.

The art of illumination continued to flourish at Bokhara, Herat, Shiraz, and Tabriz. The Boston Museum of Fine Arts has a lordly manuscript of Firdausi's *Shah-nama* signed by Arraji Muhammad al-Qawam of Shiraz (1552); the Cleveland Museum has another illuminated by Mushid-al-Kiatib (1538); and the Metropolitan Museum of Art in New York has one of the finest examples of Tabriz illumination and calligraphy in the title page from a copy (1525) of Nizami's *Khamsu*. The center of Mohammedan illumination moved to Tabriz when Bihzad chose it for his residence (*c.* 1510). During the campaign of Chaldiran Shah Ismail hid Bihzad and the calligrapher Mahmud Nishapuri in a cave as his most precious possessions.[11] Bihzad's pupil Aqa Mirak painted at Tabriz one of the master miniatures of this period, the *Khosru and Shirin Enthroned* (1539), now in the British Museum. Mirak in turn taught the art to Sultan (Prince) Muhammad Nur. Born of a rich family, Muhammad ignored the fact that he had the means to be worthless; he became the "pearl without price" at the court of Shah Tamasp, for he surpassed all his contemporaries in calligraphy and illumination, and in designing book covers and rugs. Between 1539 and 1543 he copied and illustrated the *Khamsu* of Nizami; a magnificent page in the British Museum shows King Khosru, mounted on a pink horse, peering through foliage of green, brown, and gold at Shirin bathing, half naked, in a silver pool. Even more brilliant in color is a painting of the Prophet riding through the skies on his winged horse Buraq to visit heaven and hell. The figures are grace incarnate, but deliberately and religiously without individualized features; the artist was interested in decoration rather than representation, and valued beauty, which, subjective, is sometimes attainable, more than truth, which, objective, always escapes. In these miniatures Persian illumination reached the apex of its elegance.

The same loving care and delicate designs went into textiles and rugs. No textiles survive from these reigns, but the miniatures picture them. In rugs the Safavi designers and artisans were supreme. The carpet seemed an essential of civilization in Islam. The Moslem sat and ate not on chairs but on a floor or ground covered with a rug. A special "prayer rug," usually bearing religious symbols and a Koranic text, received his prostrations in his devotions. Rugs were favored as gifts to friends or kings or mosques; so Shah Tamasp sent twenty large and many small carpets of silk and gold to Selim II on the latter's accession as Ottoman Sultan (1566). Some dominating feature of design classified the rugs as of the garden, floral, hunting, vase, diaper, or medallion type; but around these basic forms were meandering arabesques, Chinese cloud configurations, symbols conveying secret meanings to the initiate, animals lending the pattern life, plants and flowers giving it a kind of linear fragrance and joyful tone; and through the complex whole an artistic logic ran, a contrapuntal harmony of lines more intricate than Palestrina's madrigals, more graceful than Godiva's hair.

Some famous Persian rugs survive from this first half of the sixteenth century. One is a medallion rug with 30,000,000 knots in wool on a silk warp (380 to the square inch); it lay for centuries in a mosque at Ardabil, and is now divided between the Victoria and Albert Museum in London and the County Museum in Los Angeles. In a cartouche at one end is a verse from Hafiz, and beneath this the proud words: "The work of the slave . . . Maqsud of Kashan, in the year 946" after the hegira—i.e., A.D. 1539.[12] Also in the Los Angeles Museum is the immense "Coronation Carpet" used at the crowning of Edward VII in 1901. The Poldi-Pezzoli Museum at Milan, before the second World War shattered the building, counted among its greatest treasures a hunting rug by Ghiyath ad-Din Jami of Yazd, the Bihzad of rug design. The "Duke of Anhalt Rug," in the Duveen Collection, won international renown for its golden yellow ground and seductive arabesques in crimson, rose, and turquoise blue. The rug and the book are among the unchallengeable titles of Safavid Persia to a high place in the remembrance of mankind.

III. SULEIMAN AND THE WEST

Suleiman succeeded his father Selim I in 1520 at the age of twenty-six. He had won a name for himself by his courage in war, his generosity in friendship, and his efficient administration of Turkish provinces. His refined features and gracious manners made him welcome in a Constantinople tired of Selim the Grim. An Italian who saw Suleiman soon after his accession described him as tall, wiry, and strong, the neck too long, the nose too curved, beard and mustache thin, complexion sallow and delicate, countenance grave and calm; he looked more like a student than a sultan.[13] Eight years later another Italian reported him as "deadly pale . . . melancholy, much addicted to women, liberal, proud, hasty, and yet sometimes very gentle." Ghislain de Busbeq, ambassador of the Hapsburgs at the Porte, wrote almost fondly of the Hapsburgs' most persistent enemy:

He has always had the character of being a careful and temperate man; even in his early days, when, according to the Turkish rule, sin would have been venial, his life was blameless, for not even in youth did he indulge in wine or commit those unnatural crimes which are common among the Turks; nor could those who were disposed to put the most unfavorable construction on his acts bring anything worse against him than his excessive devotion to his wife. ... It is a well-known fact that from the time he made her his lawful wife he has been perfectly faithful to her, although there was nothing in the laws to prevent his having mistresses as well.[14]

It is a picture worth noting, but too flattering: Suleiman was doubtless the greatest and noblest of the Ottoman sultans, and equaled any ruler of his time in ability, wisdom, and character; but we shall find him, now and then, guilty of cruelty, jealousy, and revenge. Let us, however, as an experiment in perspective, try to view dispassionately his conflict with Christendom.

The military debate between Christianity and Islam was already 900 years old. It began when Moslem Arabs snatched Syria from the Byzantine Empire (634). It proceeded through the year-by-year conquest of that Empire by the Saracens, and the conquest of Spain by the Moors. Christendom retaliated in the Crusades, in which both sides covered with religious phrases and ardor their economic aims and political crimes. Islam retaliated by taking Constantinople and the Balkans. Spain expelled the Moors. Pope after pope called for fresh crusades against the Turks; Selim I vowed to build a mosque in Rome; Francis I proposed to the Western powers (1516) that they should utterly destroy the Turkish state and divide its possessions among themselves as infidel spoils.[15] This plan was frustrated by the division of Germany in religious war, the revolt of the Spanish communes against Charles V, and the second thought of Francis himself—to seek Suleiman's aid against Charles. Suleiman may have been saved by Luther, as Lutheranism owed so much to Suleiman.

Every government strives to extend its borders, partly to enlarge its resources and revenues, partly to create additional protective terrain between its frontiers and its capital. Suleiman supposed that the best defense was offense. In 1521 he captured the Hungarian strongholds of Szabacs and Belgrade; then, feeling safe in the West, he turned his forces against Rhodes. There the Christians, under the Knights of St. John, held a heavily fortified citadel directly athwart the routes from Constantinople to Alexandria and Syria; it seemed to Suleiman a dangerous alien bastion in an otherwise Turkish sea; and in fact the pirate ships of the Knights preyed upon Moslem commerce[16] in one end of the Mediterranean as the Moslem pirates of Algeria preyed upon Christian commerce in the other. When Moslems were taken in these Knightly raids they were usually slain.[17] Vessels carrying pilgrims to Mecca were intercepted on suspicion of hostile purposes. "Under all the circumstances," says a Christian historian, "Suleiman was in no need of justification for an assault on Rhodes"; [18] and a distinguished English historian adds: "It was in the interest of public order that the island should be annexed to the Turkish realm." [19]

Suleiman attacked with 300 ships and 200,000 men. The defenders, led by the aged Grand Master Philippe de Villiers de L'Île-Adam, fought the besiegers for 145 days, and finally surrendered under honorable terms: the Knights and their soldiery were to leave the island in safety, but within ten days; the remaining population were to have full religious freedom, and were to be exempt from tribute for five years. On Christmas Day Suleiman asked to see the Grand Master; he condoled with him, praised his brave defense, and gave him valuable presents; and to the Vizier Ibrahim the Sultan remarked that "it caused him great sorrow to be obliged to force this Christian in his old age to abandon his home and his belongings." [20] On January 1, 1523, the Knights sailed off to Crete, whence, eight years later, they passed to a more permanent home in Malta. The Sultan tarnished his victory by putting to death the son and grandchildren of Prince Djem because they had become Christians and might be used, as Djem had been, as claimants to the Ottoman throne.

Early in 1525 Suleiman received a letter from Francis I, then a captive of Charles V, asking him to attack Hungary and come to the rescue of the French King. The Sultan answered: "Our horse is saddled, our sword is girt on." [21] However, he had long ago made up his mind to invade Hungary. He set out in April 1526, with 100,000 men and 300 cannon. Pope Clement VII urged Christian rulers to go to the aid of the threatened state; Luther advised the Protestant princes to stay home, for the Turks were obviously a divine visitation, and to resist them would be to resist God.[22] Charles V remained in Spain. The consequent rout of the Hungarians at Mohács was a moral as well as a physical defeat for Christendom. Hungary might have recovered from the disaster if Catholics and Protestants, Emperor and Pope, had labored together; but Lutheran leaders rejoiced in the Turkish victory, and the army of the Emperor sacked Rome.

In 1529 Suleiman returned, and besieged Vienna with 200,000 men; from the spire of St. Stephen's, Count Nicholas von Salm, to whom Ferdinand entrusted the defense, could see the surrounding plains and hills darkened with the tents, soldiery, and armament of the Ottomans. This time Luther summoned his adherents to join in the resistance, for clearly, if Vienna fell, Germany would be the next object of Turkish attack. Reports ran through Europe that Suleiman had vowed to reduce all Europe to the one true faith—Islam.[23] Turkish sappers dug tunnel after tunnel in the hope of blowing up the walls or setting up explosions within the city, but the defenders placed vessels of water at danger points, and watched for movements that would indicate subterranean operations. Winter came, and the Sultan's long line of communications failed to maintain supplies. On October 14 he called for a final and decisive effort, and promised great rewards; spirit and flesh were both unwilling; the attack was repulsed with great loss, and Suleiman sadly ordered a retreat. It was his first defeat; yet he retained half of Hungary, and carried back to Constantinople the royal crown of St. Stephen. He explained to his people that he returned without victory because Ferdinand (who had sat the siege out safely in Prague) had refused to fight; and he promised that he would soon hunt out Charles himself, who dared to call himself emperor, and would wrest from him the lordship of the West.

The West took him seriously enough. Rome fell into a panic; Clement VII, for once resolute, taxed even the cardinals to raise funds to fortify Ancona and other ports through which the Ottomans might enter Italy. In April 1532, Suleiman marched westward once more. His departure from his capital was a well staged spectacle: 120 cannon led the advance; 8,000 Janissaries followed, the best soldiers in the realm; a thousand camels carried provisions; 2,000 elite horsemen guarded the holy standard—the eagle of the Prophet; thousands of Christian captive boys, dressed in cloth of gold and plumed red hats, flaunted lances with innocent bravery; the Sultan's own retinue were men of giant stature and handsome mien; among them, on a chestnut horse, rode Suleiman himself, robed in crimson velvet embroidered with gold, under a white turban inset with precious stones; and behind him marched an army that in its final mustering numbered 200,000 men. Who could resist such splendor and power? Only the elements and space.

To meet this avalanche Charles, after much pleading, received from the Imperial Diet a grant to raise 40,000 foot and 8,000 horse; he and Ferdinand provided 30,000 additional men at their own expense; and with these 78,000, gathered in Vienna, they awaited siege. But the Sultan was delayed at Güns. It was a small town, well fortified, but garrisoned with only 700 troops. For three weeks they fought back every Turkish attempt to break through the walls; eleven times these were pierced, eleven times the defenders blocked the opening with metal, flesh, and desperation. At last Suleiman sent a safe-conduct and hostages to the commander, Nicholas Jurischitz, inviting him to a conference. He came, and was received with honors by the Grand Vizier; his courage and generalship were sorrowfully praised; the Sultan presented him with a robe of honor, guaranteed him against further attack, and sent him back to his citadel under a handsome escort of Turkish officers. The invincible avalanche, defeated by 700 men, passed on to Vienna.

But there too Suleiman missed his prey. Charles would not come out to fight; he would have been foolish to forfeit the advantage of his defenses for the gamble of the open field. Suleiman reckoned that if he had failed to take

Vienna held by 20,000 men with no emperor or king in sight, he would hardly do better against 78,000 inspired by a young monarch who had publicly announced that he would welcome death in this contest as the noblest worldly end to which a Christian could aspire. The Sultan turned away, ravaged Styria and Lower Austria, and took stray captives to grace his retreat. It could have been no comfort to him to hear that while he was marching uselessly back and forth across Hungary Andrea Doria had chased the Turkish fleet into hiding, and had captured Patras and Coron, on the Peloponnesian coast.

When Ferdinand sent an emissary to Constantinople to seek peace Suleiman welcomed him; he would grant peace "not for seven years, not for twenty-five years, not for a hundred years, but for two centuries, three centuries, indeed forever—if Ferdinand himself would not break it," and he would treat Ferdinand as a son.[24] However, he asked a heavy price: Ferdinand must send him the keys to the city of Grau in token of submission and homage. Ferdinand and Charles were so eager to free their arms against Christians that they were ready to make concessions to the Turks. Ferdinand sent the keys, called himself Suleiman's son, and acknowledged Suleiman's sovereignty over most of Hungary (June 22, 1533). No peace was made with Charles. Suleiman recaptured Patras and Coron, and dreamed of straddling Vienna and Tabriz.

He took Tabriz, and turned west again (1536). Putting theology aside, he agreed to co-operate with Francis I in another campaign against Charles. He offered the most amiable terms to the King: peace should be made with Charles only on his surrendering Genoa, Milan, and Flanders to France; French merchants were permitted to sail, buy, and sell throughout the Ottoman Empire on equal terms with the Turks; French consuls in that realm were to have civil and criminal jurisdiction over all Frenchmen there, and these were to enjoy full religious liberty.[25] The "capitulations" so signed became a model for later treaties of Christian powers with Eastern states.

Charles countered by forming an alliance of the Empire, Venice, and the papacy. Ferdinand joined in; so short was forever. Venice bore the brunt of the Turkish attack, lost her possessions in the Aegean and on the Dalmatian coast, and signed a separate peace (1540). A year later Suleiman's puppet in Buda died, and the Sultan made Hungary an Ottoman province. Ferdinand sent an envoy to Turkey to ask for peace, and another to Persia urging the Shah to attack the Turks. Suleiman marched west (1543), took Grau and Stuhlweissenburg, and incorporated more of Hungary into the pashalik of Buda. In 1547, busy with Persia, he granted the West a five-year armistice. Both sides violated it. Pope Paul IV appealed to the Turks to attack Philip II, who was more papal than the popes.[26] The death of Francis and Charles left Ferdinand a freer hand to come to terms. In the Peace of

Prague (1562) he acknowledged Suleiman's rule in Hungary and Moldavia, pledged a yearly tribute of 30,000 ducats, and agreed to pay 90,000 ducats as arrears.

Two years later he followed his brother. Suleiman had survived all his major enemies, and how many popes had he not outlived? He was master of Egypt, North Africa, Asia Minor, Palestine, Syria, the Balkans, Hungary. The Turkish navy ruled the Mediterranean, the Turkish army had proved its prowess east and west, the Turkish government had shown itself as competent in statesmanship and diplomacy as all its rivals. The Christians had lost Rhodes, the Aegean, Hungary, and had signed a humiliating peace. The Ottomans were now the strongest power in Europe and Africa, if not in the world.

IV. OTTOMAN CIVILIZATION

1. Government

Were they civilized? Of course; the notion that the Turks were barbarians as compared with the Christians is a self-propping delusion. Their agricultural methods and science were at least as good as those of the West. The land was tilled by tenants of feudal chieftains who in each generation had to earn their holdings by serving the sultan satisfactorily in administration and war. Except in textiles, ceramics, and perhaps in arms and armor, industry had not yet developed a factory system as in Florence or Flanders, but Turkish craftsmen were famous for their excellent products, and the absence of capitalism was not mourned by rich or poor. The merchants had not reached in sixteenth-century Islam the political influence or social position then accorded to them in Western Europe. Trade between Turk and Turk was noted for its relative honesty, but between Turk and Christian no holds were barred. Foreign commerce was mostly left to foreigners. Moslem caravans moved patiently over the ancient and medieval land routes into Asia and Africa, even across the Sahara; and caravansaries, many of them set up by Suleiman, offered the merchant and traveler resting places on the way. Moslem vessels, till 1500, controlled the sea routes from Constantinople and Alexandria through the Red Sea to India and the East Indies, where exchange was made with goods borne by Chinese junks. After the opening of India to Portuguese merchants by the voyage of Da Gama and the naval victories of Albuquerque, the Moslems lost control of the Indian Ocean, and Egypt, Syria, Persia, and Venice entered into a common commercial decline.

The Turk was a man of the earth and the sea, and gave less thought to religion than most other Mohammedans. Yet he too reverenced mystics, dervishes, and saints, took his law from the Koran, and his education from the mosque. Like the Jews, he shunned graven images in his worship, and looked upon Christians as polytheistic idolaters. Church and state were one: the Koran and the traditions were the basic law; and the same ulema, or association of scholars, that expounded the Holy Book also provided the teachers, lawyers, judges, and jurists of the realm. It was such scholars who, under Mohammed II and Suleiman I, compiled the definitive Ottoman codes of law.

At the head of the ulema was the mufti or *sheik ul-Islam*, the highest judge in the land after the sultan and the grand vizier. As sultans had to die, while the ulema enjoyed a collective permanence, these theologian-lawyers were the rulers of everyday life in Islam. Because they interpreted the present in terms of past law, their influence was strongly conservative, and shared in the stagnation of Moslem civilization after Suleiman's death. Fatalism—the Turkish *qismet* or lot—furthered this conservatism: since the fate of every soul had been predetermined by Allah, rebellion against one's lot was impiety and shallowness; all things, death in particular, were in the hands of Allah, and must be accepted without complaint. Occasionally a freethinker spoke too frankly, and, in rare instances, was condemned to death. Usually, however, the ulema allowed much liberty of thought, and there was no Inquisition in Turkish Islam.

Christians and Jews received a large measure of religious freedom under the Ottomans, and were permitted to rule themselves by their own laws in matters not involving a Moslem.[27] Mohammed II deliberately fostered the Greek Orthodox Church because the mutual distrust of Greek and Roman Catholics served the Turks in countering crusades. Though the Christians prospered under the sultans, they suffered serious disabilities. Technically they were slaves, but they could end that status by accepting Mohammedanism, and millions did. Those who rejected Islam were excluded from the army, for Moslem wars were ostensibly holy wars for the conversion of infidels. Such Christians were subject to a special tax in lieu of military service; they were usually tenant farmers, paying a tenth of their produce to the owner of their land; and they had to surrender one infant out of every ten to be brought up as a Moslem in the service of the sultan.

The sultan, the army, and the ulema were the state. At the sultan's call each feudal chieftain came with his levy to form the *sipahis* or cavalry, which under Suleiman reached the remarkable figure of 130,000 men. Ferdinand's ambassador envied the splendor of their equipment: clothing of brocade or silk in scarlet, bright yellow, or dark blue; harness gleaming with gold, silver, and jewelry on the finest horses that Busbeq had ever seen. An elite infantry was formed from captive or tributary Christian children, who were brought up to serve the sultan in his palace, in administration, and above all in the army, where they were called *yeni cheri* (new soldiers), which the West corrupted into Janissaries. Murad I had originated this unique corps (*c.* 1360), perhaps as a way of freeing his Christian population from potentially dangerous youth. They were not numerous—some 20,000 under Suleiman. They were highly trained in all the skills of war, they were forbidden to marry or engage in economic activities, they were indoctrinated with martial pride and ardor and the Mohammedan faith, and they were as brave in war as they were restlessly discontent in peace. Behind these super-lative soldiers came a militia of some 100,000 men, kept in order and spirit by the *sipahis* and the Janissaries. The favorite weapons were still the bow and arrow and the lance; firearms were just coming into use; and at close quarters men wielded the mace and the short sword. Suleiman's army and military science were the best in the world at that time; no other army equaled it in handling artillery, in sapping and military engineering, in disci-pline and morale, in care for the health of the troops, in the provisioning of great numbers of men through great distances. However, the means were too excellent merely to serve an end; the army became an end in itself; to be kept in condition and restraint it had to have wars; and after Suleiman the army—above all, the Janissaries—became the masters of the sultans.

The conscripted and converted sons of Christians formed most of the ad-ministrative staff of the central Turkish government. We should have ex-pected that a Moslem sultan would fear to be surrounded by men who might, like Scanderbeg, yearn for the faith of their fathers; on the contrary, Sulei-man preferred these converts because they could be trained from childhood for specific functions of administration. Very likely the bureaucracy of the Ottoman state was the most efficient in existence in the first half of the sixteenth century,[28] though it was notoriously subject to bribery. The Diwan or Divan, like the cabinet in a Western government, brought to-gether the heads of administration, usually under the presidency of the grand vizier. It had advisory rather than legislative powers, but ordinarily its rec-ommendations were made law by a *kanun* or decree of the sultan. The judiciary was manned by *qadis* (judges) and mullas (superior judges) from the ulema. A French observer remarked the diligence of the courts and the promptness of trials and verdicts,[29] and a great English historian believed that "under the early Ottoman rulers the administration of justice was better in Turkey than in any European land; the Mohammedan subjects of the sultans were more orderly than most Christian communities, and crimes were rarer."[30] The streets of Constantinople were policed by Janissaries, and were "probably freer from murders than any other capital in Europe."[31] The regions that fell under Moslem rule—Rhodes, Greece, the Balkans—preferred it to their former condition under the Knights or the Byzantines or the Venetians, and even Hungary thought it fared better under Suleiman than under the Hapsburgs.[32]

Most of the administrative offices of the central government were located in the *serai* or imperial quarters—not a palace but a congeries of buildings, gardens, and courts, housing the sultan, his seraglio, his servants, his aides, and 80,000 of the bureaucracy. To this enclosure, three miles in circuit, admission was by a single gate, highly ornamented and called by the French the *Sublime Porte*—a term which, by a whimsy of speech, came to mean the Ottoman government itself. Second only to the sultan in this centralized organization was the grand vizier. The word came from the Arabic *wazir*, bearer of burdens. He bore many, for he was head of the Diwan, the bureaucracy, the judiciary, the army, and the diplomatic corps. He supervised foreign relations, made the major appointments, and played the most ceremonious roles in the most ceremonious of European governments. The heaviest obligation was to please the sultan in all these matters, for the vizier was usually an ex-Christian, technically a slave, and could be executed without trial at a word from his master. Suleiman proved his own good judgment by choosing viziers who contributed a great deal to his success. Ibrahim Pasha (i.e., Abraham the Governor) was a Greek who had been captured by Moslem corsairs and brought to Suleiman as a promising slave. The Sultan found him so diversely competent that he entrusted him with more and more power, paid him 60,000 ducats ($1,500,000?) a year, gave him a sister in marriage, regularly ate with him, and enjoyed his conversation, musical accomplishments, and knowledge of languages, literature, and the world. In the flowery fashion of the East Suleiman announced that "all that Ibrahim Pasha says is to be regarded as proceeding from my own pearl-raining mouth." [33] This was one of the great friendships of history, almost in the tradition of classic Greece.

One wisdom Ibrahim lacked—to conceal with external modesty his internal pride. He had many reasons to be proud: it was he who raised the Turkish government to its highest efficiency, he whose diplomacy divided the West by arranging the alliance with France, he who, while Suleiman marched into Hungary, pacified Asia Minor, Syria, and Egypt by reforming abuses and dealing justly and affably with all. But he had also reason to be circumspect; he was still a slave, and the higher he raised his head the thinner grew the thread that held the royal sword above it. He angered the army by forbidding it to sack Tabriz and Baghdad, and trying to prevent its sack of Buda. In that pillage he rescued part of Matthias Corvinus's library, and three bronze statues of Hermes, Apollo, and Artemis; these he set up before his palace in Constantinople, and even his liberal master was disturbed by this flouting of the Semitic commandment against graven images. Gossip charged him with despising the Koran. Sometimes he gave entertainments surpassing those of Suleiman in cost and magnificence. Members of the Diwan accused him of talking as if he led the Sultan like a tamed lion on a leash. Roxelana, favorite of the harem, resented Ibrahim's influence, and day by day, with feminine persistence, filled the imperial ear with suspicions and complaints. The Sultan was finally convinced. On March 31, 1536, Ibrahim was found strangled in bed, presumably as the result of a royal command. It was a deed whose barbarism matched the burning of Servetus or Berquin.

Far more barbarous was the law of imperial fratricide. Mohammed II had phrased it frankly in his *Book of Laws:* "The majority of the legists have declared that those of my illustrious children who shall ascend the throne shall have the right to execute their brothers, in order to ensure the peace of the world; they are to act accordingly"; [34] that is, the Conqueror calmly condemned to death all but the eldest born of his royal progeny. It was another discredit to the Ottoman system that the property of a person condemned to death reverted to the sultan, who was therefore under perpetual provocation to improve his finances by closing his mind to an appeal; we should add that Suleiman resisted this temptation. As against such vices of autocracy we may acknowledge in the Ottoman government an indirect democracy: the road to every dignity but the sultanate was open to all Moslems, even to all converted Christians. However, the success of the early sultans might have argued for the aristocratic heredity of ability, for nowhere else in contemporary government was so high an average of ability so long maintained as on the Turkish throne.

2. Morals

The diversity of Ottoman from Christian ways flagrantly illustrated the geographical and temporal variation of moral codes. Polygamy reigned quietly where Byzantine Christianity had so recently exacted formal monogamy; women hid themselves in seraglios, or behind veils, where once they had mounted the throne of the Caesars; and Suleiman attended dutifully to the needs of his harem with none of the qualms of conscience that might have disturbed or enhanced the sexual escapades of Francis I, Charles V, Henry VIII, or Alexander VI. Turkish civilization, like that of ancient Greece, kept women in the background, and allowed considerable freedom to sexual deviations. Ottoman homosexuality flourished where "Greek friendship" had once won battles and inspired philosophers.

The Turks were allowed by the Koran four wives and some concubines, but only a minority could afford the extravagance. The warring Ottomans, often far removed from their wonted women, took as wives or concubines, *currente thalamo*, the widows or daughters of the Christians they had conquered. No racial prejudice intervened: Greek, Serbian, Bulgarian, Albanian, Hungarian, German, Italian, Russian, Mongol, Persian, Arab women were welcomed with open arms, and became the mothers of children who were all alike accepted as legitimate and Ottoman. Adultery was hardly necessary under the circumstances, and when it occurred it was severely punished: the woman was obliged to buy an ass and ride it through the city; the man was flogged with a hundred strokes, and was required to kiss and reward the executioner who dealt them. A husband could secure a divorce by a mere declaration of intent, but a wife could free herself only by complex and deterrent litigation.

Suleiman remained a bachelor till his fortieth year. Since the wife of Bajazet I had been captured and allegedly abused by Timur and his Tatars, the Ottoman sultans, to forestall another such indignity, had made it a rule not to marry, and to admit none but slaves to their bed.[85] Suleiman's seraglio contained some 300 concubines, all bought in the market or captured in war, and nearly all of Christian origin. When they expected a visit from the Sultan they attired themselves in their finest robes, and stood in line to greet him; he saluted courteously as many as time allowed, and placed his handkerchief on the shoulder of one who especially pleased him. That evening, on retiring, he asked that the recipient should return his handkerchief. The next morning she would be presented with a dress of cloth of gold, and her allowance would be increased. The sultan might remain in the harem two or three nights, spreading his bounty; then he returned to his own palace, to live day and night with men. Women rarely appeared in his palace, and took no part in state dinners or ceremonies. Nevertheless it was considered a great honor to be assigned to the seraglio. Any inmate of it who reached the age of twenty-five without earning a handkerchief was freed, and usually found a husband of high estate. In Suleiman's case the institution did not lead to physical degeneration, for in most matters he was a man of signal moderation.

Social life among the Ottomans was unisexual, and lacked the gay stimulus of women's charms and laughing chatter. Yet manners were as refined as in Christendom, probably more refined than in any lands except China, India, Italy, and France. Domestic slaves were numerous, but they were humanely treated, many laws protected them, and manumission was easy.[86] Though public sanitation was poor, personal cleanliness was common. The institution of public baths, which the Persians seem to have taken from Hellenistic Syria, was transmitted to the Turks. In Constantinople and other large cities of the Ottoman Empire the public baths were built of marble and attractively decorated. Some Christian saints had prided themselves on avoiding water; the Moslem was required to make his ablutions before entering the mosque or saying his prayers; in Islam cleanliness was really next to godliness. Table manners were no better than in Christendom; meals were eaten with the fingers off wooden plates; there were no forks. Wine was never drunk in the house; there was much drinking of it in taverns, but there was less drunkenness than in Western lands.[87] Coffee came into use among the Moslems in the fourteenth century; we hear of it first in Abyssinia; thence it appears to have passed into Arabia. The Moslems, we are told, used it originally to keep themselves awake during religious services.[88] We find no mention of it by a European writer till 1592.[89]

Physically the Turk was tough and strong, and famed for endurance. Busbeq was astonished to note how some Turks received a hundred blows on the soles of their feet or on their ankles, "so that sometimes several sticks of dogwood are broken on them, without drawing any cry of pain." [40] Even the ordinary Turk carried himself with dignity, helped by robes that concealed the absurdities of the well-fed form. Commoners donned a simple fez, which dressy persons enveloped in a turban. Both sexes had a passion for flowers; Turkish gardens were famous for their color; thence, apparently, came into Western Europe the lilac, tulip, mimosa, cherry laurel, and ranunculus. There was an esthetic side to the Turks which their wars hardly revealed. We are surprised to be told by Christian travelers that except in war they were "not by nature cruel," but "docile, tractable, gentle . . . lovable," and "generally kind." [41] Francis Bacon complained that they seemed kinder to animals than to men.[42] Cruelty emerged when security of the faith was threatened; then the wildest passion was let loose.

The Turkish code was especially hard in war. No foe was entitled to quarter; women and children were spared, but able-bodied enemies, even if unarmed and unresisting, might be slaughtered without sin.[43] And yet many cities captured by Turks fared better than Turkish cities captured by Christians. When Ibrahim Pasha took Tabriz and Baghdad (1534), he forbade his soldiers to pillage them or harm the inhabitants; when Suleiman again took Tabriz (1548) he too preserved it from plunder or massacre; but when Charles V took Tunis (1535), he could pay his army only by letting it loot. Turkish law, however, rivaled the Christian in barbarous penalties. Thieves had a hand cut off to shorten their grasp.[44]

Official morals were as in Christendom. The Turks were proud of their fidelity to their word, and they usually kept the terms of capitulation offered to surrendering foes. But Turkish casuists, like such Christian counterparts as St. John Capistrano, held that no promise could bind the faithful against the interest or duties of their religion, and that the sultan might abrogate his own treaties, as well as those of his predecessors.[45] Christian travelers reported "honesty, a sense of justice . . . benevolence, integrity, and charity" in the average Turk,[46] but practically all Turkish office-holders were open to bribery; a Christian historian adds that most Turkish officials were ex-

Christians,[47] but we should further add that they had been brought up as Moslems. In the provinces the Turkish pasha, like the Roman proconsul, hastened to amass a fortune before the whim of the ruler replaced him; he exacted from his subjects the full price that he had paid for his appointment. The sale of offices was as common in Constantinople or Cairo as in Paris or Rome.

3. Letters and Arts

The weakest link in Ottoman civilization was its poor equipment for the acquisition and transmission of knowledge. Popular education was generally neglected; a little knowledge is a dangerous thing. Instruction was mostly confined to students intending to study pedagogy, law, or administration; in these fields the curriculum was lengthy and severe. Mohammed II and Suleiman took time to reorganize and improve the madrasas, and the viziers rivaled the sultans in gifts to these mosque colleges. Teachers in these institutions enjoyed a higher social and financial status than their counterparts in Latin Christendom. Their lectures were formally on the Koran, but they managed to include literature, mathematics, and philosophy; and their graduates, though richer in theology than in science, kept fully abreast of the West in engineering and government.

Only a small minority of the population could read, but nearly all of these wrote poetry, not excepting Suleiman. Like the Japanese, the Turks held public competitions in which poets read their offerings; Suleiman took a courtly pleasure in presiding over such Parnassian games. The Turks honored a hundred poets in this age, but our immersion in our own grandeur and idiom has left us unaware of even their greatest lyric poet, Mahmud Abdu'l-Baqi. His career spanned four reigns, for though he was forty when Suleiman died, he had another thirty-four years of life in him. He gave up his early trade as a saddler to live by his verse, and would surely have suffered want had not Suleiman befriended him with sinecures. Adding praise to profit, the Sultan wrote a poem on the excellence of Baqi's poetry. Baqi paid him back in a powerful dirge mourning Suleiman's death. Even in the translation, which loses dignity by seeking to preserve the multiple rhymes of the original, something of the poem's passion and splendor emerges:

> Prince of Fortune's cavalier! he to whose charger bold,
> Whene'er he caracoled or pranced, cramped was earth's tourney-square!
> He to the luster of whose sword the Magyar bowed his head!
> He, the dread gleaming of whose brand the Frank can well declare!
> Like tender rose-leaf, gently laid he in the dust his face,
> And Earth, the Treasurer, placed him like a jewel in the case.
> In truth he was the radiance of rank high and glory great,
> A Shah, Iskander-diademed, of Dara's armed state;
> Before the dust beneath his feet the Sphere bent low its head;

Earth's shrine of adoration was his royal pavilion's gate.
The smallest of his gifts the meanest beggar made a prince;
Exceeding bounteous, exceeding kind a potentate! . . .
Weary and worn by this sad, changeful Sphere, deem not thou him;
Near God to be did he his rank and glory abdicate.
What wonder if our eyes no more life and the world behold!
His beauty fair, as sun and moon, did earth irradiate . . .
Now let the cloud blood drop on drop weep, and its form bend low!
And let the Judas-tree anew in blossoms gore-hued blow!
With this sad anguish let the stars' eyes rain down bitter tears,
And let the smoke from hearts on fire the heavens all darkened show . . .
The bird, his soul, hath, huma-like, aloft flown to the skies,
And naught remaineth save a few bones on the earth below . . .
Eternal may the glory of the heaven-high Khosru dwell!
Blessings be on the monarch's soul and spirit—and farewell! [48]

The Turks were too busy conquering powerful states to have much time for those delicate arts that had heretofore distinguished Islam. Some fine Turkish miniatures were produced, with characteristic simplicity of design and breadth of style. Representative painting was left to the scandalous Christians, who in this age continued to adorn with frescoes the walls of their churches and monasteries; so Manuel Panselinos, perhaps borrowing some stimulus from Italian Renaissance murals, frescoed the church of Protaton on Mount Athos (1535–36) with paintings freer, bolder, more graceful, than those of Byzantine times. The sultans imported artists from West and East—Gentile Bellini from Venice, Shah Kali and Wali Jan, miniaturists, from heretical Persia. In painted tiles, however, the Ottomans needed no alien aid; they used them to dazzling effect. Iznik made a name with the excellence of its faïence. Scutari, Brusa, and Hereke, all in Asia Minor, specialized in textiles; their brocades and velvets, adorned with floral themes in crimson and gold, impressed and influenced Venetian and Flemish designers. Turkish carpets lacked the poetic brilliance of the Persian, but their stately patterns and warm colors evoked admiration in Europe. Colbert induced Louis XIV to order French weavers to copy some Turkish palace rugs, but to no avail; the Islamic mastery remained beyond the reach of Occidental skill.

Turkish art reached its peak in the mosques of Constantinople.* Not even Mashhad in its crowded architectural splendor, nor Isfahan in the days of Shah Abbas, perhaps only Persepolis under Xerxes, equaled, in Persian or Moslem history, the grandeur of Suleiman's capital. Here the spoils of Ottoman victories were shared with Allah in monuments expressing at once piety and pride, and the determination of the sultans to awe their people with art as well as arms. Suleiman rivaled his grandfather, Mohammed the Conqueror, in building; seven mosques rose to his order; and one of these (1556),

---

* Not till 1930 was the city officially renamed Istanbul.

taking his name, surpassed St. Sophia in beauty, even while imitating its assemblage of minor cupolas around a central dome; here, however, the minarets, raising their treble prayer to audacious heights, served as sparkling counterpoint to the massive base. The interior is a confusing wealth of decoration: golden inscriptions on marble or faïence, columns of porphyry, arches of white or black marble, windows of stained glass set in traceried stone, pulpit carved as if it were a lifetime's dedication; this is perhaps too sumptuous for reverence, too brilliant for prayer. An Albanian, Sinan, designed this mosque and seventy more, and lived, we are told, to the age of one hundred and ten.

V. SULEIMAN HIMSELF

It was the West that named Suleiman "the Magnificent"; his own people called him *Kanuni*, the Lawgiver, because of his share in codifying Ottoman law. He was magnificent not in appearance but in the size and equipment of his armies, in the scope of his campaigns, in the adornment of his city, in the building of mosques, palaces, and the famous "Forty Arches" aqueduct; magnificent in the splendor of his surroundings and retinue; magnificent, of course, in the power and reach of his rule. His empire marched from Baghdad to within ninety miles of Vienna, to within 120 miles of Venice, the Adriatic's quondam queen. Except in Persia and Italy all the cities celebrated in Biblical and classical lore were his: Carthage, Memphis, Tyre, Nineveh, Babylon, Palmyra, Alexandria, Jerusalem, Smyrna, Damascus, Ephesus, Nicaea, Athens, and two Thebes. Never had the Crescent held so many lands and seas in the hollow of its curve.

Was the excellence of his rule commensurate with its extent? Probably not, but we should have to say this of any spacious realm except Achaemenid Persia and Rome under the Antonines. The area governed was too vast to be well administered from one center before the coming of modern communications, transport, and roads. Laxity and corruption ran through the government; yet Luther said: "It is reported that there is no better temporal rule than among the Turks." [49] In religious toleration Suleiman was bolder and more generous than his Christian compeers: these thought religious conformity necessary to national strength; Suleiman allowed Christians and Jews to practice their religion freely. "The Turks," wrote Cardinal Pole, "do not compel others to adopt their belief. He who does not attack their religion may profess among them what religion he will; he is safe." [50] In November 1561, while Scotland, England, and Lutheran Germany were making Catholicism a crime, and Italy and Spain were making Protestantism a crime, Suleiman ordered the release of a Christian prisoner, "not wishing to bring any man from his religion by force." [51] He made a safe home in his empire for Jews fleeing from the Inquisition in Spain and Portugal.

His defects appeared more clearly in his family relations than in his government. All are agreed that despite wars—which he excused as defense by offense—he was a man of refined and kindly sentiment, generous, humane, and just.[52] His people not only admired him, they loved him. When, on Friday, he went to the mosque, they observed complete silence while he passed; he bowed to them all—Christians and Jews and Mohammedans—and then prayed for two hours in the temple. We do not hear, in his case, of that addiction to the harem which was to undermine the health and power of some later sultans. But we do find him so susceptible to the passions of love as to forget prudence, justice, and even parental affection.

In the earlier years of his reign his favorite mistress was a Circassian slave known as "The Rose of Spring," marked by that dark and chisled beauty which for centuries has characterized the women of the regions around the eastern end of the Black Sea. She bore him a son, Mustafa, who grew into a handsome, able, and popular youth. Suleiman entrusted him with important offices and missions, and trained him to merit as well as inherit the throne. But in the course of love Khurrem—"The Laughing One"—a Russian captive whom the West called Roxelana, won the Sultan away from the Circassian; and her beauty, gaiety, and wiles kept him enchanted till tragedy was consummated. Overriding the rule of his recent predecessors, Suleiman made Khurrem his wife (1534), and he rejoiced in the sons and daughters that she gave him. But as he aged, and the prospect of Mustafa's accession loomed, Khurrem dreaded the fate of her sons, who might legitimately be killed by the new sultan. She succeeded in marrying her daughter to Rustem Pasha, who in 1544 became Grand Vizier; and through this wife Rustem was brought to share Khurrem's fear of Mustafa's coming power.

Meanwhile Mustafa had been sent to govern Diyarbekir, and had distinguished himself by his valor, tact, and generosity. Khurrem used his virtues to destroy him; she insinuated to Suleiman that Mustafa was courting popularity with a view to seizing the throne. Rustem charged that the youth was secretly wooing the Janissaries to his cause. The harassed Sultan, now fifty-nine, doubted, doubted, wondered, believed. He went in person to Eregli, summoned Mustafa to his tent, and had him killed as soon as he appeared (1553). Khurrem and Rustem then found it simple to induce the Sultan to have Mustafa's son slain, lest the youth should seek revenge. Khurhem's son Selim was made prince and heir, and she died content (1558). But Selim's brother Bajazet, seeing assassination as his fate, raised an army to challenge Selim; civil war raged; Bajazet, defeated, fled to Persia (1559); Shah Tamasp, for 300,000 ducats from Suleiman and 100,000 from Selim, surrendered the contender; Bajazet was strangled (1561), and his five sons were put to death for social security. The ailing Sultan, we are told, thanked Allah that all these troublesome offspring were departed, and that he could now live in peace.[53]

But he found peace boring. He brooded over the news that the Knights whom he had ousted from Rhodes were strong in Malta, and were rivaling the Algerian pirates with their own rapacious sorties. If Malta could be made Moslem, mused the seventy-one-year-old Sultan, the Mediterranean would be safe for Islam. In April 1564, he sent a fleet of 150 ships, with 20,000 men, to seize the strategic isle. The Knights, skillfully led by the resourceful Jean de la Valette, fought with their wonted bravery; the Turks captured the fort of St. Elmo by sacrificing 6,000 men, but they took nothing else; and the arrival of a Spanish army compelled them to raise the siege.

The old Magnificent could not end his life on so sour a note. Maximilian II, who had succeeded Ferdinand as emperor, held back the tribute promised by his father, and attacked Turkish outposts in Hungary. Suleiman decided on just one more campaign, and resolved to lead it himself (1566). Through Sofia, Nissa, and Belgrade he rode with 200,000 men. On the night of September 5–6, 1566, while besieging the fortress of Szigetvar, he yielded his life, upright in his tent; like Vespasian, he was too proud to take death lying down. On September 8 Szigetvar fell, but the siege had cost the Turks 30,000 lives, and summer was fading. A truce was signed, and the army marched disconsolately back to Constantinople, bringing not victory but a dead emperor.

Must we judge and rank him? Compared with his analogues in the West he seems at times more civilized, at times more barbarous. Of the four great rulers in this first half of the sixteenth century, Francis, despite his swash-buckling vanity and his hesitant persecutions, strikes us as the most civilized; yet he looked to Suleiman as his protector and ally, without whom he might have been destroyed. Suleiman won his lifelong duel with the West; indeed, the Emperor Maximilian II in 1568 resumed payment of tribute to the Porte. Charles V had stopped the Sultan at Vienna, but what Christian army had dared approach Constantinople? Suleiman was master of the Mediterranean, and for a time it seemed that Rome remained Christian by his and Barbarossa's sufferance. He ruled his empire indifferently well, but how much more successfully than poor Charles struggling against the princely fragmentation of Germany! He was a despot, by unquestioned custom and the consent of his people; did the absolutism of Henry VIII in England or of Charles in Spain win such public affection and confidence? Charles could hardly have been capable of ordering the execution of his son on mere suspicion of disloyalty; but Charles in his old age could cry out for the blood of heretics, and Henry could send wives and Catholics and Protestants to the block or the pyre without missing a meal. Suleiman's religious tolerance, limited though it was, makes these executions look barbarous by comparison.

Suleiman fought too many wars, killed half his progeny, had a creative vizier slain without warning or trial; he had the faults that go with unchecked power. But beyond question he was the greatest and ablest ruler of his age.

CHAPTER XXXII

The Jews

1300-1564

I. THE WANDERERS

IN his *Flores Historiarum* (1228) Roger Wendover told of an Armenian archbishop who, visiting the monastery of St. Albans early in the thirteenth century, was asked about the story that a Jew who had talked with Christ was still alive in the Near East. The archbishop assured the monks that the story was true. His attendant added that the archbishop had dined with this immortal only a short time before leaving Armenia; that the man's name, Latin-wise, was Cartophilus; that when Jesus was leaving the tribunal of Pontius Pilate this Cartophilus struck the Lord in the back, saying, "Go faster"; and that Jesus said to him, "I go, but thou shalt tarry till I come." Other Armenians, visiting St. Albans in 1252, repeated the tale. Popular fiction expanded it, varied the name of the wanderer, and told how, every hundred years or so, he fell into a grave illness and deep coma, from which he recovered as a youth with memories still fresh of the trial, death, and resurrection of Christ. The story sank out of record for a while, but reappeared in the sixteenth century; and excited Europeans claimed to have seen Ahasuerus—as *der ewige Jude* or *le Juif errant* was now called—at Hamburg (1547 and 1564), Vienna (1599), Lübeck (1601), Paris (1644), Newcastle (1790), finally in Utah (1868). The legend of the Wandering Jew was welcomed, in a Europe that was losing its faith, as a reassuring proof of the divinity and resurrection of Christ, and a fresh pledge of His second coming. For us the myth is a somber symbol of a people losing its homeland in the seventy-first year of the Christian era, wandering for eighteen centuries over four continents, and suffering repeated crucifixions, before regaining its ancient habitation in the unstable flux of our time.[1]

The Jews of the Dispersion found least misery under the sultans in Turkey and the popes in France and Italy. Jewish minorities lived safely in Constantinople, Salonika, Asia Minor, Syria, Palestine, Arabia, Egypt, North Africa, and Moorish Spain. The Berbers gave them a reluctant toleration, yet Simon Duran led a flourishing settlement in Algeria. In Alexandria the Jewish community, as described by Rabbi Obadiah Bertinoro in 1488, lived well, drank too much wine, sat cross-legged on carpets like the Moslems, and removed their shoes before entering the synagogue or the home of a friend.[2] German Jews finding refuge in Turkey wrote back to their relatives enthusiastic descriptions of the happy conditions enjoyed there by the Jews.[3] In Palestine the Ottoman pasha allowed the Jews to build a synagogue on the slope of Mt. Zion. Some Western Jews made pilgrimages to Palestine, holding it good fortune to die in the Holy Land, and best of all in Jerusalem.

Nevertheless the center and zest of Jewish thought in this age were in the unforgiving West. There they were least unfortunate in enlightened Italy. In Naples they enjoyed the friendship of King Robert of Anjou. They prospered in Ancona, Ferrara, Padua, Venice, Verona, Mantua, Florence, Pisa, and other hives of the Renaissance. "Italy has many Jews," said Erasmus in 1518; "Spain hardly any Christians." [4] Commerce and finance were respected in Italy, and the Jews who served those necessities were valued as stimulating agents in the economy. The old requirement that Jews should wear a distinguishing badge or garment was generally ignored in the peninsula; well-to-do Jews dressed like the Italians of their class. Jewish youths attended the universities, and an increasing number of Christians studied Hebrew.

Occasionally some holy hater like St. John of Capistrano would excite his hearers to demand the full enforcement of all "blue law" canonical disabilities against the Jews; but though Capistrano was supported by Popes Eugenius IV and Nicholas V, the effect of his eloquence was transient in Italy. Another Franciscan friar, Bernardino of Feltre, attacked the Jews so vociferously that the civic authorities of Milan, Ferrara, and Venice ordered him to be silent or decamp. When a three-year-old child was found dead near the house of a Jew in Trent (1475), Bernardino proclaimed that the Jews had murdered it. The bishop had all the Jews in Trent imprisoned, and some, under duress of torture, said that they had slain the boy and drunk his blood as part of a Passover ritual. All the Jews in Trent were burned to death. The corpse of "little Simon" was embalmed and displayed as a saintly relic; thousands of simple believers made pilgrimages to the new shrine; and the story of the alleged atrocity, spreading over the Alps into Germany, intensified antisemitic feeling there. The Venetian Senate denounced the tale as a pious fraud, and ordered the authorities within Venetian jurisdiction to protect the Jews. Two lawyers came from Padua to Trent to examine the evidence; they were nearly torn to pieces by the populace. Pope Sixtus IV was urged to canonize Simon, but he refused, and forbade honoring him as a saint;[5] however, Simon was beatified in 1582.

In Rome the Jews for centuries enjoyed fairer conditions of life and liberty than anywhere else in Christendom, partly because the popes were usually men of culture, partly because the city was ruled and divided by Orsini and Colonna factions too busy fighting each other to spare hostility to others, and perhaps because the Romans were too close to the business side of Christianity to take their religion fanatically. There was as yet no ghetto in Rome; most of its Jews lived in the *Septus Hebraicus* on the left bank of the Tiber, but they did not have to; palaces of the Roman aristocracy rose amid Jewish dwellings, and synagogues near Christian churches.[6] Some oppression remained: the Jews were taxed to support the athletic games, and were forced to send representatives to take part in them, half naked, against Jewish customs and tastes. Racial antagonism survived. Jews were caricatured on the Roman stage and in Carnival farces, but Jewesses were regularly presented as gentle and beautiful; note the contrast between Barabas and Abigail in Marlowe's *Jew of Malta,* and between Shylock and Jessica in *The Merchant of Venice.*

By and large the popes were as generous to the Jews as could be expected of men who honored Christ as the Messiah and resented the Jewish belief that the Messiah had not yet come. In establishing the Inquisition the popes exempted unconverted Jews from its jurisdiction; it could summon such Jews only for attacks on Christianity, or for attempts to convert a Christian to Judaism. "Jews who never ceased professing Judaism were, on the whole, left undisturbed"[7] by the Church, though not by the state or the populace. Several popes issued bulls aiming to mitigate popular hostility. Pope Clement VI labored in this regard, and made papal Avignon a merciful haven for Jews fleeing from the predatory government of France.[8] Martin V, in 1419, proclaimed to the Catholic world:

> Whereas the Jews are made in the image of God, and a remnant will one day be saved, and whereas they have besought our protection: following in the footsteps of our predecessors, we command that they be not molested in their synagogues; that their laws, rights, and customs be not assailed; that they be not baptized by force, constrained to observe Christian festivals, nor to wear new badges, and that they be not hindered in their business relations with Christians.[9]

Eugenius IV and Nicholas, as we shall see, issued repressive legislation; but for the rest, says Graetz, "among the masters of Italy, the popes were most friendly to the Jews."[10] Several of them—Alexander VI, Julius II, Leo X—ignoring old decrees, entrusted their lives to Jewish physicians. Contemporary Jewish writers celebrated gratefully the security enjoyed by their people under the Medici popes,[11] and one of them called Clement VII "the gracious friend of Israel."[12] Says a learned Jewish historian:

> This was the heyday of the Renaissance period, and a succession of cultured, polished, luxurious, worldly-wise popes in Rome regarded the promotion of culture as being as important a part of their

function as the forwarding of the religious interests of the Catholic Church. . . . They tended, therefore, from the middle of the fifteenth century onward, to overlook inconvenient details of canon law and to show . . . a wide tolerance for those who were not Catholic. The Jewish loan-bankers constituted an integral part of the economic machinery of their dominions, while as broad-minded men of the world they appreciated the conversation of Jewish physicians and others with whom they came into contact. Hence the persecutory regulations that had been elaborated by the Fathers of the Church, and codified by the Third and Fourth Lateran Councils, were almost entirely neglected by them. . . . With this example before their eyes, the other Italian princes—the Medici of Florence, the Estensi of Ferrara, the Gonzaga of Mantua—acted in much the same fashion. Though they were disturbed by occasional interludes of violence or fanaticism—as for example when Savonarola obtained control of Florence in 1497—the Jews mixed with their neighbors and shared in their life to a degree that was almost unexampled. They played a distinct part in certain aspects of the Renaissance. . . . They mirrored it in their own lives and in their literary activities in the Hebrew tongue; they made important contributions to philosophy, music, and the theater; they were familiar figures in many of the Italian courts.[13]

Some once famous figures illustrate these bright days in the relations of Christians and Jews. Immanuel ben Solomon Haromi (i.e., of Rome) was born in the same year as Dante (1265), and became his friend. He was as much a Renaissance man as a loyal Jew could be: physician by profession, preacher, Biblical scholar, grammarian, scientist, man of wealth and affairs, poet, and "writer of frivolous songs that very often passed the bounds of decency."[14] A complete master of Hebrew, he introduced the sonnet form into that language; he almost rivaled the Italians in fluency and spirit, and not again before Heine would a Jewish poet show such talent for satire, such brilliance and wit. Perhaps Immanuel had imbibed some of the Averroist skepticism of the age; one of his poems expresses a distaste for heaven with all its virtuous people (he thought only ugly women were virtuous), and a preference for hell, where he expected to find the most tempting beauties of all time. In his old age he composed a weak imitation of Dante— Topheth we-Eden (Heaven and Paradise); in Judaism, as in Protestantism, there was no purgatory. More generous than Dante, Immanuel, following Rabbinical tradition, admitted into heaven all "the righteous of the nations of the world";[15] however, he condemned Aristotle to hell for teaching the eternity of the universe.

A similar spirit of lighthearted humor gave tang and verve to the writings of Kalonymos ben Kalonymos. King Robert of Naples, on a visit to Provence, noticed the young scholar of the Beautiful Name, and took him to

Italy. At first Kalonymos was all for science and philosophy; he translated Aristotle, Archimedes, Ptolemy, Galen, al-Farabi, and Averroes into Hebrew, and wrote in a high ethical vein. But he found the gay mood of Naples easy to assimilate. When he moved to Rome he became a Jewish Horace, satirizing amiably the faults and foibles of Christians, Jews, and himself. He mourned that he had been born a man; had he been a woman he would not have had to pore over the Bible and the Talmud, or to learn the 613 precepts of the Law. His *Purim Tractate* made fun of the Talmud, and the popularity of this satire among the Roman Jews suggests that they were not as pious as their more unhappy brethren in other lands.

The Renaissance revived not only Greek but Hebrew studies. Cardinal Egidio de Viterbo invited Elijah Levita from Germany to Rome (1509); for thirteen years the Jewish scholar lived in the Cardinal's palace as an honored guest, teaching Egidio Hebrew, and receiving instruction in Greek. Through the efforts of Egidio, Reuchlin, and other Christian pupils of Jewish teachers, chairs of Hebrew were established in several Italian universities or academies. Elijah del Medigo, who taught Hebrew at Padua, was so highly regarded there, despite his refusal of conversion, that when a violent controversy broke out among the Christian students over a problem in scholarship the university authorities and the Venetian Senate appointed Del Medigo to arbitrate, which he did with such erudition and tact that all parties were satisfied. Pico della Mirandola invited him to teach Hebrew in Florence. There Elijah joined the humanist circle of the Medici, and we may still see him among the figures painted by Benozzo Gozzoli on the Medici palace walls. The scholar gave no encouragement to Pico's notion of finding Christian dogmas in the Cabala; on the contrary, he ridiculed that apocalypse as a heap of stupefying absurdities.

North of the Alps the Jews were less fortunate than in Italy. They were expelled from England in 1290, from France in 1306, from Flanders in 1370. France recalled them in 1315 on condition of giving to the king two thirds of any money they might collect on loans made before their expulsion; [16] when the royal profits on these operations ended the Jews were banished again (1321). They returned in time to be blamed for the Black Death, and were again exiled (1349). They were recalled (1360) to lend financial aid and skill in raising sums to ransom the captured French king from England. But in 1394 an Israelite converted to Christianity mysteriously disappeared; the Jews were accused of killing him; some tortured Jews confessed that they had advised the convert to return to Judaism; public opinion was inflamed, and Charles VI reluctantly ordered another banishment of the harassed race.

There was a substantial community of Jews in Prague. Some of them went to hear the sermons of Huss's forerunner Milicz because he showed so much knowledge and appreciation of the Old Testament. Huss studied Hebrew, read Hebrew commentaries, and quoted Rashi and Maimonides. The Taborites who carried Huss's reforms close to communism called themselves the Chosen People, and gave the names Edom, Moab, and Amalek to the German provinces against which they waged war. The Hussite armies, however, were not averse to killing Jews; when they captured Prague (1421) they gave them not the Mohammedan choice of conversion or taxation, but the simpler choice of apostasy or death.[17]

Of all the Christian states Poland was second only to Italy in hospitality to the Jews. In 1098, 1146, and 1196 many Jews migrated from Germany to Poland to avoid death at the hands of Crusaders. They were well received, and prospered; by 1207 some of them owned large estates. In 1264 King Boleslav the Pious gave them a charter of civil rights. After the Black Death more Germans moved to Poland, and were welcomed by the ruling aristocracy as a progressive economic ferment in a nation still lacking a middle class. Casimir III the Great (1333–70) confirmed and extended the rights of the Polish Jews, and the Grand Duke Vitovst guaranteed these rights to the Jews of Lithuania. But in 1407 a priest told his congregation at Cracow that Jews had killed a Christian boy and had gloated over his blood; the charge provoked a massacre. Casimir IV renewed and again enlarged the liberties of the Jews (1447); "we desire," he said, "that the Jews, whom we wish to protect in our own interest as well as in the interest of the royal exchequer, should feel comforted in our beneficent reign." [18] The clergy denounced the King; Archbishop Olesnicki threatened him with hell-fire; and John of Capistrano, coming to Poland as papal legate, delivered incendiary speeches in the market place of Cracow (1453). When the King suffered defeat in war the cry arose that he had been punished by God for favoring infidels. As he needed the support of the clergy in further war, he rescinded his charter of Jewish liberties. Pogroms occurred in 1463 and 1494. Perhaps to prevent such attacks, the Jews of Cracow were thereafter required to live in a suburb, Kazimierz.

There, and in other Polish or Lithuanian centers, the Jews, overcoming all obstacles, grew in number and prosperity. Under Sigismund I their liberties were restored, except of residence; and they remained in favor with Sigismund II. In 1556 three Jews in the town of Sokhachev were charged with having stabbed a consecrated Host and made it bleed; they protested their innocence, but were burned at the stake by order of the bishop of Khelm. Sigismund II denounced the accusation as a "pious fraud" designed to prove to Jews and Protestants that the consecrated bread had really been changed into the body and blood of Christ. "I am shocked by this hideous villainy," said the King; "nor am I sufficiently devoid of common sense as to believe that there could be any blood in the Host." [19] But with the death of this skeptical ruler (1572) the era of good feelings between the government and the Jews of Poland came to an end.

For a time the Jews lived peaceably in medieval Germany. They functioned actively along the great river avenues of trade, in the free cities and the ports; even archbishops asked Imperial permission to harbor Jews. By the Golden Bull (1355) the Emperor Charles IV shared with the Imperial electors the privilege of having Jews as *servi camerae*—servants of the chamber; i.e., the electors were empowered to receive Jews into their dominions, protect them, use them, and mulct them. In Germany, as in Italy, students eager to understand the Old Testament at first hand learned Hebrew; the conflict between Reuchlin and Pfefferkorn stimulated this study; and the first complete printing of the Talmud (1520) provided further impetus.

The influence of Judaism culminated in the Reformation. Theologically this was a reversion to the simpler creed and severer ethic of early Judaic Christianity. Protestant hostility to religious pictures and statuary was, of course, a return to the Semitic antipathy to "graven images"; some Protestant sects observed Saturday as the Sabbath; the rejection of "Mariolatry" and the worship of saints approached the strict monotheism of the Jews; and the new ministers, accepting sex and marriage, resembled the rabbis rather than the Catholic priests. Critics of the Reformers accused them of "Judaizing," called them *semi-Judaei*, "half-Jews"; [20] Carlstadt himself said that Melanchthon wanted to go back to Moses; Calvin included Judaizing among the deadly sins of Servetus, and the Spaniard admitted that his Hebrew studies had influenced him in questioning the trinitarian theology. Calvin's rule in Geneva recalled the dominance of the priesthood in ancient Israel. Zwingli was denounced as a Judaizer because he studied Hebrew with Jews and based many of his sermons and commentaries on the Hebrew text of the Old Testament. He confessed himself enchanted by the Hebrew language:

> I found the Holy Tongue beyond all belief cultivated, graceful, and dignified. Although it is poor in the number of words, yet its lack is not felt because it makes use of its store in so manifold a fashion. Indeed, I may dare to say that if one conceives its dignity and grace, no other language expresses so much with so few words and so powerful expressions; no language is so rich in many-sided and meaningful . . . modes of imagery. No language so delights and quickens the human heart. [21]

Luther was not so enthusiastic. "How I hate people," he complained, "who lug in so many languages as Zwingli does; he spoke Greek and Hebrew in the pulpit at Marburg." [22] In the irritability of his senility Luther attacked the Jews as if he had never learned anything from them; no man is a hero to his debtor. In a pamphlet "Concerning the Jews and Their Lies" (1542) he discharged a volley of arguments against the Jews: that they had refused to accept Christ as God, that their age-long sufferings proved God's hatred of them, that they were intruders in Christian lands, that they were insolent in their usurious prosperity, that the Talmud sanctioned the deception, robbery, and killing of Christians, that they poisoned springs and wells, and murdered Christian children to use their blood in Jewish rituals. We have seen, in studying his aging character, how he advised the Germans to burn down the homes of Jews, to close their synagogues and schools, to confiscate their wealth, to conscript their men and women to forced labor, and to give all Jews a choice between Christianity and having their tongues torn out. In a sermon delivered shortly before his death he added that Jewish physicians were deliberately poisoning Christians.[23] These utterances helped to make Protestantism—so indebted to Judaism—more antisemitic than official Catholicism, though not more so than the Catholic populace. They influenced the Electors of Saxony and Brandenburg to expel the Jews from those territories.[24] They set the tone in Germany for centuries, and prepared its people for genocidal holocausts.

II. ON THE RACK

Why did Christians and Jews hate each other? Doubtless a pervasive and continuing reason was a vital conflict in religious creeds. The Jews were a perennial challenge to the fundamental tenets of Christianity.

This religious hostility led to a racial segregation at first voluntary, later compulsory, issuing in the establishment of the first ghetto in 1516. The segregation accentuated differences of dress, ways, features, worship, and speech; these differences encouraged mutual distrust and fear; this fear generated hate. The Jews turned into a glory their usual exclusion from marriage with Christians; their pride of race boasted of descent from kings who had ruled Israel a thousand years before Christ. They scorned the Christians as superstitious polytheists, a little slow of mind, mouthing gentle hypocrisies amid merciless brutalities, worshiping a Prince of Peace and repeatedly waging fratricidal wars. The Christians scorned the Jews as outlandish and unprepossessing infidels. Thomas More told of a pious lady who was shocked to learn that the Virgin was a Jewess, and who confessed that thereafter she would be unable to love the Mother of God as fervently as before.[25]

The theory of the Eucharist became a tragedy for the Jews. Christians were required to believe that the priest transformed the wafer of unleavened bread into the body and blood of Christ; some Christians, like the Lollards doubted it; stories of consecrated wafers bleeding at the prick of a knife or a pin could strengthen belief; and who would do so horrible a deed but a Jew? Such legends of a bleeding Host were plentiful in late medieval centuries. In several cases, as at Neuburg (near Passau) in 1338, and at Brussels in 1369, the allegations led to the murder of Jews and the burning of their homes. In Brussels a chapel was set up in the cathedral of St. Gudule to commemorate the bleeding Host of 1369, and the miracle was annually celebrated with a festival that became the Flemish Kermess.[26] In Neuburg a clerk confessed that he had dipped an unconsecrated Host in blood, had hidden it in a church, and had accused the Jews of stabbing it.[27] It should be added that enlightened ecclesiastics like Nicholas of Cusa condemned as shameful cruelties the legends of Jewish attacks on the Host.

Economic rivalries hid behind religious hostility. While the papal prohibition of interest was respected among Christians, the Jews acquired almost a monopoly of moneylending in Christendom. When Christian bankers ignored the taboo, firms like the Bardi, Pitti, and Strozzi in Florence, the Welsers, Hochstetters, and Fuggers in Augsburg, rose to challenge this monopoly, and a new focus of irritation formed. Both Christian and Jewish bankers charged high interest rates, reflecting the risks of lending money in an unstable economy rendered more unstable by rising prices and debased currencies. Jewish lenders ran greater risks than their competitors: the collection of debts owed by Christians to Jews was uncertain and hazardous; ecclesiastical authorities might declare a moratorium on debts as in the Crusades; kings might, and did, lay confiscatory taxes upon Jews, or force "loans" from them, or expel the Jews and absolve their debtors, or exact a share in permitted collections. North of the Alps nearly all classes except businessmen still regarded interest as usury, and condemned the Jewish bankers especially when borrowing from them. Since the Jews were generally the most experienced financiers, they were in several countries employed by the kings to manage the finances of the state; and the sight of rich Jews holding lucrative posts and collecting taxes from the people inflamed popular resentment.

Even so, some Christian communities welcomed Jewish bankers. Frankfurt offered them special privileges on condition that they would charge only 32½ per cent, while their rate to others was 43 per cent.[28] This seems shocking, but we hear of Christian moneylenders charging up to 266 per cent; the Holzschuhers of Nuremberg charged 220 per cent in 1304; the Christian lenders in Brindisi charged 240 per cent.[29] We hear of towns calling for the return of Jewish bankers as more lenient than their Christian counterparts. Ravenna stipulated, in a treaty with Venice, that Jewish financiers should be sent to it to open credit banks for the promotion of agriculture and industry.[30]

Nationalism added another note to the hymn of hate. Each nation thought it needed ethnic and religious unity, and demanded the absorption or conversion of its Jews. Several Church councils, and some popes, were aggressively hostile. The Council of Vienne (1311) forbade all intercourse between Christians and Jews. The Council of Zamora (1313) ruled that they must be kept in strict subjection and servitude. The Council of Basel (1431–33) renewed canonical decrees forbidding Christians to associate with Jews, to serve them, or to use them as physicians, and instructed secular authorities to confine the Jews in separate quarters, compel them to wear a distinguishing badge, and ensure their attendance at sermons aimed to convert them.[31] Pope Eugenius IV, at war with the Council of Basel, dared not be outdone by it in troubling the Jews; he confirmed the disabilities decreed by that Council, and added that Jews should be ineligible for any public office, could not inherit property from Christians, must build no more synagogues, and must stay in their homes, behind closed doors and windows, in Passion Week (a wise provision against Christian violence); moreover, the testimony of Jews against Christians should have no validity in law. Eugenius complained that some Jews spoke scandalously about Jesus and Mary, and this was probably true;[32] hatred begot hate. In a later bull Eugenius ordered that any Italian Jew found reading Talmudic literature should suffer confiscation of his property. Pope Nicholas V commissioned St. John of Capistrano (1447) to see to it that every clause of this repressive legislation should be enforced, and authorized him to seize the property of any Jewish physician who treated a Christian.[33]

Despite such edicts the general Christian public behaved toward the Jews with the good nature that actuates nearly all men, women, and animals when their purposes are not crossed. But there could be found in most communities a minority not averse to practicing cruelty when this might be done with collective impunity. So the Pastoureaux, originating as shepherds bound for the Holy Land, but attracting riffraff as they passed through France (1320), decided to kill en route all Jews refusing to be baptized. At Toulouse 500 Jews sought refuge in a tower; they were besieged by a wild mob, which gave them a choice between baptism or death. The governor of the city tried in vain to rescue them. Finding resistance impossible, the fugitives instructed the strongest among them to slay them; in this way, we are told, all but one died; and the survivor, though offering to submit to baptism, was torn to pieces by the crowd. In like manner all the Jews of 120 communities in southern France and northern Spain were blotted out, leaving only some destitute remnants.[34] In 1321, on a charge of poisoning wells, 120 Jews were burned near Chinon.[35] In 1336 a German fanatic announced that he had received a revelation from God commanding him to avenge the death of Christ by killing Jews. He gathered a following of 5,000 peasants, who called themselves *Armleder* from a leather band worn on the arm; they ranged through Alsace and the Rhineland, killing all the Jews they could find. A murderous mania swept through Bavaria, Bohemia, Moravia, and Austria (1337). Pope Benedict XII tried in vain to stop it, but only in Ratisbon and Vienna were the Jews effectively protected; elsewhere thousands were tortured and killed.[36]

The Black Death was a special tragedy for the Jews of Christendom. The same plague had slain Mongols, Moslems, and Jews in Asia, where no one thought of blaming the Jews; but in Western Europe a populace maddened by the ravages of the pestilence accused the Jews of poisoning the wells in an attempt to wipe out all Christians. Fevered imaginations brewed details: the Jews of Toledo, it was said, had dispatched agents with boxes of poison, made from lizards and basilisks and Christian hearts, to all the Jewish communities in Europe, with instructions to drop these concentrations into wells and springs. The Emperor Charles IV denounced the charge as absurd; so did Pope Clement VI; [37] many burgomasters and municipal councils spoke to the same effect, which was little indeed. A false belief spread among the Christians that the Jews were rarely touched by the plague. In some cities— perhaps through differences in hygienic laws or medical care—the fever did seem less fatal to them than to the Christians; [88] but in many places—e.g., Vienna, Ratisbon, Avignon, Rome—the Jews suffered equally.[89] Nevertheless some Jews were tortured into confessing that they had distributed the poison.[40] Christians closed their wells and springs, and drank rain water or melted snow. Merciless pogroms broke out in France, Spain, and Germany. In one town in southern France the entire Jewish community was cast into the flames. All Jews in Savoy, all Jews around Lake Leman, all in Bern, Fribourg, Basel, Nuremberg, Brussels, were burned. Clement VI a second time denounced the horror and the charge, declared the Jews innocent, and pointed out that the plague was as severe where no Jews lived as anywhere else; he admonished the clergy to restrain their parishioners, and excommunicated all persons who killed or falsely accused Jews. In Strasbourg, however, the bishop joined in the accusation, and persuaded the reluctant municipal council to banish all Jews. The populace thought this measure too mild; it drove out the council and installed another, which ordered the arrest of all Jews in the city. Some escaped to the countryside; many of these were killed by the peasantry. Two thousand Jews left in the city were jailed, and were commanded to accept baptism; half of them submitted, the rest refused and were burned (February 14, 1439). All in all, some 510 Jewish communities were exterminated in Christian Europe as a result of these pogroms; [41] many more were decimated; in Saragossa, for example, only one Jew out of five survived the Black Death persecutions.[42] Lea estimated 3,000 Jews killed at Erfurt, 12,000 in Bavaria.[43] In Vienna, on the advice of Rabbi

Jonah, all the Jews gathered in their synagogue and killed themselves; similar mass suicides occurred in Worms, Oppenheim, Krems, and Frankfurt.[44] A panic of flight carried thousands of Jews from Western Europe into Poland or Turkey. It would be hard to find, before our time, or in all the records of savagery, any deeds more barbarous than the collective murder of Jews in the Black Death.

Slowly the surviving Jews of Germany crept back to the cities that had despoiled them, and rebuilt their synagogues. But they were all the more hated for having been wronged. In 1385 all thirty-six towns of the Swabian League imprisoned their Jews, and released them only on condition that all debts owed them should be canceled; this was especially satisfactory to Nuremberg, which had borrowed 7,000 pounds from them ($700,000?).[45] In 1389 a number of Jews were massacred on a charge that they had desecrated a consecrated Host; on the same excuse fourteen Jews were burned in Posen (1399).[46] For diverse reasons the Jews were expelled from Cologne (1424), Speyer (1435), Strasbourg and Augsburg (1439), Würzburg (1453), Erfurt (1458), Mainz (1470), Nuremberg (1498), Ulm (1499). Maximilian I sanctioned their expulsion from Nuremberg on the ground that "they had become so numerous, and through their usurious dealings they had become possessed of all the property of many respectable citizens, and had dragged them into misery and dishonor." [47] In 1446 all Jews in the mark of Brandenburg were imprisoned, and their goods were confiscated, on charges which Bishop Stephen of Brandenburg scored as a cover for greed: "Those princes have acted iniquitously who, prompted by inordinate avarice, and without just cause, have seized on certain Jews and thrown them into prison, and refuse to make restitution of that of which they robbed them." [48] In 1451 Cardinal Nicholas of Cusa, one of the most enlightened men of the fifteenth century, enforced the wearing of badges by the Jews under his jurisdiction. Two years later John of Capistrano began his missions, as legate of Pope Nicholas V, in Germany, Bohemia, Moravia, Silesia, and Poland. His powerful sermons accused the Jews of killing children and desecrating the Host— charges which popes had branded as murderous superstitions. Urged on by this "scourge of the Jews," the dukes of Bavaria drove all Hebrews from their duchy. Bishop Godfrey of Würzburg, who had given them full privileges in Franconia, now banished them, and in town after town Jews were arrested, and debts due them were annulled. At Breslau several Jews were jailed on Capistrano's demand; he himself supervised the tortures that wrung from some of them whatever he bade them confess; on the basis of these confessions forty Jews were burned at the stake (June 2, 1453). The remaining Jews were banished, but their children were taken from them and baptized by force.[49] Capistrano was canonized in 1690.

The tribulations of the Jews in Ratisbon illustrate the age. A converted

Jew, Hans Vogel, alleged that Israel Bruna, a seventy-five-year-old rabbi, had bought from him a Christian child, and had killed it to use its blood in a Jewish ritual. The populace believed the accusation, and cried out for the death penalty. The city council, to save the old man from the crowd, imprisoned him. Emperor Frederick III ordered him released. The council dared not obey, but it arrested Vogel, told him that he must die, and invited him to confess his sins. He admitted that Bruna was innocent, and the rabbi was freed. But news came to Ratisbon that Jews under torture had confessed to killing a child in Trent. Belief in Vogel's charge rose again. The council ordered the arrest of all Ratisbon Jews, and the confiscation of all their goods. Frederick intervened, and laid a fine of 8,000 guilders on the city. The council agreed to free the Jews if they would pay this fine and an additional 10,-000 guilders ($250,000?) as bail. They answered that 18,000 guilders were more than all the property still left them; they could not possibly raise such a sum. They were kept in jail for two years more, and were then released on taking oath not to leave Ratisbon and not to seek revenge. The clergy, however, agitated for their expulsion, and threatened with excommunication any tradesman who sold goods to Jews. By 1500 only twenty-four families remained, and in 1519 these were expelled.[50]

Their expulsion from Spain has been described above, as vital to the history of that country. In Portugal their crucifixion was renewed when Clement VII, at the urging of Charles V, allowed Portuguese prelates to establish the Inquisition (1531) for the purpose of enforcing the practice of Christianity upon the *novos cristãos*—mostly Jews who had been baptized against their will. The severe code of Torquemada was adopted, spies were set to watch the converts for any relapse into Jewish religious observances, and thousands of Jews were imprisoned. Emigration of Jews was prohibited, for their economic functions were still necessary in the Portuguese economy. To prevent flight, Christians were forbidden to buy property from Jews, and hundreds of Jews were sent to the stake for attempting to leave the country. Shocked by these procedures, and perhaps swayed by Jewish gifts, Clement abrogated the powers of the Portuguese Inquisition, and ordered the release of its prisoners and the restoration of confiscated goods. His bull of October 17, 1532, laid down humane principles for dealing with the converts:

> Since they were dragged by force to be baptized, they cannot be considered members of the Church; and to punish them for heresy and relapse were to violate the principles of justice and equity. With sons and daughters of the first Marranos the case is different; they belong to the Church as voluntary members. But as they have been brought up by their relatives in the midst of Judaism, and have had this example continually before their eyes, it would be cruel to pun-

ish them according to the canonical law for falling into Jewish ways and beliefs; they must be kept in the bosom of the Church through gentle treatment.[51]

That Clement was sincere appears from a brief issued by him on July 26, 1534, when he felt death upon him; it instructed the papal nuncio in Portugal to hasten the release of imprisoned converts.[52]

Pope Paul III continued the efforts to aid the Portuguese Jews, and 1,800 of the prisoners were freed. But when Charles V returned from his apparently successful expedition against Tunis he demanded, as reward, the restoration of the Inquisition in Portugal. Paul reluctantly agreed (1536), but with conditions that seemed to King John III to nullify his consent: the accused must be confronted with the accuser, and the condemned should have the right of appeal to the pope. A fanatical convert helped the inquisitors by placarding Lisbon Cathedral with a defiant announcement: "The Messiah has not yet appeared; Jesus was not the Messiah; and Christianity is a lie." [53] As such a statement was clearly calculated to injure the Jews, we may reasonably suspect an *agent provocateur*. Paul appointed a commission of cardinals to investigate the procedures of the Portuguese Inquisition. It reported:

> When a pseudo-Christian is denounced—often by false witnesses—the inquisitors drag him away to a dismal retreat where he is allowed no sight of heaven or earth, and least of all to speak with his friends, who might succor him. They accuse him on obscure testimony, and inform him neither of the time nor the place where he committed the offense for which he is denounced. Later on he is allowed an advocate, who often, instead of defending his cause, helps him on the road to the stake. Let an unfortunate creature acknowledge himself a true believing Christian, and firmly deny the transgressions laid to his charge, they condemn him to the flames, and confiscate his goods. Let him plead guilty to such and such a deed, though unintentionally committed, they treat him in a similar manner under the pretense that he obstinately denies his wicked intentions. Let him freely and fully admit what he is accused of, he is reduced to extremest necessity, and condemned to the dungeon's never-lifting gloom. And this they call treating the accused with mercy and compassion and Christian charity! Even he who succeeds in proving his innocence is condemned to pay a fine, so that it may not be said that he was arrested without cause. The accused who are held prisoners are racked by every instrument of torture to admit the accusations against them. Many die in prison, and those who are set free, with all their relatives bear a brand of eternal infamy.[54]

Though harassed by political developments, and the danger of losing Spain and Portugal as Leo had lost Germany and Clement England, Paul did all that he could to mitigate the Inquisition. But day by day the terror went on, until the Portuguese Jews found, by whatever desperate device, some escape from their hosts, and joined the Jews of Spain in seeking some corner of Christendom or Islam where they might keep their Law and yet be allowed to live.

III. THE SECOND DISPERSION

Where could they go? Sardinia and Sicily, where Jews had lived for a thousand years past, were included with Spain in Ferdinand's edict of expulsion; by 1493 the last Jew had left Palermo. At Naples thousands of the fugitives were welcomed by Ferrante I, by Dominican friars, and by the local Jewish community; but in 1540 Charles V decreed the expulsion of all Jews from Naples.

Genoa had long had a law limiting the entry of additional Jews. When *Conversos* arrived from Spain in 1492 they were not allowed to stay more than a few days. A Genoese historian described them as "cadaverous, emaciated specters with sunken eyes, differing from the dead only in retaining the power to move."[55] Many died of starvation; women bore dead infants; some parents sold their children to pay for transport from Genoa. A small number of the exiles were received into Ferrara, but were required to wear a yellow badge,[56] perhaps as a precaution against the spread of disease.

Venice had long been a haven for the Jews. Efforts had been made to expel them (1395, 1487), but the Senate had protected them as important contributors to commerce and finance. A considerable part of the Venetian export trade was carried on by Jews, and they were active in the import of wool and silk from Spain, spices and pearls from India.[57] For a long time they had, of their own choice, occupied the quarter named after them—the Giudecca. In 1516, after consultation with leading Jews, the Senate ordained that all Jews, except a few specially licensed, should live in a section of the city known as the Ghetto, apparently from a foundry *(getto)* existing there.[58] The Senate ordered all Marranos or converted Jews to leave Venice; many Christian competitors urged the measure, some Christian merchants opposed it as threatening the loss of certain markets, especially in Islam, but Charles V threw his influence into the scale, and the expulsion decree was carried out.[59] Soon, however, Jewish merchants crept back into Venice; exiles from Portugal replaced the expelled Marranos, and Portuguese became for a time the language of the Venetian Jews.

Many Iberian exiles were kindly received into Rome by Pope Alexander VI, and prospered under Julius II, Leo X, Clement VII, and Paul III. Clement allowed Marranos to practice Judaism freely, holding that they were not obligated by any compulsory baptism.[60] In Ancona, the Adriatic port of the Papal States, where the Jews were a vital element in international trade, Clement established a haven for professing Jews, and guaranteed them against molestation. As to Paul III, "no pope," said Cardinal Sadoleto, "has ever bestowed upon Christians so many honors, such privileges and concessions, as Paul has given to the Jews. They are not only assisted, but positively armed, with benefits and prerogatives." [61] A bishop complained that Marranos entering Italy soon returned to the practice of Judaism, circumcising their baptized children almost "under the eye of the pope and the populace." Under pressure of such criticism Paul re-established the Inquisition in Rome (1542), but he "took the part of the Marranos throughout his life." [62]

His successors, caught in a reaction against the easy ways of the Renaissance, turned to a policy of making life uncomfortable for the Jews. Old canonical decrees were again enforced. Paul IV (1555–59) required every synagogue in the Papal States to contribute ten ducats ($250?) toward the maintenance of a House of Catechumens, where Jews were to be instructed in the Christian faith. He forbade the Jews to employ Christian servants or nurses, to take Christians as medical patients, to sell Christians anything but old clothes, or to have any avoidable intercourse with Christians. They were not to use any but the Christian calendar. All synagogues in Rome were destroyed but one. No Jew might own realty; those who had any were to sell it within six months; by this plan Christians were enabled to buy 500,000 crowns' worth ($12,500,000) of Jewish property for a fifth of the actual value.[63] All Jews remaining in Rome were now (1555) confined to a ghetto where 10,000 persons had to live within a square kilometer; several families occupied one room; and the low level of the quarter subjected it to the periodical overflow of the Tiber, making the region a plague-stricken swamp.[64] The ghetto was surrounded by grim walls, whose gates were shut at midnight and opened at dawn, except on Sundays and Christian holydays, when they were closed all day. Outside the ghetto the Jews were compelled to wear a distinctive garb—the men a yellow hat, the women a yellow veil or badge. Similar ghettos were established in Florence and Siena, and, by papal edict, in Ancona and Bologna—where it was called "Inferno." [65] Paul IV issued a secret order that all Marranos in Ancona should be cast into Inquisition prisons, and their goods confiscated. Twenty-four men and one woman were there burned alive as relapsed heretics (1556);[66] and twenty-seven Jews were sent to the galleys for life.[67] It was, for the Jews of Italy, a ghastly twilight to a golden age.

A handful of Jewish refugees slipped into France and England despite the excluding laws. Nearly all Germany was closed to them. Many went to Antwerp, but only a few were allowed to stay more than a month. Diogo Mendes, a Portuguese Marrano, established at Antwerp a ranch of the bank that his family had founded in Lisbon. By 1532 he was so successful that the Antwerp Council arrested him and fifteen others on a charge of practicing Judaism. Henry VIII, who employed Mendes as a financial agent, intervened, and the thirteen were released on payment of a heavy fine—the "final cause" of many such arrests. Other Jews passed on to Amsterdam, where they would prosper after the liberation of Holland from Spain (1589).

Those fugitives who sought asylum in regions of Islam not directly controlled by the Turkish sultan fared little better than in Christendom. Jews trying to land at Oran, Algiers, and Bugia were shot at by Moors, and several were killed. Forbidden to enter the cities, they built an impromptu ghetto of huts put together from scraps of lumber; one hut caught fire, and the entire settlement, including many Jews, was consumed. Those who went to Fez found the gates closed against them. They squatted in the fields and lived on herbs and roots. Mothers killed their infants rather than let them die of starvation; parents sold their children for a little bread; pestilence carried off hundreds of children and adults. Pirates raided the camp and stole children to sell them as slaves.[68] Murderers ripped open the bodies of Jews to find jewels they were believed to have swallowed.[69] After all these sufferings the survivors, with incredible courage, and under endless disabilities, developed new Jewish communities in Moorish North Africa. At Algiers, Simon Duran II repeatedly risked his life to protect the exiles and to organize them into some security. At Fez, Jakob Berab became the most famous Talmudist of his time.

Under the Mameluk and Ottoman sultans the Spanish refugees found humane acceptance in Cairo, and soon rose to leadership of the Jewish community. Selim I abolished the old office of Nagid or prince, by which one rabbi had appointed all rabbis, and had controlled all Jewish affairs, in Egypt; thereafter each Jewish community was to choose its own rabbi and manage its own internal concerns. The new rabbi of Cairo, David ibn abi-Zimra, a Spanish immigrant, ended the Seleucid method of chronology which the Jews of Asia and Africa were using, and persuaded them to adopt (as the Jews of Europe had done in the eleventh century) a calendar that reckoned by the year since creation (anno mundi), tentatively fixed as 3761 B.C.

Wherever the Sephardic or Iberian Jews went they acquired cultural—often political—leadership over the native Jews. In Salonika they became, and remained till 1918, a numerical majority of the population, so that non-Spanish Jews who came to live there had to learn Spanish. Under this Jewish hegemony Salonika was for a time the most flourishing commercial center in the Eastern Mediterranean.

Sultan Bajazet II welcomed Jewish exiles to Turkey, for they brought with them precisely those skills in handicrafts, trade, and medicine which were least developed among the Turks. Said Bajazet of Ferdinand the Catholic: "You call Ferdinand a wise king, who has made his country poor and enriched ours?" [70] Like all non-Moslems in Islam, the Jews were subject to a poll or head tax, but this exempted them from military service. Most of the Turkish Jews remained poor, but many rose to wealth and influence. Soon nearly all physicians in Constantinople were Jews. Suleiman so favored his Jewish physician that he freed him and his family from all taxation. Jews rose to such prominence as diplomats under Suleiman that Christian ambassadors had to court these Jews as an approach to the Sultan. Suleiman was shocked by the oppression of the Ancona Jews under Paul IV, and remonstrated against it to the Pope (March 9, 1556); he demanded the release of such Ancona Jews as were subjects of Turkey, and they were freed.[71] Gracia Mendesia, of the Mendes banking family, after practicing philanthropy, and suffering insult and injury, in Antwerp, Ferrara, and Venice, finally found peace in Istanbul.

The Holy Land, under Turkish rule, received again the people that had first made it holy. As Jerusalem was sacred to Christians and Moslems as well as to Jews, only a limited number of Hebrews was allowed to live there. But at Safed, in Upper Galilee, the Jews grew so rapidly in number and cultural prestige that Jakob Berab tried to establish a Sanhedrin there as a ruling congress for all Jewry. It was a bold conception, but the Jews were too divided in space, language, and ways to permit such a unification of rule. Nevertheless, in Jewish prayers throughout Islam and Christendom, Yahveh was supplicated to "gather the dispersed . . . from the four corners of the earth"; and at Yom Kippur and Passover the Jews everywhere joined in the hope that sustained them through all tragedies: "Next year we shall be in Jerusalem." [72]

IV. THE TECHNIQUE OF SURVIVAL

The ability of the Jews to recover from misfortune is one of the impressive wonders of history, part of that heroic resilience which man in general has shown after the catastrophes of life.

Segregation was not the worst indignity; they were happier and safer with one another than amid the hostile crowd. Poverty they could bear, since they had known it for centuries, and it was not their prerogative; indeed, they were more likely to be proud of their occasional wealth than conscious of their immemorial indigence. The unkindest cut of all, however motived, was the badge or distinguishing garment that marked them off as the despised and rejected of men. The great historian of the Jews writes bitterly:

The Jew-badge was an invitation to the gamin to insult the wearers and to bespatter them with mud; it was a suggestion to stupid mobs to fall upon them, to maltreat them, and even to kill them; and it afforded the higher class an opportunity to ostracize the Jews, to plunder them, or to exile them. Worse than this outward dishonor was the influence of the badge on the Jews themselves. They became more and more accustomed to their ignominious position, and lost all feeling of self-respect. They neglected their outward appearance. . . . They became more and more careless of their speech, because they were not admitted to cultured circles, and in their own midst they could make themselves understood by means of a jargon. They lost all taste and sense of beauty, and to some extent became despicable, as their enemies desired them to be.[73]

This is exaggerated and too general; many Jews retained their pride, some gloried in the splendor of their dress; we hear again and again of Jewish girls renowned for their beauty; and the *Jüdisch,* which in the sixteenth century evolved as a jargon of German with Slavic and Hebraic borrowings, was developing a vigorous and varied literature even as Graetz wrote his *History of the Jews.* But in any case the supreme crime of those centuries was the deliberate degradation of an entire people, the merciless murder of the soul.

Part and basis of the crime was the exclusion of the Jews from almost all occupations but commerce and finance. For reasons already summarized,[74] and because a tithe of agricultural produce was demanded by the Church, Jews more and more withdrew from cultivation of the soil; and finally they were forbidden to own land.[75] Since they were not admitted to the guilds (which were formally Christian religious organizations), they could not rise in the manufacturing world, and their mercantile operations were hedged in with Christian monopolies. By and large, in their dealings with Christians, they found themselves limited to petty industry, trade, and moneylending. In some regions they were forbidden to sell to Christians anything but second-hand goods. After the thirteenth century they lost their invidious pre-eminence in finance. But their fluid capital, their international languages, their international connections through scattered relatives, enabled them to achieve a high place in the foreign commerce of the Christian states. So prominent was the Jewish role that those countries which excluded them lost, and those that received them gained, in the volume of their international trade. This was one—not the main—reason why Spain and Portugal declined while Holland rose, and why Antwerp yielded commercial leadership to Amsterdam.

It was a saving consolation that the Jews, in their internal affairs, could be ruled by their own laws and customs, their own rabbis and synagogue councils. As in Islam, so in Jewry, religion, law, and morality were inextricably one; religion was held to be coextensive with life. In 1310 Rabbi Jakob ben

Asher formulated Jewish law, ritual, and morality in *Arabaah Turim (Four Rows)*; this replaced the *Mishna Torah* (1170) of Maimonides with a code in which all the legislation of the Talmud and the rulings of the Geonim were made obligatory on all Jews everywhere. The *Turim* became the accepted guide for rabbinical law and judgment till 1565.

The disasters of the fourteenth and fifteenth centuries disrupted the social organization of the Jews. The rabbis, like the priests, suffered a high mortality in the Black Death. Persecutions, expulsions, and a fugitive life almost put an end to Jewish law. The Sephardic Jews found it difficult to accept the language and customs of the Jewish communities which offered to absorb them; they set up their own synagogues, kept their own Spanish or Portuguese speech; and in many cities there were separate congregations of Spanish, Portuguese, Italian, Greek, or German Jews, each with its own rabbi, customs, charities, and jealousies.[76] In this crisis the Jewish family saved the Jewish people; the mutual devotion of parents and children, brothers and sisters, provided a haven of stability and security. These centuries of disorder in Jewish mores ended when Rabbi Joseph Karo issued from Safed his *Shulchan Aruch* (Venice, 1564-65); in this *Table in Order* the religion, law, and customs of the Jews were once more codified. But as Karo based his code chiefly on Spanish Judaism, the Hebrews of Germany and Poland felt that he had paid too little attention to their own traditions and interpretations of the Law; Rabbi Moses Isserles of Cracow added to the *Table in Order* his *Mapath ha-Shulchan (A Cloth for the Table,* 1571), which formulated the Askenazi variations on Karo's mostly Sephardic code. With this emendation the *Shulchan Aruch* remained till our own time the Justinian and Blackstone of orthodox Jews. To say of a Jew that he obeyed all the precepts of the *Shulchan Aruch* was the summit of Jewish praise.

Since all formulations of Jewish law were based on the Talmud, we can —or can we?—imagine the trepidation with which the Jews followed the vicissitudes of their second holy book. In its literary and less authoritative section—the Haggada—there were some passages that ridiculed certain Christian beliefs. Converts from Judaism paved their way into Christian acceptance by denouncing these passages, and calling for the suppression of the entire Talmud. Despite such movements, culminating in the attack of Pfefferkorn on Reuchlin, Leo X encouraged the first printing of the Talmud (Venice, 1520); but Julius III signalized the passing of the Renaissance by ordering the Inquisition to burn all copies to be found in Italy (1553). Jewish homes were invaded; thousands of copies were seized; there were bonfires of Jewish books in Rome, Bologna, Ravenna, Ferrara, Padua, Venice, and Mantua; Milan, however, refused to obey the incendiary decree.[77] Committees of Jews pleaded with the Pope to rescind his edict; he procrastinated while the volumes burned; but Pius IV ruled that the Talmud might be published after submitting to censorship. Thereafter the Jews censured their own publications.[78]

The *Zohar*, text of Jewish Cabalism, survived uninjured because some Catholic scholars thought they found in it proofs of the divinity of Christ. The *Zohar* had been written shortly before 1295 as one of a series of mystical works transmitting the Cabala or "secret tradition" of Jews who took refuge from poverty, persecution, and befuddlement in contemplating the divine and esoteric symbolism of numbers, letters, backward reading of words, the Ineffable Name of Yahveh, and so on. Sorrowing Jews gathered in private groups to seek, by fasting, weeping, ascetic austerities, and Cabalistic interpretations, some novel revelation, above all as to the coming of the Messiah who would redeem Israel from all its griefs.

Those who have tried to feel the unprecedented depth of racial suffering which the Jews experienced in the fourteenth, fifteenth, and sixteenth centuries, can understand such forgivable escapes into consolatory mysticism, and the repeated deception of the desperate Jews by belief that the Messiah had actually come. In 1524 a young and handsome Arabian Jew, calling himself David Reubeni, rode on a white horse through Rome to the Vatican, and presented himself to Clement VII as brother and envoy of a Jewish king whom he described as reigning in Arabia over the old Hebrew tribe of Reuben. His king, said David, had 300,000 soldiers, with insufficient arms; if the Pope and the European princes would provide the weapons, the tribe would drive the Moslems out of Palestine. Clement was interested, and treated David with all the courtesies due to an ambassador. The Jews of Rome were pleased to see a Jew so honored; they supplied David with the means to keep high diplomatic state; and when an invitation came to him from John III of Portugal, he sailed in a ship with a numerous retinue and under a Jewish flag.

John III was so taken with his proposals that he suspended the persecution of the Marranos. The Jews of Portugal, most of them baptized against their will, became half-hysterical with joy, and many proclaimed their belief that David was the Messiah. Diogo Pires, a converted Jew who had become secretary to the King, had himself circumcised to prove his Judaism; he changed his name to Solomon Molcho, made his way to Turkey, and announced that Reubeni was the forerunner of the Messiah, who himself would arrive in 1540. Reubeni had made no claims to be either Messiah or forerunner; he was a visionary impostor who wanted money, ships, and arms. The flight of Pires-Molcho aroused King John's suspicions; he bade Reubeni depart; David left, was stranded on the coast of Spain, and was arrested by the Inquisition. Charles V, apparently to please Clement, ordered him released. Reubeni went to Venice (1530), and proposed to the Senate that it should arm the Jews of Europe for an attack upon the Turks.

Meanwhile Molcho came to Ancona, received a passport from the Pope.

rode across Italy, and preached Judaism fervently in Rome. When the Inquisition sought to arrest him as a relapsed *Converso,* Clement rescued him and sent him safely out of the city. Although Molcho had now lost faith in Reubeni, he joined him in a rash mission to Ratisbon, where they petitioned Charles to arm the Marranos against Islam. Charles had them arrested, and brought them with him to Mantua. There Molcho was sentenced to be burned. At the last moment he was offered an Imperial pardon if he would return to Christianity; he refused, and welcomed martyrdom (1532). Reubeni was sent to Spain, was imprisoned by the Inquisition, and died about 1536, apparently by poisoning. The brokenhearted Jews of Europe crept back into their ghettoes, their mysticism, and their despair.

V. JEWISH THOUGHT

It was not to be expected that the age of the Second Dispersion should produce any high culture among the Jews; their energy was consumed in the brute task of survival. Education, in which they had excelled, was disrupted by the mobility and insecurity of life; and while Christian Europe moved with exhilaration into the Renaissance, the Jews of Christendom moved into the ghetto and the Cabala. The Second Commandment forbade them to share in the revival of art. Jewish scholars were many, but for the most part they sank themselves in the Talmud. There were grammarians like Profiat Duran and Abraham de Balmes, translators like Isaac ibn-Pulkar, who put al-Ghazzali into Hebrew, and Jakob Mantin, who rendered Avicenna, Averroes, Maimonides, and Levi ben Gerson into Latin. Elijah Levita alarmed orthodox Jews by arguing conclusively (1538) that the Masoretic text of the Old Testament—i.e., the text with notes, vowel points and punctuation—was not older than the fifth century A.D.

The Odyssey of the Abrabanels illustrates the vicissitudes of the Jewish intellect in the fifteenth and sixteenth centuries. Born in Lisbon in 1437, Don Isaac Abrabanel served Affonso V of Portugal as finance minister; but he mingled his public life with Biblical and historical studies, and made his spacious home a salon of scholars, scientists, and men of affairs. When Affonso died Abrabanel lost the royal favor, and fled to Spain (1484). He was absorbed in writing commentaries on the historical books of the Bible when Ferdinand the Catholic called him to office, and for eight years Isaac shared in managing the finances of Castile. He labored to avert the disaster that befell the Jews in 1492; failing, he joined them in their melancholy exodus. At Naples he was employed by the government, but the French invaders (1495) sacked his home, destroyed his choice library, and forced him to flee to Corfu. There he wrote as many a Jew must have written in those years: "My wife, my sons, and my books are far from me, and I am left alone, a stranger in a strange land." [79] He made his way to Venice, and was given a diplomatic post (1503). Amid these fluctuations of fortune he found time to write several philosophical or theological works, now of minor interest; but he established the principle that Scriptural events and ideas should be interpreted in terms of the social and political life of their times. He was allowed to spend his final six years in unwonted security and peace.

His sons were his decoration. Samuel Abrabanel prospered at Salonika, was made finance minister at Naples, and earned the love of his people by his many philanthropies. Judah Leon Abrabanel—Leo Hebraeus—rose to such prominence as a physician in Genoa and Naples that he became known as Leon Medigo. He studied many sciences, wrote poetry, and ventured into metaphysics. In 1505 he was appointed physician to Gonzalo de Cordoba, but two years later the "Great Captain" fell out with Ferdinand, and Leon joined his father in Venice. His *Dialoghi d'Amore* (written in 1502, published in 1535) found quite an audience among the Renaissance Italians, for whom the philosophical analysis of love served as prelude or obbligato to amorous victories. Intellectual beauty—the beauty of order, plan, and harmony—is superior to physical beauty, argued the *Dialogues*; the supreme beauty is the order, plan, and harmony of the universe, which is the outward expression of divine beauty; love rises in stages from the admiration and pursuit of physical to intellectual to heavenly beauty, and culminates in the intellectual love of God—the understanding and appreciation of the cosmic order, and the desire to be united with the Deity. The manuscript may have been known to Castiglione, who made Bembo speak to like effect in *Il cortigiano* (1528); and the printed book may have found its way across a century to influence Spinoza's *amor dei intellectualis*.[80]

To this ethereal *amour* the dispersed Portuguese Jews preferred Usque's impassioned prose poem in Portuguese, *Consolation for the Sorrows of Israel* (Ferrara, 1553). It pictured the alternate triumphs and disasters of the Jewish nation, and comforted the Jews with the assurance that they were still God's chosen people. They had been punished by God for their sins, but they were being purified by their sufferings; and no deviltry of man could cheat them of their divine destiny to happiness and glory.

Jewish contributions to science inevitably slackened in this prolonged vivisection of a people. Not only did insecurity, poverty, and instability impede scientific pursuits, but one of the most respected and influential of the rabbis, Solomon ben Abraham ben Adret of Barcelona, at the very beginning of this period (1305), had forbidden, under penalty of excommunication, the teaching of science or philosophy to any Jew under the age of twenty-five, on the ground that such instruction might damage religious faith. Nevertheless Isaac Israeli the Younger, of Toledo, summarized the astronomy of his time (1320), and clarified the Jewish calendar and chronology; Immanuel Bonfils of Tarascon drew up valuable astronomical tables, and anticipated exponential and decimal calculus; Abraham Crescas of Majorca, "Master of Maps and Compasses to the Government of Aragon," made a *mapamundi* (1377) which was so widely recognized as the best world map yet made that Aragon sent it as a distinguished gift to Charles VI of France, where it is now a prized possession of the Bibliothèque Nationale. Abraham's son Jehuda Crescas was the first director of Henry the Navigator's nautical observatory at Sagres, and helped to chart his explorations. Pedro Nuñes's *Treatise on the Sphere* (1537) opened the way for Mercator and all modern cartography; and Garcia d'Orta's *Colloquios dos simples e drogas medicināes* (1563) marked an epoch in botany and founded tropical medicine.

Abraham Zacuto was the one major figure in the Jewish science of the fifteenth century. While teaching at Salamanca (1473-78) he compiled his *Almanach perpetuum*, whose astronomical tables were used as navigational guides on the voyages of Vasco da Gama, Cabral, Albuquerque, and (after 1496) Columbus. Zacuto was among the refugees from Spain (1492). He found temporary asylum in Portugal; he was consulted by the court in preparing Da Gama's expedition to India, and the ships were equipped with his improved astrolabe. But in 1497 persecution drove him from Portugal too. For years he wandered in poverty until he settled in Tunis; and there, in his old age, he comforted himself by writing a history of his people. His pupil Joseph Vecinho, physician to John II of Portugal, was sent to chart latitudes and solar declinations along the Guinea coast, and the charts so prepared proved invaluable to Da Gama. Vecinho was one of the commission to which John II referred Columbus's proposals for seeking a western route to the Indies (1484), and shared in the negative decision.[81]

Jewish physicians were still the most sought for in Europe. Harassed with religious condemnations and official restrictions, and risking their lives in treating prominent Christians, they were nevertheless the favorites of popes and kings. Their contributions to medical science were not now brilliant, except for d'Orta's to tropical medicine; but Amatus Lusitanus exemplified the finest traditions of his profession and his people. Driven by the Inquisition from the Portugal whose Latin name he had taken, he lived passingly in Antwerp, Ferrara, and Rome, and settled in Ancona (*c.* 1549), whence he was often called to treat that same Pope Julius III who labored to destroy the Talmud. To the end of his life he was able to take oath that he had never concerned himself with compensation, had never accepted valuable presents, had served the poor without fee, had made no distinction in his practice among Christian, Jew, and Turk, and had allowed no difficulties of time or distance to interfere with devotion to his calling. His *Curiationum medicinalium centuriae septem* (1563) gave clinical records of 700 cases that he had treated; these *Centuries* were studied and treasured by physicians throughout Europe. The king of Poland invited Amatus to be his personal physician; Lusitanus preferred to remain in Ancona; but in 1556 he was compelled to resume his wandering when Paul IV demanded the conversion or imprisonment of all Marranos in Italy.

Ben Adret's moratorium on science and philosophy had less effect on philosophy than on science, and less in France than in Spain. The influence of Maimonides was still strong among the Jews who managed to survive in southern France. Joseph Kaspi dared to write treatises on logic and ethics for the guidance of his son, and defended the liberal philosophical tradition that had received its classical exposition in Maimonides's *Moreh Nebuchim*. This approach produced a major Jewish thinker in Levi ben Gerson, known to the Christian world as Gersonides. Like most Jewish philosophers, he earned his bread by practicing medicine, and realized Hippocrates's ideal of the physician-philosopher. Born at Bagnols (1288) in a family of scholars, he lived nearly all his life in Orange, Perpignan, and Avignon, where he worked in peace under the protection of the popes. There was hardly a science that he did not deal with, hardly a problem in philosophy that he left untouched. He was a learned Talmudist, he contributed to the mathematics of music, he wrote poetry.

In mathematics and astronomy he was among the lights of the age. He anticipated (1321) the method later formulated by Maurolico (1575) and Pascal (1654), of finding the number of simple permutations of n objects by mathematical induction. His treatise on trigonometry paved the way for Regiomontanus, and was so widely esteemed that Pope Clement VI commissioned its translation into Latin as *De sinibus, chordis, et arcubus* (1342). He invented, or materially improved, the cross-staff for measuring the altitude of stars; this remained for two centuries a precious boon to navigation. He made his own astronomic observations, and ably critized the Ptolemaic system. He discussed but rejected the heliocentric hypothesis, in a manner suggesting that there were quite a few adherents of it in his time. He perfected the *camera obscura*, and used it, with the cross-staff, to determine more accurately the variations in the apparent diameter of the sun and moon.

As ben Gerson's science stemmed from the Arabic mathematicians and astronomers, so his philosophy was based on a critical study of the commentaries in which Averroes had expounded Aristotle. During the years 1319–21 Levi composed commentaries on these commentaries, covering Aristotle's treatises on logic, physics, astronomy, meteorology, botany, zoology, psychology, and metaphysics; and to these studies he added, of course, repeated readings of Maimonides. His own philosophy, and most of his science, were embodied in a Hebrew work entitled, in the fashion of the age, *Milchamoth Adonai* (*Battles of the Lord*, 1317–29). It ranks second only to the *Moreh Nebuchim* in Jewish medieval philosophy, and continues Maimonides's attempt to reconcile Greek thought with Jewish faith, much to the detriment of the faith. When we consider the similar efforts of Averroes and Thomas Aquinas to harmonize Mohammedanism and Christianity with Aristotle, we might almost say that the impact of Aristotle on medieval theologies inaugurated their disintegration and the transition from the Age of Faith to the Age of Reason. Gersonides sought to soften orthodox resentment by professing his readiness to abandon his views if these should be proved contrary to Scripture—an old Scholastic dodge. Nevertheless he went on to reason at great length about God, creation, the eternity of the world, the immortality of the soul; and when his conclusions contradicted Scripture he interpreted it with such violence to the text that his critics renamed his book *Battles against the Lord*.[82] We must not take literally, said Levi, such stories as that of Joshua stopping the sun; these and similar "miracles" were probably natural events whose causes were forgotten or unknown.[83] Finally he proclaimed his rationalism without disguise: "The Torah cannot prevent us from considering to be true that which our reason urges us to believe." [84]

Gersonides derived the existence of God from what the atheist Holbach would call "the system of nature": the law and order of the universe reveal a cosmic Mind. To this he adds the teleological argument: most things in living nature seem designed as means to end, and Providence gives every organism the means of self-protection, development, and reproduction. The world as cosmos or order was created in time, but not out of nothing; an inert, formless mass pre-existed from eternity; creation gave it life and form. Between God and the created forms is an intermediary power which Gerson, following Aristotle and Averroes, calls *nous poietikos*, the Active or Creative Intellect; this emanation of divine intelligence guides all things, and becomes the soul in man. So far as the soul depends upon the individual's sensations, it is mortal; so far as it conceives universals, and perceives the order and unity of the world, it becomes consciously part of the Active Intellect, which is immortal.

Ben Gerson's philosophy was rejected by the Jews as essentially a form f Averroism, a rationalism that would ultimately dissolve religious belief. Christian thinkers studied him, Spinoza was influenced by him; but the heart and mind of thoughtful Jews were more faithfully expressed by Hasdai ben Abraham Crescas, who had imbibed the conservatism of Solomon ben Adret. Born in Barcelona in 1340, Crescas lived through a period of rabid anti-semitism. He was arrested on a charge of having desecrated a Host; he was soon released, but his son, on the very eve of marriage, was killed in the massacres of 1391. Persecution strengthened Hasdai's faith, for only by belief in a just God and a compensatory heaven could he bear a life so evil in injustice and suffering. Seven years after the martyrdom of his son he published in Spanish a *Tratado* which sought to explain to Christians why a Jew should not be asked to accept Christianity. Courteously and moderately he argued that the Christian dogmas of the Fall, Trinity, Immaculate Conception, Incarnation, Atonement, and Transubstantiation involved insuperable contradictions and absurd impossibilities. Yet when he composed his major work, *Or Adonai* (*Light of the Lord*, 1410), he took a stand from which the Christians might have defended these theories: he renounced reason and bade it surrender to faith. Though he was not officially a rabbi, he shared the rabbinical view that the renewed persecutions were a divine punishment for subjecting the revealed religion to rationalistic dilution. If he wrote philosophy it was through no admiration for it, but to prove the weakness of philosophy and reason, and to affirm the necessity of belief. He repudiated the attempts of Maimonides and Gerson to reconcile Judaism with Aristotle; who was this Greek that God had to agree with him? He protested the Aristotelian notion that God's supreme quality is knowledge; rather it is love; God is the Absolutely Good. Crescas admitted that reason cannot harmonize God's foreknowledge with man's freedom; we must therefore reject not freedom but reason. We must believe in God, free will, and immortality for our peace of mind and our moral health, and we need make no pretense to prove these beliefs by reason. We must choose between our proud, weak reason, which dissolves belief and begets despair, and our humble faith in God's Word, through which alone we can bear the indignities and inequities of life.

Crescas was the last of a brilliant line of medieval Jewish philosophers. He was not at once appreciated by his people, for his pupil Joseph Albo caught the philosophical audience with his more readable *Ikkarim* (*Fundamental Principles*); this combined Maimonides and Crescas in an eclectic system more consonant than either with orthodox Judaism, which was not prepared to admit the irrationality of faith. After Albo's death (1444) the Jews retired from philosophy, almost from history, till Spinoza. Massacres, dislocations, destitution, and restrictions of residence and occupation had broken their spirit, and had diminished their number to the lowest level since the fall of Jerusalem in 70 A.D.[85] The despised and rejected of men found refuge in the sorrowing chants and comforting fellowship of the synagogue, in hopes of divine forgiveness, earthly justification, and celestial bliss. Scholars buried themselves in the Talmud, confining their reasoning to the elucidation of the saving Law, while some followed the Cabala into a mysticism that sublimated misery into heaven-scaling delusions. Jewish poetry ceased to sing. Only a remnant lifted its head now and then defiantly against the storm, or softened the ironies of life with wistful humor and wry wit. Not till the humble Jew of Amsterdam would dare to unite Judaism, Scholasticism, and Cartesianism into a sublime merger of religion and science would the Jews wake from their long and healing sleep to take their place again in the raceless and timeless international of the mind.

BOOK IV

BEHIND THE SCENES

CHAPTER XXXIII

The Life of the People

1517-64

I. THE ECONOMY

IN one sense the drama of religious, political, and martial conflict that filled the front of the sixteenth century was superficial, for it proceeded only by permission of a deeper drama played behind the historic scenes or beneath the pompous stage—man's daily and perpetual battle with the soil, the elements, poverty, and death. What, after all, were the bulls and blasts of popes and Protestants, the rival absurdities of murderous mythologies, the strut and succession, gout and syphilis, of emperors and kings, compared with the inexorable struggle for food, shelter, clothing, health, mates, children, life?

Throughout this period the villages of Europe had to keep watch night and day against wolves, wild boars, and other threats to their flocks and homes. The hunting stage survived within the agricultural age: man had to kill or be killed, and the weapons of defense made possible the routine of toil. A thousand insects, the beasts of the forests, and the birds of the air competed with the peasant for the fruit of his seeds and drudgery; and mysterious diseases decimated his herds. At any time the rains might become erosive torrents or engulfing floods, or they might hold back till all life withered; hunger was always around the corner, and fear of fire was never far from mind. Sickness made frequent calls; doctors were distant; and in almost every decade plague might carry off some member of the household precious in the affections of the family or in the siege of the earth. Of every five children born, two died in infancy, another before maturity.[1] At least once in each generation the recruiting officer took a son for the army, and armies burned villages and ravaged fields. From the crop at last grown and harvested, a tenth or more went to the landlord, a tenth to the Church. Life on the land would have been too hard for body or soul had not happiness intervened in the gaiety of children, the games of the evening home, the release of song, the amnesia of the tavern, and the half-believed, half-doubted hopes of another and more merciful world. So the food was produced that fed the barons in the castle, the kings in their courts, the priests in their pulpits, the merchants and craftsmen in the towns, the physicians, teachers, artists,

751

poets, scientists, philosophers, and, last and least, the slaves of the soil themselves. Civilization is a parasite on the man with the hoe.

Agricultural science marked time; progress in productivity came chiefly
through the replacement of small holdings by large tracts. The new landowning merchants and capitalists brought into stagnant rural areas a lust for
profits that increased both production and misery. Enterprising importers
introduced into Europe a new fertilizer rich in phosphates and nitrogen—
the guano or dung deposited by birds off the coast of Peru. Plants and shrubs
from Asia or America were naturalized on the soil of Europe; the potato,
the magnolia tree, the century plant, the pepper plant, the dahlia, the nastur-
tium. . . . The tobacco plant was brought from Mexico to Spain in 1558; a
year later Jean Nicot, French ambassador in Lisbon, sent some seeds of it
to Catherine de Médicis; history rewarded him by giving his name to a
poison.

The fishing industry grew as population increased, but the Reformation
dealt a passing blow to the herring trade by allowing meat on Fridays. Mining
progressed rapidly under capitalistic organization. Newcastle was exporting
coal in 1549. The Fuggers multiplied the output of their mines by prodding
labor to greater and more orderly effort, and by improving the methods of
refining ore. Georg Agricola takes us into a sixteenth-century mine:

> The chief kinds of workmen are miners, shovelers, windlass men,
> carriers, sorters, washers, and smelters. . . . The twenty-four hours
> of a day and night are divided into three shifts, and each shift consists
> of seven hours. The three remaining hours are intermediate between
> the shifts, and form an interval during which the workmen enter and
> leave the mines. The first shift begins at the fourth hour in the morn-
> ing and lasts till the eleventh hour; the second begins at the twelfth
> and is finished at the seventh; these two are day shifts in the morning
> and afternoon. The third is the night shift, and commences at the
> eighth hour in the evening and finishes at the third in the morning.
> The *Bergmeister* does not allow this third shift to be imposed upon
> the workmen unless necessity demands it. In that case . . . they keep
> their vigil by the night lamps; and to prevent themselves falling
> asleep from the late hours or from fatigue, they lighten their long
> and arduous labors by singing, which is neither wholly untrained nor
> unpleasing. In some places one miner is not allowed to undertake two
> shifts in succession, because it often happens that he falls asleep in the
> mine, overcome by exhaustion from too much labor. . . . Elsewhere
> he is allowed to do so, because he cannot subsist on the pay of one
> shift, especially if provisions grow dearer. . . .
> The laborers do not work on Saturdays, but buy those things which
> are necessary to life, nor do they usually work on Sundays or annual
> festivals, but on these occasions devote the shift to holy things. How-

ever, the workmen do not rest . . . if necessity demands their labor; for sometimes a rush of water compels them to work, sometimes an impending fall . . . and at such times it is not considered irreligious to work on holidays. Moreover, all workmen of this class are strong and used to toil from birth.[2]

In 1527 Georg Agricola was made city physician of Joachimsthal. In that mining town he became between times a mineralogist; there and elsewhere he studied with zeal and fascination the history and operations of mining and metallurgy; and after twenty years of research he completed (1550) his *De re metallica*, which is as epochal a classic in its field as the masterpieces of Copernicus and Vesalius appearing in the same decade. He described in accurate detail, and engaged artists to illustrate, the tools, mechanisms, and processes of mining and smelting. He was the first to assert that bismuth and antimony are true primary metals; he distinguished some twenty mineral species not previously recognized; and he was the first to explain the formation of veins (*canales*, channels) of ore in beds of rock by metallic deposits left by streams of water flowing into and under the earth.* [3]

Mining, metallurgy, and textiles received most of the mechanical improvements credited to this age. The earliest railways were those on which miners pulled or pushed ore-carrying carts. In 1533 Johann Jürgen added to the spinning wheel, hitherto spun by hand, a treadle that spun it by foot, leaving the hands of the weaver free; production soon doubled. Watches were improved in reliability while diminishing in size; they were engraved, chased, enameled, bejeweled; Henry VIII wore a tiny one that had to be wound only every week. However, the best watches of this period erred by some fifteen minutes per day.[4]

Communication and transport limped behind commerce and industry. Postal service was gradually extended to private correspondence during the sixteenth century. The commercial revolution stimulated improvements in shipbuilding: deeper and thinner keels helped stability and speed; masts increased from one to three, sails to five or six.[5] Francis I and Henry VIII ran a race not only in war and love and dress but in shipping; each had a grandiose vessel built to order and whim, crowded with superstructure, and flaunting the pennants of their pride. In the Mediterranean a ship of the early sixteenth century could make ten miles an hour in fair weather, but the heavier vessels designed for the Atlantic were lucky to make 125 miles a day. On land the fastest travel was by the postal courier, who rode some eighty-five miles a day; yet important news usually took ten or eleven days to get from Venice to Paris or Madrid. Probably no one then appreciated the com-

---

* Agricola rejected as useless the divining rod or "forked twig" then often employed to detect metals under the soil. Our Geiger counters incline us to look with lenience upon these hopeful rods.

fort of having news arrive too late for action. Land travel was mostly on horseback; hence the heavy iron tethering ring fastened to the entrance door of a house. Coaches were multiplying, but the roads were too soft for wheeled traffic; coaches had to be equipped with six or more horses to drag them through the inevitable mud, and they could not expect to cover more than twenty miles a day. Litters carried by servants were still used by ladies of means, but simple people traveled on foot across the continent.

Traveling was popular despite roads and inns. Erasmus thought the inns of France were tolerable, chiefly because the young waitresses "giggle and play wanton tricks," and, "when you go away, embrace you," and "all for so small a price"; but he denounced German innkeepers as ill-mannered, ill-tempered, dilatory, and dirty.

> When you have taken care of your horse you come into the Stove Room, boots, baggage, mud, and all, for that is a common room for all comers. . . . In the Stove Room you pull off your boots, put on your shoes, and, if you will, change your shirt. . . . There one combs his head, another . . . belches garlic, and . . . there is as great a confusion of tongues as at the building of the Tower of Babel. In my opinion nothing is more dangerous than for so many to draw in the same vapor, especially when their bodies are opened with the heat . . . not to mention . . . the farting, the stinking breaths . . . and without doubt many have the Spanish, or, as it is called, the French, pox, though it is common to all nations.[6]

If matters were really so in some inns, we can forgive a sin or two to the traveling merchants who put up at and with them in the process of binding village with village, nation with nation, in an ever spreading economic web. In each decade some new trade route was opened—overland as by Chancellor in Russia, overseas by a thousand adventurous voyages. Shakespeare's Shylock trafficked with England, Lisbon, Tripoli, Egypt, India, and Mexico.[7] Genoa had trading colonies in the Black Sea, Armenia, Syria, Palestine, and Spain; it made its peace with the Porte, and sold arms to the Turks who were at war with Christendom. France saw the point, made her own ententes with the sultans, and, after 1560, dominated Mediterranean trade. Antwerp received goods everywhence, and shipped them everywhere.

To meet the needs of this expanding economy the bankers improved their services and techniques. As the cost of war rose with the change from feudal levies bringing their own bows and arrows, pikes and swords, to masses of militia or mercenaries equipped with firearms and artillery and paid by the state, the governments borrowed unprecedented sums from the bankers, and the interest they paid or failed to pay made or broke financial firms. The savings of the people were lent at interest to bankers, who therewith financed expensive undertakings in commerce and industry. Notes of exchange replaced cumbersome transfers of currency or goods. Rates of interest varied not with the greed of the lender so much as with the reliability of the borrower; so the free cities of Germany, controlled by merchants prompt in payments, could borrow at 5 per cent, but Francis I paid 10, and Charles V 20. Rates declined as economies were stabilized.

Gold and silver from the mines of Germany, Hungary, Spain, Mexico, and Peru provided an abundant and fluid currency. The new supplies of precious metal came just in time, for goods had been multiplying faster than coin. Imports from Asia were paid for only partly by exports, partly by gold or silver; hence, in the decades before Columbus, prices fell, to the discouragement of enterprise and trade. After the development of European mines, and the import of silver and gold from Africa and America, the supply of precious metal outran the production of goods; prices rose, business rejoiced; an economy based on mobile money dislodged the old economy rooted in the holding of land or the control of industry by the guilds.

Guilds were in decay. They had taken form in times of municipal autarky and protectionism; they were not organized either to raise capital or to buy wholesale from distant sources, or to use factory methods and the division of labor, or to reach distant markets with their products. From the thirteenth century onward they had developed an aristocratic exclusiveness, and had made conditions so hard for the journeyman as to drive him into the arms of the capitalist employer. The capitalist was animated by the profit motive, but he knew how to gather savings into capital, how and where to buy machinery and raw materials, run mines, build factories, recruit workers, divide and specialize labor, open and reach foreign markets, finance elections, and control governments. The new supplies of gold and silver cried out for profitable investment; American gold became European capital. In the resultant capital-ism there was a zest of competition, a stimulus to enterprise, a feverish search for more economical ways of production and distribution, which inevitably left behind the self-contentment of guildsmen plodding in ancient grooves. The new system surpassed the old in the quantity, not in the quality, of its product; and merchants were crying out for quantity production to pay with manufactured exports for their imports from the East.

The new wealth was largely confined to the merchants, financiers, manufacturers, and their allies in government. Some nobles still made fortunes through vast holdings with hundreds of tenants, or through enclosures that supplied wool to the textile industry; but for the most part the landowning aristocracy found itself squeezed between kings and business-controlled cities; it declined in political power, and had to content itself with pedigrees. The proletariat shared with the nobility the penalties of inflation. From 1500 to 1600 the price of wheat, with which the poor baked their bread, rose

150 per cent in England, 200 per cent in France, 300 per cent in Germany. Eggs had been 4d. for ten dozen in England in 1300; in 1400 the same quantity cost 5d., in 1500 7d., in 1570 42d.[8] Wages rose, but more slowly, since they were regulated by government. In England the law (1563) fixed the annual wage of a hired farmer at $12.00, of a farm hand at $9.50, of a "man servant" at $7.25; allowing the purchasing power of these sums to have been twenty-five times greater in 1563 than in 1954, they come to $180.00 or so per year. We should note, however, that in all these cases bed and board were added to the wage. By and large the economic changes of the sixteenth century left the working classes relatively poorer, and politically weaker, than before. Workers produced the goods that were exported to pay for imported luxuries that brightened and softened the lives of a few.

The war of the classes took on a bitterness hardly known since the days of Spartacus in Rome; let the revolt of the *Comuneros* in Spain, the Peasants' War in Germany, Ket's Rebellion in England, serve as evidence. Strikes were numerous, but they were suppressed by a coalition of employers and government. In 1538 the English Clothworkers' Guild, controlled by the masters, decreed that a journeyman who refused to work under the conditions laid down by the employer should be imprisoned for the first offense, whipped and branded for the second. The laws of vagrancy under Henry VIII and Edward VI were so savage that few workers dared to be found unemployed. A law of 1547 enacted that an able-boldied person leaving his work and roaming the country as a vagrant should be branded on the breast with a letter V, and be given as a slave for two years to some citizen of the neighborhood, to be fed on "bread and water and small drink, and refuse of meat"; and if the vagrancy was repeated the offender was to be branded on cheek or forehead with the letter S, and be condemned to slavery for life.[9] It is to the credit of the English nation that these measures could not be enforced, and had soon to be repealed, but they display the temper of sixteenth-century governments. Duke George of Saxony decreed that the wages of miners under his jurisdiction should not be raised, that no miner should leave one place to seek work in another, and that no employer should hire anyone who had fomented discontent in another mine. Child labor was sanctioned, explicitly or implicitly, by law. The lace-making industry in Flanders was entirely worked by children, and the law forbade any girl over twelve years of age to engage in that occupation.[10] Laws against monopolies, "corners," or usury were evaded or ignored.

The Reformation fell in with the new economy. The Catholic Church was by temperament antipathetic to "business"; it had condemned interest, had given religious sanction to guilds, had sanctified poverty and castigated wealth, and had freed workers from toil on holydays so numerous that in 1550 there were in Catholic countries 115 nonworking days in the year;[11]

this may have played a part in the slower industrialization and enrichment of Catholic lands. Theologians approved by the Church had defended the fixing of "just prices" by law for the necessaries of life. Thomas Aquinas had branded as "sinful covetousness" the pursuit of money beyond one's needs, and had ruled that any surplus possessions were "due by natural law to the purpose of succoring the poor." [12] Luther had shared these views. But the general development of Protestantism unconsciously co-operated with the capitalist revolution. Saints' holydays were abolished, with a resultant increase in labor and capital. The new religion found support from business-men, and returned the courtesy. Wealth was honored, thrift was lauded, work was encouraged as a virtue, interest was accepted as a legitimate reward for risking one's savings.

II. LAW

It was a cruel age, and its laws corresponded to a pitiless economy, a shameful pauperism, a somber art, and a theology whose God had repudiated Christ.

Among populations mostly fated to poverty here and damnation hereafter, crime was natural. Murder was plentiful in all classes. Every man of caliber dangled a dagger, and only the weakling relied on the law to redress his wrongs. Crimes of passion were as frequent in life as in Shakespeare, and any Othello who failed to slay his suspected wife was rated less than a man. Travelers took highwaymen for granted, and proceeded in groups. In the cities, still unlit at night, robbers were as plentiful as prostitutes, and a man's home had to be his castle. In the heyday of Francis I a gang of thieves called *mauvais garçons* despoiled Paris in full sunlight. Brantôme tells us, as unreliably as usual, how Charles IX, wishing to learn "how the cut-purses performed their arts," instructed his police to invite ten such artists to a royal ball; after the ball was over he asked to see their spoils; the money, jewelry, and garments unostentatiously acquired by them during the evening amounted to many thousands of dollars' worth, "at which the King thought he would die of laughter." He allowed them to keep the fruit of their studies, but had them enrolled in the army as better dead than alive.[13] If we classify as crimes the adulteration of goods, the chicanery of business frauds, the bribery of courts, the seizure of ecclesiastical property, the extension of frontiers by conquest, every second man in Europe was a thief; we may give some the benefit of clergy, and allow for an honest craftsman here and there. Add a little arson, a little rape, a little treason, and we begin to understand the problems faced by the forces of order and law.

These were organized to punish, rather than to prevent, crime. In some large towns, like Paris. soldiers served as guardians of the peace; city blocks had their wardens, parishes their constables; but by and large the cities were poorly policed. Statesmen weary of fighting the nature of man reckoned it cheaper to control crime by decreeing ferocious penalties, and letting the public witness executions. A score of offenses were capital: murder, treason, heresy, sacrilege, witchcraft, robbery, forgery, counterfeiting, smuggling, arson, perjury, adultery, rape (unless healed by marriage), homosexual actions, "bestiality," falsifying weights or measures, adulterating food, damaging property at night, escaping from prison, and failure in attempted suicide. Execution might be by relatively painless beheading, but this was usually a privilege of ladies and gentlemen; lesser fry were hanged; heretics and husband-killers were burned; outstanding murderers were drawn and quartered; and a law of Henry VIII (1531) punished poisoners by boiling them alive,[14] as we gentler souls do with shellfish. A Salzburg municipal ordinance required that "a forger shall be burned or boiled to death, a perjurer shall have his tongue torn out by the neck; a servant who sleeps with his master's wife, daughter, or sister shall be beheaded or hanged."[15] Julienne Rabeau, who had killed her child after a very painful delivery, was burned at Angers (1531);[16] and there too, if we may believe Bodin, several persons were burned alive for eating meat on Friday and refusing to repent; those who repented were merely hanged.[17] Usually the corpse of the hanged was left suspended as a warning to the living, until the crows had eaten the flesh away. For minor offenses a man or a woman might be scourged, or lose a hand, a foot, an ear, a nose, or be blinded in one eye or both, or be branded with a hot iron. Still milder misdemeanors were punished by imprisonment in conditions varying from courtesy to filth, or by the stocks, the pillory, the whipping-cart, or the ducking stool. Imprisonment for debt was common throughout Europe. All in all, the penal code of the sixteenth century was more severe than in the Middle Ages, and reflected the moral disorder of the time.

The people did not resent these ferocious punishments. They took some pleasure in attending executions, and sometimes lent a helping hand. When Montecucculi confessed, under torture, that he had poisoned, or had intended to poison, Francis, the beloved and popular son of Francis I, he was dismembered alive by having his limbs tied to horses which were then driven in four directions (Lyons, 1536); the populace, we are told, "cut his remains into little morsels, hacked off his nose, tore out his eyes, broke his jaws, trained his head in the mud, and 'made him die a thousand times before his death.' "[18]

To the laws against crime were added "blue laws" against recreations supposedly infringing upon piety, or innovations too abruptly deviating from custom. Fish-eating on Friday, required by common law in Catholic lands, was required by state law in the Protestant England of Edward VI to support the fishing industry and so train men to the sea for the navy.[19] Gambling was always illegal and always popular. Francis I, who knew how to amuse himself, ordered the arrest of people who played cards or dice in taverns or gaming houses (1526), but he allowed the establishment of a public lottery (1539). Drunkenness was seldom punished by law, but idleness was almost a capital crime. Sumptuary laws—designed to check conspicuous expenditure by the newly rich, and to preserve class distinctions— regulated dress, adornment, furniture, meals, and hospitality. "When I was a boy," said Luther, "all games were forbidden, so that card-makers, pipers, and actors were not admitted to the sacraments; and those who had played games, or been present at shows or plays, made it a matter of confession." [20] Most such prohibitions survived the Reformation, to reach their peak in the later sixteenth century.

It was some consolation that enforcement was rarely as severe as the law. Escape was easy; a kindly, bribed, or intimidated judge or jury let many a rascal go lightly punished or scot free. ("Scot" originally meant an assessment or fine.) The laws of sanctuary were still recognized under Henry VIII. However, laxity of enforcement was balanced by frequent use of torture to elicit confessions or testimony. Here the laws of Henry VIII, though they were the severest in the history of England,[21] were ahead of their time; they forbade torture except where national security was held to be involved.[22] Delay in trying an indicted person could also be torture; one complaint of the Spanish Cortes to Charles V was that men charged with even slight offenses lingered in prison as long as ten years before being tried, and that trials might drag on for twenty years.[23]

Lawyers bred and multiplied as the priesthood declined. They filled the judiciary and the higher bureaucracy; they represented the middle classes in the national assemblies and the provincial *parlements;* even the aristocracy and the clergy depended on them for guidance in civil law. A new *noblesse de robe*—the "furred cats" of Rabelais—formed in France. Canon law disappeared in Protestant countries, and jurisprudence replaced theology as the *pièce de résistance* in universities. Roman law sprang back to life in Latin countries, and captured Germany in the sixteenth century. Local law survived alongside it in France, "common law" was preferred to it in England, but the Justinian Code had some influence in shaping and sustaining the absolutism of Henry VIII. Yet in Henry's own court his chaplain, Thomas Starkey, composed (*c.* 1537) a *Dialogue* whose main theme was that laws should dictate the will of the king, and that kings should be subject to election and recall:

> That country cannot long be well governed, nor maintained with good policy, where all is ruled by the will of one not chosen by election but cometh to it by natural succession; for seldom seen it is

that they which by succession come to kingdoms and realms are worthy of such high authority. . . . What is more repugnant to nature than a whole nation to be governed by the will of a prince? . . . What is more contrary to reason than all the whole people to be ruled by him which commonly lacketh all reason? . . . It is not man that can make a wise prince of him that lacketh wit by nature. . . . But this is in man's power, to elect and choose him that is both wise and just, and make him a prince, and him that is a tyrant so to depose.[24]

Starkey died a strangely natural death a year after writing his *Dialogue*—but 334 years before it reached print.

III. MORALS

How did the people of Latin Christendom behave? We must not be misled by their religious professions; these were more often expressions of pugnacity than of piety. The same sturdy men who could believe so fiercely could fiercely blaspheme, and the girls who on Sunday bowed demurely before statues of the Virgin rouged their cheeks hopefully during the week, and many of them got themselves seduced, if only as a proposal of marriage. Virginity had to be protected by every device of custom, morals, law, religion, paternal authority, pedagogy, and "point of honor"; yet it managed to get lost. Soldiers returning from campaigns in which sex and liquor had been their chief consolations found it painful to adjust themselves to continence and sobriety. Students majored in venery, and protested that fornication was but a venial sin,[25] which enlightened legislators would overlook. Robert Greene declared that at Cambridge he had "consumed the flower of my youth amongst wags as lewd as myself."[26] Female dancers not infrequently performed on the stage and elsewhere "absolutely naked";[27] this, apparently, is one of the oldest novelties in the world. Artists looked down their noses at the rules and regulations of sexual behavior,[28] and lords and ladies agreed with the artists. "Among great folk," wrote Brantôme, "these rules and scruples concerning virginity are made little of. . . . How many girls I know, of the Great World, who did not take their virginity to the marriage bed!"[29] We have noted the sort of story that sweet Marguerite of Navarre seems to have heard without a blush. The bookstalls were stacked with licentious literature, for which high prices were greedily paid.[30] Aretino was as popular in Paris as in Rome. Rabelais, a priest, did not feel that he would reduce the sales of his Gargantuan epic by spattering it with such speech as would have made Aretino run to cover. Artists found a ready market for erotic pictures, even for pictured perversions;[31] masterpieces of this kind were sold by street hawkers, letter carriers, strolling players, even at the great fairs.[32] All the perversions found place in this period,[33] as in the aristocratic pages of Brantôme.[34]

Prostitution prospered in income and prestige; it was in this age that its practitioners came to be called *cortigiane*—courtesans—which was the feminine of *cortigiani*—courtiers. Some generals provided prostitutes for their armies, as a safeguard for the other women of occupied towns.[35] But as venereal disease grew almost to the proportions of a plague, government after government legislated against the unhappy *filles de joie*. Luther, while affirming the naturalness of sexual desire, labored to reduce prostitution, and under his urging many cities in Lutheran Germany made it illegal.[36] In 1560 Michel de l'Hôpital, Chancellor of France, renewed the laws of Louis IX against the evil, and apparently his decree was enforced.

Meanwhile the absurd lust of flesh for flesh begot the hunger of soul for soul, and all the delicate embroidery of courtship and romantic love. Stolen glances, billets-doux, odes and sonnets, lays and madrigals, hopeful gifts and secret trysts, poured out of the coursing blood. A few refined spirits, or playful women, welcomed from Italy and Castiglione the pastime of Platonic love, by which a lady and her courtier might be passionate friends but sedulously chaste. Such restraint, however, was not in the mood of the age; men were frankly sensual, and women liked them so. Love poetry abounded, but it was a prelude to possession.

Not to marriage. Parents were still too matter-of-fact to let love choose mates for life; marriage, in their dispensation, was a wedding of estates. Erasmus, sensitive to the charms of woman but not of matrimony, advised youngsters to marry as the oldsters wished, and trust to love to grow with association[37] rather than wither with satiation; and Rabelais agreed with him.[38] Notwithstanding these authorities, a rising number of young people, like Jeanne d'Albret, rebelled against marriages of realty. Roger Ascham, tutor to Elizabeth, mourned that "our time is so far from that old discipline and obedience as now not only young gentlemen but even very girls dare . . . marry themselves in spite of father, mother, God, good order, and all."[39] Luther was alarmed to learn that Melanchthon's son had betrothed himself without consulting his father, and that a young judge in Wittenberg had declared such a betrothal valid; this, the Reformer thought, was bound to give Wittenberg a bad name. In the university, he wrote (January 22, 1544),

> we have a great horde of young men from all countries, and the race of girls is getting bold, and run after the fellows into their rooms and chambers and wherever they can, and offer them their free love; and I hear that many parents have ordered their sons home . . . saying that we hang wives around their necks. . . . The next Sunday I preached a strong sermon, telling men to follow the common road and manner which had been since the beginning of the world . . .

namely, that parents should give their children to each other with prudence and good will, without their own preliminary engagement. . . . Such engagements are an invention of the abominable pope, suggested to him by the Devil to destroy and tear down the power of parents given and commended to them earnestly by God.[40]

Marriage contracts could be arranged for boys and girls as young as three years, but these marriages could be annulled later, if not consummated. The legal age for full marriage was generally fourteen for boys, twelve for girls. Sexual relations after betrothal and before the wedding were condoned. Even before betrothal, in Sweden and Wales, as later in some American colonies, "bundling" was allowed: the lovers would lie together in bed, but were admonished to keep a sheet between them.[41] In Protestant lands marriage ceased to be a sacrament, and by 1580 civil marriage was competing with marriage by a clergyman. Luther, Henry VIII, Erasmus, and Pope Clement VII thought bigamy permissible under certain conditions, especially as a substitute for divorce. Protestant divines moved slowly toward allowing divorce, but at first only for adultery. This offense was apparently most prevalent in France, despite the custom of killing adulterous wives. Illicit love affairs were part of the normal life of French women of good social standing.[42] A triangular ménage like that of Henry II, Catherine de Médicis, and Diane de Poitiers was quite frequent—the legal wife de convenance accepting the situation with wry grace, as sometimes in France today.

Except in the aristocracies, women were goddesses before marriage and servants afterward. Wives took motherhood in their stride, gloried in their numerous children, and managed to manage their managers. They were robust creatures, accustomed to hard work from sunrise to sunset. They made most of the clothing for their families, and sometimes took in work from capitalist entrepreneurs. The loom was an essential part of the home; in England all unmarried women were "spinsters." The women of the French court were a different species, encouraged by Francis I to prettify themselves in flesh and dress, and sometimes turning national policy by the guided missiles of their charms. A feminist movement was imported into France from Italy, but rapidly faded as women perceived that their power and prominence were independent of politics and laws. Many French women of the upper class were well educated; already, in Paris and elsewhere, the French salon was taking form as rich and cultivated ladies made their homes the rendezvous of statesmen, poets, artists, scholars, prelates, and philosophers. Another group of French women—let Anne of France, Anne of Brittany, Claude, and Renée serve as instances—stood quietly virtuous amid the erotic storm. In general the Reformation, being Teutonic, made for the patriarchal view of woman and the family. It ended her Renaissance enthronement as an exemplar of beauty and a civilizer of man. It condemned the Church's lenience with sexual diversions, and, after Luther's death, it prepared the way for the Puritanic chill.

Social morality declined with the rise of commercialism and the temporary disruption of charity. The natural dishonesty of man found fresh forms and opportunities as a money economy displaced the feudal regime. The newly rich, holding securities rather than land, and seldom seeing the individuals from whose labor they benefited, had no traditions of responsibility and generosity such as had gone with landed wealth.[43] Medieval commerce and industry had accepted moral checks in the form of guild, municipal, and ecclesiastical regulations; the new capitalism rejected these restraints, and drew men into a strenuous competition that pushed aside the old codes.[44] Commercial frauds replaced pious frauds. The pamphlet literature of the age groaned with denunciations of wholesale adulteration of food and other products. The Diet of Innsbruck (1518) complained that importers "add brick dust to ginger, and mix unhealthy stuff with their pepper."[45] Luther noted that merchants "have learned the trick of placing such spices as pepper, ginger, and saffron in damp vaults to increase their weight. There is not a single article out of which they cannot make profit through false measuring, counting, or weighing, or by producing artificial colors. . . . There is no end to their trickery."[46] The Venetian Senate branded a shipment of English woolens as fraudulent in weight, make, and size.[47]

Charity, in the Latin countries, was still administered with medieval cheerfulness. Noble families spent a considerable part of their incomes in gifts and alms.[48] Lyons inherited from the fifteenth century a complex organization of municipal charity, to which the citizens gave "with openhanded generosity."[49] In Germany and England the hands were not so open. Luther did his manful best to re-establish the charities interrupted by the princely confiscation of monastic properties, but he confessed that his efforts failed.[50] "Under the papacy," he mourned, "people were charitable and gave gladly, but now, under the dispensation of the Gospel, nobody gives any longer; everybody fleeces everybody else. . . . Nobody will give a pfennig."[51] Latimer gave a similar report in 1548: "London was never so ill as now. . . . In times past, when any rich man died . . . they would bequeath . . . great sums towards the relief of the poor. . . . Now charity is waxen cold."[52] Two Italian cities, Cardinal Pole told London, gave more alms than all England.[53] "As truth spread," concluded Froude, "charity and justice languished in England."[54] Probably it was not Protestantism, but commercialism and unbelief, that diminished charity.

Pauperism grew to the proportions of a social crisis. Evicted tenants, jobless journeymen, demobilized soldiers, roamed the highways or littered the slums, begging and robbing to live. In Augsburg the paupers were reckoned at a sixth of the population, in Hamburg a fifth, in London a fourth.[55] "O merciful Lord!" cried the reformer Thomas Lever, "what a number of poor, feeble, halt, blind, lame, sickly . . . lie and creep in the miry streets!"[56] Luther, whose heart was as kind as his tongue was harsh, was among the first to perceive that the state must take over from the Church the care and rescue of the destitute. In his address *To the Christian Nobility of the German Nation* (1520) he proposed that "every town should provide for its own poor." During his absence in the Wartburg his radical followers organized in Wittenberg a community fund to care for orphans, dower poor girls, give scholarships to needy students, and lend money to impoverished families. In 1523 Luther drew up a *Regulation of a Common Chest*, which urged that in each district the citizens and clergy should tax themselves to raise a fund from which loans were to be made, without interest, to persons in need and unable to work.[57] In 1522 Augsburg appointed six *Armenpfleger* —Protectors of the Poor—to supervise the distribution of relief. Nuremberg followed suit, then Strasbourg and Breslau (1523), Ratisbon and Magdeburg (1524).

In that year a Spanish humanist, Juan Luis Vives, wrote for the town council of Bruges a tract *On the Relief of the Poor*. He noted the spread of poverty amid growing wealth, and warned that the extreme inequality of possessions might engender a ruinous rebellion. "As it is disgraceful," he wrote, "for the father of a family in his comfortable home to permit anyone in it to suffer the disgrace of being unclothed or in rags, it is similarly unfitting that the magistrates of a city should tolerate a condition in which citizens are hard pressed by hunger and distress."[58] Vives agreed that all who were capable of work should be made to work, and that no one should be allowed to beg. But since many were really unable to work, some refuge must be set up for them in almshouses, hospitals, and schools financed by the municipality; food, medical care, and elementary education should be given them gratis, and special provision should be made for the mentally defective. Ypres combined Vives's ideas with the German precedents and organized (1525) a community chest which united all charitable endowments in one fund, and all charitable distribution under one head. Charles V asked for a copy of the Ypres plan and recommended it to all the cities of the Empire (1531), and Henry VIII sent a similar directive to the parishes of England (1536). In Catholic countries the Church retained the administration of charity.

Political morality remained Machiavellian. Spies were taken for granted; those of Henry VIII in Rome were expected to report the most secret conversations of the Vatican.[59] Bribery was traditional, and flowed more lushly after the influx of American gold. Governments competed in violating treaties; Turkish and Christian fleets rivaled each other in piracy. In the decay of chivalry the morals of war relapsed into semi-barbarism; cities that had unsuccessfully resisted siege were sacked or burned, soldiers surrendering were slaughtered or enslaved till ransomed; such international law and comity as had existed in the occasional submission of kings to arbitration by popes disappeared in a chaos of nationalistic expansion and religious enmity. Toward non-Christians, Christians recognized few moral restraints, and the Turks reciprocated. The Portuguese captured and enslaved African Negroes, and the Spanish Conquistadores robbed, enslaved, and killed American natives without abating their high resolve to make the New World Christian. Life was so bitter for the American Indians under Spanish rule that thousands of them committed suicide.[60] Even in Christendom there was a startling increase of suicides in this age.[61] Some humanists condoned self-destruction, but the Church ruled that it led straight to hell, so that the successful seeker fell out of the frying pan into the fire.

All in all the Reformation, though it ultimately improved the morals of Europe, temporarily damaged lay morality. Pirkheimer and Hans Sachs, both sympathetic with Luther, mourned that a chaos of unregulated conduct had followed the collapse of ecclesiastical authority.[62] Luther, as usual, was quite frank about the matter:

> The more we go forward, the worse the world becomes. . . . It is clear enough how much more greedy, cruel, immodest, shameless, wicked the people are now than they were under popery.[63]. . . We Germans are today the laughing stock and disgrace of all peoples; we are regarded as ignominious and obscure swine. . . . We steal, we lie . . . we eat and drink to excess, and we give ourselves to every vice.[64] . . . It is the general complaint that the young people of today are utterly dissolute and disorderly, and will not let themselves be taught any more. . . . The women and girls of Wittenberg have begun to go bare before and behind, and there is no one to punish or correct them, and God's word is mocked.[65]

Andreas Musculus, a Lutheran preacher, described his time (1560) as unspeakably immoral compared with the Germans of the fifteenth century,[66] and many Protestant leaders agreed with him.[67] "The future appalls me," moaned Calvin; "I dare not think of it; unless the Lord descends from heaven, barbarism will engulf us."[68] We hear similar notes from Scotland[69] and England. Froude, ardent defender of Henry VIII, summed up fairly:

> The movement commenced by Henry VIII, judged by its present results (1550), had brought the country at last into the hands of mere adventurers. The people had exchanged a superstition which in

its grossest abuses prescribed some shado*w* of respect and obedience, for a superstition which merged obedience in speculative belief; and under that baneful influence not only the highest virtues of self-sacrifice, but the commonest duties of probity and morality, were disappearing. Private life was infected with impurity to which the licentiousness of the Catholic clergy appeared like innocence. . . . Among the good who remained uninfected the best were still to be found on the Reforming side.[70]

We can hardly attribute this moral decline in Germany and England to Luther's unchaining of sex or his scorn of "good works," or to Henry's bad example in sexual indulgence and callous cruelty; for a similar—in some ways a more unrestrained—license ruled in Catholic Italy under the Renaissance popes, and in Catholic France under Francis I. Probably the basic cause of the moral loosening in Western Europe was the growth of wealth. A main supporting cause was the decline of faith not only in Catholic dogmas but in the very fundamentals of the Christian creed. "Nobody cares about either heaven or hell," mourned Andreas Musculus; "nobody gives a thought to either God or the Devil." [71] In such statements by religious leaders we must allow for the exaggeration of reformers disappointed to find how little their theological emendations had improved the moral life. Men had not been much better before, and would not be much better in later centuries, if we may trust the preachers. We can discover all the sins of the sixteenth century in our own age, and all of ours in theirs, according to their means.

Meanwhile both Catholicism and Protestantism had set up and strengthened two focuses of moral regeneration: the improvement of clerical conduct through marriage or continence, and the emphasis on the home as the final citadel of faith and decency. In the long run the Reformation would really reform, even to excess; and the time would come when men and women would look back with secret envy to that sixteenth century when their ancestors had been so wicked and so free.

IV. MANNERS

People then, as now, were judged more by their manners than by their morals; the world forgave more readily the sins that were committed with the least vulgarity and the greatest grace. Here, as in everything but artillery and theology, Italy led the way. Compared with the Italians the people north of the Alps, except for a thin upper crust in France and England, were fairly uncouth; the Italians called them barbarians, and many Frenchmen, charmed with their Italian conquests in field and chamber, agreed with them. But the barbarians were eager to be civilized. French courtiers and courtesans, poets and poisoners, followed Italian models; and the English limped sedulously behind. Castiglione's *Courtier* (1528) was translated into French in 1537, into English in 1561, and polite circles debated the definition of a gentleman. Manuals of manners were best sellers; Erasmus composed one. Conversation became an art in France, as later in the Mermaid Tavern in London; the duel of repartee crossed the Alps from Italy about the same time as the art of fencing. Conversation was more polished in France than in Germany; the Germans crushed a man with humor, the French punctured him with wit. Freedom in speech was the vital medium of the age.

Since the surface can be more easily made presentable than the soul, the rising classes in the rising civilizations of the North paid much attention to their clothing. Commoners dressed artlessly enough—as we see in Brueghel's multitudes: cuplike hats, loose blouses with bulging sleeves, tight trousers reaching down to comfortable shoes, with the ungainly composition centering upon a codpiece—an insolent bag, sometimes brightly ornamented, dangling before the male crotch. Moneyed males in Germany enveloped their mighty frames in voluminous folds of cloth, topped with broad hats that lay on the head like terraced pancakes; but German women were apparently forbidden to dress otherwise than as *Hausfrauen* or cooks. In England, too, the men wore more finery than their ladies, until Elizabeth outshone them with her thousand dresses. Henry VIII set a pace in extravagance of costume, prettifying his pounds with color and ornaments and precious stuffs. The Duke of Buckingham, at the marriage of Prince Arthur to Catherine of Aragon, "ware a gowne wrought of needle worke," says Holinshed, "furred with sables, and valued at £1,500" ($150,000?).[71] Sumptuary laws forbade any man lower than a knight to ape the sartorial splendor of his betters. Englishwomen covered their forms tightly, with dresses reaching from neck to floor, and sleeves to the wrist, with a trimming of fur at edges, and broad girdles buckled with metal ornaments and carrying a pendant or a rosary; in general they wore less jewelry than the men.

Under the appreciative Francis I French women opened their bodices, displayed swelling bosoms, and cut their gowns in the back almost to the last vertebra.[72] If the natural bust swelled inadequately, an artificial bust was inserted under the stays.[73] Clothing was tightened under the breasts and pinched at the waist; sleeves billowed, hidden wires spread out the skirt at rear and hem, and high-heeled shoes compelled a prancing, airy step. Women of rank—no others—were allowed to wear a train, or tail, to their dresses, the nobler the longer; if nobility sufficed it might be seven yards long, and a maid or page would follow to hold it up. In another style the woman would cover her neck with a *fraise* or ruff, stiffly supported by wires; and men in a formal mood pilloried themselves in like contraptions. About 1535 Servetus noted that "the women of Spain have a custom that would be held barbarous in France, of piercing their ears and hanging gold rings in them, often set with precious stones"; [74] but by 1550 earrings were worn by the ladies of France, and even by men. [75] Jewelry continued its immemorial sway. Frenchmen clothed themselves in silk shirts and velvet doublets, padded their shoulders, cased their legs in tight colored breeches, and protected their manhood with a *braguette* or codpiece sometimes set off with ribbons or jewelry. Reversing the custom of the fifteenth century, they wore their hair short and their beards long. Feminine hair was worn in a variety of structures discouraging to describe; it was braided, curled, netted, filled out with switches, decked with flowers, brightened with gems, perfumed with unguents, dyed to match the fashion, and raised in towers or pyramids above the head. Hairdressers were now indispensable to women of fashion, for growing old seemed a fate worse than death.

How clean were the bodies behind the frills? A sixteenth-century *Introduction pour les jeunes dames* spoke of women "who have no care to keep themselves clean except in those parts that may be seen, remaining filthy . . . under their linen"; [76] and a cynical proverb held that courtesans were the only women who washed more than their face and hands. [77] Perhaps cleanliness increased with immorality, for as women offered more of themselves to view or to many, cleanliness enlarged its area. Frequent bathing, preferably in perfumed water, became now, especially in France, part of good manners. Public bathhouses diminished in number as private bathrooms multiplied; these, however, were usually without running water, depending on bowls and tubs. Steam baths, which had come into Western Europe with returning crusaders in the thirteenth century, continued popular through the sixteenth.

The home almost replaced the church as the center of religious worship in Protestant lands. The father served as priest, leading the family in daily prayers, Bible reading, and psalms, and the mother taught her children the catechism. In the middle classes comfort went with piety. This was the age when the table evolved by joining trestles and boards into a sturdy-legged unity, benches and cushions evolved into the upholstered chair, and the four-poster bed, carved and canopied, became a symbol of moral stability and financial success. Furniture, plate, andirons, and kitchen utensils were made to endure, even sparkle, for generations. Pewter replaced wooden platters; spoons of tin or silver replaced those of wood.

Houses were big because families were large. Women bore almost annually, often in vain, for infantile mortality was high. John Colet was the eldest of twenty-two children; by the time he was thirty-two all the others were dead. Anton Koberger, the Nuremberg printer, had twenty-five children, and survived twelve of them. Dürer was one of eighteen children, of whom only three seem to have reached maturity. [78] To round out the family there were household pets almost as numerous as the progeny. Parrots had come in from the West Indies, and monkeys from India were domestic favorites.[79] A whole literature instructed women and children in the care of dogs and birds.

Meals were enormous. Vegetables were despised, and only slowly won acceptance; the cabbage, carrot, lettuce, rhubarb, potato, lima bean, and strawberry now came into common use. The main meal, or dinner, was taken at eleven in the morning; supper was deferred till seven—the higher the class, the later the hour. Beer and wine were the staple drinks at all meals, even breakfast; one of Thomas More's claims to fame was that he drank water. About 1550 the Spaniards brought in chocolate from Mexico; coffee had not yet percolated from Arabia into Western Europe. In 1512 the household of the Duke of Northumberland allowed a quart of ale per person per meal, even to boys eight years old; the average consumption of ale in sixteenth-century Coventry was a quart per day for every man, woman, and child.[80] The breweries of Munich were renowned as early as the fourteenth century.[81] Drunkenness was in good repute in England till "Bloody Mary" frowned upon it; it remained popular in Germany. The French drank more stably, not being quite so cold.

Despite poverty and oppression, many of the graces of life continued. Even the poor had gardens. The tulip, first brought to Western Europe about 1550 by Busbecq, Imperial ambassador at Constantinople, became a national passion in Holland. Country houses were a pleasant fashion in England and France. Villagers still had their seasonal festivals—May Day, Harvest Home, All Saints, Christmas, and many more; kings themselves went Maying, and crowned themselves with flowers. The amusements of the rich sometimes provided exciting pageantry for the poor, as when Henry II entered Lyons in state in 1548; and commoners might, at a respectful distance, watch lords joust at tournaments—till that sport went out of style after the death of Diane's King. Religious processions became more pagan as the age of Henry VIII moved toward the Elizabethan; and on the Continent an easy morality allowed nude women, in festival pageants, to impersonate historical or mythological characters; Dürer confessed himself fascinated by such a display at Antwerp in 1521.[82]

And there were games. Rabelais filled a chapter by merely listing them, real and imagined; and Brueghel showed almost a hundred of them in one painting. Bear-baiting, bullfighting, cockfighting, amused the populace; football, bowling, boxing, wrestling, exercised and exorcized young commoners; and Paris alone had 250 tennis courts for its blue bloods in the sixteenth century.[83] All classes hunted and gambled; some ladies threw dice, some bishops played cards for money.[84] Mummers, acrobats, and players roamed the countryside, and performed for lords and royalty. Within doors people played cards, chess, backgammon, and a score of other games.

Of all pastimes the best beloved was the dance. "After dinner," says Rabelais, "they all went tag-rag together to the willowy grove, where, on the green grass, to the sound of merry flutes and pleasant bagpipes, they danced so gallantly that it was a sweet and heavenly sport to see." [85] So in England, on May Day, villagers gathered round a gaily decorated Maypole, danced their lusty rustic measures, and then, it appears, indulged in intimacies reminiscent of the Roman festival of Flora, goddess of flowers. Under Henry VIII the May games usually included the morris (i.e., Moorish) dance, which had come from the Spanish Moors via the Spanish fandango with castanets. Students danced so boisterously at Oxford and Cambridge that William of Wykeham had to forbid the ecstasy near chapel statuary. Luther approved of dancing, and relished especially the "square dance, with friendly bows, embracings, and hearty swinging of the partners." [86] The grave Melanchthon danced; and at Leipzig, in the sixteenth century, the city fathers regularly held a ball to permit students to become acquainted with the "most honorable and elegant daughters of magnates, senators, and citizens." [87] Charles VI often led (*balait*) the ballet or dance at the French court; Catherine de Médicis brought Italian dancers to France, and there, in the later days of that unhappy queen mother, dancing developed new aristocratic forms. "Dancing," said Jean Tabourot, in one of the oldest books on one of the oldest arts, "is practiced in order to see whether lovers are healthy and suitable for one another; at the end of a dance the gentleman is permitted to kiss his mistress, in order that he may ascertain if she has agreeable breath. In this manner . . . dancing becomes necessary for the good government of society." [88] It was through its accompaniment of the dance that music developed from its vocal and choral forms into the instrumental compositions that have made it the dominating art of our time.

CHAPTER XXXIV

Music

1300-1564

I. THE INSTRUMENTS

THE popularity of music in these centuries corrects the somber note that history tends to give them; every now and then, through the excitement and bitterness of the religious revolution, we hear people singing. "I care nothing for the pleasures of food, gaming, and love," wrote the passionate printer Étienne Dolet; "music alone . . . takes me prisoner, holds me fast, dissolves me in ecstasy." [1] From the pure note of a girl's voice or a perfect flute to the polyphonic counterpoint of Deprès or Palestrina, every nation and class redeemed with music the commercialism and theology of the age. Not only did everyone sing; Francesco Landino complained that everyone composed.[2] Between the merry or plaintive folk songs of the village and the solemn High Masses of the Church a hundred forms of music lent their harmony to dances, ballets, banquets, courtships, courts, processions, pageants, plays, and prayers. The world sang.

The merchants of Antwerp were escorted daily to the Bourse by a band. Kings studied music as no feminine or mechanical prerogative but as a mark and fount of civilization. Alfonso X of Spain sedulously and lovingly collected songs to the Virgin—*Cantigas de Santa Maria*. James IV of Scotland wooed Margaret Tudor with clavichord and lute; Charles VIII of France took the royal choir with him on his campaigns in Italy; Louis XII sang tenor in the court choir; Leo X composed French chansons;[3] Henry VIII and Francis I courted and challenged each other with rival choirs on the Field of the Cloth of Gold. Luis Milan described Portugal in 1540 as "a veritable sea of music."[4] The court of Matthias Corvinus at Buda had a choir rated equal to the pope's, and there was a good school of music under Sigismund II in Cracow. Germany was bursting with song in Luther's youth. "We have singers here in Heidelberg," wrote Alexander Agricola in 1484, "whose leader composes for eight or twelve voices."[5] At Mainz, Nuremberg, Augsburg, and elsewhere the Meistersinger continued to adorn popular songs and Biblical passages with the pomp of pedantry and the jewelry of counterpoint. The German folk songs were probably the best in Europe. Everywhere music was the prod of piety and the lure of love.

Although nearly all music in this age was vocal, the accompanying instruments were as diverse as in a modern orchestra. There were string instruments like psalteries, harps, dulcimers, shawms, lutes, and viols; wind instruments like flutes, oboes, bassoons, trumpets, trombones, cornets, and bagpipes; percussion instruments like drums, bells, clappers, cymbals, and castanets; keyboard instruments like organs, clavichords, harpsichords, spinets, virginals; there were many more; and of many there were fascinating variants in place and time. Every educated home had one or more musical instruments, and some homes had special cabinets to hold them. Often they were works of art, fondly carved or fancifully formed, and they were handed down as treasures and memories from generation to generation. Some organs were as elaborately designed as Gothic cathedral fronts; so the men who built the organs for the Sebalduskirche and the Lorenzkirche in Nuremberg became "immortal" for a century. The organ was the chief but not the only instrument used in churches; flutes, pipes, drums, trombones, even kettledrums might add their incongruous summons to adoration.

The favorite accompaniment for the single voice was the lute. Like all string instruments, it had an Asiatic origin. It came into Spain with the Moors, and there, as the vihuela, it rose to the dignity of a solo instrument, for which the earliest known purely instrumental music was composed. Usually its body was made of wood and ivory, and shaped like a pear; its belly was pierced with holes in the pattern of a rose; it had six—sometimes twelve—pairs of strings, which were plucked by the fingers; its neck was divided by frets of brass into a measured scale, and its pegbox was turned back from the neck. When a pretty girl held a lute in her lap, strummed its strings, and added her voice to its tones, Cupid could save an arrow. However, it was difficult to keep the lute in tune, for the constant pull of the strings tended to warp the frame, and one wit said of an old lutanist that sixty of his eighty years had been spent in tuning his instrument.[6]

The viol differed from the lute in having its strings stretched over a bridge and played by a bow, but the principle was the same—the vibration of taut struck strings over a box perforated to deepen sound. Viols came in three sizes: the large bass viola da gamba, held between the legs like its modern replacement, the violoncello; the small tenor viola da braccio, held on the arm; and a treble viol. During the sixteenth century the viola da braccio evolved into the violin, and in the eighteenth the viol passed out of use.

The only European invention in musical instruments was the keyboard, by which the strings were indirectly struck instead of being directly plucked or bowed. The oldest known form, the clavichord, made its debut in the twelfth century and survived to be "well tempered" by Johann Sebastian Bach; the oldest extant example (1537) is in the Metropolitan Museum in New York. In the fifteenth century a sturdier variant took form in the harpsichord; this allowed modifications of tone through differences of pressure; sometimes a second keyboard extended the gamut, and stops and couplers offered new marvels of sound. The spinet and virginal were Italian and English variants of the harpsichord. These keyboard instruments, like the viol and the lute, were prized for their beauty as well as their tone, and formed a graceful element of decoration in well-to-do homes.

As instruments improved in range and quality of tone and in complexity of operation, more and more training and skill were required to play them successfully; an audience grew for performances of one or more instruments without voices, and virtuosos appeared for the organ and the lute. Conrad Paumann (d. 1473), the blind organist of Nuremberg, traveled from court to court giving recitals whose excellence knighted him. Such developments encouraged the composition of music for instruments alone. Till the fifteenth century nearly all instrumental music had apparently been intended to accompany voices or dances, but in that century several paintings show musicians playing with no visible singing or dancing. The oldest surviving music for instruments alone is the *Fundamentum organisandi* (1452) of Conrad Paumann, which was composed primarily as a guide to organ playing, but contained also a number of pieces for solo performance. Ottaviano dei Petrucci's application of movable metal types to the printing of music (1501) lowered the cost of publishing instrumental and other compositions. Music written for dances lent itself to independent presentation; hence the influence of dance forms on instrumental music; the suite of "movements" composed for a succession of dances led to the symphony and the chamber music quartet, whose parts sometimes retained dance names. The lute, viol, organ, and harpsichord were favored for solo or orchestral performances. Alberto da Ripa achieved such fame as a lutanist at the court of Francis I and Henry II that when he died (1551) the poets of France warbled dirges to his remains.

II. THE FLEMISH ASCENDANCY: 1430–1590

The songs and dances of the people were the perennial fountain from which nonecclesiastical forms of music took their origin, moods, and themes, and even Masses might stem from such ditties as *Adieu mes amours*. The chansons of France ranged from the lilting lays of street singers and the ballads of troubadours to the intricate polyphonic chants of Guillaume de Machaut and Josquin Deprès.

Machaut (*c.* 1300–77) was the lord of that *ars nova* which Philippe de Vitry had expounded in 1325—music using binary rhythms in addition to the triple rhythms sanctioned by the *ars antiqua* and the Church. Machaut was

⌐ poet, a scholar, a musician, a canon of Reims Cathedral, probably also a man of ardor, for he wrote some amorous lyrics whose warmth has not yet cooled. He excelled in a dozen musical forms—ballads, roundels, virelays, motets, Masses; to him we trace the oldest polyphonic Mass composed by one man. Though an ecclesiastic, he shared in the movement to secularize polyphonic music, to lead it from the orthodox rhythms of the motet and the High Mass to the freer, more flexible *cantilena* of secular song.

In those centuries the English were musical. They did not rival the Italians in melody (who has?), nor the Flemings in polyphony, but their songs now and then touched a strain of tenderness and delicacy equaled only in the profoundest French chansons. English singers were acclaimed at the Council of Constance, and in that generation Henry V, hero of Agincourt, composed a Mass whose *Gloria* and *Sanctus* are still preserved. The compositions of John Dunstable (*c.* 1370–1453) were sung from Scotland to Rome, and played a part in forming the style of the Flemish school.

As Flanders had set the pace in painting in the fifteenth century, so it was there, in a milieu of prosperous and art-loving nobles and burghers, that music had one of its most exuberant periods. "Today," wrote Johannes Verwere about 1490, "we have blossoming forth, quite apart from a large number of famous singers . . . an almost unlimited number of composers" whose works "excel in pleasant sound; I never hear or look at their compositions without rejoicing in them." [7] Contemporaries would probably have ranked Dufay, Okeghem, and Deprès quite on a par with Jan van Eyck, Claus Sluter, and Rogier van der Weyden in the hierarchy of genius and beneficence. Here, in Flemish polyphony, Western Europe lived the last phase of the Gothic spirit in art—religious devotion tempered with secular gaiety, forms firm in base and structure, fragile and delicate in development and ornament. Even Italy, so hostile to Gothic, joined Western Europe in acknowledging the supremacy of Flemish music, and in seeking *maestri* from Flanders for episcopal choirs and princely courts. Emperor Maximilian I, enchanted by the music of Brussels, formed a choir in Vienna on Flemish models. Charles V took Flemish musicians to Spain; Archduke Ferdinand took some to Austria, Christian II others to Denmark; "the fountain of music," said the Venetian Cavallo, "is in the Netherlands." [8] Through this Flemish ascendancy professional music escaped the narrowing nationalism of the age.

Guillaume Dufay led the way. Born in Hainaut (*c.* 1399), trained as a boy chorister in the cathedral of Cambrai, he was called to Rome to sing in the Sistine Chapel; then, back in Cambrai, he raised its choir to international renown; the Masses that he composed there were sung in all the musical centers of Latin Christendom. Those that survive sound heavy and slow to ears alert to the light celerity of modern life, yet they may have fitted well in stately cathedrals or solemn papal choirs. More to our mood is a polyphonic song of mellifluous melancholy, *Le jour s'endort*—"The day is going to sleep." We picture a robed chorus singing such a chant in the Gothic halls of Cambrai, Ypres, Brussels, Bruges, Ghent, or Dijon, and we perceive that the architecture, painting, costumes, music, and manners of that warm and colorful and pompous age made a harmonious artistic whole, being themselves variations on one pervasive theme.

Dufay's methods were developed, and were broadcast through Europe, by the most influential musical teacher of perhaps any time. Johannes Okeghem, born in Flanders (*c.* 1430), spent most of his years providing music, and musical education, at the court of France. His special passion was for the "canon"—a form of fugue in which the words and melody sung by the first voice were repeated, several bars later, by a second voice, later by a third, and so on, in a flowing counterpoint whose laborious complexity challenged the singers and charmed the composers. These ran to him from every Roman Catholic land to learn and carry off his skill. "Through his pupils," wrote an old historian, "the art" of contrapuntal and "canonical" polyphony "was transplanted into all countries; and he must be regarded— for it can be proved by [stylistic] genealogy—as the founder of all schools from his own to the present age"; [9] but since this was written in 1833, Okeghem cannot be held responsible for twentieth-century music. At his death (1495) the musicians of Europe wrote motets to his memory, and Erasmus a "Lamentation." The names of even the "immortals" are writ in water.

His pupils became the musical leaders of the next generation. Coming from Hainaut to Paris, Josquin Deprès spent years studying with Okeghem, then served as *maestro di capella*—"master of the chapel" choir—in Florence, Milan, and Ferrara. For Duke Ercole I he wrote a *Miserere* that soon resounded throughout Western Europe. After six years in the Sistine Chapel Choir he returned to Paris (1494) to serve as *maître de chapelle* for Louis XII. One of his noblest works was his *Déploration de Jehan Okeghem*, a dirge for his dead teacher. For a time he followed him in composing Masses and motets in canonic style, piling voice upon voice in almost mathematical problems of sequence and harmony. When his skill was complete, and his supremacy in "art music" was unquestioned, he tired of technique, and wrote motets, hymns, and secular songs in a simpler harmonic style, in which the music followed and illuminated the words instead of torturing them on a Protean canon, or stretching a syllable into a song. When both teacher and pupil were gone it became customary to call Okeghem the Donatello, Deprès the Michelangelo, of musical art.

The French court cultivated music as the finest flower of wealth and power. A lovely tapestry dated about 1500, and now in the Musée des Gobelins at Paris, pictures four women, three youths, and a bald monk grouped in a garden around a fountain; one lad is playing a lute, a girl plays a viol, a staid lady plays a portable organ. French poets intended their lyrics to be sung; an Académie du Palais devoted itself to promoting the union between music and poetry; and even now one without the other seems incomplete. Clément Jannequin, a pupil of Deprès', excelled in descriptive chansons; his *Chant de l'alouette*, or "Song of the Lark" (1521), still warbles over several continents.

Spanish music reflected the piety and gallantry of the people. Cross-fertilized by Arabic, Italian, Provençal, French, and Flemish influences, this art ranged from melancholy Morisco monodies to stately polyphonic Masses in the Flemish style. One of the greatest composers of the sixteenth century, Cristóbal Morales, carried polyphony to high excellence, and transmitted his art to his more famous pupil, Tomás Luis de Victoria. By contrast the Arabic heritage produced just the strains to fit the lute. Luis de Milan and Miguel de Fuenllana composed for the vihuela—and performed on it—songs that rivaled the German Lieder in range and power.

The conquest of Italy by Flemish musicians continued to the rise of Palestrina. Heinrich Ysaac, after absorbing the contrapuntal art in Flanders, was brought to Florence by Lorenzo de' Medici to teach Il Magnifico's children; he stayed there fourteen years, and composed music for Lorenzo's songs. Disturbed by the French invasion of Italy, he passed into the service of Maximilian I at Innsbruck, where he shared in giving form to the Lieder. In 1502 he returned to Italy, pensioned by the Emperor and his former pupil, Leo X. His Masses, motets, and songs—above all his *Choralis Constantinus*, fifty-eight four-part settings for the Offices of the Mass throughout the religious year—were ranked with the highest music of the age.

Orlando di Lasso brought the Flemish school to its culmination, and illustrated, in his triumphant career, the geographical range and rising social status of Renaissance musicians. As a boy chorister in his native Hainaut, he so fascinated his hearers that he was twice abducted by those who hoped to profit from his voice; finally, in his fifteenth year (1545?) his parents allowed Ferdinand Gonzaga to take him to Italy. At the age of twenty-three he became choirmaster in the church of St. John Lateran in Rome. In 1555 he settled in Antwerp, and published his *First Book of Italian Madrigals*, secular lyrics dressed in all the frills of Flemish counterpoint. In the same year he issued a miscellany of villanelles (songs of Neapolitan origin), French chansons, and four religious motets; this collection well reflected the judicious oscillation of Di Lasso's life between profane enjoyment and melodious penitence. We get a glimpse of his environment at Antwerp in the dedication of a motet to Cardinal Pole, and another to Cardinal Granvelle, minister to Philip II in the Netherlands. Probably it was Granvelle who arranged the young composer's engagement to assist in directing the ducal choir at Munich (1556). Orlando came to like Bavaria as much as Italy, took his wife from one as he had taken his name from the other, and served the Bavarian dukes till his death.

This happy Mozart of the sixteenth century doubled the 626 compositions of his counterpart. He traversed the whole gamut of current musical forms, and in each won European renown. He seemed equally at home in madrigals of refined love, chansons of amorous levity, and Masses of mystic piety. In 1563 he was made *Kapellmeister*. Now he composed for Albert V a musical setting of the seven Penitential Psalms. The Duke so admired these compositions that he engaged artists to transcribe them on parchment, adorn them with miniatures, and bind them in red morocco in two folio volumes which are today among the most prized possessions of the state library in art-loving Munich.

All Europe solicited the new star. When Di Lasso visited Paris (1571), Charles IX offered him 1,200 livres ($30,000?) per year to stay; he refused, but presented Charles and Catherine de Médicis with a book of French chansons, the most melodious, said Brantôme, that Paris had ever heard. One song chanted the praises of the French capital for its love of justice and peace—a year before the Massacre of St. Bartholomew. Returning to Munich, Di Lasso dedicated to the Fuggers a collection of Latin motets, Italian madrigals, German Lieder, and French chansons; this composer was no romantic starveling but a man adept in the ways of the world. In 1574 he traveled to Rome at Duke Albert's expense, gave Gregory XIII a volume of Masses, and received the Order of the Golden Spur. Even God appreciated Orlando's dedications; for when, on Corpus Christi day (1584), a severe storm threatened to cancel the usual religious procession through the streets of Munich, the rain stopped and the sun came out as Orlando's motet, *Gustate et videte*—"Taste and see how gracious the Lord is"—was sung by his choir; and every year thereafter, on Corpus Christi, the same music was sung to ensure propitious skies.

In 1585 Di Lasso, aging and repentant, published his *Fifth Book of Madrigals*, in which he applied the form to spiritual themes; these are among his most moving compositions. Five years later his mind began to fail; he could no longer recognize his wife, and talked of almost nothing but death, the Last Judgment, and an increase in salary. He received the increase, and died triumphant and insane (1594).

III. MUSIC AND THE REFORMATION

The Reformation was a revolution in music as well as in theology, ritual, ethics, and art. Catholic liturgy was aristocratic, a stately ceremonial rooted in inviolable tradition and standing frankly above the people in language, vestments, symbols, and music. In that spirit the clergy defined itself as the Church, and thought of the people as a flock to be shepherded into morality and salvation by myth, legend, sermon, drama, and all the arts. In that spirit the Mass was an esoteric mystery, a miraculous intercourse of the priest with God, and the music of the Mass was sung by the priest and a male choir set apart from the worshipers. But in the Reformation the middle classes asserted themselves; the people became the Church, the clergy became their ministers, the language of the service was to be the vernacular of the nation, the music was to be intelligible, and in it the congregation would take an active, finally a leading, role.

Luther loved music, appreciated polyphony and counterpoint, and wrote enthusiastically in 1538:

> When natural music is sharpened and polished by art, then one begins to see with amazement the great and perfect wisdom of God in His wonderful work of music, where one voice takes a simple part and around it sing three, four, or five other voices, leaping, springing round about, marvelously gracing the simple part, like a square dance in heaven. . . . He who does not find this an inexpressible miracle of the Lord is truly a clod, and is not worthy to be considered a man.[10]

At the same time he aspired to a religious music that would move the people by its fusion of faith with song. In 1524 he collaborated with Johann Walther, *Kapellmeister* to the Elector Frederick the Wise, to produce the first Protestant hymnal, which was expanded and improved through many editions. The words were taken partly from Catholic hymns, partly from the songs of the Meistersinger, partly from Luther's own roughly poetic pen, partly from folk songs transformed to religious themes; "the Devil," said Luther, "has no right to all the good tunes." [11] Some of the music was composed by Luther, some by Walther, some was adapted from current Catholic settings. Lutheran churches continued for almost a century to include polyphonic Masses in their ritual; but gradually Latin was replaced by the vernacular, the role of the Mass was reduced, singing by the congregation was extended, and the chants of the choir moved away from counterpoint to an easier harmonic form in which the music sought to follow and interpret the words. From the choir music composed by Luther and his aides to accompany the recitation of Gospel narratives came the noble Protestant church music of the eighteenth century, culminating in the oratorios of Handel and the Masses, oratorios, and chorales of Johann Sebastian Bach.

Not all the founders of Protestantism were so favorable to music as Luther. Zwingli, though himself a musician, excluded music altogether from the religious service, and Calvin forbade any church music except unisonal singing by the congregation. But he allowed polyphonic song in the home; and his Huguenot followers in France took part of their strength and courage from family singing of hymns and Psalms set to music for several voices. When Clément Marot translated the Psalms into French verse Calvin so liked the result that he condoned the polyphonic settings arranged by Claude Goudimel, and the fact that this Protestant composer was slain in the Massacre of St. Bartholomew made his Psalter a doubly holy book. A century after Marot a Catholic bishop expressed his envy of the role these translations and settings had played in the French Reformation. "To know these Psalms by heart is, among the Huguenots, a sign of the communion to which they belong; and in the towns in which they are most numerous the airs may be heard coming from the mouths of artisans, and, in the country, from those of tillers of the soil." [12] The democratization of religious music marked the lands of the Reformation, covering the darkness of the creed with the releasing joy of song.

IV. PALESTRINA: 1526–94

The Catholic Church remained the chief patron of music, as of the other arts. North of the Alps Catholic music proceeded along the lines set by the Flemish School. This tradition was confirmed by Ysaac in Austria, and by Di Lasso in Bavaria. One of Luther's most generous letters was addressed (1530) to Ludwig Senfl, complimenting him on the music he was composing at Munich, and praising the Catholic dukes there because "they cultivate and honor music." [13]

The choir of the Sistine Chapel was still the model on which kings and princes established their "chapels" in the fourteenth and fifteenth centuries. Even among Protestants the highest form of musical composition was the Mass, and the crowning glory of a Mass was to be sung by the papal choir. The supreme ambition of a singer was to join that choir, which was therefore able to include the best male voices in Western Europe. *Castrati*—then called *eunuchi*—were first admitted to the Sistine Choir about 1550; soon afterward some appeared at the Bavarian court. The emasculation was performed on consenting boys who were persuaded that their soprano voices would be a greater asset to them than fertility—a vulgar virtue generally supplied beyond demand.

Like any old and complex institution, which has so much to lose by an unsuccessful innovation, the Church was conservative, even more in ritual than in creed. Composers, on the contrary, were weary of old modes, as they have been in all ages, and experiment was to them the life of their art. All through these centuries the Church struggled to prevent the artificiality of the *ars nova*, and the subtlety of Flemish counterpoint, from weakening the dignity and grandeur of the High Mass. In 1322 Pope John XXII issued a stern decree against musical novelties and decoration, and ordered that the music of the Mass should keep to unisonal plain song, the Gregorian chant, as its foundation, and permit only such harmony as would be intelligible to worshipers, and would deepen rather than distract piety. The order was obeyed for a century; then it was evaded by having some of the performers sing the bass part an octave higher than written; this *faulx bourdon*—false bass—became a favorite ruse in France. Complexities in Mass music developed again. Five, six, or eight parts were sung in fugue and counterpoint, in which the words of the liturgy ran upon one another's heels in professional confusion, or were drowned in musical flourishes sometimes inserted by the singers *ad libitum*. The custom of adapting popular tunes into a Mass led even to the intrusion of profane words into the sacred text. Some Masses came to be known from their secular sources, like *The Mass of Farewell My Loves*, or *The Mass in the Shadow of the Bush*.[14] The liberal Erasmus was himself so disgusted with the artificiality of "art Masses" that he protested, in a note to his edition of the New Testament:

> Modern church music is so constructed that the congregation cannot hear one distinct word. The choristers themselves do not understand what they are singing. . . . There was no [church] music in St. Paul's time. Words were then pronounced plainly. Words nowadays mean nothing. . . . Men leave their work and go to church to listen to more noises than were ever heard in Greek or Roman theaters. Money must be made to buy organs and train boys to squeal.[15]

In this matter the reform party within the Church agreed with Erasmus. Bishop Giberti of Verona forbade the use of amorous songs or popular melodies in the churches of his diocese, and Bishop Morone of Modena prohibited all "figured" music—i.e., music adorned with the elaboration of motives or themes. At the Council of Trent the Catholic reformers urged the exclusion of all polyphonic music from church services, and a return to monodic Gregorian chant. The predilection of Pope Pius IV for Palestrina's Masses may have helped to save the day for Catholic polyphony.

Giovanni Luigi Palestrina took his name from a little city in the Roman Campagna, which in ancient days had entered history as Praeneste. In 1537 we find him listed, at the age of eleven, among the choirboys at Santa Maria Maggiore in Rome. He was not yet twenty-one when he was appointed choirmaster in the cathedral of his native town. So established, he married (1547) Lucrezia di Goris, a woman of helpful but moderate means. When the bishop of Palestrina became Julius III he brought his choirmaster to

Rome, and made him head of the Cappella Giulia, in St. Peter's, which trained singers for the Sistine Chapel. To the new Pope the young composer dedicated his *First Book of Masses* (1554), one of which presented a three-voice counterpoint accompaniment to one voice in plain song. The Pope liked these Masses enough to give Palestrina membership in the Sistine Choir. As a married man Giovanni's position in this usually tonsured group seemed irregular, and evoked some opposition. Palestrina was about to dedicate a book of madrigals to the Pope when Julius died (1555).

Marcellus II lived only three weeks after his elevation to the papacy. To his memory the composer dedicated (1555) his famous *Missa Papae Marcelli*, which was not published or so named till 1567. Pope Paul IV, a man of inflexible and puritan principles, dismissed the three married members from the Sistine Choir, allotting each a small pension. Palestrina was soon made choirmaster at St. John Lateran, but this position, though it buttered his bread, offered no patronage to cover the expense of publishing musical compositions. With the accession of Pius IV (1559) papal favor returned. Pius was impressed by the *Improperia* that Palestrina wrote for the Good Friday service, and from that time this composition became a regular part of that ritual in the Sistine Chapel. Palestrina's marriage still excluded him from the Sistine Choir, but his status rose with his appointment (1561) as choirmaster at Santa Maria Maggiore.

A year later the reassembled Council of Trent took up the problem of adjusting church music to the new spirit of reform. The extreme proposal to forbid polyphony altogether was rejected; a compromise measure was passed urging ecclesiastical authorities to "exclude from churches all such music as . . . introduces anything of the impure or lascivious, in order that the house of God may truly be seen to be . . . the house of prayer." * Pius IV appointed a committee of eight cardinals to implement this decree in the diocese of Rome. A pleasant story relates that the commission was on the verge of banning polyphonic music when one member, Cardinal Charles Borromeo, appealed to Palestrina to compose a Mass that would show the full congruity of polyphony and piety; that Palestrina wrote, and a choir sang, for the commission, three Masses, one of them the *Missa Papae Marcelli*, and that the profound union of religious elevation and chastened musical artistry in these Masses saved polyphony from condemnation. However, the *Mass of Pope Marcellus* was already ten years old, and the only known connection of Palestrina with this commission is its extension of his pension.[16] We may none the less believe that the music which Palestrina had presented in the choirs of Rome—by its fidelity to the words, its avoidance of secular motives, and the subordination of musical art to religious intent—

* Pius X (1903) and Pius XII (1955) felt it necessary to repeat these instructions.

played a part in leading the committee to sanction polyphonic music.[17] It was an added argument for polyphony that Palestrina's ecclesiastical compositions normally dispensed with instrumental adornment, and were almost always written *a cappella*—"in chapel style"—i.e., for voices alone.

In 1571 Palestrina was again made choirmaster of the Cappella Giulia, and ne kept this post till his death. Meanwhile he composed with uncontrollable fertility—in all, ninety-three Masses, 486 antiphons, offertories, motets, and psalms, and a great number of madrigals. Some of these were on secular themes, but as Palestrina aged he turned even this form to religious purposes. His *First Book of Spiritual Madrigals* (1581) includes some of his most beautiful chants. Personal misfortunes may have colored his music. In 1576 his son Angelo died, leaving to his care two beloved grandchildren, who died a few years later. Another son died about 1579, and in 1580 the death of his wife moved the composer to think of becoming a monk. However, he married again within a year.

The astonishing abundance and quality of Palestrina's product raised him to the leadership of Italian, if not of all European, music. His setting of the Song of Solomon to twenty-nine motets (1584), his *Lamentations of Jeremiah* (1588), his *Stabat Mater* and *Magnificat* (1590) confirmed his reputation and his persisting power. In 1592 his Italian competitors joined in presenting him with a *Collection of Vesper Psalms* honoring him as the "common father of all musicians." On January 1, 1594, he dedicated to the Grand Duchess Christina of Tuscany a *Second Book of Spiritual Madrigals*, combining again religious devotion with musical mastery. A month later he died, in the sixty-ninth year of his age. His tomb bore under his name the title he had earned, *Musicae Princeps*, Prince of Music.

We must not expect to appreciate Palestrina today unless, ourselves in a religious mood, we hear his music in its proper setting as part of some solemn ritual; and even there its technical aspects may leave us more marveling than moved. In a literal sense the proper setting can never return, for it was music of the Catholic Reformation, the somber tone of a stern reaction against the sensuous joyousness of the pagan Renaissance. It was Michelangelo surviving Raphael, Paul IV replacing Leo X, Loyola displacing Bembo, Calvin succeeding Luther. Our current preferences are a transient and fallible norm; and an individual's taste—especially if he be lacking in technical competence, in mysticism, and a sense of sin—is a narrow base on which to rest a standard of judgment in music or theology. But we can all agree that Palestrina carried to its completion the religious polyphony of his day. Like most high artists, he stood at the crest of a line of development in feeling and technique; he received a tradition and completed it; he accepted discipline, and through it gave structure to his music, an architectonic stability against the winds of change. Who knows but some not very distant age, tiring of orchestral sonorities and operatic romances, may find again in such music as Palestrina's a depth of feeling, a profound and placid flow of harmony, better fitted to express the soul of man cleansed of pride in reason and power, and standing again humble and fearful before the engulfing infinite.

Literature in the Age of Rabelais

1517-64

I. OF MAKING BOOKS

AFTER Gutenberg the impulse to self-display took an added form—the itch to be in print. It was a costly urge, for the only copyright then known was the "exclusive privilege" given by civil or ecclesiastical authorities to print a specified book. Such a grant was exceptional, and without it rival publishers, even in the same country, might "pirate" a work at will. If a book sold well the publisher would usually give the author an honorarium; but almost the only publications profitable enough to earn such a fee were popular romances, tales of magic or marvels, and controversial pamphlets which had to be abusive to sell. Works of scholarship were lucky to pay their cost. Publishers encouraged authors to dedicate such productions to state or Church dignitaries, or affluent magnates or lords, in the hope of a gift for the laud.

Printing and publishing were generally united in the same firm, and the man or family that engaged in them was a vital factor in his town and times. Fame through printing alone was rare. Claude Garamond of Paris managed it by discarding the "Gothic" type that German printers had adopted from manuscript lettering, and designing (*c.* 1540) a "roman" type based on the Carolongian minuscule script of the ninth century as developed by Italian humanists and the Aldine press. Italian, French, and English printers chose this roman form; the Germans clung to Gothic till the nineteenth century. Some styles of type still bear Garamond's name.

Germany led the world in publishing. There were active firms in Basel, Strasbourg, Augsburg, Nuremberg, Wittenberg, Cologne, Leipzig, Frankfurt, and Magdeburg. Twice a year publishers and booksellers met at the Frankfurt fair, bought and sold books, and exchanged ideas. One Frankfurt printer issued the first newspaper (1548)—a sheet distributed at the fair and reporting recent events. Antwerp became a publishing center when Christopher Plantin turned his bindery into a printing shop (1555); two years later he sent 1,200 volumes to the Frankfurt fair. In France the hub of the book trade was Lyons; 200 printing establishments made the city challenge Paris as the intellectual capital of the land.

Étienne Dolet, printer and humanist, was the firebrand of Lyons. Born in Orléans, schooled in Paris, he fell in love with Cicero; "I approve only of Christ and Tully." Hearing that thought was exceptionally free at Padua, he hurried there, and exchanged irreverent epigrams with skeptical Averroists. At Toulouse he became the soul of a freethinking band that laughed at "Papists" and Lutherans alike. Banished, he went to Lyons and made a name for himself with poems and articles, but he killed a painter in an argument, and fled to Paris, where Marguerite of Navarre won him a pardon from the King. He became friends—and quarreled—with Marot and Rabelais. Returning to Lyons, he set up a printing press, and specialized in publishing heretical works. The Inquisition summoned him, tried him, imprisoned him; he escaped, but was captured on a clandestine visit to his son. On August 3, 1546, he was burned alive.

The most distinguished of French publishers were the Étiennes, a dynasty as persistent in printing as the Fuggers in finance. Henri Étienne started his press at Paris about 1500; it was continued by his sons Francis, Robert, and Charles; to these four France owed her finest editions of the Greek and Latin classics. Robert compiled a *Thesaurus linguae latinae* (1532), which became the leaning-post for all later Latin-French dictionaries. To the Étiennes Latin became a second tongue; they regularly spoke it in their family life. Francis I praised their work, supported Marguerite in defending them against the Sorbonne, and on one occasion joined the coterie of scholars that met in Robert's shop; a famous story tells how the King waited patiently while Robert corrected an urgent proof. Francis provided the funds with which Robert engaged Garamond to design and cast a new font of Greek type, so beautiful that it became the model of most later printing in Greek. The Sorbonne disapproved of the King's flirtation with Hellenism; a professor warned *Parlement* (1539) that "to propagate a knowledge of Greek and Hebrew would operate to the destruction of all religion"; as for Hebrew, said a monk, it was "well known that all who learn Hebrew presently become Jews." [1] After being harassed by the Sorbonne for thirty years Robert transferred his press to Geneva (1552); and there, in the year of his death (1559), he revealed his Protestant inclinations by publishing an edition of Calvin's *Institutes*. His son Henri Étienne II upheld the repute of the family by issuing in Paris handsome editions of the classics, and compiling in five volumes a *Thesaurus linguae graecae* (1572), which is still the most complete of all Greek dictionaries. He brought the Sorbonne down upon him by publishing an *Apologie pour Herodote* (1566), in which he pointed out the parallels between Christian miracles and the incredible marvels related by the Greek. He in his turn sought refuge in Geneva, but found the Calvinist regime as intolerant as the Sorbonne.

Many publications of this age were models of typography, engraving, and binding. The heavy half-metallic bindings of the fifteenth century gave place to lighter and cheaper covers in leather, velum, or parchment. Jean Grolier de Servières, treasurer of France in 1534, had most of his 3,000 volumes so elegantly bound in Levantine morocco that they rank among the handsomest books in existence. Private libraries were now numberless, and public libraries were opened in many cities—Cracow (1517), Hamburg (1529), Nuremberg (1538). . . . Under Francis I the old royal library assembled by Charles VIII was transferred from the Louvre to Fontainebleau, and was enriched with new collections and fine bindings; this Bibliothèque du Roi became, after the Revolution, the Bibliothèque Nationale. Many monastic libraries perished in the Reformation, but many passed into private hands, and what was of value in them found its way into public repositories. Much is lost in history, but so much of worth has been preserved that not a hundred lifetimes could absorb it.

II. SCHOOLS

It was natural that the Revolution should for a time disrupt the educational system of Western Europe, for that system was almost wholly a service of the Church, and the influence of the orthodox clergy could not be successfully challenged without breaking their control of education. Luther condemned the existing grammar schools as teaching the student "only enough bad Latin to become a priest and read Mass . . . and yet remain all his life a poor ignoramus fit neither to cackle nor to lay eggs." [2] As for the universities, they seemed to him dens of murderers, temples of Moloch, synagogues of corruption; "nothing more hellish . . . ever appeared on earth . . . or ever would appear"; and he concluded that they were "only worthy of being reduced to dust." [3] Melanchthon agreed with him on the ground that the universities were turning students into pagans.[4] The opinion of Carlstadt, the Zwickau "prophets," and the Anabaptists—that education was a useless frill, a peril to morals, and a hindrance to salvation—was readily accepted by parents who grudged the cost of educating their children. Some fathers argued that since secondary instruction was largely directed to preparing students for the priesthood, and priests were now so unfashionable, it was illogical to send sons to universities.

The Reformers had expected that the revenues of ecclesiastical properties appropriated by the state would in part be devoted to establishing new schools to replace those that were disappearing with the closing of the monasteries; but "princes and lords," Luther complained, "were so busily engaged in the high and important affairs of the cellar, the kitchen, and the bedchamber that they had no time" to help education. "In the German provinces," he wrote (1524), "the schools are now everywhere allowed to go to ruin." [5] By 1530 he and Melanchthon were lamenting the deterioration of the German universities.[6] At Erfurt the enrollment fell from 311 in 1520 to 120 in 1521, to 34 in 1524; at Rostock from 300 in 1517 to 15 in 1525; at Heidelberg in that year there were more professors than students; and in 1526 only five scholars enrolled at the University of Basel.[7]

Luther and Melanchthon labored to repair the damage. In an *Epistle to the Burgomasters* (1524) Luther appealed to secular authorities to establish schools. In 1530, far ahead of his time, he proposed that elementary education should be made compulsory, and be provided at public expense.[8] To the universities, gradually reconstituted under Protestant auspices, he recommended a curriculum centered on the Bible, but also teaching Latin, Greek, Hebrew, German, law, medicine, history, and "poets and orators . . . heathen or Christian." [9] Melanchthon made the revival of education a main task of his life. Under his leadership and stimulus many new schools were opened; by the end of the sixteenth century there were 300 in Germany. He drew up a *Schulplan* (1527) for the organization of schools and universities; he wrote textbooks of Latin and Greek grammar, of rhetoric, logic, psychology, ethics, and theology; and he trained thousands of teachers for the new institutions. His country gratefully named him *Praeceptor Germaniae*, the Educator of Germany. One by one the universities of northern Germany passed under Protestant control: Wittenberg (1522), Marburg (1527), Tübingen (1535), Leipzig (1539), Königsberg (1544), Jena (1558). Professors or students who (as Duke Ulrich of Württemberg put it) were opposed to "the right, true, evangelical doctrine" were dismissed. Calvinists were excluded from Lutheran colleges, and Protestants were barred from universities still held by Catholics. Generally, after the Peace of Augsburg (1555), German students were forbidden to attend schools of another faith than that of the territorial prince.[10]

Johannes Sturm immensely advanced the new education when he set up a *Gymnasium* or secondary school at Strasbourg (1538), and published in that year an influential tract *On Rightly Opening Schools of Letters (De litterarum ludis recte aperiendis)*. Like so many leaders of thought in Central Europe, Sturm had received his schooling from the Brethren of the Common Life. Thence he went to Louvain and Paris, where he met Rabelais; the famous letter of Gargantua on education may echo a mutual influence. While making "a wise piety" the chief aim of education, Sturm laid rising stress on the study of the Greek and Latin languages and literatures; and this thoroughness of training in the classics passed down to the later *Gymnasien* of Germany to raise the army of scholars that in the nineteenth century raided and ransacked the ancient world.

The schools of England suffered even more than those of Germany from the religious overturn. Cathedral, monastic, guild, and chantry schools melted away in the heat of the attack upon ecclesiastical abuses and wealth. Most university students had been sent up by those schools; this flow ceasing, Oxford graduated only 173 bachelors of arts, Cambridge only 191, in 1548; in 1547 and 1550 Oxford had no such graduates at all.[11] Henry VIII felt the problem, but his need of funds for war or weddings limited him to establishing Trinity College, Cambridge (1546), and financing regius professorships in divinity, Hebrew, Greek, medicine, and law. Private philanthropy in this period founded Corpus Christi College, Christ Church College, St. John's College, and Trinity College at Oxford, and Magdalen College at Cambridge. The royal commission sent by Cromwell to Oxford and Cambridge (1535) to appropriate their charters and endowments for the King brought both faculty and curriculum under governmental control. The reign of Scholasticism in England was summarily ended; the works of Duns Scotus were literally scattered to the winds;[12] canon law was set aside; Greek and Latin studies were encouraged; the curriculum was largely secularized. But dogmatism remained. A law of 1553 required all candidates for degrees to subscribe to the Anglican Articles of Religion.

In Catholic France and Flanders the universities declined not in endowments or enrollments but in vigor and freedom of intellectual life. New universities were opened at Reims, Douai, Lille, and Besançon. The University of Louvain rivaled that of Paris in number of students (5,000), and in defense of an orthodoxy that even the popes found extreme. The University of Paris had a large enrollment (6,000), but it no longer attracted foreign students in any considerable number, or tolerated, as in its thirteenth-century prime, the quickening ferment of new ideas. Its other faculties were so dominated by that of theology —the Sorbonne—that this name became almost a synonym for the university. The curriculum of theology and expurgated classics seemed to Montaigne a superficial routine of memorizing and conformity. Rabelais never tired of satirizing the scholastic formalities and logical gymnastics of the Sorbonne, the waste of student years in debates carefully removed from actual concern with human life. "I am willing to lose my share of paradise," vowed Clément Marot, "if those great beasts"—the professors—"did not ruin my youth." [13] All the power and authority of the university were turned not only against the French Protestants but against the French humanists as well.

Francis I, who had drunk the wine of Italy, and had met churchmen steeped in the literature of ancient Greece and Rome, did his best to protect French scholarship from the conservative discouragements emanating from the Sorbonne. Urged on by Guillaume Budé, Cardinal Jean du Bellay, and the indefatigable Marguerite, he provided funds to establish (1529), independently of the university, a school devoted predominantly to humanistic studies. Four "royal professors" were initially appointed—two for Greek, two for Hebrew; and chairs of Latin, mathematics, medicine, and philosophy were presently added. Tuition was free.[14] This Collège Royale, later renamed Collège de France, became the warming hearth of French humanism, the home of the free but disciplined mind of France.

Spain, though passionately orthodox, had excellent universities, fourteen in 1553, including new foundations at Toledo, Santiago, and Granada; that of Salamanca, with seventy professors and 6,778 students in 1584, could bear comparison with any. The universities of Italy continued to flourish; that of Bologna, in 1543, had fifty-seven professors in the faculty of "arts," thirty-seven in law, fifteen in medicine; and Padua was the Mecca of enterprising students from north of the Alps. Poland testified to its golden age by enrolling 15,338 students at one time in the University of Cracow; [15] and in Poznan the *Lubranscianum*, founded (1519) by Bishop John Lubranski, was dedicated to humanistic pursuits. All in all, the universities suffered less in Catholic than in Protestant countries in this cataclysmic century.

The importance of the teacher was underestimated, and he was grievously underpaid. The professors at the Collège Royale received 200 crowns a year ($5,000?), but this was highly exceptional. At Salamanca the professors were chosen by the students after a trial period of sample lectures by rival candidates. Instruction was mostly by lectures, sometimes brought to life by debates. Notetaking served many a student in place of textbooks; dictionaries were rare; laboratories were practically unknown except to alchemists. Students were housed in cheap and poorly heated rooms, and became ill on unclean or inadequate food. Many worked their way through college. Classes began at six in the morning, ended at five in the afternoon. Discipline was rigorous; even near-graduates might be flogged. The students warmed themselves with street brawls and such wine and wenches as they could afford. By one means or another they achieved education, to a degree.

Girls of the lower classes remained illiterate; many of the middle classes found moderate schooling in nunneries; well-to-do young women had tutors. Holland boasted of several ladies who could be courted in Latin, and who could probably conjugate better than they could decline. In Germany the wife of Peutinger and the sisters and daughters of Pirkheimer were famous for learning; in France the women around Francis graced their flirtations with classical quotations; and in England some bluestockings—More's daughters, Jane Grey, "Bloody Mary," Elizabeth—were paragons of erudition.

Two famous teachers belong to this age. The lesser was Sir Thomas Elyot, whose *Boke Named the Governour* (1531) outlined an education by which pedigreed pupils might be fitted for statesmanship. Elyot began by berating the cultural crudity of the English nobles; he contrasted it with the learning credited to men of affairs in ancient Greece and Rome, and quoted Diogenes the Cynic, who, "seeing one without learning seated on a stone, remarked . . . 'Behold where one stone sitteth on another.' " [16] At seven the boy should be placed under a carefully selected tutor, who will teach him the elements of music, painting, and sculpture. At fourteen he is to be taught cosmography, logic, and history, and is to be trained in wrestling, hunting, shooting with the longbow, swimming, and tennis; not football, for that is plebeian, and "therein is nothing but beastly furie and external violence." The lad is to study the classics at every stage of his education—first the poets, then the orators, then the historians, then the generals, then the philosophers; to which Elyot, as almost an afterthought, adds the Bible, thereby reversing Luther's plan. For, despite his protestations, Elyot much prefers the classics to the Bible. "Lord God, what incomparable sweetness of words and matter in the works of Plato and Cicero, wherein is joined gravity and delectation, excellent wisdom with divine eloquence, absolute virtue with pleasure incredible," so "that those books be almost sufficient to make a perfect and excellent governor!" [17]

Juan Vives, humanest of the humanists, followed a larger aim and wider course. Born at Valencia in 1492, he left Spain at seventeen, never to see it again. He studied in Paris long enough to love philosophy and despise Scholasticism. At twenty-six he wrote the first modern history of philosophy—*De initiis, sectis, et laudibus philosophiae*. In the same year he challenged the universities with an attack on Scholastic methods of teaching philosophy; the scheme of promoting thought by debates, he felt, promoted only futile wrangling over inconsequential issues. Erasmus hailed the book, recommended it to More, and politely feared that "Vives . . . will overshadow . . . Erasmus." [18] Perhaps through Erasmus' influence Vives was appointed professor of the humanities at Louvain (1519). Urged on by Erasmus, he published an edition of Augustine's *City of God* with elaborate commentaries; he dedicated it to Henry VIII, and received so cordial a reply that he moved to England (1523). He was welcomed by More and Queen Catherine, his compatriot, and Henry named him one of Princess Mary's tutors. Apparently for her guidance he wrote *On the Education of Children* (*De ratione studii puerilis*, 1523). All went well until he expressed disapproval of Henry's plea for a marriage annulment. Henry stopped his salary, and put him under house arrest for six weeks. Released, Vives returned to Bruges (1528), and spent there the remaining years of his life.

Still idealistic at thirty-seven, he dedicated to Charles V an Erasmian appeal for an international court of arbitration as a substitute for war (*De concordia et discordia in humano genere*, 1529). Two years later he issued his major work, *De tradendis disciplinis* (*On the Transmission of Studies*), the most progressive educational treatise of the Renaissance. He called for an education directed "to the necessities of life, to some bodily or mental improvement, to the cultivation and increase of reverence." [19] The pupil should enter school "as if into a holy temple," but his studies there should prepare him to be a decent and useful citizen. Those studies should cover the whole of life, and should be taught in their interrelation, as they function in living. Nature, as well as books, should be studied; things are more instructive than theories. Let the student note the veins, nerves, bones, and other parts of the body in their anatomy and action; let him consult farmers, hunters, shepherds, gardeners . . . and learn their lore; these gleanings will be more useful than the Scholastic "babblement which has corrupted every branch of knowledge in the name of logic." [20] The classics, expurgated for youth, should remain a vital part of the curriculum, but modern history and geography are to be studied too. The vernaculars as well as Latin should be taught, and all by the direct method of daily use.

Vives was so far ahead of his time that it lost sight of him, and let him die in poverty. He remained a Catholic to the end.

III. SCHOLARS

The distinctive task of the universities, the academies, and the humanists in the Renaissance was to gather, translate, and transmit the old world of Greece and Rome to the young world of modern Europe. The task was grandly accomplished, and the classic revelation was complete.

Two men remain to be commemorated as oracles of this revelation. Guillaume Budé, after living sixty-two years in hopes of making Paris the heir of Italian humanism, came into his own when Francis founded the Collège Royale. He began his adult studies with law, and for almost a decade he buried himself in the *Pandects* of Justinian. To understand these texts better—Latin in language but Byzantine in bearings—he took up Greek with John Lascaris, and so devotedly that his teacher, departing, bequeathed to him his precious library of Greek books. When, at forty-one, Budé published *Annotationes in XXIV libros Pandectarum* (1508), the *Digest* of Justinian, for the first time in Renaissance jurisprudence, was studied in itself and its environment, instead of being displaced by the commentaries of the "glossators." Six years later he issued another monument of recondite research, *De asse et partibus*—on its surface a discussion of ancient coins and measures, but actually an exhaustive consideration of classical literature in relation to economic life. Still more impressive were his *Commentarii linguae graecae* (1529), a work loosely ordered, but so rich in lexicographic information and illumination that it placed Budé at the head of all European Hellenists. Rabelais sent him a letter of homage, Erasmus paid him the compliment of jealousy. Erasmus was a man of the world, to whom scholarship was only a part of life; but to Budé scholarship and life were one. "It is philology," he wrote, "that has so long been my companion, my associate, my mistress, bound to me by every tie of affection. . . . But I have been forced to loosen the bonds of a love so devouring . . . that I found it destructive to my health." [21] He mourned that he had to steal time from his studies to eat and sleep. In moments of distraction he married and begot eleven children. Jean Clouet's portrait of him (in the Metropolitan Museum of Art in New York) shows him in a pessimistic mood, but Francis I must have found some warmth in him, for he made him librarian at Fontainebleau, and liked to have the old scholar near him, even on tours. On one of these Budé caught a fever. He left precise instructions for an unceremonious funeral, and quietly passed away (1540). The Collège de France is his monument.

Paris had not yet in his time absorbed the intellectual life of France. Humanism had a dozen French hearths: Bourges, Bordeaux, Toulouse, Montpellier, and, above all, Lyons, where love and humanism, ladies and literature, made a delightful mixture. And in Agen, where no one would have looked for an emperor, Julius Caesar Scaliger ruled imperiously over the philological scene after Budé's death. Born probably at Padua (1484), he came to Agen at forty-one, and lived there till his death (1558). Every scholar feared him, for he had a masterly command of vituperative Latin. He made a name for himself by attacking Erasmus for belittling the "Ciceronians"—sticklers for a precise Ciceronian Latin. He criticized Rabelais, then criticized Dolet for criticizing Rabelais. In a volume of *Exercitationes* he examined Jerome Cardan's *De subtilitate*, and undertook to prove that everything affirmed in that book was false, and everything denied in it was true. His *De causis linguae latinae* was the first Latin grammar based upon scientific principles, and his commentaries on Hippocrates and Aristotle were remarkable for both their style and their contributions to science. Julius had fifteen children, one of whom became the greatest scholar of the next generation. His *Poetice*, published four years after his death, shared with the work of his son—and the influence of the Italians who followed Catherine de Médicis to France—in turning French humanism back from Greek to Latin studies.

A special gift of the Greek revival was Amyot's translation of Plutarch's *Lives*. Jacques Amyot was one of Marguerite's many protégés; through her he was appointed to a chair of Greek and Latin at Bourges. His translations of *Daphnis and Chloë* and other Greek love stories were rewarded, in the genial oddity of the times, with a rich abbey. So secured, he traveled widely in Italy, indulging his antiquarian and philological tastes. When he published the *Lives* (1559) he prefaced the book with an eloquent plea for the study of history as the "treasure house of humanity," a museum in which a thousand examples of virtue and vice, statesmanship and decay, are preserved for the instruction of mankind; like Napoleon, he considered history a better teacher of philosophy than philosophy itself. Nevertheless he proceeded to translate also Plutarch's *Moralia.* He was promoted to the bishopric of Auxerre, and died there in the ripeness of eighty years (1593). His version of the *Lives* was not always accurate, but it was a work of literature in its own right, endowed with a natural and idiomatic style quite equal to that of the original. Its influence was endless. Montaigne reveled in it, and turned from the France of St. Bartholomew to this select and ennobled antiquity; Shakespeare took three plays from North's virile translation of Amyot's translation; the Plutarchian ideal of the hero modeled a hundred French dramas and revolutionists; and the *Vies des hommes illustres* gave to the nation a pantheon of celebrities fit to stir the more masculine virtues of the French soul.

IV. THE FRENCH RENAISSANCE

It is customary and forgivable to call by this term, so rich in overtones, the period between the accession of Francis I (1515) and the assassination of Henry IV (1610). Essentially this colorful flowering of French poetry and prose, manners and arts and dress was less a rebirth than a ripening. By the patient resilience of men and the new growth of the new-seeded earth, the French economy and spirit had recovered from the Hundred Years' War. Louis XI had given France a strong, centered, orderly government; Louis XII had given it a fruitful decade of peace. The free, loose, fantastic creativeness of the Gothic age survived, even and most in Rabelais, who so admired the classics that he quoted nearly all of them. But the great awakening was also a renascence. French literature and art were unquestionably affected by a closer acquaintance with ancient culture and classic forms. Those forms and the classic temper—the predominance of intellectual order over emotional ardor—continued in French drama, poetry, painting, sculpture, and architecture for almost three centuries. The fertilizing agents in the new birth were the French discovery and invasion of Italy, the French study of Roman ruins, jurisprudence, and literature, of Italian letters and arts, and the influx of Italian artists and poets into France. To the happy issue many other factors contributed: printing; the dissemination and translation of classic texts; the patronage of scholars, poets, and artists by French kings, by their mistresses, by Marguerite of Navarre, by ecclesiastics and aristocrats; and the inspiration of women capable of appreciating other beauties than their own. All these elements came together in the flourishing of France.

Francis I, who inherited all this, had as a page the poet who served as a transition from Gothic to classic, from Villon to Renaissance. Clément Marot entered history as a frolicsome lad of thirteen who amused the King with jolly tales and sprightly repartees. Some years later Francis smiled upon the youth's adventures and quarrels with "all the ladies of Paris," for he agreed with Marot that they were very charming indeed:

> La Françoise est entière et sans rompeure;
> Plaisir la meine, au profit ne regarde.
> Conclusion: qui en parle ou brocarde,
> Françoises sont chef-d'oeuvre de nature—

"The Frenchwoman is flawless and complete; pleasure leads her; she does not look for profit. To conclude: whatever anyone may say to ridicule them, Frenchwomen are nature's masterpiece." [22]

Marot babbled poems like a bubbling spring. They were seldom profound, but often touched with tender sentiment; they were verses of occasion, conversation pieces, ballads, roundels, madrigals, or satires and epistles reminiscent of Horace or Martial. He noted with some pique that women (himself to the contrary notwithstanding) could be more readily persuaded by diamonds than by dithyrambs:

> Quant les petites vilotières
> Trouvent quelque hardi amant
> Qui faire luire un diamant
> Devant leurs yeux riants et verts,
> Coac! elles tombent à l'envers.
> Tu ris? Maudit soit-il qui erre!
> C'est la grande vertu de la pierre
> Qui éblouit ainsi leurs yeux.
> Tels dons, tels présents servent mieux
> Que beauté, savoir, ni prières.
> Ils endorment les chambrières,
> Ils ouvrent les portes fermées
> Comme s'elles étaient charmées;
> Ils font aveugles ceux qui voient,
> Et taire les chiens qui aboient.
> Ne me crois-tu point?

That is to say:

> When little trollops make their price,
> And find some moneyed lover bold
> Who can a sparking diamond hold
> Before their olive laughing eyes,

> Coac! They fall quite inside out.
>   You laugh? Damn him who here goes wrong!
>   For to that stone virtues belong
> That would seduce eyes most devout.
> Such gifts and boons do more avail
>   Than beauty, prayers, or wisdom staid;
>   They send to sleep the lady's maid,
> And dogs forget to bark or wail.
> Closed doors fly open to your will,
>   As if bewitched by magic mind,
>   And eyes that saw become quite blind.
> Now tell me, do you doubt me still?

In 1519 Marot became *valet-de-chambre* to Marguerite, and fell in love with her dutifully; gossip said she returned his moans, but more likely she gave him nothing but religion. He developed a moderate sympathy with the Protestant cause in the intervals of his *amours*. He followed Francis to Italy, fought like a Bayard at Pavia, had the honor to be captured with his King, and—no ransom being expected for a poet—was released. Back in France, he announced his Protestant ideas so openly that the bishop of Chartres summoned him, and kept him under genteel imprisonment in the episcopal palace. He was set free by Marguerite's intercession, but was soon arrested for helping prisoners to escape from the police. Francis bailed him out, and took him to Bayonne to sing the charms of his new bride, Eleanor of Portugal. After another session in jail—for eating bacon in Lent—he followed Marguerite to Cahors and Nérac.

Presently the affair of the placards revived the campaign against the French Protestants. News reached Marot that his rooms in Paris had been searched, and that a warrant had gone out for his arrest (1535). Fearful that even Marguerite's skirts would not suffice to hide him, he fled to Italy, to the Duchess Renée in Ferrara. She welcomed him as if a reborn Virgil had arrived from Mantua; and perhaps she knew that he liked to link his name with that of Publius Vergilius Maro. He resembled more the lighthearted, amorous Ovid, or his favorite Villon, whose poems he edited and whose life he relived. When Duke Ercole II let it be known that he was surfeited with Protestants, Clément moved on to Venice. Word reached him that Francis had offered pardon to abjuring heretics; Marot, thinking the ladies of Paris worth a Mass, abjured. The King gave him a house and garden, and Clément tried to be a *bourgeois gentilhomme*.

François Vatable, who was teaching Hebrew in the Collège Royale, asked him to translate the Psalms into French verse, and expounded them to him word for word. Marot put thirty of them into melodious poetry, and published them with a judicious dedication to the King. Francis liked them so much that he gave a special copy to Charles V, who was momentarily his friend; Charles sent the poet 200 crowns ($5,000?). Marot translated more of the Psalms, and issued them in 1543 with a dedication to his first love, "the ladies of France." Goudimel put them to music, as we have seen, and half of France began to sing them. Buc as Luther and Calvin also liked them, th Sorbonne suspected them of Protestantism; or perhaps in the ordeal of suc cess Marot had remumbled his heresies. The campaign against him was renewed. He fled to Geneva, but found the theological climate there too severe for his health. He slipped into Italy, and died in Turin (1544) at the age of forty-nine, leaving an illegitimate daughter to the care of the Queen of Navarre.

V. RABELAIS

1. Himself

The unique, inexhaustible, skeptical, hilarious, learned, and obscene author of "the most diverting and most profitable stories which have ever been told" [23] burst into the world in 1495, son of a prosperous notary at Chinon. He was entered at too early an age into a Franciscan monastery; he complained later that women who "carry children nine months beneath their hearts ... cannot bear to suffer them nine years ... and by simply adding an ell to their dress, and cutting I know not how many hairs from the top of their head, by means of certain words they turn them into birds"—i.e., they tonsure them and make them monks. The boy accepted his fate because he was inclined to study, and probably, like Erasmus, he was drawn to the books in the monastic library. He found there two or three other monks who wished to study Greek, and who were excited by the vast ancient world that scholarship was revealing. François made such progress that he received a letter of praise from Budé himself. Matters seemed to be going well, and in 1520 the future doubter was ordained a priest. But some older monks scented heresy in philology; they accused the young Hellenists of buying books with the fees they received for preaching, instead of handing the money over to the common treasury. Rabelais and another monk were put in solitary confinement and were deprived of books, which were to them half of life. Budé, apprised of this *contretemps*, appealed to Francis I, who ordered the scholars reinstated in freedom and privileges. Some further intercession brought a papal rescript permitting Rabelais to change his monastic allegiance and residence; he left the Franciscans, and entered a Benedictine house at Maillezais (1524). There the bishop, Geoffroy d'Estissac, took such a fancy to him that he arranged with the abbot that Rabelais should be allowed to go wherever he wished for his studies. Rabelais went, and forgot to return.

After sampling several universities he entered the School of Medicine at Montpellier (1530). He must have had some prior instruction, for he received the degree of bachelor of medicine in 1531. For reasons unknown he did not proceed to earn the doctorate, but resumed his wandering until, in 1532, he settled down in Lyons. Like Servetus, he combined the practice of medicine with scholarly pursuits. He served as editorial aide to the printer Sebastian Gryphius, edited several Greek texts, translated the *Aphorisms* of Hippocrates into Latin, and was willingly caught in the humanistic stream then in full flow at Lyons. On November 30, 1532, he dispatched a copy of Josephus to Erasmus with a letter of adulation strange in a man of thirty-seven, but savoring of that enthusiastic age:

> George d'Armagnac . . . recently sent me Flavius Josephus' *History* . . . and asked me . . . to send it to you. . . . I have eagerly seized this opportunity, O humanest of fathers, to prove to you by grateful homage my profound respect for you and my filial piety. My father, did I say? I should call you mother did your indulgence allow it. All that we know of mothers, who nourish the fruit of their wombs before seeing it, before knowing even what it will be, who protect it, who shelter it against the inclemency of the air—that you have done for me, for me whose face was not known to you, and whose obscure name could not impress you. You have brought me up, you have fed me at the chaste breasts of your divine knowledge; all that I am, all that I am worth, I owe to you alone. If I did not publish it aloud I should be the most ungrateful of men. Salutations once more, beloved father, honor of your country, support of letters, unconquerable champion of truth.[24]

In that same November 1532 we find Rabelais a physician in the Hôtel-Dieu, or city hospital, of Lyons, with a salary of forty livres ($1,000?) a year. But we must not think of him as a typical scholar or physician. It is true that his learning was varied and immense. Like Shakespeare, he seems to have had professional knowledge in a dozen fields—law, medicine, literature, theology, cookery, history, botany, astronomy, mythology. He refers to a hundred classic legends, quotes half a hundred classic authors; sometimes he parades his erudition amateurishly. He was so busy living that he had no time to achieve meticulous accuracy in his scholarship; the editions that he prepared were not models of careful detail. It was not in his character to be a dedicated humanist like Erasmus or Budé; he loved life more than books. He is pictured for us as a man of distinguished presence, tall and handsome, a well of learning, a light and fire of conversation.[25] He was not a toper, as an old tradition wrongly inferred from his salutes to drinkers and his paeans to wine; on the contrary, except for one little bastard [26]—who lived so briefly as to be only a venial sin—he led a reasonably decent life, and was honored by the finest spirits of his time, including several dignitaries of the Church. At the same time he had in him many qualities of the French peasant. He relished the bluff and hearty types that he met in the fields and streets; he enjoyed their jokes and laughter, their tall tales and boastful ribaldry; and unwittingly he made Erasmus' fame pale before his own because he collected and connected these stories, improved and expanded them, dignified them with classic lore, lifted them into constructive satire, and carefully included their obscenity.

One story, then current in many rural areas, told of a kindly giant named Gargantua, his cavernous appetite, his feats of love and strength; here and there were hills and boulders which, said local traditions, had dropped from Gargantua's basket as he passed. Such legends were still told, as late as 1860, in French hamlets that had never heard of Rabelais. An unknown writer, perhaps Rabelais himself as a *tour de rire*, jotted some of the fables down, and had them printed in Lyons as *The Great and Inestimable Chronicles of the Great and Enormous Giant Gargantua* (1532). The book sold so readily that Rabelais conceived the idea of writing a sequel to it about Gargantua's son. So, at the Lyons fair of October 1532, there appeared, anonymously, the *Horribles et espouvantables faictz et prouesses du très renommé Pantagruel (The Horrible and Dreadful Deeds and Prowesses of the Most Renowned Pantagruel)*. This name had been used in some popular dramas, but Rabelais gave the character new content and depth. The Sorbonne and the monks condemned the book as obscene, and it sold well; Francis I enjoyed it, some of the clergy relished it. Not till fourteen years later did Rabelais admit his authorship; he feared to endanger, if not his life, his reputation as a scholar.

He was still so wedded to scholarship that he neglected his duties at the hospital, and was dismissed. He might have had trouble buttering his bread had not Jean du Bellay, Bishop of Paris and co-founder of the Collège de France, taken Rabelais with him as physician on a mission to Italy (January 1534). Returning to Lyons in April, Rabelais published there in October *La vie très horrifique du grand Gargantua, père de Pantagruel (The Very Horrible Life of the Great Gargantua, father of Pantagruel)*. This second volume, which was later to form Book One of the full work, contained such rollicking satires of the clergy that it won another Sorbonnian condemnation. Soon the two stories, published together, outsold every publication in France except the Bible and *The Imitation of Christ*.[27] Again, we are told, King Francis laughed and applauded.

But on the night of October 17–18, 1534, the posting of insulting Protestant placards on Paris buildings and the King's own doors changed him from a protector of humanists into a persecutor of heretics. Rabelais had again concealed his authorship, but it was widely suspected, and he had good reason to fear that the Sorbonne, carrying the King in its train, would demand the scandalous writer's head. Again Jean du Bellay came to his rescue. Now a cardinal, the genial churchman snatched the endangered scholar-physician-pornographer out of his Lyons den and took him to Rome (1535). It was Rabelais' luck to find there an enlightened pope. Paul III forgave him his neglect of his monastic and priestly duties, and gave him permission to practice medicine. As *amende honorable* Rabelais expunged from future editions of his now "double-backed" book the passages most offensive to orthodox taste; and when Étienne Dolet played a trick on him by publishing, without permission, an unexpurgated edition, he crossed him from the roster of his friends. Under the protection of the Cardinal he studied again at Montpellier, received the doctorate in medicine, lectured to large audiences there, and then returned to Lyons to resume his life as physician and scholar. In June 1537, Dolet described him as conducting an anatomy lesson by dissecting an executed criminal before an assemblage of students.

Thereafter we know only snatches of his undulant career. He was in the suite of the King at the historic meeting of Francis I and Charles V in Aigues-mortes (July 1538). Two years later we find him at Turin as physician to Guillaume du Bellay, brother to the Cardinal, and now French ambassador to Savoy. About this time spies found in Rabelais' correspondence some items that raised a flurry in Paris. He hurried to the capital, faced the matter out bravely, and was exonerated by the King (1541). Despite renewed condemnations of *Gargantua* and *Pantagruel* by the Sorbonne, Francis gave the harassed author a minor post in the government as *maître des requêtes* (commissioner of petitions), and official permission to publish Book Two of *Pantagruel*, which Rabelais gratefully dedicated to Marguerite of Navarre. The volume aroused such commotion among the theologians that Rabelais judged it discreet to take refuge in Metz, then part of the Empire. There he served for a year as physician in the city hospital (1546–47). In 1548 he thought it safe to return to Lyons, and in 1549 to Paris. Finally his ecclesiastical protectors secured his appointment (1551) as parish priest of Meudon, just southwest of the capital, and the hunted, aging gadfly resumed his sacerdotal robes. Apparently he delegated the duties of his benefice to subordinates, and confined himself to using the income.[28] So far as we know he was still curé of Meudon when, a bit anomalously, he published what is now Book Four of his work (1552). This was dedicated to Odet, Cardinal de Chatillon, presumably with permission; evidently there were then in France high churchmen of the learning and lenience of the Italian Renaissance cardinals. Nevertheless the book was denounced by the Sorbonne, and its sale was forbidden by the *Parlement*. Francis I and Marguerite were now dead, and Rabelais found no favor with the somber Henry II. He absented himself for a while from Paris, but soon returned. There, after a long illness, he died (April 9, 1553). An old story tells how, when he was asked on his deathbed where he expected to go, he answered, *Je vais chercher un grand peut-être*—"I go to seek a great perhaps." [29] Alas, it is a legend.

2. *Gargantua*

The Prologue to Book One (originally Book Two) gives at once the taste and smell of the whole:

> Most noble and illustrious drinkers, and you thrice precious pockified blades (for to you and none else do I .dedicate my writings). . . . To have eyed the outside of Socrates and esteemed of him by his external appearance, you would not have given the peel of an onion for him. . . . You, my good disciples, and some other jolly fools of ease and leisure, reading the pleasant titles of some books of our invention . . . are too ready to judge that there is nothing in them but jests, mockeries, lascivious discourse, and recreative lies. . . . But . . in the perusal of this treatise you shall find . . . a doctrine of a more profound and abstract consideration . . . as well in what concerneth our religion, as matters of public state, and life economical. . . . A certain addle-headed coxcomb saith [ill] of my books, but a *bren* for him. . . . Frolic now, my lads, cheer up your hearts, and joyfully read. . . . Pull away, Supernaculum!

This is Urquhart's famed translation, which sometimes overdoes the original, but is here quite faithful to it, even with pithy words now no longer permitted in learned discourse. In these two paragraphs we have Rabelais' spirit and aim: serious satire clothed in neck-saving buffoonery, and sometimes smeared with unfumigated smut. We proceed at our own risk, thankful that the printed word does not smell, and trusting to find some diamonds in the dunghill.

Gargantua begins with a peerless genealogy Scriptural in form. The father of the giant was Grangousier, King of Utopia; the mother was Gargamelle. She bore him for eleven months, and when her pains began their friends gathered for a merry bout of wine, alleging that nature abhors a vacuum. "On with a sheep's courage!" the proud father tells his wife painlessly; "dispatch this boy, and we will speedily fall to work . . . making another." For a moment she wishes him the fate of Abélard; he proposes to accomplish this forthwith, but she changes her mind. The unborn Gargantua, finding the usual outlet of maternity blocked by an untimely astringent, "entered the vena cava" of Gargamelle, climbed through her diaphragm and neck, and "issued forth by the left ear." As soon as he was born he cried out, so loudly that two counties heard him, *À boire! à boire! à boire!*—"Drink! drink! drink!" 17,913 cans of milk were set aside for his nourishment, but he early showed a preference for wine.

When it came time to educate the young giant, and make him fit to succeed to the throne, he received as tutor Maître Jobelin, who made a dolt of him by stuffing his memory with dead facts and befuddling his reason with Scholastic argument. Driven to a desperate expedient, Gargantua turned the boy over to the humanist Ponocrates. Teacher and pupil went off to Paris to get the latest education. Gargantua rode on a tremendous mare, whose swishing tail cut down vast forests as she proceeded; hence part of France is a plain. Arrived in Paris, Gargantua alighted on a tower of Notre Dame; he took a fancy to the bells, and purloined them to hang them about his horse's neck. Ponocrates began the re-education of the spoiled giant by giving him an enormous purgative to cleanse the bowels and the brain, which are near allied. So purified, Gargantua became enamored of education; he began zealously to train at once his body, his mind, and his character; he studied the Bible, the classics, and the arts; he learned to play the lute and the virginal and to enjoy music; he ran, jumped, wrestled, climbed, and swam; he practiced riding, jousting, and the skills needed in war; he hunted to develop his courage; and to develop his lungs he shouted so that all Paris heard him. He visited metalworkers, stonecutters, goldsmiths, alchemists, weavers, watchmakers, printers, dyers, and "giving them somewhat to drink," studied their crafts; he took part every day in some useful physical work; and sometimes he went to a lecture, or a trial, or to "the sermons of evangelical preachers" (a Protestant touch).

Amid all this education Gargantua was suddenly called back to his father's realm, for another king, Picrochole, had declared war on Grangousier. Why? Rabelais steals a story from Plutarch's *Life of Pyrrhus,* and tells how Picrochole's generals boasted of the lands they would conquer under his leadership: France, Spain, Portugal, Algeria, Italy, Sicily, Crete, Cyprus, Rhodes, Greece, Jerusalem. . . . Picrochole rejoices and swells. But an old philosopher asks him: "What shall be the end of so many labors and crosses?" "When we return," answers Picrochole, "we shall sit down, rest, and be merry." "But," suggests the philosopher, "if by chance you should never come back, for the voyage is long and dangerous, were it not better for us to take our rest now?" "Enough," cried Picrochole; "go forward; I fear nothing. . . . He that loves me, follow me" (I, xxxiii). Gargantua's horse almost wins the war against Picrochole by drowning thousands of the enemy with one simple easement.

But the real hero of the war was Friar John, a monk who loved fighting more than praying, and who let his philosophical curiosity venture into the most dangerous alleys. "What is the reason," he asks, "that the thighs of a gentlewoman are always fresh and cool?"—and though he finds nothing about this engaging problem in Aristotle or Plutarch, he himself gives answers rich in femoral erudition. All the King's men like him, feed and wine him to his paunch's content; they invite him to take off his monastic robe to allow more eating, but he fears that without it he will not have so good an appetite. All the faults that the Protestant reformers alleged against the monks are satirized through this jolly member of their tribe: their idleness, gluttony, guzzling, prayer-mumbling, and hostility to all but a narrowing range of study and ideas. "In our abbey," says Friar John, "we never study, for fear of the mumps" (I, xxxix).

Gargantua proposed to reward the Friar's good fighting by making him abbot of an existing monastery, but John begged instead to be given the means of establishing a new abbey, with rules "contrary to all others." First, there should be no encompassing walls; inmates are to be free to leave at their pleasure. Second, there is to be no exclusion of women; however, only such women shall enter as are "fair, well-featured, of a sweet disposition," and between the ages of ten and fifteen. Third, only men between twelve and eighteen will be accepted, and they must be comely, and of good birth and manners; no sots or bigots may apply, no beggars, lawyers, judges, scribes, usurers, gold-graspers, or "sniveling hypocrites." Fourth, no vows of chastity, poverty, or obedience; the members may marry, enjoy wealth, and in all matters be free. The abbey is to be called Theleme, or What You Will, and its sole rule will be *Fais ce que vous vouldras*—"Do what you wish." For "men that are free, wellborn, well-bred, and conversant in honest companies, have naturally an instinct and spur that prompteth them to virtuous actions and withdraws them from vice; and this instinct is called Honor" (I, lvii). Gargantua provided the funds for this aristocratic anarchism, and the abbey rose according to specifications which Rabelais gave in such detail that architects have made drawings of it. He provided for it a library, a theater, a swimming pool, a tennis court, a football field, a chapel, a garden, a hunting park, orchards, stables, and 9,332 rooms. It was an American hotel in vacation land. Rabelais forgot to provide a kitchen, or to explain who would do the menial work in this paradise.

3. *Pantagruel*

After Gargantua had succeeded his father as king he took his turn at procreation and pedagogy. At the age of "four hundred fourscore forty and four years" he begot Pantagruel on Badebec, who died in giving birth; whereat Gargantua "wept like a cow" for his wife, and "laughed like a calf" over his robust son. Pantagruel grew up to Brobdingnagian proportions. In one of his meals he inadvertently swallowed a man, who had to be excavated by a mining operation in the young giant's digestive tract. When Pantagruel went to Paris for his higher schooling Gargantua sent him a letter redolent of the Renaissance:

> MOST DEAR SON:
>
> ... Although my deceased father, of happy memory, Grangousier, had bent his best endeavors to make me profit in all perfection and political knowledge, and that my labor and study was fully correspondent to, yea, went beyond his desire; nevertheless, as thou may'st well understand, the time then was not so proper and fit for learning as it is at present ... for that time was darksome, obscured with clouds of ignorance, and savoring a little of the infelicity and calamity of the Goths, who had, wherever they set footing, destroyed all good literature, which in my age hath by the divine goodness been restored unto its former light and dignity, and that with such amendment and increase of knowledge, that now hardly should I be admitted unto the first form of the little grammar-school boys. ...
>
> Now the minds of men are qualified with all manner of discipline, and the old sciences revived which for many ages were extinct; now the learned languages are to their pristine purity restored—viz., Greek (without which a man may be ashamed to account himself a scholar), Hebrew, Arabic, Chaldean, and Latin. Printing likewise is now in use, so elegant, and so correct, that better cannot be imagined. ...
>
> I intend ... that thou learn the languages perfectly. ... Let there be no history which thou shalt not have ready in thy memory. ... Of the liberal arts of geometry, arithmetic, and music, I gave thee some taste when thou wert yet little ... proceed further in them. ... As for astronomy, study all the rules thereof; let pass nevertheless ... astrology ... as being nothing else but plain cheats and vanities. As for the civil law, of that I would have thee to know the texts by heart, and then to confer them with philosophy ...
>
> The works of nature I would have thee study exactly. ... Fail not most carefully to peruse the books of the Greek, Arabian, and Latin physicians, not despising the talmudists and cabalists; and by frequent anatomies get thee the perfect knowledge of the microcosm, which is man. And at some hours of the day apply thy mind to the study of the Holy Scriptures: first in Greek the New Testament ... then the Old Testament in Hebrew. ...
>
> But because, as the wise man Solomon saith, wisdom entereth not into a malicious mind, and science without conscience is but the ruin of the soul; it behooveth thee to serve, to love, to fear God. ... Be serviceable to all thy neighbors, and love them as thyself; reverence thy preceptors; shun the conversation of those whom thou desirest

not to resemble, and receive not in vain the graces which God hath bestowed upon thee. And when thou shalt see that thou hast attained to all the knowledge that is to be acquired in that part, return unto me, that I may see thee, and give thee my blessing before I die. . . .

Thy father,
GARGANTUA [30]

Pantagruel studied zealously, learned many languages, and might have become a bookworm had he not met Panurge. Here again, even more than in Friar John, the subordinate character stands out more clearly than his master, as Sancho Panza sometimes outshines the Don. Rabelais does not find full scope for his irreverent humor and riotous vocabulary in Gargantua or Pantagruel; he needs this quarter-scoundrel, quarter-lawyer, quarter-Villon, quarter-philosopher as a vehicle for his satire. He describes Panurge (which means "Ready to do anything") as lean like a starving cat, walking gingerly "as if he trod on eggs"; a gallant fellow, but a little lecherous, and "subject to a kind of disease . . . called lack of money"; a pickpocket, a "lewd rogue, a cozener, a drinker . . . and very dissolute fellow," but "otherwise the best and most virtuous man in the world" (II, xiv, xvi). Into Panurge's mouth Rabelais puts his most ribald sallies. Panurge particularly resented the habit which the ladies of Paris adopted, of buttoning their blouses up the back; he sued the women in court, and might have lost, but he threatened to start a similar custom with male *culottes*, whereupon the court decreed that women must leave a modest but passable opening in front (II, xvii). Angered by a woman who scorned him, Panurge sprayed her skirts, while she knelt in prayer at church, with the effluvia of an itching pet; when the lady emerged, all the 600,014 male dogs of Paris pursued her with unanimous and indefatigable devotion (II, xxi-xxii). Pantagruel, himself a very mannerly prince, takes to this rascal as a relief from philosophy, and invites him on every expedition.

As the story rollicks on into Book Three, Panurge debates with himself and others whether he should marry. He lists the arguments pro and con through a hundred pages, some sparkling, many wearisome; but in those pages we meet the man who married a dumb wife, and the renowned jurist Bridlegoose, who arrives at his soundest judgments by throwing dice. The Prologue to Book Four catches a cue from Lucian and describes a "consistory of gods" in heaven, with Jupiter complaining about the unearthly chaos reigning on the earth, the thirty wars going on at once, the mutual hatreds of the peoples, the divisions of theologies, the syllogisms of the philosophers. "What shall we do with this Ramus and Galland . . . who together are setting all Paris by the ears?" Priapus counsels him to turn these two Pierres into stones *(pierres)*; here Rabelais steals a pun from Scripture.

Returning to earth, he records in Books Four and Five * the long Gulli-verian voyages of Pantagruel, Panurge, Friar John, and a royal Utopian fleet to find the Temple of the Holy Bottle, and to ask whether Panurge should marry. After a score of adventures, satirizing Lenten fasts, Protes-tant pope-haters, bigot pope-olators, monks, dealers in fake antiques, lawyers ("furred cats"), Scholastic philosophers, and historians, the expedition reaches the Temple. Over the portal is a Greek inscription to the effect that "in wine there is truth." In a near-by fountain is a half-submerged bottle, from which a voice emerges, gurgling, TRINC; and the priestess Bacbuc ex-plains that wine is the best philosophy, and that "not laughing but drink-ing . . . cool, delicious wine . . . is the distinguishing character of man." Panurge is happy to have the oracle confirm what he has known all the time. He resolves to eat, drink, and be married, and to take the consequences manfully. He sings an obscene hymeneal chant, and Bacbuc dismisses the party with a blessing: "May that intellectual sphere whose center is every-where, and its circumference nowhere, whom we call GOD, keep you in His Almighty protection" (V, xl. ii). So, with a typical blend of lubricity and philosophy, the great romance comes to an end.

4. The King's Jester

What sense is there behind this nonsense, and is there any wisdom in this demijohn of Falernian-Priapean hilarity? "We country clowns," Rabelais makes one of his asses say, "are somewhat gross, and apt to knock words out of joint" (V, vii). He loves words, has an endless supply of them, and invents a thousand more; he draws them, like Shakespeare, from every occu-pation and profession, every field of philosophy, theology, and law. He makes lists of adjectives, nouns, or verbs, as if for the pleasure of contem-plating them (III, xxxviii); he multiplies synonyms in an ecstasy of redun-dancy; this pleonasm was already an old trick on the French stage.[32] It is part of Rabelais' boundless and uncontrollable humor, an overflow beside which even the humor of Aristophanes or Molière is a modest trickle. His coarseness is another phase of this unmanageable flux. Perhaps some of it was a reaction against monastic asceticism, some of it the anatomical indif-ference of a physician, some of it a bold defiance of pedantic precision; much of it was in the manner of the age. Undoubtedly Rabelais carries it to excess; after a dozen pages of urogenital, excretory, and gaseous details we

---

* Book Five was published in 1562, nine years after Rabelais' death. Probably the first fifteen chapters were left by Rabelais;[81] the remaining thirty-two are of doubtful authentic-ity.

weary and turn away. Another generation of classic influence would be needed to tame such volcanic exuberance into disciplined form.

We forgive these faults because Rabelais' style runs away with us, as with him. It is an unpretentious, unliterary style, natural, easy, flowing, just the medium for telling a long story. The secret of his verve is imagination plus energy plus clarity; he sees a thousand things unobserved by most of us, notes innumerable quirks of dress and conduct and speech, unites them fantastically, and sets the mixtures chasing one another over the sportive page.

He borrows right and left, as the custom was, and with Shakespeare's excuse, that he betters everything that he steals. He helps himself to hundreds of proverbial snatches from Erasmus' *Adagia*,[33] and follows many a lead from *The Praise of Folly* or the *Colloquies*. He assimilates half a hundred items from Plutarch, years before Amyot's translation opened that treasury of greatness to any literate thief. He appropriates Lucian's "heavenly discourse," and Folengo's tale of the self-drowned sheep; he finds in the comedies of his time the story of the man who regretted that he had cured his wife's speechlessness; and he uses a hundred suggestions from the fabliaux and interludes that had rolled down from medieval France. In describing the voyages of Pantagruel he leans on the narratives that were being issued by the explorers of the New World and the Far East. Yet, with all this borrowing, there is no author more original; and only in Shakespeare and Cervantes do we find imaginative creations so lusty with life as Friar John and Panurge. Rabelais himself, however, is the main creation of the book, a composite of Pantagruel, Friar John, Panurge, Erasmus, Vesalius, and Jonathan Swift, babbling, bubbling, smashing idols, loving life.

Because he loved life he flayed those who made it less lovable. Perhaps he was a bit too hard on the monks who had been unable to share his humanistic devotions. He must have been clawed by a lawyer or two, for he tears their fur revengefully. Mark my words, he warns his readers, "if you live but six Olympiads and the age of two dogs more, you'll see these law-cats lords of all Europe." But he lays his whip also upon judges, Scholastics, theologians, historians, travelers, indulgence peddlers, and women. There is hardly a good word for women in all the book; this is Rabelais' blindest spot, perhaps the price he paid, as monk and priest and bachelor, for never earning tenderness.

Partisans have debated whether he was a Catholic, a Protestant, a freethinker, or an atheist. Calvin thought him an atheist; and "my own belief," concluded his lover Anatole France, "is that he believed nothing."[34] At times he wrote like the most irreverent cynic, as in the language of the sheep drover about the best way to fertilize a field (IV, vii). He ridiculed fasting, indulgences, inquisitors, decretals, and enjoyed explaining the anatomical requisites for becoming a pope (IV, xlviii). He had evidently no belief in hell (II, xxx). He echoed the Protestant arguments that the papacy was draining the nations of their gold (IV, liii), and that the cardinals of Rome lived lives of gluttony and hypocrisy (IV, lviii-lx). He sympathized with the French heretics; Pantagruel, he says, did not stay long in Toulouse, because there they "burn their regents alive, like red herrings"--referring to the execution of an heretical professor of law (II, v). But his Protestant sympathies seem to have been limited to those who were humanists. He followed Erasmus admiringly, but only mildly favored Luther, and he turned with distaste from the dogmatism and puritanism of Calvin. He was tolerant of everything but intolerance. Like nearly all the humanists, when driven to choose, he preferred Catholicism with its legends, intolerance, and art to Protestantism with its predestination, intolerance, and purity. He repeatedly affirmed his faith in the fundamentals of Christianity, but this may have been the prudence of a man who, in defense of his opinions, was willing to go to the stake exclusively. He loved his definition of God so well that he (or his continuator) repeated it (III, xiii; V, xlvii). He apparently accepted the immortality of the soul (II, viii; IV, xxvii), but in general he preferred scatology to eschatology. Farel called him a renegade for accepting the pastorate of Meudon,[35] but this was understood, by donor and recipient, as merely a way of eating.

His real faith was in Nature, and here, perhaps, he was as trustful and credulous as his orthodox neighbors. He believed that ultimately the forces of Nature work for good, and he underestimated her neutrality as between men and fleas. Like Rousseau, and against Luther and Calvin, he believed in the natural goodness of man; or, like other humanists, he was confident that a good education and a good environment would make men good. Like Montaigne, he counseled men to follow Nature, and possibly he looked with impish unconcern on what would then happen to society and civilization. In describing the Abbey of Theleme he seemed to be preaching philosophical anarchism, but it was not so; he would admit to it only those whose good breeding, education, and sense of honor would fit them for the trials of freedom.

His final philosophy was "Pantagruelism." This must not be confused with the useful weed Pantagruelion, which is merely hemp, and whose final virtue is that it can make appropriate neckties for criminals. Pantagruelism is living like Pantagruel—in a genial and tolerant fellowship with Nature and men, in grateful enjoyment of all the good things of life, and in cheerful acceptance of our inescapable vicissitudes and termination. Once Rabelais defined Pantagruelism as *une certaine gaieté d'esprit confite de mépris des choses fortuites*—"a certain gaiety of spirit preserved in contempt of the accidents of life" (IV, Prologue). It combined Zeno the Stoic, Diogenes the Cynic, and Epicurus: to bear all natural events with equanimity, to view without offense all natural impulses and operations, and to enjoy every sane pleasure without puritanic inhibitions or theological remorse. Pantagruel "took all things in good part, and interpreted every action in the best sense; he neither vexed nor disquieted himself . . . since all the goods that the earth contains . . . are not of so much worth as that we should for them disturb or disorder our emotions, trouble or perplex our senses or spirits" (III, ii). We must not exaggerate the epicurean element in this philosophy; Rabelais' litanies to wine were more verbal than alcoholic; they do not quite comport with a contemporary's description of him as a man of "serene, gracious, and open countenance"; [36] the wine he celebrated was the wine of life. And this pretended Lord of Dipsophily put into the mouth of Gargantua a sentence that in ten words phrases the challenge of our own time: "Science without conscience is but the ruin of the soul" (II, viii).

France has treasured Rabelais more than any other of her giants of the pen except Montaigne, Molière, and Voltaire. In his own century Etienne Pasquier called him the greatest writer of the age. In the seventeenth century, as manners stiffened under lace and perukes, and classic form became literally *de rigueur*, he lost some standing in the nation's memory; but even then Molière, Racine, and La Fontaine were confessedly influenced by him; Fontenelle, La Bruyère, and Mme. de Sévigné loved him, and Pascal appropriated his definition of God. Voltaire began by despising his coarseness, and ended by becoming his devotee. As the French language changed, Rabelais became almost unintelligible to French readers in the nineteenth century; and perhaps he is now more popular in the English-speaking world than in France. For in 1653 and 1693 Sir Thomas Urquhart published a translation of Books One and Three into virile English as exuberant as the original; Peter de Motteux completed the version in 1708; and by the work of these men *Gargantua and Pantagruel* became an English classic. Swift stole from it as if by right of clergy, and Sterne must have found in it some leaven for his wit. It is among the books that belong to the literature not of a country but of the world.

VI. RONSARD AND THE PLÉIADE

Meanwhile a veritable flood of poetry was pouring over France. We know some 200 French poets in the reigns of Francis and his sons; and these were no vapid mourners in an unheeding wilderness; they were warriors in a literary battle—form vs. content, Ronsard vs. Rabelais—that determined the character of French literature till the Revolution.

A complex ecstasy inspired them. They longed to rival the Greeks and Romans in purity of style and perfection of form, and the Italian sonneteers in grace of speech and imagery; nevertheless they were resolved to write not in Latin, like the scholars who were instructing and exciting them, but in their native French; and at the same time they proposed to mellow and refine that still rough tongue by teaching it words, phrases, constructions, and ideas judiciously pilfered from the classics. The episodic formlessness of Rabelais' romance made it, in their eyes, a crude vessel of clay hastily turned by hand, unpainted and unglazed. They would add to his earthly vitality the discipline of form carefully designed, and of feeling rationally controlled.

The classical crusade began in the Lyons of Rabelais himself. Maurice Sève spent part of his life locating, as he thought, the tomb of Petrarch's Laura, then composed 446 stanzas to his own desired Délie; and in the melancholy delicacy of his verse he cleared a path for Ronsard. His ablest competitor in Lyons was a woman, Louise Labé, who, in full armor, fought like another Joan at Perpignan, and then cooled into marriage with a rope-maker who winked in kindly Gallic fashion at her subsidiary amours. She read Greek, Latin, Italian, and Spanish, played the lute alluringly, kept a salon for her rivals and her lovers, and wrote some of the earliest and finest sonnets in the French language. We might judge her fame from her funeral (1566), which, said a chronicler, "was a triumph. She was carried through the city with her face uncovered, and her head crowned with a floral wreath. Death could do nothing to disfigure her, and the people of Lyons covered her grave with flowers and tears." [37] Through these Lyonese poets the Petrarchan style and mood passed up to Paris, and entered the Pléiade.

The very word was a classic echo, for in the Alexandria of the third century before Christ a galaxy of seven poets had likewise been named from the constellation that commemorated the seven mythological daughters of Atlas and Pleïone. Ronsard, brightest star in the French Pléiade, rarely used that term, and his models were Anacreon and Horace rather than Alexandrian Theocritus or Callimachus. It was in 1548, at an inn in Touraine, that he met Joachim du Bellay, and conspired with him to make French poetry classical. They won to their enterprise four other young poets—Antoine de Baïf, Remi Belleau, Étienne Jodelle, and Ponthus de Thyard; and they were joined also by the scholar Jean Dorat, whose lectures on Greek literature at the Collège de France and the Collège de Coqueret fired them with enthusiasm for the lyric singers of ancient Greece. They called themselves La Brigade, and vowed to rescue the French muse from the coarse hands of Jean de Meung and Rabelais, and the loose measures of Villon and Marot. They turned their noses from the riotous language and privy wisdom of Gargantua and Pantagruel; they found no classic restraint in those jumbled verbs and adjectives, those coprophilic ecstasies, no feeling for beauty of form in woman, nature, or art. A hostile critic, seeing them seven, dubbed them La Pléiade. Their victory turned the word into a flag of fame.

In 1549 Du Bellay proclaimed the linguistic program of the *Brigade* in a *Défense et illustration de la langue françoyse*. By *défense* he meant that the French language could be enabled to express all that the classic tongues had uttered; by *illustration* he meant that French could take on new luster, could brighten and polish itself, by putting aside the rough speech of prevalent French prose, and the ballad, roundel, virelay forms of French poesy, and purify and enrich itself by importing classical terms and studying classical forms, as in Anacreon, Theocritus, Virgil, Horace, and Petrarch. For to the Pléiade Petrarch was already a classic, and the sonnet was the most perfect of all literary forms.

Pierre de Ronsard realized in his verse the ideals that Du Bellay voiced in splendid prose. He came of a recently ennobled family; his father was *maître d'hôtel* to Francis I, and for some time Pierre lived at the brilliant court. He was successively page to the Dauphin Francis, then to the Madeleine who married James V of Scotland, then *écuyer* or squire to the future Henry II. He looked forward to military exploits, but at sixteen he began to grow deaf. He sheathed his sword and brandished a pen. He fell in with Virgil by accident, and saw in him a perfection of form and speech as yet unknown in France. Dorat led him on from Latin to Greek, and taught him to read Anacreon, Aeschylus, Pindar, Aristophanes. "O Master!" cried the youth, "why have you hidden these riches from me so long?" [88] At twenty-four he met Du Bellay. Thereafter he divided his time devotedly among song, woman, and wine.

His *Odes* (1550) completed the lyric revolt. They frankly imitated Horace, but they introduced the ode into French poetry, and stood on their own feet in purity of language, elegance of phrase, precision of form. Two years later, in the 183 sonnets of his *Amours*, he took Petrarch as his model, and achieved a grace and refinement never surpassed in French poetry. He wrote to be sung, and many of his poems were put to music during his lifetime, some by famous composers like Jannequin and Goudimel. He offered to the women he courted the old invitation to make play while beauty shines, but even on that ancient theme he struck an original note, as when he warned one prudent lass that she would someday regret having lost the opportunity of being seduced by so renowned a bard:

> *Quand vous serez bien vieille, au soir, à la chandelle,*
> *Assise auprès du feu, devisant et filant,*
> *Direz chantant mes vers, en vous émerveillant:*
> *Ronsard me célébrait du temps que j'étais belle.*
> *Lors vous n'aurez servante oyant telle nouvelle,*
> *Desia sous le labeur à demi soummeilant,*
> *Qui au bruit de son nom ne s'aille reveillant,*
> *Bénissant votre nom de louange immortelle.*

Je serai sous la terre et, fantôme sans os,
Par les ombres myrteux je prendrai mon repos;
Vous serez au foyer une vieille accroupie,
Regrettant mon amour et votre fier dédain.
Vivez, si m'en croyez, n'attendez à demain:
*Cueillez dès aujourd'hui les roses de la vie.**

The exaltation of style suited well the court of Catherine de Médicis, who had brought to France an Italian retinue bearing Petrarch in their books. The new poet—hard of hearing but proud of carriage, with martial figure, golden hair and beard, and the face of Praxiteles' *Hermes*—became a favorite of Catherine, Henry II, Mary Stuart, even of Elizabeth of England, who, as his seventeenth cousin, sent him a diamond ring. The Greco-Roman mythology of the Pléiade was welcomed; when the poets talked of Olympus the court acknowledged the compliment;[39] Henry became Jupiter, Catherine Juno, Diane Diana; and the sculpture of Goujon confirmed the comparison.

When Henry died, Charles IX continued to befriend Ronsard, not quite to good result, for the young monarch wanted an epic about France to match the *Aeneid*. "I can give death," wrote the royal simpleton, "but you can give immortality."[40] Ronsard began a *Franciade*, but found his muse too short of breath for so long a run; soon he gave up the pretense, and returned to lyrics and love. He passed peacefully into old age, protected from the noise of the world, safely conservative in politics and religion, revered by younger minstrels, and respected by all but death. It came in 1585. He was buried at Tours, but Paris gave him an Olympian funeral, in which all the notables of the capital marched to hear a bishop intone an *oraison funèbre*.

The poets who called him prince produced many volumes of verse, delicate but dead. Most of them, like the master, were pagans who at their ease professed Catholic orthodoxy, and scorned the moralistic Huguenots. However poor these poets might be in pocket, they were aristocrats in pride, sometimes in blood, and they wrote for a circle that had the leisure to relish form. Rabelais returned their hostility by ridiculing their pedantry, their servile imitation of Greek and Roman meters, phrases, and epithets, their thin echoes of ancient themes and Petrarchan conceits and laments. In that

---

* A prose translation seems better than an awkward forcing of rhymes and idioms into alien forms: "When you shall be very old, seated at evening beside the fire, chatting and sewing by candlelight, you will recite my poems, and marveling will say, 'Ronsard blazoned my name when I was fair.' Then no one of your helpers, though half lulled to sleep by the murmur of their looms, but, hearing these words, will rouse themselves at the sound of my name, blessing your fate to have such deathless praise. I shall be then beneath the earth, a phantom without bones; I shall be taking my repose beneath the shade of myrtle trees. You, an old woman bent before your hearth, will then regret my love and your proud disdain. Live now, believe me, wait not for tomorrow; gather the roses of life that bloom today!"

conflict between naturalism and classicism the fate of French literature was decided. The poets and tragic dramatists of France would choose the straight and narrow path of perfect structure and chiseled grace; the prose writers would aim to please by force of substance alone. Hence French poetry before the Revolution is untranslatable; the vase of form cannot be shattered and then be refashioned in an alien mold. In nineteenth-century France the two streams met, the half-truths merged, content married form, and French prose became supreme.

VII. WYATT AND SURREY

Not as a flood, but as a river flowing through many outlets to the sea, the influence of Italy passed through France and reached England. The scholarship of one generation inspired the literature of the next; the divine revelation of ancient Greece and Rome became the Bible of the Renaissance. In 1486 the plays of Plautus were staged in Italy, and soon thereafter at the rival courts of Francis I and Henry VIII. In 1508 Bibbiena's *Calandra* began the vernacular classic comedy in Italy; in 1552 Jodelle's *Cléopatre captive* began the vernacular classic tragedy in France; in 1553 Nicholas Udall produced the first English comedy in classical form. *Ralph Roister Doister*, said a critic, "smelt of Plautus"; [41] it did; but it smelled of England too, and of that robust humor that Shakespeare would serve to the groundlings at the Elizabethan theaters.

The Italian influence appeared brightest in the poetry of the Tudor reigns. The medieval style survived in such pretty ballads as *The Not-browne Mayd* (1521); but when the poets who basked in the sun of young Henry VIII took to verse their ideal and model were Petrarch and his *Canzoniere*. Just a year before Elizabeth's accession, Richard Tottel, a London printer, published a *Miscellany* in which the poems of two distinguished courtiers revealed the triumph of Petrarch over Chaucer, of classic form over medieval exuberance. Sir Thomas Wyatt, as a diplomat in the service of the King, made many a trip to France and Italy, and brought back some Italians to help him civilize his friends. Like a good Renaissance *cortigiano*, he burned his fingers in love's fire: he was, said tradition, one of Anne Boleyn's early lovers, and he was briefly imprisoned when she was sent to the Tower.[42] Meanwhile he translated Petrarch's sonnets, and was the first to compress English verse into that compact form.

When Wyatt died of a fever at thirty-nine (1542), another romantic figure at Henry's court, Henry Howard, Earl of Surrey, caught the lyre from his hands. Surrey chanted the beauties of spring, reproved reluctant lasses, and vowed eternal fidelity to each in turn. He took to nocturnal ex-

cesses in London, served a term in jail for challenging to a duel, was summoned to trial for eating meat in Lent, broke some windows with his playful
crossbow, was again arrested, again released, and fought gallantly for England in France. Returning, he toyed too audibly with the idea of becoming
king of England. He was condemned to be hanged, drawn, and quartered,
but was let off with decapitation (1547).

Poetry was an incidental ornament in this strenuous life. Surrey translated
some books of the *Aeneid*, introduced blank verse into English literature,
and gave the sonnet the form that Shakespeare was to use. Perhaps foreseeing that the paths of undue glory might lead to the block, he addressed
to a Roman poet a wistful idyl of rustic routine and peace:

> Martial, the things that do attain
>   The happy life be these, I find:
> The riches left, not got with pain;
>   The fruitful ground, the quiet mind;
> The equal friend; no grudge, no strife;
>   No change of rule nor governance;
> Without disease the healthful life;
>   The household of continuance;
> The mean diet, no delicate fare;
>   True wisdom joined with simpleness;
> The night dischargèd of all care,
>   Where wine the wit may not oppress;
> The faithful wife, without debate;
>   Such sleep as may beguile the night;
> Contented with thine own estate,
>   Ne wish for death, ne fear his might.

VIII. HANS SACHS

The mind of Germany, in the century that followed Luther's Theses, was
lost in the hundred years' debate that prepared the Thirty Years' War. After
1530 the publication of ancient classics almost ceased; in general, fewer
books were issued; they were replaced by a torrent of controversial pamphlets. Thomas Murner, a Franciscan monk with an acid pen, scourged
everybody with a chain of booklets about rascals or dolts—*Schmelmenzunft
(Guild of Rogues)*, *Narrenbeschwörung (Muster of Fools)* ... all prolifer-
ated from Brant's *Narrenschiff*.* Many of the fools lashed by Murner were
churchmen, and he was at first mistaken for a Lutheran; but then he cele-

---

* Alexander Barclay made a similar adaptation of Brant in *The Shyp of Folys* (1509), adding some Scottish darts of his own.

brated Luther as "a savage bloodhound, a senseless, foolish, blasphemous renegade."[48] Henry VIII sent him £100.

Sebastian Franck was of finer metal. The Reformation found him a priest in Augsburg; he hailed it as a brave and needed revolt, and became a Lutheran minister (1525). Three years later he married Ottilie Beham, whose brothers were Anabaptists; he developed sympathy for this persecuted sect, condemned Lutheran intolerance, was expelled from Strasbourg, and made a living by boiling soap in Ulm. He ridiculed the determination of religious orthodoxy by the German dukes, noting that "if one prince dies and his successor brings in another creed, this at once becomes God's Word."[44] "Mad zeal possesses all men today, that we should believe . . . that God is ours alone, that there is no heaven, faith, spirit, Christ, but in our sect." His own faith was a universalist theism that closed no doors. "My heart is alien to none. I have my brothers among the Turks, Papists, Jews, and all peoples."[45] He aspired to "a free, unsectarian . . . Christianity, bound to no outer thing," not even to the Bible.[46] Shocked by sentiments so unbecoming to his century, Ulm banished him in its turn. He found work as a printer in Basel, and died there in honest penury (1542).

German poetry and drama were now so immersed in theology that they ceased to be arts and became weapons of war. In this strife any jargon, coarseness, and obscenity were held legitimate; except for folk songs and hymns, poetry disappeared in a fusillade of poisoned rhymes. The lavishly staged religious dramas of the fifteenth century passed out of public taste, and were succeeded by popular farces lampooning Luther or the popes.

Now and then a man rose above the fury to see life whole. If Hans Sachs had obeyed the magistrates of Nuremberg he would have remained a shoemaker; for when, without securing the civic *imprimatur*, he published a rhyming history of the Tower of Babel, they suppressed the book, assured him that poetry was obviously not his line, and bade him stick to his last.[47] Yet Hans had some rights, for he had passed through the usual stages to become a Meistersinger, and the anomaly of his being a cobbler and a poet fades when we note that the guild of weavers and shoemakers to which he belonged regularly practiced choral song, and gave public concerts thrice a year. For this guild, and at any other opportunity, Sachs wrote songs and plays as assiduously as if he were mouthing nails.

We must think of him not as a great poet, but as a sane and cheerful voice in a century of hate. His basic interest was in simple people, not in geniuses; his plays were almost always about such people; and even God, in these dramas, is a benevolent commoner, who talks like some parson of the neighborhood. While most writers peppered their pages with bitterness, vulgarity, or ribaldry, Hans portrayed and exalted the virtues of affection, duty, piety, marital fidelity, parental and filial love. His first published poems (1516) proposed "to promote the praise and glory of God," and "to help his fellow creatures to a life of penitence"; [48] and this religious spirit warmed his writings to the end. He turned half the Bible into rhyme, using Luther's translation as a text. He saluted Luther as "the Nightingale of Wittenberg," who would cleanse religion and restore morality.

> Awake! awake! the day is near,
> And in the woods a song I hear.
> It is the glorious nightingale;
> Her music rings on hill and dale.
> The night falls into Occident,
> The day springs up in Orient,
> The dawn comes and sets alight
> The gloomy clouds of parting night. [49]

Now Sachs became the bard of the Reformation, satirizing the faults of Catholics with doggerel tenacity. He wrote plays about rascally monks, and traced the origin of their tribe to the Devil; he issued burlesques and farces which showed, for example, a priest seducing a girl or saying Mass while drunk; in 1558 he published a *History in Rhyme of the Popess Joanna*—a fable which most Protestant preachers accepted as history. But Hans satirized Lutherans too, denouncing their lives as scandalously contrary to their creed: "With your flesh-eating, your uproars, your abuse of priests, your quarreling, mocking, insulting, and all your other improper behavior, you Lutherans have brought the Gospel into great contempt." [50] He joined a hundred others in mourning the commercialism and immorality of the age.

All in all, and discounting Wagner's idealization, Hans Sachs may typify the bluff and crude but kindly German who, at least in the south, must have been in the majority. We picture him happy and melodious for forty years in his home and his poetry. When his first wife died (1560) he married, at sixty-eight, a pretty woman of twenty-seven, and survived even this trial. There is something to be said for an age and a city in which a cobbler could become a humanist, a poet, and a musician, acquire and use a large library, learn Greek literature and philosophy, write 6,000 poems, and live in reasonable health and happiness to die at the age of eighty-two.

IX. THE IBERIAN MUSE: 1515–55

This was a lively time in the literature of Portugal. The exciting stimulus of the explorations, the spreading wealth of expanding commerce, the influence of Italy, the humanists at Coimbra and Lisbon, the patronage of a cultivated court, joined in an efflorescence that would soon culminate in the *Lusiads* (1572) of Camoëns. A merry battle raged between the *Eschola Velha*—Old School—

of Gil Vicente, who cherished native themes and forms, and *Os Quinhentistas* —The Men of the Fifteenth (our Sixteenth) Century—who followed Sá de Miranda in enthusiasm for Italian and classic modes and styles. For thirty-four years (1502–36) Gil Vicente, "the Portuguese Shakespeare," dominated the theater with his simple *autos*, or acts; the court smiled upon him, and expected him to celebrate every royal event with a play; and when the king was quarreling with the pope Gil was allowed to satirize the papacy with such freedom that Aleander, seeing one of Vicente's plays in Brussels, "thought I was in mid-Saxony listening to Luther." [51] The fertile dramatist wrote sometimes in Spanish, sometimes in Portuguese, sometimes in both, with scraps of Italian and French, Church Latin and peasant slang, thrown in. Often the action of the piece was interrupted, as in Shakespeare, with lyrics that crept into the hearts of the people. Like Shakespeare, Gil was actor as well as playwright; he was stage manager as well, and directed the settings. For good measure he was one of the best goldsmiths of the age.

In 1524 Francisco Sá de Miranda returned from a six years' stay in Italy, and brought with him the classical fever of the Renaissance. Like Ronsard and the Pléiade in France, like Spenser and Sidney in England, he proposed to dignify the national literature by modeling its subjects, meters, and style on classical lines; like Joachim du Bellay, he included Petrarch among the classics, and introduced the sonnet to his countrymen; like Jodelle he wrote the first classical tragedy in his native tongue (1550); and he had already (1527) written the first Portuguese prose comedy in classic form. His friend Bernardim Ribeiro composed bucolic poetry in the style of Virgil, and lived a tragedy in the manner of Tasso: he made such a stir with his passion for a lady of the court that he was banished; he was forgiven and restored to royal favor, and died insane (1552).

A school of colorful historians recorded the triumphs of the explorers. Caspar Correa went out to India, rose to be one of Albuquerque's secretaries, denounced official corruption, and was murdered in Malacca in 1565. Amid this active life he wrote in eight volumes what he called "a brief summary" of the Portuguese conquest of India *(Lendas da India)*, full of the color of that expansive era. Fernão Lopes de Castanheda traveled for half a lifetime in the East, and labored for twenty years on his *Historia do descobrimento e conquista da India pelos Portuguezes*. João de Barros served in several administrative capacities at India House in Lisbon for forty years, and disgraced his predecessors by amassing no fortune. He had access to all the archives, and gathered them into a history which he called simply *Asia*, but which acquired the name of *Decades* because three of its four huge volumes covered periods of some ten years each. In order, accuracy, and clarity it bears comparison with any contemporary historical composition except the works of Machiavelli and Guicciardini. The proud nation would have rejected the exceptions, and gave Barros the title of "the Portuguese Livy."

The Castilian tongue had now become the literary language of Spain. Galician, Valencian, Catalonian, Andalusian dialects survived in the speech of the people, and Galician became Portuguese; but the use of Castilian as the language of state and Church under Ferdinand, Isabella, and Ximenes gave that dialect an insuperable prestige, and from their time to ours its masculine sonority has carried the literature of Spain. An infatuation with language appeared in some writers of this age. Antonio de Guevara set an example of linguistic conceits and rhetorical flourishes, and the translation of his *Reloj de principes* (*Dial of Princes*, 1529) by Lord Berners helped to mold the euphuism of John Lyly's *Euphues*, and the silly wordplay of Shakespeare's early comedies.

Spanish literature sang of religion, love, and war. The passion for romances of chivalry reached such a height that in 1555 the Cortes recommended that they be prohibited by law; such a decree was actually issued in Spanish America; had it been enforced in Spain we might have missed *Don Quixote*. One of the romances spared by the curate in the purification of the Knight's library was the *Diana enamorata* (1542) of Jorge de Montemayor; it imitated the *Arcadia* (1504) of the Spanish-Italian poet Sannazaro, and was itself imitated by Sir Philip Sidney's *Arcadia* (1590). Montemayor's prose-and-poetry romance was one of a thousand instances of Italian influence on Spanish literature; here again the conquered conquered the conquerors. Juan Boscan translated Castiglione's *Cortigiano* into prose quite worthy of the original, and accepted the suggestion of the Venetian poet Navagero to popularize the sonnet form in Spain.

His friend Garcilaso de la Vega almost at once brought the form to perfection in Castilian. Like so many Spanish writers of this period, he came of high lineage; his father was ambassador of Ferdinand and Isabella at Rome. Born at Toledo in 1503, Garcilaso was early dedicated to arms. In 1532 he distinguished himself in the repulse of the Turks from Vienna; in 1535 he was twice severely wounded in the siege of Tunis; a few months later he shared in Charles V's futile campaign in Provence. At Fréjus he volunteered to lead an attack upon an obstructive castle; he was the first to mount the wall; he received a blow on the head from which he died a few days later, aged thirty-three. One of the thirty-seven sonnets which he bequeathed to his friend Boscan struck a note that has echoed in every war:

> And now larger than ever lies the curse
>   On this our time; and all that went before
> Keeps altering its face from bad to worse;
>   And each of us has felt the touch of war—
> War after war, and exile, dangers, fear—
>   And each of us is weary to the core
> Of seeing his own blood along a spear
>   And being alive because it missed its aim.
> Some folks have lost their goods and all their gear,
>   And everything is gone, even the name
> Of house and home and wife and memory.
>   And what's the use of it? A little fame?
> The nation's thanks? A place in history?
> One day they'll write a book, and then we'll see.[52]

He could not see, but a thousand books commemorated him fondly. Historians recorded his death among the leading events of the time. His poems were printed in handy volumes which were carried in the pockets of Spanish soldiers into a dozen lands. Spanish lutenists put his lyrics to music as madrigals for the vihuela, and dramatists turned his eclogues into plays.

The Spanish drama marked time, and could not know that it would soon rival the Elizabethan. One-act comedies, farcical satires, or episodes from popular romances were performed by strolling players in a public square or the *corrale*—yard—of an inn, sometimes at a princely seat or royal court. Lope de Rueda, who succeeded Gil Vicente as chief provider of *autos* for such troupes, made his fame—and gave us a word—with his *bobos*, clowns.

Historians abounded. Gonzalo Fernández de Oviedo was appointed historiographer of the New World by Charles V, and acquitted himself indifferently well with a voluminous and ill-ordered *Historia general y natural de las Indias Occidentales* (1535). During forty years of residence in Spanish America he grew rich from mining gold, and he resented the *Brevisima relacion de la destruycion de las Indias* (1539 f.), in which Bartolomé de las Casas exposed the merciless exploitation of native slave labor in the American mines. Las Casas sailed with Columbus in 1502, became Bishop of Chiapa in Mexico, and gave nearly all his life to the cause of the Indians. In *Memorials* addressed to the Spanish government he described the rapidity with which the natives were dying under the arduous conditions of work imposed upon them by the settlers. The Indians had been accustomed by their warm climate and simple diet to only casual labor; they had not mined gold, but had been content to derive it from the surface of the earth or the beds of shallow streams, and used it only as an ornament. Las Casas calculated that the native population of the "Indies" had been reduced from 12,000,000 (doubtless too high a guess) to 14,000 in thirty-eight years.[53] Dominican and Jesuit missionaries joined with Las Casas in protesting against Indian slavery,[54] and Isabella repeatedly denounced it.[55] Ferdinand and Ximenes prescribed semi-humane conditions for the conscription of Indian labor,[56] but while these gentlemen were engrossed in European politics their instructions for the treatment of the natives were mostly ignored.

A minor debate concerned the conquest of Mexico. Francisco López de Gómara gave a very Cortesian account of that rape; Bernal Díaz del Castillo, in protest, composed (1568 f.) his *Historia verdadera de la conquista de la Nueva España*, which, while giving due praise to Cortes, condemned him for taking all the honors and profits of the conquest, leaving little for such brave soldiers as Bernal. It is a fascinating book, full of the lust of action, the joy of victory, and honest amazement at the wealth and splendor of Aztec Mexico. "When I beheld the scenes that were around me, I thought within myself that this was the garden of the world." And then he adds, "All is destroyed." [57]

The most mature Spanish history and the most famous Spanish novel of this period have been attributed to the same man. Diego Hurtado de Mendoza was born at Granada some eleven years after its conquest by Ferdinand; his father had won laurels in the siege, and had been made governor of the city after its fall. Educated at Salamanca, Bologna, and Padua, Mendoza acquired a wide culture in Latin, Greek, and Arabic, in philosophy and law; he collected classic texts with the zeal of a Renaissance prince; and when Suleiman the Magnificent bade him name his reward for certain good offices he had performed for the Porte, he asked only for some Greek manuscripts. He rose to high place in the diplomatic service of Charles V at Venice, Rome, and the Council of Trent. Rebuked by Paul III for conveying some harsh message from Charles to the Pope, he answered with all the pride of a Spanish grandee: "I am a cavalier, my father was one before me, and as such it is my duty to fulfill the commands of my royal master, without any fear of your Holiness, so long as I observe due reverence to the vicegerent of Christ. I am minister to the King of Spain . . . safe, as his representative, even from your Holiness's displeasure." [58]

Recent research questions Mendoza's authorship of the first picaresque novel in European literature—*The Life and Adventures of Lazarillo de Tormes.* Though not printed till 1553, it had probably been written many years before. That a scion of a family only less noble than the king's should make a thief his hero would be startling; more so that a man originally intended for the priesthood should include in his story such sharp satires of the clergy that the Inquisition forbade any further printing of the book until it had been expurgated of all offense.[59] Lazarillo * is a waif who, as guide to a blind beggar, acquires the tricks of petty larceny, and rises to higher crimes as servant to a priest, a friar, a chaplain, a bailiff, a seller of indulgences. Even the worldly wise young thief is impressed with some of the marvels arranged by the indulgence peddler in promoting his wares. "I must confess that I, amongst many others, was deceived at the time, and thought my master a miracle of sanctity." [60] This rollicking narrative set the *gusto picaresco*, or "style of the rogue," in fiction; it evoked innumerable imitations, culminating in the most renowned of picaresque romances, the *Gil Blas* (1715–35) of Alain Lesage.

Exiled from the court of Philip II for drawing his sword in an argument, Mendoza retired to Granada, composed incidental verses too free to be printed during his lifetime, and recounted the Moorish revolt of 1568–70 in an *Historia de la guerra de Granada* so impartial, so just to the Moors, that this too could not find a publisher, and saw print only in 1610, and then only in part. Mendoza took Sallust for his model, rivaled him, and stole a theme or two from Tacitus; but all in all, this was the first Spanish work that advanced beyond mere chronicle or propaganda to factual history interpreted with philosophical grasp and presented with literary art. Mendoza died in 1575, aged seventy-two. He was one of the most complete personalities of a time rich in complete men.

Always, in these hurried pages, conscience runs a race with time, and warns the hurrying pen that, like the hasty traveler, it is but scratching surfaces. How many publishers, teachers, scholars, patrons, poets, romancers, and reckless rebels labored for half a century to produce the literature that

---

* "Little Lazarus," referring to the beggar of that name in Luke 16; then "little beggar"; then a boy leading a blind beggar.

here has been so narrowly confined, so many masterpieces unnamed, nations ignored, once immortal geniuses slighted with a line! It cannot be helped. The ink runs dry; and while it lasts it must be enough if from its scratches and splashes some hazy picture unfolds of men and women resting a while from theology and war, loving the forms of beauty as well as the mirages of truth and power, and building, carving, painting words until thought finds an art to clothe it, wisdom and music merge, and literature arises to let a nation speak, to let an age pour its spirit into a mold so fondly fashioned that time itself will cherish and carry it down through a thousand catastrophes as an heirloom of the race.

Art in the Age of Holbein

1517-64

I. ART, THE REFORMATION, AND THE RENAISSANCE

ART had to suffer from the Reformation, if only because Protestantism believed in the Ten Commandments. Had not the Lord God said, "Thou shalt not make unto thee any graven image, or any likeness of anything that is in heaven above, or that is in the earth beneath, or that is in the water under the earth"? (Exodus 20:4) How was representative art possible after that sweeping prohibition? The Jews had obeyed, and had passed by art. The Moslems had almost obeyed, had kept their art decorative, largely abstract, often representing things, rarely persons, never God. Protestantism, rediscovering the Old Testament, followed the Semitic line. Catholicism, whose Greco-Roman heritage had overshadowed its Judaic origin, had more and more ignored the veto: Gothic sculpture had fashioned saints and gods in stone; Italian painting had pictured the Bible story, and the Renaissance had quite forgotten the Second Commandment in a blooming riot of representative art. Perhaps that old interdict had been meant to ban representation for *magical* ends; and the patrons of art, in Renaissance Italy, had the good sense to override a primitive and now meaningless taboo.

The Church, greatest patron of all, had employed the arts to form the letterless in the dogmas and legends of the faith. To the ecclesiastical statesman who felt that myths were vital to morality, this use of art seemed reasonable. But when the myths, like purgatory, were manipulated to finance the extravagances and abuses of the Church, reformers forgivably rebelled against the painting and sculpture that inculcated the myths. In this matter Luther was moderate, even if he had to revise the Commandments. "I do not hold that the Gospel should destroy all the arts, as certain superstitious folk believe. On the contrary, I would fain see all arts . . . serving Him Who hath created them and given them to us. The law of Moses forbade only the image of God." [1] In 1526 he called upon his adherents to "assail the . . . idolaters of the Roman Antichrist by means of painting." [2] Even Calvin, whose followers were the most enthusiastic iconoclasts, gave a limited approval to images. 'I am not so scrupulous as to judge that no images should be endured . . . but seeing that the art of painting and carving . . . cometh from God, I require that the practice of art should be kept pure and lawful. Therefore men should not paint nor carve anything but such as can be seen with the eye." [8] Reformers less human than Luther, less cautious than Calvin, preferred to outlaw religious painting and sculpture altogether, and to clear their churches of all ornament; "truth" banished beauty as an infidel. In England, Scotland, Switzerland, and northern Germany the destruction was wholesale and indiscriminate; in France the Huguenots melted down the reliquaries, shrines, and other vessels found in the churches that came into their power. We should have to recapture the ardor of men risking their lives to reform religion before we could understand the angry passion that in moments of victory destroyed the images that had contributed to their subjection. The demolition was brutal and barbarous, but the guilt of it must be shared by the institution that had for centuries obstructed its own reform.

Gothic art ended in this period, but the Reformation was only one cause of its demise. The reaction against the medieval Church brought with it a distaste for the styles of architecture and ornament long associated with her. And yet Gothic was dying even before Luther spoke. It ailed in Catholic France as well as in rebellious Germany and England; it was consumed in its own flamboyance. And the Renaissance, as well as the Reformation, was fatal to Gothic. For the Renaissance came from Italy, which had never loved Gothic and had travestied it even in adopting it; and the Renaissance spread chiefly among educated people whose polite skepticism could not understand the enthusiastic faith of crusading and Gothic days. As the Reformation progressed, the Church herself, which had found in Gothic architecture her supreme artistic expression, was too impoverished by the loss of Britain, Germany, and Scandinavia, and the inroads made upon her revenues by Catholic kings, to finance art as lavishly as before, or to determine taste and style. Day by day a secularizing, paganizing Renaissance asserted its classical predilections over the sacred traditions of medieval faith and form. Men impiously reached over pious and fearful centuries to grasp again the earth-loving, pleasure-loving passions of antiquity. War was declared against Gothic as the art of the barbarians who had destroyed Imperial Rome. The conquered Romans came back to life, rebuilt their temples, exhumed the statues of their gods, and bade first Italy, then France and England to resume the art that had embodied the glory of Greece and the grandeur of Rome. The Renaissance conquered Gothic, and in France it conquered the Reformation.

II. THE ART OF THE FRENCH RENAISSANCE

1. *"A Malady of Building"*

In French ecclesiastical architecture Gothic fought successfully for a reprieve. Some old cathedrals added fresh elements, necessarily Gothic; so Caen's St.-Pierre completed its famous choir; Beauvais built its south transept; and Gothic made almost its expiring effort when Jean Vast raised above that transept crossing a spire 500 feet high (1553). When, on Ascension Day, 1573, that towering audacity collapsed into the ruined choir, the disaster symbolized the end of the noblest style in architectural history.

Lesser Gothic splendors rose in this period at Pontoise, Coutances, and a dozen other cities of France. In Paris, where every glance reveals some marvel from a believing past, two handsome Gothic churches took form: St.-Étienne-du-Mont (1492–1626) and St.-Eustache (1532–1654). But Renaissance features stole into them: in St.-Étienne the magnificent stone screen overarching the choir; in St.-Eustache the compound pilasters and quasi-Corinthian capitals.

The replacement of ecclesiastical Gothic with secular Renaissance architecture reflected the taste of Francis I, and the humanistic emphasis on terrestrial pleasure rather than celestial hope. All the economic fruition, the aristocratic patronage, the pagan hedonism, that had fed the fires of art in Renaissance Italy now nourished the devotion of architects, painters, sculptors, potters, and goldsmiths in France. Italian artists were brought in to mingle their skills and decorative motives with surviving Gothic forms. Not only in Paris, but at Fontainebleau, Moulins, Tours, Bourges, Angers, Lyons, Dijon, Avignon, and Aix-en-Provence the brilliance of Italian design, the realism of Flemish painting, and the taste and bisexual grace of the French aristocracy combined to produce in France an art that challenged and inherited the Italian supremacy.

At the head of the movement was a king who loved art with abandon and yet with discrimination. The lighthearted, smiling spirit of Francis I wrote itself into the architecture of the reign. *Osez!* he told his artists—"Dare!" [4]— and he let them experiment as even Italy had not allowed. He recognized the Flemish power in portraiture, kept Jean Clouet as his court painter, commissioned portraits of himself and his entourage by Joos van Cleve. But in all the arts of refinement and decoration it was Italy that inspired him. After his victory at Marignano (1515) he visited Milan, Pavia, Bologna, and other Italian cities, and enviously studied their architecture, painting, and minor arts. Cellini quotes him as saying: "I well remember to have inspected all the best works, and by the greatest masters, of all Italy"; [5] probably the exaggeration is the ebullient Cellini's. Vasari notes in a dozen instances the purchase of Italian art by Francis I through agents in Rome, Florence, Venice, Milan. Through these efforts Leonardo's *Mona Lisa*, Michelangelo's *Leda*, Bronzino's *Venus and Cupid*, Titian's *Magdalen*, and a thousand vases, medals, drawings, statuettes, paintings, and tapestries crossed the Alps to end their travels in the Louvre.

The enthusiastic monarch, if he could have had his way, would have imported all the best artists of Italy. Money was to be lavished temptingly. "I will choke you with gold," he promised Cellini. Benvenuto came, and stayed intermittently (1541-45), long enough to confirm French goldsmithry in a tradition of exquisite design and technique. Domenico Bernabei "Boccadoro" had come to France under Charles VIII; Francis employed him to design a new Hôtel de Ville for Paris (1532); nearly a century passed before it was finished; the Commune of 1871 burned it down; it was rebuilt to Boccadoro's plan. Leonardo came in his old age (1516); all the world of French art and pedigree worshiped him, but we know of no work done by him in France. Andrea del Sarto came (1518), and soon fled. Giovanni Battista "Il Rosso" was lured from Florence (1530), and stayed in France till his suicide. Giulio Romano received urgent invitations, but was charmed by Mantua; however, he sent his most brilliant assistant, Francesco Primaticcio (1532). Francesco Pellegrino came, and Giacomo da Vignola, and Niccolò dell'Abbate, and Sebastiano Serlio, and perhaps a dozen more. At the same time French artists were encouraged to go to Italy and study the palaces of Florence, Ferrara, and Milan, and the new St. Peter's rising in Rome. Not since the conquest of ancient Rome by Greek art and thought had there been so rich a transfusion of cultural blood.

Native and Flemish artists resented the Italian seduction; and for half a century (1498-1545) the history of French architecture was a royal battle between a Gothic style affectionately rooted in the soil, and Italian modes seeping into France in the wake of conquered conquerors. The struggle pictured itself in stone in the châteaux of the Loire. There Gothic still had the upper hand, and Gallic master-masons dominated the design: a feudal castle within a protective moat, with fortresslike towers rising at the corners in majestic verticality; spacious mullioned windows to invite the sun, and sloping roofs to shed the snow, and dormer windows peering out like monocles from the roofs. But the Italian invaders were allowed to depress the pointed arch back into the older rounded form; to arrange the façades in tiers of rectangular windows buttressed with pilasters and crowned with pediments; and to decorate the interiors with classic columns, capitals, friezes, moldings, roundels, arabesques, and sculptured cornucopias of plants, flowers, fruits animals, imperial busts, and mythical divinities. Theoretically the two styles, Gothic and classical, were incongruous; their fusion by French discrimination and taste into a harmonious beauty shared in making France the Hellas of the modern world.

A fever of building—*une maladie de batir*, a wondering general called it [6] —now seized upon France, or Francis. To the old château at Blois he added (1515–19) for Queen Claude a north wing whose architect was a Frenchman, Jacques Sourdeau, but whose style was quite Renaissance. Finding it inconvenient to build a stairway within the addition, Sourdeau designed one of the architectural cynosures of the age—an external spiral staircase rising in an octagonal tower through three stages to an elegant gallery projecting from the roof, each stage richly adorned with a sculptured balcony.

After the death of his burdened Queen, Francis turned his architectural passion to Chambord—three miles south of the Loire, ten northeast of Blois. There the dukes of Orléans had built a hunting lodge; Francis replaced this (1526–44) with a predominantly Gothic château, so vast—with its 440 rooms, and stables for 1,200 horses—that it required the labor of 1,800 workmen through twelve years. Its French designers made the north façade fascinating but confused with a maze of towers, "lanterns," pinnacles, and sculptural ornament; and they distinguished the interior with a spiral staircase of great splendor, unique for a double passage that divided ascent from descent. Francis favored Chambord as a happy hunting ground; here his court loved to gather with all its trappings; and here he spent the declining years of his life. Most of the interior ornament was destroyed by revolutionists in 1793, in belated revenge on royal extravagance. Another Francis-can palace—the château of Madrid in the Bois de Boulogne, was adorned with a majolica façade by Girolamo della Robbia, and was completely demolished in the Revolution.

The extravagance was not confined to the King. Many of his aides treated themselves to palaces that still seem like importations from some fairy realm. One of the most perfect is Azay-le-Rideau, on an island in the Indre; Gilles Berthelot, who built it (1521), was not for nothing treasurer of France. Thomas Bohier, receiver-general of taxes in Normandy, built Chenonceaux (1513 f.); Jean Cottereau, finance minister, rebuilt the château of Maintenon; Guillaume de Montmorency raised a lordly palace at Chantilly (1530) —another casualty of the Revolution. His son Anne de Montmorency, Constable of France, erected the château of Ecouen (1531–40) near Saint-Denis. The château of Villandry was restored by Jean le Breton, secretary of state; Ussé was completed by Charles d'Espinay. Add to these the *hôtels* or palaces of Valençay, of Semblançay at Tours, of Escoville at Caen, of Bernuys at Toulouse, of Lallemont at Bourges, of Bourg-theroulde at Rouen, and a hundred others, all products of this reckless reign, and we may judge the prosperity of the lords and the poverty of the people.

Feeling inadequately housed, Francis decided to rebuild the château that

Louis VII and Louis IX had erected at Fontainebleau, for this, said Cellini, was the spot in his kingdom that the King loved best." The donjon and the chapel were restored, the rest was torn down; and on the site Gilles de Breton and Pierre Chambiges raised in Renaissance style a congeries of palaces connected by a graceful *Galerie de François Premier*. The exterior was not attractive; perhaps the King, like the merchant princes of Florence, thought a pretentious façade, so near the city, might draw an evil eye from the populace. He kept his esthetic flair for the interior; and there he relied upon Italians raised in the decorative tradition of Raphael and Giulio Romano.

For ten years (1531–41) Il Rosso—so named from his ruddy face—worked on the adornment of the Gallery of Francis I. Vasari describes the artist, then thirty-seven, as a man "of fine presence, grave and gracious speech, an accomplished musician, a well-versed philosopher," and "an excellent architect" as well as a sculptor and painter; [7] such were the undivided men of that expansive age. Rosso arranged the walls into fifteen panels, each adorned in High Renaissance style: a base of carved and inlaid walnut wainscoting; a fresco of scenes from classical mythology or history; a rich surrounding of stucco decorations in statuary, shells, weapons, medallions, animal or human figures, garlands of fruit or flowers; and a ceiling of deeply coffered wood completed the effect of warm color, sensuous beauty, and careless delight. All this was quite to the King's taste. He gave Rosso a house in Paris, and a pension of 1,400 livres ($35,000?) a year. The artist, says Vasari, "lived like a lord, with his servants and horses, giving banquets to his friends." [8] He gathered to his service half a dozen Italian, and several French, painters and sculptors, who formed the origin and nucleus of the "School of Fontainebleau." At the height of his success and splendor his Italian temper ended his career. He accused one of his aides, Francesco Pellegrino, of robbing him; Pellegrino, after suffering much torture, was found to be innocent; Rosso, in shame and remorse, swallowed poison and died in agony at the age of forty-six (1541).

Francis mourned him, but he had already found in Primaticcio an artist capable of continuing Rosso's work in the same style of voluptuous imagination. Primaticcio was a handsome youth of twenty-seven when he reached France in 1532. The King soon recognized his versatile ability as architect, sculptor, and painter; he gave him a staff of assistants, a good salary, and, later, the revenues of an abbey; so the contributions of the faithful were transformed into art that would possibly have shocked the monks. Primaticcio made designs for the royal tapestry works; carved a masterly chimney piece for Queen Eleonora's room at Fontainebleau, and repaid the Duchesse d'Étampes' patronage and protection by adorning her room in the château with paintings and stucco statuary. The paintings have died repeated deaths under restorations, but the statues remain in their glory; one stucco lady, raising her hands to a cornice, is among the fairest figures in French art. How could a king enamored of such demure shamelessness accept stern Calvinism in place of a Church that smiled tolerantly upon these charming nudes?

The demise of the royal satyr, and the accession of the stern Henry II, did not injure Primaticcio's status or bowdlerize his style. Now (1551–56), aided by Philibert Delorme and Niccolo dell'Abbate, he designed, painted, carved, and otherwise decorated the Gallery of Henry II at Fontainebleau. Here too the paintings have been ruined, but the grace of the female statues is alluring, and the end wall is a stately splendor of classic elements. Still finer, we are told (for it was destroyed in 1738), was the Gallery of Ulysses, which Primaticcio and his company adorned with 161 subjects from the *Odyssey*.

The château of Fontainebleau marked the triumph of the classic style in France. Francis filled its halls with sculptures and objects of art bought for him in Italy and reinforcing the classic message by their excellence. Meanwhile Sebastiano Serlio, who worked for a while at Fontainebleau, published his *Opere di architettura* (1548), which preached the Vitruvian classicism of his master Baldassare Petruzzi; it was at once translated into French by Jean Martin, who also translated Vitruvius (1547). From the School of Fontainebleau French artists trained under Rosso or Primaticcio scattered the classic norms and ideals through France; and these remained dominant there for centuries, along with the corresponding classic literary forms inaugurated by the Pléiade. Excited by Serlio and Vitruvius, French artists like Jacques A. du Cerceau, Jean Bullant, and Delorme went to Italy to study the remains of Roman architecture, and, returning, wrote treatises formulating classic ideas. Like Ronsard and Du Bellay, they condemned medieval styles as barbarous, and resolved to chasten matter into form. Through these men, their work, and their books, the architect emerged as an artist distinct from the master-mason, and standing high in the social scale. Italian artists were no longer needed in French building, for France now went beyond Italy to ancient Rome itself for architectural inspiration, and effected a superb synthesis of the classic orders with the traditions and climate of France.

In this milieu of thought and art the noblest civic building in France took form. Viewing the Louvre today from the left bank of the Seine, or standing in its majestic courts, or wandering day after day through this treasure house of the world, the spirit shrinks with awe at the immensity of the monument. If, in some universal devastation, only one building might be spared, we should choose this. Philip Augustus had raised its first form about 1191 as a fortress castle to guard Paris against invasion along the Seine. Charles V had added two new wings (1357), with an external staircase that may have suggested the gem at Blois. Finding this medieval structure, half palace and half prison, inadequate for his residence and entertaining, Francis had it torn down, and commissioned Pierre Lescot (1546) to raise in its place a château fit for a French Renaissance king. When, a year later, Francis died, Henry II bade the enterprise go on.

Lescot was a noble and a priest, Sieur de Clagny, Abbé of Clermont, canon of Notre Dame, painter, sculptor, architect. He it was who designed the rood loft in the church of St.-Germain l'Auxerrois (destroyed in 1745), and the palace that is now the Hôtel Carnavalet. In both of these tasks he enlisted the aid of his friend Jean Goujon for decorative sculpture; and when work on the new Louvre had made some progress he called upon Goujon to come and adorn it. In 1548 Lescot raised the western wing of the palaces that now enclose the Cour Carrée or Square Court of the Louvre. The style of the Italian Renaissance dictated the façade from ground to roof—exclusively, as Rabelais might say: three tiers of rectangular windows, the tiers separated by marble cornices, the windows separated by classic columns; three porches sustained by elegant classic pillars; only the sloping roof was French, and there too the moldings were of classic grace. The general aspect would have been too severe had not Goujon inserted statues in the niches of the porticoes, and carved exquisite reliefs in the pediments and beneath the cornices, and crowned the central projection with the emblem of Henry and Diana. Within this Lescot wing Goujon built the *Salle des Cariatides*—four stately females upholding a gallery for musicians; and it was again Goujon who decorated the vault of the great staircase that led to the royal chamber where slept the kings of France from Henry IV to Louis XIV. The work on the Louvre continued under Charles IX, Henry IV, Louis XIII and XIV, Napoleon I and III, always faithful to the style set by Lescot and Goujon, until today the spreading edifice is the congealed essence of 350 years of a civilization that ground the toil of the people into the splendors of art. Would the Louvre have been possible if the aristocracy had been just?

For Henry II and Diane de Poitiers Philibert Delorme created architectural Edens. As a youth Philibert studied and measured the remains of classic Rome; he loved them, but, back in France, he announced that henceforth French architecture must be French. His spirit of classic idolatry and French patriotism was precisely the program of the Pléiade. He designed the horseshoe stairway in the Cour des Adieux at Fontainebleau, and the fireplace and coffered ceiling in the Gallery of Henry II. For Diane he built at Anet (1548-53) a veritable city of palaces and formal gardens; there Cellini placed in a pediment his *Nymph of Fontainebleau,* and Goujon surpassed the Florentine with his group of Diana and her stag. Most of this costly paradise has gone to ruin; an unimpressive gateway remains in the court of the École des Beaux Arts in Paris. For the same triumphant mistress Delorme completed Chenonceaux—a little gift from her enamored King; it was Philip who conceived the idea of extending the palace across the Cher. When

Catherine de Médicis took the château from Diane, Delorme continued to labor there till the masterpiece was complete. For a time his too-mathematical style fell from favor, and he retired to write an encyclopedic *Treatise on Architecture*. In his old age he was called back to work by Catherine, and designed for her a new palace, the Tuileries (1564–70), which the Commune of 1871 destroyed. From all his patrons he received rich rewards. He became a priest, and held several fruitful benefices. He died (1570) as a canon of Notre Dame, and provided in his will for two illegitimate children.[9]

Jean Bullant completed the brilliant trio of architects who adorned France in the reigns of Catherine's husband and sons. In his thirties, at Écouen, he made his reputation by designing for Anne de Montmorency a château quite perfect in its classic lines. In his sixties he succeeded Delorme in building the Tuileries, and continued working till his death—*de jour en jour en apprenant mourant,* as he said—"From day to day, while learning dying."

It is the fashion to regret the importation of Italian styles into French building, and to suggest that the native Gothic, left undeflected by that influence, might have evolved into a civic architecture more congenial to French grace than the relatively rigorous lines of the classic orders. But Gothic was dying of old age, perhaps of senile excess and Flamboyant old lace; it had run its course. The Greek emphasis on restraint, simplicity, stability, and clear structural lines was well suited to temper French exuberance into disciplined maturity. Some medieval quaintness was sacrificed, but that too had had its day, and seems picturesque precisely because it died. As French Renaissance architecture developed its own national character, mingling dormer windows and sloping roofs with columns, capitals, and pediments, it gave France for three centuries a style of building that was the envy of Western Europe; and now that it too is passing away we perceive that it was beautiful.

2. *The Ancillary Arts*

A thousand artist-artisans adorned French life in this vivacious age of François Premier and Henri Deux. Woodworkers carved the choir stalls of Beauvais, Amiens, Auch, and Brou, and dared to decorate Gothic structures with a Renaissance play of fauns, sibyls, bacchants, satyrs, even, now and then, a Venus, a Cupid, a Ganymede. Or they made—for our mad pursuit— tables, chairs, frames, *prie-dieu,* bedsteads, and cabinets, carving them with perhaps a plethora of ornament, and sometimes inlaying them with metal, ivory, or precious stones. The metalworkers, now at the crest of their excellence, glorified utensils and weapons with damascening or engraving, and designed grilles—poems in iron tracery—for chapels, sanctuaries, gardens, and tombs, or made such hinges as those on the west doors of Notre Dame, so beautiful that piety ascribed them to angelic hands. Cellini, who had little praise left for others after meeting his own needs, confessed that in making church plate—or such domestic plate as Jean Duret engraved for Henry II— the French goldsmiths had "attained a degree of perfection nowhere else to be found." [10] The stained glass in Margaret of Austria's chapel at Brou, or in St.-Étienne's at Beauvais, or in St.-Étienne-du-Mont at Paris, proclaimed a glory not yet departed. At Fontainebleau Francis established a factory in which tapestries were woven in one piece, instead of being made, as before, in separate sections, then sewn together; and gold and silver threads were mingled opulently with dyed silk and wool. After 1530 the patterns and subjects of French tapestry ceased to be Gothic and chivalric, and followed Renaissance designs and themes from Italy.

Renaissance motives dominated ceramics in the majolica of Lyons, the faïence of southern France, the enamels of Limoges. Léonard Limousin and others painted, with brilliant fused enamel colors, elegant forms of plants and animals, gods and men, on copper basins, vases, ewers, cups, saltcellars, and other lowly utensils raised to works of art. Here too Francis took a hand, made Léonard head of the royal manufactory of enamels at Limoges, and crowned him with the title of *valet de chambre du roi*. Léonard specialized in painting portraits in enamel on copper plates; an excellent sample— portraying Francis himself—is in the Metropolitan Museum at New York; many more are in the Apollo Gallery of the Louvre, quietly attesting a golden day.

Portraiture was a fully developed art in France before the Italians came. Which of the Italians in France could have bettered the portrait of Guillaume de Montmorency painted by an anonymous master about 1520, and now in the Lyons Museum? *Voilà un homme!*—this is no pictorial compliment, it is a man. Rosso, Primaticcio, dell'Abbate, and others in the School of Fontainebleau brought to France what they had learned from Raphael, Perino del Vaga, Giovanni da Udine, or Giulio Romano, in decorating pilasters, cornices, ceilings . . . with "grotesques" or playful figures of cherubs, children, spirals, arabesques, and plants. An unnamed member of the school painted the *Diane de Poitiers* now in the Worcester, Massachusetts, Museum—sitting at her toilette, dressed in a diadem. After 1545 many Flemish painters, including Brueghel the Elder, came to France to study the work at Fontainebleau. But their own style was too deeply rooted to yield to the Italian influence; the realistic vigor of their portraiture prevailed over the feminine grace of the heirs of Raphael.

One Flemish family in France almost constituted a school by itself. Jean (Jehan, Jehannet, Janet) Clouet was attached to the court of Francis at Tours and Paris; all the world knows the portrait he painted of the King about 1525, now in the Louvre: proud, conceited, happy royalty just before a fall. Jean's son François Clouet succeeded him as court painter, and recorded the dignitaries of four reigns in chalk or oil. His *Henry II* surpasses his father's *Francis I*: we are astonished to see the chasm between the gay gallant and the somber son; we can understand how this man could sanction the *chambre ardente* for the persecution of heresy, though we do not see in the almost Borgian face any hint of his lasting devotion to Diane. For a time Corneille de Lyon, operating a rival *atelier*, challenged the Clouets in such portraits as that of Maréchal Bonnivet, lover of Marguerite. But no contemporary in France could equal the gallery of portraits that François Clouet made of Catherine de Médicis, Francis II, Mary Queen of Scots, Elizabeth of Valois, Philip II, Marguerite, future wife of Henry IV, and Charles IX as a youth—too lovely to forecast the frightened King of the Massacre. Flemish realism and veracity are in these portraits tempered with French delicacy, precision, and vivacity; the tone is subdued, the line is accurate and confident, the elements of a complex character are caught and unified; only Holbein's England would enjoy such a colorful historian.

Sculpture was a handmaiden to architecture, and yet it was the sculptors who made the architecture brilliant. Now, indeed, French sculpture poured forth masterpieces only second to those that Michelangelo and others were then cutting out of Carrara. Lordly tombs were modeled: of Louis XII and Anne of Brittany by Giovanni di Giusto Betti (Saint-Denis); of two Cardinals of Amboise by Roland Leroux and Jean Goujon (Rouen); and of Louis de Brézé, Diane's husband, in the same cathedral, of uncertain authorship. The Rouen tombs seem too ornate to befit mortality, but the cardinals are almost revived as unidealized strong administrators to whom religion was an incident in statesmanship. Francis I, his wife Claude, and his daughter Charlotte were buried in Saint-Denis in a tomb of Renaissance style designed by Delorme, with superb sculptures by Pierre Bontemps. Near by is a little *chef-d'oeuvre* by Bontemps—a funerary urn for the heart of the King. French sculptors no longer needed Italian tutelage to inherit the classic art of Rome.

Jean Goujon inherited at least the classic grace. We hear of him first in 1540, listed as a "stonecutter and mason" in Rouen. There he cut the columns supporting the organ in the church of St.-Maclou, and carved statues for the tombs of the Cardinals, and perhaps for that of Brézé. He adorned the rood screen in the church of St.-Germain l'Auxerrois with sculptures now partially preserved in the Louvre, and recalling Hellenistic reliefs in the rhythmic elegance of their lines. Goujon's characteristic quality of feminine grace approached perfection in the *Nymphs* that he contributed to the "Fountain of the Innocents" designed by Lescot (1547); Bernini thought these figures the most beautiful works of art in Paris. We have noted Goujon's *Diana and the Stag* at Anet, and his sculptures on the Louvre. His pagan deities and his idealization of the female form suggest, for France, the triumph of the Renaissance over the Reformation, of classical over Gothic ideas, of woman over her medieval detractors. However, tradition describes Goujon as a Huguenot. About 1542, as penance for attending a Lutheran sermon, he was condemned to walk through the streets of Paris in his shirt, and to witness the burning of a Protestant preacher.[11] Toward 1562 he left France for Italy. He died at Bologna before 1568, in obscurity hardly merited by the man who had brought to its culmination the art of the Renaissance in France.

III. PIETER BRUEGHEL: 1520-69

Except for Brueghel and tapestry this was a fallow age in Lowland art. Painting fluctuated between emulation of the Italians—in refined technique, rich coloring, classic mythology, nude women, and Roman architectural backgrounds —and the native flair for realistic portrayal of eminent persons and ordinary things. Patronage came not only from the court, the Church, and the aristocracy, but increasingly from rich merchants who offered their stout forms and overflowing jowls to the admiration of posterity, and liked to see reflected in painting the domestic scenes and rural landscapes of their actual life. A sense of humor, sometimes of the grotesque, replaced the lofty mood of the Italian masters. Michelangelo criticized what seemed to him a lack of discrimination and nobility in Flemish art: "They paint in Flanders only to deceive the external eye, things that gladden you . . . the grass of the fields, the shadows of the trees, and bridges and rivers . . . and little objects here and there . . . without care in selecting and rejecting." [12] To Michelangelo art was the selection of significance for the illustration of nobility, not the indiscriminate representation of reality; his solemn nature, encased in his irremovable boots and his misanthropic isolation, was immune to the glory of green fields and the affections of the hearth.

For our part we make a grateful bow to Joachim Patinir, if only for the Leonardesque landscape in his *St. Jerome;* to Joos van Cleve for his lovely portrait of Eleanor of Portugal; to Bernaert van Orley for his *Holy Family* in the Prado, his tapestry designs, and his stained glass in Brussels' St.-Gudule; to Lucas van Leyden for crowding so many masterly engravings and woodcuts into his thirty-nine years; to Jan van Scorel for the *Magdalen* cherishing the vase of ointments from which she had bathed the feet of Christ; and to Anthonis Mor for his forceful portraits of Alva, Cardinal Granvelle, Philip II, Mary Tudor, and, not least, himself.

Note how the painting craft in the Netherlands ran in families. Joos van Cleve handed down some of his skill to his son Cornelis, who painted some fine portraits before going mad. Jan Massys, inheriting the studio of his father Quentin, painted by preference nudes like *Judith* and *Suzanna and the Elders;* his son

Quentin Massys II carried on the trade, while his brother Cornelis took his art to England and painted Henry VIII in old age, bloated and hideous. Pieter Pourbus and his son Frans painted portraits and pieties at Bruges, and Frans's son Frans Pourbus II painted portraits at Paris and Mantua. And there were Pieter "Droll" Brueghel, his painter wife, his painter mother-in-law, his sons Pieter "Hell" Brueghel and Jan "Velvet" Brueghel, his painter grandsons, his painter great-grandsons. . . .

Pieter Brueghel the Elder, whose fame is among the inescapable fashions of our time, may have derived his name from either of two villages named Brueghel in Brabant; one of them was near Hertogenbosch, where Hieronymus Bosch had been born, and in whose churches Pieter might have seen several paintings of the man who influenced his work only less than nature itself. At twenty-five (c. 1545) he migrated to Antwerp, and was apprenticed to Pieter Coecke, whose landscape woodcuts may have helped to form the young painter's interest in fields, woods, waters, and sky. This lesser Pieter had begotten a daughter, Maria, whom Brueghel toddled in his arms as a child, and whom he later made his wife. In 1552 he followed the current custom of his craft and went to study painting in Italy. He returned to Antwerp with a sketchbook thick with Italian landscapes, but with no visible Italian influence on his technique; to the end he practically ignored the subtle modeling, *chiaroscuro*, and *coloratura* of the southern masters. Back in Antwerp, he lived with a housekeeper-concubine, whom he promised to marry when she stopped lying; he recorded her lies with notches cut into a stick; and having no stick for his own sins, he renounced her when the notches overflowed. In his middle forties (1563) he married Maria Coecke, now seventeen, and obeyed her summons to move to Brussels. He had only six years of life left to him.

Though his paintings led to his being dubbed "Peasant Brueghel," he was a man of culture, who read Homer, Virgil, Horace, Ovid, Rabelais, probably Erasmus.[13] Karel Mander, the Dutch Vasari, described him as "tranquil and orderly, speaking little, yet amusing in company, delighting to horrify people . . . with tales of ghosts and banshees";[14] hence, perhaps, his other sobriquet, "Droll Brueghel." His sense of humor leaned to satire, but he tempered this with sympathy. A contemporary engraving shows him heavily bearded, with a face bearing lines of serious thought.[15] At times he followed Bosch in seeing life as a heedless hurrying of most souls to hell. In the *Dulle Griet* he pictured hell as hideously and confusedly as Bosch himself; and in *The Triumph of Death* he visioned death not as a natural sleep of exhausted forms, but as a ghastly cutting off of limbs and life—skeletons attacking kings, cardinals, knights, and peasants with arrows, hatchets, stones, and scythes—criminals beheaded or hanged or bound to a wheel—skulls and corpses riding in a cart; here is one more variant of that "Dance of Death" which flits through the art of this somber age.

Brueghel's religious pictures carry on the serious mood. They have neither the grandeur nor the light grace of Italian pictures; they merely reinterpret the Biblical story in terms of Flemish climate, physiognomy, and dress. They rarely reveal religious feeling; most of them are excuses for painting crowds. Even the faces in them carry no feeling; the people who jostle one another to see Christ carry His cross seem heedless of His suffering, but only anxious to get a good view. Some of the pictures are Biblical parables, like *The Sower;* some others, following Bosch, take proverbs for their themes. *The Blind Leading the Blind* shows a succession of dull-eyed peasants, cruelly ugly, following one another into a ditch; and *Netherlandish Proverbs* illustrates, in one teeming picture, nearly a hundred old saws, including some of Rabelaisian fragrance.

Brueghel's major interest was in peasant crowds, and landscapes covering with their indifferent beneficence or maleficence the futile, forgivable activities of men. Perhaps he thought there was safety in crowds; there he need not individualize the faces or model the flesh. He refused to picture a person posing for art or history; he preferred to show men, women, and children walking, running, jumping, dancing, playing games, in all the varied animation and naturalness of life. He harked back to the scenes of his childhood, and delighted to contemplate, to join, the fun and feasting, music and mating, of the peasantry. He and a friend, on several occasions, disguised themselves as farmers, attended village fairs and weddings, and—pretending to be relatives—brought presents to bridegroom and bride.[16] Doubtless on these outings Pieter took his sketchbook, for among his extant drawings are many of rustic figures and events. He had no taste for, nor commissions from, the aristocrats that Mor and Titian found it so profitable to portray; he painted only simple people, and even his dogs were mongrel curs that could be found in any city alley or rural hut. He knew the bitter side of peasant life, and sometimes visioned it as a multitudinous confusion of fools. But he loved to paint the games of country children, the dances of their elders, the riot of their weddings. In *The Land of Cockayne* peasants exhausted with toil or love or drink sprawl out on the grass dreaming of Utopia. It is the peasant, Brueghel seems to say, who knows how to play and sleep as well as how to work and mate and die.

Against death he saw but one consolation—that it is an integral part of that Nature which he accepted in all its forms of beauty and terror, growth and decay and renewal. The landscape redeems the man; the absurdity of the part is pardoned in the majesty of the whole. Heretofore—excepting Altdorfer—landscapes had been painted as backgrounds and appendages to human figures and events: Brueghel made the landscape itself the picture, the men in it mere incidents. In *The Fall of Icarus* the sky, the ocean, the mountains, and the sun have absorbed the attention of the painter, and of the participants; Icarus is two unnoticed legs ridiculously sinking into the sea; and in *The Storm* man is hardly visible, lost and helpless in the war and power of the elements.

The art and philosophy of Brueghel culminate in the five paintings that remain of a series planned to illustrate the moods of the year. *The Wheat Harvest* schematically pictures the cutting and stacking of the sheaves, the workers lunching or napping beneath the visible heat and stillness of the summer air. In *The Hay Harvest* girls and boys bear the autumn fruit of the fields in baskets on their heads, a farmer sharpens his scythe, sturdy women rake the hay, men pitch it to the top of the wagon load, the horses champ their meal in a resting interval. *The Return of the Herd* heralds winter--the skies darkling, the cattle guided back to their stalls. Finest of the series is *The Hunters in the Snow:* roofs and ground are white; dwellings range in an amazing perspective along the plains and hills; men skate, play hockey, fall on the ice; hunters and their dogs start out to capture food; the trees are bare, but birds in the branches promise spring. *The Gloomy Day* is winter scowling its farewell. In these paintings Brueghel reached his peak, and set a precedent for the snowy landscapes of future Lowland art.

Only a painter or a connoisseur can judge these pictures in their artistic quality and technique. Brueghel seems content to give his figures two dimensions, does not bother to mingle shadow with their substance; he lets our imagination, if it must, add a third dimension to his two. He is too interested in crowds to care about individuals; he makes nearly all his peasants alike, ungainly lumps of flesh. He does not pretend to be a realist, except in gross. He puts so many people or episodes into one painting that unity seems sacrificed; but he catches the unconscious unity of a village, a crowd, a wave of life.

What does he mean to say? Is he merely jesting, laughing at man as a grotesque "forked radish," and at life as a silly strutting to decay? He enjoyed the lusty swing of the peasants' dance, sympathized with their toil, and looked with indulgent humor on their drunken sleep. But he never recovered from Bosch. Like that unsaintly Jerome, he took sardonic pleasure in depicting the bitter side of the human comedy—the cripples and criminals, the defeated or obscene, the inexorable victory of death. He seems to have searched for ugly peasants; he caricatures them, never lets them smile or laugh; if he gives their crude faces any expression it is one of dull indifference, of sensitivity beaten out by the blows of life.[17] He was impressed and hurt by the apathy with which the fortunate bear the misery of the unfortunate, the haste and relief with which the living forget the dead. He was oppressed by the vast perspective of nature—that immensity of sky under which all human events seem drowned in insignificance, and virtue and vice, growth and decay, nobility and ignominy alike seem lost in a vast and indiscriminate futility, and man is swallowed up in the landscape of the world.

We do not know if this was Brueghel's real philosophy, or merely the playfulness of his art. Nor do we know why he gave up the battle so soon, dying at forty-nine (1569); perhaps more years would have softened his wrath. He bequeathed to his wife an ambiguous picture, *The Merry Way to the Gallows*, a masterly composition in fresh greens and distant blues, peasants dancing near the village gibbet, and, perched on this, a magpie, emblem of a chattering tongue.

IV. CRANACH AND THE GERMANS

German ecclesiastical architecture went in hiding during the Reformation. No new churches were raised to art as well as piety; many churches were left unfinished; many were pulled down, and princely castles were put together with their stones. Protestant churches dedicated themselves to a stern simplicity; Catholic churches, as if in defiance, ran to excessive ornament while the Renaissance moved into the baroque.

Civic and palace architecture replaced cathedrals as dukes replaced bishops and the state enveloped the Church. Some picturesque civic structures of this period were casualties of the second World War: the Althaus in Brunswick, the House of the Butchers' Guild at Hildesheim, the Renaissance-style Rathaus or Town Hall of Nymegen. The most pretentious architecture of this and the next age took the form of immense castles for the territorial princes: Dresden Castle, which cost the people 100,000 florins ($2,500,000?); the palace of Duke Christopher at Stuttgart, so lavish in fixtures and furniture that the city magistrates warned the Duke that the luxury of his court was scandalously in contrast with the poverty of his people; and the vast Heidelberg Castle, begun in the thirteenth century, rebuilt in Renaissance fashion in 1556–63, and partly destroyed in the second World War.

The art crafts retained their excellence in the service of princes, nobles, merchants, and financiers. Cabinetmakers, woodcutters, ivory-cutters, engravers, miniaturists, textile workers, ironworkers, potters, goldsmiths, armorers, jewelers—all had the old medieval skills, though they tended to sacrifice taste and form to complexity of ornament. Many painters drew designs for woodcuts as carefully as if they were making portraits of kings; and woodcutters like Hans Lützeburger of Basel labored with the devotion of a Dürer. The goldsmiths of Nuremberg, Munich, and Vienna were at the top of their line; Wenzel Jamnitzer might have challenged Cellini. About 1547 German artists began to paint glass with enamel colors; in this way vessels and windows took on crude but rich designs, and the prosperous bourgeois could have his likeness fused into the windowpanes of his home.

German sculptors kept their preference for metal statuary and reliefs. The sons of Peter Vischer carried on his craft: Peter the Younger cast a bronze plaque of *Orpheus and Eurydice;* Hans designed a handsome *Apollo Fountain* for the court of the Nuremberg town hall; Paul is usually credited with a pretty figure in wood, known as *The Nuremberg Madonna.* Peter Flötner of Nuremberg cast excellent reliefs of Envy, Justice, Saturn, and the Muse of Dance. One of the most delightful objects in the Louvre is a bust, by Joachim Deschler, of Otto Heinrich, Count Palatine, six and a half inches high, and nearly as wide in its corpulence, with a face formed by years of *bon appétit;* this is German humor at its broadest.

The glory of German art continued to be in painting. Holbein equaled Dürer, Cranach followed on their heels, and Baldung Grien, Altdorfer, and Amberger formed a creditable second line. Hans Baldung Grien made his fame with an altarpiece for the cathedral of Freiburg-im-Breisgau; but more attractive is *The Madonna with the Parrot*—a buxom Teuton with golden hair, and a parrot pecking at her cheeks. Christopher Amberger painted some elegant portraits; the Lille Museum has his *Charles V,* sincere, intelligent, incipiently fanatical; the Chicago Art Institute's *Portrait of a Man* is a finely chiseled, gentle face. Albrecht Altdorfer stands out in this minor group by the richness of his landscapes. In his *St. George* the knight and the dragon are almost unseen in an entourage of crowding trees; even *The Battle of Arbela* loses the warring hosts in an abundance of towers, mountains, waters, clouds, and sun. These, and the *Rest on the Flight to Egypt,* are among the first true landscapes in modern painting.

Lucas Cranach the Elder took his name from his native town, Kronach, in Upper Franconia. We know almost nothing further of him till his appointment, at the age of thirty-two, as court painter to Elector Frederick the Wise at Wittenberg (1504). He kept his position at the Saxon court, there or a Weimar, for nearly fifty years. He met Luther, liked him, pictured him again and again, and illustrated some of the Reformer's writings with caricatures of the popes; however, he made portraits also of Catholic notables like the Duke of Alva and Archbishop Albrecht of Mainz. He had a good business head, turned his studio into a factory of portraits and religious paintings, sold books and drugs on the side, became burgomaster of Wittenberg in 1565, and died full of money and years.

The Italian influence had by this time reached Wittenberg. It appears in the grace of Cranach's religious pictures, more visibly in his mythologies, most in his nudes. Now, as in Italy, the pagan pantheon competes with Mary, Christ, and the saints, but German humor enlivens the traditional by making fun of safely dead gods. In Cranach's *Judgment of Paris* the Trojan seducer goes to sleep while the shivering beauties wait for him to wake and judge. In *Venus and Cupid* the goddess of love is shown in her usual nudity, except for an enormous hat—as if Cranach were slyly suggesting that desire is so formed by custom that it can be stilled by an unwonted accessory. Nevertheless Venus proved popular, and Cranach, with help, issued her in a dozen forms to shine in Frankfurt, Leningrad, the Borghese Gallery, the Metropolitan Museum of Art. . . . In Frankfurt she hides her charms revealingly behind a dozen gossamer threads; these serve again for the *Lucretia* in Berlin, who cheerfully prepares to redeem her honor with a bare bodkin. The same lady posed for *The Nymph of the Spring* (New York), lying on a bed of green leaves beside a pool. In the Geneva Museum she becomes Judith, no longer nude, but dressed to kill, holding her sword over Holofernes' severed head, which winks humorously at its mischance. Finally the lady, re-bared, becomes Eve in *Das Paradies* at Vienna, in *Adam and Eve* at Dresden, in *Eve and the Serpent* in Chicago, where a handsome stag joins and names her party. Nearly all these nudes have some quality that saves them from eroticism—an impish humor, a warmth of color, an Italian finesse of line, or an unpatriotic slenderness in the female figures; here was a brave attempt to reduce the *Frau*.

The portraits that poured from Cranach's hand or aides are more interesting than his stereotyped nudes, and some rival Holbein's. *Anna Cuspinian* is realism tempered with delicacy, gorgeous robes, and a balloon hat; the husband, Johannes Cuspinian, sat for a still finer portrait—all the idealism of a young humanist reflected in the meditative eyes and symbolized in the book fondly clasped. A hundred dignitaries were preserved in paint or chalk in this popular *atelier*, but none so well deserves survival as the child *Prince of Saxony* (Washington), all innocence and gentleness and golden curls. At the other side of life is the portrait of Dr. Johannes Schöner, terrible in features, noble in artistry. And here and there, in Cranach's work, are magnificent animals, all pedigreed, and stags so natural that—claimed a friend —"dogs barked when they saw them." [18]

Cranach might have been greater had he not succeeded so soon and well. The multiplication of his patrons divided his genius; he had no time to give all of it to any one task. Inevitably, as his eighty-one years rolled by, he tired and slacked down; the drawing, once as fine as Dürer's, became careless, details were shirked, the same faces, nudes, and trees were repeated to lifelessness. In the end we have to agree with the judgment passed on the early Cranach by the aging Dürer—that Lucas could depict the features but not the soul. [19]

In 1550, when he was seventy-eight, he painted his own portrait: a stout councilor and merchant rather than painter and engraver, with powerful square head, stately white beard, expansive nose, eyes full of pride and character. Three years later he surrendered his flesh to time. He left behind him three sons, all artists: John Lucas, Hans, and Lucas the Younger, whose *Sleeping Hercules* transmitted a theme from Rabelais to Swift by showing the giant peacefully ignoring the darts with which the pigmies around him barely pierce his ectoderm. Perhaps Lucas the Elder ignored as serenely the pricks of those who condemned him for bourgeois ideals and unconscientious haste; and under the tombstone that bears the ambiguous compliment *Celerrimus pictor*—fastest painter—he sleeps well.

With him the great age of German painting passed. The basic cause of the decline was more probably the intensity of religious dispute than the Protestant repudiation of religious imagery. Possibly a moral letdown coarsened German painting after 1520; nudes began to play a leading role; and even in Biblical pictures painters ran to themes like Suzanna and the Elders, Potiphar's wife tempting Joseph, or Bathsheba in her bath. For two centuries after the death of Cranach German art receded in the backwash of theology and war.

V. THE TUDOR STYLE: 1517–58

The reign of Henry VIII began with a Gothic masterpiece in the chapel of Henry VII, and closed with the Renaissance architecture of royal palaces; the change of style aptly reflected the conquest of the Church by the state. The attack of the government on the bishops, the monasteries, and ecclesiastical revenues put an end to English ecclesiastical architecture for almost a hundred years.

Henry VII, anticipating death, had allotted £140,000 ($14,000,000?) to build in Westminster Abbey a Lady Chapel to contain his tomb. It is a masterpiece not of construction but of decoration, from the cenotaph itself to the intricate stone skein of the fan vault, which has been called "the most wonderful work of masonry ever put together by the hand of man." [20] As the chapel is Gothic in plan and Renaissance in adornment, we have here the beginning of the Tudor or Florid Style. Henry VIII, as a young humanist, was readily won to classical architectural forms. He and Wolsey brought several Italian artists into England. One of them, Pietro Torrigiano, was commissioned to design the paternal tomb. Upon the sarcophagus of white marble and black stone the Florentine sculptor laid lavish decoration in carvings or gilt bronze: plump *putti*, floral wreaths of airy grace, reliefs of the Virgin and divers saints, angels sitting atop the tomb and extending pretty feet into space, and, over the whole, the recumbent figures of Henry VII and his Queen Elizabeth. This was such sculpture as England had never seen before, and in England it has never been surpassed. Here, said Francis Bacon, the parsimonious King, who had pinched pennies to spend pounds, "dwelleth more richly dead than he did alive in any of his palaces." [21]

Henry VIII was not the man to allow anyone to be more sumptuously buried than himself. In 1518 he contracted to pay Torrigiano £2,000 for a tomb "more greater by the fourth part" than his father's.[22] This was never finished, for the artist as well as the King had a royal temper; Torrigiano left England in a huff (1519), and when he returned he did no more work on the second tomb. Instead he designed for Henry VII's chapel a high altar, reredos, and baldachin, which Cromwell's men destroyed in 1643. In 1521 Torrigiano departed for Spain.

The mortal comedy was resumed in 1524 when Wolsey commissioned another Florentine, Benedetto da Rovezzano, to build him a tomb in St. George's Chapel at Windsor, "the design whereof," wrote Lord Herbert of Cherbury, "was so glorious that it exceeded far that of Henry VII."[23] When the Cardinal fell he begged the King to let him keep at least the effigy for a humbler tomb in York; Henry refused, and confiscated the whole as a receptacle for himself; he bade the artists replace Wolsey's figure with his own; but religion and marriage distracted him, and the funereal monument was never completed. Charles I wished to be buried in it, but a hostile Parliament sold the decoration piece by piece, until only the black marble sarcophagus remained, to serve at last (1810) as part of Nelson's shrine in St. Paul's.

Aside from these labors, and the glorious wood screen and stalls and stained glass and vault of King's College Chapel at Cambridge, the memorable architecture of this age was dedicated to glorifying the country houses of the aristocracy into fairy palaces rising amid the fields and woods of England. The architects were English, but a dozen Italians were enlisted for the decoration. An imposingly wide façade in mixed Gothic and Renaissance, a turreted gateway leading into a court, a spacious hall for crowded festivities, a massive staircase, usually in carved wood, rooms adorned with murals or tapestry and lighted with lattice windows or oriels, and, around the buildings, a garden, a deer park, and, beyond, a hunting ground—this was the English nobleman's skeptical forestalling of paradise.

The most famous of these Tudor manor houses was Hampton Court, built by Wolsey (1515) for himself, and bequeathed in terror to his King (1525). Not one architect but a coalition of English master builders created it, basically in Perpendicular Gothic and on a medieval plan, with moat and towers and crenellated walls; Giovanni da Maiano added a Renaissance touch in terra-cotta roundels on the façade. The Duke of Württemberg, visiting England in 1592, called Hampton Court the most magnificent palace in the world.[24] Only less sumptuous were Sutton Place in Surrey, built (1521–27) for Sir Richard Weston, and Nonesuch Palace, begun for Henry VIII in 1538 on an imperial scale. "He invited thither," says an old description, "the most excellent artificers, architects, sculptors, and statuaries of different nations, Italians, Frenchmen, Hollanders, and native Englishmen; and these presented a marvelous example of their art in the decoration of the palace and both within and without adorned it with statues which here recall in literal reproduction the ancient works of Rome, and elsewhere surpass them in excellence." [25] Two hundred and thirty men were constantly employed on this palace, which was intended to outshine the Chambord and Fontaine-bleau of Francis I. Seldom had English kings been so rich, or the English people so poor. Henry died before Nonesuch could be finished. Elizabeth made it her favorite residence; Charles II gave it to his mistress Lady Castle-maine (1670), who had it pulled down, and sold the parts, as the only way to transform a liability into an asset.

VI. HOLBEIN THE YOUNGER: 1497–1543

How futile are words before a work of art! Each art successfully resists translation into any other medium; it has its own inalienable quality, which must speak for itself or not at all. History can only record the masters and the masterpieces; it cannot convey them. To sit silently before Holbein's pic-ture of his wife and children is better than a biography. However . . .

He was more fortunate in his parentage than in his time. His father was among the leading painters in Augsburg. From him Hans learned the ele-ments of the art, and from Hans Burgkmair something of Italian grace and modeling. In 1512 he painted four altar panels now in the Augsburg Gallery —middling enough, but astonishingly good for a lad of fifteen. Two years later he and his brother Ambrose, also a painter, decamped to Basel. Perhaps the father had insisted too much on his own—still Gothic—style; perhaps there was not enough educated money in Augsburg to support more than a few artists; in any case youth and genius seldom love home. In Basel the lads discovered that freedom is a trial. Hans illustrated various volumes, in-cluding Erasmus' *Praise of Folly;* he did some rough painter's work, made a signboard for a schoolmaster, and decorated a table top with lively inci-dents from the story of St. Nobody—that handy nonentity who was charged with every anonymous mischief, and never said a word in his own defense. The skill shown in this work earned Hans a fruitful commission—to paint portraits of the burgomaster Jakob Meyer and his wife (1517). The fame of these portraits traveled; Jakob Hertenstein called Holbein to Lucerne, and there Hans frescoed the façade and walls of the patron's home, and painted that portrait of Benedict Hertenstein which is now in the Metropolitan Museum in New York. From Lucerne he may have passed into Italy; his work henceforth revealed Italian influence in anatomical accuracy, architec-tural backgrounds, and the management of light. When he returned to Basel, aged twenty-two, he set up his own studio, and married a widow (1519). In that year his brother died and in 1524 their father.

German realism mingled with Romanesque architecture and classic ornament in the religious pictures that Holbein now produced. Startling is the
realism—echoing Mantegna—of *Christ in the Tomb*: the body all bone and
skin, the eyes ghastly open, the hair disheveled, the mouth agape in a last effort to breathe; this seems irrevocable death, and no wonder Dostoievski
said the picture could destroy a man's religious faith.[26] About this time
Holbein painted murals for the hall of the Grand Council in Basel. The councilors were pleased, and one of them commissioned him to provide an altarpiece for a Carthusian monastery. This *Passion of Christ* suffered in the
iconoclastic riots of 1529, but two shutters were saved, and were presented
to the cathedral at Freiburg-im-Breisgau. They borrow much from Baldung
Grien, but they have their own power in the remarkable play of the light
that emanates from the Child. In 1522 the town clerk of Basel ordered another altarpiece; for this placidly beautiful *Madonna*, now preserved in the
Kunstmuseum of Solothurn, Holbein used his wife and son as models—the
wife then a woman of modest comeliness, not yet touched by tragedy. Probably near this time [27] he produced his religious masterpiece, *The Virgin and
Child with the Family of Burgomaster Meyer*—splendid in composition, line,
and color, and intense in feeling; we understand more sympathetically the
Burgomaster's prayer to the Madonna when we learn that at the time of this
painting the two sons pictured at his feet, and one of the two wives kneeling at the right, were dead.

But the fees for such religious pictures were small in proportion to the
care and labor they required. Portraits were more lucrative, and there was
a growing family to support. In 1519 Holbein painted the young scholar
Bonifacius Amerbach—a noble face, in which idealism survives a penetrating
view of the world. About 1522 he painted the great printer Froben—a man
dedicated, disturbed, creatively worn out by life. Through Froben, Holbein
came to know Erasmus; and in 1523 he painted two of his many portraits of
the saddened humanist. In the three-quarters portrait (in the Earl of Radnor's Collection at Salisbury) the artist, now in the fullness of his powers,
caught the soul of a man who had lived too long; illness and Luther had
deepened the lines in the face, the melancholy in the eyes. The profile in the
Basel Kunstsammlung shows him calmer and more alive; the nose advancing
to battle like a gladiator's sword; perhaps the manuscript under the pen is a
draft of the *De libero arbitrio* (1524) with which he was entering the lists
against Luther. Probably in 1524 Holbein painted Erasmus again, in the best
portrait of all, which hangs in the Louvre; seeing that profound and chastened face one thinks of Nisard's perceptive comment—that Erasmus was
one of those *dont la gloire a été de comprendre beaucoup et d'affirmer peu*—
"whose glory it has been to understand much and to affirm little." [28]

About 1523 Holbein painted himself, now twenty-six, and seemingly prosperous; but the cold glance suggests some fighting resentment of life's buffetings. Tradition discredits him with a moderate addiction to drink and women, and represents him as unhappy with his wife. Apparently he shared some Lutheran views; his woodcuts of *The Dance of Death* (*c.* 1525) satirized the clergy—but even the clergy did that in those days. The series showed Death dogging the steps of every man, woman, or class—Adam, Eve, the Emperor, a noble, a physician, a monk, a priest, a pope, a millionaire, an astrologer, a duchess, a jester, a gambler, a thief—all en route to the Last Judgment; it is as powerful a work as any of Dürer's in this medium. Aside from this masterpiece of drawing, and the *Meyer Madonna*, Holbein is without visible piety. Perhaps he imbibed some skepticism from Erasmus and the Basel humanists.[29] He was more interested in anatomy than in religion.

The Reformation, though he presumably favored it, ruined his market in Basel. No more religious pictures were asked of him. Payments on the paintings for the council hall were suspended. Rich men, frightened by the Peasants' War, retreated into privacy and parsimony, and thought the time unpropitious for portraits. "Here the arts are freezing," wrote Erasmus from Basel in 1526.[30] He gave Holbein letters of introduction to friends in Antwerp and London, and Holbein, leaving his family at home, sought fortune in the north. He visited Quentin Massys, and doubtless they exchanged notes about Erasmus. From Antwerp he crossed to England. Erasmus' letter assured him a cordial welcome from Thomas More, who gave him a place in his Chelsea home; and there he painted (1526) the portrait of More that is now in the Frick Gallery in New York. To the hindsight of the historian the tense and half-somber eyes foreshadow the devotion and tenacity of the martyr; to the insight of an artist the wonder will be in the fur and folds of the sleeve. In 1527 Holbein painted *Thomas More and His Family*—the oldest known group picture in transalpine secular art.

Late in 1528 Holbein, having made some pounds and shillings, returned to Basel, gave Erasmus a copy of *More and His Family*, and rejoined his wife. Now he painted one of his greatest, most honest pictures, showing his own family with a realism unsparing to himself. Each of the three faces is sad: the girl resigned, almost hopeless; the boy gazing up plaintively at his mother; she looking upon them with grief and affection profoundly mirrored in her eyes—the grief of a wife who has lost the love of her husband, the affection of a mother whose children are her only tie to life. Three years after painting this masterly self-indictment, Holbein left his family again.

During this stay in Basel he painted another portrait of Froben, and made six more of Erasmus, not as searchingly profound as those of 1523-24. The town council renewed his commission to fresco its chambers, but, yielding to the triumphant iconoclasts, it condemned all religious pictures, and ruled that "God has cursed all those who make them." [81] Commissions fell, and in 1532 Holbein returned to England.

There he painted portraits so plentifully that most of the figures dominating the English scene in those turbulent years are still alive by the magic of Holbein's hand. In the Queen's Library at Windsor are eighty-seven sketches in charcoal or chalk, some for cartoons, most of them for portraits; apparently the artist required only one or two sittings from his subjects, and then painted their likeness from such sketches. The Hanseatic merchants in London solicited his art, but did not inspire his best. For the Guildhall of the Hanse he painted two murals preserved only in copies or drawings: one represented *The Triumph of Poverty*, the other *The Triumph of Riches*; both are marvels of individualized character, living movement, and coherent design, and illustrate the motto of the Guild—"Gold is the father of joy and the son of care; he who lacks it is sad, he who has it is uneasy." [82]

Thomas Cromwell, who was to exemplify this adage, submitted his hard face and soft frame to Holbein's brush in 1534. Through him the artist found access to the highest figures at the court. He painted *The French Ambassadors*, and one of them, Charles de Saulier, he portrayed with especial success, revealing the man beneath the vestments and insignia of office. Four others—Sir Henry Guilford (controller of the royal household), Sir Nicholas Carew (royal equerry to the King), Robert Cheseman (royal falconer to the King), and Dr. John Chambers (physician to the King)—suggest the thick skins that alone could safely live near the parboiled King. Holbein became one of them about 1537 as official court painter. He received a workshop of his own in Whitehall Palace, dwelt in comfort, had mistresses and bastards like anybody else, and dressed in color and silk. [83] He was called upon to decorate rooms, design ceremonial garments, bookbindings, weapons, tableware, seals, royal buttons and buckles, and the gems that Henry presented to his wives. In 1538 the King sent him to Brussels to paint Princess Christine of Denmark; she proved quite charming, and Henry would gladly have had her, but she took Duke Francis of Lorraine instead; perhaps she preferred to hang in a gallery rather than die on the block. Holbein took the opportunity to visit Basel briefly; he arranged an annuity of forty guilders ($1,000?) for his wife, and hurried back to London. Soon thereafter came the commission to paint Anne of Cleves; Holbein almost foreshadowed the result in the sad eyes of the portrait now in the Louvre.

For the King himself he painted several large pictures, nearly all lost. One survives in the Barber Surgeons' Hall in London: *Henry VIII Granting a Charter of Incorporation to the Barber Surgeons' Company;* Henry dominates the scene in his robes of state. The artist made appealing portraits of Henry's third wife, Jane Seymour, and the fifth wife, Catherine Howard. When Henry himself sat or stood for Holbein the painter rose to the chal lenge, and produced portraits surpassed in his own work only by the Louvre and Basel pictures of Erasmus. The portrait of 1536 shows the monarch Teutonically pompous and stout. Henry liked it despite himself, and commissioned Holbein to paint the royal family as a fresco in Whitehall Palace; this mural was destroyed by fire in 1698, but a copy made in 1667 for Charles II reveals a masterly design: at the upper left Henry VII, pious and modest; lower, his son, brandishing the symbols of power and spreading his legs like a colossus; at the right his mother and his third wife; and in the center a marble monument retailing in Latin the virtues of the kings. The figure of Henry VIII was elaborated with such realism that a legend arose about persons entering the room and mistaking the portrait for the living King. In 1540 Holbein painted a still more imposing *Henry VIII in Wedding Dress*. Finally (1542) he displayed Henry in the deterioration of mind and body. Nemesis here worked leisurely, lengthening the revenge of the gods from clean or sudden death to prolonged and ignominious decay.

Two lovely pictures redeem the royal gallery: one of Prince Edward at the age of two, all innocence; the other of Edward aged six (in the Metropolitan Museum of Art). This second portrait is a delight to behold. We may judge the art of Holbein when we see him, within a year or two, portray unflinchingly the obese pride of the father, and then catch with such mysterious skill the guileless kindliness of the son.

At forty-five (1542) the artist pictured himself again, and with the same objectivity with which he had depicted the King: a suspicious, pugnacious fellow with carelessly kept graying hair and beard; and once more (1543) in a roundel showing him in a gentler mood. In that year plague came to London, and chose him as one of its victims.

Technically he was one of the supreme painters. He saw meticulously, and so portrayed; every line, color, or attitude, every incidence or variation of light, that could reveal significance was caught and pinned down upon the paper, linen, wood, or wall. What accuracy in the line, what depth and smoothness and warmth in the color, what skill in ordering details into a unified composition! But in many of the portraits, where the object was not the subject but the fee, we miss the sympathy that could see, and feel with, a man's secret soul; we find it in the Louvre and Basel *Erasmus*, and in the picture of his family. We miss, except in the *Meyer Madonna*, the idealism that ennobled the realism in the Van Eycks' *Adoration of the Lamb*. His indifference to religion kept him short of the grandeur of Grünewald, and marked him off from Dürer, who always had one foot in the Middle Ages. Holbein was neither Renaissance like Titian nor Reformation like Cranach; he was German-Dutch-Flemish-English matter-of-fact and practical sense. Perhaps his success prevented the effective entry of Italian pictorial principles and finesse into England. After him Puritanism triumphed over the

Elizabethan passion, and English painting languished till Hogarth came. At the same time the glory departed from German painting. A flood of barbarism would have to pass over Central Europe before the sense of beauty would find voice there again.

VII. ART IN SPAIN AND PORTUGAL: 1515–55

Despite El Greco and Velázquez, Cervantes and Calderón, Spain never had a Renaissance in the rich Italian sense. Her far-won wealth gave new ornaments to her Christian culture, it offered productive rewards to native genius in literature and art, but it did not flow into any exciting recapture—as in Italy and France—of that pagan civilization which had adorned the Mediterranean world before and after Christ, and which had begotten Seneca, Lucan, Martial, Quintilian, Trajan, and Hadrian on the soil of Spain itself. The remembrance of that classic era had been deeply overladen by the long struggle of Spanish Christianity with the Moors; all the glorious memories were of that protracted victory, and the faith that had won it became inseparable from the proud remembrance. While everywhere else in Europe the state was humiliating the Church, in Spain the ecclesiastical organization grew stronger with the generations; it challenged and ignored the papacy, even when Spaniards ruled the Vatican; it survived the pious absolutism of Ferdinand and Charles V and Philip II, and then dominated every aspect of Spanish life. The Church in Spain was almost the sole patron of the arts; therefore it called the tune, named the themes, and made art, like philosophy, the handmaiden of theology. The Spanish Inquisition appointed inspectors to outlaw nudity, immodesty, paganism, or heresy in art, to specify the manner of treating sacred subjects in sculpture and painting, and to direct Spanish art toward the transmission and confirmation of the faith.

And yet Italian influence was pouring into Spain. The rise of Spaniards to the papacy, the conquest of Naples and Milan by Spanish kings, the campaigns of Spanish armies and the missions of Spanish statesmen and churchmen in Italy, the busy trade between Spanish and Italian ports, the visits of Spanish artists like Forment and the Berruguetes to Italy, of Italian artists like Torrigiano and Leone Leoni to Spain—all these factors affected Spanish art in methods, ornament, and style, hardly in spirit or theme, more in painting than in sculpture, and in architecture least.

The cathedrals dominated the landscape and the towns as the faith dominated life. Traveling in Spain is a pilgrimage from one to another of these mighty fanes. Their awesome immensity, their wealth of interior ornament, the dim-lit silence of their naves, the devoted stonework of their cloisters, accentuate the simplicity and poverty of the picturesque tiled dwellings that huddle below, looking up to them as the promise of a better world. The Gothic style still ruled in the giant cathedrals that rose above Salamanca (1513) and Segovia (1522); but at Granada Diego de Siloé, architect son of a Gothic sculptor, designed the interior of the cathedral with classic columns and capitals, and crowned the Gothic plan with a classic dome (1525). The style of the Italian Renaissance completely dislodged Gothic in the palace of Charles V at Granada. Charles had reproved the bishop of Córdova for spoiling the great mosque by building within its 850 pillars a Christian church; [34] but he sinned almost as grievously when he tore down some halls and courts of the Alhambra to make room for a structure whose stern mass and dull symmetry might have passed without offense amid kindred buildings in Rome, but proved strikingly out of harmony with the frail elegance and gay diversity of the Moorish citadel.

Something of the Moors' flair for architectural decoration appeared in the "plateresque" style that marked chiefly the civil architecture of this reign. It took its name from its resemblance to the complex and delicate ornament lavished by the silversmith *(platero)* or goldsmith upon plate and other objects of their art. It topped and flanked portals and windows with winding arabesques of stone; it grooved or spiraled or flowered columns with Moorish fantasy; it pierced grilles and balustrades with marble foliage and embroidery. This *plateresco* marked the Obispo Chapel at Madrid, the church of Santo Tomás at Ávila, the choir of the cathedral at Cordova, and it disported itself without restraint on the *Ayuntamiento* or Town Hall of Seville (1526 f.). Portugal adopted the style on a portal suffused with ornament, and columns carved with decoration, in the magnificent monastery of Santa Maria at Belem (1517 f.). Charles V took the style to the Lowlands and Germany, where it flourished its signature on the town halls of Antwerp and Leyden and the castle of Heidelberg. Philip II found plateresque too florid for his taste, and under his frowns it died an early death.

Spanish sculpture yielded more readily than architecture to the swelling Italian tide. Pietro Torrigiano, after breaking Michelangelo's nose in Florence and bearding Henry VIII in London, settled in Seville (1521), and modeled in terra cotta an ungainly *St. Jerome* which Goya mistakenly judged to be the supreme work of modern sculpture.[35] Feeling poorly paid for a statue of the Virgin, Torrigiano smashed it to bits, was arrested by the Inquisition, and died in its jails.[36] Damian Forment, returning to Aragon from Italy, carried the spirit of the Renaissance on his chisel and in his boasts; he called himself "the rival of Pheidias and Praxiteles," and was accepted at his own estimate. The ecclesiastical authorities allowed him to carve likenesses of himself and his wife on the base of the reredos that he made for the abbey of Monte Aragon. For the church of Nuestra Señora del Pilar at Saragossa he cut in alabaster a spacious retable in bas-relief, combining Gothic with

Renaissance elements, painting with sculpture, color with form. To another retable, in the cathedral of Huesca, Forment devoted the last thirteen years of his life (1520–33).

As Pedro Berruguete had dominated Spanish painting in the half-century before Charles V, so his son became the leading Spanish sculptor of this age. Alonso learned the art of color from his father, then went to Italy and worked with Raphael in painting, with Bramante and Michelangelo in statuary. When he came back to Spain (1520) he brought with him Michelangelo's penchant for figures caught in tense emotion or violent attitudes. Charles appointed him court sculptor and painter. At Valladolid he worked for six years carving in wood an altar screen, forty-two by thirty feet, for the church of San Benito el Real; only fragments remain, chiefly a *San Sebastian* vividly colored, with blood pouring from the wounds. In 1535 he joined with his chief rival, Felipe de Borgoña, to carve choir stalls in the Toledo Cathedral; here too the Michelangelesque manner swayed his hand, and presaged baroque in Spain. When he neared eighty he was commissioned to erect in the hospital of St. John at Toledo a monument to its founder, Cardinal Juan de Tavera; he took his son Alonso as helper, created one of the chefs-d'oeuvre of Spanish sculpture, and died in the attempt in his seventy-fifth year (1561).

Spanish painting, still in tutelage to Italy and Flanders, produced no outstanding master under Charles V. The Emperor favored foreign painters, imported Anthonis Mor to make portraits of Spanish notables, and for himself declared that he would allow none but the great Titian to paint him. The only Spanish painter of this age whose fame crossed the Pyrenees was Luis de Morales. The first fifty years of his life were spent in the poverty and obscurity of Badajoz, painting for churches and chapels in the province of Estremadura. He was fifty-four when Philip II bade him come and paint in the Escorial (1564). He presented himself in magnificent array, which the King thought unbecoming in an artist, but Philip softened when he learned that Luis had spent his life's savings to attire himself fitly for an audience with his Majesty. Morales' *Christ Carrying the Cross* did not strike the royal fancy, and he returned to Badajoz and penury. Several of his pictures can be seen at the Hispanic Society in New York, all of them beautiful; but the best example of his work is a *Virgin and Child* in the Prado—a bit too redolent of Raphael. Philip, passing through Badajoz in 1581, allotted the artist a tardy pension, which enabled him—now disabled by palsy and failing eyes—to eat regularly during the five years left to him of life.

The artisans of Spain were often artists in all but name. Spanish lace and leather continued supreme in Europe. The woodworkers too were unsurpassed; Théophile Gautier thought that Gothic art had never come closer to perfection than in the choir stalls of Toledo Cathedral. Metalworkers made works of art out of sanctuary screens, window grilles, balcony railings, door hinges, even nails. Goldsmiths and silversmiths transformed some of the precious metal flowing in from America into ornaments for princes and vessels for the Church; famous were the *custodias* they made in filigree silver or gold to hold the consecrated Host. Gil Vicente, not satisfied to be the leading dramatist of Portugal and Spain in this period, executed a monstrance —for displaying the Host to the congregation—which has been rated "the masterpiece of the goldsmith's work in Portugal." [37] And Francisco de Hollanda, Portuguese despite his name, carried on with distinction the dying art of illumination.

All in all, this less than half a century came off with credit in the field of art despite the absorption and disruption of energies in the religious revolution. The masters in architecture, sculpture, and painting were hardly comparable to the giants who shook all Europe with theology; religion was the tune of the time, and art could only provide an accompaniment. But Il Rosso, Primaticcio, Lescot, Delorme, Goujon, and the Clouets in France, the Berruguetes in Spain, Brueghel in Flanders, Cranach in Germany, Holbein everywhere, made an honorable roster of artists for an age so agitated and so brief. Art is order, yet everything was in chaos—not religion only, but morals, social order, art itself. Gothic was fighting its losing battle with classic forms, and the artist, uprooted from his own past, had to experiment with tentatives that could not give him the grandeur of a stability mortised in confident time. In the universal turbulence faith too was hesitant, and ceased to give clear imperatives to art; religious images were attacked and shattered; sacred themes that had inspired the creator and the beholder of beauty were losing their power to stir either genius or admiration or piety. And in science the greatest revolution of all was deposing the earth from its theological throne, and losing in the endless void the little globe whose divine visitation had formed the medieval mind and generated medieval art. When would stability come again?

CHAPTER XXXVII

Science in the Age of Copernicus

1517-65*

I. THE CULT OF THE OCCULT

I T is remarkable that this age, so absorbed in theology and scholarship, should have produced two men of the highest standing in the history of science—Copernicus and Vesalius; and curious that the books that contained their lifeblood should have appeared in one *annus mirabilis*, 1543. Some conditions favored science. The discovery of America and the exploration of Asia, the demands of industry and the extension of commerce, turned up knowledge that often contradicted traditional beliefs and encouraged fresh thought. Translations from Greek and Arabic, the printing of Apollonius's *Conics* (1537) and the Greek text of Archimedes (1544) stimulated mathematics and physics. But many travelers were liars or careless; printing spread nonsense more widely than knowledge; and scientific instruments, though numerous, were almost primitive. The microscope, the telescope, the thermometer, the barometer, the micrometer, the microchronometer, were still in the future. The Renaissance was enamored of literature and style, politely interested in philosophy, almost indifferent to science. The Renaissance popes were not hostile to science; Leo X and Clement VII listened with open minds to Copernican ideas, and Paul III received without trembling the dedication of Copernicus's world-shaking *Book of Revolutions*. But the reaction under Paul IV, the development of the Inquisition in Italy, and the dogmatic decrees of the Council of Trent made scientific studies increasingly difficult and dangerous after 1555.

Protestantism could not favor science, for it based itself on an infallible Bible. Luther rejected the Copnernican astronomy because the Bible told of Joshua commanding the sun—not the earth—to stand still. Melanchthon was inclined to science; he studied mathematics, physics, astronomy, and medicine, and lectured on the history of mathematics in antiquity; but his broad spirit was overwhelmed by the forceful nature of his master, and by the predominance of a narrowed Lutheranism after Luther's death. Calvin had little use for science; Knox, none.

---

* For Islamic science, cf. Chapter XXX; for Jewish science, Chapter XXXII; for Italian science, Chapter XIX of *The Renaissance*.

A discouraging milieu of occultism continued to surround, confuse, and sometimes—as in Cardan and Paracelsus—threaten the sanity of the would-be scientist. Hermetic lore from Egypt, mystical Pythagoreanism and Neo-platonism from Greece, the Cabala from Judaism, bemused a thousand grop-ing minds. Legends and miracles infested historiography, and travelers told of fire-breathing dragons and rope-climbing fakirs. Almost any unusual event in public or private life was interpreted as contrived by God or Satan for the warning or edification, the temptation or ruination, of man. Many believed that comets and meteors were fireballs hurled by an angry deity.[1] Cheap literature entered every literate home with assurances that baser metals could be turned into gold; and (says a contemporary report) "all the tailors, shoemakers, servants, and maids who hear and read about these things give all the coins they can spare to ... perambulating and fraudulent" practitioners of such arts.[2] At a trial in England in 1549 William Wycherley, a con-jurer, said there were 500 like him in the island.[3] Itinerant students in Ger-many sold magical protections against witches and devils. Charms and talis-mans guaranteed to divert musket balls were popular with soldiers.[4] The Mass itself was often used as a charm to bring rain or sunshine, or victory in war. Prayers for rain were common, and sometimes seemed too successful; in which cases the church bells were rung to warn the heavens to stop.[5] In 1526–31 the monks of Troyes formally excommunicated the caterpillars that were plaguing the crops, but added that the interdict would be effective only for lands whose peasants had paid their Church tithes.[6]

Perhaps more events were ascribed to Satan than to God. "Scarcely a year goes by," lamented a Protestant writer in 1563, "without the most appalling news from numbers of principalities, towns, and villages, of the shameless and horrible ways in which the prince of hell, by bodily apparition and in all sorts of forms, is trying to extinguish the new and shining light of holy evangel."[7] Luther joined the commonalty in attributing most diseases to demons entering the body—which, after all, is not altogether unlike our cur-rent theory. Many believed that diseases were caused by the evil eye or other magical means, and that they could be cured by magic potions—which again is not too far removed from our present practice. Most remedies were ad-ministered according to the position of the planets; hence medical students studied astrology.

Astrology verged on science by assuming a rule of law in the universe, and operating largely through experiment. The belief that the movements and positions of the stars determined human events was not quite as general as before; yet there were 30,000 astrologers in Paris in the sixteenth century,[8] all ready to cast a horoscope for a coin. Almanacs of astrological predictions were best sellers; Rabelais parodied them in the *Pantagruelian Prognostica-tions* of Master Alcofribas. Luther and the Sorbonne here agreed with him, and condemned astrology in all its forms. The Church officially frowned upon astrological predictions, as implying determinism and the subjection of the Church to the stars; yet Paul III, one of the greatest minds of the age, "would call no important meeting of the Consistory," said an ambassador to the papal court, "and would take no trip, without choosing his days and observing the constellations."[9] Francis I, Catherine de Médicis, Charles IX, Julius II, Leo X, and Adrian VI consulted astrologers.[10] Melanchthon changed the date of Luther's birth to give him a more propitious horoscope,[11] and begged him not to travel under a new moon.[12]

One astrologer of this period is still popular. Nostradamus was, in French, Michel de Notredame. He professed to be a physician and an astronomer, and was accepted as semi-official astrologer by Catherine de Médicis; she built an observatory for him in Les Halles. In 1564 he predicted a life of ninety years for Charles IX,[13] who died ten years later at the age of twenty-four. At his own death (1566) he left a book of prophecies so wisely ambiguous that some line or another could be applied to almost any event in later history.

Because Christians of the sixteenth century believed in the possibility of obtaining supernatural powers from demons, and because the fear of demons was ingrained in their rearing, they felt an obligation to burn witches. Luther and Calvin seconded Pope Innocent VIII in urging the prosecution of witches. "I would have no compassion on these witches," said Luther; "I would burn them all."[14] Four were burned at Wittenberg on June 29, 1540; thirty-four at Geneva in 1545.[15] The Reformers, of course, had Biblical warrant for these bonfires, and Protestant dependence upon the Scriptures gave new urgency to Exodus 22:18. The Catholic practice of exorcism encouraged the belief in witchcraft by assuming the power of devils lodged in human beings. Luther claimed that his Leipzig opponent, Johannes Eck, had signed a pact with Satan; and Johannes Cochlaeus retorted that Luther was a by-product of Satan's dalliance with Margaret Luther.[16]

Accusations of witchcraft were sometimes used to get rid of personal enemies. The accused had a choice of prolonged torture to elicit a confession, or death as the result of a confession; and in sixteenth-century Europe the administration of torture was systematized "with a cold-blooded ferocity unknown ... to the heathen nations."[17] Many victims seem to have believed in their own guilt—that they had had transactions, sometimes sexual, with devils.[18] Some of the accused committed suicide; a French judge noted fifteen such cases within a year.[19] Secular magistrates often exceeded ecclesiastics in the enthusiasm of this persecution. The laws of Henry VIII (1541) punished with death any of several practices ascribed to witches,[20] but the Spanish Inquisition branded stories and confessions of witchcraft as the delusions of weak minds, and cautioned its agents (1538) to ignore the popular demand for the burning of witches.[21]

Fewer voices were raised to protect witches than in defense of heretics, and the heretics themselves believed in witches. But in 1563 Johannes Wier, a physician of Cleves, issued a treatise *De praestigiis daemonum (On Demonic Deceptions)* which timidly dared to mitigate the mania. He did not question the existence of demons, but suggested that witches were the innocent victims of demonic possession, and were deluded by the Devil into believing the absurdities that they confessed. Women, and persons suffering from illness of body or mind, were, he thought, especially subject to possession by demons. He concluded that witchcraft was not a crime but a disease, and he appealed to the princes of Europe to stop the execution of these helpless women. A few years later Wier replaced himself in his time by writing a detailed description of hell, its leaders, its organization, and its operation.

The spirit of the age spoke in the story of Faust. We first hear of Georg Faust in 1507, in a letter of Johannes Trithemius, who calls him a mountebank; and then in 1513, when Mutianus Rufus accords him no gentler term. Philip Begardi, a Worms physician, wrote in 1539: "Of late years a remarkable man has been traveling through nearly every province, principality, and kingdom . . . and has boasted highly of his great skill not only in medicine but in chiromancy, physiognomy, crystal gazing, and other kindred arts . . . and has not denied that he is called Faustus"[22]—i.e., favored or fortunate. The historic Faust seems to have died in 1539—by the Devil wringing his neck, said Melanchthon. Four years later the legend of Faust as in league with the Devil made its appearance in the *Sermones conviviales* of Johannes Gast, a Protestant pastor at Basel. Two old notions combined to transform the historical charlatan into a figure of legend, drama, and art: that man might obtain magic powers by compacts with Satan, and that secular learning is an insolent conceit likely to lead a man to hell. In one phase the legend was supposed to be a Catholic caricature of Luther; in a deeper view it expressed the religious repudiation of "profane" knowledge as opposed to a humble acceptance of the Bible as in itself sufficient erudition and truth. Goethe repudiated the repudiation, and allowed the hunger for knowledge to purify itself by its application to the common good.

The legend of Faust came to bitter life in Henry Cornelius Agrippa. Born of good family at Cologne (1487), he found his way to Paris, and fell in there with some mystics or quacks who claimed esoteric wisdom. Hungry for knowledge and fame, he took up alchemy, studied the Cabala, and became convinced that there was a world of enlightenment unattainable by ordinary perception or reasoning. He sent to Trithemius a manuscript *De occulta philosophia*, with a personal letter:

I wondered much, and indeed felt indignant, that up to this time no one had arisen to vindicate so sublime and sacred a study from the accusation of impiety. Thus my spirit was aroused, and . . . I too conceived the desire to philosophize, thinking that I should produce a work not unworthy of praise . . . if I could vindicate . . . that ancient Magic, studied by all the wise, purged and freed from the errors of impiety, and endowed with its own reasonable system.[28]

Trithemius replied with good counsel:

Speak of things public to the public, but of things lofty and secret only to the loftiest and most private of your friends. Hay to an ox and sugar to a parrot. Rightly interpret this, lest you, as some others have been, be trampled down by oxen.[24]

Whether through caution or lack of a publisher, Agrippa refrained for twenty years from sending his book through the press. The Emperor Maximilian summoned him to war in Italy; he gave a good account of himself on the battlefield, but took occasion to lecture on Plato at the University of Pisa, and to receive degrees in law and medicine at Pavia. He was appointed town advocate at Metz (1518), and soon lost that position by interfering with the prosecution of a young woman accused of witchcraft; he procured her release from the Inquisition, but he thought it wise then to change his habitat (1519). For two years he served Louise of Savoy as physician; however, he entered into so many disputes that she stopped his salary. He moved to Antwerp with his second wife and his children, was made historiographer and court librarian to the Regent Margaret of Austria, and managed to eat regularly. Now he composed his most important work, *De incertitudine et vanitate scientiarum;* he published it in 1530, and then, strangely enough, issued his youthful *De occulta philosophia,* with a preface disclaiming continued belief in the mystic abracadabra there detailed. The two books together offended all the cognizant world.

The *Occult Philosophy* urged that as the human soul pervades and governs the body, so the *spiritus mundi* pervades and governs the universe; that this great reservoir of soul-force can be tapped by a mind morally purified and patiently instructed in Magian ways. So reinforced, the mind can discover the hidden qualities of objects, numbers, letters, words, can penetrate the secrets of the stars, and can gain mastery over the forces of the earth and the demons of the air. The book circulated widely, and its many posthumous editions led to legends about Agrippa's compact with a devil, who accompanied him in the guise of his dog,[25] and enabled him to fly over the globe and sleep in the moon.[26]

The vicissitudes of life abated Agrippa's claims on supersensual experience; he learned that no magic or alchemy could feed his family or keep him out of jail for debt. He turned in angry disillusionment upon the pursuit of knowledge, and wrote at the age of thirty-nine *On the Uncertainty and Vanity of the Sciences*, the most skeptical book of the sixteenth century before Montaigne. "I well perceive," ran his exordium, "what a bloody battle I have to fight.... First of all, the lousy *(pediculose)* grammarians will make a stir, and ... peevish poets, trifle-selling historians, blustering orators, obstinate logicians ... fatal astrologers ... monstrous magicians ... contentious philosophers ..." All knowledge is uncertain, all science is vain, and "to know nothing is the happiest life." It was knowledge that destroyed the happiness of Adam and Eve; it was Socrates's confession of ignorance that brought him content and fame. "All sciences are only the ordinances and opinions of men, as injurious as profitable, as pestilent as wholesome, as ill as good, in no part perfect, but doubtful and full of error and contention." [27]

Agrippa begins his devastation with the alphabet, and upbraids it for its bewildering inconsistencies of pronunciation. He laughs at the grammarians, whose exceptions are more numerous than their rules, and who are repeatedly outvoted by the people. Poets are madmen; no one "well in his wits" can write poetry. Most history is a fable; not *une fable convenue*, as Voltaire would mistakenly call it, but an ever-changing fable which each historian and generation transforms anew. Oratory is the seduction of the mind by eloquence into error. Occultism is a sham; his own book about it, Agrippa now warns, was "false, or, if you will, lying"; if formerly he practiced astrology, magic, divination, alchemy, and other such "nesciences," it was mostly through the importunate solicitation of patrons demanding esoteric knowledge, and able to pay. The Cabala is "nothing else but a pestilent superstition." As for the philosophers, the self-canceling diversity of their opinions puts them out of court; we may leave them to refute one another. So far as philosophy seeks to deduce morality from reason, it is stultified by the irrational contrariety of morals in place and time; "whereof it cometh to pass that that which at one time was vice, another time is accounted virtue, and that which in one place is virtue, in another is vice." The arts and occupations are as vitiated as the sciences with falsehood and vanity. Every court is "a school of corrupt customs, and a refuge of detestable wickedness." Trade is treachery. Treasurers are thieves; their hands are sticky with bird-lime, their fingers end in hooks. War is the slaughter of many in the sport of the few. Medicine is "a certain art of manslaughter," and often "there is more danger in the physician and the medicine than in the sickness itself."

What is the upshot of all this? If science is transient opinion, and philosophy is the vain speculation of mental maggots on the nature of the infinite, what shall a man live by? Only by the Word of God as revealed in the Bible. This has an evangelical ring, and indeed, scattered among Agrippa's doubts, are sundry affirmations of reform. He rejects the temporal power of the popes, and even their spiritual authority when this contravenes Scripture. He denounces the Inquisition as persuading men not with reason and Scripture but with "fire and faggots." He wishes the Church would spend less on cathedrals and more on charity. But he goes beyond the Reformers when he admits that the authors of the Old and the New Testament were liable to error. Christ alone is always right and true; Him only should we trust; in Him is the last refuge of the mind and the soul.

Agrippa enjoyed the furor caused by his rampage, but he paid for the pleasure through his remaining years. Charles V demanded that he recant his criticism of the Church. When he refused, his salary was cut short. Imprisoned for debt, he laid responsibility on the Emperor, who was behind in payments to his court historiographer. Cardinal Campeggio and the Bishop of Liége secured his release, but Charles banished him from Imperial territory (1531). Agrippa moved to Lyons, where, says an uncertain tradition, he was again imprisoned for debt. Set free, he passed on to Grenoble; and there, aged forty-eight, he died. Probably he had a share in forming the skepticism of Montaigne, but his only popular book was on the occultism that he had renounced. Occult thought and practices flourished to the end of the century.

II. THE COPERNICAN REVOLUTION

Mathematical advances that now seem trivial sharpened the tools of calculation in this age. Michael Stifel's *Arithmetica integra* (1544) introduced our plus and minus signs, and Robert Recorde's *Whetstone of Wit* (1557) first used our equals sign in print. The once famous arithmetics of Adam Riese persuaded Germany to pass from reckoning with counters to written computation. Johannes Werner published (1522) the first modern treatise on conic sections; and Georg Rheticus, besides serving as midwife to Copernicus, carried on the work of Regiomontanus in trigonometry.

Astronomy had at its disposal better calculations than instruments. On the basis of these calculations some astrologers predicted a second Deluge for February 11, 1524, when Jupiter and Saturn would join in Pisces; thereupon Toulouse built an ark of refuge, and cautious families stored food on mountaintops.[28] Most of the astronomical instruments were of medieval origin: celestial and terrestrial spheres, Jacob's staff, an astrolabe, an armillary sphere, quadrants, cylinders, clocks, compasses, and several other devices, but no telescope and no photography. With this equipment Copernicus moved the earth.

Mikolai Kopernik, as Poland calls him, Niklas Koppernigk, as Germany calls him, Nicolaus Copernicus, as scholars call him, was born in 1473 at

Thorn (Torun) on the Vistula in West Prussia, which, seven years before, had been ceded to Poland by the Teutonic Knights; he was a Prussian in space, a Pole in time. His mother came of a prosperous Prussian family; his father hailed from Cracow, settled in Thorn, and dealt in copper. When the father died (1483), the mother's brother, Lucas Watzelrode, Prince Bishop of Ermland, took charge of the children. Nicolaus was sent at eighteen to the University of Cracow to prepare for the priesthood. Not liking the Scholasticism that had there suppressed humanism, he persuaded his uncle to let him study in Italy. The uncle had him appointed a canon of the cathedral at Frauenburg in Polish East Prussia, and gave him leave of absence for three years.*

At the University of Bologna (1497–1500) Copernicus studied mathematics, physics, and astronomy. One of his teachers, Domenico de Novara, once a pupil of Regiomontanus, criticized the Ptolemaic system as absurdly complex, and introduced his students to ancient Greek astronomers who had questioned the immobility and central position of the earth. Philolaus the Pythagorean, in the fifth century before Christ, had held that the earth and the other planets moved around Hestia, a central fire invisible to us because all known parts of the earth are turned away from it. Cicero quoted Hicetas of Syracuse, also of the fifth century before Christ, as believing that the sun, the moon, and the stars stood still, and that their apparent motion was due to the axial rotation of the earth. Archimedes and Plutarch reported that Aristarchus of Samos (310–230 B.C.) had suggested the revolution of the earth around the sun, had been accused of impiety, and had withdrawn the suggestion. According to Plutarch, Seleucus of Babylonia had revived the idea in the second century before Christ. This heliocentric view might have triumphed in antiquity had not Claudius Ptolemy of Alexandria, in the second century of our era, restated the geocentric theory with such force and learning that hardly anyone thereafter dared to challenge it. Ptolemy himself had ruled that in seeking to explain phenomena, science should adopt the simplest possible hypothesis consistent with accepted observations. Yet Ptolemy, like Hipparchus before him, to explain the apparent motion of the planets, had been compelled by the geocentric theory to assume a bewildering complexity of epicycles and eccentrics.† Could any simpler hypothesis be found? Nicole Oresme (1330–82) and Nicholas of Cusa (1401–64) had renewed the proposal of terrestrial motion; Leonardo da Vinci (1452–1519)

---

* A canon is a clergyman on the staff of a cathedral. He need not be a priest. No clear evidence exists that Copernicus rose from minor orders to the priesthood before his later years. In 1537 he was recommended for a bishopric, which would indicate that he was then a priest.[29]

† An epicycle is a circle whose center is borne on the circumference of a larger circle. An eccentric is a circle not having the same center as another circle contained in some measure within it.

had recently written: "The sun does not move. . . . The earth is not in the center of the circle of the sun, nor in the center of the universe." [30]

Copernicus felt that the heliocentric theory could "save the appearances" —explain the observed phenomena—more compactly than the Ptolemaic view. In 1500, now twenty-seven, he went to Rome, presumably for the Jubilee, and gave lectures there in which, a tradition reports, he tentatively propounded the motion of the earth. Meanwhile his leave of absence expired, and he returned to his duties as canon in Frauenburg. But geocentric mathematics confused his prayers. He begged permission to resume his studies in Italy, proposing now to take up medicine and canon law—which to his superiors seemed more to the point than astronomy. Before the fifteenth century ended he was back in Italy. He received the degree of law at Ferrara (1503), apparently took no degree in medicine, and again reconciled himself to Frauenburg. Soon his uncle, probably to give him time for further study, appropriated him as secretary and physician (1506); and for six years Copernicus lived in the episcopal castle at Heilsberg. There he worked out the basic mathematics of his theory, and formulated it in manuscript.

When the kindly bishop died, Copernicus resumed his place in Frauenburg. He continued to practice medicine, treating the poor without charge.[31] He represented the cathedral chapter on diplomatic missions, and prepared for King Sigismund I of Poland a plan for reforming the Prussian currency. In one of many learned essays on finance he stated what was later to be known as Gresham's law: "Bad money . . . drives the old, better money away" [32]—i.e., when a government issues a debased coinage, the good coins are hoarded or exported and disappear from circulation, the bad coins are offered as taxes, and the king is "paid in his own coin." But amid these diverse concerns Copernicus continued his astronomic researches. His geographical location was unpropitious: Frauenburg was near the Baltic, and was half the time shrouded in mists or clouds. He envied Claudius Ptolemy, for whom "the skies were more cheerful, where the Nile does not breathe fogs as does our Vistula. Nature has denied us that comfort, that calm air";[33] no wonder Copernicus almost worshiped the sun. His astronomical observations were neither numerous nor precise, but they were not vital to his purpose. He used for the most part the astronomic data transmitted by Ptolemy, and proposed to prove that all received observations accorded best with a heliocentric view.

About 1514 he summarized his conclusions in a *Little Commentary* (*Nicolai Copernici de hypothesibus motuum coelestium a se constitutis commentariolus*). It was not printed during his lifetime, but he sent out some manuscript copies as "trial balloons." He stated his conclusions with a matter-of-fact simplicity as if they were not the greatest revolution in Christian history:

1. There is no one center of all the celestial circles or spheres.

2. The center of the earth is not the center of the universe, but only of gravity and of the lunar sphere.

3. All the spheres [planets] revolve about the sun as their midpoint, and therefore the sun is the center of the universe.

4. The ratio of the earth's distance from the sun to the height of the firmament is so much smaller than the ratio of the earth's radius to its distance from the sun that the distance from the earth to the sun is imperceptible in comparison with the height of the firmament.

5. Whatever motion appears in the firmament arises not from any motion of the firmament, but from the earth's motion. The earth together with its circumjacent elements performs a complete rotation on its fixed poles in a daily motion, while the firmament and highest heaven abide unchanged.

6. What appear to us as motions of the sun arise not from its motion but from the motion of the earth and our sphere, with which [motion] we revolve around the sun like any other planet. . . .

7. The apparent retrograde and direct motion of the planets arises not from their motion but from the earth's. The motion of the earth alone, therefore, suffices to explain so many apparent inequalities in the heavens.[34]

The few astronomers who saw the *Commentariolus* paid no great attention to it. Pope Leo X, informed of the theory, expressed an open-minded interest, and asked a cardinal to write to Copernicus for a demonstration of his thesis; for a time the hypothesis won considerable favor at the enlightened papal court.[35] Luther, toward 1530, rejected the theory: "People give ear to an upstart astrologer who strove to show that the earth revolves, not the heavens or the firmament, the sun and the moon. . . . This fool wishes to reverse the entire scheme of astronomy; but sacred Scripture tells us that Joshua commanded the sun to stand still, not the earth." [36] Calvin answered Copernicus with a line from Psalm XCIII, 1: "The world also is stabilized, that it cannot be moved"—and asked, "Who will venture to place the authority of Copernicus above that of the Holy Spirit?" [37] Copernicus was so discouraged by the response to the *Commentariolus* that when, about 1530, he completed his major work, he decided to withhold it from publication. He calmly proceeded with his duties, delved a bit into politics, and, in his sixties, was accused of having a mistress.[38]

Into this resigned old age burst, in 1539, an enthusiastic young mathematician, Georg Rheticus. He was twenty-five, a Protestant, a protégé of Melanchthon, and a professor at Wittenberg. He had read the *Commentariolus,* he was convinced of its truth, he longed to help the old astronomer who, far off in an obscure Baltic outpost of civilization, was waiting so patiently for others to see, with him, the invisible rotation and revolution of the earth. The youth fell in love with Copernicus, called him "the best and greatest of men," and was deeply impressed by his devotion to science. For ten weeks Rheticus studied the big manuscript. He urged its publication. Copernicus refused, but agreed to have Rheticus publish a simplified analysis of its first four books. So in 1540 at Danzig the young scholar issued his *Narratio prima de libris revolutionum—First Account of the Books of the Revolutions* of the celestial bodies. He sent a copy hopefully to Melanchthon. The kindly theologian was not convinced. When Rheticus returned to Wittenberg (early in 1540), and commended the Copernican hypothesis in his class, he was "ordered," he says, to lecture instead on the *Sphaera* of Johannes de Sacrobosco.[39] On October 16, 1541, Melanchthon wrote to a friend: "Some think it a distinguished achievement to construct such a crazy thing as that Prussian astronomer who moves the earth and fixes the sun. Verily, wise rulers should tame the unrestraint of men's minds."[40]

In the summer of 1540 Rheticus went back to Frauenburg, and stayed till September 1541. Repeatedly he begged his master to give his own text to the world. When two prominent clergymen joined in the appeal, Copernicus, perhaps feeling that he had now one foot safely in the grave, yielded. He made some final additions to the manuscript, and allowed Rheticus to send it to a printer in Nuremberg, who assumed all financial costs and risks (1542). As Rheticus had now left Wittenberg to teach in Leipzig, he delegated to his friend Andreas Osiander, a Lutheran minister at Nuremberg, the task of seeing the book through the press.

Osiander had already written to Copernicus (October 20, 1541) suggesting that the new view should be presented as an hypothesis rather than as proved truth, and in a letter of the same day to Rheticus he had pointed out that by this procedure "the Aristotelians and the theologians will easily let themselves be appeased."[41] Copernicus himself had repeatedly termed his theories hypotheses, not only in the *Commentariolus* but in his major text;[42] at the same time his Dedication claimed that he had supported his views with "the most transparent proofs." We do not know how he answered Osiander. In any case Osiander, without appending his own name, prefaced the book as follows:

> To the reader, concerning the hypotheses of this work.
> Many scientists, in view of the already widespread reputation of these new hypotheses, will doubtless be greatly shocked by the theories of this book. . . . However . . . the master's . . . hypotheses are not necessarily true; they need not even be probable. It is completely sufficient if they lead to a computation that is in accordance with the astronomical observations. . . . The astronomer will most readily follow those hypotheses which are most easily understood. The philosopher will perhaps demand greater probability; but neither

of the two will be able to discover anything certain . . . unless it has been made known to him by divine revelations. Therefore let us grant that the following new hypotheses take their place beside the old ones which are not any more probable. Moreover, these are really admirable and easy to grasp, and in addition we shall find here a great treasure of the most learned observations. For the rest let no one expect certainty from astronomy as regards hypotheses. It cannot give this certainty. He who takes everything that is worked out for other purposes, as truth, would leave this science probably more ignorant than when he came to it. . . .[43]

This preface has often been condemned as an insolent interpolation.[44] Copernicus may have resented it, for the old man, having lived with his theory for thirty years, had come to feel it as part of his life and blood, and as a description of the actual facts of the universe. But Osiander's preface was judicious and just; it reduced the natural resistance of many minds to a disturbing and revolutionary idea, and it is still a good reminder that our descriptions of the universe are the fallible pronouncements of drops of water about the sea, and are likely to be rejected or corrected in their turn.

The book appeared at last, in the spring of 1543, with the title, *Nicolai Copernici revolutionum liber primus (First Book of Revolutions)*; later the book came to be known as *De revolutionibus orbium coelestium (On the Revolutions of the Celestial Orbs)*. One of the first copies reached Copernicus May 24, 1543. He was on his deathbed. He read the title page, smiled, and in the same hour died.

The Dedication to Pope Paul III was itself an effort to disarm resistance to a theory which, as Copernicus well knew, flagrantly contradicted the letter of Scripture. He began with pious assurances: "I still believe that we must avoid theories altogether foreign to orthodoxy." He had long hesitated to publish, wondering "were it not better to follow the example of the Pythagoreans . . . who were accustomed to transmit the secrets of philosophy not in writing but orally, and only to their relatives and friends." But learned churchmen—Nicholas Schonberg, Cardinal of Capua, and Tiedeman Giese, Bishop of Kulm—had urgently recommended that he should publish his findings. (Copernicus felt it wise not to mention the Lutheran Rheticus.) He acknowledged his debt to Greek astronomers, but, by a slip of the pen, he omitted Aristarchus. He believed that astronomers were in need of a better theory than the Ptolemaic, for they now found many difficulties in the geocentric view, and were unable to calculate accurately, on that basis, the length of the year. And he appealed to the Pope, as a man "eminent . . . in the love of all learning, and even of mathematics," to protect him against the "bites of slanderers" who, without adequate mathematical knowledge, would "assume the right to pass judgment on these things," or would "attack this theory of mine because of some passage of Scripture. . . ." [45]

The exposition begins with postulates: first, that the universe is spherical; second, that the earth is spherical—for matter, left to itself, gravitates toward a center, and therefore arranges itself into a spherical form; and third, that the motions of the celestial bodies are uniform circular motions, or are composed of such motions—for the circle is the "most perfect form," and "the intellect shrinks with horror" from the supposition that the celestial motions are not uniform. (Reason in thought would be impossible unless there were reason in the behavior of the objects of thought.)

Copernicus notes the relativity of motion: "All change in position which is seen is due to motion either of the observer or of the thing looked at, or to changes in the position of both, provided that these are different. For when things are moved equally relatively to the same things, no motion is perceived as between the object seen and the observer." [46] So the apparent daily rotation of the planets about the earth could be explained as due to a daily rotation of the earth on its axis; and the apparent annual movement of the sun around the earth can be explained by supposing the earth to move annually around the sun.

Copernicus anticipates objections. Ptolemy had argued that the clouds and surface objects of a rotating earth would fly off and be left behind. Copernicus answers that this objection would hold still more against the revolution of the major planets around the earth, since their great distances would imply vast orbits and extreme speeds. Ptolemy had further held that an object propelled directly upward from a rotating earth would not fall back to its point of origin. Copernicus replies that such objects, like the clouds, are "parts of the earth," and are carried along with it. And to the objection that the annual revolution of the earth around the sun should manifest itself in a movement of the "fixed" stars (stars beyond our planetary system) as observed at opposite ends of the earth's orbit, Copernicus answers that there is such a movement, but the great distance of the stars ("firmament") makes it imperceptible to us. (A moderate degree of such movement is now observable.)

He sums up his system in a compact paragraph:

> First and above all lies the sphere of the fixed stars, containing itself and all things, for that very reason immovable. . . . Of the moving bodies [planets] first comes Saturn, who completes his circuit in thirty years. After him Jupiter, moving in a twelve-year revolution. Then Mars, who revolves biennially. Fourth in order, an annual cycle takes place, in which . . . is contained the earth, with the lunar orbit as an epicycle. In the fifth place Venus is carried round in nine months. Then Mercury holds the sixth place, circulating in the space of eighty

days. In the middle of all dwells the sun. . . . Not ineptly some call it the lamp of the universe, others its mind, and others again its ruler . . . rightly, inasmuch as the sun, sitting on a royal throne, governs the circumambient family of the stars. . . . We find, therefore, under this orderly arrangement, a wonderful symmetry in the universe, and a definite relation of harmony in the motion and magnitude of the orbs, of a kind it is not possible to obtain in any other way.* [47]

Generally an advance in human theory carries with it many remnants of the theory displaced. Copernicus based his conceptions on observations handed down by Ptolemy, and he retained much of the Ptolemaic celestial machinery of spheres, epicycles, and eccentrics; the rejection of these would wait for Kepler. Most eccentric of all was Copernicus's calculation that the sun was not quite at the center of the earth's orbit. The center of the universe, he reckoned, would be "three sun-diameters away from the sun"; and the centers of the planetary orbits were likewise outside the sun, and not at all identical. Copernicus transferred from the earth to the sun two ideas now rejected: that the sun is the approximate center of the universe, and that it is at rest. He thought of the earth as having not only an axial rotation and an orbital revolution, but a third motion, which he supposed necessary to explain the inclination of the earth's axis and the precession of the equinoxes.

Consequently we must not smile in hindsight at those who took so long to adopt the Copernican system. They were required not only to set the earth turning and hurtling in space at an alarming speed, contrary to the direct evidence of the senses, but to accept a mathematical maze only slightly less bewildering than Ptolemy's. Not until Kepler, Galileo, and Newton should work out the mechanism of the new theory to greater simplicity and accuracy would it appear clearly superior to the old; and even then we should have to say of the sun what Galileo may have said of the earth—*eppur si muove*. Meanwhile Tycho Brahe rejected the heliocentric hypothesis on the ground that Copernicus had not convincingly answered Ptolemy's objections. More surprising than such a rejection is the relative celerity with which the new system was accepted by astronomers like Rheticus, Osiander, John Field, Thomas Digges, and Erasmus Reinhold—whose "Prutenic Tables" (1551) of celestial motions was in large part based on Copernicus. The Catholic Church raised no objection to the new theory so long as it represented itself as an hypothesis; but the Inquisition struck back mercilessly when Giordano Bruno assumed the hypothesis to be a certainty, and made explicit its consequences for religion. In 1616 the Congregation of the Index forbade the reading of *De Revolutionibus* "until corrected"; in 1620

---

* Current astronomy supposes nine planets and periods of revolution: Mercury (88 days), Venus (225), earth (365.26), Mars (687), Jupiter (11.86 years), Saturn (26.46 years), Uranus (84.02 years), Neptune (164.79 years), and Pluto (248 years).

it allowed Catholics to read editions from which nine sentences had been removed that represented the theory to be a fact. The book disappeared from the revised Index of 1758, but the prohibition was not explicitly rescinded till 1828.

The geocentric theory had fitted reasonably well a theology which supposed that all things had been created for the use of man. But now men felt tossed about on a minor planet whose history was reduced to a "mere local item in the news of the universe." [48] What could "heaven" mean when "up" and "down" had lost all sense, when each would become the other in half a day? "No attack on Christianity," wrote Jerome Wolf to Tycho Brahe in 1575, "is more dangerous than the infinite size and depth of the heavens"—though Copernicus had not taught the infinity of the universe. When men stopped to ponder the implications of the new system they must have wondered at the assumption that the Creator of this immense and orderly cosmos had sent His Son to die on this middling planet. All the lovely poetry of Christianity seemed to "go up in smoke" (as Goethe was to put it) at the touch of the Polish clergyman. The heliocentric astronomy compelled men to reconceive God in less provincial, less anthropomorphic terms; it gave theology the strongest challenge in the history of religion. Hence the Copernican revolution was far profounder than the Reformation; it made the differences between Catholic and Protestant dogmas seem trivial; it pointed beyond the Reformation to the Enlightenment, from Erasmus and Luther to Voltaire, and even beyond Voltaire to the pessimistic agnosticism of a nineteenth century that would add the Darwinian to the Copernican catastrophe. There was but one protection against such men, and that was that only a small minority in any generation would recognize the implications of their thought. The sun will "rise" and "set" when Copernicus has been forgotten.

In 1581 Bishop Kromer raised a monument to Copernicus against the inner wall of Frauenburg Cathedral, next to the canon's grave. In 1746 the monument was removed to make place for a statue of Bishop Szembek. Who was he? Who knows?

III. MAGELLAN AND THE DISCOVERY OF THE EARTH

The exploration of the earth progressed more rapidly than the charting of the skies, and with almost as disturbing influences on religion and philosophy. Geology advanced least, for the Biblical theory of creation was put beyond question by belief in its divine authorship. "If a wrong opinion should obtain regarding the creation as described in Genesis," said the Italian-English reformer, Peter Martyr Vermigli, "all the promises of Christ fall into nothing, and all the life of our religion would be lost." [49] Aside from Leonardo's scattered suggestions, the most significant work in geology in the first half of the sixteenth century was done by Georg Agricola. Note this passage from *De ortu et causis subterraneorum* (Basel, 1546) on the origin of mountains:

> Hills and mountains are produced by two forces, one of which is the power of water, the other the strength of the wind; we must add the fire in the interior of the earth. . . . For the torrents first of all wash out the soft earth, next carry away the harder earth, and then roll down the rocks, and thus in a few years they excavate the plains or slopes. . . . By such excavation to a great depth through many ages there arises an immense eminence. . . . Streams . . . and rivers effect the same result by their rushing and washing; for this reason they are frequently seen flowing either between very high mountains, which they have created, or close by the shore which borders them. . . . The wind produces hills and mountains in two ways: either . . . it violently moves and agitates the sand, or also when, after having been driven into the hidden recesses of the earth . . . it struggles to burst out.[50]

Agricola's *De natura fossilium* (1546) was the first systematic treatise on mineralogy; his *De re metallica* included the first systematic stratigraphy, and gave, as we have seen, the first explanation of ore deposits.

Ethnography produced two major works: the *Cosmographia universalis* (1544) of Sebastian Münster, and the *Descriptio Africae* (1550) of "Leo Africanus." Al-Hasan ibn-Muhammad al-Wazzan was a Moor from Granada; he traveled through Africa, and south to the Sudan, with the avidity of Ibn-Batuta; he was captured by Christian pirates and sent to Rome as a present to Leo X, who, impressed by his scholarly attainments, freed and pensioned him. He responded by accepting Christianity and Leo's name. During the next thirty years he composed his book, first in Arabic, then in Italian. Before it came from the press he returned to Tunis; and there he died in 1552, apparently in the faith of his fathers.[51]

It was an exciting age for geography. Reports poured in from missionaries, *conquistadores*, navigators, travelers, adding immensely to Europe's knowledge of the globe. The Spanish who in this period conquered Mexico, California, Central America, and Peru were first of all adventurers, tired of poverty and routine at home, and facing with pleasure the perils of distant and alien lands. Amid the hardships of their reckless enterprise they forgot civilized restraints, frankly adopted the morality of superior guns, and accomplished an act of continental robbery, treachery, and murder forgivable only because here and there—if an interested party may judge—the ultimate result was a gain for civilization. Yet there is little doubt that the conquered were at the time more civilized than their actual conquerors. Think of the

Mayan culture found in Yucatán by Hernández de Córdova (1517), and the Aztec Empire of the Montezumas conquered by Hernando Cortes (1521), and the socialistic civilization of the Incas destroyed in Francisco Pizarro's conquest of Peru (1526–32). We cannot know into what forms, noble or ignoble, these civilizations would have developed had they possessed the weapons to defend themselves.

The geographical revelation proceeded. Sebastian Cabot, under a Spanish flag, explored Argentina, Uruguay, and Paraguay. De Soto crossed Florida and the Gulf States into Oklahoma. Pedro de Alvarado discovered the empire of Texas, and Francisco de Coronado moved through Arizona and Oklahoma to Kansas. The mines of Potosi in Bolivia began to send their silver to Spain (1545). Year by year the map of the New World was charted in gold, silver, and blood. The English and French lagged behind in the great raid, because those parts of North America which the Spanish and Portuguese left to them were poor in precious metals, and forbidding in forests. John Rut sailed along the coast of Newfoundland and Maine. Giovanni da Verrazano was sent by Francis I to find a northwest passage to Asia; he landed on North Carolina, entered New York harbor (which remembers him with a statue at the Battery), and rounded Cape Cod to Maine. Jacques Cartier, under the flag of France, sailed up the St. Lawrence to Montreal, and established a French claim to Canada.

The most impressive adventure in this second generation of transoceanic exploration was the circling of the globe. Fernão de Magalhães was a Portuguese who shared actively in many Portuguese voyages and forays, but, falling into disfavor with his government, he passed into the service of Spain. In 1518 he persuaded Charles I (V) to finance an expedition that would seek a southwest passage to Asia. The young King was not yet rich, and the five ships allotted to Magellan were so weatherbeaten that one captain pronounced them unseaworthy. The largest was of 120 tons burden, the smallest, of seventy-five. Experienced sailors were loath to enlist; the crews had to be made up in large part of water-front riffraff. On September 20, 1519, the fleet sailed out of the Guadalquivir at San Lucar. It had the advantage of sailing from summer in the North Atlantic into summer in the South Atlantic; but in March 1520, winter came, and the vessels were anchored while the crews spent five weary months in Patagonia. The giant natives, averaging over six feet in height, gave the comparatively short Spaniards a condescending friendliness; nevertheless the hardships were so endless that three of the five crews mutinied, and Magellan had to wage war against his own men to compel their continuance in the enterprise. One ship stole away and returned to Spain; another was shattered on a reef. In August 1520, the voyage was resumed, and every bay was eagerly looked into as possibly the mouth of a transcontinental waterway. Or November 28 the search succeeded; the reduced fleet entered the Straits that bear Magellan's name. Thirty-eight days were spent in the 320-mile passage from sea to sea.

Then began a dreary crossing of the seemingly endless Pacific. In ninety-eight days only two small islands were seen. Provisions ran dangerously low, and scurvy plagued the crews. On March 6, 1521, they touched at Guam, but the natives were so hostile that Magellan sailed on. On April 6 they reached the Philippines; on the seventh they landed on the island of Cebu. There Magellan, to assure supplies, agreed to support the local ruler against neighboring enemies. He took part in an expedition against the island of Mactan, and was killed in battle there on April 27, 1521. He did not circumnavigate the globe, but he was the first to realize Columbus' dream of reaching Asia by sailing west.[52]

The crews were now so reduced by death that they could man only two ships. One of these turned back across the Pacific, probably seeking American gold. Only the *Victoria* remained. Juan Sebastián del Cano took command, and guided the little vessel, of eighty-five tons burden, through the Spice Islands, across the Indian Ocean, around the Cape of Good Hope, and up the west coast of Africa. Hungry for supplies, the crew anchored the ship off one of the Cape Verde Islands, but they were attacked by the Portuguese, and half of them were jailed. The remaining twenty-two managed to get away; and on September 8, 1522, the *Victoria* sailed up to Seville, with only eighteen men (the rest were Malays) of the 280 who had set out from Spain almost three years before. The ship's log recorded the date as September 7; Cardinal Gasparo Contarini explained the discrepancy as due to the westward direction of the voyage. The enterprise was one of the bravest in history, and one of the most fruitful for geography.

It remained for the geographers to catch up with the explorers. Giambattista Ramusio, the Italian Hakluyt, made the task easier by collecting, through thirty years, the accounts brought home by voyagers and other travelers; he translated and edited them, and they were published in three volumes (1550–59), thirteen years after his death. The progress made by the geographers in a decade becomes visible in comparing the 1520 globe preserved in the Germanisches National Museum at Nuremberg—which shows the West Indies but no American continent, and skips over a narrow ocean to Asia—with the three maps drawn up (1527–29) by Diogo Ribeiro, which show the coasts of Europe, Africa, and southern Asia with great accuracy, the east coast of the Americas from Newfoundland to the Straits of Magellan, and the west coast from Peru to Mexico. Probably copied from Ribeiro is the beautiful "Ramusio Map" (Venice, 1534) of the Americas in the New York Public Library. In the same alma mater is an early and faulty map by Gerhadus Mercator (1538), in which North and South America were first so named. ("Mercator's Projection" belongs to 1569.) Peter Apian

(1524) furthered the science by attempting to reduce geographical distances to precise measurements.

The effects of these explorations were felt in every phase of European life. The voyages of 1420–1560 nearly quadrupled the known surface of the globe. New fauna and flora, gems and minerals, foods and drugs, enlarged the botany, zoology, geology, menu, and pharmacopoeia of Europe. People wondered how representatives of all the new species had found room in Noah's ark. Literature was transformed: the old tales of chivalry gave way to stories of travel or adventure in distant lands; the search for gold replaced the quest of the Holy Grail in unconscious symbolism of the modern mood. The greatest commercial revolution in history (before the maturing of the airplane) opened the Atlantic and other oceans to European trade, and left the Mediterranean in a commercial—soon, therefore, in a cultural—backwater; the Renaissance moved from Italy to the Atlantic states. Europe, possessing better ships and guns, a hardier, more acquisitive and adventurous population, conquered—sometimes colonized—one after another of the newly discovered lands. Native populations were put to unwontedly steady and arduous work producing goods for Europe; slavery became an established institution. The almost-smallest continent became the richest; that Europeanization of the globe began which has been so sharply reversed in our time. The mind of Western man was powerfully stimulated by the distance, immensity, and variety of the new lands. Part of Montaigne's skepticism would root in the fascination of exotic ways and faiths. Customs and morals took on a geographical relativity that sapped old dogmas and certainties. Christianity itself had to be viewed in a new perspective as the religion of a minor continent amid a world of rival creeds. As humanism had discovered a world before Christ, and Copernicus had exposed the astronomic insignificance of the earth, so exploration and the commerce that followed it revealed vast realms beyond and ignoring Christianity. The authority of Aristotle and the other Greeks was damaged when it appeared how little of the planet they had known. The Renaissance idolatry of the Greeks declined, and man, swelling with Renaissance pride at his new discoveries, prepared to forget his lessened astronomic size in the expansion of his knowledge and his trade. Modern science and philosophy rose, and undertook the epochal task of reconceiving the world.

IV. THE RESURRECTION OF BIOLOGY

The biological sciences, which had made hardly any progress since the Greeks, now came back to life. Botany struggled to free itself from pharmacy and stand on its own feet; it succeeded, but inevitably its masters were still medical men. Otto Brunfels, city physician at Bern, began the movement with his *Herbarum vivae icones* (1530–36)—"living pictures of plants"; its text was largely filched from Theophrastus, Dioscorides, and other predecessors, but it also described the native plants of Germany, and its 135 woodcuts were models of fidelity. Euricius Cordus, city physician to Bremen, set up the first botanical garden (1530) north of the Alps, attempted an independent summary of the nascent science in his *Botanilogicon* (1534), and hen returned to his medical medium in his *Liber de urinis*. His son Valerius Cordus wandered recklessly in the study of plants, met his death in the search at the age of twenty-nine (1544), but left for posthumous publication his *Historia plantarum*, which vividly and accurately described 500 new species. Leonard Fuchs, professor of medicine at Tübingen, studied botany at first for pharmaceutics, then for its own sake and delight. His *Historia stirpium* (1542) was typical of scientific devotion; its 343 chapters analyzed 343 genera, and illustrated them with 515 woodcuts, each occupying a full folio page. He prepared a still more comprehensive work with 1,500 plates, but no printer would undertake the expense of its publication. The genus Fuchsia is his living memorial.

Perhaps the most important single idea contributed to biology in this period was Pierre Belon's demonstration, in his *Histoire . . . des oyseaux* (1555), of the astonishing correspondence of the bones in men and birds. But the greatest figure in the "natural science" of this age was Conrad Gesner, whose work and learning covered so wide a field that Cuvier called him the Pliny, and might have called him the Aristotle, of Germany. Born of a poor family in Zurich (1516), he showed such aptitude and industry that the city joined with private patrons to finance his higher education in Strasbourg, Bourges, Paris, and Basel. He made or collected 1,500 drawings to illustrate his *Historia plantarum*, but this work proved so expensive to print that it did not emerge from manuscript till 1751; its brilliant classification of plant genera by their reproductive structures reached the light too late to help Linnaeus. He published during his lifetime four volumes (1551–58), and left a fifth, of a gigantic *Historia animalium*, which listed each animal species under its Latin name, and described its appearance, origin, habitat, habits, illnesses, mental and emotional qualities, medical and domestic uses, and place in literature; the classification was alphabetical instead of scientific, but its encyclopedic accumulation of knowledge invited biology to take form. Insufficiently used up by these labors, Gesner began a twenty-one-volume *Bibliotheca universalis*, in which he set out to catalogue all known Greek, Latin, and Hebrew writings; he completed twenty volumes, and earned the title of Father of Bibliography. In an aside called *Mithridates* (1555) he attempted to classify 130 languages of the world. His *Descriptio Montis Pilati* (1541) was apparently the first published study of mountains as forms of beauty; Switzerland now knew that it was majestic. All these enterprises were accomplished between 1541 and 1565. In that year Conrad Gesner, the incarnate spirit of study, died.

Meanwhile Juan Vives's *De anima et vita* (1538) almost created modern empirical psychology. As if to elude the skepticism that Hume would expound two centuries later about the existence of a "mind" additional to mental operations, Vives advised the student not to ask what the mind or soul *is*, since (he felt) we shall never know this; we must inquire only what the mind *does*; psychology must cease to be theoretical metaphysics and must become a science based on specific and accumulated observations. Here Vives anticipated by a century Francis Bacon's emphasis on induction. He studied in detail the association of ideas, the operation and improvement of memory, the process of knowledge, and the role of feeling and emotion. In his book we see psychology, like so many sciences before it, emerging painfully from the womb of their common mother, philosophy.

V. VESALIUS

In 1543 Andreas Vesalius published what Sir William Osler judged the greatest medical work ever written.[53] His father, Andreas Wessel, was a prosperous apothecary in Brussels; his grandfather had been physician to Mary of Burgundy and then to her husband Maximilian I; his great-grandfather had been city physician at Brussels; his great-great-grandfather, a physician, had composed a commentary on Avicenna's *Kanun*; here was a social heredity outmatching Bach's. Subjected to it from birth, Vesalius soon developed a passion for dissection. "No animal was safe from him. Dogs and cats, mice, rats, and moles were meticulously dissected by him."[54] But he did not neglect other studies. At twenty-two he lectured in Latin, and readily read Greek. At Paris (1533–36) he studied anatomy under Jacques Dubois, who gave to many muscles and blood vessels the names they bear today. For a long time, like his teachers, he accepted Galen as a Bible; he never lost respect for him, but he respected much more the authority of observation and dissection. With some fellow students he made many trips to the charnel houses where were gathered the bones exhumed from the Cemetery of the Innocents; there they became so familiar with the parts of the human skeleton that, he tells us, "we, even blindfolded, dared at times to wager with our companions, and in the space of half an hour no bone could be offered us . . . which we could not identify by touch."[55] Frequently, in the classes of Dubois, the bold young anatomist would displace the "barber surgeons" to whom actual dissection was usually delegated by the physician professor, and would himself expertly expose the parts relevant to the lecture.[56]

When his sovereign Charles V invaded France (1536), Vesalius retired to Louvain. Hampered by a shortage of corpses there, he and his friend Gemma Frisius (later famous as a mathematician) snatched one out of the air. His account reveals his passion:

> While out walking, looking for bones in the place where, on the country highways ... those who have been executed are customarily placed, I happened upon a dried cadaver. ... The bones were entirely bare, held together by the ligaments alone. . . . With the help of Gemma I climbed the stake and pulled off the femur. . . . The scapulae together with the arms and hands followed. . . . After I had brought the legs and arms home in secret and successive trips . . . I allowed myself to be shut out of the city in the evening in order to obtain the thorax, which was firmly held by a chain. *I was burning with so great a desire.* . . . The next day I transported the bones home piecemeal through another gate of the city.[57]

The burgomaster saw the point, and thereafter gave the anatomy classes whatever cadaver could be released; "and he himself," says Vesalius, "was in regular attendance when I administered an anatomy."[58]

A man with such "burning desire" could not keep his temper cool. He fell into a hot dispute with a teacher about methods of venesection, left Louvain (1537), and rode down the Rhine and across the Alps to Italy. He was already so proficient that before the end of that year he received his doctor's degree at Padua *cum ultima diminutione*—"with the maximum diminution" of the fee; for the higher a student's standing the lower his graduation fee. On the very next day (December 6, 1537) the Venetian Senate appointed him professor of surgery and anatomy at the University of Padua. He was twenty-three.

During the following six years he taught at Padua, Bologna, and Pisa, doing hundreds of dissections with his own hands, and issuing some minor works. Under his direction Jan Stefan van Kalkar, a pupil of Titian, drew six plates which were published (1538) as *Tabulae anatomicae sex*. A year later Vesalius, in a *Venesection Letter*, supported Pierre Brissot of Paris on methods of bloodletting. In the course of his argument he revealed some results of his dissections of the venous system, and these observations contributed to the discovery of the circulation of the blood. In 1541–42 he joined other scholars in a new edition of the Greek text of Galen. He was astonished by Galenic errors that the simplest human dissection would have disproved—that the lower jaw had two parts, the sternum seven distinct bones, the liver several lobes. Only on the assumption that Galen's dissections had been of animals, never of men, could these errors be explained and forgiven. Vesalius felt that the time had come to revise the science of human anatomy in terms of the dissection of man. He prepared his masterpiece.

When Johannes Oporinus printed at Basel in 1543 the *De humani corporis fabrica (On the Structure of the Human Body)*, a large folio of 663 pages, what must have struck the reader at once was the title page—an engraving worthy of Dürer, which pictured Vesalius demonstrating the anatomy of an opened arm, with half a hundred students looking on. And then the illustrations: 277 woodcuts of unprecedented anatomical accuracy and high technical excellence, made mostly by Van Kalkar, with scientifically irrelevant and artistically attractive landscapes behind the figures—a skeleton, for example, at a reading desk. These cuts were so fine that some have thought they were designed in the studio of Titian, perhaps under his supervision; to which we must add that Vesalius drew several of them with his own hand. He accompanied the blocks watchfully in their journey by mule pack over the Alps from Venice to Basel. When the printing was complete the blocks were carefully preserved; later they were bought, exchanged, and lost; in 1893 they were found secreted in the library of the University of Munich; they were destroyed by bombing in the second World War.

What should have aroused more astonishment than these drawings was that the text—a triumph of typography but also a scientific revolution—was by a youth of twenty-nine. It was a revolution because it ended the reign of Galen in anatomy, revised the whole science in terms of dissection, and so established the physical basis of modern medicine, which begins with this book. Here for the first time were described the true course of the veins and the anatomy of the heart; here was the epochal statement that the most careful dissection showed none of those pores through which Galen had supposed the blood to pass from one ventricle of the heart to the other; so the way was prepared for Servetus, Colombo, and Harvey. Galen was corrected again and again—on the liver, the bile ducts, the maxillae, the uterus. Vesalius, too, made errors, even of observation, and failed to take the great leap from the anatomy of the heart to the circulation of the blood. But here were accurate descriptions of scores of organs never so well described before, and every part of the body opened to science with a confident and masterly hand.

He suffered from the defects of his qualities. The pride that upheld him through years of minute study made him quick to take offense, slow to recognize the achievements of his predecessors and the sensitivity of his rivals. He was so in love with "that true Bible . . . the human body and the nature of man" [59] that he hurt many theological toes. He referred sarcastically to the ecclesiastics who seemed most attracted to his lecture room when the reproductive organs were to be studied and shown.[60] He made many enemies; and though Gesner and Fallopio hailed his work, most of the older professors, including his former teacher Dubois, condemned him as an insolent upstart, and sedulously picked flaws in his book. Dubois explained that Galen had not been wrong, but that the human body had changed since Galen's time; so, he thought, the straight thigh bones, which, as everyone saw, were not curved in accordance with Galen's description of them, were the result of the narrow trousers of Renaissance Europeans.[61]

In a tempest of disappointment at the attitude of these men, Vesalius burned a huge volume of *Annotationes*, and a paraphrase of the ten books of al-Razi's *Kitab al-Mansuri*—an encyclopedia of medicine.[62] In 1544 he left Italy to become second physician on the staff of Charles V, to whom he had judiciously dedicated the *Fabrica*. In the same year his father died, leaving him a considerable fortune. He married, and built a handsome home in Brussels. A second edition of the *Fabrica* was issued in 1555, with augmented and corrected text. It showed that artificial respiration could keep an animal alive despite incision of its chest, and that a stopped heart could sometimes be revived by bellows. Thereafter Vesalius made no contribution to anatomy. He absorbed himself in caring for his Imperial and lesser patients, and in the practice and study of surgery. When Charles abdicated, Vesalius became second physician to Philip II. In July 1559, the King sent him to aid Ambroise Paré in an attempt to save the wounded Henry II; Vesalius applied clinical tests that showed no possibility of recovery. Later in that year he and his family accompanied Philip to Spain.

Meanwhile others advanced anatomy. Giambattista Cano noted the venous valves (1547); Servetus explained the pulmonary circulation of the blood (1553); Realdo Colombo made the same discovery (1558), and proved it by experiment on the living heart; but another seventy years passed before Harvey's epochal description of the course of the blood from heart to lungs to heart to arteries to veins to heart. The Arab physician Ibn al-Nafis had anticipated Servetus in 1285,[63] and the tradition of his doctrine may have carried down into the Spain of Servetus's youth.

Vesalius had some adventures left to him. The native physicians at the Spanish court made it a point of honor to disregard his diagnoses. When Don Carlos, Philip's only son, suffered concussion of the brain from a fall (1562), Vesalius recommended trepanning. The advice was rejected, and the youth neared death. Relics and charms were applied to the wound, and pious people flogged themselves to persuade heaven to effect some miraculous cure; to no avail. Finally Vesalius insisted on opening the skull; it was done, and a large quantity of pus was drawn off. The Prince soon improved, and eight days after the operation Philip II attended a solemn procession of thanksgiving to God.[64]

Two years later Vesalius left Spain, for reasons still in dispute. Ambroise Paré told of an anatomist who brought most of Spain down upon his head by opening the body of a woman supposedly dead from "strangulation of the uterus"; at a further stroke of the surgeon's knife, said Paré, the woman came suddenly back to life, "which struck such admiration and horror into the hearts of all her friends . . . that they accounted the physician—before of good fame and report—as infamous and detestable"; [65] relatives do not always appreciate such unexpected recoveries. "Therefore," continued the Huguenot surgeon, "he thought there was no better way for him, if he would live safe, than to forsake the country." Hubert Languet, another Huguenot, told a similar story (c. 1579), named the physician as Vesalius, and claimed that Vesalius, by dissecting a living person, had become liable to the Inquisition, which he escaped by promising to make a penitential pilgrimage to Palestine. No contemporary source mentions the incident, and Catholic historians reject it as a fable. [66] Perhaps Vesalius was just tired of Spain.

He returned to Italy, sailed from Venice (April 1564), and apparently reached Jerusalem. On the way back he suffered shipwreck, and died of exposure, far from any friend, on the island of Zante off the west coast of Greece (October 15, 1564). He was fifty years old. In that same year Michelangelo died and Shakespeare was born. The splendor that had shone for a century in Italy was passing to the north.

VI. THE RISE OF SURGERY

Despite the advances of anatomy, the science and art of medicine were still in leading strings to Greek and Arabic authorities. The evidence of the senses hardly availed against the word of Galen or Avicenna; even Vesalius, when his dissections disproved Galen, said, "I could hardly believe my eyes." Editions or translations of Galen or Hippocrates, while spreading old knowledge, discouraged new experiments—very much as the efforts of Petrarch and Ronsard to write Virgilian epics diverted and injured their natural genius. When Linacre founded what was later named the Royal College of Physicians (1518), its principal texts were his translations of Galen.

Therapy benefited from new drugs brought to Europe—cinchona, ipecacuanha, and rhubarb from America, ginger and benzoin from Sumatra, cloves from the Moluccas, aloes from Cochin China, camphor and cinnabar from China; and the development widened the use of native plants. Valerius Cordus compiled the first German pharmacopoeia (1546). The treatment of syphilis with infusions of guaiac wood from the West Indies was so popular that the Fuggers made another fortune by securing from their debtor, Charles V, a monopoly on its sale in his realms.

The poverty and uncleanliness of the masses kept diseases always ahead of cures. Open heaps of refuse or dung poisoned the air, and sometimes littered the streets. Paris had a system of sewers, which Henry II proposed to empty into the Seine; the municipal authorities dissuaded him by explaining that the river was the sole drinking water that half the people had. [67] Sewer commissions were set up in England in 1532, but as late as 1844 there were only two English towns where refuse was removed at public expense from the slums.

Epidemics were less virulent than in the Middle Ages, but they sufficed— along with high puerperal and infantile mortality, to keep the population almost stationary. Plagues swept through Germany and France repeatedly between 1500 and 1568. Typhus fever spread in England in 1422, 1577, and 1586, through the migrations of lice. The "sweating sickness"—probably a form of influenza—ravaged England in 1528, 1529, 1551, 1578; Germany in 1543–45; France in 1550–51; Hamburg and Aachen, we are told, each lost a thousand souls to it within a few days.[68] Influenza was ascribed to celestial influences—hence its name. The bubonic plague reappeared in Germany in 1562, taking 9,000 of the 40,000 inhabitants of Nuremberg [69]—though we may suspect all plague statistics as exaggerations. Brighter sides of the picture are the fading out of leprosy and such mental disorders as St. Vitus's Dance.

Medical practice progressed more slowly than medical knowledge. Quacks still abounded; despite some restrictive laws it was easy to practice medicine without a degree. Most babies were eased into the world by midwives. Specialism had hardly begun. Dentistry was not separated from medicine or surgery; barber surgeons extracted teeth, and replaced them with ivory substitutes. Nearly all physicians—Vesalius was one of the exceptions—left surgery to barber surgeons, who, however, must not be thought of as barbers; many of them were men of training and skill.

Ambroise Paré began as a barber's apprentice, and rose to be surgeon to kings. Born (1517) at Bourg-Hersent in Maine, he made his way to Paris, and set up his barber's stall in the Place St.-Michel. During the war of 1536 he served as a regimental surgeon. In treating soldiers he accepted the prevailing theory that gunshot wounds were poisonous, and (like Vesalius) he followed the current practice of cauterizing them with boiling elder oil, which turned pain into agony. One night the oil ran out, and for lack of it Paré dressed the wounds with a salve of egg yolk, attar of roses, and turpentine. On the morrow he wrote:

> Last night I could hardly sleep for continually thinking about the wounded men whose hurts I had not been able to cauterize. I expected to find them all dead the next morning. With this in view I rose early to visit them. Greatly to my surprise, I found that those whom I had treated with the salve had very little pain in their wounds, no inflammation . . . and had passed a comfortable night. The others, whose wounds had been treated with boiling elder oil, were in high fever, while their wounds were inflamed . . . and acutely painful. I determined, therefore, that I would no longer cauterize the unfortunate in so cruel a manner.[70]

Paré had little education, and it was not till 1545 that he published his little manual, now a medical classic, on the treatment of wounds (*Méthode de traicter les plaies*). In the war of 1552 he proved that ligature of the artery was preferable to cauterization to check bleeding in amputations. Captured by the enemy, he earned his release by successful operations. On returning to Paris he was appointed head surgeon at the Collège St.-Côme, to the horror of the Sorbonne, where a professor innocent of Latin seemed a biological monstrosity. Nevertheless he became surgeon to Henry II, then to Francis II, then to Charles IX; and though a professed Huguenot, he was spared by royal order in the Massacre of St. Bartholomew. His *Deux livres de chirurgie* (1573) added little to the theory, much to the practice, of surgery. He invented new instruments, introduced artificial limbs, popularized the use of the truss in hernia, improved podalic version in childbirth, made the first exarticulation of the elbow joint, described monoxide poisoning, and indicated flies as carriers of disease. Famous in the annals of medicine is his demurrer to congratulations on his success in a difficult case: *Je le pansay, Dieu le guarit*—"I treated him, God cured him." He died in 1590, age seventy-three. He had considerably improved the status and competence of surgeons, and had given France, in surgery, that lead which it was to retain for several centuries.

VII. PARACELSUS AND THE DOCTORS

In every generation men arise who, resenting the cautious conservatism of the medical profession, lay claim to remarkable cures by heterodox means, denounce the profession as cruelly laggard, perform wonders for a time, and then lose themselves in a mist of desperate extravagance and isolation. It is good that such gadflies should appear now and then to keep medical thought on its toes, and good that medicine should check hasty innovations in dealing with human life. Here, as in politics and philosophy, radical youth and conservative age unwillingly co-operate in that balance of variation and heredity which is nature's technique of development.

Philippus Theophrastus Bombastus von Hohenheim called himself Aureolus as signifying the carat of his brilliance, and Paracelsus probably as a Latinization of Hohenheim.[71] His father, Wilhelm Bombast von Hohenheim, was the illegitimate son of a hot-tempered Swabian noble. Left to shift for himself, Wilhelm practiced medicine among poor villagers near Einsiedeln in Switzerland, and married Elsa Ochsner, an innkeeper's daughter and nurse's aid, who soon afterward developed a manic-depressive condition. This ambivalent ancestry may have inclined Philip to instability, and to a resentful sense of capacities inadequately nurtured by his environment. Born in 1493, he grew up amid his father's patients, and perhaps in undue familiarity with inns, whose unbuttoned life remained always to his taste. A dubious story alleges that the boy was emasculated by a wild boar or by drunken soldiers. No woman is known to have figured in his adult life. When he was nine his mother drowned herself. Probably for that reason father and son moved to Villach in Tirol. There, says tradition, Wilhelm taught in a school of mines and dabbled in alchemy. Certainly there were mines near by, and a smelter; and it is likely that Philip learned there some of the chemistry with which he was to revolutionize therapy.

At the age of fourteen he went off to study at Heidelberg. The restlessness of his nature showed now in his quick passage from one university to another—Freiburg, Ingolstadt, Cologne, Tübingen, Vienna, Erfurt, finally (1513–15) Ferrara—though such scholastic peregrination was frequent in the Middle Ages. In 1515, without having won a degree, Philip—now Paracelsus—took service as a barber surgeon in the army of Charles I of Spain. The campaign over, he resumed his footloose life. If we may believe him, he practiced medicine in Granada, Lisbon, England, Denmark, Prussia, Poland, Lithuania, Hungary, "and other lands." [72] He was in Salzburg during the Peasants' War of 1525, treated their wounds, and sympathized with their aims. He had a socialist spell; he denounced money, interest, merchants, and advocated communism in land and trade, and equal remuneration for all.[73] In his first book, *Archidoxa* (*The Arch-Wisdom*, 1524), he rejected theology and lauded scientific experiment.[74] Arrested after the failure of the peasants' revolt, he was saved from the gallows by evidence that he had never taken up arms; but he was banished from Salzburg, and left in haste.

In 1527 he was at Strasbourg, practicing surgery and lecturing to barber surgeons. His doctrine was a confusion of sense and nonsense, magic and medicine—though God knows how the future will describe our current certainties. He rejected astrology, then accepted it; he would not give an enema when the moon was in the wrong phase. He laughed at the divining rod, but claimed to have transmuted metals into gold.[75] Animated, like the young Agrippa, by a thirst for knowledge, he sought anxiously the "philosopher's stone"—i.e., some universal formula that would explain the universe. He wrote credulously about gnomes, asbestos salamanders, and "signatures"— the treatment of diseased organs with drugs resembling them in color or form. He was not above using magical incantations and amulets as cures [76]—perhaps as suggestive medicine.

But this same man, dripping with the delusions of his time, boldly advanced the application of chemistry to medicine. Sometimes he spoke like a materialist: "Man derives from matter, and matter is the whole universe." [77] Man is to the universe as microcosm to macrocosm; both are composed of the same elements—basically, salts, sulfur, and mercury; and the apparently lifeless metals and minerals are instinct with life.[78] Chemotherapy is the use of the macrocosm to cure the microcosm. Man is, in body, a chemical compound; sickness is a disharmony not of Galen's "humours" but of the chemical constituents of the body; here was the first modern theory of metabolism. By and large the therapy of the age depended for its drugs on the plant and animal world; Paracelsus, deep in alchemy, stressed the curative possibilities of inorganic materials. He made mercury, lead, sulfur, iron, arsenic, copper sulfate, and potassium sulfate parts of the pharmacopoeia; he spread the use of chemical tinctures and extracts; he was the first to make that "tincture of opium" which we call laudanum. He encouraged the use of mineral baths, and explained their diverse properties and effects.

He noted the occupational and geographical factors in disease, studied fibroid phthisis in miners, and first linked cretinism with endemic goiter. He advanced the understanding of epilepsy, and related paralysis and speech disturbances to injuries of the head. Whereas gout and arthritis had been generally accepted as natural and incurable accompaniments of increasing age, Paracelsus claimed that they were curable if diagnosed as due to acids formed by food residues too long retained in the colon. "All diseases can be traced to a coagulation of undigested matter in the bowels." [79] These acids of intestinal putrefaction he called "tartar" because their deposits in joints, muscles, kidneys, and bladder "burn like hell, and Tartarus is hell." [80] "Doctors boast of their [knowledge of] anatomy," he said, "but they fail to see the tartar sticking to their teeth"; [81] and the word stuck. He proposed to check the formation of such deposits in the body by a healthy diet, tonics, and improved elimination; he tried to "mollify" the deposits by using laurel oil and resin compounds; and in extreme cases he advocated surgery to allow the accretions to escape or be removed. He claimed to have cured many cases of gout by these methods, and some physicians in our time believe they have made cures by following Paracelsus' diagnosis.

News of cures accomplished by Paracelsus in Strasbourg reached Basel. There the famous printer Froben was suffering acute pain in his right foot. The doctors advised amputation. Froben invited Paracelsus to come to Basel and diagnose the case. Paracelsus came, and effected a cure without use of the knife. Erasmus, then living with Froben and many ailments, consulted Paracelsus, who prescribed for him—we do not know with what success. In any case these famous patients gave the young doctor new fame, and a strange medley of circumstances brought him close to that university professorship which he coveted.

At this time the Protestants were a majority in the city council of Basel. Over the objections of Erasmus and the Catholic minority, they dismissed Dr. Wonecker, the city physician, on the ground that he had "uttered fresh words against the Reformation," [82] and they appointed Paracelsus in his place. The council and Paracelsus assumed that the appointment carried with it the right to teach in the university; but the faculty condemned the appointment, and—knowing the weakness of Paracelsus in anatomy—proposed a public examination of his fitness. He evaded the test, began practice as city physician, and gave public lectures in a private hall without university sanction (1527). He gathered students by a characteristic invitation:

> Theophrastus Bombast of Hohenheim, doctor of both medicines and professor, greetings to the students of medicine. Of all disciplines medicine alone . . . is recognized as a sacred art. Yet few doctors today practice it with success, and therefore the time has come to bring it back to its former dignity, to cleanse it from the leaven of the barbarians, and to purge their errors. We shall do so not by strictly adhering to the rules of the ancients, but exclusively by studying nature and using the experience which we have gained in long years of practice. Who does not know that most contemporary doctors fail because they slavishly abide by the precepts of Avicenna, Galen, and Hippocrates? . . . This may lead to splendid titles, but does not make a true doctor. What a doctor needs is not eloquence or knowledge of language and of books . . . but profound knowledge of Nature and her works. . . .
>
> Thanks to the liberal allowance the gentlemen of Basel have granted for that purpose, I shall explain the textbooks which I have written on surgery and pathology, every day for two hours, as an introduction to my healing methods. I do not compile these from excerpts of Hippocrates or Galen. In ceaseless toil I created them anew upon the foundations of experience, the supreme teacher of all things. If I want to prove anything I shall not do so by quoting authorities, but by experiment and by reasoning thereupon. If, therefore, dear reader, you should feel the impulse to enter into those divine mysteries, if within a brief lapse of time you should want to fathom the depths of medicine, then come to me at Basel. . . . Basel, June 5, 1527.[83]

Thirty students registered for the course. At its opening Paracelsus appeared in the customary professorial robe, but at once he cast it aside, and stood forth in the rough garb and sooty leather apron of the alchemist. His lectures on medicine were given in a Latin form prepared by his secretary Oporinus (who later printed Vesalius's *Fabrica*); on surgery he spoke in German. This was a further shock to the orthodox physicians, but hardly so disturbing as when Paracelsus proposed that "no pharmacist should act in collusion with any doctor." [84] As if to signalize his scorn of traditional medicine, he merrily threw into a bonfire—lit by students to celebrate St. John's Day (June 24, 1527)—a recent medical text, probably the *Summa Jacobii*. "I threw into St. John's Fire," he said, "the *Summa* of the books, so that all the misfortunes might go up in the air with the smoke. Thus the realm of medicine has been purged." [85] Men compared the gesture with Luther's burning of a papal bull.

Paracelsus' life in Basel was as heterodox as his lectures. "The two years I passed in his company," said Oporinus, "he spent in drinking and gluttony, day and night.... He was a spendthrift, so that sometimes he had not a penny left.... Every month he had a new coat made for him, and gave away his old one to the first comer; but usually it was so dirty that I never wanted one." [86] Heinrich Bullinger gave a similar picture of Paracelsus as a hard drinker, and "an extremely dirty, unclean man." [87] But Oporinus testified to remarkable cures performed by his master; "in curing ulcers he almost did miracles in cases which had been given up by others." [88]

The profession disowned him as a degreeless quack, a reckless empiric, incapable of dissection and ignorant of anatomy. He opposed dissection on the ground that the organs could be understood only in their united and normal functioning in the living organism. He returned the scorn of the doctors in the liveliest billingsgate. He laughed at their barbarous prescriptions, their silk shirts, finger rings, sleek gloves, and haughty gait; he challenged them to come out of the classrooms into the chemical laboratory, to put on aprons, soil their hands with the elements, and, bending over furnaces, learn the secrets of nature by experiment and the sweat of their brows. He made up for his lack of a degree by taking such titles as "Prince of Philosophy and Medicine," "Doctor of Both Medicines" (i.e., physician and surgeon), and "Propagator of Philosophy"; and he salved the wounds of his vanity with the confidence of his claims. "All shall follow me," he wrote, "and the monarchy of medicine shall be mine.... All the universities and all the old writers put together are less talented than my a——" [89] Rejected by others, he took as his motto, *Alterius non sit qui suus esse potest*—"Let him not belong to another who can be his own." [90] History rebuked his boasts by making his family name Bombast a common noun.

Whether through collusion with the university faculty, or in a spontaneous revolt of students against a dogmatic teacher, an anonymous Basel wit composed—and prominently exposed—a lampoon in dog-Latin, purporting to be written by Galen himself from Hades against his detractor, whom he called Cacophrastus—Dung-speaker. It made great fun of Paracelsus' mystical terminology, called him a madman, and suggested that he hang himself. Unable to find the culprit, Paracelsus asked the town council to question the students one by one, and to punish the guilty. The council ignored the request. About this time a canon of the Basel Cathedral offered a hundred guilders to anyone who would cure him of his disease; Paracelsus cured him in three days; the canon paid him six guilders, but refused the rest on the ground that the cure had taken so little time. Paracelsus sued him in court, and lost. He lost his temper too, denounced his critics as *Bescheisser* and

Arschkrätzer (cheaters and rear-scratchers), and published, anonymously, a pamphlet branding the clergy and magistrates as corrupt. The council ordered his arrest, but deferred execution of the order till the next morning. During the night Paracelsus fled (1528). He had been ten months in Basel.

In Nuremberg he recapitulated his experience at Basel. The city fathers gave him charge of a prison hospital; he worked impressive cures; but he inveighed against the jealous medicos of the town for their dishonesty, their opulence, and the size of their wives. Noting that the majority of the council was Protestant, he defended Catholicism. The Fuggers, who sold guaiac, were alarmed by his contention that this "holy wood" was useless in the treatment of syphilis. In 1530 he persuaded an obscure printer to publish *Three Chapters on the French Disease*, which so berated the doctors that a storm of opposition forced him to resume his wandering. He wished to publish a larger work on the same subject, but the city council forbade its printing; Paracelsus, in a letter to the council, pleaded with ineffective eloquence for the freedom of the press; the book was never printed in his lifetime. It contained the best clinical description of syphilis yet written, and advised internal doses, rather than external applications, of mercury. Syphilis became a battleground of vegetable vs. chemical therapy.

Moving to Saint-Gall, Paracelsus lived for half a year in the house of a patient. There and later he wrote his *Opus paramirum*—"the very wonderful work"—his *Paragranum*—"against the grain"?—and *Die grosse Wundartzney (The Great Surgery)*, all in rough German. They are heaps of crude ore, with here and there a gem. In 1534 he relapsed into magic, and composed *Philosophia sagax*, a compendium of the occult.

When his patient in Saint-Gall died he took to the road again, passing from place to place in Germany, sometimes begging his bread. In his youth he had uttered some religious heresies—that baptism has only symbolic significance, that the sacraments are good for children and fools, but useless for men of intelligence, and that prayers to the saints are a waste of time.[91] Now (1532), poor and defeated, he experienced religious "conversion." He fasted, gave his remaining goods to the poor, wrote essays of devotion, and consoled himself with hopes of paradise. In 1540 the Bishop of Salzburg offered him asylum, and the man who had encouraged revolution there fifteen years before accepted gratefully. He made his will, bequeathing his few coins to relatives, his instruments to the barber surgeons of the city; and on September 24, 1541, he yielded his body to the earth.

He was a man overcome by his own genius, rich in varied experience and brilliant perceptions, but too little schooled to separate science from magic, too undisciplined to control his fire, too angrily hostile to infuse his influence into his time. Perhaps his career, along with Agrippa's, helped to swell the legend of Faust. Until a century ago people suffering an epidemic in Austria made a pilgrimage to his grave in Salzburg, hoping to be healed by the magic of his spirit or his bones.[92]

VIII. THE SKEPTICS

The sixteenth century was a poor time for philosophy; theology absorbed the active thinkers, and faith, ruling every roost, kept reason in its train. Luther rejected reason as inclining to atheism,[93] but cases of atheism were rare. A Dutch priest was burned at The Hague (1512) for denying creation, immortality, and the divinity of Christ,[94] but he was not clearly an atheist. "This year," wrote an English chronicler under 1539, "there died in the University of Paris a great doctor, which said there was no God, and had been of that opinion since he was twenty years old, and was above fourscore years old when he died; and all that time he had kept that error secret." [95] Guillaume Postel, in 1552, published a book *Contra atheos*, but the word *atheist* was seldom distinguished from deist, pantheist, or skeptic.

Skeptics were numerous enough to win a blow from Luther. "For the blind children of the world," he is reported to have said, "the articles of faith are too high. That three persons are only one God, that the true Son of God was made man, that in Christ there are two natures, divine and human, etc.—all this offends them as fiction and fable"; and some, he added, doubted whether God had created men whose damnation He had foreseen.[96] In France there were some skeptics of immortality.[97] Bonaventure Desperiers, in his *Cymbalum mundi* (1537), ridiculed miracles, the contradictions of the Bible, and the persecution of heretics. His book was condemned by Calvin and the Sorbonne, and was burned by the official hangman. Marguerite had to banish him from her court at Nérac, but she sent him money to keep him alive at Lyons. In 1544 he killed himself, leaving his manuscripts to Marguerite, "prop and safeguard of all goodness." [98]

The spirit of doubt appeared in politics in the form of attacks on the divine right and inviolability of kings; and here the skeptics were usually Protestant thinkers uncomfortable under Catholic rulers, or Catholic thinkers smarting under the triumph of the state. Bishop John Ponet, resenting Mary Tudor, published in 1558 *A Short Treatise of Politique Power*, which argued that "the manifold and continual examples that have been, from time to time, of the deposing of kings and killing of tyrants, do most certainly confirm it to be most true, just, and consonant to God's judgment. . . . Kings, princes, and governors have their authority of the people . . . and men may recover their proxies . . . when it pleaseth them." [99] John Major, a Scottish professor who helped to form the mind of John Knox, argued likewise that since all secular authority derives from the will of the community, a bad king may be deposed and executed, but only by due process of law.

The most interesting opponent of royal absolutism was a young Catholic who achieved a modest immortality by dying in Montaigne's arms. Étienne de la Boétie, said the incomparable essayist, "was the greatest man, to my mind, of our age." [100] Son of a high official in Périgord, Étienne studied law at Orléans, and, before the prescribed age, was admitted as a councilor to the *Parlement* of Bordeaux. About 1549, as a youth of nineteen inspired with republican ideas by his study of Greek and Roman literature, he wrote—he never published—a passionate attack on absolutism. He called it *Discours sur la servitude volontaire*, but as it denounced the dictatorship of one over many, it came to be called *Contr'un*, Against One. Hear its flaming appeal:

> What a shame and disgrace it is when countless men obey a tyrant willingly, even slavishly! A tyrant who leaves them no rights over property, parents, wife, or child, not even over their own lives— what kind of a man is such a tyrant? He is no Hercules, no Samson! Often he is a pygmy, often the most effeminate coward among the whole people—not his own strength makes him powerful, him who is often the slave of the vilest whores. What miserable creatures are his subjects! If two, three, or four do not revolt against *one*, there is an understandable lack of courage. But when hundreds and thousands do not throw off the shackles of an individual, what remains there of individual will and human dignity? . . . To free oneself it is not necessary to use force against a tyrant. He falls as soon as the country is tired of him. The people who are being degraded and enslaved need but deny him any right. To be free only calls for the earnest will to shake off the yoke. . . . Be firmly resolved no longer to be slaves—and you are free! Deny the tyrant your help, and like a colossus whose pedestal is pulled away, he will collapse and break to pieces.[101]

La Boétie proceeded to formulate Rousseau and Tom Paine. Man naturally longs for liberty; inequalities of fortune are fortuitous, and lay upon the fortunate the obligation to serve their fellow men; all men are brothers, "made from the same mold" by the same God. Strange to say, it was the reading of this radical pronouncement that attracted the normally cool and cautious Montaigne to La Boétie, and led (1557) to one of the most famous friendships in history. Montaigne was then twenty-four, Étienne was twenty-seven; perhaps Montaigne was then young enough to harbor radical sentiments. Their friendship was soon ended by La Boétie's death at the age of thirty-two (1563). Montaigne described the final days as if remembering Plato's account of the death of Socrates. He so keenly felt the loss of the warmhearted youth that seventeen years later he spoke of it with deeper feeling than of anything else in his experience. He had not favored the printing of the *Discours*, and mourned when a Genevese pastor published it (1576). He ascribed the composition to the generous spirit of youth, and predated it to the age of sixteen. It was almost the voice of the French Revolution.

IX. RAMUS AND THE PHILOSOPHERS

Quite as romantic was the life, and more violent the death, of Petrus Ramus—Pierre de la Ramée—who undertook to overthrow the tyranny of Aristotle. Here was a one-man rule that had lasted three centuries and more, over not one nation only but many, and over not the body but the mind, almost over the soul, for had not the pagan thinker been made an official philosopher of the Church? The humanists of the Renaissance had thought to displace him with Plato, but the Reformation—or fear of it—was strangling humanism, and in Protestant Germany as well as Catholic France Aristotelian Scholasticism was still in the saddle when Luther, who had cursed it, died (1546). To depose the Stagyrite from his throne seemed to intellectual youth the most legitimate form of tyrannicide. Applying for the master's degree at the University of Paris in 1536, Ramus, aged twenty-one, took as his thesis—to be defended through a whole day against faculty and all challengers—the unequivocal proposition, *Quaecumque ab Aristotele dicta essent commentitia esse*—"Whatever was said by Aristotle is false."

Ramus's career was an ode to education. Born near Calvin's Noyon in Picardy, he twice tried to walk to Paris, hungry for its colleges; twice he failed, and returned defeated to his village. In 1528, aged twelve, he succeeded by attaching himself as servant to a rich student matriculating in the Collège de Navarre—the same that Villon had robbed. Serving by day, studying by night, Pierre made his way, for eight years, through the heavy curriculum in the faculty of "arts." He almost lost his eyesight in the process, but he found Plato.

> When I came to Paris, I fell among the subtleties of the sophists, and they taught me the liberal arts through questions and disputings, without showing me any other advantage or use. When I had graduated . . . I decided that these disputes had brought me nothing but loss of time. Dismayed by this thought, led by some good angel, I chanced on Xenophon and then on Plato, and learned to know the Socratic philosophy.[102]

How many of us have made that same exhilarating discovery in youth, happy to meet in Plato a philosopher who had wine and poetry in his blood, who heard philosophy in the very air of Athens, caught it on the wing, and sent it down the centuries still bearing the breath of life, all those voices of Socrates and his pupils still ringing with the lust and ecstasy of debate about the most exciting subjects in the world! What a relief after the prosy pages of Aristotle, after reams of middle-of-the-road, and not-so-golden mean! Of course we—and Ramus—were unfair to Aristotle, comparing his compact lecture notes with the popular dialogues of his master; only white hairs can appreciate the Stagyrite. The Aristotle that Ramus knew was chiefly the logician of the *Organon*, the Aristotle of the schools, barely surviving the ordeal of translation into Scholastic Latin, of transmogrification into a good Christian orthodox Thomist. Three years, said Ramus, he had spent studying Aristotle's logic, without ever being shown a single use or application of it in science or in life.[103]

It is to the credit of the Paris faculty, as well as to the learning and skill and courage of Ramus, that he was given his master's degree; perhaps the professors too were weary of logic and moderation. But some of them were scandalized, and felt that their stock-in-trade had been damaged by that day's debate. Enmities began that pursued Ramus to his death.

His degree entitled him to teach, and he began at once, at the university, a course of lectures in which he mingled philosophy with Greek and Latin literature. His classes grew, his earnings mounted, and he was able to reimburse his widowed mother for the savings that she had sacrificed to pay for his graduation fee. After seven years of preparation he issued in 1543 (the *annus mirabilis* of Copernicus and Vesalius) two works that continued his campaign to overthrow the Aristotelian logic. One—*Aristotelicae animadversiones*—was a frontal assault, sometimes phrased in impetuous invective; the other—*Dialecticae partitiones (Divisions of Logic)*—offered a new system to replace the old. It redefined logic as *ars disserendi*, the art of discourse, and brought logic, literature, and oratory together in a technique of persuasion. The university authorities forgivably saw some dangers in this approach. Moreover they viewed with suspicion certain propositions in Ramus that smelled of heresy, such as, "Unbelief is the beginning of knowledge" [104] —Cartesian doubt before Descartes; or his plea to replace the tomes of the Scholastics with more study of the Scriptures—this had a Protestant ring; or his definition of theology as *doctrina bene vivendi*—which threatened to reduce religion to morality. And there were Ramus's irritating ways, his pride and pugnacity, his violent controversial tone, his dogmatic superiority to dogma.

Soon after publication of these books the rector of the university cited Ramus before the provost of Paris as an enemy of the faith, a disturber of the public peace, a corrupter of youth with dangerous novelties. The trial was held before a royal commission of five men—two appointed by Ramus, two by his accusers, one by Francis I. Dissatisfied with the procedure of the trial, Ramus withdrew his appointees. The remaining three decided against him (1544), and a royal mandate forbade him to lecture, or to publish, or to attack Aristotle further. The condemnation notice was placarded through-out the city, and was sent to other universities. Students staged burlesques ridiculing Ramus, and Rabelais made heavenly fun of the fracas.

After holding his peace for a while, Ramus opened a course of lectures at the Collège Ave Maria, but he confined himself to rhetoric and mathematics, and the government winked at his disobedience. In 1545 he became assistant rector of the Collège de Presles, and his lecture room was soon crowded. When Henry II succeeded Francis I he repealed the sentence against Ramus, left him "free in both tongue and pen," and, a year later, appointed him to a chair in the Collège Royale, where he would be exempt from university control.

Having reached his pinnacle as now the most famous teacher in Paris, Ramus devoted much time and effort to reforming pedagogical methods. If he stressed "rhetoric"—which then meant literature—it was not only to revivify philosophy with poetry, but also to infuse a vibrant humanism into courses grown dry and hard with abstractions and scholastic rules. In five treatises on grammar he applied logic to language; he begged French spelling to become phonetic, but it went its reeling way; however, he succeeded in introducing into the French alphabet the letters *j* and *v* to replace conso-nantal *i* and *u*. Remembering his own penniless striving for an education, he encouraged the establishment of scholarships for poor students, and con-demned the heavy fees required for graduation. At the same time he labored to raise the remuneration of teachers.

In 1555 he published *Dialectique*, the first work on logic in French. He argued now not merely about reasoning but for reason. He was by tempera-ment a foe to traditionalism and mere authority; reason seemed to him the only authority; and he believed, with Renaissance ardor, that if reason were left free it would bring all the sciences close to perfection within a cen-tury.[105] "It was my constant study," he wrote, "to remove from the path of the liberal arts . . . all intellectual obstacles and retardations, and to make even and straight the way, in order to arrive more easily not only at intelli-gence but at the *practice and use* of the liberal arts." [106]

His character and philosophy inclined him to sympathize with the Prot-estant revolt. When, for a time, the Huguenots won toleration from the government, even participation in it, Ramus announced his adherence to the Reformed faith (1561). Early in 1562 some of his students tore down the religious images in the chapel of the Collège de Presles. The government continued to pay his salary, but his position was increasingly precarious. When civil war broke out (1562) he left Paris, with a safe-conduct from Catherine de Médicis; he returned a year later on the signing of peace. He politely refused an invitation to a chair in the University of Bologna, saying that he was too indebted to France to leave it.

The quarrel that led to his death came into the open when his chief enemy, Jacques Charpentier, frankly confessing his ignorance of mathematics, bought his way [107] into a professorship of mathematics at the Collège Royale (1565). Ramus denounced the appointment; Charpentier threatened him; Ramus appealed to the courts for protection; Charpentier was jailed, but was soon released. Two attempts were made on Ramus's life, and when the civil war between Catholics and Protestants was resumed (1567) he left Paris again. The government now ruled that only a Catholic might teach in the university or the Collège Royale. Ramus, returning, retired to private life, but Catherine continued and doubled his salary, and he was free to devote himself to study and writing.

In July 1572, Montluc, Bishop of Valence, invited him to join an embassy to Poland; perhaps the Bishop foresaw the Massacre of St. Bartholomew, and thought to protect the aging philosopher. Ramus refused, having no stomach for the enterprise of setting Prince Henry of Anjou on the Polish throne. Montluc left on August 17; on the twenty-fourth the Massacre began. On the twenty-sixth two armed men invaded the Collège de Presles, and mounted to the fifth floor, where Ramus had his study. They found him in prayer. One shot him in the head, the other stabbed him; together they hurled him through the window. Students or ragamuffins dragged the still living body to the Seine and threw it in; others recovered it and hacked it to pieces.[108] We do not know who hired the assassins; apparently not the government, for both Charles IX and Catherine seem to have continued their favor to Ramus till the end.[109] Charpentier rejoiced over the Massacre and the murder: "This brilliant sun, which, during the month of August, has brightened France. . . . The stuff and nonsense have disappeared with its author. All good men are full of joy." [110] Two years later Charpentier himself died, some say of remorse; but perhaps this does him too much credit.

Ramus seemed defeated in life and influence. His enemies triumphed; and though some "Ramists" were heard in the next generation in France, Holland, and Germany, the Scholasticism that he had fought regained its ascendancy, and French philosophy hung its head until Descartes. But if philosophy had gained little in this period, the advances of science had been epochal; modern science began with Copernicus and Vesalius. The known earth had been doubled; the world view had been changed as never before in recorded history. Knowledge was growing rapidly in scope and spread; the use of the vernacular in science and philosophy—as by Paré and Paracelsus in medicine, by Ramus in philosophy—was extending to the middle classes instruction and ideas formerly confined to tonsured scholars and priests. The "cake of custom," the mold of belief, the hold of authority, had been broken. Faith was loosed from its moorings, and flowed with new freedom into a hundred forms.

Everything was in flux except the Church. Amid the revolution she stood for a time bewildered, at first hardly realizing the gravity of the events. Then she faced resolutely the vital question that confronted her: Should she adjust her doctrine to the new climate and fluidity of ideas, or stand unmoved amid all changes, and wait for the pendulum of thought and feeling to bring men back, in humility and hunger, to her consolations and her authority? Her answer decided her modern history.

BOOK V

THE COUNTER REFORMATION

1517–65

CHAPTER XXXVIII

The Church and Reform

1517-65

I. ITALIAN PROTESTANT REFORMERS

IN climatically pagan Italy, constitutionally polytheistic, favoring a genial and artistic faith, populated with undying saints whose awesome or beloved effigies moved annually through the streets, and enriched by the gold that came to the Church from a dozen subject lands, one should not have expected to find men and women dedicated, sometimes at mortal risk, to the replacement of that picturesque and hallowed faith by a somber creed whose political support was the reluctance of northern nations to fatten Italy with the proceeds of their piety. Yet everywhere in Italy there were people who felt, even more keenly and intimately than the Germans, the Swiss, or the English, the abuses that were demoralizing the Church. And in Italy, more than anywhere else, the educated classes, though already enjoying some freedom of teaching and thought, were demanding the liberation of the intellect from even outward allegiance to the myths that so charmed and disciplined the populace.

Some of Luther's writings appeared in the bookstalls of Milan in 1519, in Venice in 1520. In St. Mark's itself a friar dared to preach the doctrines of Luther. Cardinal Caraffa reported to Pope Clement VII (1532) that religion was at a low ebb in Venice, that very few Venetians observed the fasts or went to confession, and that heretical literature was popular there. Clement himself (1530) described the Lutheran heresy as widely spread among both clergy and laity in Italy; and in 1535 the German reformers claimed 30,000 adherents in the homeland of the Church.[1]

The highest lady in Ferrara was a fervent Protestant. Renée, daughter of Louis XII, had imbibed the new ideas partly from Marguerite of Navarre, partly from her own governess, Mme. Soubise. The Princess brought this lady with her when she married (1528) Ercole d'Este, who became (1534) the second duke of that name to rule Ferrara. Calvin visited her there (1536), and intensified her Protestant convictions. Clément Marot came to her, and, later, Hubert Languet, the Huguenot publicist. Ercole accepted them all in polite Renaissance fashion until one of them shouted *Idolatria!* during the Adoration of the Cross on Holy Saturday (1536); then he let the Inquisition question them. Calvin and Marot fled; the others appear to have saved themselves by affirming their orthodoxy. But after 1540 Renée gathered a new Protestant entourage, and ceased attendance at Catholic worship. Ercole soothed the Pope by exiling her to the ducal villa at Consandolo on the Po; but there too she surrounded herself with Protestants, and brought up her daughters in the Reformed faith. Ercole, fearing that Protestant daughters would be worthless pawns in the game of political marriages, removed them to a convent. Finally he allowed the Inquisition to indict Renée and twenty-four of her household. She was convicted of heresy, and was sentenced to life imprisonment (1554). She recanted, received the Eucharist, and was restored to religious and political grace;[2] but her real opinions were silently expressed by the melancholy solitude of her remaining years. After Ercole's death (1559) she returned to France, where she made her home at Montargis a refuge for Huguenots.

Modena, also under Ercole, had a lively Protestant moment. Its *Accademia* of scientists and philosophers allowed great freedom in discussions, and some of its members, including Vesalius's pupil and successor Gabriele Fallopio, were suspected of heresy. Paolo Ricci, an ex-friar, preached openly against the papacy; Lutheran ideas were debated in the shops, the squares, the churches. Ricci and others were arrested. Cardinal Sadoleto protected the Academicians, claiming that they were loyal to the Church, and that they should, as scholars, enjoy freedom of inquiry;[3] Paul III contented himself with their signatures to a profession of faith, but Ercole disbanded the Academy (1546), and one unrepentant Lutheran was executed at Ferrara (1550). In 1568, as the Catholic reaction stiffened, thirteen men and one woman were burned for heresy at Modena.

At Lucca, Pietro Martire Vermigli, Prior of the Austin Canons, organized a learned academy, brought exceptional teachers to it, encouraged freedom of discussion, and told his large congregation that it might look upon the Eucharist as not a miraculous transformation but a pious remembrance of the Passion of Christ; this out-Luthered Luther. Summoned for questioning by the chapter of his order at Genoa, he fled from Italy, denounced the errors and abuses of Catholicism, and accepted a professorship of divinity at Oxford (1548). He took a disputed part in formulating the Book of Common Prayer (1552), left England when Catholicism returned to power, and died as professor of Hebrew at Zurich in 1562. Eighteen canons of his priory at Lucca followed him in abandoning their order and Italy.

Vermigli, Bishop Sorano of Bergamo, and many others had been turned to the new ideas by Juan de Valdés. He and his brother Alfonso, of high Castilian lineage, were perhaps the most talented twins in history. Alfonso, a devotee of Erasmus, became Latin secretary to Charles V, and wrote a *Dialogo de Lactancio* (1529) in which he defended the Sack of Rome, and contended that Luther would never have left the Church if, instead of condemning him, she had reformed the abuses that he had justly denounced. Juan contributed to the same volume a *Dialogo de Mercurio y Caron*, whose heresies were political: the rich should be made to earn their living; the poor have a right to share in the income of the rich; the wealth of a prince belongs to the people, and should not be wasted in imperialistic or religious wars.[4] Clement VII naturally preferred Juan, and made him a papal chamberlain at thirty. Juan, however, moved to Naples, where he devoted himself to writing and teaching. He remained loyal to the Church, but favored the Lutheran doctrine of justification by faith, and rated a devout mysticism above any external ritual of piety. Distinguished men and women gathered around him and accepted his lead: Vermigli, Ochino, Marcantonio Flaminio the poet, Pietro Carnesecchi, Vittoria Colonna, Costanza d'Ávalos, Duchess of Amalfi, Isabella Manriquez, sister of the Spanish grand inquisitor, and Giulia Gonzaga, whose beauty we have already acknowledged. After Juan Valdés's death (1541) his pupils scattered through Europe. Some, like Vittoria Colonna, stayed in the Church; some developed his teachings into open heresy. Three minor pupils were beheaded and burned at Naples in 1564; Carnesecchi was beheaded and burned at Rome in 1567. Giulia Gonzaga was saved by the death of the merciless Paul IV; she entered a convent (1566), and with her the Neapolitan party of reform came to an end.

Bernardino Ochino went through all the stages of religious development. Born near the birthplace of St. Catherine in Siena, he rivaled her piety. He joined the Franciscans, but finding their discipline too lax for his mood, he transferred to the severer order of the Capuchins. They marveled at his ascetic self-denial, his passionate mortification of his flesh; and when they made him their vicar-general they felt that they had chosen a saint. His sermons—in Siena, Florence, Venice, Naples, Rome—resounded through Italy; nothing like them in fervor or eloquence had been heard there since Savonarola a century before. Charles V went to hear him; Vittoria Colonna was deeply moved by him; Pietro Aretino, who had sampled almost every sin, was stirred to passing piety by hearing him. No church was large enough to hold his listeners. No one dreamed that this man would die a heretic.

But at Naples he met Valdés, and through him became acquainted with the works of Luther and Calvin. The doctrine of justification suited his spirit; he began to hint at it in his sermons. In 1542 he was cited before the papal nuncio at Venice, and was forbidden to preach. Shortly afterward Paul III invited him to Rome to discuss the religious views of some Capuchins. Ochino may have trusted the enlightened Pope, but he feared the long arm of the Inquisition, and Cardinal Contarini warned him of danger. Suddenly this saint and idol of Italy, meeting Peter Vermigli in Florence, decided, like him, to cross the Alps into Protestant terrain. A brother of Vittoria

Colonna gave him a horse; at Ferrara Renée gave him clothing. He proceeded through the Grisons to Zurich, thence to Geneva. He applauded the puritan discipline that Calvin was establishing there, but, his German being better than his French, he moved on to Basel to Strasbourg to Augsburg, trying to earn a living by tongue or pen. In 1547 Charles V, having overwhelmed the Protestants at Mühlberg, entered Augsburg as master of Germany. He learned that the Capuchin whom he had heard in Naples was living there as a married man; he ordered the magistrates to arrest him; they connived at Ochino's escape. He fled to Zurich and Basel, and then, when he seemed at the end of his food, he received a call from Archbishop Cranmer to come to England. There, as a pensioned prebendary at Canterbury, he labored for six years (1547–53); he wrote a book that strongly influenced Milton's *Paradise Lost;* but when Mary Tudor came to the throne he hurried back to Switzerland.

He secured appointment as pastor of a congregation in Zurich, but his Unitarian views offended it, and he was dismissed when he published a dialogue in which a defender of polygamy seemed to have the better of the argument against a monogamist. Though it was December (1563), he was ordered to leave the city within three weeks. Basel refused to let him stay there; he was allowed a brief sojourn in Nuremberg; soon he set out with his family for Poland, then by comparison a haven for off-color thinkers. He preached at Cracow for a while, but was expelled when the king banished all non-Catholic foreigners (1564). On the way from Poland to Moravia three of his four children succumbed to pestilence. He survived them two months, dying at Schackau in December 1564. Almost his last words were: "I wish to be neither a Bullingerite nor a Calvinist nor a papist, but simply a Christian." [5] Nothing could have been more dangerous.

It was of course impossible that Italy should go Protestant. The common people there, though anticlerical, were religious even when they did not go to church. They loved the time-hallowed ceremonies, the helping or consoling saints, the seldom-questioned creed that lifted their lives from the poverty of their homes to the sublimity of the greatest drama ever conceived —the redemption of fallen man by the death of his God. The political domination of Italy by an intensely religious Spain conspired to keep both peninsulas Catholic. The wealth of the papacy was an Italian heirloom and vested interest; any Italian who proposed to end that tribute-receiving organization seemed to most Italians to be verging on lunacy. The upper classes quarreled with the papacy as a political power over Central Italy, but they cherished Catholicism as a vital aid to social order and peaceful government. They realized that the glory of Italian art had been bound up with the Church through the inspiration of her legends and the support of her gold. Catholicism itself had become an art; its sensuous elements had submerged the ascetic and the theological; stained glass, incense, music, architecture, sculpture, painting, even drama—these were all in the Church and of her, and in their marvelous ensemble they seemed inseparable from her. The artists and the scholars of Italy did not have to be converted from Catholicism, for they had converted Catholicism to scholarship and art. Hundreds, thousands of scholars and artists were supported by bishops, cardinals, and popes; many humanists, some polite skeptics, had risen to high position in the Church. Italy loved attainable beauty too much to despoil itself over unattainable truth. And had those fanatical Teutons, or that sour popelet in Geneva, or that ruthless ogre on the throne of England, found the truth? What depressing nonsense those Reformers were shouting—just when the intellectual classes in Italy had quite forgotten hell and damnation! One could understand a quiet and private rejection of Christian theology in favor of a vague and genial deism, but to replace the mystery of transubstantiation with the horror of predestination seemed a passage from a heartening symbolism to a suicidal absurdity. Just now, when the Church had spread her forgiving wings over the pagan proclivities of the Italian people, Calvin was calling upon the world to fetter itself in a puritanism that threatened to exile all gladness and spontaneity from life. And how could Italian joy and art continue if those barbarous Teutons and Englishmen should cease to send or bring their coins into Italy?

II. ITALIAN CATHOLIC REFORMERS

Consequently the Italian argument was all for reform *within* the Church. And indeed, loyal churchmen had for centuries admitted—proclaimed—the need for ecclesiastical reform. The outbreak and progress of the Reformation gave new urgency to the need and the demand. "A vast torrent of abuse in hundreds and thousands of pamphlets and caricatures poured down upon the clergy." [6] The Sack of Rome touched the conscience and income of terrified cardinals and populace; a hundred priests pronounced the calamity a warning from God. Bishop Stafileo, preaching before the Rota (a judiciary branch of the Curia) in 1528, explained, almost in Protestant terms, why God had struck the capital of Christendom: "Because all flesh has become corrupt; we are citizens not of the holy city of Rome, but of Babylon, the city of corruption." [7] As Luther had said.

At an uncertain date shortly before 1517 Giovanni Pietro Caraffa and Count Gaetano da Thiene founded at Rome the Oratory of the Divine Love —*Oratorio del Divino Amore*—for prayer and self-reform. Half a hundred prominent men joined it, including Iacopo Sadoleto, Gainmatteo Giberti, Giuliano Dati. In 1524 Gaetano organized an order of clerks regular—i.e., secular priests subjecting themselves to monastic vows. After the Sack of Rome the Oratory was disbanded, and Caraffa and others entered the new order, which took the name of Theatines from Caraffa's episcopal see of Theate or Chieti. Men of high distinction were admitted—Pietro Bembo, Marcantonio Flaminio, Luigi Priuli, Gasparo Contarini, Reginald Pole. . . . All pledged themselves to poverty, care of the sick, and a strict moral life, "to make up," said their first historian, "what is wanting in the clergy, who are corrupted by vice and ignorance to the ruin of the people." [8] The members spread through Italy, and their example shared with papal and conciliar reforms, with Capuchin and Jesuit example, in restoring the moral fiber of the Catholic clergy and the popes. Caraffa led the way by resigning all his benefices, and distributing his substantial wealth among the poor.

Giberti was in his person and career an image of the Catholic reform. At the court of Leo X he was a leading humanist; under Clement VII he was datary or chief secretary to the Curia. Shaken by the catastrophe of 1527, he retired to his bishopric at Verona, and lived like an ascetic monk while administering his diocese. He was alarmed by the decay of religion there— the churches dilapidated, preaching rare, priests ignorant of the Latin in which they said Mass, and the people rarely using the confessional. By example, precept, and firm discipline, he reformed his clergy; soon, says a Catholic historian, "the dungeons were full of concubinary priests." [9] Giberti reestablished (1531) the *Confraternità della Carità* that had been founded by Cardinal Giuliano de' Medici in 1519; he built orphanages, and opened people's banks to rescue borrowers from usurers. Similar reforms were carried out by Cardinal Ercole Gonzaga (son of Isabella d'Este) at Mantua, by Marco Vida at Alba, by Fabio Vigili at Spoleto, and many other bishops who knew that the Church must reform or die.

Several of the heroes of the orthodox reform were later canonized by the Church they had helped to save. St. Philip Neri, a young Florentine noble, founded at Rome (*c.* 1540) a peculiar *Trinità de' Pellegrini:* twelve laymen who, after attending Mass on Sundays, would make a pilgrimage to one of the basilicas, or to some rural green, and there give or hear pious talks, and sing religious music. Many of the members became priests, and took the name of Fathers of the Oratory; from their musical propensities the word *oratorio* added to its old meaning—place of prayer—the new meaning of choral song. St. Charles Borromeo, nephew to Pope Pius IV, resigned his high place as a cardinal in Rome to cleanse the religious life of Milan. As archbishop there he maintained discipline among the clergy, and showed the way by his own austerities and devotion. There was some resistance. The Umiliati, a religious order once proud of its humility, had degenerated into a comfortable, even a licentious, life; the Cardinal ordered them to obey their rule; one of them fired a shot at him as he prayed in chapel; the result was to raise to veneration the popular awe for a man who thought that reform was the best answer to the Reformation. Within his lifetime and his archdiocese, decency was made fashionable among clergy and laity alike. His influence was felt throughout Italy, and shared in transforming the cardinals from worldly aristocrats into devoted priests.

Stimulated by such men, the popes began to give determined attention to ecclesiastical reform. Early in the pontificate of Paul III the renowned jurist Giovan Battista Caccia presented to him a treatise on the reformation of the Church. "I see," said the preamble, "that our Holy Mother the Church . . . has been so changed that she seems to have no tokens of her evangelical character; and no trace can be found in her of humility, temperance, continence, and Apostolic strength." [10] Paul showed his own mood by accepting the dedication of this work. On November 20, 1534, he appointed Cardinals Piccolomini, Sanseverino, and Cesi to draw up a program of moral renovation for the Church; and on January 15, 1535, he ordered strict enforcement of Leo X's reform bulls of 1513. Enmeshed in papal and Imperial politics, endangered by the advance of the Turks, and unwilling, in these crises, to disturb the structure or functioning of the Curia by radical changes, Paul deferred active reform; but the men whom he raised to the cardinalate were almost all known for integrity and devotion. In July 1536, he invited to a reform conference at Rome Contarini, Caraffa, Sadoleto, Cortese, Aleander, Pole, Tommaso Badia, and Bishop Federigo Fregose of Gubbio, all committed to reform, and bade them put into writing the abuses in the Church, and the means they would recommend to mitigate them. Sadoleto opened the conference by boldly stating that the popes themselves, by their sins, crimes, and financial greed, had been the prime source of ecclesiastical deterioration. [11] The conference met almost daily for three months. Its leading spirit, Gasparo Contarini, was the finest figure in the Counter Reformation. Born in Venice (1483) of aristocratic lineage, and educated in liberal Padua, he soon rose to high position in the Venetian government. He was sent as ambassador to Charles V in Germany, accompanied him to England and Spain, and then served the Senate as its representative at the papal court (1527-30). Retiring from politics, he devoted himself to study, and made his home a meeting place of the best statesmen, churchmen, philosophers, and humanists in Venice. Though a layman, he pondered ecclesiastical reform, and collaborated actively with Caraffa, Giberti, Cortese, and Pole. All Italy recognized him as a rare combination of intellect and character. In 1535, without any solicitation on his part, he was made a cardinal by Paul III, whom he had never met. [12]

In March 1537, the commission presented to the Pope its unanimous *Consilium dilectorum cardinalium de emendanda Ecclesia.* This "Counsel of the Appointed Cardinals on Reforming the Church" exposed with astonishing freedom the abuses in the papal government, and boldly ascribed them chiefly to "reckless exaggeration of the papal authority by unscrupulous canonists." Some popes, the report held, "had assumed the right to sell ecclesiastical offices, and this simony had spread venality and corruption so widely through the Church that now the great organization was on the verge of destruction through men's lack of trust in its integrity. The report urged strict supervision of all Curial activities, a check on dispensations, an end to money payments for them, a higher standard in all appointments and in eligibility to the cardinalate and the priesthood, and a prohibition of plural or absentee holding of benefices. "Throughout the whole world," the report added, "almost all the shepherds have deserted their flocks and entrusted them to hirelings." Monastic orders must be regenerated, and nunneries should be subject to episcopal supervision, for their visitaton by monks had led to scandal and sacrilege. Indulgences should be proclaimed only once a year. The report concluded with a solemn exhortation to the Pope:

> We have satisfied our consciences, not without the greatest hope of seeing, under your pontificate, the Church of God restored. . . . You have taken the name of Paul. We hope that you will imitate his charity. He was chosen as an instrument to carry Christ's name to the heathen; you, we hope, have been chosen to revive in our hearts and deeds that name long since forgotten among the heathen and by us the clergy; to heal our sickness, to unite Christ's sheep again in one fold, and to avert from our heads the wrath and already threatening vengeance of God.[13]

Paul took in good spirit this *aureum consilium*, this "golden counsel," as many called it, and sent a copy to every cardinal. Luther translated it into German, and published it as a full justification of his break with Rome; however, he judged the authors of the document to be "liars . . . desperate rascals reforming the Church with cajolery." [14] On April 20, 1537, Paul appointed four cardinals—Contarini, Caraffa, Simonetta, and Ghinucci—to reform the Dataria, that department of the Curia which had become especially venal in granting those dispensations, graces, privileges, indults, and benefices which were reserved to the papal power. The undertaking required courage, for the Dataria yielded 50,000 ducats ($1,250,000?) yearly to the Pope—nearly half his income. [15] At once a cry of anguish rose from the officials and their dependents; they complained of the high cost of living in Rome, and alleged that if they were made to keep to the letter of the law their families would soon be destitute. Paul proceeded cautiously; nevertheless, wrote Aleander to Morone (April 27, 1540), "the work of reform goes on busily." On December 13 Paul summoned eighty archbishops and bishops residing in Rome, and ordered them to return to their sees. Again a thousand objections were raised. Morone warned the Pope that haste in executing this order might drive some of the bishops, returning to now predominantly Protestant areas, to join the Lutherans. This actually occurred in several cases. Soon Paul lost himself in Imperial politics, and left reform to his successors.

The movement for internal reform triumphed when its leader, Caraffa, became Paul IV (1555). Monks absent from their monasteries without official sanction and clear necessity were commanded to return at once. On the night of August 22, 1558, the Pope ordered all the gates of Rome closed, and all vagrant monks arrested; similar procedures were followed throughout the Papal States, and some offenders were sent to the galleys. Monasteries were no longer to be assigned *in commendam* to support absentee officials with their revenues. Bishops and abbots not actually serving the Curia in a fixed office were required to return to their posts or forfeit their income. The holding of plural benefices was prohibited. All departments of the Curia were bidden to reduce their fees, and to eliminate any suspicion of simony in appointments to clerical positions. Having so diminished his own income, Paul made a further sacrifice by ending the payment of a fee for confirmation to archiepiscopal dignity. Severe papal edicts were issued against usurers, actors, and prostitutes; procurers were to be put to death. Daniele da Volterra was instructed to cover sartorially the more glaring anatomical features of Michelangelo's *Last Judgment;* and it must be admitted that that gloomy shambles of flesh damned or saved had hardly found a fitting place over the altar of the popes. Rome now assumed an uncongenial air of external piety and morality. In Italy—less visibly beyond it—the Church had reformed her clergy and her morals, while leaving her doctrines proudly intact. The reform had been long delayed, but when it came it was sincere and magnificent.

III. ST. TERESA AND MONASTIC REFORM

A moral regeneration was simultaneously taking place in the monastic orders. We may imagine their reputation from a remark of the pious and orthodox Michelangelo, who, when he heard that Sebastian del Piombo was to paint the figure of a monk in the chapel of San Pietro in Montorio, advised against it, saying that as the monks had spoiled the world, which is so large, it would not be surprising if one should spoil the chapel, which was so small.[16] Gregorio Cortese set himself patiently to reform the Benedictines at Padua; Girolamo Seripando the Austin Canons; Egidio Canisio the Augustinian Eremites; Paolo Giustiniani the Camaldolites.

New monastic orders stressed reform. Antonio Maria Laccaria founded at Milan (1533) the Clerks Regular of St. Paul, a community of priests pledged to monastic poverty; they met originally in the church of St. Barnabas, whence they came to be called Barnabites. In 1535 St. Angela organized the Ursuline nuns for the education of girls and the care of the sick or the poor; and in 1540 St. John of God established in Granada the Brothers of Mercy for hospital ministrations. In 1523 Matteo de' Bassi, in fervent emulation of St. Francis of Assisi, determined to observe to the letter the final rule that their founder had left to the Franciscans. Other friars joined him, and by 1525 their number encouraged Matteo to ask papal sanction of a new branch of the Franciscans dedicated to the strictest rule. The provincial of his order had him imprisoned for disobedience, but Matteo was soon freed, and in 1528 Clement VII confirmed the new order of Capuchins—so named because the friars wore the same kind of *cappuccio* or cowl that Francis had worn. They dressed in the coarsest cloth, lived on bread, vegetables, fruit, and water, kept rigorous fasts, dwelt in narrow cells in poor cottages, never journeyed except on foot, and went barefoot throughout the year. They distinguished themselves by their selfless care of the infected in the plague of 1528–29. Their devotion was a factor in keeping Vittoria Colonna and other incipient Protestants loyal to a Church that could still produce such ardent Christians.

The most interesting figure in this epoch of monastic reform was a frail and masterful abbess of Spain. Teresa de Cepeda was the daughter of a Castilian knight of Ávila, a man proud of his puritan rectitude and his loyalty to the Church; each night he read to his family from the lives of the saints.[17] The mother, a chronic invalid, brightened her weary days with chivalric romances, and shared, from her sickbed, the adventures of Amadis of Gaul. Teresa's childhood imagination vacillated between romantic love and saintly martyrdom. At ten she vowed to become a nun. But, four years later, she blossomed suddenly into a beautiful young woman, bounding with the joy of life, and forgetting the garb of the cloister in the colorful dresses that doubled her charms. Admirers came; she fell tremulously in love with one of them, and was invited to a tryst. At the crucial moment she took fright, and confessed the dire plot to her father. As the mother was now dead, Don Alonzo de Cepeda placed the impressionable girl with the Augustinian nuns at Ávila.

Teresa resented the solemn life and discipline of the convent. She refused to take the vows of a nun, but looked forward impatiently to her sixteenth birthday, when she would be permitted to leave. But as this goal approached she fell dangerously ill, and almost died. She recovered, but her youthful joyousness was gone. Apparently she had developed a form of hystero-epilepsy, perhaps from suppressed rebellion against constraints alien to her instincts. Attacks recurred, leaving her exhausted. Her father removed her from the convent, and sent her to live with her half-sister in the country.

On the way an uncle gave her a volume of St. Jerome. Those vivid letters described the terrors of hell, and the flirtations of the sexes as the crowded avenue to eternal damnation. Teresa read anxiously. After another severe attack she abandoned all thought of worldly happiness, and resolved to fulfill her childhood vow. She returned to Ávila, and entered the Carmelite Convent of the Incarnation (1534).

For a while she was happy in the soothing routine of Masses, prayers, and cleansing confessions; and when she took the sacrament she felt the bread as veritably Christ on her tongue and in her blood. But she was disturbed by the lax discipline of the convent. The nuns had not cells but comfortable rooms; they ate well despite weekly fasts; they adorned their persons with necklaces, bracelets, and rings; they received visitors in the parlor, and enjoyed extended vacations outside the convent walls. Teresa felt that these conditions did not protect her sufficiently from the temptations and imaginations of the flesh. Perhaps because of these, and her growing discontent, her attacks became more frequent and painful. Again her father sent her to her sister, and again, en route, her uncle gave her a religious book, *The Third Abecedarium* of Francisco de Osuña. It was an A B C of mystical prayer, prayer without words; for, said the author, "only those who approach God in silence can be heard and will be given an answer." [18] In her rural retreat Teresa practiced this silent, meditative prayer, which suited so well the trancelike state induced by her attacks.

An herb doctor tried to cure her, but his concoctions almost killed her. When she returned to the cloister at Ávila (1537) she was near death, and longed for it. The most violent of her seizures came now; she fell into a coma that was mistaken for death; for two days she lay cold and motionless, apparently without breath; the nuns dug a grave for her. She recovered, but remained so weak that she could digest no solid food, and could bear no touch. For eight months she lay in the convent infirmary in almost total paralysis. Her condition slowly improved to partial paralysis, but "the times when I was not harassed by severe pains were rare indeed." [19] She renounced medical treatments, and resolved to rely entirely on prayer. For three years she suffered and prayed. Then suddenly, one morning in 1540, the bedridden, seemingly incurable invalid awoke to find her limbs no longer paralyzed. She rose and walked. Day by day she joined more actively in the conventual regimen. Her recovery was acclaimed as a miracle, and she believed it so. Perhaps prayer had soothed a nervous system overwrought with conflicting desires, a sense of sin, and a fear of hell; and the quieted nerves, and the absence of doctors, gave her body unwonted peace.

The Incarnation Convent became famous as the scene of a miraculous cure. People came from surrounding towns to see the nun whom God had healed; they left money and gifts for the holy house; the mother superior encouraged these visits, and bade Teresa show herself when visitors came. Teresa was troubled to find that she took pleasure in these visits, this fame, and the presence of handsome men. A sense of sin returned to her. One day (1542), as she conversed in the parlor with a man who especially attracted her, she thought she saw Christ standing beside the visitor. She fell into a trance, and had to be carried to her cell in a cot.

Through the next sixteen years she continued to have such visions. They became to her more real than life. In 1558, while absorbed in prayer, she felt her soul moving out of her body and mounting to heaven, and there seeing and hearing Christ. These visions no longer exhausted, they refreshed her. She wrote:

> Often, infirm and wrought upon with dreadful pains before the ecstasy, the soul emerges from it full of health and admirably disposed for action . . . as if God had willed that the body itself, already obedient to the soul's desires, should share in the soul's happiness. . . . The soul after such a favor is animated with a degree of courage so great that if at that moment its body should be torn to pieces for the cause of God, it would feel nothing but the liveliest comfort.[20]

On another occasion she thought an "exceedingly beautiful angel" thrust "a long dart of gold," tipped with fire, "through my heart several times, so that it reached my very entrails."

> So real was the pain that I was forced to moan aloud, yet it was so surpassingly sweet that I would not wish to be delivered from it. No delight of life can give more content. As the angel withdrew the dart, he left me all burning with a great love of God.* [21]

This and other passages in the writings of St. Teresa lend themselves readily to psychoanalytic interpretations, but no one can doubt the high sincerity of the saint. Like Ignatius, she was convinced that she saw God, and that the most recondite problems were made clear to her in these visions.

> One day, being in orison, it was granted me to perceive in one instant how all things are seen and contained in God. . . . It is one of the most signal of all graces that the Lord has granted me. . . . Our Lord has made me comprehend in what way it is that one God can be in three persons. He made me see it so clearly that I remained as extremely surprised as I was comforted. . . . And now, when I think of the Holy Trinity . . . I experience an unspeakable happiness.[22]

Teresa's sister nuns interpreted her visions as delusions and morbid fits.[23] Her confessors inclined to the same view, and told her sternly, "The Devil

---

* Spanish piety celebrates in a solemn holyday, each August 27, the memory of this transfixing vision.

has deceived your senses." The townspeople thought her possessed by demons, called upon the Inquisition to examine her, and proposed that a priest should drive out her devils by exorcism. A friend advised her to send the Inquisition an account of her life and visions; now she wrote her classic *Vida*. The inquisitors scrutinized it, and pronounced it a holy document which would strengthen the faith of all who should read it.

Her position fortified by this verdict, Teresa, now fifty-seven, determined to reform the order of the Carmelite nuns. Instead of attempting to restore the old ascetic discipline in the cloister of the Incarnation, she decided to open a separate convent, to which she invited such nuns and novices as would accept a regimen of absolute poverty. The original Carmelites had worn coarse sackcloth, had gone always barefoot, had eaten frugally and fasted frequently. Teresa required of her Discalced (shoeless) Carmelites approximately the same austere rule, not as an end in itself, but as a symbol of humility and rejection of this tempting world. A thousand obstacles were raised; the townsmen of Ávila denounced the plan as threatening to end all communication between nuns and relatives. The provincial of the order refused permission for a new convent. Teresa appealed to Pope Pius V, and won his consent. She found four nuns to join her, and the new convent of St. Joseph was consecrated in 1562 on a narrow street in Ávila. The sisters wore sandals of rope, slept on straw, ate no meat, and remained strictly within their house.

The 180 nuns of the older establishment were not pleased by this simple exposure of their easy ways. The prioress, holding that Teresa was bound to her by the vow of obedience, commanded her to resume her former white robe, put on shoes, and return to the convent of the Incarnation. Teresa obeyed. She was adjudged guilty of arrogance, and was confined to her cell. The town council voted to close St. Joseph's Convent, and sent four strong men to evict its now leaderless nuns. But the sandaled maidens said, "God wants us to stay, and so we shall stay"; and the hardened officers of the law dared not force them. Teresa frightened the Carmelite provincial by suggesting that in frustrating her plans he was offending the Holy Ghost; he ordered her freed. Four nuns left with her, and the five women walked through the snow to their new home. The four original members greeted Teresa happily as *Madre*. To nearly all Spain she now became Teresa de Jesú, the intimate of God.

Her rule was loving, cheerful, and firm. The house was closed to the world; no visitors were allowed; the windows were covered with cloth; the tiled floor served as beds, tables, and chairs. A revolving disk was built into the wall; whatever food was placed by the people on its outer half was gratefully accepted, but the nuns were not permitted to beg. They eked out their sustenance by spinning and needlework; the products were placed outside the convent gate; any buyer might take what he liked and leave whatever he liked in return. Despite these austerities new members came, and one of them was the most beautiful and courted woman in Ávila. The general of the Carmelites, visiting the little cloister, was so deeply impressed that he asked Teresa to found similar houses elsewhere in Spain. In 1567, taking a few nuns with her, she traveled in a rude cart over seventy miles of rough roads to establish a Discalced Carmelite nunnery at Medina del Campo. The only house offered her was an abandoned and dilapidated building with crumbling walls and leaking roof; but when the townspeople saw the nuns trying to live in it, carpenters and roofers came, unasked and unpaid, to make repairs and simple furniture.

The prior of the Carmelite monastery at Medina, wishing to reform his relaxed monks, came to Teresa and asked for her rules of discipline. The prior was tall, but was accompanied by a youth so short and frail that Teresa, with the humor that brightened her austerities, exclaimed, as they left: "Blessed be the Lord, for I have a friar and a half for the foundation of my new monastery." [24] The diminutive friar, Juan de Yepis y Alvarez, was destined to be San Juan de la Cruz, St. John of the Cross, the soul and glory of the Discalced Carmelite monks.

Teresa's difficulties were not ended. The provincial of the Carmelites, perhaps to test her rule and courage, appointed her prioress of the Incarnation Convent. The nuns there hated her, and feared that now, in revenge, she would subject them to every humiliation. But she behaved with such modesty and kindness that one by one they were won over, and gradually the new and stricter regimen replaced the old laxity. From this victory Teresa advanced to found a new cloister in Seville.

The friars of the mitigated rule resolved to stop the extension of the reform. Some of them smuggled an agent, as a discalced nun, into the Seville convent. Soon this woman proclaimed to Spain that Teresa flogged her nuns and heard confessions as if she were a priest. The Inquisition was again called upon to investigate her. She was summoned before the fearful tribunal; it heard her testimony, and gave its verdict: "You are acquitted of all charges. . . . Go and continue your work." [25] But a papal nuncio was won over to her enemies. He denounced Teresa as "a disobedient, contumacious woman who promulgates pernicious doctrines under the pretense of devotion, who left her cloister against the orders of her superiors, who is ambitious, and teaches theology as though she were a doctor of the Church, in contempt of St. Paul, who forbade women to teach." He commanded her to retire to confinement in a nunnery at Toledo (1575).

Hardly knowing where to turn in this new vicissitude, Teresa wrote to the King. Philip II had read and loved her *Life*. He sent a special courier to invite her to an audience; he heard her, and was convinced of her saintliness.

The nuncio, royally reproved, withdrew his order of restraint on Teresa, and announced that he had been misinformed.

Amid her travels and tribulations she wrote famous manuals of mystical devotion: *El camino de la perfección* (*The Way of Perfection*, 1567), and *El castillo interior* (*The Interior Castle*, 1577). In the latter she revealed the return of her physical ailments. "It seems as though many swollen rivers were rushing, within my brain, over a precipice; and then again, drowned by the noise of the water, are voices of birds singing and whistling. I weary my brain and increase my headaches." [26] Heart attacks recurred, and her stomach found it hard to retain food. Even so she passed painfully from one to another of the many nunneries she had founded, examining, improving, inspiring. At Málaga she was seized with a paralytic fit; she recovered, went on to Toledo, and had another seizure; she recovered, went on to Segovia, Valladolid, Palencia, Burgos, Alva. There a hemorrhage of the lungs forced her to stop. She accepted death cheerfully, confident that she was leaving a world of pain and evil for the everlasting companionship of Christ.

After a shameful competition, and successive kidnapings of her corpse by Alva and Ávila, she was buried in the town of her birth. Pious worshipers claimed that her body never decayed, and many miracles were reported at her tomb. In 1593 the order of Discalced Carmelites received papal sanction. Famous Spaniards like Cervantes and Lope de Vega joined in an appeal to the Pope to at least beatify her. It was done (1614), and eight years later Teresa was pronounced, along with the Apostle James, one of the two patron saints of Spain.

Meanwhile a greater than Teresa had come out of Spain to reform the Church and move the world.

IV. IGNATIUS LOYOLA

Don Íñigo de Oñez y Loyola was born in the castle of Loyola in the Basque province of Guipuzcoa in 1491. He was one of eight sons and five daughters begotten by Don Beltran de Oñez y Loyola, a member of the higher Spanish nobility. Brought up to be a soldier, Íñigo received little schooling, and showed no interest in religion. His reading was confined to *Amadis of Gaul* and like romances of chivalry. At seven he was sent to serve as a page to Don Juan Velasquez de Cuellar, through whom he had some access to the royal court. At fourteen he fell in love with Ferdinand the Catholic's new queen, Germaine de Foix; and when, in due course, he was knighted, he chose her as his "Queen of Hearts," wore her colors, and dreamed of winning a lace handkerchief from her hand as prize in a tournament.[27] This did not prevent him from engaging in the casual amours and brawls that were half a soldier's life. In the simple and honest autobiography that he dictated in 1553-56, he made no effort to conceal these natural escapades.

His carefree youth came to an end when he was assigned to active military service at Pamplona, capital of Navarre. Four years he spent there, dreaming of glory and waking to routine. A chance came to distinguish himself: the French attacked Pamplona, Íñigo heartened the defense with his bravery; the enemy captured the citadel nevertheless, and Íñigo's right leg was fractured by a cannon ball (May 20, 1521). The victors treated him kindly, set his bones, and sent him on a stretcher to his ancestral castle. But the bones had been wrongly set; they had to be rebroken and reset. The second operation proved more incompetent than the first, for a stump of bone stuck out from the leg; a third operation set the bones straight, but the leg was now too short; and for weeks Íñigo bore the torture of an orthopedic stretcher that kept him helpless and weak and in constant pain.

During the weary months of convalescence he asked for books, preferably for some exciting tale of knighthood and imperiled princesses. But the castle library was composed of two books only: Ludolfus's *Life of Christ*, and *Flos sanctorum*, recounting the lives of the saints. At first the soldier was bored by these volumes; then the figures of Christ and Mary grew upon him, and the legends of the saints proved as wonderful as the epics of courtly love and war; these cavaliers of Christ were every bit as heroic as the *caballeros* of Castile. Gradually the thought formed in his mind that the noblest war of all was that of Christianity against Islam. In him, as in Dominic, the intensity of Spanish faith made religion no quiet devotion as in Thomas à Kempis, but a passion of conflict, a holy war. He resolved to go to Jerusalem and free the sacred places from infidel control. One night he had a vision of the Virgin and her Child; thereafter (he later told Father González) no temptation to concupiscence ever assailed him.[28] He rose from his bed, knelt, and vowed to be a soldier of Christ and Mary till his death.

He had read that the Holy Grail had once been hidden in a castle at Montserrat in the province of Barcelona. There, said the most famous of all romances, Amadis had kept a full night's vigil before an image of the Virgin to prepare himself for knighthood. As soon as Íñigo could travel he mounted a mule, and set out for the distant shrine. For a while he still thought of himself as a soldier accoutered for physical combat. But the saints he had read about had had no weapons, no armor, only the poorest clothes and the firmest faith. Arrived in Montserrat, he cleansed his soul with three days of confession and penance; he gave his costly raiment to a beggar, and donned a pilgrim's robe of coarse cloth. All the night of March 24-25, 1522, he spent alone in the chapel of a Benedictine monastery, kneeling or standing before the altar of the Mother of God. He pledged himself to perpetual chastity and poverty. The next morning he received the Eucharist, gave his mule to the monks, and set out on limping foot for Jerusalem.

The nearest port was Barcelona. On the way he stopped at the hamlet of Manresa. An old woman directed him to a cave for shelter. For some days he made this his home; and there, eager to surpass the saints in asceticism, he practiced austerities that brought him close to death. Repenting the proud care that he had once taken of his appearance, he ceased to cleanse, cut, or comb his hair—which soon fell out; he would not trim his nails or bathe his body or wash his hands or face or feet; [29] he lived on such food as he could beg, but never meat; he fasted for days at a time; he scourged himself thrice daily, and each day spent hours in prayer. A pious woman, fearful that his austerities would kill him, had him taken to her home, where she nursed him back to health. But when he was removed to a cell in a Dominican monastery at Manresa he resumed his self-flagellation. His remembrance of past sins terrified him; he waged war against his body as the agent of his sins; he was resolved to beat all thought of sin out of his flesh. At times the struggle seemed hopeless, and he thought of suicide. Then visions came and strengthened him; at communion he believed that he saw not a wafer of bread but the living Christ; at another time Christ and His Mother appeared to him; once he saw the Trinity, and understood by a flash of insight, beyond words or reason, the mystery of three persons in one God; and "at another time," he tells us, "God permitted him to understand how He had created the world." [30] These visions healed the spiritual conflict that had produced them; he put behind him all worry about his youthful follies; he relaxed his asceticism; and having conquered his body he could now cleanse it without vanity. From the experience of this struggle, almost a year long, he designed the Spiritual Exercises by which the heathen flesh could be subdued to the Christian will. Now he might present himself before the sacred shrines at Jerusalem.

He set sail from Barcelona in February 1523. En route he stayed two weeks in Rome, escaping before its pagan spirit could bend him from sanctity. On July 14 he took ship from Venice for Jaffa. He suffered a host of calamities before reaching Palestine, but his continuing visions sustained him. Jerusalem itself was a tribulation: the Turks who controlled it allowed Christian visitors, but no proselytizing; and when Íñigo proposed to convert the Moslems nevertheless, the Franciscan provincial who had been charged by the Pope to keep the peace bade the saint return to Europe. In March 1524, he was back in Barcelona.

Perhaps he felt now that though he was master of his body he was subject to his imaginations. He determined to chasten his mind with education. Though now thirty-three, he joined schoolboys in studying Latin. But the itch to teach is stronger than the will to learn. Soon Ignatius, as he was scholastically called, began to preach to a circle of pious but charming women. Their lovers denounced him as a spoil-sport, and beat him brutally. He moved to Alcalá (1526), and took up philosophy and theology. Here too he taught a little private group, chiefly of poor women, some of them prostitutes hungering for redemption. He tried to exorcise their sinful propensities by spiritual exercises, but some of his pupils fell into fits or trances, and the Inquisition summoned him. He was imprisoned for two months,[31] but he finally convinced the inquisitors of his orthodoxy, and was released; however, he was forbidden to teach. He passed on to Salamanca (1527), and went through a similar sequence of teaching, trial before the Inquisition, imprisonment, acquittal, and prohibition of further teaching. Disappointed with Spain, he set out for Paris, always on foot and in pilgrim garb, but now driving before him a donkey loaded with books.

At Paris he lived in the poorhouse, and begged in the streets for his food and tuition. He entered the Collège de Montaigu, where his sallow, haggard face, starved body, unkempt beard, and aged clothing made him a cynosure of unsympathetic eyes; but he pursued his purposes with such absorbed intensity that some students began to reverence him as a saint. Under his lead they engaged in spiritual exercises of prayer, penance, and contemplation. In 1529 he transferred to the Collège Ste.-Barbe, and there too he gathered disciples. His two roommates came by different routes to believe in his sanctity. Pierre Favre—Peter Faber—as a shepherd in the Savoyard Alps, had suffered deeply from fears superstitious or real, and under their influence he had vowed perpetual chastity. Now, aged twenty, he concealed under his disciplined manners a soul struggling feverishly against temptations of the flesh. Ignatius, though making no pretensions to intellect, had the power of sensing the interior life of others through the intensity of his own. He surmised the problem of his younger friend, and assured him that the impulses of the body could be controlled by a trained will. How train the will? By spiritual exercises, answered Ignatius. Together they practiced them.

The other roommate, Francis Xavier, came from Pamplona, where Loyola had soldiered. He had a long line of distinguished ancestors; he was handsome, rich, proud, a gay blade who knew the taverns of Paris and their girls.[32] He laughed at the two ascetics, and boasted of his successes with women. Yet he was clever in his studies; he already had the master's degree, and was aiming at a doctorate. One day he saw a man whose face was pocked with syphilis; it gave him pause. Once, when he was expounding his ambition to shine in the world, Ignatius quietly quoted the Gospel to him: "What is a man profited if he gain the whole world and lose his own soul?" Xavier resented the query, but he could not forget it. He began to join

Loyola and Faber in their spiritual exercises; perhaps his pride stirred him to equal the other two in power to bear deprivation, cold, and pain. They scourged themselves, fasted, slept in thin shirts on the floor of an unheated room; they stood barefoot and almost naked in the snow, to harden and yet subdue their bodies.

The spiritual exercises that had first taken shape at Manresa now reached a more definite form. Ignatius modeled them on the *Exercitatorio de la vida espiritual* (1500) of Don Garcia de Cisneros, Benedictine abbot at Montserrat; [33] but he poured into that mold a fervor of feeling and imagination that made his little book a moving force in modern history. Loyola took as his starting point the infallibility of the Bible and the Church; individual judgment in religion, he held, was the vain and chaos-breeding pretense of proud, weak minds. "We ought always to be ready to believe that what seems to us white is black if the hierarchical Church so defines it." [34] To avoid damnation we must train ourselves to be unquestioning servants of God, and of God's vicar on earth, the Church.

As the first spiritual exercise we should recall our many sins, and consider how much punishment they deserve. Lucifer was condemned to hell for one sin; and is not our every sin a like rebellion against God? Let us keep a daily count of our sins by marks on lines that represent the days, and let us strive each day to reduce the marks. Kneeling in our darkened room or cell, let us picture hell to ourselves as vividly as we can; we must conjure up all the horrors of that undying fire; we must vision the torments of the damned, hear their shrieks of pain and their cries of despair; we must smell the stinking fumes of burning sulfur and flesh; we must try to feel those tongues of flame scorching our own bodies; and then we must ask ourselves, How can we escape that everlasting agony? Only through the redeeming sacrifice which God Himself, as Christ, offered on the cross.* Let us then contemplate the life of Christ, and in every detail; we must make ourselves present in imagination at those profoundest events in the history of the world. We must in fancy kneel before the holy figures in that divine epic, and kiss the hem of their garments. After two weeks of such meditations we must accompany Christ through every step in His Passion, every station of the cross; we must pray with Him in Gethsemane, feel ourselves scourged with Him, spat upon, nailed to the cross; we must suffer every moment of His agony, must die with Him, lie with Him in the tomb. And in the fourth week we must picture ourselves rising triumphantly from the grave, rising at last with Him into heaven. Strengthened by that blessed vision, we shall be ready to join as dedicated soldiers in the battle to defeat Satan and win

---

* Note that Luther went through the same fears of hell, the same penitential austerities, the same release through faith in the redeeming sacrifice of Christ, that motived the career of Ignatius.

men to Christ; and in that holy war we shall gladly bear every hardship and joyfully spend our lives.

This call to lifelong devotion found nine students at Paris ready to accept it. Earnest young men feeling for the first time the unintelligibility of the world, and longing for some anchor of belief and hope in a sea of doubts and fears, may have been moved, by the very extent of the demands made upon them, to put their fate, their lives and salvation, in Loyola's plan. He proposed that in due time they should go together to Palestine, and live there a life as nearly as possible like Christ's. On August 15, 1534, Loyola, Faber, Xavier, Diego Laynez, Alonso Salmeron, Nicolas Bobadilla, Simon Rodriguez, Claude Le Jay, Jean Codure, and Paschase Broet, in a little chapel in Montmartre, took the vows of chastity and poverty, and pledged themselves, after two years of further study, to go and live in the Holy Land. They had as yet no apparent notion of combating Protestantism; Islam seemed to them the greater challenge. They had no interest in theological disputes; their aim was sanctity; their movement was rooted in Spanish mysticism rather than in the intellectual conflicts of the time. The best argument would be a holy life.

In the winter of 1536–37 they walked through France, over the Alps, and across Italy to Venice, where they hoped to find passage to Jaffa. But Venice was at war with the Turks; the trip was impossible. During the delay Ignatius met Caraffa, and for a time joined the Theatines. His experience with these devoted priests had some influence in changing his plan from life in Palestine to service of the Church in Europe. He and his disciples agreed that if, after a year of waiting, Palestine should still be closed to them, they would offer themselves to the Pope for any service that he might assign to them. Faber secured permission for all of them to be ordained priests.

By this time Loyola was forty-six. He was bald, and still limped slightly from his wound. His five feet and two inches would have left him quite unimpressive had it not been for an aristocratic refinement of features, the sharp nose and chin, the somber, deep-set, piercing black eyes, the grave, intent countenance; he was already the absorbed and almost humorless saint. He was no persecutor; though he approved of the Inquisition,[35] he was rather its victim than its agent. He was stern but kind; he willingly served the sick in hospitals and plague. His dream was to win converts not by the pyre or the sword but by catching character in malleable youth and forming it immovably to faith. Founder of the most successful educational order in history, he laid little emphasis on learning or intellect. He was not a theologian, took no part in the arguments and refinements of the Scholastics; he preferred direct perception to rational understanding. He did not have to argue about the existence of God, of Mary and the saints; he was convinced that he had seen them; he felt them closer to him than any object or person in his surroundings; in his own way he was a God-intoxicated man. Yet his mystical experiences did not make him impractical. He could combine pliancy of means with inflexibility of ends. He would not justify any means for an end that he held good, but he could bide his time, moderate his hopes and demands, adjust his methods to characters and conditions, use diplomacy where needed, judge men shrewdly, choose fit aides and agents, and manage men as if he were—as he actually thought himself—a general leading a martial company. He called his little band by a military term, *Compañia de Jesú;* they were soldiers enlisted for life in the war against unbelief and the dissolution of the Church. For their part, as a matter of course and necessity, they accepted the military discipline of co-ordinated action under absolute command.

In the fall of 1537 Loyola, Faber, and Laynez set out from Venice to Rome to ask papal approval of their plans. They walked all the way, begged their food, and lived mostly on bread and water. But they sang psalms happily as they went along, as if they knew that out of their small number would grow a powerful and brilliant organization.

V. THE JESUITS

Arrived in Rome they did not at once ask audience with the Pope, for Paul III was immersed in critical diplomacy. They took service in the Spanish hospital, tended the sick, taught the young. Early in 1538 Paul received them, and was impressed by their desire to go to Palestine and live there as exemplary monks; he and some cardinals contributed 210 crowns ($5,-250?) to pay the passage of the band When the devotees had to abandon the idea as impracticable, they returned the money to the donors.[36] Those members who had remained in the north were summoned to Rome, and the company now numbered eleven. Paul appointed Faber and Laynez to professorships in the Sapienza (the University of Rome), while Ignatius and the rest devoted themselves to works of charity and education. Loyola made a special mission of converting prostitutes; with funds collected from his supporters he founded the House of Martha to receive such women; and his fervent preaching against sexual transgressions made him many enemies in Rome.

As new candidates were received into the company, it became desirable to define its principles and rule. The vow of obedience was added to those of chastity and poverty; the "general" chosen by them was to be obeyed only next to the Pope. A fourth vow was taken: to "serve the Roman Pontiff as God's vicar on earth," and "to execute immediately and without hesitation or excuse all that the reigning Pope or his successors may enjoin upon them for the benefit of souls or for the propagation of the faith" anywhere in the world. In 1539 Loyola asked Cardinal Contarini to submit these articles of organization to Paul III, and to request the papal confirmation of the company as a new order. The Pope was favorable; some cardinals dissented, thinking the group to be unmanageable extremists; but Paul overcame their objections, and by the bull *Regimini militantis ecclesiae* ("For the rule of the Church Militant") he formally established what the bull called *Societas Jesú*, the "Society of Jesus" (September 27, 1540). The members were properly called "Clerks Regular of the Society of Jesus"; the name "Jesuit" did not appear till 1544, and then chiefly as a satirical term used by Calvin and other critics;[37] it was never used by Ignatius himself. After his death the success of the new order deprived the term of its early sting, and in the sixteenth century it was a badge of honor.

On April 17, 1541, Ignatius was elected general. For several days thereafter he washed dishes and discharged the humblest offices.[38] During his remaining years (he was now fifty) he made Rome his home, and the city became the permanent headquarters of the society. Between 1547 and 1552, after much thought and experiment, he drew up the Constitutions which, with minor changes, are the Jesuit rule today. The ultimate authority in the order was to lie in the fully "professed" members. These would choose two delegates from each province, and these delegates—together with the provincial heads, the general, and his aides—were to compose the "General Congregation." This would, when occasion required, elect a new general, and then it would delegate its authority to him as long as he should commit no grave offense. He was given an "admonitor" and four assistants, who were to watch his every act, warn him of any serious fault, and, if need appeared, convene the General Congregation to depose him.

Candidates for admission were required to pass through two years of novitiate, in which they would be trained in the purpose and discipline of the society, go through the spiritual exercises, perform menial duties, and submit to the superiors in absolute "holy obedience." They must put aside their own individual wills, and allow themselves to be ordered like soldiers and moved about "like corpses";[39] they must learn to feel that in obeying their superiors they are obeying God. They must agree to report the faults of their associates to their superiors, and to harbor no resentment against being reported themselves.[40] This discipline was rigorous but discriminating and flexible; rarely did it break the will or destroy initiative. Apparently the willingness to obey is the first step in learning to command, for this training produced a great number of able and enterprising men.

Those who survived this trying novitiate would take "simple"—revocable —vows of poverty, chastity, and obedience, and would enter the "second class." Some of these would remain in that status as lay brothers; some, as "formed scholastics," aspiring to the priesthood, would study mathematics, the classics, philosophy, and theology, and would teach in schools and colleges. Those who passed further tests would enter the third class—"formed coadjutors"; and some of these might rise into the fourth class—the "professed"—all priests, and specially pledged to undertake any task or mission assigned them by the Pope. The "professed" were usually a small minority—sometimes hardly more than a tenth—of the entire society.[41] All four classes were to live in common like monks, but in view of their many administrative and pedagogical duties they were exempted from the monastic obligation to recite the canonical hours. No ascetic practices were required, though they might on occasion be advised. There was to be moderation in eating and drinking, but no stringent fasting; body as well as mind was to be kept fit for all tasks. A member might retain title to such property as he owned when entering the order, but all income from it was to go to the society, which hoped to be the ultimate heir. Every Jesuit possession and action must be dedicated *ad majorem Dei gloriam*—to the greater glory of God.

Seldom has an institution borne so definitely the stamp of one personality. Loyola lived long enough to revise the Constitutions into a successfully functioning rule. From his small, bare room he guided with severe authority and great skill the movements of his little army in every quarter of Europe, and many other parts of the globe. The task of governing the society, and of establishing and administering two colleges and several charitable foundations in Rome, proved too much for his temper as he aged; and though kind to the weak he became cruelly harsh to his closest subordinates.[42] He was severest on himself. He made many a meal from a handful of nuts, a piece of bread, and a cup of water. Often he left but four hours of the day for sleep, and even restricted to a daily half-hour the period that he allowed himself for celestial visions and illumination.[43] When he died (1556) many Romans felt that a sharp wind had ceased to blow, and perhaps some of his followers mingled relief with grief. Men could not realize, so soon, that this indomitable Spaniard would prove to be one of the most influential men in modern history.

At his death the society had approximately a thousand members, of whom some thirty-five were "professed."[44] After disputes that showed considerable will to power in Jesuits supposedly broken in will, Diego Laynez was chosen general (1558); the fact that he had Jewish ancestors four generations back made him unacceptable to some Spanish grandees who had some influence in the order.[45] Pope Paul IV, fearful that the office of Jesuit general, because of its life tenure, might grow to rival the papacy, ordered the Constitutions revised to limit the general's term to three years; but Pius IV revoked the order, and the general became (as later generations would call him from his black cassock) the "Black Pope." After Francis Borgia, Duke of Gandia, joined the order and dowered it with his wealth, the society grew rapidly in size and power. When he became its third general (1565) it had 3,500 members, living in 130 houses in eighteen provinces or countries.

Europe was but a small sector of its activities. It sent missionaries to India, China, Japan, and the New World. In North America they were venturesome and undiscourageable explorers, suffering every tribulation as a gift of God. In South America they did more than any other group to develop education and scientific agriculture. In 1541 St. Francis Xavier left Lisbon on a Portuguese vessel, and after a year of travel and travail reached Goa. There he walked up and down the streets ringing a hand bell to gather an audience; this accomplished, he expounded the Christian creed with such sincerity and eloquence, and illustrated the Christian ethic with such cheerful sharing of his poorest listeners' life, that he made thousands of converts among Hindus and Moslems, and even convinced some hardship-hardened expatriated Portuguese Christians. His cures were probably caused by his contagious confidence or his incidental knowledge of medicine; miracles were later ascribed to him, but he himself claimed none. The papal bull that canonized him (1622) credited him with the "gift of tongues"—the ability to speak any language at need; but in truth the heroic saint was a poor linguist, who spent hours memorizing sermons in Tamil, Malay, or Japanese. Sometimes his faith was too strong for his humanity. He urged John III of Portugal to establish the Inquisition in Goa,[46] and recommended that no Hindu should be ordained unless he had several generations of Christian ancestors; he could not bear the thought of a Portuguese confessing to a native.[47] He finally left Goa as too polyglot for his purposes. "I want to be where there are no Moslems or Jews. Give me out-and-out pagans!"[48]—these, he felt, were more open to conversion, as being less ingrained in another faith. In 1549 he set out for Japan, studying Japanese on the way. Landing at Kagoshima, he and his associates preached in the streets, and were courteously heard by the people. Two years later he returned to Goa; he settled some disorder that had arisen among the Christians there, and then sailed off to convert China (1552). After much suffering he stopped on the island of Chang-Tschouen, below the mouth of the Canton River. The Chinese emperor had made it a capital crime for a European to enter China; yet Xavier would have dared it, had he been able to find passage. While he waited he fell sick. He died on December 2, 1552, crying, "In Thee, O Lord, have I hoped; let me not be confounded forever."[49] He was forty-six years old.

The same devotion which the Jesuits showed in foreign missions was displayed in their work in Europe. They kept to their posts, and tended the sick, in times of plague.[50] They preached to all classes, and accommodated their language to every situation. Their superior education and good manners made them the favorite confessors of women and nobles, finally of kings. They mingled actively in the affairs of the world, but with prudence and tact; Ignatius advised them that more prudence and less piety were better than more piety and less prudence.[51] Usually they were men of high moral quality; the faults charged against them in a later period hardly appeared in this age.[52] Though they corporately approved of the Inquisition,[53] they stood aside from it, preferring to work through education. Their limited number compelled them to leave to others the instruction of children; they concentrated on secondary education; and finding the universities preempted by other orders, or the secular or Protestant clergy, they organized their own colleges, and sought to train selected youths who would be centers of influence in the next generation. They became the greatest educators of their time.

At important points in Europe they established *studia inferiora*—corresponding to the German *Gymnasien* and the French *lycées*—and *studia superiora*—colleges. Sometimes, as at Coimbra and Louvain, they were able to take over existing universities. They shocked their competitors by giving instruction gratis. The curriculum probably owed something to the schools set up in Holland and Germany by the Brethren of the Common Life, something to the *Gymnasium* of Sturm at Strasbourg, something to the humanist academies of Germany and Italy. It was based on the classics and was given in Latin; the use of the vernacular was forbidden to the students except on holidays.[54] In the higher grades the Scholastic philosophy was restored. The education of character—of morals and manners—was given fresh emphasis, and was bound up anew with religious belief. The traditional faith was inculcated daily, and a regimen of prayer, meditation, confession, communion, Mass, and theology so imbued the students with orthodoxy that few of them, in the sixteenth century, ever strayed from that beaten path. Humanism was turned back from paganism to Christianity. The system had serious defects: it relied too much on memory, and discouraged originality. Like the other curricula of the time it was deficient in the sciences, and expurgated history to control the present. And yet so independent a thinker as Francis Bacon would soon say of the Jesuit schools, "Such as they are, would that they were ours." [55] In the next two centuries their graduates would excel in almost every walk of life except scientific research.

By the time of Loyola's death there were a hundred Jesuit colleges. Through education, diplomacy, and devotion, through fervor directed by discipline, through co-ordination of purposes and skillful variation of means, the Jesuits turned back the Protestant tide, and recaptured much of Germany, most of Hungary and Bohemia, all of Christian Poland, for the Church. Rarely has so small a group achieved so much so rapidly. Year by year its prestige and influence grew, until, within twenty years of its formal establishment, it was recognized as the most brilliant product of the Catholic Reform. When at last the Church dared to call that general council to which all Europe had so long looked for the quieting of its theological strife and the healing of its religious wounds, it was to a handful of Jesuits—to their learning, loyalty, discretion, resourcefulness, and eloquence—that the popes entrusted the defense of their own challenged authority, and the undiminished preservation of the ancient faith.

CHAPTER XXXIX

The Popes and the Council

1517-65

I. THE POPES AT BAY

WE have left to the last the difficult task, for a non-Catholic, of understanding and impartially describing the reaction of the popes to the challenge of the Reformation.

It was at first a reaction of pained surprise. The popes of the Reformation period, with perhaps one exception, were good men, so far as statesmen are permitted so to be; not selfless or sinless, but basically decent, humane, and intelligent, and sincerely convinced that the Church was an institution not only magnificent in its achievements but still indispensable to the moral health and mental peace of European man. Granting that the human ministrants of the Church had fallen into serious abuses, were there not equivalent or worse defects in every secular administration? And if one should hesitate to overthrow civil government because of the greed of princes and the peculations of officials, should one hesitate any the less to subvert a Church that had been for a thousand years, through religion, education, literature, philosophy, and art, the nourishing mother of European civilization? What if some dogmas that had been found helpful in promoting morality and order seemed difficult of digestion by the historian or the philosopher—were the doctrines proposed by the Protestants so much more rational or credible as to warrant turning Europe upside down over the difference? In any case, religious doctrines were determined not by the logic of a few but by the needs of many; they were a frame of belief within which the common man, inclined by nature to a hundred unsocial actions, could be formed into a being sufficiently disciplined and self-controlled to make society and civilization possible. Let that frame be shattered, and another would have to be built, perhaps after centuries of moral and psychical disorder; for were not the Reformers agreed with the Church that a moral code would be ineffective unless supported by religious belief? As to the intellectual classes, were they any freer or happier under Protestant princes than under Catholic popes? * Had not

---

* "Before the Lutheran revolt," says one of the Church's most powerful and erudite critics, "there was much liberty of thought and speech allowed throughout Catholic Europe." —Henry C. Lea, *History of the Inquisition in Spain*, III, 411.

art flowered under the leadership of the Church, and was it not withering under the hostility of reformers who wished to take from the people the images that fed the poetry and hope of their lives? What commanding reasons were there, to mature minds, for atomizing Christendom into countless sects, each vilifying and nullifying the others, and individually powerless against the instincts of men?

We cannot know that these were the sentiments of the Reformation popes, for the active leaders of men seldom publish their philosophies. But we may so imagine the mood of Leo X (1513–21), who found the papacy rocking under his feet so soon after he had been called to enjoy it. He was a man like many of us—guilty of sin and criminal negligence, but, all in all, forgivable. He was usually the kindest of men, feeding half the poets of Rome; yet he pursued the heretics of Brescia to the death, and tried to believe that disruptive ideas could be roasted out of mankind. He was as patient with Luther as could have been asked of a pope and a Medici; imagine the tables turned, and how Pope Martin would have blasted rebellious Leo from the earth! Leo mistook the Reformation as an unmannerly dispute among unsophisticated monks. And yet, early in 1517, at the very outset of his pontificate, Gianfrancesco Pico della Mirandola (nephew of the more famous Pico) had delivered before the Pope and the cardinals a remarkable address "painting in the darkest manner the corruption which had made its way into the Church," and predicting that "if Leo . . . refuses to heal the wounds, it is to be feared that God Himself will no longer apply a slow remedy, but will cut off and destroy the diseased members with fire and sword." [1] Despite this warning, Leo absorbed himself in maintaining, for the protection of the Papal States, a balance of power between France and the Empire; "he never gave a thought," says a Catholic historian, "to reform on the grand scale which had become necessary. . . . The Roman Curia remained as worldly as ever." [2]

The best proof that reform could come only by a blow from without was the failure of Adrian VI (1522–23). Candidly admitting the abuses, and undertaking to reform them at the top, Adrian was ridiculed and reviled by the Romans as threatening their supply of transalpine gold; and after two years of contending against this unenlightened selfishness Adrian died of frustration.

The accumulated storm burst upon the head of Clement VII (1523–34) Intellectually and morally he was among the best popes, humane and generous, defending the hounded Jews, taking no part in the sexual or financial looseness that surrounded him, and continuing to the end of his troubled life to nourish with discriminating patronage the art and literature of Italy. Perhaps he was too well educated to be a successful administrator; his intellect was keen enough to see good reasons for every course in every crisis;

his knowledge sapped his courage, and his vacillations alienated power after power. We cannot withhold all sympathy from a man so well intentioned; who saw Rome sacked under his eyes, and himself imprisoned by a mob and an emperor; who was prevented by that Emperor from seeking a reasonable peace with Henry VIII; who had to make the bitter choice between losing Henry and England or Charles and Germany; who, when he protested against the alliance of Francis with the Turks, was told by that Most Christian King that if the Pope protested further, France would divorce itself from the papacy. Never had a pope drunk the cup of office to such bitter dregs.

His errors were catastrophic. When he miscalculated the character and resources of Charles, and so invited the Sack of Rome, he dealt the prestige of the papacy a blow that emboldened northern Germany to renounce allegiance to Rome. When he crowned the man who had permitted that attack he lost the respect of even the Catholic world. He yielded to Charles partly through lack of material power to resist, partly because he feared that an alienated Emperor would call a general council of laity as well as clergy, would seize the reins of both ecclesiastical and secular authority, would complete the subjection of the Church to the rampant state, might even depose him as a bastard.[3] If he had had the courage that his uncle Lorenzo de' Medici had shown at Naples in 1479, Clement would have taken the initiative, and would have called a council that under his liberal leadership might have reformed the morals and doctrine of the Church, and saved the unity of Western Christendom.

His successor seemed at first sight to have all the requisites of both intellect and character. Born in a rich and cultured family, instructed in the classics by Pomponius Laetus, maturing as a humanist among the Medici in Florence, favored by a pope whom his sister had entangled in her golden hair, made a cardinal at twenty-five (1493), proving his mettle in difficult diplomatic assignments, rising to unquestioned pre-eminence in the college of cardinals, and unanimously elected pope in 1534, Alessandro Farnese, as Paul III, was universally recognized as the right man for the highest office in the Christian world. The esteem in which he was held suffered little from his having begotten four children before his ordination as a priest (1519). Yet his character, like his career, showed uncertainty and contradictions, partly because he stood like a shaken pillar between the Renaissance that he loved and a Reformation that he could not understand or forgive. Frail in body, he survived fifteen years of political and domestic storms. Equipped with all the learning of his time, he regularly resorted to astrologers to determine the most favorable hour for a journey, a decision, even an audience.[4] A man of strong feeling, and given now and then to bursts of anger, he was noted for his self-control. Cellini, whom he had to imprison, described him "as one who had no faith in God or aught beside"; [5] this seems extreme; and certainly Paul had faith in himself until, in his final years, the behavior of his progeny weakened his will to live. He was punished where he had sinned; he restored the nepotism that had marked the Renaissance papacy, gave Piacenza and Parma to his son Pierluigi and Camerino to his grandson Ottavio, bestowed the red hat on his nephews, fourteen and seventeen years old, and promoted them despite their notorious immorality. He had character without morals, and intellect without wisdom.

He recognized the justice of the criticisms directed by the Reformers at the administration of the Church, and if ecclesiastical amendment had been the only obstacle to reconciliation he might have ended the Reformation. In 1535 he sent Pierpaolo Vergerio to sound out Protestant leaders about attending a general council, but he would not promise to allow any substantial change in the defined faith or in the authority of the popes. Vergerio returned from Germany worse than empty-handed, for he reported that Catholics there joined Protestants in doubting the Pope's sincerity in proposing a council,[6] and that Archduke Ferdinand complained that he could find no confessor who was not a fornicator, a drunkard, or an ignoramus.[7] Paul tried again in 1536; he commissioned Peter van der Vorst to arrange terms with the Lutherans for a council, but Peter was rebuffed by the Elector of Saxony, and achieved nothing. Finally Paul made the culminating effort of the Church to reach an understanding with her critics: he sent to a conference at Ratisbon Cardinal Gasparo Contarini, a man of unquestioned sincerity in the Catholic movement for reform.

We cannot withhold sympathy from the old cardinal who braved the snows of Apennines and Alps in February and March 1541, eager to crown his life with the organization of religious peace. Everyone at Ratisbon was impressed by his modesty, simplicity, and good will. He mediated with saintly patience between the Catholic Eck, Pflug, and Gropper, and the Protestant Melanchthon, Bucer, and Pistorius. Agreement was reached on original sin, free will, baptism, confirmation, and holy orders, and on May 3 Contarini wrote joyfully to Cardinal Farnese: "God be praised! Yesterday the Catholic and Protestant theologians came to an agreement on the doctrine of justification." But on the Eucharist no acceptable compromise could be found. The Protestants would not admit that a priest could transform bread and wine into the body and blood of Christ; and the Catholics felt that to surrender transubstantiation would be to give up the very heart of the Mass and the Roman ritual. Contarini returned to Rome exhausted with failure and grief, only to be branded as a Lutheran by the rigidly orthodox followers of Cardinal Caraffa. Paul himself was not clear that he could accept the formulas that Contarini had signed; however, he gave him a friendly welcome, and appointed him papal legate at Bologna. There, five months after his arrival, Contarini died.

The politics of religion became ever more cloudy and confused. Paul wondered if reconciliation of the Protestants with the Church would give Charles V so united and peaceful a Germany that the Emperor would be free to turn south and connect his north and south Italian realms by appropriating the Papal States and ending the temporal power of the popes. Francis I, likewise dreading the pacification of Germany, charged Contarini with having shamefully surrendered to heretics, and he pledged his full support to Paul if the Pope would firmly reject peace with the Lutherans [8] —with whom Francis sought alliance. Paul seems to have decided that a religious understanding would be politically ruinous. In 1538, by brilliant diplomacy, he brought Charles and Francis to sign a truce at Nice; then, having made Charles secure in the west, he urged him to fall upon the Lutherans. When Charles neared victory (1546) Paul withdrew the papal contingent that he had sent to him, for again he trembled lest an Emperor with no Protestant problem in his rear would be tempted to subdue all Italy. The Pope became a pro-tempore Protestant, and viewed Lutheranism as a protector of the papacy—much as Suleiman had been a protector of Lutheranism. Meanwhile his other shield against Charles—Francis I—was allying himself with Turks who repeatedly threatened to invade Italy and attack Rome. Some vacillation may be forgiven to a pope so harassed and beset, armed with a handful of troops, and defended by a faith that only the weak seemed to cherish. We perceive how small a role religion played in these struggles for power when we hear the comment of Charles to the papal nuncio on learning that Paul was turning to France: the Pope, said the Emperor, had caught in old age an infection usually acquired in youth, the *morbus gallicus*, the French disease.[9]

Paul neither stopped Protestantism nor effected any substantial reforms, but he revitalized the papacy and restored it to grandeur and influence. He remained to the end a Renaissance pope. He encouraged and financed the work of Michelangelo and other artists, beautified Rome with new buildings, embellished the Vatican with the Sala Regia and the Cappella Paolina, took part in brilliant receptions, welcomed fair women to his table, received musicians, buffoons, female singers and dancers, at his court;[10] even in his eighties this Farnese was no spoil-sport. Titian transmitted him to us in a series of powerful portraits. The best (in the Naples Museum) shows the seventy-five-year-old Pontiff still strong, his face furrowed with problems of state and family, but his head not yet bowed to time. Three years later Titian painted an almost prophetic picture (also in Naples) of Paul and his nephews Ottavio and Alessandro; the Pope, now bent and weary, seems to question Ottavio suspiciously. In 1547 Paul's son Pierluigi was assassinated:

in 1548 Ottavio rebelled against his father, and entered into an agreement with Paul's enemies to make Parma an Imperial fief. The old Pope, defeated even by his children, surrendered himself to death (1549).

Julius III (1550–55) misnamed himself; there was nothing in him of the virility and power and grandiose aims of Julius II; rather, he resumed the easy ways of Leo X, and enjoyed the papacy with amiable prodigality, as if the Reformation had died with Luther. He hunted, kept court jesters, gambled for large sums, patronized bullfights, made a cardinal out of a page who took care of his monkey, and, all in all, gave Rome its last taste of Renaissance paganism in morals and art.[11] Outside the Porta del Popolo he had Vignola and others build for him the pretty Villa di Papa Giulio (1553), and made it a center of artists, poets, and festivities. He accommodated himself peacefully to the policies of Charles V. He suffered inopportunely from gout, and tried to cure it by fasting; this papal epicurean seems to have died of abstemiousness,[12] or, said others,[13] of dissipation.

Pope Marcellus II was almost a saint. His moral life was blameless, his piety was profound, his appointments were exemplary, his efforts for Church reform were sincere; but he died on the twenty-second day of his pontificate (May 5, 1555).

As if to make clear that the Counter Reformation had reached the papacy, the cardinals now raised to power the soul and voice of the reform movement in the Church, the ascetic Giovanni Pietro Caraffa, who took the name of Paul IV (1555–59). Already seventy-nine, he was immovably fixed in his views, and dedicated himself to their implementation with a firmness of will and an intensity of passion hardly becoming a man of his years. "The Pope," wrote the Florentine ambassador, "is a man of iron, and the very stones over which he walks emit sparks." [14] Born near Benevento, he carried the heat of southern Italy in his blood, and fire seemed ever burning in his deep-sunken eyes. His temper was volcanic, and only the Spanish ambassador, backed by Alva's legions, dared to cross him. Paul IV hated Spain for having mastered Italy; and as Julius II and Leo X had dreamed of expelling the French, so the first goal of this energetic octogenarian was to liberate Italy and the papacy from Spanish-Imperial domination. He denounced Charles V as a secret atheist,[15] a lunatic son of a lunatic mother, a "cripple in body and soul"; [16] he branded the Spanish people as Semitic scum,[17] and vowed never to recognize Philip as Viceroy of Milan. In December 1555, he concluded a treaty with Henry II of France and Ercole II of Ferrara to drive all Spanish or Imperial forces from Italy. If victorious, the papacy was to acquire Siena, the French were to get Milan, and to hold Naples as a papal fief; and both Charles and Ferdinand were to be deposed for having accepted the Protestant terms at Augsburg.[18]

By one of those comedies that can be seen, from a safe distance, in the tragedies of history, Philip II, the most zealous supporter of the Church, found himself at war with the papacy. Reluctantly he ordered the Duke of Alva to lead his Neapolitan army into the Papal States. In a few weeks the Duke, with 10,000 seasoned troops, overwhelmed the weak forces of the Pope, took town after town, sacked Anagni, seized Ostia, and threatened Rome (November 1556). Paul sanctioned a treaty between France and Turkey, and his secretary of state, Cardinal Carlo Caraffa, appealed to Suleiman to attack Naples and Sicily.[19] Henry II sent an army into Italy under Francis, Duke of Guise; it recaptured Ostia, and the Pope rejoiced; but the defeat of the French at Saint-Quentin compelled Guise to rush back to France with his men, and Alva, unresisted, advanced to the gates of Rome. The Romans moaned with terror, and wished their reckless Pontiff in his grave.[20] Paul saw that further hostilities might repeat the terrible Sack of Rome, and might even drive Spain to secession from the Roman Church. On September 12, 1557, he signed a peace with Alva, who offered lenient terms, apologized for his victory, and kissed the foot of the conquered Pope.[21] All captured papal territory was restored, but the Spanish domination of Naples, Milan, and the papacy was confirmed. So complete was this victory of the state over the Church that when Ferdinand took over the Imperial title from Charles V (1558), he was crowned by the electors, and no representative of the Pope was allowed any part in the ceremony. Thus ended the papal coronation of the Holy Roman Emperors; Charlemagne at last won his argument with Leo III.

Freed willy-nilly from the burdens of war, Paul IV gave the remainder of his pontificate to the ecclesiastical and moral reforms already recorded. He crowned them by tardily dismissing his licentious secretary, Cardinal Carlo Caraffa, and banishing from Rome two other nephews who had disgraced his pontificate. Nepotism, which for a century had flourished there, was at last evicted from the Vatican.

II. CENSORSHIP AND INQUISITION

It was under this iron Pope that censorship of publications reached its greatest severity and scope, and the Inquisition became a terror almost as inhuman in Rome as in Spain. Probably Paul IV felt that censorship of literature and suppression of heresy were unavoidable duties of a Church which—in Protestant as well as Catholic opinion—had been founded by the Son of God. For if the Church was divine, her opponents must be agents of Satan, and against these devils perpetual war was a religious obligation to an insulted God.

Censorship was almost as old as the Church herself. The Christians of

Ephesus, in the age of the Apostles, burned books of "curious arts" to the alleged value of "50,000 pieces of silver,"[22] and the Council of Ephesus (150) forbade the circulation of the uncanonical *Acta Pauli*.[23] At various times the popes ordered the burning of the Talmud or other Jewish books. Wyclifite and later Protestant translations of the Bible were forbidden, as containing anti-Catholic prefaces, notes, and emendations. Printing heightened the anxiety of the Church to keep her members uncorrupted by false doctrines. The Fifth Council of the Lateran (1516) ordered that henceforth no books should be printed without ecclesiastical examination and consent. Secular authorities issued their own prohibitions of unlicensed publications: the Venetian Senate in 1508, the Diet of Worms and the edicts of Charles V and Francis I in 1521, the *Parlement* of Paris in 1542; and in 1543 Charles extended the ecclesiastical control of publications to Spanish America. The first general index of condemned books was issued by the Sorbonne in 1544; the first Italian list by the Inquisition in 1545.

In 1559 Paul IV published the first papal *Index auctorum et librorum prohibitorum*. It named forty-eight heretical editions of the Bible, and put sixty-one printers and publishers under the ban.[24] No book that had been published since 1519 without bearing the names of the author and the printer and the place and date of publication was to be read by any Catholic; and hereafter no book was to be read that had not obtained an ecclesiastical *imprimatur*—"let it be printed." Booksellers and scholars complained that these measures would handicap or ruin them, but Paul insisted on full obedience. In Rome, Bologna, Naples, Milan, Florence, and Venice thousands of books were burned—10,000 in Venice in a day.[25] After Paul's death leading churchmen criticized his measures as too drastic and indiscriminate. The Council of Trent rejected his Index, and issued a more orderly proscription, the "Tridentine Index" of 1564. A special Congregation of the Index was formed in 1571 to revise and republish the list periodically.

It is hard to judge the effect of this censorship. Paolo Sarpi, ex-monk and anticlerical, thought the Index "the finest secret ever discovered for . . . making men idiotic."[26] It probably shared in causing the intellectual decline of Italy after 1600, of Spain after 1700, but economic and political factors were more important. Free thought, according to its most virile English historian, survived better in Catholic than in Protestant countries; the absolutism of the Scriptures, enforced by Protestant divines, proved, till 1750, more damaging to independent investigation and speculation than the Indexes and Inquisition of the Church.[27] In any case the humanist movement faded out, in Catholic and Protestant countries alike. The accent on life subsided in literature; the study of Greek and the love of the pagan classics declined; and the triumphant theologians denounced the Italian humanists (not without reason) as arrogant and dissolute infidels.

The censorship of books was laxly enforced until Paul IV entrusted it to the Inquisition (1555). That institution, first established in 1217, had lapsed in power and repute under the lenience of the Renaissance popes. But when the final attempt at reconciliation with the Protestants had failed at Ratisbon, and Protestant doctrines appeared in Italy itself, even among the clergy, and entire towns like Lucca and Modena threatened to go Protestant,[28] Cardinal Giovanni Caraffa, Ignatius Loyola, and Charles V joined in urging the restoration of the Inquisition. Paul III yielded (1542), appointed Caraffa and five other cardinals to reorganize the institution, and empowered them to delegate their authority to specific ecclesiastics throughout Christendom. Caraffa proceeded with his accustomed severity, set up headquarters and a prison, and laid down rules for his subordinates:

1. When the faith is in question, there must be no delay, but on the slightest suspicion rigorous measures must be taken with all speed.
2. No consideration is to be shown to any prince or prelate, however high his station.
3. Extreme severity is rather to be exercised against those who attempt to shield themselves under the protection of any potentate. Only he who makes plenary confession should be treated with gentleness and fatherly compassion.
4. No man must debase himself by showing toleration toward heretics of any kind, above all toward Calvinists.[29]

Paul III and Marcellus II restrained Caraffa's ardor, and reserved the right of pardon on appeal. Julius III was too lackadaisical to interfere with Caraffa, and several heretics were burned in Rome during his pontificate. In 1550 the new Inquisition ordered the trial of any Catholic clergyman who did not preach against Protestantism. When Caraffa himself became Paul IV, the institution was set in full motion, and under his "superhuman rigor," said Cardinal Seripando, "the Inquisition acquired such a reputation that from no other judgment seat on earth were more horrible and fearful sentences to be expected."[30] The jurisdiction of the inquisitors was extended to cover blasphemy, simony, sodomy, polygamy, rape, procuring, violation of the Church regulations for fasting, and many other offenses that had nothing to do with heresy. To quote again a great Catholic historian:

The hasty and credulous Pope lent a willing ear to every denunciation, even the most absurd. . . . The inquisitors, constantly urged on by the Pope, scented heresy in numerous cases where a calm and circumspect observer would not have discovered a trace of it. . . . The envious and the calumniator were kept hard at work snapping up suspicious words fallen from the lips of men who had been firm pillars of the Church against the innovators, and in bringing groundless accusations of heresy against them. . . . An actual reign of terror began, which filled all Rome with fear.[31]

At the height of this fury (May 31, 1557) Paul ordered the arrest of Cardinal Giovanni Morone, Bishop of Modena, and on June 14 he commanded Cardinal Pole to surrender his legatine power in England and come to Rome to face trial for heresy; the College of Cardinals, said the Pope, was itself infected with heresy. Pole was protected by Queen Mary, who prevented the papal summons from being delivered to him. Morone was charged with having signed the Ratisbon agreement on justification by faith, with having been too lenient with heretics under his jurisdiction, and with having been friendly with Pole, Vittoria Colonna, Flaminio, and other dangerous characters. After eighteen days as a prisoner in the Castel Sant' Angelo, he was pronounced guiltless by the inquisitors, and was ordered released, but he refused to leave his cell until Paul acknowledged his innocence. Paul would not, and Morone remained a prisoner until the Pope's death freed him. Flaminio cheated the Inquisition by dying, but, said Paul, "we have had his brother Cesare burned in the piazza before the church of the Minerva." [32] With impartial resolution the mad Pontiff pursued his own relatives with suspicions of heresy. "Even if my own father were a heretic," he said, "I would gather the wood to burn him." [33]

Fortunately, Paul was mortal, and went to his reward after four years of rule. Rome celebrated his death with four days of joyful rioting, during which the crowd tore down his statue, dragged it through the streets, sank it in the Tiber, burned the buildings of the Inquisition, freed its prisoners, and destroyed its documents.[34] The Pope would have retorted that only a man of his inflexible austerity and courage could have reformed the morals of Rome and the abuses of the Church, and that he had succeeded in that enterprise where his predecessors had failed. It was a pity that in reforming the Church he had remembered Torquemada and forgotten Christ.

All Western Europe was relieved when the conclave of 1559 chose Giovanni Angelo de' Medici to be Pope Pius IV. He was no Medici millionaire, but the son of a Milanese taxgatherer. He practiced law for a living, won the admiration and confidence of Paul III, was made a cardinal, and gained a reputation for intelligence and benevolence. As pontiff he kept clear of war, and reproved those who counseled aggressive policies. He did not end the Inquisition, but he let the inquisitors know that they "would better please him were they to proceed with gentlemanly courtesy than with monkish harshness." [35] A fanatic who thought him too lenient set out to assassinate him, but was palsied with awe when the Pope passed by tranquil and defenseless. Pius enforced with polite firmness the ecclesiastical reforms established by his predecessor. He proved his conciliatory spirit by allowing the Catholic bishops of Germany to administer the Eucharist in both bread and wine. He reconvened the Council of Trent, and guided it to an orderl ⁻ conclusion. In 1565, after a pontificate that had peaceably consolidated the Counter Reformation, he passed away.

III. THE COUNCIL OF TRENT: 1545–63

A thousand voices, long before Luther, had called for a council to reform the Church. Luther appealed from the pope to a free and general council; Charles V demanded such a synod in the hope of getting the Protestant problem off his hands, and perhaps of disciplining Clement VII. That harried Pope could find a hundred reasons for postponing a council until he should be beyond its reach. He recalled what had happened to the papal power at the councils of Constance and Basel; and he could not afford to have hostile bishops, or Imperial delegates, pry into his policies, his domestic difficulties, or his birth. Besides, how could a council help the situation? Had not Luther repudiated councils as well as popes? If the Protestants were admitted to a council and were allowed freedom of speech, the consequent dispute would widen and embitter the schism and would disturb all Europe; and if they were excluded they would raise a rebellious furor. Charles wanted the council held on German soil, but Francis I refused to let the French clergy attend a gathering subject to Imperial domination; moreover, Francis wanted to keep the Protestant fires burning in the Imperial rear. It was a witches' brew.

Paul III had all of Clement's fears, but more courage. In 1536 he issued a call for a general council to meet at Mantua on May 23, 1537, and he invited the Protestants to attend. He assumed that all parties in attendance would accept the conclusions of the conference; but the Protestants, who would be in a minority there, could hardly accept such an obligation. Luther advised against attending, and the congress of Protestants at Schmalkalden returned the Pope's invitation unopened. The Emperor still insisted that the council should meet on German soil; on Italian soil, he argued, it would be crowded with Italian bishops and become a puppet of the Pope. After many negotiations and delays Paul agreed to have the council meet at Trent, which, though predominantly Italian, was in Imperial territory and subject to Charles. The council was summoned to meet there on November 1, 1542.

But the King of France would not play. He forbade the publication, in his realm, of the papal summons, and threatened to arrest any French clergyman who should try to attend a council held on his enemy's terrain. When the council opened, only a few bishops, all Italian, were present, and Paul adjourned the meeting to some time when Charles and Francis would allow a full assembly. The Peace of Crépy seemed to clear the way, and Paul called for the council to reconvene on March 14, 1545. But now the renewal of danger from the Turks compelled the Emperor again to conciliate the Protestants; he asked for another postponement; and it was not till December 13, 1545, that the "Nineteenth Ecumenical Council of the Christian Church" began its active sessions at Trent.

Even that beginning was unpropitious, and far from "half the deed." The Pope, nearing eighty, stayed in Rome, and presided, so to speak, *in absentia;* but he sent three cardinals to represent him—Del Monte, Cervini, and Pole. Cardinal Madruzzo of Trent, four archbishops, twenty bishops, five generals of monastic orders, some abbots, and a few theologians made up the gathering; it could hardly claim as yet to be "ecumenical"—universal.[36] Whereas at the councils of Constance and Basel priests, princes, and certain laymen, as well as prelates, could vote, and voting was by national groups, here only the cardinals, bishops, generals, and abbots could vote, and the voting was by individuals; hence the Italian bishops—most of them indebted or for other reasons loyal to the papacy—dominated the assembly with their numerical majority. "Congregations" sitting in Rome under the supervision of the Pope prepared the issues which alone could be submitted for debate.[37] Since the Council claimed to be guided by the Holy Ghost, a French delegate remarked that the third person of the Trinity regularly came to Trent in the courier's bag from Rome.[38]

The first debate was on procedure: should the faith be first defined and then reforms considered, or vice versa? The Pope and his Italian supporters desired first a definition of dogmas. The Emperor and his supporters sought reform first: Charles in the hope of appeasing, weakening, or further dividing the Protestants; the German and Spanish prelates in the hope that reforms would reduce the power of the Pope over the bishops and the councils. A compromise was reached: concurrent commissions would prepare resolutions on dogma and reform, and these would be presented to the Council alternately.

In May 1546, Paul sent two Jesuits, Laynez and Salmeron, to help his legates in matters of theology and papal defense; later they were joined by Peter Canisius and Claude Le Jay. The unequaled erudition of the Jesuits soon gave them paramount influence in the debates, and their unbending orthodoxy guided the Council to declare war against Reformation ideas rather than seek conciliation or unity. It was apparently the judgment of the majority that no concessions to the Protestants would heal the schism; that Protestant sects were already so numerous and diverse that no compromise could satisfy some without offending others; that any substantial alteration of traditional dogmas would weaken the whole doctrinal structure and stability of Catholicism; that the admission of priestly powers in the laity would undermine the moral authority of the priesthood and the Church; that that authority was indispensable to social order; and that a theology frankly founded on faith would stultify itself by submitting to the vagaries of individual reasoning. Consequently the fourth session of the Council (April 1546) reaffirmed every item of the Nicene Creed, claimed equal authority for Church tradition and Scripture, gave the Church the sole right to expound and interpret the Bible, and declared the Latin Vulgate of Jerome to be the definitive translation and text. Thomas Aquinas was named as the authoritative exponent of orthodox theology, and his *Summa theologica* was placed on an altar only below the Bible and the Decretals.[39] Catholicism as a religion of infallible authority dates in practice from the Council of Trent, and took form as an uncompromising response to the challenge of Protestantism, rationalism, and private judgment. The "Gentlemen's Agreement" of the Renaissance Church with the intellectual classes came to an end.

But if faith was so vital was it also sufficient of itself to merit salvation, as Luther claimed? The fifth session (June 1546) heard violent debates on this point; one bishop clutched another by the beard and plucked out a handful of white hairs; hearing which, the Emperor sent the Council word that if it could not quiet down he would have a few prelates thrown into the Adige to cool them off.[40] Reginald Pole argued for a view so dangerously close to Luther's that Cardinal Caraffa (the future Paul IV) branded him as a heretic; Pole retired from the battle to Padua, and excused himself, on the ground of illness, from continued attendance at the Council.[41] Cardinal Seripando defended the compromise formula that Contarini, now dead, had offered at Ratisbon; but Laynez persuaded the Council to stress, in full opposition to Luther, the importance of good works and the freedom of the will.

Measures of ecclesiastical reform moved less actively than definitions of dogma. The Bishop of St. Mark had opened the session of January 6, 1546, by painting a somber picture of the corruption prevailing in the world, which he thought posterity would never surpass, and he had attributed this degeneration "solely to the wickedness of the pastors"; the Lutheran heresy, he said, had been caused chiefly by the sins of the clergy, and the reform of the clergy was the best way of suppressing the rebellion.[42] But the only substantial reform accomplished in these early sessions was one forbidding bishops to reside away from their sees, or to hold more than one. The Council suggested to the Pope that the reform of the Dataria should advance from theoretical recommendations to actual directives. Paul, however, wished matters of reform to be left to the papacy; and when the Emperor insisted on greater speed in reform discussions at the conference, the Pope ordered his legates to propose the removal of the Council to Bologna—which, being in the Papal States, would allow a more expeditious control of conciliar actions by Rome. The Italian bishops agreed; the Spanish and Imperial prelates protested; a minor plague conveniently appeared in Trent and killed a bishop; the Italian majority moved to Bologna (March 1547); the rest stayed at Trent. Charles refused recognition to the Bologna sessions, and threatened to convene a separate council in Germany. After two years of argument and maneuvering Paul yielded, and suspended the Bologna assembly (September 1549).

The situation was eased by Paul's death. Julius III came to an understanding with the Emperor: in return for Charles's promise to withhold support from any measure that would reduce papal authority, he summoned the Council to meet again at Trent in May 1551, and agreed that the Lutherans should be given a hearing. Henry II of France, resenting this *rapprochement* between Pope and Emperor, declined to recognize the Council. When it met it was so meagerly attended that it had to adjourn. It assembled again on September 1, with eight archbishops, thirty-six bishops, three abbots, five generals, forty-eight theologians, Elector Joachim II of Brandenburg, and ambassadors from Charles and Ferdinand.

The thirteenth session of the Council (October 1551) reaffirmed the Catholic doctrine of transubstantiation: the priest, in consecrating the bread and wine of the Eucharist, actually changes each of them into the body and blood of Christ. Thereafter it seemed useless to hear the Protestants, but Charles insisted on it. The Duke of Württemberg, Elector Maurice of Saxony, and some south German towns chose the members of a Protestant delegation, and Melanchthon drew up a statement of Lutheran doctrine to be submitted to the Council. Charles gave the delegates a safe-conduct, but these, remembering Constance and Huss, required also a safe-conduct from the Council itself. After much discussion this was granted. However, a Dominican friar, preaching on the parable of tares, in the very cathedral in which the sessions were held, pointed out that the heretic tares might be endured for a time, but in the end they would have to be burned.[43]

On January 24, 1552, the Protestant deputies addressed the assembly. They proposed that the decrees of the Councils of Constance and Basel on the superior authority of councils over the popes should be confirmed; that the members of the present body should be released from their vows of fealty to Julius III; that all decisions hitherto reached by the Council should be annulled; and that fresh discussions of the issues should be held by an enlarged synod in which the Protestants would be adequately represented.[44] Julius III forbade consideration of these proposals. The Council voted to postpone action on them till March 19, when additional Protestant delegates were expected.

During this delay military developments supervened upon theology. In

January 1552, the King of France signed an alliance with the German Protestants; in March Maurice of Saxony advanced toward Innsbruck; Charles fled, and no force could prevent Maurice, if he wished, from capturing Trent and swallowing the Council. The bishops one by one disappeared, and on April 28 the Council was formally suspended. By the treaty of Passau (August 2) Ferdinand conceded religious freedom to the militantly victorious Protestants. They took no further interest in the Council.

Paul IV thought it prudent to let the Council hibernate during his pontificate. Pius IV, a kindly old man, played with the thought that the granting of communion in both kinds might appease the Protestants, as it had done the Bohemians. He summoned the Council to reconvene at Trent on April 6, 1561, and invited to it all Christian princes, Catholic or Protestant. To this new session the French delegates brought an imposing list of the reforms they desired: Mass in the vernacular, communion in bread and wine, the marriage of priests, the subordination of the papacy to general councils, and an end to the system of papal dispensations and exemptions;[45] apparently the French government was for the moment in a semi-Huguenot mood. Ferdinand I, now Emperor, seconded these proposals, and added that "the Pope . . . should humble himself, and submit to a reform in his own person, his state, and the Curia"; the legends of the saints should be purified of absurdities, and monasteries should be reformed so "that their great wealth might no longer be expended in so profligate a manner."[46] Matters loomed perilous for Pius, and his legates looked with some trepidation to the opening of the session.

After leisurely or strategic delays the seventeenth session of the Council convened on January 18, 1562, with five cardinals, three patriarchs, eleven archbishops, ninety bishops, four generals, four abbots, and sundry lay representatives of Catholic princes. At Ferdinand's request a safe-conduct was offered to any Protestant delegate who might care to attend; none came. The Archbishop of Granada and Charles, Cardinal of Lorraine, led a movement to reduce the prerogatives of the pope by asserting that the bishops held their power not through him but by direct "divine right"; and the Bishop of Segovia repeated one of Luther's heresies by denying that the pope was supreme over the other bishops in the early Church.[47] This episcopal uprising was snuffed out by the parliamentary skill of the papal legates, the loyalty of the Italian and Polish bishops to the Pope, and some timely papal courtesies to the Cardinal of Lorraine. In the end the papal authority was not lessened but enlarged, and every bishop was required to take an oath of complete obedience to the Pope. Ferdinand was appeased by the promise that on the termination of the Council the Pope would allow administration of the Eucharist in both kinds.

This basic quarrel over, the Council quickly dispatched its remaining business. Clerical marriage was forbidden, and severe penalties were decreed against priestly concubinage. Many minor reforms were enacted to improve the morals and discipline of the clergy. Seminaries were to be established where candidates for the priesthood could be trained to habits of austerity and piety. The powers of the Curia were curbed. Rules were laid down for the reform of Church music and art; nude figures were to be sufficiently covered to avoid stimulating the sensual imagination. A distinction was drawn between the worship of images and the worship of the persons represented by them; in the latter sense the use of religious images was upheld. Purgatory, indulgences, and the invocation of the saints were defended and redefined. Here the Council frankly recognized the abuses that had sparked Luther's rebellion; one decree read:

> In granting indulgences the Council . . . decrees that all criminal gain therewith connected shall be entirely done away with, as a source of grievous abuse among the Christian people; and as to other disorders arising from superstition, ignorance, irreverence, or any cause whatsoever—since these, on account of the widespread corruption, cannot be removed by special prohibitions—the Council lays upon each bishop the duty of finding out such abuses as exist in his own diocese, of bringing them before the next provincial synod, and of reporting them, with the assent of the other bishops, to the Roman Pontiff.[48]

Pope and Emperor agreed that the Council had now reached an end of its usefulness; and on December 4, 1563, it was finally dissolved amid the happy acclamations of the wearied delegates. The course of the Church had been fixed for centuries.

The Counter Reformation succeeded in its principal purposes. Men continued, in Catholic as much as in Protestant countries, to lie and steal, seduce maidens and sell offices, kill and make war.[49] But the morals of the clergy improved, and the wild freedom of Renaissance Italy was tamed to a decent conformity with the pretensions of mankind. Prostitution, which had been a major industry in Renaissance Rome and Venice, now hid its head, and chastity became fashionable. The authorship or publication of obscene works was made a capital offense in Italy; so Niccolo Franco, secretary and enemy of Aretino, was hanged by order of Pius V for his *Priapeia*.[50] The effect of the new restrictions on art and literature was not indisputably harmful; baroque art is emerging timidly from disrepute; and from a purely literary standpoint Tasso, Guarini, and Goldoni do not fall precipitately from the level of Boiardo, Ariosto, and the dramatist Machiavelli. Spain's greatest age in literature and art came in the fullness of the "Catholic Reaction." But the joyous character of Renaissance Italy faded; Italian women lost some of the charm and exhilaration that had come from their pre-Reformation freedom; a somber and conscious morality produced an almost puritan age in Italy. Monasticism revived. From the point of view of the free mind it was a loss to mankind that the comparative Renaissance liberty of thought was ended by ecclesiastical and political censorship; and it was a tragedy that the Inquisition was restored in Italy and elsewhere just when science was breaking through its medieval shell. The Church deliberately sacrificed the intellectual classes to the pious majority, which applauded the suppression of ideas that might dissolve its consoling faith.

The ecclesiastical reforms were real and permanent. Though the papal monarchy was exalted as against the episcopal aristocracy of the councils, this was in the spirit of the times, when aristocracies everywhere, except in Germany, were losing power to the kings. The popes were now morally superior to the bishops, and the discipline required for ecclesiastical reform could be better effected by a centralized than by a divided authority. The popes ended their nepotism, and cured the Curia of its costly procrastinations and flagrant venality. The administration of the Church, according to non-Catholic students of the matter, became a model of efficiency and integrity.[51] The dark confessional box was introduced (1547) and made obligatory (1614); the priest was no longer tempted by the occasional beauty of his penitents. Indulgence peddlers disappeared; indulgences, for the most part, were reserved for pious devotions and works of charity rather than for financial contributions. Instead of retreating before the advance of Protestantism or free thought, the Catholic clergy set out to recapture the mind of youth and the allegiance of power. The spirit of the Jesuits, confident, positive, energetic, and disciplined, became the spirit of the militant Church.

All in all it was an astonishing recovery, one of the most brilliant products of the Protestant Reformation.

Epilogue

RENAISSANCE, REFORMATION, AND ENLIGHTENMENT

THE Renaissance and the Reformation are the two springs of modern history, rival sources of the intellectual and moral freshening of modern life. Men might be divided by their preference and lineage here, by their conscious debt to the Renaissance for liberating the mind and beautifying life, or their gratitude to the Reformation for quickening religious belief and the moral sense. The debate between Erasmus and Luther goes on, and will, for in these large matters such truth as men can attain is begotten by the union of opposites, and will ever feel its double parentage.

In a sense the debate is ethnic and geographical, between the Latins and the Teutons, the plein-air, sensuous South and the misty, hardy North; between peoples conquered by Rome and receiving the classic heritage, and peoples resisting Rome—some conquering Rome—and loving their own roots and climes far more than Greeks bringing gifts or Romans bearing laws. Italy and Germany divided between them the forming of the modern soul: Italy by going back to classic literature, philosophy, and art, Germany by going back to early Christian faith and ritual. Italy was almost succeeding in its second effort to conquer Germany—now through tithes and humanism; Germany resisted again, expelled the Church, and silenced the humanists. The Reformation repudiated the Renaissance and its emphasis on earthly affairs and joys, and returned to that aspect (only one!) of the Middle Ages which counted human achievements and delights trivial and vain, called life a vale of tears, and summoned sinful man to faith, repentance, and prayer. To the Italian of the Renaissance, reading Machiavelli and Aretino, this seemed a medieval reaction, a restoration of the Age of Faith in the struggling adolescence of the Age of Reason. The Italian who had heard Pomponazzi, and lived under the easy rule of the Renaissance popes, smiled to find Luther and Calvin and Henry VIII keeping all the marvelous dogmas of the medieval creed—a God-dictated Bible, a triune deity, predestination, creation by divine fiat, original sin, incarnation, virgin birth, atonement, the last judgment, heaven, and hell—and rejecting precisely those elements of medieval Christianity—the worship of the Virgin, a God of love and mercy, the invocation of intercessory saints, a ritual adorned with all the arts—which had given to that faith a tenderness, solace, and beauty warranting a wink at the myths that allowed enjoyment of the arts.

935

The sincerely believing Catholic had his own argument against the Reformation. He too resented tithes, but he could not dream of destroying the Church. He knew quite well that the monks were getting out of hand, but he felt that there should be room and institutions in the world for men dedicated to contemplation, study, and prayer. He accepted every word of the Bible with two provisos: that the law of Christ had abrogated the law of Moses, and that the Church, having been founded by the Son of God, had equal authority with the Bible, and should have the final right to interpret it and adjust it to the changing needs of life. What would happen if ambiguous and apparently contradictory passages in Scripture were left to the free interpretation and judgment of the individual man?—would not the Bible be torn to pieces by a thousand minds, and Christianity be shattered into a thousand warring sects?

The modern Catholic continues the argument through every phase of modern life. "Your emphasis on faith as against works was ruinous, and led to a religion whose coldness of heart was concealed behind the piety of its phrases; for a hundred years charity almost died in the centers of your victory. You ended the confessional and generated a thousand tensions in the soul of men struggling between instinct and civilization, and now you belatedly restore that healing institution under dubious forms. You destroyed nearly all the schools we had established, and you weakened to the verge of death the universities that the Church had created and developed. Your own leaders admit that your disruption of the faith led to a dangerous deterioration of morals in both Germany and England. You let loose a chaos of individualism in morals, philosophy, industry, and government. You took all the joy and beauty out of religion, and filled it with demonology and terror; you condemned the masses of mankind to damnation as "reprobates," and consoled an insolent few with the pride of "election" and salvation. You stifled the growth of art, and wherever you triumphed classical studies withered. You expropriated Church property to give it to the state and the rich, but you left the poor poorer than before, and added contempt to misery. You condoned usury and capitalism, but you deprived the workers of the restful holydays a merciful Church had given them. You rejected the papacy only to exalt the state; you gave to selfish princes the right to determine the religion of their subjects, and to use religion as a sanction for their wars. You divided nation against nation, and many a nation and city against itself; you wrecked the international moral checks on national powers, and created a chaos of warring national states. You denied the authority of a Church founded, on your own admission, by the Son of God, but you sanctioned absolute monarchy, and exalted the divine right of kings. Unwittingly you destroyed the power of the Word, which is the only alternative to the power of money or the sword. You claimed the right of private judgment, but you denied it to others as soon as you could; and your refusal to tolerate dissent was less understandable than ours, for we had never defended toleration; no man can be tolerant except where he is indifferent. Meanwhile see what your private judgment has led to. Every man becomes a pope, and judges the doctrines of religion before he is old enough to comprehend the functions of religion in society and morals, and the need of the people for a religious faith. A kind of disintegrative mania, unhindered by any integrative authority, throws your followers into such absurd and violent disputes that men begin to doubt all religion, and Christianity itself would be dissolved, and men would be left spiritually naked in the face of death, were it not that the Church stands firm amid all the fluctuations of opinion and argument, all the fashions of science and philosophy, and holds her regathering flock together against the time when those of you who have come to understand, and are really Christians, will submit your pride of individuality and intellect to the religious needs of mankind, and will come back to the one fold that can preserve religion despite the blasphemous ideologies of this unhappy age."

Can the Protestant answer this indictment? "Let us not forget the cause of our divergence. Your Catholic Church had become corrupt in practice and personnel, your priests were not functioning, your bishops were worldlings, your popes were the scandal of Christendom; do not your own historians confess it? Honest men called upon you to reform, and meanwhile kept their loyalty to the Church; you promised and pretended to reform, but you did not; on the contrary, you burned at the stake men like Huss and Jerome of Prague because they cried out for reform. A thousand efforts were made to reform the Church from within; they failed until our Reformation forced you to act; and even after our revolt the pope who tried to cleanse the Church became the laughingstock of Rome.

"You pride yourself on producing the Renaissance, but everyone agrees that the Renaissance was issuing in such immorality, violence, and treachery as Europe had not known since Nero; were we not right in protesting against this paganism, flaunting itself even in the Vatican? Granted that morals declined for a while after our Reformation began; it took time to rebuild a moral life whose religious foundations and ministrations had decayed; ultimately the morality of Protestant lands became far superior to that of Catholic France and Italy. We may owe our mental awakening to the Renaissance, but we owe our moral recovery to the Reformation; to the liberation of the intellect was added the strengthening of character. Your Renaissance was for the aristocracy and the intellectuals; it scorned the people, and winked at their hoodwinking by indulgence peddlers and monk-

ish profiteers on mythology; was it not good that this crass financial exploitation of human hopes and fears should be challenged? We rejected the
paintings and statues with which you had littered your churches, because you
were allowing the people to worship the images themselves, as when you required them to fall on their knees before the sacred dolls carried in procession
through the streets. We dared to base our religion on a strong and active
faith, rather than try to drug the mind of the people with liturgy.

"We acknowledged the secular authority as divine—as your own theologians had done before us—because social order requires a respected government. We rejected the international authority of the popes only after they
had flagrantly used it not to arbitrate justice among nations but to advance
their own material interests. The inability of your self-seeking popes to
unify Europe for a crusade against the Turks shows that the dishonesty of the
papacy had broken the unity of Christendom long before the Reformation.
And though we supported the divine right of kings, we also, in England,
Scotland, Switzerland, and America, favored the development of democracy,
while your priests in France, Italy, and Spain were truckling to kings; and
our rebellion against the authority of your Church broke the spell of
despotism, and prepared Europe to question all absolutisms, religious or
secular. You think we made the poor poorer. But that too was a passing
phase; the same capitalism that for a while exploited poverty learned to enrich the average man as never before; and the standard of living is surely
higher in Protestant England, Germany, and America than in Catholic
Italy, Spain, and France.

"If you are stronger today than yesterday, it is because of us. What but
the Reformation compelled you to reform the Curia, to redeem your clergy
from concubinage, to seat men of religion, instead of pagans, in the papal
chair? To whom do you owe it that your clergy today have so high a repute
for integrity? To the Council of Trent? But to what did you owe the Council of Trent, if not to the Reformation? Without that check your Church
might have continued its degeneration from Christianity into paganism until
your popes would have been enthroned over an agnostic and epicurean
world. Even with the regeneration which we forced upon your Church,
the peoples that accept your creed are more negligent of religion, more
skeptical of Christianity, than those that adopted the Reformation; compare
France with England.

"We have learned to reconcile our piety with the freedom of the mind;
and it is our Protestant lands that have seen the greatest flowering of science
and philosophy. We hope to adjust our Christianity to the progress of knowledge—but how is this possible to a Church that rejects all the science of the
last four centuries?"

Here the humanist enters the argument, and brings both houses down upon his head. "This is the honor and weakness of Protestantism, that it appeals to the intellect, which is always changing; and the strength of Catholicism lies in its refusal to adjust itself to the theories of science, which, in the experience of history, seldom survive the century in which they were born. Catholicism proposes to meet the religious demands of the people, who have barely heard of Copernicus and Darwin, and have never heard of Spinoza and Kant; such people are many and fertile. But how can a religion that speaks to the intellect, and centers around the sermon, adjust itself to an expanding universe in which the planet that claimed to have received God's Son has become a transitory speck in space, and the species for which He died is but a moment in the phantasmagoria of life? What happens to Protestantism when the Bible that it took as its sole and infallible basis is subjected to a Higher Criticism that turns it from the word of God into the literature of the Hebrews and the transformation of Christ in the mystical theology of Paul?

"The real problem for the modern mind is not between Catholicism and Protestantism, nor between the Reformation and the Renaissance; it is between Christianity and the Enlightenment—that hardly datable era which began in Europe with Francis Bacon, and hitched its hopes to reason, science, and philosophy. As art was the keynote of the Renaissance, and religion the soul of the Reformation, so science and philosophy became the gods of the Enlightenment. From this standpoint the Renaissance was in the direct line of European mental development, and led to the *Illumination* and *Aufklärung;* the Reformation was a deviation from that line, a rejection of reason, a reaffirmation of medieval faith.

"And yet, despite its original intolerance, the Reformation rendered two services to the Enlightenment: it broke the authority of dogma, generated a hundred sects that would formerly have died at the stake, and allowed among them such virile debate that reason was finally recognized as the bar before which all sects had to plead their cause unless they were armed with irresistible physical force. In that pleading, that attack and defense, all sects were weakened, all dogmas; and a century after Luther's exaltation of faith Francis Bacon proclaimed that knowledge is power. In that same seventeenth century thinkers like Descartes, Hobbes, Spinoza, and Locke offered philosophy as a substitute or basis for religion. In the eighteenth century Helvetius, Holbach, and La Mettrie proclaimed open atheism, and Voltaire was called a bigot because he believed in God. This was the challenge that Christianity faced, in a crisis far more profound than the debate between the Catholic and the Protestant version of the medieval creed. The effort of Christianity to survive Copernicus and Darwin is the basic drama of the last three hundred years. What are the struggles of states and classes beside that Armageddon of the soul?"

And now, as we look back over the meandering narrative of these thousand pages, we perceive that our sympathy can go to all the combatants. We can understand the anger of Luther at Roman corruption and dominance, the reluctance of German princes to see German collections fatten Italy, the resolve of Calvin and Knox to build model moral communities, the desire of Henry VIII for an heir, and for authority in his own realm. But we can understand, too, the hopes of Erasmus for a reform that would not poison Christendom with hatred; and we can feel the dismay of devout Roman prelates like Contarini at the prospective dismemberment of a Church that for centuries had been the nurse and custodian of Western civilization, and was still the strongest bulwark against immorality, chaos, and despair.

Nothing of all these efforts was lost. The individual succumbs, but he does not die if he has left something to mankind. Protestantism, in time, helped to regenerate the moral life of Europe, and the Church purified herself into an organization politically weaker but morally stronger than before. One lesson emerges above the smoke of the battle: a religion is at its best when it must live with competition; it tends to intolerance when and where it is unchallenged and supreme. The greatest gift of the Reformation was to provide Europe and America with that competition of faiths which puts each on its mettle, cautions it to tolerance, and gives to our frail minds the zest and test of freedom.

COURAGE, READER: WE NEAR THE END.

Bibliographical Guide

to editions referred to in the Notes

The letters C, P, J, and R after an author's name indicate
Catholic, Protestant, Jewish, and rationalist respectively

ABBOTT, G. F. (P), Israel in Europe, London, 1907.
ABRAHAMS, ISRAEL (J), Chapters on Jewish Literature, Phila., 1899.
ABRAHAMS, ISRAEL (J), Jewish Life in the Middle Ages, Phila., 1896.
ABRAM, A., English Life and Manners in the Later Middle Ages, London, 1913.
ACTON, JOHN E., LORD (C), Lectures on Modern History, London, 1950.
ADAMS, BROOKS (P), Law of Civilization and Decay, N. Y., 1921.
ADDISON, JULIA, Arts and Crafts in the Middle Ages, Boston, 1908.
AGRICOLA, G., De re metallica, tr. Herbert and Lou Hoover, London, 1912.
ALLEN, J. W. (P), History of Political Thought in the Sixteenth Century,
          London, 1951.
ALLEN, P. S. (P), The Age of Erasmus, Oxford, 1914.
ALTAMIRA, R., History of Spanish Civilization, London, 1930.
AMEER ALI, SYED, Short History of the Saracens, London, 1934.
ARCINIEGAS, GERMAN, Amerigo and the New World, N. Y., 1955.
ARETINO, PIETRO, Works: Dialogues, N. Y., 1926.
ARMSTRONG, EDWARD (P), The Emperor Charles V, 2v., London, 1910.
ARNOLD, SIR THOS., and GUILLAUME, ALFRED, Legacy of Islam, Oxford, 1931.
ARNOLD, SIR THOS., Painting in Islam, Oxford, 1928.
ARNOLD, SIR THOS., The Preaching of Islam, N. Y., 1913.
ASCHAM, ROGER, The Scholemaster, London, 1863.
ASHLEY, W. J., Introd. to English Economic History, 2v., N. Y., 1894 f.

BACON, FRANCIS, Philosophical Works, ed. J. M. Robinson, London, 1905.
BACON, FRANCIS, Works, ed. Spedding, Ellis, and Heath, 6v., London, 1870.
BAEDEKER, KARL, Belgique et Hollande, Paris, 1910.
BAEDEKER, KARL, Munich, N. Y., 1950.
BAINTON, ROLAND (P), Here I Stand: A Life of Martin Luther, N. Y., 1950.
BAINTON, ROLAND (P), Hunted Heretic: The Life of Michael Servetus, Boston,
          1953.
BAINTON, ROLAND (P), The Reformation of the Sixteenth Century, Boston, 1953.
BAKELESS, JOHN, The Tragicall History of Christopher Marlowe, Harvard, 1942.
BALDASS, LUDWIG VON, Hans Memling, Vienna, 1942.
BALDASS, LUDWIG VON, Jan van Eyck, Phaidon Press.
BARNES, H. E., Economic History of the Western World, N. Y., 1942.
BARON, S. W. (J), Social and Religious History of the Jews, 3v., N. Y., 1937.
BATIFFOL, L., The Century of the Renaissance, N. Y., 1935.
BAX, BELFORT, German Society at the Close of the Middle Ages, London, 1894.
BAX, BELFORT, The Peasants' War in Germany, London, 1899.
BEARD, CHAS. (P), Martin Luther and the Reformation, London, 1896.
BEARD, CHAS. (P), The Reformation of the Sixteenth Century in Relation to
          Modern Thought and Knowledge, London, 1885.

BEARD, MIRIAM, History of the Business Man, N. Y., 1938.
BEAZLEY, C. R., Prince Henry the Navigator, London, 1901.
BEBEL, AUGUST, Woman under Socialism, N. Y., 1923.
BEER, M., Social Struggles in the Middle Ages, London, 1924.
BELL, GERTRUDE, Poems from the Divan of Hafiz, London, 1928.
BELLOC, H. (C), How the Reformation Happened, London, 1950.
BEUF, CARLO, Cesare Borgia, Oxford, 1942.
BLOK, P. J., History of the People of the United Netherlands, 3v., N. Y., 1898.
BLOMFIELD, SIR R., History of French Architecture from the Reign of Charles
    VIII till the death of Mazarin, 2v., London, 1911.
BLOMFIELD, SIR R., Short History of Renaissance Architecture in England, 1500–
    1800, London, 1893.
BOCK, ELFRIED, Geschichte der Graphischen Kunst, Berlin, 1930.
BOER, T. J. DE, History of Philosophy in Islam, London, 1903.
BOISSONNADE, P., Life and Work in Medieval Europe, N. Y., 1927.
BOND, FRANCIS, Westminster Abbey, London, 1909.
BOYD, CATHERINE, The French Renaissance, Boston Museum of Fine Arts.
BRANTÔME, SIEGNEUR DE, The Lives of Gallant Ladies, London, 1943.
BRIFFAULT, ROBERT, The Mothers, 3v., N. Y., 1927.
BROWNE, EDWARD, A Literary History of Persia, 4v., Cambridge, England, 1929 f.
BRUNETIÈRE, Ferdinand, Manual of the History of French Literature, N. Y., 1898.
BRYCE, JAMES, The Holy Roman Empire, N. Y., 1921.
BUCKLE, HENRY T., History of Civilization in England, 4v., N. Y., 1913.
BULLETIN OF THE AMERICAN INSTITUTE FOR IRANIAN ART AND ARCHAEOLOGY,
    N. Y., 1938.
BURCKHARDT, JACOB, Civilization of the Renaissance in Italy, London, 1914.
BURKE, U. R., History of Spain, 2v., London, 1940.
BURNET, GILBERT, History of the Reformation of the Church of England, 2v.,
    London, 1841.
BURTON, R. F., The Jew, the Gypsy, and El Islam, Chicago, 1898.
BURY, J. B. (R), History of Freedom of Thought, N. Y., n.d.
BURY, J. B. (R), History of the Later Roman Empire, 2v., London, 1923.

CALVERT, A. F., Cordova, London, 1907.
CALVERT, A. F., Moorish Remains in Spain, N. Y., 1906.
CALVIN, JOHN (P), Institutes of the Christian Religion, 2v., Phila., 1928.
CAMBRIDGE HISTORY OF ENGLISH LITERATURE, 14v., N. Y., 1910 f.
CAMBRIDGE HISTORY OF POLAND, 2v., Cambridge, England, 1950.
CAMBRIDGE MEDIEVAL HISTORY, 8v., N. Y., 1924 f.
CAMBRIDGE MODERN HISTORY, 12v., N. Y., 1907 f.
CAMÕES, LUIZ DE, Lusiads, tr. Leonard Bacon, N. Y., 1950.
CAMPBELL, THOS., Life and Times of Petrarch, 2v., London, 1843.
CAMPBELL, THOS. (C), The Jesuits, N. Y., 1921.
CARLYLE, R. W., History of Medieval Political Theory in the West, 6v., Edin-
    burgh, 1928 f.
CARLYLE, THOS. (P), Heroes and Hero Worship, in Works, N. Y., 1901.
CARPENTER, EDWARD (R), Pagan and Christian Creeds, N. Y., 1920.
CARTER, THOS., The Invention of Printing in China, and Its Spread Westward,
    N. Y., 1925

CASTIGLIONI, ARTURO, History of Medicine, N. Y., 1941.
CATHOLIC ENCYCLOPEDIA, N. Y., 1912.
CELLINI, BENVENUTO, Autobiography, tr. Symonds, N. Y., 1948.
CHAMBERS, E. K., The Medieval Stage, 2v., Oxford, 1903.
CHAPIRO, JOSÉ, Erasmus and Our Struggle for Peace, Boston, 1950.
CHAPMAN, CHAS., History of Spain, N. Y., 1930.
CHENEY, EDWARD, The Dawn of a New Era, N. Y., 1936.
CHENEY, SHELDON, A World History of Art, N. Y., 1937.
CLAPHAM, J. H., and POWER, EILEEN, Cambridge Economic History of Europe,
        Cambridge, England, 1944.
CLAVIJO, GONZALEZ DE, Embassy to Tamerlane, N. Y., 1928.
COKER, F. W., Readings in Political Philosophy, N. Y., 1938.
COMINES, PHILIPPE DE, Memoirs, 2v., London, 1900.
CONWAY, SIR MARTIN, The Van Eycks and Their Followers, N. Y., 1921.
COPERNICUS, N., Commentariolus, in Rosen, Three Copernican Treatises.
COULTON, G. G. (P), Art and the Reformation, N. Y., 1925.
COULTON, G. G. (P), The Black Death, N. Y., 1930.
COULTON, G. G. (P), Chaucer and His England, London, 1921.
COULTON, G. G. (P), Five Centuries of Religion, 3v., Cambridge, England, 1923.
COULTON, G. G. (P), From St. Francis to Dante, a tr. of the Chronicle of Salim-
        bene, London, 1908.
COULTON, G. G. (P), Inquisition and Liberty, London, 1938.
COULTON, G. G. (P), Life in the Middle Ages, 4v., Cambridge, England, 1930.
COULTON, G. G. (P), Medieval Panorama, N. Y., 1944.
COULTON, G. G. (P), The Medieval Scene, Cambridge, England, 1930.
COULTON, G. G. (P), The Medieval Village, Cambridge, England, 1925.
COULTON, G. G. (P), Social Life in Britain from the Conquest to the Reforma-
        tion, Cambridge, England, 1938.
CRAVEN, THOS., A Treasury of Art Masterpieces, N. Y., 1952.
CREASY, E. S., History of the Ottoman Turks, London, 1878.
CREIGHTON, MANDELL (P), Cardinal Wolsey, London, 1888.
CREIGHTON, MANDELL (P), History of the Papacy during the Reformation, 5v.,
        London, 1882 f.
CRUMP, C. G., and JACOB, E. F., The Legacy of the Middle Ages, Oxford, 1926.
CUNNINGHAM, WM., Growth of English History and Commerce, Cambridge,
        England, 1896.
CUST, LIONEL, The Paintings and Drawings of Albrecht Dürer, London, 1897.

D'ALTON, E. A. (C), History of Ireland, 6v., Dublin, n.d.
D'ARCY, M. C. (C), Thomas Aquinas, London, 1930.
DAVID, MAURICE (J), Who Was Columbus?, N. Y., 1933.
DAVIS, F. H., The Persian Mystics: Jami, N. Y., 1908.
DE VAUX, BARON CARRA, Les penseurs de l'Islam, 5v., Paris, 1921 f.
DE WULF, MAURICE (C), History of Medieval Philosophy, 2v., London, 1925.
DE WULF, MAURICE (C), Philosophy and Civilization in the Middle Ages, Prince-
        ton, 1922.
DIAZ DEL CASTILLO, BERNAL, True History of the Conquest of Mexico, N. Y.,
        1938.
DIEHL, CHAS., Manuel d'art Byzantin, Paris, 1910.

DIEULAFOY, MARCEL, Art in Spain and Portugal, N. Y., 1913.
DIMAND, M. S., Guide to an Exhibition of Islamic Miniature Painting, N. Y., 1933.
DIMAND, M. S., Handbook of Muhammadan Art, N. Y., 1944.
DIMIER, L., French Painting in the Sixteenth Century, London, 1904.
DIVALD, KORNEL, Old Hungarian Art, Oxford, 1931.
DOMANOVSZKY, SANDOR, et al., Magyar Muvelodestortenet (History of Hungarian Civilization), 3v., Budapest.
D'ORLIAC, JEHANNE, The Lady of Beauty: Agnes Sorel, Phila., 1931.
D'ORLIAC, JEHANNE, The Moon Mistress: Diane de Poitiers, Phila., 1930.
DOUGHTY, CHAS., Travels in Arabia Deserta, 2v., N. Y., 1923.
DOZY, REINHART, Spanish Islam, N. Y., 1913.
DRAPER, J. W. (R), History of the Intellectual Development of Europe, 2v., N. Y., 1876.
DUBNOW, S. M. (J), History of the Jews in Russia and Poland, 3v., Phila., 1916.
DUHEM, PIERRE, Études sur Léonard de Vinci, 3v., Paris, 1906 f.

ECKARDT, HANS VON, Russia, N. Y., 1932.
EINSTEIN, ALFRED, The Italian Madrigal, 3v., Princeton, 1949.
EINSTEIN, LEWIS, The Italian Renaissance in England, N. Y., 1935.
ELLIS, HAVELOCK, The Soul of Spain, Boston, 1937.
ELYOT, SIR THOS., The Boke Named The Governour, Everyman's Library.
EMERTON, EPHRAIM, The Defensor Pacis of Marsiglio of Padua, Harvard, 1920.
ENCYCLOPAEDIA BRITANNICA, 14th ed. unless otherwise specified.
ENGLISH HISTORICAL REVIEW, London.
ERASMUS, D., Colloquies, 2v., London, 1878.
ERASMUS, D., Education of a Christian Prince, N. Y., 1936.
ERASMUS, D., Epistles, 3v., London, 1901.
ERASMUS, D., In Praise of Folly, N. Y., Brentano, n.d.

FAGUET, ÉMILE, Literary History of France, N. Y., 1907.
FERRARA, ORESTES, The Borgia Pope, Alexander VI, N. Y., 1940.
FIGGIS, J. N. (P), From Gerson to Grotius, Cambridge, England, 1916.
FINKELSTEIN, LOUIS (P), ed., The Jews: Their History, Culture, and Religion, 2v., N. Y., 1949.
FOSDICK, H. E., Great Voices of the Reformation, N. Y., 1952.
FOXE, JOHN, Acts and Monuments (Book of Martyrs), 8v., London, 1841.
FRANCE, ANATOLE (R), Life of Joan of Arc, 3v., London, 1925.
FRANCE, ANATOLE (R), Rabelais, N. Y., 1928.
FRANCKE, KUNO, History of German Literature as Determined by Social Forces, N. Y., 1901.
FREEMAN, E. A. (P), Historical Essays, First Series, London, 1896.
FRIEDELL, EGON (R), Cultural History of the Modern Age, N. Y., 1930.
FRIEDLÄNDER, LUDWIG, Roman Life and Manners under the Early Empire, 4v., London, 1928.
FROISSART, SIR JOHN, Chronicles, Everyman's Library.
FROISSART, SIR JOHN, Chronicles, 2v., London, 1848. All references are to this edition unless otherwise stated.
FROUDE, J. A. (P), The Divorce of Catherine of Aragon, N. Y., 1881.
FROUDE, J. A. (P), Lectures on the Council of Trent, N. Y., 1896.

FROUDE, J. A. (P), Life and Letters of Erasmus, N. Y., 1894.
FROUDE, J. A. (P), Reign of Edward VI, Everyman's Library.
FROUDE, J. A. (P), Reign of Elizabeth, 5v., Everyman's Library.
FROUDE, J. A. (P), Reign of Henry VIII, 3v., Everyman's Library.
FROUDE, J. A. (P), Reign of Mary Tudor, Everyman's Library.
FÜLÖP–MILLER, RENÉ (C), Saints That Moved the World, N. Y., 1945.

GANZ, PAUL, The Paintings of Hans Holbein, Oxford, 1950.
GASQUET, FRANCIS CARDINAL (C), Eve of the Reformation, London, 1927.
GASQUET, FRANCIS CARDINAL (C), Henry VIII and the English Monasteries, 2v., London, 1888.
GIBB, E. J. W., Ottoman Literature, N. Y., 1901.
GIBBON, EDWARD (R), Decline and Fall of the Roman Empire, 7v., ed. J. B. Bury, London, 1900. Same, Everyman's Library, 6v.
GIBBONS, H. A., Foundation of the Ottoman Empire, N. Y., 1916.
GIERKE, OTTO, Political Theories of the Middle Ages, Cambridge, England, 1922.
GILSON, ÉTIENNE (C), La philosophie au Moyen Age, 2v., Paris, 1922.
GILSON, ÉTIENNE (C), Reason and Revelation in the Middle Ages, N. Y., 1938.
GLÜCK, GUSTAV, Brueghel, Details from His Pictures. Vienna, 1936.
GLÜCK, GUSTAV, Die Kunst der Renaissance in Deutschland, Berlin, 1928.
GLÜCK, GUSTAV, Pieter Brueghel le Vieux, Paris, 1936.
GOTTHEIL, R. J., ed., The Literature of Persia, N. Y., 1900.
GRAETZ, H. (J), History of the Jews, 6v., Phila., 1891 f.
GRAVES, F. P. (P), History of Education during the Middle Ages, N. Y., 1931.
GRAVES, F. P. (P), Peter Ramus, N. Y., 1912.
GREEN, J. R. (P), Short History of the English People, 3v., London, 1898.
GREEN, MRS. J. R., Town Life in the Fifteenth Century, 2v., N. Y., 1907.
GREGOROVIUS, FERDINAND (P), History of the City of Rome in the Middle Ages, 8v., London, 1900.
GROUSSET, RENÉ, The Civilization of the East: The Near and Middle East, London, 1931.
GROVE'S DICTIONARY OF MUSIC, 5v., N. Y., 1928.
GUICCIARDINI, FR., History of the Wars in Italy, 10v., London, 1753.
GUIZOT, FR. (P), History of France, 8v., London, 1872.

HACKETT, FR., Francis I, N .Y., 1935.
HAFIZ: The Tongue of the Hidden. Paraphrase by Clarence Streit, N. Y., 1928.
HALLAM, HENRY (P), Introd. to the Literature of Europe in the Fifteenth, Sixteenth, and Seventeenth Centuries, 4v. in 2, N. Y., 1880.
HAMMERTON, J. A., ed., Universal History of the World, 8v., London, n.d.
HARE, CHRISTOPHER, Life of Louis XI, London, 1907.
HARVARD CLASSICS, N. Y., 1938.
HASTINGS, JAS. (P), ed., Encyclopedia of Religion and Ethics. 12v., N. Y., 1928.
HAUG, HANS, Grünewald, Paris, Éditions Braun, n.d.
HAYDN, HIRAM, The Counter-Renaissance, N. Y., 1950.
HAYES, CARLTON, J. H. (C), Political and Social History of Modern Europe, 2v., N. Y., 1919.
HEADLAM, CECIL, The Story of Nuremberg, London, 1911

HEARNSHAW, F. J. (P), ed., Medieval Contributions to Modern Civilization, N. Y., 1922.

HEARNSHAW, F. J. (P), ed., Social and Political Ideas of Some Great Thinkers of the Renaissance and the Reformation, N. Y., 1919.

HEFELE, K. J. VON (C), Life and Times of Cardinal Ximenez, London, 1885.

HENDERSON, E. F. (P), History of Germany in the Middle Ages, London, 1894.

HISTORY, Quarterly Journal of the Historical Association, N. Y.

HITTI, P. K., History of the Arabs, London, 1937.

HOLINSHED, RAPHAEL, Chronicle, Everyman's Library.

HOLZKNECHT, KARL, Backgrounds of Shakespeare's Plays, N. Y., 1950.

HORN, F. W., History of the Literature of the Scandinavian North, Chicago, 1884.

HUGHES, PHILIP (C), The Reformation in England, 2v., London, 1952 f.

HUGHES, T. P., Dictionary of Islam, London, 1935.

HUIZINGA, J., Waning of the Middle Ages, London, 1948.

HUME, MARTIN (P), Spain: Its Greatness and Decay, Cambridge, England, 1899.

HUME, MARTIN (P), The Spanish People, N. Y., 1911.

HUSIK, I. (J), History of Medieval Jewish Philosophy, N. Y., 1930.

HUSS, JOHN, De ecclesia, tr. Schaff, N. Y., 1915.

IBN BATUTA, M., Travels in Asia and Africa, tr. Gibb., N. Y., 1929.

IBN KHALDUN, ABD-AL-RAHMAN, Les prolegomènes, traduit en français par M. de Slane, 3v., Paris, 1934.

IBN KHALDUN: An Arab Philosophy of History, Selections from the Prolegomena by Chas. Issawi, London, 1950.

IGNATIUS LOYOLA, St., Autobiography, N. Y., 1900.

INGE, W. R. (P), Christian Mysticism, London, 1899.

JAMES, WM. (P), Varieties of Religious Experience, N. Y., 1935.

JAM'I, M. N., Salaman and Absol, tr. Edw. Fitzgerald, Boston, 1899.

JANELLE, PIERRE (C), The Catholic Reformation, Milwaukee, 1949.

JANSSEN, JOHANNES (C), History of the German People at the Close of the Middle Ages, 16v., St. Louis, Mo., n.d.

JOYCE, P. W. (C), Short History of Ireland, London, 1924.

JUSSERAND, J. J., English Wayfaring Life in the Middle Ages, London, 1891.

JUSSERAND, J. J., Literary History of the English People, 2v., N. Y., 1926.

KASTEIN, JOSEF (J), History and Destiny of the Jews, N. Y., 1934.

KAUTSKY, KARL (R), Communism in Central Europe in the Time of the Reformation, London, 1897.

KEMPIS, THOS. À. (C), The Imitation of Christ, N. Y., 1932.

KESTEN, HERMANN (R), Copernicus and His World, N. Y., 1945.

KITTREDGE, G. L., Harvard Studies and Notes in Philology and Literature, 2v., Harvard, 1896.

KLUCHEVSKY, V. O., History of Russia, 3v., London, 1912.

KNOX, JOHN (P), History of the Reformation in Scotland, 2v., N. Y., 1950.

KNOX, JOHN (P), Works, ed. David Laing, 6v., Edinburgh, 1854 f.

LACROIX, PAUL, Arts of the Middle Ages, London, n.d.

LACROIX, PAUL, History of Prostitution, 2v., N. Y., 1931.

Lacroix, Paul, Manners, Customs, and Dress During the Middle Ages, N. Y., 1876.

Lacroix, Paul, Military and Religious Life in the Middle Ages, London, n.d.

Lacroix, Paul, Science and Literature in the Middle Ages, London, n.d.

La Fargue, John, Great Masters, N. Y., 1903.

Lamb, Harold, Tamerlane, N. Y., 1928.

Lane-Poole, Stanley, Cairo, London, 1895.

Lane-Poole, Stanley, Saladin, London, 1926.

Lane-Poole, Stanley, Story of the Moors in Spain, N. Y., 1889.

Lane-Poole, Stanley, Story of Turkey, N. Y., 1895.

Lang, Andrew, Ballads and Lyrics of Old France, London, 1872.

Lang, Andrew (R), History of Scotland, 4v., Edinburgh, 1902.

Lang, P. H., Music in Western Civilization, N. Y., 1941.

Langland, Wm., Vision of William Concerning Piers the Plowman, Oxford, 1906.

La Tour, P. Imbert de (C), Les origines de la Reforme, 4v.:
    I. La France moderne, Paris, 1905.
    II. L'église catholique: La Crise et la Renaissance, Paris, 1909.
    III. L'évangelisme, Paris, 1914.
    IV. Calvin et l'institution chrétienne, Paris, 1935.

Lea, H. C. (P), Historical Sketch of Sacerdotal Celibacy, Boston, 1884.

Lea, H. C. (P), History of Auricular Confession, 3v., Phila., 1896.

Lea, H. C. (P), History of the Inquisition in the Middle Ages, 3v., N. Y., 1888.

Lea, H. C. (P), History of the Inquisition in Spain, 4v., N. Y., 1906.

Lea, H. C. (P), Studies in Church History, Phila., 1883.

Lecky, W. E. H. (R), History of European Morals, 2v., N. Y., 1926.

Lecky, W. E. H. (R), History of Rationalism, 2v., London, 1910.

Ledderhose, C. F. (P), Life of Philip Melanchthon, Phila., 1855.

Lednicki, Waclaw, Life and Culture of Poland, N. Y., 1944.

Lees-Milne, James, The Tudor Renaissance, London, 1951.

Leonardo da Vinci, Notebooks, ed. Edward MacCurdy, 2v., N. Y., 1938.

Lewinski-Corwin, E. H., Political History of Poland, N. Y., 1917.

Lewis, D. B. Wyndham, François Villon, N. Y., 1928.

Lingard, John (C), History of England, 9v., London, 1855.

Lippmann, Walter, The Public Philosophy, N. Y., 1955.

Locy, W. A., Biology and Its Makers, N. Y., 1915.

Longridge, W. H., The Spiritual Exercises of Ignatius Loyola, London, 1919.

Lounsbury, Thos., Studies in Chaucer, 3v., N. Y., 1892.

Luther, M., Table Talk, ed., Wm. Hazlitt, London, 1884. References are by item.

Luther, M., Werke, Weimar ed., 1883 f.; this is the edition usually referred to.

Luther, M., Werke, Erlangen ed., 1826 f.

Luther, M., Werke, Walch ed., St. Louis, Mo.

Luther, M., Works, 6v., Phila., 1943.

Lützow, Count von, Bohemia, Everyman's Library.

McCabe, Jos. (R), Candid History of the Jesuits, N. Y., 1913.

McCabe, Jos. (R), Crises in the History of the Papacy, N. Y., 1916.

Machiavelli, N. (R), Discourses, Modern Library.

McKinney, H. D., and Anderson, W. R., Music in History, Cincinnati, 1940.

Madariaga, Salvador de, Christopher Columbus, London, 1949.

Maitland, S. R. (P), Essays on the Reformation, London, 1849.

Malory, Sir Thos., Le Morte d'Arthur, 2v. in 1, London, 1927.

Mantle, Burns, and Gassner, John, A Treasury of the Theater, N. Y., 1935.

Mantzius, Karl, History of Theatrical Art, 6v., London, 1903 f.

Marcus, Jacob (J), The Jew in the Medieval World, Cincinnati, 1938.

Margaret, Queen of Navarre, Heptameron, London, n.d.

Maritain, Jacques (C), Three Reformers: Luther—Descartes—Rousseau, London, 1950.

Marx, Karl, Capital, 2v., Chicago, 1919.

Mattingly, Garret, Catherine of Aragon, London, 1942.

Maulde La Clavière, R. de, The Women of the Renaissance, N. Y., 1905.

Mendoza, Diego Hurtado de, Life and Adventures of Lazarillo de Tormes, London, 1881.

Merriman, R. B., Suleiman the Magnificent, Harvard, 1944.

Michelet, Jules (P), Histoire de France, 5v., Paris, n.d. References are by volume and page.

Michelet, Jules (P), History of France, 2v., N. Y., 1880. References are by book and chapter.

Milman, H. H. (P), History of Latin Christianity, 8v., N. Y., 1860.

Monmarché, M., ed., Châteaux of the Loire, Paris, 1919.

Montalembert, Comte de (C), Monks of the West, 2v., Boston, n.d.

Montesquieu, Chas. de, Spirit of Laws, N. Y., 1899.

More, Sir Thos., Utopia, Burt Library, N. Y., n.d.

Morison, Samuel Eliot, Admiral of the Ocean Sea: A Life of Christopher Columbus, Boston, 1942.

Motley, J. L. (P), Rise of the Dutch Republic, 2v., N. Y., n.d.

Muir, Edwin (P), John Knox, London, 1920.

Müller-Lyer, F., Evolution of Modern Marriage, N. Y., 1930.

Müntz, Eugène, Leonardo da Vinci, 2v., London, 1898.

Murray, Robt. H. (P), Erasmus and Luther, London, 1920.

Nekam, Louis, The Cultural Aspirations of Hungary, Budapest, 1935.

Newman, Louis I. (J), Jewish Influence on Christian Reform Movements, N. Y., 1925.

Nock, A. J., and Wilson, C. R., Francis Rabelais, N. Y., 1929.

Nosek, Vladimir, The Spirit of Bohemia, N. Y., 1927.

Noyes, Ella, The Story of Ferrara, London, 1904.

Nussbaum, F. L., History of the Economic Institutions of Modern Europe, N. Y., 1937.

O'Brien, George (C), Essay on the Economic Effects of the Reformation, Westminster, Md., 1944.

Ogg, Frederic, Source Book of Medieval History, N. Y., 1907.

Oman, Chas., The Great Revolt of 1381, Oxford, 1906.

Ouseley, Sir Gore, Biographical Notices of Persian Poets, London, 1846

Owen, John (P), Evenings with the Skeptics, 2v., London, 1881.

OWEN, JOHN (P), Skeptics of the French Renaissance, London, 1893.
OXFORD HISTORY OF MUSIC, 7v., Oxford, 1929 f.

PACHTER, H. M., Magic into Science: The Story of Paracelsus, N. Y., 1951.
PANOFSKY, ERWIN, Albrecht Dürer, 2v., Princeton, 1948.
PASTON LETTERS, 2v., Everyman's Library.
PASTOR, LUDWIG (C), History of the Popes, 14v., St. Louis, 1898, and London, 1910 f.
PAULSEN, FRIEDRICH (P), German Education, N. Y., 1908.
PAUPHILET, ALBERT, ed., Jeux et sapience du Moyen Age, Paris, 1940.
PAUPHILET, ALBERT, ed., Poètes et romanciers du Moyen Age, Paris, 1943.
PAYNE, E. A. (P), The Anabaptists of the Sixteenth Century, London, 1949.
PENROSE, BOIES, Travel and Discovery in the Renaissance, Harvard, 1952.
PERCY, THOS., Reliques of Ancient English Poetry, 2v., Everyman's Library.
PERNOUD, REGINE, La poésie mediévale, Paris, 1947.
PIRENNE, H., Belgian Democracy, Manchester, England, 1915.
PIRENNE, H., Economic and Social History of Medieval Europe, N. Y., n.d.
PIRENNE, H., Histoire de Belgique, 4v., Bruxelles, 1909.
POKROVSKY, M. N., History of Russia, N. Y., 1931.
POLLARD, A. F. (P), Henry VIII, London, 1925.
POOLE, R. L., Illustrations of the History of Medieval Thought and Learning, N. Y., 1920.
POOLE, R. L. (P), Wycliffe and Movements for Reform, London, 1909.
POPE, ARTHUR UPHAM, Catalogue of a Loan Collection of Early Oriental Carpets, Chicago, 1926.
POPE, ARTHUR UPHAM, Introduction to Persian Art, London, 1930.
POPE, ARTHUR UPHAM, Masterpieces of Persian Art, N. Y., 1945.
POPE, ARTHUR UPHAM, Survey of Persian Art, 8v., Oxford, 1938.
POST, C. R., History of Spanish Painting, 8v., Harvard, 1941.
POWER, EILEEN, Medieval People, Boston, 1924.
PRESCOTT, H. F. M. (C?), Mary Tudor.
PRESCOTT, WM. H. (P), History of the Reign of Ferdinand and Isabella the Catholic, 2v., Phila., 1890.
PUTNAM, GEO. H. (P), Books and Their Makers During the Middle Ages, 2v., N. Y., 1898.
PUTNAM, GEO. H. (P), The Censorship of the Church of Rome, 2v., N. Y., 1906.

RABELAIS, FR., Gargantua; Pantagruel; ed. Cluny, Paris, 1939.
RABELAIS, FR., Works, London, n.d.
RAMBAUD, AFLRED, History of Russia, 3v., Boston, 1879.
RANKE, LEOPOLD (P), History of the Popes, 3v., London, 1878.
RANKE, LEOPOLD (P), History of the Reformation in Germany. London, 1905.
RASHDALL, HASTINGS, Universities of Europe in the Middle Ages, 3v., Oxford 1936.
RÉAU, LOUIS, L'art russe, 2v., Paris, 1921.
REYNAUD, PAUL, Unite or Perish, N. Y., 1951.
RICHARD, ERNST (P), History of German Civilization, N. Y., 1911.
RICKARD, T. A., Man and Metals, 2v., N. Y., 1932.
RIEDL, FREDERICK, History of Hungarian Literature, N. Y., 1906.

ROBERTSON, J. M. (R), Short History of Freethought, 2v., London, 1914.
ROBERTSON, WM. (P), History of the Reign of Charles V, 2v., London, 1878.
ROBINSON, D. S., Anthology of Modern Philosophy, N. Y., 1931.
ROBINSON, J. H., Readings in European History, Boston, 1906.
ROCKER, RUDOLF (R), Nationalism and Culture, Los Angeles, 1937.
ROEDER, RALPH, Catherine de' Medici and the Lost Revolution, N. Y., 1937.
ROGERS, JAS. E. T., Economic Interpretation of History, London, 1891.
ROGERS, JAS. E. T., Six Centuries of Work and Wages, N. Y., 1890.
ROPER, WM., Life of Sir Thomas More, in More, Utopia, N. Y., n.d.
ROSCOE, WM. (P), Life and Pontificate of Leo X, 2v., London, 1853.
ROSEN, EDWARD, ed., Three Copernican Treatises, N. Y., 1939.
ROTH, CECIL (J), History of the Marranos, Phila., 1941.
ROTH, CECIL (J), The Jewish Contribution to Civilization, Oxford, 1945.
RUSSELL, BERTRAND (R), History of Western Philosophy, N. Y., 1945.

SALADIN, H., and MIGEON, G., Manuel d'art musulman, 2v., Paris, 1907.
SALZMAN, L. F., English Industries of the Middle Ages, Oxford, 1923.
SANGER, WM., History of Prostitution, N. Y., 1910.
SANTOS Y OLIVERA, D., Guia de la cathedral de Sevilla, Madrid, 1930.
SARTON, GEORGE, Introduction to the History of Science, 3v. in 5, Baltimore, 1930 f.
SAUNDERS, J. B., and O'MALLEY, CHAS., The Illustrations from the Works of Andreas Vesalius, Cleveland, Ohio, 1950.
SCHAFF, PHILIP (P), History of the Christian Church:
        The German Reformation, 2v., Edinburgh, 1888; pagination continuous.
        The Swiss Reformation, 2v., Edinburgh, 1893; pagination continuous.
SCHAPIRO, J. SALWYN (J), Social Reform and the Reformation, N. Y., 1909.
SCHEVILL, FERDINAND, History of the Balkan Peninsula, N. Y., 1922.
SCHOENFELD, HERMANN, Women of the Teutonic Nations, Phila., 1908.
SCHOENHOF, J., History of Money and Prices, N. Y., 1896.
SCHULTZ, ALWIN, Deutsches Leben in XIV and XV Jahrhundert, 2v., Vienna, 1892.
SCHUSTER, M. LINCOLN, ed., Treasury of the World's Great Letters, N. Y., 1940.
SCOTT, WM. B., Albert Dürer, London, 1869.
SEDGWICK, HENRY D., Ignatius Loyola, N. Y., 1923.
SEEBOHM, FREDERIC (P), The Oxford Reformers, London, 1869.
SELLERY, G. C., The Renaissance, Madison, Wis., 1950.
SHAKESPEARE, Plays.
SICHEL, EDITH (P), Catherine de' Medici and the French Reformation, London, 1905.
SICHEL, EDITH, Michel de Montaigne, N. Y., 1911.
SICHEL, EDITH, Women and Men of the French Renaissance, London, 1903.
SIGERIST, H. E., The Great Doctors, N. Y., 1933.
SINGER, CHAS., ed., Studies in the History and Method of Science, 2v., Oxford, 1917 f.
SISMONDI, J. C. L., History of the Italian Republics, ed. Wm. Boulting, London, n.d.

SMITH, PRESERVED (R), The Age of the Reformation, N. Y., 1920.
SMITH, PRESERVED (R), Erasmus, N. Y., 1923.
SMITH, PRESERVED (R), History of Modern Culture, 2v., N. Y., 1930.
SMITHSON, R. J. (P), The Anabaptists, London, 1935.
SOMBART, WERNER, The Jews and Modern Capitalism, Glencoe, Ill., 1951.
SPECULUM: A Journal of Medieval Studies, Cambridge, Mass.
SPENCE, LEWIS, Cornelius Agrippa, in Waite, Three Famous Alchemists.
STANGE, ALFRED, German Painting, XIV–XVI Centuries, N. Y., 1950.
STIRLING-MAXWELL, SIR WM., Annals of the Artists of Spain, 4v., London, 1891.
STRAUSS, D. F. (P), Ulrich von Hutten, London, 1874.
STRIEDER, JACOB, Jacob Fugger, N. Y., 1931.
STUBBS, WM., Constitutional History of England, 3v., Oxford, 1903.
SWINBURNE, A. C., Poems, Phila., n.d.
SYKES, SIR PERCY, History of Persia, 2v., London, 1921.
SYMONDS, J. A. (P), The Catholic Reaction, 2v., London, 1914.

TAINE, HENRI, Italy: Rome and Naples, N. Y., 1889.
TAINE, HENRI, Lectures on Art, N. Y., 1884.
TAWNEY, R. H. (P), Religion and the Rise of Capitalism, N. Y., 1926.
TAYLOR, RACHEL, Leonardo the Florentine, N. Y., 1927.
THATCHER, O. J., and MACNEAL, E., Source Book for Medieval History, N. Y., 1905.
THOMAS AQUINAS, Summa Theologica, 22v., London, 1920.
THOMPSON, JAS. W., Economic and Social History of Europe in the Later Middle Ages, N. Y., 1931.
THORNDIKE, LYNN, History of Magic and Experimental Science, 4v., N. Y., 1929 f.
THORNDIKE, LYNN, Science and Thought in the Fifteenth Century, N. Y., 1929.
TICKNOR, GEORGE, History of Spanish Literature, 3v., N. Y., 1854.
TILLEY, ARTHUR, Studies in the French Renaissance, Cambridge, England, 1922.
TIMUR (?), Autobiography, tr. Stewart, London, 1830.
TORNAY, STEPHEN C., Ockham: Studies and Sketches, La Salle, Ill., 1938.
TOYNBEE, ARNOLD J., A Study of History, 10v., 1935–54.
TRAILL, H. D., Social England, 6v., N. Y., 1902.
TRATTNER, ERNEST R., Architects of Ideas, N. Y., 1938.
TREND, J. B., The Civilization of Spain, Oxford, 1952.
TREVELYAN, GEO. M. (P), England in the Age of Wycliffe, London, 1925.
TREVELYAN, GEO. M. (P), English Social History, London, 1947.
TROYES, JEAN DE, Chronique scandaleuse, or Secret History of Louis XI, in Comines, Memoirs, Vol. II.
TURNER, E. S., History of Courting, N. Y., 1955.

UEBERWEG, F. (P), History of Philosophy, 2v., N. Y., 1871.
USHER, ABBOT P., History of Mechanical Inventions, N. Y., 1929.

VACANDARD, E. (C), The Inquisition, N. Y., 1908.
VAMBÉRY, ARMINIUS, The Story of Hungary, N. Y., 1894.
VASARI, G., Lives of the Painters, etc., Everyman's Library, 3v.
VASILIEV, A. A., History of the Byzantine Empire, 2v., Madison, Wis., 1929.

VERNADSKY, GEO., History of Russia, Yale U. P., 1929.
VERNADSKY, GEO., Kievan Russia, Yale U. P., 1948.
VILLARI, PASQUALE, Life and Times of Girolamo Savonarola, N. Y., 1896.
VILLARI, PASQUALE, Life and Times of Niccolò Machiavelli, 2v., N. Y., n.d.
VILLON, FR., Poems, tr. John Payne, Modern Library.
VILLON, FR., Poems in Pauphilet, Poètes et romanciers du Moyen Age.
VOLTAIRE, F. M. A. DE (R), Selected Works, tr. Jos. McCabe, London, 1911.
VOLTAIRE, F. M. A. DE (R), Works, 22v., N. Y., 1901.

WALISZEWSKI, K., Ivan the Terrible, Phila., 1904.
WALKER, WILLISTON (P), John Calvin, N. Y., 1906.
WALPOLE, HORACE, Letters, 8v., London, 1880.
WALSH, J. J. (C), The Popes and Science, N. Y., 1913.
WALSH, J. J. (C), The Thirteenth, Greatest of Centuries, N. Y., 1920.
WARD, W. H., Architecture of the Renaissance in France, 2v., London, n.d.
WATSON, FOSTER, Luis Vives, El Gran Valenciano, Oxford, 1922.
WATSON, PAUL B., The Swedish Revolution under Gustavus Vasa, Boston, 1889.
WAXMAN, MEYER (J), History of Jewish Literature, 2v., N. Y., 1930 f.
WEBER, SIR HERMANN, On Means for the Prolongation of Life, London, 1914.
WEBER, MAX, The Protestant Ethic and the Spirit of Capitalism, London, 1948.
WHITCOMB, MERRICK, Literary Source-Book of the German Renaissance, Phila.,
        1899.
WHITE, ANDREW D. (P), History of the Warfare of Science with Theology in
        Christendom, 2v., N. Y., 1929.
WILKINS, C. A. (P), Spanish Protestants in the Sixteenth Century, ed. Rachel
        Challice, London, 1897.
WOLTMANN, ALFRED, Holbein and His Times, London, 1872.
WRIGHT, THOS., ed., The Book of the Knight of La Tour-Landry, London, 1868.
WRIGHT, THOS., History of Domestic Manners and Sentiments in England Dur-
        ing the Middle Ages, London, 1862.
WRIGHT, THOS., The Home of Other Days, London, 1871.
WRIGHT, THOS., Womankind in Western Europe, London, 1869.
WYCLIFFE, JOHN, English Works, ed. F. D. Matthew, London, 1880.

Notes

NOTES ON THE USE OF THIS BOOK

1. Coulton, *Chaucer*, 62.
2. Michelet, x, 3.
3. Müntz, *Leonardo da Vinci*, I, 22.

CHAPTER I

1. Coulton, *Life in the Middle Ages*, I, 205.
2. Pastor, *History of the Popes*, I, 71, 66.
3. Ibid.
4. Bryce, *The Holy Roman Empire*, 226; *Cambridge Medieval History*, VIII, 623.
5. Sarton, *Introduction to the History of Science*, III-1, 1034.
6. Pastor, I, 91.
7. Sismondi, *History of the Italian Republics*, 328.
8. Gierke, *Political Theories of the Middle Ages*, 52, 59; Hearnshaw, *Medieval Contributions to Modern Civilization*, 67.
9. Emerton, *The Defensor Pacis of Marsiglio of Padua*, 70-2.
10. Milman, *History of Latin Christianity*, VII, 328-31.
11. Ogg, *Source Book of Medieval History*, 391.
12. Creighton, *History of the Papacy during the Reformation*, I, 297; *Camb. Med. Hy*, VIII, 8n.
13. Pastor, I, 241.
14. Pastor, III, 269.
15. Ibid., 324.
16. For a candid Catholic summary of ecclesiastical abuses *c.* 1500 cf. Janelle, *The Catholic Reformation*, Chapters I-III.
17. *Cambridge Modern History*, I, 388.
18. Montalembert, *The Monks of the West*, I, 81.
19. Coulton, *Inquisition and Liberty*, 45.
20. Coulton, *Five Centuries of Religion*, I, 465.
21. Beard, Chas., *Martin Luther and the Reformation*, 42.
22. Machiavelli, *Discourses*, iii, 1.
23. Robertson, *History of the Reign of Charles V*, I, 402.
24. Hayes, *Political and Social History of Modern Europe*, I, 126.
25. La Tour, *Les origines de la Reforme*, I, 361.
26. Cf. Pastor, V, 361-2.
27. *Camb. Mod. Hy*, I, 670.
28. Ibid.
29. Ibid.
30. Coulton, *Five Centuries of Religion*, II, 411.
31. Erasmus, Mar. 5, 1518, in *Epistles*, III, 287
32. Pastor, VIII, 124.
33. *Camb. Mod. Hy*, I, 670.
34. Ibid., 659.
35. Smith, Preserved, *History of Modern Culture*, I, 19.
36. *Camb. Mod. Hy*, I, 674.
37. Coulton, *Five Centuries of Religion*, I, 410 f.; II, 429.
38. Ibid., 400.
39. Erasmus, Epistle 94 in Froude, *Life and Letters of Erasmus*, 352.
40. Blok, *History of the People of the Netherlands*, II, 299.
41. Coulton, *Life in the Middle Ages*, IV, 354.
42. Coulton, *Five Centuries*, II, 399.
43. Lea, *History of the Inquisition in Spain*, I, 427.
44. Coulton, *Five Centuries*, I, 410.
45. La Tour, *Les origines*, II, 297 f.
46. Coulton, *Medieval Panorama*, 150, 160.
47. Ibid., 177.
48. Lea, *Inquisition in Spain*, IV, 95 f.
49. Lea, *Historical Sketch of Sacerdotal Celibacy*, 429-32; Kautsky, *Communism in Central Europe in the Time of the Reformation*, 268.
50. *Camb. Mod. Hy*, I, 672.
51. Pastor, V, 457 f.
52. Lea, *Inquisition in Spain*, I, 394.
53. Ibid., 402.
54. Ibid.
55. 406.
56. 407.
57. Gascoigne, *Seven Rivers of Babylon*, in Coulton, *Social Life in Britain*, 203.
58. Lea, *Auricular Confession*, III, 277; Beard, *Luther*, 299.
59. Lea, *Auricular Confession*, III, 74.
60. Ibid., 179.
61. 343 f.
62. Pastor, VII, 338, 340.
63. Ranke, *History of the Reformation in Germany*, 153.
64. *Camb. Mod. Hy*, 660.
65. Pastor, VII, 305.
66. Coulton, *The Black Death*, 114.
67. Erasmus, *Militis Christiani enchiridion*, in Lea, *Auricular Confession*, III, 429.

68. Lea, ibid.
69. Coulton, *Five Centuries*, I, 410.

CHAPTER II

1. Stubbs, *Constitutional History of England*, II, 331.
2. Headlam, *Story of Nuremberg*, 164.
3. Coulton, *Chaucer and His England*, 173.
4. Froissart, *Chronicles*, I, 77, 89.
5. Froissart, Everyman ed., 124.
6. Trevelyan, *England in the Age of Wycliffe*, 28.
7. Stubbs, III, 385.
8. Power, *Medieval People*, 78.
9. Ibid., 68.
10. Green, Mrs. J. R., *Town Life in the Fifteenth Century*, I, 351 f.
11. Rogers, *Economic Interpretation of History*, 75.
12. Cheyney, *Dawn of a New Era*, 186.
13. Poole, R. L., *Wycliffe and Movements for Reform*, 88; Id., *Illustrations of the History of Medieval Thought*, 254.
14. Wyclif, *De civili dominio*, i, 30, in Poole, *Wycliffe*, 89.
15. Poole, *Illustrations*, 264.
16. Poole, *Wycliffe*, 65.
17. *Camb. Med. Hy*, VII, 489.
18. Thompson, J. W., *Economic and Social History of Europe in the Later Middle Ages*, 499.
19. Trevelyan, *England in the Age of Wycliffe*, 82.
20. Wyclif, "On the Pope," in *English Works*, 477.
21. Wyclif, "Of Prelates," in *English Works*, 80-1.
22. Ibid., 81.
23. Ibid., 100.
24. 143-63.
25. 96-104.
26. Wyclif, "Of Prelates," v, 66; vi, 68.
27. "On the Popes," iii.
28. *De officio pastorali* in *English Works*, 457.
29. I John, ii, 18.
30. Rev., xi, 7.
31. Janssen, *History of the German People*, IV, 119.
32. Wyclif, "On Dominion" (English), i.
33. *English Works*, 47-57.
34. "On Dominion," iv; *De officio pastorali*.
35. *English Works*, 469-70.
36. "On Dominion," ii, in Poole, *Illustrations*, 261.
37. *English Works*, 452.
38. Ibid., 328
39. 330-1.
40. Trevelyan, *England in the Age of Wycliffe*, 173.
41. *English Works*, 465.
42. Ibid., 227-9.
43. 276 f.
44. Coulton, *Medieval Panorama*, 685.
45. Poole, *Wycliffe*, 110; Trevelyan, *Wycliffe*, 316.
46. Coulton, *Black Death*, 68; *Medieval Panorama*, 89.
47. Mrs. Green, *Town Life*, I, 54.
48. Stubbs, III, 617-8.
49. Mrs. Green, I, 141.
50. Abram, A., *English Life and Manners*, 191.
51. Lounsbury, *Studies in Chaucer*, I, 14.
52. Abram, 191-3.
53. Coulton, *Black Death*, 96; *Camb. Med. Hy*, VII, 442.
54. Coulton, *Social Life*, 350.
55. Ashley, *Introd. to English Economic History and Theory*, II, 333.
56. Poole, *Wycliffe*, 106.
57. Oman, *The Great Revolt of 1381*, 42.
58. Ibid., 51.
59. Froissart, ii, 73.
60. Ibid.
61. Oman, 38-43.
62. *Speculum*, Jan., 1940, 25.
63. Oman, 68-77.
64. Ibid., 84.
65. Stubbs, II, 428 f.
66. Chambers, *Medieval Stage*, II, 185.
67. Langland, *Vision of William . . . concerning Piers the Plowman*, i, 73 f.
68. Ibid., i, 68-99, 144-94; vi, 169 f.; xiii, 4 f.
69. Jusserand, *Literary History of the English People*, 401.
70. Coulton, *Chaucer*, 30.
71. Lounsbury, I, 74; Coulton, *Chaucer*, 54.
72. Ibid., 36.
73. Lounsbury, II, 228.
74. Chaucer, *Troilus*, i, 463.
75. Ibid., iii, 1373 f.
76. The Nun's Priest's Tale, 413 f.
77. *Legend of Good Women*, 1-9.
78. Knight's Tale, 444 f.
79. Coulton, *Chaucer*, 60.
80. Lounsbury, I, 87.
81. Shakespeare, *Richard II*, iii, 3.
82. Holinshed, iii, 507.

CHAPTER III

1. Pirenne, *Economic and Social History of Medieval Europe*, 187, 207; Ashley, II, 101; Salzman, *English Industries of the Middle Ages*, 337.
2. Coulton, *The Medieval Village*, 126;

Boissonade, *Life and Work in Medieval Europe*, 310.
3. Pirenne, op. cit., 198.
4. Milman, VII, 65-6; Thompson, *Economic History ... of Later Middle Ages*, 53.
5. Michelet, *History of France*, bk. vi, ch. 1.
6. Campbell, *Life and Times of Petrarch*, xxv.
7. Guizot, *History of France*, I, 616 f.
8. Encyc. Brit., XIX, 880b.
9. Froissart, i, 115.
10. Ibid., 127-8.
11. Sarton, III-1, 38.
12. Hammerton, *Universal History of the World*, VI, 3394.
13. Froissart, i, 151.
14. Boissonade, 284.
15. Bury, *History of the Later Roman Empire*, II, 65.
16. Sarton, III-2, 1653.
17. Castiglioni, *History of Medicine*, 359.
18. Coulton, *Black Death*, 68.
19. Sarton, III-2, 1654.
20. Thompson, *Economic History*, 383.
21. Michelet, vi, 3.
22. Froissart, i, 178.
23. Carlyle, R. W., *History of Medieval Political Theory*, VI, 213.
24. Clapman and Power, *Cambridge Economic Hy of Europe*, 559.
25. Froissart, I, 181, 183.
26. Michelet, vi, 3.
27. Michelet, vii, 1.
28. Guizot, *History of France*, II, 245.
29. Boissonade, 330.
30. Nussbaum, *History of the Economic Institutions of Modern Europe*, 108.
31. Boissonade, 315.
32. Wright, *Book of the Knight of La Tour-Landry*, ch. 2.
33. Michelet, xi, 1.
34. En. Br., IV, 857b.
35. Huizinga, *Waning of the Middle Ages*, 144-7.
36. Lacroix, *History of Prostitution*, I, 793.
37. Ibid., II, 1114.
38. Sanger, *History of Prostitution*, 106.
39. Huizinga, *Waning*, 145.
40. Ibid., 97.
41. Lacroix, *Prostitution*, I, 911.
42. Huizinga, 103, 108.
43. *Le menagier de Paris*, in Power, *Medieval People*, 85.
44. Coulton, *Life in the Middle Ages*, III, 152.
45. Huizinga, 133.
46. Ibid., 21, 175.
47. Thompson, *Economic History*, 105.
48. Huizinga, 140.

49. *Speculum*, April, 1940, 148.
50. Friedländer, *Roman Life and Manners*, II, 196.
51. France, A., *Joan of Arc*, II, 254.
52. In Jusserand, *English Wayfaring Life in the Middle Ages*, 400.
53. Froissart, Everyman ed., 368, 292, 1.
54. In Pernoud, *La poésie médiévale*, 80.
55. In Faguet, *Literary History of France*, 147. Margaret came to France in 1436; there is no trace of Chartier after 1434.
56. In Pauphilet, *Poètes et romanciers du moyen age*, 774.
57. Tr. in Lang, *Ballads and Lyrics of Old France*.
58. In Faguet, 151.
59. In Pauphilet, 792.
60. Michelet, x, 3.
61. Ibid.; France, *Joan of Arc*, I, 25.
62. Trial process in Michelet, x, 3.
63. Ibid.; France, *Joan of Arc*, 139 f.
64. Michelet, 1.c.
65. Ibid.
66. France, *Joan*, II, 250.
67. Ibid., I, xlvii.
68. Michelet, xi, 1.
69. Ibid., xi, 2; D'Orliac, *The Lady of Beauty*, 17-35.

CHAPTER IV

1. Guizot, *History of France*, II, 407.
2. Ibid.; Hare, *Life of Louis XI*, 69.
3. Comines, *Memoirs*, i, 10.
4. Ibid., ii, 1; Hare, 241.
5. Hare, 204.
6. Comines, vi, 2.
7. Ibid., iv, 10.
8. Ibid., vi, 7, 11; *Camb. Med. Hy*, VIII, 296.
9. Troyes, *Chronique scandaleuse*, in Comines, II, 379, 395.
10. Comines, vi, 12.
11. Lacroix, *Prostitution*, II, 116.
12. Ferrara, *The Borgia Pope*, 184; Beuf, *Cesare Borgia*, 42; Michelet, *Histoire de France*, III, i, 1.
13. Lacroix, *Prostitution*, II, 1117.
14. Batiffol, *Century of the Renaissance*, 22.
15. Guizot, *France*, II, 627.
16. Michelet, iii, 109.
17. Ward, *Architecture of the Renaissance in France*, II, 16-17.
18. Boyd, *French Renaissance*, 9.
19. Cf. the handsome reissue of *Les heures d'Anne de Bretagne*, Editions Verve, Paris, 1946.
20. Addison, J. D., *Arts and Crafts in the Middle Ages*, 265.
21. Comines, v, 18.

22. Ibid., iii, 8-9; ii, 6.
23. Mantzius, *History of Theatrical Art*, II, 134.
24. Pauphilet, *Jeux et sapience du moyen age*, 332.
25. Villon, *Ballade de la grosse Margot*; Lewis, *François Villon*, 6, 301.
26. Villon, *Le petit testament*, xxiii, xxxi, x.
27. Tr. by John Payne. Ruskin's version, less agreeable as a whole, rendered better the final line: "But where are the snows of yester-year?"
28. Villon, *Poems*, tr. John Payne, 128.
29. Ibid., 189.
30. Ibid., 191.
31. Tr. by Swinburne, *Poems*, 265-6.
32. In Lewis, 209.

CHAPTER V

1. *Camb. Med. Hy*, VIII, 375n.
2. Holinshed, iii, 541.
3. Walsingham in Stubbs, III, 79.
4. Michelet, ix, 3.
5. Comines, ii, 12.
6. Ibid., vi, 2.
7. Holinshed, iii, 712; cf. Shakespeare, *3 Henry VI*, iii, 2; *Richard III*, i, 1.
8. Bacon, *Works*, VI, 240.
9. Coulton, *Medieval Village*, 136.
10. More, *Utopia*, 175.
11. Coulton, *Social Life in Britain*, 321.
12. Rogers, *Six Centuries of Work and Wages*, 73; Schoenhof, *History of Money and Prices*, 311-2.
13. From Sir E. Dudley, *Tree of the Commonwealth* (1509), in Coulton, *Social Life in Britain*, 354.
14. Green, J. R., *Short History of the English People*, II, 568; Mrs. Green, *Town Life*, II, 70.
15. *Camb. Med. Hy*, VIII, 441-2.
16. Ibid.
17. Holinshed, iii, 632.
18. Ibid., 636.
19. Coulton, *Social Life*, 37.
20. Lounsbury, II, 346; Wright, *Homes of Other Days*, 429.
21. Paston Letters, I, 70.
22. Holinshed, iii, 508.
23. Cf. Percy's *Reliques*, II, 88 f.
24. Salzman, 230.
25. Mrs. Green, *Town Life*, I, 212-5; Coulton, *Chaucer*, 200.
26. *Camb. Med. Hy*, VIII, 365.
27. In Coulton, *Medieval Panorama*, 304.
28. Sarton, III-1, 158.
29. Wright, *Homes*, 379.

30. Hammerton, *Universal History*, VI, 3443.
31. Hearnshaw, *Social and Political Ideas of . . . the Renaissance and the Reformation*, 75.
32. Chaucer, Parson's Tale, lines 415-30.
33. Stubbs, III, 288.
34. Hearnshaw, op. cit., 82.
35. Coulton, *Medieval Panorama*, 126.
36. Id., *Black Death*, 112.
37. Catholic Encyclopedia, X, 334; Sarton III-2, 1046; Trevelyan, *England in the Age of Wycliffe*, 179, 317, 321, 327.
38. Coulton, *Medieval Panorama*, 490.
39. Trevelyan, *Wycliffe*, 334.
40. Shakespeare, *2 Henry IV*, Epilogue.
41. Cath. Encyc., X, 335.
42. Trevelyan, *Wycliffe*, 347-9.
43. In Sellery, *Renaissance*, 207.
44. Jusserand, *English Wayfaring*, 192.
45. Mantle, Burns, and Gassner, *A Treasury of the Theater*, 1345.
46. Putnam, G. H., *Books and Their Makers during the Middle Ages*, II, 104.
47. Kittredge, G. L., *Harvard Studies . . . in Philology and Literature*, II, 87 f.
48. Malory, *Morte d'Arthur*, iii, 15.
49. Ibid., x, 5.
50. Paston Letters, I, 81.
51. Gasquet, *Eve of the Reformation*, 220.
52. Einstein, Lewis, *Italian Renaissance in England*, 36.
53. Ibid., 38.
54. Smith, P., *Erasmus*, 95-6.
55. Seebohm, *The Oxford Reformers*, 70-1, 74-6, 110.

CHAPTER VI

1. Blok, *History . . . of the Netherlands*, II, 289.
2. Pirenne, *Histoire de Belgique*, II, 471; Michelet, x, 4; Blok, II, 289.
3. Pirenne, *Histoire*, II, 471.
4. Huizinga, 289.
5. Ibid., 203.
6. Hastings' *Encyclopedia of Religion and Ethics*, II, 843a.
7. Janssen, *History of the German People*, I, 88.
8. Kempis, Thomas à, *Imitation of Christ*. i, 1, 3, 10, 22, 9, 20.
9. In Michelet, xii, 2.
10. Baldass, *Jan van Eyck*, 273.
11. Cheney, *World History of Art*, 623.
12. Conway, *The Van Eycks and Their Followers*, 141.
13. Comines, *Memoirs*, v, 9; Freeman, E. A., *Historical Essays*, 338.
14. Comines, ii, 3-4; Michelet, xv, 2-4.

15. Conway, 185.
16. Ibid., 194.
17. Baedeker, *Belgique et Hollande*, 129.
18. Baldass, *Memling*, 148.
19. Isaiah, xl, 6.

CHAPTER VII

1. Boissonade, 285.
2. Rickard, *Man and Metals*, II, 525.
3. Boissonade, 325.
4. *Camb. Med. Hy*, VII, 736 f.
5. Beard, Miriam, *History of the Business Man*, 63.
6. Headlam, *Nuremberg*, 32.
7. Thompson, *Later Middle Ages*, 402.
8. Janssen, IV, 132-6.
9. Freeman, *Historical Essays*, 360.
10. Gregorovius, *History of the City of Rome in the Middle Ages*, VI, 116; *Camb. Med. Hy*, VII, 120, 283 f.
11. Emerton, 66.
12. Gregorovious, VI, 151.
13. Emerton, 17; Ueberweg, *History of Philosophy*, I, 462; Owen, *Evenings with the Skeptics*, II, 357.
14. *Camb. Med. Hy*, VII, 130-1.
15. *Camb. Mod. Hy*, II, 602.
16. Lea, *Sacerdotal Celibacy*, 395.
17. Pastor, II, 48.
18. Kautsky, 102-3.
19. In Inge, *Christian Mysticism*, 160; James, Wm., *Varieties of Religious Experience*, 417; Huizinga, 203.
20. In Francke, *History of German Literature*, 110.
21. De Wulf, *Philosophy and Civilization in the Middle Ages*, 294-7; Id., *History of Medieval Philosophy*, II, 130; Coulton, *Medieval Panorama*, 522.
22. Inge, 162.
23. Coulton, *Medieval Scene*, 126.
24. Headlam, *Nuremberg*, 29.
25. Cheney, *History of Art*, 665.
26. In Walsh, J. J., *Thirteenth, Greatest of Centuries*, 158.
27. As supposed by Carter, *Invention of Printing in China*, 24.
28. Sarton, III-1, 830.
29. Putnam, *Books*, I, 352-6.
30. En. Brit., XI, 12c.
31. Putnam, *Books*, I, 359.
32. Janssen, I, 19.

CHAPTER VIII

1. Lützow, *Bohemia*, 59.
2. Ibid., 68.
3. Milman, VII, 487.
4. Kautsky, 46.

5. Huss, *De Ecclesia*, 114.
6. Ibid., 3, 16 f.
7. Ibid., xvi, 127.
8. 220-1.
9. Kautsky, 47.
10. In Creighton, *History of the Papacy*, I, 359.
11. Kautsky, 48.
12. Bax, *German Society at the Close of the Middle Ages*, 43.
13. Kautsky, 58 f.
14. Nosek, *Spirit of Bohemia*, 76 f.
15. Kautsky, 61-4.
16. Creighton, *Papacy*, II, 471; Reynaud, *Unite or Perish*, 185.
17. Burton, *The Jew, the Gypsy, and Islam*, 123.
18. Lewinski, *Political History of Poland*, 58.

CHAPTER IX

1. Vasiliev, *History of the Byzantine Empire*, II, 395.
2. Ibid., 388.
3. 419.
4. In Diehl, C., *Manuel d'art Byzantin*, 761.
5. Gibbons, H. A., *Foundation of the Ottoman Empire*, 134.
6. *Camb. Med. Hy*, IV, 546.
7. Lane-Poole, *Story of Turkey*, 52.
8. Froissart, iv, 90.
9. Gibbons, H. A., *Foundation*, 132.
10. *Camb. Med. Hy*, IV, 620 f.
11. Ibid.
12. Ibid., 693; Pastor, II, 252.
13. The remainder of this section follows the incomparable narrative of Gibbon, *Decline and Fall of the Roman Empire*, ch. lxviii.
14. Voltaire, *Essai sur les moeurs*, in Works, XIV-1, 297.
15. *Camb. Med. Hy*, IV, 691.
16. Gibb, *Ottoman Literature*, 203.
17. Sismondi, *History of the Italian Republics*, 630.
18. Janssen, II, 198.
19. Vambéry, *Story of Hungary*, 221.
20. Ibid., 23.
21. Réau, *L'art russe*, I, 235; Riedl, F., *History of Hungarian Literature*, 27.
22. Domanovsky, S., *Magyar Muvelodestortenet*, I, 160.
23. Szoni, *Regi Magyar Templomok*, 203.
24. Cf. Divald, *Old Hungarian Art*, figs. 123, 145.
25. Riedl, 34.
26. Nekam, *Cultural Aspirations of Hungary*, 88.
27. Vambéry, 251.

28. Riedi, 28-9.
29. Vambéry, 272-5.

CHAPTER X

1. Camões, *Lusiads*, iii, 132.
2. *Camb. Mod. Hy*, I, 12.
3. Beazley, *Prince Henry the Navigator*, 213.
4. *Camb. Mod. Hy*, I, 10, 16.

CHAPTER XI

1. Thompson, *Economic and Social History*, 349, 422, 449.
2. Michelet, III, 348; *Camb. Mod. Hy*, I, 651; Belloc, *How the Reformation Happened*, 69.
3. Chapman, C. E., *History of Spain*, 139, 163.
4. Ibid., 216.
5. Burke, U. R., *History of Spain*, I, 404; Prescott, *Ferdinand and Isabella*, I, 338; Lea, *Inquisition in Spain*, I, 16.
6. Carpenter, Ed., *Pagan and Christian Creeds*, 25.
7. Graetz, *Hy of the Jews*, IV, 77.
8. Lea, op. cit., I, 64.
9. Graetz, IV, 79-84.
10. Michelet, vi, 4.
11. Roth C., *Hy of the Marranos*, 28.
12. Lea, *Inquisition in Spain*, I, 120.
13. Graetz, IV, 566.
14. Ibn Batuta, *Travels*, 315.
15. Ameer Ali, S., *Short History of the Saracens*, 570.
16. In Chapman, *Hy of Spain*, 200.
17. Pedraza in Prescott, *Ferdinand and Isabella*, I, 314.
18. Lane-Poole, *The Moors in Spain*, 232.
19. Ibid., 267.
20. Prescott, *Ferdinand*, I, 169.
21. Cf. Lea, *Inquisition in Spain*, I, 560-6.
22. Prescott, II, 340, note 46.
23. Lea, *Spain*, IV, 362.
24. Guizot, *Hy of France*, II, 564.
25. Letter to Fr. Vettori in Machiavelli, *Hy of Florence*, Appendix, p. 498; cf. *The Prince*, ch. xxi.
26. Guicciardini, *History*, IV, 108.
27. Hefele, K., *Cardinal Ximenes*, 40-4.
28. Graetz, IV, 315.
29. Lea, *Spain*, II, 511-13.
30. Ibid., III, 2; Ellis, H., *Soul of Spain*, 42.
31. Lea, *Spain*, I, 268, 100, 193; II, 323, 385.
32. Ibid., I, 235.
33. Ibid., I, 233-6; Pastor, IV, 400.
34. Lea, I, 178; II, 104-9, 401 f.; III, 184; Lacroix, P., *Military and Religious Life in the Middle Ages*, 433.

35. Graetz, IV, 313.
36. Lea, *Spain*, IV, 517.
37. Ibid.
38. Beginning of Psalm CXIV in the Vulgate translation.
39. Lea, *Spain*, I, 133.
40. Ibid.
41. Ibid., I, 134.
42. Prescott, *Ferdinand*, I, 514.
43. Graetz, IV, 391.
44. Ibid., 369.
45. Ibid., 370.
46. Ibid., 371; Abbott, *Israel in Europe*, 167.
47. Graetz, IV, 372.
48. Ibid., 376.
49. Marcus, *The Jew in the Medieval World*, 56-9.
50. Dozy, *Spanish Islam*, 268.
51. Arnold, T. W., *The Preaching of Islam*, 143.
52. Lea, *Spain*, III, 325.
53. Lane-Poole, *Moors in Spain*, 279.
54. Coulton, *Inquisition and Liberty*, 315.
55. Vacandard, *The Inquisition*, 198.
56. Santos y Olivera, *La cathedral de Sevilla*, 8.
57. Calvert, *Moorish Remains in Spain*, 383.
58. Post, C. R., *History of Spanish Painting*, VIII-2, 705.
59. In Ticknor, *Hy of Spanish Literature*, I, 227.
60. Prescott, *Ferdinand*, II, 448-9.
61. Ibid., 327.
62. Ibid., 332.

CHAPTER XII

1. France, A., *Joan of Arc*, II, 17.
2. Lacroix, *Prostitution*, II, 1040 f.
3. Thorndike, Lynn, *History of Magic and Experimental Science*, III, 18.
4. Lacroix, *Science and Literature in the Middle Ages*, 187.
5. Thorndike, III, 520.
6. Sarton, III-2, 1246.
7. Coulton, *Social Life*, 505.
8. Singer, C., *Studies in the History and Method of Science*, 191.
9. Lea, *Inquisition in the Middle Ages*, III, 461-5; Jusserand, *English Wayfaring Life*, 333.
10. Smith, P., *Age of the Reformation*, 655.
11. Sanger, *Prostitution*, 104.
12. Lea, *Inquisition in the Middle Ages*, III, 519.
13. Ibid., 543.
14. Sprenger, *Malleus maleficarum*, in Ibid., 502.
15. Michelet, III, 36.
16. Lea, *Middle Ages*, III, 549.

17. Cf. Thorndike, IV, ch. LI.
18. Id., III, 11.
19. III, 30, 33.
20. 454.
21. 398-469.
22. Jusserand, *Wayfaring Life*, 328.
23. Abram, *English Life and Manners*, 205.
24. In Seebohm, *Oxford Reformers*, 211.
25. Paston Letters, I, 117.
26. De Wulf, *Hy of Med. Philosophy*, II, 168.
27. Thorndike, *Science and Thought in the Fifteenth Century*, 254.
28. *Cambridge Hy of Poland*, I, 274.
29. *Camb. Mod. Hy*, II, 117.
30. Duhem, *Études sur Léonard de Vinci*, III, 388.
31. Gilson, *La philosophie au Moyen Age*, II, 135.
32. Kesten, *Copernicus*, 91.
33. Penrose, *Travel and Discovery in the Renaissance*, 19.
34. In Morison, S. E., *Admiral of the Ocean Sea*, 93.
35. Thorndike, IV, 102.
36. Ibid., 108.
37. Gilson, *La philosophie au Moyen Age*, II, 129; Sarton, III-1, 543-4; Duhem, III, chs. IX-X.
38. Ibid., 181 f.
39. Sarton, III-2, 1429-31.
40. Thompson, *Social and Economic History*, 503.
41. Usher, A. P., *Hy of Mechanical Inventions*, 127.
42. Lacroix, *Science and Literature in the Middle Ages*, 186.
43. Thorndike, III, 483.
44. Walsh, J. J., *The Popes and Science*, 79.
45. Froissart, iv, 51.
46. In Sarton, III-1, 870.
47. Castiglioni, *Hy of Medicine*, 381.
48. Coulton, *Social Life*, 330.
49. Ashley, *Introd. to English Economic Hy*, II, 318.
50. Lecky, *Hy of European Morals*, II, 86.
51. Ibid.
52. Beard, C., *Luther*, 56.
53. De Wulf, *Hy of Med. Philosophy*, II, 172.
54. Ockham, *Super IV Lib. Sentent.*, I, 27, 2, K, in Tornay, *Ockham*, 9.
55. *Summa totius logicae*, I, 12, in Tornay, 9.
56. Thomas Aquinas, *Summa theologica*, I, ii, 3.
57. Ockham, *Super IV Lib. Sentent.*, IV, 12, K, in Tornay, 119.
58. Ibid., I, ii, 6, in Owen, *Evenings with the Skeptics*, II, 375.
59. Ibid., I, iii, 2, in Owen, II, 378.
60. Tornay, 63.
61. Gilson, *Philosophie au Moyen Age*, II, 104; Tornay, 58, 191-2.
62. Tornay, 186; Owen, II, 377.
63. De Wulf, *Med. Philosophy*, II, 184; Crump and Jacob, *Legacy of the Middle Ages*, 251.
64. Owen, II, 392.
65. Gilson, *Reason and Revelation in the Middle Ages*, 86.
66. Ockham, *Centiloquium theologicum*, ix, in Owen, II, 395.
67. Owen, II, 386.
68. Ibid., 396, 399.
69. Allen, J. W., *Hy of Political Thought in the Sixteenth Century*, 124.
70. Beer, *Social Struggles in the Middle Ages*, 112; Tornay, 81.
71. Carlyle, R. W., *Medieval Political Theory*, VI, 44.
72. De Wulf, *Med. Philosophy*, II, 187.
73. Jacobs, E. F., in *History*, XVI, no. 63, p. 218.
74. Rashdall, *Universities of Europe in the Middle Ages*, III, 265.
75. Owen, II, 410.
76. Duhem, *Études*, in Tornay, 51, 165.
77. Cunningham, W., *Growth of English Industry and Commerce*, 359.
78. Marsilius of Padua in Emerton, 35, 45, and *passim*.
79. Ibid., 39; Pastor, I, 78; Coulton, *Medieval Panorama*, 656.
80. Coker, F. W., *Readings in Political Philosophy*, 246-52.
81. Ibid., 25; Emerton, 22.
82. *Defensor Pacis*, i, 15, in Carlyle, R. W., *Medieval Political Theory*, VI, 41.
83. Coker, 257; Duhem, II, 106-7.
84. Thorndike, IV, 388.
85. Id., *Science and Thought in Fifteenth Century*, 296.
86. Ibid., 296, 136-7.
87. Nicholas of Cusa, *De concordantia Catholica*, in Hearnshaw, *Thinkers of the Renaissance and Reformation*, 44n.
88. Figgis, J. N., *From Gerson to Grotius*, 67.
89. In Pastor, II, 137.
90. Coulton, *Med. Panorama*, 528.
91. In Janssen, I, 3.

CHAPTER XIII

1. Morison, 24. The account henceforth follows this fascinating biography.
2. The evidence is presented in the early chapters of Madariaga, S. de, *Christopher Columbus*, esp. pp. 53-9, and 184.

3. Beazley, C. R., in En. Brit., VI, 78.
4. Penrose, 10.
5. Seneca, *Medea*, 364 f.
6. Morison, 72.
7. Roth, C., *Jewish Contribution to Civilization*, 74.
8. Lea, *Spain*, I, 259.
9. Morison, 229.
10. Ibid., 231-3.
11. 115.
12. David, M., *Who Was Columbus?*, 70.
13. Morison, 576.
14. Ibid., 617.
15. En. Brit., XXIII, 107c. For a recent defense of Vespucci cf. Arciniegas, G., *Amerigo and the New World*.

CHAPTER XIV

1. Froude, *Erasmus*, 11n.
2. One of many *bon mots* appropriated from Mrs. Will Durant by the laws of community property.
3. Letter to Wm. Gauden in Froude, *Erasmus*, 32-3.
4. In Smith, P., *Erasmus*, 28.
5. Erasmus, *Colloquies*, II, 326 f.
6. Id., *Epistles*, I, 127.
7. Smith, *Erasmus*, 60; Froude, *Erasmus*, 45.
8. Smith, *Erasmus*, 63.
9. Erasmus, *Epistles*, II, 117.
10. Froude, *Erasmus*, 80.
11. Smith, 32.
12. *Epistles*, I, 301, 307.
13. Froude, 80-1.
14. *Epistles*, I, 370.
15. *Colloquies*, II, 13-35.
16. In Froude, 91.
17. Erasmus, *In Praise of Folly*, 14, 30, 33.
18. Ibid., 51.
19. 127.
20. 138.
21. 67.
22. 131-4.
23. 86-8.
24. 175.
25. 169-74.
26. 207.
27. *Epistles*, II, 168.
28. On Erasmus' authorship cf. Allen, P. S., *The Age of Erasmus*, 185-9, and Chambers, R. W., *Thomas More*, 114-5.
29. In Froude, 150-68.
30. *Epistles*, III, 418.
33 *Colloquies*, I, 298.
32. Ibid., 391; II, 13, 34.
33. *Colloquies*, I, 298.
34. Ibid., 229, 236.
35. Ibid., II, 161.

36. I, 22.
37. I, 24, 35.
38. Smith, 299.
39. Froude, 121 and Smith, 171.
40. In Froude, 126.
41. Smith, *Age of Reformation*, 58.
42. *Epistles*, II, 400.
43. Ibid., 464.
44. 249.
45. Erasmus, *Education of a Christian Prince*, 173; Smith, *Erasmus*, 201, 217.
46. *Epistles*, II, 201.
47. *Education*, 253.
48. *Epistles*, II, 517.
49. "Peace Protests!" in Chapiro, J., *Erasmus and Our Struggle for Peace*, 153-65.
50. Ibid., 168.
51. 81.
52. *Epistles*, II, 120.
53. Letter to Zwingli, Sept. 5, 1522.
54. *Epistles*, II, 421.
55. "Peace Protests!" in Chapiro, 173, 183.
56. Tract "On the Immense Mercy of God" in Bainton, *Reformation of the Sixteenth Century*, 218.
57. Froude, 195.
58. Erasmus, *In Praise of Folly*, 48.
59. Froude, 108.
60. *Folly*, 215.
61. Froude, 130-1, 144.
62. Beard, *Luther*, 97.
63. Erasmus, *Encheiridion*, in Beard, 98.
64. Letter of March 25, 1520, in Murray, *Erasmus and Luther*, 83.
65. *Colloquies*, I, 98.
66. Ibid., 182.
67. Letter of Jan. 5, 1523, in Chapiro. 105.
68. *Epistles*, II, 143; Froude, 171-2.
69. *Epistles*, II, 163, 327.
70. Smith, *Erasmus*, 150.
71. *Epistles*, III, 1.
72. Smith, 155.
73. Cf., e.g., Smith, 176-9.
74. *Epistles*, I, 42.
75. In Froude, 172.
76. *Epistles*, II, 176.
77. Ibid., III, 186.
78. Ibid., 94.
79. Letters to Fabricius Capito, Feb. 26, 1517, and to Leo X in *Epistles*, II, 505, 521.
80. *Epistles*, III, 48.

CHAPTER XV

1. Bax, *German Society at Close of the Middle Ages*, 54-6.
2. Rickard, *Man and Metals*, II, 562.
3. Janssen, II, 39, 41; Kautsky, 91.

4. Adams, B., *Law of Civilization and Decay*, 56.
5. Strieder, J., *Jacob Fugger*, 124.
6. Ibid., 86-9.
7. Crump, *Legacy of Middle Ages*, 449; Janssen, II, 87; Schapiro, J. S., *Social Reform and the Reformation*, 32.
8. Janssen, II, 85.
9. Ibid., 88.
10. Bax, *German Society*, 234-5; Schapiro, 29.
11. In Schapiro, 30.
12. Janssen, II, 88; Boissonade, *Life and Work in Medieval Europe*, 299.
13. Schapiro, 30.
14. Ibid., 31.
15. Schoenhof, *Money and Prices*, 72.
16. Janssen, II, 82.
17. Ibid., 3.
18. Adams, B., *Civilization and Decay*, 56.
19. Janssen, II, 60; Francke, *Hy of German Literature*, 103.
20. Janssen, I, 140.
21. Erasmus, *Epistles*, II, 175.
22. Comines, *Memoirs*, v, 18.
23. Ranke, *Reformation*, 100, 108-9.
24. In Villari, *Machiavelli*, I, 444; Janssen II, 202.
25. Creighton, *Hy of the Papacy*, IV, 94.
26. Janssen, II, 260.
27. Schoenfeld, *Women of the Teutonic Nations*, 188 f.
28. Beard, *Luther*, 147.
29. Müller-Lyer, *Evolution of Modern Marriage*, 57.
30. En. Brit., XVIII, 598b.
31. Schoenfeld, 181.
32. Schultz, A., *Deutsches Leben in XIV und XV Jahrhundert*, I, 277, 283.
33. Lacroix, *Prostitution*, I, 165-7.
34. Coulton, *Medieval Village*, 248; Headlam, *Nuremberg*, 163-4.
35. Ibid., 164-8.
36. *Camb. Mod. Hy*, I, 638.
37. In Whitcomb, *Literary Source Book of the German Renaissance*, 63.
38. Richard, E., *Hy of German Civilization*, 219.
39. Janssen, II, 64.
40. Ibid., 6.
41. Janssen, I, 168.
42. *Speculum*, Jan. 1931.
43. In Headlam, *Nuremberg*, 208.
44. Cf. Glück, *Die Kunst der Renaissance in Deutschland*, 100-1; Haug, H., *Grünewald*, 1-3, 13-18.
45. Cf. Bock, *Geschichte der Graphischen Kunst*, 260-1.
46. The ascription of this picture to Grüne-

wald follows Haug. Stänge assigns it to the Master of the House Book.
47. N. Y. *Times*, April 7, 1928.
48. In Cust, *Paintings and Drawings of Albrecht Dürer*, 17.
49. Camerarius in La Fargue, *Great Masters*, 197.
50. Panofsky, *Dürer*, I, 43.
51. Ibid., 11.
52. Ibid., 8.
53. Cust, 59; Janssen, XI, 94.
54. N.Y. *Times* magazine, April 8, 1928, p. 11.
55. Cust, 31.
56. In Panofsky, I, 44.
57. Panofsky, II, fig. 171.
58. Id., I, 6.
59. Ibid., 208.
60. In Scott, W. B., *Albert Dürer*, 136.
61. Ibid., 154-6.
62. Janssen, I, 301.
63. Hughes, P., *The Reformation in England*, I, 100; Beard, *Luther*, 53.
64. In La Tour, *Les origines de la Réforme*, II, 340.
65. In Janssen, I, 78.
66. In Thompson, *Social and Economic Hy*, 604.
67. Janssen, I, 108.
68. Schoenfeld, *Women of the Teutonic Nations*, 218.
69. In Smith, *Age of the Reformation*, 54.
70. Strauss, D., *Ulrich von Hutten*, 22.
71. Creighton, *Hy of the Papacy*, VI, 32.
72. Robertson, J. M., *Hy of Freethought*, I, 435.
73. Creighton, VI, 31.
74. Ibid., 32.
75. Acton, *Lectures on Modern History*, 84.
76. Ranke, *Reformation*, 135; Beard, *Luther*, 85.
77. In Janssen, I, 104.
78. Strauss, *Hutten*, 112 f.
79. Henderson, E., *Hy of Germany in the Middle Ages*, 131.
80. Janssen, I, 278.
81. *Camb. Mod. Hy*, I, 675.
82. Lacroix, *Prostitution*, 960.
83. Strauss, 89.
84. Janssen, III, 74.
85. Ibid.
86. Strauss, 83.
87. Janssen, III, 72.
88. Letter of Nov. 1519 in Froude, *Erasmus*, 252.
89. Lea, *Inquisition in the Middle Ages*, III, 89.
90. Janssen, II, 298; Ranke, 140; Beard, *Luther*, 48.
91. Preface to Luther's edition of Wessel's *Farrago*, in Creighton, *Papacy*, VI, 7.

92. Ranke, 120.
93. Beard, *Luther*, 35.
94. *Camb. Mod. Hy*, II, 106.
95. Tawney, R. H., *Religion and the Rise of Capitalism*, 138.
96. *Camb. Mod. Hy*, II, 106.
97. Janssen, II, 292-6; cf. III, 77, and Catholic Encyclopedia, IX, 446.
98. Thompson, 500.
99. Pastor, VII, 326.
100. In Pastor, II, 413; italics mine.
101. Pastor, III, 194; 98 f.; *Camb. Mod. Hy*, I, 689.
102. Pastor, VI, 85.
103. Pastor, I, 157-8.
104. *Camb. Mod. Hy*, I, 690.

CHAPTER XVI

1. Acton, *Lectures on Modern Hy*, 91; Thompson, *Social and Economic Hy*, 425, 428; Ranke, *Reformation*, 151.
2. Friar Myconius in Thatcher, O. J., *Source Book for Medieval Hy*, 339.
3. In Robertson, W., *Charles V*, I, 372.
4. Pastor, VII, 349.
5. Luther, *Works*, I, 26; Thesis 75.
6. Beard, *Luther*, 257.
7. Acton, 97.
8. *Camb. Mod. Hy*, II, 127.
9. Ranke, *Reformation*, 154.
10. Beard, 121; Smith, P., *Luther*, 2.
11. In D'Arcy, M. C., *Thomas Aquinas*, 254.
12. Ranke, 144; Beard, 156.
13. Beard, 165.
14. Luther, *Tischreden*, lxxvii, in Gregorovius, *Hy of Rome*, VIII-1, 249.
15. Ganss, H. G., in Cath. En., IX, 441.
16. In Janssen, III, 97.
17. Ibid., 89.
18. Cath. En., IX, 442.
19. In Pastor, VII, 354.
20. Cath. En., IX, 443.
21. In Beard, 231-3.
22. *Camb. Mod. Hy*, II, 132.
23. Ranke, 160.
24. Roscoe, Wm., *Leo X*, II, 95, 105-7.
25. Pastor, VII, 367.
26. H. von Schubert in Smith, *Luther*, ix.
27. In Pastor, VII, 378.
28. Smith, *Reformation*, 700.
29. Beard, 270.
30. Ibid., 273-4; Ranke, 195; Cath. En., IX, 443; Acton, 94-5.
31. Pastor, VII, 382; Beard, 272.
32. Smith, *Luther*, 56.
33. Cath. En., IX, 444.
34. Smith, *Luther*, 71.
35. Letter of Aug. 20, 1531, in Froude, *Erasmus*, 397.
36. In Ledderhose, *Life of Melanchthon*, 30.
37. In Beard, 279.
38. In Strauss, *Hutten*, 263.
39. In Pastor, VII, 389; Janssen, III, 111.
40. Strauss, 225.
41. *Werke*, VIII, 203, in Beard, 352.
42. Pastor, VII, 384; Smith, *Luther*, 75.
43. Luther, *Works*, II, 63.
44. Ibid., 69-70.
45. 76.
46. 78.
47. 83-99, italics mine.
48. 110-42.
49. 138-9.
50. *Babylonian Captivity*, in *Works*, II, 188.
51. Ibid., 257.
52. In Janssen, III, 129.
53. *Works*, II, 269-71.
54. Ibid., 293.
55. 302-10.
56. 299.
57. 331.
58. 318.
59. Ranke, 215; Pastor, VII, 400-8; Janssen, III, 30.
60. Ranke, 220; Beard, 375.
61. Hume, M., *The Spanish People*, 331.
62. Adams, Brooks, *Civilization and Decay*, 98.
63. Strieder, *Jacob Fugger*, 153.
64. Michelet, III, 174.
65. Thompson, *Social and Economic History*, 428.
66. Armstrong, E., *Charles V*, I, 69.
67. Janssen, III, 173.
68. Pastor, VII, 423.
69. Lingard, *Hy of England*, IV, 225.
70. In Janssen, III, 172; Bainton, *Here I Stand*, 175.
71. Strauss, 276 f.
72. Beard, 421-3.
73. Janssen, III, 182.
74. Beard, 432.
75. Bainton, *Here I Stand*, 185.
76. Ibid.; Schaff, *German Reformation*, 29.
77. Bainton, *Here I Stand*, 185; cf. Cath. En. IX, 446d, and the Protestant authors there cited.
78. Creighton, *Hy of the Papacy*, VI, 176.
79. Carlyle, Thos., *Heroes and Hero Worship*, 360.
80. Bainton, *Here I Stand*, 186.
81. Acton, 101.
82. Bainton, 189.
83. Ibid., 195.
84. Taylor, H. O., *Thought and Expression in the 16th Century*, II, 213.
85. Bax, *German Society*, 142; Lecky, *History of Rationalism*, I, 22.
86. Janssen, III, 246-8.

87. Bainton, 200.
88. Ibid., 205-6; Ranke, 251.
89. Luther, *Works*, III, 206-7.
90. Ibid., 211.
91. Ranke, 254.
92. Bainton, 208.
93. Janssen, III, 259.
94. Ibid., 263.
95. Bainton, 214.
96. Beard, 127.
97. Janssen, IV, 98.
98. Smith, *Luther*, 155.
99. Ibid., 168.
100. 380.
101. Froude, *Erasmus*, 294.
102. Janssen, XIV, 408.
103. Luther, *Table Talk*, 118.
104. *Werke* (Walch), VIII, 2042, in Beard, *The Reformation of the 16th Century in Relation to Modern Thought and Knowledge*, 161.
105. Luther, *Table Talk*, 353.
106. Luther, *Werke* (Erlangen), VI, 142-8, in Maritain, *Three Reformers*, 33, and Beard, *Reformation*, 156.
107. In Paulsen, *German Education*, 47.
108. In Janssen, III, 240.
109. Schaff, *German Reformation*, 35-6.
110. Luther, *T.T.*, 24.
111. Smith, *Luther*, xi.
112. *T.T.*, 2.
113. Ibid., 91, 96.
114. 67.
115. 15.
116. 797; Smith, *Luther*, 362.
117. *T.T.*, 574.
118. Sermon of March 6, 1521; Janssen, XII, 316.
119. Maritain, *Three Reformers*, 30.
120. Smith, *Reformation*, 653.
121. Lecky, *Rationalism*, I, 22.
122. *T.T.*, 577, 597; Janssen, XIV, 87.
123. Janssen, XII, 317.
124. Lecky, *Rationalism*, I, 23.
125. *T.T.*, 579-86, 608.
126. Luther, *Works*, III, 235-7.
127. *Works*, II, 391.
128. Ibid., 316.
129. *T.T.*, 283.
130. Romans, x, 9.
131. Mark, xvi, 16.
132. *Works*, II, 316.
133. *Werke*, XL, 436; XXV, 330, 142, 130; *Werke* (Erlangen), XVIII, 260.
134. *Werke* (Erlangen), XX, 58; LX, 107-8; *Werke* (Weimar), X-2, 276.
135. O'Brien, G., *Economic Effects of the Reformation*, 41.
136. *Works*, II, 328-9.
137. Ibid., 331.
138. Romans, ix, 18.
139. Luther, *De servo arbitrio*, in Janssen, IV, 104.
140. *De servo arbitrio*, in Lecky, *Rationalism*, I, 140.
141. In Fülöp-Miller, R., *Saints That Moved the World*, 291.
142. Janssen, IV, 114.
143. *T.T.*, 96.
144. Ibid., 178.
145. *Works*, II, 188.
146. *Werke*, XXVIII, 142-201, in Bax, *German Society*, 188-90.
147. *Works*, III, 258-61.
148. In Janssen, III, 268.
149. In Allen, J. W., *Political Thought*, 330.
150. *Works*, IV, 25.
151. Ibid., 26, 29.
152. *Works*, II, 160.
153. Ibid., IV, 35.

CHAPTER XVII

1. Richard, E., *German Civilization*, 250.
2. Janssen, III, 214.
3. Pastor, IX, 134.
4. Schapiro, J. S., *Social Reform*, 34-5.
5. Richard, 250; *Camb. Mod. Hy*, II, 174.
6. Luther, *Works*, III, 204-5.
7. *Camb. Mod. Hy*, II, 183.
8. Janssen, III, 221; Schapiro, 103-14.
9. Janssen, III, 223; *Camb. Mod. Hy*, II, 177.
10. Janssen, III, 342.
11. *Camb. Mod. Hy*, II, 193.
12. Kautsky, 116-119.
13. Ibid., 121.
14. 130.
15. Ranke, *Reformation*, 338.
16. In Kautsky, 139.
17. Ibid., 144.
18. Luther, *Works*, IV, 210-16.
19. Ibid., 220-1.
20. 240.
21. 244.
22. Ranke, 459.
23. Janssen, IV, 166; Bax, *Peasants' War*, 79-84.
24. Ranke, 348-9.
25. Robinson, J. H., *Readings in European Hy*, 289 f; Bax, *Peasants' War*, 156-60.
26. Ranke, 344.
27. Bax, *Peasants' War*, 101.
28. Ibid., 118-30.
29. In Janssen, IV, 208
30. Bax, 76, 224.
31. Ibid., 205.
32. 229.
33. Luther, *Works*, IV, 248-54.
34. Bax, 265-6.
35. Ibid., 312-5.

36. 303.
37. *Camb. Mod. Hy*, II, 191.
38. Bax, 336-7.
39. Armstrong, *Charles V*, I, 222.
40. Ranke, 360.
41. Schapiro, 86; Smith, *Luther*, 164.
42. Ibid., 165.
43. 164.
44. *Works*, IV, 261.
45. Ibid., 261-72.
46. *Camb. Mod. Hy*, II, 192.
47. Ranke, 728.
48. Payne, E. A., *Anabaptists*, 11.
49. Kautsky, 164.
50. Ibid., 166.
51. Allen, *Political Thought*, 43.
52. Ranke, 732-3.
53. Schaff, *Swiss Reformation*, 82.
54. Janssen, IV, 114.
55. Kautsky, 176.
56. Ibid., 185.
57. 187.
58. Ranke, 729.
59. Kautsky, 192.
60. Ranke, 757.
61. Kautsky, 255-6.
62. Ibid., 257.
63. 260.
64. 273.
65. Ranke, 745-6.
66. Smithson, R. J., *Anabaptists*, 179-80.
67. Kautsky, 290; Ranke, 755.
68. Smithson, 181.
69. Fosdick, *Great Voices of the Reformation*, 285.
70. Payne, *Anabaptists*, 16.

CHAPTER XVIII

1. Cath. En., XV, 773.
2. Schaff, *Swiss Ref.*, 6.
3. Ibid.
4. Hughes, *Reformation*, I, 124.
5. Schaff, 24.
6. *Camb. Mod. Hy*, II, 713.
7. Schaff, 32.
8. Ranke, 513.
9. Schaff, 52-3.
10. Fosdick, 183.
11. Ibid., 173, 191.
12. Lea, *Auricular Confession*, I, 519.
13. Fosdick, 190.
14. Schaff, 59.
15. *Camb. Mod. Hy*, II, 321, 334.
16. Smith, *Erasmus*, 391.
17. Schaff, 94.
18. Bainton, *Hunted Heretic*, 36-8.
19. Erasmus, Epistle of May 9, 1529, in Schaff, *Swiss Reformation*, 112.
20. *Camb. Mod. Hy*, II, 207-10.

21. In Janssen, V, 231.
22. Schaff, 177.
23. Ibid.
24. Bossuet, *Variations*, II, 29.
25. En. Brit., XXIII, 998.
26. Schaff, 188.
27. Smith, *Luther*, 290.
28. *T.T.*, 801.

CHAPTER XIX

1. Kauffmann Collection, Berlin.
2. *Werke*, XLII, 582, in Maritain, 171.
3. *Werke*, X-2, 304, in Maritain, 171.
4. *T.T.*, 715.
5. Ibid., 752.
6. Maulde, *Women of the Renaissance*, 467.
7. *Werke*, X-2, 301, in Maritain, 184.
8. Bainton, *Here I Stand*, 299.
9. *T.T.*, 715.
10. Bainton, 301.
11. *T.T.*, 737.
12. Ibid., 751.
13. In Schaff, *Swiss Reformation*, 417.
14. In Fosdick, 71.
15. Smith, *Luther*, 354.
16. Schaff, *German Reformation*, 465.
17. Bainton, 304.
18. Smith, 320.
19. Letter to Pope Leo, 1520.
20. Luther, *Works*, I, 7.
21. Janssen, XI, 349; Luther, *Works*, II, 231; Bainton, 295.
22. Bainton, 295.
23. Janssen, III, 242.
24. *Werke*, VIII, 624, in Maritain, 188.
25. In Carpenter, *Pagan and Christian Creeds*, 207.
26. *T.T.*, 462.
27. *Werke*, XXV, 108, in Cath. En., IX, 447b.
28. *T.T.*, 319.
29. Gasquet, *Eve of the Reformation*, 173.
30. Smith, *Luther*, 407; Bainton, *Here I Stand*, 295.
31. Smith, 355.
32. Ibid., 326.
33. In Janssen, XI, 253.
34. Bainton, 225.
35. *T.T.*, 100.
36. Smith, *Luther*, 322.
37. Ibid., 349.
38. Ibid.
39. Janssen, XII, 16; *T.T.*, 114.
40. Ibid., 257.
41. 91, 96.
42. 780.
43. Jusserand, *Literary History of the English People*, II, 167

44. *T.T.*, 841.
45. Ibid., 413.
46. Luther, *Works*, I, 76.
47. Ibid., 142.
48. *Works*, III, 251.
49. Bainton, *Here*, 314.
50. *Works*, III, 204, 207.
51. Preface to the Shorter Catechism.
52. *Werke* (Erlangen), XXIX, 46-74, in Jewish Encyc., VIII, 213.
53. *T.T.*, 275.
54. *Werke* (Erlangen), XXXII, 217-33, in Janssen, III, 211-12.
55. *Werke* (Erlangen), XXVIII, 144, in Maritain, 15.
56. Letter of Aug. 26, 1529, to Jos. Metsch, in Smith, *Luther*, 218.
57. In Froude, Erasmus, 389.
58. *T.T.*, 61.
59. Putnam, *Books*, II, 244.
60. *Werke*, XXXI-1, 208 f.
61. *Werke* (Erlangen), XVI, in Allen, *Political Thought*, 27.
62. Bax, *Peasants' War*, 352.
63. Smith, *Luther*, xiv.
64. Id., *Reformation*, 645.
65. Janssen, IV, 140-1.
66. Murray, *Erasmus and Luther*, 366.
67. Janssen, XIV, 503.
68. Janssen, V, 290.
69. Luther, Commentary on Psalm LXXXII.
70. Janssen, V, 491, 502, 505.
71. Janssen, VI, 46-63, 181, 190, 208-14, 348-9; Lecky, *Rationalism*, II, 15.
72. Janssen, IV, 232 f.
73. Lea, *Studies in Church History*, 492.
74. *T.T.*, 389.
75. Smith, *Reformation*, 104; Panofsky, Dürer, I, 233; Cath. En., IX, 447c.
76. Janssen, III, 198.
77. Ibid., 342.
78. Robertson, J. M., *Freethought*, I, 455.
79. Erasmus, letter to Pirkheimer, Feb. 21, 1529.
80. Janssen, III, 361.
81. Strauss, *Hutten*, 290.
82. Smith, *Erasmus*, 233.
83. In Michelet, III, 170.
84. Smith, *Erasmus*, 334.
85. Letter of March 5, 1518.
86. Letter of October 17, 1518.
87. In Froude, *Erasmus*, 139.
88. Smith, *Erasmus*, 219.
89. Ibid., 221.
90. Ibid., 22; Froude, *Erasmus*, 233-4.
91. In Murray, *Erasmus*, 76.
92. Froude, 270-2.
93. Smith, *Erasmus*, 241.
94. Ibid., 255.
95. Erasmus, *Epistles*, I, ep. lxxxv.

96. Ibid., ep. ccclxvi.
97. Froude, 308.
98. Letter of Feb., 1523, in Froude, 310.
99. Acton, 105; Lecky, *Rationalism*, I, 140.
100. Ibid.
101. Bainton, *Here I Stand*, 254-5.
102. Froude, 340, 381.
103. In Allen, *Political Thought*, 80.
104. Froude, 403.
105. Ibid., 352.
106. In Froude, 400.
107. Erasmus, *Hyperaspistes*.
108. In Froude, 352.
109. Walpole, H., *Letters*, III, 184.
110. Beard, *Luther*, 93.
111. Acton, 89.

CHAPTER XX

1. Janssen, IV, 62.
2. Cf. *Camb. Mod. Hy*, II, 159.
3. Janssen, VI, 534.
4. Janssen, V, 277.
5. Lea, *Clerical Celibacy*, 530.
6. Janssen, VII, 247.
7. Id., IV, 47.
8. Id., IX, 130.
9. Id., XIII, 24.
10. Froude, *Erasmus*, 387.
11. Vambéry, 283.
12. Janssen, IV, 119.
13. Ibid., 109-11.
14. En. Brit., XI, 288.
15. Janssen, V, 271; Ranke, 614.
16. Cath. En., XI, 453.
17. *Camb. Mod. Hy*, II, 219.
18. Janssen, V, 423.
19. Luther, *Works*, V, 128; Pastor, XI, 69, 81-7.
20. Janssen, V, 495 f; *Camb. Mod. Hy*, II, 233.
21. Pastor, XI, 362-3.
22. Ibid., 375-98.
23. Ledderhose, 177-82.
24. Ibid., 188.
25. Cath. En., IX, 452d.
26. In Bainton, *Here I Stand*, 346.
27. Pastor, XI, 67.
28. Smith, *Luther*, 309.
29. *Werke* (Walch), XX, 223, in Cath. En., IX, 456d.
30. Luther, *Works*, V, 163.
31. In Tawney, *Religion and the Rise of Capitalism*, 101; Bainton, *Here I Stand*, 238.
32. *Werke*, XIX, 626, in Allen, *Political Thought*, 22.
33. Bax, *Peasants' War*, 351.
34. *Werke*, XV, 276, in Bax, 352.
35. Smith, *Luther*, 374.

36. Letter of Sept. 3, 1531.
37. Smith, 196.
38. In Bebel, *Woman under Socialism*, 68.
39. Janssen, VI, 81-6.
40. *Camb. Mod. Hy*, II, 241.
41. Ledderhose, 170.
42. Janssen, VI, 122.
43. *Camb. Mod. Hy*, II, 241.
44. In Smith, *Luther*, 399 f.; Pastor, XI, 215 f.
45. *Werke*, XXV, 124-55, in Janssen, VI, 271-2, and Pastor, XII, 216 f.
46. Weber, Hermann, *On Means for the Prolongation of Life*, 48.
47. Smith, *Luther*, 405.
48. Ibid., 409.
49. James, Wm., *Varieties of Religious Belief*, 137.
50. Ibid.
51. *T.T.*, 633.
52. Ibid., 15.
53. 19.
54. 235.
55. In Robertson, *Charles V*, II, 158n.
56. Smith, *Luther*, 419.
57. Armstrong, *Charles V*, I, 138.
58. *Camb. Mod. Hy*, II, 276.
59. Ibid., 278.
60. Schaff, *Swiss Reformation*, 387, 548; Janssen, XIV, 149.
61. Id., VII, 139.
62. Id., IV, 362-3; Schapiro, 78; Allen, *Political Thought*, 33.
63. In La Tour, IV, 161.
64. In Janssen, VII, 139.

CHAPTER XXI

1. Cath. En., III, 196.
2. Beza in Schaff, *Swiss Ref.*, 302.
3. La Tour, IV, 11.
4. Calvin, *Institutes*, Preface, 20-2, 39-40.
5. *Institutes*, I, viii, 1.
6. Ibid., II, v, 19.
7. Ephesians, i, 3-7.
8. *Institutes*, III, xxi-xxii.
9. Romans, ix, 15.
10. *Institutes*, II, xxi, 7.
11. Consensus Genevensis in Schaff, *Swiss Ref.*, 554.
12. *Institutes*, III, xxi, 1.
13. Ibid.
14. III, xxiii, 7.
15. IV, i, 10.
16. IV, i, 4.
17. Allen, *Political Thought*, 61; Hearnshaw, *Thinkers of the Renaissance and the Reformation*, 211.
18. *Institutes*, IV, xix, 3.
19. III, xxi, 1.
20. Schaff, 558.

21. *Institutes*, III, ix, 4.
22. Ibid.
23. III, ix, 6.
24. For: La Tour, IV, 32, and *Camb. Mod. Hy*, II, 358; against: Cath. En., III, 196a.
25. *Camb. Mod. Hy*, II, 360.
26. Robinson, *Readings*, 299.
27. Schaff, 361.
28. Ibid., 414.
29. 412.
30. 426.
31. 437.
32. Robinson, *Readings*, 300.
33. La Tour, IV, 178.
34. Villari, *Savonarola*, 491.
35. Schaff, 492.
36. Beard, *The Reformation*, 250.
37. Ibid., Schaff, 491.
38. Ibid., 492.
39. O'Brien, *Economic Effects*, 101.
40. As by Weber, Max, *The Protestant Ethic and the Spirit of Capitalism, passim*; Barnes, *Economic Hy of the Western World*, 201-2; and O'Brien, 129.
41. *Institutes*, III, vii, 5.
42. Cf. O'Brien, 100.
43. Ibid., 20.
44. Tawney, 119.
45. Barnes, *Economic History*, 201.
46. Schaff, 644.
47. Beard, *The Reformation*, 252: Muir, *John Knox*, 108.
48. Smith, *Reformation*, 174.
49. Schaff, 519.
50. Ibid., 839.
51. La Tour, IV, 206.
52. Schaff, 739.
53. La Tour, IV, 200; Schaff, 594.
54. Schaff, 618.
55. Ibid., 502.
56. Robertson, J. M., *Freethought*, I, 443-4.
57. Servetus, *De Trinitatis erroribus*, i, 94b, in Bainton, *Hunted Heretic*, 48.
58. Servetus, ibid., i, 34; Newman, L. I., *Jewish Influence on Christian Reform Movements*, 584.
59. Bainton, *Hunted Heretic*, 144.
60. Ibid.
61. Ibid., 147.
62. Schaff, 733.
63. Bury, J. B., *History of Freedom of Thought*, 64.
64. Schaff, 770.
65. Ibid., 764, 773; Bainton, 191.
66. Bainton, 188.
67. Schaff, 777.
68. Ibid., 778.
69. Bainton, 185.
70. Ibid., 209-11; Schaff, 710, 781-4.
71. Schaff, 784.

72. Walker, *John Calvin*, 425.
73. Schaff, 707-8.
74. Ibid.
75. 709.
76. In Allen, *Political Thought*, 87.
77. Castellio in Allen, 90-4; Haydn, *Counter-Renaissance*, 104.
78. In Allen, 98.
79. *Time* magazine, Feb. 22, 1954.
80. Schaff, 652n.

CHAPTER XXII

1. In Lacroix, *Prostitution*, II, 1142.
2. Ibid., 1141.
3. 1130.
4. Taylor, R., *Leonardo*, 444.
5. Sichel, *Catherine de' Medici and the French Reformation*, 38.
6. Erasmus, *Colloquies*, II, 54.
7. Erasmus, *Epistles*, II, 468.
8. Michelet, III, 175.
9. E.g., Aretino, *La cortigiana*, in *Dialogues*, 228.
10. Batiffol, *Century of the Renaissance*, 44.
11. Lacroix, *Prostitution*, II, 1131.
12. Cellini, *Autobiography*, ii, 10.
13. Guizot, *Hy of France*, III, 81.
14. Ibid., Michelet, III, 218.
15. Michelet, III, 148.
16. Sichel, *Women and Men of the French Renaissance*, 87.
17. Ibid.
18. Michelet, III, 135.
19. Sichel, *Women*, 193.
20. Faguet, *Literary History of France*, 281.
21. Margaret, Queen of Navarre, *Heptameron*, xli.
22. In Maulde, 354.
23. Margaret, *Heptameron*, 36.
24. In Maulde, 53.
25. Ibid., 297.
26. In Sichel, *Women*, 195.
27. Ibid., 371.
28. 180.
29. Boyd, *French Renaissance*, 25.
30. Sichel, *Catherine de' Medici and the French Reformation*, 138.
31. Sichel, *Women*, 104.
32. Michelet, III, 136.
33. *Camb. Mod. Hy*, I, 659.
34. Ibid.
35. Lacroix, *Prostitution*, II, 1247.
36. Margaret, *Heptameron*, Tale 22.
37. Ibid., xlii.
38. In Guizot, III, 187.
39. Ibid., 196.
40. 197.
41. Roeder, *Catherine de' Medici*, 54.
42. La Tour, II, 237 f.

43. Michelet, III, 216.
44. Guizot, III, 216.
45. Schaff, *Swiss Reformation*, 320.
46. Ibid., 320; La Tour, II, 556-7.
47. Sichel, *Women*, 18.
48. Guizot, III, 220.
49. La Tour, II, 612.
50. Michelet, III, 319; Guizot, III, 229; *Camb. Mod. Hy*, II, 289.
51. Guizot, III, 15.
52. Ibid., 73.
53. Ibid., 91; Michelet, III, 239.
54. Guizot, III, 95.
55. Ibid., 91.
56. Michelet, III, 244.
57. Robertson, W., *Charles V*, 538.
58. Guizot, III, 105-6.
59. Ibid., 116.
60. *Camb. Mod. Hy*, III, 105.
61. Guizot, III, 129; Robertson, *Charles V*, II, 57-60.
62. Michelet, III, 316; *Camb. Mod. Hy*, II, 77.
63. Janssen, VI, 358.
64. Michelet, III, 293-4.
65. Hackett, *Francis I*, 428.
66. Brantôme in Guizot, III, 192.
67. Sichel, *Catherine*, 51.
68. D'Orliac, *The Moon Mistress*, 186.
69. Janssen, VI, 359.
70. Michelet, III, 366.
71. Guizot, III, 281.
72. Pastor, XII, 486.
73. Batiffol, 175.
74. Robertson, *Charles V*, II, 351.
75. Guizot, III, 261.

CHAPTER XXIII

1. Pollard, *Henry VIII*, 39.
2. Froude, *Erasmus*, 142.
3. Chambers, *Thomas More*, 99.
4. Erasmus, *Epistles*, I, 457.
5. Froude, *Henry VIII*, I, 30; Ep. 447 in Froude, *Erasmus*, 107.
6. Seebohm, *Oxford Reformers*, 261-6.
7. Erasmus, *Epistles*, II, 546.
8. Guicciardini, VIII, 126.
9. Pollard, 67.
10. Creighton, *Cardinal Wolsey*, 48.
11. Gasquet, *Henry VIII and the English Monasteries*, I, 69.
12. Robinson, J. H., *Readings*, 303.
13. Burnet, *History of the Reformation*, I, 6.
14. Chambers, *More*, 158; Hughes, *Reformation*, I, 60.
15. Ibid.
16. Creighton, *Wolsey*, 59.
17. Burnet, I, 15.
18. Lingard, IV, 192.

19. Robinson, *Readings*, 303.
20. Pollard, 110.
21. Robinson, l.c.
22. Lingard, IV, 193; Chambers, *More*, 173-4; Hughes, I, 109.
23. Froude, *Henry VIII*, I, 60; but cf. Hughes, I, 58 f.
24. Hughes, I, 103n.
25. Belloc, *How the Reformation Happened*, 117.
26. Seebohm, 230-46.
27. Coulton, *Panorama*, 718.
28. Froude, *Henry VIII*, II, 114-5.
29. Hughes, I, 49-50.
30. Froude, I, 350.
31. Hughes, I, 50-66.
32. Gasquet, *Monasteries*, II, 237; Trevelyan, *English Social Hy*, 73.
33. Ibid.
34. Hughes, I, 57-8.
35. Coulton, *Panorama*, 554.
36. Hughes, I, 150.
37. Ibid., 127-9.
38. 202.
39. Smith, *Luther*, 193.
40. Coulton, *Life in the Middle Ages*, II, 143; Gasquet, *Eve*, 213.
41. *Camb. Mod. Hy*, I, 640.
42. Beard, *Reformation*, 305.
43. Ibid.
44. Hughes, I, 146.
45. Froude, I, 319, 336.
46. Burnet, I, 16.
47. Gasquet, *Monasteries*, I, 85-8.
48. Froude, I, 81.
49. Burnet, I, 26.
50. Hughes, I, 67-70.
51. Pollard, 174.
52. Burnet, I, 27.
53. Pollard, 76, 176.
54. Froude, I, 74n.
55. Pollard, 183.
56. Ibid., 135.
57. Froude, *Divorce of Catherine of Aragon*, 47.
58. Pastor, X, 241.
59. Froude, *Divorce*, 47.
60. *Camb. Mod. Hy*, II, 431.
61. Pastor, X, 244.
62. Pollard, 207.
63. Ibid., 208.
64. Pastor, X, 257-8; Hughes, I, 175-9; Acton, 139.
65. Hughes, I, 176.
66. Pastor, X, 267.
67. Pollard, 225.
68. Burnet, I, 55.
69. Froude, *Reign of Elizabeth*, III, 259.
70. Froude, *Divorce*, 190.
71. Hughes, I, 181.
72. Cavendish, *Life of Wolsey*, in Froude, *Henry VIII*, III, 115.
73. Creighton, *Wolsey*, 186.
74. Pollard, 223-4.
75. Creighton, 185.
76. Burnet, I, 61.
77. Creighton, 194.
78. Froude, *Divorce*, 138.
79. Creighton, 205.

CHAPTER XXIV

1. Froude, *Divorce*, 166, 81.
2. Pollard, 250-1.
3. Trevelyan, *Social Hy*, 102.
4. Pollard, 237.
5. Froude, *Henry VIII*, I, 128-35.
6. Ibid., 139.
7. 162.
8. Sichel, *Women*, 176.
9. Lingard, IV, 273.
10. Prescott, H. F., *Mary Tudor*, 38.
11. Schuster, M. L., *Treasury of the World's Great Letters*, 77.
12. Froude, *Henry VIII*, I, 218.
13. Ibid., 265.
14. Pollard, 187.
15. Ibid., 300.
16. Gasquet, *Monasteries*, I, 122, 129, 134 f.
17. Pollard, 304-5.
18. Chambers, *More*, 323, 326; Lingard, IV, 19.
19. Froude, *Henry VIII*, II, 82.
20. Burnet, I, 123-5.
21. Erasmus, *Epistles*, II, 186.
22. Pollard, 305; Froude, *Council of Trent*, 116-7.
23. Chambers, *More*, 334.
24. Prescott, *Mary Tudor*, 60.
25. Roper, *More*, 46.
26. Hughes, I, 345.
27. Cf., e.g., Chambers, *More*, 191, 193.
28. Erasmus, *Epistles*, II, 427.
29. Jusserand, *Wayfaring Life*, 354.
30. Froude, *Erasmus*, 103-7; Chambers, *More*, 75.
31. Chapiro, 36.
32. Erasmus, *Epistles*, II, 423.
33. Chambers, *More*, 125.
34. More, *Utopia*, 168.
35. Ibid., 213.
36. 247.
37. Ibid.
38. 303.
39. 322-5.
40. 323.
41. 320.
42. 335.
43. 290-1.
44. 215 347, 209.

45. 178-9.
46. 343-4.
47. Froude, *Henry VIII*, I, 347.
48. Chambers, *More*, 276.
49. Ibid., 281.
50. Cf. Coulton, *Panorama*, 709.
51. More, *English Works*, 586, in Taylor, *Thought and Expression*, II, 68.
52. Roper, 89.
53. Ibid., 109.
54. Hearnshaw, *Thinkers of the Renaissance*, 146.
55. Roper, 126.
56. Chambers, *More*, 349.
57. Froude, *Henry VIII*, II, 95.
58. Erasmus, Letters of Aug. 24 and 31, 1535.
59. Roper, 127.
60. Chambers, 277.
61. Burnet, I, 143.
62. Prescott, *Mary Tudor*, 50; Pollard, 304.
63. Froude, *Henry VIII*, II, 142.
64. Burnet, I, 143.
65. Prescott, *Mary Tudor*, 70.
66. Pollard, 343.
67. Ibid.
68. Froude, *Henry VIII*, II, 159.
69. Lingard, V, 37.
70. Froude, II, 171.
71. Pollard, 346.
72. Ibid., 305.
73. Froude, *Henry VIII*, III, 26n.
74. Ibid., II, 204.

CHAPTER XXV

1. C. R. Beazley in Traill, *Social England*, III, 49.
2. Gasquet, *Eve*, 397-8.
3. Montesquieu, *Spirit of Laws*, xii, 10.
4. Froude, *Henry VIII*, II, 116.
5. Ibid., 240.
6. Pollard, 337; Gasquet, *Monasteries*, I, 254-336.
7. Pollard, 339.
8. Froude, II, 119-26.
9. Ashley, *Economic Hy*, II, 312.
10. Gasquet, I, 341-3.
11. Ibid., 291-5.
12. Froude, II, 240.
13. Gasquet, II, 82.
14. Ibid., I, 408-9.
15. Froude, II, 56.
16. Gasquet, I, 363; II, 33, 323.
17. Ibid., II, 386-7, 438.
18. Hughes, I, 328.
19. Gasquet, II, 447-8.
20. Traill, III, 129.
21. Salzman, *English Industries*, 232; *Camb. Mod. Hy*, II, 467.

22. Lecky, *Rationalism*, II, 126; Ashley, II, 316; Trevelyan, *Social Hy*, 112.
23. Traill, III, 128.
24. D'Alton, E. A., *Hy of Ireland*, II, 382-7; Joyce, *Short Hy of Ireland*, 317-20.
25. D'Alton, 530 f.; Froude, *Henry VIII*, III, 166.
26. Pollard, 438.
27. Froude, III, 280.
28. Pocock in *English Historical Review*, Vol. X, p. 421.
29. Froude, III, 280.
30. Id., II, 363.
31. III, 23-4; Pollard, 390-1.
32. Lingard, V, 73-4; Pollard, 400; Froude, III, 104.
33. Froude, *Edward VI*, 68.
34. Ashley, II, 351.
35. Froude, *Edward VI*, 69.
36. Froude, *Henry VIII*, I, 52-5; II, 137; Traill, III, 250; Marx, *Capital*, I, 806.
37. Trevelyan, *Social Hy*, 137.
38. Froude, *Henry VIII*, I, 16n.
39. Rogers, J., *Six Centuries of Work and Wages*, 78.
40. Hughes, I, 29.
41. Traill, III, 127.
42. Hughes, I, 159.
43. Lingard, V, 61.
44. Pollard, 403.
45. Lingard, V, 76.
46. Lees-Milne, *Tudor Renaissance*, 21.
47. Froude, *Henry VIII*, III, 281-2.
48. Ibid., 402-6.
49. *Camb. Mod. Hy*, II, 459; Traill, iii, 65.
50. In Coulton, *Medieval Village*, who disagrees. Cf. Froude, *Henry VIII*, I, 43.
51. Rogers, 79 f.

CHAPTER XXVI

1. Stow's *Chronicle*, in Froude, *Edward VI*, 21.
2. Ibid., 34.
3. Hughes, II, 162; *Camb. Mod. Hy*, II, 490-1.
4. Rogers, 89.
5. Froude, *Edward*, 165.
6. Ibid., 183; Prescott, *Mary Tudor*, 25.
7. Hughes, II, 192-3.
8. Robertson, *Freethought*, I, 459.
9. Froude, *Edward*, 98-101.
10. Ibid., 163.
11. *Camb. Mod. Hy*, II, 502.
12. Froude, *Edward*, 156.
13. Ibid., 278.
14. Ibid.
15. 163.
16. 176; Lingard, V, 228.
17. Froude, 176.

18. Ibid., 209.
19. *Camb. Mod. Hy*, II, 301.
20. Froude, 226.
21. Cf. Prescott, *Mary Tudor*, 17.
22. En. Brit., XIV, 1001.
23. Chapuys in Prescott, 50, 54.
24. Ibid.
25. En. Brit., XIV, 1000b.
26. Prescott, 122.
27. Ibid., 209.
28. Pastor, XIV, 399.
29. Froude, *Mary Tudor*, 44.
30. Prescott, 191-2.
31. Ibid., 194.
32. 196.
33. Froude, *Mary Tudor*, 66.
34. Hughes, I, 18.
35. Froude, 56.
36. Ibid., 50.
37. 56.
38. Prescott, 285.
39. Ibid., 247.
40. 266.
41. 284.
42. 315.
43. Froude, 325.
44. Prescott, 325.
45. Lingard, V, 230.
46. Prescott, 206.
47. Ibid., 302.
48. 304.
49. Pastor, XIV, 360.
50. Froude, 119.
51. Prescott, 307.
52. *Camb. Mod. Hy*, II, 543.
53. Froude, 110.
54. Prescott, 311.
55. Foxe, *Acts and Monuments*, I, 231 f.; Maitland, S. R., *Essays on the Reformation*, 409; Smith, *Reformation*, 586; Lee, Sidney, *Dictionary of National Biography*, XX, 146.
56. Hughes, II, 258-9.
57. Froude, *Mary Tudor*, 199.
58. Lingard, V, 231.
59. Pastor, XIV, 370.
60. Froude, 202.
61. Ibid., 233.
62. Foxe, VIII, 82-3.
63. Ibid., 88.
64. 90.
65. Froude, 235.
66. Beard, *Reformation*, 182.
67. Hughes, II, 198.
68. Hume, *Spain: Its Greatness and Decay*, 117.
69. Prescott, 332.
70. Ibid., 381.
71. 390.

CHAPTER XXVII

1. Cf. Buckle, *Hy of Civilization*, II, ch. ii.
2. Ibid., I, 150; Belloc, *How the Reformation Happened*, 188.
3. Ibid., 189.
4. Lang, *Hy of Scotland*, I, 425.
5. Froude, *Elizabeth*, I, 73.
6. Knox, *Hy of the Reformation*, Introd. by W. C. Dickinson, xvii.
7. Lang, I, 300.
8. Ibid., 476.
9. Froude, *Henry VIII*, III, 298.
10. Ibid., 295, 300.
11. Knox, *History*, I, 76.
12. Ibid., 78.
13. 8.
14. 55.
15. Lang, I, 484.
16. Knox, I, 84-5.
17. Muir, *Knox*, 119.
18. Ibid., 133.
19. 120.
20. 202.
21. Froude, *Elizabeth*, I, 257.
22. Allen, *Political Thought*, 110.
23. Knox, *History*, Introd., lxxiii; Muir, 67.
24. Knox, I, 194 and note 2.
25. Knox, Introd., xlv; cf. Muir, 300.
26. Muir, 157.
27. Lang, II, 37.
28. Knox, II, 18.
29. Ibid., 4.
30. I, 6.
31. Knox, Introd., xli.
32. Ibid., xxxix.
33. Knox, *Works*, IV, 365, 373-7.
34. Ibid., 418-20.
35. Knox, *Book of Discipline*, in Allen, *Political Thought*, 113n.
36. Ibid., 113; Lecky, *Rationalism*, II, 16.
37. Knox, Introd., xlii, and Allen, 113.
38. In Muir, 142.
39. Ibid., 148-9.
40. Lang, II, 45.
41. Knox, I, 161-2.
42. Ibid.
43. 163.
44. Lang, II, 51-3.
45. Knox, I, 164.
46. Ibid., 171-2.
47. 182; Lang, II, 54-5.
48. Knox, I, 191.
49. Knox, II, Appendix VI.

CHAPTER XXVIII

1. *Camb. Mod. Hy*, II, 602; En. Brit., VII, 210a.
2. Watson, P. B., *Swedish Revolution under Gustavus Vasa*, 123.

3. Ibid., 162.
4. 169.
5. Horn, *Literature of the Scandinavian North*, 147.
6. In Lednicki, *Life and Culture of Poland*, 107.
7. Kesten, *Copernicus*, 144.
8. *Camb. Hy of Poland*, I, 322-4.
9. Ibid., 329.
10. Lützow, *Bohemia*, 206n.
11. Tawney, 75.
12. Blok, II, 331.
13. *Camb. Mod. Hy*, II, 63; Taine, *Lectures on Art*, 272.
14. Pirenne, H., *Belgian Democracy*, 218.
15. Motley, J. L., *Rise of the Dutch Republic*, I, 101.
16. Smith, *Reformation*, 240.
17. Blok, II, 314.
18. In Kautsky, 283.
19. Smith, 244.
20. Kautsky, 285 f.; Ranke, 75 f.
21. Motley, I, 222-5.
22. Smith, 245.
23. Draper, J. W., *Intellectual Development of Europe*, II, 226.
24. Smith, 245.
25. Armstrong, *Charles V*, II, 382-3; Robertson, *Charles V*, II, 137; Michelet, III, 293.
26. Ibid., 363.
27. 349.
28. Robinson, *Readings*, 317-9.
29. Altamira, *Hy of Spanish Civilization*, 135.
30. Hume, *Spanish People*, 222-3.
31. Vernadsky, G., *Kievan Russia*, 243.
32. Wilkins, *Spanish Protestantism in the 16th Century*, 19.
33. Lea, *Inquisition in Spain*, IV, 8-12.
34. Wilkins, 26; *Camb. Mod. Hy*, I, 403.
35. Lea, IV, 431-8.
36. Ibid., 441.
37. Prescott, W. H. in Robertson, *Charles V*, II, 648.

CHAPTER XXIX

1. Waliszewski, *Ivan the Terrible*, 95.
2. Rambaud, *Hy of Russia*, I, 286.
3. Waliszewski, *Ivan*, 68.
4. Eckhardt, Russia, 29.
5. Réau, *L'art russe*, I, 244.
6. Kluchevsky, *Hy of Russia*, I, 275.
7. Pokrovsky, *Hy of Russia*, 104.
8. Vernadsky, *Hy of Russia*, 55.
9. Rambaud, I, 253.
10. Kluchevsky, I, 75, 95.
11. Pokrovsky, 144.

12. Rambaud, I, 266; Waliszewski, *Ivan*, 267.
13. Ibid., 268, 272.
14. Pokrovsky, 157.
15. Waliszewski, 258.
16. Rambaud, I, 300.
17. Réau, I, 272.
18. Waliszewski, 374.
19. Roeder, *Catherine de' Medici*, 495.
20. Waliszewski, 381.

CHAPTER XXX

1. Browne, E. G., *Literary Hy of Persia*, III, 43.
2. Lamb, H., *Tamerlane*, 293.
3. Clavijo, *Embassy to Tamerlane*, 153.
4. *Bulletin of the American Institute for Iranian Art*, June, 1938, 248-52.
5. Arnold, T. W., *Painting in Islam*, 93.
6. Browne, III, 289.
7. Ibid., 277.
8. Hafiz, tr. Streit, 80.
9. In Gottheil, ed., *Literature of Persia*, I, 408.
10. Hafiz, tr. Streit, stanzas 10, 11, 19, 21, 49.
11. Bell, G. L., *Poems from the Divan of Hafiz*, xxiii.
12. Ouseley, G., *Biographical Notices of Persian Poets*, 23 f.
13. In Grousset, R., *Civilizations of the East*, I, 338-9.
14. Hafiz, tr. Streit, 65.
15. Ibid., stanza 38.
16. Bell, stanza xliii.
17. Clavijo, 181.
18. Ibid., 137.
19. Browne, III, 185. Some assign Timur's lameness to a later period; so Clavijo, 210, and Sykes, P., *History of Persia*, II, 121.
20. Timur, *Mulfuzat*, v. 26.
21. Browne, III, 186.
22. Ibid., 178; Lamb, 150.
23. Browne, III, 189.
24. Ibid., 190.
25. Clavijo, 132.
26. Ibid., 151, 278.
27. Ibid., 249.
28. Pope, A. U., *Masterpieces of Persian Art*; 149.
29. Dawlatshah in Browne, III, 501.
30. Ibn Khaldun, *Les Prolegomènes*, I, p. lxxii.
31. Lane-Poole, S., *Cairo*, 50.
32. Gibbons, H. A., *Foundation of the Ottoman Empire*, 150.
33. Froissart, J., *Chronicles*, iv, 90.
34. Lane-Poole, S., *Story of Turkey*, 97.

35. *Cambridge Modern History*, IV, 705.
36. Vambery, A., *Story of Hungary*, 282.
37. Gibb, E. J., *Ottoman Literature*, 3.
38. Ibid., 209 f.
39. Browne, III, 455.
40. *Jami, Mulla Nuru' d-Din*, tr. E. Fitz-gerald, 69.
41. Pope, *Masterpieces*, 146.
42. Davis, F. H., *Persian Mystics: Jami*, 71.
43. Clavijo, 153.
44. Saladin, H., et Migeon, G., *Manuel d'art musulmane*, I, 357.
45. Cf. Pope, A. U., *Survey of Persian Art*, IV, 428 f.
46. Ibid., III, 1324.
47. Sykes, II, 155.
48. In Dimand, M. S., *Handbook of Muhammadan Art*, 42.
49. Arnold, T., and Guillaume, A., *Legacy of Islam*, 96.
50. Ibn Battuta, M., *Travels*, tr. H. A. Gibb, 148.
51. Ibid., 57.
52. Sarton, G., *Introd. to the History of Science*, II-2, 1100.
53. Arnold, *Legacy of Islam*, 340.
54. Ibn Khaldun, *Prolegomènes*, I, p. xxx.
55. Ibid., lxxiii.
56. Ibid., 4.
57. 71.
58. 12.
59. 67.
60. Boer, T., *History of Philosophy in Islam*, 203.
61. Ibid., 205.
62. De Vaux, C., *Les penseurs de l'Islam*, I, 288.
63. Ibn Khaldun, I, **175**.
64. Ibid., 176 f.
65. 170 f.
66. Ibid., Introd., **xxxii**.
67. Ibid., 95.
68. Introd., xxxii.
69. Ibid., 324.
70. Ibid., III, 44.
71. I, 303.
72. I, 345; III, 300-5.
73. I, 333, 354.
74. III, 227, 233, 240.
75. III, 115-20, 184, 188; I, **218**.
76. De Vaux, I, 282.
77. Ibn Khaldun, III, 249; I, 347.
78. III, 456.
79. III, 125.
80. Issawi, C., *An Arab Philosophy of History*, 21.
81. Toynbee, A., *A Study of History*, III, 321.
82. Sarton, III-2, 1770.

CHAPTER XXXI

1. *Cambridge Mod. Hy*, III, 112.
2. Sykes, II, 164; Browne, IV, 21.
3. Browne, IV, 62.
4. Ibid., 51.
5. Hughes, T. P., *Dictionary of Islam*, 572.
6. Doughty, Chas., *Arabia Deserta*, I, 59.
7. Sykes, II, 163.
8. Pope, A. U., *Introduction to Persian Art*, 224.
9. Browne, IV, 93.
10. Sykes, II, 168-9.
11. Dimand, M. S., *Guide to an Exhibition of Islamic Miniature Painting*, 34.
12. Pope, A. U., *Catalogue of a Loan Exhibition of Early Oriental Carpets*, 39.
13. Merriman, R. B., *Suleiman the Magnificent*, 33.
14. Ibid., 190.
15. *Camb. Mod. Hy*, I, 92.
16. Guicciardini, F., *History of the Wars in Italy*, VIII, 12; Schevill, F., *History of the Balkan Peninsula*, 217; *Camb. Mod. Hy*, I, 93.
17. Merriman, 60.
18. Ibid., 61.
19. Bury, J. B., in *Camb. Mod. Hy*, I, 93.
20. Merriman, 72.
21. *Camb. Mod. Hy*, 94-5.
22. Ibid., 95.
23. Ranke, L. von, *History of the Reformation in Germany*, 579.
24. Merriman, 124.
25. Ibid., 141-2.
26. *Camb. Mod. Hy*, III, 123.
27. Gibbons, *Foundation of the Ottoman Empire*, 81; Schevill, 240.
28. Schevill, 233.
29. Merriman, 171.
30. Bury in *Camb. Mod. Hy*, I, 101.
31. Merriman, 202.
32. Ibid., 165.
33. *Camb. Mod. Hy*, I, 101.
34. Creasy, E. S., *History of the Ottoman Turks*, 113; Merriman, 148.
35. Robertson, Wm., *History of the Reign of Charles V*, II, 367.
36. Schevill, 238.
37. Creasy, 109.
38. Lane-Poole, S., *Saladin*, 36.
39. Hitti, P. K., *History of the Arabs*, 19.
40. Merriman, 203.
41. Gibbons, 74; Creasy, 106.
42. Bacon, Fr., *Philosophical Works*, ed. Robertson, 749.
43. Creasy, 113.
44. Gibb, *Ottoman Literature*, 233.
45. *Camb. Mod. Hy*, VI, 420.
46. Creasy, 108.

47. Ibid., 109.
48. Gibb, 123-8.
49. Luther, *To the Christian Nobility*, in *Works*, II, 149.
50. Froude, J. A., *The Reign of Henry VIII*, II, 184n.
51. Lang, A., *History of Scotland*, II, 78.
52. Gibb., 218.
53. Merriman, 185-93; Robertson, *Charles V*, II, 365-73.

CHAPTER XXXII

1. Percy, Thos., *Reliques of Ancient English Poetry*, II, 116; Jewish Encyc., XII, 462.
2. Marcus, J., *The Jew in the Medieval World*, 395-7.
3. Graetz, H., *History of the Jews*, IV, 272.
4. Erasmus, Letter to Capito, March 13, 1518.
5. Graetz, IV, 296-9; Abbott, G. F., *Israel in Europe*, 198-9.
6. Abbott, 203.
7. Baron, Salo, *Social and Religious History of the Jews*, II, 58 f.
8. Sarton, *Introduction to the History of Science*, III-1, 57.
9. Graetz, IV, 220.
10. Ibid., 407.
11. Pastor, L., *History of the Popes*, VIII, 444.
12. Id., X, 372.
13. Roth, C., in Finkelstein, L., ed., *The Jews*, 239.
14. Waxman, M., *History of Jewish Literature*, II, 66.
15. Roth, C., *The Jewish Contribution to Civilization*, 92.
16. Thompson, J. W., *Economic and Social History of Europe in the Later Middle Ages*, 30.
17. Newman, L. J., *Jewish Influence in Christian Reform Movements*, 436-50.
18. Dubnow, S. M., *History of the Jews in Russia and Poland*, I, 61.
19. Ibid., 85-7.
20. Abrahams, Israel, *Jewish Life in the Middle Ages*, 403.
21. Newman, 483.
22. Ibid., 473.
23. Graetz, IV, 549-51.
24. Finkelstein, 241.
25. Coulton, G. G., *Medieval Panorama*, 185.
26. Sarton, III-2, 1059.
27. Coulton, G. G., *From St. Francis to Dante*, 110.
28. Janssen, J., *History of the German People at the Close of the Middle Ages*, II, 73.
29. Roth, *Jewish Contribution*, 25.
30. Graetz, IV, 286.
31. Ibid., 245.
32. Cf. e.g., Coulton, *Life in the Middle Ages*, II, 147.
33. Graetz, IV, 253.
34. Ibid., 55-7; Baron, II, 29.
35. Monmarché, M., ed., *Châteaux of the Loire*, 190.
36. Graetz, IV, 98.
37. Lea, *Inquisition in Spain*, I, 101; Abbott, 103; Graetz, 103.
38. Ibid., 101.
39. Abrahams, *Jewish Life*, 331.
40. Marcus, 44.
41. *Cambridge Medieval History*, VII, 657.
42. Baron, II, 29.
43. Lea, *Inquisition in the Middle Ages*, II, 379.
44. Graetz, 109-10.
45. Thompson, *Economic and Social History*, 214.
46. Kastein, J., *History and Destiny of the Jews*, 321.
47. Janssen, II, 78.
48. Ibid., 76.
49. Jew. Encyc., III, **554.**
50. Graetz, 302-7.
51. Ibid., 513.
52. Ibid., 515.
53. Ibid., 520-1.
54. Ibid., 523.
55. Prescott, W. H., *History of the Reign of Ferdinand and Isabella*, I, 517; Abbott, 191.
56. Burckhardt, J., *Civilization of the Renaissance in Italy*, 488.
57. Sombart, W., *The Jews and Modern Capitalism*, 17.
58. Finkelstein, 240.
59. Roth, *Jewish Contribution*, 210.
60. Graetz, 500.
61. Ibid., 515.
62. Ibid., 525-7.
63. Ibid., 567; Pastor, XIV, 271-4.
64. Abbott, 203; Abrahams, *Jewish Life*, 67.
65. Pastor, XIV, 274.
66. Abbott, 204; Robertson, W., *History of the Reign of Charles V*, I, 206-7.
67. Pastor, i.c.
68. Graetz, 361-2.
69. Ibid.
70. Ibid., 356.
71. Robertson, W., *Charles V*, I, 207.
72. Burton, R. F., *The Jew, the Gypsy, and El Islam*, 65.
73. Graetz, III, 511.
74. Durant, W., *Age of Faith*, 375.
75. Finkelstein, 229.
76. Abrahams, *Jewish Life*, 160.

77. Abbott, 202.
78. Marcus, 170 f.
79. Abrahams, I., *Chapters on Jewish Literature*, 226.
80. Waxman, II, 258.
81. Jew. Encyc., XII, 404.
82. Baron, II, 132.
83. Husik, I., *History of Medieval Jewish Philosophy*, 360; Waxman, 256.
84. Jew. Encyc., VIII, 29.
85. Baron, 85.

CHAPTER XXXIII

1. Mattingly, G., *Catherine of Aragon*, 109.
2. Agricola, *De re metallica*, 99, 100.
3. Ibid., xiii, 46-7, 52.
4. Usher, 274.
5. Toynbee, A., *A Study of History*, IX, 365-6.
6. Erasmus, "Diversoria," in *Colloquies*, I, 288 f.
7. *Merchant of Venice*, III, iv, 271.
8. Smith, *Reformation*, 473.
9. Froude, *Edward VI*, 41-2; Marx, *Capital*, 808.
10. Smith, *Reformation*, 554-5.
11. Ibid., 469.
12. Thomas Aquinas, *Summa theologica*, II IIae, lxvi, 7; cxviii, 1.
13. Lacroix, *Manners, Customs, and Dress during the Middle Ages*, 479.
14. *Camb. Mod. Hy*, II, 436.
15. Kesten, *Copernicus*, 33.
16. Coulton, *Medieval Village*, 338.
17. Lecky, *Rationalism*, II, 113.
18. Hackett, *Francis I*, 406.
19. Smith, *Reformation*, 483.
20. Beard, *Luther*, 126.
21. Froude, *Edward VI*, 2.
22. Pollard, *Henry VIII*, 432.
23. Armstrong, *Charles V*, I, 59.
24. Starkey, Thos., *Dialogue between Reginald Pole and Thomas Lupset*, London, 1871, in Allen, *Political Thought*, 149.
25. Smith, *Erasmus*, 27.
26. Bakeless, *Tragicall Hy of Christopher Marlowe*, 50.
27. Friedländer, *Roman Life and Manners*, II, 93.
28. Janssen, XI, 239.
29. Brantôme, *Lives of Gallant Ladies*, 65, 68.
30. Maulde, 391.
31. Lacroix, *Prostitution*, II, 1151.
32. Janssen, XI, 233.
33. Lacroix, II, 1162 f.
34. Brantôme, 133.
35. Lacroix, II, 1189.
36. Smith, *Reformation*, 321.
37. Erasmus, *Colloquies*, I, 342.

38. Rabelais, iii, 48.
39. Ascham, *The Scholemaster*, 50.
40. In Smith, *Reformation*, 412.
41. Turner, *Hy of Courting*, 45-7; Briffault, *The Mothers*, III, 415; Smith, *Modern Culture*, I, 531.
42. Sichel, *Catherine de' Medici*, 6.
43. Cf. Lippmann, W., *The Public Philosophy*, 117.
44. Cf. O'Brien, *Economic Effects of the Reformation*, 75.
45. Schapiro, *Social Reform*, 31.
46. Ibid.
47. Froude, *Edward VI*, 166.
48. Maulde, 66.
49. Sichel, *Women*, 230.
50. O'Brien, 55.
51. Janssen, III, 367.
52. Froude, *Edward VI*, 69.
53. Prescott, *Mary Tudor*, 327.
54. Froude, 1.c.
55. Smith, *Reformation*, 559.
56. Ashley, II, 369.
57. Ibid., 342.
58. Watson, F., *Luis Vives*, 61.
59. Froude, *Henry VIII*, II, 372.
60. Lecky, *Hy of European Morals*, II, 54.
61. Ibid., 55.
62. Janssen, IV, 60 f.
63. *Werke* (Erlangen), I, 14, in Maritain, *Three Reformers*, 186.
64. O'Brien, 51, transposed.
65. Janssen, VI, 275; Smith, *Luther*, 416.
66. Janssen, VII, 301.
67. Lea, *Auricular Confession*, III, 428.
68. Calvin, Preface to the Geneva Catechism.
69. Lang, *Hy of Scotland*, II, 402.
70. Froude, *Edward VI*, 265.
71. Traill, III, 160.
72. Lacroix, *Prostitution*, II, 1213-4.
73. Maulde, 217.
74. Schaff, *Swiss Reformation*, 722.
75. Wright, Thos., *Womankind in Western Europe*, 325.
76. Lacroix, *Prostitution*, II, 1205.
77. Ibid., 1204.
78. Allen, P. S., *Age of Erasmus*, 203-4; Smith, *Reformation*, 510.
79. Wright, Thos., *Domestic Manners*, 491.
80. Coulton, *Social Life*, 376; *Medieval Panorama*, 313.
81. Baedeker, *Munich*, 12.
82. Huizinga, *Waning of Middle Ages*, 289.
83. Smith, *Reformation*, 500.
84. Wright, *Domestic Manners*, 485-8.
85. In Nock & Wilson, *Rabelais*, 41.
86. In Bainton, *Here I Stand*, 343.
87. Rashdall, *Universities*, III, 422.
88. In Lacroix, *Manners*, 241.

CHAPTER XXXIV

1. Sichel, *Women*, 246.
2. Lang, *Music in Western Civilization*, 300.
3. Einstein, A., *The Italian Madrigal*, I, 7.
4. Grove, *Dictionary of Music and Musicians*, III, 459.
5. Whitcomb, *Literary Source Book of the German Renaissance*, 22.
6. Grove, III, 254.
7. McKinney and Anderson, *Music in History*, 210.
8. Blok, II, 377.
9. Kiesewetter, *Hy of Music*, in Grove, III, 684.
10. Bainton, *Here I Stand*, 343.
11. McKinney, 303.
12. Guizot, *Hy of France*, III, 123.
13. Bainton, *Here I Stand*, 344.
14. Janelle, *Catholic Reformation*, 218.
15. Froude, *Erasmus*, 122.
16. Grove, IV, 20 f.
17. Cf. *Oxford Hy of Music*, II, 243.

CHAPTER XXXV

1. Putnam, *Books*, II, 40-1.
2. Luther, *Works*, IV, 128.
3. Janssen, III, 355.
4. Ibid., 356.
5. 363.
6. Luther, IV, 156.
7. Richard, *German Civilization*, 289; Janssen, III, 358.
8. Paulsen, *German Education*, 56-7.
9. Luther, IV, 128.
10. Janssen, XIII, 260, 264.
11. *Camb. Mod. Hy*, II, 468; Gasquet, *Eve*, 42.
12. Traill, III, 93.
13. Owen, J., *Skeptics of the French Renaissance*, 438.
14. Graves, F., *Peter Ramus*, 15.
15. *Camb. Hy of Poland*, I, 274.
16. Elyot, *The Governour*, i, 12.
17. Ibid., i, 11.
18. Watson, F., *Luis Vives*, 33.
19. In Haydn, *Counter-Renaissance*, 242.
20. Ibid., 199.
21. Sichel, *Women*, 47.
22. Marot, Rondeau 13, in Maulde, 165.
23. France, A., *Rabelais*, 6.
24. Smith, *Erasmus*, 414; France, *Rabelais*, 38.
25. Faguet, 211.
26. Rabelais, *Gargantua*, ed. Cluny, Introd., xxi.
27. Michelet, III, 300.
28. Rabelais, Introd., xxiii.
29. Owen, *French Renaissance*, 619.
30. Rabelais, *Works*, bk. ii, ch. 8.
31. Tilley, *Studies in the French Renaissance*, 85 f.
32. Nock, *Rabelais*, 105.
33. Brunetière, *Manual of French Literature*, 46n.
34. France, *Rabelais*, 216.
35. Smith, *Reformation*, 195n.
36. France, 124.
37. Sichel, *Women*, 239.
38. Sichel, *Catherine de' Medici*, 245
39. La Tour, *Origines*, IV, 413.
40. Roeder, *Catherine de' Medici*, 510.
41. Holzknecht, *Backgrounds of Shakespeare*, 270.
42. *Camb. Hy of English Literature*, III, 189.
43. Richard, *German Civilization*, 151.
44. Janssen, XIII, 467.
45. In Bainton, *Reformation*, 129.
46. En. Brit., IX, 675.
47. Putnam, *Books*, II, 243.
48. Janssen, XI, 317 f.
49. In Friedell, *Cultural Hy of the Modern Age*, I, 232.
50. Janssen, XII, 324 f.
51. En. Brit., XXXIII, 1192.
52. In Trend, *Civilization of Spain*, 101.
53. Prescott, *Ferdinand*, II, 568n.
54. Ibid., 569n; *Camb. Mod. Hy*, V, 495.
55. Hefele, *Ximenez*, 101; Hume, *The Spanish People*, 348.
56. Allen, *Political Thought*, 119.
57. Diaz del Castillo, *True Hy of the Conquest of Mexico*, xi.
58. Mendoza, *Lazarillo de Tormes*, Introd., 3.
59. Ticknor, *Spanish Literature*, II, 512.
60. Mendoza, 71.

CHAPTER XXXVI

1. In Coulton, *Art and the Reformation*, 408.
2. Janssen, XI, 56.
3. Calvin, *Institutes*, I, xi, 12.
4. Michelet, III, 295.
5. Dimier, *French Painting in the Sixteenth Century*, 51.
6. Tavannes in Sichel, *Catherine*, 294.
7. Vasari, II, 355.
8. Ibid.
9. Blomfield, *Hy of French Architecture*, I, 81.
10. Lacroix, *Arts of the Middle Ages*, 151.
11. Ward, *Architecture of the Renaissance in France*, II, 125.
12. Sichel, *Catherine*, 394.
13. *Réalitiés* magazine, March, 1954, p. 27.
14. Conway, *The Van Eycks*, 494.
15. Glück, *Pieter Brueghel le Vieux*, 7.
16. Conway, 492.

17. Glück, *Brueghel: Details from His Pictures*, 10-11.
18. Craven, *Treasury of Art Masterpieces*, 112.
19. Smith, *Luther*, 176.
20. Bond, Fr., *Westminster Abbey*, 131.
21. Bacon, Fr., *Henry VII*, in *Works*, VI, 245.
22. Blomfield, *Renaissance Architecture in England*, 8; Lees-Milne, *Tudor Renaissance*, 31.
23. Ibid.
24. 45.
25. Blomfield, 11.
26. Ganz, P., *The Paintings of Hans Holbein*, 218.
27. So Stange, *German Painting*, 28; but Ganz, 223, assigns it to 1528-30.
28. En. Brit., VIII, 679a.
29. Stange, 22.
30. Janssen, XI, 48.
31. Ibid.
32. Ganz, 284.
33. Woltmann, *Holbein and His Time*, 454.
34. Calvert, *Cordova*, 97.
35. Dieulafoy, *Art in Spain and Portugal*, 230.
36. Calvert, *Sculpture in Spain*, 125; but Stirling-Maxwell, *Annals of the Artists of Spain*, I, 126, questions the story.
37. Dieulafoy, 336.

CHAPTER XXXVII

1. Schaff, *Swiss Reformation*, 182.
2. Janssen, XII, 292.
3. Traill, III, 269.
4. Janssen, XII, 307.
5. Thorndike, *Hy of Magic and Experimental Science*, V, 231.
6. Coulton, *Medieval Village*, 268.
7. Janssen, XII, 372.
8. Bainton, *Hunted Heretic*, 112.
9. In Kesten, *Copernicus*, 96.
10. Lacroix, *Science and Literature in the Middle Ages*, 211; Thorndike, V, 175, 255-9.
11. Bainton, *Hunted Heretic*, 112.
12. Smith, *Luther*, 310.
13. Roeder, *Catherine de' Medici*, 368.
14. Lecky, *Rationalism*, II, 3.
15. Lacroix, *Military and Religious Life*, 444; Smith, *Reformation*, 656.
16. Friedell, I, 283.
17. Lea, *Studies in Church Hy*, 588.
18. Lea, *Inquisition in Spain*, IV, 220.
19. Lecky, *Hy of European Morals*, II, 54.
20. Traill, III, 326; Froude, *Henry VIII*, III, 191.
21. Lea, IV, 212-25.

22. Janssen, XII, 355.
23. Spence, *Cornelius Agrippa*, 84.
24. Ibid.
25. Thorndike, V, 136-7.
26. Spence, 79.
27. Owen, *Evenings with the Skeptics*, II, 495-6.
28. Kesten, 196; Thorndike, V, 178 f.
29. Cath. En., IV, 352.
30. Leonardo, Notebooks, I, 310, 298.
31. Gassendi in Kesten, 109.
32. Kesten, 132.
33. Ibid., 153.
34. *Commentariolus*, in Rosen, *Three Copernican Treatises*, 58.
35. Trattner, *Architects of Ideas*, 28.
36. Luther, *Table Talk*, 69, in Fosdick, *Great Voices of the Reformation*, xviii
37. In Russell, B., *Hy of Western Philosophy*, 528.
38. Kesten, 233.
39. Ibid., 382.
40. 309.
41. 295-6.
42. Rosen, 30.
43. Kesten, 297-8.
44. E.g., Kesten, 299; Trattner, 31.
45. *Prefaces and Prologues*, in Harvard Classics, XXXIX, 52 f.
46. Copernicus, *De revolutionibus*, i, 5.
47. Ibid., i, 10.
48. Josiah Royce in Fletcher, J. B., *Dante*, 236.
49. In White, *Warfare of Science with Theology*, I, 212.
50. In Agricola, *De re metallica*, 595.
51. Penrose, *Travel and Discovery*, 306.
52. R. I. Mantiri of Indonesia has argued unconvincingly that Magellan was not killed on Mactan, but chose to remain behind and to found a kingdom in the Celebes.
53. Castiglioni, *Hy of Medicine*, 421.
54. Sigerist, *The Great Doctors*, 125.
55. In Saunders & O'Malley, *The Illustrations from the Works of Andreas Vesalius*, 14.
56. Locy, *Biology and Its Makers*, 28.
57. Saunders, 14; italics mine.
58. Ibid., 15.
59. In Haydn, *Counter-Renaissance*, 198.
60. Vesalius, *De humani corporis fabrica*, v, 15, in Thorndike, V, 526.
61. Locy, 35.
62. Letter of Vesalius of June 13, 1546, in Thorndike, V, 529.
63. Sarton, III-1, 267.
64. Saunders, 37.
65. Ibid., 39.

66. Walsh, *Popes and Science*, 117.
67. *Speculum*, April, 1928, p. 193.
68. Castiglioni, 466.
69. Janssen, XIV, 68.
70. Sigerist, 131.
71. Ibid., 111. The usual interpretation of *Paracelsus* as meaning "Beyond Celsus" is stultified by the very minor rank of Celsus (1st cy A.D.) in the history of medicine.
72. Pachter, *Magic into Science: the Story of Paracelsus*, 92.
73. Ibid., 105-6.
74. Cf. passage in Robinson, D. S., *Anthology of Modern Philosophy*, 13-14.
75. Pachter, 67, 112, 116.
76. Thorndike, V, 628.
77. *Opus Paramirum*, in Pachter, 129.
78. Thorndike, V, 665.
79. In Pachter, 210.
80. Ibid., 211.
81. Ibid.
82. 147.
83. 152-3.
84. 163.
85. 158.
86. 155.
87. 168.
88. 187.
89. 167.
90. Inscription on engraving of Paracelsus in Vienna State Library.
91. Pachter, 108, 229.
92. Ibid., 4.
93. Commentary on Galatians, iii, 6, in Janssen, XIV, 121.
94. Robertson, *Freethought*, I, 399
95. Ibid., 389.
96. *Table Talk*, 66.
97. La Tour, IV, 417.
98. Sichel, *Women*, 225.
99. In Hallam, *Introd. to the Literature of Europe*, II, 140.
100. Montaigne, Letter to M. de Mesmes in Sichel, *Montaigne*, 21.
101. In Rocker, R., *Nationalism and Culture*, 134.
102. In Taylor, *Thought and Expression in the 16th Cy*, I, 381.
103. *Speculum*, Oct. 1933, p. 431.
104. Owen J., *Skeptics of the French Renaissance*, 505.
105. Ibid., 539.
106. Graves, *Peter Ramus*, 108. Italics mine.
107. Owen, 529.
108. Ibid., 534-5; Michelet, III, 474; Graves, 106-7.
109. Ibid., 106.
110. Michelet, III, 474.

CHAPTER XXXVIII

1. Pastor, X, 310; XII, 494; Robertson, *Freethought*, I, 408.
2. Noyes, *Ferrara*, 203-19.
3. *Camb. Mod. Hy*, II, 386.
4. Trend, *Civilization of Spain*, 123.
5. Schaff, *Swiss Reformation*, 651.
6. Pastor, XI, 3.
7. Ibid., X, 444.
8. Carpacciolus in Ranke, *Hy of the Popes*, I, 131.
9. Janelle, *Catholic Reformation*, 64.
10. Pastor, XI, 134.
11. Ibid., 155 f.
12. Ranke, *Popes*, I, 117.
13. In Pastor, XI, 164 f.
14. Ibid., 192.
15. McCabe, *Crises in the History of the Papacy*, 319.
16. Voltaire, Selected Works, ed. McCabe, IV, 216.
17. Fülöp-Miller, *Saints That Moved the World*, 333.
18. Ibid., 350.
19. 354.
20. James, *Varieties of Religious Experience*, 414.
21. Fülöp-Miller, 375.
22. James, 411.
23. Fülöp-Miller, 367.
24. Ibid., 396.
25. 405.
26. 419.
27. 274.
28. Ignatius, St., *Autobiography*, 28.
29. Ibid., 40.
30. 54.
31. Cath. En., VII, 640.
32. Fülöp-Miller, 302.
33. *Camb. Mod. Hy*, II, 657; McCabe, *Candid Hy of the Jesuits*, 8; Ranke, *Popes*, I, 173n.
34. Longridge, *The Spiritual Exercises of St. Ignatius Loyola*, 119.
35. Sedgwick, *Ignatius Loyola*, 350; McCabe, *Candid Hy*, 40.
36. Sedgwick, 182.
37. Belloc, 228, 234.
38. McCabe, 32.
39. Sedgwick, 221.
40. Ibid., 215.
41. Symonds, *The Catholic Reaction*, I, 215.
42. Report of Father Gonzalez in Sedgwick, 344.
43. Fülöp-Miller, 319-20.
44. Cath. En., VII, 643.
45. Sedgwick, 111.
46. Penrose, *Travel and Discovery*, 69.
47. Campbell, Thos., *The Jesuits*, 77-8.

48. Ibid., 78.
49. 84.
50. McCabe, 84.
51. Acton, *Lectures*, 115.
52. Robertson, *Charles V*, II, 78
53. Pastor, XIII, 222.
54. Graves, *Hy of Education during the Middle Ages*, 214.
55. Smith, *Reformation*, 666.

CHAPTER XXXIX

1. Pastor, VII, 6.
2. Ibid., 5.
3. Pastor, X, 385.
4. XI, 40.
5. Cellini, *Autobiography*, i, 123.
6. Pastor, XI, 50.
7. *Camb. Mod. Hy*, II, 233
8. Ranke, *Popes*, I, 125.
9. Froude, *Council of Trent*, 213.
10. Pastor, XI, 356.
11. XIII, 61 f.
12. Ibid., 154.
13. Robertson, *Charles V*, II, 401.
14. Pastor, XIV, 72.
15. Armstrong, *Charles V*, II, 361.
16. Pastor, XIV, 126.
17. Ranke, *Popes*, I, 218.
18. Pastor, XIV, 345.
19. Ibid., 142-3.
20. Ranke, I, 226.
21. Ibid., 227.
22. Acts, xix, 19.
23. Putnam, *Censorship of the Church of Rome*, I, 1.

24. Draper, *Hy of Intellectual Developmen.*, II, 214.
25. Pastor, XIV, 277 f.
26. Sarpi, *Istoria del Concilio Tridentino*, II, 91, in Symonds, *Catholic Reaction*, I, 154.
27. Robertson, *Freethought*, I, 456-7.
28. Pastor, XII, 503.
29. Ranke, I, 159.
30. Pastor, XII, 508.
31. XIV, 286.
32. Ibid., 300
33. Ibid
34. 414 f.; Ranke, I, 235.
35. Ibid., 245n.
36. Admitted by Janelle, 78.
37. Ibid., 71.
38. *Camb. Mod. Hy*, II, 664, 678
39. Sarton, II-2, 916.
40. Ranke, I, 153; *Camb. Mod. Hy*, II, 667; Froude, *Edward VI*, 9 f.
41. Ranke, I, 155; *Camb. Mod. Hy*, II, 668.
42. Lea, *Sacerdotal Celibacy*, 518.
43. Froude, *Council of Trent*, 283.
44. Pastor, XIII, 116.
45. *Camb. Mod. Hy*, II, 675; Ranke, I, 252.
46. Ibid., 251.
47. *Camb. Mod. Hy*, II, 680.
48. Session XXV; Cath. En., VII, 787.
49. For Italy cf. Symonds, *Catholic Reaction*, I, 234, 333; for Spain, Lea, *Auricular Confession*, II, 426.
50. Lecroix, *Prostitution*, II, 1156.
51. Figgis, *From Gerson to Grotius*, 43; Robertson, *Charles V*, II, 515-6, Taine, *Italy: Rome and Naples*, 240.

Index

Dates are of birth and death except for kings and popes, where they are of the reign. A single date indicates a *floruit*. A footnote is indicated by an asterisk. Italicized page numbers indicate principal treatment.

About the Authors

WILL DURANT was born in North Adams, Massachusetts, on November 5, 1885. He was educated in the Catholic parochial schools there and in Kearny, New Jersey, and thereafter in St. Peter's (Jesuit) College, Jersey City, New Jersey, and Columbia University. New York. For a summer he served as a cub reporter on the New York *Journal*, in 1907, but finding the work too strenuous for his temperament, he settled down at Seton Hall College, South Orange, New Jersey, to teach Latin, French, English, and geometry (1907–11). He entered the seminary at Seton Hall in 1909, but withdrew in 1911 for reasons he has described in his book *Transition*. He passed from this quiet seminary to the most radical circles in New York, and became (1911–13) the teacher of the Ferrer Modern School, an experiment in libertarian education. In 1912 he toured Europe at the invitation and expense of Alden Freeman, who had befriended him and now undertook to broaden his borders.

Returning to the Ferrer School, he fell in love with one of his pupils—who had been born Ida Kaufman in Russia on May 10, 1898—resigned his position, and married her (1913). For four years he took graduate work at Columbia University, specializing in biology under Morgan and Calkins and in philosophy under Woodbridge and Dewey. He received the doctorate in philosophy in 1917, and taught philosophy at Columbia University for one year. In 1914, in a Presbyterian church in New York, he began those lectures on history, literature, and philosophy that, continuing twice weekly for thirteen years, provided the initial material for his later works.

The unexpected success of *The Story of Philosophy* (1926) enabled him to retire from teaching in 1927. Thenceforth, except for some incidental essays Mr. and Mrs. Durant gave nearly all their working hours (eight to fourteen daily) to *The Story of Civilization*. To better prepare themselves they toured Europe in 1927, went around the world in 1930 to study Egypt, the Near East, India, China, and Japan, and toured the globe again in 1932 to visit Japan, Manchuria, Siberia, Russia, and Poland. These travels provided the background for *Our Oriental Heritage* (1935) as the first volume in *The Story of Civilization*. Several further visits to Europe prepared for Volume 2, *The Life of Greece* (1939), and Volume 3, *Caesar and Christ* (1944). In 1948, six months in Turkey, Iraq, Iran, Egypt, and Europe provided perspective for Volume 4, *The Age of Faith* (1950). In 1951 Mr. and Mrs. Durant returned to Italy to add to a lifetime of gleanings for Volume 5, *The Renaissance* (1953); and in 1954 further studies in Italy, Switzerland, Germany, France, and England opened new vistas for Volume 6, *The Reformation* (1957).

Mrs. Durant's share in the preparation of these volumes became more and more substantial with each year, until in the case of Volume 7, *The Age of Reason Begins* (1961), it was so great that justice required the union of both names on the title page. And so it was on *The Age of Louis XIV* (1963), *The Age of Voltaire* (1965), and *Rousseau and Revolution* (winner of the Pulitzer Prize in 1968).

The publication of Volume 11, *The Age of Napoleon*, in 1975 concluded five decades of achievement. Ariel Durant died on October 25, 1981, at the age of 83; Will Durant died 13 days later, on November 7, aged 96. Their last published work was *A Dual Autobiography* (1977).